The Most Excellente Hugo Grotius
The Reverend W. Evats B.D. Ætat: Suæ 77.
The Most Excell^t:
HUGO GROTIUS
OF
the rights of
Peace & Warr
Translated into
English by the
Reverend
William Evats B.D:
Printed for Ralph
Smith under the Piaz-
zà of ye Royall Exch:
in Cornhill.
T. Cross Senior Sculpsit.

THE MOST EXCELLENT HUGO GROTIUS HIS THREE BOOKS Treating of the RIGHTS OF WAR & PEACE.

In the First is handled,
Whether any War be Juſt.
In the Second is ſhewed,
The Cauſes of War, both Juſt and Uujuſt.
In the Third is declared,
What in War is Lawful; that is, Unpuniſhable.

With the ANNOTATIONS digeſted into the Body of every CHAPTER.

Tranſlated into ENGLISH by
WILLIAM EVATS, B.D.

With a new introduction by William E. Butler
Pennsylvania State University; University College London

THE LAWBOOK EXCHANGE, LTD.
Clark, New Jersey

ISBN 978-1-61619-317-1

Lawbook Exchange edition 2013

The quality of this reprint is equivalent to the quality of the original work.
The irregular pagination is reproduced as it was found in the original work.

THE LAWBOOK EXCHANGE, LTD.
33 Terminal Avenue
Clark, New Jersey 07066-1321

Please see our website for a selection of our other publications and fine facsimile reprints of classic works of legal history:
www.lawbookexchange.com

Library of Congress Cataloging-in-Publication Data

Grotius, Hugo, 1583-1645.
[De jure belli ac pacis libri tres. English]
The most excellent Hugo Grotius, his three books treating of the rights of war & peace: in the first is handled, whether any war be just : in the second is shewed, the causes of war, both just and unjust : in the third is declared, what in war is lawful, that is, unpunishable : with the annotations digested into the body of every chapter / translated into English by Williams Evats, BD ; with a new introduction by William E. Butler, John Edward Fowler, Distinguished Professor of Law, Pennsylvania State University, Dickinson School of Law, Emeritus Professor of Comparative Law at University College London, Academician, National Academy of Sciences of Ukraine, National Academy of Legal Sciences of Ukraine, and Russian Academy of Natural Sciences. -- Lawbook Exchange edition.
pages cm
Includes bibliographical references and index.
ISBN 978-1-61619-317-1 (hardcover : alk. paper) -- ISBN 1-61619-317-4 (hardcover : alk. paper)
1. International law. 2. War (International law) 3. Natural law. I. Evats, William, translator. II. Butler, William Elliott, 1939- Evats translation of Hugo Grotius. III. Title. IV. Title: Of the rights of war & peace.
KZ2093.A3D313 2013b
341--dc23 2013012836

Printed in the United States of America on acid-free paper

INTRODUCTION

THE EVATS TRANSLATION OF HUGO GROTIUS

W. E. Butler

Hugo Grotius was a formidably productive writer whose works ranged from the law of nations, to Dutch law, to poetry, history, theology, philosophy, literature, and other disciplines. Throughout the remainder of the seventeenth century following his death, a veritable "Grotiana factory" operated throughout Europe, devoted to translations of his works into the principal European vernacular languages. English was amongst them, although Latin editions continued to find an audience. Among those contributions is the present work, the second English translation of Hugo Grotius, *De jure belli ac pacis* (1625), completed not later than 1677 and published at London in 1682.

The Author

Hugo Grotius (1583–1645) remains after more than four and a quarter centuries from his birth perhaps the single most recognizable name in the history of international law. Sometimes (quite wrongly) labeled the "father of international law", his works on the subject – above all the present work – became classics in the field even during his lifetime.[1] In some works on the history of international law, "Grotius" is singled out as a period in its development.[2]

Grotius was born at Delft into a Calvinist family. His intellectual abilities manifested themselves early on, composing Latin verses at the age of seven (said by Eyffinger to be "… the only man in world history acclaimed a child prodigy by virtue of his juvenile poetry")[3] and entering the University of Leiden at the age of eleven. He graduated at the age of fourteen, having satisfactorily performed in the fields of law, philosophy, and mathematics. By the age of fifteen he had

---

[1] See L. E. van Holk, "Hugo Grotius, 1583–1645: A Biographical Sketch", in L. E. van Holk and C. G. Roelofson (eds.), *Grotius Reader: A Reader for Students of International Law and Legal History* (1983), pp. 23–44; J. L. de Burigny, *The Life of the Truly Eminent and Learned Hugo Grotius* (London, 1754); E. Dumbauld, *The Life and Legal Writings of Hugo Grotius* (1969); W. S. M. Knight, *The Life and Works of Hugo Grotius* (1925).

[2] See W. E. Butler, "Periodization and International Law", in A. Orakhelashvili (ed.), *Research Handbook on the Theory and History of International Law* (2011), pp. 379–393.

[3] See A. Eyffinger, "In Quest of Synthesis: An Attempted Synopsis of Grotius's Works According to Their Genesis and Objective", *Grotiana*, IV (N.S., 1983), pp. 76–88.

accompanied a Dutch Embassy to Henry IV of France. The King described him as the "miracle of Holland"; the University of Orléans conferred the degree of Doctor of Laws on him. Admitted to legal practice at the age of sixteen, he continued to excel in the humanities, publishing a dramatic tragedy in 1601. At twenty years of age he was appointed Historiographer of Holland.[4]

His first known work on the law of nations originated in a commission from the Dutch East India Company to prepare an opinion of the legality of the seizure of a Portuguese ship, the carrack *Sta. Catarina*, by the Company flotilla during the War in February 1603 between the Netherlands and Spain. A substantial manuscript was produced, one chapter of which was published in 1609 as *Mare liberum*[5] (the full text was not discovered until 1864 and published in 1868).[6] Grotius rose rapidly in the Dutch firmament, being appointed to influential legal posts and continuing his sundry writings on history, theology, and Dutch law. His political career in Holland ended when he was sentenced to life imprisonment for his role in a dispute among Calvinists in 1619 that Maurice of Nassau, Prince of Orange (1568–1625) equated to treason.[7] His tenure in prison and ultimate escape were known to every schoolboy throughout Europe.[8] During two years of confinement, he wrote two major works, one an introduction to Dutch jurisprudence and the other an exposition of the central doctrines of the Christian faith intended for seafarers. He was allowed to have books in quantities while in prison and the companionship of his wife. He trained himself to lie in the closed chest in which books were conveyed and eventually was clandestinely removed in that receptacle in March 1621 to the safety of friends, who assisted him in escaping to France in disguise. There he was received by the King of France,

---

[4] See A. Nussbaum, *A Concise History of the Law of Nations* (rev. ed., 1954; reprint ed. Gryphon, 2008).

[5] We are blessed with two recent published versions, one originally made by Richard Hakluyt but never fully published in its time. See Grotius, *The Free Sea*, transl. R. Hakluyt; ed. D. Armitage (2004); and Grotius, *Mare Liberum 1609-2009*, ed. R. Feenstra (2009), a sumptuous edition. Also see on this book W. E. Butler, "Grotius and the Law of the Sea", in H. Bull, B. Kingsbury, and A. Roberts (eds.), *Hugo Grotius and International Relations* (1990), pp. 209–220. On Hakluyt in this connection, see D. Pirillo, "Balance of Power and Freedom of the Sea: Richard Hakluyt and Alberico Gentili", in D. Carey and C. Jowitt (eds.), *Richard Hakluyt and Travel Writing in Early Modern Europe* (2012), pp. 177–186.

[6] The most recent edition, attended by new supporting materials, is H. Grotius, *Commentary on the Law of Prize and Booty*, ed. & intro. Martine Julia van Ittersum (2006).

[7] On a later assessment of the trial based on access to sealed records of the proceedings, see G. G. Brandt, *Brandts Historie van de Rechtspleging gehouden in de Jaeren 1618 en 1619. Ontrent de dry gevangene Heeren Mr. Johan van Oldenbarnevelt Mr. Rombout Hoogerbeets Mr. Hugo de Groot* (Rotterdam, 1708). On Oldenbarnevelt's defense of his conduct, see Jan van Barnevelt, *Barnevelt's Apology of Holland's Mysterie, with Marginall Castigations* (1618). Also see John L. Motley, *The Life and Death of John of Barneveld, Advocate of Holland; with a View of the Primary Causes and Movements of the Thirty Years' War* (London, 1874). 2 vols.

[8] Recounted in Burigny, note 1 above and greatly embellished by "that literary larcenist", Charles Butler in what one reviewer called his "indifferent life" of Grotius. See C. Butler, *The Life of Hugo Grotius with Brief Minutes of the Civil, Ecclesiastical, and Literary History of the Netherlands* (London, 1826).

awarded an allowance, and during 1622–1624 commenced and completed the Latin version of his monumental work here reproduced.[9] Dedicated to Louis XIII, the book, it was hoped, might contribute to a resolution of the Thirty Years War, then fully in progress.[10]

The work, well received at the time, disappointed in that its appearance did not enable him to return home or to secure a position consistent with his stature and ambition. Eventually, in 1634 he was appointed by the Court of Sweden to become the Swedish Ambassador to Paris. He held the post for a decade, but not without difficulties. In manner he was not diplomatic, and his continued preoccupations with matters of theology and literature were seen by his Swedish patrons as detracting from the proper performance of his duties. In 1645 he perished in the aftermath of a shipwreck on the coasts of modern Germany.

There have been more than fifty editions of the original Latin text, including several during Grotius' lifetime with his emendations. There are translations into Chinese, Dutch, French, German, Japanese, Russian,[11] Spanish, Swedish, and Church Slavonic,[12] among others. Although Grotius was well regarded in France and Spain, his fame was greatest in Protestant countries. The Vatican placed his book on the Index in 1626, where it remained until 1899.

There are several translations of Grotius's work in English. William Whewell referred to a "small and worthless abridgement" published in 1654 by C.B., whom he believed (correctly) to be Clement Barksdale (1609–1687).[13] Whewell is actually referring to a biography of Grotius cobbled together by Barksdale and published in its own right in 1654 and then appended to the full translation of Grotius *De jure belli ac pacis* published under the initials "C.B." in 1654 and

---

[9] Intellectually, Tuck suggests, *De Iure Belli ac Pacis* really grew out of Grotius's time in prison". See R. Tuck, "Introduction", in H. Grotius, *The Rights of War and Peace* (2005), p. xv.

[10] On that War and references to Grotius, see P. H. Wilson, *The Thirty Years War: Europe's Tragedy* (2009), pp. 134, 318, 389, 463, 553, and 675.

[11] The most comprehensive bibliography of foreign translations of Grotius is Jacob Ter Meulen and P. J. J. Diermanse, *Bibliographie des écrits imprimés de Hugo Grotius* (The Hague, 1950). Published more than six decades ago, it requires some correction and augmentation. With respect to the Russian versions, for example, it is unaware of the 1902 St. Petersburg edition, which seems to be so far the first appearance of Grotius' treatise on the law of war and peace in printed form in Russia, although heavily censored. The later editions mentioned in Ter Meulen and Diermanse are not editions at all, but merely an enumeration of the table of contents from Grotius or extremely abbreviated extracts on certain topics (for example, ambassadorial immunity). The first full edition of Grotius in the Russian language appeared in 1956, after the Ter Meulen/Diermanse bibliography had been published. It is entirely possible that the reaction of the Russian Orthodox Church to Grotius was not dissimilar from that of the Vatican.

[12] See W. E. Butler, "Grotius' Influence in Russia", in Bull, et al., note 5 above, pp. 257–266.

[13] See Hugo Grotius, *De jure belli ac pacis libri tres. The Illustrious Hvgo Grotius Of the Law of Warre and Peace. With Annotations. III. Parts. And Memorials of the Author's Life and Death* (London, 1654). 39 p. A fuller edition appeared in 1654. Harvard Law School has both printings which, but for the designation of dates, are much the same, together with the extremely short version. The versions are compared in Ter Meulen and Diermanse, note 11 above, pp. 271–272.

1655.[14] Apparently Whewell was unaware of the full 1654 translation. A second version reprinted herein appeared three decades later, translated by William Evats.[15] Another, in folio, was published in 1738.[16] However, Whewell was unaware of the 1715 version, whose text differed to some extent from that of 1738, although both are now known to have been translated principally by John Morrice (1686–c. 1740).[17] There also was an 1814 London edition with notes by A. C. Campbell.[18] Given the wealth of translations of Grotius over the centuries, it remains to collate and compare them to determine how much our comprehension of Grotius may depend upon the particular merits of one or the other.

The Translator

The early English translations of the works of Hugo Grotius on the law of nations are not the product of legal scholars or legal scholarship. We are indebted primarily to theologians for their appearance, either because Grotius figured prominently in theological discourse at various periods after his death or because his legal writings were espoused by dons dedicated to the cause of peace who considered the Grotian contributions to the law of nations to be a constructive step in the direction of a more peaceful world community.

William Evats (c.1606-07–1677), the second English divine to translate Grotius' on the law of war and peace, remains a man of mystery. A contemporary of Barksdale, it is unclear whether they knew one another or were in contact with one another. According to the "Epistle to the Reader" below, Evats began his translation of Grotius about 1670, some fifteen years after the Barksdale version already had appeared. Whether he was unaware of the Barksdale version, or the Barksdale version was no longer available on the market, or Evats believed that he could produce a superior version remains unclear.

What little is known about Evats we glean from his translation of Grotius. An added copper-engraved title page contains in the top left and right corners

[14] C[lement] B[arksdale] (transl.), *The Illustrious Hugo Grotius of the Law of Warre and Peace with Annotations. III. Parts. And Memorials of the Author's Life and Death* (London, 1655; reprinted by Lawbook Exchange, 2013). [78], 660, [98] p.

[15] H. Grotius, *Three Books Treating of the Rights of War and Peace. In the First is handled, Whether Any War be Just. In the Second is shewed, The Causes of War, both Just and Unjust. In the Third is declared, What in War is Lawful; that is, Unpunishable. With the Annotations Digested into the Body of Every Chapter*, transl. William Evats (London, 1682). 572 p.

[16] H. Grotius, *The Rights of War and Peace, in Three Books: Wherein are Explained, the Law of Nature and Nations, and the Principal Points Relating to Government* (London, 1738).

[17] See R. Tuck, "A Note on the Text", in Grotius, note 9 above, p. xxxv.

[18] H. Grotius, *The Rights of War and Peace: Including the Law of Nature and of Nations*, transl. from the Original Latin of Grotius, with Notes and Illustrations from Political and Legal Writers by A. C. Campbell, A. M. (London, 1814). 3 vols. This version, with notes by Archibald Colin Campbell, was reprinted in 1901 with an introduction by David Jayne Hill and the 1901 version again in 1979.

respectively oval portraits of Hugo Grotius and William Evats. The lettering encircling the Evats portrait discloses that he died in the year 1677. The Epistle to the Reader describes Evats as a "Divine", "Eminent for Learning, and well skill'd in the Civil Laws". A "great Admirer" of Grotius' works, especially his "Treatise of the Rights of War and Peace", he thought it "worth his time" to translate—a formulation which suggests that Evats may have been unaware of the Barksdale translation but equally may be disingenuous in ignoring the Barksdale translation.

Some sources suggest that there were Evatts at Sutton Courtenay and that "The Rev. William Evatts, of Berks., translator of the Works of Grotius into English, held livings in Lincolnshire, died 1683".[19]

Until demonstrated otherwise, the more plausible candidate for William Evats (sometimes: Evatts) is the individual recorded as having matriculated at Oriel College Oxford on 8 February 1621–1622, aged 15. The B.A. was conferred on 26 June 1622 and an M. A. from St. Mary Hall on 30 June 1627. There is no reference to the B.D. mentioned on the title page of the Evats translation of Grotius. This Evats was vicar of Rauceby, co. Lincoln, 1636; rector of Thorganby, 1640; and vicar of Ashby-de-la-Laund, 1642.[20] Others have speculated that "this William Evatts may be the translator of Grotius "De Jure Belli ac pacis" published after his death in 1682".[21]

No other works are recorded by Evats. According to The Epistle to the Reader below, Evats devoted the last seven years of his life to perfecting the translation. The text was found in his study after his death and published by his executors, John Nelham and Thomas Whitfield, as a "... more durable Monument to preserve his Memory, than any other we could raise unto him". The Epistle is dated November 1681.

Of John Nelham there is no trace. Thomas Whitfield may be the "Minister of the Gospel" who published several works at London between 1646 and 1657. These describe him at various times as "minister of the Gospel at Great Yarmouth in Norfolk" and "minister of the gospel at Bugbrook in Northampton-shire"; some of these works are attacks on Arminianism, a subject that would have concerned Grotius.

---

[19] *The Berkshire Archaeological Journal*, XIX–XX (1913), p. 31, which indicates that the "main line of the Evatt family is in Leicestershire and Lincolnshire". The date of death given in this source is unlikely. Equally unlikely is the William Evett, son of John, of Hallow, co. Worcester, who matriculated at Balliol College Oxford on 15 June 1632, aged 19 and later became rector of Little Yeldham, Essex, 1643, and of Grafton Flyford, co.Worcester, 1645.

[20] J. Foster (1844–1905), *Alumni oxonienses: The Members of the University of Oxford, 1500-1714* (1891-92), II.

[21] *Lincolnshire Notes & Queries*, XII (1912), p. 31. I am indebted to Sir John Baker for this and other genealogical sources on Evats.

The Book

Although international lawyers are well aware that Grotius wrote widely in theology, philosophy, history, and sundry components of the humanities, they are inclined to treat his works on the law of nations quite separately from his other writings.[22] Recent approaches to Grotian intellectual history suggest any such "compartmentalization" may be misleading and that the seventeenth English translations of Grotius on the law of nations in aggregate were part of a dialogue quite different in nature and direction. Barksdale's version of Grotius is perceived to be part of a larger movement in England aimed partly at setting out an ideological alternative to reformation proposals under discussion and to clarifying the relations between civil and ecclesiastical authority in England. Whether Evats intended his work to be part of that larger movement (he, according to his executors, had intended to publish it) is unknown but an intriguing question given Barksdale's messianic quest to publicize Grotian works widely.

The first English translation of Grotius, *De veritate religionis Christianae* (1629) appeared in an English version by Franciscus a Sancta Clara (1598-1680)[23] under the title *True Religion Explained and Defended against ye archenemies thereof in these Times* (London, 1632). Given Grotius' close association with the law of the sea, it is entirely appropriate, if not serendipitous, that *De Veritate* should have been intended for the ordinary seaman with time on his hands during lengthy voyages to fortify his Christian faith or, if opportunity presented itself, to convert pagans, Muslims, or Jews.[24]

Barksdale became a veritable "Grotian" factory, the full measure of which has never been appreciated. In his own collection of verses, *Nympha libethris, or, The Cotswold Muse* (London, 1651), Barksdale had praised Grotius. That same year Barksdale pursued the cause of disseminating Grotius' thinking with his translation of *De imperio summarum potestatum circa sacra* (1647). Grotius had begun to compose the work as early as 1614, completing the first draft by 1617, but its appearance in print was posthumous, in 1647. John Selden was greatly impressed with the version which he first read in manuscript ('that golden book' which he praised as 'than which there is nothing more learned').[25] Copies were

[22] A pioneering effort to synthesize the totality of Grotius is found in Eyffinger, note 3 above, pp. 76-88.

[23] Born Christopher Davenport, he entered the Franciscan order of friars in 1617 and eventually after periods of time in France and Spain, returned to England as a missionary, where he became chaplain to Queen Henrietta Maria (1609-1666), wife of King Charles I. Franciscus a Sancta Clara devoted himself to reconciling the Church of England with Rome. Author of more than ten major works on theology, his translation of Grotius is commonly ignored in many Grotian circles.

[24] Maria Rose Antognazza (intro.), to H. Grotius, *The Truth of the Christian Religion,* transl. J. Clarke with Notes by J. Le Clerc (2012), p. xiii.

[25] Grotius shared a high opinion of Selden. Upon learning that Selden was walking about London and mistakenly believing him to have been released from prison. Grotius wrote in 1630 that Selden was "the best of men and a very brave citizen". G. J. Toomer, *John Selden: A Life in Scholarship* (2009), I, p.333.

circulating in manuscript as early as 1617 in England, and John Selden acquired at least two manuscript versions.[26] Although widely seen as a theological work and included in an early collection of Grotian theological writings,[27] *De imperio* has been characterized as "… a political response of the Dutch Arminian party led by Oldenbarnevelt, and to the independent and decentralized system of churches advocated by the 'Counter-Remonstrants'". In this perception, Grotius was said to have conceived his role and his work as a "… manifesto of State-sponsored Erastian Arminianism,[28] whose main purpose was to affirm the supremacy of the State of Holland in the Dutch Government, and of the Arminian party in the Dutch church".[29] These are both facets of Grotius's works that would have appealed to the reconciliation inclinations of Barksdale within an English milieu.

It is instructive for international lawyers to consider the larger proposition that the Barksdale and Evats translations of Grotius, including his work on the law of nations,

> publicized the idea expounded in it, and by placing it in a context other than the one in which it had been originally written, imparted a different meaning to it … in doing so, the translator evaded authorial responsibility and the risk of being charged for positions put forward in the edited work … By selecting from Grotius' output of over fifty works and translating his selection, Barksdale implicitly imparted his ideological interpretation of their meanings and purposes … The study of translations and editions of texts should therefore be a feature of the philological approach to the history of ideas, pointing to the link between the author, the work, and its social and cultural circulation or reception ….[30]

Barducci's comment on Barksdale's implicit ideological interpretations of Grotius was a criticism specifically addressed in the early eighteenth century to the Evats translation of Grotius. The author of the criticism was Jean Barbeyrac (1674–1744), sometime Professor of Public Law at the University of Gronigen and widely admired as the most knowledgeable commentator on the works of Grotius, Samuel Pufendorf, and the history of the law of treaties. Evats, said

---

[26] Toomer, ibid., II, p. 717.

[27] H. Grotius, *Opera omnia theologica* (London, 1679). 3 vols.

[28] "Erastian" refers to Thomas Erastus (1524–1583), a Swiss medical doctor and religious figure whose name is associated with a doctrine which he never supported, namely, that the State is superior to the Church in ecclesiastical matters. "Arminianism" has in view the teachings of Jacobus Arminius (1560–1609), who attempted to reform certain tenets of Calvinism. His followers became known as Remonstrants after issuing Five Theses disagreeing with central tenets of Calvinism. Arminian teachings continue to have vitality through their acceptance by mainstream Methodism.

[29] M. Barducci, "Clement Barksdale, Translator of Grotius: Erastianism and Episcopacy in the English Church, 1651–1658", *The Seventeenth Century*, XXV, no. 2 (2010), p. 270. On Erastian elements and influences in Grotian thought, see E. Nelson, *The Hebrew Republic: Jewish Sources and the Transformation of European Political Thought* (2010), pp. 97–107.

[30] Barducci, ibid., pp. 268–269.

Barbeyrac,[31] took great liberties with the Grotian text, inserting things in the text itself and in the Notes that were contrary to Grotius' intention. These also interrupted the flow of the narrative. Barbeyrac's observation is worthy of quotation in full in the original[32] and in translation:[33]

> [The] "Translator, William Evats, Bachelor in Theology, ... allowed himself great liberties: as not only did he insert into the Text itself, the author's Notes, against the intention of the author himself, & and thus causing the loss of the thread of discourse, which was already too often interrupted by the Quotations; but on top of that he stuck in some of his own comments, which is unforgiveable. One can only distinguish these foreign Additions by comparing straight away the Translation with the Original: because nowhere does one warn, & never is there an indication of differentiation, only in some places where a bracket features, and which is even, most often, only at the beginning of the words added by the Translator. The confusion is especially great, & more elusive, that in other places one finds some marginal Notes, in smaller character, which this way differentiate themselves, preventing the suspicion that there are other similar Additions placed in the Text but without any differentiation. These Additions in themselves do not contain anything substantial. They are only very common thoughts, & examples or passages, based on "Livres Anglois", or others in which the Translator had found something that he judged suitable to clarify or confirm certain areas of his Author. As far as this Translation is concerned, although I have only discussed some areas here and there (as it only arrived in my possession when mine was almost completed) I noticed several areas where the meaning of the Original was

[31] The criticisms were contained in H. Grotius, *Le droit de la guerre, et de la paix*, transl. Jean Barbeyrac (Amsterdam, 1724), I, p. xvii. They did not appear in the Barbeyrac preface to the 1738 English translation of Grotius. They are reprinted in Ter Meulen and Diermanse, note 11 above, pp. 272–273.

[32] [Le] "Traducteur, Guillaume Evats, Bachelier en Théologie, ... s'est donné de grandes libertez [libertés]: car non seulement il a inséré dans le Texte même, les Notes de l'Auteur, contre l'intention de l'Auteur même, & en faisant perdre ainsi le fil du discours, qui n'étoit [était] déjà que trop souvent interrompu par les Citations ; mais encore il y a fourré de ses propres remarques, ce qui est impardonnable. On ne peut même distinguer ces Additions étrangéres[è], qu'en comparant de suite la Traduction avec l'Original : car on n'en avertit nulle part, & il n'y a aucune marque de distinction, qu'en quelques endroits où l'on a mis la figure d'une parenthése [è], qui n'est même le plus souvent qu'au commencement des paroles ajoûtées par le Traducteur. La confusion est d'autant plus grande, & plus imperceptible, qu'en d'autres endroits on trouve des Notes marginales, en plus petit caractére [è], qui par là se distinguant elles-mêmes, empêchent de soupçonner seulement qu'il y aït [i] de pareilles Additions placées dans le Texte sans aucune distinction. Ces Additions en elles-mêmes ne renferment rien de considérable. Ce ne sont que des pensées fort communes, & des exemples ou des passages, tirez [tirés] de Livres Anglois [Anglais] ou autres dans lesquels le Traducteur avoit [avait] trouvé quelque chose qu'il jugeoit [jugeait] propre à éclaircir ou confirmer certains endroits de son Auteur. Pour ce qui est de la Version, quoi que je n'en aie conferé que quelques endroits par ci par là (car elle n'est parvenuë[e] entre mes mains, que lors que la mienne étoit [était] presque achevée) j'y ai remarqué plusieurs endroits, où l'on a mal rendu le sens de l'Original. Il m'en est même tombé un sous les yeux, où le Traducteur prête ses pensées à l'Auteur, par un désir manifeste d'insinuer certains principes de son Systême [è] favori de Théologie ...

[33] Translation from the French by Alice Butler, Anna Butler, and Stephanie Butler.

> badly expressed. I even noticed one area where the Translator lends his thoughts to the Author, through an obvious desire to insinuate some principles of his favourite system of Theology …".

The book was printed by "M.W." [Margaret White], bookseller and printer in London, for Thomas Bassett[34] and Ralph Smith.[35]

The copper-engraved frontispiece contains portraits of Hugo Grotius,[36] William Evats, figures of peace and war, and a battle in progress below. It is signed by Thomas Cross, Senior (fl. 1632–1682), a superior engraver who did numerous title pages, book illustrations, and some bookplates. He engraved shorthand, inventing his own system, and undertook scripts for Josiah Ricraft (fl. 1645–1679), *The Peculiar Characters of the Oriental Languages and Sundry Others* (London, [1645]). The frontispiece in Samuel Collins, *The Present State of Russia* (1671) is signed by him.

---

[34] Bassett included law books among his specialties. A broadside survives: *An Exact Catalogue of the Common & Statute Law Books of this Realm, and Some Others Relating Thereunto* (London, Collected by Thomas Bassett, 1654), reissued numerous times. He was based at the George in Fleet Street. See *A Catalogue of Books printed for Thomas Basset, and are to be sold at his shop at the George near Cliffords Inne in Fleet-Street* (London, Printed by R. Battersby for Thomas Bassett, 1672). He published Sir Edward Coke (1552–1634), Rastell, yearbooks, John Selden (1584-1654), and Ben Jonson (c. 1573–1637), among others.

[35] Ralph Smith, London bookseller from 1642 and still in business in 1684. See Plomer, *A Dictionary of the Printers and Booksellers Who Were at Work in England, Scotland and Ireland from 1668 to 1725* (1922), p. 275.

[36] See E. A. van Beresteya (1876–1948), *Iconographie van Hugo Grotius* (1929).

THE MOST EXCELLENT

HUGO GROTIUS

HIS THREE

BOOKS

Treating of the

RIGHTS

OF

WAR & PEACE.

In the Firſt is handled,

Whether any War be Juſt.

In the Second is ſhewed,

The Cauſes of War, both Juſt and Uujuſt.

In the Third is declared,

What in War is Lawful; that is, Unpuniſhable.

With the ANNOTATIONS digeſted into the Body of every CHAPTER.

Tranſlated into ENGLISH by

WILLIAM EVATS, B. D.

LONDON,

Printed by M. W. for Thomas Baſſet at the *George* in *Fleetſtreet*, and Ralph Smith at the *Bible* under the *Piazza* of the *Royal Exchange* in *Cornhill*. M DC LXXXII.

THE PREFACE.

THE Civil Law, whether that, proper to the Romans, *or that appertaining to any other people, many have endeavoured either to expound by large Commentaries, or to expose to present view by Epitomies : But of that Law, which governs most Nations, and the Rulers of diverse People, whether it arise from Nature, or be Instituted by Divine Authority, or whether it be introduced by Custome or Tacite Consent, few have hitherto treated ; and none at all either Universally or Methodically : though such a Treatise would highly conduce to the Benefit of Mankind.* The Excellency of this Science, *saith* Seneca, is seen in Leagues, Covenants, Articles of Agreement, and Conditions made between diverse free people, and between Kings of Foreign Nations, and in all the Rights of War and Peace. *Insomuch, that* Euripides *prefers it before all other knowledge of things either Divine or Humane ; saying,* The usefulness of this Treatise.

It's vain, of Things, of Gods, or Men, to boast,
Past or to come : unless what's Just thou know'st.

And indeed, such a Treatise would be so much the more necessary, by how much we find many as well in this, as in former Ages, contemning this part of Justice, as if there were nothing in it but an Empty Name. There is nothing more frequent in every mans mouth, than that of Euphemus *in* Thucydides, *To Kings and Cities Imperial, there is nothing Unjust, that is Profitable. And that also which the* Athenians *(being then the most Potent Party in all* Greece *) told the* Metians, To humane reason, those things are Just, which an Equal Necessity on both sides imposeth : otherwise, whatsoever the stronger Party can and will do, the weaker Party must suffer. *As if it were in the power of Fortune to make Oppression just ; or, that no Common-wealth could be well governed without Injustice. Whereunto* The Vulgar Error concerning the Rights of War. *Lib. 6.*

they

they usually add, That the Sword is the Common Judge or Arbiter of all differences arising between Kings and Foreign Nations. Neither is this the opinion of the Vulgar only, That all Laws are silenced by War; but some such like sayings do often fall from Men otherwise Learned and Prudent, whereby this Opinion gathers strength. There being nothing more frequently opposed one to another, than Law and Arms: Thus we find them opposed in Enneus,

—to gain their Right,
Not at the Law, but with their Arms, they fight.

The like we find in Horace, *who speaking of* Achilles, *saith,*

Nothing by Law, but All, by Arms, he claims.

Old Antigonus *laught at him, who beholding him busied in battering the* Alber. Gent. *Forts and Cities of his Enemy, presented him with some Commentaries of Justice.* Marius *was wont to say,* That he could not hear the Cry of the Laws, for the Clashing of Arms. Lysander *in* Plutarch, *laying his hand upon* Plut. Lys. *his Sword said,* He that knows how to use This, is the best Judge of the Bounds of Empires. *To the same purpose was that of* Cæsar, Non est Idem tempus Armorum, quod Legum; Arms and Laws do never flourish at one and the same time. Kings, *saith* Seneca, grant many things blindfold, especially in times of War: for no one man, though Just, can possibly satisfie the desires of so many Armed Men; neither can any one man at the same time perform the Office of a Good Man, and of a Good General. *Nay, even* Pompey *himself, though otherwise very Modest, yet would say,* Armatus ut Leges cogitem? What do ye tell me of Laws, that am in Arms? *Or as* Plutarch *frames his Answer to the* Mamertines, What, will ye never cease to upbraid us with your Laws, whom ye see begirt Lib. 9. with Swords? So easily, *saith* Curtius, doth War pervert and destroy even the very Laws of Nature. *Even among Christian Authors, we find many such like sayings: That of* Tertullian *shall suffice instead of the rest,* Dolus, Asperitas, Injustitia, propria sunt Præliorum negotia; Fraud, Cruelty and Oppression are the proper Imployments of War. *Now they that favour this Opinion, will doubtless object against me, that of the Comœdian,*

If Things uncertain, thou with certain Rules
Wilt Guide, thou'lt undertake a Task as Bad,
As he that would with Reason run stark Mad.

Seeing then it would be to no purpose to treat of Right, if there be no such thing; It will very much concern us, to commend and defend this ensuing Discourse, by a brief, but sound Confutation of this Error.

But

But that we may avoid Confusion in disputing with a Multitude, let us allow them an Advocate; and who fitter than Carneades, *who arrived at that heighth and perfection of Eloquence, that he could plead as strongly for Error, as for Truth: This man having undertaken to decry Justice, especially that part of it which we now defend, could find no Argument more forceable, than this,* Men, *saith he,* have ordained unto themselves Laws for Profits sake, various, according to their several manners, which also they often change with the Times: whereas indeed, there is no Natural Law or Right at all. For all, both Men and other living Creatures, are by the meer Guidance of Nature, led to such things, as to themselves are profitable: Wherefore there is either no Justice at all; or if there be any, it is extream folly, because it robs it self to enrich others. *But what the Philosopoer here saith, and the Poet after him:*

This Error confuted.

Carneades his Argument against Justice.

What's Just, or Unjust, Nature can't discern.

must by no means be admitted: For man indeed, is a living body, but far more excellent than all others, and much more differing from the rest, than they do one from another; as may easily be demonstrated by many actions, which are proper only to mankind. Amongst which, this is one, that he greedily affects Society, that is, Community; yet not any but that which is peaceable, and according to the Model of his Understanding, Regular, with those of his own kind; which the Stoicks *term* οἰκείωσιν, *Familiarity.* Men, *saith* Chrysostom, with men have Society naturally; and why not, seeing that Beasts with Beasts have the same. *And in another place he tells us,* That Nature hath instill'd into our minds the very seeds of Vertue. *This also* M. Antoninus (*that Emperour who was so highly famed for his Philosophy*) *thus testifies,* That we were born for Communion, was long since apparent: For, Is it not plain, *saith he*, That Nature frames all things in order, when we see the worser things made for the better, and the better things one for another? *That therefore which* Carneades *affirms, That every Creature is by Natural Instinct led to such things, as are to it self only profitable, if universally taken, is not to be granted: for some of the rest are content to abate somewhat of their own profit, partly to their young ones, and partly to others of their own kind: The Proverb intimates as much, when it saith,* Canis Caninam non est; One Dog will not eat another. *And the Poet confirms it,*

Man differs from all other Creatures, and how.

Tygers, though fierce, at Peace with Tygers are:
And every Beast will its own Kindred spare.

Juvenal.

It was therefore Philo's *advice,* Let men, *saith he*, learn Gratitude from Dumb Beasts: The Dog will defend his Masters house that feeds him, and oft-times will expose himself even to death for him, upon

Upon the Fifth Commandment.

on the approach of any Danger that threatens him. Is it not then the greatest of all shames, that a Dog should be more thankful than a Man? And that a Creature naturally Fierce and Ravenous, should in Gratitude excell the Mildest and Meekest of all Creatures? But if we scorn to learn our duty from Creatures Terrestrial, let us yet observe the Nature of Birds, those Aereal Travellers: The Stork being Feeble through Age, and not able to fly abroad, rests in her Nest, whilst her young ones travelling o're Sea and Land, seek for Food for their aged Parents, who being worn and spent with Age and Travel, deservedly enjoy ease, plenty of necessaries, nay, of delicates; whereas their young ones comfort themselves with this, That they have conscientiously performed that duty, which Piety exacted from them, together with an expectation of the like to be paid unto them hereafter, when they also shall grow old, and through age, feeble. Thus do they in due time discharge a necessary debt, by restoring that, to their Parents in their old Age, which in their Infancy they received from them. Now from whence think ye, do they learn this duty of fostering their young, but from Nature; being in the same manner fostered themselves when they are young? And how can they hear this, *saith* Philo, and not hide their heads for shame, that take no care of their aged Parents, but wilfully neglect them, whom either alone or before all others they ought to sustain? Especially considering, that in so doing, they cannot be said properly to give, but only to repay what they owe them: For Children have nothing of their own, but what they derive from their Parents, who either gave it them, out of what was theirs, or by some means or other enabled them to get it.

Whence this proceeds.

Now in Beasts, this care of their young, proceeds (as I conceive) from some Extrinsick Intelligent Principle, Because as to other Acts, not more difficult than these, the same Intelligence doth not appear in them. The like may be said of Infants, In whom, *as* Plutarch *well observes,* there is a Natural Propensity to do good unto others, even before they are capable of Instruction, and whom Nature it self teacheth to be Compassionate. *But in a man of perfect Age, when knowingly he doth the same in like cases, having withal an exceeding great desire after Society, whereof he alone of all other Creatures hath the proper Organ, I mean, Speech: In him, I say, it is fit that we should admit a Faculty of knowing and doing things according to some General Rules, whereunto whatsoever is agreeable, is not so to all living creatures, but peculiarly to mankind only.* Homo ad id natus est, bene ut aliis faciat, &c. Man, *saith* M. Antoninus, was born for this end, to do good unto others. *And again,* Sooner may we find Bodies Terrestrial not tending to the Earth, than a sound and perfect man, not affecting the society of men. *For as he speaks in another place,* Quod ratione utitur necessario Cœtum appetit; Whatsoever hath the Faculty of Reason, must necessarily affect

Man only hath the faculty of Speech.

And of knowledge by General Rules.

L. 6 5.

affect Society. *To the same purpose is that also of* Nicetas Coniates, Nature her self hath insculpt and ingenerated in us, a mind easily consenting and agreeing with those of our own kind. *Neither can I here omit that excellent saying of* Seneca, That thou maist understand, how desiderable a thing of it self it is, to have a thankful mind; and how odious a thing Ingratitude is: Know that there is nothing sooner dissolves and disjoints Humane Society, than this Vice of Unthankfulness. For wherein otherwise consists our security, if not in those mutual good offices, that we do one to another, by which Commerce and Exchange of Courtesies only, our lives are strongly guarded and fortified against all violent Incursions whatsoever. Take us singly, and what are we but a prey to all other creatures; and as so many sacrifices, to appease the hunger or rage of ravenous beasts? No Blood so vile, none so easily purchased as ours. All other creatures are sufficiently guarded against all violence. Whatsoever is born wild and unsociable, comes into the world armed; only man comes naked and infirm, having neither Hoofs, Horns, Claws nor Teeth, to make him to appear terrible to the rest; only two things Nature hath given him, whereby both to offend others, and to defend himself, namely, Reason and Society. By these, he that being single, is weakest of all, becomes Lord and Master of all: It is Society that gives him the dominion over all other creatures; it is Society that transfers Empire from one Nation to another, extending it self over the Seas also; it is this that mitigates the violence of Diseases; it is this that yields Comfort to old age; this asswageth grief and pain; this makes us strong, valiant, nay, invincible: For as much as we may lawfully crave its assistance, even against Fortune her self. Take away this, and you break asunder that Unity that there is between mankind, whereby our lives are sustained: And it is certainly taken away, if Ingratitude be not in it self odious. *Thus far* Seneca.

Lib. 10. See *Aug. de Doctr. Christ. lib.* 3. *c.* 14.

Now this very conservation of Society, as it is agreeable to humane understanding, though but crudely here exprest, is the foundation of that which is properly called Right. From whence ariseth our abstinence from that which is anothers, and our restoring of that which we have detained, together with the full profits we have made of it: As also our obligation to perform our promises, our satisfaction for damages done unto others through our default, and the merit of punishment among men. For Justice is by Porphyry *thus described,* Ut abstineretur alienis, neque noceatur non nocentibus; To abstain from what is anothers, and not to harm them that are harmless.

Concerning the great care that Doves have over their young, see *Porphyry de non esu l.* 3. Society the foundation of Law. 1. Of Nature strictly taken. *De non esu l.* 3.

From this signification of the word Right, there flows another of a larger extent. For seeing that man above all other living bodies, hath not only such a laudable Faculty as is described, but Judgement also to discern, as well

2. More largely.

what is pleasant and delightful, as what is hurtful unto it self: And that not only at present, but for the future, and what may lead unto either. Is is therefore agreeable most to humane Nature, according to the measure of humane understanding, to be guided in those things by a Judgement rightly informed; I mean, such a Judgement, as is not mis-led, either by vain fear, or by the sweetness of some instant pleasure; nor yet violently carried away by any Inconsiderate Rashness. For what is manifestly repugnant unto such a Judgement is also understood to be contrary to the Law of Humane Nature. And hereunto also appertains that Prudent dispensation in the distribution of such things as properly belong to every person or Society, which sometimes prefers the wise before the Ignorant, a neighbour before a stranger, and sometimes the poor before the rich, so far forth as every mans Acts, and the nature of the thing will bear: Which many of old reckoned as a part of Right, properly and strictly so called; whereas notwithstanding that Right, properly so named, may have a far different nature, namely in this, That those things which are now one mans, may be permitted to, or accomplisht by another.

Of the Divine Law.

Now these things which we have already said would hold true, though we should grant, what without great wickedness we cannot, That there is no God, or that he takes no care of humane affairs. *But since we are instructed to the contrary, partly by reason, and partly by perpetual and universal Tradition, and are therein also confirmed by so many Irrefragable Arguments and miracles, attested by and through all ages: It now follows, That we ought to obey God in all things without exception, as our Soveraign Lord and Maker, to whom we owe both our selves, and all we have; especially since he hath many ways shewed himself to be the best, and most powerful of all beings. So that he is both most able, and most willing to reward our obedience with the greatest Rewards, even with such as are like unto himself, Eternal; especially, since he hath confirmed it, and bound himself thereunto by his Word and Promise; as we Christians being so convinced by Infallible Testimonies, do strongly believe.*

From whence springs up another Law beside that which is Natural, namely, from the Free Will and Pleasure of God, whereunto (as our own understandings direct us, we must be subject: And therefore we may conclude with M. Antoninus, *Qui Injustè agit Impius est*; He that is Unjust is also Impious. *But even that Law of Nature, whereof we have already treated, Whether it be that which springs from Society, or that which is of a larger extent, although it flow from principles internal as to man, yet may deservedly be ascribed unto God. Because it was originally his will, that such principles should be instilled into us. So* Chrysostome *understood it,* Cum Naturam dico, Deum dico, ipse enim Naturæ Artifex; When I say Nature, I mean God, who is the Author of Nature. Neither can we (*say* Chrysippus *and the Stoicks*) derive Justice from any other Root than from *Jove* himself. *From which Word* Jove, *the* Latin *word* Jus *was very probably at first derived; Unless haply we had rather*

Lib. 9.

The Law of Nature in some sense the Law of God.

Chrys. de Diis lib. 3.

rather deduce it from Jussum, *by cutting off the last Syllable, as of* Ossum *anciently is now made* Os.

Moreover, God by the express Laws that he hath given us, hath made those very principles yet more conspicuous to them that are of weak understanding, restraining the wandring and otherwise exorbitant passions of those who consult their own, or the safety of others, by curbing those that are most violent with a stronger Rein, and keeping them within his own bounds, both in respect of the manner and of the end. And explained by the Laws given by God. *Besides, even the very Sacred History (setting aside what consists in Precepts) doth not a little provoke us to Mutual Love, by teaching us that we are all of us born of the same first Parents.* All mankind of one stock. *In which sence, what* Florentinus *saith, is very true,* That Nature hath constituted all mankind of one stock or Kindred; *whence it follows, That for one man to betray or defraud another, is Impiety. Therefore our Parents are as Gods,* Θεοὶ ἐπίγειοι, *Earthy Gods, as* Hierocles *calls them, conspicuous and visible Gods, who do imitate the invisible and unbegotten God, in giving life unto others. And therefore* Plato *calls Parents Gods Images or Representatives.* De Leg. 9. *To whom we owe our Reverence as to the Gods themselves, saith* Aristotle; *yet not such an obedience as is infinite and unlimited.* Nic. l.9. c. 11

Again, Seeing that it is a Dictate of the Law of Nature to fulfil all Covenants and Agreements, (for it is necessary that there should be some means of obliging men among themselves, nor can there be any other means found that is Natural;) from this very spring flow all Civil Laws. The Civil Law from whence it ariseth. *For they that listed themselves into any Society, or otherwise subjected themselves to any one man, or to any Society of men: These have also either expresly promised, or from the very nature of the thing it self, ought so to be understood, as if they had tacitely promised to observe and fulfil whatsoever the major part of that Society, or they unto whom their power was transferr'd, had constituted or ordained for the general good. What therefore, not* Carneades *only, but others also have said,* Carneades confuted, who held that all was lawful that was profitable.

What's Just and Equal doth from Profit spring,

if spoken properly is not true; For the Law of Nature is the product of Humane Nature it self: Which although we should want nothing, yet would, of it self, carry us to a desire of Humane Society. The Civil Law then acknowledgeth no other Mother, than that very obligation which ariseth from Consent, which because it derives its Authority from the Law of Nature; Therefore may Nature be said to be (as it were Grand-mother to this Law. But even from the very Law of Nature there ariseth some profit; For God who is the Author of Nature, was willing that every man in himself singly considered, should be infirm and defective of many things conducing to a good life, the more strictly to engage us to affect Society. But it was common profit, I grant, that occasioned the Civil Law: For that very Consociation or Subjection (whereof we have spoken) was first instituted for some utility: yea, and they that prescribe

Laws unto others, either do, or should propose something of profit even therein. But as the Municipal Laws of every City do mainly regard the benefit of that City, even so among all, or at least the most Cities, there may, nay certainly are, some Laws by common consent agreed on, which respect the benefit not of those particular Cities, but of all in general. And this that we call the Law of Nations, so often as we distinguish that Law from the Law of Nature, which in that Partition Carneades *made of all Laws into Natural and Civil only, was omitted. Whereas notwithstanding being to treat of that Right which was between Nations (for he subjected his discourse to War and things got by War) he ought most especially to have mentioned this Law. But whereas he traduceth Justice, by calling it folly, he doth ill. For as by his own Confession, That Citizen is no Fool who observes the Civil Laws of the City he lives in, although he (for the reverence he bears unto those Laws) omits some things that would be profitable to himself: So neither is that a foolish people who have not so great an esteem for their own private gain, as for it, to trample upon the Laws Common to all, or to most Nations: There being the same reason for both. For as he that for his present profit, shall violate the Laws of the Countrey he lives in, doth as much as in him lies, but destroy that, which should perpetually defend both him and his, in whatsoever he hath or shall acquire; so also a people in violating the Laws of Nature and Nations, do but pull down those Bulwarks, that should thenceforth secure their own peace and safety. For as* M. Antoninus *well observes,* Whatsoever Action it is, that aims not, either directly or mediately at the good of the Common-wealth, takes away the life of it, by dissolving the connexion of all its parts, and is no less seditious than he that Heads a Party separate from the body of the people : For one man separated from another, cannot but be separated from mankind in general. *For,* Quod examini expedit idem & Api; As what is good for the Hive, is good for the Bee; so what is profitable to the Common-wealth, is so likewise to every Citizen. *So then, Although by our Conformity to the Law, we could expect no profit at all to our selves, yet would it be a point of wisdom rather than folly, to suffer our selves to be carried thither, whither we may perceive our selves to be led by the manuduction of Nature. Wherefore neither is that altogether true,*

The Law of Nations.

To neglect our own profit in obedience to the Laws of Nature or Nations, is Wisdom.

And why. *Lib. 9.*

Prov.

For fear of wrongs, good Laws invented were.

As if men were enforced to be just for fear of punishment only; for this belongs to such Laws and Constitutions, as are found out to be most expedient for the better execution of this Law. As when a multitude of men, finding themselves singly and apart, unable to defend themselves, shall unite and conspire with their common and joynt forces, to institute and to defend such Laws and Courts of Judicature, as should punish those who should attempt to oppress them; so that what they cannot do singly, they may be able to do with an united force. And in this sence that may very well be understood, which is usually said, That

Coercive Laws invented for mutual defence.

is

is just which pleaseth the most powerful party. *Whereby we may understand, that the Law it self without a power to defend it, loseth its external force, and so becomes fruitless: which made* Solon *to boast what gallant things he had done,* *Jus est illud quod validiori placuit.* Laws without power to defend them are fruitless.

By coupling Might, in equal yoke, with Right.

But yet neither is the Law, though it want a force sufficient to abett it, altogether fruitless; because it begets Peace and Tranquillity of Conscience: whereas on the contrary, Injustice doth wound and torment it, as Plato *instanceth in those of Tyrants. Besides, Justice is approved of and Injustice condemned by the consent of all good men, yea, and what is the greatest comfort of all, This, hath God for its Avenger, That, God for its Patron, who so reserves his Judgments after this life, that he ofttimes gives a taste af them, even in this; as we are taught by many examples in Histories. But whereas there are many that think it superfluous, to require that Justice from a free people or their Governors, which they exact daily from private men; the ground of this error is this, Because these men respect nothing in the Law, but the profit that ariseth from it, which in Private Persons, being single and unable to defend themselves, is plain and evident: but for great Cities that seem to have within themselves, all things necessary for their own well-being, it doth not so plainly appear, that they have any need of that virtue (called Justice) which respects Strangers. But not to insist upon what hath been already said, namely, That all Laws were not ordained for Profit only, there is no City so strong and of it self sufficient, but may sometimes stand in need of Foreign Aid, either by way of Commerce or to defend it self, against the united forces of many Foreign Nations confederate against it: Therefore we see, that the most potent Princes and States, have always been desirous of Leagues, which would be of little use or force were all Laws and Justice confined within the bounds of any one City only.* Externally. Not Internally. The Law of Nations how beneficial.

Most true it is, That as soon as we recede from the Law, there is nothing that we can certainly call ours: If no Community can possibly subsist without Laws (which Aristotle *proves by that notable example of Thieves) surely, that which knits together either all mankind, or divers Nations among themselves, had need of some Law to preserve it; which he well knew, who held that a man ought not to do a wicked act, no not for his Country.* But some may say (*saith* Chrysostom) How comes it to pass then that Thieves live in peace? But when? I pray tell me, *saith he*; Surely when they cease to act as Thieves: For when they observe not the Rules of Justice in dividing the spoil, in not giving to every one his equal share, thou shalt quickly see them engaged in War and Combats among themselves. Plutarch *reciting that Saying of King* Pyrrhus, That he would leave his Kingdom to that Son who had the sharpest Sword; *saith, That it was so said, only to excite them to enrich his House with Blood and Rapine: Whereupon he breaks out into this exclamation,* Adeo insociabile No Community can subsist without Laws. *Ad Eph.* 4. No not of Thieves.

bile, ferinumque est propositum plus suo habendi; So wild and unsociable a thing is Covetousness. Aristotle *seems exceedingly to blame them, who though they are not willing to admit of any King, or Governor, over themselves, but him that hath the true Right; yet regard neither Right nor Wrong in the Government of Foreigners.* The *Lacedæmonians (saith* Plutarch) place the greatest part of Honesty in their Country's profit: Jus aliud nec norunt, nec discunt, quam unde *Spartam* putant posse augeri; They will neither know or learn any other Law, than how to enlarge their Territories. *The like Character do the* Athenians *give of them in* Thucydides, That among themselves, and to their own Civil Laws, they were very just; but as to Strangers, they esteemed every thing honest that was pleasant, and every thing just that was profitable. *But yet when one of the* Spartan *Kings pronounced that Common-wealth happy, which was bounded by the Sword and the Spear;* Pompey *correcting him, said,* Yea rather that Common-wealth is truly happy, that is on every side bounded with Justice. *For which he might also have produced the Authority of another* Spartan *King, who preferred Justice even before Military Prowess. Upon this very ground, because all Martial Power ought to be regulated by Justice, for in case all men were just, there would be no need of valour.*

Plut. Agef.

The *Lacedæmonians* prefer publick profit before honesty.

Which *Pompey* reproves.

Even Fortitude it self is by the Stoicks *thus defined, to be Valour contending for Justice: When* Agesilaus *in* Plutarch *heard the* Persian *King stiled Great, He demanded,* Quomodo me major, nisi sit & justior? How is he greater than my self, unless he be more just? Themistius *in his Oration that he made to the Emperor* Valens, *elegantly discoursing how Kings should be qualified, if Wisdom were to chuse them, saith,* Not such as should think themselves entrusted with the care of one single Nation only, but of all mankind; neither should he profess himself to be a Friend to the *Macedonians* only, or to the *Romans*, but to all Men and all Nations whatsoever. *As* M. Antoninus *sometimes said of himself,* Civitas & Patria mihi est, ut *Antonino*, *Roma*; ut Homini, Mundus: As I am *Antoninus*, *Rome* is my Country; as I am a Man, the World. *So also* Porphyry, He that is guided by reason carries himself inoffensively towards his own Subjects, yea and towards Strangers, yea and towards all men. Quanto ratione præstans, tanto Divinior; The more he partakes of Reason, the more he partakes of the Divine Nature. *The very Name of* Minos *was odious to Posterity, for no other reason, but, because he extended his Justice no farther than his Dominions:*

Justice preferred before fortitude.

And to be extended to all Nations.

De non esu Animal. l. 3.

See *Cyril* against *Julian, l.* 6.

Each Country groaned under *Minos* Yoke.

Now what some have fansied, namely, That, Inter Arma cessant Leges, In War all Laws lye asleep, *is so far from truth, that no War ought to be undertaken, but for the prosecution of a mans Right; nor any that is undertaken, managed beyond the bounds of Justice and Faithfulness: It was very well said*

That even in War some Laws are in force.

said of Demosthenes, That War might justly be made against those, who cannot be compelled to do us right in a judicial way. *Now against such as are sensible of their own weakness, Judgments are forceable enough, and so no need of War: But against such as are, or think themselves of equal strength, if they will not do right, War may be justly undertaken, which also that (they may be altogether righteous) must be managed with as much Conscience, as judgments are usually passed. Admit then that Laws may sleep in the midst of Wars, yet they must be those only that are Civil and Judicial; such I mean as are proper to peace, but not such as are perpetual and fitted unto all times. It was very well said therefore by* Dion Prusæensis, That written Laws are of no force amongst Enemies, but such as are unwritten: *That is, Such as Nature her self dictates, or the consent of Nations constitutes, are in force even in the midst of Arms. When one asked King* Alphonsus, Whether he thought himself most indebted to Books or Arms; he readily answered, That he was beholding to his Books, both for the knowledg of his Arms, and also for his knowledge of the Laws of Arms. *So also* Plutarch, Sunt apud bonos viros quædam & belli jura; Amongst good men there are some Laws to be observed, even in War: *Neither are we so to prosecute Victory, as to enrich our selves by base and dishonest gain. This appears by that ancient form of the* Romans, These things I judge ought to be acquired by a just and pious War. *These very ancient* Romans (*as* Varro *notes*) *were very slow in making War, and not very licentious when they did make it, because they approved of no War but what was pious.* Camillus *was wont to say*, That War was to be waged with no less Justice than Valour. *The like Testimony doth* Scipio *the* African *give of the People of* Rome *in his time, namely, that they always began and finished their Wars justly: And another Author tells us*, That there are Laws for War as well as for Peace. *A third admires* Fabritius *for a gallant Soldier, but principally for that which in War was very rarely found, namely, his Innocence; as believing that some things usually done against an Enemy were impious: What great power and efficacy the justness of a Cause hath, Historians do every where declare, whilst they ofttimes ascribe the Victory to this, as to its principal cause. From whence arise these Proverbial Sayings*, The Courage of Soldiers do either rise or fall, according to the equity of their Cause. He seldom returns in safety, that willingly engageth himself in an unjust War. A good Cause is never unattended with hopes. *Thus* Pompey *in* Appian *cheers up the Spirits of his Soldiers*, We, *saith he*, must place all our confidence in the Gods, and in the goodness of our Cause; as having entred into this War upon honest and just grounds, for the defence of the Common-wealth. *Thus likewise doth* Cassius *encourage his Soldiers by telling them*, That the greatest hopes were always, where there was the best Cause. *The like we may read in* Josephus, Abs quo stat Jus, ab eo Deus; Where the Right is not, God is not. *Many such like sayings we find in* Procopius: *As that of* Belisarius *upon his expedition*

But such only as are Civil and Judicial.

There are Laws in the midst of Arms.

Eas res puro pioque duello quærendas censeo.

The goodness of a Cause is of great efficacy in war. Proverbial Sayings.

Antiq. hist. lib. 15.

dition into Africk, *where he tells his Army*, That Valour never gets the Victory, unless accompanied with Justice. *And in another Speech of his, before the Battel fought near* Carthage, We appeal, *saith he*, to God for witness, the smallest Atome of whose Power is able to overballance all humane strength: He, as we believe, weighing Justly the Causes of the War, will give successes to this Battel that are due to both Parties. *The truth of which saying, the Admirable Event of that Fight, did presently after undoubtedly prove. Thus likewise* Totilas *bespeaks his* Goths, It cannot be, *saith he*, it cannot possibly be, I say, that they that use Violence and Injustice, should gain Honour in Battel.

Lib. 2. *Sed pront vita cuique est, ita ei obtingit belli fortuna*; But according to every mans Life, so is his fortune in the War. *It was therefore well advised by* Agathias, Injustice and the Contempt of God is at all times to be abhorred as dangerous; but then most, when the Fortune of the War is to be determined by a Battel. *Neither should any man be discouraged by reason of the prosperous successes of some wicked designs: For it suffices, That the righteousness of the Cause, hath a very great efficacy to excite Valour, and stir up to Action, although that Power (as it often falls out in humane affairs) be sometimes hindered and frustrated in its effects by the intervention, or opposition of some other Causes. Besides the Opinion that men have, that the War is neither rashly begun, nor unjustly managed, is very prevalent to contract Friendship, whereby as private men, so Nations and Kingdoms reap infinite advantages. For no man will willingly associate himself with those, who have no regard to Justice, to Piety, to Fidelity.*

The good success of wicked designs should not discourage us.

The Justice of our Cause sometimes begets friends.

Now upon the Reasons above recited, concluding with my self, that there was a certain Law common among Nations, guiding them as well to, as in the Wars, I had many, and those very weighty motives, that induced me to compile this Treatise of it. For I very well saw throughout the Christian World so great a licence of making War, and of running into Arms upon every light cause, and sometimes upon none at all, that even the Barbarians *would have been ashamed to have owned it. And also, that Arms being once taken up, there was no reverence at all had to Laws, either Divine or Humane; but just as if some Fury had been sent out to kill and destroy: so War, being begun, a general licence was granted to work all manner of Mischief whatsoever. The consideration of which barbarous Cruelty, gave occasion to many men, not evil, to teach, That it is not lawful for a Christian (whose Religion principally consists in promoting Love and Charity amongst all men) to take Arms: With whom* Ferus *and our Countrey-man* Erasmus *seem sometimes to accord; both of them being great Lovers of Peace, Ecclesiastical and Civil. But, as I suppose, with that intent only as we usually have, when we bend a stick, in it self crooked, so far to the other side, as may probably upon its return make it straight. But this very design of too much contradiction, is so far from doing good, that it doth much hurt; because that we may easily perceive, that their urging of these things too far, doth detract from their Authority in other things,* though

The Authors motives to undertake this work.

1. A general licence in making War; and in managing it without restraint.

Erasmus & Jo. Ferus.

though haply true. We ought therefore to moderate between these two, as well, that all things may not be admitted to be lawful in War, as that nothing.

Moreover, another design I had, namely, that being unworthily banished mine own Countrey, which with so many of my Labours I have honour'd, I might promote now by my private Studies, the knowledge of the Laws, which heretofore I practised in publick Offices, with as much Integrity as I possibly could. Many have endeavoured heretofore, to reduce this into the form of an Art; but none, as yet, have done it. Neither indeed can it be done, unless (what no man hath yet taken sufficient care of) those Laws which are established by Humane Authority, be rightly separated from those that are Natural. For the Laws of Nature being alwayes the same, may easily be collected into an Art: But those that arise by Constitution, seeing that they are both often changed, and are also diverse in diverse Nations, are put without Art, as the Collections of such things as are singular. But if the Doctors of true Justice, would but undertake to treat of the parts of Natural and Perpetual Jurisprudence, setting aside what hath its rise from the Freedom of the Will; so that one would treat of Laws, another of Tributes, another of the Office of a Judge, another of the Conjecture of Wills; and another, of the proofs of Matters of Fact. Then by a Collection of all these parts, a Body may be composed. 2. Motive, To promote learning, especially in the Laws.

But what Method we thought fit to use, we have shewed rather in deeds than words, in this Treatise, which contains that part of Jurisprudence, which is by far the most Noble. For in the first Book, having discovered the Original of Right; we have handled this General Question, Whether there be any War that is Lawful? *And next, to the end that the difference between a publick and private War, may be the more easily discovered, we thought fit to explain the Just Rights of the Supream Power, what People may have it, and what Kings: and which of these have it, either fully, or in part only. And again, which of them may have it with a Power of Alienation, and which otherwise: And then we were to speak of the Duty of Subjects towards their Lawful Prince, or to their Superiours.* The Author's Method. The Subject of the First Book.

Our second Book, undertaking to expound all the Causes from whence a War may arise, shews at large, what things are common, and what private; what Right persons may have over persons; what obligation ariseth from Dominion; by what Rule Kingly succession is guided; what Right ariseth from Covenants and Contracts; what Interpretation is to be made of Leagues; what Force, and what Interpretation is to be made of Oaths, both publick and private; what may be due for damages done; what Sanctimony is due to Embassadors; what Right to bury the dead; and what the nature of punishments are, and the like. Of the Second.

Our third Book, treating of that which is in War lawful, and having distinguished between that which is not punishable, or that which among foreign Nations is defended as lawful, and between that which is altogether blameless, descends afterwards to the several kinds of Peace; and to all Covenants or Agreements made in War, which appears for this reason to be worth our pains, Of the Third.

pains, because (as I have said) no man hath ever yet treated upon this subject; and they that have handled the parts of it, have left very much to other mens Industry. There is nothing of this subject extant from the old Philosophers, neither of the Græcians, (*among whom,* Aristotle *indeed, had composed a Book, Intituled* δικαιώματα πολέμων, The Rights of War): *nor among the Christians, which yet, is a work very desiderable. Nay, of those Books wrote by the Ancient* Romans *concerning their* Fecial Laws, *there is nothing traduced unto us, but the bare Name. They that collected the summs of such Cases as they call Cases of Conscience; have, as of other things, so also of War, of Promises, of Oathes, and of Reprizals wrote whole Chapters. I have also seen some special Books written of the Rights of War, partly by Divines, as by* Franciscus de Victoria, Henricus Gorichemus, Willielmus Mathæus, Johannes de Carthagena; *and partly by Doctors of the Law, as by* Johannes Lupus, Franciscus Arius, Johannes de Lignano, *and* Martinus Laudensis. *But on so Copious an Argument, they all of them said but very little: And most of them so, that they have confounded things due by the Law of Nature, things appertaining to the Divine Law, things due by the Law of Nations, and things due by the Civil and Canon Laws, mixing them altogether, without either order or distinction. But what all these were most defective in, namely, the Light of Histories, the most Learned* Faber, *in some Chapters of his* Semestria (*but so far only, as conduced to his purpose, and alledging Testimonies only*) *hath endeavoured to supply. So also, did* Balthazar Ayala, *but somewhat more fully: and* Albertus Gentilis *yet more fully than* Ayala, *whose Labours, as I know they may be helpful to others, and confess have been to me; so what may be wanting in him, either in the way of Teaching, or in his Method, or in distinguishing of questions, and of the kinds of diverse Laws, I leave to the Readers Judgement. This only I shall say, That in his decision of Controversies, he usually follows either some few examples, not altogether to be allowed; or he is led by the Authority of some Modern Lawyers in their Answers; many whereof, were framed in favour to their Clients, more than to the Nature of Justice and Equity.*

The Causes that render a War either Just or Unjust, are not by Ayala *so much as touched:* Gentilis *hath indeed described some general Heads, in such a way as pleaseth himself. But many places of such Controversies, as are both Noble and very frequent, he hath not so much as glanced at. Now lest any such should escape us, we have adventured to discover the very foundation, whereupon we may build our judgement, so that it may be easie to decide any such question, as shall happen by us, to be omitted.*

The Law of Nature how proved, and how distinguished from other Laws.

It remains now, that we briefly declare, by whose assistance, and with what care we undertook this Work. And in the first place, My care was, to refer the proof of such things as belong to the Law of Nature, to such Notions as are so certain and undoubtedly true, that no man without wronging his own judgement, can deny them. For the principles of that Law, if rightly observed, are as plain and evident of themselves almost as those we discern

with

with our outward Senſes, which if our Organs be rightly diſpoſed, and other things (thereunto neceſſary) not wanting, cannot deceive us: Therefore Euripides *brings in* Polynices *aſſerting the righteouſneſs of his own Cauſe, thus.*

> Theſe things being plain and regularly due,
> Both Learn'd and Unlearn'd muſt confeſs are true.

Whereunto he preſently adds the Judgment of the Chorus (*which after the manner of the* Barbarians, *conſiſted all of Women*) *acknowledging the truth of what* Polynices *had ſaid. The ſame Author in another place brings in* Hermione *ſaying,*——

> We live not like *Barbarians* here, I trow.

Whereunto Andromache *anſwers,*

> Yet what with them is ill, with us is ſo.

For the proof alſo of this Law, I have likewiſe produced the Teſtimonies of Philoſophers, Hiſtorians, Poets, and in the laſt place Orators: Not that they are all either equally, or raſhly to be believed, for they ſpeak many things in favour to their own Sect, and to the Argument or Cauſe they undertake to defend; but that which many wiſe men, living in ſeveral Ages and in ſeveral places, do all of them affirm to be true and certain; that, I ſay, ought to be referred to ſome univerſal cauſe, which in theſe Queſtions brought by us, can be no other than either ſome inference directly drawn from the very Principles of Nature, or from the common conſent of all Nations. The former ſhews the Law of Nature, the latter the Law of Nations. The difference between theſe is not to be underſtood by the Teſtimonies themſelves, (for the Laws of Nature and Nations are every where by Writers promiſcuouſly uſed) but by the quality of the matter; for that which cannot be deduced from certain Principles, by certain and concluding Arguments, and yet every where appears to be obſerved, we may conclude hath its riſe or beginning from the freedom of the Will: And therefore I alone have endeavoured to diſtinguiſh theſe two, not only one from another, but both of them from the Civil Law. So alſo in the Law of Nations, I have diſtinguiſhed that which is truly, and in every reſpect Right, from that which hath only got a certain outward effect like unto that of Primitive Right, namely, that it may not lawfully be reſiſted, or, that it ought every where to be defended even by publick force, either by reaſon of ſome profit, or that ſome greater inconveniences may be eſchewed; which how neceſſarily it is to be obſerved, will appear in the contexture of this enſuing Treatiſe. Nor have I been leſs careful to diſtinguiſh between thoſe things that are Right, ſtrictly and pro-

The Laws of Nature and Nations how diſtinguiſhed.

In the Law of Nations that which is perfectly right, diſtinguiſhed from that which hath ſome effects of right.

perly taken, whence ariseth the obligation to Restitution: And those things that are so accounted; because to do otherwise would be repugnant to some other dictate of Right Reason; of which diversity of Right, we have said somewhat already both here and above.

Aristotle commended. *Among Philosophers,* Aristotle *deservedly claims the Preheminence, whether we consider the order of his Treatise, his acute distinctions, or the strength and weight of his Reasons. Only I wish that this Principality of his, had not for some Ages past, degenerated into Tyranny; so that Truth (for the discovery whereof* Aristotle *took so great pains) finds no greater Oppressor than the very Name of* Aristotle.

I, as well here as elsewhere, do challenge to my self the liberty of the ancient Christians, who would espouse no Sect of Philosophers: Not that they were of their Opinion, who held, That nothing could be known, *(than which nothing can be more absurd) but that there was no Sect that could discern all Truth, nor any but what held something that was true: Wherefore to collect Truth thus scattered, and through so many Sects disperst into one Body, this, they conceived to be nothing else, but to deliver a Doctrine truly Christian. Thus thought* Justin Martyr, *as appears by the first of his Apologeticks,* The Doctrines of *Plato* were not much different from those of Christ, nor were they altogether the same: So neither were the opinions of the *Stoicks,* Poets, or Historians; for every one of them having some impress of Reason, saw in part, what was consentaneous thereunto, and so far they said what was right. For those very manners, *saith* St. Augustin, which *Cicero* and other Philosophers so highly commended, are both taught and learned in all our Churches now flourishing through the world. *And in another place speaking of the* Platonists, *he saith,* That some few things being corrected, they might pass for Christians.

Ep. 96. De ver. rel. c. 3.

De Conf. l. 7. c. 9. lib. 8. c. 11.

It was not without cause that some of the Platonists, *and ancient Christians dissented from* Aristotle *in this, That he placed the very nature of Virtue in a mediocrity of Affections and Actions, which being thus placed, drove him to this, That he compacted two several virtues, namely, Liberality and Parsimony, into one: And gave unto Truth two Opposites, not equally distant from it, namely, Vain-boasting and Dissimulation; and imposed the name of Vice upon some Things, either not existing, or which of themselves are no vices, as the contempt of Pleasure and Honour, and a vacuity of Anger against men. But that this foundation of his, if taken universally, is not rightly laid, will appear even from Justice it self, whose opposites (being too much or too little) when he could not find in the affections and their subsequent Actions, he was inforced to seek for both in the very things themselves, about which Justice was conversant. Which very thing is in the first place to leap from one* Genus *to another, which he deservedly blames in others: And in the next place, To receive less than what is our due, may have somewhat of Vice adhering unto it as Circumstances may happen. For it may be, that what any man so abates,* he *he may owe to the relief of either himself, or of his Relations. But certainly it cannot be repugnant to Justice, which wholly consists in abstaining from what is another mans: Such another fallacy is this, that he would not have Adultery proceeding from Lust, and Murder proceeding from Anger, to belong properly to Injustice; whereas notwithstanding Injustice is nothing else but the detention of another mans Right, whether out of Lust or out of Anger, or out of an unadvised Charity, or out of an Ambition or Vain-glory (from whence the greatest injuries do usually arise) it matters not. For to trample upon all temptations whatsoever, rather than to dissolve Humane Society, this truly is the proper work of Justice.*

But to return from whence we came, True it is that to some virtues, it falls out so, that the affections must be moderated, but not because it is proper and perpetual to all virtues that they should be so; but because Right Reason, whereupon Virtue always and every where attends, doth in some prescribe a measure to be followed, whereas in others it excites to the highest degree of what we can do. It was well said of Agathias, Of the motions of the Mind, those are simply and altogether to be embraced, in which that which is agreeable to our duty, and worthy our choice, is sound and sincere. But in those which may haply decline unto evil, we must not simply and absolutely follow, but so far only as is convenient: Prudence is a pure and uncorrupted good, which none will deny. In Anger, that which stirs us up to action is commendable, but that which exceeds moderation, to be avoided as being damagable. *Love God too much we cannot; for Superstition sins not in this, that it worships God too much, but in that it worships him perversely: Neither can we be said excessively to desire things that are good, and that are eternal, or excessively to fear those torments which are everlasting, nor too much to hate sin: It was therefore truly said of* Gellius, Some things there are of so vast extent, that they will admit of no bounds or moderation, and that are so much the more praise-worthy as they are greater and larger. Lactantius *when he had largely discoursed of the Affections, said,* Non in his moderandis sapientiæ ratio versatur, *&c.* True Wisdom consists not in the moderation of these, but in the causes of them; because these are moved by some things that are without us: Neither should a restraint be put principally upon them, because they may be but small in the greatest crime, and they may be very great without any crime.

Some vertues require the moderation of our affections.

Others not.

Lib. 5.

Our purpose is to magnifie Aristotle, *but with the same freedom as he himself took against his Masters in favour to Truth: Histories have a double use as to the matter in hand; for it supplies us with examples and Judgments in most cases. As for examples, The better the Times and the People were, the greater was their Authority; for which reason we make choice of the ancient* Grecians *and* Romans, *rather than of others: Neither do I despise their judgments, especially when they agree: For the Law of Nature (as we have said)*

Histories have a twofold use in this Treatise.

is

is in some measure from hence proved; but the Law of Nations cannot be proved otherwise. The Opinions and Sentences of Poets and Orators, are not of so great Authority; but yet we sometimes make use of them, not so much because we count them Authentick or Authoritative, but rather as Ornaments to Confirm what otherwise we do prove. Of the authority of such Books, as holy men by the afflate of Gods Spirit, have written or approved, we often make use, yet with some difference between the Old and New Testament: The former is by some quoted for the very Law of Nature, but without doubt erroneously, for many things therein do proceed from the free-will and pleasure of God, which notwithstanding is no whit repugnant to the truth of the Law of Nature; and so far Arguments may be rightly drawn from thence, so that we carefully distinguish that Law of God, which God by men doth sometimes execute, and that which men execute among themselves. We have, as nearly as we could, avoided both this error and another contrary unto it, which is, that after the times of the new Covenant, there is no use at all to be made of the Old. As to this we are of a contrary Judgment, as well for what we have already said, as because such is the Nature of the New Law, that whatsoever is commanded in the Old, appertaining to Virtue and good manners, the same or much greater is commanded in the New. And after this manner do the ancient Christian Writers make use of the Testimonies drawn from the Old Testament. But to the right understanding of the sence of the Books of the Old Testament, we have no small help from the Hebrew *Writers, especially those who were throughly instructed in the language and manners of their own Country. The New Testament I do also make use of, to instruct Christians in what is lawful for them to do, which cannot be elsewhere learned; which notwithstanding (contrary to what some have done) I have distinguished from the Law of Nature: Being most assured that in that most holy Law, a greater sanctity is commanded, than that which the Law of Nature doth of it self require. Neither have I omitted to observe, what is rather commended unto us than commanded, that so we may understand that to do contrary to that which is commanded, is impiety, and renders us lyable to punishment; but eagerly to aspire to that which is most excellent, as it argues a noble and generous mind, so shall it not want its due reward.*

The holy scriptures.

Not repugnant to the Law of Nature.

The Old Testament not useless since the New was published.

A greater sanctity requir'd by the Gospel than by the Law of Nature.

Precepts distinguished from Counsels.

Synodical Canons if they be right, are nothing but Collections drawn from the general sayings of the Divine Law, and fitted to particular cases which do usually happen: These also do either point out what the Divine Law doth enjoyn, or exhort us to that which God commends unto us: And this is the office of the true Christian Church, faithfully to traduce unto others what God hath delivered unto her, and after the same manner as they were delivered. *But even the Customs used among those ancient Christians, and that were worthy of that Great Name, being either generally received, or praised, are deservedly to be ranked with the Canons.*

Canons Ecclesiastical.

After these, the second Authority is of those who were in their times famous among Christians, for either their pious lives or doctrines, and were as yet never

The Fathers.

ver noted for any great error. For even these men also ought to be had in good esteem, as to what, with great asseveration, they affirm, and have found out to be true in the interpretation of such places of Scripture as seem to be obscure: And the more, by how much both their consent is the greater, and they draw nearer to the times of the first purity, long before any Supremacy was usurped, or any Sects or Factions known to adulterate the Primitive Truth.

The School-men that succeeded to these, do often shew the strength of their Wits; But they happened to live in very unhappy times, being altogether ignorant of good Arts: No marvel then, if amongst many things which are in their Writings Commendable, there are some that are Pardonable. And yet when they agree in matters of Morality, they seldome err, being very quick-sighted to discern what in the sayings of other men was to be reproved: And yet, even in this very endeavour of theirs to defend their diverse opinions, they furnish us with great examples of Modesty, whilest they contend among themselves with Reasons and Arguments; and not, as the Custome now begins, to deface our Books with Reproaches, the spurious issue of weak and effeminate minds. *The School-men.*

There are three sorts of those that profess the knowledge of the Roman Laws: The first are they whose pains appear in the Pandect, the Codes of Theodosius and Justinian, and in the Novel Constitutions. The Second sort are they who succeded to Irnerius; as Acursius, Bartolus, and many more, who at that time governed the Courts of Justice. The Third sort are of those who joyned Humane Learning, with the study of the Laws. To the first I confess I owe much, as well for the solidity of their Arguments to prove that which appertains to the Law of Nature; as also for the Testimonies they often give, both to that Law, and not much less to that of Nations: yet so, that even they, as well as others, do often use these names promiscuously, misapplying that to the Law of Nations which is in force, but among some people only; and that not by any Consent or Agreement, but because they take it one from another by Imitation or by Chance: Yea, and even those things that belong truly to the Law of Nations, they oft-times handle confusedly and indiscreetly, with those that belong to the Roman Laws, as appears by the Chapters of Captives and Postliminy. To distinguish these I have taken great pains. *The sorts of Lawyers. 1. The Pandect. 2. Codes. 3. Novel Constitutions.*

The Second sort, regardless of the Divine Law and Ancient Histories, endeavour to determine all Controversies between Kings or People out of the Roman Laws, assuming some things from the Ecclesiastical Canons. But these also were often frustrated by the infelicity of the times, so that they could never attain to the right understanding of those Laws, although otherwise acute enough, to search into the Nature of what was Good and Right: Whereby they often became good Law-makers, though not so good Expositors of Laws already made. These, therefore, are then to be hearkened unto, when they give Testimony *Second sort.*

ſtimony to ſuch a Cuſtome as now paſſeth for the Law of Nations.

Third ſort. *But of thoſe of the Third Form, who confine themſelves wholly within the bounds of the* Roman *Laws, and never, or at leaſt very ſeldome, expatiate into that Law that is common, there is but very little uſe to be made to our purpoſe: Theſe men having joyned their School-ſubtilties with the knowledge of the Laws and Canons, abſtain not from the deciding of all Controverſies between Kings and People. Amongſt whom are two* Spaniards, *namely,* Covarruvia *and* Vaſquius: *This latter uſing great Boldneſs; the former much more Modeſty, and not without ſound Judgement. The* French *chuſe rather to interſert Hiſtory with the ſtudy of the Laws: The chief whereof are* Bodine *and* Hottoman: *The former in a continued Treatiſe; the latter in ſome ſcattered Queſtions; whoſe Judgements and Reaſons will often ſupply us with matter to find out the Truth.*

Three things the Author propoſeth to himſelf eſpecially. *In this whole Treatiſe I chiefly propoſe to my ſelf Three things: Firſt, To make the Reaſons of my Definitions as evident as I can. Secondly, To diſpoſe the things I am to treat of, into a certain Order and Method. And Thirdly, Clearly to diſtinguiſh thoſe things which ſeem to be the ſame, but are not. I have purpoſely abſtained from that which belongeth to another Treatiſe: As from thoſe things which teach us what is of Common uſe to be done; becauſe theſe have an Art peculiar to themſelves, to wit, the Politicks; which* Ariſtotle *rightly ſo handled by it ſelf, that he mixt nothing of any other Art with it; whereas* Bodine *on the contrary, confounds that Art with this of ours. Yet in many places, I have glanced at that which is profitable: But on the by, and only that I may the more clearly diſtinguiſh it from that which is juſt. Whoſoever thinks that I have any regard to the Controverſies of this age, either thoſe already on foot, or thoſe that may be eaſily foreſeen, will ariſe, do me wrong. For I confeſs truly, That as Mathematicians conſider Forms abſtracted from Bodies; ſo I, in treating of Right, have withdrawn my mind from all ſingular facts.*

His Stile. *As to the Stile, I was unwilling to oppreſs my Reader with a multitude of Words, added to a multitude of Things, to be treated of, whom my purpoſe is only to Inſtruct. Therefore I choſe rather to expreſs my ſelf in as plain and conciſe a way as I could, as being moſt convenient for him that would Teach others: That ſo, they that are to tranſact Publick Affairs, may at one view, ſee both what kind of Controverſies do uſually ariſe, and by what principles, their Judgements may be guided to determine them: Which once known, it will be no difficult thing to fit their Diſcourſes to the ſubject matter, and to enlarge themſelves upon it as they pleaſe. I have alſo brought in the Ancients ſometimes ſpeaking their own words, whereſoever they ſeem to be ſpoken, either with ſome Gravity, or with ſome ſingular Elegancy: Which I have alſo ſometimes done the* Greeks; *But then eſpecially, when the Sen-*

tence

tence was either brief, or when I could not so gracefully translate it into Latine: *Which notwithstanding I have always subjoined, for the benefit of those who are not expert in that Dialect. The same Liberty that I have herein taken, in judging of the Sentences and Writings of others, the very same, I say, do I heartily beg and intreat all, into whose hands this Book of mine shall come, to take in judging of me, and mine. They shall not be more ready to Admonish me of mine Errors, than I shall be to Retract them, and to follow their Advice. And even now at this present, If there have fallen from me in this Treatise, any thing that is dissonant to Piety, to Good Manners, to the Holy Scriptures, if any thing disagreeing from the consent of the Catholick Church; or from any Truth whatsoever, I wish, with all mine Heart, it had never been spoken.*

Hugo Grotius.

THE

CHAPTERS

Of the First

BOOK.

The Chapters of the Second Book.

XVII. Of

The Chapters of the Third Book.

Places of SCRIPTURE in this TREATISE either Explained, Examined, or Amended.

2 Samuel.

A Table of Scriptures.

John.

A Table of Scriptures.

John.

Acts.

Romans.

1 Corinthians.

2 Corinthians.

Galatians.

Epheſians.

Philippians.

Coloſſians.

1 Theſſalonians.

1 Timothy.

Titus.

Hebrews.

James.

1 Peter.

1 John.

HUGH

THE EPISTLE TO THE READER.

THE Author of this Tranſlation was by Profeſſion a Divine, Eminent for Learning, and well skill'd in the Civil Laws. He was a great Admirer of the Works of *Hugo Grotius*, and valued him particularly upon this Treatiſe of the Rights of War and Peace; wherein finding matter fit for a general communication, he thought it well worth his time to Tranſlate. It was the Labour, or rather Paſtime of the laſt Seven Years of his Life to perfect it; which he intended to Print during his Life: And ſo we found it in his Study after his death. And although it added nothing to the value of his Eſtate; yet we (to whom he committed the care of all the reſt) thought it our duty to make this Publick, believing it

would

would prove a more durable Monument to preſerve his Memory, than any other we could raiſe unto him.

Whileſt it was in the Original, it was a Jewel, but hid from Vulgar Capacities; it is no leſs a Jewel now it is made intelligible to every Capacity.

We ſhall not enlarge this Epiſtle in Praiſe either of the Work or the Author, the Tranſlation being ſufficient for both, if thou wilt take the pains to Read it.

Nov. 1681.

John Nelham.

Thomas Whitfield.

Hugh Grotius

OF THE RIGHTS OF PEACE & WAR.

BOOK I.

CHAP. I.

What War is, And what Right is.

I. *The order of the whole Treatise.*
II. *The Definition of War, and the original of the word,* Bellum.
III. *Right, as it is Attributed to Action, defined, and divided into that which concerns Governours, and that which concerns Equals.*
IV. *Right taken for a Quality, divided into Faculty and Aptitude or fitness.*
V. *Faculty strictly taken divided into Power, Dominion and Credit.*
VI. *Another division of Faculty into that which is vulgar, and that which is High and Eminent.*
VII. *Aptitude what.*
VIII. *Of Expletive and Attributive Justice, not rightly distinguished by Geometrical and Arithmetical proportions, nor in that this is conversant about things common, that about things private.*
IX. *Right as taken for a Law, how defin'd and divided into Natural and Voluntary.*
X. *The Law of Nature defin'd, divided, and distinguisht from such as are not properly so called.*
XI. *That Natural Instinct, either common with other living Creatures, or proper to men, doth not constitute another distinct Law.*
XII. *How the Law of Nature may be proved.*
XIII. *The Voluntary Law divided into that which is Humane and that which is Divine.*
XIV. *Humane Law divided into that which is Civil, that which is more strict than Civil, and that which is more large, which is also called the Law of Nations, how explained, and how proved.*
XV. *The Divine Law divided into that which is Universal, and that which was peculiarly given to one only Nation.*
XVI. *That the Law peculiarly given to the* Hebrews *did not oblige strangers.*
XVII. *What Arguments Christians may draw from the Hebrew Law, and how.*

ALL Controversies between such as are not associated under one Civil Law, as between those who never yet entred into any Civil Society, or that are among themselves of several Nations, whether they are private Subjects, or such as are invested with Soveraign Power, whether Kings, Nobles, or Free people; All such Controversies, I say, are to be referred to the times, either of Peace, or War. But because the end of War is Peace, and that there is no such Controversie but may produce War, therefore what differences soever do arise by the occasion of the Rights of War, shall in the first place be exactly discuss'd: That so War it self, being duly prosecuted, may lead us unto Peace, as to its proper end. (I. The order of this whole Treatise.)

II. War defin'd. Being therefore to treat of the Rights of War, it concerns us in the first place to know what that War is, whereof we are to treat, and then, what that Right is that we search for. War (as *Cicero* defines it) is *Certatio per vim, a Debate by force*: But custom hath Translated the signification of the word, from the Act it self, to the state and condition of those that make War; for as *Philo* well observes: *They only are not Enemies that are actually engaged in Battle whether at Sea, or Land, but they also, that raise Forts, plant Ordnances, or such like Engines of War on their Walls, or Ports, though at present they fight not. Servius* upon those words of *Virgil*, concerning *Æneas*,

In War and Arms None greater was than He,

makes this distinction, By War we understand all consultations and Preparations for War: but by Arms only the use or exercise of them. Therefore in another place he concludes, *that all that may be reckoned a time of War, wherein either things necessary for fight are preparing, or the fight it self lasts; so that* War may be defined to be the State or Condition of those that contend by force as such: Which general acception of the word comprehends all the kinds of War whereof we are to treat, not excluding that which sometimes happens between private persons as Duels or single Combats, which certainly are precedent to those Wars that are publick, and being of the same nature, may well be comprized under the same proper name. Which sense the Original word will very well bear, for from the Old word *Duellum* is made this new word *Bellum*, as of *Duonus* is made *Bonus*, and of *Duis*, *Bis*. Now *Duellum* signifies a contest between two, in the like sence as we express Peace by *Unity*, or as the *Greeks* do *War* by πόλεμος, in respect of the Multitude of people that are engaged in it; as also they sometimes do by the words λύη and δύη, in respect of those direful effects that attend it. Now as the Original of the word will justifie this large signification, so will the common use thereof bear it. But if it be objected, that this word is taken generally for that contest by force of Arms, that is publick, I answer, that this argues not that single Combats may not be also so called; For most certain it is that the name of the Genus doth often peculiarly adhere unto that of its Species, which is most excellent. As to Justice, I do not admit of it in this definition, because it is the Subject of this whole Treatise to enquire, Whether any War be Just, and what War is so. But that which we seek, must be distinguisht from that concerning which we seek.

III. Right, as it relates to *Action*, defined and divided. Whereas the subject of this whole Treatise is The Right of War, we are in the first place to understand, (what we said just now) whether any War be just? And in the next place, what it is in War that is just? For we understand in this place by the word, *Right*, that which is just: And that also, rather in the Negative, than in the positive sence, so as we here term that just, which is not unjust. Now that we account unjust which is repugnant to the Nature of a Rational Society: As for example, to rob another to enrich our selves, is (as *Cicero* observes) contrary to Nature, which he thus proves; *De off. l. 3.* If this, saith he, were allowed, all Society and Communion between men, would quickly be dissolved. So for one man to betray or deceive another is unjust, as *Florentinus* proves, because it breaks that bond of Alliance, wherein Nature hath linkt together all mankind for mutual defence. *De Ira l. 2. c. 32.* Which *Seneca* thus Illustrates: *Just as all the members of the body ought to be equally solicitous one for another, because in the preservation of each part, consists the welfare of the whole; so ought all men to forbear each other, because they are born for Society. For it is not possible for any Society long to stand, unless every part thereof be cherished and defended by the whole.* *Ep. 48.* So in another place: *That Society is Faithfully and religiously to be preserved, which so Unites us one to another, that we all agree in this, That there is somewhat whereunto all mankind hath a Common Right.* But as of Societies, some consist of Persons that are equal, as that of Brothers, of Citizens, of Friends and Allies: and some consist of Persons that are unequal, (and these also vary according to their degrees of Excellency) as that of Parents and Children, of Masters and Servants, of Kings and their Subjects, God and Man (for such a Society there is, if *Philo* and *Plutarch* *Numa.* deceive us not.) Even so things may be said to be just or unjust respectively; for one thing may be just in respect of those that live together being Equals, and another thing may be just in respect of the persons Governing, and the persons Governed as such; whereof this shall be said to be the Right of Rulers, and that the Right of Equals.

IV. Right as it is a quality divided into faculty and fitness. There is also another signification of the word, Right, which though different from this, doth notwithstanding arise from it, and respects the qualification of the person; in which sence it signifies a moral Quality in any person, sufficient to enable him justly to have or to do something. Now this Right appertains to the Person, though it be sometimes but in relation to the thing he holds, as services for Land held of a chief Lord, and these are called real Rights, comparatively to those that are merely personal not because even these belong not to the person, but because they belong to no other but

but to him that enjoyes the thing whereunto that service is annexed. This moral Quality, if perfect, we call Faculty; If imperfect, an Aptitude or fitness only: Answerable whereunto in things Natural are, to That, an Act done; to This, a Power to do it.

V. Faculty divided into Power, Dominion and Credit.

Which Faculty Civilians call that Right which a man hath of his own; but we henceforth call it Right properly and strictly taken: Under which are comprehended, First, a Power over our selves, which we call Liberty; Then a Power over others, such as Fathers have over their Children, Lords over their slaves: Secondly, Dominion, and that either full and Absolute, or Limited: As that which a Tenant hath in the profits of his Farm, for his Rent; the Right that a man hath to a thing Pawned. And Credits, to which are opposed Debts.

VI. This Right is twofold, either Common or Eminent.

Now this Faculty is also twofold, that is to say, either vulgar, as that which every man hath over his Goods, to dispose of them as he pleaseth; or that which is more eminent, being superiour to that which is vulgar, as that which every Society hath over the persons and Estates of all its members, so far as conduceth to the preservation of the whole. Thus doth Regal Power comprehend as well that of a Father, as that of a Master; so that a King, as he is a King, hath a greater Right in the Goods of his Subjects, so far as is necessary for the publick safety, than any private Subject hath in his own. Of this opinion was *Philo* the *Jew*, *Surely both the Silver, and the Gold, and whatsoever else is held dear and precious to Subjects, are more in the Power of those that govern, than of those that possess them*: Of the same mind also was *Pliny*, as appears by his Panegyrick, where speaking of a King he saith: *Cujus est quicquid est omnium, what all men have, is his.* And again: *Is there any thing that* Cæsar *can see, that is not his? that is, whensoever the Commonwealth doth necessarily require it.*

This is grounded on the Law of Nature, which makes that to be just, which is necessary for the preservation of Humane Society, which our blessed Saviour takes as granted; and therefore speaking of Taxes, he saith not, Offer or give as of a thing Arbitrary, which was in our Power either to do or not to do: But *render*, as of a thing that we owe or are trusted with for the benefit of another, which we are bound to restore whensoever we are thereunto required. And such indeed is that portion of every mans Goods, which is necessary for the defence of the Commonwealth, not ours, but *Cæsars*. St. *Paul* calls these *Debts*, which being joyned with the word, *Render*, makes it as clear as the Sun, that our Taxes are not Donatives, but just Debts: Nay they are the Greatest of Debts, due upon the strictest account, and therefore justly to be preferred before all other Debts, and in the first place to be discharged; And good reason, for the Non-payment of this Debt, may occasion the loss of the whole Estate, not private only, but publick.

VII. Aptness what it is.

That which before I called Aptitude or Fitness, *Aristotle* expresseth by the word, Worthiness, *Michael Ephesius* by another word implying Fitness or convenience. As for example, *If a Question should be put To whom in duty we stand most obliged? The Answer,* saith Cicero, *should be, to our Prince, to our Country, to our Parents; Because from them we receive the greatest Blessings we enjoy; next to those, we stand engaged to our Children, to whole Families, whose dependence is upon us alone: Then to our nearest relations, who for the most part do claim a share in our fortunes. Wherefore all these we are bound to relieve with all things necessary for life, but especially those above named: But to Eat, to Drink, to Converse with, to exhort, to advise, to comfort and sometimes to reprove, these are the proper Offices of Friendship.* So being to make our will, we consider who hath best deserved of us, *Quærimus dignissimos quibus nostra tradamus, we seek out such as are most worthy to whom to bequeath our Estates.*

De offic. l. 1.

See Book 2. ch. 7. § 9, 10.

Sen. de Ira lib. 4. c. 2.

VIII. Of Expletive and Attributive Justice.

Expletive Justice, which hath now gotten the name of Justice strictly taken, hath a respect to that which is our own, which Justice, *Aristotle* by too narrow and pincht a word, calls Commutative Justice; For that he that is possest of what is mine, should restore it to me, is not by Commutation, and yet it belongs to this Branch of Justice: And therefore in another place he finds out a more apt and pertinent word to express it by, calling it ἐπανορθωτικὴν, A Justice that makes the ballance even, or that repairs and restores to the full. Attributive Justice, which is called by *Aristotle*, *Distributive Justice*, hath a respect to aptness, worthiness or convenience, and is usually the Concomitant of such Vertues as are beneficial to others, as mercy, liberality, and State Providence But whereas the same *Aristotle* saith, that Expletive or Commutative Justice hath respect unto a simple and Arithmetical proportion; but Atributive, to a Comparative, which he calls a Geometrical proportion, as being the only proportion owned by Mathematicians; and which *Cassiodore* calls the comparing of mens habits or dispositions, and not unfitly by *Homer* described in this verse,

ἐν συναλλάγματος.

διανεμητικῆς

Things best to best, he gave, mean things to mean.

This may hold in some cases, but not in all; neither doth Expletive Justice of it self differ from Attributive in such use of Proportions, but in the matter whereabout it is Conversant, as is before shewed. Therefore as in all Elections made by Societies, if there be several Competitors the Choice is made by a Comparative Proportion, for *Datur dignitati;*

digniori; *the worthieſt is choſen*: ſo if there be no Competitor, and one only be found worthy of ſuch a publick office, it is Attributed to him by a ſimple proportion. Neither is that more true which ſome affirm, that Attributive Juſtice is Converſant only about things Common, but Expletive about things private, that is, appertaining to particular men. For on the contrary, If a man ſhall go about to bequeath his Eſtate by Will, he doth it by Attributive Juſtice, diſpenſing it according to the worthineſs of the perſons that are to receive it: And a City which renders out of that which is Common, what ſome of her Citiziens have beſtowed in publick, doth it by the Rule of Expletive Juſtice, not regarding the worthineſs of the perſons, but the bare Right of him that ought to receive it. This young *Cyrus* learnt of his Tutor in this caſe: There were two boyes that had two Coats, both of different Dimenſions, the bigger Boy had the leſſer Coat, and the leſſer Boy had the bigger Coat, which the bigger Boy took from him, being fit for himſelf, leaving him the leſſer Coat, which alſo was fit for him; whereof *Cyrus* being made Judge, and regarding more what was fit and convenient, than what was juſt and Right; adjudged the greater Coat to the bigger Boy, and the little Coat to the leſſer Boy: But his Tutor told him, *That he had done amiſs*: *For had he been to judge what was fitteſt, he had done well: But being to judge, whoſe each Coat was, he was to regard who had the beſt right to it, he that by force took the great Coat away, or he that made it, or bought it.* This is it that *Moſes* in his Law forbids, ſaying: *Thou ſhalt not regard the Poor in judgment, but ſhalt judge thy Neighbour with Righteouſneſs.* Which cannot be done, unleſs we do (as *Philo* adviſeth) *A perſonis litigantibus res abſtrahere*, *Conſider the matter, without regarding the parties contending.*

Aulus Gell.

Cyrus his miſtake.

Exod. 23. 3. Levit. 19. 15.

IX. Right as taken for a rule or Law defined.

There is alſo a Third ſignification of the word *Jus*, or Right, whch makes it Equivalent to the word, *Lex*, that is Law, when taken in its largeſt ſenſe; that is to ſay, as it is a rule to Moral Actions, obliging us to do that which is right: In which ſenſe it was that *Horace* took it where he ſaith,

For fear of wrong, ſtrict Laws invented were.

So in another place: *Jura neget ſibi data*;

He may deny that Laws for him were made.

Which the Scholiaſt thus expounds: He was a man that deſpiſed all Laws. In which Definition we ſay firſt that it muſt oblige, and herein it differs from Counſels and other preſcriptions, which though honeſt, yet fall not under this Notion of Law. And as for permiſſion, to ſpeak properly, it is not the Action of Law, but the denyal or Reſtriction of that Action, unleſs it be, as it obligeth another not to give him to whom ſuch permiſſion is granted, any lett or impediment. Beſides, it muſt oblige us to that which is Right, and not ſimply to what is juſt, becauſe Right in this ſence, doth not belong to Juſtice alone, (ſuch I mean, as we have heretofore explained) but unto the matter of other Vertues: An example whereof we have in that Law made by *Zeleucus*, who ordained a puniſhment to be inflicted upon him who contrary to the advice of his Phyſician preſumed to drink Wine. And therefore that Right which this Rule guides us unto, muſt needs be of a larger ſignification than that which is ſimply juſt. Of this Right ſo taken, the beſt partition is that of *Ariſtotle*'s, into that which is Natural, and that which is Voluntary, or as he there calls it Legitimate; the word Law being taken in the ſtricter ſenſe; which difference is acknowledged both by the *Hebrews*, and the Grecians, who when they would ſpeak properly, diſtinguiſh them by their proper names.

For many things may be juſt according to the letter of the Law, which notwithſtanding are not Right. Neither is it poſſible that any Lawgiver ſhould foreſee all the defects of his own Law: So that that which being agreeable to the Law ſtrictly taken, may ſeem juſt, is not ſo ſafe a Rule to walk by, as that which is juſt in this larger ſenſe, that is, Righteous and honeſt.

δικαίωμα. ἐντολή.

X. This Law of nature defined & diſtinguiſht from that which is not properly ſo.

That which we call natural Right, or the Law of Nature, is the dictate of Right reaſon, ſhewing the Moral Malignity, or the Moral Neceſſity that there is in any Act, by either the Repugnancy, or Congruity, it hath to Rational Nature it ſelf, and conſequently, that ſuch an Act is either commanded or forbidden by God, who is the very Author of Nature. Or as † *Philo* deſcribes it: *Right reaſon is a Law that cannot lie, it is not Mortal, nor given by any thing that is Mortal, it is not liveleſs, nor written in Paper, or inſculpt on Pillars that are liveleſs, but it is an immutable and immortal Law, being engraven by an immortal hand, on a mind that is immortal.* Cicero, as * *Lactantius* quotes him, gives this excellent deſcription of it: *Right reaſon is a perfect Law that will not lie, it is moſt agreeable to humane Nature, and Univerſally diffuſed throughout all mankind: It is incorruptible, immortal, which ſummons us to our duty by commanding it, and drives us from all fraud by forbidding it; neither are its Injunctions or prohibitions in vain to the Righteous:* though

† *Tit. omnem virum bonum eſſe liberum.*

* *Lib. 6. c. 8.*

though with the wicked they prevail not. To this Law nothing must be added, nor any part thereof detracted; and wholly to abrogate it, is impossible. It is not in the power either of the Senate or the people to absolve us from our obedience to this Law, neither need we to seek after any other Expositor than the Law it self: Neither is it one Law at Athens, *and another at* Rome, *one now, and another hereafter: But this one Law, being both Eternal and Immutable, shall bind all Nations and in all Ages: As there will ever be one Common Lord and Governour of all, which is God. He is the sole inventour, judge and giver of this Law, which he that refuseth to obey, must fly from (and so unman) himself, and although he may fly from, and haply avoid all other (which are thought) punishments; yet for the wilful contempt of this only, he shall be severely punished.* Now the Acts whereupon Right reason gives her Dictates, are such as are either good or evil, lawful or unlawful, simply and of themselves, and therefore must necessarily be understood to be either commanded or forbidden by God himself: And herein, the Law of Nature is different not from humane Laws only, but from the Voluntary Divine, for they do not command or forbid such things as are of themselves, and in their own Nature either due or unlawful; But by commanding them, they make them the one, and by forbidding them, the other. But for our better understanding of this Law of Nature, we must observe, That some things are said to belong unto the Law of Nature, not properly, or immediately, but (as the Schoolmen love to speak) by way of reduction, that is, for as much as the Law of Nature doth not prohibit them: As some things are said to be just, because they have nothing in them of injustice. And somethings are said to be lawful, which the Laws do neither prohibit nor punish. And sometimes by the abuse of the word, those things which our Reason approves to be honest, or at least, are so Comparatively to those that are opposed unto them, though they are not enjoyned us, yet are said to be due by this Natural Law: Moreover we must observe, that this Natural Law doth not determine of such things only, as have no dependence upon Mans will, but of many things also which the Common consent of mankind hath already moulded (as it were) into a Law. Thus was Dominion, as now in use, by Common consent, introduced as by a Law: But being introduced, this very Law of Nature doth instruct us, that to take away from any man that which is his own without his consent, is Impious; And from hence it is that *Paulus* the Lawyer concludes Theft to be prohibited by the Law of Nature; and *Ulpian*, that it is dishonest; And *Julian* tells us, *That after that which concerns the Worship of God, there is a Second Law in its own Nature holy, and of Divine Extraction, that enjoyns us at all times, and in all places, to abstain from Theft and Rapine; and that forbids us either in word, in deed, or in our most retired thoughts to mix or confound each others Properties.* For as *Cicero* out of *Chrysippus* well observes: *For any man to gain to himself what is necessary for his own lively hood, is not unjust; but to take it away by force from any other, is not Right. Euripides* also condemns this as hateful to God himself:

Some things belong to the Law of Nature by way of Reduction.

Julian.

De off. l. 3.

Námque odit ipse vim Deus: Nec divites
Nos esse rapto, sed probe partis cupit;
Spernenda, si non pure veniat, Copia est.
Communis Æther hominibus, Tellus quoque
In qua Ampliare cuique sic fas est domum,
Ut ab alienis rebus, ac vi temperet.

For God himself hates force, nor would that we
Grow rich by fraud, but Goods got honestly;
Riches unjustly gain'd, we should disdain:
The Earth, the Air, and eke the Ocean main,
Stand free to all, each may his House maintain
By these, so that from Rapine he abstain.

The Law of Nature is so Immutable, that God himself cannot alter it; for though the power of God be Immense, yet may somethings be said, whereunto this great power doth not extend it self, because what are so said, are said only, but have no sense which can express the thing, but they must contradict themselves: As therefore that twice two should not be four, God himself cannot effect; so neither can he, that what is intrinsecally evil, should not be evil. For as the being of things after they are, and as they are, depends not upon any other; so do the proprieties that necessarily follow that being: But such is the Malignity of some acts, compared with Nature as it is guided by Right reason. And therefore doth God himself suffer himself to be judged of according to this Rule, as appears by that of *Abraham* to God: *Shall not the Judge of all the world do Right?* Such a contradiction it is to say, that he that is the judge of the whole Earth

God himself cannot alter the Law of Nature.

Gen. 18. 25.

Earth should not do Right, that though it may be spoken, yet do the words though spoken bear no sense, but rather imply a manifest contradiction. The like we may find in other places of the holy Scriptures; it sometimes notwithstanding so falls out, that in these acts concerning which the Law of Nature hath determined something, there is some shew or appearance of change, which may easily deceive the unwary, whereas indeed the change is not in that Law which (as I have already said) is immutable, but in the things about which that Law is conversant; As for example, If he to whom I owe a just Debt, shall freely discharge me of it, I am not bound to pay it; not that the Law of Nature doth cease to command me to pay what I owe; but because that which I did owe, ceaseth to be my Debt being so discharged. For as *Arrianus* in *Epictetus* rightly argues, *To make a just Debt it is not enough, that the money was lent, but it is required that the Obligation remains uncancelled.* So when God commands any man to be put to death, or his Goods to be taken from him, Murther and Theft do not thereby become lawful, for these very words do imply sin; and no sin can be lawful. But those acts will not amount to Murther or Theft, which are done by the express command of him who is the Soveraign Lord both of our Lives and Fortunes. Lastly there are somethings justifiable by the Law of Nature, not simply, but so long as the condition of affairs stand thus: So till dominion was introduced the use of things was Naturally common; so before Laws and Courts of Judicature were established, by the Law of Nature, it was Lawful to recover by force what was our own, but not since.

Es. 5. 3. Ez. 18. 25. Jer. 2. 19. Mich. 6. 2. Rom. 2. 6, 3, 6.

XI. Natural instinct.

That distinction which we may read of in the books of the Roman Laws, is, namely that this immutable Law is either that which is common to men with beasts, which they call the Law of Nature in the stricter sense; and that which is peculiar unto men only which they sometimes call the Law of Nations, is of very little use. For nothing is properly capable of a Law, but that Nature that is capable of making use of General precepts, which was well observed by *Hesiod*, when he said:

> *To men hath God given Laws to be rul'd by:*
> *But Fish, and Beasts, and Fowls that soar on high,*
> *Having no Law, do on each other prey;*
> *But in good Laws doth all our safety lay.*

We say not of Horses and Lyons, saith *Cicero, that they are just; neither* as *Plutarch* observes, *do we by Nature make use of Law or justice against any other Creatures but man. Among all other Creatures not endued with reason,* saith *Lactantius, Nature is permitted to be her own Carver, Nocent aliis, ut sibi prosint; They destroy others to preserve themselves: And in so doing they are ignorant, that they do amiss. But man who hath a faculty to discern good from evil, wisely abstains from hurting others, though thereby he sometimes incommodate himself. Polybius* having declared upon what grounds men at first entred into Society, adds, That when the rest saw some men abusing their own Parents, and others behaving themselves injuriously towards their Benefactors; they could not chuse but grieve at it, whereof he gives this Reason: For mankind, saith he, *being endued with understanding and reason above all other Creatures, it is not credible, that they should behold acts so abhorrent from Nature without expressing some sign of discontent.* So likewise *Chrysostom, This we learn from Nature herself, that when we see one man abusing another, we cannot but sympathize with the injured Person, and swell with indignation against the injurer: although those injuries do not the least touch us.* And the greater the wrong is, the greater is our indignation against him that did it. *No man is equally incensed against him that cuts a purse only, as he is against him that commits a Murther.* But if at any time Justice be attributed to Brute Beasts, it is improperly, and only by reason of some Analogy or Resemblance that it hath to Humane Justice: As was that of the 30 *Elephants* recorded by *Pliny*, who could not by any means be provoked to be instrumental to the Cruelty of King *Bacchus* in worrying 30 other *Elephants* which he had bound to so many Trees on purpose to have them destroyed. And that also of the Aspe, recorded by the same *Pliny*, who having been fed daily at a mans table, killed one of her own young ones for killing the mans son, by whom he had been so fed; and would never afterwards come into the same house. These are said to be just acts, not properly, but only as they have some faint resemblance of Justice, and some light impressions of Reason. *Seneca* therefore denies *that Dumb Beasts partake any thing of Humane passions; yet he acknowledgeth that they have somewhat that is like unto them:* They cannot properly be said to be angry, yet have they some violent impulses like unto anger. *Non vitia sed vitiorum simulachra; they have no vices, but somewhat like unto Humane vices,* as *Origen* pleads against *Celsus.* But whether the act it self whereupon the Law of Nature hath decreed, be common to us with other living creatures, as the education of our Issue, *&c.* or proper unto us only, as that God should be Worshipped; doth nothing appertain to the very Nature of Right.

Off. lib. 1. Vita. Cat. M. Lib. 5. Lib. 6. De statuis. 13. Pliny l. 8. c. 5. Lib. 10. De ira l. 5. c. 3.

But

XII. The Law of Nature how proved.

But that any thing may be due by the Law of Nature, is uſually proved two waies, either by Arguments drawn *à priori*, or by ſuch as are drawn *à poſteriori*: Whereof the former ſort are more convincing; the latter more vulgar and plauſible: the proof by the former way is by ſhewing the neceſſary convenience or repugnancy that there is in any thing, with rational and Social Nature; for whatſoever can be proved to be neceſſary to the conſervation of Humane Nature, and Humane ſociety, muſt needs be inſtituted as a Law by the author of Nature, who is the God of order. That proof which is *à poſteriori* is, when we can though not demonſtratively, yet with very great probability, collect and conclude that to be a Dictate of the Law of Nature, which is unanimouſly believed to be ſo by all, or at leaſt, by the moſt Civilized of all Nations. For if the effect be Univerſal the cauſe muſt needs be ſo too: But of ſo Univerſal a perſwaſion there can be no other cauſe probably given, than that ſenſe it ſelf which is called common: That of *Heſiod* hath been highly celebrated by many;

> *What Nations have avow'd,*
> *Ought not by private men be diſallow'd.*

Quæ communiter ita videntur fida ſunt; that which to moſt men ſeems true, may be believed, ſaith *Heraclitus*. For we can have no ſtronger proof, or evidence of the truth of any thing that cannot be demonſtrated, than the general conſent of the wiſeſt in all Nations that it is ſo. This *Ariſtotle* took to be of *all others, the moſt powerful and convincing proof*: *Si in id quod dicimus omnes conſentiunt; If to what we ſay all men give their conſents.* Of the ſame mind was *Cicero, Whatſoever all Nations do grant, muſt needs be the voice of Nature*: [1 Tuſc.] So *Seneca* alſo, *What appears the ſame to all men, muſt undoubtedly be true. He that derogates* [Ep. 117.] *from this faith can never expect to be believed himſelf*, ſaith *Ariſtotle*: ſo likewiſe *Tertullian*, [Nic. l. 10, 11.] *Quod apud multos unum invenitur, non eſt erratum, ſed traditum; What is approved of by the moſt, is not error but Tradition.* I ſaid before that that muſt needs be a Dictate of Nature that was acknowledged to be ſo by all, or at leaſt, by the moſt Civilized Nations, and deſervedly; *for ſome people are ſo fierce and ſavage that they have hardly any humanity among them*, as *Prophyrie* rightly obſerved. *Now no man of ſound judgment ſurely, will impute this as a general reproach to all mankind: Surely this Law of Nature is immutable, and the ſame with all mankind that are of ſound and perfect mind: But if it appear other-* [Andr. Rhod.] *wiſe to ſuch as are of diſtempered and perverſe ſpirits, or have been ſo corrupted through an evil Education, that they have loſt even common ſenſe, and all natural Notions, it doth not in the leaſt weaken the authority of this Law, no more than it would evince, That Honey is not ſweet, becauſe it doth not ſeem ſo to ſuch as are ſick, or of diſtempered Pallates.* Not much diſcrepant from this is that of *Plutarch* in the life of *Pompey, There neither is, nor ever was, any man, by Nature wild and unſociable; many have indeed been made ſo by accuſtoming themſelves to live like Beaſts, beyond the bounds of Natures Laws; and yet even theſe, by changing their manner of life, or the place of their abode, are eaſily reduced to become gentle, and ſociable.* And therefore *Ariſtotle* in the deſcription that he gives of man, makes [Top. l. 5. c. 3.] this as it were his proper paſſion, *That he is by Nature a Creature mild and Tractable*; Eſpecially if we judge of him, according to that general rule, that the ſame *Ariſtotle* laies down, *Quid naturale ſit, ſpectandum in his quæ bene ſecundum naturam ſe habent, non in depravatis*; [Pol. l. 1. c. 5.] *What is the true nature of any thing, is beſt known by thoſe that are perfect in their own kind, and not by thoſe that are depraved and corrupted. For if we ſteer our judgments by this Rule, we cannot but acknowledge man to be in his own nature, the moſt meek, gentle, and peaceable creature of all others: as having nothing, by nature given him, whereby either to offend others or to defend himſelf*: Beſides as Nature hath made him the gentleſt of all other living Creatures; *So* (as *Philo* obſerves) *hath ſhe made him ſociable, nay greedy of Society, and hath alſo fitted him thereunto by giving him that excellent Ornament of ſpeech, wherewith his Paſſions, though never ſo fierce and raging, are ſuddenly, as if by ſome ſpell or incantation, becalmed.*

XIII. Voluntary Laws.

Another ſpecies of *jus*, as taken for a Law, there is, which we call voluntary, becauſe it is derived from the will; which is either Divine or humane.

XIV. Humane Laws divided.

We ſhall begin with that which is humane; becauſe it is more generally known, and this is either Civil, or that which is more extended, or that which is more contracted than Civil. The Civil Law is that which ariſeth from the Civil power. The Civil power is that which governs any City: Now a City is a compleat company of free-men, aſſociated for the defence of their own Rights, and for their common profit. That Law that is of leſſer extent, and ariſeth not from the Civil Power, though ſubject unto it, is various, comprehending under it that of a Father over his Children, that of a Maſter over his Servants, and the like. That Law which is more extenſive than that which is Civil, is that of Nations, which derives its authority from the joynt conſent of all, or, at leaſt, of many Nations: I ſay of many, becauſe there is hard-

hardly any Law besides that of Nature (which also is usually called the Law of Nations) that is common to all Nations; yea oft-times that which is accounted the Law of Nations in one part of the world, in another is not, as we shall shew hereafter, when we treat of Captivity and Postliminy. Now the Law of Nations is proved in the same manner as the unwritten Civil Law is, namely by continual use, and the testimony of men skilful in the Laws; and therefore *Dio Chrysostome* calls it the daughter of time and experience, and to this purpose are the Annals of former ages of singular use.

XV. The Divine voluntary Law divided.

The divine voluntary Law is that which is warranted by the express will of God, (as may be understood by the very word it self) whereby it is differenced from the naturall Law, which in some sense may be termed Divine also. And here that which was said by *Anaxarchus* in *Plutarch* (though somewhat confusedly) may take place, namely, That God doth not will things because they are just; but things are therefore just, that is, rightly due, because he wills them. Now this Law was given by God either to all mankind, or to one Nation; to all mankind we find that God gave Laws thrice. First, Immediately after the Creation of man. Secondly, in the Restauration of mankind after the Floud; and Thirdly, in that more perfect reparation by Christ. These three Laws do doubtless oblige all mankind, as soon as, and as far forth, as men arrive at the knowledge of them.

That this voluntary Divine Law was as obliging before the writing of it in Books or Tables, as it was or is since, is clear; for first, if the obliging power were only from the time when it was written by *Moses*, they that lived before *Moses* were no waies obliged by it, because till then it was not written. Secondly, then the obligation must needs extend it self to all the parts of the Law so written, and so to every circumstance of the Judaical Sabbath, as well as to the acknowledgement of the only true God. Neither is it sufficient to say, it was written in the times of *Adam* and *Noah*, it being uncertain unto us now, whether there were so Ancient a Record or not, much more, * whether that which was written, were as the Tables of the Law, written by the finger of God. * Dr. *Hammond.*

The Six Laws given by God to *Adam* and *Noah*, as First, that against strange and false worship. Secondly that of blessing the name of God, (that is, of adoring, invocating and praising God) Thirdly, that of judgment, (that is) of erecting of Magistrates and requiring administration of Justice. Fourthly, That of disclosing Nakedness (*i. e.*) setting bounds to lust and prohibiting Marriages, within such degrees. Fifthly, That of shedding blood against *Homicides.* And Sixthly, That against Theft and Rapine, and of doing to all as they would be done unto, are no where recorded in holy Writ, yet were they as obliging to the *Jews* that knew them, as any of the written Laws of *Moses*; we shall find them toucht at *Act.* 15. 20. But so surely, that had it not been for those writings of the *Jews* that were never within their Canons, nor in ours; we of these times had never known to what that reference belonged. And as all the Laws that were given to *Adam*, *Noah* and the rest of the Patriarchs, although not committed to writing, nor traduced to us, yet lost nothing of their obliging power to them, to whom they were given: so in the times of the new Law, although Christ revealed much of his Fathers will in Sermons, and other occasional discourses, very few whereof are written, and those that are, were not so written, until many years after his Resurrection; yet will no man say, that because they were not left written, therefore they did not oblige his Auditors.

XVI. The Law given to the *Jews* did not oblige strangers. Psalm 147.

Of all the Nations of the Earth there was but one to whom God vouchsafed to give Laws peculiar to themselves, which was that of the *Jews*: *What Nation*, saith *Moses*, *so great to whom God hath given Statutes and judgements, so righteous, as this whole Law?* Deut. 4. 7. So likewise *David*, *The Lord hath shewed his word unto* Jacob, *his Statutes and ordinances unto* Israel: *Non ita fecit genti ulli*; *He hath not done so to any Nation, neither have the Heathen knowledge of his Laws.* Doubtless then those *Jews* (and among them *Tryphon* himself in his disceptations against *Justine*) do grosly err, who hold, That even Foreigners, if they would be saved, must submit to the yoke of the Mosaical Law. For that Law binds none but those to whom it was given, and who these are, the Preface to the Law it self will plainly declare; *Audi Israel*, *Hear O Israel*, saith the Text: And every where we read, that the Covenant was made with them, and that they were chosen to be the peculiar people of God; which *Maimonides* acknowledgeth to be true, and proves it out of *Deut.* 33. 4. But even amongst the *Jews*, there always lived some Foreigners being holy men; and such as feared God, as the *Syrophœnician* Woman, *Mat.* 15. 22. Cornelius, *Acts* 10. 2. The Grecians mentioned *Acts* 18. 4. whom they called *the pious among the Gentiles*; such as are termed strangers, *Lev.* 22. 25. and a sojourner, *Lev.* 25. 47. whom the *Chaldee* Paraphrast calls an inhabitant that is uncircumcised, whereof we may read, *Exod.* 12. 45. who was distinguished from a Proselyte; who, though a Foreigner, yet was circumcised, as appears by comparing this place with that of *Numb.* 9. 14. These uncircumcised Sojourners *Maimonides* admits may be partakers of the blessings of the life to come.

Rom. 2. 9, 10. St. *Chrysostome* upon the *second* to the *Romans*, where St *Paul* mentions the *Jew*, and *Gentile*, writes thus: *What Jew, and what Gentile doth St.* Paul *here mean? surely those*, saith he, *that lived before Christ*, as Job, *the* Ninevites, Melchisedeck, Cornelius, *&c. And what Græcians doth he discourse of? Surely not such as were Idolaters, but such as worshipped God according to the Law of Nature, who setting aside the Jewish Ceremonies, religiously observed all things that appertained to an holy life.* And again, *The Græcian he calls, not him that worshipped Idols, but him that was pious and devout, though he submitted not to the Jewish Rites.* And thus likewise doth he expound that of St. *Paul*: *To him that is without Law, as being free from the Law.* And in another place,

A

A Greek he calls not him, that was given to Idols, but him that invoked the true God, and yet observed not the Jewish Ceremonies, as their Sabbaths, their Circumcision, their ablutions and the like; but yet endeavoured to steer the whole course of his life, according to the Rules of wisdom and true piety. Now these, as the Hebrew Doctors themselves testify, were bound to live in conformity to the Laws given to *Adam* and *Noah*, abstaining from Idols and Blood, and from other things hereafter exprest, but not to the Laws peculiar to the *Jews*; and therefore, whereas it was not lawful for the *Jews* to eat the flesh of any thing that dyed of it self, yet it was lawful for the stranger living among them so to do, *Deut.* 14. 21. unless it were to some particular Laws wherein it was expresly provided that as well the stranger as the home born was bound to observe them. For we read that it was lawful to the stranger, that never submitted to the Mosaical Law, to worship God even in the Temple at *Jerusalem*; yet so, that he stood in a particular place by himself, separate from that of the *Hebrews*, as you may read 1 *Kings* 8. 41. *Jo.* 12. 20. *Act.* 8. 27. Neither did *Elisha* enjoin *Naaman*, nor *Jonas* the *Ninevites*, nor *Daniel Nebuchadnezzar*, nor the other Prophets perswade the *Syrians*, *Moabites*, or *Ægyptians*, unto whom they wrote, that there was any necessity at all for them to submit to the yoke of the Jewish Law. And what I say here of the whole Law is true also of Circumcision, which was as it were, the introduction unto it, with this only difference, That to the whole Law of *Moses*, the Israelites only were bound, but to that of Circumcision all the posterity of *Abraham*: And from hence it was, that the *Idumeans* being the off-spring of *Esau*, *Ismael*, or *Cetura*, were compelled by the Israelites to be circumcised as both the Jewish, and Grecian Histories inform us. Besides of all other Nations, that of St. *Paul* holds true, *Seeing that the Gentiles who have not the Law, do by Nature, the things of the Law*; (that is, by their own manners and Customs, flowing from the original fountain of reason) (unless any man had rather referr the word, *Nature*, to the words foregoing, thereby opposing the Gentiles to the *Jews*, who as soon as they were born had their Law instilled into them), *these having not the Law, are a Law unto themselves, as shewing the work of the Law written in their hearts, their thoughts and Consciences mutually accusing or excusing themselves.* And that also in the 26*th* verse of the same Chapter, *If the uncircumcision keep the Law, shall not his uncircumcision be accounted for Circumcision.* Thus doth *Chrysostome* expound that place of St. *Paul* before cited, *The Gentiles by Nature*, that is, *by the very Dictates of Right reason:* And presently after *in this*, saith he, *are they to be admired, That they stood in no need of the Law to guide them. And that instead thereof, they were guided only by the use of reason and the light of their own Consciences.* Thus also doth *Tertullian* argue against the *Jews* of his age; *Long*, saith he, *before* Moses *wrote the Law in the Tables of stone, there was (as I will justifie) a Law naturally understood and observed by the Patriarchs.* And therefore *Ananias* the *Jew* in *Josephus* did rightly inform *Izates Adiabenus*, *That God might be duly worshipped and well pleased with us, Although we were not circumcised.* And *Triphon* himself grants this to *Justin*, *That there was some hopes left him of a better condition, though he did persist in the way of his own Philosophy.* Now the reasons why so many strangers among the *Jews* were circumcised, and thereby obliged to keep the Law, (as St. *Paul* expounds it) were, partly that they might partake of the priviledges of the Jewish Commonwealth, for Proselytes enjoyed the same Rights with the Israelites, as may be gathered out of *Numb.* 15. and is plainly asserted *Exod.* 12. 27. And partly, that thereby they might be made capable of those Promises which were not common to all Nations, but peculiar to the *Jews* only: Although I cannot deny but that there grew up afterwards an erroneous opinion, affirming that without the pale of the Jewish Church there could be no Salvation. From hence then we may collect; that we Gentiles stand obliged to no part of the Mosaical Law, as a Law properly so called, because all obligation beyond that which ariseth from the Law of Nature, is derived from the will of the Lawgiver. But that it was the will of God, that any other Nation besides the *Jews* should be bound by that Law, cannot be made out by any solid arguments; we need not therefore, as to ourselves, prove the abrogation of that Law, because it cannot be said to be abrogated as to them, whom it never bound: yea even to the *Jews* themselves the obliging power was abolished, as to the Ceremonial Law, as soon as the Evangelical Law began to be promulgated; which was plainly revealed to St. *Peter*, *Acts* 10. 15. And as to the rest, after that people ceased to be a people by the destruction of their City, and that general desolation that succeeded, without any hopes of restitution; but we who are strangers are not freed from that Law, by the advent of Christ, but by Christ we who before had nothing but a faint and obscure hope, placed only in the goodness of God, are now strengthened by a clear and firm Covenant, assuring us that we also may grow up together with the *Jews*, (being the sons of the Patriarchs) into one Church, the Judaical Law, (which was that Partition-wall that kept us asunder) being now taken away, as St *Paul* testifies to the *Ephesians*.

Orat. 2. de statuis.

Rom. 2. 14.

Ant. lib. 20. *c.* 2.

The reason why strangers were circumcised.

Gal. 5. 3.

Acts 10. 15.

Eph. 2. 14.

C Since

XVII. What Christians may learn from the Moſaical Law.

Since the Moſaical Law cannot directly oblige us (as hath been already proved) let us now ſee of what other uſe it will be to us, as well in this caſe of War, as in the like doubtful caſes; the knowledge of this being very neceſſary for the clearing of diverſe caſes: For in the firſt place, from hence we may be aſſured, that what was heretofore commanded in that Law, is not repugnant to the Law of Nature. For ſince the Law of Nature is (as I have already ſaid) perpetual, and immutable, nothing can be commanded us by God contrary to this Law, because God can never be unjuſt. Beſides the Law of *Moſes* is (as the Pſalmiſt ſpeaks) pure and right, and as the Apoſtle ſaith, *Holy juſt and good*; which places are to be underſtood of the precepts of the Law only. But as to the permiſſions of the Law we muſt ſpeak of them more diſtinctly: Now legal permiſſion (for that which reſpects the bare fact and ſignifies the removal of impediments only, I ſhall not here meddle with) is either full and perfect, which gives us a right to do ſomethings altogether lawfully; or leſs full and imperfect, which gives us only an impunity with men, and a Right that no man ſhall give us any lawful lett, or impediment in the doing of it. Concerning the former of theſe, the ſame may be ſaid as is of poſitive precepts, namely, That what the Law thus permits, cannot be contrary to the Law of Nature, but of what is permitted in the latter ſenſe, the caſe may be otherwiſe: but this collection takes place very rarely. Becauſe where the words permitting are ambiguous, it is much more convenient for us to judge of whether of theſe two Permiſſions, it is to be underſtood by the Law of Nature, than by arguing from the manner of the permiſſion, to proceed to judge of the Law of Nature: In the next place, Soveraign Princes, being Chriſtians, may from hence learn, to form their Laws according to thoſe given by *Moſes*; unleſs it appear that thoſe Laws were ſuch as did wholly relate either to the coming of Chriſt, or to the Evangelical Law not then revealed; or that ſuch Laws are contrary to what Chriſt did, either in general, or particularly, command. For excepting theſe three caſes, no other can be imagined, why what *Moſes* commanded ſhall now be unlawful. Again we may hence learn, that whatſoever was enjoyned by *Moſes*, which may ſerve to the improvement of thoſe vertues which Chriſt exacted from his Diſciples, ought now to be as ſtrictly (if not more) obſerved by us than heretofore it was by them: The reaſon whereof is this, becauſe what vertues ſoever Chriſt requires of us, as humility, patience, love, *&c.* are to be performed in an higher degree, than they were under the ſtate of the Jewiſh Law: And not without good reaſon, becauſe of thoſe Celeſtial promiſes that are held forth unto us in the Goſpel, which are more clear than under the Law. *Our Chriſtian liberty*, ſaith *Tertullian*, *is no way injurious unto innocency, for the whole Law as to piety, truth, conſtancy, chaſtity, juſtice, mercy, benevolence, and modeſty, ſtands yet unrepealed.* Nay, *a larger proportion of theſe* (ſaith *Chryſoſtome*) *is expected from us, becauſe the graces of the ſpirit are more plentifully poured down upon us, than they were upon them. Athanaſius* alſo tells us, *That Chriſt makes the precepts of the Law to be of a larger extent than* Moſes *did: For* Moſes *ſaid only Thou ſhalt not kill; but Chriſt ſaith, Thou ſhalt not be angry unadviſedly:* Moſes *ſaid, Thou ſhalt not commit Adultery; but Chriſt ſaith, Thou ſhalt not look to luſt after a woman.* And therefore the Old Law in compariſon to the New is ſaid *to be weak, and not without blemiſh.* And Chriſt is ſaid to be *the end of the Law.* But the Law, *our School Miſtriſs*, or *our guide to lead us unto Chriſt*, Gal. 3. 25. So the Law of the Sabbath, and that of Tithes, do oblige us Chriſtians, not to yield a leſſer proportion of time for the worſhip of God, than a ſeventh day, nor a leſſer proportion of the fruits of the Earth for the Prieſts Alimony, and other the like ſacred uſes, than the tenth part.

Pſal. 19. 8. Rom. 7. 12.

Vid. Chryſoſt. ad 7 ad Rom. juxta finem.

Chriſtian Princes may frame their Laws according to thoſe of *Moſes*, unleſs in three caſes.

De Pudicitia.

De Virginitate 94.

On the firſt of St. Mat.

Heb. 7. 19. 8. 4. Rom. 10. 5. Gal. 3 25.

CHAP.

CHAP. II.

Whether it be lawful at any time to make War.

I. *That to make War, is not repugnant to the Law of Nature, proved by reason.*
II. *By Histories.*
III. *By consent.*
IV. *That it is not repugnant to the Law of Nations.*
V. *That the voluntary Divine Law, before Christ, was not against it, proved; and the objections to the contrary, answered.*
VI. *Certain precautions concerning this question: whether War be repugnant to the Law of the Gospel?*
VII. *Arguments for the negative opinion out of the holy Scriptures.*
VIII. *The arguments out of Scripture for the Affirmative, answered.*
XI. *The consent of the primitive Christians concerning this, examined.*

I. The Law of Nature is not against it.

HAving thus taken a view of the springs from whence all Rights flow, let us now begin with the most general Question, Whether any War be just, or whether it be lawful at any time to make War? But this very question with others that follow are to be discust in the first place by the Law of Nature. *Cicero* in several places very learnedly proves, out of the books of some *Stoicks*, That there are some principles instill'd into us by Nature her helf, as soon as we are born; as to love our selves, and to hold nothing dearer unto us, than our selves; and in order to the conservation of that being, that she hath given us, to love and rejoyce in those things which conduce to the safety of the whole body, and of every member thereof: and to abhor those things that tend to its destruction. Hence it comes, that there is no man but being left to his own choice, had rather that all his members should be proportionable and entire, than by use broken or crooked. Therefore our first duty (according to Natures instinct) is to desire those things most, that are most agreeable to our own Nature, and to avoid those that are destructive unto it. But these things thus known, and reason beginning to sprout forth from her latent seeds, then our second duty is to follow such things as are agreeable to reason it self, which is ever more to be preferred before those that are convenient to the body; and consequently to embrace those things that accord with justice and honesty, rather than those whereunto we are led by sense and appetite; because the Principles of our Nature do chiefly commend us to right reason, as to our best guide and protectrix. *For as Nature in all other things never produceth her best and choicest, fruits until she arrives at maturity; so neither doth humane nature her self produce her best operations, until reason grows up to perfection.* And therefore should Reason it self be much dearer unto us, than those things whereby we arrive unto it. Now these things being undeniably true, and without any farther demonstration by all men of sound judgment granted; it follows that in examining the Law of Nature, we find out, what is agreeable to those beginnings or first principles of Nature: and then that we proceed to that, which though in order of time later, yet is much more worthy to be followed; and that not as accepted only, if it may be granted; but as that, which by all means is to be required. Moreover that which we call, honest, according to the diversity of the matter, is sometimes taken strictly; so as to consist (as I may say) in a very point, from which if a man deviate on either side, he falls into vice; and some times largely, for that which may be commendably done, and yet blamelesly either left undone, or done otherwise. Now concerning things honest in this latter sense, are all Laws, both divine and humane, conversant, making those things due Debts, which of themselves are commendable only. Above, when we treated of the Law of Nature, it was questioned whether any thing might be done, not unjustly: But that we understood to be unjust, which had a necessary repugnancy to rational and social Nature. Now amongst the first principles of Nature we do not find any thing repugnant to War; nay all things seem highly to favour it, for both the ends of War (being the conservation both of our lives and Limbs, and the acquiring or retaining of what doth necessarily conduce thereunto) are most agreeable to Natural instinct. And to do this by force, if necessity require it, is a like natural; for why else hath nature given unto every Creature strength, to help and to defend it self? All sorts of Annimals, saith *Xenophon*, are expert in some kind of War, having no other instructer than Nature.

Right reason is Natures best guide. *Sen. Ep.* 124. Ep. 76. 121. 128.

Honesty considered two waies strictly, as in a point, or largely. For whatsoever may be commendably done, and yet may be blamelesly undone.

Each

Each, both its enemy, and preserver knows;
She weapons gives, and how to use them shews.

So likewise *Horace*:

Who taught the Woolf *to bite, the* Oxe *to gore,*
The Horse to kick? all's set on Natures score.

But *Lucretius* yet more fully:

All beasts, their power to hurt, full well can tell;
Calves, ere they sprout, know'ng where their Horns should dwell;
With angry Brows, their urging foes repel.

To the like purpose is that of *Martial*:

The Calfe *with unhorn'd brows to fight prepares.*

De non esu. Animal. *Every living creature*, saith *Porphyry*, *is taught by Nature wherein its strength, and wherein its weakness lies: and accordingly to expose the one; to defend the other: the* Libard *makes use of his teeth, the Lyon of his claws and teeth; the Horse defends himself with his Hoofes, and the Oxe with his Horns.* Wherewith accords that of *Galen*, *We see every living Creature making use of that part for its own defence, wherein it conceives it self strongest; the young Colt will kick with his Hoofs before they be hardened; and the* Calfe *threaten with its head, though it have no Horns.* (*De usu partium.*) And in his book of the use of the members, he tells us, *That man is a creature, fitted by Nature either for War, or peace; for although he be born unarmed, yet hath Nature given him hands apt to provide, and to make use of Arms: which Infants, we see, do of their own accord without instruction.* It was well observed of St. *Chrysostome*, (*De statuis.* 11.) *That to all Creatures who want the use of reason, Nature hath affixed Arms to their bodies, as to the Oxe horns, to the Boar Tusks, to the Lyon claws: But to me*, saith he, *hath God assigned Arms not affixt to my body, but without it, hereby shewing that he intended man for a gentle creature, and that it was not lawful for me at all times to make use of such Arms. For as I often lay them aside, so I sometimes assume them, that therefore I may be the more free and at liberty, and not alwaies compell'd to go armed; God though he hath given me Arms, yet hath placed them without me.* *Aristotle* also tells us, That hands were given unto man instead of a Sword, a Spear, or any other weapon; because he can thereby make use of all. Hence then we may conclude, That in the first principles of Nature, there is nothing that is repugnant to War. But if we will examine the Lawfulness of War by right reason, and the Nature of humane Society, which is the second and most perfect rule to judge by; we shall plainly perceive that all manner of force is not thereby forbidden, but that only which is repugnant to humane Society, that is, which invades another mans Right: for the main end whereunto such Societies were at first entred into, was that the whole should engage it self, that each part thereof should freely enjoy its own, which without much difficulty may be presumed to have been in force; although that which we now call Dominion had not been introduced. Because our lives, our limbs, and our liberties, had even then been our own, and could not without manifest injury have been invaded, or taken from us. So likewise, to have made use of such things as were then in common, and to have consum'd as much of them, as was necessary to sustain Nature, had been even then the right of the Occupant. But since Dominion hath been either by Law, or custom established, this is much easier to be admitted and understood, which I shall take leave to express in *Cicero*'s own words*: *To purloyn from another that which is his, or to enrich our selves by the spoil of others, is more repugnant to Nature, than sickness, poverty, imprisonment, banishment, yea than death it self: For it dissolves that Contignation that there is, or should be betwixt mankind; for if this be admitted, it must necessarily disjoynt, and break in pieces, that sweet consociation that there is between man and man; than which nothing can be more agreeable to humane Nature. If every member of the body should be possest with this opinion, That it should enjoy better health, if it could attract unto it self the nourishment of the member next unto it, and should thereupon do it, would not the whole body languish presently and die? So if it were permitted that what one man soweth, another should reap, that what one man planted, another should receive the fruits of, or that one man should enrich himself by the spoils of another; it is impossible that that Society should long stand. For as it is most natural for every man to love himself best, and to feed and support himself rather than another, with what is*

To rob another is more against Nature than sickness, imprisonment, or than death.

* *De offic. l.* 3.

his

his own; so there can be nothing more unnatural, or abhorring from right reason, than for a man to take away from his neighbour that wherewith he should sustain himself; or to improve his own Estate by the ruin of his Neighbours. Neither is this more agreeable to the Laws of Nature and Nations, than it is to the municipal Laws of every City; for to this point do they all steer, at this they chiefly collime, this they all of them strictly command and enjoyn, That every member of that Society should freely enjoy his own without fear or disturbance: For by this means is that excellent conjunction and Confederation between them preserved sound and intire. And he that willingly breaks this Golden Chain of humane Society, is by the general consent and astipulation of all people, adjudged as unworthy of humane Society: and therefore like some noxious beast is deservedly prosecuted to Banishment, bonds, imprisonment, yea and even to death it self. This then being agreeable to the Laws of Nature, and Nations, and being the end of all municipal Laws, must needs be the Dictate of right reason, and so the voice of God himself: whereunto whosoever willingly conforms himself, will certainly so moderate his desires, that he will never covet what is not his own; nor either by force or fraud impoverish others for his own private gain; than which nothing can be more unnatural, nothing more unreasonable, nothing more destructive to humane Society. Neither is it against the Nature of humane Society, for a man to provide for himself so as he do not damnifie his Neighbour; and by consequence that force which doth not violate another mans right is not unjust: which the same *Cicero* thus expresseth, *Since there are but two sorts of decertations, the one by arguments, the other by plain force: the former being proper to men, the other to beasts, we ought to make the latter our refuge, when by the former we cannot prevail.* And in another place, *Quid est, quod contra vim fieri sine vi posset? What remedy can we have against force, but by force?* So *Vulpian, To repel force with force, is a right that Nature ordains for all creatures.* *Ep. Fam. l.12. ep. 3.*

Arms against Arms, all Nations do allow. *Ovid.*

II. This proved by Histories. What I have already laid down, namely, that it is not every War that is repugnant to the Law of Nature, may be farther justified out of the Sacred Story. For God by his High-Priest *Melchisedeck*, did approve of the War made by *Abraham*, and his Confederates, upon those four Kings that came to plunder *Sodom*. Yea and *Melchisedeck* blesseth God for the Victory; *Blessed*, saith he, *be the most high God who hath delivered thine enemies into thine hand*, Gen. 14. 20. And yet had *Abraham* no special Commission from God for it; but was excited and perswaded thereunto by the mere Law of Nature, being himself a man not only exceedingly holy, but very wise, according to the Testimony that *Berosus* and *Orpheus* give of him. The War made by the Israelites upon the seven Nations whom God delivered up unto them, I purposely omit; because they had a special warrant from God to make War upon that people, who had highly provoked him: and therefore those Wars are in holy Writ called The Wars of the Lord, being undertaken by Divine not humane authority. More to our purpose was that War made by the Israelites under the conduct of *Moses* and *Joshua* against the *Amalekites*, who had forceably opposed them in their passage towards *Canaan*; which though it was not commanded to be done, yet being done was approved of by God, *Exod.* 17. Nay farther God himself prescribed unto *Moses* certain general and lasting Rules and Ordinances how he should make War, whereby he sufficiently testified, That War might sometimes be just, though we have no special command from God to make this or that War; for there *Moses* makes a manifest difference between the case of the seven Nations, and the case of other people: For these they might receive to mercy, but not them. And seeing he doth not prescribe, for what particular causes they might make a just War, it may reasonably be presumed, that those causes may easily be discerned by the very light of Nature: such was the cause of the War that *Jephtha* made against the *Ammonites*, for the defence of their boundaries, *Judg.* 11. And that which *David* was enforced upon, against those who had violated the rights of his Ambassadors, 2 *Sam.* 10. And it is worthy to be observed what the Author to the *Hebrews* records, concerning those pious Heroes, *Gideon*, *Baruck*, *Sampson*, *Jephtha*, *David*, *Samuel*, &c. That by faith, they subdued Kingdoms, and put whole Armies of the aliens to flight, *Heb.* 11. 34. Where under the notion of faith, is included a full assurance they had, that what they then did, was acceptable to God. And upon this presumtion also it was, that *David* is said, by a wise woman, to fight the Lords battle, and made a pious and just War, which could not be if all manner of War had been utterly unlawful. Exod. 17. 14. Deut. 20. 10, 15. Heb. 11. 34. 1 Sam. 25.28.

III. By examples. To the authority of Sacred Story, we may add for greater confirmation, the universal consent of all, or at least, of the wisest of all Nations, concerning that force whereby our lives are defended. *Cicero* gives us the Testimony of Nature it self, *Est hæc, non scripta sed nata lex; This*, saith he, *is no written Law, but a Law that is born with us, that if* Pro Milone *if our lives be endangered, either through force, or Treachery; all means we can use for our safety are just and honest.* And again, *This, the learned are taught by reason; the unlearned by necessity; the Nations by custom, and the very beasts themselves by natural instinct, to repel by all means whatsoever, all force and violence that shall be offered us whereby our bodies, our members, or our lives shall be endangered.* So *Cajus* the Lawyer, *Against all imminent dangers, natural reason teacheth us to defend our selves.* And *Florentinus*, *Whatsoever any man doth in his own defence is just and lawful.* *Josephus* also informs us, *That to preserve life is a Law that Nature her self hath imprinted in all living Creatures. And for this cause it is, that they who endeavour to dispoil us of our lives, are justly accounted our enemies.* Which indeed hath so much of natural equity, that even amongst beasts, who (as I have said already) have nothing of Justice or Law among them, more than a faint shadow or resemblance of it, we distinguish between that beast, which of his own accord assaults us, and that which assaults us in its own defence. And *Ulpian* notwithstanding that he had said before, That Beasts wanting the use of reason, could not be said properly to do wrong; yet he presently subjoyns, that when Rams or Bulls fight and kill each other, by the Law of *Qu. Mutius*, they were to distinguish between them, so, that if he perished, that was the aggressor, the action was null; but if he perished, that was provoked, the action was good. The ground of which Law is set down by *Pliny*, *Because*, saith he, *there is no sensible Creature, but what is impatient of an injury, and being assaulted, will assault again. For as he well observes,* Lyons *will not prey upon* Lyons, *nor Serpents bite or sting Serpents: yet if any violence be offered them; there are none but will express somwhat that is like unto anger: none so stupid but being hurt, will to his utmost power defend himself, so that in all contests that which is defensive is the most just, because Natura potior est salus nostra, quam adversarii pernities* *; *Our own preservation is more agreeable to Nature, than the destruction of an enemy.*

De Bello Jud. l. 3. c. 25.

* *Quintil. l. 7. c. 2.* See *Philo* in the Preface upon the fifth Commandment.

IV. That War is not repugnant to the Law of Nations.

By the Law of Nature then, (which may likewise be called the Law of Nations) it is evident, that all War is not to be condemned; nor yet by the voluntary Law of Nations, as Histories will sufficiently instruct us, wherein the Laws, Customs, and manners of all people are faithfully recorded. Nay by the very Law of Nations were Wars introduced, saith *Hermogenianus*; so he that wrote the lives of men, famous in their several ages, in that of the life of *Themistocles*, tells us, *That he acknowledged that it was by his advice, that the* Athenians *surrounded their City with Walls; which notwithstanding by the common right of all Nations they might do, whereby to defend their publick and private Gods from the fury of their enemies.* Yet whereas I said before, that by the Law of Nations War was at the first introduced, the words will as I conceive, admit of a better sense, than what at the first view they seem to import; as namely, that there are some certain forms and Ceremonies introduced by the Law of Nations, which by the consent of Nations do give such and such peculiar effects to such Wars as have them: whence ariseth that distinction whereof we shall hereafter make use; between a War that is solemn by the Law of Nations (which also is said to be just, that is, full and absolute) and a War that is not solemn, yet ceaseth not therefore to be just, that is, congruous to Right: for even other Wars (so as the cause be good) the Law of Nations doth neither approve of, nor yet impugne, as shall be shewed more at large hereafter. *It is ordained as a Law amongst all Nations*, saith *Livy*, *that Arms may be repelled with Arms.* With whom agrees *Florentinus*, *It is generally consented unto by all Nations, that we may forceably drive away all violence and wrongs offered unto us, whereby our lives are endangered.* Which justifies all Wars that are merely defensive; for as much as Nature is much better pleased with its own preservation, than with the destruction of enemies.

Lib. 43.

V. Nor to the Voluntary divine Law before Christ.

But the main question is, Whether it be agreeable to the divine voluntary Law to make War? And here if any shall object, that the Law of Nature being immutable, nothing can be decreed by God himself contrary to it. I answer, that this is true in such things as the Law of Nature doth expresly either command, or forbid: But not in such things as by the Law of Nature are only lawful, only, that is, tolerated: for such as these, because they belong not properly to the Law of Nature, but are without its jurisdiction, may be either commanded, or forbidden. The first objection that is brought out of the holy Scriptures against War, is that Law given to *Noah* and his posterity, *Gen.* 9. 5, 6. Where God speaks thus: *Surely the blood of your lives will I require, at the hands of every beast will I require it; and at the hands of man, at the hand of every mans brother will I require the life of man. Whosoever shed mans blood, by man shall his blood be shed: for in the image of God made he man.* Some there are that would have the former words of requiring blood, understood in the largest sence; and the latter words of shedding blood, they would have to be a commination, and not an approbation; but I like neither. For the prohibition to shed blood is of no larger extent, than that in the Moral Law, Thou shalt not kill: which doth neither prohibit a Magistrate,

Objections answered.

Gen. 9. 5, 6.

giſtrate, from putting to death an obſtinate Malefactor, nor doth it forbid a lawful war. Neither doth the one or the other ſo much enjoyn any new thing, as revive and proclaim that old Law of Nature, which through evil cuſtom had been almoſt defaced; where by killing and ſhedding of blood, we are to underſtand ſuch a manner of putting a man to death, as implies ſome vice: As by the word *Homicide* or *Murther*, we underſtand not every putting a man to death, but the wilful deſtroying of an innocent perſon. But that which follows concerning the ſhedding of blood for blood, is to be underſtood (as I conceive) not ſo much of the bare fact, as of the right to do it, which I thus explain; That every man ſhould ſuffer as much evil from others, as he hath done unto others, is not naturally unjuſt, according to that old *Rhadamanthæan* Law,

To ſuffer as we do, is juſt and right.

That *Phalaris* ſhould be tormented in his own Bull, *That he that intended miſchief to another, ſhould ſuffer the ſame miſchief from another*, is *juſtiſſima patiendi norma*, as *Seneca* ſpeaks; *The moſt equal rule of ſufferance that can be ordained.* Out of a deep ſence of this natural Equity it was, that *Cain* (his hands yet reeking in his brothers blood) paſt this ſentence upon himſelf; *And it ſhall come to paſs, that whoſoever finds me, ſhall kill me.* But God in the infancy of the world, either by reaſon of the ſcarcity of men, or becauſe this ſin was rarely practiſed, and ſo the leſs need of exemplary puniſhments to deter them, did by an Edict repreſs that which ſeemed naturally to have been lawful, and adjudged the Homicide to wander as a vagabond, forbidding all men to have any commerce, or to make any contract with him, yet would he not have his life taken from him. Thus alſo did *Plato* ordain among his Laws; and that this puniſhment was much uſed among the ancient Greeks, *Euripides* teſtifies in theſe words: Gen. 4. 14.

How wiſely did our Anceſtors decree,
That he that guilty was of blood, ſhould flee
Far from Commerce, or ſight of men, that he
Puniſh'd by flight, rather than death, might be?

To the ſame purpoſe is that of *Thucydides: It is very probable that anciently ſmall puniſhments were awarded to great crimes; but at length thoſe being ſlighted, they proceeded to death.* *Servius* upon the firſt book of *Virgil*, deſcanting upon theſe two words, *Solvetis*, *Luetis*, ſaith: That theſe words were derived from the payment of money, *Antiquorum enim pœnæ omnes pecuniariæ fuêre: For among the Ancients all puniſhments were pecuniary.* The like we find in *Lactantius*, *Hitherto it was accounted impious to put men to death, though never ſo wicked*; grounding their conjecture upon that one notable example of *Cain*, That it was not the will of God that *Homicides* ſhould be ſo puniſhed, whereupon it grew at length into a Law; ſo that *Lamech* not long after having committed the like ſin (or rather (if he did commit the like) for *Moſes* his words will bear this ſence) yet by this one example promiſed to himſelf the ſame impunity, *Gen.* 4. 24. Nevertheleſs, though before the Flood, in the age of the Giants, through the remiſneſs of puniſhments men grew ſavage and outragious, killing each other like beaſts; yet when after the flood, the earth was fully ſtockt with men, leſt the ſame licenſe ſhould again increaſe, God thought fit to reſtrain it by a more ſevere puniſhment: So that correcting the lenity of the former age, what nature before judged not unjuſt, he himſelf permitted to be done, namely, that he that ſheds mans blood, ſhould himſelf be put to death, and that he that killed an Homicide, ſhould be held innocent. But afterwards Tribunals being erected, this power for many weighty reaſons was transferred to Judges only; yet ſo, that ſome prints of that ancient cuſtom were to be ſeen, even after *Moſes* his law was given (whereof more ſhall be ſaid anon) as may appear by that right which was granted unto him that was next of kin unto him that had been ſlain. We have *Abraham*'s practice to juſtifie this gloſs, who though he very well knew the Law that God gave unto *Noah*, *Gen.* 9. 6. yet took Arms againſt the four Kings, preſuming on that principle of Nature, that to deſtroy the deſtroyer, was not diſpleaſing to the God of Nature: Thus *Moſes* commanded the Iſraelites to fight the Amalekites, who with Arms oppoſed their paſſage into *Canaan*, having no other warrant for ſo doing, than the bare Law of Nature: For it appears not that in this, as in other like caſes, he conſulted with God at all, *Exod.* 17. 9. Exod. 17. 9.
Whereunto we may likewiſe add, that Capital puniſhments were executed not againſt murther only, but againſt other great crimes; and that not amongſt the Gentiles only, but even among the Patriarchs, as the ſtory of *Judah* and *Thamar* doth clearly evince, *Gen.* 38. 14. rationally conjecturing by an Argument drawn from like to like, that it was agreeable to Gods will, that the puniſhment ordained againſt Homicides, might juſtly be inflicted on ſuch as were notoriouſly criminous. For ſome things there are that we equally Gen. 38. 14.

value,

value, as we do our lives, such are our Honour, our Virgin Chastity, our Matrimonial Faith, and such things without which our lives cannot be well secured; as our reverence to our Prince, without which no society can be preserved. Now they that offend against any of these, are no better than Homicides, and are therefore to be equally punished with them. Hence ariseth that ancient Tradition among the Hebrews, that God gave more laws to *Noah* than were recorded by *Moses*, who thought it sufficient to insert them among those laws which God gave to the Hebrews by himself. Incestuous Marriages were certainly forbidden by some Law before *Moses* his time, for which God is said to visit the Heathen, and to cast them out; for it had not been accounted as a sin, and so not punishable by desolation had there been no law to forbid it; and yet we do not find it in any place expresly prohibited, until *Moses* records it as punished, *Lev.* 18. Among those things that were commanded by God to the Sons of *Noah*, they reckon this, that not only Murther, but Adultery, Incest, and violent Rapes were to be punished with death, which seems to be confirmed as well by the story of *Abimelech*, *Gen.* 20. 6. as by the words of holy *Job*, *Job* 31. 11. But the law given by *Moses* adds the reasons of these Capital punishments which were no less in force among the Gentiles, than among his own people, as it is most apparent, *Lev.* 18. 24, 25. and the 27, and 28. verse. And elsewhere he tells us, that the Land being defiled with blood, could not be cleansed but by the blood of him that shed it, *Numb.* 35. 31, 33. And it were unreasonable to think, that God should indulge this favour to the Jews only, that they might defend themselves by war and punish malefactors with death, and at the same time forbid it to other Nations: Neither doth it appear that the Prophets were at any time sent by God, to admonish or reprove either Kings or People for either inflicting Capital punishments on Malefactors, or for undertaking a war, merely, as war, as they were to reprove other sins. But on the contrary, who would not think but that seeing *Moses*'s judicial laws were observed to carry the stamp of the divine Law, those Nations did wisely and piously, who formed their laws according to that original? As questionless the Greeks, especially the Atticks did, and from them the Romans in their Laws of the twelve Tables. But let this suffice to prove that the laws of *Noah* are not so to be understood as they conceive, who by them would evince all wars to be unlawful.

Incestuous marriages forbidden before Moses.

Gen. 20. 6. *Job* 31. 11. *Psal.* 101. 5. *Prov.* 20. 8.

VI. Cautions, concerning the lawfulness of war by the Gospel law. 1. Caution.

But much more specious are those Arguments which are drawn out of the New Testament against war: In the examination whereof I shall not take that as granted which some do, that there is nothing in the New Testament commanded (except matters of Faith and the Sacraments) but what is commanded by the Law of Nature: For this, in that sense wherein they take it, I cannot admit it. But this I willingly grant, that there is nothing commanded in the Gospel but what is naturally honest: But that the laws of Christ do not oblige us further than to what the Law of Nature doth by it self bind us, I see no reason why I should admit: And for them that approve of this opinion, it is a wonder to see what pains they take to prove that Polygamy, Divorce, Fornication, which we find forbidden in the New Testament, were by the law of Nature unlawful. Hence is that of St. *Jerome*, *Aliæ sunt leges Cæsaris, aliæ Christi, aliud Papinianus, aliud Paulus noster præcipit: The Laws of* Cæsar *are one, and the Laws of Christ another, it is one thing that* Papinian *prescribes unto us, and another what St.* Paul *commands.* 'Tis true, these are such as right reason tells us, to abstain from, is more agreeable to the rules of honesty; but not such as are in themselves impious, but only as they are by the Divine Law forbidden. But as to that which the Christian Law enjoyns us, namely, *That we should lay down our lives one for another*, who can say that we are obliged thereunto by the Law of Nature: *It is for those that do not yet believe the Gospel, to be guided by the Law of Nature*, saith *Justin Martyr*, of which opinion likewise was *Origen*. Neither can I assent unto those who hold that Christ in his Sermon on the Mount, did only interpret, and (as it were) embowel the Law of *Moses*: For those words so often repeated, (*Ye have heard that it hath been said to them of old; But I say unto you:*) do plainly signifie another thing, yea and the Syriack and other Translations do clearly shew, that by *veteribus* is understood not *by*, but *to them of old*; as in the opposite word, *vobis*, is not meant *by*, but *to you*. But those of old were none other, but such as lived in *Moses* his time, and those sayings that are there rehearsed, as spoken to them of old, were meant as spoken by *Moses* himself, not by the Lawyers either in the same words, or to that sense; as *Thou shalt not kill, whosoever killeth shall be in danger of judgment; Thou shalt not commit adultery, whosoever shall put away his Wife, let him give her a Writing of Divorcement: Thou shalt not forswear thy self, thou shalt perform unto the Lord thine oaths: An eye for an eye, and a tooth for a tooth*, (that is, thou mayst exact this in judgment) *so thou shalt love thy Neighbour* (that is an Israelite) *and hate thine enemy*; that is, those seven Nations with whom they were forbidden to contract friendship, or to whom they ought to shew no mercy; unto whom we may add the Amalekites, with whom they were bound to have a perpetual war, *Deut.* 25. 19. Now the better to understand the words of Christ, we must necessarily understand that the

John 3. 16. *Ad Zenam.* Caution 2.

Exod. 20. 13. *Levit.* 20. 21. *Exod.* 20. 14. *Deut.* 24. 1. *Exod.* 20. 7. *Lev.* 24. 20. 19. 18. *Exod.* 34. 2. *Deut.* 7. 1. *Exod.* 27. 19.

the Law given by *Moses* will admit of a twofold construction, either in such a sense, as is common with all humane Laws, namely as it restrains men from gross sins by the fear of publick punishments, *Heb.* 2. 2. And so it was given by *Moses* to restrain the Hebrews in the state of a Civil Government, *Heb.* 7. 16. Where it is called the Law of a carnal Commandment, as it is also in another place called the Law of Works, *Rom.* 3. 27. Or it is taken in a sense more proper to a Divine Law, namely, as it requires also the purity of the mind, and such duties, the omission whereof, no humane Laws do punish. In which sense, it is called a spiritual Law, *Rom.* 7. 14. Comforting the soul, *Psal.* 19. 9. (which the Latins make the 18th.) The *Pharisees* and Lawyers contenting themselves with the Carnal part of the Law, wholly neglected the spiritual as superfluous; and therefore never instructed the people therein, as not our own writers only, but *Josephus* and many of their own Doctors do testifie against them. But as to the spiritual part also we must know, That those vertues which are required from us Christians, were either commanded or commended unto the Hebrews also, although not in that degree and Latitude, as they are unto us, which we have already proved. For a more perfect and exact obedience is now required from us, than was formerly from the *Jews*; because the coming of Christ doth heighten our hopes, by far more precious promises. And the graces of his spirit which descended unto them but as a little dew upon the Herbs, falls on us as showrs on the Grass. *Under the Law God did not bind us up to so great a measure of vertue as he now doth under the Gospel; then it was permitted to take some revenge for injuries done, as to revile them that reviled us, we might exact an eye for an eye, a tooth for a tooth; it was then permitted unto us to swear, though not to forswear, and to hate our enemies: It was not as yet forbidden to be angry, to put away a Wife that offended us, or to marry another; nay, nor to have diverse at the same time. Great was the Indulgence of the Old Law in these and the like cases. But since the coming of Christ, the way to heaven is made much straiter, and narrower than before, both by the addition of many new precepts not given in the old Law, and also by straining up those that were so given, to a much higher Key.* Christ therefore opposeth his own doctrine to the doctrine of the ancients, in both these senses; first because his own took not hold of the outward man only, to restrain it by pure negatives, as other Laws did; but restrained the inward man also obliging to positive duties, whose omission was not punishable by *Moses* his Law. But also in the second place because it enjoyned spiritual duties, in that heighth of degree, that neither *Moses*, nor any other Law-giver, did ever reach; whence it is plain, that what Christ delivered, was not a bare interpretation of *Moses* his Law, as some would have it. But yet that these things should be known, is not only pertinent to the matter in hand, but to many other purposes, lest we should attribute greater authority to *Moses* his Law than indeed is fit or due unto it.

A twofold sence of *Moses* his Law. Carnal.

Rom. 3. 27.

Spiritual.

Supra. ch. 1. §. *ult.*

Chrysost. de virg. c. 44.

VII. That it is not repugnant to the Gospel to make War.

Omitting such arguments as are less convincing, the first and principal Testimony whereby it may easily be proved that all right of making War is not fully taken away by the Evangelical Law, is that of St. *Paul* to *Timothy*: *I exhort you*, saith St. *Paul*, *that above all things, Prayers, and suplications, Intercessions, and giving of thanks, be made for all men, for Kings and such as are in authority; that we may lead a quiet and peaceable life in all Godliness, and honesty, for this is good and acceptable in the sight of God our Saviour, who would have all men to be saved, and to come to the knowledge of the truth.* From whence these three things are to be learned; first, that it is acceptable unto God that Kings be made Christians: Secondly, that being made so, yet they cease not to be Kings; Which *Justin Martyr* thus expresseth, *We pray*, saith he, *that Kings and Princes may together with their Regal Power, retain a sound and perfect mind.* And this also in the third place we may learn, that Christian Kings should use their utmost endeavours, That other Christians may lead under them godly and Christian lives. But you will happily say, How? Surely the same Apostle explains himself elsewhere thus, *He is the Minister of God for thy good, and if thou do ill then fear: Non enim frustra gladium gerit; For he beareth not the sword in vain, for he is Gods Minister, an avenger to execute wrath upon them that do evil.* Under the right of the Sword, is comprehended all manner of restraining or coercive authority, and so it is also sometimes understood by Lawyers; yet so, that the chief and principal part, that is, the true and proper use of the Sword is not excluded. The Second *Psalm* doth very much conduce to the understanding of this power, which Psalm, though verified of *David*, yet was much fuller and clearer understood of Christ, as we may collect out of *Acts* 4. 25. and *Acts* 13. 33. and out of *Heb.* 5. 5. Now that Psalm exhorts all Kings to kiss the Son of God with reverence, that is, to express themselves his servants as they are Kings; for so St. *Aug.* rightly expounds that place, whose very words as being pertinent to our purpose, found thus, *Herein*, saith he, *do Kings serve God according to his command, as Kings, when they encourage vertue, and depress vice not only in things appertaining to humane Society, but in things appertaining also to the worship of God.* And so in another place: *How*, saith he, *do Kings serve the Lord*

1 Tim. 2. 1, 2, 3.

Arg. 1.

The right of the Sword.

Psalm 2.

How Kings serve God as Kings.

in

Ad Bonif. Ep. 50. *in fear, unless it be in prohibiting, and by a Religious austerity punishing all manner of impiety? For to serve God as a man, is one thing, but to serve him as a King is another.* And a little after, *Herein do Kings serve God, as Kings, when in zeal to his service, they do those things which none can do but Kings.*

Arg. 2. Rom. 13. Kingly Government asserted by St. *Paul.* The second Argument, whereby we prove that all Wars are not unlawful, is drawn from that place of St *Paul* before cited in the 13th to the *Romans*; where it is said, That the highest powers, and such are those of Kings, are ordained of God, and that power is therefore called *Gods ordinance.* From whence we inferr the necessity of our subjection, together with that honour and reverence we owe unto them, and that, not so much out of fear, regarding the power they have to hurt, and punish; as out of Conscience, as it is Gods ordinance, and out of a strong perswasion, that in resisting it, we resist God himself. Now if the thing understood by the word, *Ordinance,* were only that which God permits, and will not hinder, as all actions that are vitious, then would there follow no obligation of honour or obedience, especially that extended to the Conscience; and therefore the Apostles whole Argument, would instantly fall to nothing, whose main scope was to extol this Regal power, which if wicked, he could never do, but by the same Argument he might as well have commended Theft, and Robbery. It must necessarily follow then, that by this ordained power, we understand such a power, as God doth especially approve of; and then we may safely inferr, That seeing that God cannot will things contrary to himself, that this power is no ways repugnant to that will of God, which is revealed in the Gospel, and which obligeth all men to honour and obedience: neither doth it at all weaken the force of this Argument, That at that time, when St. *Paul* wrote, all Kings and Princes were strangers to the Christian Faith. For in the first place, this is not Universally true; for even at that time *Sergius Paulus* being *Propraetor* of *Cyprus* had given up his name to Christ long before, *Acts.* 13. 12. Besides, this dispute is not concerning persons, whether pious, or impious, but concerning the Kingly function, whether it be ordained of God, or usurped by men, which St. *Paul* seems here to determine, plainly asserting, That ordinance to be from God: and thereupon concludes, That it ought to be honoured and obeyed, and that, not outwardly, only for fear, but even in the inmost recesses of the mind, where God alone doth properly reign. Christianity then doth not abolish Soveraignty; *Nero* and *Agrippa,* though they had received this faith, yet had still remained, the one an Emperor, the other a King; which necessarily inferrs the power of the Sword. For as under the Law, the Sacrifices were reputed holy, though offered by *Hophni* and *Phineas,* Priests unholy: so *Pia res est imperium, quamvis ab impio teneatur*; *The Function is Sacred, though the person be never so wicked*: *Saul* was anointed King, as well as *David.*

(Margin: Act. 13. 12. — 26. — See *Chrysost. in locum supra citatum.*)

Arg. 3. A Third Argument is drawn from the words of St. *John* the Baptist, who being demanded by the Jewish Souldiers, what they should do to flee from the Wrath to come, did not command them presently to lay down their Arms, and desert their calling, though they fought then under the Roman Banners, as in all probability they would have done, had it been contrary to the Christian Law to make War: but allowing their calling, he only labours to reform the abuses of it, exhorting them to abstain from acts of unlawful violence, and from false accusing, and to rest content with their wages, *Luk.* 3. 14. But here, some object, That there was so great a difference between the precepts of Christ, and the prescriptions of the Baptist, that the Baptist seems to preach one Doctrine, and Christ another; but this we cannot admit, first because both of them declare the sum and substance of the Doctrine they intended to preach, in the same words, *Repent for the Kingdom of Heaven is at hand*; so begins the Baptist, *Mat.* 3. 2. And so Christ, *Mat.* 4. 17. And Christ himself saith, The Kingdom of Heaven, that is, the new Law (for it is the manner of the Hebrews, to call their Law by the name of Kingdom) began to suffer violence from the daies of *John* the *Baptist, Mat.* 11. 12. *John* is said to preach repentance for the remission of sins, *Mark* 1. 4. So did the Apostles in the name of Christ, *Acts* 2. 38. *John* required fruits worthy of repentance, and threatens destruction to those that do not produce them, *Matth.* 3. 8, 10. He requires also works of Charity beyond the Law, *Luke* 3. 11. The Law also is said to continue till the days of *John,* that is, until the new and more perfect Law should with him begin, *Mat.* 11. 13. And for this cause it is that *John* is said to be *Prophetis major, Greater than the Prophets, Mat.* 11. 9. *Luk.* 7. 26. and that he was sent to give knowledge of Salvation unto the people, *Luk.* 2. 77. and to preach the Gospel, *Luk.* 2. 18. Neither did *John* ever distinguish *Jesus* from himself, by any difference that there was in their Doctrines, (but only, thus, that what *John* declared generally and confusedly, was more distinctly delivered by Christ, who was the true light) but by this, That *Jesus* was the *Messias* that was promised, the King of an heavenly Kingdom, who should give the power of the holy Ghost to those who should believe on him.

(Margin: Luke 3. 14. — The *Jews* call their Law, Kingdom. — Acts 19. 4. Joh. 1. 29. Mat. 3. 11. Mar. 1. 8. Luk. 3. 16.)

The

The Fourth Argument, and which ſeems to me of no ſmall force is this; That if by the Goſpel all power were taken away from the Magiſtrate to execute capital puniſhments, together with that of the Sword, to defend their Subjects from Thieves and Robbers: how ſoon would the Chriſtian world be over-run with Rapin and violence, and what a Deluge of wickedneſs, of all ſorts would break in upon us? That this muſt needs be the conſequence, we ſhall eaſily grant; if we either remember what ſad effects this remiſneſs brought upon the old world; or if we do but obſerve, how hardly theſe ſins of Rapin, Cruelty, and the like are reſtrained now, even by capital puniſhments: *For the ſuppreſſing whereof Tribunals, Laws, and ſo many kinds and degrees of puniſhments are invented,* ſaith *Chryſoſt. in ſerm ad Patrem fidelem* Wherefore if Chriſt had intended to have introduced a new, and never before heard of form of Government; without doubt he would have declared it in ſuch diſtinct terms, and in ſuch a plain dreſs of words, as ſhould have been liable to no miſpriſion; as, Let no man hereafter adjudge Malefactors to death, Let no man take Arms to defend himſelf, or the like, which we no where read that ever he did: but whatſoever words are wreſted from the Scriptures to this purpoſe, are either very general, or very obſcure. But equity it ſelf, and common reaſon will inſtruct us thus much, That in publiſhing new Laws we are to reſtrain words too general, and to explain terms too ambiguous; and rather to decline a little from the common acception of the words, than to admit of ſuch a ſenſe of them, as may introduce ſo many miſchiefs and inconveniences with it.

Arg. 4. An Argument drawn from the ill conſequences that would follow.

The Fifth Argument is this, That it cannot be concluded by any probable argument, that the Judicial Law of *Moſes* was ever aboliſhed, till their City *Jeruſalem* was burnt, and with it, not the form only, but the very hopes of a Commonwealth did utterly vaniſh. For neither doth *Moſes* prefix any term or period to this Law, nor doth Chriſt or his Apoſtles any where declare the ſurceaſing of it; unleſs as it ſeems to be comprehended in the deſtruction of the Commonwealth: yea rather on the contrary, St. *Paul* ſaith, That the High Prieſt was conſtituted, that he might judge according to the Law of *Moſes, Acts,* 24. 3. And Chriſt in the Preface to his precepts, *Mat.* 5. ſaith, That he came to fulfil the Law, and not to deſtroy it; which words if we referr to the Ceremonial Law, are not difficult to be underſtood: for when the Picture is finiſhed, what need we the foul draught? The Ceremonial Law was fulfilled in him, it conſiſting in Types and ſhadows, whereof the ſubſtance was Chriſt; but how could Chriſt be ſaid to fulfil the Judicial Law, if (as ſome hold) he took it away? And if the *Jews* were obliged by the Judicial Law, till the diſſolution of their Commonwealth, it will follow, That the *Jews*, though Chriſtianized, in caſe they had been called to be Magiſtrates, could neither have avoided it, nor have judged otherwiſe, than as *Moſes* had preſcribed. I, truly, having throughly weighed all that can be ſaid, can find no ground at all, why any pious man ſhould expound thoſe words of Chriſt in any other ſenſe: This I acknowledge, that many things were tolerated among the *Jews* before the coming of Chriſt, (whether as to outward impunity, or in reſpect of inward purity alſo, I ſhall not now determine) which Chriſt would not permit in his Diſciples, as for a man to put away his Wife for every offence, and for a man injured, to require revenge by way of Retaliation: but yet between Chriſts precepts, and *Moſes* his permiſſion, there may be ſome difference, but no repugnancy; for, under the Law, if a man did retain his Wife, or if he did remit revenge privately due, he could not be ſaid to break the Law, but to do that which the Law did chiefly require of him. But it is far otherwiſe in a Judge, whom the Law doth not permit, but enjoyn to puniſh a Murtherer with death; which if he do not, he himſelf ſhall be found guilty before God. Now if Chriſt had commanded ſuch a Judge, that he ſhould not adjudge any Malefactor to death, this being contrary to Law, he had diſſolved, and not fulfilled it.

Arg. 5. Mat. 5. 17.

The Sixth Argument is drawn from *Cornelius* the Centurion, who received the Holy Ghoſt (an undeniable ſign of Juſtification) from Chriſt himſelf, and was baptized into the name of Chriſt by St. *Peter*; yet do we no where read that he laid down his Commiſſion, or that he was admoniſhed by St. *Peter* ſo to do. But ſome may ſay, That being inſtructed by St. *Peter* in the Chriſtian Religion, it may be preſumed, that at the ſame time he did reſolve to deſert his calling: whereunto I anſwer, That if it could be any where found amongſt the precepts of Chriſt, or infallibly proved, that Chriſt did forbid to make War, then what they ſay were to the purpoſe. But ſeeing no ſuch precept is extant; certainly it is much more probable, that in this caſe of *Cornelius*, ſomewhat would have been ſaid againſt it, if it had been held unlawful, that ſo in after ages, men of that profeſſion might not have pleaded ignorance of the danger incident to that function. Neither is it likely that in caſe the Centurion had then renounced his Military profeſſion, St. *Luke* would have omitted the recording of it, as uſually he did in like caſes, as will appear by ſeveral places, but eſpecially *Acts* 19. 19.

Arg. 6 From the example of *Cornelius.*

Arg. 7. And of *Sergius Paulus*. The Seventh Argument we deduce from *Sergius Paulus*, of whom after his conversion there is not the least mention made of his renouncing his Proprætorship, or of any admonition given him by St. *Paul* to do it: that which is not recorded, (being most expedient to have been so) may be presumed not to have been done at all.

Arg. 8. And of St. *Paul*. The Eighth Argument is drawn from the practice of St. *Paul*, who understanding that the *Jews* had laid wait to kill him, acquainted the chief Captain therewith, who sent him a strong guard of Souldiers to secure his person; which St. *Paul* did not refuse, nor did he admonish either the chief Captain, or the Souldiers, that it was not acceptable to God to repel force with force, which he had been apt enough to have done, had he believed it to have been unlawful.

Arg. 9. From Tribute which was to have been paid. Rom. 13. 6. The Ninth Argument is taken from St. *Pauls* precept, for paying tribute for conscience sake, for of every thing that is honest and just, its proper end must needs be so; now the proper end of paying of Tribute, is to maintain the power of the Sword, whereby the innocent are protected, and the nocent corrected or cut off. But that we render unto Princes their Tribute due, is a precept of the new Law, and bindeth the Conscience, as St. *Paul* testifies to the *Romans*; therefore it follows, that by the precepts of Christianity, the power of the Sword in the hands of the chief Magistrate is honest and just: very pertinent to this purpose, is that of *Tacitus*, *There can be no peace amongst Nations without Arms, no Arms without pay, nor pay without taxes.* So St. *Aug*. *For this cause pay we Tribute, that Souldiers may have their wages to buy necessaries.* (*Hist. l. 4. lib. 22. contra Faustum c. 74.*)

Arg. 10. Acts 25. Apolog. 2. Act. 28. 18. The Tenth Argument is taken from St. *Pauls* speech, *Acts* 25. *If I have wronged any man, or if I have done any thing worthy of death, I refuse not to die.* So *Act*. 28. 18. *They found no cause of death in me*, saith St. *Paul*: Whereupon *Justine Martyr* thus glosseth, *If there be any amongst us that live not conformably to those precepts, being only in name Christians, that such should be punished, and that, by you, is our desire, as well as yours.* From whence we may collect, that it was St. *Pauls* opinion, even after the Gospel was published, that there were some crimes which in common equity deserved death: which very thing is granted by St. *Peter* also, 1 *Pet*. 2. 19, 20. But if it had been Gods will that no Capital punishment should have been executed after Christs coming, St. *Paul* might have purged himself; but he thought it not convenient to instil such principles into the minds of his hearers, as though it had not been as lawful then, as formerly, to punish Criminals with death; wherefore he waveth this Plea, and submits to the ancient Law, If I have done any thing worthy of death, I refuse not to die. Now, having thus proved, that after the Christian Law was given, it was lawful to punish obstinate Malefactors with death; I take it to be sufficiently proved that it is Lawful for Princes to make War, namely against such a multitude of offenders, as shall by force of Arms infest a Nation, who unless they be by force subdued will never acknowledge their own guilt. For though the power of these offenders, and their obstinate resolution may be a prudent consideration to perswade Princes sometimes not to execute it; yet certainly, it diminisheth nothing of their right so to punish.

Arg. 11. The last Argument may be this, that the Christian Law did abrogate that Law of *Moses* only, that did separate the *Gentiles* from the *Jews*, *Eph*. 2. 14. But those things which have the reputation of being honest either by the Law of Nature, or by the unanimous consent of all Civilized Nations, the Christian Law is so far from taking away, that it comprehends them under that general precept of all honesty and vertue, *Phil*. 4. 8. 1 *Cor*. 11. 14. And as to the Capital punishments of Malefactors, and the repelling of injuries by force, these may be ranked among things laudable, and may well be referred unto those two excellent vertues, Justice and beneficence. But here, on the by, we are not to omit the error of some, who wholly attribute the lawfulness of the *Jewish* Wars against the seven Nations to the grant, that God made unto them long before of the Land of *Canaan*: whereas this, indeed, may be one, but not the only cause. For as well before, as after the possession of that Land, many pious and just men did make War, by the guidance of meer natural reason upon several other occasions. As King *David* did, for the affronts offered unto his Ambassadors; neither are those things which every man enjoys by the right of humane Laws less his own, than that which is given him by God himself, nor is that right either lessened or taken away by the Christian Law.

VIII. The Arguments for the adverse opinion answered. Esay 2. 4. Now by poising these arguments with those brought on the adverse part, the judicious may easily find whether of them are weightiest. And in the first place, they urge that of *Esay*, *And it shall come to pass, that the people shall break their Swords into Ploughshares, and their Spears into pruning hooks, Nation shall not lift up Sword against Nation, neither shall they learn War any more.* Which words of *Esay*, St. *Chrysostome* applies unto that universal peace that the world enjoyed under the Roman Empire; *Neither was it foretold only*, saith he, *that this new Religion should be firm, stable and unshaken; but that therewith there should come peace to the whole earth.* But this Prophecy of *Esay* (as I take it) is (*Orat. Christum esse Deum. Eusib. de prap. lib. 1. c. 10.*)

to

to be underſtood, either under ſome condition as many others are, as that ſuch ſhould be the ſtate of affairs, in caſe all Nations ſhould ſubmit to the yoke of Chriſt, and live according to his Law, whereunto there ſhall nothing be defective on Gods part: for moſt certain it is, that if all were Chriſtians, or all that call themſelves ſo, would live after the rules of Chriſt; there would be no occaſion for Capital puniſhments, and conſequently no uſe at all of the Sword. So *Juſtin* writes of the Chriſtians in his time, *Non pugnamus in hoſtes, We,* ſaith he, *fight not againſt enemies: and thus Philo* teſtifies of the Eſſeni, *There is none among them, that make either Javelins, Arrows, Swords, Helmets, or any other inſtruments of War.* So *Chryſoſtome, Si eſſet inter homines qualis oportet dilectio, nullas fore pœnas capitales; If there were that perfect love among men that there ſhould be, there would be no need at all of Capital puniſhments. Then alſo* as *Arnobius* ſpeaks, *would Iron and Steel be converted into more innocent and profitable inſtruments, than for men therewith to kill and deſtroy each other.* Or this place of *Eſay* is to be underſtood ſimply and purely, as the words import; and then it is apparent that this prophecy is not as yet accompliſhed, but the fulfilling thereof, as that of the general converſion of the *Jews*, is yet to be hoped for; but take it, as we pleaſe, in either ſenſe nothing can be from thence concluded againſt the lawfulneſs of War, ſo long as they that heartily endeavour to live in peace, are not ſuffered to enjoy it: Or as the Pſalmiſt hath it, whilſt ſome are endeavouring after peace, others are preparing themſelves for battel. Many arguments are uſually drawn from the fifth of St. *Matthew*. For the reſolving whereof, it is convenient that we ſhould remember what a little before was ſaid, that had our great Law-giver intended to have aboliſhed all Capital puniſhments, and this Right of making War, he would certainly have done it in moſt plain and expreſs terms, the matter being ſo weighty, and ſo new; and the rather, becauſe none of the *Jews* could conceive or imagin but they were obliged to *Moſes* his judicial Laws, ſo long as their Commonwealth ſhould ſtand. This being thus premiſed, let us orderly examine what plain and concluding power, theſe places of Scripture have to evince the thing they are brought for. The Second place they urge is this, *Ye have heard it ſaid, an eye for an eye, and a tooth for a tooth; but I ſay unto you, do not reſiſt him that doth thee an injury, but if any man ſtrike thee on the one cheek, turn to him the other alſo.* From hence ſome do infer, That it is unlawful either to repel, or to avenge an injury, whether publickly or privately. But this cannot be enforced from the words of Chriſt, who doth not there addreſs his diſcourſe to the Magiſtrate, but to the perſon injured; neither doth he there ſpeak of every injury, but of ſuch ſlight ones, *as a box on the eare*, and the like: the precept following ſeems to reſtrain the words preceeding, as if they were too general, *If any man will ſue thee at the Law, to take away thy Coat, let him have thy Cloak alſo*; which words *Cyprian* thus expounds, *What is taken away from thee unjuſtly, ſeek not to recover.* And ſo likewiſe *Irenæus, If any man ſhall take away thy Coat, do not grieve, as if thou wert deprived of it againſt thy will; but rather rejoyce, as if thou hadſt given it voluntarily. And if any man ſhall compel thee to go with him a mile, go with him not grudgingly but willingly, not following him as a ſervant, but going before him as a guide.* It is not every conteſt in Law that is therefore forbidden, as St. *Paul* ſeems to interpret that place in 1 *Cor.* 6. 4, 5, 6, 7. But he forbids Chriſtians to go to Law for every trifle, or to convent their brethren before the Tribunals of the Heathen, contrary to the cuſtom of the *Jews*, amongſt whom it was a received opinion, *Qui adducit negotia Iſraelitica ad extraneos, polluet nomen Dei; He that makes a ſtranger Judge of any controverſie between Iſraelites, pollutes the name of God*: but Chriſt to exerciſe the patience of his diſciples would not have them cavil in judgment for things eaſily recoverable, as for a Coat or Cloak. For though they might do it *Optimo jure, with the greateſt Right*, yet was it much more acceptable to God rather to ſuffer ſuch loſſes with patience, than to proſecute the Law for them. *Apollonius Tyanæus* denies it to be the part of a wiſeman, to ſue for a little money. *There is no judge,* ſaith *Ulpian, that can diſapprove of that man, who ſets ſo little by his loſs, as not to vex himſelf for it with many ſutes, for that mans diſpoſition that hates contention, is no waies to be diſallowed.* What *Ulpian* there ſaith is approved of by all good men, and is no more than what Chriſt there commands, collecting the ſum and ſubſtance of his precepts out of theſe things that are moſt honeſt and vertuous. But yet, thou canſt not hence well conclude, that for a Parent or a Tutor to defend, or recover by Law, that which his Child or Pupil hath been wrongfully deprived of, and without which he cannot ſubſiſt, being thereunto compelled, is any violation of this precept of Chriſt. For it is one thing to contend for a Coat which haply we may ſpare, and another thing to contend for that, without which we cannot live. In the Conſtitutions of *Clement*, it is ſaid concerning a Chriſtian, *If he have a ſute at Law, let him endeavour as ſoon as he can to end it, though it be to his loſs.* What therefore is uſually ſaid of moral duties, may alſo be ſaid of theſe precepts, that they conſiſt not in a point, like the negative precepts of the Law, from which we cannot deviate in the leaſt without ſin; for theſe have their *huc uſque*, their certain Latitudes, wherein we may walk ſafely. So, in that

Mat. 5. expounded.

Anſwered.

Lib. de patientia.

Lib. 4. *c.* 27.

Philoſt. 2, 15.

For trifles it is better to suffer than to contend.

that precept that follows, *If any man shall compel thee to go with him a mile, go with him two.* He saith not, he that compels thee to go with him one hundred miles, this had been hard, because haply it would draw us too far from our own necessary concernments, and so the injury or damage done would be greater to our selves, than the benefit to him: But he mentions a mile or two only, which cannot much endamage us. The sense of the words then must needs be this: In such things as are not very damageable to our selves, we are not too strictly to insist upon our own right, but rather to grant more than is required from us, that our patience and readiness to do good may be known unto all. Thus *Justin Martyr* expounds these words, What Christ there said, tends only to this, that we should behave our selves towards all men patiently, obligingly, and not prone to anger. But it follows, *Give unto him that asks, and from him that would borrow turn not away*: Than which words, if not understood with some limitation, nothing sound harsher. *He that takes no care for his Family*, saith St. *Paul*, *is worse than an Infidel*: Let St. *Paul* himself be Judge who was best able to expound his Masters Law, and who exhorting the Corinthians to extend their liberality to the poor at *Jerusalem*, saith, *Not that others should be eased and you burdened, but that by an equality, your abundance should supply their wants*: that is, (to borrow the words of *Livy*, in a case not unlike to this) *that out of your store ye may relieve the necessities of others.* Dabo egenti, sed & ipse non egeam, *I will give to the poor, but so, as that thereby I make not my self poor*, saith Seneca. So also *Chrysostom*, *God requires those things of us that are in our power to give*: *According to what a man hath*, saith St. *Paul*, *and not according to what a man hath not.* And he commends the Thessalonians, *that they gave above what they were able*; but yet he doth not exact the same from the Achaians: To the like purpose is that of *Cyrus* in *Xenophon*, *What I find superabundant in mine own estate, will be sufficient to relieve the wants of my friends.* By all which we may conclude, That this precept of our Saviours (as all the rest which follow in this Chapter) are to be understood with some equitable limitation, and not barely as the words import:

The indulgence of the Hebrew Law.

The Hebrew law to prevent the cruelty of Husbands to their Wives, did indulge unto them the liberty of Divorce; and to prevent private revenge, whereunto that Nation was too much addicted, gave liberty to the injured person to avenge himself, not by his own hand, but by requiring it from the Judges, according to the Rule of Retaliation;

Which Christ reforms.

which Law was so pleasing to the Romans, that they inserted it among those in the 12 Tables, *Si membrum rupit talio esto*, *He that breaks a limb shall suffer the like.* But Christ being Master of much more patience, was so far from approving this Law, that he would not permit his disciples to repel some injuries either by force or judgment.

But what injuries were these? Surely such as might easily be born, not that patience was not commendable even in the greatest, but that he was content with somewhat a more limited patience: And therefore he instanceth only in a box on the Ear, which neither endangers life nor limb, but implyes only a slighting or contemning of us, which doth not at all damnifie us. *Seneca* in his Book entituled, *Of a wise mans Constancy*, distinguisheth between an injury and a reproach: *The former*, saith he, *is naturally more grievous; the latter more light, and to such only as are nicely bred, troublesome: Qua non læduntur, sed offenduntur; whereby they are offended, but not hurt. Such is the weakness and vanity of mens minds, that they esteem nothing worse than a reproach; so we may find some servants, that had rather be beaten with stripes, than to take a box on the Ear.* So in another place, *A reproach* (saith he) *is much less than an injury, which we rather complain of than revenge, there being no punishment assigned unto it by the Law* So he in *Pacuvius*, *Patior facile injuriam, si absit contumelia*; *An injury I can easily digest, provided that it be without contumely.* To the same purpose also is that of *Demosthenes*, *The Tongue wounds deeper than the Sword, and stripes though grievous, yet are more easily born, if not accompanied with reproaches.* And the same *Seneca* a little after tells us, That grief arising from reproach, is an affection or passion occasioned by the humbleness of a mind contracting it self, by reason of some word or deed tending to our disparagement. Against all these passions which seem to invade the tranquillity of the mind, Christ fortifies his disciples only with patience; so that in case the wrong offered us either in word or deed, do not much hurt us, it is more magnanimous to overcome them with sufferance and patience, than to seek revenge either by force or Law. And lest we should be discouraged by that vulgar saying, *Veterem ferendo injuriam invitas novam*; *By over calmly bearing an old injury, we do but invite a new*: Our blessed Saviour adds, that even the second is rather to be endured, than the first either repelled or revenged; because such kind of injuries leave no evil Characters behind them,

De Statuis 1.

besides what consists in our own foolish conceits. For what St. *Chrysostom* observes is very true, *Contumelia non ab inferentis animo sed ex judicio eorum qui patiuntur, aut fit aut perit*; *A reproach doth either vex or vanish, not according to his intention that inferred it, but according to the apprehension of him that suffers it. To offer the Cheek* is an Hebrew phrase, implying the bearing of a thing patiently, as may be collected from *Esay* 30. 6. and from *Jeremy*

Tacitus hist. 3.

3. 3. whence the Latines borrowed it, as appears by that Phrase so often used by *Tacitus*, *Terence*,

Terence, and others, *Præbere os contumeliis*, is, *To bear reproaches patiently.* *Ter. Adelph.*

The third Objection is taken from the words following, *Ye have heard that it hath been* Obj. 3. *said, Thou shalt love thy Neighbour and hate thine enemy: But I say unto you, Love your enemies, bless them that curse you, and pray for them that despitefully use you, and persecute you.* Matth. 5. 43. There are some that think that these duties of Dilection and Beneficence to our enemies, are directly opposite to War and Capital punishments: But this objection will easily vanish, if we do but understand the very words of the Hebrew Law; for the Jews were commanded to love their Neighbours, that is Jews or Hebrews (equal unto whom were Proselytes; but those laws which forbad them to do hurt, reached even unto those Strangers that lived among them, being uncircumcised, as the Talmudists note) for in this Whereof before, ch. 1. §. 16. sence is the word *Neighbour* there taken, as appears *Levit.* 19. 17. being compared with the Verse there following. And yet notwithstanding were the Magistrates commanded to inflict Capital punishments upon Homicides, seducers of the people to Idolatry, and other hainous and obstinate Malefactors: So notwithstanding this precept of loving their Neighbours, the 11 Tribes did justly make war against the Tribe of *Benjamin*, for their more than barbarous inhumanity, *Judg.* 21. so notwithstanding this Precept, did *David*, who is said to fight the Lords battels, by force of Arms recover the Kingdom (being promised to him) from *Ishbosheth*. But admit that the word, *Neighbour*, doth now extend it self to all mankind, for as much as all are now fellow Denizens, all received into the Covenant of Grace, and no one people accursed from God; yet what was heretofore lawful for the Israelites, will be as lawful for us, both being obliged to the same duties of Love and Beneficence. But you may haply say, That the Evangelical Law requires an higher degree of love than the Mosaical Law did: Even this also I grant with this allowance, that all are not equally to be beloved, our Parents and our Children are certainly to be preferred before Strangers, and our Neighbours before our Enemies. *'Tis true,* *Adv. Pelag. dialog.* 1. saith St. *Hierom*, *I am commanded to love mine enemies, and to pray for my persecutors; but yet is it just that I should love them equally as I do my Neighbours and kinsmen? Is it equal that I should make no difference between my Friends and mine Adversaries? Surely the Laws of a well* There are degrees of Dilection. *ordered Affection do command me to prefer the Righteous before the wicked, and the publick safety before the safety of any private person.* Now out of the very love we bear to the righteous do we put the wicked to death; and out of our care to the publick peace, do we make war upon those that disturb it: If therefore our Saviours precepts do admit of degrees, and if the greater obligation do tye us to the stricter duty; then are we not bound to preserve the nocent, when in so doing we endanger, if not destroy the innocent. That of *Seneca* is very well known, *Tam omnibus ignoscere crudelitas est, quam nulli*; *Lib.* 1. *de clem.* *It is as great a cruelty to pardon all, as to pardon none.* *Chrysostom* speaking of such humane punishments as are inflicted on the obstinate, saith, *that they proceed not from cruelty, but from goodness.* And St. *Augustine* affirms, That as there is sometimes *crudelitas parcens, a cruelty in pardoning*, so there is sometimes *misericordia puniens, mercy in punishing.* *Those protections*, therefore, *that ripen sin by giving too great encouragement to sinners, are to be removed:* For as *Totilas* in *Procopius* speaks, *Peccare, & prohibere pœnas peccantium in pari* *See Bo.* 2. *ch.* 21. §. 2. *ponto: He that commits a crime, and he that hinders a Criminal from due punishment, are alike faulty.* Besides we are commanded to love our Enemies by the example of God himself, who causeth the Sun to shine and the Rain to fall, as well on the Evil as on the Good: And yet doth the same God put a manifest difference between them, visiting the sins of such as are incorrigible with heavy judgments in this life, and yet reserving much heavier for them to be inflicted in the life to come. And thus are all those Objections drawn from those precepts, enjoyning Christians to mercy, lenity, beneficence, against war and Capital punishments; easily answered. For Almighty God though he pleased to make himself known unto us principally by these Attributes of Gentleness, Long sufferance, Godspatience doth not hinder his justice. and Patience, *John* 4. 2. *Exod.* 34. 6. yet do the holy Scriptures almost in every page set forth, and declare his indignation and wrath against obstinate and contumacious sinners, as *Numb.* 14. 18. *Rom.* 2. 8. whereof the Magistrate is designed to be the Minister, *Rom.* 13. 4. *Moses* was highly celebrated for his meekness and gentleness, yet did he punish Malefactors with death; and Christ himself the most absolute pattern and mirror of meekness and patience, being provoked by the obstinacy of the Jews ingratitude, is said by a Parable to send out his Armies to burn up their City, and to destroy her Citizens, *Mat.* 22. 7. the like we may read *Mat.* 21. 44. and *Luke* 19. 12, 14, 27. And although the Roman Army were (as *Chrysostom* observes) the Axes and the Hammers, yet was it *Chrys. in* 1 *Cor.* 4. 21. Christ himself that brought these calamities upon them, according to his own predictions, as well by Parables, as plainly and expresly. Nearest unto their Master, came the Apostles themselves in imitation of his meekness and gentleness, who notwithstanding made use of the power given them from above, in the punishment of incorrigible sinners, *Aug. Ser. Dom. in mont. l.* 1. *Grat. c.* 23. *q.* 8. as is plain, 1 *Cor.* 4. 21. 1 *Cor.* 5. 5. 1 *Tim.* 1. 20.

Their

Object. 4.

Rom. 12. 17.

Their fourth Objection that is brought against the lawfulness of war, is extracted from *Rom.* 12. 17. *Render unto no man evil for evil, provide things honest in the sight of all men: If it be possible, as much as in you lyeth, live peaceably with all men: Dearly Beloved,* * *avenge not your selves, but rather give place unto wrath: For it is written, Vengeance is mine, I will repay it saith the Lord: Therefore if thine enemy hunger feed him, if he thirst give him drink; for in so doing thou shalt heap coals of fire upon his head: Be not overcome of evil, but overcome evil with good.* But here also the same answer will serve, as was given to the former: For at the very same time when God impropriated to himself the Sword of Vengeance as his prerogative, saying *Vengeance is mine*; at the self same time were Malefactors put to death by the Magistrate, and laws prescribed for making of war, and yet it was at the same time enjoyned to the Jews to do good to their enemies (if their own Country-men) as *Exod.* 23. 4, 5. which notwithstanding did no ways diminish either the right of making a just war, or the execution of incorrigible malefactors, wherefore neither can these or the like Precepts now (though never so much enlarged) be wrested to such a sense; much less if we consider, that the dividing the Scriptures into Chapters and Verses, was not done by the Apostles, nor in their age, but long after, for the more easie quotation of the Text when fit to be brought for confirmation: so that what begins the 13*th* to the *Romans, Let every Soul be subject to the higher powers*; and what there follows, was annexed to those precepts foregoing, against taking revenge. But in this dissertation, St. *Paul* saith expresly, that the higher powers are constituted Gods Ministers, and the executioners of his wrath (that is as to punishments) upon those that do ill; thereby clearly distinguishing between that revenge, which the Magistrate instead of God exacts for the publick good, being a part of his prerogative; and that which every private man takes upon his enemy with his own hands, merely to gratifie his own passion, which the Apostle had a little before interdicted. For if we include in that negative precept, that Revenge that is taken by the Magistrate for the publick good, what can be more absurd than after he had charged the Romans, not at all to execute capital punishments, to have immediately subjoyned, that to this very end God had ordained the higher powers, that they in his stead, should execute even Capital Judgments upon Malefactors? for so the power of the Sword must needs signifie, if any thing.

* The vulgar Interpretation is, *Defend not your selves*: But this word is often put by Christian Authors, in this sence of Avenging: *Aug.* expounds this place very well, where he saith *Resist not evil, lest ye delight in revenge, which feeds the mind fat with other mens misfortunes. Vide infra* Bo. 2. ch. 20. §. 5. and 10.

The first verse of *Rom.* 13. was annexed to the precepts in the Chapter foregoing against taking revenge.

Object. 5.

2 Cor. 10. 3. expounded.

A fifth Objection is by some brought out of the 2 *Cor.* 10. 3. *Although we walk in the flesh, we do not war according to the flesh; for the weapons of our warfare are not carnal, but mighty, through God, to the pulling down of strong holds.* Where by the way, we must understand that by carnal weapons, are meant Riches, Glory, Power, Eloquence, and such like (as *Chrysostom* expounds that place) in which sence, this place is quoted to little purpose, for both the words preceding and subsequent do plainly shew, that St. *Paul* by the word *Flesh* understood his mean appearance as to the outward, which rendred him to those who looked no further contemptible. Whereunto St. *Paul* opposeth his own weapons, that is, the power committed to him as an Apostle, to compel such as were obstinate and refractory, which power he exercised on *Elymas* the Sorcerer, on the incestuous Corinthians, and on *Hymenaus* and *Alexander* the Coppersmith. This power he denyes to be carnal, that is, weak, nay rather he asserts it to be most strong and forceable. Now what doth this belong to the rights of War or Capital punishments? yea rather on the contrary, because the Church of Christ was at that time utterly destitute of all manner of tutelage or protection from the publick powers: therefore did God for a while supply this defect by that prodigious power which began to cease, almost as soon as the Church had gained the protection of Christian Emperors; even as *Manna* then began to cease, so soon as he had brought his people out of the barren Wilderness into a fruitful Country.

Object. 6. out of Eph. 6. 12. expounded.

The sixth place they produce, is out of *Eph.* 6. 12. *Put ye on the whole Armour of God, that ye may be able to stand against the wiles of the Devil; for ye wrestle not against flesh and blood* (only) as the Hebrews understand it, *but against Principalities, &c.* In which place the Apostle discourseth only of that spiritual warfare, which Christians, as Christians, have with their spiritual enemies, and not that which Christians as men may make against men upon just grounds.

Object. 7. from James 4. 1.

The seventh place objected against the lawfulness of war, is that of St. *James*, *From whence are Wars and Fightings among you? Come they not hence, even from your Lusts that war in your members? Ye lust and have not, ye kill and desire to have, and cannot obtain; ye fight and war, yet ye have not because ye ask not; ye ask and receive not, because ye ask amiss, that ye may consume it upon your lusts.* But in these words there is nothing universal, for St. *James* here condemns only those unnatural wars which the dispersed Jews then had among themselves, whereby they were miserably shattered and torn in pieces, (some part whereof

whereof is recorded by *Josephus*) which arose from no other causes but what were unjust: the like we may see among Christians in these days, though not without remorse; whereof *Tibullus*,

> *This is the vice of Gold, no Wars were then,*
> *When nought at Feasts but Beechen Bowls were seen.*

So we often read in *Strabo*, how innocently they lived who contented themselves with a single and simple diet; wherewith agrees that of *Lucan*,

> ——— *O Luxury, of things the wast,*
> *That not contented art with mean repast;*
> *Ambitious hunger, which for to appease,*
> *Both Lands and Seas are sought for rarities:*
> *Learn with how little Life sustain'd may be,*
> *And what by Nature's due.*———

Whereunto we may add that of *Plutarch*, *There is no War among men, but what ariseth from some vice; some through inordinate lust, others from covetousness, some through ambition, and immoderate love of Glory.* *Justin* commending the manners of the *Scythians* saith, *They affect not Gold and Silver as other Nations do:* And presently after he adds, *This Contentation of theirs begat in them so much justice, that they coveted nothing that was not their own; for there only are riches inordinately sought after, where they serve for inordinate uses.* Memorable is that saying of *Taxiles* the Scythian to *Alexander*, *What necessity is there that we, O* Alexander, *should make War one upon another, seeing that thou comest not to abridge us of our Water, or of our necessary sustenance; in the defence of which things only, men endued with reason make War?* Much to the same purpose was that of *Diogenes*, *Thieves and Incendiaries to War, are never found among such as are contented with homely fare.* For as *Porphyry* observes, *That which is easily got and at small charge, much conduceth to the perpetual Piety, even of all. Whereas Tyrants and such as devast Kingdoms, do not raise Wars either Foreign or Civil, to feed coursely on Herbs, Roots, or Apples; but to pamper themselves with Flesh, Fowl, and such like delicious Fare.* Therefore *Chrysostom* speaking of such as were rich and opulent, saith, *Do not Seditions, Wars, Combats, Bondage, Slavery, Captivity, Murthers, and innumerable other such like mischiefs and inconveniences commonly arise from these men?* I may conclude these and many other such wise sayings of the best men, with that one of *Polybius*, *Animus necessariis contentus alio ad sapiendum magistro non eget; That mind which can be contented with necessaries only, needs no other Tutor to learn wisdom.* Our wish therefore shall be the same with *Justin's*, who having commended the Scythians for their temperance, wisheth the like moderation among all Nations: Then might we hope that that Prophecy of *Esay* would soon be fulfilled, that our Swords should be turned into Coulters, and our Spears into Pruning-hooks; Nation would not then rise against Nation, neither should we learn war any more. For what is it that fills the world so full of blood and rapine, that the Sword devours more than those that dye by natural deaths, but only our exorbitant Lusts, whereby we are violently hurried to things unjust and dishonest. Now that which Christ sometimes said to St. *Peter*, *He that takes the Sword shall perish by the Sword*, not properly belonging unto War in its vulgar acception, but to private quarrels (for Christ himself gives this as a sufficient reason, why we should neglect our own defence, rather than study revenge; because his Kingdom was not of this world, *Jo.* 13. 36.) shall be more fully handled in its proper place.

In Stoicor. contradictionibus.

Just. de Scythis.

De non edendis animal. l. 2. Hieron. adv. Jov. l. 2.

Ad Patrem fidelem.

IX.

What the Primitive Christians held as to this.

When there ariseth any doubt concerning the sence of things written, we have two main helps, namely, the common practice of that Age, and the authority of the most prudent men, both which are of singular use for the right understanding of the holy Scriptures: According to that ancient rule, *Sanctorum praxis, optimus est præceptorum interpres; The practice of the Saints, is the best interpreter of our Saviours precepts.* For it is not probable, that the Apostles did commit all things so clearly to Writing, that might or did concern the Oeconomy of the Church; but that some things were delivered by words only: Neither is it probable, that all the Churches by them established, should quickly forget what was so delivered unto them and practised by them. Now they that dispute against the lawfulness of War, do usually justifie themselves by the opinions of some of the ancient Christians, against whom I have these things to urge: First, That from their sayings, nothing can be concluded more than that it was the opinion of some private men, but not the general Doctrine of the Chnrch in that Age; especially if it be granted, that those Fathers affected to be singular, and to introduce somewhat that was more sublime, than what was generally approved of by those Churches; yea and (which in those times was ordinary)

Concerning the ancient Fathers three things observable.

Observ. 1.

Clem. Alex. Strom. l. 7. ordinary) to cloath their own Fancies with that generous Notion of an *Apostolical Tradition*, as may be observed by *Origen*, and *Tertullian*: (so *Clemens Alexandrinus* saith, That it was delivered by a certain secret Tradition from the Apostles, That it was not lawful for Christians to go to Law, either before the Saints, or before the *Gentiles*: or for a perfect Christian to swear:) yet are not these Fathers constant to what they say; for *Origen* brings in Bees, as a Document, *That it was lawful for Christians to make a just and well ordered War, as often as necessity required.* And the very same *Tertullian*, who in another place seems to disapprove of Capital punishments, yet saith, *None can deny, but that it much conduceth to the publick safety, that Malefactors should be punished.* And again, *Who*, saith he, *would not rather preferr humane Justice (than see a Righteous man opprest) which as the Apostle testifies, is not begirt with the Sword in vain, and which even in persecuting is Religious.* So also to the Proconsul *Scapula*, *We* (saith he) *do not terrifie others, neither are we terrified by others. But as we would have all men saved by admonishing them not to fight against God: So thou mayst both faithfully perform the duty that belongs to thy jurisdiction, and yet not be unmindful of that, of humanity, especially considering that ye also are under the power of the sword.* And as concerning the lawfulness of War he speaks doubtfully; For in his book concerning Idolatry, he saith, *It is much questioned whether Christians may take arms, or whether Souldiers may be admitted to Christianity*: and in that place he seems to favour the Negative; but in another place, after he had a while disputed against the lawfulness of War, he at length distinguisheth between him that entred into Arms before he was baptized, and him that listed himself after Baptism. For saith he, *Their condition is plainly otherwise, who being first Souldiers were afterwards converted to the faith, as theirs whom St.* John *admitted to his Baptism; or that faithful Centurion's whom Christ approved of, and whom St.* Peter *instructed*: *Provided that having once embraced the Christian Faith, and being sealed up thereunto by Baptism, they either renounce the War presently, as some have done; or take special care that they do nothing therein that may offend God.* Whereby it is evident, That some Christians did, or at least might continue in Arms after Baptism, which certainly would not have been permitted, had Warfare been by Christ absolutely forbidden; no more than Southsayers, Magicians, and the professors of such like prohibited Arts, were permitted after Baptism to persist in their Diabolical Professions. *Tertullian* tells us, *That they who professed such Arts as the Christian Discipline did not allow of, were not to be admitted into the Church of Christ.* And St. *Aug. instances*, amongst others, *in common Whores, Bauds, and Stage-Plaiers, none whereof until they had removed their professions would he admit unto the Sacrament.* Of the same opinion also was St. *Cyprian*.

Origen. *Tertullian.* *De Anima.* *De Coron. Militis.* *De Idol.* *De fide & op.* *Ep. 65.*

Obser. 2. War declined not as in it self unlawful, but to avoid Acts repugnant to Christianity. As the *Jews* did.

Secondly, We may observe, that in the Primitive times, Christians did either disapprove or avoid the Wars, not because it was in it self unlawful, but in respect of some circumstances incident to those times, which would not admit of the exercise of War without the doing of some acts which were repugnant to Christian Religion. Thus *Tertullian* forbids a Christian to go to War, not that it was unlawful, but because the Discipline of War did sometimes enjoyn such acts, as the Discipline of Christ could not allow of: In the Epistle of *Dolobella* to the *Ephesians*, as it is recorded by *Josephus*, the *Jews* desire to be exempted from all military expeditions, not simply as being unlawful, but that being mixt with strangers, they could not sufficiently perform the Rites and Ceremonies of their own Law, nor would their Religion permit them to make long marches, or to perform acts of Hostility on the Sabbath day: and the same *Josephus* tells us that for these very reasons, the *Jews* got leave of *L. Lentulus* to be discharged the Army: The same Historian also relates, that the *Jews* being banished *Rome*, some betook themselves to the Wars, others were punished for refusing to take Arms in reverence to their Country Laws, and for the reasons above mentioned; whereunto they sometimes added a third, namely, *Because they thought it a sin to make War against their own Counrty-men, especially being persecuted for observing their own Country Laws.* But being freed from these inconveniences they refused not to take Arms, and that under foreign Kings, but still *under condition, that they might enjoy their own Laws, and worship God after the manner of their Fore-fathers.* Unto these dangers that the Wars exposed them unto may be added, that which *Tertullian* objects, That they were sometimes commanded to swear by the Gods of the *Gentiles*, *Mars*, *Jupiter*, *&c.* Which unto Christians was a very great scandal, as well as to the *Jews*. Whereupon the same *Tertullian*, in another place thus Apologizeth for them, *Shall*, saith he, *a Christian watch to guard the Temples of those gods whom he hath renounced? Shall he sup there where he is forbidden to eat? Shall he defend those spirits by night which he exorciseth by day?* And a little after, *How many other great offences may be seen in military-duties, which cannot be otherwise interpreted, but as breaches of our Christian Laws.*

Jos. Ant. l. 11. *Lib. de Idol.* *De Coron Militis.*

Obser. 3. The Fathers

A third thing observable is this, That many Christians in the primitive times were inflamed with so great a zeal to an holy life, that they oft-times embraced the Godly Counsels

ſels of wiſe-men, with the ſame fervor of devotion, as if they had been the commands of Chriſt. *Chriſtians,* ſaith *Anaxagoras, will not contend in judgement with thoſe that rob them.* And *Salvianus* was of opinion, that it was the command of Chriſt, that we ſhould rather yield up our own right, than proſecute the Law for it. But this, if taken generally, may be imbraced as good and Fatherly Counſel tending to Evangelical perfection, but was never digeſted into a Chriſtian precept.

gave it as their Counſel but not as Chriſts precept.

In like manner the Fourth Council of *Carthage* decreed *That a Biſhop though provoked, ſhould never ſue for things tranſitory.* So moſt of the ancient Fathers condemned *all Oaths,* as unlawful, without any exceptions; whereas St. *Paul* himſelf to gain belief in a ſerious matter, *did ſwear. A Chriſtian* in *Tatian, refuſed the* Prætorſhip; and *Tertullian* tells us *that a Chriſtian ſhould not affect Magiſtracy. Lactantius* * alſo denies that a juſt man (and ſuch he would have a Chriſtian to be) ought *to make War*; but denies alſo that he ſhould *navigate the Seas.* How many of the ancient Fathers do diſſwade Chriſtians from *Second Marriages*? yet no wiſe man will from thence conclude, that any of theſe are in themſelves unlawful: for though they are all of them excellent Ornaments to our Chriſtian profeſſion, and very acceptable to God; yet are they not impoſed on us by the neceſſity of any Law. (Nay farther, admit that there were ſome places of Scripture which did ſeemingly reſtrain the political uſe of the Sword, yet ſince it hath been accounted by all good men a means ſufficient for the avoiding of perſonal inconveniences, (as mutilation, *&c.*) to admit of any ſenſe rather than the literal, as of the plucking out of the right eye, the cutting off, of the right hand, *&c.* Much rather ſhould thoſe places of Scripture, that are urged againſt the power of the Sword, admit of any ſenſe; than that it ſhould be thought, that Chriſtianity ſhould deſtroy that, which is the chiefeſt inſtrument of juſtice, the only curb to vice, and one of the main pillars of humane Society. For if it be granted, that the World cannot ſubſiſt without Government, nor any Government without Laws, and that the Laws themſelves ſignifie but little without Coercion: then it is as certain that that Religion cannot be good, that holds forth ſuch doctrine whoſe conſequence will deſtroy all Government; and therefore ſuch a doctrine is to be ſuppreſt with all care and prudence, as the greateſt peſt and nuſance to a Commonwealth: and thoſe very men that did firſt intend by this doctrine to exauctorate Princes and Magiſtrates, would (it is to be feared) be the very firſt, that would take up Arms to abett and eſtabliſh their own wild and exorbitant fancies: And thoſe Princes who ſuffer themſelves to be deluded by them, will quickly find the conſequences to be inconſiſtent with Government; when being diſarmed, they ſhall be diſabled to defend themſelves againſt their Neighbours, to ſuppreſs mutinies and ſeditions at home, or to give that protection unto their own ſubjects againſt rapine and violence, which in honour and Conſcience is due unto them. But let theſe ſuffice to diſſolve thoſe objections that are uſually brought out of holy Writ againſt the lawfulneſs of War; and now let us ſee what may be brought to confirm our opinion, namely, That all War is not unlawful.

Vid. Amb. de Off. lib. 2. c. 21. Greg. M. l. 2. Indict. 11. ep. 58.

* *Lib. 5. c. 18.*

Arguments proving ſome Wars lawful

And here in the firſt place, we may alledge many Authors and thoſe more antient, who hold, That Chriſtians may lawfuly put to death incorrigible Malefactors, and conſequently may make a juſt War; of which *Clemens Alexandrinus* ſhall lead the van, *A Chriſtian,* ſaith he, *being called to be a Supream Magiſtrate, as was* Moſes, *is to be unto his Subjects a living Law, encouraging the juſt with rewards, and reſtraining the unjuſt by ſevere puniſhments.* And in another place deſcribing the habit of a Chriſtian, he ſaith, That it would become him to be unſhod unleſs he be a Souldier. In thoſe Conſtitutions, that are fathered upon *Clemens Romanus,* we read, *That every putting of men to death is not unlawful: but that only which deſtroys an innocent perſon, yet ſo notwithſtanding that the Magiſtrate alone is to determin who are innocent.* But ſetting aſide theſe private authorities, let us proceed to thoſe that are publick, that is, of the Church, which in this caſe is of greateſt moment. And this I affirm, That no man was ever rejected from Baptiſm, or Excommunicated the Church becauſe he was a Souldier; which certainly ought to have been done, had War been inconſiſtent with the precepts of the new Law. The ſame Author elſewhere ſets down, who anciently were to be admitted to, and who were to be rejected from Baptiſm; *Let the Souldier,* ſaith he, *that deſires Baptiſm be inſtructed, to abſtain from wrong doing, and from oppreſſion, and to content himſelf with his pay: If he be willing to obey, let him be admitted.* *Tertullian* in his Apology, ſpeaking in the perſon of Chriſtians, ſaith, *Navigamus & nos, vobiſcum, & militamus; We both ſail and fight together with you in the ſame Fleet.* A little before he had ſaid, *We, though ſtrangers, do notwithſtanding ſupply all your places and Offices, we fill your Cities, Iſlands, Caſtles, Towns, Councils, yea, and your very Camps.* And in the ſame book, he tells the Emperour *M. Aurelius,* That the prayers of his Chriſtian Souldiers had procured from God, Rain in the time of Drought. And in his book, *De Corona,* he commends the Gallantry and Magnanimity of that Souldier, before all his brethren, that had thrown away the Garland when he had won it; intimating unto the ſaid Emperor, that he had many other ſuch Chriſtian Souldiers. Whereunto

Invitis pedibus.

Conſt. l. 8. c. 32.

unto we may add, That some Souldiers there were that endured Torments even to death for the Christian Faith; and were therefore worthily admitted by the Church to the same honour with other Martyrs, amongst whom he makes mention of three of *Pauls* Companions, one *Cerealis* under *Decian*, *Marinus* under the Emperor *Valerian*, 50 Souldiers under *Aurelian*, *Victor*, *Maurus*, and *Valentinus* with diverse others. *Cyprian* concerning *Laurentinus* and *Ignatius*, both *African* Souldiers, writes thus, *They were once Souldiers fighting under secular Princes, but they were also true Souldiers of God when by the confession of their faith in Christ, they vanquished the Devil, and by their invincible patience under the Cross were ennobled with the Crown of Martyrdom.* Whereby it is plain what esteem the Primitive Christians had of Souldiers, even before any of their Emperors under whom they served, became Christians. And if the Christians of those times did express an unwillingness to be spectators at the execution of Capital punishments; it is not to be wondred at, considering that those punishments were but too frequently executed upon their fellow Christians: especially if we add thereunto some grains of allowance, for that the Roman Laws were far more severe and cruel, than would consist with Christian Lenity: As sufficiently appears by that one *Silanian* Decree of the Senate; the Rigor whereof was somewhat mitigated by the Emperor *Adrian*, as *Spartianus* records it. Amongst which severe Laws we may place that which forbad the Testimony of any servant to be taken unless he were tortured. But after that *Constantine* the Great began not only to approve of, but to advance Christianity, even then also were Capital punishments frequently executed. For even *Constantine* himself (amongst many others) enacted this Law of sowing up of Paracides in a sack, which is yet extant in the Code, under the Title of Murtherers of their own Parents or Children; though he was otherwise so remiss in punishing, that by several Historians, it was imputed unto him as a Blemish. Yet *Zonaras* gives this Testimony of him, That he was very merciful to such as reformed their evil lives: for he would often say, *Abscindendum est membrum ægrotans ac putridum, ne sana contagio corrumpat, non id, quod aut sanatum jam sit, aut sanescat; That member that is putrid and incurable is to be cut off, lest the sound should be infected, but not that which is either healed, or healing.* Besides *Constantine* had a multitude of Christians in his Army, and (as Historians tell us) had the name of Christ embroydered on his Banners, and from him it was that the Military Oath was changed into that form extant in *Vegetius*, namely, *By God, by Christ, and the Holy Ghost, and by the Majesty of the Emperor, who according to Gods Ordinance is to be beloved, and reverenced by all mankind.* Neither was there at that time any one Bishop (that we read of among so many that were great sufferers for Religion) that did ever reprove *Constantine* for putting Malefactors to death, or for making of War; or that did upon the account of Religion, deterr Souldiers from their Military duties, though many of them were severe Disciplinarians, sparing neither Prince nor people, that were defective in their duties. Such was in the Reign of *Theodosius* the Emperor St. *Ambrose*, who thus declares his opinion concerning War, *Non Militare Delictum est, sed propter prædam Militare, Simply to go to War: is no sin, but to fight for spoil and plunder is wicked.* So likewise in his Offices, *That force whereby either our Country is defended from our enemies by War, or the weak and innocent defended at home, or our Associates from Pirats and Robbers, is perfect Justice.* This Argument is of so great force; that I shall need no other. And yet I am not ignorant that sometimes Bishops and other good Christians have often by their Intercession turned Capital punishments, into Pecuniary Mulcts, or some lesser punishments not reaching to life: *Officium sacerdotis est intervenire pro reis*; It is the duty of a Priest to interceed for the guilty, saith *Aug.* And there is a right introduced by Custom, That they that flee to the Altar for Sanctuary, are not to be delivered up until faith be given for the saving of their lives; and that such as were for misdemeanors delivered to Prison, should at *Easter* be freely released; but he that throughly perpends these and such like Customs, shall find, That they proceed rather from minds full fraught with Christian Charity, which watcheth all opportunities and occasions to do good, than from minds quarrelling at the equity of Capital punishments: whence it was that the priviledges of those times and places, yea and the very intercessions themselves were moderated with some exceptions, as we may learn by *Cassiodore*. But here some will object against us the 12th. Canon of the Council of *Nice*, which sounds to this sence, *If any being by the grace of God called, shall first express their faith by deserting the War, and afterwards returning to their vomit shall by money or favor, seek to be re-admitted into the War; these after the three years allowed them to hear the word, shall remain among the Penitentials for ten years. But in this case a strict observation must be taken, how such persons stand affected, and what fruits of Repentance they bring forth; for whosoever among them shall shew forth their sincere conversion by fear, by tears, by Patience and good works without dissimulation, these fulfilling their three years of hearing shall at length communicate in prayers, and afterwards it shall be lawful for the Bishop to deal more tenderly with them. But if any of them*

Spartianus.

Paracides

Serm. 7.

Lib. 11. c. 40.
12 Can. of Nicen Council.

them shall bear it but indifferently, and shall think that their very entrance into the Church is sufficient, these shall fulfil their whole time. Whereunto I answer, that by the time of 13 years Penance we may collect, That the sin was neither small nor dubious; for so great a punishment must needs be inflicted for some Crimes that were both to God abominable, and to all good men scandalous, which without question was Idolatry. For the words preceeding in the elventh Canon do manifestly referr us to the times of *Licinius*, which gives a very great light to the understanding of the sense of this Canon. This *Licinius* as *Eusebius* relates, in his War against *Constantine*, first turned all Christians out of their houses, and made sale of their goods; then drew out all the Christian Souldiers and Officers both out of his Armies and Cities from the rest: and then commanded, *That unless they would of their own accord sacrifice to Devils, they should all of them be cashiered from their Offices.* (Which fact of his was afterwards imitated by *Julian*,) whereupon many renounced their commands, and among them, one *Victricius*; so did 1104 more in *Armenia* under *Dioclesian*, concerning whom, there is honourable mention made in our *Martyrologies*: and so in *Ægypt* did *Menna*, and *Hesychius*. So also in the times of *Licinius*, did many renounce their Commands, amongst whom was *Arsacius*, mentioned among the Confessors, and one *Auxentius* afterwards made Bishop of *Mopsuestia*. Now they, that out of tenderness of Conscience had formerly renounced their Commands, had no possible means to be re-admitted under *Licinius*, but by a publick Abjuration of the Christian Faith: wherefore as they that were so admitted, committed much the greater sin (being against knowledge and Conscience) so they deserved a much greater punishment, than those mentioned in the foregoing words of the Canon, namely, that without any danger either of life or goods had renounced their Christianity. But to interpret this Canon so generally, as if it comprehended all manner of going to War, is infinitely against reason. For the same Historian testifies, That many of them that under *Licinius* had laid down their Arms, and whilst *Licinius* Reigned, did never reassume them, because they would not abjure their faith in Christ, being by *Constantine* left to their own choice, were upon their request, re-admitted. There are likewise, that urge against us the Epistle of Pope *Leo*, where it is said *to be against the Ecclesiastical Canons to return into a Secular War, after the Act of Repentance.* But here we must understand, That from Penitentiaries as well as from Priests and Monks, there was required a more strict, and austere course of life, than what was required from other Christians: That they might be as great examples to others, of Contrition and Humiliation; as they had been before, of prevarication. For as *Leo* well observes, *Illicitorum veniam postulantem, oportet etiam multis licitis abstinere*; *It is but just that he that begs pardon for his unlawful acts, should abstain from some things otherwise lawful.* So in an Epistle wrote by some Bishops to King *Lewis* we read, *Quilibet tanto à se licita debet abscindere, quantò se meminit & illicita perpetrasse*; *Every man ought so far to abridge himself of things lawful, by how much he remembreth that he hath committed some things unlawful.* So in those ancient Customs of the Church which to gain the greater reverence are commended unto us under the name of the Apostles Canons, It is decreed *that no Bishop, Priest or Deacon should addict himself to the War, so as to retain the dignity of both Functions, both Civil and Sacerdotal*; But *leaving unto* Cæsar *the things that are* Cæsars, *they should give unto God, the things that are Gods.* Whereby it appears that they who were not thought worthy to be admitted to Ecclesiastical dignities, were not interdicted those that were Military: with this also, That none who after Baptism had obtained any Office Civil or Military, could be admitted into the Clergy. As may also be collected from the several Epistles of *Syncius*, *Innocentius*, and from the *Toletan* Council. For Clergy men were not chosen out of any sort of Christians, but out of such as were likely to be exemplary unto others in austerity of life and manners. Besides upon Military Officers, as also upon some Civil Magistrates, there lies a perpetual obligation: But such as put themselves into Holy Orders, ought not to be entangled with any other care, nor diverted by any other daily Labour. For which cause, it was provided by the 6th Canon, *That no Bishop, Priest or Deacon should take upon them, any secular imployment, nor thrust themselves into any publick Office.* And by the 6th. Canon of the *African* Council, They were forbidden to be Sollicitors of other mens affairs, or to defend other mens causes. But that which gives the greatest reputation to our opiniou is, the judgement of the Church which we have set down in the third Canon of the first Council of *Arles* which was held under *Constantine*: The words sound thus, *Concerning those that cast away their Arms in the time of peace, it pleaseth the Synod, that they should be debared from the Communion*: that is, They that lay aside their Arms when there is no persecution that threatens them, for by the word, *Peace*, the Primitive Christians understood *only a vacancy from persecution*, as appears by *Cyprian* and others; *Nostræ paci, quod est bellum quam persecutio? As to the peace of the Church, What greater War can there be than persecution?* So St. *Cyprian*

Hist. Eccl. l. 10. c. 8.

Can. Apost. 6. 8. *Vid Ep. Hier. ad nepot.*

Tertul.

Cyprian. *Cyprian, when God began to give peace unto his Church*; That is, when he freed it from Persecution. Next we have the example of *Julians* Souldiers, who were no mean proficients in the School of Christianity; for they were ready to testifie their faith in Christ by the effusion of their blood, of whom St. *Ambrose* speaks thus, *The Emperor* Julian *though an Apostate, yet had many Christians that fought under his Banner; to whom when command was given to march against the enemy in defence of their Country, they readily obeyed: But being commanded to march against the Christians, then they acknowledged no Emperor but the King of Heaven.* Such also were long before them the *Thebæan* Legion, which in the Reign of the Emperor *Dioclesian* was converted to the Christian Faith, by *Zabda* the Thirtieth Bishop of *Jerusalem*, which Legion did afterwards leave behind them a singular pattern to all future Generations of Christian patience and constancy; whereof I shall have occasion to speak more at large hereafter. It shall suffice in this place to rehearse that excellent speech they made to the Emperor, which doth both solidly, and summarily represent unto us the Duty of a Christian Souldier: *Against any Foreign Power we freely offer our hands, which yet we dare not embrew in the blood of Innocents. Our Arms which have been long practised in suppressing vice, and in vanquishing Foes, never yet knew how to oppress the Righteous, or to cut the Throats of our Neighbours and fellow-Citizens. When first we engaged in War we remember, it was to protect and not to destroy them: we have hitherto fought for Justice, for Piety, for the defence of Innocence: For these prizes we have slighted all dangers, we have fought for the defence of our faith; which should we have broke with God, How canst thou, O Emperor, expect that we should keep with thee?* *Basil* also gives this Testimony of the Primitive Christians, *That their Ancestors never accounted that execution that was done in War as Murther; but alwaies held them excused, that fought for the defence of Chastity and of Piety.*

CHAP.

CHAP. III.

War divided into Publick and private. The Supream Power explained.

THE first and most necessary division of War is this, That some are Publick, and some Private, and some mixt. Publick is that which is made by publick Authority; and Private is that when the Authority is so; and mixt when it is in part Publick, and in part Private: and First, Let us treat of that which is Private, as being most ancient, That by the Law of Nature some Private War may lawfully be waged is, as I suppose, sufficiently proved by what hath been already said, where it was shewed, That to repel force with force, was no ways repugnant to Natural equity. But the Question will be, Whether since the erection of Courts of Justice, it be now lawful to repel force with force? Whereunto I answer, That although Courts of Judicature were not instituted by Nature, but by humane Authority: yet doth natural reason, and Common equity instruct us, That it is more agreeable to common Honesty, and to the conservation of peace and tranquillity amongst men, that all differences should be publickly scanned, and determined by persons that are unconcerned; rather than by them, who being blinded with self-love, do oft-times mistake right for wrong, and will do that only which seems good in their own eyes: *Non est singulis concedendum quod per magistratum publice possit fieri, ne occasio sit majoris tumultus faciendi; That is not to be granted to every private man, that may be done publickly by a Magistrate, lest for every petty injury men run into Tumults.* And hence it is, saith King *Theodorick, That so great a reverence is due to the Law, that no man ought to revenge himself with his own hand, or by the suggestion of his own passions. For if all differences may be determined by plan force, wherein would a calm peace differ from the tumults of War?* And therefore the Laws call that Force, *When any man takes that which is his due with his own hands, without the determination of a Judge.*

I. War divided.

Paulus Jurisconf.

Cassiod. l. 4. Var. Ep. 4.

Most

II. That Tribunals being erected, all war is not unlawful.

Most certain it is, That the Licence which before Tribunals were established publickly, was permitted, is since much restrained: And yet in some places the same Licence still remaineth, namely, where Judgment cannot be had against offenders. For the Law in prohibiting a man to take his own, unless it be judicially, doth tacitely imply that it be in such a place, and at such a time where an ordinary course of Justice may be had.

Now Judgment ceaseth either for a while only, or for continuance: For a while, when the Judge cannot be so long waited for without certain danger and damage. *Servius* upon these words of *Virgil*, *Injicere manum parcæ*, The Fates have snatcht him hence, tells us, That the Poet makes use of a Phrase borrowed from the Law: for it is called *Injectio manus*, the snatching away of a thing, as it were by force, when without attending the warrant of Authority, we suddenly seize upon something that is our due, which is usually done when the Laws do for a while cease, And sometimes there is a total and continued cessation of Judgment, and that either by Right or in Fact. By Right, as in places that are desert and unoccupied, on the Seas and in Islands not inhabited, and in any other such places wherein are not civil Societies. In Fact, as when Subjects do not regard the Sentence of the Judge, or the Judge publickly refuses to examine the case. Now what we said before, namely, that since publick Judicatories were established, all Private Wars are not repugnant to the Law of Nature; is clearly evinced by the Law given to the Jews, where God gives this charge by *Moses*, *If a Thief be found breaking up (i. e. by night) and be smitten that he dye, there shall be no blood shed for him; but if the Sun be risen upon him, there shall be blood shed for him.* Certainly this Law so accurately distinguishing of the time when the offence was committed, seems not only to induce an impunity, but serves to explain even the Law of Natnre; being not so much grounded on any one particular Divine Precept, as indeed upon common equity, which guided other Nations also to do the like. The old Attick Law was this, If any man shall steal in the day time, to above the value of fifty Drachmaes, let him be tryed by eleven men: But if a man shall steal to the smallest value in the night, he may lawfully be killed. This ancient Law of *Solon* doubtless occasioned that of the twelve Tables among the *Romans*. *Si nox furtum faxit, si furem aliquis occisit, jure cæsus esto*; *If any man shall kill a Thief robbing in the night, he shall be held innocent.* So by the Laws of all Nations that as yet we have known, He that by Arms shall defend himself against him that attempts to take away his life, is accounted guiltless; which so plain a consent doth evidently assure us, that there is nothing in it repugnant to the Law of Nature.

Exod. 22. 2.

Solon's Law.

Vide infra Bo. 2. ch. 12.

III. Neither is it repugnant to the Evangelical Law.

But whether this private war be justifiable by the more perfect Law of the Gospel, is somewhat more doubtful: I dare not but grant that Almighty God, who hath a much greater power over lives than we have, might have imposed upon us such an unlimited patience, that even privately, in a case of imminent danger, we ought rather to be killed than to kill. But whether it be his pleasure thus strictly to tye us up, is the thing in question. There are two places of Scripture that seem to favour the Affirmative, which we quoted above when we handled the general question: The former was that in the fifth of *Mat. v.* 39. *Resist not him that doth thee an injury*: And the latter that in the twelfth to the *Rom. v.* 19. *Dearly Beloved, Avenge not your selves*; which the Latin Translation renders, *Defend not your selves.* But a third may be added, namely that of Christ to *Peter*, *Put up thy Sword into the Sheath, for they that take the Sword shall perish by the Sword.* Some there are likewise that urge the example of Christ himself, who dyed for his enemies, *Rom.* 5. 8, 10. Neither are there wanting among the Ancients, some, who although they do not disallow of publick War, yet believed that all private, even that which is defensive was forbidden. Some places out of St. *Ambrose* for war we alledged above, but many more and much clearer, and more generally known, may be produced out of St. *Augustine*: But yet the same *Ambrose* in another place saith, *That haply therefore Christ said unto* Peter, *when he shewed him two Swords, It is enough: As if till the Gospel came it had been lawful, that so there might be, as in the Law the doctrine of Equity, so in the Gospel the doctrine of Verity.* And in another place he tells us: That a Christian though assaulted by Robbers, ought not to strike again; *Ne dum salutem defendit, pietatem contaminet: Lest whilst he seeks to preserve his own safety, he sin against piety.* And St. *Augustin* himself speaking of Thieves and Robbers, saith, *Legem quidem non reprehendo, quæ tales permittit interfici, sed quomodo istos qui interficiunt, defendam, non invenio. The Law that adjudgeth these men to death, I disallow not; but how to justifie the Executioners, I find not.* And in another place, *But as to them that give advice, that some men are to be put to death, lest others by them should be destroyed, I cannot subscribe, unless he that kills him be either a Soldier or a publick Executioner, who doth it not by his own, but by publick Authority.* And of the same opinion was *Basil*, as appears in his second Epistle to *Amphilochius*, whereunto we may add the last Canon of the Council of *Orleans*, cited by *Gratian*. But the opposite opinion, as it is more Catholick, so it seems to be more agreeable to truth, namely, That Christians are not

Mat. 5. 39.

Mat. 26. 52.

In Luc. 10.

De off. l. 3. *c.* 3.

Lib. 1. *de lib. Arb.* 15.

Ep. 154. *ad Publ.*

Cap. 43. & 55.

C. 13. *q.* 2.

not obliged to ſuch an height of patience: We are indeed commanded by the Chriſtian Law, to love our Neighbours as our ſelves, but not above our ſelves; ſo that when we are both of us involved in the ſame, or in equal danger, we are no where forbid to prefer our own ſafety before anothers; as we have already proved by the Rules St. *Paul* gives to Chriſtian Beneficence, and which *Caſſiodore* in the duties or offices of Friendſhip likewiſe confirms. *There is,* ſaith he, *neither Law nor Reaſon, that can oblige us to redeem another mans ſoul with the loſs of our own; or to procure the preſervation of his body (ſetting aſide our hopes of eternal ſalvation) with the certainty of our own ruine.* But if any man ſhould object, that we are bound to prefer our ſelves before others in dangers that are equal, but not in ſuch as are unequal; and therefore I ought rather to give up mine own life, than to ſuffer him that invades me to fall into eternal damnation. To this we anſwer, That it is probable that he that is aſſaulted may ſtand in as much need of time to repent in; and that the Aggreſſor may alſo have ſpace ſufficient before he dye, to do the ſame. Beſides, That danger into which a man wilfully caſts himſelf, and out of which he may (if he pleaſe) redeem himſelf, ſeems not in any Moral Judgment to be much eſteemed. Certain it is, That ſome of the Apoſtles even to the laſt time, and in the preſence and in the very ſight of Chriſt, ſeemed to travel begirt with Swords; and ſo alſo did other Galilæans journeying out of their own Country towards *Jeruſalem,* (the High-ways being much infeſted with Thieves, as *Joſephus* informs us;) So alſo did the Eſſenes, the moſt harmleſs of all men, as the ſame Hiſtorian records it. And hence it came, That when Chriſt told his Diſciples that the time was at hand, when they ſhould ſell their Veſts to buy themſelves Swords, *Luke* 22. 36. ſome of the Apoſtles readily made anſwer, That there were in their company two Swords: But at that time there were none in that company but the Apoſtles; ſo that it muſt needs follow that ſome of them did go, even in Chriſts own preſence, armed with Swords. Beſides, what Chriſt then ſaid, although in truth it was not a Precept but a Prophecy, foretelling thoſe many dangers that were then at hand, (as appears by that oppoſition which theſe words have unto thoſe in the 35th verſe, which ſpeaks of the firſt times which were ſecure and proſperous times, wherein they needed neither Money nor Swords, whereas in theſe later times that were approaching, they ſhould have need of both) yet was it ſuch, as ſeems to be taken from that which was then wont to be done, and which the Apoſtles might lawfully do. It was well ſaid of *Cicero, Gladios habere certe non liceret ſi uti illis nullo pacto liceret; Surely it were utterly unlawful for Chriſtians to have Swords, if it were altogether unlawful for them to uſe them.*

Caſſ. de Amicitia.

Some of the Apoſtles in Chriſts preſence travelled with Swords.

Luke 22. 36.

But as to the other Objection taken from *Mat.* 5. 39. namely, *That we reſiſt not him that doth us an injury;* It is no more of univerſal obligation than that which follows, *Give unto every man that asks:* Both which do certainly admit of ſome exceptions, otherwiſe we ſhould too far neglect our ſelves: Nay that precept of *giving to every one that asketh,* hath nothing ſubjoyned unto it to reſtrain it, but is left to the judgment of common equity; whereas this of *non-reſiſtance,* ſeems to be both explained and reſtrained by the ſubſequent inſtance of a Box on the Ear; that we may underſtand that that precept doth *then* oblige us, when the injury done us is but ſlight and eaſily born, ſuch as is a blow on the Cheek, or ſomewhat that is like unto it; which rather argues a contempt in the ſtriker, than infers any conſiderable damage to him that is ſtruck: For otherwiſe it had been much better to have ſaid, Reſiſt not him that injures thee, no though he ſhould attempt to kill thee. And as to thoſe words of St. *Paul* to the *Romans, Avenge not your ſelves,* the word ἐκδικεῖν there uſed, doth not properly ſignifie to *defend,* as the Latin Tranſlation renders it, but to *revenge,* as appears by other places where the ſame word is uſed: As *Luke* 18. 7, 8. *And ſhall not God avenge his own Elect?* So alſo, *Luke* 21. 22. *Theſe be the days of Vengeance:* The like we find 2 *Theſſ.* 1. 8. 1 *Pet.* 2. 14. And this the connection of the words will plainly ſhew, for the words preceding are theſe, *Requite no man evil for evil:* which is the proper deſcription of *Revenge,* but not of *Defence.* Beſides, St. *Paul* ſtrengthneth this advice with that place of *Deut. Vengeance is mine, I will repay it:* which muſt neceſſarily be underſtood of returning injury for injury: For neither can the Hebrew word there uſed be in propriety of ſpeech, nor the congruity of the Sentence in that place poſſibly underſtood of a bare Defence.

2. Object. anſwered. Mat. 5. 39. expl.

Private war in our own defence lawful.

Rom. 12. 19. expl.

Rom. 13. 4. 1 Theſſ. 4. 6

Now as to that which was ſaid to St. *Peter, Put up thy Sword, &c.* It doth indeed prohibit the uſe of the Sword at that time for revenge, but not at other times in caſes of neceſſary defence: Neither indeed had *Peter* at that time any need of Defence; for Chriſt had already interceded for his Diſciples, ſaying, *Suffer theſe to go away, Jo.* 18. 8, 9. Nor had Chriſt himſelf any need of St. *Peter's* Sword: *For thinkeſt thou,* ſaith he, *that I cannot now pray to my Father, and he ſhall ſend me more than ten Legions of Angels?* Neither would he then be defended, for he thus infers, *Shall I not drink of the Cup that my Father hath given me? ver.* 11. And ſo in *Mat. How then ſhall the Scriptures be fulfilled, that thus it muſt be?* Whence we may conclude, That St. *Peter* was at that time tranſ-

Put up thy Sword, expl.

ported with an eager desire of Revenge, (being very hot and zealous) and not of Defence only: Whereunto we may add, That *Peter* did make use of his Sword against those that came armed against Christ with publick Authority. Now whether any case will justifie our resistance of those that are thus armed, is a peculiar question hereafter to be particularly handled: And whereas Christ adds these words, *They that take the Sword shall perish by the Sword*; it was either Proverbially spoken, to shew that blood requires blood, and consequently that the use of Arms was never without peril; or rather as *Origen*, *Theophylact*, and others interpret the place, it shews that we should not be too rash in taking the Sword of Vengeance out of Gods hands, who will certainly in his own time repay blood with blood. And in this sence it is expresly said, *Apoc.* 13. 10. *He that leadeth into Captivity, shall go into Captivity*; *He that killeth with the Sword, shall be killed by the Sword*; *Here is the patience and faith of the Saints*; very consonant whereunto is that of *Tertullian*, *So fit is God to be trusted with thy patience*; *that if thou shalt commit thy sufferings unto him, he will be thine Avenger: If thy grief and pain, he will be thy Physician*; *If thou trust him with thy Death, he will raise thee up again*: *O how great a power hath patience, that is able to make God himself to become our Debtor*! Besides, In these words of Christ, there seems to be coucht a Prophecy of those punishments, which God would take of the blood thirsty Jews by the Sword of the Romans. But as to the example of Christs dying for his enemies, it may be thus answered: Though all Christs actions upon Earth were full of vertue and goodness, and such as may be (so far forth as humane frailty will permit) laudably imitated by us, and that cannot want their reward; yet were they not all such as were done, either in obedience to any Law; or being done, are obliging, as a Law unto us. For that Christ dyed for the wicked, and for his enemies, was not by the Command of any Law, but by a special agreement and Covenant with the Father, who had promised that for his so doing, *He would not only exalt him in glory, far above all Principalities and Powers in Heaven or Earth*; but that he would build him also a Church, an holy Seed, that should endure for ever, *Esay* 53. 10. But this fact of Christ was otherwise singular, and not to be parallel'd, as St. *Paul* testifies, *Rom.* 5. 7. And Christ indeed bids us to expose our lives to peril, yet not for every man, but only for the Brethren, that is, for those that profess the same Faith with our selves, 1 *Jo.* 3. 16.

Patience to be preferred before Revenge.

The Objections out of the Fathers answered.

Can. 45.

And as to those Sentences that are quoted out of the Fathers, they were partly good Fatherly Counsels, and Exhortations to an holy life, tending to perfection rather than any strict precepts to oblige us; and partly their own private opinions, rather than the doctrine of the whole Church: For in those ancient Canons called the Apostles, *He was to have been excommunicated, that in a Fray had slain his Adversary at the first blow for his too much heat or rashness.* And St. *Augustin* himself whom we before quoted in the defence of the contrary opinion, seems notwithstanding to approve of this in his 84th question upon *Exodus*: So also doth St. *Ambrose*, *O Lord*, saith he, *Why dost thou command me to buy a Sword, if thou forbiddest me to strike? Why dost thou bid me to have one, if having it, I may not use it? Unless perhaps thou wouldst have us to be armed for defence, but not for revenge.*

Christians may bear Arms for Defence, not for Revenge.

IV.

Solemn War what it is.

Of publick Wars some are solemn according to the Law of Nations, and some are less solemn: That which I here call solemn, is usually and for the most part called just, in the same sence as a Testament is being opposed to a *Codicil*; or as a solemn Marriage between such as are free, compared to a Clandestine between such as were bond: Not that it was not lawful to bequeath Goods by a *Codicil*, or for a Servant to have his married woman with him in the same house; (for even among Freemen there are some marriages not just, and some children not just, as *Paulus* the Lawyer notes, and some liberty not just, as *Seneca* observes:) But that a solemn Testament and a solemn Marriage, hath by the Civil Law some Rights and Effects peculiar to themselves, which others have not; which is very useful to be observed: For that many misunderstanding the word *just*, condemn all wars as unrighteous and unlawful, that are not solemn. Now that a war be solemn according to the Law of Nations, two things are requisite: First, That it be on both sides made by the Authority of those who in their respective Cities have the Soveraign power: And next, That it be waged with such Rites and Formalities as the Law of Nations requires, whereof we shall discourse in its proper place. And because these are joyntly requisite, therefore the one without the other is not sufficient: That publick war which we call less solemn, may be both defective in these rites, and also be made against private men, and that by the Authory of any Magistrate. And truly if we consider the thing it self without regard to the Civil Law, every Magistrate as he is entrusted with the peoples safety, so (in case any violence be offered) is he entrusted with the exercise of that power and jurisdiction, and consequently hath a power to make war. But because by war the whole City is endangered, therefore it is provided by the Laws of almost all Nations, That no war be made but by the Authority of him who hath the supreme power in that City. Such a Law we find extant in *Plato*, and by the Roman Laws

Paul. Sent. l. 2. *c.* 74. *tit.* 19. *L. si uxor D. ad L. Juliam de Adult.*

Sen. de vit. beat. c. 24. *Suet. Octav. c.* 40.

Less Solemn.

De legibus ult.

Laws, whosoever should presume to make War, list Soldiers, or Muster an Army, without special warrant from the Prince, was held guilty of Treason: Or as the Cornelian Law, instituted by *L. Cornelius Sylla*, saith, without warrant from the people, placing the Soveraign Power in them only. There is an ancient Constitution extant in the Code of *Justinian*, made by *Valentinianus* and *Valens*, which runs thus: *Let no man presume to raise an Army without special warrant, or to make War without our knowledg and advice.* Pertinent whereunto is that of St. *Augustin*, *That Natural Order which is best accommodated to the preservation of humane peace, requires that the Counsel and determination of raising of War, should remain in the power of Princes.* Now as all other Rules, be they never so general, must admit of equity to be their Interpreter, so must this Law. First then, It cannot well be doubted, but that it is lawful for him to whom the Lieutenancy of any City is committed, to reduce into obedience, by his Officers, some few Rebels; so as it require not any great force to do it, nor much endangers the City wherein he presides. Or in case the danger threatning the City be very great, and so imminent that it will not admit of so much time as to consult the Supreme Magistrate, pure necessity will plead strongly for exemption. Upon the presumption of this Right it was, that *L. Pinarius* Governor of *Enna*, a Garrison in *Sicily*, being certainly informed that the Townsmen had designed to revolt to the Carthaginians; preserved the said Town, by putting to death the chief Conspirators. Nay even beyond these cases of Necessity, If a King do neglect to revenge the injuries of his Subjects, *Franciscus de Victoria* is so bold as to transfer the right of making War upon the Citizens: But herein he walks by himself, for by all judicious Writers this opinion is rejected as dangerous.

He that lists Soldiers, or Musters an Army without warrant from his Prince, is a Traitor.

V. Whether a War waged by a Magistrate, that hath not an Authority from the Supreme power, be publick? And when?

But by what event soever it happens, that the power of making war is manifestly in inferior Magistrates, whether such a War may be said to be publick, Lawyers agree not: For some affirm it, and some deny it: Surely if by publick we understand nothing else but what is done by the right of a Magistrate, such Wars are publick: And therefore he that in such a case shall set himself in opposition to the Magistrate, incurs the punishment due unto those who behave themselves contumaciously against such as are set over them. But if we take the word Publick in the better sence, for that which is solemn, as without question it is usually taken; then are not such wars publick: For to the legitimating of such a War there must go, as well the judgment of the Supreme Authority, as other Rites and Ceremonies which the Law of Nations have made necessary. Neither doth it at all stagger me that even in such wars, the goods of such as make resistance are lawful prize, and given to encourage the Soldiers; for this doth not so peculiarly belong to a solemn war, but that the same may be done in any other. Besides, It frequently happens that in Empires of large extent, the Lieutenants of Provinces are impowered by their Prince to begin a War; which if so, then it is all one as if the Supreme Magistrate had immediately done it: *Quod faciendi jus quis alii dat, ejus ipse auctor censetur*; *Look, What right any man gives to another to do, that he himself is reputed the Author of.* But that which admits of a larger dispute is, Whether in case no such power be given, the subordinate Magistrate by conjecturing at the will of his Prince, may make War. But this I cannot admit of, for it sufficeth not to foresee what the will of the Prince would be, in case he were consulted withal; but we are to consider, what a Prince would have a Magistrate to do without advising with him, in case the matter be important, and will admit of time enough for a serious debate, if a general Law were to be made thereupon. For though the reason that moves a Princes will, being particularly inspected, may in some particular fact cease; yet the reason universally taken, ceaseth not, which is, That all dangers should be timely prevented: which could not possibly be, if every inferiour Magistrate should assume unto himself the Right of making War. *Cn. Manlius* was not therefore unjustly accused by his Lieutenants, that without order of the people of *Rome* he had made war against the Gallo-Græcians. For although there were certain Legions of the Gauls in *Antiochus* his Army, yet having concluded a League with *Antiochus*, whether that injury were to have been revenged on the Gallo-Græcians, was not in the choice of *Cn. Manlius*, but of the people of *Rome*: *Cato*'s opinion was, That *Cæsar* should be delivered up to the Germans, for making a War against them without order: But (as I believe) not so much regarding the equity of the thing, as indeed to free the City of the fear they had of so potent a Master; for the Germans had given assistance to the Gauls, being then enemies to the Romans; and therefore had no reason to complain of any wrong done them; in case that war with the Romans against the Gauls were just: But *Cæsar* should have been contented to have beaten the Germans out of *Gallia*, which was the Province allotted to him, and not have prosecuted the War into *Germany*, without first consulting the people of *Rome*; especially considering that there was no danger then imminent: The Germans therefore could have no right to demand *Cæsar*, considering that they had given the Romans just cause to make War upon them; but the Romans had just cause to punish *Cæsar* for transgressing his

No Inferior Magistrate can make a Solemn War, without special warrant.

Liv. 48.

Commission; as the Carthaginian Embassador told the Romans plainly, in the very like case, *I do not think it fit for you,* saith he, *to enquire whether* Saguntum *were besieged by the publick Edict of the City of* Carthage, *or by the private Authority of our General; but whether it were done justly or unjustly? For it concerns us only to call our own Subject to an account, by whose order he did it. The only dispute between us and you is, Whether it might be done without breach of our League with you or not?* *Cicero* defends the fact both of *Octavius* and of *Decimus Brutus*, who upon their own private judgments made war upon *Anthony*: But although it had been as clear as the Sun, that *Anthony* had deserved it, yet should they have consulted the Senate and the people of *Rome*, before they had begun it. For although it were granted, that the affront given, did manifestly deserve an hostile invasion; yet ought they to have expected the judgment of the Senate and People of *Rome*, whether it had not been more expedient for the Common-wealth, at that time, to have dissembled it, than to have revenged it; to have treated with him about Articles of Peace, than to have rush'd presently into Arms: For no man ought to be compelled to pursue his own Right, when it cannot be done without fear of a greater loss. Besides, Suppose that *Anthony* had been declared an enemy, yet ought the Senate and People of *Rome* to have had their free choice, under whose conduct that War should be carried on. Thus the Rhodians answered *Cassius*, demanding *Agdes* of them according to their League, That they were ready to send them if the Senate should command them. By this and the like examples (for many such we shall meet with) we may learn, not to approve of every thing that Historians (though of never so good fame) seem to commend unto us: For sometimes they are awed by fear, sometimes byassed by affection; fitting their Stories to their own occasions: wherefore in such cases we should endeavour to be guided by our own uncorrupted Judgments, and not rashly to make those Actions our Precedents, which deserve rather to be excused than applauded; whereby we may be drawn into pernicious errors. Now whereas it hath been said, That a publick War cannot justly be undertaken without the Authority of the Supreme Magistrate; it will be necessary for the better understanding as well of this Question, and of that of a Solemn War, as of divers others, to enquire what that Supreme Power is, and in whom it rests: And the rather, because the Learned of this Age, do not so well determine it; for whilst each of them pursues this Argument, rather according to present use and custom, than according to truth; they have rendred that which, of it self, was not very easie, much more dark and obscure than it was before.

Liv. l. 31.

Though a just cause of War be given, yet should it be left to the Superiors to judge, whether it were safer at that time to have dissembled, or to have revenged it.

Historians not always to be approved.

VI. The Civil Power, what?

That Moral Power whereby Common-wealths are governed, which *Thucydides* calls the Civil Power, he describes by three things; where he calls a City, that is truly so, αὐτόνομον, αὐτόδικον, αὐτοτελῆ, that is, 1. That it should have a power to make or abolish Laws. 2. That it should have a power to pass Judgments. And 3. To create Magistrates, or which the word will likewise bear, to raise Taxes; for every Common-wealth ought to have a Moral Power in these things. *Aristotle* divides the administration of this power into three parts: The first is, The consultation about things common; as about Peace, War, Leagues to be either made or broken. The second is, The choice of fit Persons for Magistrates. And the third is, A power to determine all Controversies. *Dionysius Halicarnassensis* makes the Civil Power to consist in these three things: 1. The Creation of Magistrates, 2. The Legislative Power, And 3. The power of concluding either Peace or War. And elsewhere he adds this fourth, namely, A power to determine all differences, by passing definitive Sentences; and by and by he adds, The care of setling Religion, and the power of calling Assemblies. But he that would rightly divide this power, so that nothing be either defective or redundant, may do it thus: He that rules in any Common-wealth, doth it partly by himself, and partly by others. What he doth by himself concerns either Universals or Particulars: what concerns Universals, are the making of Laws or the abrogating of them; and these are either sacred (so far forth as concerns the Civil State) or prophane. This *Aristotle* calls the Art of building up a City: Those singulars about which this power is conversant, are either things directly Publick, or Private, yet such as are in order to Publick. Those that are directly Publick, are either Actions, as Peace, War, Leagues; or Things, as Taxes, Customs, Tributes, and such like: Wherein also is comprehended that eminent Dominion, that every Common-wealth hath over the Persons and Goods of its own Subjects, so far as concerns the publick safety: And this Art *Aristotle* terms by its general name, Political, that is Civil, or the Art of Counselling and well Advising. Or (as I said) they are things private; namely, things controverted between singular persons, the determination whereof doth much conduce to publick peace and safety; and this Art *Aristotle* terms judicial. But those things which he dispatcheth by another, he doth either by Magistrates or by Procurators, among whom we are to place Embassadors, and Envoyes. And in these things do principally consist the Civil Power.

Pol. l. 4.

That

That we call the Supreme Power, whose Acts are not subject to the power of another, nor can by any Humane Authority be made void; when, I say, by another, I exclude him who hath this Supreme Power, in whose power it is to change his own Will; so also I exclude his Successor who hath the same right, and so the same power and no other. This therefore is that which we call the Supreme Power: Now let us see in whom it rests, the Subject wherein this Soveraign Power remains, is either common or proper: As the common Subject wherein Sight rests is the Body, the proper Subject is the Eye; so of this Supreme Power, the common Subject is the City or Common-wealth, which, as I said before, is a perfect company or society of men. Hence then we exclude those who have given themselves up to the power of another people, as those Nations that were conquered by the Romans, were no longer called Kingdoms, but Roman Provinces: For such a people cannot be called a City, in that sence wherein we now take the word, but the unworthy Members of that City that conquered them, as Servants are the meanest Members of a Family. Again, It sometimes happens, that of divers people there is but one and the same head, and yet every one of these people do constitute one perfect Society; for it is not so in the Moral, as it is in the Natural Body, where it is not possible that one Head should govern two Bodies: For in the Moral, one and the same person diversly considered, may be the head of divers and distinct Bodies, whereof this is a most infallible sign; for whensoever the Regal Family of him in whom the Soveraign power over divers Nations was united, shall be extinct; the power it self separates, and each reverts to its own people. So it may fall out, that many Cities may be linkt in so strait a confederacy, that (as *Strabo* speaks) they may constitute but one well governed Body; and yet doth each of them still retain the state of a perfect City; as is well observed both by others, and also by *Aristotle* in divers places; so then the common Subject wherein this power resides, is a City so understood as I have already exprest. But the proper Subject of this power is either one person or many, according to the several Laws, Customs, and Manners of every Nation.

VII. Power Supreme what it is? In whom it is.

And here first we must disclaim their opinion, who affirm the Supreme Power to be (every where, and without any exception) in the People; and that so fully that it is in their power, either to inforce or to punish their King, if he govern amiss: What great mischiefs this opinion, being once fixed in the minds of the Rabble, already hath, and hereafter may introduce, there is no wise man but may easily discover. For confutation of which opinion, we offer these Arguments to the more ingenious Reader. By all the Laws both of the Hebrews and Romans, it will appear; that it is lawful for every man that hath power over himself, to bind himself as a Servant, or an Apprentice to whom he pleaseth. And why then should it not be as lawful, for any people naturally free, to give themselves up to any one person or Society to be governed wholly by them, without retaining any part of their liberty to themselves? Neither will it suffice to say, this is not to be presumed; for the question is not what in a doubtful case is to be presumed, but what by Right may be done; and it is as vain and frivolous to urge the inconveniences that may arise from hence: For there is no form of Government whatsoever, be it never so well fansied and framed in the Brain, but upon the exercise of it will produce some inconveniences and some dangers with it; so that we must, do what we can, resolve to take the advice of the Comedian, *Aut hæc cum illis sunt habenda, aut illa cum his mittenda sunt*; *either to accept of the inconveniences with the conveniences, or to renounce both*; and so live like Beasts without Government, which is the greatest inconvenience of all. As there are several kinds of Trades or Callings for men to live by, some better, some worse, and every man is permitted to chuse which he pleaseth; so there being several sorts of Government, it is in the peoples choice which of them they will be governed by: Neither is the right to Govern to be measured by the excellency of the Form, whereof divers men judge diversly, but by the freedom of their own will: What *Cato* sometimes said of Laws, may as well be said of Governments; *There are none so perfect, but have some defects.* But what the same *Cato* observed is very true, It is sufficient to commend any Government, that it produceth good effects in the general, and profiteth the greater part of mankind. Now, as *Cicero* speaks, *To reckon up all the inconveniences only in any Government, and to pass over with silence all the conveniences is unjust, because the good that we seek for we cannot obtain, without the evil which we would avoid.* But of these several kinds of Government our choice being made, and the right thereby transferred to another, to reassume it at our pleasure upon what pretence soever is unjust. Many causes there may be for which a people may be induced to renounce, and yield up unto others all right of Government: As namely, when they shall be reduced into so great danger of their Lives, that no other way can be found whereby to defend themselves; or when they shall be opprest with so much want, as that they cannot otherwise sustain themselves. Thus the Israelites being distrest by the Ammonites, sent for *Jephtha*, and rather then be opprest by a Foreign enemy, they transferred the Government

VIII. Not in the people. This proved. Exod. 21. 6. *Gell. l.* 21. *c.* 7. No form of Government without some Inconvenience. *De leg.* 3. Many reasons there may be, why a people may yield up themselves to be Governed by another.

vernment upon him, whom before they had banished, *Judges* 11. This also was the condition of the *Campanes*, when they surrendred themselves unto the *Romans*, in this Form; *We*, say their Embassadors, *in the name of all the people of* Campania, *do freely surrender and give up our selves, our City* Capua, *our Fields, Temples, together with all that we have, both divine and humane, into your power, O Conscript Fathers.* And some people we may read of who have offered themselves to the *Romans* upon condition of protection only, and have been rejected: as the *Falisci*, and the *Samnites*. And if so; what then should hinder, but that some people may in like manner surrender all power and right over themselves to some one man, by whose wisdom and power, they expect protection? Also it may so happen, that a man having vast possessions, will not admit of any to inhabit his Countrey, but under condition to submit to his Jurisdiction: or, It is possible, that a man having large Territories, and a multitude of servants, may manumit them, giving to each a proportion of Land, on condition, that they yield him their subjection with some kind of Tribute. Precedents of this nature we want not; *Tacitus* speaking of the *Germans*, saith, *That every servant hath his several house, and peculiar estate, and governs his own Family: his Lord imposing upon him what proportion of Corn, Cattle and Garments he pleaseth, which he readily payes, and as a servant, hitherto, obeys.* Add hereunto what *Aristotle* observed, That some men are naturally servants; that is, so apt for servitude, as if Nature had made them for no other use: and so are some people too of so servile a disposition, that they know better how to obey, than how to govern; such were the *Cappadocians*, who told the *Romans* plainly, when they offered them Freedom, that they could not live without a King. So *Philostratus* in the Life of *Apollonius*, It is but folly to set at liberty the *Thracians*, *Mysians* and *Getes*, for they value it not. Besides, there were not a few people who have been perswaded to admit of Kingly Government by the example of other Nations, who for many Ages have been observed to live very happily under it. *Seneca* speaking of *Brutus*, saith, *Though he were in other matters a gallant man, yet in this he seemed to me to err, Not to have behaved himself like a Stoick: That he was either affrighted at the Name of a King, when the best Form of Government is that which is under a good King: Or hoped for Liberty there, where the rewards due to Empire and Subjection were so great: Or that he could believe it possible to recall the Primitive Government, unless he could restore the Citizens to their ancient Manners: or that he could reduce them to an equality of Civil Rights, and put in force their ancient Laws, when he saw so many thousands of men to fight,* Non utrum servirent sed utri, *Not whether they should obey or not, but whom they should obey. Some Cities,* saith *Livy*, *were so well pleased with the Government of* Eumenes, *that they would not have changed their condition with the Freest Cities in the world.* The like is recorded by *Isocrates*, *That many deserted the Free Cities of* Greece, *to live in* Salamina *a City in* Cyprus, *under the Mild Government of* Evagoras. Again, such may be the condition of a City, that there remains no probable hopes of safety, unless they put themselves under the Dominion of one single person. Such was the state of the City of *Rome*, which most wise men thought could not have been preserved, had not *Augustus Cæsar* assumed to himself the sole Government of the whole Empire. Such cases, I say, not only may, but do usually happen, as *Cicero* observes in the second of his *Offices*: But (as hath been already said) like as private Dominion may by a Just War be lawfully acquired, so also may Civil Dominion, or the right of Empire, if it depend not upon some other. Nor would I be thought to speak this of Monarchical Government only, where that is received; but the same Arguments will hold for the acquiring of an Oligarchical Government, where the Nobles have excluded the Commons, and assumed the Government upon themselves. What, that there is any Commonwealth so popular, wherein some, as the poor, the stranger, women and youths are not excluded from publick Counsels? Even now there are some people also that have others truckling under them, and who are no less subject unto them, than they could be unto Kings. Whence ariseth that Question in *Livy*, *Are the Collatine people under their own Jurisdiction, or have they any power that is their own?* And the *Campanes* when they surrendred themselves unto the *Romans*, are said to be under the Jurisdiction of the *Romans*. *Acarnania* as also *Amphilochia* are said to be subject to the *Ætolians*: so are *Peræa* and *Caunus* to the Dominion of the *Rhodians*. The Emperour *Otho* gave all the Cities of the *Moors* to the Province of *Granado* in *Spain*, as *Tacitus* testifies: So did *Philip* the City *Pydna* to the *Olynthians*. Many other examples are here produced, all which were absolutely Null, if it be granted, That the Right of Government be at the disposal of them that are governed. Again, some Kings there are, that are not subject to the whole body of the people, as Histories both Sacred and Prophane do testifie. *If thou shalt say,* saith God to the *Israelites*, *I will set a King* supra me, *above me*, Deut. 17. 14. And unto *Samuel* saith God, *Shew them the right or manner of the King that shall reign over them*, 1 Sam. 8. 4. The like we may read, 1 *Sam.* 9. 16. and 1 *Sam.* 10. 1. still it is *super eos*; not under my people, but over them: not under them, to serve them; but over them, to save, defend and deliver them. Thus *David* and *Solomon* are said to be anointed over the people,

App. *Liv. lib.* 5. *lib.* 8.

Some people naturally servile.

Strab. lib. 12. *Just. l.* 38.

Lib. 2. *de Benef.*

The best Government is under a good King.

Liv. lib. 1.

Lib. 7.

Some Kings are so absolute, that they are not subject to the whole body of the people. Deut. 17. 14.

people, over the Lords anointed, and over *Israel.* And *David* gives thanks, that God had subdued his people under him. Christ also declares as much, where he saith, *The Kings of the Gentiles exercise dominion over you,* Luke 22. 25. 2 Sam. 5. 2. 1 Kings 4. 1. Psal. 144. 2.

> *The Power of Kings o're Subjects is their own:*
> *But none can Kings command, but God alone.* Horace.

The three Forms of Government are by *Seneca* thus described: *Sometimes the people are most to be feared; sometimes, if the Government be such, those most in favour with the Senate; and sometimes, those particular persons upon whom the whole power of the people, and over the people is devolved. For such,* saith *Plutarch, have power to govern, not only according to the Laws, but even the Laws themselves for the publick good.* Thus *Otanes* in *Herodotus* describes a King, *That he may do even what he will, without being accountable to any.* So doth *Dion Prusaensis, That he may so rule, as not to render an account to any. Pausanias* to the *Messenians,* opposeth Kingly Government to that which is lyable to give an account of his Acts to others. *Aristotle* affirms, *That there are some Kings who are invested with as much power as elsewhere a whole Nation hath over it self, or whatsoever it hath.* So, as soon as the *Roman* Generals began to assume unto themselves Regal power, the people are said to confer upon them all their power and authority over themselves, as *Theophilus* expounds it. Hence is that excellent saying of *M. Antoninus, None but God himself is the Judge of Kings.* Ep. 14. Flav.

Uno minor Jove, That Kings Inferiour to God alone, is no less Christian, than Ethnick Philosophy. For in this, and in nothing more, are Kings like unto God, that they depend upon none: He whom God hath placed in his Throne, is accountable to none, but unto him who placed him there. He is *Solutus Legibus,* above the lash of humane Laws: He judgeth all, but is judged of none. When *Herod* was accused to *M. Anthony* for the Murder of *Aristobulus, Anthony* makes this Apology for him, *It was neither Just nor Equitable, to require an account from Kings for what they do as Kings: For if that were permitted, they could be no longer Kings.* Kingly Power then must needs be the highest, because there lyes no Appeal from him, or against him, but unto God. And as it is subject to no other power; so it is bounded by no humane Law, as other powers are. 'Tis granted, that *Moses* indeed seems to prescribe Laws unto Kings, and tells them what they should do. And good Princes will say with the Emperour *Theodosius, Tantum mihi licet, quantum per Leges licet; That only is lawful for me to do, which the Laws account so.* But as *Moses* teacheth us what a King should do, so *Samuel* tells us what a King may do: *Moses* tells us his duty, *Samuel* his power. The Law consists of two distinct parts, the one Direct, the other Coercive: the former points at the rationability of the Law; the latter at the danger we run into, if we break the Law. Now Laws serve to direct Kings, because they mind them of their duty: But they have no power to force them to that duty, much less to Un-King them if they do it not.

Dion Prusaensis speaking of such a King, saith, *He is free and absolute in power, both over himself, and over the Laws; what he will, he doth; and what he will not, he doth not.* Such anciently in *Greece* was the Kingdom of the *Inachidæ* at *Argis,* whom *Moses* terms the *Anakims, Deut.* 2. 10. For the *Argives* in *Æschylus* thus bespeak their King;

> *Our State and City is in thee,*
> *Thou need'st not fear Laws Tyranny;*
> *Sacred as Altar, is thy Throne,*
> *For all are Rul'd by thee alone.*

The *Lacedæmonians* in the Story of the *Macchabites,* claim to be of Kin to *Abraham*: they had two Kings; but *Magis Nomine quam Imperio, More in Name than Power,* as *Corn. Nepos* testifies.

Much different from what *Theseus* himself, though a King, speaks in *Euripides,* concerning the Common-wealth of *Athens,*

> ———————Athens *being Free,*
> *Enslav'd by any one disdains to be;*
> *The People there are Kings, who Annually*
> *The Government to this, or that decree.*

For *Theseus,* as *Plutarch* informs us, was not their King, but their General in War, and the Guardian of their Laws in peace, in other matters he was but equal with the rest of the Citizens. Hence it comes, That those Kings that are accountable to the people, as those after *Lycurgus;* but especially as the *Ephori* were to the *Lacedæmonians,* are by *Polybius, Plutarch* and others, said to be Kings in Name only, but not in Power: which example of the *Lacedæmonians,* notwithstanding most of the *Græcian* Cities followed. *Pausanius* to the *Corinthians,* thus testifies of the *Argives, That they were so far addicted to parity and liberty, that at length they reduced the power of their Kings to almost nothing; for to the Sons and Posterity of* Cisus, *they left not any thing, but the bare Name and Title of a Kingdom.* And therefore *Aristotle* denyes, that such Kingdoms do constitute any special Form of Government, allowing them but as parts, either of Optimacy or Democracy. Nay, even among such people as were not perpetually governed by Kings, we may find some footsteps of a Temporary Monarchy, not at all subject unto the People. *M. Livius Solinator* in his Censorship disfranchised all the Tribes but one in *Rome* for their Ingratitude; thereby shewing his

Lib. 3. Vit. Cleom. Vit. Agef.

Corinthiacis. Kings in name only, not in power.

Some have for awhile the power, but not the name.

his power over the whole body of the people. And ſuch was the power of the Dictators in *Rome*, from whom there was no Appeal, no not unto the People; whence it came to paſs, that as *Livy* informs us, An Edict from the Dictator was as Authoritative as an Oracle from God: Neither was there any ſafety at all but in obedience. For though Kings were baniſhed, yet was the Regal Power comprehended in the Dictatorſhip.

Dictators in *Rome* temporary Kings.

1. Arg. anſwered. The Thing that conſtitutes, not always greater than the thing conſtituted.

The Arguments produced for the contrary opinion, are eaſily anſwered: For in the firſt place, Whereas they ſay, the Thing that conſtitutes is greater than the Thing conſtituted; and therefore the people that make the King, muſt needs be greater than the King they have made: I anſwer, That it is true, where the Authority of the thing conſtituted doth always depend on the will of the Conſtitutors; but not where the Authority once freely given, doth ever after fully remain in the perſon that received it. As for example, A woman being free, may chuſe whom ſhe will for her Husband; but having once choſen, the woman is perpetually bound to obedience: (So he that reſolves to put himſelf as an Apprentice, hath a freedom to chuſe his own Maſter; but having choſen, cannot free himſelf when he pleaſeth.) It was well ſaid of *Valentinian*, who being firſt choſen Emperor by the Army, and afterwards denying them a requeſt, which ſeemed unto him unreaſonable, told them, *That it was indeed in their power to have choſen, or not to have choſen him; but being choſen, what ye demand is in my power to grant, but not in yours to exact: It is your duty to obey, and mine, being your Emperor, to conſider what conduceth to the General Safety.* Neither is it altogether true, what they ſeem to take as granted, that all Kings are conſtituted by the people; as may eaſily be proved, as well by ſome Fathers of Families, who admit of Strangers under the condition of Subjection, as of ſome Nations conquered by the Sword.

The wiſe Anſwer of *Valentinian*.

Theodoret lib. 4. c. 5.

2. Arg.

Another Argument they draw from that maxim of Philoſophers, That all Government is granted for the benefit of the people, and not of the Governors; and therefore the end being more noble than the means, they for whoſe good Rulers are conſtituted, are above the Rulers themſelves. But neither is this univerſally true, That Government is for the good of the perſons governed; for ſome are for the ſole uſe of the Governors, as that of a Maſter over his Servant, is chiefly and principally for the good of the Maſter; but the good of the Servant is but extrinſecal and adventitious, as the Phyſicians gain is but accidental to the Phyſick he gives. There are alſo ſome Governments that are for the mutnal benefit of both parties, as that of an Husband over his Wife: So of Empires, ſome are gained by the Sword, and thoſe doubtleſs are for the benefit of the Conqueror; neither is it therefore to be accounted tyrannical, which word (as now taken) implyes ſomewhat of injuſtice: And ſome Empires are for the mutual good, both of him that governs, as of them that are governed; as when *Jephtha* was made King to defend the oppreſſed Gileadites. Yet notwithſtanding I cannot deny, but that in moſt Empires, what was long ſince ſaid by *Heſiod*, *Herodotus*, and *Cicero*, is very true, That Kings are conſtituted to adminiſter Juſtice to their people. But to infer from thence, that the people are above their King, will be no good conſequence; for the Guardian is appointed for the good of his Pupil, and yet hath he a right and a power over him. But you will farther ſay, That in caſe a Guardian perform not his duty he may be removed, and why then may not a King? Whereunto I anſwer, That the caſe is not the ſame, for a Guardian hath a power above him, by whom he may be judged, but ſo hath not a King; for that there may be certain bounds ſet to all humane power, it is neceſſary that we admit of one to be Supreme; and That one muſt be either a ſingle Perſon or an Aſſembly, unto whom are referred the laſt Appeals; whoſe faults becauſe they have no Superior upon earth, God himſelf is ſaid to puniſh: And if he do not, yet is that very toleration intended, either as a puniſhment or as a Tryal of the People. It was excellent advice that *Tacitus* gives in this caſe, *The Luxury and Covetouſneſs of Princes, are to be endured with the ſelf ſame neceſſary patience, as we do ſtorms and tempeſts at Sea, or drought and ſcarcity by Land, or the like natural inconveniences which are not to be avoided: For vices there will be as long as there be men; but this is our comfort, that as they are not perpetual, ſo they are ſometimes recompenced with great advantages.* It was well ſaid of *M. Aurelius*, *That if private perſons offended, the Magiſtrate is to judge; If the Magiſtrate offend, the Prince: But of Princes God alone is the proper Judge.* Thus doth *Vitigis* (being himſelf a King) plead in *Caſſiodore*, in the behalf of Kings, *Cauſa Regiæ poteſtatis ſupernis eſt applicanda Judiciis quandoquidem illa è cœlo petita eſt, & ſoli cœlo debet innocentiam; The miſcarriages of Princes are to be referred to Gods Tribunal, for receiving their power from Heaven, to Heaven alone they owe their innocence.* And preſently after he ſubjoyns, *Neither can we be accountable to any other, becauſe upon Earth we have no Judge, nor within our Dominions any Peers.* Another notable place we have in *Gregory Turonenſis*, where he (being a Biſhop) thus beſpeaks the King of *France*, *If any Subject deal unjuſtly with us, it is in thy power, O King, to puniſh him: But if thou oppreſs us, who ſhall judge thee? We may complain unto thee, and if thou wilt, thou mayſt hear us; but if not who, ſhall condemn thee, but he only that is Juſtice it ſelf?* Among other

Jer. 25. 12.

The extravagancies of Princes are to be born with patience.

other opinions of the Essenes, *Porphyry* commemorates this, *That Empires fall not to any man by chance, but by the special Providence of God. Cujus jussu homines nascuntur, hujus jussi reges constituuntur, apti iis qui in illis temporibus ab ipsis regnantur*; *Look*, saith Ireneus, *by whose providence it is that men are born, by the same it is that Kings are ordained*: Not by chance or peradventure, but by Gods special appointment; *as being fitted for such times, in which, and for such persons, over whom they are to rule*, (according as it doth best advance those great designs of Gods Wisdom and Counsels, whose instruments they are.) Thus is he said to raise up *Pharaoh* to manifest his power in him, *Exod.* 9. 16. *Rom.* 9. 17. These were the sober thoughts of the Egyptians themselves, as *Diodorus* observed, *Existimant non sine divina providentia pervenisse Reges ad summam omnium potestatem*; *They are perswaded, that it is not without a divine providence, that Kings ascend to the highest power.* So St. *Augustine, He that gave the Roman Empire to* Augustus, *gave it afterwards to that monster of men*, Nero: *He that setled the same Empire in* Vespasian *and his Son* Titus, *did afterwards transfer it on* Domitian. That Constitution of *Clement* is very pertinent to this purpose, *Regem timebis gnarus à domino electum*; *Thou shalt fear the King, knowing that his choice is from God*: Neither will it avail to say, that we read of some people who have been punished for the sins of their Kings; for this happens, not because the people do not restrain and punish their Kings, but because they tacitely consent to their vices: Or haply without regard to this, he makes use of that supereminent power that he hath over the lives of every of his Creatures, whereby to punish those Kings by taking away their Subjects, it being the proper punishment of Kings to be thus weakned *.

Lib. 5.

Ireneus.

It is Gods providence that fits Kings to such times, and to such a people.

De Civit. Dei lib. 5. *c.* 21.

Lib. 7. *c.* 17.

1 Kin. 4. 16.
2 Kin. 10. 17.
2 Sam. 24. 17.

It is one and the same God that sets up one and pulls down another, and that transfers Crowns and Scepters from one Nation to another People, and that rules the People by whom he pleaseth. Now to such as judicially peruse the Writings of the Prophets, they will appear most evident; for they do not only foretel the Counsels of God: but the very Kings and Princes, by whom God intends to bring about his secret purposes, are therein described, yea and sometimes named, long before they were born, as *Josias* by name, 1 *Kin.* 13. 2. *Cyrus* by name, *Es.* 45. 3. Which plainly argues, that God doth not only foresee what will come to pass, but pre-ordains such and such persons, by whom he intends to effect his purposes; yea and fits them with habits and graces accordingly. * The proper punishment of Kings is to be deprived of their Subjects.

IX. Mutual Subjection refuted.

Others there are that seem to fansie to themselves mutual subjection, as in case the King shall govern well, then the whole body of people should obey; but in case he govern ill, then he ought to be subject unto the people. Now if what they say do amount to no more than this, That our obedience to Kings binds us not to do any thing that is manifestly wicked; they say no more than what all sober men will grant: Yet doth not this imply any compulsion or any right of Empire that is in the people. But in case they had a purpose to divide the Government with the King (whereof we shall have occasion hereafter to speak somewhat) they ought to assign bounds and limits to the power of either party, which may easily be done by making distinction of either Places, Persons, or Affairs. But the well or ill management, especially of Civil Affairs, being apt to admit of great debates, are not so fit to distinguish the parts; for great confusions must necessarily arise, where the right of power is to be judged of by the pretensions of good or evil acts, some judging of these Acts in favour to the King, others in favour to the people; which confusion no people, that I as yet know, were ever so imprudent as to introduce.

X. Cautions in judging of the Supreme Power.

These errors being thus refuted, It remains that we set down some Cautions, which may guide us to give a right judgment, to whom in every Nation the Supreme Power belongeth; whereof the first is this, That we suffer not our selves to be deceived by such names as are ambiguous in sence, nor with the shew of outward things. As for example, Although amongst the Latins, a Kingdom and a Principality are usually opposites; as when *Cæsar* said, the Father of *Vercingetorigis* having got the principality of *Gallia*, was slain for his affecting the Kingdom: And when *Piso* in *Tacitus* said, that *Germanicus* was indeed the Son of a Prince of the *Romans*, but not of the King of the *Parthians*. And when *Suetonius* said that *Caligula* wanted but a little of changing his Principality into a Kingdom; yet we find these Titles of times promiscuously used. For both the *Lacedæmonian* Generals, who derived themselves from *Hercules*, though afterwards they were subjected to the *Ephori*, yet were still called Kings. And some ancient Kings of *Germany* there were (as *Tacitus* relates) who Reigned, *magis suadendi, quam jubendi potestate*; *more by perswasions, than by power.* And as *Livy* speaks of King *Evander*, that he governed rather as a prudent Magistrate, than as a King. Thus *Solinus* calls *Hanno* the King of the *Carthaginians*: And he that wrote the Life of *Hannibal* saith, *That as the* Romans *chose every year two Consuls, so the* Carthaginians *chose two Kings*, (meaning their Suffetes or Judges.) Among these Kings, improperly so called, we may likewise reckon their Sons, whom their Fathers were pleased to honour with the Title of Kings, though they reserved unto themselves the Regal Power. Such was that *Darius*, whom his Father *Artaxerxes* commanded to be killed, being first condemned for plotting his Fathers death, as *Plutarch* relates the Story. So on the contrary, The Roman Emperors, after they had openly assumed unto themselves Regal Power, contented themselves with the Names

Kingdoms and Principalities promiscuously used.

Lib. 1.

Lib. 15.

Plut. Artax. ad finem.

and

and titles of Generals or Princes. Nay, the Ensigns of Regal Power are in some Free Cities usually given to Princes. But now the assembly of States, that is, of those that represent the whole body of the people, digested, as *Gunther* speaks, into three orders; namely, Prelates, Nobles, and the Principal Burgesses of Cities, do in some places indeed serve to this end only, to be the Kings Greater Council, whereby the grievances of the people, which are oft-times concealed by his Privy Council, may come to the Kings knowledge, who have also power to determine them, as it shall seem good unto them, according to Custome. But in other places they have power to call into question the Actions of the Prince, and also to prescribe Laws which shall be binding even to the Prince himself. There are many also that place the difference between the Supreme and the Lesser Powers, in the translation of the Empire by Election or Succession: Attributing the Supreme Power to this latter, but not unto the former. But this holds not universally true: For Succession assigns not the Form of Government, but the Continuation of a Form in the same Family. For the right which began in the Election of such a Family is by Succession continued. Among the *Lacedamonians* the Kingdom, even after the *Ephori* were constituted, was hereditary: And of such a Kingdom or Principality it is that *Aristotle* speaks, where he saith, *That some pass by the right of Blood, and some by Election.* And such in the time of the Ancient Heroes were most of the Kingdoms of *Greece*, I mean successive; as both *Aristotle* and *Thucydides* observed; so doth *Dionysius Halicarnassensis.* Whereas on the contrary, the *Roman* Empire, even after all power was taken as well from the Senate as people, was always transferr'd by Election.

Parliaments why called.

XI.

The Second Caution.

The thing it self distinguisht from the manner of holding it.

A Second Caution shall be this, It is one thing to enquire concerning the thing, and another to enquire concerning the manner of holding it, which holds good not in things Corporeal only, but in things Incorporeal. For as a Field is a Thing, so also is a Passage, an Act, or Way. But these some may have by a full right of propriety, others by a right usufructuary (as a Farmer hath a right to his Farm,) and some others by a Temporary Right: As the Roman Dictator the Soveraignty but by a Temporary Right. So Kings, as well those that are first Elected, as also those that succeed to them in a right line, hold their Kingdoms by an Usufructuary right; (that is, they hold them as to all the rights and profits, but not to alienate them.) But others hold their Kingdoms by a full Right of Propriety, as they that by a just War have conquered them: Or he to whom any people, to prevent greater mischiefs, have yielded themselves Subjects for protection, so as they reserve nothing unto themselves. Neither do I agree with those who hold that the Roman Dictator during his time could not have Supream Power, because it was not perpetual. For the Nature of all Moral things are best known by their operations: Wherefore those powers that have the same effects are to be called by the same name. But a Dictator during his time, exerciseth all Rights that a King doth, who holds his Kingdom by a full right. Neither can any Act of his be made void by any other, as may appear by the Case of *Fabius Rutilianus*, whom when the people would have preserved, they could deal with the Dictator by no other means but by Petition: Whence we may conclude, That he had the same supreme power. Now the Duration or Continuation of a thing, alters not the nature of it; yet if question be made concerning the dignity which is usually called, *Majesty*: doubtless, he that hath it perpetuated unto him hath the greater Majesty, than he that hath it for a time limited only; because the manner of holding it adds much to the Dignity of him that holds it. Now what hath been said of Kings, may also be said of such as are, either during the Minority of Kings, or during their Captivity, or Lunacy, appointed Protectors: For neither are those subject unto the people, nor is their power revocable before the time come, appointed by the Laws. But it is otherwise with those who have a Right which is at any time revocable: As they who reign only during the pleasure of others, such was the Kingdom of the Vandals in *Africa*, and of the *Goths* in *Spain*, who were as often deposed as they displeased the people. And every act of theirs might be made void, because they who gave them that power, gave it under condition of Revocation: And therefore not having the same effect, they could not be said to have the same Right.

Protectors have absolute power during their time.

Some Kingdoms held during the pleasure of the people. *Procop. Vand. lib. 1.*

XII.

Some Soveraign powers are held fully, with a right of alienation.

Hottom. Cont. illust. quaest. 1. *Diog. Laert.* 1 Sam. 22. 28. 2 Sam. 10. 2. 1 King. 9. 22. *Liv. lib. 1. Lib. 2.*

Against what I have before said, That some Kingdoms are held in full right of propriety, that is, as Patrimonial: There are very learned men that make this objection, That Men being free, are not to be trafficKt away from one to another, (as things that are bought and sold:) But as the power of a Master is different from that of a King; so is personal liberty from that which is Civil: And the freedom of singular persons, from the freedom of States. The Stoicks themselves confess, That there is a kind of servitude in subjection, and the Subjects of Kings are sometimes in Holy Writ called their Servants: As personal liberty excludes the power of a Master, so also doth civil liberty that of Empire, and all manner of Soveraignty properly so called. *Livy* thus opposeth them, *Before men had tasted the sweetness of liberty, they desired a King.* And again, *What a shame is it for the people of* Rome, *who when they served under*

under Kings, were never straitned by War, nor besieged by an enemy, being now a free people to be besieg'd by the Hetruscans. And in another place, *The people of* Rome *live not now under Kingly Government, but in liberty.* And elsewhere he opposeth those Nations that were free, unto those that lived under Kings. So also *Seneca* the Father, *We ought not to give our opinions in a Free state, in the same manner as we did under Kings.* Yea, and *Cicero, Either we did not well to expel Kings, or we ought to restore the people to liberty, not in words only, but in deeds.* After these comes *Tacitus, The City of* Rome, saith he, *was at first governed by Kings, but it was* L. Brutus *that instituted Liberty and Consular Authority.* And to be short, every where among the Roman Laws, when they treat of War and recuperatory Judgements, all Foreigners are distinguisht into Kings and Free people. The question then here put, respects not personal, but civil subjection. In which sense, some Nations are said not to have power over themselves. Hence is that in *Livy, Which Cities, Fields, and Men were sometimes under the power of the Ætolians.* And that also, *Are the people of* Collatia *a free people ? (i. e.)* have they any power over themselves ? Nevertheless, to speak properly, when any people are said to be alienated, it is not the men, but the perpetual right of governing themselves, as they are a people, that is alienated. As vain and frivolous is that Inference, which concludes, That because Kings conquer Nations by the blood and sweat of their Citizens, therefore what is so conquered, ought of right to belong rather to them than to him : For possible it is, That that King may pay his Army out of his own private estate ; as *M. Anthony* did in his Bohemian Wars, who when the Roman Treasury was exhausted, being unwilling to impose any more Taxes upon the people, brought into *Trajans* Court, and made sale of all his Vessels of Gold, Silver, Crystal and Myrrh, together with his own and his wives Robes of Silk and Gold, and all other their Ornaments and Jewels for the maintenance of the War. Or he may pay his Army out of the rents and profits of that patrimony which attends the Principality : And therefore *Ferdinando* claimed to himself all that part of the Kingdom of *Granada* which he had gained, with the rents and profits he had raised out of *Castile*, during the time of his Marriage, as *Mariana* testifies. For although a King have but the mean profits arising out of that Patrimony, in the same manner as he hath the right of governing the people who have elected him, yet are those profits properly his own. As it is also in the Civil Law, where though the Inheritance be judged to be restored, yet the profits are not, because they are perceived, not from the inheritance, but from the thing it self. Possible therefore it is, that a King may be so possest of the Government over some people in his own proper right, that it is in his own power to alienate it. As it was granted to *Baldwin*, by those that accompanied him in his expedition to the Holy Land, That the half of all the Cities, Provinces, Tributes and Prizes that should be taken in that War, should be his. *Strabo* tells us, That the Isle *Cythara* lying against *Tenarus* did belong to *Eurycles*, one of the *Lacedæmonian* Princes, in his own Right. So we read that *Solomon* gave *Hiram* of *Tyre* twenty Cities, not of those that belonged to the *Hebrews* : For *Cabul* (which was the name imposed on those Cities) was seated without the *Hebrew* bounds, *Jos.* 19. 27. But out of those, which the people that were enemies to the *Jews*, had held till the days of *Solomon*, and were partly conquered by the King of *Egypt*, and given unto *Solomon* in dowry with his daughter, and partly conquered by *Solomon* himself. For that these Cities were not at that time possest by the *Hebrews* is evident from this, That as soon as King *Hiram* had restored them to *Solomon*, he then planted in them a Colony of the *Jews*. So we read that *Hercules* gave the Kingdom of *Sparta* which he had conquered by arms, unto *Tindareus*, on this condition, That if *Hercules* should have any children of his own, she should restore it to them : And having conquered the *Epirots*, he gave them to *Apollo*. So we read that *Ægimus* King of *Doris*, having called to his assistance *Hercules*, in his War against the *Lapithæ*, gave him a part of that Kingdom as his reward. *Cychreus* King of *Salamine*, having no children, left his Kingdom by his Testament unto *Teucrus*. *Amphipolis* was given in a Marriage dowry to *Acamantes*, the Son of *Theseus*. And in *Homer*, *Agamemnon* promises to give unto *Achilles* seven Cities. So King *Anaxagoras* freely bestowed two parts of his Kingdom upon *Melampus*. So again in *Homer*, we read that *Jobates* gave his daughter to *Bellerophon*, with a part of his Kingdom in Dowry. And *Justin* tells us, That *Darius* bequeathed by his Testament his Kingdom to *Artaxerxes*, but the Cities whereof he was governour only, to *Cyrus*. And probable it is, That the successors of *Alexander* every one for his part, did succeed him in that full Right of Governing the Nations, which were either formerly under the Persian Empire, or which they afterwards gained, by the right of their own Conquests. And therefore it is not to be wondred at, that they claimed unto themselves the Right of Alienation. So when King *Attalus* the Son of *Eumenes*, had by his Testament made the people of *Rome* heir to all his goods, they under the name of goods, possessed themselves of his Kingdom, whereof *L. Florus* speaks thus, *The Word,* Heir, *implying an Inheritance, the people of* Rome *held his Kingdom as a Province, and not as gained by War or by force of Arms : But*

Marginal notes: *Lib.* 45. — *Suas.* 1. — *De leg.* 3. *Ann. l.* 1. — When a Kingdom is alienated, it is not the people, but the right of governing them that is alienated. — *Lib.* 28. *Hist. Hispan.* — *Lib.* 8. — 1 Kings 19. — 1 King. 9. 6, 12. — 1 Chron. 8. 14. — *Diod. l.* 4. — *Serv. ad* 4. *Ænead.* — *Apollod.* — *Vid. Serv. ad* 6. *Eclog.* — *Lib.* 5. — *Lib.* 2. *Epit. Liv.* 58.

by what, was yet more righteous, by a Testamentary Right. So when afterwards *Nicomedes* (the King of *Bithynia* dying) made the Romans his heir. They presently reduced his Kingdom into the form of a Province: Whereof *Cicero* thus, *We have added to our Inheritance the Kingdom of* Bithynia. So that part of *Libia*, wherein the Cities *Berenice, Ptolomais* and *Cyrene* stood, was by King *Appio* given by Testament to the same people. And *Tacitus* makes mention of some Fields, which belonging formerly to King *Appio*, were by him left together with his Kingdom, to the people of *Rome*. *Procopius* likewise tells us, That King *Arsaces* by his Testament divided the Kingdom of *Armenia*, leaving the greater *Armenia* to *Arsaces*, and the lesser to *Tigranes*. And hence it was, That King *Herod* having obtained from *Aug. Cæsar* a Power to leave his Kingdom to which of his Sons he pleased, was so often observed to alter his Testament. This custom also was much in use amongst the *Goths* and *Vandals*, in those Kingdoms which they held by Conquest. The same we may observe much practised among the Turks: Sultan *Aladine* bequeathed by his Will many Cities to *Osman*: *Bajazet* also gave diverse of the Cities of *Servia* to *Stephanus*, in favour to his own Wife, being Sister to *Stephanus*. Sultan *Mahomet* bequeathed his Kingdom by his Testament to Sultan *Morat*: and *Mahomet* the Turk intended to have divided his Empire, and to have left the Asian Empire to *Mustapha*, and the European to *Amurat*. This also was frequently used in many other Nations. To rehearse them all would be no less troublesome to me, than it would be tedious to the Reader. But these may suffice to prove, That where Kingdoms are held by a full and absolute Right, they may be alienated: Yet so, That though the Right of Empire may be transferred, yet doth every singular person enjoy his own Liberty.

Orat. 2. In Rullum. — *Epitom. Livy l. 43.* — *Ann. l. 41.* — *Josephus.* — *Procopius.* — *Leunclavius lib. 2.* — *Idem, lib. 4.*

XIII. Some are held not so fully.

But in those Kingdoms wherein the people have any power, by way of Election or Confirmation, I confess it cannot be presumed, That it was ever their Mind to suffer the King to alienate his Kingdom. Wherefore what *Crantzius* observed, *in Unguinus*, as an Act without any Precedent, That he had by his Testament given away *Norway*, we ought not to disapprove: For haply he regarded only the Customs of the *Germans*, amongst whom there was no such Right permitted, as to bequeath Kingdoms. For as *Vopiscus* in *Tacitus* saith, Empires cannot be bequeathed, as goods and bond-slaves may. *Nor can a King*, as *Salvian* observes, *by his Testament, bequeath the people whom he hath governed, to the poor.* Now whereas *Charles* the Great, *Lewis* the Good, and others afterwards among the *Vandals* and *Hungarians*, are said to dispose of Kingdoms by their Testaments: These afforded rather matter of praise among the people, than argued the force of a true Alienation: And as to that of *Charles*, *Ado* makes special mention, that he desired his Testament might be confirmed by the Peers of *France*. The like we find in *Livy*, concerning *Philip* King of *Macedon*, who endeavouring to expel *Perses* out of his Kingdom, and settle *Antigonus* his own Brothers son in it, went throughout the Cities of *Macedon* solliciting the Princes on his behalf. Neither is it to the purpose to object, That the same *Lewis* restored the City of *Rome* to Pope *Paschal*: Considering that the French having before received the Soveraignty over that City from the people, might very well restore it back again to the same people, in the person of the Pope, being their chief Citizen, and a Prince of the first order.

XIV. Some power not Supreme, yet fully held.

What we have hitherto admonisht, namely, That we are carefully to distinguish between the supreme power it self, and the manner of holding, it is so true, That as many Soveraign Empires are not held by a full and absolute Right; so there are many that are not supreme, that are fully and compleatly held: whereby it falls out that Marquisates and Earldoms are much more easily either sold or bequeathed by Testaments, than Kingdoms are.

XV. This appears by the assigning Tutors and Protectors in Kingdoms.

There is also another mark whereby this distinction may be seen, namely, in the Tutelage or Protection of Kingdoms, when Kings and Princes are hindered or disabled either by some disease, or through old age, or the like, from performing their duty. For where the Kingdom is not Patrimonial, the Protectorship is theirs to whom the publick Laws, or if they are silent, the people shall consign it. But if the Kingdom be Patrimonial, then to them whom the Father, or the nearest of kin shall chuse. Thus did *Ptolomy* King of *Ægypt*, appoint by his Testament the people of *Rome* as Guardians to his Son, who to perform that trust sent *M. Æmilius Lepidus* who was their Chief Priest, and had been twice Consul, unto *Alexandria* to take care of the Government, and of the Childs Education: By whose care, not only the Kingdom was preserved, but the Child in his youth so well disciplin'd, that it was hard to judge whether he received more glory by his Fathers great fortunes, or by the Majesty of his Guardian. So we read that in the Kingdom of *Epirus*, which first depended on the suffrages of the people, Tutors were publickly assigned unto their young King *Ariba*: The like was done by the Nobility of *Macedon* to the Posthumous son of the Great *Alexander*. But in *Asia* the Lesser which was gained by the Sword, King *Eumenes* dying, appointed his Brother Protector to his young son *Attalus*. So did *Hiero* King of *Sicily*, by his Testament constitute unto his son *Hieronymus* what

Val. Max. lib. 6. Tit. 6. c. 1.

what Tutors he pleased. But whether the King be also in his own private right Lord of the soil, as the Kings of *Ægypt* were after the times of *Joseph*; or as the Kings of the *Indians* were, as *Diodorus* and *Strabo* testifie; or whether they are not, it makes no difference. For these are extrinsick to the Empire, and therefore can neither constitute another kind of Government, nor alter any thing as to the manner of holding it.

The Third observation shall be this, That an Empire ceaseth not to be supreme, though he that is to govern do by promise oblige himself either to his Subjects or to God, unto such things as do properly appertain unto his manner of Government. I mean not here, such things as appertain to the Laws of God, Nature, or Nations: For unto these every Prince stands obliged, though he promise not: But I mean though he do promise to confine his own power within certain Laws and Rules, whereunto nothing can bind him but his oath or promise. The Emperour *Trajan* did solemnly imprecate vengeance on his own head and right hand, in case he knowingly failed in what he had promised. And the Emperour *Adrian* sware, that ye would never punish a Senator without a decree of the Senate. *Anastasius* bound himself by oath to observe the decrees of the Synod of *Chalcedon*. And all the Greek Emperours did likewise oblige themselves to observe the Canons and Constitutions of the Church. But by none of these Oaths or Promises doth the Power of an Emperour cease to be supreme. This may clearly be illustrated by comparing the power of a King with that of a Master in his own Family: For although a Master do promise to observe such orders as he conceives to be most conducing to the welfare of it; yet doth he not thereby cease to be supreme in his own Family. Nor doth a husband cease to have power over his wife, though he have obliged himself to the contrary by some promises that he hath made to her: yet I must acknowledge that where such Oaths and Promises are made, the soveraignty is thereby somewhat straitened; whether the obligation do only restrain the exercise of the Act, as that of *Adrian*'s abovementioned, or the very power it self. If it restrain the exercise only, then the act that is done contrary to promise, is said to be unjust; because as we shall shew anon, every promise gives a right to him to whom it was made. But if it restrain the faculty it self, then the Act will be void, for want of a Right or Faculty to do it. And yet will it not necessarily follow, that he that thus promiseth hath any power superiour to himself; for his Act is not made void by any power above him, but by very right. Among the Persians no man can say but that their Kings were supreme and absolute in power, and not liable to give an account, as *Plutarch* testifies: Nay their Kings were adored as Gods own Image; and as *Justin* tells us, were never changed but by Death. He was a King indeed, that said to the Nobles of *Persia*, *Ne viderer meo tantummodo usus consilio, vos contraxi; cæterum, mementote parendum vobis, magis quam suadendum*: *Lest I should be thought to govern by mine own counsels only, I have called you together, but otherwise remember, that it is your duty rather to obey, than to perswade.* And yet did this very King at his Coronation swear not to alter the Laws of that Kingdom made after such a form, as both *Xenophon* and *Diodorus* testifie: and as the Histories of *Daniel*, and *Plutarch* in the life of *Themistocles* inform us. So *Josephus* tells us, That *Vashti* could not be reconciled to the King because the Royal Decree was gone out, which could not be broken. And long after them, *Procopius* confirms as much, where we may read a notable example to this purpose. The very same doth *Diodorus Siculus* relate of the Kings of *Æthiopia* and *Ægypt*, who without doubt, as all other Eastern Kings, had in their respective Kingdoms absolute Power; and yet were they all at their admission obliged to many things by Oaths or Promises: Which if they performed not, though whilest they lived, they could not be questioned; yet being dead, their memories might be accused, and being condemned, their carcasses might be denyed solemn Funeral. This *Apion* records, *Leges Tyrannorum Corpora insepulta extra fines projici jubent*; *The Laws*, saith he, *command the bodies of Tyrants to be cast out of their Territories unburied.* In obedience to the like Law, the Emperour *Andronicus* deprived his own Father *Michael* of Christian Burial, because he followed the Faith of the Latin Churches. And such another Law there seemed to be amongst the Hebrews, who would not permit the dead bodies of their wicked Kings to be interr'd among their good Kings. The like we may find in *Josephus* concerning the two *Jorams*, the one King of *Juda*, the other King of *Israel*. By which excellent temperament of reverence and justice, they both preserved the Majesty of their Kings inviolable whilest they lived, and also deterred them from breaking their oaths and promises by the fear of a dishonourable Interrment being dead. The Kings of *Epirus* were wont to make oath, That they would rule according to the Laws: And their Subjects likewise bound themselves by Oaths to defend both him and the Kingdom according to the same Laws; as *Plutarch* informs us in the life of *Pyrrhus*. Nay further, suppose a King should accept of his Kingdom upon these terms, That in case he should falsifie his promise, he should lose his Kingdom; yet were his power supreme only, the manner of holding it would be so much impaired by such a condition, as would make that Government not much better than that

XVI. Soveraignty not lost by any promise made of any things which belong not to either the Law of God or Nature.

Val. Max. lib. 9. c. 5.

Ch. 6, 8, 12, 15.

Pers. l. 1.

Civilium 3.

Gregoras l. 6.

2 Chr. 24. 25. & Ch. 28. 27. *Jos. Ant. l. 8. c. 3. 5.*

that which is Temporary. It was said by *Agatharchides*, concerning a King of the *Sabæans*, That he was not liable to give any account of his Actions as King, and yet if ever he were seen out of his own Palace, he might be stoned to death justly: Which *Strabo* also notes out of *Artemidorus*. So that Land which is held upon condition of some Trust to be performed, is held as fully during the performance of that Trust, as that which is held absolutely. But yet it is possible that it may be lost, and such a conditional Law may be added, not only in conferring of a Kingdom, but in any other Contract. For some Leagues with our Neighbour Princes we see entred into under such penalties. As in case a King being at his admission sworn, shall break his Articles of Agreement, his Subjects shall not help him, no nor obey him. So *Crommerus* testifies in his Treatise concerning the affairs of *Poland*, *Ch.* 19, & 21.

XVII. It may sometimes be divided.

The Fourth thing is this, That though the Soveraign Power be but one, and of it self indivisible, consisting of those parts above-mentioned, adding thereunto Supremacy; that is, the being accountable to none: Yet it may so fall out, that sometime it may be divided, either by Parts which they call *Potential*, or by Parts which they term *Subjective*. As though the *Roman* Empire were but one entire thing, yet it so fell out sometimes that one held the Eastern, and another the Western part of it, or that three sometimes divided the whole between them. So also it may fall out, that the People electing a King may reserve some Acts to themselves, and transfer others to their King to be held in full Right: Which notwithstanding is not done (as I shewed before) whensoever the King shall oblige himself by some promise: But then only when either the Partition is expresly made; as in the time of the Emperour *Probus*, when it was agreed, That the Senate should confirm the Princes Laws, and that they might take cognizance of Appeals, appoint Proconsuls, and give Legates unto the Consuls: Or when the people, being as yet free, shall require it from him whom they chuse to be their King, by way of a permanent Law or Precept: Or if some such thing be added, whereby it may plainly be understood, that their King may be compelled or punished if he refuse. For a Precept or Command is commonly from a Superiour, at least in that which is commanded; but to compel, doth not always argue a superiour: For naturally every man hath power to compel his Debtor to do him justice, but it is repugnant to the nature of an Inferiour. And therefore from Compulsion there must naturally follow at least a parity, and consequently a division of the Soveraign Power. Many Allegations are usually brought against this bipartite state. But as we have already said, *In civilibus nihil est, quod omni ex parte incommodis caret, & Jus, non quod optimum est huic, aut illi, videtur, sed ex voluntate ejus, unde jus oritur, metiendum est*; *In Civil matters it is not possible to provide against all Inconvenience* (no one Law can exactly fit every mans case, no more than any one Shooe can fit every mans Foot) *neither is any thing accounted Right, by seeming so, to this or that person, but by the will of him who was the Law-maker.* An excellent example of this is brought by *Plato* in the third Book of his Laws: For when the *Heraclidæ* had built *Argus*, *Lacedæmon*, and *Messena*, they obliged their Kings to govern them according to Laws prescribed them; which whilest they did, the people also were obliged to continue their Kingdoms unto them and to their posterity, and not to suffer any man to take them from them: And for the better assurance of this Agreement, not only the Kings bound themselves by Oath to their Subjects, and the Subjects to their King; but the Kings bound themselves each to other, and the people of their respective Kings one to another, and the Kings gave their faith to their neighbouring people, and those people to their neighbouring Kings, each King and people promising their mutual aid and assistance in defence of the Government established amongst them. Many examples of this kind may be collected out of the Histories of our Northern Nations, as in *Johannes Magnus* his History of *Sweden*, and in *Crantzius* of the *Swedes*, and *Pontanus* of the *Danes*.

Vid. Gail. lib. 2. *Obs.* 157.

To command argues a superiour, but not to compel.

XVIII. Which is ill collected from this, That some Princes will have their Acts confirmed by the Senate.

True it is, that some Kings will not permit that some Acts of theirs shall be of force, until they are confirmed by the Senate or some other Commissioners. Yet he that shall hence inferr, That there is a Partition of power, will be mistaken: For whatsoever Acts are thus rescinded, ought to be understood as though they were made void by the King himself, who by this means provides, that nothing fraudulently gained from him shall pass to his disadvantage. This was the scope of that Rescript sent by *Antiochus* the Third to his Magistrates, That in case he commanded them to do any thing contrary to Law, they should not obey him: And of that of *Constantine* to his, That Widows and Orphans should not be compelled to come for Judgement to the Court of the Emperour, although the Emperours own Letters should be produced for it. This is very like unto those Testaments unto which this clause is added, That no Testament hereafter to be made shall be of force: For such a Clause would have it believed, that the latter Testament proceeded not from the will of the Testator. But as that clause in the Will, so the first Act of a Prince may by any after-Act of his, or by any special Indication of his later Will, be easily rescinded.

Neither

Neither am I at all swayed by the authority of *Polybius*, who would fain have the *Romans* to be a mixt Common-wealth; which if we regard not so much the Acts themselves, as the Power whereby they were done, was doubtless at that time, meerly popular: For as well the Authority of the Senate which he refers to Optimacy, as that of the Consuls, which he refers to Monarchy, were both of them subject to the power of the people. Now the self same may be said, in answer to all other the Opinions of those that write of Politicks, who haply think it more agreeable to their purpose, to gaze on the extern face and daily administration of the Soveraignty, than unto the very Right of it, it self. XIX. Some other examples hither ill drawn.

Much more pertinent to the matter, is that of *Aristotle*, who saith, That between a full and absolute Monarchy, and that like unto the *Laconian*, being but a meer Principality, there are some of a Mixt kind; whereof we have an example, as I conceive, in the *Israelitish* Kings, who doubtless in most things governed by a full power. For such a King the people required, as their Neighbour Nations had: Supposing, as *Josephus* testifies, *That if they were governed like unto their neighbours, they should suffer no Inconveniencies*: not considering, that all the Eastern Nations, except themselves, were under a Slavish Government. So *Atossa* in *Æschylus*, speaking to the *Persians* of their King, saith, That he is not accountable to the City for what he did. That of *Virgil* is well known, XX. True examples. Mixt Governments.

———————*Nor* Ægypt, *nor vast* Lydia,
Nor Medes, *nor* Parthians, *thus their Kings obey.*

Livy gives this Character of the *Syrians*, and all the *Asian* people, *That they were a kind of men born to be Slaves.* Not much unlike is that of *Apollonius* in *Philostratus*, *The* Assyrians *and* Medes *do adore their Kings*: nor that of *Aristotle*, *All the* Asians *do patiently submit to Monarchy.* And to the same sense is that *Civilis Batavus* to the *Gauls* in *Tacitus*, *The* Syrians *and* Asians *might well serve, because all the Oriental people were accustomed to be governed by Absolute Monarchs.* Not but that there were even at that time Kings also both in *Germany* and *France*; but as the same *Tacitus* there observes, They were such as governed for the most part in a Precarious way: or as I said before, more by a Perswasive, than by a Coercive Power. We observ'd before, that the whole body of the people of *Israel* was under their King. And *Samuel* describing the Government of Kings sufficiently proves, That against the Injuries done by them, there remained no power at all in the people, either to resist, or revenge. Which the Ancients did rightly gather from those words of King *David*, Tibi soli peccavi, *Unto thee only have I sinned*; because as St. *Hierom* upon that place glosseth, David *being a King, stood in fear of none but God, as having no other Judge but him*: So likewise St. *Ambrose*, David *was a King, and so subject to no Laws*; *For Kings are Free from those shackles, wherewith their Subjects crimes do entangle them*: *They Fear no punishments, being secured by the power of the Empire.* To Man therefore he sinned not, because to him, he was not accountable for his Actions. Apposite to this, is that of *Vitiges* in *Cassiodore*, Causa regiæ potestatis supernis est applicanda judiciis, quandoquidem illa cœlo petita est, ita soli cœlo debet Innocentiam: *The cause of a King is to be referred to Gods Tribunal*; *for from whence he derives his power, to him only he owes his Innocence.* And in cases of such oppressions, God himself prescribes the only Remedy that the people can have against their Kings, namely, Prayers and Tears; *And ye shall cry out in that day, because of the King whom ye have chosen*, 1 Sam. 8. 18. (He doth not encourage them to Rebel, nor doth he prescribe any Legal way of proceeding against them; only they may cry unto the Lord, and if he heard them not, they must suffer with patience. Nor doth *Samuel* insinuate this to the *Jews* as if it were *nudum factum*: that is, *That Kings abusing their power would do so*; but as if it were *Jus Regium, a Right proper to Kingly Government to do so.*) The *Jews* themselves grant, that if their Kings did transgress those Laws which *Moses* prescribed unto them, they were to be beaten with Rods. But this was no reproach unto them, neither was it by compulsion, but by a voluntary susception, as a sign of their penitence: Nor was it done by any publick Officer; but as he imposed it upon himself freely, so he chose whom he pleased to do it; and prescribed both the manner and measure of his own punishment. But from all Coercive punishment their Kings were so free, that even that Law of Excalciation, *Deut.* 25. 9. because it was not without some reproach, was not in force against them. Yet notwithstanding all this, there were some Cases whereof their Kings had no Right at all to judge, but they were reserved to the Great Sanhedrim, or Council of the 70. Elders; which being Instituted by *Moses* at Gods special Command, continued by a perpetual supply of Election, until the dayes of *Herod*: For which cause, they are by *Moses* and *David* frequently called Gods, and their Judgement, Gods Judgement. And those Judges are likewise said, to judge not for man, but for God, 2 *Chron.* 19. 6, 8. Nay, there is a plain distinction made between the things of God, and the things of the King, 2 *Chron.* 19. 11. where by the matters of the Lord (as the most Learned among the *Jews* no interpret it) are

Pol. l. 3. c. 14. *Hist. l. 4.* All the *Asian* Kings Absolute. Deut. 1. 17. Psal. 82. 1, 6.

are meant, the Administring of Judgement according to the Laws of God. That the Kings of *Judah* did by themselves sometimes inflict Capital punishments, I cannot deny: wherein *Maimonides* prefers those Kings before the Kings of *Israel*: which is sufficiently cleared by many examples both in Holy Writ, and also in other *Hebrew* Authors. But yet the Cognizance of some Causes was not permitted unto them, as that of the Tribes, that of the High Priests, that of a Prophet. *For it cannot be* (saith our Saviour) *that a Prophet perish out of Jerusalem*, Luke 13. 33. And this is evident by the story of *Jeremy*, whom when the Princes demanded to death, the King answered them, *Behold he is in your power; for against you, the King can do nothing*, Jer. 38. 5. Yea, and in another place, he that was condemned by the Sanhedrim, could not be released by the King himself. And therefore *Hircanus*, when he saw he could not hinder the Sanhedrim from passing Sentence against *Herod*, advised him by Flight to secure himself. In *Macedonia*, they that derived their Pedegree from *Caranus*, as *Calisthenes* in *Arianus* reports, *obtained the Government not by Force, but by Law. Now the* Macedonians *though they were accustomed to Regal Goverment, yet had a greater smack of liberty than other Nations.* For it was not in the power of the King himself to take away the life of any Citizen. *It was the Antient custome of the* Macedonians *in criminal matters to be judged by the Army; but in times of peace by the People: The Kings power availed nothing farther than his Authority reached.* There is in another place of the same Author another sign of the same mixture mentioned, namely this, *The Macedonians*, saith he, *ordained that according to the custome of their Nation, Their King should never hunt on Foot, but in the company of some of his select Friends or Princes.* The like doth *Tacitus* write of the *Gothones*, *That they were under a stricter Government than others of the* German *Nation, yet not altogether without liberty.* For whereas he had before described a Principality thus, That it governed rather by a Perswasive than Coercive Power. He now describes a Kingdom in these words, *When*, saith he, *One person rules without any limitation or exception; and that not by entreaty, but by absolute command. Eustathius* upon the Sixth of *Homer's Odysses*, describing the Common-wealth of *Corcyra*, saith, *That it was a kind of mixt Government, having something of Kingly, and something of an Aristocratical Government. Laonicus Chalcocondylas* makes mention of the like Government in *Hungary* and in *England*, in *Arragon* and in *Navarr*, where the Magistrates are not created by the King; nor are any Garrisons imposed on them against their will, nor any thing commanded them by their King contrary to their Laws and Customs. Not much different was the Government of the *Romans* in the time of their Kings: For although almost all publick affairs were then transacted by the Regal Power. *Romulus*, saith *Tacitus*, governed us as he pleased. And it is plain, *That in the Infancy of their City, all power was in the King*, saith *Pomponius*; yet even at this very time, were some few fragments of that power reserved in the people, if we may give credit to *Dionysius Halicarnassensis*: but if we had rather believe the *Romans*, in some Cases, Appeals might be made from the King unto the people, as *Seneca* collects out of *Cicero's* Books *de Rep.* as also out of some Pontifical Books, and *Fenestella*. By and by after *Servius Tullius* being advanced to the Empire, not so much by Right, as by popular Favour, did much more impair the Majesty of the Kingdom. For to gratifie the people for their kindness, he ordained some Laws, whereunto the Kings themselves stood obliged. No marvel then, if *Livy* puts this only difference between the power of the first Consuls and of Kings, that it was but Annual. The like mixture of Popular and Aristocratical Power there was in *Rome* in the Vacancy of their Kings, and in the times of their first Consuls. For in some things, and those of moment, what ever the people commanded was established as a Law, if the Fathers were made the Authors. But as *Plutarch* observes, The People had no Right, either to make a Law, or to command any other thing, unless proposed by the Authority of the Senate. The like Mixture of Government *Chalcocondylas* notes to have been in the Common-wealth of *Genoua* in his time. But afterwards in *Rome*, the power of the people increasing, though the Fathers began and proposed, as anciently they were wont to do; yet as *Livy* and *Dionysius* observe, the people would decree what they pleased. But yet even after this, there remained some of this Mixture, whilst (as the same *Livy* speaks) the Soveraign Power was in the Patricians, that is, the Senate; and the Auxiliary power in the Tribunes, *i. e.* the Plebeians, who had a Right to either forbid or intercede when they pleased. And of this mixt Government, between Democracy and Aristocracy, *Isocrates* would have the Common-wealth of *Athens* to consist in the time of *Solon*. Now these things being premised, let us examine some doubtful Questions which do frequently arise about this matter.

Jer. 38. 5. *Jos. Ant. l.* 14. *c.* 17. In Criminal Cases the King of *Macedon's* power availed nothing. *Curt. lib.* 4. *Curtius lib.* 6. *Curt. lib.* 8. *Ep.* 100. *Tacit. l.* 3. *Vit. camilli. lib.* 5.

XXI. A Confederate on unequal terms may have the Supream Power.

The first thing that falls under dispute, is this, Whether that Nation can be said to have Supream Power that is in League with another Nation upon terms unequal? Where, by Unequal, I do not mean, where the Confederate Nations are of Unequal power; as when the City *Thebes* made a League with the *Persian* Monarch in the time of *Pelopidas*, or the *Romans* with the *Massilians*, and afterwards with *Massanissa*. Neither do I mean such a League,

League, as implyes some one transient Act that seems dishonourable; as when an Enemy paying the Charges of the War, or performing some such thing, is reconciled, and becomes a Confederate. But where by the express Articles of the League there is some permanent and lasting Prelation given from one to the other. As when one Nation is bound to maintain the honour of another; as in that League between the *Ætolians* and the *Romans*, whereby the *Ætolians* were bound to use their endeavours, to preserve as well the dignity, as the safety of the *Roman* Empire: which dignity is sometimes called the *Majesty*, and by *Tacitus*, *the Reverence of the Empire*; which he thus expresseth: *Though they are separate from us in place, and live within their own bounds, yet in their minds and understanding they act with us.* So likewise *Florus*, *As for the rest of the Nations though free, yet perceiving the vastness of their Empire, they did highly reverence the people of* Rome, *being Conquerors of so many Nations.* Whereunto we may also refer some Rights due to them that undertake the Patronage and defence of others. And those Rights, the Mother Cities have over smaller Cities and Colonies amongst the *Gracians*. *For such Colonies*, saith *Thucydides*, *enjoy the same Right of Liberty as their Mother Cities do: But yet they owe a Reverence to their Mother City, and ought to send her presents, as an acknowledgement of the honour they have for her.* *Livy* concerning that ancient League of the *Romans*, who had received all the Rights of *Alba*, and of that which the *Latines* derived from *Alba*, saith, *In that League the* Roman *State was superiour.* *Andronicus Rhodius* following *Aristotle*, did well observe, that in contracting amity between Nations of equal power, *It was but reasonable, that the weaker should give the greater honour, and the stronger afford the greater succours.* *Proculus* in his Answer to this Question we very well know, namely, That that is a Free Nation, which is not subject to the power of another, although it be comprehended in the League, that that Nation shall faithfully uphold the Majesty of the other. If therefore a Nation bound by such a Covenant, do yet remain free, and not subject to the power of another. It follows, that that Nation doth yet retain its Soveraignty; the like may be said of a King. For of a free-people, and of a King that is truly so, there is the same reason. *Proculus* adds further, that such a Clause is added in the League, to declare, that one Nation is superiour to another; and not to declare that the other is not free. By superiour, we understand not in power, (for he had said before, that a free Nation should not be subject to the power of another) but in Authority and Dignity: which the words following by a very fit Simile do clearly illustrate; *For as we know our Clients to be free, though neither in Dignity, nor in Authority, nor in all Right our equals: so they that are obliged faithfully to uphold our Majesty, are notwithstanding to be understood our equals in liberty.* Clients are free, though under the defence of their Patrons or Advocates; so is an Inferiour people free, though in League with a people superiour unto them in dignity. For they may be under their protection, though not under their jurisdiction, as *Sylla* speaks in *Appian*. An example we have in the *Dilimnites*, who as *Agathias* tells us, were αὐτόνομοι, *Free to live by their own Laws, though they served the* Persian *in his Wars.* This was the design of the Empress *Irene*, *so to divide the Empire among the Sons of her Husband, that the younger Sons should be Inferiour to the Eldest in dignity; but otherwise they should be Independent and Absolute in Power.* *Cicero* speaking of that Golden Age of the *Roman* Empire, saith, *Patrocinium Sociorum penes eos esse, non Imperium*; *The* Romans *gave protection to their Friends and Allies, but claimed no dominion over them.* With whom agrees that of *Scipio Africanus*, *The People of* Rome *had rather oblige their Neighbours unto them by Courtesies, than by Fear; and to win foreign Nations unto them by Faith and Friendship, than to subject them to an ungrateful bondage.* And what *Strabo* reports of the *Lacedæmonians*, after the arrival of the *Romans* in *Greece*, saying, *They enjoyed their own Freedom, contributing nothing unto the* Romans, *but the mutual offices of love and friendship.* As private Protection takes not away personal Liberty, so neither doth publick take away Civil, which without Soveraign Power cannot consist. And therefore *Livy* wisely opposeth to be under protection unto, to be under Jurisdiction. *Augustus Cæsar* (as *Josephus* relates) threatned *Syllæus* King of *Arabia*, that if he abstained not from injuring his neighbours, he would quickly make him, of a Friend, a Subject; which was the condition of the Kings of *Armenia*, who being under the *Roman* Jurisdiction, retained only the Title of Kings, but not the Power: As did also the Kings of *Cyprus* and some others, though in name Kings, yet were they Subjects to the *Persian* Monarchy, as *Diodorus* calls them. But here it may be objected what *Proculus* adds, *But some who belong to our Confederate Cities, are with us found guilty, whom being condemned we may punish.* But that we may understand these words, we must know, that there are four kinds of differences that usually arise among Confederates. As in the first place, If the Subjects of the King or State under protection, are said to have done any thing against the League: Secondly, If the King or States themselves are accused: Thirdly, If the Associates that are under the protection of the same King, do quarrel one with another: Lastly, If Subjects complain of Injuries done them, by those under whose Jurisdiction they are.

[Margin notes: *Lib.* 4. — Colonies. — *Nic.* 9. 18. The weaker should give the greater honour, and the stronger the greater succours. — Some Nations are equal in liberty, though not in dignity with others. — *Ap. Mithridat.* — *De Off. l.* 2. — *Liv. l.* 26. — Protection. — *Lib.* 16. Four kinds of differences usually arise between Confederates.]

if the Controversies be of the first kind, the King or State are obliged either to punish, or to deliver up the Offender to the person injured. And this ought to be done, not only between unequal Confederates, but between equals, even between such as are not linked together by any League, as shall be shewed anon. Nay farther, He is obliged to endeavour that satisfaction be made to the injured person, which in *Rome* was called the Recuperators office: *For the Law* (saith *Ælius Gallus* in *Festus*) *doth determine between King and People, Nations and Foreign Cities, how things by the Recuperator may be restored, and how they may be received, and how private mens cases may be prosecuted in each Nation.* For one of the Confederates can have no right directly to apprehend or to punish the Subjects of the other Confederate; and therefore *Decius Magius*, a *Campane*, being apprehended and bound by *Hannibal*, and so conveyed to *Cyrene*, and from thence sent to *Alexandria*; pleaded, that he was bound by *Hannibal*, contrary to the Articles of the League, whereupon he was presently set at liberty. As to the second kind of Controversies, One of the Kings or People Confederate hath power to compel the other to keep the Articles of the League, and in case of refusal to punish him; but neither is this peculiar to a League that is unequal, but may be done in one that is equal: For it is enough to justifie any man for seeking a revenge against him that hath wronged him, that he is not subject unto him, as shall be proved anon; wherefore this is also in force even among such people as are not confederated. The third sort of Controversies are amongst such as are equally confederated, and these are usually referred to a Dyet or Convention of the States associated, yet not therein concerned: For so the *Greeks*, the *Latins*, and the *Germans* were wont to do, or otherwise referred to Arbiters, or even to the Prince of the League as to a common Arbiter. So in an unequal League it is usually agreed, that the things in controversie shall be discust in that Nation which is superior in the League, wherefore neither doth this argue a superiority in power; for even Kings themselves refuse not to have their own causes sometimes tryed before such Judges, as even themselves have constituted. But of the last kind of Controversies, Associates have no right at all to judge; and therefore when *Herod* did vehemently accuse his two Sons before *Augustus Cæsar* for conspiring against his life, they took it as a favour he
Jos. Ant. lib. 16. c. 7, 8. had done them: *Poteras de nobis Supplicium sumere tuo jure, tum qua pater, tum qua Rex; Thou mightest have inflicted what punishment upon us thou wouldst by thine own Right, both as a Father and as a King.* And when *Hannibal* was accused at *Rome* by some *Carthaginians*,
Val. Max. lib. 4. c. 1. for stirring up Sedition amongst the Citizens, *Scipio* told the Senate, *That it did not become them to intermeddle with that which properly belonged to the City of* Carthage. And here-
Pol. lib. 1. c. 9. in it is that *Aristotle* puts a difference between a Society and a City, for it concerns confederate Societies to take care, that no injuries be committed against them; but not that the Citizens of any one of the Confederates do not injure one another. But here again it may be objected, That in unequal Leagues, he that is superior in the League is sometimes said to command, and he that is inferior to obey; but neither should this move us: for this is when the things in controversie concern either the common good of both parties confederate, or the private profit of him that is superior in that League. As to
Dan. 11. 22. the things of common concernment, the Assembly not sitting, He that was the Prince of the League (though it were an equal League) did usually command his Associates, as *Agamemnon* in the *Trojan* Expedition, did the *Gracian* Princes, and as afterwards the *Lacedemonians* did the *Gracians*, and after them the *Athenians*. *Thucydides* in that Oration made by the *Corinthians*, saith, *It very well becomes the Prince of the League, in private matters to deal equally; but in publick to be more than ordinarily sollicitous.* *Isocrates* commending that excellent conduct of the ancient *Athenians*, in the managing of their social Wars, saith, *That they took care for all, without intrenching upon the liberty of any.* And in another place he allows them, *to Command*, but not *to Domineer*. It is well worth our observation, that what the *Latins* express by the word *Imperare, to command*, the *Greeks* more modestly express by the word *τάσσειν, to dispose or set in order.* The *Athenians*, to whom the conduct of the War against the *Persians* was committed, *ἔταξαν*, saith *Thucydides, did order which City should contribute Money, and which Ships:* And they that were sent
Liv. lib. 3. c. 24. from *Rome* into *Greece*, are said *to be sent to give orders for the well governing of the free Cities.* Now if he that is the principal party in an equal League do thus, it is not to be wondred at, if he that in an unequal League is superior in honour and dignity, do the same: For the word *Imperium*, that is, *Empire*, taken in this sence as it signifies only an Ordinance and Appointment, equally conducing to the common good, doth not at all imply the
Liv. l. 37. loss of the others liberty. The *Rhodians*, in their Oration to the *Roman* Senate, thus bespake them, *The* Gracians *were wont to defend their Empire with their own forces: But their Empire where now it is, they wish that it may remain for ever: They are now well contented to*
Ibid. 23. *defend their liberties with your Arms, being no longer able to do it with their own.* So *Diodorus* tells us, that after the taking of the *Cadmean* Fort by the *Thebans*, many of the *Gracian* Cities met and agreed among themselves, *That every City in* Greece *should enjoy its own freedom*,

freedom, yet the conduct of the War should be given to the Athenians. And yet *Dion Prusaensis* speaking of those very *Athenians*, in the times of *Philip* of *Macedon*, saith, *That having at that time lost their command in the War, they retained only their own liberty.* So those people which *Cæsar* reckoned to be under the command of the *Suevians*, he by and by calls his Confederates. But in such things as appertain to his own particular profit, the request of him that is Superior in the League, are usually taken for Commands; not that they are so indeed, but that they are in respect of their usual effects, equivalent to Commands; for he needs no force, who knows himself to be feared. *Armatæ sunt Regum praces; The Requests of Kings have the same power as Commands.* And a denyal how just soever, shall be by them as ill digested as an injury. *It was never heard of,* saith Livy, *before* Caius Posthumius, *that any Consul was either chargeable or burdensome to our Associates in any thing; and therefore were our Magistrates supplyed abundantly with Mules, Pavilions, and all other Instruments of War, that so they might not require them from our Associates.* In the mean time, it sometimes so falls out, That if he that is superior in the League, be much more potent than the rest of the Confederates, he may by degrees at length usurp the Soveraignty over them; especially if the League be perpetual, and that he hath thereby a right to place Garrisons in any of their strong Towns, as the *Athenians* sometimes did, when they suffered themselves to be appealed unto from their Associates, which by the *Lacedemonians* was never done: wherefore *Isocrates* equals the Government that the *Athenians* exercised in those days over their Associates, with that of Kings and absolute Princes. So the *Latines* in *Livy* complain against the *Romans*, that under the specious Title of being Associates in War, they were reduced into a mere Subjection; which Society in Arms, *Plutarch* in the Life of *Aratus*, calls *a Gentle Slavery.* So *Festus Rufus* in *Tacitus*, concerning the *Rhodians*, *At first they lived in great freedom, till afterwards the* Romans *gently urging them, they were brought by little and little into an habit of Subjection.* So the *Ætolians* likewise complained, *That they had nothing left them but the bare shadow and empty name of Liberty.* So likewise afterwards the *Achaians* complain, *That they had indeed a League in appearance, but were at length brought into a Precarious Servitude.* The like complaint *Civilis Batavus* in *Tacitus*, makes against the same *Romans*, *That they used them not as formerly, like Companions, but usurped and insulted over them as mere Slaves.* And in another place, they falsely called that peace, which was indeed but a miserable Slavery. Thus *Eumenes* also in *Livy*, concerning the Confederates of the *Rhodians*, that they were their Associates in Name, but their Vassals indeed. Thus also *Magnetes* in *Polybius* saith, That *Demetrias* was in shew free, but in effect all things were done there at the will of the *Romans*. The *Thessalians* likewise were in appearance free, but indeed under the dominion of the *Macedonians*, as the same *Polybius* testifies. Now when these things are done, and so done as by patient endurance they may by mistake be said to be rightly done, (whereof we shall elsewhere discourse more fully;) then either of Companions they are made Subjects, or certainly there must be a partition of the Supremacy, which (as I have said before) may sometimes happen.

The weaker Associates sometimes reduced unto subjection.

Hal. l. 6.
Livy l. 34.
Hist. 4.

XXII. Of such as pay Tribute.

They that pay any thing either in satisfaction of wrongs past, or to be protected against injuries to come, are by *Thucydides* called tributary Associates, such were the Kings of the *Hebrews*, and of their Neighbour Nations after the time of *M. Anthony*, free; though under a certain tribute: Nor do I see any cause to doubt but that they that Reigned so, had Supreme Power within their respective Dominions, and had a full right to punish delinquents, according to their own Laws. Thus *M. Anthony* defends King *Herod*, being accused for murthering *Aristobulus*, *That it was neither just nor right to call a King to an account for what he doth as a King; for if so, he could not be a King: For common equity requires that they that gave him that honour, should permit him the free use of that Soveraign Power, which was appendent unto it.* So Chrysostom, *When the Empire of the* Jews *began to decline, and they made Tributaries to the* Romans; *They neither enjoyed that full liberty which they did formerly; nor were they in that pure subjection as now they are: But were indeed honoured with the Title of Associates, yet they paid Tribute to their Kings, and received Governors from them. Moreover, they had the free use of their own Laws, so that if any of their Countrymen offended, they themselves punished them by their own Laws.* And yet I deny not but even this very acknowledgment of their own weakness and insufficiency, doth somewhat abate and detract from the Majesty of their Empire.

XXIII. Of such as hold their dominions in Feud.

But that which seems to some to be more difficultly to be answered, is, when one Prince holds his Dominion from another, as being Lord of the Fief; which yet may be sufficiently answered by what hath been said before. For in this Contract (which is peculiar to the *German* Nation, and no where found but where they have planted themselves) two things are especially to be observed. 1. The personal Ob-

ligation. 2. The Right in the Thing so held. The Personal Obligation is the same, whether a man possesseth the very Right of Soveraignty, or any thing else though lying elsewhere, by vertue of the Fief: but such an Obligation as it takes not from a private man the right of Personal Liberty; so neither doth it diminish any thing in a King or State of the Soveraignty, which is Civil Liberty; which is easily to be understood by those Lands which are called Free-holds, which consist in Personal Obligations only, but gives no right in the thing so held: for these are no other than a species of that unequal League whereof we have discoursed before, wherein the one promiseth Fealty, and the other safeguard or protection. But admit they do swear Faith and Allegiance against all men, yet would this detract nothing from the Right of Soveraignty over their own Subjects. Not at all in this place to mention, that there are ever reserved in these Oaths, a tacite Condition that the War be just, whereof we shall treat elsewhere. But as to the Right in the thing so held, it may be such, that the very Right of Governing, if held in the right of the Fief or Fee, may be lost, and so return unto him that gave it; as well in case the Family be extinct, as also for some notorious crimes; and yet notwithstanding in the mean time, it ceaseth not to be the Supreme Power: For as I said before the thing it self is one thing, and the manner of holding it is another. And by this Right I find many Kings constituted by the *Romans*, so that the Royal Family failing, the Empire did escheat unto themselves, as *Strabo* observes
Lib. 12. of *Paphligonia* and some others.

XXIV. *A mans right distinguisht from the exercise of that right.* *Vide Bo.* 3. *ch.* 20. §. 3.

Lastly, We must also distinguish as in Private Dominion, so in Empire, between the Right it self, and the exercise of that Right; or between the first act and the second. For as a King (though an Infant) hath a Right to govern, but is not permitted to exercise that Right; so he that is mad, or a Prisoner, or that so lives in a Foreign Country, that he is not permitted freely to act in such matters, as concern the good of that Empire that is remote from him: For in all such cases, they have their Lieutenants or Viceroys to act for them; wherefore *Demetrius* living under restraint with *Seleucus*, did forbid any credit to be given to his Letters or
Plut. Demetr. unto his Seal; but commanded that all things should be so governed as if he were dead.

CHAP.

CHAP. IV.

Of a War made by Subjects against their Superiors.

PRivate Men may without doubt make war against private men, as the Traveller against the Thief or Robber; so may Soveraign Princes and States against Soveraign Princes, as *David* against the King of the *Ammonites*: Private men may make war against Princes, if not their own, as *Abraham* against the King of *Babylon* and his Neighbours; so may Soveraign Princes against Private Men, whether they be their own Subjects, as *David* against *Ishbosheth* and his party; or Strangers, as the *Romans* against *Pyrates*. The only doubt is, whether any person or persons, publick or private, can make a lawful war against those that are set over them, whether as supreme or as subordinate unto them. And in the first place, It is on all hands granted, That they that are commissionated by the highest powers, may make war against their Inferiors; as *Nehemiah* did against *Tobia* and *Sanballat*, by the Authority of *Artaxerxes*. But whether it be lawful for Subjects to make war against those who have the Supreme Power over them, or against such as act by and according to their Authority, is the thing in question. It is also by all good men acknowledged, That if the Commands of a Prince shall manifestly contradict either the Law of Nature, or the Divine Precepts, they are not to be obeyed; for the Apostles when they urged that Maxim, *Deo magis quam hominibus obediendum, That God is rather to be obeyed than man*; unto such as forbad them to Preach in the name of *Jesus*, did but appeal to a Principle of right reason, which Nature had insculpt in every mans breast, and which *Plato* expresseth in almost the very same words. But yet if either for this, or for any other cause, any injury be offered unto us, because it so please him that hath the Soveraign Power, it ought rather to be patiently tolerated, than by force resisted: *For although we do not owe an active obedience to such Commands of Princes, yet we do owe a passive: though we ought not to violate the laws of God or of Nature, to fulfil the will of the greatest Monarch; yet ought we rather patiently to submit to whatsoever he shall inflict upon us for not obeying, than by resistance to violate our Countries peace: The best and safest course we can steer in such a case, is either by Flight to preserve our selves, or resolvedly to undergo whatsoever shall be imposed on us.* I. The Question stated.

And naturally all men have a right to repel Injuries from themselves by resisting them, (as we have already said.) But Civil Societies being once instituted for the preservation of Peace, there presently succeeded unto that Common-wealth a certain greater Right over us and ours, so far forth as was necessary for that end. And therefore that promiscuous Right that Nature gave us to resist, the Common-wealth, for the maintaining of good order and the publick peace hath a right to prohibit, which without all doubt it doth, seeing that otherwise it cannot obtain the end it proposeth to it self. For in case that promiscuous II. War against Superiors as such unlawful.

promiscuous Right of forceable resistance should be tolerated, it would be no longer a Common-wealth, that is, a Sanctuary against Oppression, but a confused Rabble, such as that of the *Cyclops*, whereof the Poet thus:

——————Where every Ass
May on his Wife and Children Judgment pass.

A dissolute Company where all are speakers and no hearers: Like unto that which *Valerius* records of the *Bebricii*——————

——— Who all Leagues and Laws disdain,
And Justice, which mens minds in peace retain.

Salust makes mention of a wild and savage people, living like Beasts in Woods and Mountains without Laws and without Government, whom he calls *Aborigines:* And in another place of the *Getuli*, who had neither Laws, good Customs, nor any Princes to govern them. But Cities cannot subsist without these, *Generale pactum est societatis humanæ regibus obedire*; *All humane Societies*, saith St. Augustine, *unanimously agree in this, to obey Kings*: So Æschylus,

Kings live by their own Laws, subject to none.

And *Sophocles*,

They Princes are, obey we must, what not?

To the same Tune sings *Euripides*,

Folly in Kings must be with patience born.

Whereunto agrees that of *Tacitus*, *Principi summum rerum arbitrium Dii dederunt,&c. Subditis obsequii gloria relicta est*; *God hath invested a Prince with Soveraign Power, leaving nothing to Subjects but the glory of Obedience.* And here also,

Sen. *Things base seem Noble, when by Princes done;*
What they Impose, bear thou, be't right or wrong.

Wherewith agrees that of *Salust*, *Impunè quid vis facere, hoc est Regem esse*, *To do any thing without fear of punishment, is peculiar to Kings*; for as *Mark Anthony* urged in *Herod*'s case, *If he were accountable for what he hath done as a King, he could not be a King.* Hence it is, that the Majesty of such as have Soveraign Power, whether in one or more, is fenced with so many and so severe Laws, and the licentiousness of Subjects restrained with such sharp and exquisite torments; which were unreasonable, if to resist them were lawful. If a Souldier resist his Captain that strikes him, and but lay hold on his Partisan, he shall be cashiered; but if he either break it, or offer to strike again, he shall be put to death: for as *Aristotle* observes, *If he that is an Officer strike, he shall not be struck again.*

An Officer striking must not be struck again.

III. The unlawfulness of making war against our Superiors proved by the Jewish Law. Jos. 1. 18. 1 Sam. 8. 11. Deut. 17. 14.

By the *Hebrew* Law, He that behaved himself contumaciously against either the High-Priest, or against him who was extraordinarily by God ordained to govern his people, was to be put to death; and that which in the eighth Chapter of the first Book of *Samuel*, is spoken of the right of Kings, to him that throughly inspects it, is neither to be understood of their true and just rights, that is, of what they may do justly and honestly (for the duty of Kings is much otherwise described, *Deut.* 8: 11.) nor is it to be understood barely, of what he will do: for then it had signified nothing that was singular or extraordinary, for private men do the same to private men: But it is to be understood of such a fact, as usurps or carries with it the priviledge of what is right, that is, that it must not be resisted although it be not right; for Kings have a Right peculiar to themselves, and what in others is punishable, in them is not. That old Saying, *Summum jus, summa injuria*, Extreme right is extreme wrong, is best fitted to the case of Kings, whose absolute power makes that seem right, which strictly taken is not so. There is a main difference between Right in this sence taken, and Just; for in the former sence, it comprehends whatsoever may be done without fear of punishment: but Just, respects only things lawful and honest. And though some Kings there be, who are (what *Servius* in *Cicero's Philippicks* is commanded to be) *magis Justitiæ quam Juris Consulti*; More regardful of their honour and duty, than of their power and prerogatives: Yet this doth not diminish their Soveraign Right; because if they will, they may do otherwise without the danger of

Right differenced from Just.

of being resisted. And therefore it is added in that place of *Samuel* before cited, That when the people should at any time be thus oppressed by their Kings, as if there were no remedy to be expected from men, they should invoke his help who is the Supream Judge of the whole Earth. So that whatsoever a King doth, though the same done by an inferiour person would be an Injury, yet being done by him is Right. As a Judge is said *Jus reddere*, to do right, though the sentence he gives be unrighteous.

When Christ in the New Testament commanded, to give *Cæsar* his due, doubtless he intended, that his Disciples should yield as great, if not a greater obedience, as well active as passive, unto the higher Power, than what was due from the *Jews* to their Kings: which (St. *Paul*, who was best able to Interpret his Masters words) expounding *Rom.* 13. doth at large describe the duty of Subjects; charging those that resist the power of Kings, with no less Crime *than Rebellion against Gods Ordinance*; and with a Judgement as great as their sin. For saith he, *They that do so resist, shall receive unto themselves damnation.* And a little after, he urgeth the necessity of our subjection, *Not altogether for fear, but for Conscience*, as knowing, that *He is the Minister of God for our good.* Now if there be a necessity of our subjection, then there is the same necessity for our not resisting; because, he that resists is not subject. Neither did the Apostle mean such a necessity of subjection as ariseth from an apprehension of some worse inconvenience that might follow upon our resistance: But such as proceeds from the sense of some benefit that we receive by it, whereby we stand obliged in duty, not unto man only, but unto God; (so *that he that resists the power of the Supream Magistrate, incurs a double punishment*, saith *Plato*, *First, From God, for breaking that good order which he hath constituted amongst men: and Secondly, From the Common-wealth, whose righteous Laws, made for the preservation of the publick peace, are by resistance weakned, and the Common-wealth thereby endangered. For canst thou believe*, saith *Plato*, *that any City or Kingdom can long stand, when the publick Decrees of the Senate shall be wilfully broken, and trampled upon by the over-swelling power of some private men; who in strugling against the execution of the Laws, do as much as in them lyes, dissolve the Common-wealth, and consequently bring all into confusion.* The Apostle therefore fortifies this necessity of publick subjection to Princes with two main Reasons: First, Because God had constituted and approved of this Order of Commanding and Obeying; and that not only under the *Jewish*, but under the *Christian* Law: wherefore the Powers that are set over us are to be observed (not servilely, superstitiously or out of fear, but with free, rational and generous Spirits) *tanquam à Diis datæ, as being given by the Gods*, saith *Plato*: or as St. *Paul*) *tanquam à Deo ordinatæ, as if ordained by God himself.* Which order, as it is originally Gods, so by giving it a Civil Sanction, it becomes ours also; for thereby we add as much authority unto it as we can give. The other reason is drawn *ab utili*, from profit: Because this order is constituted for our good, and therefore in Conscience is to be obeyed and not resisted. But here some men may say, That to bear Injuries, is not at all profitable unto us, whereunto some men (haply more truly, than appositely, to the meaning of the Apostle) give this answer, That patiently to bear Injuries, conduceth much to our benefit; because it entitles us to a reward far transcending our sufferings, as St. *Paul* testifies. But though this also be true, yet is it not (as I conceive) the proper and genuine sense of the Apostles words, which doubtless have respect to that universal Good, whereunto this order was at first instituted, as to its proper end; which was the publick Peace, wherein every particular man, is as much concerned, if not much more than in his private. (For what protection can good Laws give, if Subjects may refuse to yield their obedience to them; whereas by the constant observance of good Laws, all estates, both publick and private do grow up and flourish together.) And certainly these are the good Fruits that we receive from the Supream Powers, for which in Conscience we owe them obedience. For no man did ever yet wish ill to himself. (But he that resists the power of the Magistrate, and wilfully violates the Laws established, doth in effect (as far as in him is) dissolve his Countreys peace, and will in the end bury himself also in the ruines of it.) Besides, the Glory of Kings consists in the prosperity of their Subjects. When *Sylla* had by his Cruelty, almost depopulated, not *Rome* only, but all *Italy*, one seasonably admonisht him, *Sinendos esse aliquos vivere, ut essent, quibus imperet*; *That some should be permitted to live, over whom he might rule as a King.* It was a common Proverb among the *Hebrews*, Nisi potestas publica esset, alter alterum vivum deglutiret; *Were it not for the Soveraign Powers, every Kingdom would be like a great Pond wherein the greater Fish would alwayes devour the lesser.* Agreeable whereunto is that of *Chrysostome*, *Unless there were a power over us to restrain our Inordinate Lusts, men would be more fierce and cruel than Lyons and Tygers, not only biting, but eating and devouring one another. Take away Tribunals of Justice, and you take away all Right, Property and Dominion: No man can say, this is mine House, this my Land, these my Goods, or my Servants: but* Omnia erunt fortiorum, *the longest Sword would take all.* The mighty man could be no longer secure of his Estate, than until a mightier than he came to dispossess him; the weaker

IV. By the Gospel Law.

Rom. 13. 2.

Plato.

Plato.

Plut. Florus. Aug. de Civ. Dei, lib. 3. *c.* 28.

Chrys. de Statuis 6. *Ad Eph.* 5.

weaker must alwayes give place to the stronger; and where the strength was equal, the loss would be so too. And this would at length introduce a general Ataxy, which would be far more perilous than a perfect Slavery. Wherefore seeing that God hath established, and humane reason upon tryal, approved of Soveraign Empire, as the best preservative of humane Societies, that every man should yield obedience thereunto, is most rational. For without Subjection, there can be no Protection. But here it will be objected, *That the Commands of Princes do not alwayes tend to the publick good, and therefore when they decline from that end for which they were ordained, they ought not to be obeyed.* To which I answer, That though the Supream Magistrate doth sometimes, either through Fear, Anger, Lust, Covetousness, or such like inordinate passions, baulk the ordinary path of Justice and Equity; yet are these, (happening but seldome) to be passed over as personal blemishes, which (as *Tacitus* rightly observes) are abundantly recompensed by the more frequent example of better Princes. (Besides, the Lives of Princes are to be considered with some grains of allowance, in respect of those many provocations and opportunities they have to offend, which private men have not: All men have their Failings, we our selves have ours; and in case we will admit of none in Kings, we must not rank them amongst men, but Gods. The Moon hath her spots, *Venus* her Mole; and if we can find nothing under the Sun without blemish, Why should we expect perfection in Kings? He is very uncharitable, that judges of Rulers by some few of their Evil deeds, passing over many of their Good ones. Seeing therefore, that there is in all mens lives, as in our best Coin, an Intermixture of Good and Evil, it is sufficient to denominate a Prince Good, if his Virtues excel his Errors. Besides, to charge the Vices of Princes upon the Government, as they usually do who affect Innovation, is but a cheat: For what is this, but to condemn the Law for the Corruption of some Lawyers: Or Agriculture, because some Husbandmen do curse God for a Storm? *Si mentiar, ego mentior, non negotium; If I do lye,* (saith the Merchant in St. *Augustine*) *it is I that am to be blamed, not my Calling.* And if some Princes do prevaricate in some things, they and not their Function are to be blamed.) But as to Laws, though they cannot be so made, as to fit every mans Case, yet it sufficeth to denominate them good, if they obviate such disorders as are frequently practised, and so do good to the generality of the people. But as to such cases, which, because they rarely happen, cannot so easily be provided against by particular Laws, even these also are understood to be restrained by general Rules. For, though the reason of the Law being particularly applyed to that special Case, hold not; yet in the general, under which special cases may lawfully be comprehended, it may. And much better is it so to do, than to live without Law, or to permit every man to be a Law to himself. Very apposite to this purpose, is that of *Seneca, Better it is not to admit of some excuses, though just, from a Few, than that All should be permitted to make whatsoever they please.* Memorable is that of *Pericles* in *Thucydides, Better it is for Private men, that the Common wealth flourish, though they thrive not in it, than that they should abound and grow rich in their own private estates, and the Common-wealth pine and wither. For if the whole be ruined, every private mans Fortunes must needs be ruined with it: But if the Common-wealth flourish, every private mans estate, though in it self weak, may in time be repaired. Wherefore since the State, if well ordered, can easily support any private mans fortunes; but a private mans estate, though never so well ordered, cannot repair the loss of the Publick State: Why do ye not rather Contribute your utmost care to advance the Publick, than (as ye now do) seek to build your own private Fortunes upon the publick Ruines?* Wherewith agrees that of *Ambrose,* Eadem est singulorum utilitas, quæ universorum; *The Profit which the Common-wealth receives, redounds to every private man.* And that also in the Law, *Semper non quod privatim interest uni ex sociis, sed quod communi societati expedit, servari debet; Evermore, not that which particularly availeth any one party, but that which conduceth to the benefit of the Common society is to be observed.* (When the common people in *Rome* began to Mutinee by reason of some Taxes extraordinarily imposed on them, *Lævinus* the Consul exhorted the Senate, to encourage the people by their own example: And to that very end advised every Senator to bring into the Senate-house all the Gold, Silver and Brass money he had, that it might be delivered to the *Triumviri* for the publick service: adding this Reason, If our City overcome, no man needs to fear his own estate; but if it fall, let no man think to preserve his own.) For as *Plato* rightly observes, *What is common strengthens a City; but what enricheth Private Families only, weakens and dissolves it: And therefore it concerns both Princes and Subjects, to prefer the affairs of the Common-wealth, before their own private, (either pleasure or profit.)* It is a very true Observation of *Xenophon's, He that in an Army behaves himself seditiously against his General, sins against his own life.* And no less true is that of *Jamblicus, No man should think himself a Loser by what the Common wealth gains; for every private mans loss is sufficiently recompensed in the Publick Profit. For as in the Natural body, so doubtless in the Civil,* In totius Salute, Salus est partium; *The well being of every part consists in the safety of the whole.* But without doubt, among those things that are

Object.

Kings to be censured with some favour.

Lib. 7. de bene. cap. 16.

Lib. 2.

In the general safety each particular is included.

De Off. lib. 3.

Liv. l. 26.

are publick, the chief and principal is that aforesaid Order of well Commanding and well Obeying; which cannot consist where private Subjects assume that Licence of resisting the publick Magistrate: which is excellently described by *Dion Cassius*, whose words sound much to this sense, *I cannot conceive it seemly for a Prince to submit to his Subjects; for there can be no safety, where the Feet are advanced above the Head, or where they undertake to govern whose duty it is to be governed. What a dismal confusion would it introduce in a Family if Children should be permitted to despise their Parents, or Servants to dispute the commands of their Masters? In what a desperate condition is that patient, that will not be ruled in all things by his Physician? And what hopes can there be of that Ship, where the Marriners refuse to obey their Pilot? Surely God hath ordained, and humane reason upon tryal hath found it necessary, that for the preservation of humane Society some should Command, and some Obey.* To the Testimony of St. *Paul*, we shall add that of St. *Peter*, whose words are these, *Honour the King. Servants be ye subject to your Masters with all Fear, and not only to the good and gentle, but also to the froward: For this is Thank-worthy if a man for Conscience towards God endure grief, suffering wrongfully. For what glory is it, if when ye be buffetted for your faults ye take it patiently? But if when ye do well, and suffer for it, ye take it patiently, this is acceptable with God.* And this he by and by confirms by Christs own example. Which *Clemens* also in his Constitutions thus expresseth, *The servant that feareth God*, saith he, *will serve his Master also with all faithfulness, yea, though he be impious and unjust.* Whence we may observe two things: First, That under the subjection that servants are in, even to hard Masters, is also couched that of Subjects unto Kings, though Tyrannical. And therefore, as a little before, he commanded subjection to every humane ordinance; that is, to the Laws and Constitutions of Princes without distinction, (for when that Epistle was written, there were very few Princes that were not Idolaters,) yet submit we must, saith St. *Peter*, for all that, and that *Propter Dominum, For the Lords sake.* So what follows in the same Chapter being built upon the same Foundation, respects the duty as well of Subjects as of Servants. And so requires the same Obedience, as well Passive as Active; Such as we usually pay to our Parents, according to that of the Poet,

The General safety consists chiefly in well commanding and well obeying.

1 Pet. 2. 17, 18, 19.

Thy Parents Love if Good: If Bad, yet bear.

And that also of *Terence*,

To bear with Parents, Piety commands.

And that likewise of *Cicero*, in his Oration for *Cluentius*, *Men ought not only to conceal the Injuries done unto them by their Parents, but to bear them with patience.* A young man of *Eretria*, that had been long educated under *Zeno*, being demanded, What he had learned? Answered, *Meekly to bear his Fathers wrath.* So *Justin* relates of *Lysimachus*, *That he endured the reproaches of the King with the same calmness of Spirit, as if he had been his Father.* Ferenda sunt Renum Ingenia, *The humours of Kings must be endured*, saith *Tacitus*: And in another place he tells us, *That good Emperours are to be wished for, but whatsoever they are, they must be obeyed.* So also *Livy*, *As the rage of our Parents, so the cruelty of our Countrey are no ways to be becalmed, but by patience and sufferance:* For which *Claudian* highly extols the *Persians*, who obeyed all their Kings equally, though never so cruel.

Lib. 15. *Lib.* 27.

Ann. 16. *Hist.* 6.

V. The practice of the Primitive Christians.

Neither did the Practice of the Primitive Christians swerve from this Law of God, which is an undeniable argument that they so understood it. For though the *Roman* Emperours were sometimes the very worst of men, and deadly enemies to the Christian Faith; yea, though there wanted not such under their Government, who under the specious pretence of freeing the Common-wealth from Tyranny and Oppression, took Arms against them, yet could they never perswade the Christians to joyn with them. In the Constitutions of *Clemens* we read, *Regiæ potestati resistere nefas*; *To resist the power of a King is Impious.* *Tertullian* in his Apology writes thus, *What was that* Cassius *that conspired against the life of* Julius Cæsar? *What was that* Poscennius Niger *that in love to his own Countrey, took Arms in* Syria, *as* Clodius Albinus *did in* France *and* Britain, *against that bloody Emperour* Septimius Severus? *Or what was that* Plautianus, *who to set the Common wealth free from Tyranny attempted the life of the same Emperour in his own Pallace? What was that* Ælius Lætus, *who having first poysoned that Infamous Emperour* Commodus, *fearing it should not take that effect which he desired, did afterwards hire* Narcissus, *a strong Wrestler, to strangle him? Or what was that* Parthenius (*whose fact* Tertullian *doth so much detest,*) *who being Chamberlain to that execrable Tyrant* Domitian, *yet killed him in his own Chamber? What* (*saith* Tertullian) *were all these? Surely not* Christians, *but* Romans: *Nay so abominated they were by Christians,* that *Tertullian* seems to glory in this, *That though Christians were every where reproached as Enemies, nay Traytors to the Imperial Crown, yet could they never find any of them either stained with that crime, or so much as favouring those Treasonable practices of*

I either

either Callius, Niger, *or* Albinius. When St. *Ambrose* was commanded by the Emperour *Valentinus* to give up his Church to be Garrison'd by Souldiers, though he took it to be an Injury done, not only to himself, and to his Congregation, but even unto Christ himself; yet would be not take any advantage of the commotions that it made among the people, to make resistance. *If the Emperour,* saith he, *had commanded what was in my power to give, were it mine House, Land, Goods, Gold or Silver, how readily should I obey; whatsoever is mine I would willingly offer: But the Temple of God I cannot give away, nor can I yield it up to any man:* Cum ad custodiendum non ad tradendum illud acceperim, *Since it was committed unto me to defend and to keep, but not to betray.* And whereas the people being enraged thereby, did offer their assistance to repel the Souldiers, he refused it, saying, *Coactus repugnare non novi; Though provoked and compelled thereunto, yet withstand or resist I cannot: Grieve, and weep, and mourn I can: Against Arms, Souldiers, and* Goths, *I have no other Weapons but Tears: For these are the only Forts and Muniments of a Priest:* Aliter nec debeo nec possum resistere, *otherwise I neither ought, nor can resist.* And presently after, being commanded to appease the Tumult, he replyed, *That not to excite them was in his power; but being exasperated and enraged, to appease them was in the sole power of him, who when he pleased, could still the ragings of the Seas, and the madness of the people.* And in another place he writes thus, *Will ye hale me to prison, or cast me into chains, I am willing to suffer, neither shall I guard my self with multitudes of people who offer themselves to defend me.* Neither would he make use of the Forces of *Maximus* when offered against the Emperour, though an *Arian*, and a grievous persecutor of the Church. In imitation of whom, *Gregory* the Great in one of his Epistles confesseth, *That if he would have engaged himself in the death of the* Lumbards, *that Nation had at that day had neither King, Dukes, nor Earls; but had been reduced into extreme confusion. Nazianzen* informs us, That *Julian* the Apostate was diverted from some bloody designs he intended against the Church, by the tears of Christians: Adding withal, *That these are our best preservatives against Persecutions.* And because a great part of his Army were Christians, therefore his cruelty towards them would have been not injurious to the Church of Christ only, but would at that time have much endangered the Commonwealth: Unto all which we may also add that of St. *Augustine*, where expounding those places of St. *Paul*, he saith, *Even for the preservation of our own lives, we ought to submit to the Supreme power, and not to resist them, in whatsoever they shall take away from us.*

See *Gratian* c. 23. q. 8. — *Lib.* 5. *orat. in Auxen.* — *Epist.* 33. — *Greg. l.* 6. *Ep.* 1. — *Theodoret. Hist. Eccl. lib.* 5. c. 4. — *Naz. Orat.* 1. *in Julian.* — *Prop.* 74.

VI. Inferiour Magistrates ought not to resist the Supreme.

Some very learned men there are even in this age, who accomodating themselves too servilely to the times and places wherein they live, do perswade themselves first, and then others, That though this Licence of resisting the Supreme Power be inconsistent with the condition of private men, yet it may agree with the Rights of Inferiour Magistrates; nay further, that they sin in case they do it not: which opinion is to be exploded, as Seditious. For as in Logick there is a Genus which is called Subalterne, which though it be comprehensive of all that is under it, as a living creature comprehends both man and beast; yet hath it a Genus above it, in respect whereof it is but a species: As a living creature is to a body, which comprehends all sorts of bodies, both animate, and inanimate. The like we may say of Magistrates, some are Supreme, who rule all and are ruled by none; others are subordinate, who in respect of private men are publick persons, governing like Princes: But in respect of the Supreme Magistrate are but private men, and are commanded as Subjects. For the power or faculty of Governing as it is derived from the supreme power, so it is subject unto it, and whatsoever is done, by the Inferiour Magistrate, contrary to the will of the Supreme is null, and reputed but as a private act, for want of the stamp of publick Authority. All order (say Philosophers) doth necessarily relate to somewhat, that is first and highest, (from whence it takes its rise, or beginning. Now they that are of this opinion, that Inferiour Magistrates may resist the Supreme, seem to introduce such a state of things, as the Poets fansied to have been in Heaven before Majesty was thought on, when the lesser Gods denyed the Prerogative of *Jupiter*. But this order or Subordination of one to another is not only approved of by common experience, as in every Family the Father is the head, next unto him the Mother, then the Children, and after them the Servants, and such as are under them: So in every Kingdom, *Each power under higher powers are*——And, *All Governours are under Government*——To which purpose is that notable saying of St. *Augustine*, *Observe*, saith he, *the degrees of all humane things: if thy Tutor enjoyn thee any thing, thou must do it; yet not, in case the Proconsul command the contrary: Neither must thou obey the Consul, if thy Prince command otherwise. For in so doing thou canst not be said to contemn Authority, but thou chusest to obey that which is highest: Neither ought the lesser powers to be offended that the greater is preferred before them, (For God is the God of order.)* And that also of the same Father concerning *Pilate*, *Because*, saith he, *God had Invested him with such a Power as was it self subordinate to that of* Cæsar's. But it is also approved of by Divine Authority: For St. *Peter* enjoyns us to be subject unto Kings otherwise, than unto Magistrates: To Kings as Supreme, that is, absolutely, without exceptions to any other com-

Grat. c. 11. *q.* 3. *Qui resistit.* — *In Johan.* — 1 Ep. 2. 1.

commands than those directly from God; who is so far from justifying our resistance, that he commands our passive obedience: But unto Magistrates, as they are deputed by Kings, and as they derive their Authority from them. And when St. *Paul* subjects every soul to the higher Powers, doubtless he exempts not Inferiour Magistrates. Rom. 13. Neither do we find amongst the *Hebrews* (where there were so many Kings utterly regardless of the Laws both of God and Men) any Inferiour Magistrates, among whom some without all question there were both Pious and Valiant, that ever arrogated unto themselves this Right of resisting by force the Power of their Kings, without an express command from God, who alone hath an unlimited power and jurisdiction over them. But on the contrary, what duties Inferiour Magistrates owe unto their Kings though wicked, *Samuel* will Instruct us by his own example, who though he knew that *Saul* had corrupted himself, and that God also had rejected him from being King, yet before the people, and before the Elders of *Israel*, he gives him that reverence and respect that was due unto him. 1 Sam. 15.3. And so likewise the state of Religion publickly profest, did never depend upon any other humane Authority, but on that of the King and *Sanhedrim*. For in that after the King, the Magistrates with the people, engaged themselves to the true worship and service of God, it ought to be understood, so far forth as it should be in the power of every one of them. Nay, the very Images of their False Gods which were publickly erected, (and therefore could not but be scandalous to such as were truly Religious) yet were they never demolished, so far as we can read of, but at the special command either of the people, when the Government was Popular; or of Kings, when the Government was Kingly. And if the Scriptures do make mention of any violence sometimes offered unto Kings, it is not to justifie the fact, but to shew the equity of the Divine Providence in permitting it. And whereas they of the contrary perswasion do frequently urge that excellent saying of *Trajan* the Emperour, who delivering a Sword to a Captain of the *Prætorian* Band, said, *Hoc pro me utere, si rectè impero; si malè, contra me*: *Use this Sword for me, if I govern well; but if otherwise, against me.* We must know, That *Trajan* (as appears by *Pliny*'s Panegyrick) was not willing to assume unto himself Regal power, but rather to behave himself as a good Prince, who was willing to submit to the Judgement of the Senate and people; whose decrees he would have that Captain to execute, though it were against himself. Whose example both *Pertinax* and *Macrinus* did afterwards follow, whose excellent Speeches to this purpose are recorded by *Herodian*. The like we read of *M. Anthony*, who refused to touch the publick Treasure, without the consent of the *Roman* Senate.

VII. Of resistance in case of inevitable necessity.

But the Case will yet be more difficult, whether this law of not resisting do oblige us when the dangers that threaten us be extreme, and otherwise inevitable. For some of the Laws of God himself, though they sound absolutely, yet seem to admit of some tacite exceptions in cases of extreme necessity: For so it was, by the wisest of the *Jewish* Doctors, expresly determined concerning the Law of their Sabbath, in the times of the *Hasmonæans*: Whence arose that famous saying among them, *Periculum animæ impellit Sabbatum*, *The danger of a mans life drives away the Sabbath.* When the *Jew* in *Synesius*, was accused for the breach of the Sabbath, he excuseth himself by another Law, and that more forcible, saying, *We were in manifest jeopardy of our lives.* When *Bacchides* had brought the Army of the *Jews* into a great strait on their Sabbath day, placing his Army before them and behind them, the River *Jordan* being on both sides; *Jonathan* thus bespake his Souldiers, *Let us go up now and fight for our lives, for it standeth not with us to day, as in times past.* 1 Macc. 9 43, 44, 45. Which case of necessity is approved of even by Christ himself, as well in this Law of the Sabbath, as in that of not eating the Shew-bread. And the *Hebrew* Doctors pretending the authority of an Ancient Tradition, do rightly Interpret their Laws made against the eating of meats forbidden, with this tacite exception; Not that it was not just with God to have obliged us even unto death, but that some Laws of his are conversant about such matters as it cannot easily be believed that they were intended to have been prosecuted with so much Rigour as to reduce us to such an extremity, as to dye rather than to disobey them, which in humane Laws doth yet further proceed. I deny not but that some acts of vertue are so strictly enjoined, that if we perform them not, we may justly be put to death: As for a Sentinel to forsake his station. But neither is this to be rashly understood to be the Will of the Law-giver. Nor do men assume so much Right over either themselves or others, unless it be when, and so far forth, as extreme necessity requires it. For all humane Laws are so constituted, or so to be understood as that there should be some allowance for humane frailty. The right understanding of this Law, of resisting or not resisting the highest Powers in cases of inevitable necessity, seems much to depend upon the Intention of those who first entred into Civil Society, from whom the right of Government is devolved upon the persons Governing: Who had they been demanded, Whether they would have imposed such a yoke upon all Mankind as death it self, rather than in any case by force to repel the Insolencies of their Superiours; I much question, whether they would have granted it, unless it had been in such a case, where such resistance could not be made without great commotions in the Common-wealth, or the certain destruction of many Innocents; for what Charity commends in such a case to be done, may, I doubt not, pass for an humane Law. But some may say, that this rigid obligation to dye, rather than at any time to resist injuries done by our Superiors, is not imposed on us by any humane, but by the Divine Law. But we must observe, That men did not at first unite themselves in Civil Society, by any special Command from God, but voluntarily out of a sence they had of their own impotency, to repel force and violence whilst they lived solitarily, and in Families apart; whence the Civil Power takes its rise: For which cause it is, that St. *Peter* calls it an humane ordinance, although it be elsewhere called a Divine Ordinance, because this wholesom constitution of men was approved of by God himself. But God in approving an humane Law, may be thought to approve of it as an humane Law, and after an humane manner. *Barkley* (who was the stoutest Champion in defending Kingly Power) doth notwithstanding thus far allow, That the People or the nobler part of them, have a right to defend themselves against cruel Tyranny, and yet he confesseth that the whole body of the people is subject unto the King. Now this I shall easily admit, That the more we desire to secure any thing by Law, the more express and peremptory should that Law be, and the fewer exceptions there should be from it; (for they that have a mind to violate that Law, will presently seek shelter, and think themselves priviledged by those exceptions, though their cases be far different;) Yet dare I not condemn indifferently either every private man, or every, though lesser, part of the people, who as their last refuge, in cases of extreme necessity, have anciently made use of their Arms to defend themselves, yet with respect had to the common good. For *David*, who (saving in some particular Facts) was so celebrated for his integrity, did yet entertain first four hundred, and afterwards more armed men; to what end, unless for the safeguard of his own person, against any violence that should be offered him? But this also we must note, That *David* did not this until he had been assured, both by *Jonathan*, and by many other infallible Arguments, that *Saul* sought his life; and that even then, he neither invaded any City, nor made an Offensive War against any, but lurked only for his own security, sometimes in Mountains, sometimes in Caves, and such like devious places, and sometimes in Foreign Nations, with this resolution, to decline all occasions of annoying his own Countrymen. A Fact parallel to this of *Davids*, we may read of in the *Maccabees*: For whereas some seek to defend the Wars of the *Maccabees* upon this ground, That *Antiochus* was not a King, but an Usurper; this I account but frivolous: For in the whole Story of the *Maccabees*, we shall never find *Antiochus* mentioned by any of their own party, by any other Title than by that of King; and deservedly: For the *Hebrews* had long before submitted to the *Macedonian* Empire, in whose Right *Antiochus* succeeded. And whereas the *Hebrew* Laws forbad a Stranger to be set over them, this was to be understood by a voluntary Election, and not by an involuntary Compulsion, through the necessity of the times. And whereas others say, That the *Maccabees* did act by the peoples right, to whom belonged the Right of Governing themselves by their own Laws, neither is this probable: For the *Jews* being first conquered by *Nebuchadonosor*, were by the right of War subject unto him, and afterwards became by the same Law, subject to the *Medes* and *Persians* as Successors to the *Chaldeans*, whose whole Empire did at length devolve upon the *Macedonians*. And hence it is, that the *Jews*, in *Tacitus*, are termed *The most servile of all the* Eastern *Nations*; neither did they require any Covenants or Conditions from *Alexander* or his Successors, but yielded themselves freely without any limitations or exceptions, as before they had done unto *Darius*. And though they were permitted sometimes to use their own rites, and publickly to exercise their own Laws, yet was not this due unto them by any Law that was added unto the Empire, but only by a precarious Right, that was indulged unto them by the favour of their Kings. There was nothing then that could justifie the *Maccabees* in their taking of Arms, but that invincible Law of extreme necessity, which might do it so long as they contained themselves within the bounds of self-preservation, and in imitation of *David*, betook themselves to secret places, in order to their own security; never offering to make use of their Arms unless violently assaulted. In the mean time, Great care is to be taken, that even when we are thus enforced to defend our selves in cases of certain and extreme danger, we spare the Person of the King; for they that conceive the carriage of *David* towards *Saul*, to proceed not so much from the necessity of duty, as out of some deeper consideration, are mistaken. For *David* himself declares, that no man can be innocent that stretcheth forth his hand against the Lords anointed: Because he very well knew that it was written in the Law, *Thou shalt not revile the Gods*, that is, the Supreme Judges: *Thou shalt not curse the Rulers of thy people.* In which Law, special mention being made of the Supreme Power, it evidently shews that some special duty towards them is required of us: Wherefore *Optatus Milevitanus* speaking of this fact of *David*, saith, *That Gods special command coming fresh into his memory, did so restrain him, that he could not hurt* Saul, *though his mortal enemy.*

[Margin notes: *Barkley Lib.* 3. *contra Monarchomach. c.* 8. — *David's* example. — The *Maccabees.* — The *Jews* a conquered Nation. — The Kings Person to be spared in the defence of our selves. — 1 Sam. 26. 9. — Exod. 22. 28. — *Lib.* 2.]

enemy. Wherefore he brings in *David* thus reasoning with himself, *Volebam hostem vincere, sed prius est divina præcepta observare*; *Willingly I would overcome mine enemy, but I dare not transgress the Commands of God.* And *Josephus* speaking of *David*, after he had cut off *Sauls* Garment, saith, *That his Heart smote him*: So that he confest, *Injustum facinus erat Regem suum occidere, It was a wicked act to kill his Soveraign.* And presently after, *Horrendum Regem quamvis malum occidere, Pœnam enim id facienti imminere constat, ab eo qui Regem dedit*; *It is an horrid act to kill a King, though wicked; for certainly he, by whose Providence all Kings reign, will pursue the Regicide with vengeance inevitably.* To reproach any private man falsly is forbidden by the Law, but of a King, we must not speak evil though he deserve it; because as he that wrote the Problems (fathered upon *Aristotle*) saith, *He that speaketh evil of the Governor, scandalizeth the whole City.* So *Joab* concludes concerning *Shimei*, as *Josephus* testifies, *Shalt thou not dye, who presumest to curse him whom God hath placed in the Throne of the Kingdom? The Laws* (saith *Julian*) *are very severe on the behalf of Princes, for he that is injurious unto them, doth wilfully trample upon the Laws themselves.* Now if we must not speak evil of Kings, much less must we do evil against them: *David* repented but for offering violence to *Saul*'s Garments, so great was the Reverence that he bare to his Person, and deservedly; for since their Soveraign Power cannot but expose them to the general hatred, therefore it is fit, that their security should especially be provided for. *This*, saith Quintilian, *is the fate of such as sit at the Stern of Government, that they cannot discharge their duty faithfully, nor provide for the publick safety, without the envy of many.* (And for this cause are the persons of Kings guarded with such severe Laws, which seem, like *Draco*'s, to be wrote in blood,) As may appear by those enacted by the *Romans*, for the security of their Tribunes, whereby their persons became inviolable. Amongst other wise Sayings of the *Esseni*, this was one, That the persons of Kings should be held as sacred. And that of *Homer* was as notable,

Kings must not be reviled, much less killed, though wicked.

Misopogoris.

The Laws are severe in the defence of Kings.

> *His chiefest care was for the King,*
> *That nothing should endanger him.*

And no marvel: For as St. *Chrysostom* well observes, *If any man kill a Sheep, he but lessens the number of them; but if he kill the Shepherd, he dissipates the whole Flock.* The very name of a King, as *Curtius* tells us, among such Nations as were Governed by Kings, was as venerable as that of God: So *Artabanus* the *Persian*, *Amongst many and those most excellent Laws we have, this seems to be the best, which commands us to adore our Kings as the very Image of God, who is the Saviour of all.* And therefore as *Plutarch* speaks, *Nec fas, nec licitum est Regis corpori manus inferre, It is not permitted by the Laws of God or Man, to offer violence to the person of a King.* But as the same *Plutarch* in another place tells us, *The principal part of valour is, to save him that saves all. If the Eye observe a blow threatning the Head, the Hand, being instructed by Nature, interposeth it self, as preferring the safety of the Head (whereupon all the other members depend) before their own*: Wherefore, as *Cassiodore* notes, *He that with the loss of his own life, redeems the life of his Prince, doth well; if in so doing he propose to himself the freeing of his own soul, rather than that of another mans body: for as Conscience teacheth him to express his fidelity to his Soveraign; so doth right reason instruct him to prefer the life of his Prince, before the safety of his own body.* But here a more difficult question ariseth; as namely, whether what was lawful for *David* and the *Maccabees*, be likewise lawful for us Christians? Or whether Christ who so often enjoyns us, to take up our Cross, do not require from us a greater measure of patience? Surely, where our Superiors threaten us with death upon the account of Religion, our Saviour advised such as are not obliged by the necessary duties of their calling to reside in any one place, to flee, but beyond this, nothing. St. *Peter* tells us, *That Christ in suffering left us an ensample, who though he knew no sin, nor had any guile found in his mouth, yet being reviled he reviled not again; when he suffered, he threatned not, but remitted his cause to him that judgeth righteously.* Nay he adviseth us to give thanks unto God, and to rejoyce when we suffer persecution for our Religion: And we may read how mightily Christian Religion hath grown and been advanced, by this admirable gift of patience, wherefore how injurious to those ancient Christians, (who (living in or near the times of either the Apostles themselves, or men truly Apostolical) must needs be well instructed in their Discipline, and consequently walked more exactly according to their rules, yet suffered death for their Faith;) how injurious I say, to these men, are they, who hold that they wanted not a will to resist, but rather a power to defend themselves at the approach of death? Surely *Tertullian* had never been so imprudent, nay impudent, as so confidently to have affirmed such an untruth, whereof he knew the Emperor could not be ignorant, when he wrote thus unto him, *If we had a will to take our private revenge, or to act as publick Enemies, could we want either numbers of Men, or stores of warlike Provisions? Are the* Moors, Germans, Parthians, *or the People of any one Nation, more than those of the whole World? We, though Strangers, yet do fill all places in your Dominions, your Cities, Islands, Castles, Forts, Assemblies, your very Camps, Tribes,*

1 Tim. 1. And why.

Plut. Them.

De Amicitia.

We are to prefer his life before our own.

Whether *Davids* example and the *Maccabees*, be sufficient to justifie Christians in like cases.

1 Pet. 4. 12, 13, 14, 15, 16.

Christs advice is to flee, where the duties of our calling will permit, but beyond that nothing.

So [illegible]

Courts,

Courts, Palaces, Senates; only your Temples we leave to your selves: For what war have not we always declared our selves fit and ready, though in numbers of men we have sometimes been very unequal? How cometh it then to pass, that we suffer death so meekly, so patiently, but that we are instructed by our Religion, that it is much better to be killed than to kill? *Cyprian* also treading in his Masters steps, openly declares, *That it was from the Principles of their Religion, that Christians being apprehended made no resistance, nor attempted any revenge for injuries unjustly done them, though they wanted neither numbers of men, nor other means to have resisted: But it was their confidence of some Divine Vengeance that would fall upon their Persecutors, that made them*
Lib. 5. *thus patient; and that perswaded the Innocent to give way to the Nocent.* So *Lactantius*, *We are willing to conside in the Majesty of God, who is able as well to revenge the contempt done to himself, as the injuries and hardships done unto us: Wherefore though our sufferings be such as cannot be exprest, yet do we not mutter a word of discontent, but refer our selves wholly to him*
Lib. 6. Qu. 10. in Joshua. *who judgeth righteously.* And to the same Tune sings St. *Augustin*, *When Princes err, they presently make Laws to legitimate their errors, and by those very Laws they judge the Innocent who*
Ep. 166. *are at length Crowned with Martyrdom.* And in another place, *Tyrants are so to be endured by their Subjects, and hard Masters by their Servants, that both their temporal lives (if possible) may be preserved, and yet their eternal safety carefully provided for:* Which he illustrates by the examples of the Primitive Christians, *Who though they then sojourned upon earth as Pilgrims, and had infinite numbers of Nations to assist them, yet chose rather patiently to suffer all manner of torments, than forcibly to resist their Persecutors: Neither would they fight to preserve their temporal lives, but chose rather not to fight, that so they might ensure unto themselves an eternal. For they endured Bonds, Stripes, Imprisonment, the Rack, the Fire, the Cross; they were flea'd alive, killed, and quartered, and yet they multiplied; they esteemed this life not worth the fighting for, so that with the loss of it they might purchase what so eagerly they panted after, a better.* Of the same opinion was *Cyril*, as may appear by many notable sayings of his

The *Thebean* Legion. upon that place of St. *John*, where he treats of *Peter's* Sword. The *Thebean* Legion, we read, consisted of six thousand, six hundred, sixty six Soldiers, and all Christians, who when the Emperor *Maximianus* would have compelled the whole Army to sacrifice to Idols, first removed their Station to *Agaunus*; and when, upon fresh orders sent after them, they refused to come, *Maximianus* commanded his Officers to put every tenth man to death, which was easily done, no man offering to resist: At which time, *Mauritius* (who had the chief command in that Legion, and from whom the Town *Agaunus* in *Switzerland* was afterwards called St. *Mauritz*, as *Eucherius*, Bishop of *Lyons*, records) thus bespake his Fellow Soldiers, *How fearful was I lest any of you under the pretence of defending your selves (as was easie for men armed as ye are to have done) should have attempted by force to have rescued from death those blessed Martyrs? Which had you done, I was sufficiently instructed by Christs own example to have forbidden it, who expresly remanded that Sword into its sheath, that was but drawn in his own defence; thereby teaching us that our Christian Faith is much more prevalent than all other Arms.* This Tragick Act being past, the Emperor commanding the same thing to the Survivors, as he had done before to the whole Legion, they unanimously returned this answer, *Tui quidam,* Cæsar, *Milites sumus, &c. We are thy Soldiers,* O Cæsar, *we took Arms for the defence of the* Roman *Empire; we never yet deserted the War, nor betrayed the trust reposed in us; we were never yet branded with fear or cowardise, but have always observed thy commands, until being otherwise instructed by our Christian Laws, we refuse to worship the Devil, or to approach those Altars that are always polluted with blood. We find by thy Commands, that thou resolvest either to draw us into Idolatry, or to affright us by putting every tenth man of us to death: Make no farther search after those that are willing to lye concealed; but know that we are all of us Christians; all our Bodies thou hast indeed under thy power, but our Souls are subject only to Christ our Redeemer.* Then *Exuperius* being the Standard-bearer to that Legion, thus bespake them, *Hitherto, Fellow Soldiers, I have carried the Standard before you in this secular War, but it is not unto these Arms that I now invite you, it is not unto these Wars that I am now to excite your valour, for now we are to practise another kind of warfare; for with these weapons ye can never inforce your way into the Kingdom of Heaven.* And by and by he sends this message to the Emperor, *Against thee, O* Cæsar, *Desparation it self (which usually makes even Cowards valiant) cannot prevail with us to take Arms. Behold we have our weapons fixt, yet will we not resist; because we chuse rather to be killed by thee than to overcome thee, and to dye innocents, than to live Rebels to either God or thee.* And a little after he adds, *Tela projicimus, &c. We abandon our Arms, O Emperor, and will meet thy Messengers of Death with naked breasts, yet with hearts strongly munited with Christian Faith.* And presently after followed that General Massacre of the *Thebean* Band, whereof *Eucherius* gives this Narrative, *It was neither their Innocence, nor their Numbers, that could exempt them from death, whereas in other more dangerous tumults, a multitude though offending, are rarely punished.* The same story in the old Martyrology we find thus recorded, *They were every where wounded with Swords, yet they cryed not out; but disdaining the use of their Arms, they exposed their Breasts naked to their persecutors: It was neither their numbers, nor*

their

their experience in War, that could perswade them to assert the Equity of their cause by their Swords, but placing his example always before them, who was led to the slaughter dumb, and like a Lamb to be Sacrificed, opened not his mouth; they also in imitation of him, like the Innocent Flock of Christ suffered themselves to be worried and torn in pieces by an herd of Persecuting Wolves. Thus also do the *Jews* of *Alexandria* testifie their Innocency before *Flaccus*, *We are, as thou seest, unarmed, and yet we are accused unto thee as publick enemies to the State. These hands which nature hath given us for our defence, we have caused to be pinnacled behind us, where they are of little use, and our breasts we expose naked to every man, that hath a mind to kill us.* And when the Emperour *Valens* cruelly Persecuted those Christians, which according to the Holy Scriptures, and the Traditions of the Ancient Fathers, profest Christ to be ὁμέσιον, that is, *Co essential with the Father*; though there were every where great multitudes of them, yet did they never attempt by Arms to secure themselves. Surely, wheresoever patience in times of persecution is commended unto us, there we find Christs own example held out unto us (as we read it was to the *Thebean* Legion) for our Imitation. As therefore his Patience, so ours, should have no bounds nor limits but death it self. And he that thus loseth his life, is truly said by Christ himself to find it. Thus having sufficiently proved, That he that is invested with the Supreme Power ought not to be resisted. Now I must admonish our Reader of some things, wherein he may mistake, by judging that those men do dash their Feet against this stone, who indeed do not.

1 Pet. 2. 21. Mat. 10. 39. Luk. 12. 33.

VIII. That a free people may make War against their Prince.

In the first place therefore, Those Princes that are under the body of a people, whether they originally retained such a power, or by some after contract or agreement made with them, as in *Lacedæmon*; if they do violate the Laws, or wrong the Commonwealth, may not only be by force resisted, but if it be necessary, may be punished with death: As it befel *Pausanias* King of the *Lacedæmonians*, of whom *Plutarch* thus, The *Spartans* taking to heart the death of *Lysander*, sentenced their King to death, because leaving *Lysander* out of Cowardise, whom he was sent to relieve, he had fled for safety to *Tegra*. The like he records in the life of *Sylla*, The *Spartans*, saith he, deposed some of their Kings, as being unfit for Government, because they were of low and abject Spirits: Yea, and of *Agis* he reports, That being their King, yet was condemned, though unjustly. Now seeing that there were in *Italy* diverse such Kingdoms, it is no marvel that *Virgil*, having first recorded those many wicked Acts done by *Mezentius*, adds,

Plut. vit. Lysand.

Th' Hetrur'ans *therefore, all in a just rage,*
To bring their Kings to Judgement do engage.

Of whom an old *Hetrurian* South-sayer, spake thus,

———*Whom their just Woe*
Arms, as against a Foe.

IX. Or against a King that hath renounced his Kingdom.

Secondly, If a King or any other shall renounce his Empire, or manifestly forsake it; against such a Prince or King, after that time, any thing is lawful, that may be done to a private man. But this then we must observe, That he that is careless and negligent only in his Government, cannot thereby only be judged to have forsaken it.

X. Or against a King that would alienate his Kingdom.

Thirdly, It was the opinion of *Barkley*, That if a King would alienate his Kingdom, or subject it to another, he lost it. But here I make a stand, For if the Kingdom be Elective, or descend by succession, such an Act of Alienation is in it self null. And whatsoever is in it self null can have no effects of a just Right. Wherefore, as also of that Kingdom that is barely usufructuary, whereunto I have likened such a King, the opinion of the Civilians is to me more probable, That in yielding up his Kingdom to a stranger he confers nothing: And whereas it is said that the fruits and profits revert to the Lord of the propriety; It is to be understood, after such a time as is prefixed by the Law. Yet notwithstanding, if a King shall really endeavour to deliver up, or subject his Kingdom to another, I doubt not but that in this case he may be resisted: For Empire is one thing, and the manner of holding that Empire another. The alteration whereof the people may hinder; for that is not comprehended under the notion of Empire. Whereunto may that of *Seneca* be not unfitly applyed: Although our Father be in all things to be obeyed, yet not in those things wherein he ceaseth to be a Father.

XI. Or a King that Invades the whole body of the people in an hostile way.

Fourthly, as the same *Barkley* observes, If a King shall endeavour, with a mind truly hostile, the destruction of the whole body of the Nation over which he is set to govern, he loseth his Kingdom and may be resisted: Which I grant. For the end of all Government being for mutual conservation, he that wilfully resolves to destroy, can have no right to Govern. Wherefore he that openly, either in word or deed, professeth himself an enemy to the whole Nation, is in that very act presumed to abjure and renounce the

the Government of it. When *Sylla* had depopulated not *Rome* only, but almost all *Italy*, one seriously advised him, that it was fit to spare some, that he might have some to govern; *Ut essent quibus Imperassent*. But this case can hardly be found in any King that is of sound mind, and that governs one only Nation. But in case he govern more than one, it may so happen, that in favour to one, he may endeavour to destroy the other, that so he may plant it with new Colonies. *Gracchus* his Arguments are very Ingenious, whereby he proves, that a Tribune of the people (being therefore accounted sacred and Inviolable, because he is consecrated by the people to defend them) in case he shall endeavour to oppress them, to diminish their power, and to take from them their rights of suffrage; doth thereby actually degrade himself, in not performing that for which that honour was conferr'd on him. For to admit (saith *Gracchus*) that the Tribunes of the people may in some cases imprison their Consul; and yet to deny that the people have a power to take away the Tribunitial power from him that abuseth it, even against those from whom he received it, seeing that both the Consul and the Tribune were by the people created; would be very absurd. The like we find asserted by *Johannes Major*, namely, That a people cannot abdicate their power of deserting their Prince, in such cases as tend to their manifest destruction. Both which may be very well expounded by what hath been herein already delivered.

Plut. vit. lib. Grac.

XII. And against him who breaks the condition upon which he was admitted.

Fifthly, In case a Kingdom be confiscate either by Felony committed against him whose the Fief is, or by any clause or condition expresly made and agreed on at his admission to the Kingdom. As in case the King shall do this or that, his Subjects shall then stand absolv'd from all obligation of duty and obedience unto him †. In this case also a King may recede into the condition of a private person.

† *Vid. Marian. de regno Arragon.*

XIII. And against him who having but one part of the Soveraign power, Invades the other.

Sixthly, If a King having but one part of the Soveraign power, and the Senate or people the other, if such a King shall Invade that part which is not his own, he may justly be by force resisted, because in that part he hath not the Soveraign power: Which I believe may take place, although it be said, That the power of making War is in the King. For this is to be understood of a Foreign War; since otherwise, whosoever hath any part of the Supreme power, cannot be denyed a Right to defend his own even by force, which when it happens, even the King himself may justly by the Right of War, lose even his own part of the said Empire.

XIV. And against him, who grants such a Licence in certain cases.

Seventhly, If in the Translation of the Empire it be expresly said, That upon some certain events that may happen it may be lawful to make resistance. For although it could not then be conceived that by that agreement any part of the Soveraign power was intended to have been retained; yet certainly it may be conceived, that some kind of natural Liberty was thereby understood to have been reserved to the people, and exempted from the power of the King *. For possible it is for him that alienates his own Right, to diminish and decurt the Right that he gives by certain clauses or Articles of Agreements, whereof we may find in Histories many examples †.

* *Thuan. l. 131. in anno 1604. Id. l. 133. an. 1605. de Hungaris.*
† *Meierum in anno 1339. de Flandr. & Brab &c.*

XV. An Usurper how far to be obeyed. The Acts of an Usurper binding, and why.

We have hitherto treated of him who hath or had a Right to Govern; now something we must say of him that Invades or Usurps the Government, not after he hath either by long possession, or by Consent or Agreement obtained a Right unto it, but so long as the cause of his unjust acquisition continues. And certainly during the time that he possesseth the Empire, his Acts may have power to bind: But yet, not as they are his, for Right to command he hath none, but upon this presumption, That he who of Right should govern, whether King, People or Senate, had rather that his Laws for that time should be binding, than that the people should live altogether without Laws, and without Judgements, which must necessarily introduce the greatest disorder and confusion. *Cicero* condemns *Sylla*'s Laws as too cruel against the children of those that were proscribed, in making them uncapable of suing for Honours; yet he thought fit, that those Laws should be observed: Affirming (as *Quintilian* tells us) that the state of the Common-wealth was so contained in those Laws, that if they were not kept, the Common-wealth at that time could not have subsisted. *Florus* also concerning the Acts of the same *Sylla*, saith thus, Lepidus *went about to rescind the Acts of this so great a man, and indeed not without cause, if at least, he could have done it, without the ruine of the Common-wealth.* And by and by, *It was expedient for the Common-wealth, being then sick and wounded, to be governed by any Laws whatsoever, rather than to fret and scarrifie her Wounds by attempting an untimely Cure.* Yet notwithstanding at such times, and in such Cases wherein our obedience is not so exquisitely necessary, and yet may help to confirm the Usurper in his unjust possession; If by our disobedience we incur no great danger, we must not obey. But whether it be lawful for the people by force of Arms to deject him that shall thus usurp the Soveraign power, or to kill him, is disputable.

XVI. An Usurper may be killed, during the War, if no contract be made with him.

And in the first place, If he that usurps another mans dominion have not gained it by a Just War, that is, by such a War as hath all the Rights required by the Law of Nations; nor by any contract or agreement made with him, or Faith given to him, but that he holds

holds his possession by force only: The Right of War seems in this case to continue; and therefore what may lawfully be done against an enemy may lawfully be done against him, whom any private man that hath not given his Faith to him, may lawfully kill. *In reos Majestatis, & publicos hostes omnis homo miles est; Against Traytors and publick Enemies every private man,* saith *Tertullian, is a Souldier.* So against such as desert their Colours in the time of War, it is indulged unto every man to take publick revenge in order to the common safety. By the Right of the War continued. *Tertul. Apolog.*

XVII. Or by vertue of some antecedent Law.

The same may be said if before such an Invasion there were extant any such Law, authorizing any private man to kill him who dares in his presence commit such or such a fact. As for example, If being but a private man he shall go with a guard about him, or if he shall attempt a Fort, or kill a Citizen uncondemned, or illegally condemned, or if any man shall presume to create a Magistrate without just suffrages. Many such Laws we may read of to have been in force among the Cities of *Greece,* with whom it was also thought lawful to kill such Tyrants. Such was that Law of *Solon* in *Athens,* renewed after his return from *Piræus,* against such as had abolished Popular Government, or that after such abolition had born any office. The like Law there was also in *Rome,* called the *Valerian* Law, against any man that should assume the office of a Magistrate without the peoples consent, making it lawful for any man to kill such a man uncondemned, as *Plutarch* relates, where he thus distinguisheth *Solon*'s Law from that of *Publicola*'s: *Solon* would have such a man legally convicted; but *Publicola* permitted any man to kill him that usurped the office of a Magistrate without any formal Process. And such was the Consular Law, immediately after the *Decemviral* Government, That no man should dare to create a Magistrate without an Appeal; and he that created such, might by the Laws both of God and Man be killed. *Plut. Public.*

XVIII. By his Commission who hath Right to the Empire.

No less lawful it is for him to kill an Usurper, that hath an express Warrant so to do from him to whom the just Right of Government belongeth, whether it be in the King, the People, or the Senate. Amongst whom likewise we may place the Protectors or Guardians of Kings during their nonage: Such as was *Jehojada*'s to King *Joas,* at whose command *Athalia* was deprived at once both of her Life and Kingdom, 2 *Chron.* 23.

XIX. Why an Usurper may not be killed, but in one of these cases.

Now unless it be in one of these Cases, I cannot perceive how it should be lawful for any private man by force either to deject, or to destroy him that usurps the Imperial Dignity: Because possible it is, that he who hath the true Right had rather prefer the peace and tranquillity of his Subjects, though under the Usurpers power, than embroil his Countrey in blood, or to vex his Subjects with Civil War, which are the sad and bloody effects and consequences that attend the Murther or Expulsion of Kings, especially if his quarrel be espoused, by either a strong Faction at home, or powerful Friends abroad: Or because it is at least doubtful, Whether that King, People, or Senate, in whom the Right of Empire is, are willing that the matter should be brought to so desperate an issue. And without the precise knowledge of this, all violence of this kind is unjust. It is very true, what *Favonius* in *Plutarch* observes, *Pejus est Bellum Civile Dominatu Illegitimo; An Intestine War is more destructive than any Tyranny.* For though the Rage of Incensed Tyrants may produce more Tragical effects upon some particular Families, yet the Deluge of a Civil War spreads farther, continues longer, and leaves more dreadful prints behind it, than any Tyranny. *Give me any peace,* saith *Cicero, rather than a Civil War. Titus Quintus* told the *Lacedæmonians,* That it would be much better for them to bear with the Tyranny of *Nabis,* than by endeavouring by Arms to recover their lost Liberty, to make the Tyrants Grave in the ruines of their City. And to this purpose was that prudent advice of *Aristophanes,* Leo in Civitate non est alendus; si alitus sit, ferendus est: *Either not to nourish a Lion, or being nourisht, not to provoke him.* It is indeed a very difficult case, and will admit of a strong debate, Whether Peace or liberty be most acceptable: *Cicero* makes this question, the most difficult of all others in the Politicks to be resolved, *Whether our Countrey being opprest by Tyranny, we may attempt to redeem it, although with the danger of its desolation.* But it is not for private men to determine what the Common Judgement of the people would be in this case, but this we abominate as being grosly unjust: to make our Countries Liberty a cloak for our own Ambition; and to pretend to deliver her, when we intend to inslave her. *Sylla* being demanded, Why he marcht into his own Countrey so strongly Armed: answered, *Ut eam à Tyrannis liberem; To deliver it from Tyrants:* When he that pretended so to do, was himself the greatest Tyrant. So *Antiochus* brought a Mighty Army into *Greece,* alledging that he came to set *Greece* at Liberty, when indeed it wanted none. His pretence, was Liberty, but his Intent, Tyranny. *Crudelitatem Damnat & crudelitatem init; By condemning Tyranny, he trapans them into it:* It was much better Counsel, that *Plato* gave to *Perdiccas,* which *Plato* thus renders, *That he should attempt no more in the Common-wealth, than he could justifie to his Subjects: For that nothing savouring of force or violence should be obtruded upon either our Parents or our Countrey.* To the same sense is that of *Salust, Though thou couldst govern thy Countrey or thy Parents by force,* *Vita Bruti.* *Liv.* 34. Whether Peace or Liberty be most eligible. *App. Civil.* 1. *Plut. Catone Major.* *Cicero Ep. Fam. l.* 1. No alterations of Government without violent commotions.

Bello Jug. *force, and correct at thy pleasure every small offence, yet would it seem harsh and troublesome, especially considering that no violent thing can be permanent, nor any Mutations of Government, without violent Commotions, War, Rapine, and such like acts of hostility.* Not much different

Vita Beat. from this is that of *Statius* in *Plutarch*, *It becomes not a wise or a prudent man to endanger himself in Popular Tumults, amongst either Fools or Knaves.* Whereunto we may also not

To deliver the poor from oppression, so it be without raising Tumults or Sedition, is commendable. impertinently refer that of St. *Ambrose*, *This also will highly advance thy Credit and Reputation, if thou canst rescue the poor out of the hands of the Oppressors, and deliver him that is wrongfully condemned to dye; so that thou do it without raising Tumults or moving Sedition: Lest otherwise thou shouldst seem to do it rather out of an affectation of Popularity and Vain-glory, than out of Pity and Commiseration, and so consequently make those wounds deeper which thou shouldest heal.* It was the opinion of *Aquinas*, That the pulling down of Government though Tyrannical, was sometimes Seditious. Neither are we much moved to the contrary, by that fact of *Ehud* to *Eglon* King of the *Moabites*. For the Scriptures plainly

Judg. 3. 15. tell us, *That God raised up* Ehud *to deliver* Israel: What *Ehud* did was done by the special Warrant of God himself. Neither doth it appear, That this King of the *Moabites*

Nehem. 9. 27. had by Agreement no right of Soveraignty. For God we read did execute his Judgements even against other Kings by such Instruments, as he himself was pleased to raise up to that purpose, as may be collected by *Jehu* against *Joram*, 2 *Kin.* 9.

XX. **No private man to be Judge in this case.**

But it is especially to be noted, That no private person ought to determine Controversies of this nature, but should rather obey the present possessor. As Christ commanded to pay Tribute to *Cæsar* †, because his Image made the Money currant; which was a convincing argument that he was in full possession of the Empire at that time: For the Coining of Money was ever the most certain sign of the Possession of the Empire.

† Mat. 22. 20.

CHAP. V.

Who may lawfully make War.

I. *The Efficient Causes of War are either the Principals in their own cause:*
II. *Or in the Cause of another.*
III. *Or Instrumental as Servants and Subjects.*
IV. *By the Law of Nature none are prohibited from War.*

I. **The principal efficient Cause.**

AS in all other things, so in Actions that are voluntary there are three sorts of Causes efficient, that is to say, Principal, Auxiliary, and Instrumental. The Principal efficient cause in a War is for the most part he whose the quarrel is: In a private War, any private person: In a publick, he that hath the publick Power, especially if it be Supreme. Whether a War may be justly undertaken in the behalf of another, not making War, shall be discust hereafter. In the mean time this is most certain, That naturally every man hath a Right to revenge his own quarrel, and for this cause were hands given unto us.

II. **Auxiliary.**

Nihil utilius homini homine altero.

Neither have we a Right to vindicate our own quarrels only, but we may both lawfully and laudably improve our Right to the vindication of other mens also. They that treat of Offices say truly, That there is nothing so usuful and profitable unto man, as another man. There are several obligations, wherein we stand bound to one another for mutual help and assistance; For kinsmen do usually combine to help one another: So one Neighbour being opprest invokes the help of another: So also do Citizens the aid of their fellow-Citizens. *Aristotle* thought it a duty incumbent to every man to assume Arms, either to defend himself, in case an injury were offered him; or to assist his Kinsmen, his Benefactors, or his Companions, in cases of oppression. And in *Solon's* esteem, That was the best Common-wealth, wherein every man was as sensible of Injuries offered to another, as if they had been offered to themselves: Hence is that of *Plautus*, Prætorquete Injuriæ prius Collum quam ad vos perveniat: *Break the Neck of an Injury before it comes at us.* But though all other obligations should fail, yet it is sufficient that we are linkt together in the common stock of humanity. For, *ab homine nihil humani alienum*; *Nothing that is incident to humane nature, should be to any man strange. Democritus* tells us, *That it is a duty incumbent upon every man, so far as he is able, to succour all that are oppressed with wrong, and not at all to neglect it: For this,* saith

It was well said of *Menander*:

Injuriarum si Improbis Auctoribus
Recurreremus ultionem singuli,
Nobis putantes fieri, quod fit alteri,
Inter nos juncti, Conspiratis viribus,
Non prævaleret Innocentiæ Impetus
Audax Malorum: Qui custoditi undique
Justique pœnas quas merentur penderent,
Aut nulli penitus essent, aut pauci admodum.

faith he, *is both just and honest:* Which *Lactantius* thus expresseth, *God,* saith he, *who denyed to all other creatures Wisdom, furnisht them with such natural Muniments, as were sufficient to defend them from violent incursions and sudden dangers: But unto man, being sent into the world naked and unarmed; the better to instruct him in Wisdom, hath God, besides other endowments, given him Natural affection, whereby we are taught to love, cherish, and defend each other, and readily to give and receive aid and assistance one to, and from another, against all outward assaults and dangers whatsoever.*

III. Or Instrumental, as Servants, &c.

By Instruments here, we mean not Arms or such like, wherewith we either offend others, or defend our selves: But such voluntary Agents, as are contented to receive directions from others. Such as a Son is to his Father, being a part of himself naturally; or as a Servant to his Master, of whom he is legally a part. For as a part doth not only refer to the whole in the same relation, as the whole is the whole of the part; but this very thing That it is, is the whole: So Possession is said to be something of him that possesseth it. And *Servants,* saith *Democritus, are to be used as we do the members of our body, some to one purpose and some to another.* Now what Servants are to a Family, the same are Subjects to a Common-wealth, and so are as Instruments to him who hath the Supreme power.

IV. Naturally no man excused from War.

Without doubt, Naturally all that are Subjects may be employed in the War, though some special Laws may excuse some; as heretofore Servants among the *Romans,* and now every where the Clergy: As the *Levites* among the *Jews* were not liable to the duties of War (as *Josephus* testifies) which Law notwithstanding, as all others of that nature, must admit of the exception of extreme necessity. And let this suffice to be spoken in general concerning Subjects and Servants: For what more especially concerns them, shall be handled in their proper places.

Hugo Grotius OF THE RIGHTS OF PEACE & WAR.

BOOK II.

CHAP. I.

Of the Causes of War, And, First, of War made in our own defence.

I. *What Causes may be said to justifie a War.*
II. *That they arise either from our own defence, or from requiring what is our own, or is due to us, or from punishment.*
III. *War made for the defence of our Lives, lawful.*
IV. *Against the Aggressor only.*
V. *In such dangers as are imminent and certain, not in such as are opinionative only.*
VI. *War made in defence of our Limbs, lawful.*
VII. *Especially in defence of Chastity.*
VIII. *War made in defence of our selves, may sometimes be omitted.*
IX. *Our defence made against a Person publickly very profitable, sometimes unlawful by the Law of Charity.*
X. *To kill a man for a box on the ear, or for some such reproach, or rather than flee; not lawful for a Christian.*
XI. *To kill a man in defending our Goods, by the Law of Nature not unlawful.*
XII. *How far permitted by the Law of* Moses.
XIII. *Whether, and how far permitted by the Evangelical Law.*
XIV. *Whether the Civil Law, permitting a man to kill another in defence of himself, do give a right so to do, or only an impunity, explained by a distinction.*
XV. *When Duelling may be lawful.*
XVI. *Of defence in a War that is publick.*
XVII. *If only to weaken the growing power of a Neighbour Prince, the War be to be reputed unlawful.*
XVIII. *The defence of him who hath given just cause of a War, is likewise unlawful.*

LET Us now proceed to the Causes of War: I mean those that justifie a War; for there are others that excite men to War under the notion of Profit, which are sometimes distinct from those which excite upon the account of Justice; which as well between themselves, as from the beginnings of War, (such as was the Hart in the War between *Turnus* and *Æneas*) *Polybius* doth accurately distinguish. And though the difference between these are manifest, yet are the terms usually confounded: For even these causes which we call justifying, *Livy*, in the Oration of the *Rhodians*, calls the beginnings of the War; *Surely ye* (say the *Rhodians*) *are those very* Romans, *who pretend that your Wars are therefore successful, because they are just; and that glory, not in the event, that ye can conquer, but in the beginnings, that ye never make War but upon just cause.* And indeed there was hardly ever any Nation that

I. 3 *Hist.* *Lib.* 45.

that did so long pride themselves in the justice of their Quarrels, as the *Romans* did. *The* Romans, saith *Polybius, took very great care not to begin a war with their Neighbours; and would have all men believe that they never made war but to repel Injuries.* This *Dion* testifies in that notable comparison he makes between the *Romans*, and *Philip* of *Macedon*, and *Antiochus*. And elsewhere he tells us, *That the* Romans *took special care that their Wars should be just, nor did they ever decree a War rashly, or without just cause.* In the same sence Lib. 12. c. 53. doth *Ælian* call the Causes of War, the beginnings of War: And *Diodorus* discoursing of the war between the *Lacedemonians* and the *Ælians*, makes the pretences and the beginnings of the War to be the same. These justifying Causes of War are the proper Argument of our present discourse, whereunto that of *Coriolanus* in *Halicarnassensis* is pertinent, Lib. 8. *Let your first and principal care be, that the ground of all your Wars be pious and just.* So is that likewise of *Demosthenes*, Olynth. 2. *As in the building of houses, Ships, and such like, the Foundation or Ground-work should be firm and lasting, (otherwise the Superstructures will soon decay and totter:) So in all our Enterprizes, Justice and Truth should lay (as it were) the first stone, if we expect that the success should be honourable.* No less pertinent to this purpose is Lib. 12. that also of *Dion Cassius, In all our Wars let our chief regard be to Justice; for if she lead up the Van, true valour may bid fair for the victory: But if she be wanting, though our first attempts flatter us, yet will the end prove inglorious.* And that also of *Cicero*, De rep. l. 3. *Those wars are unjust that are undertaken without cause.* And therefore in another place he sharply reproves *Cassius* for passing with his Army over *Euphrates*, when there was no just cause of War given, which holds true no less in publick wars than it doth in private. Hence ariseth that complaint of *Seneca, Do we restrain Homicides, and punish Murderers, and yet esteem the depopulation of whole Nations glorious? Covetousness and Cruelty know no moderation, Commissions are every day sent out by the Senate and People to execute Acts of Cruelty, and what we privately forbid, we publickly commend. Homicidium cum admittant singuli, crimen est; virtus vocatur, cum publice geritur; When a private man commits a murder he is punished as a Criminal, but when thousands are publickly taken away and destroyed, it is instantly canonized for virtue and valour.* It is true indeed, That War being undertaken by publick Authority, like the definitive Sentence of a Judge, hath some effects of Right (whereof more anon:) But yet are they not altogether blameless, unless there be a just cause to warrant it. Thus was *Alexander* for invading the *Persians* and other Nations without cause given, deservedly censured by the *Scythians* in *Curtius*, and elsewhere by *Seneca*, for a Robber, and by *Lucan* for a Thief, by the wise men of *India* as a Scourge to all Nations, and the common pest of mankind; and before that by a Pirate, for the greater Pirate of the two. So *Justin* speaking of his Father *Philip*, saith, That two Kings of *Thrace* were thrust out, and deprived of their Kingdoms through the fraud and villany of a Thief: Whereunto we may likewise refer that of St. *Augustin, Remotâ Justitiâ, quid sunt Regna nisi magna Latrocinia; Take away Justice, and what are Kingdoms but great Robberies.* With whom accords that of *Lactantius, Inanis gloriæ specie capti, sceleribus suis virtutis nomen imponunt, Being blinded with self-love and vain glory, they miscal all their vices vertues.* Nor was *Justin Martyr* much amiss, when he said, *What Thieves do in desert places, the very same do such Princes who prefer Opinion before Truth.* Now other just causes of making war there can be none, but injuries: So St. *Augustin, The wrongs done on the one side, make the war done on the other side just.* So also saith the *Roman* Herald, *I do testifie and declare, that such a people are unjust and have not done us right*; thereby intimating, that the people of *Rome* might justly make war upon them.

II. War made, 1. For Defence. 2. For Redemption. 3. For Punishment, lawful.

Now look how many causes there are of civil Actions, so many there are of a just war; for *Ubi desinunt Judicia, incipit Bellum; Where Judgments cease, War begins.* Now at the Law, Suits arise either for prevention of Injuries not yet done, as when Cautions and Securities are required, that no acts of violence shall be offered, nor any damages done us; or for injuries already done, as namely, that they may be recompenced, or the person injuring punished. But as to that which comes under the notion of Reparation, it refers either to that which is, or was ours, from whence arise vindications and some personal Actions; or to something that is owing and justly due unto us, whether by some contract or agreement, or for some hurt done unto us, or by the Law, whither also we are to refer those things, which are said to arise, as if they were due by contract or by some wrong done unto us; from which heads arise the other condictions: That which concerns Facts to be punished, requires, First, An Accusation, Secondly, Courts of Judgment. Most men assign three just causes of a War, namely, for Defence, for recovery of what is ours, and for punishment: which three we shall find summ'd up by *Camillus* in his denouncing War against the *Gaules, Omnia quæ defendi, repetique & ulcisci fas sit; All which may lawfully be defended, recovered, and revenged.* In which enumeration, unless we take the word, *Recovered*, in its larger signification, it will not include the exacting of that which is due unto us; which was not omitted by *Plato*, when he said, That war might be justly made, not only when a man is oppressed by violence, or when he is pillaged, but when

when he is fraudulently dealt with, and ſo deceived of what is his due. Wherewith accords that of *Seneca*, *Æquiſſima vox eſt, & jus Gentium pre ſe ferens, Redde quod debes*; *This is a righteous ſaying, and conſonant to the Law of Nations, Pay what thou oweſt.* And it was a clauſe always inſerted in that form uſed by the *Roman* Heralds, *Quas nec dederunt, nec ſolverunt; nec fecerunt, quas dari, fieri, ſolvi oportuit*, *That they neither gave, did, nor paid, what they ought to have given, paid, and done.* So likewiſe *Saluſt* in his Hiſtory, *Jure Gentium res repeto, According to the Law of Nations, I require what is mine own.* *Servius* upon *Virgils Æneads* tells us, That *When the King of the Heralds was ſent to denounce war, he came to the borders of the enemies Country; and after ſome ceremonies, cryed out with a loud voice, That he denounced War againſt them for ſuch or ſuch cauſes; either becauſe they had wronged their Aſſociates, or becauſe they had not reſtored ſomething unjuſtly taken away, or that they had not delivered up offenders to be puniſhed.* And when St. *Auguſtin* ſaith, That juſt Wars are uſually thus defined, *Quæ ulciſcuntur injurias, Which revengeth injuries*: He takes the word [to revenge] in its general ſignification, for that which includes alſo, To take away; as may appear by the words following, which do not expreſs an enumeration of parts, but an illuſtration by examples. So *That Nation* (ſaith he) *or City may by Arms be aſſaulted, which ſhall neglect either to puniſh their own Subjects for injuries by them done, or to reſtore that which by force was taken away.* And by this light of Nature it was, that the King of the *Indies* (as *Diodorus* relates) accuſed *Semiramis* for the breach of the Law of Nations *for making war upon him; without any injury at all done her.* For, as *Joſephus* ſaith, *They that offer violence to them that live peaceably, do but enforce them into Arms to defend themſelves.* Thus do the *Romans* plead with the *Senones*, that they ought not to have invaded them, having no ways wronged them: *For men*, ſaith *Ariſtotle*, *do not uſually make war, but upon them who have firſt injured them.* As *Curtius* teſtifies of the *Abian Scythians*, the moſt innocent of all the *Barbarians*; *Armis abſtinebant niſi laceſſiti, They never made war, unleſs highly provoked.* And *Plutarch* of *Hercules*, *That being throughly provoked, he ſubdued all in his own defence.* The firſt cauſe then of a juſt war are injuries not yet done, that threatens imminent danger to our Perſons or our Eſtates.

De beneſ. l. 3. c. 14.
Livy l. 1.
Lib. 6.
Ad 9. Æn.
10 Queſt. upon *Joſ.*
War defenſive.
Ant. l. 17.
Livy l. 5.
Lib. 2.

III. War in defence of our ſelves lawful.

That it is lawful for us to deſtroy him by war, that would otherwiſe deſtroy us, or at leaſt draw us into imminent peril of our lives, hath already been proved. Now it is to be obſerved, That this right of defending our ſelves doth principally and primarily ariſe, not from the malicious attempt of the Aggreſſor, but from the right that Nature gives unto every creature to preſerve it ſelf: So that although he by whom our lives are ſo endangered be without blame, as the Souldier in doing but his duty, or haply a man miſtaking me for another, or being mad, or in a dream (as we have read of ſome to whom it hath thus happened) yet ſhall not my right to defend my ſelf be thereby taken away. For to juſtifie me it ſufficeth that I am not bound to ſuffer that which he attempts to do againſt me, no more than if a wild beaſt ſhould attempt to worry me.

IV. Yet againſt the Aggreſſor only.

But what if ſome innocent perſons are ſo interpoſed, that I cannot preſerve mine own life either by flight or juſt defence, unleſs I either kill or trample upon them, may I juſtly do it? There are ſome (even among Divines) that hold I may †: And certainly if we hearken to the dictates of Nature alone, ſhe will perſwade us to prefer our own ſafety before our reſpect to ſociety. But the Law of Charity, eſpecially the Evangelical Law, which commands us to love our Neighbour as our ſelves, doth not permit it: It was notwithſtanding very well ſaid of *Aquinas*, if it be rightly underſtood, that in a true defenſive war, we do not intentionally kill others; not but that it may ſometimes be lawful, if all other means of ſafety fail to do that purpoſely whereby the Aggreſſor may die. But that this death was not our choice, nor intended primarily (as in capital puniſhments) but our laſt and only refuge, there being no other viſible means then left to preſerve our own lives, but by killing him that ſeeks to kill us; nay and even then, he that is thus violently aſſaulted ought to wiſh rather that ſome other thing would happen, whereby the Aggreſſor might be either affrighted or ſome ways diſabled, than that he ſhould be killed.

† Cajet. 2. 2. Art. 6, 7, q. 2.
2. 2. q. 64. Art. 1.

V. And where the dangers are certain, and imminent, and not opinionative only.

It is alſo here required, that the danger be preſent and ready inſtantly to fall upon us: As when a man ſhall furiouſly aſſault another with a drawn Sword, or ſnatch up any weapon with a manifeſt purpoſe to kill him, I confeſs that in this caſe he may lawfully, by way of prevention, kill him. Thus *Phrynichus* in *Thucydides* pleads *, *He muſt needs be void of malice, who being reduced by them into ſo great jeopardy, did attempt this, or that, or any way to free himſelf, rather than ſuffer himſelf to be deſtroyed by thoſe malicious men*: For as well in Morals as Naturals, it is not poſſible to find a point without ſome latitude; but they are much miſtaken, and ſo apt to miſlead others, who think their own fears, how ever occaſioned, ſufficient to juſtifie the killing of any man by way of pre-occupation, as though it were in their own defence. For it was well ſaid of *Cicero*, *That many inconveniences do uſually ariſe from vain and idle fears, and much miſchief we oft-times do unto others, whilſt we fanſie that the like was intended againſt us.* So *Clearchus* in *Xenophon*, *I have known many ſo far tranſported, either through calumny or ſuſpicion, againſt thoſe they feared, that chu-*

* *Thucydides* l. 8.
De off. lib 1.

ſing

sing rather to prevent dangers than to undergo them, they have most miserably afflicted those who never intended them hurt, nor entertained a thought of evil against them. To the same purpose is that of *Cato* in his Oration for the *Rhodians, What we object that they intended to have done against us, shall we by way of Anticipation do against them?* It was notably said by *Aulus Gellius, To Gladiators preparing for fight, this was the condition proposed; either to kill his Adversary or to be killed by him: But the life of man,* saith he, *is not beset with such hard and unavoidable necessities, as that thou must either do, or suffer wrong inevitably.* For as the same *Cicero* speaks in another place, *Who did ever enact such a Law, or what Common-wealth could ever without manifest danger to it self, so much as tolerate so great an inconvenience, as that one man might lawfully kill another, and then justifie the fact by his own unnecessary fears,* as namely, *lest otherwise he should have been killed by him?* Very appolite whereunto is that of *Thucydides,* *Lib. 1.* *What is to come is as yet in the Clouds, uncertain whither it will fall or not; neither ought any man to be so far incensed thereby, as to undertake a present and certain war, for that which is as yet future, and so uncertain.* And in another place elegantly describing the many inconveniences that were likely to ensue upon those seditions which then began to vex the *Gracian* Cities, adds this as one, *That they strove which of them should first commit those villanies,* *Lib. 3.* *which they feared another would do before them.* *Cæsar* when he had possest himself of the Common-wealth, pleaded in his own defence, *That it was the fear of his Adversaries that had enforced him thereunto. Cavendo ne metuant homines metuendos ultro se efficiunt, &c.* *Lib. 3.* saith *Livy, Pretending to free themselves and their Country from the fear of other men, they voluntarily made themselves formidable; and as if there had been a necessity of either doing, or suffering wrong, we ease our selves of our burdens but oppress others.* But against these, that saying of *Vibius Crispius,* so much celebrated by *Quintilian,* may be well applyed: *Quis te sic timere permisit? Who permitted thee thus to fear?* Or that of *Livia* in *Dion, Infamiam eos non effugere, qui facinus quod timent occupant, They can never wipe off the stain from their honours, who commit that wickedness which they fear another would act before them.* But what if the dangers that threaten us be not imminent, but future, by conspiracy, or by treachery, as by poison, or false accusation, or by false witnesses to procure an unjust Sentence, or the like; I deny that in such cases it is lawful to kill any man, that is, if either the danger may by any other means be avoided, or that it be not sufficiently clear, that it cannot otherways be avoided: For commonly delays afford us many remedies, and produce many accidents which are unexpected, whereby these dangers may be avoided: *Inter os & offam,* as it were, *between the Cup and the Lip.* Although there be many, I know, both Lawyers and Divines, that give a larger Indulgence in these cases, yet this other opinion doth not want the defence of good Authors, as being indeed the better and safer of the two.

VI. *Or for the defence of our Limbs.* But what if the danger threaten the maiming of our limbs only? Surely since the loss of a limb, especially if it be any of the principals, is very grievous and equivalent to the loss of life it self, and such also as may bring us into the danger of death, if it cannot be otherwise avoided, he that shall certainly endanger it may lawfully be killed.

VII. *Or for the defence of our Chastity.* And without doubt the same may be done in defence of our chastity, seeing that not only in the general repute of the world, but by the Law of God himself, Chastity is æquiballanced with life. *The Law* (saith St. *Augustin*) *gives power to the Traveller to kill the Thief, who would otherwise kill him; and to a man or woman to kill him that shall attempt to ravish them, or after the Rape is committed if they can.* *Aug. lib. 1. de lib. Arb.* So *Paulus* the Lawyer, He that shall slay a Thief or a Ravisher, ought not to be punished, for by a publick and heroick Act, the one defends his Life the other her Chastity. Amongst women that have thus defended their Chastity with the death of him that attempted it, *Heliodorus* records the noble act of *Heraclea*, which he calls a *Just defence of her honour.* Another amongst men we *Plut. vit. Marii.* have recorded by *Plutarch*, of one *Trebonius*, who slew *C. Lusius* a Tribune of the Souldiers, and *Marius* his own Sisters Son, for attempting to bugger him; for which fact he was by *Marius* honoured with a Crown.

VIII. *Yet may this defence sometimes be laudably omitted.* Although (as we have said) it be lawful to kill him that is ready to kill me, yet is it more commendable to chuse rather to be killed than to kill, which some grant; yet so that it be with this limitation, that it excepts that person upon whom the safety of many doth much depend. But I cannot judge it safe to impose this so contrary a Law to patience upon all those whose lives are beneficial unto others; and therefore I think it more convenient to restrain the exceptions to such only, whose office and duty it is to defend others from violence. As to those whom we have contracted with as our Guards, to defend us in our Journeys either by Sea or Land, and to such as are publick Governors, unto whom that of *Lucan* may not unfitly be applied.

Cum

Cum tot ab hac anima populorum vita salusque
Pendeat, & tantus caput hoc sibi fecerit orbis,
Sævitia est voluisse mori:

Since on thy life so many lives depend,
And wast made Head the Members to defend,
To wish to dye were madness.

As also that of *Curtius*, *Whilst thou unadvisedly exposest thy life to so many perils, thou dost not remember how many of thy Subjects lives thou endangerest, which thou oughtest to defend.* *Lib.* 10.

On the contrary, It may so fall out, That the life of him that endangers ours, is so beneficial to others, that he cannot without sin be killed; and that not only because it is forbidden by Gods Law both in the Old and New Testament, which we have already proved, where we shewed that the Person of a King is sacred, but by the very Law of Nature: For the Right of Nature as it signifies a Law, doth not only respect those things which are agreeable to that which we call Expletive Justice, but it comprehends also the Acts of Fortitude, Temperance and Prudence, as being in some certain circumstances, not only honest and laudable, but strictly due. But unto this that we have said we stand obliged by Charity. Neither am I at all startled from this opinion of mine by what *Vasquius* urgeth, That the Prince that shall Insult over an Innocent person, doth *ipso facto* cease to be a Prince; than which, nothing can be said less true, or more dangerous. For as Right and Property, so Soveraignty is not lost by mis-government, unless some Law doth so determine it. But by what Law was it ever yet decreed, that Kings should lose their Soveraignty, by an offence committed against a private person? Surely there was no such Law ever yet found, nor I believe ever will be: For the condition of Princes would then be very slippery, and the Common-wealth soon fall into Confusion. And as to that which *Vasquius* layes as his ground-work, whereupon he erects this and many other such dangerous conclusions; as namely, that all Soveraignty was granted, for the benefit of the Subjects, and not of the King; were it universally true, yet were it nothing to the purpose: For the thing it self doth not then wholly cease, although the benefit or profit thereof doth in some part cease. And whereas he adds, That every man wisheth well to the Common-wealth for his own sake; and therefore every man should prefer his own safety, before that of the Common-wealth, it doth not follow. For although we do wish the preservation of the Common-wealth for our own sakes, because our own safety is included in it; yet do we not wish it only for our own sakes, but for the good of others also. For the opinion of those Philosophers, who hold, that true friendship doth arise out of some Indigency or Insufficiency, is rejected as false and pernicious, seeing that Man, being a creature naturally sociable, is promptly and of its own nature inclined unto it. But that I should prefer the common safety before mine own, Charity doth sometimes perswade, and sometimes command me. *Plutarch* will tell us, *That the principal part of Valour is, to defend our Defender.* And *Cassiodore* illustrates this, by a very fit comparison, *If the hand,* saith he, *by its intelligence from the eye, perceive a blow threatning the head, without regard to its own safety, it will interpose it self between it and danger*: From whence he infers, *That they who to redeem their Prince his life, hazard, nay lose their own, do but the same in the Politicks, which the hand by Instinct doth in the body Natural. It is no marvel,* saith *Seneca*, *if Kings and Princes being the Guardians of publick States, be dearer unto us than our own Relations: For if in the Judgement of the Wise, the Publick Good be to be preferred before any private mans; It will easily follow, That he that is the Father of our Countrey, deserves to be dearer unto us than the Father of any one Family.* Or as St. *Ambrose* speaks, *He that delivers a Nation from desolation, merits more love, than he that delivers us from particular dangers.* And therefore the same *Seneca* doth highly commend *Calistratus* and *Rutilius, the one an* Athenian, *the other, a* Roman, *who refused to have their own estates restored unto themselves by the publick ruines: esteeming it much better to perish by themselves, than to redeem their own lives and fortunes with the destruction of their Countrey.*

IX. Our defence against a person publickly useful, unlawful by the Rule of Charity.

Soveraignty not lost by mis-government.

The errors of *Vasquius* confuted.

Vita Pelop.

Lib. 1. *de Clem. c.* 4.

De Off. l. 3. *c.* 3.

Lib. 6. *de Ben. c.* 17.

There are also, that hold it lawful to defend our selves from any slight Injuries, as a box on the ear or the like, even by killing him that attempts it. But respect being herein had to Justice meerly Expletive, I cannot dissent from them. For although the Inequality be very great between a box on the ear and death, yet he that shall attempt to injure me, doth therein give me a Right, that is, a kind of Moral power to oppose him without any limitation, so far forth as I cannot otherwise repel or avoid the Evil intended against me. Neither doth Charity by it self seem to restrain us herein, in favour to the Nocent; Linus *the Musician, provoking his Disciple* Hercules *with a slight blow, had his brains beaten out by*

X. To kill any man for a slight Injury not lawful for Christians.

Hercules *with his own Harp: and being by some arraigned for the Murder, appeals for his Indempnity to that Law of* Rhadamant, *whereby he that wounded another, being by him first assaulted, was declared Innocent.* But the Christian Law doth clearly forbid it: and Christ himself doth expresly charge his Disciples patiently to suffer any such slight injury though reiterated, rather than to hurt our adversary: How much more doth he forbid them to kill him, to avoid a box on the ear? By which particular Instance, we are sufficiently cautioned against that of *Covarruvias,* That Mans understanding being well Instructed in what is naturally Right, will not endure, that any thing should in natural reason be permitted, that is not also permitted by God, who is very Nature it self. For God, who is so the Author of Nature, that he sometimes acts Freely above Nature, hath a right to bound and to limit us by Laws, even in such things as are in their own nature, Free and Indefinite; much more hath he power to oblige us to that which is naturally honest, though not due. But a wonder it is, That since Gods will is in this point so expresly declared in the Gospel, there should yet be found so many Christians, yea, and those Divines, who maintain, not only that for the avoiding of a box on the ear, or such like slight Injury, we may lawfully kill our adversary: But that in case he that hath smitten us do fly, yet may we pursue him even to death, for the vindication of our own honor, which seems to be as equidistant from natural reason, as from Christian piety. For, *Honor est opinio de excellentia,* Honour is an opinion of some Excellency in the person honoured. But he that can bear such an Injury, doth express himself eminently patient, and by that means doth rather magnifie than diminish his own honour. Neither is it much material, That some men of corrupt Judgements do reproach this Vertue by the name of Cowardice. For those shallow heads can neither alter the thing it self, nor lessen the reputation of it. Neither was this the Judgement of the Primitive Christians only, but of the Ancient Philosophers also, who ever accounted it an argument of a weak and pusillanimous Spirit, Not to be able to digest an Injury, as we have elsewhere shewed. And from hence we may collect, how deservedly their Opinion is to be exploded, who hold it lawful by even Divine Right, (for that it may be so by the Right of Nature I deny not) to defend our selves even from mean and slight Injuries by even the death of the person Injuring, although we may without any danger avoid him by Flight, or otherwise; Because it is accounted dishonourable in a Person of Quality so to do: whereas indeed, the scandal is not justly given, but by a popular misprision unjustly taken, and by all those who understand wherein true Wisdom and Valour do consist, to be contemned. And it doth not a little rejoyce me, that herein I have the concurrent opinion of that Excellent Lawyer *Charles Moline* amongst others to abett me. Now what is said of a blow on the cheek, and of Flight, the very same may also be said in all such cases wherein our honour or reputation is not greatly wounded. But what if a man shall speak that of us, which being believed, may blast our credit and esteem with men? Some there are that would perswade us, that we may lawfully kill him also, but very erroneously, and against the Law of Nature: For this is no fit means whereby we may hope to clear our Fame, or to repair our good Name being sullied.

Navarr. c 15.4 Henr. de Irregul. c.11. Vict. de Jure Belli, n. 5. — Honor, what? — Seen more in patience, than an over-hasty revenge. — To kill a man for a slight Injury, tho' naturally lawful, yet is contrary to the Laws of God, and of Charity. — *In addit. ad Alex. Cons. 119.* — *Pet. Navar. l. 2. c. 3. n. 376.*

XI. To kill any man in defence of our goods, by the Law of Nature not unlawful.

Let us now proceed to those Injuries, whereby we are damnified in our Goods or Estates. And if we respect Expletive Justice only, I shall not deny, but that for the conservation of them, the Robber, if need be, may be killed: For as there is some Inequality between a righteous man and a Thief; so in the judgement of the Law, the Goods of the Innocent are evenly ballanced with the Life of the Nocent: Whence it follows, That if we respect this Right only, a Thief flying away with stoln Goods, if those Goods cannot otherwise be recovered, may be killed. So *Demosthenes* in his Oration against *Aristocrates, Is it not,* saith he, *a very sad Case, and contrary to all Law and Equity, that I should not be permitted to use violence against him, who by violence hath dispossest me of my Goods?* Neither doth common charity (setting aside the Laws of God and men) hinder me by way of precept, unless it be for things of so small value, as deserve rather to be slighted, than with such eagerness to be prosecuted; which is an exception that some Writers do admit of.

XII. How far lawful by the Law of *Moses*. — The Day-Thief and the Night-Thief distinguished.

Let us now see in what sense the *Mosaical* Law is to be understood, whereunto that old Law of *Solon* was parallel, which *Demosthenes* commemorates against *Timocrates,* from whence was taken the Law of the 12. Tables; and that of *Plato* also in his Ninth *de Legibus.* All which Laws do agree in this, That they put a great difference between a Night, and a Day-Thief. But concerning the reason of this Law there is some question; Some are of opinion, that the only reason of this Law is, because by Night it cannot well be discerned, whether he that breaks into an house, be a Thief or a Murderer; and therefore to prevent the worst, he may be killed as a Murderer. Others place the difference in this, That in the night a Thief cannot be known, and consequently the Goods stoln cannot be recovered, and therefore he may be killed. But in mine opinion, the Law-makers had no regard to either of these properly; but rather, that none ought to be killed

led for stealing of Goods directly; yet, that in some cases, the Goods stoln might occasion the death of him that stole them; namely, when the Goods stoln cannot otherwise be recovered, but by killing him who is flying away with them. But if I my self in pursuing after my Goods, shall be brought into danger of my life, then it may be lawful for me to redeem mine own life out of danger, though with the hazard or loss of another mans: Neither can it be justly objected against me, that I brought my self into that danger, because I proposed nothing to my self, but either to defend or recover what was mine own, or to take the Thief, which to me is lawful: nor do I injure any in the use of lawful means to a lawful end. But the difference between a Nocturnal and a Diurnal Thief consists in this, That in the Night there can hardly be found witnesses sufficient to testifie the matter of Fact. Therefore in case a Thief be found slain, we do easily give credit to him, who shall confess that he slew him in his own defence; especially if the slain Thief be found with any offensive weapon by him.

In the Night Witnesses cannot prove the Theft.

For this is by the *Hebrew* Law required, That the Nocturnal Thief was found digging through an house, as some have translated the *Hebrew* word; or as others better, with a digging Instrument about him; as the most Learned of them have expounded that place of *Jer.* 2. 34. I am the more easily guided to this Exposition by the Law of the Twelve Tables, whereby it is forbidden to kill a Thief that robs by day, with this exception, Unless he shall defend himself with some weapon. Now it is to be presumed, that a Thief that robs by Night, hath weapons about him to defend himself. By Weapons the Lawyer *Cajus* understands, either Iron, a Club or a Stone: on the contrary, it is the opinion of *Ulpian*, That whereas it is provided by the Law, that he that kills a Thief by Night shall be indempnified, it ought to be understood, in case, that in defending his Goods, he could not otherwise free himself from danger.

A Nocturnal Thief may be killed, if he have any Weapons about him.

There is therefore (as I said) a strong presumption for him that kills a Nocturnal Thief: But if there were sufficient witnesses to prove, that he that killed such a Thief, was in no such danger, then the presumption would instantly cease, and he that should kill the said Thief, should be held guilty of Homicide. It is likewise provided by the Law of the Twelve Tables, That he that apprehends a Thief, whether by Day or Night, should publish it with an Out-cry (as *Cajus* instructs us:) that so, if it might be, both the Magistrate and the people may be called in to assist, and give testimony to the matter of Fact. But because such a Concourse cannot so easily be procured in the Night, as in the Day, therefore is more credit given unto him that shall affirm, that he killed the Nocturnal Thief in his own defence.

A Nocturnal Thief must be assaulted with an Out-cry.

Not unlike is that *Hebrew* Law in the case of Ravishment, which if committed in the Field, the person ravished was to have been believed; but not so, if in the City: Because there she both might and ought by her clamour, to have called in the Neighbours to her assistance. Not that the Case of Ravishment is alwayes to be determined by this Rule, as *Philo* well expounds this place: For possible it is, that such a fact may be committed in a City without clamour, by stopping the mouth: and that in the Field, it may be done with Consent (as in his Book of Special Laws he affirms). But that this Rule is to guide us in ordinary cases of Ravishment, moreover admitting the dangers to be equal; yet in the Night, because we cannot so well descry what the dangers are, either for Quality or Quantity, therefore though the dangers may be less, yet the terror must needs be more.

A Rape committed in the Field, and in the City, differenced.

Let this also be observed, that both the *Hebrew* and *Roman* Laws, though they appear severe, yet are they usually addulced by Charity. For they would not willingly punish Theft with death; there being so great a disproportion between Life and Goods, unless the Injured person in striving to recover his Goods, shall be brought in jeopardy of his Life. And *Moses Maimonides* hath left this Charitable Rule for our Guide, whilst he gives no private man power to take away the life of another, unless it be in the defence of that, which being lost, is irreparable; such as are Life and Chastity.

XIII. How far forth Lawful by the Evangelical Law.

But the Question is, Whether the Evangelical Law, being more Sublime and Spiritual, than either the *Jewish* or *Roman* Laws, do not require a more strict and perfect obedience, than those Laws do? And clearly it doth. For if our Blessed Saviour do enjoyn us to part with our Coat and our Cloaks, and if St. *Paul* admonish us to suffer our selves to be dispoiled of our Goods, rather than contend in Law for them, which is a kind of unbloody strife: How much more doth that Law expect, that we should rather forbear and forego things though of a greater value, than embrew our hands in our Neighbours blood, he being Gods own Image, and of the same nature with our selves? Wherefore if our Goods, being stoln, may be recovered or defended without the danger of bloodshed, we do well so to do: But if not, we ought rather willingly to lose them, than to stain our hands with the blood of him that robs us: unless the things stoln, be such as are necessary for the sustentation of our selves or our families, and which cannot by any Courts of Justice be recovered; because haply the Thief is not known, and that there is some fear, that without bloodshed, the thing will be gone. And although almost all both Divines and Lawyers, do at this day maintain, That to kill him that shall attempt to rob us of

Forte quia fur sit ignotus, & Spes sit aliqua sine cæde rem abituram.

of our Goods is lawful, even beyond thoſe limited bounds, wherein the *Jewiſh* and *Roman* Laws permitted it; as namely, in caſe the Thief being poſſeſt of our Goods do fly; yet that this was the ſenſe of the Holy Scriptures in the Primitive Times, I cannot doubt. Neither did St. *Auguſtin* think otherwiſe, as may appear by theſe his own words, *Quomodo apud divinam providentiam à peccato liberi ſunt, qui pro his rebus, quas contemni oportet, humana cæde polluti ſunt? How can they appear Innocent before Gods Tribunal, who for things not worthy a Chriſtians care, can pollute themſelves with humane blood?* But doubtleſs in this, as in many other things of the like nature, *Cum tempore laxata eſt diſciplina; The ancient diſcipline of the Church is through age grown feeble;* and by little and little, inſtead of fitting our lives to the ſtrict Rules of the Goſpel, we expound thoſe Evangelical Precepts, in favour to the Corruptions of the Age we live in. This ancient diſcipline although almoſt forgotten among the Laity, yet was wont heretofore to be ſtrictly obſerved by the Clergy; but now it is almoſt, if not altogether laid aſide by theſe alſo. Thus St. *Jerom* complains in the Life of *Malchus* †, *After the Church of Chriſt began to be governed by Chriſtian Princes, ſhe grew outwardly indeed, more Splendid, but inwardly, leſs vertuous.*

De lib. Arb. l. 1.

† *Vid. C. ſuſcepimus, de homicid. voluntario: & Canon. de his Diſt. 1.*

XIV. Whether the Civil Law doth permit only, or approve of this kind of Interfection.

It is queſtioned by ſome, Whether the Law, at leaſt the Civil Law, as it hath power of life and death, in ſuch caſes wherein it ſuffers a private perſon to kill a Thief, doth ſo far legitimate the Fact, as to make it altogether blameleſs? But this I cannot grant. For in the firſt place, The Law it ſelf hath not the power of death over all its ſubjects for every offence; but for ſuch Crimes only as deſerve death. And very probable is the opinion of *Scotus*, That it is not lawful to adjudge any man to death, unleſs it be for ſuch Crimes, as the *Moſaical* Law puniſhed with death; with this addition only, or for ſuch Crimes, as may be equally emballanced with them. Neither doth the knowledge of the will of God, which alone can ſatisfie the mind, concerning this ſo great and weighty a matter, ſo plainly elſewhere appear, as it doth in that Law of *Moſes*, whereby the Thief is not adjudged unto death. Beſides, the Law neither ought, nor uſually doth give unto any man a Right to put a Malefactor to death privately, though he deſerve it, unleſs it be for ſome great and horrible Crime. Otherwiſe the Authority of Magiſtrates and Courts of Judicature would ſoon dwindle to nothing. Wherefore when the Law licentiates a man to kill a Thief, it is to be underſtood, that it rather tolerates, than approves of the Fact; and that it acquits him only of the puniſhment, but not that it gives him a Right to do it.

XV. Single Combats when lawful.

From what hath been already ſaid, we may collect, that in two caſes ſingle Combats may be undertaken by private men without ſin. In the firſt place, If the Challenger ſhall grant his adverſary a licence to fight, and otherwiſe threatens to kill him immediately in caſe he refuſe. In the next place, when a King or a Magiſtrate ſhall give licence to two Malefactors equally deſerving death, to try it out by Combat, whether of them ſhall live: And he that doth ſo, doth not ſo rightly perform his duty as he might: For it were much better, if he intended to ſatisfie himſelf with the death of one only, to determine, which of them ſhall dye by Lot.

XVI. Of Defence in a publick War.

Lib. 23.

Lib. 5.

What we have hitherto ſaid concerning the Right we have to defend our Perſons and Goods, belongs principally to private War, yet ſo, as it ought alſo to be applyed to a publick, ſome reſpect being had to the difference that is between them. So ſaith *Ammianus*, *To all that are Invaded by a Foreign Power, there is but one Law, and that perpetual; namely, by all poſſible means to defend their own ſafety, notwithſtanding the force of any Cuſtom.* For as *Alexander* in *Herodotus* told his Souldiers, *He that is the Aggreſſor, hath no colourable excuſe for his Injuſtice: But he that defends himſelf only, gathers Courage from a good Conſcience, and fortifies his hopes in this, that he doth not infer an injury, but repel one.* Now in a private War, this Right of killing another, is but momentany, and determines as ſoon as the matter may be brought before a Judge. But in a publick War, which beginneth not, till Juſtice and Judgement ceaſe, there this Right laſts long, being fomented and perpetuated by ſuch accidents, damages and wrongs, as are every day renewed in the proſecution of the War. Beſides, in a private War, we have ſcarce any other end, than our own defence: But the Supream Powers have a Right, not only to defend themſelves, but to be avenged on others; whence it is likewiſe lawful for them, not only to reſiſt certain and preſent dangers, but to prevent ſuch as ſeem to threaten afar off: Not directly, for that (as I have already ſaid) were Injuſtice; but indirectly, by revenging ſuch wrongs as are already begun, although not fully conſummate; concerning which, we ſhall have cauſe to ſpeak anon.

XVII. When only to curb the power of a Neighbour Prince unlawful.

Alb. Gent. lib. 1. c. 14.

Neither can we approve of that which ſome Authors do affirm for truth; namely, That by the Law of Nations, it is a ſufficient ground of a Juſt War, to ſuppreſs the over-ſwelling Power of ſome ambitious Prince, who if let alone, may exceedingly annoy us. That in our ordinary Councils of War, this uſually comes in debate, I grant. But not ſo much under this Notion, becauſe it is Juſt, but as it is profitable: So that in caſe the War for

for other cauſes be Juſt; for this cauſe it may prudentially be undertaken: And this is all that the Authors before cited do in effect ſay. But from a meer poſſibility, that we may hereafter ſuffer wrong, to conclude a preſent Right, or a neceſſity of doing wrong, will prove no good Inference in a Court of Equity. For all humane affairs are obnoxius to ſo many contingencies, that no ſecurity can be expected in this life. Againſt all uncertain and Ignote dangers, our ſafety conſiſts not in our Arms, but in our Innoxious prudence, co operating with the Divine Providence. *Bal. lib. 3. de re milit.*

XVIII. Defence in ſuch as have given juſt cauſe of War unlawful.

Nor leſs unſatisfied am I with their Reaſons, who affirm, That their Defence is Juſt, who have given an occaſion of a Juſt War. Becauſe, ſay they, There are very few that will be contented with ſuch a meaſure of revenge, as is proportionable to the Injuries they have received. For this very Fear of what is to come, being uncertain cannot juſtifie us, in the defence of Injuries already done. For ſo, the malefactor may juſtifie his reſiſtance of the publick Miniſters of Juſtice, by his fear, that they will inflict a greater puniſhment upon him, than his Crime deſerves. But he that gives juſt cauſe of offence, ought in the firſt place to tender ſuch ſatisfaction, as in the judgement of unbyaſſed men, is equivalent to the wrong done; which if refuſed, then is his defence Juſt. Thus did *Hezekiah*, who for breaking the League which his Anceſtors had made with the Kings of *Aſſyria*, being threatned with War, confeſt his fault, and promiſed to pay whatſoever the ſaid King ſhould impoſe upon him; which being done, when notwithſtanding he was afterwards Invaded with a powerful Army, truſting to the Juſtice of his Cauſe, he made his defence, and had the Moſt High God for his Protector. *Pontius Samnis* after he had made reſtitution to the *Romans* of their Goods, and delivered up the Authors of the War, pleads thus with them, *We have I hope appeaſed the juſt wrath of Heaven againſt us for our breach of the League, and am confident that the ſame Incenſed Deities, who have conſtrained me to make full reſtitution of whatſoever we have formerly taken away from the* Romans, *will alſo plague the* Romans *for deſpiſing the expiation we offer, for the breach of ſo Inſolent a League.* And by and by after, *What more, O ye* Romans, *do I owe to you, or to your League, or to the Gods, that are the Impartial Arbiters of Leagues? To whom ſhall I appeal? Whom will ye accept of to judge of the Cauſes of your Anger, and of the meaſures of my ſufferings? I refuſe no people, no perſon.* So when the *Thebans* had offered to the *Lacedæmonians*, all the ſatisfaction that in equity they could require, and were by them rejected; *Ariſtides* told them, That the Juſtneſs of the War was thereby tranſlated from the *Lacedæmonians* to the *Thebans*. The like we read of the *Switzers*, who in revenge for a Load of Sheep-skins taken from a Merchant of theirs, by the Earl of *Romont*, having ſpoiled his Countrey, did afterwards (being threatned by the Duke of *Burgundy*) offer to reſtore all they had taken from the ſaid Earl, and to give what further ſatisfaction the ſaid Duke ſhould require: The refuſal of which offer, coſt the Duke his life, and the loſs of almoſt all his Jewels and Treaſure, as *Comines* teſtifies.

2 Kings 18. 7, 14. & c. 19.

Lib. 5. *ch.* 1.

CHAP.

CHAP. II.

Of such things wherein Men have a Right in Common.

I. The division of what we call Ours.

THat War may be undertaken for Injuries not done, we have seen proved. Now it follows, that according to the order we proposed, we discourse of the Second Branch of the causes justifying a War, namely, for Injuries actually done. And herein, first of Injuries done against that which is ours: Now of that which is ours, Some things are ours by a Right common with all Mankind, and some things are ours, in our own particular Right. We shall begin with that which is ours in common with others. This Common Right is either directly in some Corporeal thing, or to some Acts. Things Corporeal are either such as do admit of no propriety, or such as properly belong to some persons. Of things whereof there is as yet no propriety, some there are that cannot be impropriated, and some there are that may. Now that this may be rightly understood, we must search into the rise or beginning of propriety, which Lawyers call Dominion.

II. The original and growth of Propriety. Gen. 1. 29, 30. 9. 2.

Almighty God, as soon as he had created the World, did immediately confer a Right generally to all mankind in things of this Inferiour Nature. And so again when he had renewed the world after the Flood, as may be seen *Gen.* 1.29,30. and *Gen.* 9.2. *All things at first* (saith *Justin*) *were promiscuously common and undivided to all, and as it were one intire Patrimony bequeathed unto all.* Whence it came to pass, that every man did catch whatsoever he would to his own use, and consume what could be consumed. And the free exercise of this Universal Right was then instead of Propriety: For whatsoever any man did thus catch unto himself, no man could take from him without injury. This may be very fitly illustrated by that Simile which we find in *Cicero* concerning a *Theatre*, which we know *is a publick place, and common to all that come; yet may that particular place which I possess be rightly called mine. There are Seats that are common to all* Roman *Knights, but that amongst them is mine own,* saith *Seneca, which I actually possess.* Which state of things might very well have lasted, had men either persisted in the same inoffensive simplicity, or could they have embraced each other with the same mutual endearments of charity. An experiment

De finibus l. 3.

De benefic. l. 7. c. 12.

ment of the former we have in some people of *America*, who have continued in that happy Communion for many ages, with admirable simplicity: And for those that lived in the like Communion, through Charity, we have the like precedents in the *Esseni*, and in the Primitive Christians at *Jerusalem*, and their followers, the *Pythagoreans*; and now also in not a few, who lead lives purely Monastical. The nakedness wherein our first Parents were created, did sufficiently evidence their simplicity, which consisted rather in their Ignorance of Vice, than in their knowledge of Vertue: As *Trogus* testifies of the *Scythian*. *The men of the first age* (saith *Tacitus*) *were free from inordinate affections, untainted with wickedness, clear from any thing that might occasion reproach; and consequently without restraint or punishment.* Thus *Seneca* also testifies of them, *They were*, saith he, *ignorantly Innocent: And afterwards*, speaking of the four Cardinal vertues, he adds, *Some resemblances of all these, there were in that plain and simple life they led: As having their minds distracted with no manner of Cares*: As *Josephus* testifies. And to the same purpose writes *Macrobius*, *At the first the Conversation of men was with such an Innocent Simplicity, as had no commixture at all of evil in it, being altogother unacquainted with that guile and subtilty that now rageth in the World.* The Wise man terms it *Sincerity*; and so doth St. *Paul*, *Eph.* 6. 24. and sometimes it is called singleness, which is opposed to *craft and subtilty*. They then made the worship of God their only care, which was symbolized by the Tree of Life or Divine Wisdom, *Prov.* 3. 18. As *Philo*, and the learned among the *Jews* explain it; with whom agrees St. *John*, *Apoc.* 22. 2. Their dyet was as simple as their lives; for they fed on nothing but what Nature liberally afforded them, without Cultivation. But in this Innocent Simplicity they continued not long, but wandring in devious paths, and making every day new experiments, they became by degrees acquainted with Sin, which stands Emblem'd out in Scripture by the Tree of Knowledge of Good and Evil, that is, of those things which they had power to use well or ill: which *Philo* calls φρόνησιν μέσην, an Intermediate Prudence; or a Prudence which is conversant about things in themselves Indifferent. Whereunto *Solomon* had respect, when he tells us, *That God made man upright, that is, Simple, but he hath found out many Inventions*: Which *Philo* expounds, *Many subtle Devices*; *Which*, as *Dion Prusaensis* observes, *were no whit to those that succeeded to our first Parents, advantageous as to Life; For they made use of their Sagacity not so much to fortifie themselves with Justice and Temperance, as to corrupt themselves by voluptuousness.* Those most ancient Arts, as the Tilling of the Earth, and the depasturing of Cattle were first exercised by the first brethren, not without some kind of distribution of the Fruits. This diversity of Arts begat a kind of Emulation, and this ended in Murther. And afterwards, when by Conversation the bad infected the good, there grew up a Race of men, who for their violence and oppression, were called Gyants; which the *Greeks* called χειροδίκας, because they observed no other rule of Justice but their own strength, and therefore thought all to be their own, which they could conquer. But the World being cleansed from blood and rapine by the Deluge; Lust, inflamed with Wine, succeeded to Cruelty, and brought forth Incest, and such like unnatural Coitions. But that which especially blew the Coals of discord among Princes and Nations, was that Heroick Sin of Ambition, whose Emblem was the Tower of *Babylon*; whence the division of Tongues caused their dispersion into several Countreys; some possessing one part of the Earth, and some another. But yet still among Neighbours there remained a Communion not of Cattle, but of Pasturage; for so large a proportion of ground (being but thinly peopled) might without any Inconvenience, sufficiently supply all their necessities.

A Community of all things.

Gell. l. 1. *c.* 5. *ad finem.*
Porphyr. Diog. Laert.

The Simplicity of the first age, wherein it consisted.
Ep. 90.

ἀφθαρσία.
Wisd. 3. 24.
πανουργία.
Arbor vitæ.
See Ecclus. 40. 17. And of the four Rivers.
Ecclus. 24. 55.
The Tree of Knowledge of Good and Evil, what it signified.
Eccl. 7. 29.

The Age of the Giants.

Ambition.
Gen. 13.

> *To mark their own, and trench out others Land*
> *Was not yet Lawful.*

Virg. Georg. 1.

Until at length, the numbers both of Men and Cattle encreasing, the Land also became sub-divided, not into Nations and Provinces as before, but into single Families. And whereas in dry and sandy regions, Springs though very necessary, yet were not able to supply a multitude; Therefore did every man strive by taking the first possession of them to make them his own. All these things we may trace out of the Sacred story, whereunto we might add the concurrent Testimonies both of Philosophers and Poets, who have treated of the first state of things held in common, and of the subsequent distribution of them, but that I have done it elsewhere. From hence we learn the true cause why men departed from that Primitive Community of things, first of movables, and afterwards of immovables: Namely, because repining to be at Natures bare allowance, that is, to feed on Roots and Herbs, to make their habitations in Caves, to go naked, or clad with barks of Trees, or Skins of Beasts (as the *Scritefinni* described by *Procopius* did) they made choice of a more delicate kind of living, which would roquire industry, which every particular man was in every thing to use for himself. Now that the Fruits of the Earth could not be conveniently

Gen. 13.
Gen. 21.

Mari libero, c. 15.

Got. 2.

ently laid up or disposed of in common, will easily be granted; First, by reason of the vast distance of the places inhabited, the one from the other. And Secondly, because of the great defect of Love and Charity among men: By reason whereof, no due equality could be observed, either of Labour in their Acquisition, or of Temperance in their Consumption. And from hence we may further learn, for what causes things were reduced into Propriety: Not by the sole act of the Mind; for no one man could possibly know what another would have to be his own, that he might forbear it. Besides, possible it is, that diverse men might be competitors for one and the same thing. But things became proper by compact or agreement, and that either express, or by partition; or tacite, as by present occupancy: But as soon as experience had taught them the inconveniencies of holding things in common, and yet before Division was first instituted, it is very probable, that they unanimously agreed, That what every man possest at that time should be his own. Thus *Cicero, To the end that of what nature had made common, each man might call something his, it was agreed, That look what every man had in possession, he might hold as his own.* And in another place †, *It is generally granted,* saith he, *neither doth nature her self envy it, That as to things appertaining to life,* Quisque sibi malit quam alteri acquiri; *Every man had rather enjoy them himself, than that another should have them.* Whereunto we may add that of *Quintilian, If this be the state and condition of things, That whatsoever is useful to Men, belongs properly to him that possesseth it; then surely whatsoever is justly ours, cannot justly be taken from us.* Which very thing *Cicero* illustrates by a Similitude borrowed from *Chrysippus* of a race, *Ubi currendo licet adversarium vincere, non detrudendo*; Wherein a man might overcome his adversary by running, but not by detrusion. This was wise *Solon*'s wish,

See as to this matter what the honour of the *English* Nation, *Selden* hath traduced unto us out of the *Gemara* and the *Alcoran*, in his *Thalassocratico*.

† *De finib. l.* 3.

Riches I fain would have, but if ill got
(Let them be ne're so great) I wish them not.

And when the Ancients stiled *Ceres* the Law giver, and called her holy Mysteries *Thesmophoria*, they doubtless insinuated that the division of the Earth into Corn-fields, was as it were, the Creation of a new Right. *For as an house or field unoccupied is common, but if possest, the possessors.* So the Earth is divided into several parcels, that each man may till, and hold his own.

III. Now these things being admitted, we say, That the Sea, considered either Universally, or as to its principal parts, cannot be held in propriety by any: This, because granted by some, as to private persons only, but not unto people or nations, I shall endeavour to prove, first, by moral reason. For the cause that moved men to decline their tenure of Lands in common, doth not at all hold in the Sea, which being so vast and boundless, and Ships and Men thereon imployed, so few, must needs be abundantly sufficient to all nations, and for all uses; whether for Water, Fishing, or Navigation. The very same may be said of the air, if any such use could be made thereof; whereunto the use of the Earth under it were not necessary; as in the sport of Hawking, and in the Right of Habitation; both which do receive Laws from him who is the Lord of the Soyl: For as *Pomponius* observes, *Tam Soli quam Cœli mensura facienda est*: And again *Cajus*, Cujus est Solum ejus est usque ad Cœlum; *Whose is the Soyl, his is all that is above it, even unto Heaven.* The very same may be said of Shelves and Quick-sands, where nothing can be made to grow, and whereof there can be made no other use, but to ballast Ships, and whereof there is such store, that it cannot possibly be exhausted. There is also a Natural reason, why the Sea so taken, cannot be held in propriety: because *Occupatio non procedit nisi in re terminata*; *Nothing can be said to be possest, that is not bounded.* Hence it is that *Thucydides* calls Land unoccupied, Lands unbounded: And *Isocrates*, of some Land occupied by the *Athenians*, saith, That that Land is by us bounded and limited. Now *Aristotle* tells us, *That Liquid things cannot be contained within their own bounds.* And if so, then they cannot be possest, unless they be contained in somewhat that is solid and comprehensive of them; as Ponds, Lakes, and Rivers are theirs properly whose the Land is, wherewith they are embanked. Now the Sea cannot properly be said to be contained in the earth, being equal to it, *Nay greater than the Earth*, as *Jarchas* in *Philostratus* thought of the Ocean: And therefore the Ancients held that the Sea did contain the Earth. *What* (saith *Gellius*) *can be said to be about the Ocean, when the Ocean doth every where circumscribe, and encompass the Earth?* And a little after, *Since that every where, and in all manner of ways it flows about the Earth, nothing can be said to be about it: But all regions being entrenched and environed with its Waves, whatsoever is enclosed within the brinks of the Ocean, are in the midst of it.* So likewise speaks *Livy* of the Ocean, *Qui orbem terraram amplexu finit*; *Which encircles with its Waves the terrestrial globe. Seneca* calls the Ocean, *Vinculum totius orbis, custodiaque terrarum*; *The bond or ligament of the earth, and the safeguard of the Nations.* Neither is a division of that vast body of Waters

That some things will not admit of Propriety; as the Sea, taken Universally.

The Ocean not bounded.

Paneg.

De gener. l. 2. *c.* 2.

Greater than the Earth.

Lib. 3. *c.* 11.

ters to be imagined: For when at the first, Lands were divided, the Sea, at least, the greatest part thereof, was unknown; and therefore no means can possibly be invented whereby the nations so far distant should agree about the division of that which they know not: wherefore it is probable, that what then was the Common Right of all, and in the first division was left undivided, is not now the proper Right of any, either people or person by division, but by occupancy, neither can be divided until they have first been occupied.

IV. Places not inhabited are his that first possesseth them.

Let us now descend unto such things wherein we may have a Right of Propriety, though as yet we have none: Such are many places which are as yet desart and unoccupied; Islands in the Sea, Wild Beasts, Fish, and Birds. Concerning which, two things are observable; First, concerning places unpeopled: There is a two fold Right of the occupancy of Lands, the one Universal, or of the whole; the other Partial, as that of Mannors and Farms. The former is usually gained at the charge, and for the benefit of the Common-wealth, or of him who hath the Soveraignty over the people: The other by private Lords or Farmers, which is done, rather by assignation from the former, than by any free and unlimited occupancy. But in case there be any part or parcel of that Countrey or Island, (so universally occupied) that is not yet assigned to particular persons, it is not therefore to be reputed as waste, but it is still supposed to be in the possession of the first occupants, be they King or People. Such are usually Rivers, Lakes, Ponds, Woods, steep Mountains, and the like.

V. Birds, Beasts and Fish, the first occupiers, unless restrained by Law.

Secondly, As to Wild Beasts, Fish, and Birds, this is to be observed, That he that hath the dominion over the Lands and Waters, may by his Laws interdict others from taking them; or being taken, from carrying them away: And by this Law shall strangers also be obliged. The reason whereof is, That to the Government of the people it is morally necessary, That whosoever shall sojourn among the people, though but for a while, yet as soon as he shall enter into their dominions, he shall render himself Conformable to the Laws and Customes of that people. Neither doth it avail to the contrary, to say, That in the *Roman* Law we often read, that by the Laws of Nature and Nations, it is free for any man to hunt such kind of creatures: For this might be, whilest there was no Civil Law to prohibit it, as indeed there were many other things that were left free and arbitrary, by the *Roman* Laws in the Infancy of their Common-wealth, which the Laws of other Nations did severely restrain. But when the Civil Law shall otherwise decree it, then the very Law of Nature doth require that we should observe it. For although the Civil Law can enjoyn nothing that the Law of Nature forbids, nor forbid any thing that it commands; yet notwithstanding it may limit and circumscribe that which the Law of Nature leaves free, and forbid that which naturally may be lawful. And so the Civil Law may by interposing her authority, prevent that dominion which naturally might be acquired.

Though the Civil Law can enjoyn nothing that the Law of Nature forbids, yet it may bound that which the Law of Nature leaves Free.

VI. In times of necessity what is properly ours, may be common to others.

Let us now examine, Whether in what is properly ours, there may yet remain a Right in Common to others. Which question may by some be thought strange, considering that Property seems to swallow up all Right, which was at first held in Common. But it is not so; for our better understanding whereof, we must look back to the true meaning of those who first introduced particular dominion: which may be presumed to be such as did (as little as might be) recede from natural equity. For if even our written Laws oblige us but to a *Quatenus fieri potest*; *To what in natural equity may be done* (as appears by our frequent Appeals from our Statute, and Common Laws, unto our Courts of *Chancery*:) much more may our Customes admit of such an exposition, which are not fitted to Words and Syllables. Hence then it follows, that in cases of extreme necessity that ancient Right of using every particular mans goods, as if they remained yet in Common, stands in force: For as in all humane Laws, so in this very Law of Dominion, cases of absolute necessity are generally excepted. Hence it is, that in Navigation, If the Common stock of Victuals be spent, what every particular man hath is held as Common. So in the case of Fire, If I cannot otherwise avoid it, I may pull down my neighbours house to preserve mine own: And on the Seas, If my Ship fall foul, or be intangled with another, I may cut their Cables to free my self. All which are not Introduced, but expounded by the Civil Law: But this (as *Ulpian* tells us) never holds, unless it be in cases of extreme and manifest necessity, where this case is added of the blowing up of another mans house to save mine own. For even among Divines, it is a received opinion, That in a time of absolute necessity, if a man shall take away from another that without which he that takes it cannot live, he doth not commit Theft: Not, as some think, because it is to be presumed, that the right owner by the rule of Charity, is bound to give it to him that so wants it; but, that it may be presumed, that the reducing of things originally Common into private dominion, was to be understood with some grains of allowance in such Cases. For if they that first divided such things, had been demanded, What they would to have been done in such a case, they would certainly have been

In Navigation.

In the case of Fire.

of this mind. *Necessity* (saith *Seneca* the Father) *being a most benign Patroness to humane frailty, will not be bound up by any Law, i. e. Humane, or that is made after the manner of Humane Laws. Quicquid coegit, defendit; Whatsoever it commands, it also defends,* saith the same *Seneca. In a Storm it disburthens the Ship with the loss of the Goods, in a Fire it quencheth the flame with the ruine of the Fabrick: Necessity is indeed the Law of time.* Thus *Cicero*, Cassius (saith he) *passed over into* Syria, *another mans Province: If men might freely enjoy the benefit of our written Laws, but these being by Arms supprest into his own Province by the Law of Nature.* So *Curtius, In a common calamity every man must bear his portion, and be content with the fortune that befalls him.*

Philip 11.

VII. But not if the necessity be otherwise avoidable.

But some Cautions ought to be admitted, lest this License stray too far, the first whereof is this, That all ways and means are in the first place to be tryed, whether this necessity may be otherwise avoided, that so it may appear unto all men that this necessity is extreme: As we should first make our application to the Magistrate, and try whether he will relieve us; then to the owner of the Goods, whether we may by entreaty obtain that which we stand in need of. *Plato* would not permit any man to require water from anothers well, that had not dug for water in his own grounds, *usque ad cretam, even till he came to chalk, but could find none. Solon* required that he should dig forty Cubits in his own Lands, whereunto *Plutarch* adds, *Subveniendum necessitati, non instruendum pigritiam; It is fit that mens necessities should be relieved, but not that idleness should be encouraged.* And it was *Xenophon*'s plea to the *Sinopenses, Wheresoever we are denyed the common right of buying necessaries, there, whether from* Græcians *or* Barbarians, *we will take them by force, yet not out of perverseness but necessity.*

Cyr. exped. l. 5.

VIII. Nor if there be the like necessity in the right owner.

2. This is not to be allowed, if the right owner be prest by the like necessity, for when the case it equal, *Possidentis melior est conditio* *, *The condition of the present Occupant is to be preferred. A wise man will rather dye* (saith *Lactantius*) *than be unjust: He will not dispossess the Shipwrackt of the plank he bestrides, though he might thereby save his own life; nor unhorse his wounded Comrade, although by betraying his life, he might save his own. Will not then a wise man* (saith *Cicero*) *being famished with hunger, take away meat from him whom he knows to be good for nothing? No surely, for life it self is not dearer unto me, than this resolution of mine, Neminem ut violem commodi mei gratia, Not to injure another to benefit my self.* So *Curtius, Melior est causa suum non tradentis, quam alienum poscentis; For better is his condition that gives not what is his own, than his that requires that which is another mans.*

* *Lactant. l.* 5. *c.* 17.

Off. l. 3.

IX. Things thus taken are to be restored when we are able.

Thirdly, When the danger incumbent is past, restitution is to be made, if we are able: Some there are that think otherwise, being swayed by this argument, because he that useth his own right only, is not obliged to restitution. But to speak truly, this right is not his own fully and absolutely, but restrained and clog'd with the duty of restitution, when that necessity shall cease; for such a limited right sufficeth to preserve natural equity, against the rigour of absolute dominion.

X. An example of this right in war.

Hence we may collect, By what Right he that wageth a Just War, may lawfully surprise and hold some strong place in a Country that is at peace with him, being but weakly guarded; that is to say, if there be no imaginary but a certain danger that his enemy may possess himself of it, and thereby do him an irreparable damage, especially if nothing be taken but what is necessary for his own Security: As namely, the bare custody of the place, leaving the jurisdiction and profits thereof unto the right owner. And lastly, If it be done with a full purpose to restore even the custody of the place also, as soon as the necessity of keeping it for his own indemnity shall cease. *Enna,* saith *Livy, was detained either by fraud or out of pure necessity:* For whatsoever here doth in the smallest degree decline from necessity, is injury. The *Gracians* that stood in great danger for want of Ships, by the advice of *Xenophon*, seized such as passed by, yet so, that the Goods were preserved entire for the Owners, and the Seamen well fed and paid. The First Right therefore, that since propriety was introduced, pleads for exemption, is this of Necessity.

Livy l. 24.

De exped. Cyri lib. 5.

XI. In cases of innocent profit.

The next is, That of Innocent profit. *What should hinder us* (saith *Cicero* †) *from communicating with others, when we may do it without any detriment to our selves, especially in those things that are profitable to those that receive them, and not damagable to us that give them? Seneca* will not admit of this to be a courtesie, to kindle a Coal at our Fire, or to light a Torch or a Candle by ours: *Plutarch* accounts it *an act of impiety, to cast away what we cannot eat, to seal up a Fountain when we have drank our selves full, to remove Land or Sea-marks which have been useful unto us*: For, saith he, in these things after that we have satisfied our selves, every man hath a common Right.

† *De off. l.* 1.
*De benef. lib.*4.

So a River, as it is a River, is the propriety of those people whose the Banks are, or his, who hath the Soveraign Power over them, in whose power it is to make Dams or Mills in it, and whatsoever is bred in that River is his: But that River as it is a flowing Stream remains common, every man hath a Right to drink or to draw water out of it, as well as he that owns it.

Quis

Quis vetat apposito lumen de lumine sumi?
Atque cavum vastas in mare servet aquas?

Who at his Torch, light to a Torch denyes?
And wh'would engross the Seas vast Cavities?

saith *Ovid*, who also brings in *Latona* thus bespeaking the *Lycians*:

Quid prohibetis Aquas? usus communis aquarum.

Why water d'ye deny?
Whose use should common lye.

Where also he reckons water among those publick Gifts that Nature bestows upon all men alike, the word Publick being improperly taken, in which sence some things are said to be publick by the Law of Nations: *Virgil* tells us the water is open and common to all, as well Strangers as Natives.

XIII. A right to travel by Land or Sea, common to all.

Thus both Lands, Rivers, and such parts of the Sea as are held by any Prince or People in propriety, ought to lye open and free to all such as have occasion to pass over them upon any just and lawful cause; as namely, either because being expelled their own, they seek after some other Country that lyes waste, or because they desire to traffick with some people remote from them; or even because they seek to recover what is their own by a just war. The reason is the same here as above, because it is very probable, that dominion was introduced at the first with this limitation, that such things should remain in common use, which might be profitable to some and not hurtful to others: And therefore the first Authors of Propriety are conceived to have thus agreed it. A signal example whereof we have in the History of *Moses*, *Numb.* 20. 21. who being to march through the borders of the *Edomites* and *Amorites*, offers these Conditions, *That he would travel only through their high-ways, without trespassing upon any private mans possessions; if he had need of any thing that was theirs, he would pay the just price of it.* Which being rejected, was ground sufficient for that War which he made against the *Amorites*: Whence St. *Augustin* thus, *An innocent passage was denyed them, which ought by the Laws of humanity to lye open and free to all who require it.* Whereupon St. *Augustin* concludes, *That the war made by the* Israelites *against the* Amorites, *was just. Hercules* slew *Amyntor* King of the *Orchomenians*, because he denyed him a free passage: So did the *Græcians* make War against *Josephus*, because he refused to give them leave to pass through the borders of his Country. Thus also do the *Græcians*, which were under *Clearchus*, plead; *We* (say they) *are travelling towards our own Country, peaceably, if none molest us; but if any shall hinder us, we will endeavour by the assistance of the Gods to force our way.* So likewise *Agesilaus* returning out of *Asia*, when he came to *Troas*, demanded, *An ut Amicum se an ut hostem transire mallent? Whether they desired that he should pass through their Country as a Friend or as an Enemy?* The like demand was made by *Lysander* to the *Bœotians*, *Rectis se hastis se transire vellent, an inclinatis? Whether they would have him to pass in a peaceful or in a warlike posture?* Thus do the *Batavians* remonstrance to the *Bonnenses* in *Tacitus*, *If none oppose us, our march shall be innocent; but if we find resistance, we will force our passage with our Swords. Cimon* carrying Succours to the *Lacedæmonians*, led them through the Territories of *Corinth*; and being blamed by the *Corinthians*, that he had not first acquainted the City with his purpose, (for they that knock at other mens doors (say they) enter not but by permission) returns this answer, *But ye* (saith he) *have not knockt at the doors of the* Cleonæans *and of the* Megarenses, *but have broken them open: Censentes omnia potere debere plus valentibus, Conceiving that all places ought to lye open to the strongest.* But the most moderate opinion is the best: Leave is first to be demanded, according to that of *Aristophanes*,

Numb. 20. 21.

Li. quæst. 4. sup. Numb. c. 20.

Apollodor.

Scholiast. in Hor. carmen in Canidiam.

Plut. Ages.

Hist. l. 4.

Leave to be first asked.

Whilst toward Delphos *we our Army lead,*
First from Bœotians *we free passage crav'd.*

Which if denyed may be forced.

But if it be denyed, then may our passage be justly forced by Arms: When the *Germans* and the *French* made war one against the other for *Maranus*, the *Venetians* gave free passage to them both, whereof when the *Germans* complained, they were answered that they could not hinder it but by Arms, which it was not their custom to use, but against their publick Enemies. *Agesilaus* in *Plutarch* returning out of *Asia*, and demanding free passage for his Army through *Macedon*, was answered by the King that he would consult about it: Whereunto *Agesilaus* replyed, *Consultet nos interea intrabimus, Let him consult; and we in the mean time will enter.* Neither may it be justly objected, that the multitude of those that

Paral. lib. 11.

are

Remedies against this fear.

are to pass, may give just cause of fear; for *Jus meum metu tuo non tollitur, My Right is not taken away by thy fear:* And the rather, because there are certain Remedies provided against this fear; as that they shall march in smal parties, that they shall march unarmed, or that they shall give security to repair all damages that shall be done, which was required from *Isacius* for his passage through *Germany*, (which custom, as *Strabo* notes, was anciently observed in the Country of the *Æleans*) or that he through whose Country the Army is to pass, may at the charge of him that demands leave, hire sufficient Forces to guard his own Subjects; or that Hostages may be given, which *Seleucus* required of *Demetrius*, to suffer him to stay a while within the borders of his Empire. Many notable Cautions and Remedies we may read of in *Nicetas*, made and agreed on by *Frederick Barbarossa*, and *Isacius Angelus*, concerning the free passage of an Army: Yet *Cæsar* we read denyed the *Switzers* passage through his Province, because he believed them to be a people so rapacious that they could not abstain from acts of violence. So likewise neither is the fear of him, against whom he that craves passage makes a just War, any sufficient reason to deny passage: Nor is it sufficient to say he may pass some other way, for so may any other say, and consequently by that means all right of passage shall be taken away. But it is enough that without any fraud or ill meaning, passage is demanded the nearest or most convenient way; yet certainly if he that craves passage do make an unjust war, or shall lead with him such as are mine enemies, I may deny them; for it is lawful for me to meet him even in his own Territories, to intercept his passage into mine: Neither is there only a Right in common due for persons to pass to and fro about their lawful affairs, but for their merchandises; for to hinder any one Nation from maintaining commerce and traffick with another that is remote from them, is unjust. For that this freedom may be admitted and maintained, is for the common interest of humane society, neither can it bring damage unto any: For although a man do sometimes fall short of that gain, which was not due, but hoped for only, we ought not to register this among the number of our losses. To these Testimonies which we have already produced to this purpose, we shall add this one out of *Philo, Merchants Ships do sail over the Seas without danger, with such Goods as Nations, out of a desire to participate of each others Commodities, do carry for exchange, whilst they mutually relieve the wants of the one, with the superfluities of the other.* And another out of *Plutarch*, who concerning the Sea, speaks thus, *Our life, which is otherwise wild and unfit for commerce, this Element perfects and makes sociable, supplying whatsoever is wanting in one Nation, out of the stores of the other; and by the exchange of Merchandises, contracting a friendly consociation.* Wherewith accords that of *Libanius, God,* saith he, *Hath not made any one part of the World, the Storehouse of all his blessings, but hath wisely distributed them through all Nations, that so each needing anothers help, he might thereby lead men to Society: And to this end he discovered unto them the Art of Merchandising, that so whatsoever any Nation produced, might be communicated unto others.* And therefore *Euripides* reckons Navigation amongst those things, which humane reason had found out for a publick good: So *Theseus* speaks very pertinently,

Nicetas l. 2.

De bell. Gall. lib. 1.

To hinder traffick with remote Nations is unjust.

In legatione ad Cajum.

> *What, to one Nation, Nature doth deny,*
> *That, She from others, doth by Sea supply.*

XIV.
Whether Tolls may be imposed on Merchandises.

But a Question will arise, whether upon such Merchandises as are thus transported either on Land, or in a River, or in some small parts of the Sea, which may be called Accesses to Land, Tolls may be imposed by him who hath the Soveraign Power in that Land. And doubtless if such Impositions have no respect to the Goods, there can be no colour of equity to impose them on the Goods: As if a Tax be laid by the Pole upon Subjects, to defray the charges of the Common-wealth; it cannot be required of Merchants, who pass as Strangers. But if either for the better securing of their Merchandises, or if for this among other things, the Prince shall be at any great charge, then to recompence that charge, Tolls may be imposed upon those goods that shall be thus secured, so that they be not excessive; for hereupon depends the Justice of Taxes and Tributes. Thus we read that King *Solomon* received Tolls for Horses and Linen Thred, passing by the *Syrian Isthmus*: So *Pliny* of Frankincense, that it could not be transported by any but the *Gebanites*; therefore there was a Toll paid unto the King for them: So the people of *Marselles* being exceedingly enriched by a Channel or Trench, which *Marius* caused to be made out of the *Rhine* into the Sea, *imposed a Toll for all Ships importing or exporting any kind of Merchandises,* as *Strabo* notes. And in another place he tells us, that the *Corinthians* did by a very ancient custom, require Toll for all such Goods as were carried over Land from Sea to Sea, to avoid that dangerous passage of *Malea*. The like did the *Romans* receive for passing the *Rhine*. Thus did the King of *Denmark* exact a quarter of an ounce of Gold, for every Ship passing the *Sound*, and as much for the Lading, with some other smaller Sums to maintain Fires, and Barrels to guide Merchants, that they might avoid Rocks and Shelves,

1 Kin. 10. 28. 12. 14.

Lib. 4.
Lib. 8.

as

as Mr. *Cambden* relates. *Nay for passing over Bridges is Toll in some places paid,* saith *Seneca. Yea and for passing over Rivers, as all our Law Books testifie.* But these Tolls are sometimes very excessive, whereof *Strabo* complains thus, *Difficile est ut inter validos & feroces definiatur modus mercatori non gravis*; *It is very hard to find amongst fierce and warlike Nations, such Impositions as are not to the Merchants grievous.*

There is likewise a common Right for all that travel as well by Sea as by Land, to stay and rest for a while, in any Foreign parts, either for health or for any other just cause. This being comprehended among things innocently profitable, and therefore *Ilioneus* in *Virgil* being forbidden to stay on the *African* Shore, presumed to invoke the Gods as Judges, and the complaint of the *Megarenses* against the *Athenians* for denying them admittance into their Ports, was allowed by the *Græcians* to have been just, as *being against common Right*, as *Plutarch* notes. The Shore is his that occupies it, and therefore they must needs be cruel who deny us things that are common. *Hercules* slew *Laomedon* for denying him the benefit of his Port: And the *Lacedæmonians* thought no cause of War could be more just, than to be denyed the benefit of the Shore. And consequently it is likewise lawful to erect a little slight Cottage on the Shore for present shelter, notwithstanding that, we do grant that shore to be possest by the people that are Natives: For whereas *Pomponius* requires an Order from the People or Prætor, to license any man to erect any thing upon the common shore or in the Sea, it is to be understood of such Edifices, as are lasting and permanent; whereunto tends that of the Poet, XV. A right in common to stay for a time. *Vit. Pericl.*

Contracta pisces æquora sentiunt,
Jactis in altum molibus.

——*Whilst Hills in Seas are cast,*
Fish frighted from their Holds, do stand agast.

Neither may we justly deny such Strangers as are driven from their own Seats, a right of perpetual cohabitation, whilst they shall submit to the Government established, and to other things necessary to avoid Sedition, which was very well observed by the Poet, where he brings in *Æneas* tendring these reasonable Conditions, XVI. A right to inhabit for such as are expelled their own Country.

——*Socer arma* Latinus *habeto,*
Imperium solenne socer.

And *Latinus* himself in *Halicarnassensis* adjudged *Æneas* his cause to be just, if being destitute of any other place of habitation, he were inforced thither. *Barbarum est hospites pellere*; *To drive those from us who come like Friends to visit us, or to dwell amongst us is barbarous.* Neither are the *Spartans* herein to be approved of: So St. *Ambrose*, *Their advice is not to be followed who would not have Strangers to live among them.* Thus did the *Græcians* receive the *Colophonians*, the *Rhodians Phorbantes* with his Associates, the *Lacedæmonians* the *Minyans*, as the *Cumæans* did others that came to cohabit with them. But when the same *Minyans*, being so received, demanded to share with the *Lacedæmonians* in their Government, *Herodotus* justly condemns them as ungrateful, *for pretending to that whereunto they could have no Right*; *whereby* (as *Valerius Maximus* observes) *that was turned into an injury, which was intended as a Courtesie.* *Lib. 1.* *Lib. 17.* *De off. l. 3. c. 7.* *Herod. l. 1. & 4.* *Pauf. l. 7.* *Oros. l. 7.* *Diod. l. 5.* *Lib. 4. c. 6.*

And if there be within the Territories of any Prince or People, any Land that is desart and incultivated, that also is to be granted unto Strangers if they request it, or they may lawfully possess it, because that which is not cultivated is reputed as desart, unless it be in respect of the Soveraignty, which remains notwithstanding with the people or Prince within whose Territories it lyes. *Servius* notes, that seven hundred Furlongs of Land being barren and hard, was by the old *Latines* granted to the *Trojans*: And we read in *Dionysius Prusæensis*, that *Nihil peccant qui partem terræ incultam colunt, They do no wrong that are willing to inhabit places desert and unoccupied.* The *Ansibarii* of old (in *Tacitus*) cry out against the *Romans*, for denying them some grounds that (as they conceived) lay waste. Thus, *As the Gods have reserved Heaven to themselves, so have they given the Earth to Mankind, every part whereof that lyes unoccupied, is common.* And then looking up to the Sun, and the Stars, he thus demands of them, *Vellent ne intueri inane solum? Whether they were willing to behold the Earth to lye desolate, and not rather that the Sea should overflow it, than to suffer such destroy-* XVII. Especially places desart and untilled. *Ad xi. Æn.* *Orat. 7.* *Annal. l. 13.*

ers

ers of the Earth to engross it, and to make no use of it? But these general sayings, though true, yet were ill applyed to the matter then in question: For those Lands did not at all lye waste, but served for the depasturing of all manner of Cattle belonging to the Souldiers, and might therefore justly be denyed them. No less just was that Query which the ancient *Romans* made to the *Gallisinones*, *By what Right they exacted Land from the Right owners, and in case of refusal threatned War?*

Livy l. 5.

XVIII. A right to such acts without which men cannot well live.

After the Right that is Common to things, follows that which is Common to some acts: And this Right is granted either simply, or upon supposition. Simply, This Right in Common is granted to such Acts, whereby those things may be acquired, without which we cannot conveniently subsist. I mean not here, such a necessity as justifies us in the taking away of another mans goods: For we discourse not here, of things taken away against the will of the right owner, but of the means how to obtain things convenient, with the consent of the owner; at least, that no impediment be given either by a publick Law, or any private Conspiracy: For in such things whereof we have spoken, such an Impediment is repugnant to humane Society. Thus *Plutarch* concerning the *Megarenses*, *They bitterly complained, that contrary to the Law of Nations, they were denyed traffick, and driven from all Ports which were held by the* Athenians. *What every Countrey abounds with,* saith *Seneca*, *is made known to all Nations, that all men might see the necessity there was of maintaining commerce among themselves, in case any Nation did want what another Nation had.* And again, *Whatsoever any people hath, that doth Commerce give to all, and those Countreys that are disperst and distant from each other, Traffick unites and knits together.* I speak not here, as to things superfluous or voluptuous, but of such only as conduce to the preservation of our Lives, as Aliment, Vestments, Medicaments, and the like.

Pericle.

The Right of Traffick common to all.

Ep. 87.

XIX. A right of buying necessaries.

To procure those things at an equal rate, every man (we say) hath a Common Right; unless they from whom such things are required, do themselves stand in need of them: As in the time of a Common dearth we usually forbid the transportation of Corn; *For, that the Natives should first be fed with the fruits of their own Land is but reasonable.* And yet in so necessitous a time, the strangers whom we have once admitted, we cannot expel. For, *Commune Malum communiter tolerandum*; *Common Calamities must be born in Common.*

Cassiod. l. 1. Ep. 34.

XX. But not always to sell.

But to sell their Commodities, it is not fit to allow every man the same Right; For every man is free to prescribe what he will buy, and what he will not. So the *Belgians* of old would not admit of Wine, and other exotick Commodities, to be sold amongst them. The like *Strabo* testifies of the *Arabians*, amongst whom some things might be imported, and others not.

XXI. A Right to contract Matrimony.

By this right it is Lawful for the people of one Nation to contract Matrimony with the people of another; especially, if being driven out of their own Countrey, they shall come to inhabit another. For though some men may live without the use of Women, yet others cannot. They are men of excellent tempers that can content themselves to lead single lives: And therefore to abridge them of the liberty of Marriage is an Injury offered to humane Nature. *Romulus*, in *Livy*, makes it his request to his Neighbours, That they would not disdain by Interchangable Marriages to mix generations with them. And *Canuleius* in the same Author pleads thus, *We*, saith he, *require but lawful Wedlock, which to Neighbour Nations and Foreigners is usually granted. What is unjustly denyed, may by the right of War be justly taken*, saith *Aug.* Now whereas the Civil Laws of some people do carefully provide against such Marriages; they seem to be grounded upon this reason, Because in the times when those Laws were made, there was hardly any Nation or People but were sufficiently stored with Women, or that those Laws were not intended to interdict all such Marriages, but such only as were Legitimate or Just; that is, which should produce some special effects of a Civil Right.

Lib. 1.

De Civit. Dei lib. 2. c. 17.

XXII. A Right to do such acts as were permitted to all strangers.

Among such acts whereunto a Right in Common is given by supposition, we are to reckon those which a Prince or People do promiscuously permit to all strangers; for that Nation is injured which is excluded. Thus if it be permitted in any place for strangers to Hunt, Fish, Hawk, gather Pearls; If it be allowed them to receive Legacies, to sell Commodities, if (even where there is no scarcity of Women) to contract Marriages, these cannot be denied to any one people, unless they have some ways abused their Liberty; for which cause it was, that the rest of the *Hebrews* denied to inter-marry with the *Benjamites*.

Judg. 20.

XXIII. I mean such as are permitted by the Right of nature, not out of grace and favour.

But this is to be understood of such Acts only, as are permitted, as it were, by vertue of that liberty which nature gives, being restrained or taken away by no Law: but not of such as are indulged to any Nation as acts of Grace, dispensing with the Laws; For to deny a Courtesie is no Injury.

Another

Another Queſtion is frequently ſtarted, which is this, Whether it be lawful for one Nation to contract with another for all their Fruits of ſuch a kind, which are no where elſe to be found, ſo that they ſhall ſell none to any other Nation. This in mine opinion may be lawful: If that people that ſhall ſo buy them, be willing to communicate to others at a reaſonable price. For it concerns not other Nations much by whom they are ſupplied with their Natural wants, ſo as they are ſupplied. And it is lawful for any to anticipate others in matters of profit, eſpecially if there be any ſpecial cauſe for it; as in caſe the people making this Contract, ſhall undertake the protection of the other people, and ſhall for that cauſe be at ſome expence or charge. For ſuch an Ingroſſing made with ſuch an Intent, as I have ſaid, is no way repugnant to the Natural Right; although it be ſometimes prohibited by the Civil Law, for the benefit of the Commonwealth. XXIV. Whether to engroſs all the fruits of one kind be lawful.

CHAP.

CHAP. III.

Of the Original Acquisition of things; where also of the Sea, and of Rivers.

I. *That things were originally acquired, either by division or occupancy.*
II. *Other ways refuted as the concession of Right Incorporeal.*
III. *As that also of Specification.*
IV. *Occupancy two-fold, either of Empire, or of Dominion: This explained.*
V. *That the Right of Occupancy, as to things movable, may by Law be prevented.*
VI. *The Dominion of Infants and Mad-men, by what Right held.*
VII. *That Rivers may be acquired by Occupancy.*
VIII. *Whether the Sea also may be so.*
IX. *Anciently in some parts of the* Roman *Empire, that was not lawful.*
X. *But as to such parts of the Sea, as are Included by Land on each side, the Law of Nature doth not Impugn it.*
XI. *How such a Right of Occupancy may be made, and how long it lasts.*
XII. *That such an Occupancy gives no Right to Impede an Innocent passage of Ships upon them.*
XIII. *That Empire over some part of the Sea may be gained by Occupancy, and how.*
XIV. *That Toll for certain causes may be Imposed on such as traffick by Sea.*
XV. *Of Agreements which forbid some people to sail beyond certain bounds.*
XVI. *A River changing its course, whether it change the bounds of the territory; explained by a distinction.*
XVII. *What is to be determined in case a River do manifestly change its course.*
XVIII. *That the whole River doth sometimes pass with the Territory.*
XIX. *That things clearly deserted become the next Occupants, unless the Propriety be held in general by some Prince or People.*

I. **How things become ours originally.** THings may become ours by a particular Right, either by an Originary, or by a Derivative Acquisition. Originary Acquisition (when men began first to associate together) might also arise by Division, as we have said; but now by Occupancy only.

II. **Other means refuted.** But some man may haply say, That somewhat of Originary Right may also be acquired by some service done, or by reason of some Pledge, *&c.* But to him that throughly weighs the matter, it will appear, That this is no new Right unless it be in respect of the manner; for it was first virtually in the dominion of the Lord.

III. *Paulus* the Lawyer, to the Causes of Acquisition, adds this, which indeed seems most natural, if we our selves have given being to that which we claim as ours. But since nothing can naturally be made without some pre-existing matter: Now if that be ours, the Species being introduced, the dominion will be continued. But if the matter pre-existing belong to none, then shall the Right be acquired by a kind of Occupancy: But if it it belong to another, then that the Right of Propriety descends not naturally unto us alone, will appear by what follows.

IV. **Occupancy two-fold, of Empire or Dominion.** Now let us examine, Whether that Occupancy, which after those first times, is the only natural means of gaining Propriety, be also the Originary. Of things that properly belong to none, two things are subject to be held in Propriety; namely, Empire and Dominion, as it is distinguisht from Empire: Which *Seneca* thus differenceth, *Ad Reges potestas omnium pertinet, ad singulos Proprietas*; *To Kings appertain the Soveraignty over all, to private men the Propriety or Dominion of what is theirs.* (*Ch. 5.*) And a little after, *Rex omnia Imperio possidet, singuli Dominio*; *Kings hold all by their Soveraignty, and private men what is theirs by Dominion.* And again, *Cæsar omnia habet, Fiscus autem privata tantum & sua*; Cæsar *hath all, yet is his Exchequer private only, and his own.* (*Lib. 10. Ep. 54.*) So *Symmachus concerning Kings, Ye Rule all, but preserve to every one his own.* Of the same mind was *Dion Prusæensis*, *Regio civitatis est, at non eo minus in ea suum quisque possidet*; *The whole Countrey is under the command of the City, yet in it every man enjoys his own.* (*Paneg.*) So saith *Pliny*, *The Empire of a Prince is much greater than his private Patrimony.* Now there are commonly two things that are subject to Empire; First, Persons, which alone sometimes sufficeth; as in an Army of Men, Women and Children, seeking new Plantations. Secondly, Lands, which are called Territories. And although both Empire and Dominion are usually gained by one and the same Art, yet are they in themselves distinct: So we find in *Apollodorus*, That the Lands as well in *Arcadia* as in *Attica* were divided, yet the Empire remained in one only. And therefore although the Dominion or Property of things do usually pass not to Subjects only, but sometimes

ſometimes to ſtrangers, yet may the Soveraignty ſtill remain where it was before. *Siculus*, in the Book that he wrote concerning the condition of Lands, tells us, *That the Fields belonging to their own Colonies being inſufficient, they that took the care to aſſign and divide the Land, did apportion to ſuch of their Citizens as came afterwards, ſuch Fields as they had taken out of the Neighbouring Territories*; contenting themſelves with the bare poſſeſſion, *but leaving the Juriſdiction over them unto thoſe whoſe the Territory was*. *Demoſthenes* calls thoſe Fields which lay within their own Territory, *Inheritances*; but thoſe that lay in anothers, *Poſſeſſions* only.

V. But in a place whoſe Empire is already poſſeſt, the right of Occupancy, as to things movable may by the Civil Law be anticipated, as we ſaid above. For this Right proceeds from the Law of Nature, rather permitting it, than commanding that it be always lawful: Neither indeed doth Humane Society require it. And if any man ſhould object, That the Law of Nations ſeems to juſtifie it; I ſhall anſwer, That although in ſome parts of the World it commonly is, or hath been ſo received, yet did it never amount to a Compact, or general Argument among all Nations, that it ſhould be ſo: but is rather from the Civil Law of many Nations diſtributed, which notwithſtanding may by any particular Nation be rejected. As indeed there are many other things which our Civil Lawyers ſeem to juſtifie by the Law of Nations, when they treat of the diviſion of things, and of the manner of acquiring Propriety and Dominion.

That the Right of Poſſeſſing things movable may by Law be prevented.

VI. This alſo muſt be obſerved, That if we reſpect the Law of Nature only, no right of Propriety can be admitted to thoſe who have not the uſe of reaſon. But the Law of Nations; for the common good, doth indulge this favour unto Infants, Ideots, and Mad-men, that they may lawfully receive and retain the propriety of things. All Mankind in the mean time favouring, and as it were ſuſtaining their perſons: For humane Laws may conſtitute many things that are preternatural, but not any thing that is againſt nature. And therefore that Right of Dominion that, in favour to ſuch, is by the unanimous conſent of all Civilized Nations thus introduced, may haply conſiſt with the firſt act of Dominion, which is a power to have and to hold things in propriety; but not with the ſecond Act, which is freely and voluntarily to diſpoſe of them by themſelves without a Guardian. For as to the Right of alienation and the like, becauſe in their own nature they imply the act of a *Will* guided with reaſon, which Infants and Mad-men have not: Therefore doth not the Law permit theſe acts unto them. Whereunto the Apoſtle alludes *Gal.* 4. 1. *The Pupil though he be Lord of all the Inheritance, yet during his nonage is no better than a Servant*; that is, as to the uſe and free exerciſe of his Right. We have heretofore begun to treat of the Dominion of the Sea, which we ſhall now compleat.

Upon what Right the Dominion of Infants and Mad-men is grounded.

Gal. 4. 1.

VII. Rivers may be held in Propriety, though neither the Water above nor beneath be included within our Territories, but do co-here with both, or with a part of the Sea. It is ſufficient to denominate them ours, that their greater part, that is, their banks on both ſides, wherein they are included are ours, and that that River, in reſpect of the Land adjoining, is but a ſmall thing.

That Rivers may be poſſeſt in our own proper Right.

VIII. But by this it ſhould alſo appear, that the Sea might have been held poſſeſt by him that on both ſides poſſeſſeth the ſhoar; yea, although it be open above, as a Gulf, or both above and below, as a branch of the Sea, ſo as it be not ſo great a part of the Sea, that being compared with the Lands, it cannot reaſonably be thought to be a part or portion of them. Now what is lawful to any one King or People, may alſo be lawful to two or three, in caſe they are willing to poſſeſs the Sea running alike, between them. So we have ſeen ſome great River gliding between two Territories, occupied by both at firſt, but at laſt divided.

Whether the Sea may be ſo.

IX. It is granted, That in thoſe parts of the Sea which were ſubject to the *Roman* Empire, from the former ages, till the Reign of the Emperour *Juſtinian*, the Law of Nations did forbid that any one people ſhould challenge any Right peculiar to themſelves in the Sea, though it were only the Right of Fiſhing. Neither can we approve of their opinions, who think, That when the *Roman* Laws do tell us, That the Sea is the Common Right of all, it is to be underſtood only of all the *Roman* Citizens: For firſt, the words are ſo general, that they cannot admit of ſuch a limitation; For what the *Latines* render in theſe words, *Omnium Commune*; *The Common Right of all*: *Theophilus* expounds by theſe, *κοινὸν πάντων ἀνθρώπων*, *Common to all men*. And *Ulpian* tells us, That the Sea is by nature as open and free for all men as the Air. And ſo doth *Celſus* aſſure us, That the uſe of the Sea is to all men alike Common. Beſides, Civilians do manifeſtly diſtinguiſh the publick things of the people, among which they reckon Rivers, from thoſe that are Common to all men: For ſo we read in the Conſtitutions, *That ſome things are by the Law of Nature, Common to all, and ſome things are Publick: By Natural Right theſe things are alike Common to all, The Air, Running Water, the Sea, and the ſhoar adjoyning: But all Rivers and Ports are Publick.* The very ſame alſo we read in *Theophilus* and others. Concerning the Sea Coaſts, *Neratius* was of opinion, That they were not ſo publick as thoſe things which are in the Patrimony of the people; but as thoſe which Nature at the firſt

Not ſo of old in ſome parts of the Roman Empire.

discovered, but were never ſince in the occupancy of any, no not of any one people: Which ſeems to contradict that of *Celſus*, who ſaith, *That to what place ſoever the* Roman *Empire did extend it ſelf, there the ſhoars are, as I conceive, the people's of* Rome: *But the Sea, as to the uſe thereof lies Common to all Men.* Which

The Seas and Shoars how Common, and how held in Propriety.

ſeeming Contradiction may be thus eaſily reconciled: *Neratius* ſpeaking of the Shoar, as to the neceſſary uſe thereof to Mariners, and to ſuch as paſs by, ſaith, That it is naturally Common; but as to any benefit or profitable Improvement of it, by erecting Forts, or other durable Buildings, ſo, as *Celſus* well obſerves, it is peculiar to the People of *Rome*. For, as *Pomponius* likewiſe informs us, ſuck Buildings could not be erected without ſpecial Licence from the Prætor, either on the Shoar, or in any part of the Sea, which was contiguous to the Shoar, and ſo reputed as part of it.

X.
That the Law of Nature doth not hinder, but that part of Sea cloſed by Land may be occupied.
Camd. Eliz. anno 1600.

Though theſe things be true, yet doth it ariſe from Cuſtome and Conſent, and not from the Law of Nature, that the Sea, in that ſence taken as is before declared, is not occupied, nor by right could be. So the King of *Denmark* having ſeized and confiſcated ſome Merchants Ships of *Hull*, for Fiſhing on the Coaſts of *Norway*, near *Iſland*, without leave, our moſt wiſe Queen *Elizabeth* pleaded, That the beſt Lawyers had adjudged the Sea to be free, and by the Law of Nations, Common to all; nor could be Interdicted by any Prince. And as to Cuſtome, ſhe anſwered, That neither his Great Grand-father, nor his Grand-Father, nor his Father had ever exacted it: But on the contrary, That his Father had granted, That the *Engliſh* abſtaining from Injuries, ſhould have freedom of Fiſhing without leave. For Rivers alſo are publick we know, and yet the right of Fiſhing in ſome corner or creek of the ſame River may properly belong to ſome private perſon. Nay, even of the Sea it ſelf, it is ſaid by *Paulus* the Civilian, That where it is the proper Right of ſome particular perſon, he may have an Injunction to quiet his poſſeſſion: for this is now a private caſe, for as much as it concerns the Right of Poſſeſſion, which properly appertains to private, not publick cauſes; where doubtleſs, he treats of ſome ſmall portion of the Sea let into ſome private mens ground: Which we read was uſually done among the *Romans*, as by *Lucullus*, and others; And, as *Saluſt* teſtifies, by many private men in his time, *who had ſubverted many mountains, and made Seas out of dry Land.* Whereunto *Horace* thus alludes:

Whileſt Mountains into Seas are caſt,
Fiſh frightned from their holds, do ſtand agaſt.

The like is recorded by *Paterculus*, *We*, ſaith he, *inject huge hills of earth into the Sea; and when we have made Mountains hollow, we let in the Sea to fill up the Concave. Pliny* likewiſe ſpeaking of the earth, ſaith, *That it muſt be embowelled to let in the Sea. With what great Bulwarks,* ſaith *Caſſiodore, are the Sea banks decently Invaded? How far doth the Earth encroach into the Bowels of the Sea?* So that as *Tibullus* writes:

Th' untam'd Seas with Mountains are immur'd,
That Fiſh from Winters ſtorms may lye ſecur'd.

Varro writing of *L. Lucullus*, ſaith, *That having cut through a Mountain near* Naples, *and thereby made a paſſage for the Maritine Rivers into his Ponds, he had ſo great plenty and variety of Sea Fiſh, that* Neptune *himſelf had not more.*

Vita Luculli.
Lib. 9. c. 54.

Plutarch alſo records the fame of *Lucullus*, *That having ſurrounded his Villages with Trenches and Channels even from the Sea, and ſo ſtored them with Fiſh; he made his Banqueting-houſe within the Sea it ſelf.* So doth *Pliny*, *That having at a vaſt charge dugg through a Mountain and let in the Sea, he was by* Pompey *the Great, called* Xerxem togatum. The very like doth *Valerius Maximus* record of *C. Sergius Orata*, *Who by letting in the Sea at Spring-tides, and intercepting its going out, made Seas peculiar to himſelf.* But the very ſame we find afterwards produced by the Emperour *Leo*, in oppoſition to the opinions of the Ancient Lawyers, about the paſſages of the *Thracian Boſphorus*; namely, That they might be incloſed within certain bounds, and poſſeſt as a private

vate

vate estate. Now if any part of the Sea may be annexed to a private mans estate, as being environed by it, and in respect of the Land, so small in proportion that it may be deemed as a part of it, and that the Law of Nature did not oppose it; why may not that part of the Sea which is contiguous to the Shoar, be reckoned as a part of his, or their dominions whose the Shoars are? Especially whilest that part of the Sea being compared with the Territory, is no greater than a small creek of the Sea, compared with the greatness of a private mans Land, wherewith it is encompassed. Neither will it much alter the case, to say, That those Seas are not on all sides surrounded, as may be easily illustrated by the example of a River, that is not every where begirt with Banks; or by the example of the Sea, that for conveniency of Importation is let into some Town, adjoyning to the Shoar. But there are many things indulged unto us by nature, which the Law of Nations, by common consent do prohibite: wherefore where this Law is in force, and not by common consent repealed, no one part of the Sea, though for the most part surrounded by the Shoar, can be claimed by any people as their peculiar Right.

And questionless, though the Seas be naturally free, yet as to any profit that may arise from that part of the Sea, that is contiguous to the Shoar, as by Fishing or otherwise, it may by custome or consent be possest by the Prince whose the Territories are. For the distinct dominion of that part of the Sea bordering on the Territorie of any Prince is best seen by the Taxes and Tributes which those Princes take of strangers for Fishing, whereof we have many precedents: As in *Russia*, where the Tax for Fishing is very great; insomuch that the *Hollanders* gave the tenth Fish. *Denmark* takes great Tribute at *Ward-house* and in the *Sound*: As also for Fishing in the North Sea, and even for Navigating that Sea between the Coasts of *Norway* and *Island*; as the Merchants of *Hull* lately found by sad experience: as *Sweden* also did heretofore when *Norway* was theirs. All the Princes of *Italy* do the like for Fishing on their respective Coasts in the *Mediterranean*. The Earls of *Orkney* in *Scotland* took the tenth Fish for the Isle of *Orcades*. So do the Lords of Mannors in the West of *England*, for *Pilchards*, *Hake* and *Conger*. The States lay Impositions upon the Fish taken within the Seas and Streams of other Princes, also on those taken on their own Coasts. *Edward* the Third of *England* took 6 *d. per* Tun in his time, which is now as much as 18 *d. H.* 7. resolved to set up the Fishing Trade in *England*, considering that it was most proper for him so to do, in respect of his domiuion in the North Sea. Queen *Mary* let a Lease of the Fishing of the North parts of *Ireland* for twenty one years for a certain Fine, and 1000 *l.* yearly Rent to be paid into the Treasury of *Ireland*. The *Hans-towns* had liberty of Fishing granted them in those Seas 1 *Mar.* upon some conditions, as appears by the Rolls of Chancery. And for the Fishing in the North Seas, Licences were usually granted at *Scarborough* Castle. King *James* set out a Proclamation 1609. to restrain all strangers from Fishing on the Coasts of *England*, *Scotland*, and *Ireland*, without Licence to be yearly granted.

Whether strangers may fish in those parts of the Sea that joyn to the Shoar of another Prince.

Natures Law Merchant.

XI. How such possession is gained, and how long it lasts.

But this also is to be observed, That where this Law of Nations is not yet received, or now abolished, the bare possession of the Coasts is not sufficient to entitle any people to a Right in the Seas adjoyning. Nor is it enough for a Prince to conceive, or to write himself Lord of the Seas, unless by some Overt Act he proclaim himself to be so. Besides, That Dominion that is acquired by occupancy may be deserted, and then the Sea returns to its pristine nature; and is Common to all, as the Shoars are, being destitute of buildings: and as the Right of Fishing in Creeks of a River, as *Pomponius* notes.

XII. Such Occupancy hinders not our Right to Traffick innocently by Sea.

But most certain it is, That the Right that is gained by Occupancy, extends not so far, as to give a Right to Impede any Nation from the benefit of a free passage; so as it be meerly for Innocent Commerce and Traffick, but not for depredation, or such like acts of Hostility; seeing that even by Land we allow the like freedom of passage, which usually is less necessary, and more offensive.

XIII. That the Soveraignty over some parts of the Sea may be possest, and how.

But that the sole Soveraignty over some parts of the Sea, without any other Propriety, may be held, may more easily be evinced: Neither (as I suppose) can the Law of Nations, whereof I have spoken, gain-say it. The *Argives* charge it upon the *Athenians*, as a manifest breach of their League, For that they had suffered the *Spartans*, being their enemies, to pass through their Seas unmolested; whereas it was expresly provided against in the said League, That neither party should permit the others enemies to pass διὰ τῆς ἑαυτῶν, *through any part of their dominions.* And (as *Thucydides* records it) when the *Grecians* had made a truce for some years in the *Peloponesian* War, it was allowed to the *Megarenses*, That they might freely and safely pass through their own, and their Confederates Seas. So likewise *Dion Cassius* describing some part of the Sea, doth it thus,

Lib. 6.

thus, *All that Sea belonging to the* Roman *Empire.* And *Themistius* also concerning the *Roman* Emperour, saith, That his dominion reacheth over Sea and Land. And to the same purpose is that of *Oppianus* to the Emperour,

The Seas do know no others Laws but thine.

Dion Prusæensis, among the many priviledges given by *Augustus* unto the City of *Tarsis*, adds this, That he gave them the dominion over the River *Cydnus*, and over the Sea adjoining thereunto. *Demosthenes* saith, That the *Lacedæmonians* governed all, both by Sea and Land: And he that wrote the life of *Timotheus* relates, That after such a time, the *Lacedæmonians* laid down their long continued claim, and voluntarily yielded unto the *Athenians* the Soveraignty over the Sea. *Curtius* of the City of *Tyre*, saith much to the same purpose, *That she sate as Queen in the midst of the Sea, extending her dominion not to her Neighbouring Seas only, but to all others whithersoever her Fleet should ride.* *Philo* the *Jew*, discoursing of Kings, saith, *That they add to their possessions Seas infinite in number and extent.* So he that penn'd that Oration concerning *Halonesus*, which is inserted amongst those of *Demosthenes*, speaking of *Philip* of *Macedon*, saith, *All that he desires of us is, That we would confess our selves unable to defend the Seas without him, and therefore that we would put him into the possession of them.* And the Emperour *Julian* speaking of *Alexander*, saith, *That he endeavoured by that War to make himself Lord both of Sea and Land.* Now what *Alexander* endeavoured to do, his Successor *Antiochus* claimed as his right, as appears by that Speech of his in *Gorionides*, Nonne terra & mare mea sunt? *Are not both the Sea and the Land ours?* So also did his other Successor *Ptolomy*, if *Theocritus* deceive us not:

Philip 2.

O're many Seas and Lands his Empire reacht.

And again,

All Lands and Seas, and roaring Rivers, lye
Under the Empire of King Ptolomy.

Now let us us descend to the *Romans*: *Hannibal* himself thus bespake *Scipio* the Greater, *We* Carthaginians *are confined within the Coasts of* Africk, *whilest ye* Romans *are known to lord it over Foreign Kingdoms, both by Sea and Land.* And of the Lesser *Scipio*, *Claudian* writes thus,

With Rome's *great Power, first in Revenge, he awes*
The Spanish *Ocean, under* Roman *Laws.*

All the *Roman* Historians do every where call the *Mediterranean* Sea their own: As *Salust*, *Florus*, *Mela*, and others. But *Dionysius Halicarnassensis owns them as Lords, not of the inland Seas only, which he bounds with* Hercules *Pillars, but of the Ocean, as far as it is not impossible for men and Ships to sail.* And *Cassius* grants, That their Empire extended *almost as far as there was either Sea or Land.* *Appian* describing the vastness of their power, assigns unto them the *Euxine*, the *Propontis*, the *Hellespont*, the *Ægæan*, the *Pamphilian*, and the *Ægyptian* Sea. And *Plutarch* makes *Pompey* Lord of all that Sea that lay within *Hercules* Pillars: So doth *Appian*. This also doth *Philo* against *Flaccus* acknowledge: *Since which, saith he, the Family of the* Cæsars *have got the Empire both of Sea and Land.* *Ovid* also speaking of *Augustus Cæsar*, saith,

——*Even*

—Pontus quoque ſerviet illi.

———*Even the Seas ſhall him obey.*

And *Suetonius* likewiſe records it in honour to the ſame *Auguſtus*, *That during his Reign the Temple of* Janus *was twice ſhut up, he having ſo often made peace with all Nations both by Sea and Land.* And in another place he tells us, That the ſame *Auguſtus kept conſtantly two great Fleets, the one at* Miſenus, *the other at* Ravenna, *for the defence of the Upper and the Nether Seas.* So alſo *Valerius Maximus* tells *Tiberius*, *That by the unanimous conſent of both Gods and men, the Soveraignty of the Seas was committed to him.* The very ſame doth *Philo* teſtifie of the ſaid *Tiberius*, *That his Empire comprehended both Sea and Land.* And therefore *Joſephus* ſtiles *Veſpaſian*, *Terræ Mariſque dominum*; *The Lord of Sea and Land.* The like doth *Ariſtides* in many places attribute to *Antoninus* the Emperour. *Procopius* tells us of ſeveral Statues of the Emperour *Juſtinian* erected in many places, as holding in his hand a Globe, thereby intimating, *That both the Earth and the Sea were ſubject unto him.* And *Conſtantinus Monomachus* is ſaid in Hiſtory to be *Terræ Mariſque Imperator & Dominus*; *Emperour and Lord both of Land and Sea.* Thus was the *Ægean* Sea made a part of the *Roman* Empire: And yet *Procopius* gives the Dominion of the Sea, at and about *Marſelles* to the *French*. The like do other Hiſtorians give to the *Venetians* in the *Adriatique* Sea. Now the Dominion in any part of the Sea may in the ſame manner be obtained, as other Empires are; namely, as is above ſaid, either by the numbers of men, as when their Fleet (which is nothing elſe but *Exercitus Maritinus, a Sea Army*) doth uſually ride in ſuch a part of the Sea: Or by reaſon of their Territory, when from the Land they can command thoſe parts of the Seas adjoyning as fully, as if it were all dry Land.

Goth. 3.
Of the right of the *Venetians* to the Soveraignty of the Sea: See *Paruta*.
How it is claimed.
Camden 1602.

XIV.
Of the lawfulneſs of taking Tolls by Sea.
Plin. l. 19. *c.* 4.
Strabo l. 17.

Wherefore it cannot be thought repugnant either to the Laws of Nature or Nations, for ſuch Princes as ſhall undergo the Charge of maintaining Fleets, to ſecure Paſſengers from Pyrates, or of Sea-Marks or Land-Lights, to guide Merchants through dangerous places, to impoſe equal and indifferent Tolls upon ſuch as ſhall receive benefit by them. Such was that which the *Romans* impoſed on all Merchants that failed by the *Red Sea*, to compenſate the Charge they were at, in ſending out every year a Fleet with certain Bands of Archers to ſecure them from Pyrates that infeſted thoſe Seas. And that Toll, which the *Byzantines* required from thoſe that paſſed through their Seas, whereof *Herodian* makes mention in the Life of the Emperour *Severus*. And that alſo which the *Athenians* did anciently exact, when they held *Chryſopolis* in the ſame Sea, as *Polybius* teſtifies: and that which the ſame *Athenians* required from thoſe that paſſed the *Helleſpont*, when they had taken *Byzantium*, as *Demoſthenes* records. The like doth *Procopius* mention in his Secret Hiſtory of the *Romans* in his time. The *Rhodians* alſo exacted Toll from the Iſlanders, for ſecuring the Seas from Pyrates; yea, and from *Pharo* at *Alexandria*, as we read in *Ammianus*. The like doth *Cæſar* teſtifie of the *Venetians*, *whoſe Seas being Tempeſtuous, and having but few Ports which they themſelves held, they made all that traffickt in thoſe Seas pay Toll.* So likewiſe *Florus* concerning the *Romans*, *That having loſt the Soveraignty of the Sea, and the Iſlands being taken from them, they were aſhamed to pay that Tribute, which they themſelves were wont to command.* The ſame *Procopius* above mentioned, as well in his Publick, as Secret Hiſtories, ſpeaks of an ancient Tribute paid in the *Helleſpont*, as alſo of a new Impoſition exacted in the Streights of the *Euxine* and *Byzantine Seas*, the one paid at *Blackhern*, the other at *Abydôs*, which was called δεκατευτήριον, that is the tenth of the Fraight, which was afterwards leſſened by the Empreſs *Irene*, and laſtly by the Emperour *Immanuel Comnenus* granted unto certain Monaſteries, as *Balſamo* informs us upon the Fourth Canon of the Council of *Chalcedon*, and upon the Twelfth Canon of the Seventh Synod. The *Danes* in Queen *Elizabeth*'s Reign, required a Roſe Noble of every Ship: and one piece of Money in the hundred, and laſtage for ſecuring the *Engliſh* Sailers through their Seas, to *Muſcovy*. Neither would they permit the *Engliſh* to fiſh in thoſe Seas, without leave, or an yearly Toll.

Camden Eliz. Anno 1582. *&* 1602.

XV.
Some people by agreement forbidden to ſail beyond ſuch bounds.

Some precedents alſo we find of Leagues, whereby one Nation is bound to another, that they will not ſail beyond ſuch bounds. So it was of old Articled between

tween the Kings bordering on the *Red Sea* and the *Egyptians*, that the *Egyptians* ſhould not come into that Sea with any long Ship, or with above one Ship of Burden. [*Philoſt. de vit. Apol. l. 3. c. 11.*] So it was agreed between the *Athenians* and the *Perſians* in the time of *Cymon*, [*Plut. Cymo.*] That no *Median* Ship armed ſhould ſail between the *Cyanea* and the Promontories of the Mountain *Taurus*. [*Diod. l. 11.*] This was that moſt honourable Peace mentioned by *Plutarch*, wherein it was alſo agreed, That the *Perſians* ſhould not approach nearer unto the Sea, than the length of an Horſe Race, that is, than forty Furlongs. And in thoſe Annual Truces of the *Peloponeſian* War, it was Articled, That the *Lacedæmonians* ſhould not ſail with long Ships, but with other Veſſels, which ſhould not carry above the weight of Five Hundred Talents. [*Thucyd. l. 4.*] And in the firſt League which the *Romans* (immediately after the expulſion of their Kings) made with the *Carthaginians*, [*Polyb.*] it was agreed, That neither the *Romans*, nor their Aſſociates, ſhould ſail beyond the Promontory called *Pulchrum*; but if at any time they ſhould either by diſtreſs of Weather, or by their Enemies, be driven beyond it, they ſhould carry nothing from thence but neceſſaries, and ſhould alſo depart within five dayes. Whereupon *Servius* upon that of *Virgil*,

—*Littora Littoribus contraria*—

obſerves, that *in that League it was provided, that neither the* Romans *ſhould approach the* Carthaginian *Shoar, nor the* Carthaginians, *the* Roman *Shoar.* Such another League there was made, between the *Romans* and the *Tarentines*, whereby it was provided, *that the* Romans *ſhould not ſail beyond the Promontory* Lacinium. So in the ſecond League that was made between the *Romans* and the *Carthaginians*, it was agreed, that the *Romans* ſhould neither traffick, nor take any Prizes beyond the ſaid Promontories *Pulchrum*, *Maſſia*, or *Tarſeium*; as alſo, that the *Romans* ſhould not touch upon the Coaſts either of *Africa* or *Sardinia*, unleſs it were to receive ſafe Conduct, or to repair their Ships. [*Liv. l. 48. c. 59.*] And after the Third Punick War, we find the *Carthaginian* Senate blamed, for that contrary to their League, they had raiſed an Army, and were making Naval Proviſions. The like we may read of the Sultan of *Egypt*, that by a League made with the *Gracians*, he had obtained liberty to ſend two Ships every year, through the Streights of *Boſphorus*. But yet were not all theſe ſufficient to prove, that either the Seas or the Right of Navigating them, may be held in Propriety by any one or more people. For, Nations as well as perſons, may by contract and agreement among themſelves, relinquiſh not only what is properly their own, but what belongs unto them in common with all other Nations, in favour to thoſe who may reap benefit by it. And yet in this caſe we ſay not, that the Seas could loſe their freedom; but that the people contracting and their ſucceſſor are obliged to perform their contract and agreement; that ſo the Law of buying and ſelling may be preſerved. And therefore both the preſent Occupants, and they that ſhould ſucceed in their Right, ſtand obliged by that contract.

XVI. *Whether a River changeing its courſe, changes the bounds of the Territories.* [*Jul. Frontin.*]

Controverſies do frequently ariſe between neighbouring Nations, whoſe Territories are ſeparated by the Intervention of ſome great River, whether ſo often as that River ſhall change its courſe, the bounds of both Empires do change with it; and whether, what that River, by altering its courſe, takes from the one, doth of right belong to the other: which diſpute cannot be determined, without firſt knowing the nature and the manner of the Tenure. Surveyors tell us, that Lands are of three ſeveral kinds; ſome are divided and incloſed with artificial Fences: ſome again are aſſigned by meaſure in groſs, as by hundreds of Acres or Furlongs; and others are called *Arciſinia*, becauſe (as *Varro* hath obſerved) Nature hath fenced them with ſuch bounds as are ſufficient to ſecure them from the Incurſions of an Enemy; as with Mountains, Woods and Rivers. *Pliny* ſpeaking of the *Alpes*, ſaith, *We carry away ſuch things as Nature ordained for Boundaries to ſeparate Nations.* And ſuch Lands are alſo called Occupatory, becauſe commonly they are ſuch, as being waſte and deſart, or being gained by the Sword, are held by occupancy. In the two former kinds, although the River do change its courſe, yet is nothing changed of the Territory, but what is gained by the River, is the Occupants. But in thoſe that are Arciſinious, that is, which Nature hath thus bounded, the River in altering by little and little its courſe, doth alſo alter the borders

Borders of the Territories. And whatſoever the ſaid River ſhall caſt to the adverſe part, ſhall be accounted his, to whoſe Territory it is added: becauſe it is very credible, that both people did at the firſt agree, that the midſt of that River ſhould be the Natural Boundary of both Empires. *Tacitus* accounts the Channel of the *Rhine* ſufficient to bound the *German* Empire. But *Spartianus* tells *Adrian*, *There are many places wherein the Barbarians are divided, not by Rivers, but by Land-marks.* And *Conſtantine* calls the River *Phaſis*, σύνορον, *the common boundary.* *Diodorus Siculus* reciting the Controverſie that there was between the *Egeſthenes* and the *Selinuntii*, ſaith, *That the River parted both their Territories.* And *Xenophon* calls the like River, ſimply τ̀ ὁρίζοντα, i. e. *the Horizon or Boundeer.* The Ancients record it of the River *Archelous*, that becauſe it kept no ſetled or conſtant courſe, but ſometimes branched it ſelf into ſmaller Streams, and ſometimes (like a Serpent) running in an oblique or indented Channel, it gave frequent occaſion of War between the *Ætolians* and the *Acarnanians* concerning the Lands adjacent, until *Hercules* immur'd it with Banks: For which ſervice *Oenus* King of *Ætolia* gave him his Daughter in marriage.

XVII. What if the waters do wholy forſake the Channel.

What I have hitherto ſaid holds true, in caſe the ſtream do not change its Channel. For a River as it divides Nations, is not to be underſtood barely as a Current of Waters, but as waters running in ſuch a Channel, and included within ſuch banks. Wherefore though in ſome particular places, it may gain or loſe, on either ſide, by reaſon of the weakneſs of the banks, or the violence of the Stream, and thereby beget ſome ſmall alteration: yet whileſt the whole body of the River retains its wonted form, the River ſeems to be the ſame. But if the whole River do at once change its Channel, then it is another thing. And therefore as when the old Channel is dammed up with banks of earth, above, and the waters thereby turned into a new one, which is dugg purpoſely to receive them, the old ceaſing, it is called a new River: So, if the old Channel ſhall be forſaken by reaſon that the waters have found out a new paſſage, it is not the ſame River that it was; but the old being loſt, the River is to be accounted new. And as a River, though dried up in a time of extream drought, yet is each Territory bounded with that mediety of the Channel that is next unto it; becauſe it may be ſafely preſumed that it was the will and intention of either people, to be naturally ſeparated by the midſt of that River: And that in caſe the River ſhould dry up, that either of them ſhould hold what they held before, ſo it is likewiſe, if the water ſhall wholly forſake the Channel. When queſtion is made of the bounds of an Empire, thoſe Territories that do reach unto ſome great River, are always reckoned to be Arcifinious, (that is) naturally bounded, becauſe nothing is ſo fit to bound Nations, as that which cannot eaſily be paſſed over; But that Kingdoms ſhould be bounded by either Land marks, or by admeaſurement is rarely ſeen; and where they are ſo, it cannot be thought to be done by Original acquiſition, but by conſent.

XVIII. The whole River ſometimes belongeth to one Territory, and none to the other.

Although where the bounds of Empires are doubtful, (as I have ſaid) each Territory is preſumed to extend to the midſt of the Channel, yet it may and ſometimes doth ſo fall out, that the whole River belongs to one Empire only; namely, when either the River was preoccupyed, before the Empire on the adverſe bank began; or when the matter was ſo determined by the conſent of both Nations.

XIX. That things clearly deſerted become the next occupants.

Neither ſhould it eſcape our obſervation to know, That ſuch things as have been occupyed, in caſe they be deſerted by the occupants, and have then no owner, may be held by him that ſhall next ſeiſe them, as by primary acquiſition; becauſe what no man can claim a right to, returns to its priſtine condition, and are really his, that can firſt apprehend them. But this alſo muſt be conſidered, That new diſcoveries are ſometimes ſo made at the charge of the Prince or people, That not only the Empire and Soveraignty, (wherein conſiſts that eminent right whereof we have already diſcourſed) but the private and full Dominion thereof, ſhould in the firſt place be generally veſted in themſelves; and after ſuch inveſtiture, then that it may be ſo diſtributed by parcels to private Families, that their Title ſhould ſtill depend upon the right of the firſt diſcoverers, if not as that of a Vaſſal upon his Patron, nor as that of a Fee-farmer upon his chief

chief Landlord, yet in some other more mild, and easie manner, as there are many ways, whereby we may claim a right to a thing. Amongst which is the right, of a man that hath but an estate expectant, committed to him though but in trust for another. Thus *Seneca*, *It follows not, because thou canst neither sell, waste or exchange what thou hast, that therefore it is not thine.* Tuum enim est, quod sub certa lege tuum est; *For that also is thine, which is but conditionally thine.* And again, *Quædam quorundam sunt sub conditione*; *To some things men may have a Right, though with some restraint and limitation.* To the same sense is that of *Dion Prusaensis*, *There are many ways and those very discrepant, whereby things may be called ours; for a right we may have to a thing, although we can neither alienate it, nor use it at our own pleasure.* The like I find in *Strabo*, *Dominus fuit dempto vendendi jure*; *It was his by right, yet had he no power to sell it.* now very opposite to what hath been here said, is that which *Tacitus* records of the *Germans*, *Who consigned to such a number of people, such a proportion of their fields to inhabit, which they presently divided, apportioning to every man, according to the honour and esteem they had of him.* By which means seeing that every mans Estate depended on the publick; if at any time it should fall out that any part of the whole wanted an owner, it was not his that could next seize it; but it escheated, either to the people in general, or to some Superiour Lord. And thus we read that in some places, the goods of such as died without children, were seized to the use of the people; and that there were certain Magistrates appointed to administer them. For so *Eustathius* interprets that of *Homer*,

De benef. l. 7. c. 12. & l. 8. c. 12.

De moribus Germ.

Partiebanter opes rectores urbis;

The City Rulers did his wealth divide.

Some such Law (as Histories inform us) there was anciently in force in the Kingdom of *Mexico*: and haply the Civil Law may have introduced such a kind of right in some other such like cases, as we have now begun to observe.

CHAP.

CHAP. IV.

Of a Presumed Dereliction and the following Occupancy: And wherein it differs from Prescription and Usucapion.

Note, Usucapion respects things moveable; Prescription, things immoveable. The former must be three years possest: the latter ten; but if the party be absent, twenty.

I. *Why Usucapion or Prescription strictly taken, is of no force among diverse Nations or their Governours.*
II. *Yet among these are usually pleaded, long Possessions.*
III. *The reason drawn from humane conjectures, and those not from words only.*
IV. *But from deeds done.*
V. *And from some left undone.*
VI. *How Time, joyned with non possession, and a non-claim is sufficient to ground our conjectures of a Dereliction.*
VII. *Ordinarily Time out of Mind sufficeth for such a conjecture; and what that time is.*
VIII. *An Objection answered.*
IX. *That setting aside conjectures, even by the Law of Nations, Dominion may seem to be transferred by possession time out of mind.*
X. *Whether the Right of such as are unborn, may be thus taken away.*
XI. *That even the Right of Soveraign Power, may be thus gained by either King or People.*
XII. *Whether the Civil Laws concerning Usucapion and Prescription, do bind them that have the Supream Power, explained by a distinction.*
XIII. *What Rights do either separably, or communicably adhere to the Supream Power, may be either got or lost by Usucapion or Prescription.*
XIV. *That Subjects may at any time lawfully assert their own liberty, refuted.*
XV. *Those Rights that are meerly in our own power, no time can take away.*

I. Long possession of no force among different Nations.

A Notable Question doth here arise concerning a long continued possession; For seeing it is the Civil Law that gives life and being to this Right, (For Time in its own nature hath no effective power: For nothing is done by time, although there is nothing that is not done in time †), it can be of no force, as *Vasquius* observes, between two free Nations or Kings, nor between a King and a Free People, no nor between a King and the Subject of another Prince, nor yet between two private Subjects of two several Kings or people. Thus were the *English* Commissioners answered, demanding *Calice* upon the Prescription of Two Hundred and Thirty years, *That Prescription of Time took no place amongst Princes. Camd. An. Reg. Eliz.* 10. For as we read amongst the Laws of the Twelve Tables, *Æterna Authoritas cum hoste isto; Our claim against an Enemy, i. e.* a foreigner, *is everlasting*: (So likewise in things stoln, the right Owner never loseth his property. For the word *Authority*, in that place signifies the Right of Dominion) which holds true, unless it be when either the Thing or Act is held, by the Laws of the Territory. But yet in admitting this, one main inconvenience would ensue; namely, that Titles to Kingdoms, and Controversies concerning their bounds, would never be at an end: which would not only procure much trouble and perturbation of mind among many, and occasion matter for War, but is repugnant to the common sense of all Nations.

† *Nihil fit à tempore, quamvis nihil non fit in tempore.*

II. Yet it is sometimes pleaded by them.

For, both *Jephtha* in the Sacred Story defends his Title against the Claim of the King of the *Ammonites*, unto all that Land lying between *Arnon* and *Jabock*, and from the *Arabian* Desarts unto *Jordan*, by an uninterrupted possession for three hundred years, and demands of him, why in so long a time, neither he, nor his Ancestors did ever challenge those Lands. And the *Lacedæmonians* also in *Isocrates* urge it, as a thing most certain and granted by all Nations, That publick possessions as well as private, might by long continuance take so deep root, and be so strongly confirmed, that they could never be recovered. By which Right they dismissed those that came to demand *Massena*. And thus doth the same *Isocrates* urge it against King *Philip*, *That length of time had rendred the Title Indisputable.* And upon this very account, it was that the latter *Philip* told *Titus Quintius*, *That as for those Cities which he had taken by the Sword, he was willing to set them free: but for those that he had received from his Ancestors by a just and hereditary right of possession, he would not relinquish them. Sulpitius* pleading against *Antiochus*, shews, That because the *Græcians* had sometimes served in *Asia*, therefore to endeavour by War, after so many years past, to reduce them again into bondage, was very unjust. And nothing among Historians *Tac. Ann. l. 6.*

O

τὰ πρὸ Εὐκλείδου. *De off. l.* 2.

Lib. 3. *c.* 13.

storians is reputed more vain and foolish, than to require things *long out of possession.* To the like purpose is that of *Cicero, With what colour of Justice, can we deprive him of those Lands, whereof for so many years, nay, ages past, he hath been quietly possest?* And that also of *Florus, Their Countrey notwithstanding which their Ancestors had left them, they held as firmly by prescription, as if it had descended unto them by an hereditary Right.*

III.

How things may be said to be forsaken.

Not by words only.

What then shall we say? The effects of Right that depend upon the mind, cannot notwithstanding by the sole acts of the mind be obtained, unless that act be declared by some overt signs: For to attribute so much of efficacy to the bare acts of the mind, as to create a Right, had been inconvenient to humane Nature, which cannot possibly understand them, unless exprest by some outward signs; whence it is, that those bare internal acts are not subject to Humane Laws. But there are no signs that can so clearly demonstrate those inward acts, as to render us infallible; for a man may dissemble his thoughts, and both mean and intend otherwise than he either speaks, or by some deeds pretends to do. And yet will not the nature of humane society admit, that these internal acts of the mind, being sufficiently exprest, should have no efficacy; wherefore whatsoever is so sufficiently signified, shall be held for truth, and be admitted of as a good plea against him, that shall so express his mind, which if done by words, the case is plain.

IV.

But by deeds done.

By deeds that is understood to be forsaken, which is cast away, unless it appear by some circumstance that it was so cast away only for a time, and with a mind to require it again. Thus a debt is said to be forgiven, when the bond is delivered up to be cancel'd: A man, saith *Paulus,* may renounce his inheritance, not by words only, but by any other indication of his will; as if he, who being the right owner of a thing, shall knowingly contract with him that usurps it from him, he may very well be judged to have released his own interest in it. And why this should not take place, as well amongst Kings and free people, as amongst private persons, no reason can be assigned: The like may be said, when a Prince shall give leave, or command his Subject to do that which cannot with safety be done, unless he be exempted from the penalty of the Law; it may be presumed that he is so exempted, for this ariseth not from the Civil, but from that natural right which every man hath to renounce what is his own; and from a natural presumption, whereby every man is believed to will that, which by signs he sufficiently declares. In which sence that of *Ulpian* may rightly be understood, where he saith, It is agreeable to the Law of Nations, that whatsoever a man accepts of in full of his debt, is a good discharge.

Whatsoever is accepted in full of a Debt is a discharge.

V.

And deeds not done.

Things given for lost, cease to be ours.

Under things done, are morally comprehended things not done, being considered with due circumstances; so he that is knowing and present yet is silent, seems to give his consent, which the *Hebrew* Law seems likewise to acknowledg, *Numb.* 30. 5, 12. that is, unless by some circumstance it appear, that either fear or some other accident, did restrain him from speaking; so is that given for lost, whereof there is no hopes of recovery, as a Lamb in the paws of a Lyon: So if a Merchant suffer shipwrack, his Goods cease to be his own, though they be afterwards driven to shore, yet not immediately (as *Ulpian* notes) but when he gives them for lost, and useth no outward means to recover them: For in case he send out and make enquiry after them, or promise a reward to those that shall find and restore them, the case is otherwise to be judged. So he that knows his own things to be by another man detained, and makes no claim unto them in a long time, unless some cause do manifestly appear; seems to do it to no other purpose, but to shew that he is willing to renounce them. And this is it that *Ulpian* elsewhere intends, where he saith, That an house possest for a long time by another, and no claim made nor rent demanded for it, seems to be deserted by the right owner. *To exact Interest long since due,* saith that good Emperor, *Antoninus, is hardly just; for the not demanding it in so long a space, makes it probable that thou wert willing to remit it; and that by not so much as demanding it, thy purpose was to make thy self the more beloved and honoured, and thy Debtor the more thankful.* Something like unto this will appear in custom, for even this setting aside the Civil Laws which are willing to admit it, (though limited to a certain time, and after a certain manner) may be introduced by a people that are Subjects, being long tolerated by him who hath the Supreme Power. But how long time is required to entitle it to the effects of a just right, is not determined, but left Arbitrary; yet so much is required, as is sufficient to signifie a consent. Now that silence should be of so great force, as to justifie our presumption of a Dereliction, two things are requisite: First, That he that is silent, knows that he hath a Right; for him that knows it not, silence cannot prejudice. Secondly, That his silence be free and voluntary, and not occasioned by fear or any other such cause, which if it appear, makes our conjectures at the Will, of no force.

Int. mony long forborn, presum'd to be forgiven.

That silence should argue a consent, two things necessary.

Vide infra Bo. 2. *c.* 22. §. 11.

VI.

Of what force time without possession is to prove a Dereliction.

That both these therefore may be thought to concur (though other conjectures may avail) yet is that of time most prevalent: For, in the first place, it is hardly possible that in a long time, a man should not by some means or other, arrive to the knowledg of his own Right; time usually administring many occasions to the discovery of truth. Now

if

if the right owner be present, much less time sufficeth to ground our conjectures, than if he be absent, setting aside what is determined by the Civil Laws: So fear once imprinted, cannot suddenly be cast off, yet can it not be perpetual; length of time supplying us with many occasions and remedies, both by our selves and from others against fear; and for providing for our own safety, even by going out of his dominions whom we fear: or at least by making our protestation concerning our Right, or which is better, by offering to refer our cause to indifferent Arbiters.

But because that time which exceeds the memory of man, is in a moral sence, infinite; therefore if claim be not made within such a time to any thing out of possession, it is a sufficient presumption that it is forsaken, unless some very strong reasons be brought to the contrary. And here it is very well observed by our most prudent Lawyers, That Time out of mind is not altogether the same with a Century of Years, though it be true that there is not much difference between them: For one hundred years is commonly reputed the term of a mans life, which doth well nigh make up three Ages or Generations; which the *Romans* seem to object against *Antiochus*, to prove the injustice of his demands, in requiring those Cities, which neither he, nor his Father, nor his Grandfather, ever enjoyed. Thus Queen *Elizabeth* pleaded against the King of *Denmark*, for the fishing upon the coasts of *Norway*, and *New Island* without leave, That neither his Great Grandfather, nor his Grandfather, nor his Father, had exacted it; and therefore concluded it to be unjust: Seeing also that the Sea is free for all by the Law of Nations. VII. Time out of mind, what it is. Time out of mind, not the same with a Century of years, though not much different from it. *Cambd. Eliz. an. 1600.*

Porphyry accounts thirty years for an Age, and *Herodian* in the life of *Severus*, accounts three Ages for a Century: *Philo* also reckons in three hundred years, ten Kings to Reign in *Egypt*, so *Plutarch* records fourteen Kings to have Reigned in *Lacedæmon* in five hundred years: And therefore the Emperor *Justinian* wisely forbad that any Title should be set on foot, that had been discontinued for four Ages. An Age what.

But here it may be objected, That seeing that men do naturally love themselves and whatsoever is theirs, it is not easily to be presumed, that they will cast away what is their own; and therefore such Negative Acts though long continued, can be no sufficient ground to conclude a Dereliction. But we ought also to believe so charitably of men, that they would not suffer one another to live perpetually in a sin unrepented of, for any thing that is vain and perishable, which cannot oft-times be avoided, unless we do grant such a dereliction. As concerning Empires, though they are held in great esteem among men, yet are they not without their burthens; for if they be not well administred, they expose the Governor to the wrath of the Supreme Judge: And as the case were sad, when they that are Tutors and Guardians should waste the Orphans Estate with needless Suits at Law, about the Right of Tutelage, or (to use *Plato*'s similitude to this very purpose) when Mariners in a Storm shall contend (to the endangering of the Ship) whether of them can best steer her; so they are not always the best Patriots, who can be content to sacrifice the publick peace to their own private ambition, and not without the vast expence of innocent blood, dispute, which of them can best provide for the peoples safety. Highly extoll'd by our Ancestors was that act of *Antiochus*, who being driven out of a great part of his Empire by *Scipio*, and confined to that only which lay beyond Mount *Taurus*, *gave hearty thanks to the People of* Rome, *for easing him of so great a burden, and for contracting his Dominions within moderate bounds.* Of the very same mind seemed *Jonathan* to be, willing rather to forego his right to the Crown, than to destroy his Country with Civil Wars, so that he might be but next unto *David*, whom he loved as his own Soul, 1 *Sam.* 23. 17. (It is said of *Otho*, the Emperor, that in his life he was as dissolute as *Nero*, but in his death as honourable as any of the *Roman* Emperors; for rather than harass his own Country with intestine wars, he chose to dye resolutely by his own hands.) Among those many grave Sayings bequeathed unto us by *Lucan*, this in mine opinion, is not the least: VIII. An Objection answered. *Cic. pro Dejot.* *Lib. 1.* *Val. Max. lib. 4. c. 1.* *Plut. vit. Othon. ad finem.*

——Cantone novorum
Proventu scelerum quærunt, uter imperet Urbi?
Vix tanti fuerat, Civilia bella movere
Ut neuter——

——Shall they my praises have,
Who seek by broils, which shall the State enslave?
'T had scarce been so much worth to expect whether,
As to provide by Civil Wars that neither.

But howsoever seeing that it much conduceth to the conservation of humane society, that Titles to Empires should at length become fixt and undoubted; therefore whatsoever proofs (though but conjectural) shall be brought in reference to that end, must be embraced Titles to Empires should be fixt and certain.

braced with ſome grains of favour: For if *Aratus Sicyonius* thought it ſevere to loſe what for fifty years he had quietly enjoyed; how much more was that of *Auguſtus*, who eſteemed him for a good man and a true Citizen, who would by no means alter the preſent State of the Common-wealth, but as *Alcibiades* in *Thucydides* ſpeaks, would help to defend that form of Government which was then in being. Of the ſame mind was *Iſocrates*, as appears by his Oration againſt *Calimachus*: And ſo was *Cicero*, who in his Oration againſt *Rullus*, tells the people of *Rome*, That it concerned him that would preſerve peace to defend the preſent ſtate of the Common-wealth, whatſoever it was. And *Livy* alſo who ſaith, that every good Subject ought to rejoyce in the preſent Government of publick affairs: But if there be any thing defective in what I have here ſaid, yet againſt that preſumption whereby it is believed that every man hath a will to preſerve that which is his own, there is another more ſtrong, that it is not credible that any man that would ſo preſerve what is his, ſhould not in ſo long a time lay ſome manifeſt claim thereunto by ſome fit ſignification of his Will.

The preſent ſtate of Government not to be altered.

Lib. 35.

IX.

Dominion hath been transfer'd by poſſeſſion immemorial.

But here it may be ſaid, and haply not improbably, that this depends not upon a bare preſumption, but that it was a Law introduced by the voluntary Right of Nations, that an immemorial and an uninterrupted poſſeſſion without any claim or appeal made to Arbiters, ſhould be of force to transfer an undoubted Dominion: And therefore when *Phocaa* was given to the Elders of *Catana* by the *Græcian* Emperors, *Gregoras* tells us, That there was a Law added, that every of their Succeſſors ſhould declare in writing that they held it under the Title of Adminiſtrators, leſt by a long continued omiſſion, the right of the Emperour ſhould be excluded: For it may eaſily be admitted, that what did ſo highly conduce to the publick peace and common benefit of mankind, might by the conſent of all Nations paſs into a Law. But this muſt be underſtood of an uninterrupted poſſeſſion, that is, as *Sulpitius* in *Livy* ſpeaks, *Such a poſſeſſion as is held by one and the ſame perpetual form of Right, always continued and never intermitted.* And as the ſame *Livy* in another place expreſſeth it, *A continued poſſeſſion that was never controverted*: For if it be inconſtant and deſultory, it avails nothing, as the *Numidians* ſometimes pleaded againſt the *Carthaginians*, *That ſometimes the* Numidian *Kings, and ſometimes the* Carthaginians, *held the poſſeſſion, as opportunities and advantages offered themſelves to either of them, and at all times he that was ſtrongeſt held it longeſt.*

Lib. 35.

Lib. 34.

X.

Whether the Right of thoſe unborn, may be thus loſt.

But a more knotty Queſtion yet remains, namely, Whether the right of ſuch as are unborn, may by ſuch a dereliction tacitely paſs from them? If we ſay it cannot, then neither can a long uninterrupted poſſeſſion, add any certainty to Dominion or Empire, becauſe there are few of them, but ſome that are unborn may pretend a Title to: If we ſay it may, then will it ſeem as ſtrong, how ſilence can prejudice them that could never ſpeak, as having as yet no exiſtence; or how the fact of one man may damnifie another. To reſolve this, we muſt know, that he that hath no viſible being, can have no right; as that which hath no exiſtence can have no accidents: wherefore if the people, from whoſe will all right of Soveraignty did originally proceed, may change their will; ſurely they cannot be ſaid to injure thoſe that are as yet unborn, ſeeing they have as yet no acquired right. But as the people may change their will expreſly, ſo may they be believed to do it tacitely; and therefore it being granted, that the people have changed their will, and that the right of thoſe who are as yet unborn, doth not exiſt, but that the Parents of whom they may be born, and who had a right in the mean time to have preſerved it for them did relinquiſh it; what ſhould hinder but that what is thus deſerted, may be occupied by another. Many examples we find in Hiſtories of ſuch Derelictions, the moſt eminent is that of *Lewis* the Ninth of *France*, whom we find renouncing for himſelf and his children, all that right which, by his Mother *Blanch*, he might have claimed to the Kingdom of *Caſtile*. *And thoſe renunciations, which the Infanta's of* Spain *do uſually make, whenſoever they marry to the Kings of* France, *are of force to debar them, and their Children, from all pretenſions to the Crown of* Spain. And thus much may ſuffice to be ſpoken of that right which is natural. For by the Civil Law, as many other Fictions, ſo this alſo may be introduced, that the Law may, in the mean time, ſuſtain the perſons of ſuch as are unborn, and may ſo provide, that nothing ſhall be poſſeſt by any other, to their prejudice; as the Civil Law doth for the inheritances of Infants and Ideots: But whether the Law will do it or not, is not raſhly to be preſumed, becauſe what thus conduceth to the particular benefit of theſe, may haply much endanger the Common-wealth. There is no doubt, but that ſuch a right may be eſtabliſhed by the Civil Law, as cannot lawfully be alienated by any one act, which, notwithſtanding, for the avoiding of the uncertainty of Dominion, may by the neglect of claim in ſome certain time be loſt, yet ſo, that they that ſhall afterwards be born, may have their perſonal Action againſt thoſe by whoſe neglect they have loſt their Right, or againſt their heirs.

He that hath no viſible being, can have no right.

Many examples of Derelictions.

*Mariana l.*13. *c.* 18.

XI.

That the Title to Empires may be got or loſt by Preſcription.

By what hath been already ſaid, it is plain; that a juſt Title may be gained by one King againſt another, and by one free people againſt another, not only by expreſs conſent,

sent, but by dereliction and the occupancy following it, creating (as it were) from thence a new Right or Title unto it: For as to that general maxim, *Quæ ab initio non valent, ex post facto convalescere non possunt, Those Titles which were originally naught, cannot by any post fact be made good,* is to be understood with this exception, unless some new cause do intervene, which, of it self, is apt and able to form a new right: And by this means, that is, by a manifest dereliction and a long possession, he that is a true King, may lose his Kingdom and become a Subject to the people, and he that was really no King, but a Prince, may become an absolute King: And that Soveraign Power which was once wholly in either King or People, may at length come to be divided among them.

XII. Whether Kings are obliged by those Civil Laws of Usucapion or Prescription.

But here it is not altogether unworthy our pains to enquire, Whether the Law of Usucapion or Prescription, having the stamp of the Soveraign Power, may bind him also that made it; or whether the very rights of Empires, or their necessary parts, which we have elsewhere explained, are subject to this Law of Prescription, and uninterrupted possession. Some *Civilians* are of opinion that they are, and those not a few, especially of such as handle questions concerning Soveraign Empire according to the Civil Law of the *Romans*. But we, with some others, are of another opinion; for that a man should be bound up by Laws, it is required, that in the Law Maker there should be both a power, and a will (at least strongly presumed) so to do. But no man can properly impose a Law upon himself, as a Superior upon an Inferior; for then the person commanding and the person commanded, would be one and the same: And from hence it is, that he that hath power to make a Law, hath also a power to change that Law, (and consequently not only to command according to Law, but to command sometimes the Laws themselves for the general good.) And yet a King may stand obliged by his own Laws, though not directly, yet by reflection, namely, as he is a part of the Body Politick, and so in natural equity ought to be conformable to the whole, as *Saul* in the Infancy of his Reign is said to do, 1 *Sam.* 14. 40. *So in a Ship, the Captain sustains two persons, one common with the rest, being carried also along with them, the other proper, as he is Governor, both of the Ship and those that are in it.* But here we look at the Law-giver, not as apart, but as one in whom the power of the whole is contracted: For in this place we treat of Soveraign Power as such: Neither is it easily to be believed, that it was the will of the Law-maker to comprehend himself under the Law he makes, unless it be where the matter and reason of the Law is universal, as in the apprising of Commodities, and the like. For there is not the same reason, that the Soveraign Power should be bounded and limited by the Law, as other things are, it being in dignity far above it; (for if we once admit it to be absolute and supreme, we must also grant it some Priviledges and Prerogatives above and before others.) I never yet found any Civil Law that treated of Prescriptions, that could with any probability be understood to include the highest powers: Hence then we may conclude, that neither the time limited by the Civil Law, can suffice to acquire a Soveraign Empire, or any of its necessary parts, in case these natural Conjectures, whereof we have here treated, be wanting: Nor is such a space of time required, if within that time sufficient conjectures of Dereliction shall appear. Nor lastly, doth the Civil Law, which forbids things to be acquired, within such a certain time, at all appertain to the things belonging to the Supreme Power: Yet might the people in the first Creation of the Empire have exprest their will, by what means, and in what space of time, the Government by not using it should be lost, which Will so exprest, ought without doubt to have been followed: Nor could it then have been infringed by the King himself, though invested with Supreme Power, because it appertains not to the Empire it self, but to the manner of holding it, as we have elsewhere explained it.

Kings not always bound by their own Laws directly.

Though indirectly they may.

Vide infra Bo. 2. ch. 20. §. 22.

Sen. Epist. 85.

No Prescription without strong conjectures of Dereliction can lye against a King as such.

XIII. What is not inseparable from Soveraignty may be got or lost by Prescription.

But what things soever are not essential to the Soveraign Power, nor belongs unto it, as its natural proprieties, but may naturally be either separated from it, or at least communicated with others, are also subject to the Civil Laws of every people, which are in force concerning Usucapion and Prescription. So we read of some Subjects who have gained by Prescription, that it cannot be appealed from them; yet so that always some appeal may be made from, namely by Petition, or some such like way: For that there should be no Appeal at all from any, is not consistent with the condition of a Subject, and therefore must needs appertain to Soveraignty, or to some essential part of it; nor can it otherwise be obtained, than according to the Law of Nature, to which the highest powers themselves are subject.

XIV. That Subjects may at all times assert their own Liberty refuted. *Vasquius* refuted.

Hence it is easie to discern, how far forth we may admit of that which *Vasquius* and others maintain, namely, that Subjects may at all times endeavour, if they can, to recover that liberty which belongs to a free people; because what was by force got may by force be regained: And of that which at first proceeded from the will, it is lawful to repent and to change the will; for both that Empire that was at first gained by force, may in time by the tacite consent of the people, yielding thereunto a willing obedience, receive a firm and established Right: As also that will, either at the first establishment of the

the Empire, or by a postnate fact, might be such as should give such a Right, as should not afterwards depend upon that will. It was an excellent Speech that *Josephus* records of King *Agrippa*, to those *Jews*, who from their preposterous endeavours to recover their lost liberty, were called Zealots: *Intempestivum est, nunc libertatem concupiscere, olim ne ea amitteretur certatum oportuit*; *To contend now for your liberty is unseasonable, this ye should have done before ye had lost it. To be enslaved to another is grievous, the miseries of War are to be preferred before it: But if being by the fortune of the War reduced into bondage, ye attempt to free your selves, Non amantes libertatis dicendi estis, sed servi contumaces*; *Ye will not be thought to affect liberty but rebellion.* So *Josephus* himself to the same *Jews*, *Honestum est pro patria pugnare, &c. To fight in defence of our Liberty whilst we have it, is honest, nay honourable*; *but having long since lost it, now to endeavour by Arms to recover it, is to make our condition, which was before tolerable, now desperate.* Thus did *Cyrus* in *Xenophon* answer King *Armenius*, who would fain have excused his defection by his earnest desire of his lost liberty, yet notwithstanding I make no question, but that a long continued patience in a King (as I have above described) may be sufficient for the people to recover their liberty upon a presumption of a Dereliction.

De Cyri Inst. lib. 3.

XV. **Things merely in our power are not lost by Prescription.**

Neither are those Rights lost by Prescription, that are not exercised frequently, but may be once at a time convenient; as the right of redemption of things morgaged or given in pledge: As also those Rights of our free liberty to do such other acts, whereunto that act already executed is not directly contrary, but is rather comprehended in it, as a part is in its whole. As in case a man hath entred into an Association with one of his Neighbours only, and continued the same for an hundred years, whereas he was at liberty to have done the like with others also within that time; those rights of his liberty, I say, are not by Prescription lost, until being prohibited to exercise it, or compelled to forego it, he obeys it, and sufficiently signifie his consent thereunto; which being congruous not only to the Civil Law, but to natural reason, may also be in force even amongst men of the highest fortunes.

CHAP.

CHAP. V.

How a Right over Perſons was originally gained: Where alſo the Rights of Parents over their Children, of Matrimony, of Colledges or Societies, of Kings over Subjects, and of Maſters over Servants, are diſcuſt.

I. The Right of Parents over their Children.

A Kind of Right may be gained over Perſons as well as things, and that either by Generation, by Conſent, or by way of Puniſhment, for ſome delinquency: By Generation, ſo both the Parents have equal right over their Children, yet ſo, that if they differ in their Commands, the Father, as being of the more noble Sex, is to be obeyed before the Mother. Of this mind was St. *Chryſoſtom*, *It is expedient*, ſaith he, *that the Wife ſhould be ſubject unto her own Husband, for equality in honour begets quarrels.* And St. *Auguſtine* alſo, *A Son born in lawful wedlock, is more at the command of his Father than of his Mother.* (1 Cor. 11. 3. — Ep. 191.)

II. This right differs according to the age and diſcretion of their Children. (*Vide ſupra c.* 3. §. 6.)

In Children, we muſt diſtinguiſh their three different times: The firſt is that of their Infancy, whilſt they are of unripe judgment, not able to know good from evil, not to diſtinguiſh truth from error. The ſecond is, When they grow to ripe judgment, but yet continue in their Fathers Family. The third period is this, When they are ſeparate from their Fathers and have Families of their own: During the firſt of theſe, all the actions of the Child ought to be regulated by the Parents; for it is but equal, that he that cannot govern himſelf ſhould be governed by another, and naturally there is none ſo fit to govern the Child as the Parents. And yet by the Law of Nations, the Child is then capable of inheriting an eſtate, though he be juſtly reſtrained from managing of it by reaſon of his immature judgment. This was *Plutarch*'s obſervation, where he ſaith, *That Children have a Right,* (*De fort. Alex. lib.* 2.)

Right, ἐν κτήσει but not ἐν χρήσει: to the Inheritance, but not to the use of it. Neither is it from the Law of Nature that all that is the Childs, ſhould be diſpoſed of by the Parents; but from the Laws of ſome people, which do in this caſe ſometimes diſtinguiſh the Father from the Mother, as they do alſo between their bond, and free children, and between the natural iſſue and legitimate: of which diſtinction the Law of Nature takes no Cognizance, except only of the priviledges of Sexes, where both Parents contend who ſhall command the Child.

III. The Second Period. Whileſt the Child is a part of the Parents Family.

In the ſecond period, when the Childs Judgement is ripened with his years, yet abiding in his Fathers houſe, thoſe actions of the child only are ſubject to the commands of his Parents, that are of moment to the well ordering of the eſtate of his Father, or of his mothers Family. For it is but reaſonable, that every part ſhould endeavour the welfare of the whole. But in his other actions he hath a moral power to do whatſoever his own judgement ſhall guide him to, provided that in all things he endeavour as far as in him lies, to pleaſe his parents. But becauſe this is a debt ariſing not by vertue of that moral faculty, as thoſe above, but from the duty of piety, reverence, and gratitude; it cannot make void thoſe actions of his that are otherwiſe done, no more than it will ſuffice to avoid any grant or gift, given by the right owner, to ſay, That it was againſt the Rules of Parſimony.

IV. Of Parents coercive power.

During both theſe ſpaces of time, Parents have a Right not to govern only but to puniſh, and to enforce obedience from their children, ſo far forth, as they ought to be either compelled to their duty, or to reform what is amiſs. But as to greater puniſhments, we ſhall diſcourſe elſewhere.

V. Their power to ſell them. *Hiſt. Goth.* *Lib.* 2.

Although the Paternal Right be ſo inherent in the Fathers perſon, as that it can no ways be either taken from him, or transferr'd to another, yet naturally, if the Civil Laws do not reſtrain, the Father hath power to pawn, or (if neceſſity ſo require) to ſell his ſon, if he have no other way or means to maintain him: *Thus the* Goths (as *Jornandes* records) *ſolicitous of their Childrens ſafety, chuſe rather to preſerve their lives than their liberties; and therefore in Compaſſion, thought it better to ſell them to be kept and nouriſhed as ſlaves, than to ſuffer them to dye in defence of their freedome.* Which Right other Nations ſeem to have borrowed from that old *Theban* Law (recited by *Ælian*) which alſo ſeems to be derived from the *Phœnicians*, and alſo from the *Hebrews*, and by them to the *Grecians*, as *Apollonius* obſerves in his Epiſtle to *Domitian*: For Nature it ſelf is preſumed to give us a right to all that, without which that which ſhe commands, cannot be obtained.

VI. Their power over them when ſeparate from them.

In the Third ſpace or period, that is, when the Children are grown to maturity, and in another Family by themſelves, then they are free to do what pleaſeth themſelves, always paying the duty of piety and reverence to them, which is an obligation never to be cancelled; whence it follows, that the acts of Kings are not therefore null'd, becauſe their parents are living.

VII. The Rights of Parents are either Natural or Civil. The *Romans* gave as much power over their Sons as over Slaves. *Pyrrhoniorum*, 3. *In legatione.*

What power Parents have over their children more or leſs than this, they derive from the poſitive Laws of men, which in all Nations are not the ſame. So by that right that God gave unto the *Hebrews*, the power of a Father to null the vows of his Sons and Daughters was not perpetual, but only during their abode in their Fathers family: As may appear *Numb.* 30. 2, 3, 4, 5 verſes. For otherwiſe the Son being parted from his Father, had power at thirteen years of age to bind himſelf without the conſent of his parents. The *Roman* Citizens, being Fathers, had a peculiar power over their Sons, though they were heads of their own Families, before they were made free: which power they themſelves confeſs that other people had not over theirs. So ſaith *Sextus Empericus*, *The* Roman *Law-givers gave as much power to parents over their children as over their ſlaves; for the goods of the Children were not reputed theirs, but their Parents, until they were mannmitted in the very ſame manner as their ſlaves were*: Which other Law-makers rejected as Tyrannical. The like doth *Philo* record of them, *All manner of power over the Son was by the* Romans *given to the Father.* The ſame doth *Simplicius* teſtifie, *The Ancient* Roman *Laws reſpecting as well the dignity of the Father, as their great pains and care in the education of their children, the better to tye them up in the ſtricteſt bonds of obedience without exceptions; yet* (as I believe) *preſuming upon their natural affection*, Et venundandi ſi vellent, & impune interficiendi, parentibus jus dederunt; *Gave the Parents abſolute power either to ſell, or if they would, to kill their own children.* The like Power given to Parents over their Children by the *Perſians*, *Ariſtotle* condemns as Tyrannical: Which I was therefore willing to inſert, that ſo we might the more exactly diſtinguiſh between the Natural and Civil Rights of Parents over their Children.

VIII. A Right over perſons by conſent. Of an Husband over his Wife.

The Right that is gained over perſons by conſent, is gained either by Conſociation, or by Subjection. Of that which ariſeth from Conſociation, the moſt natural is that of Wedlock, wherein all things are Common: Yet the Right of Command, which is the Prerogative of the Husband, as being of the nobler Sex, is not Common. For he is the head of the Wife, as well in Conjugal, as in houſhold affairs: For the Wife is but a

part

part of the Husbands Family: And therefore it is the Husbands Right to appoint Laws in his own house. But what Power soever it is that is given to the Husband beyond this, as by the *Hebrew* Law, the Husband had power to make void all the Vows made by his Wife, and by the Laws of some people, he had power to sell away all his Wives goods: This ariseth not from the Law of Nature, but from the voluntary Laws of men. And here it is requisite that we enquire into the nature and essence of Matrimony. And we find Marriage (taken naturally) to be nothing else, but such a co-habitation of a man with a woman, as placeth the Woman, as it were, under the eye, (that is) under the safeguard of the man. For such a Consociation we may observe to be among dumb creatures. But because men are governed by reason, therefore it is required from the Woman that she be faithful and obedient unto her Husband, (for Subjection is rationally due to Protection.) Matrimony what.

IX. Whether the tie of one man to one woman inseparably be by the Natural or Evangelical Law only.

Surely Nature seems to require no more to the constitution of Marriage than Cohabitation and Protection. Neither did the Law of God require more before the publishing of the Gospel: For diverse holy men before the Law, had several Wives at the same time. St. *Chrysostome* speaking of *Sarah* saith, *That it was some comfort against her barrenness, to have children by her husband, though begotten on her hand-maid*; *Nondum enim talia tunc vetita erant*; For such things were not as yet forbidden. So St. *Augustine* †, *There was then no Law given against the having of many Wives for propagation sake.* And in another place, *Erat uxorum plurium simul habendarum tunc inculpabilis consuetudo*; *The Custome of having many Wives at once, was then unblameable.* And even under the Law we find some Precepts given to those that should have many Wives at once. And we find it expresly forbidden to their Kings to be excessive in accumulating either Wives or Horses, wherefore the *Hebrew* Doctors upon that place do limit their Kings to eighteen Wives and Concubines, and no more. And *Josephus* acknowledges, That to have many Wives at once was *Mos patrius*, The Custome of his Countrey. Therefore God himself seems to upbraid *David*, For that he had given him his Masters Wives and Concubines, *Quas justè & legitimè habere posset*; *Whom he might justly and lawfully enjoy*, saith *Josephus*. Neither was this knot of Marriage under the Law indissoluble as now it is; For we find a prescript Form to him that was willing to put away his Wife. . Neither was any man forbidden to marry the person repudiated, but he only that put her away, and the Priest, who also is in the same place forbidden to marry a Widow or an Harlot. Now whereas *Philo*, and many modern Interpreters, do understand this to be meant of the High Priest only, by reason of that which follows, *ver.* 10. It is evident by that of *Ezek.* 44. 22. That every Priest was thereby forbidden; as may also be easily collected from the connexion of this seventh verse, with the verses preceding. But yet this liberty that was thus given to the woman that was repudiated to become another mans Wife, was by the Law of Nature, restrained to a certain time after her Divorce, to avoid confusion about her issue. To prevent which, the *Jews* did require, That there should be three months interval, between the Divorce and the second Marriages; whence arose that question in *Tacitus*, *Whether a Woman having conceived, might be married before her delivery.* But the Christian Law hath reduced this, as many other things besides, to a more perfect rule, whereby both he that puts away his Wife, unless for the act of Uncleanness, and he that marries her that is put away, are both pronounced guilty of Adultery. And St. *Paul*, who was both his Apostle and Interpreter, doth give not only to the Husband the power over his Wives body, which he had before under the state of Nature, (For he that joins himself to a Woman in Marriage, *in corpus ejus habet dominium*; *hath power over her body*, saith *Artemidorus*) but to the Wife likewise power over the body of her Husband, thereby making the obligation mutual, and the transgression, on either part, equal. So *Lactantius*, *The Divine Law doth so conjoin two persons in Matrimony, that is, into one body, on such equal terms, that whosoever shall violate this bond, or cut asunder this knot, shall be reputed an Adulterer.* And therefore he presently subjoyns, *By thine own example thou art to teach thy wife Chastity.* Iniquum est, ut id exigas, quod ipse præstare non possis; *It is very unjust to exact that from her, which thou canst not perform thy self.* To the same sense, and almost in the same words, speaks *Nazianzene*, *Being equally bound*, Quomodo exigis, quod non rependis? *With what Conscience canst thou exact that which thou refusest to pay?* To the same purpose is that of St. *Jerome* to *Oceanus*, *The Laws of* Cæsar *are one thing, and the Laws of* Christ *another*; Papinian *commands one thing, and St.* Paul *another: By the former, the Reins of our unbridled lusts are let loose; and Adultery only being condemned every where, Men are permitted to frequent the Stews and Brothel-houses without restraint*, Quasi dignitas culpam faciat, non voluntas; *As if it were the Sex that made the crime, not the will. But with us what is unlawful for women is equally unlawful for men.* The same yoke binds both to the like conditions.

†*De Civit. Dei lib.* 16. *c.* 38.
De Doct. Christ. lib. 4. *c.* 12.
Deut. 21. 15. 17. 16, 17.
2 Sam. 14. 8.
Ant. Hist. l. 17. *c.* 1.
Nor was this knot indissoluble.
Lev. 21. 7.
Whether a Woman having conceived might marry before delivery.
The Christian Law.
Inst. l. 6. *c.* 23.

There are some that are of opinion, That our blessed Saviour in the fore-cited places, namely, *Mat.* 5. 32. and *Mat.* 19. 9. did not ordain a new Law, but only restore the old; Objection.

P

old: Alledging for themſelves the very words of our Saviour, which ſeem to reduce us to the Original Inſtitution, *Ab initio non fuit ſic*; *From the beginning it was not ſo.*

Anſwered.

Whereunto we may anſwer, That from our firſt condition, when God to one man gave but one Woman; we may well collect what was beſt for man, and what moſt acceptable to God: And from thence conclude, That to walk by the ſame Rule was ever moſt ſafe and commendable. But we cannot from thence infer, That to have many Wives was ſinful: For where there is no Law, there can be no tranſgreſſion. But in thoſe times there was no ſuch Law extant. So alſo, when God ſaid, whether by *Adam* or by *Moſes*, That this League of Matrimony was ſo ſacred and ſtrict, that the Husband was obliged to ſeparate himſelf from his Fathers houſe, and together with his Wife plant another family: It was no more than what was ſaid to *Pharaoh*'s daughter, *Pſal.* 45. 11. *Forget alſo thine own people, and thy Fathers houſe.* And although we may collect from this ſtrong conſignation, how acceptable it would be to God that it ſhould be perpetual, yet it cannot from hence be evinced, That even then it was commanded that this knot ſhould not be, for any cauſe whatſoever, diſſolved. St. *Ambroſe*, in the caſe of Polygamy, diſtinguiſheth that which God commends in Paradiſe from condemning the contrary. But Chriſt forbids any man to ſeparate thoſe, whom God by his firſt Inſtitution did conjoyn, making that a matter worthy of his new Law, which he knew to be beſt for men, and moſt acceptable to God.

Lib. 1. *c.* 14. *de Abraham.*

*Grat.c.*33. *q.*4.

Moſt Nations tolerated Divorce and Polygamy.

De moribus Germ.

Herodian l. 2.

Certain it is, that moſt Nations in ancient times did both indulge unto themſelves the liberty of Divorces, and alſo of enjoying plurality of Wives. Of all barbarous Nations the *Germans* were well nigh the only people, recorded by *Tacitus*, that were contented with one Wife: But the *Perſian*, *Indian*, and *Thracian* Hiſtories do clearly teſtifie the lawfulneſs among them both of Polygamy and Divorces. Amongſt the *Ægyptians* their Prieſts only were reſtrained to one Wife. And amongſt the *Grecians*, as *Athenæus* tells us, *Cecrops* was the firſt that allowed to one man but one Wife. And yet, that this was no long-liv'd practice among the *Athenians*, we are taught by the example of *Socrates* and others. And if haply any people did live more abſtemiouſly, as the *Romans*, who never admitted of Bigamy, nor in a long time, of Divorces, they were certainly highly to be commended, in that they drew near unto that which was moſt perfect. And yet will it not hence follow, That they who did otherwiſe before the promulgation of the Chriſtian Law did therein ſin: For as St. *Auguſtine* rightly obſerves *, *Quando mos erat, crimen non erat*; Whileſt it was a Cuſtome it was no Crime, (at leaſt not imputed as ſo.)

**Contr. Fauſt. lib.*22.*c.* 47.

Every Nation hath its ſeveral qualites wherein they differ no leſs than in their peculiar Language, which diſagreeing conditions to govern aptly, no one and the ſame Law can ſuffice. The moſt high God permitted ſome things in the *Iſraelites* for the hardneſs of their hearts, which were not conſonant to the rules of perfection; where therefore nature or cuſtome have entertained a vicious, yet not intolerable habit, with ſo long and publick approbation, that the oppoſite vertue would ſeem as uncouth as it would be to walk naked in *England*: There may a wiſe and upright Law-giver conceal for a while his inward diſlike, till time make way for a more compleat Reformation.

Eſt aliquid prodire tenus, ſi non detur ultra.

For want of diſcretion in this caſe, the Kingdom of *Congo* in *Africa* was unhappily diverted from Chriſtianity, which it willingly at firſt embraced; but afterwards with great Indignation rejected, for no other reaſon, but becauſe Plurality of Wives, was (I know not how neceſſarily but I am ſure) more contentiouſly, than ſeaſonably denied unto them. For where a vice cannot be rooted out, without the ruine of a ſtate, it is acceptable to God, for a time to connive at it.

See Rawl. p. 293.
See 2 *Chron.* 30. 18, 19.
Hiſtory of the Council of Trent, p. 63.

X.
What Marriages are juſtifiable by the Law of Nature.

Now let us ſee what Marriages are good by the Law of Nature. To direct our judgements herein we muſt remember, *That not every thing that is repugnant to the Law of Nature, is made void by the Law of Nature*; As appears by things prodigally given away: but thoſe only wherein that principle is wanting, which ſhould give life and vigour to the act; or in which, all its effects are vitiated and tainted. Now that principle which gives life to this and all other humane acts, is that Right which we expounded to be a moral power or faculty to do it, together with a will ſufficiently declared. But what Will may be ſufficient to produce a Right, we ſhall have occaſion to declare more fully when we ſhall diſcourſe of promiſes in general. But concerning this moral power, the firſt queſtion is, Whether the conſent of Parents be by the Law of Nature requiſite to a perfect Marriage, which ſome affirm. But herein they are miſtaken: For all their Arguments do enforce no more than this, That it is agreeable to the duty they owe to their Parents, to crave their conſents: Which we ſhall eaſily grant them, provided that the will of their Parents be not manifeſtly unjuſt. For if Children be to reverence their Parents in all things, ſurely they ought to do it moſt eſpecially in ſuch things wherein the whole Nation is concern'd, as in Marriages. And yet it cannot hence be inferred, That a Son hath not a Moral Right to diſpoſe of himſelf, if they conſent not. For he that marries, ought

Whether the conſent of Parents be requiſite to a perfect Marriage, by the Law of Nature.

ought to be of mature age and judgement, and he is to forsake his Fathers house, so that he is herein exempted from his Fathers domestick discipline. (*And becomes from thence* αὐτεξούσιος , *Master of himself.*) And although the duty of love and reverence do oblige him to ask the good will of his Parents, yet doth not the breach of that duty null the act of his Marriage. That the *Romans* and such other Nations did make void such Marriages was not from the Law of Nature, but from the will of their Law-makers. For by the same Law, the mother to whom notwithstanding the children do naturally owe reverence, could not by her descent, make the Marriage void ; no, nor the father of a Free-man: And if the Father himself be under the power of his own Father, then the consents of both Father and Grand-father, are required to the Sons Marriage : But to the Marriage of a Daughter, the Grand-fathers consent alone sufficeth. Which differences being altogether unknown to the Law of Nature, doth evidently prove, that they arise not from the Natural, but from the Civil Laws.

We find in Sacred story, That many holy men, and much more, women (who by reason of their modesty and bashfulness ought especially in this case to be governed by others) have in contracting Marriages submitted themselves to the authority of their Parents : *Non est virginalis pudoris, eligere maritum* ; It becomes not a Virgins modesty, saith *Ambrose* †, to chuse an Husband for her self. And yet was not *Esau's* Marriage declared null, nor his Children held as Illegitimate, because in his Marriage he had not the consent of his Parent: It is true, *That as to Daughters, the chief power of disposing them is in the Father.* So in *Euripides Hermione*,

Virgins not to chuse Husbands for themselves. 1 Cor. 7. 36. *Lib.* 1. *de Abrah. c. ult.* † *Grat. c.* 32. *q.* 2.

My Nuptial I to Parents care alone
Commit ; for free choice therein have I none.

But as to Sons, If we respect strict and Natural Right, that of *Quintilian* will be found true, *That if it be lawful for a Son at any time to do things otherwise unreprovable, without, yea against his Fathers will* ; *surely that liberty is never more justifiable than in Marriage :* For as *Cassiodore* truly observes, *Durum est, libertatem liberam non habere in Matrimonio, unde liberi procreantur* ; *To be debarr'd of our free choice in Matrimony, from whence our Children should be born, is hard* ; *nothing is more plain than that a Son in his Marriage should please himself.*

Lib. 7. *c.* 4. *Ter. Andr. Act.* 1. *sc.* 5.

XI. *It is a void Marriage that is contracted with anothers Wife or Husband.*

That Marriage that is contracted with another mans Wife, is doubtless null by the Law of Nature, unless her former Husband have dismist her : For so long doth his power last over her, which by the Evangelical Law is not dissolved but by death. The latter Marriage therefore is null, for want of a moral power in the woman to dispose of her self, which being lost by her former Marriage doth vitiate all those subsequent effects that attend it ; because every Act is but the invading of anothers Right. So likewise on the other side by the same Law, a Marriage contracted with the Husband of another Woman is alike void, by reason of that power that Christ gives a chaste Wife over the body of her Husband.

XII. *Of Marriages between kindred.*

Concerning Marriages between such as are nearly allied, or of the same blood, many difficult questions arise, which are often with much zeal and animosity agitated on both sides. Because he that shall undertake to assign certain and natural reasons, why these Marriages (that are by Law or Custome thus forbidden) are unlawful, should experimentally find how hard, nay how impossible, it is to effect it. That alledged by *Plutarch* in his *Roman* Questions, by St. *Augustine* in his Book *De Civitate Dei*, by *Philo* in his Special Laws, and by St. *Chrysostome* on 1 *Cor.* 13. 13. as the contracting of new Friends, and the strengthning our selves with new Alliances, favours more of Policy than true Piety : Nor are they of that force and energy as to conclude the contrary Acts to be either unlawful or void. Whereunto may be added, That some cases there may be, wherein such prohibited Marriages may be more profitable and politick than others, as may be collected, not only from that which God himself in his Law given to the *Jews* excepts, of raising Seed to a deceased Brother having no issue : But from that also of a Virgin left by her Father, as sole heir of all his estate, who by the *Grecian* and *Hebrew* Laws, was to be Married to the next of kin, to preserve the name and Estate in their own Tribe and Family ; and from many such like cases which do, or may occur.

The Marriage of kindred sometimes profitable and politick.

Incestuous Marriages forbid by the Law of Nature, and why.

But yet from this general rule, we must except the Marriages of Parents with their Children in what degree soever, the reason whereof is sufficiently evident. For neither can the Husband, who by the Law of Matrimony, is the head of the Wife, pay that respect and reverence, that Nature binds him to give to his Mother, nor the Daughter to her Father : For though she be subordinate to her Husband by Matrimonial Right, yet doth her Marriage allow her so great a Familiarity with her Husband, as is altogether inconsistent with the duty of a Child. *Paulus* the Lawyer was in the right, when having said before, That

That in contracting Marriages the Law of Nature and Modesty were chiefly to be regarded; he added, That it was against modesty for a man to take his own Daughter to be his Wife. And *Philo* in his Special Laws condemns it as an execrable wickedness to pollute the bed of his deceased Father, which as a thing Sacred, ought not to be toucht, and without regard to either the age, or the reverence of a Mothers name, to make himself both Son and Husband to the same Woman, and to make her both Mother and Wife to the same Man. Wherefore such Marriages are doubtless not illegal only, but void, by reason of something that is vicious, which perpetually cleaves to the effects of it. Neither is that Argument of *Diogenes* and *Chrisippus*, which is drawn from the practice of Cocks, and such like dumb creatures, sufficient to prove, that such commixtures are not repugnant to the Law of Nature. For (as I have already said) it is enough to conclude any thing unlawful, That it is repugnant though but to humane nature. This is that Incest which the Lawyers, *Paulus* and *Papinian*, wrote to be by the Law of Nations committed, between the degrees ascendent and descendent. And this is that Law of Nature, which, as *Xenophon* notes, is no less a Law, because it was contemned by the *Persians*, *Medes*, *Indians* and *Æthiopians*; for which they were punished with perpetual Wars, Parricides, Fratricides, as *Philo* first, and after him St. *Hierome* observed: For as *Michael Ephesius* well interprets it, That is Natural, which is of common use amongst such Nations, as are uncorrupted; *And that live most agreeable unto Nature.* And therefore *Hippodamus* the *Pythagorean calls these incestuous commixtures, inordinate and unnatural lusts, unbridled passions, and abominable pleasures.* Such were those of the *Parthians*, whereof *Lucan* thus complains,

That is unlawful which is repugnant to Humane Nature.
Lib. 2. Contr. Jovin.

——— Epulis vesana, meroque
Regia non ullos exceptos legibus horret
Concubitus ——— ——

With Wine and dainty fare, the Court inflam'd,
Of their unbridled Lusts are not asham'd.

And a little after,

——— Cui fas implere parentem,
Quid reor esse nefas? ———

Who fears not with his Mother t' lye,
To him, what can be Villany?

Orat. 20.

The execrable Custome particularly among the *Persians*, *Dion Prusaensis* prudently attributes to their evil education. But here we cannot without wonder pass by that vain conceit of *Socrates* and *Xenophon*, who could find nothing reprovable in these incestuous Marriages, besides the disparity in age, whence barrenness, or mis-shapen children must necessarily follow. For if there were no other reason than this to hinder such Marriages, surely it could no more invalid these, than the like disparity in years could render other Marriages unlawful. But that which is much more worthy of our enquiry is this, Whether among men, unbyassed by an ill education, there be not (besides that which, as I have said, is conceived in the mind and understanding) a natural abhorrency, even in our affections to commix, either with our own parents, or with the children issuing out of our own Loyns; especially when we find the like even in some brute beasts. For so amongst others, *Arnobius* testifies, where speaking of the horrour of such unnatural Coitions, he saith, *Quem non hominibus solis, sed animalibus quoque nonnullis natura ipsa subjecit, & ingeneratus ille communiter sensus*; *Which Nature and common sense have instilled not into men only, but into some beasts.* *Aristotle* records a notable experiment of this in a Camel, who could not be induced to cover his own Dam, until his Keeper had covered her head over with an Hood, and so deceived him, but the Hood falling off whilest he was upon her, though he did the act; yet remembring what he had done, presently after so tore his Keeper that he killed him. The like he relates of a generous Colt in *Scythia*, which refused to cover his Dam, but being in like manner deceived, brake his own neck for very horrour of the fact. The like Stories we read in *Pliny*, of an Horse that for the same cause killed himself: and of a Mare that being likewise deluded, worried her Keeper to death. For, saith the Historian, these Beasts are not without some knowledge of their own kindred. Not much unlike unto this is that of *Oppianus*, in his first Book of Hunting; and of *Varro* in his Second Book and Seventh Chapter *de re rustica*: And to the like purpose is that of *Seneca* in his *Hippolitus*,

Some Beasts abhor such Coitions.
Lib. 5. adv. Gent.
Hist. Animal. l. 9. c. 47.
Nat. Hist. Lib. 8. c. 42.

Fera

Feræ quoque ipſæ Veneris evitant nefas,
Generiſque leges Inſcius ſervat pudor.

Ev'n Beaſts themſelves do from their Dams refrain,
And taught by Nature, chaſter Laws maintain.

XIII. Another Queſtion ariſeth here, concerning the degrees of Affinity and Conſanguinity in the croſs line, eſpecially of thoſe mentioned *Lev.* 18. For though we ſhould grant, that they are not interdicted by the meer Law of Nature, yet it is manifeſt, that they are forbidden by the expreſs Will of God: And that not only to the *Hebrews*, but to all mankind, as may be collected from the very words of God himſelf, to *Moſes*, *Defile not your ſelves in any of theſe things; for in all theſe things the Nations are defiled, which I caſt out before you, and the Land is defiled: Therefore do I viſit the Iniquity thereof upon it; and the Land it ſelf ſpeweth out her Inhabitants.* For if the *Canaanites* and their Neighbours did ſin in all theſe things, and were puniſhed for ſo doing; certainly they had a Law given them, which forbad the doing of them: Which Law, ſince it was not meerly Natural, muſt needs be given by God, either peculiarly to them (which is not very probable, nor will the words bear that ſenſe) or to all mankind, either at the Creation to *Adam*, or after the Flood to *Noah*. Now, ſuch Laws as were given to all mankind, Chriſt did no where abrogate, but thoſe only, which as an Hedge or Partition wall, did ſeparate that Nation from all others. Beſides, when St. *Paul* did ſo ſeverely cenſure the *Corinthian* for marrying his Mother-in-Law; as he had no peculiar command from Chriſt ſo to do, ſo he uſeth no other argument to juſtifie his ſeverity, than this, *That it was reputed unclean even among the profane Gentiles*: Witneſs *Carondas* his Law, which branded ſuch Marriages with infamy. And that of *Cicero*, in a caſe not much different from that of the *Corinthian*: For having firſt laid open the matter of fact, and proved the Marriage of the Mother-in-law with her Son-in-law, in deteſtation of ſo foul a crime, he crys out, *O mulieris incredibile ſcelus, & præter hanc unam, in omni vita inauditum! O the incredible wickedneſs of a Woman, and but in this never heard of!* When King *Seleucus* had a mind to give his Wife *Stratonice* to his Son *Antiochus*, Verebatur ne ipſa offenderetur ut re illicita; *He was afraid*, ſaith *Plutarch*, *leſt ſhe ſhould take offence at it as a thing unlawful.* For ſo it was in *Virgil*'s account,

The degrees of Affinity and Conſanguinity forbidden.
Lev. 18. 24, 25, 27.
Inceſtuous Marriages forbidden by God, to *Adam* or *Noah*.
Eph. 2. 14.
1 Cor. 7. 25.
Pro A Cluentio.

Thalamos auſum inceſtare novercæ.

His Fathers Bed with Inceſt durſt pollute.

Which general deteſtation of theſe Inceſtuous Marriages, if it derive not its origine from an immediate dictate of Nature, it muſt neceſſarily deſcend by ancient tradition from ſome precept given by God, to *Adam*, or *Noah*. The Ancient *Hebrews*, who herein were no mean Interpreters of the Divine Law, and *Maimonides*, who had read and with ſound Judgement weighed all they wrote, do aſſign two cauſes of thoſe Laws concerning Marriages, mentioned *Lev.* 18. The firſt is, A certain Natural modeſty which will not endure that Parents ſhould mix with their own iſſue, either by themſelves, or by ſuch perſons as either in Blood or Alliance are neareſt unto them: The Second is for prevention of Fornications and Adulteries, which too much Familiarity and daily Converſation, without any watchful eye to reſtrain them, may occaſion; eſpecially if ſuch wanton dalliances may be made good by lawful Marriages. Now if we would judiciouſly adapt theſe two cauſes unto thoſe Divine Laws before-mentioned, *Lev.* 18. it will eaſily appear, That in thoſe that are allied in the right line, either Aſcendent or Deſcendent, (for we do not here mention that of Parents with their Children, which Natural Reaſon without any other Law, teacheth us to abhor) and in thoſe the firſt degree of the oblique line, which becauſe of its immediate deſcent from the common ſtock, is uſually accounted the ſecond degree, by reaſon of that freſh and lively Image of the Parents in the Children; The former of the two cauſes above-mentioned is very forceable, as iſſuing from that which Nature her ſelf doth, if not command, yet at leaſt commend unto us as the more honeſt: Of which kind there are many which afford abundance of matter, for Laws both Divine and Humane. And therefore the *Hebrews* do not preciſely tye themſelves to the degrees of the right line, that are expreſt in the Law, but comprehend under them many degrees, that are not there mentioned by a manifeſt parity of reaſon. The names whereof, with them, are theſe, The Mother of his Mother, the Mother of his Mothers Father, his Fathers Mother, the Mother of his Fathers Father, the Wife of his Fathers Father, the Wife of his Mothers Father, his Sons Wife, the Wife of his Sons Son, the Wife of his Daughters Son, the Daughter of his

The *Hebrews* aſſign two reaſons of thoſe Laws.

Sons

Sons Daughter, the Daughter of his Sons Son, the Daughter of his Daughters Daughter, the Daughter of his Daughters Son, the Daughter of his Wives Sons Daughter, the Daughter of his Wives Daughters Daughter, the Mother of his Wives Fathers Mother, the Mother of his Wives Mothers Father: That is to say, according to the *Roman* Dialect, all Grand-mothers and Great Grand-mothers, the Grand, and Great Grand-mothers-in-law, the Nephews, and Neeces Daughters, the Daughters of the Son-in-law, the Nephews Wife, and the Wives Mother and Grand-mothers; because there is the same reason for the kindred on the Mothers side, as for that on the Fathers: And so under the first degree is comprehended the second, and under the second the third. Beyond which it is not likely that any Controversie should arise, which might otherwise proceed *in infinitum*.

The six Precepts given by God to *Adam* and *Noah*'s Sons.

Now these Laws, together with that which prohibits Brothers and Sisters to marry one another, the *Hebrews* reckon among those which God gave unto *Adam*, which were these, First, That, Enjoyning the worship of God. Secondly, That, Commanding the ordaining of Magistrates, and the administration of Justice. Thirdly, That, Against the shedding of Innocent Blood. Fourthly, That, Against Images or Idol-worship. Fifthly, That, Against Rapine: And Sixthly, This, against Incest. Yet so, that this last was not to be in force till the world was well replenished with mankind, which in the beginning could not be avoided. Neither do they think it to the purpose to say, That *Moses* makes no relation of any such Laws given to *Adam*, forbidding such Marriages. For he thought it sufficient tacitely to couch it in the Law it self, wherein he declares, That the Nations were punished for these very sins: Which they could not justly have been, had there not been a Law given them, that did forbid them. There being many things recorded in the Law, not in order of time, but as occasion served to express them. It will nothing avail then to say, That these Incestuous Marriages were not sins, because there was no Law against them before *Moses*; for no more was there any Law then extant to punish Adultery with death: yet we find *Thamar* sentenced to death for it by *Judah*. So the punishment of the *Sichemites* by *Simeon* and *Levi* was just for ravishing their Sister *Dinah*, though we read of no Law then published against it. And the Incest of *Reuben* deserved his Fathers Curse, though the Law forbidding it be not recorded: For it was sufficiently condemned in this, That the Nations were cast out by God for these things; whereby it may probably be concluded, That God had given such Laws to mankind before *Moses* his time, though they are but obscurely glanced at by him.

Gen. 38. 24. No Laws extant to punish Incest, Rapes, or Adultery; yet we find these punished before *Moses*, in the stories of *Thamar*, *Dinah* and *Reuben*.

In the *Jewish* Law there is neither *prius*, nor *posterius*.

And indeed the *Jews* have a notable wise saying, which gives some light to those dark times, namely, that in their Law there is neither *Prius* nor *Posterius*, *First nor Last*; for many things are recited without order. As touching the marriage of Brothers and Sisters, the very words of *Michael Ephesius* are these, *For Brothers and Sisters to lye together, was at the first indifferent; but when there was a Law that forbad such Coition, then whether that Law should be observed or not, was not to be questioned.* And therefore *Diodorus Siculus* notes, that *to abstain from such Commixtures, was the common custom of all men, the* Egyptians *only excepted:* though *Dion Prusaensis* excepts also the *Barbarians*. *Seneca* wrote thus, *We*, saith he, *joyn the Gods in marriage, but with very little piety; for we marry together Brothers and Sisters.* *Plato* calls such marriages, prophane and abominable before God. Whereby we may discern, how mean an opinion other Nations as well as the *Jews*, had of these Incestuous Marriages, which they seldom mention without a *Nefas*, to testifie their dislike of them. All Brothers and Sisters, as well on the Mothers side, as on the Fathers side, that is, as well of the half, as whole blood are comprised within this Law, whether they are educated at home or abroad, as is manifest by the *Chaldee* Paraphrast.

Lib. 1.

L. 8. de Leg.

XIV. Remote degrees seem not forbidden.

† Hist. l. 12. Jos. Ant. Hist. lib. 12. and lib. 75.

Now these marriages being expresly forbidden, seem to justifie, or at the least to tolerate those in more remote degrees. For to marry an Aunt, that is, his Fathers Sister, is expresly prohibited: but yet to marry his Brothers Daughter, which is equal in degree, is not. Such was *Sarah* to *Abraham*, as *Josephus* thought †. Nay, there are diverse Precedents for this among the *Jews*: And after the Law given, the same *Josephus* gives us examples in *Herod*, who married his Brothers Daughter, and gave his own Daughter to his Brother *Pheroras*. *There are certain marriages lately contracted* (saith *Tacitus*) *which to us are strange, though not so with other Nations, because forbidden by no Law*: Namely, that a man should marry his Brothers Daughter, this was held *lawful among the Athenians*, as *Isæus* and *Plutarch* in the Life of *Lysias* record; whereof the *Jews* give this reason, Because young men do daily frequent, and are more usually brought up in their Grand-fathers and Grand-mothers houses amongst their Aunts, than their Aunts are in their Brothers amongst their Nephews, neither have they there so much Right. Which if we do admit, as it is indeed very agreeable to reason, then we must acknowledge, that the Law which Interdicts Marriages with Kindred in the right degree, and with Sisters (from

whence

whence sprung the whole race of mankind at first) is now perpetual, and obligeth all men, being grounded upon natural honesty: So that whatsoever is done against this Law, may be made Null, by reason of the Impediment, that is lasting and permanent; but what is done against other Laws, is not so, as being but cautionary against this, which may be otherwise provided against. Sure I am, that by the Nineteenth Canon of those that are called the Apostles, they that marry two Sisters successively, or their Brothers or Sisters Daughters, are only driven from the Clergy. And as to the sins for which God is said to extirpate the *Canaanites* and their Neighbours, the answer is easie. For though the charge be general, yet it may be restrained to some principal heads in the charge; as to Sodomy, to Carnal Copulation with Beasts, with Parents, Sisters, other mens Wives, &c. And that other Laws were added but as Fences and Retrenchments, to restrain men from violating these Laws, as the *Hebrews* thought. For that it was not to be understood of every particular in that charge is sufficiently proved, in that they were forbidden to have two Sisters, as Wives, at the same time; which that it was not at the first made to all mankind, the example and great piety of *Jacob* will not suffer us to believe; whereunto may be added that of *Amram* the Father of *Moses*, who married his own Aunt, as did diverse others, both among the *Grecians* and *Romans*. And yet I cannot but commend the great modesty of the Primitive Christians, who did not only of their own accord observe those Laws, which were given in common, to all Nations, but those also which were given to the *Jewish* Nation only; yea, and did enlarge the bounds of their modesty, beyond those degrees forbidden them: that as in other vertues, so in this also, they might be seen to excel them. And that this was done with a general consent, will appear by the Canons of the Councils. *Common use and practice is of great power, to commend or discommend any thing to humane sense* (saith St. *Augustine* speaking in dislike of the marriage of Brothers and Sisters) which, saith he, *now by Custome most Nations, though Heathenish, do abhor.* And although those marriages are sometimes permitted, by some wicked Laws, yet hath a better Custome at length introduced an Abhorrence of them: *Now since this Custome hath so far prevailed, as to curb and restrain this Licence, to endeavour to infringe, or corrupt this Custome, is little less than Impiety: For if it be unjust, out of covetousness to remove the Land-marks of our neighbours grounds, how much more unjust is it, out of an inordinate lust, to subvert so profitable and so laudable a Custome? We have observed*, saith St. *Augustine, how rare it is to see Brothers and Sisters Children to be joyned in marriage in these times of ours, by reason of their propinquity in blood, being the next in degree to Brothers and Sisters; which though by the Law is lawful, because neither Divine nor Humane Laws have yet forbidden it, yet hath Custome introduced such a dislike of it, that it is seldome done.* Factum etiam licitum propter vicinitatem horrebatur Illiciti; *That which is in it self lawful, is prudently avoided for its vicinity to that which is unlawful:* whereunto he presently subjoyns, *That though it were the Religious Care of our Fore-fathers, after two or three descents, to renew their Allyances, by Interchangeable marriages, abstaining only, after the world was sufficiently stockt with men, from that of Brothers with Sisters; yet who can doubt, but that,* honestius hoc tempore etiam consobrinarum prohibita esse conjugia; *The marriage of Brothers and Sisters Children, is now more modestly forbidden. And that, not only for strengthening our selves with new allyances; but also by reason of a certain natural and commendable bashfulness, which should restrain us from committing such libidinous-acts with her, (of whom by reason of the nearness of blood, we should have a reverend esteem) as even conjugal modesty we see doth even blush to own.* And therefore *Æschylus* calls the marriage of Cousin Germans such a Conjunction as the Law forbids, because by this means the Stock is corrupted and tainted. Now this natural Shamefacedness, many Kings and Free People have by their Laws cherished and upheld. The Emperour *Theodosius*, as *Victor* reports, *did so highly esteem of it, that he expresly forbad the marriage of Cousin Germans, making but little difference between that, and that of Brothers and Sisters*: Which Law St. *Ambrose* highly commends, as being full of Piety. Such another Law we find made by *Arcadius* and *Honorius*. The like *Cassiodore* relates of the *Goths*, who prudently following this example, did reserve the priviledge of contracting marriages with Cousin Germans to their King only. And yet we must still remember, That not every thing that is forbidden to be done by Humane Laws, being done, is presently void, unless it be so signified by the Law it self. In the Council of *Agatha*, among other prohibited marriages, that of Cousin Germans also is mentioned; whereunto it is added, That the Council did not at that time, so prohibit them, as to dissolve those that had been made. So *Paulus* the Lawyer saith, That marriages without the consent of Parents, was unjust, but yet not to be dissolved. So in the *Eliberine* Council it was decreed, That if a man after the death of his Wife, should marry her Sister, and she be faithful, he shall be debarred from the Communion five years; thereby shewing, that the band of marriage was to remain undissolved. And by the aforesaid Canon of the Apostles it was likewise concluded, That if a man did marry two Sisters successively, or his Brothers Daughter, he

Marriage of two Sisters.

Other Marriages forbid to restrain men from contracting these.

The Primitive Christians exceeded the *Jews* in modesty.

De Civit. Dei, lib. 15. *c.* 16.

Ibid.

Concerning the marriage of Cousin Germans.

Not every thing that is done contrary to Law, is presently made void. *Quod fieri non debuit, factum valet.*

Can. 6[illegible].

he was only not to have been admitted into Sacred Orders, but the marriage was not void.

XV. Some Concubinary Contracts may amount to marriage.

But that we may proceed to other marriages, it is to be obſerved, That ſome Concubinary Contracts may amount to true and authentick marriages: although they may be deprived of ſome effects peculiar to marriages by the Civil Law, or loſe ſome effects that are natural, by reaſon of ſome impediment ariſing from the Civil Law. As for example, the accompanying of a Bond-man with a Bond-woman, was called by the *Romans*, *Contubernium*, a Conſociation, and not a marriage; yet it had nothing wanting requiſite to the nature of marriage: And therefore in the Ancient Canons, it is called by the name of Wedlock. So the accompanying of a Free-man with a Bond-woman, is not honoured with the Title of Matrimony, but of Wedlock: which by Imitation, is ſince derived to other perſons that are of unequal Conditions; as that in *Athens* between a Citizen and a Stranger. So *Servius* upon *Virgil*, calls thoſe Baſtards, that are born of obſcure Mothers. And yet even theſe ſervile conjunctions were in *Greece*, *Carthage* and *Apulia*, reckoned as marriages, though the *Hebrews* would not honour them by that name, nor legitimate them without the conſent of thoſe whoſe ſervants they were. For ſo they expound that place of *Exod.* 21. where mention is made of marriages. And *Caſſiodore* will inform us, that they were not to marry any woman of unequal condition to themſelves, without leave obtained from their Prince. But certainly in the ſtate of Nature, ſuch unequal marriages may be Authentick, if the woman be under the cuſtody and ſafeguard of her husband, and have plighted her troth unto him. So alſo, under the ſtate of the Evangelical Law, a marriage between two Servants, or between a Free-man and a Servant, is a firm and lawful marriage; much more that between a Citizen and a Stranger, a Senator and a Free-woman, if thoſe things which are neceſſarily required by the Divine Chriſtian Law, to the accompliſhment of a marriage be added, namely, an indiſſoluble joyning together of one man to one woman, although ſome effects properly due by the Civil Law to other marriages, do not attend theſe, or which of their own accord would follow theſe, were they not by ſome Law hindered. And thus are the words of the firſt *Tolitane* Council to be underſtood, *He that hath no Wife, but inſtead of a Wife hath a Concubine, may not be driven from the Communion, ſo as he content himſelf with one woman, whether ſhe be his Wife or Concubine, as he pleaſeth.* Concerning ſuch a Concubine, St. *Auguſtine* writes thus, *If ſhe ſhall ſolemnly profeſs, that ſhe will never know any other man, although he to whom ſhe is at preſent ſubject, ſhould diſmiſs her: It may be worthy our pains, to enquire whether ſhe ſhould not be admitted to Baptiſm.* So in another place, *A queſtion doth often ariſe, In caſe a man and a woman being neither husband nor wife to any other, ſhall agree to lye together, not for procreation ſake, but only to avoid Incontinency, and ſhall give faith each to other, never to enjoy any elſe, whether that may be be called a marriage or no? And haply* (ſaith he) *it may not abſurdly be ſo called, if they both agree, that this conjunction ſhall continue until death; and although the procreation of children were not the main end they propoſed to themſelves in their lying together; yet if they do not purpoſely avoid it, nor do any wicked act, to the intent that children ſhould not be born unto them: But if a man have a Wife, he ought not to keep a Concubine, leſt ſhe eſtrange his heart from his Wife.* Hereunto likewiſe we may refer, that *Theodoſius* and *Valentinianus* do call an unequal marriage a kind of Fornication; and that from thence, an Accuſation of Adultery is ſaid to ariſe.

Exod. 21.
Lib. 7. *c.* 40.
Concubines.
De fide & oper.
Lib. de bono Conjugii.
Concerning Concubines, St. *Aug.*
Gen. 38. 9.

XVI. Some marriages though forbid to be done, yet being done are valid.

Though the Laws of men do forbid ſome certain perſons to be joyned in marriage, yet it follows not, that being married, their marriage is void. For it is one thing to forbid the doing of a thing, and another to make that void that is done: For the Prohibition may extend its force no farther than to ſome penalty, either expreſt or arbitrary; which ſort of Laws *Ulpian* calls Imperfect Laws: *Quæ fieri quid vetant, ſed factum non reſcindunt; Which prohibit the doing, but reſcind not the fact done.* Such was the *Cincian* Law among the *Romans*, that reſtrained men from giving more than unto ſuch a proportion, but did not make void that which was given beyond it. *The* Valerian *Law* (ſaith *Livy*) *when it forbad the whipping with Rods, or the killing with the Axe, him that had provoked or challenged another, impoſed no penalty upon the breaker of the Law, but adjudged it to be* improbe factum, *diſhoneſtly done* (*ſuch was the modeſty of thoſe times, when Infamy only was thought a ſufficient guard to the Laws*) *whereas now, there is ſcarce any that will ſo mildly threaten his ſervant.* By the *Fuſian* Law, none except ſome few particular perſons was to receive by way of Legacy more than ten thouſand Aſſes, (which reduced to our Coyn, amount to about one and thirty pounds ten ſhillings, reckoning every As to an Half Penny Farthing): and he that received more, was to forfeit the Quadruple ſumm. *Amongſt thoſe Laws that were called Imperfect,* Macrobius *reckons thoſe which had no penalty annexed to the breach of them.* Such was that reſcript of *D. Marcus*, *That Heir who forbad him to perform Funeral Rites, who was thereunto appointed by the Teſtator, did not rightly; howbeit he ordered no puniſhment to be inflicted upon him that did it.* We do acknowledge, that

Inſtit. Tit. 1.
Liv. lib. 10.
Ulpian.
Mille aſſ. m.
Ad Somn. Scipionis.
See *Sect.* 14. of this Chapter towards the end.

that amongst the *Romans*, it was afterwards introduced by the *Theodosian* Law, That whatsoever was prohibited only by the Law, although it was not expresly said, that what was done contrary unto it should be as null; yet if it proceeded to Judgment, it should be constrned as unprofitable, void, and of no force: But this strained construction arose not from the force of the bare prohibition, but from the vertue of the new Law, which other Nations were not obliged to follow. For sometimes there is greater indecency in the act doing, than there can be in the effects that proceed from it; and sometimes also the inconveniences which do follow upon the Recession, or making void of the fact, are more than could ensue upon the doing of it.

Besides this of marriage (which of all Consociations is the most natural) there are divers others as well private as publick; and those either over the people, or of the people: But all of them have this in common, that as to those things for which such a Society is instituted, the whole, or the major part in the name of the whole, do oblige every particular in that Society. For it may well be presumed that it was the mind of those that first entred into that Society, that the power to determine all matters therein treated, should rest somewhere. But because it would be apparently unjust, that some few Persons should impose upon the rest, where every Person hath equal power; therefore by the Right of Nature (setting aside those Orders and By-Laws which do prescribe a Form or Method to the whole Society, in the handling and discussing of matters that are brought before them) the major part should have the power of the whole. So *Thucydides*, *That which the Multitude, or the greater part thereof, shall decree, is Authoritative. Appianus* was of the same mind, *As well in publick Elections, as in Courts of Judgment, the greater part rules the rest.* So also was *Dionysius Halicarn. That which seems best to the most, must prevail:* that is, Unless it be otherwise provided by some former Law or Agreement, that of such a number of persons, such and such shall be of the *Quorum*, whereof any two or more have power to determine: Yea, though their judgment be not altogether so righteous as it might be, yet, *Eo quod major pars decrevit, stetur*; *Because the major part hath decreed it, it must stand.* Whereas on the contrary,

XVII. Of the right of the major part of a Society.

Lib. 5. Quod pluribus visum id valere.

Curtius l. 10.

——In paucis jam deficiente caterva,
Nec persona sita est patriæ, nec curia constat.

The Assembly being dissolv'd in two or three,
No face of Country nor of Court can be.

And by and by after,

Prudentius.

————Infirma minoris,
Vox cedat numeri, parvaque in parte quiescat.

Of the same Opinion was *Xenophon, Who would have all things done according to the vote of the major part of the Suffragans:* And in this sence doth, as well the *Chaldee Paraphrast*, as the *Jewish Rabbins*, understand that of *Moses, Exod.* 23. 2. Neither shalt thou speak in a cause to decline after many to wrest Judgment, which the said *Paraphrast* renders thus, *Neither shalt thou cease to speak thine own mind in judgment. Juxta Sententiam plurimorum perfice judicium*; *According to the opinion of the most, give Judgment.*

But if the Sentences be equally ballanced, nothing can be done; because there is not any thing of moment sufficient to cast the scale: In which case if the Sentences be equal, the accused shall be held innocent: And this the *Greeks* call the suffrage of *Minerva*, as *Æschylus* and *Euripides* inform us. So where the Judges are equally divided in opinion, *Possessor rem tenet*; *The Right goes with the Possession*, saith *Aristotle:* And *Seneca* in one of his Controversies saith the same, *One Judge condemns and another absolves: Where the Judges are equal, and their Judgment so unequal, the milder Sentence must prevail. Neither is there any reason*, saith *Seneca*, *that any man should envy that Power which overcomes only by shewing mercy.* Nay the *Jews* go yet further: For if the condemning Part had but one single Vote more than the absolving part, it stood for nothing; as may be collected from the *Chaldee Paraphrast*, upon that place of *Exodus* before cited, and by others; for so also in all Logical Collections, the Inference follows that part which is least grievous.

XVIII. Which part carries the sentence when the Votes are equal.

Orestes. Electra. Arist. Probl. Sect. 29. Non est invidiosa potestas quæ misericordia vincit. Sen.

But here another Question ariseth, namely, when and what sentences are to be conjoyned, and what to be divided? Wherein if we consider the Law of Nature only, that is, if no Law or Covenant have otherwise determined, we ought to distinguish between such Opinions or Sentences, as are altogether inconsistent and differ in the whole, and such as differ only in part, that so these latter may conjoyn in that wherein they agree, though the former cannot. And therefore where the Question to be argued wraps up many things together, it is to be divided and discuss'd in parts. Thus *Seneca*, when ano-

XIX. Where the question is not agreed unto, what is to be conjoyned and what divided.

Q ther

ther man delivers his opinion in a Question, whereunto I consent in part only, I desire him to divide that wherein I agree with him from that wherein I disagree, and I shall then joyn with him. As for example, they that adjudge a delinquent to pay twenty pounds, and they that adjudge him to pay but ten pounds, may unite in the ten against them that would acquit him. But they that censure a Malefactor to death, and they that censure him to banishment, cannot be reconciled, because death and banishment are inconsistent; neither can that part that would absolve him, joyn with those that would banish him. For though they both agree that he deserves not death, yet is not that exprest in the sentence, but deducible from it by consequence: For he that would banish doth not absolve. It was therefore well observed by *Pliny*, that when there shall happen to be such a diversity of opinions in a free Assembly, concerning one and the same thing, that they cannot be included in any one question, they must divide the matter into several and distinct questions; for it avails but little that two are displeased with the third, if in nothing they agree between themselves. *Polybius* justly taxeth *Posthumius* the Prætor with fraud, when in demanding the Judgment of the Senate, concerning the *Græcian* Captives, he joyns together those that condemned them, and those that would have had them detained as Prisoners for a while only, against those that would have released them. Such a question as this we shall find in *Gellius*, and another in *Quintilian*, where it being agreed that of seven Judges, what punishment the major part should think fit to decree, the Malefactor should suffer; two adjudged him to Banishment, and two to be branded with Infamy, and three to Death: And when the Person so adjudged, pleaded, that four of his Judges agreed that he should live, and three only that he should dye; *The Accuser desired him to recite the Judgment of the four: And when he began to say, Two sentenced me to Banishment and two to Ignominy; he was presently answered by his Adversary, That of two Sentences he made but one, and that that number which being united had preserved him, being divided, destroyed him, and how can they be united, that so expresly divide themselves?*

Where the Question is not assented unto, it is to be disputed in parts.

Lib. 8. Ep. ad Aristonem.

Lib. 9. c. 15. Declam. 365.

XX. The Right of the Absent remains with the Present.

Whereunto also we may add this, That in all Assemblies, the Right of those that either by absence, or any other means, are hindred from making use of their Right, is devolved on those that are present, yea, sometimes even to one single person, whose sole act shall be reputed the act of the whole. So saith *Seneca, Think thy self to be the common servant, yet shalt thou serve that Master that is present:* Yet herein also, as well as in that general rule of plurality of Votes, humane Laws do make some exceptions; as namely, when they require that so many shall be present to make a Court (as in our House of Commons;) or that the Persons absent, may give their Vote by their Proxies (as in our House of Peers.)

De Conser. l. 3.

XXI. What order is to be used among persons equal.

The order of Nature is this, that amongst equals he should be esteemed the first, that first entred into that Society: For so we find it is among Brethren, the Eldest always precedes the rest, and after him the second, &c. Notwithstanding all other qualifications. *All Brothers are equal* (saith *Aristotle*) *it is only their Age that makes them unequal. Theodosius* and *Valens*, in designing the order that should be observed among Consuls, say, *Of those who are in the same degree of honour, who should precede, but they that were first thought worthy of that honour.* And the ancient custom among Christian Kings and States was, that they always preceded in such Councils as were called concerning Christian affairs, who first profest themselves Christians, as *Æneas Sylvius* records in his History of the Council of *Basil.*

XXII. Where divers societies claim unequal shares how Votes are to be reckoned.

But yet so often as the ground and main reason of entring into this Society, was the preservation of something held by them in common, but not in equal proportions: As in an Inheritance, or in a Field, wherein one hath half, another a third, another a fourth part. Then not only the order, but the suffrages of that Assembly shall be, not by the plurality of single Votes, but by the proportions that they severally have in the thing held in common; which as it is most agreeable to natural equity, so it is approved of by the *Roman* Laws. So *Strabo* tells us, That when *Lybica* with three other adjoyning Cities, did unite themselves, as it were, in one Body; it was agreed, that each of the three was to have one voice, but *Lybica*, two; because it contributed much more to the common benefit than the rest: And the same Author tells us, that in *Lycia* there were twenty three Cities combined, whereof some had three voices, some two, and some but one, and accordingly all charges were divided and paid. *And this is but just*, saith *Aristotle, if the defence of their common possessions were the chief cause of their Consociation.*

Pol. l. 3. c. 9.

XXIII. The right of societies over their Citizens.

Of all Societies, that of divers Masters of Families embodyed in one City or Nation, as it is the most perfect, so it gives a greater right or power to the whole over every part thereof, than any other Society whatsoever. Neither is there any outward act done by any one Citizen, but what either by it self doth, or by circumstance may, refer to the conservation of that Society: For as *Aristotle* tells us, *The Laws do rule us in things of all sorts.*

And

XXIV. Whether Citizens may desert their City.

Mariana lib. 28. c. 13.

And here it may be questioned, whether it be lawful for Citizens to forsake their City without leave given. *There was an ancient Custom,* saith *Servius, that he that transplanted himself into another Family or Nation, did first renounce that wherein he formerly dwelt, and then was received.* And trne it is, that in some Countries it is not lawful to forsake the City without leave; as in the City of *Mosco*: Neither do I deny that it is possible for a Civil Society to be entred into under some such Agreements; and that Customs may introduce the force of such an Agreement. Yet by the latter *Roman* Laws, it was lawful for any Citizen to remove his Habitation, yet not so, but that he stood still obliged to execute such Offices in the City, as should be imposed on him: Neither were these to depart out of the *Roman* Territories, and special care was taken by the Law it self, that they should pay their Contributions. But setting aside these municipal Laws and Constitutions, let us discuss this question according to natural Right; and that not of any one part, but of the whole City, though under the Supreme dominion of one Person. And surely that they cannot recede by Flocks or great Companies, is easily collected from the necessity of the end, which in moral things is able to create a Right: For if this should be lawful, there might instantly follow a dissolution of that Civil Society. *Zonoras* speaking of King *Lazus,* who revolted from the *Persians* to the *Romans,* makes it the cause of a just War between the *Persians* and the *Romans,* that the *Roman* General had drawn unto himself the Subjects of the Kings of *Persia.* But as touching the departure of some particular persons from a City, it is much otherwise: As it is one thing to draw water out of a River, and another thing to turn the course of it. *Every Citizen* (saith *Triphonius*) *is free either to stay in, or to depart from his own City.* And *Cicero,* in his Oration for *Baldus,* commends this Law, *That no man should be enforced to stay in a City against his will, and this he lays down as the foundation of Liberty, that every Freeman hath absolute power over himself, either to remain in it or to recede from it.* And yet herein also we are to submit to natural equity, which was the Rule that the *Romans* walked by, in dissolving private Societies; that it should not be lawful, when the publick was damnified by it: For as *Proculus* rightly observes, Always not that which is profitable to some one of a Society, is usually to be observed, but what is expedient for the whole. But it is expedient for the whole Society, that in case any great publick debt be contracted, no Citizen should forsake the City, unless he have first paid his proportion of it: Also if upon confidence of the number of their Citizens, they have begun a War, but especially if they are in danger to be besieged, no Citizen ought to forsake the City, till he have first provided a Person as able as himself, to defend the Common-wealth. But unless it be in these cases only, it is probable enough that the people do give their consent that any Citizen may freely depart, because even from this liberty, they may make no less advantages to themselves some other ways.

To live where we please is the foundation of liberty.

XXV. A City hath no power over her banished.

Lib. 3. c. 20. §. 41.

So likewise no City can have any Right over those whom she hath banished, as we shall shew anon*. The *Heraclidæ* being banished *Argos* by *Eurystheus,* and afterwards persecuted by him, do thus plead by their Advocate *Jolaus*: By what Right doth he prosecute us now, whom he banished his City, for now we are no Subjects of his. And *Alcibiades* his Son speaking of the times of his Fathers banishment, tells the *Athenians,* that *The welfare of their City did nothing concern his Father.* So likewise *Nicetas* speaking of *Isaac Angelus,* saith, *It is no new thing for any man to court and flatter his Enemy, that is but sensible that his own Countrymen do persecute him as their Enemy.* But now the consociation of several Nations (whether by themselves or their Governors) are called Leagues; of the nature and effects whereof we shall have occasion to speak, when we shall treat of Obligations which arise from Contracts and Agreements.

XXVI. What Right a man hath over his adopted Son.

There are also voluntary subjections, and those either private or publick, the private vary according to the several sorts of Government: that which is most noble is that of Arrogation or Adoption, whereby a man translates himself into the Family of another; so as he behaves himself with that duty and reverence, as a Son of mature Age should do towards his own Parents. No Father can possibly transfer his Paternal Right over his Son to another man so fully, as to be altogether discharged of the duty incumbent on him as a Father: Nature it self will not admit of such an alienation, but yet he may commit his Son to another man to be fed and educated by way of Substitution.

XXVII. What power Lords have over their Slaves.

The most ignoble of all Subjections is that, whereby a man gives himself up to perfect slavery: Such were they among the *Germans,* of whom *Tacitus* speaks, *That sold themselves for food and rayment.* And of such there were great numbers among the *Græcians,* who (as *Dion Prusæensis* notes) *of Freemen became Slaves, and performed their service according to Articles of Agreement.* Now that we call perfect Bondage, which tyes a man during life to perform all manner of work, for no other reward but food and cloathing; which if it extend it self to whatsoever conduceth to the preservation of Nature, is not much to be grieved at: For our continual labour is indifferently well recompensed with a constant supply of things necessary for life, which they that hire out themselves by the day only, do often want. This the Stoick *Possidonius* observed out of Histories, that many in ancient times, conscious of their own weakness to maintain themselves, voluntarily submitted themselves to be commanded by others, *Constantly performing what they were able, and receiving from their Lords whatsoever was necessary for them.* Like him in *Plautus*.

> *If I were free, the charge were mine;*
> *But being bound, that charge is thine.*

XXVIII. Whether this power extend to life and death.

De benef. lib. 3. c. 22.

No Lord can have absolute power over the life and death of his Slave, if we respect internal Justice: For no man can take away the life of another, and be guiltless, unless it be for some capital crime committed; and yet by the Laws of some Nations, he that shall kill his Slave for what cause soever, is indemnified, as Kings are in all Nations by reason of their vast and unlimited power. For as *Seneca* notes, *If a Servant dare not plead with his Master for fear of suffering the worst of torments, no more dare Subjects with their Prince, nor Soldiers with their General, who have all of them equal Right, though under unequal Titles.* No Master then hath a just power to injure his Slave, but only as *That is sometimes improperly called Just, which being done, is not punishable.* Such a Right did *Solon* give to Parents over their own Children, and so did the ancient *Roman* Laws, witness that of *Sopater*, *It was lawful for him, being a Father, to kill his own Children, if they offended; for the Law (presuming upon the Fathers Integrity) had permitted such a Right unto him: The like power,* saith *Dion*, *we find permitted in many Nations famous for wise and wholesom Laws.*

XXIX. Of the Children of Slaves that are born and bred in their Masters family.

Vide infra Ch. 8. §. 18.

Pliny l. 10. c. 34. de columbis.

Lex Visigothica.

The *Sclavonian* Law judgeth the Children by the Father.

The Laws of *England.*

Littleton de Villanagio.

The *Roman* Laws.

What the Law of Nature is in this case.

If the Parents cannot maintain the Child but at the Lords charge, the Child is a Slave.

Otherwise not.

But of the children of Captives, which are born of Slaves in their Lords Family, there is yet a more difficult question: For by the Laws of the *Romans*, and of other Nations, concerning Captives (as we shall elsewhere shew) as of brute Beasts, so of people of a servile condition it holds true, that, *Partus sequitur Ventrem; As is the Mother, so is the Child.* But this notwithstanding is not altogether congruous to the Law of Nature, especially where the Father of the Child may be sufficiently known: For since even among dumb creatures, as *Pliny* observes of Doves, *Amor utrique sobolis aequalis;* Both Parents are equally concerned for their own young, thereby acknowledging their common interest in them. So also had not the Civil Law otherwise determined, the Child had followed the condition of the Father, no less than that of the Mother: *For if the Son* (saith the *Visigothick* Law) *be born and created by both Parents, why should he follow the condition of the Mother only, who without the Father could not beget him?* Among the *Sclavonians*, as also in some parts of *Italy*, among the *Lombards* and *Saxons*, the children are accounted either bond or free from their Father. *The Laws of* England *judge of the Child, not by the Mother, but by the Father; for the Husband and Wife, being but one person in our Law, and the Wife marrying a Freeman, by the common Law of* England, *the Issue is free:* Which Laws, though different from the *Roman* Civil Law, yet, as *Aquinus* notes, doth not much deviate from the Law of Nature. And why not, since among the *Romans*, by their *Mensian* Law, if both the Parents were Aliens, the Child born of them were so too, as *Ulpian* tells us. Now let us admit that both the Parents are Slaves, it is worth our pains to know whether naturally the Child be so or not? And certainly if the Parents have no other means to breed up the Child, but in their Lords family, or at his charge, they have a power to deliver him up to the Lord for a Slave. For although the Child were ingenuous and free-born, yet in such a case they have power by the Law to sell him: And in case the Parents were Servants to several Masters, then by the Law of Nature the Children were to be divided between their respective Lords. But if they had but one Child, then of right it belonged to him whose Slave the Father was, the Lord of the Mother being first satisfied for his half part; and yet of the Children of him that was born in the house of his Lord, two parts did accrew to his Lord, and but one to the Lord of the Mother, according to the Edict of *Theodoric*, as *Cassiodore* records. Now whereas I said before, that the Parents, if they had not any means to breed up their Children, but at the charge of their Lord, might deliver them up unto him as his Slaves; it may seem that this Power doth naturally arise from their supplying them with food and other necessaries, and therefore where there is no such necessity, as where there are other means to breed them, they have no right to sell them: And so it was adjudged by *Charles* the Bald, wherefore the Right that these Lords have in the Children of their bond-servants, springs from the many years Alimony that is given them by the Lord, before they could be serviceable to him, which they are to recompense by their future labour. And for this cause, the Parents cannot dispose of them to any other man, neither may the Servant flee from his Lord, until full satisfaction be given unto that Lord for the charge of their education: But if the Lord be too unmercifully cruel, then that even they who have surrendred themselves as Slaves, may provide for their own safety by flight, is the most probable opinion, notwithstanding the charge given by the Apostle, and by the ancient Canons, forbidding Servants to flee from their own Masters; because those Precepts were general, and oppo-

Gal. 6. 5. Tit. 2. 9. 1 Pet. 2. 18.

sed

sed only to that error which was then growing, namely, that denyed all manner of subjection, whether publick or private, as being inconsistent with Christian Liberty.

XXX. There are divers kinds of Servitudes.

Besides that slavery which is perfect, there are others imperfect; as those that are limited to a certain time, or to certain things, or upon conditions: Of such there were divers among the *Romans*, as that of their *liberti, nexi, addicti, asscripti glebæ, statu liberi*: As also among the *Jews*, there were those that served seven years, and that bound themselves until the next *Jubilee*, and then were free: And such were the *Penestæ* among the *Thessalonians*, and all Mercenaries, amongst whom are to be reckoned our Apprentices here in *England*, who for a certain number of years are under so hard a discipline, as doth but little distinguish them from those of a servile condition, and such like. All which differences do depend, either upon some Laws or upon some Contracts, his servitude also seems to be naturally imperfect, who is born of Parents, whereof one of them is bond and the other free, for the causes aforesaid.

XXXI. Publick Subjection by consent.

Publick Subjection is, when any one Nation or People do give themselves up to the power and command of another, either of one man or many, or of another people or Nation: The form of such a voluntary rendition, we have already set down in that of *Capua*: The like is that of the people of *Collatia*, *Do ye give up unto me, and unto the jurisdiction of the People of* Rome, *the* Collatine *People, with their City, Fields, Water, Bounds, Temples, Utensils, with all things else whether Divine or Humane? We do*, say they: *And I accept thereof.* Whereunto *Plautus* seems to allude in his *Amphitryo*. All which the *Persians* comprehend under the general names of Earth and Water: This is an absolute Subjection; but there are some likewise that are not so full and absolute, in respect either of their manner of holding it, or of that arbitrary power of command, of the several degrees whereof we have already elsewhere discoursed. *Lib. 1. c. 3.*

XXXII. What Right is gained over persons by way of punishment.

There is likewise an involuntary subjection, when by reason of some delinquency, we forfeit our liberty, and are forcibly reduced into servitude, by such as have a right to punish us; and who those are we shall shew hereafter. And thus may not only private men be brought into slavery, as at *Rome*, *Qui ad delectum non respondebat*; *He that refused to perform an Office, being thereunto chosen*, and they that were not enrolled or registred in the number of Citizens; and afterwards women, who though otherwise ingenuous, yet if they married another mans servant, lost their own freedom. But the publick things of a Nation may be thus subjected, for some publick injuries done; but with this difference, that if the State be brought into captivity, it is perpetual. For, as in the Laurel, though the leaves dye, yet is the Tree always green; so though every person in that Nation be mortal, yet doth Succession make the people immortal: But in personal bondage, *Noxa sequitur caput*, The punishment never exceeds the person offending; but both these servitudes, as well private as publick, being penal, may be either perfect or imperfect, according to the offence and punishment thereunto due. Now of that servitude, whether private or publick, that ariseth from the voluntary Law of Nations, we shall have occasion to treat, when we come to the direful effects of War.

CHAP.

CHAP. VI.

Of that Right which is derivatively acquired, by the voluntary Fact of a man, wherein is handled the Right of Alienation of Empires, and Things thereunto belonging.

I. *To make an Alienation valid, what is required from the Giver.*
II. *What is required from the Receiver.*
III. *That Empires may be alienated, sometimes by the King, sometimes by the People.*
IV. *That the Government over one part of a Nation, cannot be alienated by the people, if that part dissent or be unwilling.*
V. *Neither can one part alienate the Government over themselves, unless in case of unavoidable necessity.*
VI. *The Causes or Reasons of this.*
VII. *That the Empire over some place, may be alienated.*
VIII. *That no part of an Empire may be alienated by the King, either for profit or necessity.*
IX. *Under this Title of Alienation, all Feoffments and Morgages are comprehended.*
X. *So under Empires, are all lesser Jurisdictions which cannot be alienated but by the special consent of the People, or by Custom.*
XI. *No more can the Peoples Patrimony be alienated by the King.*
XII. *That the fruits and mean profits of the Patrimony, must be distinguished from the Patrimony it self.*
XIII. *Some parts of the Peoples Patrimony may be engaged by the King for debts, how far, and why.*
XIV. *That a mans Testament is a kind of Alienation, and is warranted by the Law of Nature.*

I. What is requisite to a perfect Alienation.

Hitherto we have spoken of Original Right: Now we are to treat of that Right which we derive from another, and this may be done either by the fact of the Person that gives it, or by some Law that warrants it; for that the right owners of things should have power to assign their interests, either wholly, or in part, unto others (propriety being once introduced) is most agreeable to the Law of Nature: And therefore *Aristotle* places it in the very definition of Dominion, *As if that only were truly and simply ours, which we have a Right to alienate.* Wherein two things only are to be observed, one in the Donor, the other in the Donee: First in the Donor, the internal act of the Will only is not sufficient, unless it be declared by some overt act, as by words, or some other external signs. For of the inward acts of the mind, we are no competent Judges; neither is it congruous to the nature of humane society: But that there should be also a publick delivery of the thing transferred, is required by the Civil Law, which being now received by most Nations, is (though improperly) said to be required by the Law of Nations. So in some places it is required that every Alienation should be published, either before the People, or before the Magistrate, and that it should be also recorded; all which do certainly proceed from the Civil Law. But because every Alienation of a mans Right ought to be done with sound Judgment, therefore the acts of the Will, that are exprest by some overt signs, are to be understood the acts of a mind endued with Reason.

1 *Rhet.* 5.

II. What in the Receiver.

So likewise in the Receiver, setting aside the Civil Law, it is naturally requisite that he should express his willingness to accept of it, by some outward signs; which though it be usually subsequent to the tender of the giver, yet may it also precede it: As when a man requires that such a thing should be given him, in this case it is presumed, that he is willing to receive it, unless it do appear that he hath altered his mind; as to other things requisite, as well to the transferring, as to the acception of a Right in things, and how both may be safely done, we shall shew more fully, when we treat of promises; for concerning both these, Nature hath prescribed the same Rules.

III. Empires whether alienable.

As other things, so are Empires alienable by him, in whose dominion they truly are; that is, as we have said before, by a King whose Kingdom is Patrimonial: But otherwise by the people, yet not without the Kngs consent, because he hath a kind of Right in it, though but to the present revenue, which cannot without his own act, be taken from him: Thus it stands with a whole Soveraign Empire.

IV. That the whole cannot alienate the parts that consent not to the Alienation.

But as to the Alienation of any one part of the whole, it is further requisite that that part that is to be alienated, consent thereunto. For they that first entred into that society, did (as may be presumed) contract a firm and immortal League among themselves, for the defence of all those parts which are called Integrants: Whence it follows, that these

these parts are not ſo under their own body, as the members of a natural body, which cannot live without the life of the body; and are therefore for the preſervation of the body ſometimes juſtly cut off. But this body whereof we now ſpeak, is conſtituted after another manner, namely, by mutual conſent and agreement; and therefore its power over its parts depends wholly upon the will and intention of them who firſt inſtituted that ſociety, who without doubt would never have granted ſuch a power to the whole, as to abſcind from it ſelf any of its parts, and to give them up into the power of another.

V. Nor any part over themſelves, but in caſes of neceſſity.

Neither is it, on the other ſide, in the power of any part to recede from the whole, unleſs it be evident, that it cannot otherwiſe ſubſiſt: For, as we have ſaid already, *In omnibus quæ ſunt humani inſtituti, excepta videtur neceſſitas ſumma, quæ rem reducit ad merum jus naturæ; All humane conſtitutions give place to the Law of Nature, in caſes of unavoidable neceſſity. Almoſt all Nations* (ſaith St. *Auguſtin*) *are taught by the very voice of Nature, to ſubmit to the will of the Conqueror, rather than to hazard an utter devaſtation.* And therefore, as *Herodotus* notes, *In that Oath, wherewith the* Grecians *bound themſelves to be faithful to the* Perſians *as to the Conquerour*, this *Salvo* was added, *Niſi planè coacti; Unleſs they were manifeſtly forced to the contrary.* Thus we read that *Anaxilaus* was deſervedly acquitted by the *Spartans*, for delivering up the City *Byzantium*, being diſtreſſed more by famine within, than by the Sword without. And *Xenophon* tells us, that the Emperour *Anaſtaſius* returned thanks to his Commanders, for their timely ſurrender of the City *Martyropolis*, thereby preventing the unneceſſary effuſion of blood, ſince it was impoſſible to be defended. *Cum fame habitare virtus recuſat; Valour will not cohabit with famine,* ſaith *Procopius, neither can we expect that Nature ſhould act vigorouſly, when ſhe wants nouriſhment.* So *Cephalas* (in his Epiſtle to the Emperor *Alexius*) being ſtraitly beſieged in *Lariſſa, Yielding to neceſſity we muſt deliver up the Town to thoſe, who not only beſiege us, but manifeſtly ſtarve us, (for what can valour do againſt the force of Nature?*

Vide infra c. 24. §. 6.

Goth. l. 4.

An. Commen. lib. 6.

VI. The cauſes of this different power.

Now the reaſon why, in caſes of abſolute neceſſity, every part of the ſociety hath more right to defend it ſelf, than the body of that ſociety can have over its parts, is; becauſe that part that is ſo neceſſitated, may uſe that Right which Nature gave it, before that ſociety was inſtituted, which the whole ſociety cannot: Neither let any man ſay, that the Right of Empire is in the whole ſociety, as in its ſubject, and therefore may be alienated by it as things held in propriety may; for the Government is indeed in the whole body as in its adequate Subject, (but not diviſibly in many bodies) as the Soul is in perfect Bodies. But that neceſſity that enforceth us to flee back to the Original Right of Nature for defence, cannot here have place: For under that Right the free uſe of Nature is comprehended, as eating, and detaining what is ours, which are natural, but ſo is not the Right of Alienation, which receiving its authority from humane inſtitution, is from it to receive its bounds.

VII. That the Empire over ſome place may be alienated.

But as to the Empire over ſuch a place, being a part of the Territory that lies uninhabited and deſart, I cannot diſcern any reaſon at all, why it may not be alienated either by a free people, or by a King with his peoples conſent. For as every part of the people have equally freedom of Will, ſo have they equally a Right to gainſay whatſoever any other would have; but the Territory it ſelf, whether wholly, or in its part, conſidered, is the peoples Common undivided, and therefore wholly at their diſpoſe; but as to the ſoveraignty over any part of the people, if, as I have ſaid, it cannot be alienated by the whole body of the people; much leſs can it be done by a King, who though he have the full power, yet he hath it not fully.

VIII. No part alienable either for profit or neceſſity by a King alone.

And here I muſt crave leave to diſſent from thoſe *Civilians*, who hold that no part of an Empire can be alienated by a King, unleſs it be for publick profit or out of neceſſity; unleſs they underſtand it in this ſence, that where the profit doth equally accrew, both to the whole Nation, and to that part which is to be alienated, the conſent of both may eaſily be collected from their ſilence, though of no long time, which may much more eaſily be preſumed, if there appear likewiſe a neceſſity for it: But if either part do manifeſtly declare againſt it, there can be no Right to alienate, unleſs the part be evidently enforced either to ſeparate from the whole, or ſuffer themſelves inevitably to be deſtroyed.

IX. Infeudations and Morgages of the parts of the Empire, unlawful.

Under Alienation is deſervedly compriſed even Infeudations, under penalty of confiſcation for breach of Faith, given to the Lord of the Feoff; or when the Family is extinct *: For even this is a conditional Alienation, wherefore we often ſee, that as thoſe Alienations, ſo theſe Infeudations of Kingdoms which Kings have made without the peoples conſent, yea, and the Remiſſion of Homage too, have by many people been made void. Now the people are ſaid to conſent, either when the whole body of them do meet to expreſs it, as the *Germans* and *Gauls* were wont; or when the ſeveral Provinces do it by their Deputies, being thereunto ſufficiently authoriſed. As in the *German* Empire, the conſent of the Princes Electors doth both by Cuſtom and Covenants, conclude all the orders thereof in any Alienation: for, *Whatſoever we do by another, is reputed our own act; Id facimus quod per alium facimus.* So neither can any part of an Empire be morgaged, without the like conſent;

* *Sub onere commiſſa ex felonia aut deficiente familia. Vide l.* 1. *c.* 4. §. 12.

consent; not only because it usually introduceth an Alienation, but for that Kings are bound to their Subjects, to exercise the Soveraign Power by themselves, and so are the people in general to their respective parts, to conserve the administration of the Empire entire, this being the chief end of their Consociation.

X. Inferior Jurisdictions not alienable by the King.

But as to other lesser Civil Functions, I see no reason why the people may not, by an hereditary right, grant them at their pleasure, because they do not thereby diminish the intire body of the Empire; yet cannot a King do it without the consent of the people, if we confine our selves within the bounds of nature, because the effects of a temporary power, such as Elective, and legally successive Kingdoms are, can be but temporary; yet may the people, as well by their express consent, as by their long continued silence, give that Right to their Kings. For so the Histories of the *Medes* and *Persians* do inform us, that their Kings usurping this Right, did anciently give away whole Towns and Provinces, to be held by a perpetual right.

XI. Nor the peoples patrimony.

That part of the peoples Patrimony (being amongst the ancient *Grecians* a part of the common Fields) the fruits whereof were designed for the maintenance either of the publick charge of the Common-wealth, or of the Royal dignity, cannot either in the whole, or in any the least part thereof, be alienated by Kings without the consent of the three States, that is, the Clergy, Nobles, and Commons; because they have no right to any thing more than to the present profits, no not to the smallest part of it, as I have said: For, *Quod meum non est, ejus nec exiguam partem alienare mihi jus est*; *Of that which is not mine, I cannot alienate the smallest part.* Yet the people may sooner be presumed to consent by their knowledge and silence, in such small matters than in greater: And the like may be presumed in cases of common profit or danger, concerning the alienation of some parts of the Empire, if it be not of any great moment, for that Patrimony was at first instituted for the good of the Empire.

XII. The patrimony to be distinguished from the mean profits.

But many are deceived in that they do not rightly distinguish between the things arising from the Patrimony as its fruits or profits, and the Patrimony it self. As for example, the washing of the banks of a River is patrimonial, but the increment which the Flood produceth is but the fruits and profits of it: so the power and right of raising a Tax is patrimonial, but the mony so raised is but the profits of that Right. The right to confiscate is patrimonial, but the Lands confiscated are but the profits of that right.

XIII. How far forth that part of the peoples patrimony may be pawned by the King, and why.

Those parts of the peoples patrimony, which are so designed as aforesaid, may upon just cause be pawned or morgaged by Kings, that have full and absolute power, that is, that have power upon occasion to raise new Taxes upon their Subjects: For as Subjects are bound to pay such Taxes, so are they likewise bound to satisfie that, for which any part of their patrimony is for the publick good pawned, the redemption whereof is some kind of Tribute. For the very patrimony of the people is a kind of pawn given to the King for the payment of the publick debts, and any thing that is thus pawned to me, I also have a right to pawn to another: Yet what hath hitherto been said is of force, unless it be where the Laws of the Land do either enlarge or contract the power either of the Prince or the people.

XIV. Testaments a kind of Alienation. *Arist. Pol. l.* 2. *c.* 7.

This also must be observed, That under this Title of Alienation, we comprehend likewise Testaments: For though Testaments, as some other acts also, are beholding to the Civil Law for their form, yet is the matter of it nearly allyed to dominion; and it being granted to the Law of Nature. For a man may by Testament give away his Estate, not only fully, but under certain conditions, nor irrevocably only, but with a power to revoke; and yet he may still keep the possession of what he so gives, with a full right of enjoying it: For a Testament is an Alienation of a mans Estate at his death, and revocable till then, and yet reserving in himself the full possession, and absolute fruition during life. And therefore *Solon*, in permitting his Citizens to make their Testaments, *Made them absolute Lords and Proprietors of what they had. Surely our Estates would be but burthensom unto us, if the power we have in it during life, should be taken away from us at our deaths.* *Abraham* in pursuance of this Right (had he dyed childless) had left, by his Testament, all his Estate to *Eliezer*, as we may collect from *Gen.* 15. 2. And the making of Testaments was of frequent use among the *Hebrews*, as may appear, *Deut.* 21. 16. *Ecclus.* 33. 25. But that in some places it is not permitted to Strangers to make their Wills, is not to be attributed to the Law of Nations, but to the municipal Laws of some Countries, and if I mistake not, enacted in such an Age, when all Strangers were accounted enemies; and therefore amongst the more civilized Nations hath long since been worn out of use.

Quint. Patr. Vide supra Bo. 1. *ch.* 3. §. 12.

CHAP.

CHAP. VII.

Of that Right that is acquired by Law, and of Succession from an Intestate.

Having thus shewed what Right may be derived from another by his Act, now we are to treat of the Right that is derived from another by Law: And this is, either by the Law of Nature, or by the voluntary Law of Nations, or from the Civil Law. It were endless to treat here of the Civil Law, neither are the main Controversies concerning War thereby determined; and therefore we shall purposely omit it. Yet is it worth our Observation to know, that some of the Civil Laws are apparently unjust; as that which adjudgeth goods Shipwrackt unto the Kings Coffers. For to take away anothers Right and Propriety without any preceeding cause, that is probable, is a manifest injury. Thus pleads *Helen* in *Euripides*, I. Some of the Civil Laws unjust.

R Wreckt,

Helen.

Wreckt, and a Stranger came I in,
Such to despoil, is horrid sin.

Lib. 1. C. de Nauf. l. 12.

For what Right, saith *Constantine, can the misfortunes of another create to a King, that he should be enriched by a calamity so much to be pitied.* And therefore *Dion Prusæensis*, in an Oration of his concerning Shipwracks, crys out, *Absit, O Jupiter, ut lucrum captemus tale, ex hominum infortunio*; *Far be it, O* Jupiter, *from me to take such advantages by other mens misfortunes.* And yet such a Right do the Laws of Nations very unjustly give; as amongst the *English*, the *Sicilians*: And such an ancient Law *Sopater* mentions to be in force in *Greece*. *Christian* King of *Denmark*, upon the abrogating of this Law, complained, That he lost an hundred thousand Crowns yearly. *Nicetas* speaking of this Law, calls it a Custome so barbarous as is not to be named. What then was *Bodines* meaning to defend this Law? He, namely, who reprehended *Papinian* for chusing rather to dye, than to act against his own Conscience.

II. A man may have a Right to that which he takes from another, and when. See *Book.* 3. *ch.* 7. §. 6.

Propriety or Dominion being introduced, it follows, by the Law of Nature, That things are alienable two ways: First, By commutation; which consists in the making up of that Right which I want, whereby the ballance of Justice may be made even: or Secondly, By Succession. Now Alienation by way of Commutation or Expletion is when for something that is, or ought to be mine, which I cannot receive in kind, I take from him that detains it or somewhat in lieu thereof, that is, some other thing of equal value. Thus *Irenæus* excuseth the *Hebrews* for robbing the *Ægyptians* of their goods, *Which,* saith he, *they might take and keep in compensation of their labour.* Now that Dominion may be thus transferred, is easily proved from the end, which in moral things is the best proof. For how otherwise can I be said to receive my full Right, unless I become the right owner of it? Seeing that it is not the bare detention, but the full power to use and dispose of it at my pleasure, that makes the Scales of Justice even. An ancient example of this we have in *Diodorus*, where *Hesionæus* in lieu of those things which being promised to his Daughter by *Ixion*, but not given, took away his Horses. For Expletive Justice, when it cannot recover what is the same, endeavours to get the value of it, which in a moral estimation is the same. By the Civil Law no man, we know, can do himself Right: Nay, if any man shall with his own hands take away from another, though but what is his due, it shall be imputed unto him as Rapine, and in some Countreys, he shall lose his debt. And although the Civil Law did not diectly forbid this, yet from the very institution of publick Tribunals, it may easily be concluded to be unlawful. But where there are not publick Courts to appeal unto (as on the Seas and in Desarts) there the Law of Nature must be our guide. So it should sometimes, when the Laws cease but for the present, that is, if the debt can never be got otherwise: As, if the Debtor be ready to fly the Countrey before the Courts can be open; in which case the Creditor may lawfully have recourse to the Law of Nature: Yet so, that the Judgement of the Court must afterwards be expected, before the Right of Propriety can be assured, as in the case of Reprizals; as shall be said hereafter. But yet, if the Right be certain, and it be also morally as certain, That a man cannot by a Judge receive satisfaction for want of due proof, the best opinion is, That the Law concerning Judgements ceaseth, and that a man may have recourse to the ancient Law of Nations.

III. The Estate of an Intestate to whom it naturally descends.

Dominion being once introduced, that which naturally guides the Succession to the estate of a person dying intestate, setting aside the Civil Law, is our conjecture at the Will of the deceased. For seeing that the force of Dominion is such, that it may be transferred at the will of the right owner, unto another: Therefore in case a man dyes possest of an estate, leaving nothing to testifie his mind after his death; because it is not credible that he would leave it to him that could next catch it, therefore shall it succeed to him to whom it is probable he would have left it, had he lived to have declared it. *Defunctorum voluntatem intellexisse, pro jure est*, saith *Pliny Junior*; *To have understood the Will of the deceased, is sufficient to create a Right.* Now to the dead this favour is indulged, That in cases that are doubtful, it is presumed, That every man would do that which is most just and honest; whereof in the first place is the payment of his just debts, and in the next, that which, though not due, yet is most agreeable to our duty: And therefore *what is committed to a mans trust may be restored*, saith *Paulus*, *(the person dying Intestate that trusted it) to those that succeed him, because it may be believed, That his Will was freely to leave the lawful Inheritance unto them.*

IV. Whether Parents do owe unto their Children any part of their goods.

It is much controverted by Lawyers, Whether Parents may be said to owe their children Aliment: Some of them hold it to be agreeable to Natural Reason, but deny it to be a Debt. But we think it fit here to distinguish of the word Debt, which may be taken either strictly, for that which by Commutative Justice we are obliged to do; or largely, for that which cannot with honour or honesty be left undone, as being a duty arising from

First Reason.

from another spring, but not from that of Justice. Now Aliment is due to Children (if Humane Laws do not otherwise determine of it) in this looser sense. In which, I conceive, that of *Val. Maximus* is to be understood, *Our Parents by nourishing us, have laid this obligation upon us to nourish our Children.* And that also of *Plutarch*, in that most elegant Oration of his, concerning the Love of Parents towards their Children, *Liberi hæreditatem, ut sibi debitam, expectant*; *Our Children look for our estates, as due unto them after our death.* So great was the Equity of this, That St. *Augustine would not admit that the goods of such as had exheredated their own Children, should be received by the Church.* And as *Procopius* in his *Persian* Wars observes, *Though Humane Laws do in other things extreamly differ one from another, yet all Nations, as well* Romans *as* Barbarians, *in this agree, That Children should succeed to their Parents, as the right owners of what they leave.* Again, *Qui formam dat, dat quæ ad formam sunt necessaria*; *He that gives the form gives things necessary to that form*, saith *Aristotle.* Therefore he that gives man his existence, ought, as much as in him lies, to provide for him all things necessary for a Natural and Social life; for hereunto he was born. There needs no Law to bind us to this duty; for all other creatures, even by Natures instinct, do feed their young: As *Pliny* observes of Swallows, *That with great equity they feed their little ones by turns*; (*Summa æquitate alternant cibum.*) Hence it is, that the Ancient Civilians do refer the Education of Children to the Law of Nature. And *Euripides* comprehends all Creatures under one and the same Law, *Which*, saith he, *is common as well to men among themselves, as to them, with all other sensible Creatures.* For that which Natural Instinct commends to them, the same doth Reason prescribe unto us. *Of such force is Natural affection, that it easily perswades us to nourish our Children*, saith *Justinian. Nature is an Indulgent Mistress to all living creatures, equally instructing them how to conserve not only themselves, but those that are born of them*; *that so by this successive Charity she may aspire to make her self immortal. Quintilian* brings in the Son claiming a Portion of his Fathers Estate *by the Law of Nations.* And *Salust* condemns that Testament as impious and unnatural, by which the Son is excluded from his part of the Inheritance. And because this is a debt that we owe to Nature, therefore is the Mother bound to nourish the Child that hath no certain Father. And though the *Roman* Laws made no provision for Children *ex damnato legibus Concubitu*, *that were illegitimate*; and that by *Solons* Laws it was provided, That no man should leave any thing to his Natural Issue‡: yet do the Canons of our Religion correct the severity of these Laws, by teaching us, That our Children, however begotten by us, should be a part of our care; and that in case it be needful, we ought to leave them enough to preserve that life which we gave them: but beyond necessaries, is no man bound by the Law of Nature to provide for them. Neither are we bound to nourish our Sons only, but those also that proceed from them, yea, even to the third generation, according to *Justinian*, and that for humanity sake: Neither should our Charity rest here, but it should extend it self even unto those who issue out of our Loins, and are born unto us by strange women, if they cannot otherwise be maintained.

Lib. 2. de vita cler. & ser. 52. ad frat. in eremo.
Gratian. c. 13. q. 2. & c. 17. q. 4. in fine.
Pers. l. 1.
Second Reason.

Partem jure gentium peto.

The *Roman* Laws made no provision for Bastards.

Beyond necessaries no man bound to provide for them.

V.

In Succession the Children of the deceased are to be preferred before their Parents, and why.

Children ought also to nourish their Parents; not only in obedience to many wholsome Laws, but in common gratitude, like the Storks, who when their Parents are spent with age, feed them, and being faint, receive them on their backs, and carry them from place to place: And therefore in fostering those, who when we were Children fostered us, we are Proverbially said, To imitate the Stork†. *Solon* is highly commended for setting a brand of infamy upon those that did it not: Yet is not this so ordinary as that which we have said of Children. Because Children when they are born, bring nothing into the world with them whereby to live; and have probably a longer time to live here than their Parents have. And as honour and obedience is properly due to Parents, and not to Children: So is Sustentation due rather to Children than to Parents: And thus is *Lucian* to be understood, when he tells us, *That it is more agreeable to the dictates of Nature, for Parents to love their Children, than for Children their Parents.* And that also of *Aristotle*, *That which begets, is always better affected to the thing begotten, than that which is begotten, can be to the begetter*: *For that is properly said to be our own, which derives its being from us.* Whence it comes, That without the favour of the Civil Law, the first Succession to the goods of the Parents is transmitted to their Children; it being presumed, That next after themselves, they would that those born of them (as being part of their own body) should be plentifully supplied with all things, not only necessary for life, but for a more honest and comfortable livelihood. *Insomuch, that were all humane Laws asleep, yet*, as *Paulus* the Lawyer observes, *would natural Reason, which is as it were a silent Law, adjudge the Fathers Inheritance unto his Children, and invest them in it, as their due, by an undoubted Succession.* But yet, as *Papinianus* notes, *cannot Parents claim the estates of their Children, by the same Right as Children do the Inheritance of their Parents: For Parents are admitted to their Childrens goods meerly out of Commiseration*; *but Children to the estate of their Parents by the common vote, that is, both* of

† ἀντιπελαργεῖν.

Reverence to Parents, and sustenance to Children.

Nic. 8.

of Nature and of their Parents. *Philo* in his third Book of the life of *Moses*, gives this Reason why *Moses* made no provision for Parents out of their Childrens Estate, *Because seeing that the Law of Nature did provide that Children should succeed their Parents in their Estates, and not Parents their Children; therefore did* Moses *pass over in silence, what was contrary to the desires of all Parents, and might prove unlucky.* Hence we may observe, That the Inheritance of Parents descends upon their Children, by a twofold Right; partly, as a meer debt of Nature; and partly, out of a Natural Conjecture, That it is the Will of their Parents, that their own Children should be best provided for. *Lib.* 5. *c.* 9. *Sanguini honorem relinquit*, saith *Val. Max.* of *Quintus Hortensius*; *His honour he bequeathed to his Blood.* For though he detested the wicked life of his Son, yet dying, *Ne ordinem naturæ confunderet, non nepotes, sed filium hæredem scripsit*; *To preserve the order of Nature, he made his Son, and not his Nephews, heir to his Estate:* Thinking it enough, that he had declared his dislike of his Sons ill manners whilest he lived. And *Ib.* therefore dying, he left him the honour due to his Blood. The like he records of *Fulvius*, who causing his own Son to be apprehended for conspiring his death, did not only forbear to prosecute him whilest he lived, but dying, *Dominum omnium esse voluit, quem genuerat hæredem instituens, non quem fuerat expertus*; *Made him heir of all he had, regarding his Birth and Blood, and not his Crimes.* And to this purpose is that of St. *Paul*, 2 Cor. 12. 14. *Children do not lay up for their Parents, but Parents for their Children.*

VI. Of Representative Succession.

Now because it is thus natural and ordinary for Parents to take care of their Childrens Education, therefore whilest they live, there lyes no obligation upon the Grand Parents to give them maintenance: Yet in case the Father or the Mother dye, or be otherwise disabled, then it is a duty, which in all equity the Parents of the deceased Son or Daughter are obliged unto, to see their Nephews or Neeces virtuously brought up. And by the same reason, is the same duty incumbent on the Parents of more remote degrees if these fail. And from hence ariseth the Right of the Nephew to inherit the Estate, instead of a deceased Son, as *Ulpian* speaks. Which gave occasion to that *Hebrew* saying, *Filius etiam in Sepulchro succedit*; *That the Son succeeds, though in his Grave.* Because *Filii filiorum sunt quasi filii*; *The Sons of that dead Son, are reputed Sons.* And as *Modestinus* speaks, *Shall fill up the vacant place of their dead Father.* *Justinian* thought *nothing more unreasonable than this, That the Nephew should succeed instead of the deceased Father, in the Estate of his Grand-father in case he dyed Intestate.* And this kind of Vicesuccession, our Modern Civilians do affectedly call Representative; when the Sons claim an Estate, by representing the person of their Father being dead. And that that manner of Right was approved of amongst the *Hebrews*, the division of the Land of *Canaan* amongst the Children of *Israel*, doth sufficiently demonstrate. As our Sons and Daughters are nearest unto us in blood, so are those who are born of either of them, as *Demosthenes* observes in his Oration against *Macartatus*.

VII. Abdication or exheredation.

What we have hitherto said concerning the Right of Succession, arising from our Conjectures at the Will of the Intestate, is of force, if there appear no certain sign, that he was otherwise minded. Such in the first place was among the *Grecians* an Abdication, or a manifest renouncing, or casting off of the person claiming: And among the *Romans* an open disinheriting of him; yet so, that if that person did not by his crime deserve to be put to death, he was to be allowed sufficient to sustain Nature, for the Reasons aforesaid.

VIII. The Right of Bastards.

And here we may add another exception to this general Rule, that is, If it do not sufficiently appear that such a Son or Daughter was begotten by him: But yet we know that of such matters of fact there can be no certain knowledge: But of such acts as are publickly done before men, there may be some certainty upon the Testimony of such as beheld them. In which sense the Mother may be certain that the Child is hers, by those who were present at its Birth and Education; but thus certain cannot a Father be. Which *Homer* first, and after him *Menander* thus intimates:

> *Know directly no man can*
> *From what stock himself first sprang.*

And so in another place he thus distinguisheth between the Parents,

> *Fathers do love their Children, Mothers dote:*
> *She knows them hers; but this he takes by rote.*

Therefore some way was thought fit to be found, whereby it might probably appear, who the Father of every Child was: And this was Marriage taken in its Natural terms, that is, for such a cohabitation, as placeth the woman under the custody or safeguard of the man. But whether by this, or some other way, the true Father of the Child be known,

known, or that any man doth own the Child as his; by the Law of Nature, that Child, as well as that born in Marriage shall inherit. Neither is this strange, seeing that we see meer strangers (being adopted for Sons) to succeed in the Inheritance, only by conjecture at the owners will. And the Nephew instead of the Father; as old *Jacob* adopted *Ephraim* and *Manasses* into the number of his Sons, in the stead of their Father *Joseph*. But our Natural Issue is differenced from our Legitimate by Law only. So *Euripides*,

> *Bastards, no less than those in Wedlock born,*
> *Are ours, although by Laws they're left forlorn.*

And yet may those also be adopted Sons, if the Laws forbid not, as it was anciently permitted among the *Romans*, by the Laws of *Anastasius*: But afterwards in favour to lawful Marriage, there was a more difficult way found, to make Bastards equal to such as were Legitimate, namely, by the free offer of the Court (when they say cause) or by the subsequent Marriage of the Mother of the Child. Thus did old *Jacob* adopt his Natural Son s, making them equal to his Legitimate, and giving them equal shares in his Inheritance. But the contrary may sometimes happen, not only by the prohibition of the Law, but even by agreement, when it is agreed on by both parties before, That they that are to be born by that Wedlock shall receive only Aliment, but no part of the Ancient Inheritance. And such a Marriage the *Hebrews* call **Concubinary**, although made with a Free-woman: Such was that of *Abraham* with *Keturah*, called therefore his Concubine, *Gen.* 25. 6. whose Children, together with *Ishmael* the Son of *Agar* his Bond-maid, are said to have received gifts, that is, Legacies; but no part of the Ancient Inheritance. So it was anciently among the *Mexicans*, who gave all to the eldest son, but nothing to the rest but sustenance only: And not much better are second Marriages in *Brabant*, where the Children by the second Venter, have no Propriety in the Estate which the Father held at the death of his former Wife. The like Law we find among the ancient *Burgundians*.

IX. *If a man dye Childless and Intestate, to whom shall the Estate descend. The Fathers Estate to his Relations, the Mothers to hers. The ancient Estate to be continued in the same Tribe.*

If a man dye Childless, and withal Intestate, on whom the Succession should descend, is not easily to be determined. There being no one thing wherein the Laws do more differ. All which differences may notwithstanding be reduced under two Heads, whereof the one hath respect to the nearest of kin, the other to the several Spring-heads from whence it descended: That which came by the Father, to his Relations; and that which came by the Mother, to hers. But here we must distinguish between the ancient Inheritance, and that lately purchased: That of *Plato* must be understood of the former, *Ego Legum conditor*, &c. *I being a Law giver*, saith he, *do ordain, That neither your Persons nor Patrimonial Estates are in your own power fully, but your stock and lineage have a Right thereunto; as well they that now are, as they that are to come.* Whereby it seems that *Plato* would have κλῆρον πατρῷον, *the Ancient Inheritance* preserved intire for that Tribe or Kindred by which it came: Which I would not have so to be understood, as though it were not naturally lawful to dispose of any goods that descend unto us, from either Parents or Ancestors otherwise. (For sometimes to relieve the wants of a Friend, who hath well deserved of us, is not only commendable, but necessary.) But (that in a case ambiguous) it may appear what we ought to believe the will of the Intestate was. For we take it as granted, That he that dies hath at his death a full Right to dispose of his Estate. But since it is impossible for him to retain this Right being dead, and that it may be presumed, That he would not altogether lose that Right, whereby he might gratifie his Friends: It concerns us to enquire in what order this benefit should naturally descend. Wherein that of *Aristotle* is most rational, *Potius est gratiam referri ei qui benefecit quam amico conferre beneficium; That it is better to return thanks to our Benefactor, than to oblige new Friends.* For as *Cicero* saith truly, *There is no duty so necessary as that of Gratitude: For since Liberality hath but two Branches, whereof one is to do good, the other to repay good; the former we may do if we will, but the latter we must do if we would be honest, and can do it without injuring any.* So St. *Ambrose*, *It becomes every man to have a greater respect unto him from whom we have received a Courtesie, than unto others.* And presently after, *What can be more against our duty, than not to return what we have received?* Now our Gratitude is exprest either to the living or to the dead, as *Lisias* observes in his Funeral Oration, It is shewed in doing good to their Children, being naturally the surviving parts of them, and unto whom their parents, if living, would have been most beneficent. *In me conferes quicquid in liberos meos contuleris*, saith the Fisher-man, in *Procopius*, who was about to adventure his life against a Dog-fish, to gain a very great Pearl for the Emperour *Cosroe*, *That is the best Gratitude that is shewed to the dead: For what, O Emperour, thou shalt confer on my Children, if I perish, thou bestowest upon me.* And according to this rule did they walk who framed the *Justinian* Laws, in that question concerning whole and half Brothers, and in that concerning Cousins in Blood, and in some others. *Brothers*, saith *Aristotle*, *do love each*

Our Benefactors are first to be gratified, and then our Friends obliged.

Procop. Pers. 1.

each other, being born of the same Parents: Ortus communis ipsos quasi eosdem facit; *One common blood whereof they are made, makes them almost one and the same.* Whence *frater* is *quasi fere alter*, A Brother is but *almost another, or as one cast in the same mould.* For *as the highest bond of Love is deservedly that which Children owe their Parents, from whom they receive the most and the greatest benefits, as their lives and livelihoods: So the next is that of Brethren to each other, as having received the same benefits together from the same Parents.* And therefore for Brethren dying Childless and Intestate, to succeed one another, is (according to *Justin*) *the Common Right of Nations.* But in case he, from whom the goods last descended, be not to be found, nor any of his Children; it remains that the thanks be paid to them, to whom, though not so much, yet next after him they are notwithstanding due; namely, to the Parents of the next degree above him, and to his Children: Especially, seeing by this means it may be continued between the Kinsmen, both of him whose inheritance it was, and of him from whom the said goods first descended. So the same *Aristotle, Cousin Germans, and the rest of our Kinsfolks, are linked together by their Parents, as being born of one common stock; yet so, as some are more nearly allyed than others, according to their respective birth.* Thus by the Law of *Moses*, the Unkle succeeded after the Brothers, as being nearer unto the first Owner, than the Brothers Children, *Numb.* 27. 10, 11.

Val. Max. lib. 5. c. 5.

X. An estate lately gained to the next of kin.

But as to that part of the estate that is but lately acquired, because there lyes no obligation of thankfulness to our Ancestors for them, it remains that the succession should pass to him, that was dearest to the person deceased, which is presumed to be his nearest Kinsman, who is as it were his own Flesh, *Prov.* 11. 17. or his Brother, *Deut.* 15. 11. *For our love to our kindred should be proportionable to the nearness they are unto us in blood, so that after our Parents, they are best to be provided for, who are by nature in the nearest relation unto them.* And therefore among the *Grecians*, as *Isæus* tells us, *The Goods of the deceased, did alwayes descend unto the next of kin.* Whereunto he adds, *What can be more just, than that the estate that was a kinsmans, should descend unto a kinsman? How well would this conserve Humane Society,* saith *Cicero, and promote the honour of private Families, if the nearer any man were allyed unto us, so much the more benign and bountiful we would be unto him?* Next unto our children, the same *Cicero* placeth our loving kindred, who as they are nearest, so ought they to be dearest unto us; *and to provide for these especially, is a debt that we owe them,* not by Commutative Justice, but by Distributive, as being most worthy, for the honour that is due unto our own blood. And therefore the same *Cicero*, speaking elsewhere of that natural affection which every man bears to his own Relations, tells us, *That from thence ariseth the Testaments and Legacies of dying men*: It being much more equitable, to leave our estates to our own kindred, than unto strangers. This is the Charity that is most acceptable to God, as *Esay* tells us, *To feed the hungry, to clothe the naked, and that we hide not our selves from our own flesh.* And St. *Ambrose* highly commends that *liberality that is shewn to our brethren and kinsfolks, as being next in blood to us.* Now that succession that thus descends from a person dying Intestate, is but as it were a silent Testament, which the Laws of Nature and Nations make Authentick, by guessing at the will of the deceased. Thus *Quintilian* also, *Next unto them who claim a Right by the Testators Testament, are his kindred in case he dye Intestate and Childless: not because the Goods of the deceased are in Justice due unto them, but because being deserted, and as it were left without any certain Owner, none can pretend so much right to them as they, being the next of kin.* And what hath been said of Goods newly purchased by the person dying Intestate, That they naturally descend to his nearest Relation; may as truly be said of such Goods as descend unto him from his Father or Grand-father, in case neither they, from whom they descended, nor any of their children do survive, to whom in point of Gratitude they should return.

Esay 58. 7. De Off. l. 1. c. 30.

XI. Diversity of Laws as touching succession.

Now though what we have here said, be most agreeable to Natural Conjectures, yet are they not by the Law of Nature necessary: wherefore, from divers causes moving mens wills, successions do usually vary, according to the diversity of Agreements, Laws or Customs rationally grounded; some whereof will admit of substitution in some degrees; others not. The Ancient *Germans* were altogether ignorant of that kind of succession which we call Representative, even among their children; as that the Eldest Brothers Son should succeed in the room of his deceased Father: which Right first took place in *France* by an Edict of *Childebert*; and was first introduced into those parts beyond the *Rhine* by *Otho*. So the Ancient *Scottish* Right of succession went according to the sole proximity in blood, and not by substitution, it being so decreed by the King of *England*, who was chosen as Arbiter, to decide that difference. In some places regard is had to the first Purchaser; in others, this is neglected. There are some Countreys, where the first-born carries away the greatest part of the estate, as among the *Hebrews*; but in some others, all the Children share alike. In some the kindred by the Fathers side, only succeed; in others, those by the Mothers, have an equal portion. In some, regard is had to

Pontanus 7. Danicor.

to the Sex ; in others, none at all. In some, the kinsfolks in the next degree only are admitted ; in others, they admit those in degrees more remote. To trace all, would be tedious ; neither is it my purpose so to do. But this we must grant, That where the deceased hath declared nothing of his Will, it must be presumed, that the Estate should pass, as the Law or Custome of the place doth order it ; but not so much by the power of the Empire, as by the force of this Conjecture, which also takes place against those in whom the Supream Power resides. For it is very probable, that what they by their Laws command, or by their Customs approve of in their Subjects, the same in their own affairs, they hold to be most Equitable, so as no great damage ariseth to them by it.

As concerning the Succession to Kingdoms, we must distinguish between those that are Patrimonial, and in a full and absolute manner possest, and those that are held in such a manner as pleaseth the People. The former sort may be divided even between the Sons and Daughters ; as in the Kingdoms of *Egypt*, as *Lucan* testifies, XII. How succession to Kingdoms patrimonial ought to be guided. Daughters capable to succeed in *Egypt* and *Britain*.

——Nullo discrimine Sexus
Reginam scit ferre Pharos.

——In Ægypts Throne
Difference of Sexes there is none.

The like doth *Tacitus* record of the *Brittish* Empire. In *Asia* after *Semiramis*, many Women were permitted to Reign, saith *Arrianus* ; as *Nitocris* in *Babylon*, *Artimissa* in *Halicarnassus*, and *Tomyris* amongst the *Scythians* : yea, and such Kingdoms may be divided, as in *Asia*, all the Brothers Reign together, though one only hath a principal Right to the Crown ; which Custome the Empress *Irene* would without any precedent have introduced into the *Constantinopolitan* Empire in the Reign of *Andronicus Palaologus*, as *Gregoras* notes, *That*, saith he, *which is most strange and to be admired, was, That she was not willing, that any one should obtain the whole, according to the Ancient Custome of that Empire, but according to the Examples of the Western Princes, the Cities and Regions should be divided amongst her Sons, that so each of them might hold his Kingdom as his Patrimony, just as the estates of private men are divided among their children ; so that each part of the Empire should descend perpetually to each of her Sons, and to their Heirs after them. For being her self of a Western Extraction, she indeavoured to introduce their Custom without example.* Neither are adopted Sons less capable of Succession, by guessing as the Will of the Intestate, than true Sons : Thus did *Hyllus* the Son of *Hercules* succeed to *Æpalius* King of the *Locrians* by Adoption ; as also did *Molossus* the Bastard in the Kingdom of *Epirus*, by the Judgement of his Father *Pyrrhus*, having no lawful Issue. The *Tartars* make no difference between Bastards and them that are Legitimate. So *Herodotus* of the *Persians*, *Mos est illis ut Nothus regnet dum legitimus aliquis reperitur ; Who admit of Bastards, till one that is legitimate may be found.* And we read in *Justine* of a Treaty between King *Atheas* and *Philip* concerning the Adopting of *Philip* to succeed him in the Kingdom of *Scythia*. *Jugurtha*, though a Bastard, yet succeeded in the Kingdom of *Numidia* by Adoption. The like we read of those Kingdoms which the *Goths* and *Lombards* conquered, that the succession often passed by Adoption. Nay, the succession to the Kingdom shall pass to the nearest of kin to him that last possest it, though he were nothing of kin to the first King. If any such succession be in force in those places : Thus did *Mithridates* in *Justine* plead, That *Paphlagonia* became his Fathers Inheritance, by the death of all its domestick Kings.

Neque enim Sexum in Imperiis discernunt, Tac. *Lib.* 7. *Strab. l.* 9. *Pausl. l.* 1. *Salust. bell. Jugurth.* *Paul. Diac. l.* 6. *de gest. Longob.*

But in case express caution be given, that the Kingdom shall not be divided, and yet it be not exprest who shall succeed, then the Eldest, whether Son or Daughter, shall enjoy the Kingdom. So saith *Nicetas Coniates*, *Nature indeed observing her own order, gives the greatest honour to the first-born ; But God hath a Prerogative above Nature, and acts not alwayes by her order.* And speaking of *Isaacius*, he saith, *That by his birth-right, the succession to the Kingdom was his.* The like is said of *Hircanus* in *Josephus*. In the *Talmud*, under the Title of Kings, we read, *That he that hath the best title to an estate of inheritance, hath also the best title to the possession of a Kingdom ; and therefore the eldest Son is alwayes preferred before the younger.* *Herodotus* makes it *the custome of all Nations for the eldest Son to succeed in his Fathers Throne.* And in another place, he terms it, *the Law of Kingdoms.* *Livy* makes mention of two Brethren, *Allobrogi*, contending for a Kingdom, whereof the younger had the worst Title, but the greatest Power. Of all *Darius* his Sons, *Artabazanes being the first-born claimed the Kingdom as his birth-right* : Quod Jus & ordo nascendi & Natura ipsa gentibus dedit ; *Which Right*, saith *Justine*, *both the order of birth, and Nature it self hath given to Nations* : which in another place he calls, *the Law of Nations.* As *Livy* also saith, It is a priviledge due by the order both of Age and Nature ; yet must this be understood with this restriction, unless the Father by his Testament do otherwise dispose XIII. In Kingdoms that are Indivisible, the eldest succeeds. *Lib.* 2. *Lib.* 40.

dispose of the succession, as *Ptolomy* in *Justin*, did his Kingdom to his youngest Son. But yet he that shall thus succeed, is bound to gratifie his Brethren for their shares with all respect and honour, if (and as far forth as) he shall be able to do it.

XIV. A Kingdom by the peoples consent hereditary, if in doubt, is presumed to be indivisible. *Lib.* 21. A Kingdom united is stronger, than when divided.

But those Kingdoms that by the Peoples free consent are made hereditary, may by guessing at the will of the people be transferred. Now, because it may easily be presumed, that the people will give their consent to that which is most expedient; therefore in the first place it will follow, That unless some Law or Custome do otherwise determine, (as in many it hath and may do) the Kingdom should stand entire and undivided; because whilest so, it will be the better able, both to defend it self, and to conserve the people in peace and unity. Of this opinion was *Justin*, *Firmius futurum esse regnum, si penes unum remansisset, quam si portionibus inter filios divideretur, arbitrabantur*; *They judged that the Empire would be more firm, being intirely possest by one, than it could possibly be, if divided amongst many Sons.*

XV. The succession not to last beyond the line of the first King. * *Lib.* 8.

Again, it being granted, that the peoples consent is easily gained to what shall be most expedient, it will in the next place follow, That the succession should descend from the first King in a right line: Because that Family was then elected, as being thought the most Noble; which Family being extinct, the Kingdom doth return back to the people. Thus *Curtius* adviseth *, *That the Soveraign Power be strongly fixt to one Royal Family, which ought to claim by an hereditary Right. For the people being so accustomed, will not only reverence his person, but will have the very name of their King in great esteem: And therefore no man ought to usurp that dignity, but he that was born unto it.*

XVI. Natural Issue not concerned in it.

Thirdly, It will thence likewise follow, That none should be admitted to succeed in the Royal Throne, but he that is born Legitimate: Not the Natural Sons, because they are subject to be reproacht, to whose Mother the Father did never vouchsafe the honour of marriage. And therefore of such, there can be no certainty, who was the Father. But in the succession to Crowns, the people ought to have the greatest assurance that in such a case can be given to avoid Controversies. For which cause it was, that the *Macedonians* preferred *Demetrius* the younger Son to the Throne, rather than *Perseus* the elder, because he was born in lawful Wedlock. Not Sons by Adoption, because the people are apt to conceive greater hopes, and to have their Kings in greater esteem and veneration, when they know them to be descended from a Royal Stock.

Est in Juvencis, est in equis patrum
Virtus.

In Horse and Oxe we may descry
The Syre's Generosity.

XVII. Males preferred before Females in the same degree.

Fourthly, That of those that have equal Title to the Inheritance, either as being in the same degree, or as succeeding to their Parents who were in the same degree, the Male Issue be preferred before the Female; because Men are fitter for War, and to administer other Regal duties, than Women can be.

XVIII. The elder before the younger.

Fifthly, That of Sons, or of Daughters, if there be no Sons, the elder be preferred before the younger; because it may easily be believed, that as he is of more years, so he either then is, or may sooner arrive to be of sounder Judgement than the younger. So *Cyrus* in *Xenophon*, Imperium relinquo majori Natu; *I bequeath my Kingdom to my Eldest Son, as being of most experience*, and consequently best knowing how to govern. And because our green years will sooner ripen, than our Sex change; therefore the prerogative of our Sex is much to be preferred, before the priviledge of our Age. Wherefore *Herodotus* where he tells us, that *Persis* the Son of *Andromede* the Sister of *Cepheus* did succeed *Cepheus* in his Kingdom, gives this as the reason, *Because* Cepheus *had no Male Children.* And *Diodorus* assigns the same reason, why *Teuthras* left the Kingdom of *Misia* unto his Daughter *Argiope*, *Because as to Male Issue he was childless.* And *Justin* tells us, That the Empire of the *Medes* did of right belong to the Daughter of *Astyages*, because *Astyages* had no Son. So doth *Cyaxares* in *Xenophon*, declare his Daughter Heiress to the *Median* Empire: *For*, saith he, *I have no Son that is legitimate.* So *Virgil* concerning King *Latinus*,

(*Lib.* 7. — *Lib.* 4.)

He had no Son, no Issue Male was left,
In prime of youth, Both being of Life bereft;
And by one Daughter this vast State possest.

Iliad. n. — *Lib.* 2.

Homer discoursing of the Kingdom of *Crete*, doth very wisely assign the reason why in successions the Elder is commonly preferred before the younger, namely, *first for their priority of Age; and secondly, for their greater knowledge and experience.* *Zozimus* also mentions

mentions a *Persian* Law, *which gave their Empire to their Kings eldest Son.* Thus did *Periander* succeed his Father in the Kingdom of *Corinth* by order of Birth, as *Damascene* testifies. Whence we are given to understand, that although the Children of deceased Parents in some degrees from them, may succeed in the room of their Parents; yet is it to be understood with this Proviso, That they are as capable as the rest, which Bastards are not. Provided also, That of such as are capable, regard be had first to their Sex, and then to their Age; for the qualities of Sex and Age (as they are in this case by the people considered) are so adherent to their persons, that they cannot be pluckt asunder.

XIX. Whether such a Kingdom be part of an Inheritance.

But here it may be demanded, Whether a Kingdom thus conveyed, be a part of an Inheritance: whereunto the most probable Answer is, That it is a kind of an Inheritance, yet separate from that of other Goods. And therefore *Innocent* the Third thought that the succession to such a Kingdom might be lost, if he who was to succeed, did not fulfill the last Will of the deceased. Such peculiar and separate Inheritances, we may see in some Fee-Farms and Copyholds, (which were originally given for the meliorating of Lands barren and desart, under some small Rent, which were not to return back to the Donor.) The like may be seen in the Rights of Patronages and Royalties. Whence it follows, That a Kingdom may belong to him, who if he will, may be heir to the Goods; yet so, that if he will, he may also enjoy the Kingdom, and not inherit the Goods, nor subject himself to the charge that attends them. Now the reason hereof is, because it is probable, that the Kingdom by the peoples consent, should be setled on the King, in the best manner of Right that could be: Neither did they much regard, whether he would accept of the Inheritance or not, since it was not for this, that they made choice of an hereditary order, but that the Title to the Kingdom might be clear; and that their Kings being extracted from a Royal Stem, might attract the more reverence from the people, who were apt from their High Birth and Princely Education, to conceive the greater hopes of their Heroick Vertues; and that the Prince in possession, might receive the greater encouragement to be careful of the Kingdom, and with the greater Courage and Magnanimity to defend it; as knowing that he was to leave it to such, as were either in gratitude or love most endeared unto him.

Fee-Farms and Copy-holds why first given.

Why the people would have their Kingdoms hereditary.

XX. The succession to Kingdoms is the same as that to other estates. Whether absolute.

But where the custome of succession to Lands absolutely free, and to Lands held from another is diverse, if the Kingdom be not held of another, or was not at first certainly held, (although it do appear, that homage hath been since done for it) yet shall the succession, by the Law go in such manner, as the succession of Free-hold Lands went, at such time when that Kingdom was at the first Instituted.

XXI. Or held from another.

But in such Kingdoms as were at first given to be held from another, as being the chief Lord of it, the manner of succession shall by the Law be such as the succession to Lands held in Fee-Farm within that Kingdom was at such time as the Investiture into that Kingdom was at first given; and that not alwayes according to that Law of the *Lumbards* which we have prescribed. For the *Goths*, *Vandals*, *Almains*, *French*, *Burgundians*, *English*, *Saxons* and all the *German* Nations, which have by War possest themselves of the best parts of the *Roman* Empire, have every one of them their own Laws and Customs, concerning things held in Fee, as well as the *Lumbards*.

XXII. Of a Lineal Cognatical succession, and what manner of transmission of right is therein.

But there is another kind of succession much used in some Kingdoms, not hereditary, but as they call it, lineal; wherein is observed not that Right which is called Representative, but a Right to transmit the future succession, as though it were already conveyed; the Law, namely, out of an hope, (which naturally and of it self worketh nothing) raising a certain true Right, namely, such a Right as ariseth from a Conditional Stipulation, which at present gives only an hope, that it will be due; which very hope they transmit unto the Children springing from the Loins of the first King, but in an order that is certain: so that in the first place, the Children of the last possessor of the first degree, as well of those that live, as of those that are dead are to be admitted, with regard had as well among the living as the dead; to the Sex first, and then to the Age. But if this Right descend on the deceased, then this Right shall pass to such as are descended from them: amongst equals alwayes observing the like prerogative of Sex, and then of Age, and the transmitting of the Right of the dead upon the living, and of the living upon the dead. And in case their children fail, it descends unto those who are, or if they lived should have been, by the like transmission next unto him; the same distinction of Sex and Age among equalls, being alwayes observed in the first Line; so that no transition by reason of Sex or Age should be made from one Line to another, so long as any remain of the first Line, of what Sex or Age soever. And consequently the Daughter of a Son, shall be preferred before the Son of a Daughter, and the Daughter of a Brother, before the Son of a Sister; so the Son of an elder Brother, before the younger Brother. This is the order of succession in the Kingdom of *Castile*, and of *Norway* (as *Pontanus* testifies in his *Danish* History): and such is the succession in many Dutchies, Counties

Cognatical succession.

See *Argentraeus* in his *Brittish* History, *l. 6. c. 4.*

This is the succession of the Kingdom of *England.*

and Baronies that are held by Homage or Fealty to the chief Lord. As in the Counties of *Artoise, Champane, Tolouse* and *Brittany:* This was the order of succession prescribed unto the Dutchy of *Mantua* by the Emperour *Sigismund, Anno* 1432. and by *Charles* the Fifth Emperour and King of *Spain*, to *Philip* the Second in his Kingdoms and Principalities. But the proof of this Lineal Succession, though there were no Law or Example to guide us, may be taken from the order that is observed in Publick Assemblies. For if in that order, regard be had to lineal descents, it will be a sign that the hopes conceived of the children of the deceased, was by Law quickened into a Just Right, so that it may well pass from the dead to the living. This is that Lineal Cognatical succession, wherein women, and those that are born of them, are not excluded, but only post-pon'd in the same line. So that recourse is had unto them, in case the Males that are nearer, or that those born from Males in an equal line should fail. The ground whereof, as it differs from an hereditary succession, is the hopes which the people conceive of them who are nearest related to the Prince in possession, and who have the justest hopes to succeed him, that they have Educations answerable to their high birth and hopes; such are the Children of those Parents, who had they lived, must have succeeded.

XXIII. The lineal succession of the Males only. Agnatical succession.

There is likewise another lineal succession of Males only which is called Agnatical, which differs from the Cognatical, in that it excludes Females, and admits only of Males; which, from the Kingdom of *France* takes its rise, and is therefore called the *French* succession. Though the Kingdom of *Israel* seems to have been thus setled, 2 *Chron.* 13. 5. And the chief reason of this, is to debar Strangers from the Crown, by marrying the Kings Daughters. In both these lineal successions all are admitted that are any wayes allyed, though in degrees never so remote from the last possessor, whilst they can derive themselves from the first King. And in some places where the Agnatical Succession is deficient, recourse is had to the Cognatical. Nay, and this latter is sometimes preferred before the former; as in *Æthiopia*, where the Kings Sisters Son did alwayes succeed him; which *Bede* records also of the *Picts*, where the kindred of the women were preferred to the succession. The like we read of the *Indians*; So *Tacitus* of the *Germans*, That their Kings gave the greatest honour to their Sisters Son, as being nearest in blood to them.

XXIV. A succession that alwayes respects the proximity to the first King. *Livy, lib.* 29. *Vand. l.* 1.

Other manner of successions may be introduced, either by the people, or at the pleasure of him, who holds the Kingdom in a patrimonial right, so that he may alienate it. For he may so settle the succession, that they that are next to himself at all times, may be preferred before others; as it was anciently among the *Numidians*, where for the like cause, the Unkle did succeed in the Kingdom, before the Children of the last King. This Custome was introduced in *Africk* by the Testament of *Gizerick*, wherein amongst many other things, he chargeth his *Vandals, That they should admit of him only into the Throne, that should be at any time nearest unto himself, in a right Masculine line, and of them still the eldest, and then the next in order, wherein he regarded not the present possessor, but the first Acquisitor:* Which order, whether *Gizerick* himself learnt from the *Africans*, among whom it had been long observed; or whether they learnt it from some of our Northern Nations, is a question. The like was of old in use among the *happy Arabians*, as may be gathered out of *Strabo*. And the later Historians report the same of *Taurica Chersonesus*: Neither is it so long since the Kings of *Fesse*, and *Morocco* did the like. *Livy* speaking of *Massinissa*, saith, *That whilst he made War in* Spain *for the* Carthaginians, *his Father dying, the Kingdom fell according to the custome of the* Numidians *unto* Desalces *the deceased Kings Brother.* The same Custome is in force throughout all *Mauritania*, as *Mariana* testifies: and in the Kingdom of *Mexico* and *Peru*, as the Histories of those parts record. Now the same if in doubt, is to be observed in things committed to trust, if it be left to the Family. And this agrees best with the *Roman* Laws, though some Interpreters do wrest it otherwise. These things premised, it will be no hard matter to resolve all Controversies which do arise, concerning the Right of Kingdoms, which the different opinions of Lawyers have made so intricate.

Lib. 16.

XXV. Whether the Son may be so exheredated, that he shall not succeed in his Fathers Kingdom.

He may, if the Kingdom be Patrimonial.

And in the first place, this Question ariseth, Whether a Father may exheredate his Son, so that he shall not succeed in his Kingdom? Where we must distinguish between Patrimonial Kingdoms which are Alienable, and such as are not Alienable. In the former there is no doubt, but that exheredation is lawful; for such Kingdoms differ nothing from other Goods: and therefore in such places, where by Law or Custome Exheredation is in force, it is practicable even in the case of Kingdoms: yea, though there were no Law or Custome to warrant it, yet naturally it is lawful for a Father to exclude his Son from all but bare Alimony; yea, and from that also, if he have committed any Crime worthy of death, or have been otherwise notoriously wicked, and have of his own whereby otherwise to subsist. Thus was *Reuben* punished by *Jacob* with the loss of his Birth-right, and *Adonija* by *David* with the loss of his Kingdom: For *David*'s Kingdom was in a manner Patrimonial, though not by the right of War, yet by special donation

donation from God himſelf. Now where the Kingdom is Patrimonial, the King may nominate which of his Sons he will to ſucceed him, as the Kings of *Mexico* now do. Nay, if the eldeſt Son have provoked his Father by any hainous crime, and there be no manifeſt ſign that he hath forgiven him, he ſhall be as one tacitely exheredated. But it is otherwiſe in Kingdoms not alienable, though they be hereditary, becauſe the people are beſt pleaſed that the Kingdom ſhall deſcend in an hereditary way, eſpecially from an Inteſtate. Much leſs ſhall it be in the power of a Father to exheredate his Son where the Kingdom is to paſs in a lineal deſcent: For there without any imitation of an Inheritance, it was agreed in its firſt Inſtitution, That the Kingdom ſhould by the peoples gift paſs to every perſon of the Royal Family, in ſuch order as was then preſcrib'd.

Otherwiſe in Kingdoms not alienable.

XXVI. Whether a King may renounce his Kingdom. In a Kingdom meerly hereditary he may, but not in a Lineal Succeſſion.

Another Queſtion is this, Whether a King may ſo abdicate his Kingdom as to deprive his Son of his Right to ſucceed, which is reſolved by the ſame diſtinction. For in Kingdoms meerly hereditary, he that renounceth his Kingdom, cannot transfer it to his Son. But in lineal deſcents the Fathers act cannot null his Sons Right that is born: For as ſoon as the children begin to exiſt, the law makes proviſion for them; yea, and for thoſe that are to be born ſo, becauſe that right which, by the peoples conſent is entailed upon them, muſt in due time deſcend upon them. Neither doth that which I have already ſaid concerning tranſmiſſion, contradict this. For that tranſmiſſion is *Neceſſary*, as to the Parents, and not Voluntary. But yet a difference there is between thoſe Children that are born before the Renunciation, and thoſe born after: For they that are already born, have by the Law a full Right to the Kingdom, though they that are not permitted to enjoy that Right during the life of their Parent; but to thoſe not born, there cannot as yet be any Right acquired: and therefore it may be taken away by the will of the people, if the Parents alſo to whom it belongs to transfer that Right unto them, be willing to releaſe it. And to this purpoſe is that we have already ſaid concerning dereliction.

XXVII. Whether the King, or the People only, have a Right to judge of the Succeſſion.

Another Queſtion doth ſometimes ariſe, namely, who ſhall be judge of the Right of Succeſſion to a Kingdom: Whethet the King then reigning, or the people by themſelves, or by ſuch Judges as they ſhall appoint. If the Queſtion be put of ſuch a Judgement as is Authoritative, neither of them have any Right to judge. For Juriſdiction there cannot be, but in a ſuperiour, who ſhould have reſpect not barely to the perſon, but to the matter alſo, which is to be poiſed with its due circumſtances. But the caſe of Succeſſion is not properly under the juriſdiction of the preſent King: becauſe he cannot of himſelf by any Law bind his Succeſſor. For the Succeſſion to the Empire lies not under the juriſdiction of the Empire, but remains in the ſtate of Nature, wherein there was no juriſdiction at all. But yet notwithſtanding, if the Right of Succeſſion be controverted, the pretenders unto it will do very piouſly and juſtly, if they can agree between themſelves upon ſome indifferent perſons, to whoſe arbitrement they can be contented to refer themſelves; whereof we ſhall diſcourſe hereafter. But the people have transferred all their Juriſdiction from themſelves into the King and the Royal Family; during which, they cannot challenge to themſelves any reliques of it. This I mean of a true Kingdom, and not of every Principality. But yet, if in the diſcuſſing of this Right any queſtion do ariſe concerning the primary will and intention of the people at the firſt inſtitution of the Kingdom, it were not amiſs to take the advice of the people in preſent, that is, of all the three States; I mean, of the Nobles, Clergy, and Commons in Parliament aſſembled, as is uſual in *England* and *Scotland*, as *Camden* teſtifies in his Hiſtory of Queen *Elizabeth*: For the people in preſent may be judged to be the ſame they anciently were. Or by Delegates purpoſely choſen, as in the Kingdom of *Arragon*, unleſs it do ſufficiently appear, That the people then were clearly of another will, and that thereupon the Right of Empire was obtained: Thus did King *Euphaes* ſuffer the *Meſſenians* diligently to enquire which of the Royal ſtock of the *Æpytidæ* had moſt Right to the Kingdom. But the conteſt between *Xerxes* and *Artabazanes* was determined by their Uncle *Artaphernes*, to whom it was amicably referr'd, as to a Domeſtick Judge.

1571, 1572.

Plut. de fratrum amore. Pauſ. lib. 4. *Juſtin. lib.* 2.

XXVIII. The Son born before his Father was King, to be preferred before him that was poſtnate.

But let us proceed to other caſes, It hath been often controverted which of the two Sons hath the beſt Right to the Succeſſion: He that was born before the Father gained the Kingdom, or he that was born after: Whereunto the moſt Rational Anſwer is, That he that was firſt born, ſhall firſt ſucceed, if the Kingdom be indiviſible, which holds true in every kind of Succeſſion. (Yet did *Henry* the Firſt, youngeſt Brother to *Rufus*, aſſume the Crown of *England*, whileſt his elder Brother *Robert* was in the Holy Land, upon this pretence, That he was born to his Father after he was Crowned King of *England*, whereas his Brother *Robert* was born whileſt his Father was Duke of *Normandy* only; yet was *Henry* juſtly branded as an Uſurper of his Brothers Right, by *Mat. Pariſienſis*.) But in caſe the Kingdom be diviſible, without doubt the latter ſhall have his ſhare, as well in this as in other goods, concerning which it matters not when they were got.

Now if he that of a divisible Estate may have his share; and in that which is indivisible, is preferred by the priviledge of his birth: Surely even the Inheritance must follow that Son which was born before his Fathers first Investiture. But even in a Lineal Succession, a Kingdom is no sooner got, but the Children which are antenate, do immediately conceive an hopes of Succession. For admit that there are none born after, surely no man will say, That those before born are to be excluded. But in this kind of Succession *an hope once conceived begets a Right:* Neither doth it by any post fact determine, unless it be in a Cognatical Succession, where it may be for a while suspended, by reason of the priviledge of Sex. Thus was the case decided in *Persia*, between *Cyrus* and *Artaxerxes*; in *Judæa*, between *Antipater*, the Son of *Herod* the Great, and his Brethren; In *Hungary*, when *Geissa* began his reign; and in *Germany* (though not without Blood) between *Otto* the
Mariana l. 24. first, and *Henry*; and in *Turky*, between *Bajazet* the antenate, and *Gemes* the postnate, to the Empire. And though haply it may be true, that the choice of the Kings of *Persia* did much depend upon the suffrages of the people; yet were those suffrages always li-
Lib. 23. mited to the Royal Family: For thus much doth *Mariana* testifie of the *Arsacidæ*, who being *Parthians* reigned in *Persia*. And the like doth *Zonaras* in *Justin*, of those *Persians* that succeeded those *Parthians*.

XXIX. Unless otherwise provided by some Law.

But that it was otherwise in *Sparta*, we attribute to the Laws proper to them only, which gave the Sons that were postnate the Preheminence, for their more Heroick Education. The like may also happen by some peculiar Law made upon the first Investiture, If a Soveraign Lord shall give unto his Vassal, and to those that shall be born of him, an Empire, to be held of him in Fee: upon the strength of which Argument, *Lewis* (in the contest that arose between him and his Brother *Galeatius* for the Dutchy of *Millain*) did principally rely. For in *Persia*, That *Xerxes* the Postnate Son was preferred before *Artabazanes* the Antenate, was more by the power of *Atossa* his Mother, than by true right, as *Herodotus* observes. For in the same Kingdom when the same Controversie afterwards arose between *Artaxerxes*, *Mnemon* and *Cyrus*, the Sons of *Darius* and *Parisardis*, *Artaxerxes* the first-born, though begotten by his Father in his private condition, was notwithstanding saluted King. Unless we take that as granted, which *Ammianus* hath delivered unto us, That the Succession to that Monarchy did much depend upon the suffrages of the people, confined only within the Royal stock.

XXX. Whether the Nephew by the elder Son be to be preferred before the younger Son.

It is no less disputed both by Wars and single Combats, whether the elder brothers Son, his Father being dead, should succeed before the second Brother. But this in a lineal descent will hardly admit of a dispute. For herein are the dead reckoned as living, in that they are able to transfer a Right to their Children; therefore the Son of the deceased, shall doubtless in such a Succession be preferred, without any exception made to his age; yea, and where the Succession is cognatical, the Daughter of the eldest Brother shall be preferred before the Uncle: because in such Successions neither Sex nor Age should make us to decline the right line. But in such Kingdoms as are hereditary, yet divisible, there shall each have a share, unless it be where the Right of Representation is not as yet received: as of old among many of the *German* Princes: For it is but of late that Nephews have been admitted before their Uncles. But where it once comes into debate, surely the Nephews case is to be preferr'd, as being most pleasing to humane Nature. And where by the Civil Laws of any Nation, representative Succession is once openly admitted, there the Son of the deceased Brother shall succeed in the room of his Father; though in that Law the word *Proximus*, that is, *Next of kin*, be only mentioned. The Reasons that are extracted out of the *Roman* Laws for this, are but weak; as is evident to such as inspect them. But this is the best reason, That in matters that are to be favourably understood, the sense of words must be extended to all propriety, not only vulgar, but artificial. So that under the name of *Sons*, may be comprehended those of Adoption; and under the word *Dead*, may in included those that are dead in Law, because the Laws do usually speak thus. And thus he may deservedly be said to be *Proximus*, whom the Laws present in the next degree. But yet in Kingdoms that are hereditary, and withal individual, and where this Representative Succession is not excluded: Neither is the Nephew always preferred to the Succession, nor always the second Son, but as amongst equals; because by an effect of Right, as to degrees that are adequate, his
Diod. l. 6. case is best that is eldest. For as we have said before, in hereditary Kingdoms, Succession is guided by the priviledge of age. Among the *Corinthians*, the eldest Son of the
Procop. Vand. lib. 3. deceased King did succeed in his Fathers Throne. So among the *Vandals* it was provided, That the next in Blood to the first King, and the eldest should be declared Heir. So that the second Son, because of his maturity of years, was preferred before the Son
Vid. sup. §. 24. of the eldest Brother. So in *Sicily*, *Robert*, being the Second Son, was advanced to the Throne before *Martell*, his elder Brothers Son, not properly for the reason fansied by *Bartolus*, because *Sicily* was held in Fee (as it were) by a Superiour Lord; but because that Kingdom was hereditary. There is in *Crantzius* an ancient example, of such a Succession

Succession in the Kingdom of the *Francks*; but that proceeded rather from the peoples choice, which at that time did not fully cease: But since that Kingdom ceased to be Elective, and that the line of Agnatical Succession was there established, the matter admits of no dispute. As anciently among the *Spartans*, where as soon as the Kingdom came to the *Heraclida*, the same Agnatical Succession was introduced. And therefore *Areus*, the Son of the elder Brother *Cleonymus*, was preferred to the Crown before his Uncle. But even in a Lineal Cognatical Succession, the Nephew hath been preferred: As in *England*, *John*, the Nephew of King *Edward* by his eldest Son, was preferred before *Hemon* and *Thomas*: Which also is setled by Law in the Kingdom of *Castile*.

By the same distinction we may resolve another doubt, between the surviving Brother to the last King, and the Son of the elder Brother: But that we must know, that in many places, where among children, the living may succeed in the room of the dead in the right line, they are not permitted so to do in the transverse. But where the Right is not clear and undoubted, it is most rational to incline to that part which favours the Child in the Right of his Father; because we are thereunto guided by natural equity, namely, in that Estate which descended from his Ancestors. Neither is it any Impediment, that *Justinian* calls the Right of Brothers Children, Depredatory: For this he doth in relation to the ancient *Roman* Laws, but not to natural equity. Let us now proceed to examine the other cases proposed by *Emanuel Costa*. XXXI. Whether the younger Brother living, be to be preferred before the Kings elder Brothers Son.

The Son of the deceased Brother, or even his Daughter, he saith is to be preferred before the Kings Uncle: This is true, not in a Lineal Succession only, but even in an hereditary, in such Kingdoms where Representative Succession takes place; but not in such Kingdoms which in express terms do bind us up to the degrees that are Natural. For there they are to be preferred, which have the precedency of Sex and Age. XXXII. Whether the Son of the Brother be to be preferred before the Kings Uncle.

He further adds, That the Nephew from the Son is to be preferr'd before the Daughter: It is true, By reason of his Sex; yet with this exception, Unless it be in such a Nation, which even amongst Children respects only the Degree. XXXIII. The Nephew by the Son preferred before the Daughter.

He farther adds, That the younger Nephew from the Son is to be preferr'd before the elder from the Daughter; which is likewise true, where a Lineal Cognatical Succession is in use, but not in an hereditary, without the warrant of some Special Law. Neither do we approve of the Reason alledged, namely, because the Father of the one, was to be preferred before the Mother of the other: For that was by reason of his dignity, which was meerly personal, and descended no farther. And yet on the contrary, we read that *Ferdinando*, the Son of *Berengaria*, the younger Sister of King *Henry* deceased, was preferred to the Kingdom of *Castile* before *Blanch*, the elder Sister of the same King: But this, as *Mariana* notes, was done in hatred to the house of *France*, into which *Blanch* married. XXXIV. The younger Nephew from the Son, before the elder from the Daughter.

That which he adds, as seeming to him most probable, namely, That the Neece from the elder Son excludes the younger Son; cannot hold in hereditary Kingdoms, although Representative Succession be there in force. For that gives only a capacity to succeed: But of those that are capable, regard is to be had to the priviledge of the Sex. XXV. The Neece from the elder Son preferred before the younger Son.

And therefore in the Kingdom of *Arragon*, the Sisters Son was preferr'd before the Brothers Daughter: And as *Mariana* observes, It is credible, that in that Kingdom in times long since past, The Kings Brother, and not his Daughter, had the Right of Succession: But afterwards they were so well pleased with a Lineal Succession, that they preferred the Sisters Son before those that, in a more remote degree, descended from the Brother. And in another place, speaking of *Alphonsus*, he saith, That unto the Inheritance of the Kingdom of *Arragon*, after his Son *Ferdinando*, he appointed his Nephews by his Sons; and for want of such, then the Nephews by his own Daughter were to be preferred before the Daughters of the said *Ferdinando*: Whereunto he adds, *Sic sæpe ad Arbitrium Regum jura regnandi commutantur*; They are Titles to Kingdoms ofttimes fann'd about by the breath of Kings. XXXVI. The Sisters Son preferred before the Brothers Daughter.

After the same manner, In Kingdoms that are hereditary, the Daughter of the eldest Son shall give place to the Kings younger Brother. XXXVII. Whether the Daughter of the elder Brother be to be preferred before the younger Brother.

CHAP.

CHAP. VIII.

Of Dominion vulgarly said to be acquired by the Law of Nations.

I. That many things are said to belong to the Law of Nature that properly do not.

NOw our Method leads us to treat of that Dominion, which is vulgarly said to be acquired by the Law of Nations, which being distinct from that gained by the Law of Nature, we have therefore termed the voluntary Law of Nations. Such is that Dominion which is got by the Right of War: But of this we shall discourse better hereafter, where the effects of War shall be explained. The *Roman* Lawyers, where they treat of the gaining of the Dominion of things, do reckon up many ways whereby it may be acquired, which they seem to justifie by the Law of Nations. But to him that diligently examines them, there is hardly any, except that gained by War, that will appear to be gained by that Law of Nations whereof we now speak. But are either such as are to be referred to the Law of Nature, not that which is meerly so, yet to that which follows close upon it, Dominion, being first introduced, and so antecedes all Civil Law; or they are such as may be referred to the very Civil Law, not that of the sole people of *Rome*, but of many other Nations: Which I rather believe, because this Civil Law or Custome came originally from the *Greeks*, whose Institutes, as *Dionysius Halicarnassensis* observes, with some others, all *Italy* and some other adjoyning Nations followed. But this is not the Law of Nations, properly so called. For it serves not to conglutinate all Nations mutually among themselves; but rather to preserve peace and tranquillity between the Subjects of every Nation: And was therefore alterable by any one people without consulting the rest, so that it may also come to pass, That in other places and in other ages, a far different common custom; and so, another Law of Nations, improperly so called, may be introduced: Which we have found really done, as soon as the *German* Nation had invaded all *Europe*. For as of old the

the *Gracian* Laws, so then, the *Germans* were almost every where received, and do as yet flourish. The first way of gaining Dominion by the Law of Nations, as the *Romans* call it, is by the primary seizure or occupancy of such things as have no owner, which without doubt is natural in that sense which I have declared, that is, Dominion being first introduced, and so long as no Law did otherwise determine. For Dominion may also be gained by the Civil Law.

II. As Fish in Ponds, Deer in Parks.

And hitherto in the first place we may refer the taking of Wild Beasts, Birds and Fish. But how all these may be said to belong to none, will afford matter of debate. *Nerva* the Son was of opinion, That Fish, if in a Pond, were possest, but not in a great Lake: And that Wild Beasts, if in a Park or Warren, had an owner; but ranging in Woods hedg'd about, not. As though Fish inclosed in a greater Pond could not be as well owned as in a lesser; and Deer and Conies as well possest in a well fenced Wood, as in a Park or Warren: Seeing that there is no more difference between them, than that in the one they are close Prisoners, and in the other Prisoners at large. Wherefore in this age of ours, the contrary opinion is most prevalent, That both Deer in private Woods, and Fish inclosed in Lakes may be, as possest, so also held in Propriety.

III. That out-lying Deer cease not be the owners, could they be known.

In Wild Beasts, as soon as they recover their Natural Liberty, we lose our Property, say the *Roman* Lawyers. But in all other things the Dominion that is got by Possession, is not lost with the loss of Possession; nay, it gives us also a Right to recover our Possession: And whether it be taken away from us by another, or stray away of it self, as in the case of a Fugitive Servant, it matters not much. (The Title we may retain though the Possession be lost.) Wherefore it seems more agreeable to truth, That our Property is not lost meerly because the Beasts that were wild have escaped our custody; but because it may probably be conjectured, That by reason of the difficulty of recovering them, we have utterly deserted them; especially when it cannot be known unto others that they were ours; But this conjecture may easily be wiped away by other conjectures, as namely, by affixing unto them *γνωείσματα*, some things whereby it may be known whose they are, as is usually done to Harts, Hawks, and the like. To acquire a full Dominion in things naturally wild, it is necessary that we should have a Corporal Possession: It is not enough to entitle our selves to a Deer, that we have wounded him; but we must catch him too, lest the Proverb upbraid us with folly, *In starting an Hare for another to eat*: According to that of *Ovid*,

Et lepus hic aliis exagitatus erit.

By the Law of the *Lumbards*, He that killed a Wild Beast, being first Wounded by another, might take away the Shoulder with the Ribs; the rest belonged to him that wounded him, if he claimed it within twenty four hours, otherwise not. For as *Ovid* well observed, It is one thing to know where a thing is, and another to find it. *Met. 5.*

IV. Possession how got by Instruments, as Nets, &c.

Now this Possession may be gained, either by Hands only, or by Engines, as by Traps, Nets, Snares, Ginns, *&c.* Provided, first, That those Instruments are under our own power: And secondly, That the Beast so taken cannot escape. And thus is the question decided, concerning a Wild Boar that is fallen into a Snare or Toyl.

V. That Wild Beasts should be the Kings, is not against the Law of Nature.

These things are thus to be understood, where no Civil Law intervenes, wherefore our Modern Lawyers are much mistaken, who think these Rights to be so Natural, that they cannot be changed: For they are not simply or absolutely so, but as things at that time were, before the Civil Law did otherwise determine of them. The people of *Germany* consulting about some allowances to be given to their Kings and Princes, whereby to support their Regal Dignities, thought it prudence to begin with such things as no private man could claim as his own: Which prudential course the *Ægyptians* also anciently took; where the Kings Attorney seized on all such things to his Masters use. But the Law of it self is sufficient to transfer a Propriety in any thing that is not already occupied. The Whales that are cast upon the Shoar, the *Portugals* give unto their King.

VI. Possession of things not owned, how gained.

After the same manner as Wild Beasts are possest, are all other things that have no owner. For Nature doth indifferently adjudge all such things to the first finder and possessor of them. Thus was the Island *Acanthos* * being desart, adjudged to the Inhabitants of *Chalcis*, who first entred upon it; and not unto the *Andrians*, who had first thrown their Darts into it. Because Possession is taken either by the apprehending of a thing, if movable, mostly by the hand; or if immovable, as of Land, by setting our feet upon it. For as the Poet tells us, *Scire ubi res est, non est invenire; It is not enough to know where a thing is, unless we can find it.*

* *Plut. Græc. Qu. 29.*

Among

VII. Mony found whose it is. Among such things as are ἀδέσποτα without an owner, are Treasures reckoned, that is, Mony, the owner whereof is unknown, *For things that appear not, are as if they were not*; wherefore such treasures are naturally his that finds and apprehends them, yet not so but that Laws and Customs may dispose otherwise of them. *Plato* would have the finder to give notice thereof to the Magistrate, or to take advice of an Oracle. *Apollonius* looked at such treasure, as being an especial gift of God, and adjudged it to him that was best beloved of him. It is Scripture Law, *Quod non posuisti ne tollas*; *Take not away what thou didst not lay down*: The *Hebrews* gave such treasures to him that was Lord of the ground wherein it was found, as may be collected from that parable of our Saviour, concerning Treasures hidden in the ground, which being found, he that found it sold all he had, and bought the Field, *Mat.* 13. 44. So did the *Syrians*, as may be gathered out of *Philostratus*: And it seems that in *Plautus* his time, this was approved of by the *Romans*. The Laws of the Empire do much vary about this, as may appear partly by their constitutions, and partly by the Histories of *Lampridius*, *Zonoras*, *Cedrenus*, and *Tacitus*, who writing of the great Treasures found in *Africa*, saith, *Which* Nero *in his hopes devoured.* The *Germans* gave such (as also they did all other ἀδέσποτα) to their Prince, which is now so common every where, that it may well pass for one of the Laws of Nations: For it is this day observed in *Germany*, *France*, *England*, *Spain*, and *Denmark*. But this very same custom we read of among the *Goths*, witness King *Theuderick* in *Cassiodore*: *Non est cupiditas eripere, quæ nullus se dominus ingemescat amisisse*; *It cannot be imputed as Covetousness, to take that which no man hath just reason to complain for the loss of.* And in another place, *Those riches which having lain so long hid have lost their Masters, by thy diligent inquisition are now ours: For since we permit every man freely to enjoy his own, what is no mans ought to be ours. He may well be content to lose what he hath found, who knows that in so doing he loseth nothing that is his own.*

Philostr. D. 15. *Bibliorum Lex.* *Annal l.* 16. *Lib.* 4. *c.* 34. What is no mans is the Kings.

VIII. Of Islands and Inundations. Let us now proceed to Inundations or Increments by Rivers, whereof the ancient Lawyers have written much, but the Modern whole Commentaries: But what they have written is for the most part grounded not on the Law of Nature, but on the Laws of some Nations, though to gain the greater authority they oft-times put them off under that name. Most of their determinations being built upon this foundation, That the banks of the River are his who possesseth the adjoyning soil, and that the Channel, as soon as it is forsaken by the waters, is his also; and consequently, those Islands which are cast up in the River. There they distinguish of Inundations, a small one alters not the property of the ground, but a great one doth; yet so that if it come by reason of some sudden and violent force of waters, and so recede, the ground overflown shall, upon the return of the waters, as if by postliminy, remain to its right owner: But if by a continual beating upon it, it wash it away by degrees, it is lost for ever. Now that all these might be introduced by some Law, to make men more carefully to defend their own banks, I deny not; but that they be so by a Natural Right (as they would have it) I cannot grant.

IX. Whose they are naturally. See above, ch. 3. towards the end. For if we respect that which mostly happens, the soyl is first possest by the people, and that, not only under a Soveraign power or Empire, but under dominion also, before the Fields were distributed among private persons. *The boundaries of the* Athenians *or Campagnes*, saith *Seneca*, *are those whereby their Fields (which before lay in common) are by private agreement between themselves and their Neighbours, distinguished.* So also *Cicero*, *Privata natura nulla sunt*; *There is nothing naturally private, but either by primary possession, as they that first set footing in a place that is desart; or that which comes by conquest or by Law, consent, condition, or by Lots; whereby it comes to pass, that the fields about* Arpinum *are said to belong to the Inhabitants of* Arpinum; *and the Fields of* Tusculum, *to the Inhabitants of* Tusculum: *And thus is every private mans estate described.* So *Dion Prusæensis*, *There are many things which a City in general challengeth as her own, though they are divided by parcels amongst private Lords.* After the same manner speaks *Tacitus* of the *Germans*, *That their Fields were first occupied by the people in common by Villages, according to the number of the Inhabitants, and afterwards distributed among themselves, according to every mans reputation and dignity*: Wherefore whatsoever was thus originally possest by the people, and never afterwards distributed, doth as yet properly belong unto the people. And as in private Rivers, those Islands which the waters cast up, and that part of the Channel which the waters forsake, are properly his who owns the River; so in publick are both of them the peoples, or his, to whom the people hath given them. Now what is here said concerning the Channels, may also be said of the Banks, which are but the extreme parts of the Channel, wherein the River naturally runs; and thus it is every where taken. In *Holland* and the Countries adjacent, many such disputes did anciently arise, by reason of the lowness of the ground, the greatness of their Rivers, and their nearness to the Sea, receiving and casting up by alternate tides, mud and sand: Those that were Islands, truly so called, were always adjudged to be part of the peoples patrimony; as also the whole Channel of the *Rhine* and of the *Mase*, which the Waters have left, as it hath been frequently determined, and with very

De benef. l. 7. *c.* 4. *De Off. lib.* 1. *Or. Rhodiaca.*

very good reason: For as the *Roman* Lawyers themselves do grant, that the Islands which float in a River, being upheld by the young sprouts that grow in it, of right belong to the Common-wealth; because, *Cujus juris est flumen, ejus est & insula in flumine nata*; *Whose the River is, his is the Island that is in it.* And surely there is the same reason for a River, as for the Channel wherein it runs, not for the reason which they bring, namely, because the Channel is covered by the River; but for the reason aforesaid, because it was originally possest with the River, and was never since transferred into any private mans dominion. Neither can we admit of that as true naturally, which they averr, that if the Fields be bounded, the Islands are the first Occupants; for that indeed were true, in case that neither the River, nor with it the Channel, were at all possest by the people: for then they were like those Islands which are raised in the Seas, his only that did first seize them.

Of Floating Islands see *Sen* his Nat. Quest *lib.* 3. *c.* 25. *Pliny lib.* 2. *c.* 95.

X. That naturally the Land is not lost because drowned.

Neither is that more to be admitted, which they write of a great Inundation, namely, that it gives away the property of the Land overflowed, if we respect only natural reason: For admit we do grant, that the superficies of the Land may be dissolved into Sand; yet do the lower parts thereof remain firm and solid, and though somewhat of the quantity be changed, yet is not the substance changed at all, no more than that part of a Field is, which is devoured by some Lake, the property whereof (as the *Roman* Lawyers themselves do rightly acknowledge) doth still remain. Neither is that natural that they write, that an Inundation performs the office of a Judge or Censor, making that private which was publick, and that publick which before was private: as *Cassiodore* speaks of a surveyor, *More vastissimi fluminis aliis spatia tollit, aliis concedit*; *That he was like a great River taking away from some that which of right was theirs, and giving unto others that wherein they had no right.* Much better were it to follow that which *Strabo* reports of the *Egyptians*, *To take an exact survey of the Fields, and so divide unto every man his own by Admeasurement: Because the River* Nilus *by her frequent floods and rapid streams, adding here and taking away there, and changing the form and marks of the Fields, doth so confound their bounds and limits, that it is hard for a man to distinguish between his own and another mans; therefore are Fields to be often surveyed.* Whereunto agrees that tradition of the *Roman* Lawyers, *Quod nostrum est, nostrum esse non desinit, nisi facto nostro*; *That which is ours ceaseth not to be ours without our own fact, or by some Law.* Now under things done are (morally) comprehended things left undone, as we have said already, that is to say, so far forth as we may thereby guess at the will of him that should do them. We may therefore grant, that where the Inundation is very great, and where there are no visible signs of the owners intention to retain his dominion; it may well be presumed, that he gives his Land for lost: Now as our conjectures in this case cannot but be naturally uncertain, by reason of the variety of circumstances, which are herein considerable, and to be referred to the Judgment of some prudent man; so ought it to be determined by Civil Laws: As in *Holland*, That ground is given for lost which hath for ten years been drowned, in case there appear no signs that the possession is still claimed; which with them is sufficiently done by fishing in it only, though the *Romans* do not allow thereof. But among other Princes the ancient occupants are prescribed a certain time wherein to drein their Lands, which if they do not, then are the morgagers of that Land (if engaged) admonish'd to do it; but if they delay it, then the Magistrates, either Civil or Criminal, are to do it; and if they neglect it; then it is forfeited unto the Prince, who may either drein it at his own charge, or transfer it to some other, reserving a part of it unto himself.

Where the Inundation is very great and no visible sign that the owner endeavours to recover what is to be done.

XI. That the Increments of Rivers if in doubt, are the peoples.

Whatsoever the floods do add to the soil, because it cannot be known from whence it came, cannot be claimed by any; (for if it could, naturally the property should not be changed) wherefore it is adjudged to be his whose the River is, and if the River be the peoples, consequently the increment is so too.

XII. But if granted, then theirs whose fields have no other bounds but the River.

But it is in the peoples power to grant it, as unto others, so unto those who enjoy the Lands next adjoyining; and doubtless they are presumed so to do, if those Lands have no other bounds but the River on that side: And although that distinction which the *Romans* make between Lands bounded, and Lands measured, be of good use; yet have both of them in this case equal right. For what we have said before concerning the bounds of Empires *, is of force here also with this only difference, that the bounds of Kingdoms (if in doubt) are presumed to be arcifinious, because those are most agreeable to their nature: But private possessions are rather believed to be set out and bounded, either by Landmarks or by measure, as being most suitable to theirs. But yet we deny not but that the people may grant their Land as fully as they themselves enjoy it, that is, even unto the River; which if they do, then is the increment of that River theirs also. This was a judged case in *Holland*, not many Ages since, of grounds bordering upon the Rivers *Izal* and *Maze*; because both by the deeds of purchase, and by the books of rates, they were always mentioned as bounded by the River: And although in the sale of these Lands, somewhat of the measure be exprest, yet shall it retain its own nature, and have right to whatsoever the River shall add unto it.

* *Ch.* 3. *§.* 16.

XIII. So are the banks if forsaken by the River and left dry.

What hath been said concerning that which the Floods do add to the soil, is likewise verified of that part of the shore, or of the Channel, which the River forsakes: For where there is no Occupant, there the next Occupyer hath the best Title; but in Rivers that are possest, whatsoever is so gained from the Channel is the peoples or theirs, to whom they have assigned the Lands next adjoyning, as being bounded by the River.

XIV. What is to be held as Increment, and what as an Island.

Now because there is one manner of right proper to Islands, and another to the increments of Rivers, Controversies do often arise how to distinguish them, especially when a little rising ground lyes near the Fields adjacent, yet is separated from them by the intervention of a little water that covers the Plain; as is often seen in the Low Countries where the ground is not level, where also the customs do somewhat vary: For in *Gildria*, if a loaden Wain can pass through the Waters interjacent, then is the rising ground judged to belong to the adjoyning Fields; so is it also in the Fields of *Puttene*, if a man standing upon the bank, can with his Swords point touch the ground that lyes beyond the water. Thus the *German* Histories record of *Autharis*, King of the *Lombards*, *That sitting on Horseback upon the Shore, and touching with the point of his Lance a certain Pillar*, said, *Usque hic erunt Longobardorum fines*; *Hitherto came King* Autharis, *and this shall be the bounds of* Lombardy. The like story we read of the Emperor *Otto*, who standing on the bank, threw his Javelin into the *Baltick Sea*, assigning that to be the limits of his Empire: But it is most agreeable to Nature, that if, for the most part, the passage over be by boat, it should be judged an Island..

XV. When the Increment belongs to the Vassal.

Another Question doth no less frequently arise between a Prince that fully enjoys the peoples right, and his Vassals or Lieutenants, who, under him, are intrusted with the Government: But it is sufficiently evident, that the bare grant of the Government doth not intitle the Vassal to the increment of Rivers. But yet we must note, That many that are thus intrusted with these limited Governments, do together with them receive the profits of all the * Lands in general, except such as are in the possession of private men: Upon this presumption, that those Fields were anciently either the peoples, or the Princes, or at least drained by the Prince; and if so, then doubtless whatsoever either the Prince or the people did so enjoy, their Vassals have a good right unto. Thus we see that in in *Zealand*, those Vassals that have power to appoint Judges, though but in civil affairs, do pay a tribute to the State for their common Fields, whereof every man according to the tenure of his private possession, bears his proportion. Now that these Vassals have a right to the increment of the Rivers, there can be no doubt: Others there are to whom the Rivers themselves are granted, who may therefore justly claim the Islands thereunto belonging, whether they be of mud heaped up together, or made out of the Channel, if surrounded by the River. Others again there are, in whose grants neither the one nor the other is included, and these have but an ill cause to defend against the publick Exchequer, unless either the custom of the Country do favour them, or a long uninterrupted possession (with such adjuncts as are requisite) give them a right. But in case the Lands only and not the Government be granted unto them, then we must look unto the nature of the Land, as is abovesaid: For if its bounds be arcifinious, then are the Increments granted with the Land; not so much by any Right properly belonging to the Prince, as by the quality of the Land; for in such a case, he that holds the Fee hath the benefit of what the Floods cast up.

* *universitatem agrorum.*

XVI. The Arguments whereby the *Roman* Lawyers would prove their Law to be as it were the Law of Nature, answered.

The *Roman* Lawyers, to prove the Laws by them used to be natural, do often alledge this Maxim, That it is most natural, that his should be the profit of any thing, whose is the disprofit; whereupon they infer, that since the River wasts a part of my Land, it is but reasonable that of what it adds to mine, mine should be the benefit. But this rule holds not, unless it be where the benefit ariseth from what is mine own, but in this case it ariseth from the River which is anothers: But that that which perisheth, should perish to the owner of it, is natural; besides, neither is that universally true that they alledge, as may appear by the exception of grounds limited, which themselves admit: Not now to insist upon that which often comes to pass naturally, that Rivers do sometimes impoverish, and sometimes enrich their Neighbours Fields: Whence *Lucan* thus,

Illos terra fugit dominos, his rura colonis
Accedunt, Donante Pado:

Old Lords forsook, the Earth doth gliding go
New to enrich, thanks to the River Po.

Whereby it appears, that some are enricht and impoverisht by one and the same River.]

But

But whereas also they say, that a publick way doth not put a stop to the increment of a River, it hath nothing of natural reason in it, unless it be where the Field is private, through which such a way ought to pass.

XVII. Whether an High-way do stop the Increment of a River.

Among other means whereby propriety (by that which is called the Law of Nations) is acquired, one is Procreation, wherein that, which (as well the *Romans* as) some other Nations have determined, namely, That the Child should follow the condition of the Mother only, is not (as we have already said *) natural, but only as the Father is unknown: For if the Father, by any probable means could be discovered, why the Child should not as well be reputed his as hers, no natural reason can be given; since it cannot be denyed but that what is so begotten, is a part of him that did beget it. But whether of them do contribute most to the production of the Child, Natural Philosophers do not accord: Whereof notwithstanding *Plutarch* speaks thus, *Nature*, saith he, *doth mix the Seed of both Sexes, and so confounds them; that what is thereby born should be common to them both, and that neither of them should be able to distinguish that which is theirs from that which was the others.* And hereupon are the Laws both of the *French* and *Lumbards* grounded.

XVIII. That the Child should follow the condition of the Mother only, is not natural.

* See ch. 5. §. 29.

Vid. Gall. l. 2. de femine.

If the matter belong to one, and the form given by another, the *Sabinians* give the property to him whose the matter was; but *Proculus* to him that gave the form, because he gave it such an existence as before it had not. At length a middle opinion crept in, namely, that if the matter could be reduced to its pristine form, then should the thing be his who gave the matter; but if it could not, then should it be his that gave the form: But this opinion pleased not *Connanus*, who would have no respect but to the value, so that whether of them was of greater value, should attract unto it that which was of lesser value, by an Argument drawn from those things which are delivered unto us by the *Roman* Lawyers, concerning Accession. But if we look to the naked truth, as by a commixture of several matters there ariseth a community to each, according to proportion, because it cannot otherwise be determined; so when a thing is compounded of matter and form as of its parts, if the matter or substance belong to one, and the form to another, (which cannot be divided) there must naturally follow a community to each, according to their respective proportions; for the form is a part of the substance but not the whole, which was acknowledged by *Ulpian*, in saying, that the form being changed, the substance was almost destroyed.

XIX. Community may arise by giving a new form to another matter.

But although it be not altogether unjust, that he that abuseth the matter, being another mans, shall lose the form he gives it, yet we must know that this is penal, and therefore not natural: For though it be natural that every delinquent should be punished, yet doth not Nature determine how, nor doth she of her self take away any mans property for his offence.

XX. Yea though the matter be abused.

But that the greater part should swallow up the lesser, whereupon *Connanus* grounds his opinion; though it be natural in respect of the Fact, yet is it not of Natural Right: Wherefore he that hath but the twentieth part of a Field, hath as much right in that, as he that hath the other nineteen. Therefore what the *Roman* Lawyers have decreed concerning an acquisition gained by way of prevalence, or what they have or may decree in other the like cases, is not justifyable by the Law of Nature, but by the Civil Law for the better dispatch of business; yet is it not repugnant unto Nature, because the Laws have a power to create dominion. There is scarce any one question in the Law, more variously handled among Lawyers than this: For who can grant, that if Brass and Gold were mixed together, they could not be separated, as *Ulpian* writes; or that if Metals were soldred together, they must needs be confounded, as *Paulus, &c.* or that there is one rule for a Picture, another for a Scripture, that the Table should carry away this but not that.

XXI. That the lesser should yield to the greater, by reason of its prevalence, is not natural.

Naturale est facti, non juris.

Ferruminatione.

That things planted or sown should go with the soyl, is a dictate likewise of the Civil Law, grounded on this reason, because they are nourished by it; and therefore it is a material question concerning a Tree whether it have taken root: But in case we look unto Nature only, we must confess, that the nourishment of a thing that had existence before, gives but augmentation to the thing nourished, which is but an additional part of it. And therefore as there is a Right due to the Lord of the Soyl, in respect of that nourishment; so surely there remains a Right naturally to him that owned the Plant or the Seed, without which the Soyl could not produce such fruits: So that here also Nature admits of a Community, no less than in an House built upon anothers ground, whose parts are the Soyl and the Superstructure, and in which, were it moveable, the Lord of the Soyl could have no right at all: Of which opinion was *Scævola*.

XXII. Of things planted or sowed on anothers ground, the fruits are naturally to be communicated.

He that ignorantly sows another mans ground, thinking it to be his own, cannot by the Law of Nature, appropriate all the fruits thereof to himself; but he may charge the owner of the ground with his costs, and with his profitable labour, and pay himself out of the profits either already perceived, or retain those that are extant, if he cannot otherwise get satisfaction.

XXIII. The Possessor cannot claim the fruits, but may his charges.

XXIV. Yea, though he possess it unjustly.

And the very same, it seems, may be said of him that is possest of another mans Estate, unjustly, where no penal Law interposeth. *For though he that possesseth mine Estate be an intruder, or an Usurper,* (saith *Paulus* the Lawyer) *yet ought I to satisfie him for his just expences: For he that seeks only to recover his own, ought not to enrich himself by the loss of another.*

XXV. That naturally the delivery is not requisite to transfer dominion.

The last means of acquiring dominion by the Law of Nations is by Tradition: But (as I said before) this is not required to the transferring of dominion by the Law of Nature, which the *Roman* Lawyers themselves acknowledge in some cases: As when the property of any thing is given away, but the profits of it reserved; or when it is bestowed on him that may hereafter possess it; or when being but lent, it may be kept; (and in such like cases:) Yea and even now a man may in some cases transfer Dominion to another, before he hath gained possession himself. As of an Inheritance expectant, of Legacies to be received, of things given to Churches and to pious places, or to Cities, *&c.* whereof it may be said, *Then the delivery of possession seems to be good, when the deeds of gift are in a mans own possession.* And thus did the ancient *Romans* use to aliene things sold by striking the Scales with a piece of Brass, and then giving it to him that made the sale.

Godwin's Rom. Ant. p. 240.

XXVI. What use may be made of what hath been said.

These things have I observed, lest any man finding, among the *Roman* Authors, the Law of Nations often quoted, should presently understand that Law to be such as could not be changed: But rather that he should be able to distinguish between such Laws as are purely natural, and those that are for some certain state, natural; and between such Laws as are in force amongst many Nations apart, and such as knit together all humane societies. And this likewise is to be observed, That if either by the Law of Nations, improperly so called, or by the Law of any Nation or People, any one way of acquiring a Right or Property be agreed on, without making any distinction between Natives and Strangers; there Foreigners also shall have and enjoy the same Right: And in case they shall be hindred in the consecution thereof, they have such wrong done them as may give occasion to a just War.

CHAP.

CHAP. IX.

How Empire and Dominion may Ceaſe and Determine.

I. *Dominion and Empire determine, when he that had the Right dies, and leaves no Succeſſor in being.*
II. *So the Right of a Family dies, when that Family is extinct.*
III. *The like of a People, when they ceaſe to be a free people..*
IV. *Which falls out, when their neceſſary parts are taken away.*
V. *And when the whole Body of a People are ſwept away.*
VI. *And when their Form is loſt, whereby they become a People.*
VII. *But not by the change of Place.*
VIII. *Nor upon their change of Government, where alſo is diſcuſt, what place a new King or free People are to take in general Aſſemblies.*
IX. *What if two People be united.*
X. *What if a People be divided.*
XI. *In whom now are, what once belonged to the* Roman *Empire, ſince there appears no Alienation.*
XII. *Of the Right of Heirs.*
XIII. *Of the Right of Conquerors.*

I. When the owner dying, leaves no Succeſſor.

HOw as well Propriety as Empire were at firſt introduced, and how they may be transferred, is ſufficiently diſcuſt: Now let us underſtand how they may end; And firſt, that they may determine by a voluntary dereliction hath been already demonſtrated: For, *Ceſſante voluntate non manet dominium; Where the Will diſclaims, Propriety vaniſheth.* Again, they may ceaſe when the Subject wherein they are, is taken away before any Alienation be made of them, either expreſs or preſumptive, as in Succeſſions from him that dyes inteſtate, and leaves no Kindred behind him; wherefore all the right that he had in any thing, dyes alſo with him: Wherefore his Servants (unleſs the Laws do otherwiſe ordain) are immediately free, and the people that were in ſubjection to him are at their own liberty; becauſe theſe are not in their own nature occupyable, but as they are willing to ſurrender themſelves, but all his other goods are naturally his that hath them.

II. So of a Family.

The very ſame holds true, if a Family happen to be extinct, whatſoever right it had ceaſeth with it.

III. When the people that were free, ceaſe to be ſo.

So alſo if a People fail, *Iſocrates* firſt, and from him the Emperour *Julian*, tells us, *That Cities are immortal*; meaning that ſo they may be, becauſe the people are a Body conſiſting of Members remote one from another, yet united under one name, as having but one order or form of Government, as *Plutarch* calls it; or one Spirit, as *Paulus* the Lawyer, which animates and informs all the parts of it; and is therefore (as *Ariſtotle* terms it) the life of it. But this Spirit in the people is a full and perfect conſociation tending to a civil life, whereof the ſupreme power is the firſt product: This is the bond that knits all the parts together, the Vital Spirit, as *Seneca* terms it, *Quem tot millia trahunt*, which animates ſo many thouſands at once; for plainly the Artificial Bodies have ſome reſemblance with the Natural. The Natural Body though it every day waſtes a little, yet whilſt that which waſtes, is every day repaired, and the ſame form or figure continued, ceaſeth not to be the ſame body. And therefore that of *Seneca*, where he ſaith, *That no man is the ſame being old, as he was when he was young*, may very fitly be interpreted, as if underſtood of the matter only: As alſo that of *Heracleus* in *Plato* verified, *That no man can deſcend twice into the ſame River*; Which *Seneca* thus expounds, *Manet idem fluminis nomen, aqua tranſmiſſa eſt*; *The Name only continues, but the Waters glide away.* So *Ariſtotle* comparing a River to the people, ſaith, *That the River is ſtill called by the ſame Name, though the Waters are not the ſame.* Neither doth it retain its name in vain, for it hath the ſame form, figure, and ſpirit, (as they call it) as formerly it had: So is it in Cities, though the Citizens are not the ſame that they were an hundred years ſince, *Yet whilſt there remains the ſame conſociation and communion, which both conſtitutes a People, and continues them in the ſame Mould, Form, and Figure, as they were ſo many Years or Ages ſince; it may juſtly be called the ſame City, though not one of the Citizens thereof may be now living. As the Ship wherein* Theſeus *ſayled with the principal young men of* Athens, *and ſafely returned, being by the* Athenians *(by repairing whatſoever was decayed in her) preſerved, till the time of* Demetrius Phalerenſis, *gave occaſion to Philoſopher, to diſpute, Whether ſhe were the ſame or another.* Which though much controverted by them, yet is by Lawyers prudently adjudged to be the ſame. For, as

Lib. 1. declementia cap. 4. *Ep. 58.*

Pol. 13. c. 2.

Plut.

In the life of *Theſeus.*

Philo

Philo. *Philo* obſerves of the World, Not every thing whoſe parts do ſucceſſively periſh, muſt certainly be diſſolved; but that only, all whole parts do at one and the ſame time periſh together. Hence ariſeth that cuſtom uſed in Hiſtories, as well ſacred as profane, of attributing unto the people which now are, thoſe things which were done by the people of the ſame City many Ages paſt: As may be ſeen, *Mat.* 23. 35. *Acts* 3. 22. *Mark* 10. 3. *Tacitus.* *Jo.* 6. 32. and 7. 19. So in *Tacitus* we read, That *Antonius Primus* ſerving under *Veſpaſian*, puts the Soldiers of the *Tertian* Legion in mind, *That it was their valour that routed the* Parthian *Army under the Conduct of* M. Anthony; *and that it was their valour that under* Corbuto, *had put to flight the* Armenians: Whereas there was not one of that *Tertian* Legion that fought under *M. Anthony*, then living when he ſaid it, it being done an hundred *Alberic. Gent. lib.* 1. *c.* 23. *L.* 2. years before. It was therefore more out of hatred than truth, that *Piſo* in the ſame Author, *denyes the* Athenians *of his time to be natural* Athenians, *whom the Wars* (as he pretends) *had totally deſtroyed, but the very ſcum and outcaſts of other Nations.* Whereas in truth, theſe mixing with the *Athenians*, might haply detract ſomewhat from their ancient honour, and repute, but not make them another people: Neither was *Piſo* ignorant of this, for in the ſame place, *He objects againſt the ſame* Athenians, *thoſe Injuries which had been done many Ages before, namely, how they had aſſiſted* Mithridates *againſt* Scylla, *and* M. Anthony *againſt* Auguſtus, *and how unſucceſsfully they had made war againſt the* Macedonians, *and what cruelty they had exerciſed over their own Subjects.* Now as there may be many particular changes in a Nation, and yet the people continue the ſame, they were a thouſand years ſince and more; ſo it cannot be denyed, but that there may happen ſo univerſal a change, as that they may utterly ceaſe to be a people; which may be done two ways, either when the whole body of the People is deſtroyed, or when that order, form, or ſpirit, that unites them together, is totally aboliſhed.

IV. As when their neceſſary parts are taken away. See *Sen.* Nat. Queſt. *lib.* 5. *c.* 23. 32. *Epiſt.* 92. *Lib.* 17. *rerum. geſt.* The few remaining may retain their propriety as a private perſon, but not as a State.

The Body periſheth, either when all its Members are at once deſtroyed, without which it cannot ſubſiſt; or when, though the parts be entire, yet the frame is disjoynted and its parts diſſipated: *By theſe two ways is an Army deſtroyed; either by an univerſal Slaughter, or by a total Diſperſion.* Among ſuch as ceaſe to be a people the former way, are thoſe that periſh univerſally by ſome deluge; as did the people of the *Atlantick* Iſlands, whereof *Plato* makes mention in his *Timæo*; and ſuch as are ſwallowed up by ſome great Caſme, occaſioned by Earthquakes: Examples we may read of in *Seneca*, in *Ammianus Marcellinus*, and elſewhere; and ſuch as have voluntarily deſtroyed themſelves, as the *Sydonians* and *Saguntines*. But what if, of ſuch a people, ſo few remain alive, as that they cannot be ſaid to be a people, yet may they retain that propriety which that people had, as private perſons; though what they had as being a people, they cannot: The ſame is alſo to be underſtood of Corporations and Colledges.

V. When the whole people are ſwept away. *Ariſt. Pol. l.* 3. *c.* 2. *Philo de mundo.*

The frame or manner of being a Body is taken away, when the Citizens do either of their own accord diſſipate themſelves, by reaſon of ſome general contagion or ſedition; or when they are by force ſo ſcattered and diſperſt, as that they cannot unite again, as it often happens in times of War: *All Bodies conſiſting of remote parts, as Flocks, Herds, Armies, being knit together no leſs than members of the ſame body, if they be forced aſunder, vaniſh, and are diſſolved, as a Ship that is torn in pieces.*

VI. Or when the Form or Spirit is loſt. *Lib.* 26.

The form and ſpirit of a people periſheth, either when all or a perfect community of Right is taken away; which is done either when every perſon is brought into captivity, as when the *Mycenæans* were by the *Argives*, the *Olynthians* by King *Philip*, the *Thebans* ſold by *Alexander*, and the *Brutii* condemned by the *Romans* to their publick works; or when enjoying community of Right, yet they are utterly deprived of all Government. So *Livy* of *Capua*, *It pleaſed the* Romans *that their Town ſhould be inhabited, but that there ſhould be no Corporation of Citizens, no Senate, no Common Council, no Magiſtrates, but a multitude of Folks without any publick Aſſemblies, and without any Juriſdiction Civil or Military; all cauſes among them being to be decided by a Governor ſent from* Rome. So that as *Cicero* obſerved, in his Oration againſt *Rullus*, *There was not left in* Capua *ſo much as the face or ſhadow of a Commonwealth.* In the very ſame condition are thoſe people, who being once a free Nation, are reduced by force into a Province; and thoſe alſo who are ſubjected to the power of another people, as *Byzantium* was by the Emperor *Severus* to *Perinthus*, and *Antioch* by the Emperor *Theodoſius* to *Laodicea*.

VII. But not by the change of their Seat. *Plut. Ageſilao.*

But if the people ſhall change their habitation, either voluntarily, through ſcarcity of things neceſſary, or any ſuch inconvenience, or being thereunto compelled, as the *Carthaginians* were by the third *Punick* War; if the form or ſpirit of Polity do yet remain, they do not ceaſe to be a people, much leſs if their City Walls only be caſt down: And therefore when the *Lacedæmonians* refuſed to admit of the *Meſſenians*, among the reſt of the *Grecian* Cities, to ſwear the conſervation of the peace of *Greece*, becauſe their Walls were deſtroyed, it was carried againſt them by the common ſuffrage.

VIII. Nor by the change of Government.

Neither doth it much alter the caſe, under what Form of Government the people are, Monarchical, Oligarchical or Democratical; that is, of King, Nobles or People. The

Romans

Romans were but the same people, whether under Kings, Consuls, or Emperors: yea, though the Government be never so absolute, yet are the people the same they were, as when they were free, so long as he that governs, governs as the Head of that people, and not as the Head of another. For that Soveraign Power, which resides in the King as Head, rests in the people, as in the whole body, whereof the King is the Head; so that if the King being elected, should dye, or if the Royal Family be extinct, the Right of Government recedes back to the people, or to whom they grant it. Neither is that of *Aristotle* to be objected against me, who denyes that to be the same City, the form of whose Government is changed: As the Harmony cannot be said to be the same, that is changed from the *Dorick* to the *Phrygian* way: For we ought to know, that of any one artificial thing, there may be several forms: As of a Legion or Regiment, there is one form, whereby the Souldiers are governed, and another wherein they fight: So there is one form consisting in a Consociation of Right and Empire, and another, in relation to the parts between themselves, as those that are governed, and of those that govern. This latter, the Politician respects, as the Lawyer doth the former: Neither was *Aristotle* himself ignorant hereof, who presently adds, *But whether the Form of Government being changed, all debts and reckonings be discharged or not, is a question belonging to another Art*, which *Aristotle* would not confound with his Politicks; lest what he blamed in others, he should practise himself, making a transition *from one kind of Treatise to another.* Surely a debt contracted by a free people ceaseth not to be a debt, because they have admitted of a King; for the people are the same, and do still retain the Right and Dominion of those things, that formerly were theirs, yea, and the Empire too, though now it be not exercised by the body, but the head: whence we may easily determine that Controversie, which is sometimes started, concerning his place in General Councils, who is newly made a King over a Nation formerly free; namely, that he is to be admitted into that very place which that Nation enjoyed, whilst it was free: as *Philip* of *Macedon* in the Great Council of *Amphictyon*, took that place that was due to the *Phocenses*; so on the other side, That place which formerly belonged to the King, the people shall succeed in, being made free.

Pol. l. 2. c. 3.

A King newly admitted shall take that place in General Councils that the Nation, when free formerly enjoyed.

IX.

But if two people or Kingdoms be united, the Rights shall not be lost, but communicated; as the rights of the *Sabines* first, and afterwards of the *Albanes* were transferred into the *Romans*, and so were made one Common-wealth, as *Livy* records. The same may be said of Kingdoms being conjoyned, not in League, nor as having but one King, but being perfectly made one.

X. Or one be divided.

But if a Nation or Kingdom be divided, either by mutual agreement, or by the Sword, as the *Persian* Kingdom was by *Alexander*'s Successors, then of one entire Empire there shall be made two or more; and each shall enjoy its peculiar right over its particular parts: Or if any thing shall be held in common, it shall be either ratably divided between them, or else be administred in common. Hither we may refer those who are sent out to plant Colonies: For this is usually the rise of a new free people; *For we do not* (as *Thucydides* notes) *send them out as our servants, but as those who have equal right with our selves.* And thus did King *Tullius* in *Dionysius Halicarnassensis* judge this case, *That the Mother Cities should govern their Plantations abroad absolutely, as if by the Law of Nature, we conceive to be neither true nor righteous; yet ought they to reverence them, as the* Carthaginians *did the* Tyrians *their first Founders*, as *Curtius* testifies.

Colonies usually the Rise of a free State. *Vid. sup.* B. 1. C. 3. §. 1. L. 4.

XI. Where the old *Roman* Empire now resides.

It is also a famous Question much controverted both by Historians and Civilians, To whom the rights belonging formerly to the *Roman* Empire do now appertain: Some say, to the *German* Emperor, which by I know not what deputation, they place in the room of it. But it is sufficiently known, That the *Great Germany*, namely, that which lyes beyond the *Rhine*, was but a little while within the pale of the *Roman* Empire: And to translate the rights of Kingdoms from one to another without certain and evident proofs, seems to me to be too great a presumption. Wherefore, I am of opinion, that the *Roman* people are now the same they were of old, though somewhat mixt by the access of Foreigners; and that the Empire doth still remain with them as in a Body Politick wherein it was and should live. For whatsoever the people of *Rome* had of old a right to do before they had Emperors, that they had the same right to do in their *Interregna*, or vacancy of their Emperors. Yea, and the very Choice of their Emperors was their right; who were often made either by the people by themselves, or by the Senate; yea, and those Elections which were made by the *Roman* Legions, (as such there were, sometimes by these, and anon by others) were not firm nor stable by any right that those Legions had: (for from a Fleeting power no right can be certain), but by the approbation of the people. (When the two *Roman* Generals *Publ.* and *Cn. Scipio* were both slain, and the Army had chosen *L. Martius*, a valiant young Gentleman their Captain General, though he had vanquished two several Armies of the *Carthaginians*, and forced their Camps;

From a Fleeting power, no Right can be certain. It is of dangerous consequence for Soldiers to elect their Generals.

Camps; yet notwithstanding when in his Letters to *Rome* he had assumed that Honourable Title of Pro-Prætor, the Senate (considering that his Command was neither granted by the people, nor allowed of by themselves) were much offended at his presumption in usurping it; fore-seeing well, that it was a matter of dangerous consequence, for Soldiers abroad to make choice of such as should command Armies and Provinces: And that the solemnity of Elections, so devoutly begun in the name of their Gods, should now be transferr'd into Camps, far from Laws and Magistrates.) But yet we have many examples of Elections made by their Armies; but so, as they were afterwards approved of, and confirmed by the Senate: as were those of *Adrian*, *Pertinax*, *Julian*, *Severus*, *Macrinus*, *Maximinus*, *Baldinus*, *Aurelian* and others. *Capitolinus* records an Epistle of *Albinus* concerning the right of the Senate in the Election of their Emperour, and another of the Senate concerning the *Gardiani*. *Macrinus* in an Oration thus bespeaks the Senate concerning the *Roman* Legions, *They have conferred the Empire on me, the defence whereof, O Fathers Conscript, I do in the mean time undertake: and if it be as pleasing to you, as it hath been unto them, I shall also undertake the Government.* So also doth the Emperour *Tacitus* in *Vopiscus*, *Me*, saith he, *hath the Senate made their Prince, according to the prudent advice of the Army.* To the like purpose is that of *Majorinus* to the Senate, *Remember that I was made Emperour as well by your own Free Suffrages, as by the appointment of your puissant Army. The Roman Empire* (as *Maximinus* in *Herodian* tells his Soldiers) *is not the possession of any one man, but the Ancient Inheritance of the whole people of* Rome; *upon whose safety the Empire depends. And we together with you are to this purpose chosen, that they through our Care and Courage may live securely.* Neither doth it avail to the contrary, to say, That by the Constitution of *Antoninus* the Emperour, all that lived within the Verge of that Empire, were made *Roman* Citizens: For by that Sanction, all the Subjects of that Empire, were only made capable of such rights and priviledges, as the *Roman* Colonies and such other Towns and Cities anciently had, that were made free; namely, that they might use the same Laws, and be governed by such Magistrates, as the people of *Rome* had. But the Foundation of the Empire was not so in any other people, as it was in the people of *Rome*; for this was not in the power of the *Roman* Emperors to grant, who could neither change the state of the Empire, nor its manner of holding it. Neither did it at all detract from the right of the Citizens of *Rome*, that their Emperours changed the place of their residence from *Rome* to *Constantinople*: For even then also was the choice of their Emperours made by such of the *Roman* Citizens, as were resident at *Constantinople*, whom *Claudian* calls the *Byzantine Romans*: yet so, as that choice was to be confirmed by the whole body of the people of *Rome*; who like Princes, jealous of their own Soveraignty, alwayes preserved the prerogative of their City, and the honour of their Consuls, (the first whereof did constantly reside at *Rome*) as the Trophies of their own incommunicable right; wherefore all that right which those *Byzantine Romans* pretended to have in those Elections, depended wholly on the people of *Rome*. *Nero* in the fourteenth of *Tacitus* his Annals, *accuseth his Mother for endeavouring to divide the Empire with him, by swearing to her self the Prætorian Bands, and for hoping to put the same reproach upon the Senate and people*: Whereas (as *Priscus* notes) *the Soveraignty of the* Roman *Empire appertained not to women, but men.* For after the death of *Heliogabalus*, *it was especially provided, that no woman should ever after be admitted into the Senate, and that he that should do it, should be accursed to Hell.* And it was observed by *Tribellius* as a matter of reproach, *That* Zenobia *usurped the Empire, and governed the Common-wealth, longer than was fit for a woman to do it.* When the *Byzantine Romans* contrary to the mind and custome of the *Romans*, had subjected the whole Empire to the Empress *Irene*, they deservedly revoked that Grant, which they had either expresly or tacitly given them, and by their own power chose *Charles* the Great, Emperour; which they publickly declared by their chief Citizen, the Bishop of *Rome*: For so also was the High Priest among the *Jews* alwayes accounted, during the vacancy of their Kings. Now *Charles* the Emperour and his Successors did always very prudently distinguish between the right they had to the Kingdoms of the *Francks* and *Lumbards*, and the right they had to the Empire; the former being their Ancient Inheritance, the latter being entrusted unto him upon a new account: but afterwards the Kingdom of the *Francks* being divided into the Western, which is now called *France*, and the Eastern, which is *Germany* or *Almany*, seeing that the Oriental *Francks* did then begin to set over themselves Kings by Election, (for even at that time the succession to the Kingdom of the *Francks*, being as it were Aquatical, depended not so much upon any certain Law, as upon the choice of the people:) The *Romans* that they might enjoy a most assured protection, chose not a King of their own, but him whom the *Germans* had admitted for their Emperour; yet still reserving unto themselves, the right of either approving or rejecting him, so far as concerned their own affairs. And this approbation is in their name solemnly witnessed by their chief Citizen the Bishop,

For *Rome* over all her Colonies, appeared as a Lady or a Queen, *Zon.*

The change of the Imperial Seat did not change the Empire.

The Empire continued in the people of *Rome*, though the Emperor resided at *Constantinople*.

The Bishop of *Rome* the Principal Citizen in the Vacancy of the Empire.

ſhop, by a peculiar Coronation. Wherefore as he that is admitted or elected by the ſeven Princes of *Germany*, being the Repreſentatives of the whole Nation, hath according to their cuſtoms the beſt title to the Empire: So is the ſame perſon by the approbation of the people of *Rome*, made King or Emperour of the *Romans*, or as Hiſtorians ſometimes call him, King of *Italy*. As in the excommunication of the Emperour *Henry*, the Pope makes expreſs mention of the Kingdoms of *Germany* and *Italy*; and in the Oath that the Pope adminiſtred unto the Emperour *Otto* (as *Gratian* records) the Emperour ſwears, *That he will make no Decree or Ordinance concerning any thing belonging to the Pope or to the* Romans *without his Counſel.* So that the Emperour under the Title of being King of the *Romans*, hath a right unto all that did formerly belong unto the *Roman* Empire, that hath not been otherwiſe alienated or granted away, either by agreement, or by occupancy, upon a preſumption of being deſerted, or by the right of Conqueſt. From whence it is an eaſie matter to determine, by what right the Biſhop of *Rome* in the vacancy delivers to the ſucceeding Emperour, the ornaments of the *Roman* Empire; namely, becauſe at ſuch time, the people being free, the Primacy belongs to him. And it is uſual for Bodies Politick, to diſpatch all their affairs by the chief perſon, in the name of the whole. So that as the *Prince Palatine* and the Duke of *Saxony* do deliver the Royal Diadem to the Emperour Elect, thereby giving him poſſeſſion of the *German* Empire: So doth the Biſhop of *Rome* in the name of all the *Romans*, give unto the ſame perſon being by them approved, the ornaments of the *Roman* Empire. So it is alſo in *Poland*, the Arch-Biſhop of *Gueſsne* during the vacancy, ſits on the Royal Throne, and adminiſters the publick affairs of the Kingdom, as being of all the Orders, the chief. Neither is it much amiſs, what *Cynus* and *Rainerius* have delivered unto us, That if the Emperour either by Sickneſs or by Captivity be diſabled to perform his duty, it is in the power of the *Roman* people to appoint a Deputy or Vice-Roy in his room.

By what right the Pope in the Vacancy delivers the Ornaments of the *Roman* Empire, to the Emperour of *Germany*.

The Arch-Biſhop of *Gueſſne* in *Poland*.

That the perſon of the Heir ſucceeding to the perſon deceaſed, is ſufficient to preſerve the propriety in any thing, either private or publick, is of undoubted right. XII.

But how far forth the Conquerour ſhall ſucceed to the conquered, when we come to treat of the effects of War, ſhall be explained. XIII.

CHAP. X.

What Obligation ariseth from Dominion.

I. *The obligation to restore that which is anothers, from whence, and what manner of Obligation it is.*
II. *An obligation to restore the profits of what is anothers: this proved by many examples.*
III. *He that makes use of what is anothers, thinking it to be his own, is not bound to restitution, if the thing perish.*
IV. *Yet is the same person bound to restore the fruits in being.*
V. *Yea, and those that are spent, unless it appear that otherwise he had not spent them:*
VI. *But not those that he neglected to gather:*
VII. *Nor those that he hath given away to others; this explained by a distinction.*
VIII. *Nor if he sell only what he bought; explained by a like distinction.*
IX. *When he that honestly buyes of one man what is really anothers, may reserve the price, or part of it.*
X. *Another mans Goods being bought cannot be restored to him that sold them, but to the right Owner.*
XI. *He that is possest of a thing, that no man can justly claim, is not bound to yield it up to any.*
XII. *What is received, being due, though for some bad cause or otherwise, is not to be restored naturally.*
XIII. *The opinion, That what consists in number, weight or measure, may be alienated, without the Consent of the Owner, refelled.*

I. Restitution. Having thus sufficiently, as to our purpose, unfolded what Right or Dominion we may have over things or persons, let us now consider, What obligation lyes against us upon this account. Now this ariseth either out of things extant (wherein also I include persons, if profitable unto us) or out of things not yet extant. Out of things, or persons appearing, there naturally ariseth this obligation, That he that hath in his power, that which of right, is mine, should endeavour (as much as in him lyes) that it may be restored unto me. Among other Precepts of the Law given to the *Jews*, this is one, *That things found should be restored to their right Owner:* which is grounded as well upon Natural Equity, as upon that in *Deuteronomy*, where we read thus, *Thou shalt not see thy Brothers Oxe or his Ass go astray, and hide thy self from them, but thou shalt in any wise bring it home again unto thy Brother,* &c. [Deut. 22. 1.] *Many there are* (saith *Hierom*) *who think that what they find, though of another mans, they may keep without offence*; that say, *Deus mihi dedit, cui habeo reddere? God hath given it me, to whom shall I restore it? But let them know,* saith he, *it is a sin next to that of Theft, not to restore what we have so found.* [*In Lev.*] So likewise St. *Augustine*, Si quid invenisti & non reddidisti, rapuisti; *If what thou hast found, thou restore not, thou hast robbed thy neighbour.* [*Ser. 9. de verb. Domini.*] And in another place he tells us, *That so long as a man enjoyes that, which he knows not to belong to another, he may be honest; for his Ignorance is the cause of his detention: but being once convinced of his error, then if he restore not, he may justly be reputed an Usurper.* [*Grat. c. 14. q. 5.*] *As for my part,* saith *Bellisarius*, *I make but little difference between him that knowingly detains what is another mans, and him that is a Thief or a Robber; Pari loco habeo, res alienas non reddentem, cum raptore.* [*Proc. Goth. l. 2.*] Yet doth this obligation reach no farther, than as far as in us lyes; for no man is bound to impossibilities, nor to restore any thing that is lost at his own charge: but to declare his knowledge to the right Owner, that so if he please, he may recover them. For as there is an equality to be observed, where any thing is held in common, that it may be made use of no less by one than another; So Dominion being once admitted, this is mutually agreed on between the Proprietors, That if a man be possest of another mans Goods, he should restore them to their right Owner. Now if this obligation extended no farther than to restore upon demand, it would both too much weaken the future property, and aggravate the charge of keeping the thing lost. Neither is it in this place regarded, whether a man hath got the possession of another mans Goods honestly or dishonestly: For there is one manner of obligation arising from the crime, and another arising from the thing held and detained by that crime. The *Lacedæmonians* thought they had expiated the Injury done to the *Thebans*, by laying an heavy Fine upon *Phœbidus*; who contrary to the League between them and the *Thebans*, had possest himself of the *Cadmæan* Fort, though they restored it not. But (as *Plutarch* observes) all Grace stood amazed at their Injustice, *Quod cujus Facinoris Authorem pœna affecissent, Facinus tamen reipsa approbarent*; *In that they punished the offendor, yet in effect justified his offence.* The like we may read of *Bajazet* recorded by *Leunclavius*: The former, *Plutarch* attributes

attributes to the advice of *Agesilaus, who perswaded the City, to transfer the blame upon him; but to preserve the Fort to themselves.* But this kind of Injustice being singular, is usually, as *Xenophon* notes, punished by the especial Providence of God. Thus were *M. Crassus* and *Qu. Hortensius* much blamed by *Cicero*, for detaining part of an Inheritance which was got by a Testament that was forged, though not by any fault of theirs. But because this obligation as by an universal Contract binds all men, and creates a certain right to the Owner of the thing, hence it comes to pass, that all singular Contracts, as being post-nate, do from hence receive their exception, which seems to illustrate that of *Tryphoninus: A Thief delivers that whereof he hath robbed me, to* Sejus *to keep for him, who is altogether ignorant of the theft. Now the Question is, To whom is* Sejus *bound to restore it? If we look only to the Giver and Receiver, it is just that the thing intrusted, should be restored to him that gave it. But if we respect the equity of the matter, which takes in all the persons concerned, it ought to be restored doubtless to me, from whom it was fraudulently taken.* Whereunto he adds, *Et probo hanc esse Justitiam, quæ suum cuique ita tribuit, ut non distrahatur ab ullius personæ justiore repetitione; And this I approve of to be Justice, which so gives to every man his own, that it be not withheld from the juster claim of any other person that hath a right unto it.* Now his must needs be the juster title, that claims by a right as ancient as propriety it self: Whence it likewise follows, That he that ignorantly accepts of that from another in trust, which afterwards he knows to be his own, cannot be bound to restore it. And the case which the same *Tryphoninus* puts, concerning Goods deposited by him whose whole Estate was before confiscate, is better determined by this rule, than by that which he there produceth, concerning the profits gained by punishments. For if we look strictly to the nature of the propriety, it matters not whether it arise from the Law of Nations, or from the Civil Law; for either way it carries with it all things natural unto it self, whereof this is one, That every person being possest of another mans goods, is bound to make restitution thereof to the right Owner. And this is the meaning of *Martianus*, where he tells us, that Goods may by personal actions at Law be required from those, who without any just cause are possest of them. And from hence also springs that in *Ulpian*, He that finds what is anothers, is so strictly bound to restore it, that he cannot so much as require a reward for the finding of it; but he is to restore it with its fruits, if any be, saving only to himself his reasonable charges.

Plut. Agesilao.

Hist. Cyr. l. 5.

Restitution to be made to the right Owner, and not to him who hath usurped anothers Right.

Res condici possunt ab iis qui non ex justa causa possident.

II. Of the profit of what belongs to another.

Of things not extant the Law of Nations runs thus, That if another be enriched by what is mine, I not enjoying mine own, he stands obliged to restore to me so much, as he is made the richer by what is mine: Because as to that which he hath gained by what is mine, he hath the more, and I for want of what is mine own, have the less, by so much as he hath gained. For dominion was therefore generally agreed on, that every man according to his proportion, should enjoy his own. *Contra naturam est, ex hominis Incommodo suum augere Commodum; For one man to enrich himself by that, which is another mans loss, is unnatural,* saith *Cicero*. And in another place, *That we should build up our own Power, Fortunes or Wealth, upon the ruine of other mens, nature it self will not permit.* There is so much of natural reason in this saying, that the Lawyers are enforced to decline the prescript Rules of their Laws, and to determine many Cases by this of equity, as being the most convincing. A Contract made by a Servant, being a Factor, shall bind his Master, unless Proclamation be first made, that no credit shall be given unto him. But yet, although such Proclamation be made, if that Servant makes any profit thereby, either to himself, or puts it to his Masters account, it shall be judged a Fraud; *Videtur enim dolum malum facere, qui ex aliena jactura lucrum quærat: For he seems to deal deceitfully, that makes himself rich by another mans loss.* Where the words *Dolus malus* signifie whatsoever is repugnant to natural right and equity. If a Wife shall give unto her Husband money, which by the Law, she may require of him again, the Wife shall have either a personal Action against her Husband, or shall relieve her self by that which was bought with her money: Because it cannot be denyed, but that the Husband is made the richer by it; and therefore enquiry shall be made, what he possesseth that was bought with her money. So again, if thou hast spent or otherwise disposed of money, which my Servant hath stoln from me, conceiving it to be his; I have a good Action against thee, for this reason, because my Goods came into thy possession without any just cause. Pupils, according to the *Roman* Laws, are not bound to pay what they borrow; yet if it appear, that they are the richer by what they borrowed, an Action shall lye against them. So likewise, if thou contractest with my debtor, not as mine, but supposing him to be another mans, and borrowest my money of him, Thou standest bound to pay me; not because I trusted thee with my money, (which could not be without mutual Consent) but because my money coming into thy possession, it is both just and righteous, that thou shouldst restore it to me, as to the right Owner.

Cicero Off. 3.

Our modern Lawyers do prudently judge of other the like Cases by these, as namely, that he whose Goods, whilst he lay concealed had been sold, when he might have had an exception should be admitted to receive the money that was raised by the sale of them. And that he that accommodates the Father with money for his Sons maintenance, if the Father be not able to discharge the debt, should have his Action against the Son, if he enjoy any Goods that were his Mothers. These two Rules being throughly understood, may guide us to give satisfaction in such Cases of Conscience, as are usually by as well Lawyers as Divines, proposed.

III. He that useth anothers, thinking it his own, not bound to restore if the thing perish.

For in the first place it hence appears, That he that is possest of what is anothers, yet thinks it to be his own, is not bound to make any restitution, if the thing it self so possest do perish; because he hath neither the thing it self, nor any gains by it. But he that knowingly possesseth what is anothers, is bound not only by reason of the thing it self, but for his fact in detaining it.

IV. Yet is he bound to restore the fruits in being, if any be.

Secondly, He that through Ignorance possesseth anothers right, is bound to restore not only the thing, but the fruits of the thing that are extant: The fruits, I say, of the thing, but not the fruits of his own labours. For though without the thing, those fruits could not be perceived, yet are they not due to the thing it self, which without his labour could not have produced them. Now the ground of this obligation ariseth from propriety; for he that is the Owner of the thing, is naturally the Owner of the Fruits arising from the thing.

V. Yea, and those that are consumed, unless otherwise he had not spent them.

Thirdly, He that unknowingly possesseth another mans Goods, is bound to make restitution both of the thing, and of the fruits that are spent, if it appear that he must otherwise have spent as much of what was his own; because he is by that so much the richer. This *Suetonius* highly commends in *Caligula*, *That those whom he restored to their Kingdoms, he likewise restored to the Fruits and Profits of them for half the time they stood exiled.*

VI. But not for those which he neglected to perceive.

Fourthly, That he is not bound to make good that which he neglected to perceive, because he neither hath the thing it self, nor any thing that succeeds in the place of it.

VII. Nor those that he hath given away, this explained.

Fifthly, If such a possessor shall give to another that which was given to him, he is not bound to restore it, unless in case he had not given that, he must have given as much other wayes; by sparing which, he is so much the richer.

Sixthly, If he sell the thing he bought he is not obliged, unless it be for the overplus of the price it was bought for: But if he sell the thing that was given, he is bound to restore the price, unless he have prodigally spent it, which had it not been so given, he had not so spent.

VIII. Nor if he sell what he bought.

IX. When he that sells what is anothers, may reserve the price or a part of it.

Seventhly, That another mans goods, though *bona fide* bought, must be restored: neither may the price given for them be required from the Owner; unto which rule, we think it not amiss to add this exception, unless it be where the Proprietor could not probably recover the possession of what was his, without some charges; as when things are possest by Pyrates †. For in this case, what the Owner would willingly have spent to have recovered his Goods, may be deducted by him that delivers them. For the very regaining of the possession being not to be done without charge and difficulty, is accordingly to be valued; which charge and trouble being saved, the right Owner (having thus lost his thing) is reputed by so much the richer. And therefore since the buying this thing in the ordinary judgement of the Law be of no value; yet as *Paulus* the Lawyer saith, It is valuable, if from the beginning it be agreed, that the possession of what is ours (being at present in another mans power) may be bought. And where things so bought, are strictly required by the Owner without any moderate allowance, though it may stand with the Rigour of the Law, yet hath this Rigour so much of Injustice in it, as the one is a gainer by the others loss. Nor do I here require, that the thing should be bought with an intent to restore it to the Owner. In which case, That an Action of Negotiation may arise, as there are some that affirm, so there are others that deny. For such an Action ariseth from the Civil Law. Neither hath it any of those grounds or principles, whereupon Nature introduceth this obligation. Not much unlike is that which *Ulpian* relates of Funeral charges, wherein a prudent Judge doth not alwayes walk by the same rule, as in meer actions of Negotiation, but gives himself a looser Rein which the nature of such an Action will very well bear. And that which the same *Ulpian* in another place saith, If any man mis-wage mine affairs, not so much regarding me, as his own profit, and shall disburse money, in so doing he shall recover by his Action, not according to what he laid out, but according to the benefit that I receive by it. So the Owners of such Goods, as in a Tempest to secure the rest, are cast over-board, shall recover a part of their losses from those whose Goods remain entire: because he whose Goods are so preserved by the loss of mine, is by my damage made the richer.

† *Ter. Heaut. Act.* 4. *Scen.* 4, 5.

Summum Jus summa Injuria. Ter. loc. supradicto.

Negotiorum actionem.

Eighthly,

X. Another mans goods being sold, cannot be restored, but to the right Owner.

Eighthly, He that buyes another mans Goods, cannot restore them back to him that sold them, to recover the price he paid for them; because as soon as those goods did come under his power (as we said already) the obligation began to restore them to the right Owner.

XI. Where the right Owner is not known, we are not bound to restitution.

Ninthly, He that is possest of a thing, and is ignorant whose it is, is not by the Law of Nature bound to give it to the poor; though it be very pious so to do, and in many places is well ordered to be so disposed: the reason is, because by the Right of Propriety, no man can claim an interest in it, but the Proprietor. But to him that is ignorant who that is, it is all one as if it had none. For, *De non entibus & non apparentibus eadem est ratio*; Of things that are not, and of things that appear not, there is the same reason, as to him to whom they appear not.

XII. What is received if due, whether the cause be honest or dishonest, is not to be restored, naturally.

Tenthly, By the Law of Nature whatsoever is received, which another is bound to pay, be the ground of that Obligation honest or dishonest, is not to be restored; although even this also be introduced by some Laws, and that not without cause. The reason whereof is, because in respect of the thing it self, no man is obliged to restitution, unless that thing belong to another man. But in this case, he that was the right Owner before, hath willingly transferred his right to another. But it will be another thing, where the manner of receiving it is vicious, as in the case of Extortion. For this is another kind of Obligation, whereof we discourse not at present †.

† *Vid.* St. *Aug.* *Ep.* 54.

XIII. The opinion confuted, that holds, That things consisting in number, weight and measure may be transferred without the consent of the Owner.

Neither is that true, which is delivered by *Medina*, namely, that the property of other mens Goods may come unto us without the Owners consent, in case they are such things as are usually valued by weight, number or measure. For things of this nature may be restored in others of the same kind, which is true, if it be done with consent, or if either by Law or Custome such a Consent may be reasonably presumed; as when we restore what we borrow, or when the thing it self being spent or consumed, we restore the like, in quantity and quality. But without such a Consent, either exprest or presumed, and setting aside cases of necessity, this giving of one thing for another is not to be allowed of.

CHAP.

CHAP. XI.

Of Promises.

I. That Naturally a Right may arise from Promises.

BY our Method formerly designed, we are now to treat of obligations made by Promise; where we find *Franciscus Connanus*, a man eminently learned, opposing us, who holds, That those Promises that are not made for a valuable consideration, oblige not, either by the Law of Nature or Nations. And yet he confesseth, That they might justly be performed, in case the thing promised be such as might justly and honestly be fulfilled, though no such Promise had been made. To confirm which opinion, he produceth not only the testimonies of some Lawyers, but these Reasons also: First, That he who believes every rash Promise causlesly made, is no less to be blamed than he that believes none at all. Secondly, That it would endanger most mens Fortunes, were men bound to perform all their Promises, which for the most part are made more out of ostentation, than a premeditated Will and Purpose to fulfil them. Lastly, That it is fit that some things should be left to every mans honesty, and not to reduce all promises to a necessity of Performance. And whereas it is said, That it is dishonest not to perform what we have promised, the meaning is not that it is unjust, but that it argues lightness and inconstancy in the Promiser. Thus pleads *Connanus*, urging besides the Testimony of *Cicero*, who denies that those promises are to be performed, which are to them to whom they are made, unprofitable; or that infer more damage to him that made them, than benefit to them to whom they are made. But yet in case the matter be not entire, (something having been performed by the one party) then he would have the other party obliged, not unto all that was promised, but unto that only that is in difference between them: And for those agreements that of themselves are not binding, they receive their obliging power, either from the Contract wherein they are, or whereunto they are adjoyned, or from the delivery of the thing: From whence arise, partly Actions, partly Exceptions, and prohibited Reclaims. But as to those that may have their obligatory power according to the Laws, as those made by stipulation, with some others, they receive their binding faculty from the benefit of the Laws, whose efficacy is such as to make that which in it self is only honest, to be even

even necessary. But this opinion of *Connanus*, taken so generally as he seems to express it, cannot be current: For in the first place it would thence follow, That those Articles of Agreement that are made between Kings, and between the people of diverse Nations, so long as nothing was on either side performed, were of no force; especially, in such places where are no set Forms of Leagues or Sponsions found. Besides, no Reason can possibly be given why Laws (which are but as it were so many common Covenants or Promises of the people, for so both *Aristotle* and *Demosthenes* term them) should add such an obliging force unto Agreements. And yet that every mans own Will endeavouring by all means to oblige it self, cannot do the same thing; especially where the Civil Law gives no restraint or Impediment unto it. Whereunto add, That the Dominion of a thing may be transferred by the Will being sufficiently declared: And why therefore may not the Will have the same Right over a person, either to transfer Domiminion (which Right is less than Dominion it self) or to do something, seeing that we have the same power over our Actions, as we have over our Goods? And herein likewise we have the consent of the learned. Nay, the *Hebrews* hold that where the thing consulted about, will not admit of delay, our silence is equivalent to a Sponsion. For as the Lawyers say, No Title can be naturally more assured, than that which the Proprietor doth willingly transfer to another: In the same manner it is said there is nothing so fit to preserve faithful dealing among men, as to observe and perform whatsoever is promised and agreed upon between themselves. So a Decree for the payment of Money promised, though there were no other reason assigned why it should be due, but the free consent of him that promised it, is said to be agreeable to Natural equity. He, saith *Paulus* the Lawyer, doth naturally owe, and by the Law of Nations must give, upon whose word and promise we have relied: Where in the first place we must observe, That this word [*Oportet*] *Must*, implies a kind of necessity: Neither may we admit of that which *Connanus* takes as granted, That we are then said to rely upon a mans faith, when the thing ceaseth to be entire (that is, when something is already performed by one party.) For *Paulus* in that place treats of a personal Action brought for a thing not due, which presently ceaseth as soon as something (upon what agreement soever) is paid: Because, even before, when nothing was as yet performed on either side, by the Laws of Nature and Nations, what was promised, ought to be given; although the Civil Law, to prevent the occasions of unnecessary suits, do give little or no encouragement to exact it. But *Tully* in his Offices attributes so great a power to Promises, that he makes Faithfulness to be the very foundation of Justice; which *Horace* also calls the Sister of Justice: As the *Platonists* also do oft-times express Justice by ἀλήθειαν, Truth: Which *Apuleius* renders by the word Fidelity: And *Simonides* calls it Justice, not only to restore what we have received, but even to speak Truth, (that is, to perform what we have promised.) But to clear this yet better, we must carefully distinguish between the three degrees of speaking concerning things to come, which either are, or at least are reputed to be hereafter in our own power.

Condictione Indebiti.

Lib. 1.

Apul. de Plat.
Plat. lib. 1. de rep.

Three degrees of speaking of things to come.

II. 1. That a bare assertion obligeth not.

The first consists in a bare assertion of what we purpose for the future, things thus standing, and in the same mind we now are: And hereunto it is required, that we speak sincerely, and without guile, what at that present time we think: But not with any resolution to continue in that thought, if the face of things change, or if other chances happen, which though we then foresee not, yet may otherwise incline us. For the mind of man hath not only a Natural Power, but a Right and Freedome to alter its counsels; and if there be any weakness or error in the change, as it often happens, that is not intrinsick to the change, but to the matter, in that we change from the better to the worse.

See Q. *Elizabeth*'s dealing with the *Hollander*, *B. 2. c. 14. §. 12.*

III. 2. A Promise though naturally obliging, yet transfers no Right to another.

The Second degree is when the will confines it self for the time to come, giving some sign whereby the necessity of its perseverance is sufficiently declared, and this may be called a Pollicitation, or a Promise; which setting aside the Civil Law obligeth either absolutely, or under some condition, yet gives no peculiar Right to another. For in many cases it happens, that there may be an obligation within our selves when there is no Right given to another, as may appear by those debts of mercy and gratitude, whereunto we may refer those of Constancy and Fidelity; and therefore no man can by the Law of Nature require the thing promised from the right owner by vertue of such a Pollicitation, nor can the Promiser be compelled by that Law to perform what he hath so promised.

IV. 3. What that Promise is that gives a Right to another.

Thirdly, When the Will to the confinement adds some outward sign whereby its consent to transfer its own proper Right to another is sufficiently declared: Which is a compleat Promise, as having the like effect to the alienation of a mans Property. For it is the way to alienate a thing, or, at least, the alienation of some part of our Liberty or Freedome. Unto the former belongs our Promises to give, unto the latter our Promises to do something. And hereof the Scriptures do give us a notable

Neh. 9. 8.
1 Cor. 1. 19.
10. 13.
Prov. 6. 1.

Stipulatus & sponsio are such Promises as are made with solemnity.
Numb. 30. 4, 5, 6.
Vox mea, facta tua est.

Sent. lib. 2. tit. 14.

De Promisso non Sponso; jam non promittunt de te, sed spondent. Seneca Ep. 19.

Rash Promises bind not.

table example, where they tell us, That God himself, who cannot be bound by any Law; yet professeth it to be contrary to his own Nature, not to perform what he promiseth, *Heb.* 6. 17, 18. From whence it is plain, That to perform our Promises is a duty springing from the Nature of Immutable Justice; which as it is in God, so is it in some measure, common to all such as have the use of right Reason. Let us hear the opinion of *Solomon* in this case, *My Son, if thou hast been surety for thy Friend, thou hast given thy Faith to a stranger*; or (as the *Septuagint* translate it) *to thine Enemy: Thou art ensnared by the words of thy mouth: Thou are taken and bound by thine own Speech.* Whereunto may be added that of *Thales* the Philosopher, *Sponde noxa presto est*; *Engage freely, and thou art not far from harm.* And that also of *Chilo, Sponsioni non deest jactura*; *Engagements are seldome made to loss.* Hence it is, that the *Jews* term a Promise, *Vinculum, A Bond*, which also in the Scriptures is compared to a Vow; as if by Vows and Promises we did contract (as it were) with God himself. From the same Root ariseth the *Greek* word ὑπόχεσις, which likewise signifies a Promise, namely, from ἔχω, which signifies *To have or to hold*:. Because he to whom any thing is promised, doth hold fast, and, as it were, bind the Promiser. These things promis'd, *Connanus* his Arguments are easily answered; For what the Lawyers say, *De nudo pacto non oritur actio*; *A bare Promise will bear no Action*: hath respect only to what was introduced by the *Roman* Laws, which made *Stipulation* to be an infallible sign of a deliberate mind. *Paulus* the Lawyer speaks very warily of such Promises, *If* (saith he) *we make a bare Promise to pay use, it avails nothing; for among* Roman *Citizens no Action ariseth from a bare Promise.* The like Laws we grant to be in force among other Nations, *Quæ lex ad id præstandum, nos quod alicui promisimus, obligat? What Law* (saith *Seneca*) *binds us to perform all our Promises?* Where he speaks of humane Laws and of rash and inconsiderate Promises. But if we respect the Law of Nature only, there may be other signs of a mind perfectly resolv'd, besides that which the *Romans* introduced by Stipulation, or if there be any other such like, which the Civil Law requires to beget an Action. But as to that Promise which is made rashly, and without due consideration, neither do we admit it to have any obliging power, as *Theophrastus* hath well observ'd. Yea, and as to that which is deliberately done, but not with a purpose thereby to transfer our own proper Right to another, we deny that from thence there ariseth Naturally a Right to any man to exact the performance of it. Although we do acknowledge, That from such a Promise there may arise an obligation, not in honesty alone, but in a moral necessity to do it. And as to that of *Cicero* we shall treat hereafter, when we shall discourse of the manner how Contracts are to be understood. But now let us see what Conditions are required to make a Promise valid.

V. To make a Promise compleat, the use of Reason is required in the Promiser.

And in the first place it is requisite that he that promiseth should be endued with Reason, which renders the Promises of Mad-men, Ideots, and Infants void, and of no force; but the case of Minors is somewhat different: For although they are believed to be but of weak judgement, as Women also are; yet neither is this weakness of Judgement lasting, nor is it of it self sufficient to invalid their acts. At what years a young man or woman arrives at the use of Reason cannot certainly be determined, but must be guessed at, either by their daily Actions, or by the Customes of every Nation: Among the *Jews*, a young man after thirteen years of age might oblige himself by any solemn Promise he should make, and a young woman after twelve. But the Civil Laws, upon better reason, thought good to make void many of their Promises, not only among the *Romans*, but among the *Grecians*. And against some they introduced the benefit of Restitution: But these are the peculiar effects of the Civil Law, and do no whit appertain to the Laws either of Nature or Nations; except only in this, that where they are received, it is agreeable to Nature that they should be observ'd. Insomuch that if a Foreigner shall contract with a Citizen, he shall be bound up by the Laws of that City, as if he were, for that time, a Subject of that Nation. But it were otherwise in case such a Contract were made either on the Seas, or in some desart Island, or by Letters between two persons inhabiting diverse Nations. For then such Agreements should be regulated by the Law of Nature only, as are the Agreements made between such as are invested with the Supreme Power, as they are such: For in these, what they do privately, may by their Laws be made void, when it is done in favour to those powers, but not when done to their Punishment.

VI. A Promise made through error, how far Naturally it obligeth.

Concerning a Promise made by an error or mistake in the person promising, the question is yet more difficult. For we are to distinguish between that Error which is about the substance of the thing promised, and that which concerns not the substance; and then we are to consider whether the Fraud gave occasion to the Promise or not. Again, whether he with whom we have to do be guilty of the Fraud or not. And lastly, Whether the Act be strictly due, or binds only in Honesty and Conscience. For the opinions of Lawyers do vary according to the variety of these cases, declaring some acts to be void

and

and others valid. But so, that according to his will and pleasure that is injured, the promise may be either revoked or reformed. But most of these distinctions proceed from the *Roman* Laws; as well from the old Civil Law, as from the Prætorian: And some of them are either not altogether true, or not well digested. But yet it sufficeth to chalk out a way for us to find out the natural truth; for as concerning the force and efficacy of Laws, this hath ever been allowed of by the general consent of almost all Nations, That when a Law is enacted upon the presumption of such a Fact as was not really so done as was suggested, and believed, that Law is not obliging, because the truth of the Fact failing, the foundation of that Law faileth with it. But when a Law is grounded upon such a presumption, may be gathered from the matter of that Law, from the Words, and from other Circumstances. The like may be said in this case, if a Promise be made upon the belief of such a fact as indeed never was done, that Promise naturally is of no force; because the Promiser did not give his consent absolutely to the thing promised, but upon such a condition (if not exprest, yet presumed) as really was not: As in that case mentioned by *Cicero*, of him who falsly believing his own Son to be dead, appointed a stranger to be his heir. And yet in case the Promiser were neglective, either in his diligence to examine and search out the truth of his Sons death, or in his care of expressing his own sense, and did thereby occasion any damage to the person to whom he made that Promise, he shall be obliged to repair it: Not upon the account of his Promise made, but for the damage, which through his neglect, was sustained by him to whom it was made; whereof we shall speak more anon. But if there were an error or mistake in the person promising, and yet that Error was not the cause of the Promise made, the act shall be valid, because there was nothing wanting of a true consent: But if in this case also the person to whom the Promise was made, did by any fraud of his, directly or indirectly, occasion that error, what damage soever shall accrue to the Promiser by reason of that Error, shall be by him repaired. But if the Promise were but in part occasioned by an Error, then as to the other part the Promise shall stand good.

VII. A Promise made through fear obligeth.

Concerning those Promises that are made through Fear, questions do arise no less perplext. For herein they do usually distinguish of Fears, which are either great and vehement, or light and slender: If great, then they consider whether it be so absolutely, or in respect only of the person fearing: Then whether it be occasioned justly or unjustly; and whether by him to whom the Promise was made, or by some other: As also they distinguish of the Acts, whether free and generous, or grievous and burdensome; and according to this diversity, are some Acts said to be void, others revocable at the pleasure of the Promiser, and others to be wholly renewed. Concerning every one of these cases, there are great differences in opinions. But I do wholly incline to those who hold, That setting aside that Authority of the Civil Law, which sometimes takes away, and sometimes moderates the binding power of such promises: He that promiseth any thing through Fear, is obliged to perform what he hath so promised; because the consent he gave was not conditional, as in the case of Error, but absolute. For as *Aristotle* well observes, He that for fear of being shipwrackt, throws his goods overboard, *Eth. Nic.* 3. would willingly preserve them on condition that he might not be wreckt; but upon a serious consideration of the present danger he is in, he absolutely resolves that his goods rather than himself, shall perish. But yet we must also crave this allowance, That if he to whom the Promise was made, did occasion not a just, but an unjust Fear, though but slight; and that thereupon the Promise was so made, he is bound to discharge the Promiser if he desire it: Not that the Promise is in it self void, but for the damage that he sustained who made it, by reason of the injury done him. But what exceptions the Law of Nations admits herein, shall in its proper place be hereafter explained. See *Chap.* 17. §. 19. and *B.* 3. *ch.* 19. §. 1. But that some Acts are rescinded, which were made through Fear, being occasioned not by him with whom we have to do, but by another, is an effect of the Civil Law, which doth often either null or revoke Acts, though freely done, if they that do them be of weak Judgement. *Seneca* argues according to the Law of Nature, when he tells us, *That whatsoever either Force or Fear or Necessity makes us to grant, may be* *Lib.* 4. *cont.* 26. *revoked, if that Force or Necessity be imposed on us by him to whom the grant is made. But what,* saith he, *is that to me, what thou art compelled or necessitated to do, if not by me?* Meam culpam oportet esse, ut mea pœna sit; [*It is necessary that the Fault should be mine own, if the Punishment be so.* Now what we have before said concerning the force and efficacy of the Civil Law, were not amiss to be here repeated: But what force or strength Oaths do add unto Promises to confirm them, shall be shewed anon. See *B.* 3. *c.* 19. §. 4.

VIII. What is promised ought to be in the power of the Promiser.

Again, That a Promise may be strong and binding, it is necessary, That the thing promised either now is, or hereafter may be in the power of the Promiser. Wherefore in the first place, we may be sure, That no Promise can bind us to that which is in it self unlawful: For, *Id possumus quod jure possumus*; *That only we can do, which we can do, do, which we can lawfully do.* All promises receive their vigor from his Right that makes them, beyond which they are of no force. *Agesilaus* being once challenged upon his promise, answered, *Benè si justum sit, seu minus dixi tantum, non & promisi; Ye do well to urge it, if what I promised were just; but if not, I only said it but did not promise it.* But if the thing promised be not now in our power, but may be, then doth the strength of that Promise hang in suspence; because the Promise was but conditional, namely, if at any time it shall lye in my power. But if that condition whereby the thing may be in our power, be also in our power, then is he that made the Promise, obliged to do whatsoever is morally fit, that his Promise may be fulfilled. But the Civil Law nulls many Promises of this kind also for profit, which the Law of Nature would bind us unto: As when a man or woman shall promise to marry another hereafter, being now already married: And not a few other Promises made by Minors and Children, whilest under their Parents tuition.

XI. Whether a Promise made to do an act simply evil obligeth.

But here it may be demanded, Whether a Promise for the performance of an act in it self vicious, doth naturally oblige: As if a man should Promise a Reward to him that should kill another. That this is a wicked Promise doth sufficiently appear by this, That it was made to excite a man to do a wicked Act. But yet not every thing that is viciously done, doth lose the effect of a just Right, as is manifest in things prodigally given, wherein notwithstanding there is this difference, That so soon as the gift is prodigally given, the obliquity ceaseth: For the gift contracts no soil from the giver, and therefore it may without sin be possest by those to whom it is given. But in Promises made to a vicious end, the vice remains so long till the crime be perpetrated: For so long the very fulfilling of the Promise being an incentive to vice, must needs be sinful; which begins to cease, when the crime is committed. Whence we may conclude, that the force and efficacy of such a Promise until that time did hang in suspence, as I said before, concerning the thing promised, being not in our own power. But the crime being done, then the obligation arising from that promise breaks forth, which from the beginning was not intrinsically wanting, but hindred by a vice that was accidental. An example hereof we have in *Judah* the Son of *Jacob*, who performed his Promise unto *Thamar*, whom he dealt with as with an Harlot, by sending her the reward which by the Law of Nature, then in force, was due unto her. Though it be otherwise by the Civil Law, as may appear by the sentence which *C. Aquilius* past in the like case. But in case that Promise were occasioned by the fraud or injustice of the person to whom it was made, or if it were made upon any unequal terms or conditions, how it is to be rectified, is another Question, whereof we shall speak anon.

Things prodigally given may lawfully be retained.

Judah's Promise to *Thamar*. Gen. 38. *Val. Max. l.* 8. *lib.* 2. *n.* 2. *Ch.* 12. §. 9. 10, 11.

X. Concerning a Promise of that which was formerly due. See *Book* 2. *c.* 6. §. 2.

But when any Promise is made for some cause formerly due, it is not thereby the less due, if we look unto Natural Right, according to what we have already said concerning our acceptance of that which is anothers: Because Promises are Naturally debts, though there be no cause preceding; but here also, if any damage accrue by extortion, or if there be any inequality in the agreement made, that damage is to be repaired, according to such Rules as shall be set down anon.

XI. The manner of a firm Promise made by our selves.

Now as to what appertains to the manner of promising, it requires, as I said before, concerning the Alienation of Dominion, some external Act or Sign sufficient to testifie the consent of the Will which may be done, sometimes by a beck or nod, but is usually done either by voice or writing.

XII. Of the like made by others.

But we may also be bound up by another mans act, if it appear that we have deputed and empowred him to act for us, either as our Instrument in that particular business, or under some general notion or qualification. And it may likewise happen, that where the Commission is to act in general, he that is so commissionated, may oblige us, by acting contrary to his private Instructions: For here are two distinct Acts of the Will, the one whereby we oblige our selves to confirm and ratifie whatsoever our Agent shall do in such a business; the other, whereby we oblige our said Agent, that he shall not act beyond our secret Instructions: This we observe, in relation to those things which Ambassadours do Promise for their Masters, by vertue of their Instructions or Letters of Credence, but exceeding their secret Commands.

Of Ambassadours exceeding their private Commands.

XIII. The obligations of Masters of Ships and Factors, how far they naturally extend.

From hence also we may conclude, That such Actions as are brought against Masters of Ships and Factors (who have the charge of goods transported by Sea into foreign parts) which are not so much Actions, as qualities of Actions) are grounded upon the very Law of Nature. And here we cannot but note the error of the *Roman* Laws, which by the fact of the Master do bind every one of the Mariners for and in the whole, which is both repugnant to Natural Equity, which seems to be satisfied if every Mariner be bound for what concerns himself: And also damagable to the Commonwealth; for men would thereby be deterred from Navigating the Seas, fearing to be so strictly, and, as it were, infinitely bound by the fact of the Master. Insomuch,

much, that in *Holland*, a Countrey of late famous for Merchandizing, this *Roman* Law both of old was, and now is of no force: Nay, rather on the contrary, it is decreed, That the Master and Mariners in general, shall each of them be bound no farther than to the value of the Ship, and the goods that are therein transported.

XIV. To a good Promise acceptation is requisite. A pretending demand argues an acceptance, if no alteration appear.

But that a Promise should transfer a Right in the thing promised, the acceptance of him to whom it is promised, is no less requisite, than it was in the case aforesaid of Alienation: And herein *Tertullian* in his Book of Fasts, speaks like a Civilian, *Votum cum à Deo acceptatum est, Legem in posterum facit*; *A Vow*, (though freely made, yet) *when it is by God accepted, is as binding as a Law.* And here also a preceding demand of a thing promised, (if no alteration appear) shall be judged an acceptance. Neither doth that which the Civil Law hath introduced concerning such Promises as are made to Cities hinder this: Which notwithstanding hath so far prevailed with some, that they hold that the sole Act of the Promiser is by the Law of Nature sufficient to transfer a Right: For the *Roman* Law saith not, That the Promise is fully compleat, and of force before it be accepted; but that it is not lawful to revoke such a Promise, but that it may be always accepted, which effect is not from the Law of Nature, but meerly from the Civil Law. Not much unlike unto that which the Law of Nations hath introduced in favour to Infants, Ideots and Madmen. For, for these, as the will and purpose of possessing things that are gained by occupancy, so the will and purpose to accept of things promised creates a Right.

XV. Whether it be requisite that the acceptation should be made known to the Promiser.

It is also sometimes controverted, Whether to make a Promise fully effective, it be requisite that the thing promised be not only accepted, but that the acceptance be also made known to the Promiser, before it can obtain its full effect. And certain it is, that either way the Promise made may be binding: As for Example, either thus, This will I do if it shall be accepted; or thus, This I will do, if I shall understand that it will be accepted. And if the Promise do imply a mutual obligation on both sides, then it is to be understood in the latter sense. But if the Promise be free and spontaneous, then it is best to believe that it was meant in the former sense, unless it shall appear otherwise.

XVI. Whether a Promise made may be revoked before it be accepted.

Again, Hence it follows, That such a Promise made before Acceptance (for till then no Right passeth) may be revoked, without the imputation of either Injustice, yea, or Levity, if it were really so intended, when made, That it should not be of Force, till it were accepted, so till then it could transfer no Right. It may also be revoked, in case the person shall dye to whom such a Promise was made, before he hath accepted of it. Because the Acceptance was referred to his own choice, and not to his heirs. For it is one thing, to be willing to give away my Right to such a man, to be by him transferred to his Heirs; and another thing, to be willing to give it unto his Heirs immediately: It is very material to consider on whom we bestow a benefit. Of this opinion was *Neratius*, who could not believe that a Prince would have granted that to him being dead, which he had granted unto him, believing him to be alive.

XVII. Whether it may be revoked, if the party dye who was authorized to make it. Explained.

A Promise may also be revoked upon the death of the person who was authozed to make it; because the binding power was in his words: But not so, if the grant be sent by a Messenger or a Carrier, because the obliging power is not in him, but in the Instrument he carries. And therefore those Letters importing the consent of the party may be conveyed by any man. We must also distinguish between him that is deputed only to signifie the Promise we make, and him that is authorized by us to make that Promise himself. In the former case a revocation shall take place, although it be not so exprest to him that carries the Promise or Grant: In the latter case, the revocation is of no force; because the obliging power depended upon the Will of him that is sent to make it; who if he do make it whilest it is in his power so to do, that is, before the revocation be made known unto him, the grant shall be valid, and the person that made it justified. So also in the former case, though the Donor dye, yet may the gift be accepted, as being on his part perfect and compleat, although subject to a revocation: which is apparent in Ambassadours. But in the latter case it cannot, because the gift is not actually given, but only commanded to be given. But where the matter will admit of a debate, it may be presumed, that the will of the Prince was, That his Commands should be executed, unless some great alteration should happen in the mean time: As namely, the death of the person commanding. 'Tis true, there may be many conjectures that may be of force to perswade us to think otherwise, which may easily be admitted, That so what was in a good cause commanded to be given, may notwithstanding abide with us. And thus may that question that hath been heretofore muted, be answered, Whether the heir of him that was so commanded, may be sued at Law.

XVIII. Whether a Promise be revocable after it hath been accepted of by another.

Controversies also do usually happen, concerning the accepting of a thing in the behalf of another: Wherein also we must distinguish between that Promise that is made to me of something to be given to another, and that promise which is made in the name of him to whom the thing is to be given. If the Promise be made to me (setting aside that Query introduced by the *Roman* Law, Whether any benefit do accrue unto me by it.) The Right of accepting the thing seems naturally to be given to me, and the power of transferring that Right unto another, if he also will accept thereof; so that he that made the Promise hath no Right in the mean time to revoke it; but I to whom the Promise was made may remit it. For this sense, as it is no whit repugnant to the Law of Nature, so is it most agreeable to the words of such a Promise: Neither can it be said, not at all to concern me, That another by me should receive a benefit. But if the Promise be made in his name to whom the thing is to be given, we must then enquire, Whether he that accepts of what is promised, hath a Special Command so to do, or an order so general, as may be thought sufficient to include it; or whether he hath no such order at all. If it do appear that he hath such order or authority to accept thereof, I do not then conceive it necessary to enquire any farther, Whether the person so impowred be a Free-man or not, as is usually done by the *Roman* Laws; but conclude rather, That the Promise is fully compleat by that acceptance: For it sufficeth to signifie our consent, though by a Servant, whose will is reputed ours, if we authorize him, and he accept thereof. But if he that accepts of the Promise, have no such order from him to whom the Promise is made, but is deputed by the Promiser, then hath the Promiser no power to revoke the Promise, until he whom it concerns, do either accept thereof, or reject it. Yet so, notwithstanding, That he, who in the mean time, hath accepted of the Promise made, hath no power to remit it, because he is not deputed to accept of any Right to the thing promised, but to bind the Promiser to observe and perform his Promise, in sustaining the thing promised: So that if the Promiser shall retract, he may be said to break his Faith, but he cannot be said to invade any mans Right or Propriety.

XIX. In what time a charge may be added to a Promise.

By what hath been already said, it may easily be conceived, what we are to judge concerning such a charge as is usually added unto a Promise. For such a charge may be imposed, as long as the Promise is not yet made perfect by acceptance, nor the Faith of the Promiser given, that it shall be irrevocable. But yet this charge added for the use and benefit of a third person is also revocable, until it shall be by that third person accepted: Although some there be, that, as well in this, as in other the like questions, are otherwise perswaded. But he that throughly considers the matter, will quickly discern so much of natural reason and equity in what hath been said, that he will judge all farther proofs to be needless and superfluous.

XX. A Promise in it self invalid, how it may be made firm.

It is also sometimes Controverted, How a Promise occasioned by an error (or mistake) in the Promiser may be made good, if, the truth being known, the Promiser notwithstanding his mistake, be willing to stand to his Promise. The like question may be put concerning Promises occasioned by fear, force, or the like, when the cause thereof shall afterwards cease, as in the case of Matrimony, and the like. For the confirmation of which Promises, some are of opinion, that nothing is requisite but the internal acts of the mind, which being conjoined with the former external act, sufficeth to contract a firm obligation. Others disallowing this, because they cannot admit that any outward Act should be a competent sign of an internal act subsequent to it, do require a new verbal Promise and Acceptance. But the middle opinion is the safer, which requires some outward act, but not such as is verbal, seeing that the retaining of the thing promised by the person to whom it was promised, and the relinquishing of it by the person promising, or some such like act, are sufficient to testifie the mutual consent of both parties.

XXI. Promises made without cause not naturally void.

They also must not be omitted, lest we should confound the Civil Law with the Law of Nature: That by the Law of Nature, Promises as well as Gifts may be good and valid, though there be no cause or consideration exprest, wherefore they were made.

XXII. He that promiseth for the fact of another how far he standeth bound.

Neither is any man bound by his Promise that he makes for the fact of another man, to make good all that wherein they differ, so as he omits nothing of that which on his part may be done, to procure that man to do it, unless either the words of the Promise or the nature of the business do naturally require a stronger obligation. So *Livy* in the like case, *He thought himself discharged of his Promise, forasmuch as he left nothing unattempted that lay in him, to have had it performed.*

CHAP. XII.

Of Contracts.

I. *The Division of humane Acts unto others profitable: And first of simple and mixt.*
II. *Simple are either purely liberal, or with mutual obligation.*
III. *Or into such as are permutatory, as well such as separate the parts.*
IV. *As those that introduce Community.*
V. *Those that are mixt are either so principally,*
VI. *Or by way of Accession.*
VII. *Which of these Acts are called Contracts.*
VIII. *In all Contracts there should be an equality, and that first in such Acts as are Præcedaneous.*
IX. *As an equality in knowledge.*
X. *An equal freedom of Will.*
XI. 2. *In the very act, if it be by way of Exchange.*
XII. 3. *In the things contracted for, explained.*
XIII. *That this equality takes place, even in such Acts as are either meerly or in part beneficent.*
XIV. *How things are to be valued, and for what causes the prices are either increased or diminished.*
XV. *When things are perfectly bought, and when the Dominion is transferred.*
XVI. *What Monopolies are contrary to the Law of Nature, or Rules of Charity.*
XVII. *How mony receives its function.*
XVIII. *Of Lands hired, nothing of the Rent is to be abated by reason of the sterility or the like: And if the first Tenant be disabled to use the Land or thing, may it not be let to another.*
XIX. *How the just hire of mens Labours may be increased or diminished.*
XX. *By what Law Usury is forbidden.*
XXI. *What profit falls not under the notion of Usury.*
XXII. *What the Civil Law determines of Usury.*
XXIII. *In Contracts, what value we are to put upon the peril we run, in securing the main stock.*
XXIV. *In social Contracts how the profits are to be proportioned, and of its several kinds.*
XXV. *Of Naval Confederations.*
XXVI. *If there be an inequality in the terms agreed upon, as to Acts external, the Law of Nations allows no remedy; and in what sence this is said to be Natural.*

I. The division of humane Acts to others profitable.

OF such humane Acts as are to others profitable, some are simple, others mixt or compounded.

II. Of those that are simple, some are meerly beneficent, some mutually obligatory.

Of those that are Simple, some are Beneficent, others Permutatory: Such as are Beneficent, are either merely gratuitous or infer a mutual obligation: Such as are merely gratuitous, are either presently done, or such as extend to the time to come. Those that are presently done, are either some fact or deed that yields profit to another, whereof there is no necessity that we should discourse, since though it doth produce profit, yet it hath no effects of Right: Or some donative or free gift, which also is a profitable act and presently done, whereby Dominion is transferred, and whereof we have treated above, when we discourst of the acquiring Dominion. Those gratuitous acts that extend to the time to come, are promises, either to give or to do somewhat, whereof we discourst in the Chapter preceding. Those beneficent Acts which infer mutual obligation, are such as dispose either of things without alienating them, or of some Fact; yet so, as that some effects remain to another. Such, as to things, is the concession of the use of them, which is called lending: And as to Facts, the performance of some work that is costly or obligatory, which is called a Mandate or Charge, whereof one *species* is, something deposited or committed to our trust, as namely, our labour in the keeping of the thing. Now like unto these Acts, are our Promises of these Acts, but that these, as I have already said, do extend to the time to come; which also we would have to be understood of those Acts, which are now to be explained.

III. And into such as are permutatory.

Of such Acts as do infer Profit by exchange, some divide and dissipate the parts, others unite them, and so introduce Communion: Those which divide and separate the parts, the *Roman* Lawyers rightly distinguish into these three heads: *Do ut Des, Facio ut Facias, Facio ut Des.* First, when we exchange one thing for another, the agreement runs thus; I'll give you this, if you'll give me that. 2. When we truck Deeds, then it runs thus; I'll do this for you, if you'll do that for me. The 3d. is mixt, as when we agree, That if I do this for you, then you shall give me that as the price or reward of my pains. But the *Roman* Lawyers do exempt from this Division, some Contracts, which they call *Nominati*;

Nominati; not so much because they have proper names (for so have those Contracts which are made by exchange also, which they will not admit amongst their Nominate Contracts) But because by reason of their more frequent and ordinary use, they had received some certain force, and were of such a Nature, that though nothing at all had been particularly said, yet by their very name they might have been sufficiently understood. Hence it was, that to those there were certain set forms of Actions appointed; whereas to others that were less ordinary, that common form was not sufficient: But the plea must be made in a form fitted to the fact, and therefore it was said to be in prescript words. Neither is there any other cause but this of frequent use, why in these nominate conventions, if some things requisite to a Contract were by both parties assented unto: As in the sale of any thing, if the price were on both sides agreed on, yea, though the matter were yet entire, (that is, if there were no mony paid, nor any thing performed on either side) yet was there enjoyned a necessity of fulfilling the Contract on both sides; whereas in Contracts not so frequent, whilst things stood entire, and nothing on either sides performed, there was indulged unto them a liberty to retract, that is to say, they might without any penalty revoke. For the Civil Law restrained all coercive power from such Contracts, and left them wholly to the Faith and Honesty of the Contractors: But the Law of Nature takes no cognizance of these distinctions; for neither are those Contracts which they call Innominate, either less natural or less ancient. Nay even Bartering, which they reckon among those that are Innominate, is both more simple and more ancient, than those made by bargain and sale. Thus *Tacitus* testifies of the *Germans*, *That they used the more simple and ancient way of Traffick, that is, by exchange of Commodities.* For as *Servius* rightly observed, *Our Ancestors did only exchange one thing for another.* *How much more happy was that Age,* saith *Pliny*, *when men exchanged Goods for Goods, the Native Commodities of one Country for those of the growth of another.* The like he relates of the *Seres*, a people of *Scythia*, *Who having exposed their Native Commodities to sale on the farther bank of the River, they take away what they find to be set by it, if they are pleased with the exchange.* Which kind of bartering of Commodities is yet in use in some parts of *Africk*: We therefore taking Nature for our best guide, do reduce all diremptory Contracts (without taking any cognizance of that *Roman* distinction of Nominate and Innominate agreements) unto these three heads before named. When we give to receive, we either barter one thing for another, which doubtless was the ancient way of Traffick, or we receive mony for mony, as by Bills of Exchange; or we receive goods for mony, as in the case of buying and selling; or we receive the use of a thing for another thing, or the use of one thing for the use of another, or the use of a thing for mony, as in things let and taken to hire. By the use of things we are to understand, not only the bare use of a thing, but also the fruits, profits, or proceeds of it, whether temporary, personal, hereditary, or any other way however limited or circumscribed, as among the *Hebrews*, that which was held until the next Jubilee. Some things are given, that after some Intervals of time, are to be restored either in kind or to the same value, as in things that are lent; and this kind of Permutation is chiefly used, where the things exchanged do consist in number, measure, o weight, whether it be mony or other things. The exchange of deeds for deeds do infinitely vary, according to the no less infinite variety of humane actions. But when we do that we may receive, it is either work done for mony, as when for our daily labour we receive wages; and this also is a kind of letting our selves to hire for profit in our several callings: Or when by our voluntary act, we undertake to secure another mans goods from all casualties or contingent misfortunes, which manner of contract was hardly known to former ages, though now of frequent use; or when we do somewhat to receive either things, or the use of things for our pains.

Ensurance.

IV. As into such as are communicatory.

But such Acts as are communicatory, do contribute either deeds or things, or on the one side things, and on the others deeds, towards some publick benefit: All which are comprised under the notion of Society or Confederacy, under which also we comprehend that of war, when private men combine together, to equip a Fleet at their own charge, against Pyrates, or against such as invade them, and such a combination is vulgarly called the Admiralty.

V. Acts mixt are either so principally.

But such Acts as we call mixt, are either principally and originally so, or are made so, by the accession of some other: As if I shall knowingly give more for a thing than it is worth, or than I can buy it for of another, it is a mixt Act, partly a Gift and partly a Buying. So if I do contract with a Goldsmith, for so much mony, to make me so many Rings of his own Gold, it is a mixt Act, for I buy the Gold and hire the Workman. And thus it happens also in Societies, as that one part should contribute deeds and mony, but the other mony only: So likewise the grant of Land to be held in Fee Farm, is a benefit or a gift, but the binding of him to whom this Grant is made to serve in the wars for our defence, is, *faciam ut facias*, to do somewhat for him that he may do somewhat for us: So the Gain, by mony lent to traffick by Sea, is mixt; partly for the loan of my mony, and partly for running the danger of the Seas.

Acts

VI. *Or by accession.*

Acts are mixt by accession, when we strengthen our own Acts by the Acts of another; as by Sureties, or by delivering Pledges or Hostages: For Suretiship, if we respect only the matter between the principal Debtor and the Surety, is for the most part a Command, or bidding the Surety to engage his credit for him: But if we respect the business between the Creditor and the Surety, who receives nothing at all from him, it is an Act purely free; yet because it confines upon such Contracts as are burdensom, therefore it is to be reckoned as such: So the giving of a thing to pawn or as a pledge, seems of it self to be a free act, whereby the detaining of the thing pawned becomes lawful; but this also derives its nature from the contract, which is thereby strengthned and secured.

VII. *Which of these are called Contracts.*

All such Acts as are profitable unto others, besides those that are merely bountiful and beneficent, are comprehended under the name of Contracts.

VIII. *Equality is requisite in Contracts and first in Acts precedaneous.*

In all Contracts Nature requires an equality, and that so strictly that she gives a right to him, that through inequality hath less than his due. This Equality doth consist partly in the Act of Contracting, and partly in that about which the Contract is made: And in the Act of Contracting, as well in those Acts that are precedaneous, as in those that are principals.

IX. *As Equality in knowledge.* *Cicero offic. l. 2. 10.* *Val. Max. lib. 8. c. 11. 1.* *Lact. l. 5.*

It appertains to these Acts that precede any Contract, that he with whom we have to deal, should discover unto us all the faults and defects which he knows to be in the thing contracted for, which is not only required by the Civil Law, but is most agreeable to the nature of the Act, there being a nearer relation between the persons contracting, than that which is common to all mankind. And thus may that of *Diogenes Babylonius* be answered, handling this Argument, namely, that all things are not hid which are not spoken: Neither is it necessary for me to express all that is profitable for thee to hear, as in matters celestial; for the nature of a Contract being invented for gain and profit, requires something that is more proper. To this purpose *Valerius Maximus* brings in an excellent example in *Claudius Contumatus*, whose house standing near the Capitol, and so hindring the Augurs in the prospect of the Birds, and consequently in their divination, was ordered to be demolished; which *Claudius* knowing, but concealing, went immediately and sold his House to *Calphurnius Lanarius*, who understanding the cheat, appealed to *Cato*; who prudently condemned *Claudius*, alledging that *bonæ fidei venditor, nec commodorum spem augere, nec incommodorum cognitionem obscurare oportet*; *And that with a great deal of Equity*, saith *Valerius*, *for an honest Seller should neither heighten the Buyers hopes of gain, nor hide from him his knowledge of the incommodities of what he sells.* It was a good observation of St. *Ambrose*, *In contractibus etiam vitia eorum quæ veneunt prodi jubentur; ac nisi intimaverit venditor, quamvis in jus emptoris transcripserit doli actione vacuantur*: *In ordinary Contracts, whatever defects are in the thing exposed to be sold, ought to be discovered to the Buyer; which if not faithfully done, though the right of the thing be transfer'd to the Buyer, yet ought the Contracts to be null'd, by reason of the fraud in the concealment of the defects. As in case a man should sell an House that is haunted with Devils, or infected with the Plague, or a Servant that is a Fugitive, and doth not discover it, regarding only his own profit and not natural equity. Non est ille sapiens, sed callidus & astutus, That man is not wise*, saith *Carneades*, *but crafty and knavish.* But if the thing concealed, do not immediately concern the thing contracted for, we are not bound to reveal it: As if I expose to sale such things, whereof I know a greater quantity is coming in after to be sold, I may safely conceal mine own knowledge; yet even to discover this is commendable, and in some cases not to be omitted without breach of charity; yet I dare not say it is unjust, I mean any violation of his Right with whom we have to do. So that what the same *Diogenes* saith in the same place (as *Cicero* quotes him) is very true, and to the purpose. *Advexi, exposui, vendo meum; non plures quam cæteri: Fortasse erunt minoris, cum major sit copia, cui sit injuria? Hither have I brought my goods, I expose them to sale, I sell but mine own, and at no dearer rates than others: Perhaps when there is greater plenty they will be cheaper, and in so doing whom do I injure?* Whence then we may observe, that of *Cicero* is not generally to be admitted, that to hide a thing is, when thou wouldest have them whom it concerns, to be ignorant of what thou knowest, thereby to gain profit to thy self. For then only is this concealment unjust, when it immediately concerns the thing that is to be contracted for; as in Houses infected with the Pestilence, or ordained by the Magistrates to be pulled down, or the like: For of these things there should be, between the Buyer and Seller, an equal knowledg, for that makes them both equal.

Celare quid. *Par scientia.*

X. *And in freedom of Will.*

And as there should be an equality in knowledge between both the Contractors, so should there also be a like freedom of Will between them; not that in case the Seller be prepossest with an unjust fear, no Contract can be made with him till that fear be removed, for that is a thing extrinsick to the Contract. But that no man ought to be constrained through fear to consent to the sale of what he would not otherwise part withal, and if such an occasion of fear be given him to that end, that it should be first taken away, that so as well the Seller as the Buyer may have a like freedom of Will. When the

the *Ælians* had bought ſome Lands of their Neighbors, who durſt not deny to ſell it them on any terms. The *Lacedæmonians* made no ſcruple to make void the Contract, and therefore cauſed the *Ælians* to make reſtitution; alledging, *That there was as much injuſtice in taking away the Goods of their Inferiors, under the ſpecious pretence of Purchaſe, as in extorting from them by mere force,* which are the very words of *Xenophon.* But what exceptions the Law of Nature admits of in theſe caſes, ſhall be diſcourſed of in its proper place.

Greek Hiſt. l. 3.

XI. Equality in the act it ſelf if it be permutatory.

In the very principal act of Contracting, there is alſo required this equality, that no more be exacted than what is fit, which rule is of no force in ſuch acts as are beneficent: For if I will give ſomewhat more by way of reward, either for work done at my command, or for things lent me, or for preſerving things depoſited, than is juſtly due; I do no man wrong, I do but mix the act by making it partly permutatory, and partly gratuitous. But in all permutatory Contracts, this equality is punctually to be obſerved: Neither is it to the purpoſe to pretend, that what is either promiſed or given by either party more than is due, may be accounted as a donative; for this is not the uſual meaning of Contractors, nor is it to be ſo preſumed, unleſs by ſome act or word it be ſo declared. For whatſoever either party doth either give or promiſe, is but in proportion to what they expect to receive, and as it were to even the Ballance; inſomuch that St. *Chryſoſtom* was of opinion, and not without reaſon, *That in Contracts as often as we ſtrive earneſtly to buy any thing for leſs than it is worth, or to have more than our juſt meaſure or weight, there was in that Fact a kind of Theft.* He that writes the Life of *Iſidore* in *Photius,* tells a Story of one *Hermias,* who having bought any thing that was judged more worth than he paid for it, would of his own accord add as much as it wanted of the true value, holding it a kind of Injuſtice to detain it, but ſuch an injuſtice as few men then underſtood (and as few now adays would ſcruple at.) And in this ſence do the *Jewiſh* Doctors interpret that Law of *Moſes, If thou ſelleſt ought to thy Neighbor, or buyeſt ought of thy Neighbors hand, ye ſhall not oppreſs one anoeher.*

A juſt proportion to be obſerved between the Giver and the Receiver.

Lev. 25. 14. and 17.

XII. And in the things contracted for.

Yet farther, Though both parties have equal knowledge of the thing contracted for, and alſo equal freedom of Will, ſo that there is nothing concealed that ſhould be diſcovered, nor a greater price exacted than is thought to be due; yet if there prove to be any inequality in the things themſelves, which the parties themſelves could not diſcern, or that there were a miſtake of the juſt price or value, then that error or miſtake is to be rectifyed by the *Roman* Laws: And he that hath too much muſt impart to him that hath too little, becauſe in that Contract it was or ought to have been the mind and meaning of both parties, That there ſhould be an even ballance in a right eſtimation. And yet do not the *Roman* Laws require this in every unequal Contract, In caſe the inequality be but ſmall, the Law takes no cognizance of it to prevent multitudes of ſuits; but only where the inequality is weighty, as where it exceeds half of the juſt value: For the Law (as *Cicero* ſaith) reſtraineth iniquity by pinnacling the hand, but Philoſophy by Reaſon and Underſtanding. But they that are not ſubject to Civil Laws, ought to follow that which by the dictates of right reaſon ſeems unto them righteous; yea and they alſo that are ſubject to Laws, ſo oft as they have to do with ſuch things as are agreeable to Piety and Religion, if the Laws do neither give nor take away Right, but only deny their aid and aſſiſtance unto it for ſome certain reaſons.

Minima non perſequitur Lex.

XIII. What Equality takes place in Acts merely or in part beneficent.

But here alſo it is to be obſerved, that ſome equality ought to be had even in ſuch Contracts as are beneficent, yet not altogether ſo ſtrict as are in thoſe that are permutatory, but as the caſe of ſuch Contracts may be ſuppoſed, namely, leſt any man ſhould be damnifyed by the good he doth. For example, That he who doth any thing in obedience to anothers Command, ſhould be ſaved harmleſs and indemnifyed, as well in reſpect of his charges, as of any loſs ſuſtained by reaſon of the execution of that command. Again, That he to whom any thing is freely lent, ſhould ſatisfie the juſt value, if the thing periſh in his cuſtody, becauſe he ſtands obliged to the owner not only for the thing it ſelf, but to be thankful for the courteſie done him in the loan thereof, unleſs it be evident that the thing ſo lent had certainly ſo periſhed, had it continued in the poſſeſſion of the right owner: For in this caſe he loſeth nothing by the Loan. But on the contrary, He with whom any thing is depoſited, receives nothing but a bare truſt; and therefore if the thing miſcarry he is not bound to repair the loſs: Neither in reſpect of the thing truſted, there being no ſuch in being, neither is the Truſtee any thing the richer for it; nor in reſpect of his acceptance of the truſt, becauſe thereby he receiveth no courteſie but doth one. And as to things pawned, as alſo in things let out to hire, a middle way is to be taken; for in every caſe of loſs the receiver is not bound to reſtitution, as he is to whom a thing is lent; yet is a much greater care required from him to preſerve it, than of that which is committed barely to truſt, becauſe the acceptance of it though gratuitous, yet uſually comes very neer unto ſuch Contracts as are burdenſom. All which do agree with the *Roman* Laws, but were originally extracted from natural equity; and are therefore found

Things lent.

Things depoſited.

found to be of force amongst other Nations: As (amongst others) of the *Hebrews*; for so *Moses Maimonides* testifies. And hereunto hath *Seneca* respect*, when he saith, *That some owe fidelity and others Tutelage and Protection.* And by these rules we may easily pass our judgments upon other Contracts: But now having (as far as is requisite to our purpose) sufficiently discours'd of Contracts in general, we shall briefly handle some more particular questions concerning them.

See Exod. 22, 6, 10, 11, 12, 13.
* *De benef. l.* 7. *c.* 19.

XIV. Concerning the price of things, how they may be dearer or cheaper.

The most natural measure whereby the true value of every thing is known, is by the want of it, as *Aristotle* rightly observes; which rule the barbarous Nations do very strictly walk by: Yet is not this the only rule that guides the value of things, for the mind of man, like an Empress, covets many things for their rarity, which are not purely necessary. *Margaritis pretia Luxuria fecit, It is Pride that gives the price to Pearls,* saith *Pliny* †. And in another place, *Look,* saith he, *what value we put upon the* Indian *Pearls, the same do the* Indians *put upon our Coral; for these things are valued by the opinion that Nations have of them.* And no marvel, saith St. *Augustin* *, *For in the esteem of these men, an Horse is sometimes bought at a far dearer rate than a Servant, and a Jewel than a Slave,* &c. So *Cicero, Qui modus est in his rebus cupiditatis, idem est æstimationis; Nothing so much heightens the prices of these things, as the longing desire that men have after them.* So likewise on the contrary, *Those things that are most necessary, are least prized where there is great plenty of them:* Which *Seneca* illustrates by many examples, where also he adds this, *The price of every thing varies with the times, when thou hast sufficiently praised these things, they are so much worth as they cannot advance to more.* So likewise *Paulus* the Lawyer, *That which gives a just value to any thing, is not the affection of any one person, or the profit that this or that particular man can make of it, but what it may be commonly sold for.* And this cannot be at all times alike and certain, but it riseth and falls according to the pains, expences, and hazards, that Merchants are at in their importation. Neither doth St. *Augustin* disapprove of it, who upon the Seventieth *Psalm*, brings in the Merchant pleading thus, *Affero è longinquo merces, mercedem laboris mei unde vivam, peto, Dignus enim est Mercenarius mercede sua,* &c. *I bring my Merchandises from far, I require but a reward for my pains that I may live, the Labourer is worthy of his hire.* But saith the good Father there, *De mendacio & perjurio agitur, non de negotio; It is not thy Calling but thy Lying and Perjury that we condemn.* Moreover the prices of things may rise or fall by reason of the plenty or scarcity, either of Buyers, of Mony, or of the Merchandises themselves. Besides, such Accidents do sometimes fall out, as may justly enhance or lessen the prices of things, as namely, we may haply sustain some future loss by the sale of them, or for want of them; or our gains we make by them may cease, or we may be unwilling to part with them for some affection we particularly bear, either to the things themselves or to him that gave them: And therefore we would not willingly sell them but in favour to him that buyes them. All which ought to be declared to him with whom we are to Contract: Regard also may be had unto that damage or surceasing profit, which is occasioned by either the delaying or anticipating the payment of the price agreed on.

† *Lib.* 32.
Pearls and Coral.
* *De Civit. Dei l.* 11. *c.* 16.
De benef. l. 6. *c.* 15.
Aug. in Psal. 70.
Of Merchants.

XV. When a sale is perfected by the Law of Nature, and when dominion passeth.

As to buying and selling, we must know that the bargain and sale is good, from the very minute of the Contract: For though the thing bought be not actually delivered, yet may the property by a bare mutual consent of both parties be transferred, and this is the most simple and innocent way of bargaining. So *Seneca, Venditio alienatio est, & rei suæ jurisque sui in alium translatio; Selling is the alienation of a thing and the translation of it, together with our right and property in it to another.* But if it be so agreed that the property shall not pass presently, then shall the Seller be bound to transfer his dominion, and in the mean time both the profit and peril shall be the Sellers: And if it happen that one and the same thing be twice sold, that sale shall be most valid which hath the property first translated, either by delivery of possession or otherwise; for hereby doth the moral power pass away from the seller to the buyer, and that which is made by promise only shall stand for nothing.

XVI. What Monopolies are against the Law of Nature or the Rule of Charity.

Monopolies are not all of them repugnant to the Law of Nature, for they may be permitted by the Supreme Magistrate upon some just cause and at a certain rate, as may appear by the example of *Joseph* in his Government of *Egypt*. So also under the *Romans*, the *Alexandrians* had the Monopoly of all *Indian* and *Æthiopick* Commodities. The like may be instituted by private men, so that they retail them for moderate gains. But they that, like the Oylmen in *Velabrum*, shall purposely combine, and either by fraud or force stop the importation of Goods, that they may enhanse the price of those they have, which is already at the highest; or that agree to buy all the Goods of that kind that come in, to the end that they may sell them at what rate they please; are very injurious to the Common-wealth, and are bound to make reparation. But if by any other means they shall hinder the bringing in of such merchandises, or shall therefore engross the whole to themselves, that they may vend them at a price (respect being had to the time in which they sell them) not unreasonable, they infringe the Bonds of Charity (as St. *Ambrose* proves

The History of *Thales* is well known.

Off. l. 3. c. 6. by many Arguments, though to ſpeak properly, they violate no mans Right.

XVII. How Money receives its value.

As for Money, the office it performs it naturally receives, not from the ſole matter, or metal, nor from its form or appellation, but from a more general relation, namely, as we counterpoiſe it with other things, eſpecially, with thoſe that are moſt neceſſary: Now the value that is put upon it, if it be not otherwiſe agreed on, muſt be according to the rate, that it bears at the time, and in the place, where payment is to be made. *Ad. 5. Nicom.* Now as *Michael Epheſius* rightly obſerves, *Money it ſelf varies as all other things do, according to the plenty or ſcarcity of it; for as we have not always a like occaſion to uſe other things, and according to our deſire of them, ſo the prices riſe or fall: So Money doth not always retain the ſame value, but ſometimes it is more and ſometimes leſs worth. But yet the price of Money is moſt laſting: Which we uſe chiefly as a counter-ballance to all other things wherewith it is compared.* Now that which is the meaſure or ſtandard to all things ought in it ſelf to be conſtant. And therefore Gold, Silver, and Braſs by themſelves are of the ſame value almoſt always and in all places. And as other things that are uſeful or neceſſary, are either rare, or abounding, ſo the ſame Money in weight, and made of the ſame Metal is ſometimes more, and ſometimes leſs worth.

XVIII. Rents not to be remitted for barrenneſs or ſuch like chances.

Next to buying and ſelling (as *Cajus* notes) is letting and taking to hire, and ſteered by the ſame Rules. That which anſwers to the price is the rent or hire, and that which anſwers to the Propriety, is the poſſeſſing and enjoying of the benefit of it. Wherefore as when the thing periſheth, the owner bears the loſs: So when the thing hired proves ſteril or barren, or by any other accident proves fruitleſs and unprofitable; the loſs is naturally the preſent occupiers: Neither hath the Lord any thing the leſs Right to the rent or hire agreed for, becauſe when he delivered the thing to him to uſe, it was ſo much worth as was contracted for. Although that may be changed, either by general Laws, or by Covenants between themſelves; yet notwithſtanding if he that firſt hired the thing be diſabled to make uſe thereof, and thereupon the owner let it to another, whatſoever he ſhall gain thereby, more than the hire firſt agreed for, he ſhall repay to him that firſt took it, leſt he ſhould enrich himſelf by that which is due to another man.

XIX. How the reward of mens labours may be encreaſed or diminiſhed.

Again, what was before ſaid in the caſe of ſelling, namely, that the price may be more or leſs if the thing were only ſold to gratifie the buyer, but otherwiſe was neither to be bought nor ſold: The very ſame may be underſtood of any thing, or of any work let or taken for hire, in favour of him that requires it. But if a man by one and the ſame pains may accommodate diverſe perſons, as in conveying them from place to place, if he that undertakes it ſhall oblige himſelf entirely to every one of them, he may require the ſame reward from every one, as he exacted from the firſt, if the Law do not otherwiſe provide; becauſe that, by my labour a ſecond, third or fourth perſon receives a benefit doth no whit prejudice the Contract made with the firſt. And if the benefit be equal, ſurely the reward ought to be ſo too.

XX. By what Law Uſury is forbidden.

As concerning Money lent, it is frequently queſtioned by what Law Uſury is forbidden: and although it be the moſt received opinion, That it is prohibited by the Law of Nature, yet was *Albulenſis* of a contrary Judgement, neither are thoſe arguments which are brought to prove the adverſe part of ſuch weight as to turn the Scale. For whereas it is ſaid of things lent, that they are lent freely, as much may be ſaid of things delivered to another to uſe; and yet if any thing be required for the uſe of either, it may haply cauſe the Contract to paſs by another name, but it cannot make the taking of a moderate price for the uſe of a thing unlawful. Neither is that argument which they draw from the ſterility of Money any thing more perſwaſive. For mans Induſtry is able to make Houſes, Lands or any other thing, which in themſelves are barren, to become fruitful. But that which ſeems to be the moſt plauſible Argument is this, That here one thing is given for another, as an Houſe for Rent. But the uſe of a thing *Uſus in abuſu conſiſtit.* cannot be diſtinguiſhed from the thing it ſelf, where the thing it ſelf *periſheth by the uſing of it*: And therefore for that nothing ought to be exacted. But here we muſt note, That when by the decree of the Senate, the fruits ariſing from the uſe of things, that either by their uſe periſh, or are transferred into the dominion of another was introduced by the Name of *Uſusfructus*, (which properly ſignifies the profit that is gained by the uſe of anothers mans goods, the property remaining his own) they intended not by that word *Uſusfructus*, that it ſhould obtain the ſame effect of right with that which was properly ſo called. For certainly the word ſo taken could not according to its Propriety agree with ſuch a Right. Neither will it thence notwithſtanding follow, That ſuch a Right is nothing, or not valuable: Since, on the contrary, it is certain, That if any man would yield up ſuch a Right to the Proprietor, Money may be required upon that account. So alſo the Right of not paying either Money or Wine borrowed, till after ſuch a time, is valuable: *Minus enim ſolvit, qui tempore minus ſolvit; For he pays not his due that pays not in due time.* And therefore in Lands mortgaged for Money, the profits of the Land ſhould anſwer for the uſe of the Money. Now what Arguments are brought by *Cato*, *Cicero*, and *Plutarch* againſt Uſury, do not ſo much reſpect

respect the intrinsick nature of the thing, as the adjuncts and consequences of it. What we are to do in this case, we may collect from the Law given by God to the *Hebrews*; which forbids them to lend money each to other upon Usury. The subject matter of which Law, if it be not necessary, yet it is morally honest: And therefore in *Psal.* 15. it is enumerated among such as are highly Moral; as also in *Ezech.* 18. Some there are (saith *Hierom*) who place Usury in the gain by money only; but the Scriptures do providently take away all Immoderate Gain by any thing; and do require, that thou shouldst take no more than thou gavest. Now such Precepts as these are, do as well oblige Christians as *Hebrews*, we being called to be more excellent patterns of Vertue than they. Wherefore look what Moral duties the Law then enjoyned the *Jews*, and all that were circumcised, for they were both herein equally obliged, the same ought now to be observed by all Nations, the partition-wall being now taken away by the promulgation of the Evangelical Law, which under the notion of *Neighbour*, comprehends all mankind; as by that excellent Apology of our Saviour concerning the *Samaritan*, most evidently appears. So *Arnobius* testifies of the Christians of his time, *That they were communicative of their goods with all men, loving all men as if they were their brethren.* And therefore *Lactantius* treating of Christian duties, makes this one, *He shall not* (saith he) *give his money upon usury, for this is to seek gain by anothers wants.* So also St. *Ambrose*, *Subvenire non habenti humanitatis est, Duritiæ autem, plus extorquere quàm dederis*; *To relieve the wants of others is humane, but to require more than was lent, cruel.* And *Augustus Cæsar* himself blamed some who took up money at an easie rate, to lend it to others upon harder terms. St. *Chrysostome* speaking of Fasting, gives this Caution, *If thou fast, take heed that thou lend not thy money upon Usury, but break the bonds of all unjust Contracts.* And on the last Chapter of the first Epistle to the *Corinthians*, he saith, *That he that offers unto God money gained by Usury, is as if a woman should offer out of her Meretricious Gain.*

See Psal. 102. The good man is merciful and lendeth, and will guide his words with discretion.

Lib. 4.

Epit. Instit. c. 2.

De Off. 13. *c.* 2

See *Grat. c.* 14. *quæst.* 3, 4.

XXI.

What Gain falls not under the Notion of Usury.

It is notwithstanding to be observed, that there are some Contracts which have some resemblance of Usury, and are vulgarly so accounted, which yet are of another kind: As when the lender requires somewhat to repair the damage he hath sustained, either by reason of the long detention of his money lent; or being frustrated of the hopes of gain that he might have made by it, deducting notwithstanding somewhat in respect of the incertainty of those hopes, and also for the labour and hazard he must have run for it. So likewise, to defray the charges of him that lends money to many, and to that purpose keeps his money ready (with his Books of Account); and for the danger he runs of losing the Principal where it is not sufficiently secured. If any thing in these Cases be required, it is not to be reputed Usury. And if we would know, what opinion the *Roman* Lawyers had of it, we shall find, that as they hated the word *Fœnus*; so they would easily admit of *Usura*. *Usura, non propter lucrum petentium, sed propter moram solventium*; *Not that the lender desired to make a gain by the wants of the borrower, but because his money is not paid at the time agreed on.* The difference being only this, [*Fœnus*] *is that which we contract for, more than the principal, meerly out of a desire of gain*: But [*Usura*] *is that which is given more than the principal, lest the lender should be damnified by the detention of the principal.* But since this word *Usura* being abused by some, hath gotten an ill report; therefore hath this latter Age substituted in its room the word *Interest*. *Demosthenes* in his Oration against *Pantænetus*, denyes peremptorily, that he deserves to be branded with the name of an Usurer, that lends what he hath got either by merchandizing, or by his honest labour, *sub modico lucello*, *for some moderate gain*: partly that he may keep what he hath so got; and partly, that thereby he may gratifie another. It is recorded of *Germanus* Kinsman to *Justinian*, That he lent money to every man that needed it, to be imployed; but never took any thing that deserved the name of Usury. (True it is, that the Scriptures, the Fathers, the Canon Law and the Decretals do all declaim against Usury, so do the Civilians: *Baldus* calls it a profitable Theft or Piracy. *Bartolus* condemns all Usury, so do the *Roman* Emperours, and most Common-wealths; yet are they contented to tolerate it, being restrained and moderated. The *Hebrew* word *Nishech*, signifies a biting or grinding Usury, such a lending of money, as under the pretence of Charity, devours the poor borrower. The matter that binds the Conscience, is the Debtors gaining nothing by the money lent, and not the taking of much or little Interest. It is a more biting Usury, to take 2 or 3 *per Cent.* of him that gets nothing, than to receive 6 or 8, of him that makes thereof a greater gain: which was the cause, that among the *Romans*, he that took Usury of the poor, was more punished, than he that robbed the rich. No man is by the Law bound, or so much as admonished to lend to those who have no need: And in case another man gain by what is mine, Natural equity requires that I should be a gainer, by so much as he, by my means, is made the richer. Again, If to a man that stands in present want, I lend freely until such a time prefixt, if he fail then of payment, and I thereby incur any damage, it is reason that he should satisfie the damage, and so Interest may be due *ex damno habito*, for the loss I sustain. Also, if a Tradesman lend his money which he

Fœnus and *Usura* how distinguisht.

Goth. l. 3.

can ſpare till ſuch a Mart to be then paid, and the borrower fail in his payment, whereby he is diſabled to drive on his Trade for the next year; then ſhall he be bound to ſatisfie the damage the lender ſuſtaineth *propter lucrum ceſſans*, by reaſon that our hope of gain ceaſeth. Again, four men are Partners in one Shop, two being Aged ſupply Money, the other two being young and active, do take pains to improve it; if they by their labour and care gain 20 or 30 *per Cent.* and pay the other two being paſt their labour, 6 or 8 *per Cent.* for their Maintenance, Can this be called Biting Uſury? If it be objected, That the two lenders take no pains, nor run any hazard; I anſwer, Yes, they did doubtleſs take pains when they were able, and they do now run an hazard by lending their money to them that are painful, but have nothing. It is recorded by *Procopius*, to
Proc. Got. l.3. the honour of *Germanus*, a Kinſman of *Juſtinian's*, That he lent great ſums of money, to be imployed by ſuch as needed it, but never took any thing that deſerved the name of Uſury. Our King *Edgar* forbad Uſury, and *Edward* the Firſt ſent away all the Bankers whom *Gregory* the Tenth had ſent out of *Italy* into *England*, and placed in *Lumbard-ſtreet*: *Henry* the Eighth allowed 10 *per Cent.* for one year, which *Edward* the Sixth repealed. Queen *Elizabeth* tolerated 10 *per Cent.* ſo did King *James*, which *Charles* the Firſt reduced to 6 *per Cent.* which yet continues.

XXII. What power the Civil Laws have determined in the caſe.

But theſe humane Laws that tolerate a moderate gain, for the uſe of money or any other thing (as in *Holland* they permit 8 *per Cent.* to ſome, and 12 *per Cent.* to Merchants for a year, as a reaſonable compenſation for that loſs which the lender doth or may ſuſtain by the forbearance of his money) are no way repugnant to the Laws, either Natural or Divine: But if they exceed this rate, thoſe Laws may afford Impunity, but no juſt Right.

XXIII. How Contracts concerning enſurances are to be valued.

A Contract for the enſuring of Goods from Caſualties either by Sea or Land, is altogether void, if either of the Contractors do know, that the Goods are already ſafely arrived at the Port or place whither they were bound, or that they are periſhed by the way: not only in reſpect of that parity or equality of knowledge, that there ſhould be, between ſuch Contractors; but in reſpect of the ſubject matter of ſuch a Contract, which is a loſs, but uncertain, which in reſpect of both parties may, or may not be. But at what rate theſe Goods are to be ſecured, depends upon common eſtimation.

XXIV. How in Societies: with their ſeveral kinds.

In ſocial Negotiations where traffick is maintained by the joint Stock of a Company, if every member contribute an equal proportion in money, their gain or loſs, ſhall alſo be equal; but if their proportions be unequal, every member ſhall be rated according to his proportion: The like is to be obſerved, where the traffick is to be maintained by joint ſervice, accordingly as the ſervice is by agreement, either equally or unequally to be performed. But yet, in ſuch Negotiations, ſervices may be ſet againſt money, or againſt ſervice and money, ſo that they may anſwer one another, as it is uſually ſaid, *Par pari datum hoſtimentum eſt opera pro pecunia*; *To give like for like, is to even the ſcales.* But this may be done diverſe wayes; for, either ſervice may counterballance the bare uſe of money, in which caſe the principal ſtock whether preſerved or loſt, is entirely his gain or loſs that owns it, or the work or ſervice may counterballance the whole ſtock of money; in which caſe, he that doth the work, is partaker of the whole ſtock. In the former of theſe caſes, the work is ſet againſt, not the ſtock, but the danger of loſing it, or the gains that probably might be expected from it. In the latter caſe, the price of the labour is added unto the ſtock of money, and he that performs it, ſhall have a ſhare in the ſtock equivalent to it. But that either of the parties aſſociated, ſhould ſhare in the profit, and yet be indemnified in caſe of loſs, is preternatural to ſocieties; yet ſuch an Agreement there may be without injury: As when there is a mixt contract, partly by the ſociety, and partly for enſurance, wherein ſuch an equality may be obſerved, as that he that aſſumes to make good the loſs, ſhall receive a greater proportion of the gain, than otherwiſe he ſhould have had. But that any man ſhould bear the loſs, that partakes not of the gain, is inconſiſtent with a ſociety, whoſe principal end is common profit, without which it cannot conſiſt. Now, whereas the Lawyers ſay, That where the proportions are not expreſly named, they are to be underſtood as if they were equal, this holds true only where other things contributed are alſo equal.

XXV. Of Naval Societies.

Where a Fleet is ſent out by the joint Stock of a Society againſt Pyrates, there the common Profit is the common Defence; and ſometimes the Prizes taken from the Enemy: And then the Ships and all that are in the Ships are to be apprized, and drawn into one groſs ſumm, out of which, all charges and damages are to be deducted, and born by the Owners of the Ships and Goods, according to the parts they have in that ſumm; and among thoſe charges, that of the wounded, is to be reckoned. And what we have hitherto ſaid, we judge to be moſt agreeable to the Law of Nature.

XXVI. The Law of Nations takes no notice of Inequalities, if conſented unto.

Neither do the Voluntary Laws of Nations alter any thing of it; except only in this, That where the Contributions are unequal, yet conſented unto, if no lye be in the caſe, nor any thing concealed which ſhould have been declared, in all external Actions they

ſhall

shall be held as equal: So that as by the Civil Law, before that Constitution made by *Dioclesian*, no action would be admitted of in a Court against such an Inequality; so now by those that are consociated by the sole Law of Nations, no exaction or constraint can be admitted for that cause. Of this opinion was *Pomponius*, That naturally in buying and selling, it was lawful for one man to circumvent another: where the word *Licitum* is not the same with *Fas*; but it was so permitted, that there was no Remedy provided against it for him that was willing to justifie him by his Agreement: In which sense that is termed Natural in this, and some other places, which is every where customarily received. In which sense, St. *Paul* saith, that some men are naturally vain, and that it is against nature, that *a man should nourish his hair*, when it was only *against Custome*, and that not of all, but of those Nations wherein he had lived. So the same Apostle speaking not in his own, but in the person of the *Romans*, with whom he converst, saith, *That they were by Nature the Sons of wrath*: so that *Nature* is nothing but Custome, or that which hath been of long continuance. In which sense *Galen* is to be understood, where he saith, That Custome is an acquired or adventitious Nature. So likewise *Thucydides*, *Humana natura Legum victrix*; *Humane Nature cannot be bound up by any Laws.* So the *Grecians* called both Vertues and Vices, πεφυσιωμένα, when by long Custome they are made natural unto us. Now how great the advantage of such a Law if introduced, would be to the General Peace, is evident: for it would prevent infinite contests which would arise, concerning the uncertain prizes of Commodities, which could not possibly be determined or avoided, where there was no common Judge, if every man might break off from his agreement, upon pretence of such an inequality. *Hæc est Emptionis & venditionis substantia*, (say the *Roman* Emperours, calling a perpetual Custome by the name of Substance) *This is the perpetual manner of buying and selling, the buyer beating the price as low as he can, and the seller drawing up the buyer as high as he can, till at length they agree in an equal and just value.* And *Seneca* respecting this very Custome saith, *What matter is it what any thing cost, if the buyer and seller are agreed about the price? He owes nothing to the seller, that gets a good bargain.* And much after the same Copy writes *Andronicus Rhodius*, *That which by the mutual consent of the Contractors is gained, is neither unjust, nor should it be amended: For the Laws do indulge a licence in these things.* And he that writes the Life of *Isidore*, calls the selling of any thing at too dear a rate, or the buying of any thing at too cheap a rate, *An Injustice tolerated by the Law. Harum rerum licentiam Lex dedit*, saith *Andronicus Rhodius*; *The Law gives a Licence in these things.* But yet such a permission it is, as will at length undermine and easily pervert Justice.

And how this is said to be Natural.

1 Cor. 11. 14. 13. 1.

Eph. 2. 3.

φύσις.

CHAP.

CHAP. XIII.

Concerning Oaths.

I. *The great Authority given unto Oaths by the Heathens.*
II. *Great deliberation required in him that would take an Oath.*
III. *Oaths oblige in that sense which he to whom they are made, is thought to understand them.*
IV. *An Oath procured by Fraud, when binding.*
V. *The words of an Oath not to be wrested beyond their ordinary sense.*
VI. *An Oath binds not to things unlawful.*
VII. *Nor to things that impede a greater moral good.*
VIII. *Nor to things impossible.*
IX. *What if the Impossibility be but for some certain time?*
X. *To be sworn by the Name of God, and in what sense.*
XI. *By other things in respect to God.*
XII. *It is an Oath though it be sworn by False Gods.*
XIII. *The effects of an Oath: whence ariseth a twofold obligation, one at the time of the taking of it, and another after. This explained.*
XIV. *When by an Oath a Right is gained to God and Man, and when to God only.*
XV. *The opinion, That an Oath, given to a Pyrate, or a Tyrant, binds not before God, refuted.*
XVI. *Whether an Oath given to the Perfidious, be to be kept: explained by a distinction.*
XVII. *He that is bound to God alone, doth not bind his heir after him.*
XVIII. *It is no perjury not to fulfil that, which he for whom it should be fulfilled, is willing to remit it; nor when the quality ceaseth whereunto it was sworn.*
XIX. *When that is made void, which is done against a mans Oath.*
XX. *How far the Princes power prevails, concerning what either his Subjects have sworn to strangers, or strangers to them, explained by distinction.*
XXI. *Of what manner of Oaths the words of Christ are to be understood, when he forbids us to swear at all.*
XXII. *What Gestures or manners of Speech, have by Custome the force of an Oath, though not the Form of one.*

I. The Credit given to Oaths by Heathens.

IN all Contracts, Vows and Promises, the greatest assurance that any Age or Nation could ever either give or require, of their Faith and Sincerity, is by Oath. This is an indissoluble bond, which whoso violates, is deservedly reputed as an execrable and accursed thing both before God and men, whereof *Sophocles* speaks thus,

The mind that's startled by a sacred Oath,
Will carefully avoid two smarting Rods;
The blame of Friends, and th' Anger of the Gods.

Nullum vinculum ad astringendam fidem, majores nostri jurejurando arctius esse voluerunt; Our fore fathers, saith *Cicero, never knew any thing stronger than an Oath, whereby to bind us to perform our promises:* and to violate this bond, they alwayes accounted a sin of the greatest magnitude; neither did they believe any other sin to be so severely punished, as this of perjury: so *Hesiod* testifies,

Whence is't that mortal men thus plagued are?
Surely, because fallaciously they swear.

This is one of those sins which draws down vengeance on our posterity after us, and wherein the bare Will is punished, without the deed. Of both which, *Herodotus* hath given a clear example in one *Glaucus*, a man highly famed by the *Lacedamonians* for his Vertues, but especially for his Justice; with whom a Citizen of *Miletum* (confiding in a man of so great a repute) left deposited a very great sum of money, with a writing, desiring him to keep both; and to pay the money to such, as should hereafter bring him a duplicate of that writing. *Glaucus* accepts of the money and condition; but when the money was demanded by his Sons, and the duplicate shewed, he denyed that he knew any thing of it; yet he told them, that he would rub up his memory, and in case he could retrieve it there, he would repay it: otherwise, he threatned to proceed against them according to the *Grecian* Laws. So dismissing them for four months, and in that time consulting the Oracle of *Delphos*, whether he might by his Oath make prey of the money, he received this stabbing Answer: *Lib. 6.*

A

A nameless Brat, stumpt both in Hands and Feet,
False Oaths bring forth; which yet in furious rage,
Consumes the House, and blasts the Heritage.

Glaucus hearing this, devoutly implores the Gods to forgive him; but is again answered, That it was the same thing to tempt the Gods in this case, by the Will, as by the Deed. And though *Glaucus* did restore the money, yet the Curse denounced by the Oracle did fall upon him: For in the third Age, *Glaucus* had neither Child, nor House, nor any to inherit his Name, which also had been forgotten long since, but that his example might (like *Lots* Wifes pillar) deter others from the like attempt. *Juvenal* also reciting this story, concludes thus,

Has patitur pœnas peccandi sola voluntas.

The bare intent to Sin, such Plagues attend.

So true is that of the Prophet *Zachary, I will bring the Curse into the house of him that sweareth falsely by my Name (saith the Lord), And it shall remain in the midst of his house, and shall consume it, with the Timber thereof, and the Stones thereof,* Zach. 5. 4. *Cicero* was in the right, when he termed *an Oath, a Religious Asseveration or a Divine Attestation of the truth of what we say: For what we seriously affirm or promise, and call God to witness of, that we are bound to make good and to perform, under the greatest penalty that can be.* But whereas he adds, *Not for fear of the Anger of the Gods, which is none at all, but for Truth and Justice sake.* If by Anger he means a passion, or perturbation of the mind, we deny it not: But if he understand by Anger a will to punish or revenge, it can by no means be admitted, as *Lactantius* rightly observes. Now let us see from whence this Sacred Power of an Oath ariseth, and how far forth it extends.

See *Chrysost.* upon this place.

Lib. de ira Dei.

II. It requires a deliberate mind.

And in the first place, What we have already said of Contracts and Promises, is true also in the case of Oaths, namely, That he that swears, should be of sound mind, and should use great deliberation before he takes it. (The *Romans* would not permit any man to swear by *Hercules* till he had gone out of the Court for a while, and seriously considered with himself what he was to do.) Wherefore if a man not intending to swear, shall rashly utter words importing an Oath (as it is recorded of *Cydippe*) that may be true, which *Ovid* affirms of him,

Quæ jurat mens est: nil conjuravimus illâ.

It is the Mind that swears: we swear not there.

Sed si nil dedimus præter sine pectore vocem,
Verba suis frustra viribus orba tenes.
Non ego juravi, legi jurantia verba, &c.

And what before him *Euripides* said in his *Hippolitus*:

Jurata lingua est, Mente juravi nihil.

It was our tongue that sware, our minds were free.

But he that willingly swears, yet is not willing to be bound by that Oath, is notwithstanding strongly obliged to what he hath sworn; Obligation being inseparable from an Oath, and its necessary effect.

III. The words of an Oath are to be understood in that sense that he is believed to understand to whom we swear.

There are some who hold, that though a man do seriously pronounce the words of an Oath, yet if it be not with a purpose to swear, he shall not be bound by that Oath: But that in speaking the words of that Oath he sins, by swearing rashly. But it accords more with Divine truth, that he is bound to make good his words, whereof he hath called God for a witness: For that Act which of it self was Obligatory, did proceed from a serious and deliberate mind: Wherefore though what *Cicero* saith, be for the most part true, *Quod ex animi tui sententia juraveris, id non facere perjurium est; That not to perform, what we have deliberately sworn, is Perjury*: Yet is it to be understood, with this limitation, unless he that swears, knows, or at least believes, that he with whom he converseth, doth otherwise understand the words of the Oath. For he that calls God to witness the truth of what he saith, is obliged to perform his word in that sense, wherein he thinks himself to be understood. That Soldier, who being a Prisoner to the *Carthaginians* had gotten his Parole upon the credit of his Oath, when being departed a little from the Camp, he upon some pretence made his return unto it; and supposing that he was thereby discharged from his Oath, fled immediately to *Rome*, was by the Senate immediately sent back.

For

The reverend esteem of Oaths among the *Romans.* *For they regarded not what he intended that sware, but what the* Carthaginians *expected from him to whom he had sworn.* For after this Rule doth God himself judge.

> *Qui non ut juras, sed ut jurasse putavit*
> *Cui juras, audit: sic es utrique reus.*

This is that which the same *Cicero* asserts, *What is sworn must be so done as he that imposed the Oath conceived must be done.* And it was the observation of *Tacitus, That they who swear timorously, craftily changing the words of their Oaths, had their Consciences polluted with wickedness.* Wherefore St. *Augustine brands them with Perjury, who though they perform what is exprest by the bare words of the Oath, do yet delude the expectation of those to whom that Oath was given. But* (as *Isidore* well observes) *though the words of the Oath be never so craftily penned, yet God, who is the Judge and Witness of the Conscience, doth judge of it, as he to whom we swear understands it.* Wherefore *Metellus* did wisely, in refusing to swear to the *Apuleian* Law, though he was told that that Law was unduly enacted, and that the Oath was not binding, unless the Law whereunto it referred, was rightly gained. For although in other Promises it be no hard matter to suppose some tacite condition, which if admitted, may absolve the Promiser; yet in Oaths, such tacite conditions are by no means to be admitted, but if we do swear, we must *liquido jurare, swear clearly and apertly*: For *such an Oath for confirmation, is the end of all Controversies*; as St. *Paul* testifies to the *Hebrews*, and proves by the example of God himself: *Who to shew to the Heirs of the Promise the immutability of his Counsels, confirmed it by his Oath, that by two immutable things, namely, his Promise and his Oath, wherein it is not possible that God should de-*
ψεύδεσθαι. *ceive us* (For so the word ψεῦδος is best expounded in this place, as Plain Speaking is else-
Heb. 4. 17. where called Truth) *we might have a sure Consolation.* For the clearer understanding of
Dan. 7. 16. 8. 26. 10. 1. which words, we must know, That the Pen-men of the Sacred stories do often speak of God, ἀνθρωποπαθῶς, after the manner of men: Not properly, as he is in himself, but as he appears unto us to to be. For God doth not really change his Decrees and Counsels: And yet he is sometimes said to change his sentence and to repent, as often as he doth otherwise than his words seemed to import, by reason of some condition tacitely un-
Jo. 4. 2. derstood, though not exprest, which ceaseth to be. So we read in *Jonah, Yet forty days and* Nineveh *shall be destroyed.* This was the Sentence that was denounced against their Impenitency; but that ceasing, the Sentence was reverst, yet Gods Counsel did even then remain unchargable. That such a condition is tacitely to be understood, will evidently appear by that of the Prophet *Jer.* 18. 8. And, that this was true, not in the case of *Jonah* and the *Ninevites* only, *Jon.* 3. 5. is plain, by the like proceedings in the case of *Abimelech, Gen.* 20. 3. Of the *Israelites, Exod.* 32. 14. Of *Ahab,* 1 *Kings* 21. 29. In which sense, God may, though improperly, be said to deceive us, foras-
ψεύδεσθαι. much as the word ψεῦδος, sometimes imports an event deluding our hopes or expecta-
Hos. 1. 2. tion, as it doth *Heb.* 6. 17; 18. *Levit.* 6. 2. Now this may easily be admitted of in
Abac. 3. 17. Comminations, because they confer not a Right to any: And sometimes in Promises,
Jos. 24. 27. namely, when some condition is understood, though not exprest. And therefore the
Esa. 58. 11. Apostle in the place recited, doth instance in two things, which do necessarily infer an
Job 41. 6. immutability in God: First, *His Promise,* which confers a just Right. Secondly, *His*
Hos. 9. 2. *Oath,* which will not admit of any conditions tacite, or any ways latent. As may also be seen *Ps.* 89. 30, 31, and so to the 36 verse. But it is another case, where the very nature of the business doth clearly discover some conditions to be performed. Whereunto some do refer that of *Numb.* 14. 30. where God tells the *Israelites, That they shall not come into the Land, concerning which he sware, to make them dwell therein, save* Caleb *the Son of* Jephunne, *and* Joshua *the Son of* Nun. Though this Promise of the Land of *Canaan* be much better understood, as sworn to the People and Nation of the *Jews,* than to any of their persons, as is evident by verse 23. *Surely they shall not see the Land, which I sware unto their Fathers, neither shall any of them that provoke me, see it.* Whence we may observe, That the Oath that was made to their Fathers was not to be fulfilled to them, but to their Children: For such a Promise might at any time be fulfilled, which was not affixt to any particular persons, like as it was afterward to *Caleb* and *Joshua.*

IV. An Oath by fraud procured, when binding. From whence we may also learn what to think of an Oath by fraud gained; for certainly, in case he that swears, supposeth somewhat to be done that really is not, or somewhat to be true that is false: And unless he did so believe, he would not have so sworn, that Oath binds him not. But if it be doubtful, whether he would not have bound himself by Oath, though he had not been so deceived, then shall he stand to his agreement,
Josh. 9. *For there is nothing that naturally so well becomes an Oath, as plain meaning.* And hereunto
Joshua's Oath. we may refer the Oath of *Joshua* to the *Gibeonites,* which though it were gained by fraud, yet doth it not thence necessarily follow, That had *Joshua* known that they dwelt amongst

amongst the *Canaanites* he would not have spared them. And whereas the *Israelites* say, *Perhaps ye live amongst us, and how then shall we make a League with you?* It may be understood of the manner of the League which the *Gibeonites* desired, Whether of Alliance only, as amongst equals; or of Dedition, as with such who to preserve their lives, did willingly surrender all things else to the pleasure of the Conquerour: Or it was so spoken, to shew, That as it was not lawful for them to enter into any *League* with some people, (meaning that of Alliance;) so also it was not prohibited them to save the lives of such as should freely surrender themselves to mercy. For that Divine Law that commanded them to destroy the Nations, *Deut.* 7. 4. *Exod.* 23. 33. being compared with another charge given by God, concerning them, *Deut.* 20. 10. will admit of this limitation, That if they yielded upon the first summons, they might be received to mercy. As is clear by the Histories of *Rahab*, who for securing the Spies was saved: Of the Inhabitants of *Gezer*, who were suffered to live among the *Ephramites*, and to serve them: Of the *Gergezites*, of whom St. *Matthew* records, that there were some living even until his time. Neither shall we find these ennumerated among those that were to have been extirpated, as you may read *Deut.* 20. 17. *Jos.* 9. 1. And lastly, It is clear, by that Act of *Solomon*, 1 *King.* 20. 20, 21. whereby he is said to have received the remainder of the *Canaanites*, whom the Children of *Israel* could not destroy, as his Tributaries and Bond-Servants unto that day. Yea, and if we examine the cause of that severe charge given unto *Moses* for their extirpation, as it is exprest *Exod.* 23. 33. *Deut.* 7. 4. we shall find that in case (as the *Hebrew* Doctors observed) they would submit to the Commandments given to *Noah*, and his Sons, and pay Tribute, the cause of their extirpation being taken away, they might live. Now, why *Joshua* might not as well spare the *Gibeonites* upon their Dedition, as he did *Rahab*, and the *Canaanites* of *Gezer*, upon theirs, no solid Reason can be assigned. And yet that the *Gergezites* being the Off-spring of the Inhabitants of *Gezer*, were spared and lived as Tributaries to the *Israelites* till Christs time, is most evident by the Sacred story. The immediate cause of the destruction of all the rest of the *Canaanites*, was not any inexorable Command given by God to *Moses*; for that left them a possibility to live, because a power to submit: But the *hardness of their hearts, which*, proceeded from God as a punishment for all their great provocations, *Jos.* 11. 19, 20. *that so, he might destroy them utterly, without any mercy, as the Lord commanded* Moses. Wherefore, considering that in case the *Gibeonites* had dealt plainly with *Moses*, which they durst not do for fear of him, and had voluntarily given themselves up as Bond-servants; It is probable, that he would have spared their lives, under the same condition as he did the Inhabitants of *Gezer*. Therefore *Valuit juramentum, The Oath was to remain inviolable:* Yea, and the breach of this Oath (three hundred years after, when *Saul*, either forgetting the Oath of his Forefathers, or out of a well-meant zeal, slew some of these *Gibeonites*) cost the lives of many thousand *Israelites*, in the three years Famine which God brought upon *Israel*. Of this opinion was St. *Ambrose*, who handling this Question, saith, Joshua *did not think it safe to break the Peace with the* Gibeonites, *because he had confirmed it by Oath:* Ne, dum aliorum perfidiam arguit, suam fidem solveret; *Lest whilest he punished others for their perfidiousness, he should be found guilty of Perjury.* Neither did this fraud of theirs go altogether unpunished: For whereas had they dealt plainly, they had been admitted upon paying of Tribute only; now their Corporal Slavery is at once the price of their lives, and the just Punishment of their Craft and Subtilty. So were the *Brutiani* served by the *Romans*, as *Gellius* relates.

Jos. 16. 10.

Mat. 8. 28.

2 Sam. 21. 6

De Off. l. 3. *c.* 10.

Lib. 10. *c.* 3.

V. The words of an Oath not to be too far extended.

Neither should the meaning of an Oath be wrested to any other sense, than the words do usually bear. Wherefore, when the Children of *Israel*, having sworn not to give their Daughters in Marriage to the *Benjamites*, did notwithstanding suffer the *Benjamites* to take the Daughters of *Shiloh* by force, and to enjoy them, they were not guilty of Perjury. For it is one thing to give, and another, not to require what is already lost. Whereof St. *Ambrose* speaks thus, *This Indulgence of theirs was not without a Punishment suitable to their Intemperance, whilest they were permitted only to enjoy those whom they had ravished, without the solemnity of Marriage.* Nec hortabantur Israelitæ, nec prohibebant, saith *Joseph*; *The* Israelites *did neither encourage the* Benjamites, *nor forbid them. Now the Law,* saith *Seneca, may punish him, that succoureth an exile, but not him that only suffers him to be relieved.* Not much unlike was that request which the *Achaians* made to the *Romans*, (who were highly displeased at some things by them done, and confirmed by Oath, namely, That the *Romans* would be pleased to alter what they would, but not to bind them by any Religious Vow, to null those things which they had already established by Oath.

VI. Oaths bind not to things unlawful.

Secondly, That an Oath be binding, it is necessary that it refer to things lawful. For, if the thing promised upon Oath be forbidden either by the Law of Nature, or by the Divine Law, or interdicted by humane Laws, (whereof more anon) it hath no

power at all to oblige us. That which is unlawful to be ſworn, is unlawful to be done being ſworn, and that which is unlawful for us to do, is unlawful to be ſworn. All Oaths have a tacite exception of the higher powers, and of former Oaths: Now God is greater than man, and therefore having firſt bound our ſelves unto him, no Oath made againſt him or againſt our duty to him, ought by us to be performed, but repented of. *No Weapon formed againſt him ſhall proſper*, ſaith the Prophet, *Eſ.* 54. It is good counſel that *Philo* gives in this caſe, *Let him that goes about to do an unjuſt act by reaſon of his Oath, know, That he doth not thereby perform his Oath but break it. For an Oath is a ſacred thing, which deſerves our greateſt care and devotion, to preſerve; whereby we ſtand obliged to do ſuch things only, as are juſt and honeſt. For he doth but accumulate one ſin upon another, who to a wicked Oath, adds a diſhoneſt action. Wherefore let him that hath enſnared his own Soul by a raſh Vow, yet refrain from doing wickedly, That God who is rich in mercy may forgive him. For wilfully to contract a double guilt, when we may be diſcharged from a ſingle one, is an incurable madneſs.* Raſh Vows are ill made and ſometimes worſe kept. Our Tongues muſt
1 Sam. 25. not bind our hands to do wickedly. *David* was leſs ſinful in breaking his Oath, and ſparing the life of *Nabal*, whom he had ſworn to kill, than *Herod* was in killing the Baptiſt, or *Agamemnon* in ſacrificing *Iphigenia*, for their Oaths ſake. Surely Oaths were never invented to be the Bonds of Iniquity.

Præſtare fateor poſſe me tacitam fidem,
Si ſcelere careat; interim ſcelus eſt fides.

My Faith perform I can, I do confeſs,
If void of Sin; elſe Faith's but Wickedneſs.

Some Promiſes cannot be performed, ſaith *Ambroſe*, *nor ſome Oaths kept, without the violation of our duties to God or Man.* And if we have pawn'd our Faith to commit a Sin (the beſt way to preſerve our Faith is to break our Promiſe.) For that is not properly called Faith, that engages us to do wickedly. Wherefore take the Advice of *Iſidore*,
Gratian. In malis Promiſſis reſcinde Fidem, in turpi voto muta decretum, impia eſt Promiſſio quæ ſcelere impletur; *Make no ſcruple of breaking that Oath, that would bind thee to a diſhoneſt or unjuſt action, for that Promiſe muſt needs be wicked that cannot be fulfilled, but by making thee wicked.*

VII. Nor that impede a greater moral good.

Yea, though that which is promiſed upon Oath be not unlawful, yet if it cannot be performed without the omiſſion of ſomething that is a greater moral good, it loſeth its binding faculty: For we owe unto God our growth in goodneſs, and we cannot abridge our ſelves of this liberty without ſinning againſt him. *Some there are*, ſaith *Philo*, *of ſo harſh and unſociable a nature, either as bearing hatred to all mankind, or ſo enſlaved to their own inordinate paſſions, that they even ſtrengthen themſelves in their churliſh humours by raſh and inconſiderate Vows; as namely, That they will never admit ſuch a man either to bed or board; or that they will never do ſuch a man good, nor ever receive any thing from him till death.* (St. *Auguſtine* being conſulted with about one *Hubaldus*, who (to ſave his own life being threatened) had bound himſelf by Oath to marry his own Concubine, and to thruſt his own Mother and Brethren out of doors, and never to relieve them, gives this reſolution of the Caſe, *That as to his marriage with his Concubine, whom he had long enjoyed, his Oath was binding, for that was no ſin: But as to his not relieving his Mother and Brethren, it could not bind him:* For *Qui non alit necat*; *To deny them neceſſaries, was no better than to kill them:*
The Error of the *Jews* concerning Oaths. See *Godw. Jewiſh* Ant. *pag.* 274. *And no Oath can oblige to a ſin ſo unnatural.*) Such a kind of Oath was called among the *Jews* an Oath concerning beneficence or doing good: The form whereof we have ſet down, *Mat.* 15. 5. δῶρον ὃ ἐὰν ἐξ ἐμοῦ ὠφεληθῇς· That is, By the gift upon the Altar thou ſhalt never receive any good from me. Which Oath was always to be ſo underſtood as if ſome direful Execration were at the tail of it. As, *So do God to me, and more alſo*, if thou ever receive any good from me, which Oath was among the *Jews* thought to be the moſt binding of any, yea, though it were againſt our own Parents. Such corrupt Interpreters of the Law of God, were the *Jewiſh* Doctors in thoſe ſuperſtitious times: Which Chriſt there confutes, making no diſtinction between honouring our parents and relieving them, as appears by comparing that of *Matthew* with the like in *Mark*, and with 1 *Tim.* 5. 3, 17. and *Numb.* 23. 11. Yea, though it be not made againſt our Parents, but againſt others, yet doth it not bind, becauſe it is a duty we owe unto God to do good unto all men, which is altogether inconſiſtent with ſuch an Oath.

VIII. Nor to impoſſibilities.

To things manifeſtly impoſſible, no Oath can oblige us.

IX. If the impoſſibility be only for the preſent, how the Oath obligeth.

But as to things that are for a certain time impoſſible, or ſuppoſed at preſent to be ſo, the obligatory power of that Oath hangs in ſuſpenſe, inſomuch that he that ſwears ſuppoſitively, ought to endeavour, as far as in him lies, to make that which he hath ſworn poſſible.

The

X. *The form of Oaths.*

The forms of Oaths may be different, but the ſubſtance of all are alike: For all invoke God as a Witneſs, or as an Avenger, both which in him are one and the ſame. For in calling him to Witneſs, who hath a Power and a Right to puniſh, we do but beſpeak him to a Revenge due to our Perfidiouſneſs. And he that is omniſcient is therefore an Avenger, becauſe a Witneſs. *What is to ſwear* (ſaith *Ambroſe* to the Emperour *Valentinian*) *but to acknowledge that Divine Power which thou invokeſt, to witneſs and defend thy truth? Every Oath,* ſaith *Plutarch, ends in ſome Curſe in caſe we Swear falſely.* *Queſt. Rom.* And therefore the ancient forms of making and ſwearing Leagues was uſually by killing of Sacrifices, as appears *Gen.* 15. 9, *&c.* and by that of the *Romans* in *Livy*, Tu Jupiter, ita illum ferito, ut ego hunc porcum; *And do thou, O* Jupiter, *deſtroy him that breaketh this league, as I do this Hogg.* And in another place, the Prieſt killing a Lamb, *Prays the Gods to kill him that violates that Oath, as he doth that Lamb.* So in *Polybius* and *Feſtus* we read, *If I knowingly deceive, let God caſt me away from him, as I do this Stone.*

XI. *Oaths not by God only, but by others alſo in relation to God, oblige.*

It was the cuſtom of the Ancients, not only to ſwear by God, but by other both things and perſons, thereby either wiſhing thoſe creatures might be noxious unto them in caſe they ſware falſely, as when they ſware by the Sun, the Moon, the Heavens, the Earth, *&c.* or wiſhing they might be puniſhed in them; as when they ſware by their Head, by their Lives, by their Children, by their Prince, *&c.* Neither did the prophane and barbarous people only ſwear thus, but the *Jews* themſelves. *Philo* the *Jew* among his Special Laws, tells us, *That it is not fit for us upon every ſlight occaſion, to have recourſe to the Creator and Preſerver of all things.* And *Homer*'s Interpreters do teſtifie the ſame of the ancient *Grecians*, that they were not eaſily induced to ſwear by God, but by other things that were preſent, as by the Scepter, *&c.* Thus *Apollonius* teſtifies of *Socrates*, *That he ſware by ſuch things, Non ut per Deos, ſed ne per Deos; Not as by Gods, but leſt he ſhould ſwear by the Gods*) And this cuſtom (as *Porphyry* records) was introduced by that Prince, who was ſo famous for his Juſtice, King *Rhadamanth.* So did *Joſeph* according to the cuſtom of that Nation among whom he lived, ſwear by the Life of *Pharaoh*, *Eliſha* by the Life of *Elias*, and the *Shunamite* by the Life of *Eliſha.* Neither doth our Saviour (as ſome think) declare ſuch Oaths to be leſs lawful, or leſs binding, than thoſe whereby God himſelf was invoked: But obſerving that the *Jews* did not ſo regard ſuch Oaths (in an opinion, haply, not unlike to his who ſaid, *Sceptrum non putat eſſe Deos, That he did not believe the Scepter to be the Gods.* He ſhews, that even theſe are true Oaths, and as binding as thoſe that are made in the name of the true God. It was very well ſaid of *Ulpian, He that ſwears by his own ſafety, ſeems to ſwear by God, becauſe he hath reſpect to ſome Divine power that preſerves him.* So our Bleſſed Saviour tells us, *That he that ſwears by the Temple, ſwears by him that preſides therein; and he that ſwears by Heaven, ſwears by God who dwelleth there.* But the *Jewiſh* Rabbins in Chriſts time, were of opinion, That an Oath made by the Creatures did not bind, unleſs when ſome puniſhment was added thereunto, as if the thing by which they ſware were conſecrated unto God; ſo that an Oath by the Temple was nothing, but an Oath by the Gold of the Temple was binding: An Oath by the Altar was invalid, but an Oath by the Gift on the Altar was inviolable: And this Oath they called κοϱβᾶν, or an Oath by the Gift, whereof mention is made, not only in the Story of *Matthew*, but amongſt the *Tyrian* Laws, as *Joſephus* writes in his Diſputes againſt *Appian.* But this opinion of the *Phariſees* being erroneous, our Saviour refutes in *Mat.* 5. And *Tertullian* informs us, *That the ancient Chriſtians were wont to ſwear by the Life of their Prince, which in their eſteem was more reverenced than all their Genii.* And in *Vegetius* we find the form of the Oath given unto the Soldiers that were Chriſtians, wherein they ſware, *Not only by God, but by the Life of their Emperours*, which according to the Ordinance of God, is a thing to be deſired and prayed for by all mankind.

Oaths by the Creatures oblige. — 2 King 4. 30. Cant. 2. 7. Mat. 5. — See Wiſd. 14. 20. — *The Error of the Jews concerning Oaths.* — κοϱβᾶν.

XII. *And by falſe Gods.* See Wiſd. 14. 30, 31.

Yea if a man ſwear by ſuch as are falſe Gods, yet is he thereby bound, becauſe though under a falſe Notion, yet in the general he invokes the Deity: And therefore the True God in caſe he forſwear, doth ſo interpret it as if done in contempt of himſelf. And although we ſee that holy men have ſeldom admitted of Oaths in that form, and much leſs have taken ſuch Oaths themſelves, yet if we cannot prevail with thoſe with whom we have to do, to ſwear by the True God, we may enter into League with them, taking for confirmation their Oaths in ſuch a form as is uſual among them. An Example whereof we have in the League made between *Jacob* and *Laban*, *Gen.* 31. 53. Whereupon St. *Auguſtin* thus infers: *Et qui per lapidem jurat, ſi falſum jurat, perjurus eſt; He that invokes a Pillar or a Stone as witneſs, if to what he knows to be falſe, is guilty of Perjury.* For though *Non audit te lapis loquentem, puniet te Deus fallentem; The Stone hears thee not when thou ſpeakeſt, yet God will certainly judge thee when thou deceiveſt.* (Moreover, *He that ſwears by a falſe God, yet thinks the God he ſwears by to be the True God, may be believed upon that Oath; and if that Oath refer to things juſt and honeſt, he that makes a League with him upon that Oath, Non peccato illius ſe ſociat* (ſaith St. *Auguſtin*) *doth not partake with him of his ſin though he swear by Devils*; *but of that good agreement which by that Oath is confirmed.* And therefore St. *Augustin* in the same place concludes, that *Minus malum est, per falsos Deos veraciter jurare, quàm per Deum verum fallaciter*; *It is a lesser sin to swear truly by false Gods, than to swear falsely by the True God.* For the more holy the Person is by whom we swear, the more execrable is the sin, and the greater is the punishment if we forswear.

Ad Publicol.

XIII. The principal effect of an Oath.

The principal effect of an Oath is to determin all strifes: So the Author to the *Hebrews*, *An Oath for Confirmation is the end of all Controversies.* Not much unlike is that of *Philoneus*, *An Oath is the Testimony of God in cases that are doubtful.* And to the same purpose is that of *Dionysius Halicarnassensis*, *The greatest assurance of Faith, that either* Græcians *or* Barbarians *can give, and which no Age can cancel, is when to their sworn Contracts and Promises, both parties bring in the Gods for their Sureties.* *An Oath*, saith *Procopius*, *is the greatest and strongest pledge that can be given by men, both of their fidelity and veracity.* He therefore that swears, ought to be careful of two things: First, That his Heart consents to what his Tongue utters, *Chrysippus* terms ἀληθορκεῖν. Secondly, That his deeds be suitable to his Promises, which he calls εὐορκεῖν: He that offends in the former, is said ψευδορκεῖν: which is forbidden *Exod.* 20. And he that offends in the latter, is said ἐπιορκεῖν, forbidden likewise, *Lev.* 19. As the same *Chrysippus* distinguisheth them, acutely enough, though sometimes they are confounded.

Pers. l. 2.

XIV. When by an Oath a right is given to God and Man, and when to God alone.

And truly if the matter be such, and the words so conceived, that they be referred not only to God, but unto Man, without doubt a Right will be gained to a man through that very Oath, even as by any promise or agreement, which ought to be understood in the most plain and simple way of Construction. But if the words of the Oath do not refer to man by conferring a Right to him, or if it do, yet such a Right only as may be questioned; then such is the force of an Oath, that though he to whom it is sworn, cannot acquire that Right (because the words will not clearly carry it) yet is he that swears obliged before God to make good his Oath. As for example, He that by some unjust terror or affright, shall extort a promise of something; which promise binds with an Oath, though the Promiser cannot thereby claim his Right to the thing promised; or if he do, is bound to restore it, because he gave the occasion of the damage unjustly: Yet as St. *Augustin* well observes, *Etiam vi extortum jusjurandum, ob Dei reverentiam servandum est*: *Even that Oath so extorted, ought for the reverence that we owe to the Name of God, to be carefully observed.* We read that the Kings of *Israel* were sharply reproved by the Prophets and punished by God himself, for not keeping their faith sworn to the King of *Babylon*, *Ezek.* 17. 12, 13, 14. and so by *Jeremy*, *Jer.* 29. 7. And *Cicero* highly commends *Pomponius* the Tribune for observing his Oath, though wrested from him by terror: *Tantum temporibus illis jusjurandum valebat*, saith he; *So great was the reverence which in those times was given unto Oaths.* So that not only *Regulus* did well in rendring himself a Prisoner to the *Carthaginians*, but those ten men also (recorded by *Cicero*) in returning to *Hannibal*, by reason of their Oaths given in both cases.

XV. An Oath given to a Pyrate or a Tyrant valid.

Neither is this practised among publick enemies only, but generally amongst all: For it is not the quality of the persons to whom we swear, but the fear and reverence of God whom we invoke, as a Witness and an Avenger of what we swear, that creates this Obligation. It was an error in *Cicero* to hold it no perjury, *Si prædonibus pactum pro capite pretium non attuleris, nulla fraus est, ne si juratus id non feceris. de Offic. lib.* 3. Though a man did not pay the mony, which he promised by Oath to Robbers for saving his life: Because a Pyrate is not a particular enemy to this or that Nation, but a common enemy to all mankind, *Cum quo nec fides esse debet, nec jusjurandum commune*; *With whom*, saith he, *we ought not to keep either faith or common Oath.* The very same he elsewhere saith of Tyrants, namely, that the *Romans* were not obliged by any Oaths or Promises they made to or with them: For though the difference be vast between an Enemy and a Pyrate, yet will not that difference much alter the case, where we have to do with God and not with men. And though the condition of the person be such, as that he cannot claim a Right in what is so promised, yet to perform it being sworn, is a duty that we owe to God: And therefore is an Oath termed a *Vow*, because being made to God, we stand obliged before him to keep it. Neither can we grant what *Cicero* asserts, That there is no Society of Right with a Pyrate or Robber: For by the Law of Nations, whatsoever is deposited with us by a Pyrate, ought to be restored to him, if the right owner of it doth not appear, as *Triphonius* rightly states this Question. Wherefore neither can we approve of their opinion, who think it sufficient to lay down the ransom which he hath sworn to pay: So that it is lawful for him to take it away again, because when we have to do with God, we ought to deal simply and sincerely, so that it may have some effect. And better it is to bear a temporal loss, than to provoke God by the breach of our Vow: For as *Plutarch* observes, *Qui juramento hostem circumvenit, is ostendit hostem a se metui, Deum contemni*; *He that circumvents an Enemy by a false Oath, plainly discovers that he fears his enemy, but despiseth God.* (Yet that what is so paid, may by a due course of Law be recovered, notwithstanding

It is compared to a Vow.

Vita Lysand.

ſtanding our Oath, was the opinion of *Aquinas*.) And therefore the Soldier who having leave to depart upon his Oath given to return, though he came privately back, and then departed, did not thereby in the judgment of the *Roman* Senate, ſatisfie his Oath. (Yet if a man do haply break his Faith with a Pyrate or a Robber, whether ſworn or unſworn, he ſhall thereby incur no penalty amongſt other Nations : For generally all Nations in deteſtation of theſe men, whom they account as common enemies to Humane Society, are pleaſed to connive at whatſoever is (though unjuſtly) done againſt them : For they that break the Communion and League that there is between all mankind, are common enemies, and can have no right by the Law of Nations.) *2da 2dæ q. 89. Art. 7.*

But it is farther queſtioned, whether we ought to keep Faith with them who keep not theirs with us? To which I anſwer, that of *Accius* may be in this ſence approved of, namely, XVI. Whether Faith be to be kept with the Faithleſs.

T.———— *Thy Faith thou broken haſt*,
A. *Which I nere gave, nor to the Faithleſs give.*

If our promiſe made and confirmed by Oath, were manifeſtly grounded on ſome other promiſe, which was as a condition whereunto ours related, then that condition being not performed, makes void our promiſe though confirmed by Oath. But if the two promiſes were of ſeveral kinds, and did not mutually reſpect each other, then each promiſe is to be kept by him that ſware it, without any reſpect had to what the other doth. And hence it is, that *Silius* ſo highly extolls the Fact of *Regulus*, in that he kept his Faith with the *Carthaginians*, who had been ſo often known to break theirs with the *Romans*. A manifeſt inequality in Contracts, doth naturally afford cauſe ſufficient either to reform or reſcind them, as I have already proved. And although the Law of Nations hath changed ſomewhat herein, yet by the Civil Law, which is in force where both parties are of the ſame people, recourſe is often had to that which by the Law of Nature is allowed, as we have alſo elſewhere ſhewed. But yet if the Contract be bound up by an Oath, notwithſtanding this inequality, our Faith given unto God muſt be obſerved. The Pſalmiſt gives this Character of a good man, *Pſal.* 15. *That if he ſwear to his Neighbour, he diſappointeth him not, though it be to his own diſadvantage.*

And here alſo it is to be noted, that where no Right is transferred to the perſon with whom we have to do by reaſon of ſome ſuch defect as is aforeſaid, but only in reſpect of the Oath that we have made to God, there the hire of him that made the Oath is not bound : For although, *Tranſeunt bona cum onere*, The Goods of the deceaſed do deſcend upon the heir with the debts which he owed ; I mean thoſe Goods which are uſed in commerce with men ; yet do not the debts of mere Piety, Gratitude, or Fidelity, oblige his Children : For theſe do not appertain unto that Right, which among men is ſtrictly ſo called, as I have elſewhere ſhewed. XVII. How far the Heir of that Promiſe ſtands obliged.

Moreover where the Promiſe confers no Right to the Perſon, yet if being ſworn it ſeems to reſpect anothers profit, if that man will not accept thereof, or if he be willing to releaſe the Promiſer, the Oath ſhall not bind him : So alſo if the quality of the Perſon ceaſe in reference whereunto a man ſware, then the Oath made to that Perſon in relation to that Quality, is of no force. As if a Magiſtrate ſhall recede from his dignity, and become a private man, the Obligation made by Oath to him ceaſeth : As *Curio* rightly informs *Domitius* his Soldiers, who ſcrupled at the Oath they had formerly taken. *How is it poſſible that you* (ſaith he) *ſhould be bound by Oath unto him, who having thrown away the Enſigns of Soveraignty, and renounced his Kingdom, is now become a private man and a Priſoner to a ſtrange Prince :* And by and by he adds, That the Oath had loſt its obliging power by the loſs of the Princes freedom. XVIII. Two caſes wherein the Obligation ceaſeth.

Another Queſtion is ſometimes made, Whether an Act done contrary to an Oath, be unlawful only or void? Where we muſt diſtinguiſh : For if our Faith only be engaged, the Act that is done contrary to our Oath ſhall ſtand good as in Teſtaments and Bargains and Sales. But in caſe the Oath be ſo framed, that it comprehends an utter abdication of any power to do that Act, then ſhall the Oath prevail, and the ſubſequent Act be made void. Now theſe things do naturally attend any Oath, whereby we may eaſily judge of the Oaths of Kings, and of Foreigners one to the other, when the Act is not ſubject to the Laws or Cuſtoms of the place. XIX. When that which is done againſt an Oath is void.

Now let us ſee what power our Superiors, namely, Kings, Princes, Maſters, and Husbands, have, in things that concern them in their reſpective Rights, over their ſeveral Relations : And firſt we muſt know, That the Acts of our Superiors cannot make an Oath that is truly obligatory, void ; ſo that it ought not to be fulfilled : For this would be repugnant both to Natural and Divine Right ; but becauſe all our Actions are not fully in our own power, but ſo as they have ſome dependance on our Superiors, therefore we grant that our Superiors have a twofold power over us, concerning that which is ſworn ; the XX. How far the Prince's power prevails over his Subjects Oaths.

the one directed upon the perſon ſwearing, the other upon the perſon to whom he ſwears. The act of our Superiours may reſtrain the perſon ſwearing either before he ſwears, making ſuch an Oath void, ſo far as the Right of an Inferior is ſubject to the power of his Superior; or after he hath ſworn, by forbidding the performance of it. For an Inferior, as ſuch, could not bind himſelf without the approbation of his Superiour: beyond which he had no power. And after this manner, by the Jewiſh Law the Husband had power to null the Vow of his Wife, ſo had the Father the Vow of his Children, ſo long as they were under the power of his government. *Seneca* ſtarts this queſtion, What if there ſhould be a Law enacted, that no man ſhould do that which I have promiſed my friend to do for him? Which he thus reſolves, *Eadem lex me defendit quæ vetat*; *The ſame Law defends me, that forbids me.* There are alſo ſome mixt acts between both, as when the Superior doth appoint, that his Inferior ſhall bind himſelf by Oath in this or that caſe, namely through fear, or want of judgment, but with this limitation, that the Oath ſhall bind if his Superiour ſhall approve thereof; And upon this foundation are built all diſpenſations and abſolutions from Oaths, which Princes in former times did exerciſe by themſelves, as *Suetonius* teſtifies in the Reign of *Tiberius*, and *Vaſquius* records to have been long uſed in *Spain*; which power they now remit, that it may be with more piety executed, unto the Eccleſiaſtical juriſdiction. So the act of a Superiour may be directed againſt the perſon to whom it is ſworn, either by taking away that Right which by that Oath he hath gained; or if as yet he hath no Right, by forbidding him from claiming any Right by vertue of that Oath. And this he may do two ways, either by way of puniſhment, or for a more publick good by vertue of his Soveraign power. And from hence we may learn what power Princes have over their Subjects Oaths, where he that ſwears, and he to whom it is ſworn, are of ſeveral Nations. But he that upon his Oath hath promiſed any thing, to a Nocent perſon, as to a Thief, or to a Pirate, as ſuch, cannot by way of puniſhment take away from him, that Right he hath given him: For then the words of his promiſe or of his Oath, ſhould have no effect at all, which inconvenience is to be avoided. For the like cauſe, the Right of that which is promiſed cannot be compenſated, with the Right of that which was before controverted, in caſe the agreement were made after that Controverſie began. Yet may an humane Law remove that impediment which it had put in acts of ſome certain kind, in caſe an Oath either of what kind ſoever, or in ſome certain form be added: As the *Roman* Laws have done, in ſuch impediments as reſpect not the publick directly, but the private benefit of him that ſwears; which if it may be done, the act ſworn ſhall ſtand in force in the ſame manner as naturally it would, if ſuch an humane Law were not, either in obliging his faith only, or in giving alſo a Right to another, according to the diverſe natures of acts, which we have already elſewhere handled.

cap. 35.

The power to abſolve from Oaths in whom anciently.

XXI.

What manner of Oath Chriſt forbad.

James 5. 12. Rom. 1. 9. 9. 1. 2 Cor. 1. 23. 11. 31. Phil. 1. 8. 1 Theſ. 11. 9. 1 Tim. 11. 7.

And here by the way we muſt obſerve, that what is ſaid in the Precepts of Chriſt, and by St. *James*, concerning our not ſwearing at all, doth not properly belong to aſſertory Oaths, whereof we have ſeveral examples in St. *Paul*; but unto ſuch as are promiſſory for a time to come, which is uncertain. And this is evident by the oppoſition in the very words of Chriſt, *Ye have heard it ſaid to them of Old, Thou ſhalt not forſwear; but thou ſhalt pay thy vows unto the Lord. But I ſay unto you, ſwear not at all.* And by the reaſon that is added by St. *James*, That ye be not found to be deceivers. For ſo the word ὑπόκρισις ſounds among the Greeks, as will appear by *Job* 34. 30 and *Mat.* 24. 57. The ſame may eaſily be evinced by our Saviours ſubſequent words, *Let your ſpeech be Yea yea, Nay nay*: which St. *James* thus expounds, *Let your yea, be yea, and your nay, be nay*: which is a plain Figure, which the Rhethoricians call πλοκή. The former yea, ſignifying the promiſe made, the latter yea, the fulfilling of that promiſe. For this word ναὶ, (*i. e.*) yea, is an Adverb of yielding, granting, or promiſing, and is expreſt by Amen, *Apoc.* 1. 7. The *Roman* Lawyers expreſt it by μάλιστα and *Quidni*, which is an affirming, or an aſſenting to that which is asked of us. It is uſed for the fulfilling of a promiſe by St. *Paul*, 2 Cor. 1. 20. Where he ſaith that all the promiſes of God in Chriſt are yea, and Amen. Hence ariſeth that old Heb. Adage, An honeſt mans yea, is yea, and his no, is no: But on the contrary, he whoſe

Cor. 1. 17.

words and deeds do not accord, is by them ſaid to be ναὶ καὶ οὔ· ſometimes off, and ſometimes on, as 2 *Cor.* 1. 18, 19. That is, their ναὶ is οὔ, and their οὔ ναὶ, their yea is no, and their no is yea; the meaning whereof is, that they are inconſtant, unſetled, always changing. So St. *Paul* himſelf expounds it; for when they *charged him with levity*, he excuſeth himſelf ſaying, that his ſpeech to them was not yea and no, but as to himſelf it was always yea. *Feſtus* among the various ſignifications of the word *Naucum* writes thus, Some there are that think that it is derived from the Greek, ναὶ καὶ οὐχὶ, and ſo ſignifies a wavering man. Now if ναὶ καὶ οὐχὶ, yea and no, ſignifies lightneſs or inconſtancy; it will follow, that yea, yea, and no, no, ſignifies ſtayedneſs, or conſtancy. So that our Saviours words ſignifie no more than what *Philo's* the *Jew* did, *It is an excellent*

lent thing (saith he) *and most agreeable to Rational men, so to accustom themselves to speak truth, That their bare words may carry as much authority as other mens Oaths.* And in another place he saith, *That a good mans word is as firm, immutable, and void of deceit, as if he had confirmed it with an Oath.* So likewise *Josephus* testifies, of the Esseni, *That whatsoever they affirmed upon their words, was as true as if they had affirmed it upon their Oaths. And therefore to swear, was unto them superfluous.* And from these Esseni, or from those *Jews* that followed them, *Pythagoras* seems to have learnt it where he saith, *We must not swear by the Gods; but every man should be so careful of his word and credit, that he may be believed without an Oath.* It was the advice of *Chrysostome*, If thou dost believe that he with whom thou hast to deal, is honest and faithful, urge him not to swear; but if thou suspect him for a lyar, urge him not to forswear. The *Scythians* in *Curtius* told *Alexander*, *That it was not the custom of the Scythians*, Gratiam jurando sancire, *to purchase his favour or establish their own peace by Oaths. For,* saith *Curtius*, Colendo Fidem, Scythæ jurant; *The* Scythians *are so great admirers of truth and Fidelity, that their bare words do oblige them as firmly as (and their deeds confirm their promises, more than) their Oaths.* *Cicero* in his Oration for *Roscius Comœdus* tells us, *that look what punishments the Gods awarded to a perjured person, the same they awarded to a Lyer. For it was not the form of words, wherein the Oath was comprehended, that provoked the Gods unto vengeance; but the malice and perfidiousness of the heart, wherein all Treacheries and forgeries are minted.* It is excellent Counsel that *Solon* gives us, *That we should have so great a regard to our own honesty, that our words may be as Authoritative and convincing as our Oaths.* Thus *Clemens Alexandrinus* describes a just man, *to be one, that evidenceth the truth of his promises, by the sincerity and constant stability of his words and actions.* *Cicero* records it of a certain Citizen of *Athens*, that being known to be of a Religious, and upright conversation; and being to give his publick testimony upon Oath, was not permitted so to do; but as he approached near the Altar to that purpose, all the Judges with one voice cryed out, That he should not swear, being unwilling to give more credit to his Oath, than to his word. Very pertinent to the meaning of our Saviour where he saith, *Swear not at all*, is that saying of *Hierocles*, *He that in the beginning said, Thou shalt reverence an Oath; did therein enjoyn us to abstain from swearing, concering such thing as are contingent, and of uncertain events. For such things are so mutable, and of so small an account, that they are not worth an Oath, neither is it safe to swear about them.* And *Libanius* inserts this amongst many other Vertues, for which he highly extols a Christian Emperor, *That he was so far from Perjury, that he feared to swear to what he knew to be truth; A perjurio tantum abest, ut etiam vera jurare vereatur.*

De Decal.

De stat. 15.

Orat. pro Baldo.

XXII. Faith may be given without an Oath.

Therefore in some Nations, instead of Oaths, they give unto each other their right hands; which among the *Persians* is the strongest assurance of Faith that can be given. And amongst other people they oblige themselves by other signs, and that so strongly, that unless he that shall so oblige himself, do fulfill his promise, he is held as execrable, as if perjured. But especially of Kings and Princes, it is usually said, that their faith given is as good as an Oath. For such they should be, that they may say with *Augustus*, *Bonæ fidei sum*, I have a clear Reputation: And with *Eumenes*, I had rather lose my life than break my Faith. Whereunto *Gunther* alludes, where he saith:

——*No Oath more Sacred than the word of Kings.*

Whereunto we may add that of *Alexis Comicus*:

——*If I but nod 'tis firm, as though I sware.*

This testimony *Isocrates* gives of King *Evagrius*, That he kept his word as Religiously as he did his Oath. *Cicero* in his Oration for King *Dejotarus* highly commends *Cajus Cæsar* for this, That if he gave to any man his right hand, it was sufficient to confirm any Promise that he made, whether in Peace or War. And in those Heroick times, The elevation of the Royal Scepter was equivalent to the Oath of a King, as *Aristotle* notes.

CHAP.

CHAP. XIV.

Of the Promises, Contracts and Oaths of Soveraign Princes and States.

I. The opinion of some, who hold that Restitutions to the full, arising from the Civil Law, appertain to the acts of Kings as such, refuted: as also this, that Kings are not bound by their own Oaths.
II. To what Acts of Kings, the Laws extend: explained by distinction.
III. When a King is bound by his Oath; and when not.
IV. How far forth a King is bound to what he hath promised without cause.
V. The use of what hath been said concerning the force of the Laws, about the Contracts of Kings.
VI. In what sense a King may be said to be obliged to his Subjects by the Law of Nature only, or even by the Civil Law.
VII. A Right gained to Subjects, how it may lawfully be taken away.
VIII. The distinction of Things, gained by the Law of Nature, and by the Civil Law, rejected.
IX. The Contracts of Kings, whether they be Laws, and when.
X. How by the Contracts of Kings, they that inherit all his Goods, stand bound.
XI. How by those Contracts, they that succeed in the Kingdom may stand bound:
XII. And how far.
XIII. The free Grants of Kings, when revocable, and when not.
XIV. Whether the true Kings be bound by the Contracts of them that invade, or usurp the Kingdom.

I. Whether Kings may rescind their own Acts.

THE Promises, Contracts, and Oaths of Kings, and of such others as have the like Soveraign power, have some questions peculiar to themselves, as well concerning what power they have over their own Acts, as concerning what they have over their Subjects, as that which they have over their Successors. As to the first of these, it is questioned, Whether the King himself hath the same power to restore himself to the full, or to make void his own Contracts, or to absolve himself from his Oath, as he hath, his Subjects. *Bodine* was of opinion that a King being circumvented by another mans fraud, by fear or error, may for the same causes be restored to his own Rights, as well in things appertaining to the lessening of his Prerogative as a King, or in things appertaining to his private Estate, as his Subjects may. Whereunto he addes, That a King is not bound by his Oath, if the Contract agreed on be such, as by the Civil Law may be revoked, although the Contracts be agreeable to honesty. And that a King is not therefore bound, because he hath sworn; but as every man may be bound by such just covenants, so far as it concerns the other Party. But we, as we have elsewhere distinguished, so do we here, between the acts of Kings which they do as Kings, and the private acts of the same Kings. For what they do as Kings in their politick Capacity, is so esteemed, as done by the consent of the whole Nation: But over such acts, as the Laws made by the whole body of the people could have no power, because the Community cannot be superiour to it self; so neither can the Prerogative Laws of a King null his own publick acts; because a King cannot be Superiour to himself. Wherefore restitution which receives its vigor from the Civil Law only, is of no force against such Contracts. Neither are those Contracts to be exempted which Kings make in their Minority.

II. To what Acts of Kings the Laws extend.

Without all question, if the people elect a King, yet not with full and absolute Right, but restrain him with some Laws; then what acts he shall do contrary to those Laws, may by those Laws be made null, either altogether, or in part, because the people did reserve that Right unto themselves. But if the King do Reign in full Right, (*i.e.*) not bounded by any Law, yet holds not his Kingdom in propriety, (*i.e.*) hath no power to alienate it, or any part of it, or of its Revenues: all such acts of his that shall tend to such an alienation, are by the Law of Nature void, because what he so alienates, is not his own. But the private acts of a King, are to be considered, not as the acts of the Community, but as the acts of a Part, and are therefore made with a purpose, that they may follow the common rule of the Laws. Whence it is that even the Laws, which make void some acts either simply, or if the person damnified will, shall take place even here also, as if it had been contracted upon this condition: So we have seen some Kings, who have consulted the Laws for remedies against extortion. Yet may a King, if he please, exempt from those Laws, his own acts as well as other mens: but whether he will so do, or not, must be gathered from Circumstances. If he do, then shall the mere Law of Nature

Nature determine the case; yet with this Proviso, That where the Laws do make void any private mans act, not in favour to the person acting, but as his punishment; those Laws are of no force against the acts of Kings, nor indeed, any other Penal Laws, nor any thing else that implies *vim cogendi*, a power Coercive. For to punish and to compel, cannot proceed but from two different and distinct wills, and so from distinct persons; neither can the compeller, and the compelled, be any one person, though under diverse respects.

III. When Kings are bound by their Oaths, and when not.

A King may make void his own Oath, as a private man, *antecedenter*, *i.e.* If by a former Oath, he hath deprived himself of the power to oblige himself by Oath, to any such thing: but consequently he cannot, for herein also is required a distinction of persons. Besides, to every such absolution it is requisite, that in the very Oath before taken there should have been this limitation or exception (either exprest or implied) *Nisi superior voluerit, Unless my Prince comand the contrary:* Which in the Oath of a King cannot be admitted, because this were to make a King superior to himself, or to make his Oath still to depend upon his own will, which is contrary to the nature of an Oath. And whereas an Oath, though made, may confer no Right to another, by reason of some default in that person; yet is he that sweareth, bound before God, to make good what he hath so promised, as is before said. And thus also are Kings bound by their Oaths, which they make, no less than private men: though *Bodinus* thought otherwise.

IV. How far a King is bound by those Promises which he makes without cause.

We have likewise already shewed, That full and absolute Promises being accepted of, do naturally transfer our Right to another. Now this holds as well in Kings as in private men. Their opinion therefore is not to be admitted, who say that Kings are not bound by their promises which they make without good cause; which notwithstanding may in some sense be true, as we shall shew anon.

V. Of what use that which hath been said of the power of the Law about the Contracts of Kings.

That the Civil Laws of a Kingdom have no power over the Covenants and Contracts of a King, is well acknowledged by *Vasquius*. But that which he would thence infer, namely, that what is by him bought or sold for no price certain, or what is by him let or taken to hire without any Rent agreed on; or what he shall give away in Fee, without any Writing or Grant under his hand, shall be of force, we cannot admit: For these acts are done by him, not as a King, but as any private person; and over such acts as these, not only the Civil Laws of that Nation, but even the Municipal Laws of that City wherein the King resides, have power: because the King for some special reason placeth himself there as a Member of that Corporation, unless it shall appear by good circumstances, that it was his will, that those acts of his should be exempted from the power of those Laws. But that other example brought by the same *Vasquius*, concerning a promise any way made, doth very well agree, and may be explained by what hath been before said.

VI. In what sense a King may be obliged to his Subjects by the Law of Nature only, or by Civil Law.

That which Civilians do generally affirm, that the Covenants which a King entreth into with his Subjects, do oblige by the Law of Nature only, and not by the Civil Law, is somewhat obscure. For that is sometimes corruptly said by the Law-givers, naturally to oblige, which is only agreeable to the rules of honesty, but yet cannot properly be said to be due: As for an Executor to pay the entire Legacies without Defalcation, though he have not the fourth part of the Testators Estate left him; or to pay a just Debt, though the Creditor be made by the Law uncapable of receiving it; or to requite a Courtesie received: all which can no ways be recovered by any action at Law. Sometimes again, That is more properly said naturally to oblige, which is indeed truly obligatory, whether it be such as transfers a Right unto another as in Contracts; or such as transfers none, as in a full and firm Pollicitation. *Maimonides* the *Jew* doth very aptly distinguish between these three: Whatsoever cometh more than is due, falls under the notion of mercy, which is but the overflowings of a good nature, such are good works done meerly out of bounty and munificence. Secondly, To perform what we are strictly bound to do, which the *Hebrews* call judgment; but to do that which in honesty and Conscience only we ought to do, this they call Righteousness or Equity. Which three some Expositors upon that of *Mat.* 23. 23. render by mercy, judgment, and fidelity, whereby the word, πίστις, the Greeks do commonly understand Righteousness; and by the word κρίσις, judgment, that which we are strictly obliged to do, as we may find, 1 *Mac.* 7. 18, & 32. Moreover a man may be said to be civilly obliged by his own act, either in this sense, that the Obligation spring not from the mere Right of Nature, but from a Civil Right, or from both; or in such a sense, as that an action at the Civil Law may lie against him. We conclude therefore, that from the Covenants and Promises which a King makes with his people, there may arise such a true and proper Obligation, as may confer a Right unto them: For such is the Nature both of Promises and Contracts, even between God and Men, as we have shewed already. If the acts of a King be such as may be done by any other man, the Civil Laws shall bind him; but if they be such as are done by him merely as a King, the Civil Laws do not reach him, which difference was

Mercy, Judgment and Righteousness distinguisht.

not by *Vasquius* sufficiently observed. Nevertheless an action may arise from either of these acts, so far forth as to evidence the Right of the Creditor; but no enforcement there can be, by reason of the quality or condition of the adverse party. For that Subjects should compel him whose Subjects they are, is not lawful, which Equals may do against Equals by the Right of nature, and Superiours against Inferiours by the Civil Laws.

VII. How a Right gained by Subjects may lawfully be taken from them.

But this also must be noted, that a King may take away the Right of his Subjects two ways, either by way of punishment, or by Vertue of his Soveraign Power. But if he do it this latter way, it must be (in the first place) for some publick profit, and then also the Subject must receive, if it be possible, a just satisfaction out of the Common stock for the loss he shall sustain; this therefore as it holds in other things, so also in that Right, that is gained, by either Promise or Contract.

VIII. The distinction of things gained by the Natural and Civil Law rejected.

Neither doth it make any alteration in the case, whether the Right of the Subject were acquired by the Law of Nature, or by the Civil Law. For the King hath an equal Right to both, nor can either of them be taken away from the Subject without cause. For it is against natural Right that what Dominion or other Right a man hath lawfully gained to himself, he should be causelesly deprived of. And if a King should do it, he ought without doubt to make restitution, and to repair the damage that the Subject hath sustained, because he doth thereby violate the true Right of his Subject. And herein is the Right of Strangers much different from that of Subjects; for the Right of Strangers, and of such as in no respect are Subjects, can by no means be under that superеminent Dominion of a King; as the Rights of Subjects are for the publick good: unless by way of Punishment, whereof hereafter.

IX. The Contracts of Kings whether they be Laws, and when.

From whence we may collect, upon how sandy a Foundation they build, who hold all the Contracts of Kings to be Laws. For from the Laws there ariseth no Right against a King to any man. Therefore if the King should think fit to repeal those Laws, he cannot be said to injure any man: Yet if he do it without good cause, he gives just cause of offence. But from Promises and Contracts a man may claim a Right. For by Contracts the Contractors only are bound; but by the Laws, all that are Subjects. Yet may some things be of a mixt nature: Partly by Contracts, and partly by the Laws, as when a King contracts with a Neighbour King, or with Farmers of his Revenues, which he presently proclaims a Law, so far forth as it contains what is by his Subjects to be observed.

X. How by the Contract of a King, his Heirs may stand bound.

Let us now proceed to the Successors, concerning whom we are to distinguish between those that are to inherit all the goods of the deceased King together with his Kingdom; as he that receives a Patrimonial Kingdom, either by his Testament, or from an Intestate: and between those that succeed in the Kingdom only, either by a new Election, or by Prescript; and that either in imitation of other vulgar inheritances, or otherwise; or whether they succeed by any mixt Right. For they that inherit all the goods, with the Kingdom, are without doubt obliged to perform all the Contracts and Promises of the deceased King. And that the goods of the deceased should stand obliged for his personal Debts, is as ancient as Dominion it self.

XI. And how his Successors.

But how far they that succeed to the Kingdom only, or to the goods in part, but to the Kingdom entirely, are obliged by the Covenants and Contracts of their Predecessors, is as worthy to be discust, as it hath hitherto been confusedly handled. They that succeed in the Kingdom but not as Heirs, are not immediately bound by the Covenants and Contracts of their Predecessors; because the Title they have, they receive not from him but from the people; whether that Succession fall like other vulgar inheritances, to him that is nearest of kinn to the deceased, or to those that are more remote. But mediately (*i. e.*) by the City that chose him, such Successors also are bound: which shall be thus understood. Every Society, no less than every particular person hath a power to oblige it self, either by it self, or by its Major part. This Right every Society may transfer, either expresly, or by necessary consequence, that is, by transferring the Empire: for in Morals he that gives the end, gives all things conducing to the end.

XII. And how far.

And yet should not this be boundless; neither is it at all necessary to the good Government of a Nation, that this obliging power should be infinite, no more than that of a Guardian is, but so far forth only as the Nature of that power requires. *Tutor Domini loco habetur, cùm rem administrat, non cum pupillum spoliat*; *The Guardian* (saith *Julian*) *hath a power equal to the Lord, whilest he orders the estate prudently, but not, when he wastes it.* And in this sense is that of *Ulpian* to be understood, Every Society shall be bound by the acts of their Governours, be the agreement profitable, or damagable to that Society: yet notwithstanding, is not he that negotiates the publick affairs, to be strictly tyed up to this rule as some hold, so that his act shall then only be held firm, and ratified, when the Commonwealth is meliorated by it. For to reduce a Prince to such straits would be dangerous to the Commonwealth. Neither is it likely, that when the people transferr'd the Government

ment upon him, they intended so to retain him. But what the *Roman* Emperors answered in the cause of their City, That what was transferred by the Magistrate, should be of force in doubtful matters, but not, when that which is clearly due to the City is rashly given away or forgiven; the same answer may and ought to be given to this question, in the behalf of the whole body of the people, observing a due proportion. For, as it is not every Law that obligeth Subjects; for besides those which command things unlawful, some Laws are evidently absurd, and foolish, as that Law of *Cabades* King of *Persia*, recorded by *Procopius*, and *Agathias*. Neither is it congruous to reason, (as *Peter* Ambassador of *Justine* the Second, told *Cosroes* King of *Persia*, treating about some things, which *Justinian* seemed long before to promise to the *Saracens*, *That a Commonwealth should forever be condemned, for one simple Law or custome introduced, or enacted by one man, although an Emperor.* So also the Contracts of Princes do bind their Subjects, if they have any probable reason to justifie them, which in doubtful cases ought to be presumed, in respect of the wisdom, and authority of those that made them. And it is much safer thus to distinguish of them, than (as some do) by the greater or lesser damage, that ariseth to the Commonwealth by them. For we are not so much to regard the event of such Contracts, as the reasons whereupon they were grounded; which if probable the people shall be bound by them, if by any accident they shall begin to a be free people; and so shall they that are Successors as being for the time, the heads of the people: For if the people being free, shall make any Contract or agreement, their Kings that shall afterwards Reign, shall thereby be bound, although he receive the Kingdom in the fullest Right. The Emperor *Titus* is highly commended for this, That he would not endure to be sollicited to confirm any thing that his Predecessors had granted, thinking it but reasonable, That if he expected that his Successors should be bound by his acts, he also should be obliged by the acts of their Predecessors: Whereas *Tiberius* (and they that succeeded him) did never hold the Grants of his Predecessors to be good, unless they themselves had granted the same, to the same persons. That excellent Emperor *Nerva*, following the example of *Titus*, in that Edict recorded by *Pliny*, speaks thus, *Let not any man conceive, That what he hath got from any of my Predecessors either privately, or publickly, shall by me be so far rescinded, as that they shall be indebted to me though but to confirm it, neither shall they need any mans Intercession to obtain it.* But when *Tacitus* had declared, how *Vitellius* had torn the Empire in pieces, without any regard had to Posterity, (the Common people flocking about him, and courting him for his profuse gifts; and some others hoping for a good purchase, tempting him with ready money) at length adds this, *Apud sapientes, cassa habebantur, quæ neque dari neque accipi, salva republica poterant; That such gifts were always by wise men accounted void, which could neither be given, nor received without endangering the Commonwealth.* Which very saying of *Tacitus*, is much commended by *Mariana*, and applyed to the vast and unbounded Beneficence of *Frederick* King of *Naples*, who gave away, as *Philip de Comines* relates, not his own Crown Lands only, but other mens also, according as his fancy led him. The same may very fitly be applyed to the question in hand, and therefore *Galba* made no scruple of revoking the Grants of *Nero*, even from those that had purchased them, leaving the Tenth part only unto them: as *Tacitus* and *Plutarch* testifie. So did *Basilius* the *Macedonian* Emperor, recover all that the Emperor *Michael* had given away. Whereof *Zonaras* thus: That it was unanimously agreed, that They that had received moneys without any probable cause, should restore it, some wholly, and others one half. The like did *Charles* the Eighth of *France*, revoke all that *Lewis* the Eleventh had prodigally, given not excepting his Donatives to the Church: As *Commineus* testifies. This also may here be added, if any such accident fall out wherein a Contract made by a King is discovered to be not only damagable, but pernitious to the Commonwealth, so that at the time, when the said Contract was so made, had it been applyed to that case, it had been judged unlawful and unjust; Then may that Contract be not so much revoked, as declared to be no longer binding, as if made with condition, of being void in that case, without which condition it could not have been justly made. Thus did that wise Queen *Elizabeth* revoke some priviledges granted to the *Hans-Towns*, by her Predecessors, when they began to exact them as due by rigour of Law, and not as granted them by the meer favour of the Prince: Alledging that priviledges granted by Princes to their subjects, much more to strangers, might according to the times for the benefit of the Commonwealth and other causes be lawfully suspended, yea revoked and made void. And when the same Queen had drawn a dangerous War upon her self, for assisting the *Hollanders*, who refused to repay her those vast sums expended for their ten years defence, upon pretence that by her Contract with them, that money was not due till the War was ended, and that till then she could not recede from her contract: She prudently replyed, That all Contracts between Princes, were to be understood to admit of an interpretation of sincere fidelity. Neither is any Prince bound by his Contracts, when for just

Suet. c. 8.
The Grants of good Princes shall bind their Successours.

But not of prodigal Princes.

Comines lib. 9.

See *Camdens Elizab. Anno.* 1595, 1597. *in Controversia Hansiatica.*

just cause that Contract turneth to the publick Detriment. That the peace is not broken, though a Prince recede from his Contract, when it is done by an accident of a new case, or when it comes to a new case, which had it been thought on had otherwise been provided against. Lastly, That a Prince is not bound by any Contract though solemnly made, if it tend to the Detriment of the Commonwealth: For that a Prince is more strongly bound to the Commonwealth, than to his own Promise, as Mr. *Camden* records. And what is here said of Contracts is true also in the Alienation of the peoples money, and of any other things, which the King hath by Law a power to alienate, for the publick good. For herein also is this distinction to be observed, where there is any probable reason for giving, or otherwise alienating what is the peoples. But in case the King shall by any Contract go about to alienate any part of his Kingdom, or of the Royal Patrimony, beyond what is permitted unto him, such a Contract shall be of no force, as being made of that which was not his to dispose of. As much may be said of such Kingdoms as are limited and restrained, if the people have exempted any, either matter or kind of acts from the power of their King. For to make such acts valid, the consent of the people, or their Representatives, is necessarily required; as we have already shewed when we discourst of alienations. Now these distinctions being observed, it is no difficult matter to judge, Whether the exceptions of Kings who refuse to pay their Predecessors Debts, whose Heirs they are not, be just or unjust; whereof we may read many examples in *Bodine*.

Vide Camd. Eliz. 1595, 1597.

XIII. Of the Grants of Kings which are revocable and which not.

Neither is that which some affirm, to be admitted without a distinction, namely, that the benefits of Princes which are freely and liberally granted, may at any time be revoked. For some benefits, a King may give out of what is his own; and which were it not for this clause, at the prayer or request of the Grant, might well pass for a perfect Donative. Now these cannot be revoked unless from Subjects by way of punishment, or for publick good, for which also satisfaction must be given out of the publick stock, if possible. But other benefits there are which only take away the binding power of the Law, without any Contract; and these are revocable. For as a Law universally taken away, may always be universally restored; so also being particularly taken away, it may be particularly restored. For no Right is here acquired against the Law-maker.

XIV. Whether the right King be bound by Contracts of an Usurper.

But by such Contracts as are made by Usurpers, or such as without any just title invade a Kingdom, neither the people nor their lawful Prince are obliged. For such have no right at all to bind them: Yet even these also shall be bound by those Contracts, so far as they are enriched by those Contracts.

CHAP.

CHAP. XV.

Of Leagues and Sponsions.

I. *Publick Agreements what they are:*
II. *Divided into Leagues, Sponsions, and other Conventions.*
III. *How these differ, and how far Sponsions oblige.*
IV. Menippus *his division of Leagues rejected.*
V. *Leagues divided into such as oblige unto things agreeable to the Law of Nature, and from whence this ariseth.*
VI. *And unto things thereunto added, which are either equal:*
VII. *Or such as are unequal, which again are divided.*
VIII. *Leagues made between those of a different Religion, by the Law of Nature, are lawful.*
IX. *Nor are they universally forbidden by the* Hebrew *Law:*
X. *Nor by the Christian Law.*
XI. *Cautions concerning such Leagues.*
XII. *All Christians are obliged to enter into a League against such as are enemies to Christianity.*
XIII. *If diverse of our Confederates are at War, which we ought to assist; explained by a distinction.*
XIV. *Whether a League may be understood to be renewed tacitely.*
XV. *Whether the breach by one Party, do free the other from being obliged.*
XVI. *How far the Sponsors stand obliged, in case what they undertake for, be refused.*
XVII. *Whether a Sponsion being known, but not refused, do oblige by silence: This explained by a distinction.*

ALL agreements are by *Ulpian* divided into such as are publick or private. The publick he expounds, not as some think, by a Definition, but by Examples. The First whereof is, that whereupon a Peace is concluded. The Second is, that whereon the Generals on both sides do agree among themselves about some things touching the War. By Publick Agreements he understands those which cannot be made, but by such as have the Right of Empire either Greater or Lesser, whereby it is distinguished not only from the Contracts of private persons, but from the Contracts which Kings make in their private affairs; although even from these private Contracts, a War is sometimes occasioned, but oftner from the publick. Wherefore since we have sufficiently treated of Conventions in general, we will add thereunto some things concerning this kind, which of all others is the most excellent. I. Publick Conventions what they are.

Now these publick Conventions which the *Greeks* call συνθήκας, we may divide into Leagues, Sponsions, and other Pactions. II. How divided.

The difference between Leagues and Sponsions we may learn out of the ninth Book of *Livy*, where he tells us, That Leagues are such agreements as are made by the Command of the Supreme power, and whereby the whole Nation is made liable to the wrath of God, if they infringe it. And this among the *Romans* was wont to be performed by Heraulds in the presence of the King of the Heraulds: But a Sponsion is where the Generals having no order from the Supreme Power to conclude any thing about such a matter, do yet promise and undertake something concerning it. In *Salust* we read thus, *The Senate (as it is very fit) have decreed, That without their, and the peoples Command, no League shall be made.* *Hieronymus* King of *Syracuse* (as *Livy* relates) contracted friendship with *Hannibal*; but he sent afterwards to *Carthage* to make of that Alliance, a perfect League. Wherefore that of *Seneca* the Father, where he saith, [*In that the Emperour struck up a League, the* Roman *people may be said to strike it up, and to be concluded by it*] must be referred to those ancient Consuls or Generals who had received special Order from the Senate and People of *Rome* so to do. But in Monarchical Estates, the sole power of making Leagues is in the King. According to that of *Euripides*, III. The difference between them. *Lib.* 24. *Cont. l.* 4. *c.* 29. See *Book* 3. *ch.* 20. §. 2.

———*Adrastum hunc opus*
Jurare: Namque is jus habet regni potens,
Ut civitatem fœdere obstringat suo.

———*This* Adrastus *ought to swear, I say,*
Who being their Soveraign, the whole City may
Oblige, this League for ever to obey.

Now

Now as Inferiour Magistrates cannot oblige the people, so neither can the minor part of the people oblige the whole: But let us here enquire how far forth they are bound, who not having the peoples Right, shall yet undertake that, which the people only have a Right to do. Some may think that if the Sponsors use their utmost endeavour to effect that which they have undertaken, they have preserved their Faith, according to what we have already said, of Promises made for the fact of a third person. But the nature of the business concerning which this Contract is made, requires a stricter obligation: For no man in Contracts, will either give or promise any thing of his own, but expects that something shall be performed unto him in lieu thereof. Whence it is, that by the Civil Law, which will not admit of one mans Promise for another mans fault, such a Promise shall amount unto a Confirmation of the things agreed on, and shall bind the Promiser to make good what the Prince or People refuse.

Vid. sup. ch. 11. §. 22.

IV. *Menippus* his division of Leagues rejected.

IV. *Menippus* King *Antiochus* his Embassadour to the *Romans*, (as it is recorded by *Livy* and *Diodorus Siculus*) being led more by his own use and custome than by the rules of Art, divided Leagues into three sorts: The first whereof is, When the Conquerour gives Laws to the Conquered, where it is in the Victors power to determine what the Conquered shall have, and how far he shall be punished. The Second is, When both parties being of equal power and success in the War, do agree in an amicable League on equal conditions. And then by agreement, things taken are on either side to be restored: And in case any man hath been disturb'd in his possessions during the War, the difference is to be composed, either according to ancient Right, or according to the mutual Profit and Convenience of both parties. The Third is, When they that never were Enemies do enter into a Social League between themselves, without either giving or receiving Laws on either side.

V. Leagues divided into those that bind to things agreeable to the Law of Nature.

V. But we are to distinguish somewhat more accurately: As, in the first place, we may say that some Leagues require such things only as are congruous to the Law of Nature, others add something thereunto. Leagues of the former kind are usually made, not only between Enemies at the end of a War, but of old, were both often made, and in some sort necessary amongst those who before had never contracted for any thing. The ground whereof was, That that Principle of Natural Right, (which instructed us, that Nature had prudently linked together all mankind in a kind of strict Alliance: And therefore for one man to hurt another was impiety) was, as of old before the flood, so again some times after, by an universal corruption of manners so obliterated, that it was held lawful to rob and spoil Foreigners; yea, though there were no Wars proclaimed. So *Cæsar* of the *Germans*, *Latrocinia nullam habent Infamiam, quæ extra fines cujusque civitatis fiunt*; *Look what Spoil and Robberies they committed without the bounds of their City, they held as no dishonour*. The like Testimony *Tacitus* gives of them, with whom agrees that of *Plutarch* touching the *Spaniards*, *Who* (saith he) *till that time thought it an honourable imployment to spoil and plunder out of their own Territories*: Nay, the *Jews* themselves refused to make satisfaction for damages done, unless to a *Jew* or a Confederate. whence that question in *Homer* (*An Prædones estis? Are ye Forragers (i. e.)* such as live by the spoils of strangers) was an innocent and friendly Interrogation: For, saith the Scholiast upon that place, *To prey upon strangers was then held an honourable imployment.* The very same we find in *Thucydides*, with this addition, *For this kind of life was not at that time infamous, but commendable.* No more was Pyracy upon the Seas until the Reign of *Tarquine*, as *Justin* testifies. And this the *Roman* Laws seem to justifie. For if any thing had been taken by the *Romans* from any Nation with whom they had no commerce, hospitality, nor League of Amity, (for these were not accounted enemies) it was held by them as lawful prize: So if a *Roman* Citizen were found among them, or brought unto them they were immediately made Slaves. And in this case did their Law of Postliminy take place: The same and no better quarter had those people being taken by the *Romans*. Thus we read that the *Corcyrenses* before the *Peloponnesian* War, were no Enemies to the *Athenians*; but neither had they Peace with them nor any Truce, as by the Oration of the *Corinthians* in *Thucydides* appears. So *Salust* speaks concerning *Bocchus*, *Nobis nec pace nec bello cognitus*; *That he was altogether unknown to the* Romans *by either Peace or War.* And to rob and spoil such, was, in the opinion of *Aristotle*, laudable: And is so far warrantable by the *Roman* Laws, that the word *Hostis*, which signifies *an Enemy*, did in the old *Latin* dialect signifie nothing but a Stranger or Foreigner. Now under this kind of League, I comprehend those also, whereby Freedome of Commerce and the reception of strangers are on both sides assented unto, as being agreeable to the Law of Nature, whereof we have treated above. And thus we shall find these Leagues distinguisht by *Livy* in that Oration which *Arco* makes to the *Achaians*, where he insists not upon any League of Society, but upon that of Commerce, which consisted in giving and receiving that from each other which was due by the Law of Nature; namely, That the *Achaians* would forbear to receive into their protection the fugitive Servants of the *Macedonians*

No sin to rob strangers.

De moribus Ger. lib. 14. In the Life of *Minus.*

Hostis taken anciently for a Foreigner.

Lib. 41.

Macedonians. Now all such Conventions the *Greeks* do strictly include under the word εἰρήνη (*i. e.*) Peace, whereunto they oppose the word σπονδὴ, which is a League made by Sacrifices.

Those Agreements which contain those additaments to those of Natural Right, are either equal or unequal; equal, when the Articles are the same on both sides: Whereunto *Virgil* alludes, VI. And into those that add unto it, which are either things equal;

> *Nec mihi Regna peto, paribus sub Legibus ambas*
> *Invictas gentes Æterna in Fœdera mittam.*

> *Empire I claim not, but with equal Right,*
> *Both Nations will with lasting Leagues unite.*

And these the *Greeks* sometimes term συνθήκας, *Leagues* simply, sometimes Leagues upon equal conditions, as we read in *Appian* and *Xenophon*: But those that are made upon unequal conditions they call σπονδὰς, because made by Sacrifices: And as they respect the weaker party, προστάγματα, because imposed upon them upon hard conditions, which (as *Demosthenes* adviseth) are carefully to be avoided by all such as love their liberty, because they approach too near to subjection. Now both these kinds of Leagues are made either for Peace or for Society sake. Those equal Leagues of Peace are usually made for the restitution of Prisoners or Goods taken in War, or for mutual security, whereof we shall speak more at large anon, when we have occasion to speak of the effects and consequences of War. Those equal Leagues of Society respect either mutual commerce, or an equal participating of the charge of a War, or some other matters. Concerning Commerce, equal Covenants may be various, as namely, That no Customs be paid on either side, which we find to be one of the Articles agreed on in that ancient League made between the *Romans* and the *Carthaginians*, except only what was given to the Notary and to the Cryer: Or that no more should be exacted than what was at present paid, or not beyond such a rate. So also in a Social War, That each party should contribute a like number of Foot or Horse or Ships, and that, either against all Nations, and in all Wars, whether offensive or defensive, which the *Greeks* called ξυμμαχίαν, as having the same both Friends and Enemies; Examples whereof we often read in *Livy*: Or for the defence of their own bounds only, or limited to such a War only as is exprest, or against such an enemy, or against all except their Allies, as in the League concluded between the *Carthaginians* and *Macedonians*, recorded by *Polybius*: Or as the *Rhodians* covenanted with *Antigonus* and *Demetrius* against all Enemies whatsoever, *Ptolomy* only excepted. The like equal Leagues may be made, in respect of other things: As, That neither party should build any more Forts, confining on the Borders of the others Territories; or that neither of them shall protect the others Subjects; or that neither of them shall permit the others Enemies to march through their Countreys.

By what hath been said of Leagues that are equal, we may easily discover what is meant by such as are unequal. Which inequality may respect either the more powerful party, or that which is weaker: From the stronger, as, when succours are promised, but none required, or when more is granted, than is exacted. From the weaker, as when harder conditions are imposed on them than are just, and these we call Mandatory: And of these, some tend to the weakening of the Empire, as in the second League made between the *Romans* and the *Carthaginians*, wherein it was provided, That the *Carthaginians* should make no War without leave from the *Romans*. And from that time were the *Carthaginians* by that League, little better than Servants to the *Romans*. And to this also we may refer those conditional surrenders, saving that this is not so properly a diminution of the Empire, as a full translation of it to another. Yet is such an Agreement sometimes sweetned with the name of a League, as *Livy* testifies, *The* Teates *in* Apulia *made suit to the* Romans, *That they might enter into a League with them, not upon equal conditions, but that they might be under the dominion of the* Romans. Some again tend not to the undermining of the Empire, but only impose grievous burthens upon the weaker party, and that either for a certain time only, or for continuance. For a certain time, as the defraying the charge of the War, the demolishing of their Walls, the quitting of certain places of strength; Or to give Hostages to deliver so many Elephants, Ships, or the like. Others are permanent, as, That they bear all reverence to the Majesty and Empire of the other party, which how far it extends, we have elsewhere shewed. Confining upon this is, That they account those as Friends or Enemies which the other party declares to be so; also, that they permit no Army free passage through their dominions that are the others Enemies. There are also some lighter burthens sometimes laid upon them, as, That they shall not raise any Fort, nor build any City, nor lead an Army, nor traffick by Servants to such and such places; That they shall not keep above such

VII. Or unequal, which are again divided.

Lib. 9.

B.1. c.3. §.21.

ſuch a number of Ships, That they ſhall make no War with ſuch a people being Aſſociates with the other party, That they ſhall not ſupply the others enemies with any manner of proviſions, nor receive them though they come from other places; That they ſhall break their League, though formerly made with ſuch a people: For examples of all theſe we find very frequently in the beſt Hiſtorians. Moreover, unequal Leagues are often made, not only between the Conquerors and the Conquered, as *Menippus* conceited, but alſo between people of unequal power, yea, amongſt thoſe Nations that never were at War againſt each other.

VIII. Leagues with ſuch as differ from us in Religion, naturally not unlawful;

Concerning Leagues, it is frequently diſputed, Whether they may be lawfully made with a people that are enemies to the true Religion: which if we reſpect the Law of Nature only, is not to be doubted. For that Law is ſo equally indulgent to all men, that it will not admit of any difference upon the ſcore of Religion. The queſtion then is, whether by the Law of God, it be lawful, or not? And thus we find it often controverted, by not only Divines, but ſome Lawyers, amongſt whom are *Oldradus* and *Decianus*.

IX. Nor univerſally forbidden by the *Hebrew* Law.

Let us therefore firſt look into the Old Teſtament, where we find, that ſuch Leagues if Inoffenſive, were before *Moſes*'s time lawful: For *Jacob* we find making ſuch a League with *Laban* *. We purpoſely omit that of *Abraham* and *Abimelech*, becauſe it doth not clearly appear, that *Abimelech* was an Idolater. Neither did the Law given by *Moſes* change any thing herein. But we find a ſtrict prohibition given to the *Hebrews* concerning the *Egyptians*, That they ſhould not treat with them as enemies, and yet without doubt they were Idolaters. But here we muſt beware, that we draw not the ſeven Nations which God had decreed to caſt out of the Land of *Canaan* for their Idolatry, into a precedent, and from their and the *Amalekites* examples, create a general rule. For the reaſon why *Joſhua* might not make a League with them, was not ſimply becauſe they were Idolaters, for ſo were the *Egyptians*; but becauſe God had long before declared his purpoſe to caſt them out, and to plant his own people in their room, according to his promiſe formerly made to *Abraham*, of which ſentence the *Iſraelites* were but the Executioners. And as to the League of Commerce, either for mutual, or either parties advantage, that ſuch might be made with Heatheniſh people, we may ſafely conclude from thoſe made by *David* and *Solomon* with King *Hiram*: Where this is worthy our obſervation, That it is ſaid in Holy Writ, *That this League was ſo made according to the wiſdom that God had given him.* And *David* being perſecuted by *Saul* fled to *Achis*, nor was he ever reproved for ſo doing. 'Tis true, that *Moſes* doth every where command them to do good to their Countrey-men, and ſpecial care is taken to preſerve them in love one with another: And as true it is, that their very diet, and the whole manner of their lives was ſuch, that it would not ſuffer them to have any familiarity with ſtrangers. For as *Juvenal* obſerves, They were ſo moroſe, that they would not direct a ſtranger in his way; that is, they would not do a ſtranger the leaſt of courteſies, though they might do it without the ſmalleſt pains or charge:

* Gen. 31.44.

Deut. 23.7.

Joſhua might not make a League with the *Canaanites*, not becauſe Idolaters, but becauſe God had declared his purpoſe to caſt them out.

2 Sam. 5. 11.

1 Kings 5. 12.

Non monſtrare viam, eadem niſi ſacra colenti.

——Strangers ſhall not direct
Into their way; if not of their own Sect.

Hiſt. 6.

The like doth *Tacitus* record of them, *Apud ipſos, fides obſtinata, miſericordia in promptu, adverſus omnes alios hoſtile odium*; Between themſelves they were very faithful, and apt to ſhew mercy, but to all others they bare a mortal hatred. But becauſe they were commanded to be thus charitable to their Brethren, therefore to conclude, that it was not lawful for them to do good unto ſtrangers, will prove but ill conſequence. But yet ſuch were the corrupt Gloſſes of the *Hebrew* Doctors, that they perſwaded the *Jews*, that if they performed thoſe duties of Juſtice and Charity to thoſe of their own Nation, they had ſufficiently fulfilled the Law; though to all others they were not uncivil only, but barbarous, as indeed they were. For we find it recorded of them by the Evangeliſt, that it was not their cuſtome to eat, to drink, or to have any familiarity with Strangers. And thus through all Ages they have continued, as appears by the Characters given of them by all Hiſtorians. *Apollonius Molo* objects againſt them thus, *They admit of none amongſt them, that agree not with them in matters of Religion, neither will they communicate with them in any thing.* Thus do the Friends of *Antiochus* in *Diodorus* brand them, *A people they are of all others the moſt unſociable to ſtrangers; for they account all ſuch as enemies:* And a little after, *They will not eat with any other people, nor ſo much as ſalute or bid them farewel; ſuch a general hatred they bear to all mankind.* The like teſtimony doth *Philoſtratus* give of them: And in *Joſephus* we find it every where objected againſt them, That they were a *people of all others the moſt uncivil, and the moſt unſociable.* But Chriſt, who was every where moſt obſervant of the Law, did by his own example teach them, that this was not the

the scope of *Moses*, nor the sense of the Law, when he preferred the good *Samaritan* before the *Levite*, and asked and received water from the woman of *Samaria*. In that prayer which King *Solomon* made at the Dedication of the Temple, we find this Petition, *That God would vouchsafe to hear the prayers of the strangers, which they should offer up unto him in that house:* whereunto *Josephus* adds these words, *For we are not of so Inhumane a nature, as to stand ill affected to strangers.* Yet herein we are to except, not only the seven Nations above mentioned, but the *Ammonites* and the *Moabites*, of whom we find it written thus, *Thou shalt not seek their prosperity nor their good all thy dayes for ever.* In which words the *Israelites* are forbidden to make any League of society or amity with them; yet it gives them no right to make war against them. Or haply this place of *Deuteronomy* may be better understood, according to the opinion of some of the *Hebrew* Doctors, as if to seek a peace from them were forbidden, but not to accept thereof, when offered. Certain it is, they were forbidden to make War upon the *Ammonites*, *Deut*.2. 19. neither did *Jephtha* accept it till they had obstinately refused equal conditions of Peace; nor *David* till he was provoked thereunto by unsufferable injuries. The Question then resteth here, Whether it be lawful to enter into a Social War with Infidels? Before the Law given, that this was not unlawful, appears by the practice of *Abraham*, who assisted the wicked *Sodomites* in their War. Neither did *Moses* change any thing herein, that we can read. Of the same perswasion were the *Asmonæans*, who were both very skilful in the Law, and very strict observers of it, witness their religious observation of the Sabbath, whereon notwithstanding they made use of their Arms to defend themselves, but not otherwise: and yet we find them entring into Confederacy with the *Romans* and the *Lacedæmonians* by the consent both of Priests and people; and instituting solemn Sacrifices for their safety. These *Asmonæans*, we find highly commended in the *Chaldee Targum*, in the Books of the *Maccabees*, and in the Epistle to the *Hebrews*, whose example both Emperours and Christian Kings following, made Leagues with such as were either not at all Christians, or at least not sound Christians: as *Constantine* with the *Goths* and *Vandals*, *Justinian* with the *Lumbards*, the *Saracens*, the *Francks*, the *Scythians*. So did *Theodosius*, *Honorius*, *Leo*, *Heracleus*, *Basilius*, *Isacius* and others with the *Vandals*, and the King of *Spain* with the *Moors*. Now the examples that are brought out of the Scripture for the defence of the contrary opinion, have causes peculiar to themselves. For certainly some Kings and people there were (beside those forbidden by the Law) who were so wicked, that God by his Prophets declared his purpose to destroy them; now to joyn in Confederacy with these, was doubtless unlawful. Thus did the Prophet reprove *Jehosophat*, for joyning in League with *Ahab*; yea, and seems to threaten him for it, *Shouldst thou help the ungodly, and love them that hate the Lord? therefore is wrath upon thee from before the Lord.* For the Prophet *Micah* had before told the unhappy success of that War. So did another Prophet reprove *Amasia*, for waging a War with an Army hired out of *Israel*, *Let not the Army of Israel go with thee, for the Lord is not with them* But this was not by reason of the unlawfulness of the League, but by reason of the quality of the persons; as may be evinced by this, that God did sharply rebuke and threaten *Jehosophat*, for associating himself with *Ahaziah* King of *Israel*, though it were but for traffick. And yet when *David* and *Solomon* did the like with *Hiram*, God did not only not reprove, but in part commend them for it: For in that *Ahaziah* is said to do very wickedly, it is to be understood of the whole course of his life, which was aggravated, in that being an *Israelite*, he had forsaken the God of his Fathers; and therefore was God provoked to blast all his enterprises. For this also is to be observed, That the case of those, who being *Israelites*, forsook the Lord whom they knew, was far worse than of those that were strangers. For against those that made this defection, the rest of the people might take Arms, and destroy them and all they had, *Deut*. 13. 13. Sometimes again where the Leagues are blamed, it is not for the Leagues sake, but for the wicked intention of him that makes it: So God reproves *Asa*, for betaking himself to the *Syrian*, namely, out of diffidence; which he had declared by sending the Vessels consecrated to God unto the *Syrian*. So when he was sick, he placed more confidence in his Physician, than in God; whereby we can no more conclude, that it is generally and of it self unlawful to make a League with such as this *Syrian* was, than it would be to consult a Physician about a mans health. *Multa enim non illicita, vitiat animus*; *The mind sometimes makes that unlawful, which in it self is not:* As that Act of *David*'s in numbring the people, and that of *Hezekiah*'s in shewing his treasure to the King of *Babylon*. So *Es*. 31. 1. the vain confidence of Gods people in the *Egyptians* is sharply reproved, whereas it was lawful for *Solomon* to contract a League with them, 1 *Kings* 3. 1. And good reason; for the *Hebrews* under the Old Law, had the express promises of God for victory; in case they observed the Law, and therefore they had no reason to fly to humane succours in times of danger. Besides, there are many excellent Sentences in *Solomons Proverbs*, that disswade us from the society of the wicked. But these are rather *Prudentis monita*

John 4. 9. *Ant. lib.* 8. *c.* 2. Deut. 23. 6. Judg. 11. 16.

Whether we may joyn with Infidels in a Social War.

2 Chr. 19. 2. 2 Chr. 25. 7. *Constit. Clem. lib.* 6. *c.* 18. Esay 8. 6. 1 Chr. 16. 12. *Ambr. ad Rom.* 3. 1 Chr. 16. 12. 2 King. 20. 13.

monita quam legis pracepta, Wise mens counsel, than Dictates of the Law : And these admonitions have many exceptions, as most Morals have.

X. Nor by the Christian Law. But the Gospel gives a greater encouragement to Leagues made with such as are strangers in Religion, whereby they may in a just cause be relieved, than the Law doth; for as much as we are commanded to do good unto all men, yea, even unto our enemies; and this too, not as a thing commendable only, as to be thankful; but as a thing necessary: For we are enjoyned thereunto, under this penalty of being reputed Bastards, and not Sons of our Heavenly Father, who in causing the Sun to shine, and the Rain to fall promiscuously upon the good and bad, would have all his Children, to do good unto

Matth. 5. 45. all men. 'Twas very well said of *Tertullian, As long as God restrained his Covenant to Israel only, he enjoyned them to shew mercy to their Brethren. But when he enlarged his Kingdom over all, giving unto Christ the utmost parts of the Earth for his possessions, he extends the Law of brotherly love unto all men, so that as he exempts no Nation from his Calling, so we*

Gal. 6. 10. *should exempt none from our Charity.* Which notwithstanding must be understood with

Off. l. 3. some grains of allowance to those who are of the same Faith. So *Clemens* in his Constitutions, *We are to communicate of our labours to all, but especially to the Saints.* For as *Ari-*

Nic. 4. *stotle* observes, *There is no reason that we should take as much care of strangers as we do of friends.* Our eating and drinking with men of another Religion, is no where forbidden us; neither are we interdicted all manner of commerce with such as are Apostates from the true Religion, but only all familiar conversation with them, beyond what is necessary, but not such as may haply beget hopes of their Conversion. And by that of

2 Thess. 1. 15. St. *Paul* to the *Corinthians, Be not unequally yoked with unbelievers,* &c. It appertains unto those who communicated with them in their Idol Feasts, and were thereby drawn either to commit Idolatry, or at least to seem to do so. And this is evident by what follows,

2 Cor. 6. 14. *What fellowship hath the Temple of God with Idols?* like unto what he said before, *Ye cannot partake of the Table of the Lord, and of the Table of Devils,* 1 Cor. 10. 21. And yet we may not conclude, That because we may contract Leagues with them, therefore we may also willingly put our selves to live under the Government of Infidels, and contract Marriages with them: For in both these cases, there may be a great deal of danger and many hinderances to the free exercise of the true Religion. Besides, these bonds are more lasting: And a greater freedom of choice there is in our marriages, whereas Leagues are usually made, according to the occasions of time and place. And as to do good even to profane persons is not evil, so neither is it, to implore help from them: For St. *Paul,* we read, sought aid from the Tribune, and appealed unto *Cesar.*

XI. Cautions about such Leagues. In contracting Leagues with Infidels then, there is no Intrinsick or Universal Evil, but what evil there is, must be collected from circumstances: For special care must be taken, that by our too near alliance with them, we do not scandalize the weak: And therefore where there is a mixture of men of diverse Religions, as in an Army, it is very convenient, that their habitations be distinct, as the *Israelites* were from the *Egyptians*: where-

Book 1. Ch. 2. unto also appertains what we have elsewhere delivered concerning the Religion of *Jews* and *Christians,* when they jointly warred against the *Pagans.* And although by such Contracts, great improvement of prophane wealth may be made, yet were it better to abstain, unless it be upon great necessity. In which case, that of *Thucydides* takes place, *They that are treacherously assaulted, as we are by the* Athenians, *are not to be envyed, if they*

Lib. 1. *seek to preserve themselves by the aid, not of the* Grecians *only, but of the* Barbarians. For, it is not the defence of every thing that is our right, that can justifie us in the committing of that, which may, if not directly, yet indirectly prejudice our Religion. For we are taught in the first place, to seek the Kingdom of God, that is, the propagation of the Gospel: And it is seriously to be wished, that many Princes and people at this day, would be mindful of that free and devout admonition, which *Fulk* sometimes Arch-Bishop of *Rhemes* gave to *Charles* the Simple; *Whose heart doth not melt within him, to think that your Majesty should go about to contract friendship with Gods enemies, and to the ruine and subversion of Christians, to make use of the Arms of Pagans. Nihil enim distat, utrum quis Paganis se sociat, an abnegato Deo, Idola colat; For,* saith he, *there is but small difference between confederating with Pagans, and by denying God, to worship Idols. Alexander* in *Arrianus, thought those men unworthy of the name of* Grecians, *who being so, did notwithstanding fight for the* Barbarians *against the* Grecians, *for that which did by right belong to* Greece. Much more worthy of Imitation, was the Piety of *Emanuel* Duke of *Savoy,* who when he might have recovered *Cyprus* by the help of the *Turks,* refused it. I would to God, that all Christian Princes would follow the Example of this Generous Duke, and not implore the Aid of *Pagans* against their Brethren, nor assist them to enlarge their Empires, and consequently to darken the Light of the Gospel.

XII. All Christians obliged to confederate themselves against the enemies of Christianity. Hereunto I shall add, That since all Christians are but Members of one Body, which are commanded to have a fellow-feeling of each others sufferings; as that Command extends to every singular person, so should it to every Nation as they are a Nation, and all

Kings

Kings as they are Kings, ſhould ſympathize with their Neighbour Nations, and Kings that are oppreſſed. Neither is every perſon more bound to defend his own members, than Princes are (in obedience to Chriſt) to defend each other with that power which he hath given them. But this duty neither Kings nor People can well perform, whilſt Chriſtendom is invaded by the Enemies of Chriſt, unleſs they do mutually aſſiſt each other; which can never be done ſucceſsfully, unleſs they ſtrongly confederate together for that end: And ſuch a General League between Chriſtian Princes hath heretofore been made, whereof the *Roman* Emperor was by general conſent choſen General, whereby all Chriſtians were obliged to contribute either Men or Mony, according to their power, as to the defence of Religion, which is or ought to be the common cauſe: for the neglect whereof, I cannot ſee how any people can plead excuſe, unleſs it be ſuch as are engaged in an inevitable War, or afflicted with ſome other general calamity at home.

XIII. If our Confederates are ingaged in ſeveral Wars, which we ought to aſſiſt.

Another Queſtion doth often ariſe, namely, in caſe two Nations are engaged in War one againſt the other, and both are our Confederates, whether of them we are bound to help? Where in the firſt place, we muſt remember what we have already ſaid, that *ad Bella injuſta nulla eſt obligatio*; *No League can bind us to a War that is unjuſt.* He therefore is to be preferred, that hath the juſter cauſe, if the War be againſt a ſtranger Prince, yea, if it be againſt another Confederate. The words of him that ſwears Fealty to another, are theſe, *Si ſcivero velle te aliquem juſte offendere, & inde generaliter, aut ſpecialiter fuero requiſitus, meum tibi ſicut potero, præſtabo auxilium*; *If I ſhall underſtand, that thou wilt make an offenſive War againſt any man upon a juſt ground, and that I am either generally or ſpecially required to give thee mine aſſiſtance, I ſhall do it to my utmoſt power.* Thus *Demoſthenes* in his Oration concerning *Megalopolis*, The *Athenians* are bound by their League to aid the *Meſſenians* their Confederates, againſt the *Lacedæmonians* their Confederates, if the *Lacedæmonians* were the firſt Aggreſſors: which holds true, unleſs in our Articles it ſhall be expreſly forbidden, to ſend out any aid againſt ſuch a Confederate. In that Agreement which *Hannibal* made with the *Macedonians*, there is this Clauſe, *Hoſtes erimus hoſtium, exceptis Regibus, Civitatibus, &c. Quibuſcum fœdus nobis & amicitia eſt*; *Enemies we ſhall be to thine Enemies, except only ſuch as are in League and Amity with us.* If two Nations be at War, and both our Confederates, and neither of them have a juſt cauſe (which may ſo happen) we are to ſtand Neuters, and to aſſiſt neither. So *Ariſtides*, *If either of our Confederates had required our aid againſt ſtrangers, it had been readily granted; but if againſt one another, we deſire to ſtand Neuters.* If both our Confederates be engaged in a juſt War againſt ſtrangers, and both ſend for Aid; if we are able, we muſt ſend to both either Men or Money: But if a Prince ſhall be required by both to aid them in his own perſon, having ſo promiſed; then becauſe his perſon cannot be divided, it is but reaſonable that he ſhould prefer him, with whom he hath contracted the ancienter League: As the *Epirots* anſwered the *Lacedæmonians* in *Polybius*: The like anſwer was given to the *Campanes* by the *Roman* Conſuls, *In contracting friends, it is fit that we take care, that the new do not ſupplant the old: The Ancienter the Leagues are, the more Inviolable.* Thus *Ptolomy* anſwered the *Athenians* in the like caſe, *Amicis ferenda Auxilia contra hoſtes, non contra amicos*; *We are to aid our Friends againſt Enemies, but not againſt our Friends.* Which alſo will admit of this exception, unleſs the latter League do bind us farther than our bare promiſe; for it may include a tranſlation of the Government, and imply ſomewhat of ſubjection. And thus we ſay, that in ſelling of Goods, the firſt ſale is the beſt, unleſs the latter ſhall alſo transfer the property and dominion. So *Livy* of the *Nepeſines*, That the faith given upon their ſurrender, bound them faſter, than that given by former Leagues as to their Aſſociates. Some there are that do more nicely diſtinguiſh between theſe: But what I have ſaid, I take to draw neareſt as to ſimplicity, ſo alſo to truth.

See Book 3. chap. 25. §. 4.

Polyb. l. 6.

Leuctrica.

Deditionis quam ſocietatis fides ſanctior.

XIV. When renewed.

A League for a certain time prefixt, is not eaſily preſumed to be renewed through ſilence, unleſs ſuch acts intervene, which cannot otherwiſe be underſtood; for a new obligation is not eaſily to be preſumed.

XV. The League is void, if either party break it.

If either party violate the League, the other party is freed: becauſe each Article of the League, hath the force and vertue of a Condition. Thus *Thucydides* determines it; *They, (ſaith he) are not the firſt breakers of the League, who being deſerted, ſeek for aid to others; but they that perform not by their deeds, what they have promiſed to do upon their Oaths.* And in another place, *Si vel tantillum ex dictis, pars alterutra tranſgrederetur, rupta ſunt pacta*; *If either party ſhall tranſgreſs the Articles they have ſworn unto, never ſo little, the League is broken.* This alſo is true, unleſs it be otherwiſe provided by the League, as it uſually is, leſt what is ſeriouſly debated and ſolemnly ſworn, ſhould be adjudged to be broken upon every raſh offence.

XVI. How far Generals engaging are bound, if the Prince refuſe.

Sponſions are ſuch promiſes or undertakings, as Generals make without the conſent of their Soveraign; for the performance whereof they engage themſelves, or give hoſtages till it be confirmed by their Prince or Senate. The ſubject matters whereof are as

 diverſe,

diverse, as of Leagues. They differ from Leagues, in the dignity of those that make them. Concerning these Engagements, two Doubts usually arise: The first is, If the matter engaged for, be refused by the King or State, how far forth are the parties engaged, bound? Whether to make up what the King or State shall not think fit to grant, or to restore all things to the same state and condition as they were in before such agreement was made, or to deliver up their own bodies and the hostages to the Will of the Enemy. The first whereof is most agreeable to the Civil Law of the *Romans*: The second to Equity and Reason; which we find urged by the Tribunes of the people in the *Caudine* Controversie: The third is most approved of by Use and Custome, as appears by the examples of the two notable Sponsions made at *Caudis* and *Numantia*. But by no means may we admit, that either the King or the people are thereby obliged. *Posthumius* therefore was in the right, when he told the *Romans*, *That they stood not engaged to the enemy for any thing; neither had they commanded any of their Citizens to undertake for them. And therefore, saith he to the Senate, ye have nothing to do with us, to whom ye gave no such command; nor with the* Samnites, *with whom ye contracted nothing.* And again, *I utterly deny that any Contract can bind the people, that is made without their approbation.* And therefore neither are they engaged to make good that wherein they and the *Samnites* do differ, nor to put the Army into the same condition it was in, before the Contract made by the Sponsors. But if the *Samnites* would have engaged the people of *Rome*, they should have kept the Army within the Streights of *Caudis*, until they had sent to the Senate and people, to treat with them concerning a League and a Peace, that they might have judged how much the safety of the Army did concern them. And then in case they had not stood to their Agreement, they might justly have said what *Velleius* reports, both they and the *Numantines* did alledge, *That the violation of the Publick Faith ought not to be expiated with the blood of one single person.* Whereas now they may with more equity plead, that the whole Army is bound by that Agreement: For so the *Numantines* understood it; namely, that if the Sponsion was not approved of by the people of *Rome*, the whole Army which was thereupon set at liberty, should have been delivered unto them; which certainly had been most just, had that Agreement been made by the Sponsors in their Name, and at their Command: As we read that was which *Hannibal* made with the *Macedonians*. But if the *Samnites* were satisfied in the Faith of the persons engaging, being the two Consuls and six hundred hostages whom they had in custody, they might take their satisfaction from them, and blame themselves for accepting them: But from the Senate and people of *Rome*, they could expect nothing, being no way obliged unto them. But yet in case the Sponsors here had pretended to have received power from the people of *Rome*, to contract on their behalf, then had they been bound to have made restitution and satisfaction for the damage, which by their fraud, the *Samnites* had received: But if that appear not, then were they obliged to make good that which was in difference by force of the Negotiation. And in this case, not their bodies only had been obliged, but all that their estates would have amounted unto; unless some other penalty had been in that agreement exprest, in lieu of that wherein the *Samnites* and the people of *Rome* did differ. For as to the hostages, it was expresly agreed, that if the peace should not be confirmed as it was promised, they should be put to death. But whether the same punishment were to have been inflicted upon the Sponsors is very doubtful. But the stipulation of a punishment after such a manner made hath this effect, that in case that fact engaged for, may not be performed, nothing else can be exacted by that Obligation; for of that which is in difference between them, something that is certain is agreed on, in lieu of something that is uncertain. It was the common opinion of those times, that their Lives were also engaged; but amongst us, it is thought more agreeable to Reason, that to satisfie for that which the people did not think fit to grant, the Estates of the Sponsors, should in the first place be sold: And if that were not enough, their persons were to be delivered up as Slaves. It is recorded by *Plutarch* of *Fabius Maximus*, That when the Senate refused to confirm an agreement made by him with their enemies, he sold his own Land to preserve his Faith: But the *Samnites* delivered up *Brutulus Papius* to the Enemy together with all he had, for breaking a Truce with the *Romans*.

The Sponsions made at *Caudis* and *Numantia*.

The two Consuls, the two Questors, four Præfects, 12 Tribunes, all which were delivered up, upon the *Caudine* Engagement, but upon the *Numantine*, the Consul only: the rest were spared for *Tib. Gracchus* his sake; as *Plutarch* in the Life of *Tib. Gracchus* records. With us the Sponsors Estates to satisfie the damage, and their persons to be made Slaves.

Val. Max. l. 4. c. 8.

XVII. Whether the Articles of agreement being made known to the Prince, do bind him in case of Silence.

There is yet another Question to be resolved, namely, Whether after notice given to the Supream Power, of an agreement so made, silence may suffice to prove a consent. And here we are in the first place to distinguish, whether the Sponsion were purely and simply made, or whether it were upon condition, that it be ratified by the Supream Power; for if it were conditional, that condition being fulfilled, the Sponsion is of no force. like as that of *Luctatius*, which he made with the *Carthaginians*, which the people of *Rome* denyed to have been made by their Authority: And therefore another League was by common consent agreed upon. In the next place, requisite it is to know, whether any thing were by the Decree of the people acted, which might probably argue their acceptance

ceptance of the agreement so made. For silence of it self, is not sufficient to prove a consent, without some other thing or deed which in all probability would not have been, had not that engagement been approved of, as hath been already declared when we treated of the relinquishing of our propriety. But if any such thing or deed happpen, which cannot probably be referred to any other cause, then it may justly argue a Consent and Confirmation, as *Cicero* well observes in the case of the *Gaditans*. The *Romans* pleaded Silence against the *Carthaginians*, when they understood the Agreement made by *Asdrubal*: but because that agreement was made in Negative terms, namely, That no *Carthaginian* should pass the River *Iber*, it would hardly be admitted, that a bare silence should be sufficient to ratifie the fact of another; because no Act properly theirs, could suffice to prove the ratification of that agreement, until some *Carthaginian* did attempt to pass the said River; but being prohibited by the *Romans*, the *Carthaginians* did obey the Order. For such an act, hath the force of a positive act, and is not to be ranked among those which are barely Abnutive. Now, if that Accord made by *Luctatius*, had consisted of many parts; and if it had constantly appeared, that the *Romans* had observed the rest of the parts which did abridge them of their Common Right, this had been sufficient to justifie, that that Agreement in all probability was firmly ratified. It remained now that we should speak of such agreements as Captains and Soldiers make among themselves, not concerning those things which belong to the Supream Power, but to their own private concerns, and which are permitted unto them to do one to another: But we shall have a fitter opportunity to treat hereof, when we come to speak of such accidents as usually happen in War. *Orat. pro Balbo.*

CHAP.

CHAP. XVI.

Concerning the True meaning, and Interpretation of Leagues and Promises.

I. How Promises bind externally

* *De off. l.* 1.

IF we respect the person alone that promiseth, he is obliged to perform that freely, whereunto he was willing to be bound. What *Cicero* saith in this case is true *, *In fide quid senseris, non quid dixeris cogitandum*; In things depending upon faith, what thou meanest is more to be considered, than what thou saiest. But because our inward thoughts are not discernible, and that there would be no obligation at all by Promises, were every man left at liberty, to frame what interpretation he pleased of them, therefore some certain Rule must be agreed upon, whereby we may know to what our Promises do bind us;and surely natural reason will inform us, That he to whom any thing is promised, hath a power to enforce the Promiser to that which his Promise rightly interpreted, doth suggest. For otherwise, no treaty would have an end, which in things appertaining to Morality is held impossible. And perhaps in this it was that *Isocrates* treating of agreements in his prescription against *Calimachus* saith, We men do all of us, whether *Greeks* or *Barbarians*, dispatch affairs, using this common rule: hence it was that in ancient Leagues, this form was usual, saith *Livy*, Without any evil fraud, according to the usual sence and true meaning of the words here at this time. Thus do the *Hebrew* Doctors

Doctors upon the 30. of *Numbers* interpret *Vows* in that ſence, as the words are commonly then underſtood. The beſt rule of interpretation is that which gueſſeth at the will, by the moſt probable ſigns. Now theſe ſigns are of two ſorts, as words and other conjectures: and theſe conſidered ſometimes a part, and ſometimes conjoyned.

II. According to the ſenſe of the words, if other conjectures do not hinder.

If there be no conjecture that guides us otherwiſe, the words are to be underſtood according to their propriety; not that which is Grammatical or Primitive, but that which is vulgar and moſt in uſe,

Quem penes arbitrium eſt & jus & norma loquendi;

Which gives at pleaſure, Rules and Laws to ſpeech.

It was very well ſaid by *Procopius*, Long time doth not alway preſerve words in the ſame ſignification as *they were at firſt given. For the very things themſelves are turned in ſenſe according to mens pleaſure, without regard to thoſe names that were originally impoſed on them.* It was but a ſimple refuge that the *Locrians* made uſe of againſt Perjury, when having put ſome of their enemies earth into their Shooes, and carrying ſome heads of Garlick covertly on their ſhoulders they ſware, they would keep the Articles of the League (which were very grievous) ſo long as they carried thoſe heads on their Shoulders, and trod upon that earth: But having caſt away the earth out of their ſhooes, and thrown away thoſe heads of Garlick from their Shoulders, they thought themſelves abſolved from their Oaths; which ſtory we find in *Polybius*: not much unlike is that of the *Bœotians* in *Thucydides*, Who having promiſed to reſtore a certain City, thought it ſufficient to preſerve their faith, if they reſtored it not ſtanding, but demoliſht. So *Sultan Mahomet*, having taken *Eubœa*, cut the Governours body aſunder, whoſe head he had promiſed to preſerve. But (as *Cicero* well obſerves) this is not a way to prevent Perjury, but to confirm it.

Vand. l. 1.

Lib. 12.

III. Words of Art according to Art. *Referunt ad ſtatum finitivum.*

If in a League, there be an occaſion to make uſe of Terms of Art, which the people underſtand not, thoſe terms are to be defined and explain'd by the moſt skilfull in that Art, as what Majeſty is, what Parricide, *&c.* wherewith Rhetoricians uſe to limit the matter treated of. For what *Cicero* ſaith is very true, *That the terms of Logick are not vulgar, but proper to themſelves only, as indeed are the terms of every art.* As when the word *Army* is uſed, it is to be underſtood of ſuch a number of Souldiers, as dare openly invade anothers Dominions. For Hiſtorians do diſtinguiſh between thoſe that make ſpoil of anothers Territories, ſecretly and like Robbers, and thoſe that do it openly, with a juſt Army. Now the beſt way to judge what numbers make an Army, is by the ſtrength of him againſt whom it is ſent out. In *Cicero*'s account Six Legions with Auxiliaries was an Army. *Polybius* was of opinion, that One hundred and ſixty thouſand *Romans*, and Twenty thouſand of their Aſſociates, made a compleat Army; but a leſſer nember may alſo ſometimes do it. *Ulpian* gives him the title of General that had the charge of a *Roman* Legion, with ſome Auxiliaries: Which as *Vegetius* expounds it, conſiſted of Ten thouſand Foot and Two thouſand Horſe. *Livy* ſeems to contract an Army to Eight thouſand. The like may be ſaid of a Fleet, which a certain number of men of War make up ſometimes more, ſometimes leſs. A Fort is a place ſo fortified that it may hold out againſt an Army for a time; *Arx* from *arceo* to repel or drive away, becauſe by forts the enemy is reſtrained and driven back.

IV. Interpretation by conjectures.

Conjectures are uſeful when words or ſentences will admit of diverſe ſences, which Rhetoricians term *Amphibologies*; but Logicians do more ſubtilly diſtinguiſh, for if one word will admit of diverſe ſignifications, they call it an *Homonymy*; if a ſentence will admit of a double ſence, they term it an *Amphiboly*. So likewiſe when in any Contracts, there appears any ſeeming repugnancy. Then muſt we fly to conjectures; as alſo where its ſeveral parts ſeem to claſh one againſt the other, we muſt by gueſſing at the ſence, reconcile them if poſſibly we can; but if not, then ſhall that be admitted which pleaſed the Contracters laſt: Becauſe it is not poſſible that at one and the ſame time, the will ſhould imbrace two contraries, and in things that depend upon the will, the latter act derogates from the former, whether it be the act of one Party only, as in a Law, or a Teſtament; or of more, as in Contracts or agreements: in which caſes, the evident obſcurity of the words and ſentences do juſtifie our conjectures. Sometimes again the conjectures themſelves are ſo plain and evident, that they carry us to a ſence contrary to thoſe of the words. The common heads whence theſe conjectures ariſe are chiefly, either from the matter, or from the effect, or from other things conjoyned.

V. From the matter.

Firſt from the matter: as the word *Day* (if a truce be made for Thirty days) ought to be underſtood of natural days, but not of Civil, being moſt agreeable to the ſubject matter. So the word *donare* (*i.e.*) to give freely is taken to tranſact according to to the quality of the affairs. The word, *Arms*, ſometimes ſignifying inſtruments of War, and ſometimes armed Souldiers, is to be underſtood in ſuch a ſence, as is moſt congruous to the matter whereunto it is conjoyned. So when men are promiſed to be delivered, it is to be underſtood of living men, not of dead, contrary to the Cavil of the *Platæans*. So where Souldiers are required to lay down their Iron or Steel, it is enough if they lay down their weapons, and not their Steel Buttons, as *Pericles* would have it. And by a free departure out of a City, is meant a ſafe conduct to the place agreed on, contrary to that fact of *Alexander*. And by leaving half a Fleet, is meant the one half of the number of Ships whole, not diſſected, contrary to what the *Romans* dealt with *Antiochus*. The ſame judgement may paſs upon the like caſes.

VI. From the effect;

Then from the effect, the chiefeſt whereof is this, If the word taken in the moſt uſual ſence do infer an effect contrary to reaſon; then may we fly to conjectures. For where the word is ambiguous we muſt take it in ſuch a ſence, as will admit of no incongruity. It was therefore but a fooliſh Cavil of *Braſidas*, who having promiſed to depart with his Army out of the fields of the *Bœotians*, denyed afterwards that the place where his Camp was pitcht, belonged to the *Bœotians*; as if that promiſe had been made, in reference to the poſſeſſion which the preſent fortune of the War had given him, and not to the ancient bounds of the *Bœotians*: in which ſenſe the agreement had been void.

VII. Or from other things conjoyned ariſing from the ſame will. *Symp.* 9. 13. *Ad Adimant.*

Laſtly, from other things conjoyned; and thoſe either ſuch as ſprang from the ſame root (*i. e.*) from the ſame evil, though haply in ſome other place, or upon other occaſion declared, whereupon we ground our conjectures. For it is to be preſumed that in a caſe that is dubious, the will doth conſtantly adhere to one ſence. As in *Homer* where it is ſaid it was agreed between *Menelaus* and *Paris* that *Helen* ſhould be his that ſhould be the Victor; it was afterwards judged who ſhould be the Victor, namely he that killed the other. For, ſaith *Plutarch*, Judges are guided by that which is plain, and not by that which is obſcure. It was an excellent obſervation of *Auguſtine* concerning ſome Hereticks, That they cull'd out ſome ſentences of Scripture, whereby they deluded the ſimple by their not obſerving the Coherence of it, to that which went before, and that which followed after, whereby the meaning of the Writer was to have been diſcovered.

VIII. And in the ſame place.

Or from ſuch things as are alſo conjoyned in the ſame place, amongſt which the moſt forceable is the reaſon of a Law, which ſome confound with the mind of the Law, whereas it is but one of thoſe ſigns, whereby we gueſs at the mind of the Law. So *Cicero* in his Oration for *Cæcina*, Whether I am thrown out of my poſſeſſion by your lawful Attorney in your abſence, or by your Tenant, Farmer, or Servant, who forceth me out in your name, and by your command, it makes a difference; for reaſon of the Law holds in any of theſe caſes. Now of all conjectures this is the ſtrongeſt, when it evidently appears, That the Will was excited to ſuch a thing, by ſome one reaſon, as its ſolitary cauſe, for oft-times there may be many conſiderations moving us to do a thing: And ſometimes beſides reaſon, the Will to ſhew its freedom determines it ſelf, and this alone is ſufficient to beget an Obligation. Thus things given in reference to a Marriage, alter not their property, in caſe the Marriage ſucceed not.

IX. By a ſtrict or large ſignification of words.

Moreover, many words will admit of divers ſignifications, as being taken ſometime ſtrictly, ſometimes largely; which proceeds from many reaſons, either becauſe the name of the Genus doth adhere to one of the ſpecies, as in thoſe words of Cognation and Adoption; and in words of the Maſculine gender, which are taken for the Common, where the Common is wanting; or becauſe words of Art are more extenſive, than thoſe that are vulgar: As Death in the Civil extends to baniſhment, but in the vulgar acception implies only a ſeparation of the ſoul from the body.

X. Of Promiſes, ſome are favorable, ſome grievous, and ſome mixt.

It is alſo to be obſerved, That of thoſe things that are promiſed in any League, ſome are friendly and favourable, as thoſe that are on both parts equal, and to both profitable, which the farther it extends, the greater is the favour in the Promiſe; as in thoſe that belong to Peace, the favour is greater than in thoſe that belong to War; and in War, thoſe that repect defence are more favourably to be interpreted, than thoſe that are made for other cauſes. Some alſo are odious, as thoſe that are impoſed on one Party only, or which are more burthenſome to one Party than to the other; and thoſe that are impoſed by way of puniſhment, or which make ſome acts void, or alter what hath been agreed on formerly. But in caſe any are mixt, as thoſe which do alter ſomewhat formerly agreed for the ſetling of Peace, that according to the greatneſs of the good, or of the alteration ſhall be judged either favourable or odious; yet ſo as if other things are equal, thoſe made in favour ſhall be preferred before others.

XI. As to the acts of Kings or people, the diſtinction between Contracts due in equity and ſtrict Law, rejected.

The difference of acts due in equity and thoſe due in ſtrictneſs of Law, if we mean only the *Roman* Law, appertains not to the Law of Nations: Yet may it in ſome ſence be better applied, as namely, If in any Regions there be ſome acts which have one certain common

common form, that form so far forth, as it is not changed may be understood to be in the very act. But in other acts, by themselves, indefinite, such as are a free Donative, or a free Promise, we should more adhere to the very words.

XII. By these rules we may frame Interpretations of words and promises. See *Book* 3. c. 20. §. 11.]

These distinctions being thus observed, we are to guide our conjectures by these rules, in things not odious, the words are to be understood in their full propriety as they are vulgarly taken; and in case there be any Ambiguity in them, then are they to be taken in the largest sence: As when the Masculine only is exprest, both Sexes are to be understood; and where things are mentioned indifferently, they shall be understood universally. So these words *unde quis dejectus est*; *From whence one is thrust out*, shall be understood so as to imply the restoring him to the possession of that which hath been forceably detained from him: For the words in their largest signification will admit of this construction, as *Cicero* pleads in his Oration against *Cæcina*. But in such as are yet more favourable, if he that promiseth any thing be verst in the Law, or use the advice of Lawyers, the words shall then be yet more largely understood, so as to include the signification of Art, or that sense which the Law hath given it. But to have recourse to such Interpretations as are plainly improper, we ought not, unless it be where some absurdity would otherwise ensue, or when somewhat would render the Agreement unprofitable. On the contrary, if necessity shall so require, to avoid either some manifest injustice, or some as evident absurdity, we may not interpret the words more strictly than their Propriety will bear. And though there be no such necessity, yet if there appear either manifest equity, or very great utility in the restriction, we are to confine our selves within the strictest bounds of Propriety, unless other circumstances forbid it. But in such as are odious, that the burthen may be moderated, even Figurative Speeches are sometimes admitted: And therefore in voluntary grants, and in the remission of that which is a mans Right, though the words be general, yet are they to be restrained unto those things, to which in probability they were intended. And amongst things of this kind, that is sometimes understood to be possest, which we have hopes may be recovered. So succours promised by one party only, are presumed to be raised at the charge of that party that requires them.

XIII. Under the name of Associates, whether those at present only be comprehended.

But here a notable Question is sometimes started, Whether by Friends mentioned in a League, we are to understand those only who are so at the League making, or those also which shall afterwards be admitted. In that League made between the *Romans* and the *Carthaginians* after the *Sicilan* War, it was Covenanted thus, *Utriusque populi socii ab utroque populo tuti sunto*; *That the Friends of either party should not be molested by either party.* Hence the *Romans* would infer, That though the League made with *Asdrubal*, of not passing the River *Iberas*, did nothing avail them, because the *Carthaginians* refused to sign it; yet in case the *Carthaginians* should own that fact of *Hannibal*'s in besieging the *Saguntines*, who had been admitted into League with the *Romans*, though after the said League with the *Carthaginians*, they might justly denounce War against them, as having first broken the League. *Livy* thought *the* Saguntines *well enough provided for, in that the Allies on either side were excepted. For neither was this clause added, They that were at that time Friends, nor were they excluded that should afterwards be admitted*, (Which was added in the *Peloponnesian* League, between the *Lacedæmonians* and the *Athenians*). And *seeing that it was lawful for them to admit of new Confederates, who could conclude it reasonable, either that no Nation should be received upon any merit whatsoever; or that being admitted, they should not accordingly be defended. Provided always, That none of the Allies of the* Carthaginians *should be either sollicited to revolt, or received into Protection, in case they voluntarily did so.* Which are the very words almost of *Polybius*, and from him by *Livy* borrowed. There is no question at all, but that the words of the League might admit of either, (*i. e.*) either to restrain them to those then in League only, or to enlarge them to those who should hereafter be received, and that without any incongruity of speech. But the best interpretation may easily be guessed at by the precedent rules: According to which we say, That they who were to be admitted were not comprehended; for the matter in Treaty now is of the breaking of a League, which is *Res odiosa*; *A thing in it self odious.* And Secondly, It concerns the abridging of the *Carthaginians* of their liberty, in taking a just revenge upon those who had injured them) which by the Law of Nature was their due, and so not rashly to be understood as given away. What then shall we hence conclude, That the *Romans* might not admit of the *Saguntines* as their Friends; or being so admitted, might not defend them? Yea, certainly they might, but not by vertue of the League, but by the Law of Nature, which that League had not abrogated: So that the *Saguntines* were at that time both to the *Romans* and to the *Carthaginians* in such a state, as if in that League there had been no mention at all made of Friends: In which case, both the *Carthaginians* might revenge the injuries done them, and the *Romans* might also justly defend them, without breaking their League one with the other. Thus the *Romans* answered the *Samnites*, who desiring that they might have liberty to make

Lib. 21. The case of the *Saguntines* discust.

Hist. l. 3.

The breach of a League being a thing odious, and the taking of a just Revenge natural; the *Carthaginian* League with the *Romans* must be understood in the strictest sense.

C c

make War upon the *Sidicines* without offence to them, *That they knew nothing to the contrary, but that the* Samnites *had power to make Peace or War upon whom they pleased.* And in the League made with *Antiochus, It was provided, That if any of the Allies of the* Romans *should make War against* Antiochus, *it might be lawful for him by force to repel them: So as he held not any of their Cities from them by the Right of War, nor contracted any Alliance with them.* In the time of King *Pyrrhus* it was thus covenanted in a League between the *Romans* and the *Carthaginians*, That in case either of the two Cities should make Peace with *Pyrrhus*, it should be with a reservation of Liberty to send succours unto that City against which *Pyrrhus* should at any time make War. I do not say that the War on both sides in these cases could be just: But I deny that if either party did send succours unto the other, they did therein violate the League made between them: As *Polybius* rightly distinguisheth concerning the succour sent to the *Mamertines*, Whether it were just, and whether it were lawful so to do, without violating the League. Thus doth *Alamandarus* King of the *Saracens* plead for himself, *That none of the Articles of the Agreement made between the* Romans *and the* Persians *had been by him violated, for as much as he was not so much as named in them by either party.* Thus also did the *Corcyrians* tell the *Athenians*, That notwithstanding their League made with the *Lacedæmonians*, they might send them succours, because it was in their own power notwithstanding that League, to admit of any new Friends at their own pleasure. And the *Athenians* did afterwards assume this Liberty, commanding their Generals not to make War against the *Corinthians*, unless they saw the *Corinthians* ready to invade the *Corcyrians* in any of their Territories, lest they should seem to break their League with the *Corinthians*. For, it is no breach of a League, that they who are injured by others, should by others be defended, so long as the Peace in other things is preserved. And so after these times the *Corcyrians* decreed, *That they would assist with their Arms the* Athenians *their Allies, according to their Covenants, and yet preserve the Rights of Friendship with the* Lacedæmonians. *Justin* writing of those very times, saith, *That the* Athenians *broke that Truce in the name of their Allies the* Corcyrians, *which they made in their own name with the* Corinthians, *thinking it a lesser Perjury to help their Friends being invaded, than to engage against the* Corinthians *in a Solemn War.* So the *Athenians* making a Peace with King *Philip*, did expresly provide that those *Grecian* Cities that were not comprehended in that Peace might remain free: And if any man did molest them, it might be lawful for those that were included in that Peace to defend them. And let this example suffice for equal Leagues.

Liv. l. 38. *Pol. l. 1.* *Procop. Pers.*

XIV. What is meant by this clause, That one party shall not make War without the consent of the other.

In such Leagues as are unequal we shall give another: If it be agreed that one of the Confederates shall not make War without the others Consent; as it was in that between the *Romans* and the *Carthaginians* after the second *Punick* War; and as it was also in the League between the *Romans* and the *Macedonians*, before the reign of King *Perseus*: Since under the notion of making War, all Wars may be comprehended, as well that which is Defensive as that which is Offensive. The word is to be taken in its strictest signification, lest the liberty of defending our selves, being Natural, should be too much straitened.

XV. That *Carthage* should be free, how meant.

Of the same kind is that which the *Romans* promised, namely, *That* Carthage *should be free*; which though it could not reasonably be understood of Absolute Power, from the very Act, for they had long before lost the Right of making War, and diverse other priviledges, yet was it to be presumed, That some kind of Liberty should be left them, and so much, at least, that they should not be obliged to translate the Seat of their dwelling into a Foreign Countrey, and to have their own City demolished. It was therefore a foul gloss which the *Romans* did afterwards put upon that Promise, when they urged, That by *Carthage* they meant the multitude of their Citizens, and not their City, (which, though improper, may be granted, because of that attribute, *Free*, which is more agreeable to their Citizens than to their Town). For, in these words, Carthage *shall be left free*, was meant that it should be governed by its own Laws. And as *Diodorus Siculus* expounds it, *That they should enjoy their own Laws and Territories, their own Religious Rites, their own Sepulchres, and their own Liberties.* For so much was granted in leaving them free. So that what the *Romans* objected was a meer cavil, in making them free, yet taking their City from them.

XVI. What Arguments are Real, and what Personal.

Another Question likewise doth usually arise concerning Contracts real and personal. When we have to do with a free people, there is no question, but that the Contract that is made with them, is in its own nature real, because the subject is a thing permanent. Yea, though that popular State should turn into a Monarchy, yet would the League hold, because the body of the people is still the same, though the head be changed; neither doth the Supreme Power cease to be the power of the People, because exercised by the King: where we must except this case, namely, where it appears, that the cause was proper to that State only, as when Free Cities enter into a Social League for defence of their own Liberties. But if a League be contracted with a

King

King, it is not instantly to be accounted Personal: Because, as *Ulpian* well observes, for the most part the person is inserted in the League: Not that the League is personal, but that it may appear by whom that League was made. But if it be inserted in the League, That it should stand for ever; or that it is so made for the general good of the kingdom; or that it is made with him and his Successors: (For this addition ϗ τοῖς ἐκγόνοις is usual, saith *Libanius*, in his defence of *Demosthenes*:) Or to continue for such a limited time, (as mostly some of these are inserted:) It will from hence sufficiently appear that the League is real. Such was the League made between the *Romans*, and *Philip* King of *Macedon*, which when his Son *Perseus* denyed to bind him, was the cause of the War ensuing. There are also other words that may serve to prove a League to be real, yea, and sometimes the matter it self may administer ground for probable conjectures. And where the conjectures are equally probable, there we may conclude, That those Leagues which are favourable and equal, shall be accounted real, those that are grievous and hateful, Personal: Leagues made for the preservation of mutual Peace or Commerce are favourable; those that are made for War are not always odious, as some hold; but if they are made for mutual defence, they draw near to such as are favourable: But those that are for a Social War do too nearly approach to those that are burthensome. Besides, in those that are made for any War, great respect is to be had to the Prudence and Justice of those with whom we contract: That they be such as will not engage us in a War, either unjustly, or too rashly, when it may be avoided. And as to that saying, *That Societies are dissolved by Death*, I alledge it not here; for this appertaineth to Private Societies, and is determinable by the Civil Law: And therefore whether the *Fidenates*, *Latines*, *Etrusians* and *Sabines*, did right or wrong in departing from their League upon the death of *Romulus*, *Tullus Ancus*, *Priscus* and *Servius* cannot rightly be determined by us, because the words of the League it self are not extant. The Queen of *Scots* being deposed by the Estates of the Realm, and imprisoned in *England*, and her Son an Infant solemnly Crowned: The *French* refused to own any but the deposed Queen, saying, *That the ancient League between her and the* French *King was to be observed.* Whereunto the *English* replyed, *That she being deposed, and her young Son inaugurate, the* French *King ought by that League to defend him; for that ancient League was not contracted betwixt the persons, but betwixt the Kingdoms of* France *and* Scotland: Which was plain by the very words of that League, wherein it was provided, *That if the Crown of* Scotland *should be at any time controverted, the* French *King should defend him to whom the Estates of* Scotland *should adjudge it.* Whereunto not much different is that controversie in *Justin*, Whether the Cities of the *Medes*, which had been Tributary, did change their condition with the change of their Empire. For it is to be considered, Whether in that Convention they had committed themselves to the protection of the *Medes*. And here we must note, that *Bodine*'s Argument is by no means to be admitted, That the Leagues of Princes bind not their Successors, because the obligatory power of an Oath dyes with him that takes it. For an Oath sometimes binds the person only, and yet may the Promise made and confirmed by that Oath, bind the Heir. Neither is it altogether true, that all Leagues are grounded upon Oaths; for usually there is power enough in the very Promise to bind, though for the more reverence, those Promises are confirmed by Oaths. *Publius Valerius* being Consul, the people of *Rome* bound themselves by Oath to assemble at the Summons of the Consul; he dying, and *Lucius Quintus Cincinnatus* succeeding him, the Tribunes of the people began to cavil, alledging that *Valerius* being dead, the people were freed from that Oath. Whereupon *Livy* gives his Judgement thus, *That general contempt of the Gods that now rageth, had not then corrupted that age: Neither were men then so audacious, as to give unto their Oaths what Interpretation they pleased, and thereunto to adapt their Laws: But they chuse rather to compose their manners unto that, whereunto they had so religiously sworn.*

Camden Eliz. anno 1572.

XVII. A League holds with a King, though expelled his Kingdom.

Surely a League made with a King is valid, though that King or his Successor be expelled his Kingdom by his own Subjects. For though he hath lost his possession, yet doubtless the Right and Title to the Kingdom remains in him, according to that of *Lucian* concerning the *Roman* Senate:

——Non unquam perdidit Ordo
Mutata sua jura loco——

Though the Imperial Seat be changed quite,
Yet must the Empire still retain its right.

XVIII. But not so with an Usurper.

But on the other side in case a War be made against him that usurps the Kingdom, with the consent of the true King, or if it be made against him that oppresseth a free people, before he hath been established by their general and free consent, it shall not be be interpreted as a breach of any former league: Because these men, though they have got possession, yet they have no Right to what they hold. And therefore the Emperour *Justinian* denyed that he had broken the League made between him and *Gizerich*, by making War against *Gelimer*, who had at once deprived the lawful King *Ildericbus* both of his Liberty and his Kingdom. Thus doth *Titus Quintius* also plead against *Nabis*, on the behalf of the *Romans*, *We made no League or Confederacy with thee, but with* Pelops, *the just and lawful King of* Sparta. Now in Leagues, these qualities of a King, a Successor, and the like, are favourably to be interpreted, as being properly their Right, whereas the cause of an Usurper is odious.

XIX. A Promise made to him that shall perform such an act, if more do it together, to whom is the Promise due?

Another Question we find handled of old by *Chrysippus*, namely, Whether a Reward promised to him that shall first arrive at such a place, is to be given to both, if both arrive together, or else to neither. Where we must observe, that the word First is ambiguous: For either it signifies one that preceeds all the rest, or one before whom, none. But because the Rewards due to vertue are to be construed with favour, both of them that shall arrive together, shall share the Reward between them: Although the Liberality of *Scipio*, *Cæsar*, *Julian*, and others, was more honourable, who to each of them that first scaled the Walls, if more than one did it together, gave the entire Reward promised. And let these suffice to be said concerning the proper and improper signification of words.

XX. A conjecture offering it self either extends the signification, and when.

There is also another way of interpreting by conjectures beyond the signification of the words wherein the Promise is contained: And this also is two-fold, either by extending them farther than the words signifie, or by restraining them. But that Interpretation which restrains the signification of words is easie, but that which enlargeth them, more difficult. For as in all humane things, the want of any one cause is enough to make all the rest ineffectual: But to produce an effect, all the causes must concur; so also in this case of obligation, that conjecture that shall extend the Obligation is not rashly to be admitted: But with much more caution than in the case before mentioned, where we admit of words in their largest signification, though not much in use. For here we raise our conjectures without regard had to the words promising, which cannot introduce an obligation, unless the Conjectures be very certain; for here a parity of Reason is not sufficient, unless it be the very same: Neither is the same Reason at all times sufficient; because, as I said before, Reason doth often so move us, that to shew our own freedome, our will is of it self a sufficient cause of our Promises, without any other Reason. Now to justifie such an extended conjecture beyond the words of the Promise, it is necessary that it should plainly appear, That the Reason under which that case which we would comprehend falls, was the only and most efficacious cause which moved the Promiser; and that that Reason was in its generality so considered by him, because otherwise the Promise would prove either unjust or unprofitable. As for Example, An agreement that such a place should not be surrounded with walls, being made at such a time when no other Fortifications were in use, should doubtless extend to all Muniments, though but of Earth, in case it do appear, that the only reason why Walls were prohibited, was, That that place should not be fortified. Another Example is usually brought of a man, who believing his Wife to be with Child, disposeth his Estate to such a man in case that Child should dye, which by all probable conjectures should be extended to this sense, Or if such a Child should not be born: For certain it is, That the Will of the Testator was moved with this only consideration, That then he should have no Child of his own to inherit it: This case we shall find, not among the Lawyers only, but in *Cicero*, and in *Valerius Maximus*. *Cicero* in his Oration for *Cæcina*, pleads this case thus, *What? Is this sufficiently provided for in words? No. What then was of force to do it? The Will: Which if it could be understood by silence, we should have no need of Words: But because that cannot be, therefore were words invented, but such as should not hinder the Will, but declare it.* And a little after, in the same Oration, he adds, *Idem jus esse, ubi perspicitur una atque eadem causa æquitatis; Where there manifestly appeared but one and the same cause of Equity,* (*i. e.*) where there was the same solitary cause moving, *It may be presumed there is also one and the same Right.* Thus *Philo* in his Special Laws proves that it is Adultery to lye with a woman that is betrothed to another, and he adds this reason, *Quia idem valent sponsalia quod Nuptiæ*; *Because*, saith he, *such Espousals are equal to Marriages.* (So likewise in the *Mosaical* Law, under the name of Oxen, are all gentle Beasts comprehended; so is every Pool or Pond under the name of a Well:) So likewise an Injunction, though it run in this form, *Unde me vi dejeceris hominibus coactis, armatisve*; *Whence thou hast thrust me out by force and arms*, takes place also against all manner of force that threatens our life and limbs. *For that which is usually done by armed men, if by any other counsels or means we are brought into the same danger, the Law affords us the same Right and Remedy.* *Quintilian* the Father, in one of his Declamations brings in this Example, *Murther doth usually signifie the effusion of humane blood by the Sword: But if a man be killed by* *any*

Lib. 1 & 2. de Orat. Bruto & pro Cæcina.

Exod. 21, 28, 35.

any other means we have recourse to the same Law: For if a man shall fall among Thieves, or if he be thrown into a River, and there drowned, or if he be tumbled headlong from an high Precipice, his death shall be revenged by the same Law as if he had been killed by the Sword. The like Argument we find used by *Isaus*, concerning the Inheritance of *Pyrrhus*, where because by the Laws of *Athens*, a Father having no Son could not make his Testament if his Daughter were unwilling; he infers, that neither had he, without her consent, the power of adopting one.

XXI. Whether a Command given for one thing, be fulfilled in doing another as profitable, if not more: *Lib. 1. c. 13.*

And from hence that famous Question in *Gellius* may easily be answered, concerning a Command given by our Superiour, Whether it may be fulfilled, though not by the same, yet by another thing equally profitable, or haply more than that which was commanded. *Servants,* saith *Quintilian, act some things more freely out of a good mind; and even our Slaves bought with our Money, do sometimes think it an Argument of their Fidelity to do otherwise than they are commanded.* Which may be done, if it appear, That what was so particularly described, but only under some general consideration, which might also be otherwise obtained: But if that do not sufficiently appear, then we are to follow *Gellius* his advice in that place, For the Authority of a General would quickly be contemned, if what he commands should be disputed, and not obeyed.

XXII. Or restrained, and that either by reason of some defect in the Will:

That Interpretation that restraineth the sence from what the signification of the words, wherein the Promise is contained, will bear, is derived either from an originary defect of the Will, or from the repugnancy of some emergent case with the Will. The originary defect of the Will is understood, either from some absurdity which would otherwise evidently ensue; or from failing of the main Reason which alone did fully and effectually move the Will; or from a defect of matter. The first whereof is grounded upon this, That no man is to be believed to will things that are absurd.

XXIII. Or when the main Reason ceaseth:

The Second is grounded on this, That what is contained in the Promise whereunto such a Reason is added, or where it is plainly understood, is not considered barely or simply, but as it falls under that Reason.

XXIV. Or when there is a defect in the matter:

The Third is grounded on this, That the matter so restrained is always observed to be in the mind of him that promiseth, although the words of the Promiser do admit of a large signification.

XXV. (An observation concerning the last recited Conjectures.)

But as concerning the Reason that moves the Will we must observe, That under it are comprehended not only things actually existing, but sometimes things that morally considered, may be; which when it takes place, no restriction ought to be admitted. As when it is in any League provided, That no Army or Fleet shall be sent to such a place, they ought not to be led thither, though there be no intention thereby to do harm, because in that agreement not so much the present damage, as all future dangers whatsoever are regarded. But here it is also sometimes questioned, Whether Promises are to be understood with this tacite condition, That things remain so as they were when the Promise was made; Which we deny, unless it do manifestly appear, That that present condition of things was included in that only Reason which we have said. And we read of nothing more frequently in Histories than of Ambassadours, who understanding so great an alteration made in the State, as would render the whole matter and cause of the Embassie frustrate, have returned home without attempting any thing.

XXVI. Or from the repugnancy of some emergent case with the Will: Which is taken either from something that is unlawful. Courts of Equity necessary.

The Repugnancy of some emergent case with the Will is of two sorts: For the Will is guessed at, either by Natural Reason, or by some other sign of the Will. The proper office to judge at the Will by Right Reason, *Aristotle* assigns to Prudence in the understanding, and in the Will, to Equity, which he very fitly defines to be the Correction or Moderation of that wherein the Law by Reason of its generality is deficient: Which ought to take place, as well in Testaments as in Contracts respectively. For seeing that all emergent cases could neither be foreseen by the Law-giver, nor excepted in the Law; therefore there is a necessity that some liberty should be granted for the exempting of such cases, as he that made the Law would have exempted, had he been present, or could he have foreseen it: And yet is not this rashly to be admitted, for that were to make himself Lord over another mans act; but then only, when we have sufficient signs to justifie our Conjectures. Whereof none can be more just than this, when they would binds us to things repugnant to the Laws either of God or Nature. For such Laws having no power to oblige, are necessarily to be exempted. *Quadam etiamsi nulla significatione Legis comprehensa sint, natura tamen excipiuntur; There are some things* (saith *Quintilian*) *that naturally are exempted, although they are not comprehended by any signification of the Law.* As he that hath promised to restore a Sword to him who entrusted him with it, if the man to whom the Promise was made, be mad, he ought not to deliver it, lest he thereby create danger to himself, or to some others that are innocent. So neither are we to restore a thing to him that deposited it with us, if the right owner demand it. *This I approve of* (saith *Triphonius*) *to be Justice,*

that

that so gives to every man his own, that he detracts not from the juster claim of another. The Reason whereof is, because such is the force of Propriety, being once introduced, that not to return a thing to the right owner, when known, is altogether unjust.

XXVII. Or when some too great a charge ariseth to the Promiser in comparison of that act. The Second sign shall be this, When strictly to follow the words of the Promise or Contract is not of it self and altogether unlawful. But when it binds to such things as to a prudent and well-balanced Judgement are too grievous and intollerable: And that whether we respect humanity it self absolutely, or by comparing the person promising, and the thing promised, with the end for which such a Promise or Contract was made. So he that lends a thing for such a time, may require it before that time, if he stand in great want of it: Because it is presumed, that no man would willingly do his Friend a courtesie in that, wherein he should do himself a manifest injury. So he that shall promise succours to his Allies, shall be excused in case he be engaged in War at home, so far forth as he shall stand in need of those Forces. In like manner, he that promiseth immunity from Tributes and Taxes, means only from ordinary and annual Taxes, not from those that may be imposed in times of greatest danger, for the defence of the Common-wealth. Wherefore it was too loosely said of *Cicero, That those Promises were not to be performed, which were unprofitable to him to whom they were made; nor those which did more endamage the Promiser, than benefit him to whom they were made.* For the person promising is no competent Judge whether the thing promised will be profitable to him to whom it is promised, unless it be in such a case as is before instanced of apparent madness: Neither is every damage sufficient to absolve the Promiser from the performance of his Promise, but the damage must be such, as even from the very nature of the act it may be believed, That could it have been foreseen, it would have been exempted. So he that is engaged to do so many days service for another, is acquitted from his engagement, if either his Father or his Son be affected with some dangerous sickness: This was *Cicero*'s opinion in this case, *If being retained to plead the cause of thy Client, thy Son should in the mean time fall desperately sick,* Off. l. 1. Non est contra officium, non facere quod dixeris; *Thou art not in duty bound to attend that Cause.* And in this sense is that of *Seneca* to be understood, *Then do I break my word, then* De Benef. l. 4. c. 35. *may I be justly charged with levity, when all things remaining in the state they were in when the Promise was made, I do not perform what I promised. But in case there fall out any unexpected change concerning that whereupon the Promise was made, it gives me liberty to consult anew, and yet I preserve my Faith. I am haply retained in a cause, wherein I do afterwards conceive that my Father may be damnified; I have promised to take a Journey into the Countrey with such a Companion, but I understand since that the way is infested with Robbers; I have engaged my word to be present, and to assist in such a business, but am with-held by the unexpected sickness of my Son, or by my Wives falling into labour:* Omnia esse debent eadem, quæ fuerunt cum promitterem, ut promittentis fidem teneas; *All things ought to be in the same condition as they were when I promised, to oblige me to do what I did promise.* Where by *All things*, we must understand all things relating to the nature of that Act which See Camd. anno 1595. is in question. The *English* did frequently make use of these politick Maxims both with the *Hollanders* and with the *Hans-towns*, as *Camden* records: For when Queen *Elizabeth*, by assisting the States of *Holland*, had drawn down the whole power of *Spain* against herself, and therefore, for her necessary defence, demanded those vast summs lent them to prosecute their War: They urging, That that Money was not due, by their Contract, till the end of the War; and that until then, she was obliged in Honour to assist them. She Answered, *That a Prince was not bound by his Contract, when for just causes it manifestly turned to the publick detriment; or when it was done by the accident of a new case; or when a new case ariseth, which had it been foreseen, would have been provided against. For that every Contract, though sworn, is understood with this reserved condition, if matters continue in the same state, but not if they be changed.* Which that wise Queen grounded upon the Authority of *Seneca*, *A wise man changeth not his resolution, all things continuing as they were at the time when he made it: nor can he be said to Repent, because, at that time, and as the case then stood, no better counsel could be followed than was then resolved on.* And when the Hans-towns complained against her to the Emperour, That their priviledges were broken in *England*, and their customes much enhansed: She Answered, *That those Priviledges were by Authority of Parliament abrogated, as being not convenient for the times, being granted when Traffick and Merchandizes lay dead among the* English. *And for her Customes,* she said, *that the Common-wealth could not subsist, if no other Customes should now be paid by the Hans-towns than what were paid three hundred years before.* And much to this purpose is that of *Seneca*, *Being invited to a Feast, I'll go because I have promised, although it be cold: I will arise to a Wedding because I have promised, although I am not sufficiently refresht with sleep; but not if I am Feverish, although I have*

I have promised: Nor will I stand bound with thee for any thing that is uncertain, though thou biddest me, in case thou art indebted to the Exchequer. For in all these Promises there are some tacite exceptions to be understood; namely, if I can, or if I ought so to do, if things be then as they now are: Effice ut idem status sit cum exigitur, qui fuit cum promitterem; *Make the case the same when thou exactest my Promise, as it was when I made it: If any new thing intervene, it is not levity or inconstancy in me if I fail. What wonder is it if a man change his mind and counsel, when his condition is changed.* Eadem mihi omnia præsta, & idem sum; *Make all things the same, and then I also am the same.*

XXVIII. Other signs whereby we may guess that such a case ought to be exempted.

There are also (as we have said) other signs of the Will, whereby we may conjecture, That that case was to have been exempted: Among which there are none more convincing, than words spoken or recited, in some place, not where they do directly contradict each other, which is ἀντινομία, whereof we made mention above. But when (as it were) unexpectedly from the very event of things they seem to clash one against another, which the *Greeks* call τὴν ἐκ περιστάσεως μάχην.

XXIX. What Rules should then guide our conjectures.

Now when such a case happens, which part of the Writing ought to prevail with us, we may be instructed by some rules that *Cicero* * hath left us out of some ancient and approved Authors, which are by no means to be slighted, yet in mine opinion are they not digested into a right order. And therefore I think fit to place them thus, That that which is permitted do always give place to that which is enjoyned: For, as *Quintilian* saith, *Semper potentior lex est quæ vetat, quàm quæ permittit; That Law that commands is always stronger than that which permits.* Because he that permits any thing is conceived to permit it, unless somewhat else do hinder, than what is then treated of; and therefore *Plus valet sanctio, quam permissio, A Decree or Sanction is more prevalent than a Toleration.* Secondly, That what is to be done at a time prefixt be always preferred before what may be done at any time. From whence it follows, That for the most part, that which forbids, is to be preferred before that which enjoyns: Because what prohibits, binds us at all times, but so doth not that which commands, unless it be either when the time is exprest, or that the command comprehends under it some tacite prohibition. Again, that in such agreements as are in their qualities before-named, equal, That should be preferred, which is most proper, and comes nearest to the matter in question: For Particulars are always more efficacious than Generals. And in things prohibited, that those which have a penalty affixt, be preferred before those that have none; and those that have a greater penalty, before those that have a lesser. As also that those be preferred that have causes affixt, either more honest or more profitable: And in the last place, that that which was spoken last be more valid than that which was spoken before. Of what hath been already said, this also must be here repeated, That look what Agreements are sworn unto, must be understood in the most usual Propriety of Speech: And that all secret reservations and restrictions, more than the very nature of the thing doth necessarily require, be altogether disowned. Wherefore also in case an Agreement sworn shall in effect clash with that which is not sworn, that which was bound by an Oath shall be preferred.

* De Invent. 2. Verina 2.

XXX. In a case that is dubious, a Writing is not required to compleat the Contract.

It is also usually questioned, Whether in a doubtful case a Contract ought to be accounted perfect and compleat, before the Writings are signed and delivered. For this *Muræna* alledgeth against the Agreement made between *Sylla* and *Mithridates.* To me it is very plain, That unless it be otherwise agreed on, the Writings stand but as the lasting Monument of the Contract, and not as any part of the substance of it: If otherwise it must be so exprest, as in that made with *Nabis*: Where it was provided, That those conditions should be of force, *From that day whereon they should be published by* Nabis.

XXXI. The Contracts of Kings not always to be interpreted by the *Roman* Laws.

But I cannot admit of their opinion, who hold, That the Contracts of Kings and Free States are to be interpreted, as far as is possible, by the *Roman* Laws; unless it appear, That among those people the Civil Law, in such things as concern the Right of Nations, hath ever been received for the Law of Nations, which is not rashly to be presumed.

XXXII. Whether his words that offers, or his that accepts, are most binding.

As to that Question moved by *Plutarch* in his *Symposiacks*; namely, Whether the words of him that proposeth conditions, or of him that accepts of them are most binding. It appears to me, That seeing it is he that accepts that promiseth, they are his words, if absolute, and in themselves, that gives form and being to the Contract. For if he regards the words of him that offers conditions affirmatively, he shall be thought to repeat those very words in his Promise, according to the Nature of Relatives. But certain it is, That before the conditions be accepted, even he that offers them is not bound to perform them. For until they are accepted, there is no Right acquired, as appears by what hath been already said concerning Promises. And this offering of conditions, is less binding than a Promise.

CHAP. XVII.

Of the Damage done to one man, through the default of another, and the Obligation thence arising.

I. *He that occasioneth the Damage is bound to repair it.*
II. *A Damage is that which is repugnant to a mans Right strictly taken.*
III. *A mans Aptitude or fitness for a thing is exactly to be distinguisht from his Right strictly taken.*
IV. *That Damage extends to even the fruits or profits of what was his;*
V. *And to the surceasing of gain, and how.*
VI. *Of Damage Primarily occasioned:*
VII. *And of such as are occasioned secondarily.*
VIII. *Of Damages occasioned by omission primarily:*
IX. *And secondarily.*
X. *What they must contribute to the act that are thus far bound.*
XI. *In what order they are bound to reparation.*
XII. *This Obligation is to be extended to the Damage that shall ensue.*
XIII. *An example in a Man-slayer:*
XIV. *In him that offers violence otherwise:*
XV. *In an Adulterer or Fornicator:*
XVI. *In a Thief, Robber, and others:*
XVII. *And in him that giveth the occasion of a Promise, either by fraud, or by fear that is unjust.*
XVIII. *What if that fear be naturally Just.*
XIX. *What if that fear be by the Law of Nations deemed just.*
XX. *How far the Civil Powers are bound for Damages done by their Subjects; where the question, concerning Prizes taken by Sea, from Confederates, contrary to publick command, is handled.*
XXI. *That by the Law of Nature no man is bound to repair damages done by his Beast, or Ship, without his knowledge.*
XXII. *Damages sustain'd in a mans credit or honour, how to be repaired.*

I. He that occasioneth the Damage, is bound to repair it.

WE have already shewed, that a Right unto a thing may accrue unto us from another, three several ways; either by Contract, or by injuries done us, or by Law. Concerning Contracts I have spoken sufficiently. Let us now come unto that which is naturally due unto us, by reason of wrong done unto us. For every fault (whether it be by Commission, or Omission) that is repugnant to that which men, either in respect to common humanity, or in respect to their particular qualities or callings ought to do, we here call a wrong: From such a default their naturally arises this Obligation (in case any Damage be done us,) namely, that reparation be made us.

II. Damage is that which is repugnat to Right strictly so taken.

Damage is haply derived *à demendo (i. e.)* from something that is taken away from us. It is τὸ ἔλαττον, when a man receives less than what is his Right, or his own, whether that Right do accrue unto him by Nature meerly, or by the access of some humane fact, as by Dominion, by Contract, or by Law; by Nature a mans own is his life, (not to destroy it, but to preserve it,) his Limbs, his Reputation, his Honour, and his peculiar actions. By Dominion and by Contracts, how any thing becomes our own, we have been taught, by what hath been already said, and that in respect, as well to things, as to other mens actions. So likewise by Law, there ariseth to every man his own Right; for that the Law claimeth the same or a greater right over the persons, and Estates of Subjects, than any private man can have over his own. Thus hath a Pupil a Right to exact from his Guardian his utmost care; so hath the Commonwealth from the Magistrate; and not only the Commonwealth, but every Citizen so far forth as the Law shall warrant it either expresly, or by sufficient consequence. But from any mans Aptitude or fitness only, because it is not so properly called a Right, and that it belongs to that kind of Justice which is Distributive, no true Dominion or property can arise; and therefore no obligation to restitution: Because that is not instantly his own, for which he is fit or capable. For as *Aristotle* well observes, *He cannot be said to transgress the rules of Justice properly so called, who out of parsimony relieves not a poor man with his mony.* *This*, saith Cicero, *is the condition of*

Nic. v. c. 4. Orat. pro. Cn. Planco.

of a free State, that they can by their Votes, either give to, or take away from any man what they please. And yet he presently subjoyns, That it sometimes happens that the people may do even what they will, not what they ought, where the word, *Ought*, is taken in its larger signification.

III. A strict Right distinguisht from a bare fitness.

But here we must take heed, that we do not confound things that are of diverse kinds. For, He to whom the choice of Magistrates is committed, is obliged to the Commonwealth to chuse a man that is worthy; and to exact this of him, the Commonwealth hath a peculiar Right, in so much that if by his evil choice, The Commonwealth sustain any damage, he is bound to repair it: so any Citizen that is not unworthy, though he have no proper Right to any Office, yet hath he this true Right, that he may be a Competitor for it as well as others. And in case he shall be either by fraud or force hindred in this his Right, he may sue for satisfaction, though not to the value of the Office he sought, yet to the value of his uncertain damage. The like may be said of him to whom a Testator would, but being by fraud or force hindred, cannot give a Legacy. For a capacity to receive a Legacy is a certain Right; and consequently to hinder the Testator of his freedom to bequeath it, is an injury that requires reparation.

IV. A Damage extends to the fruits and profits;

A man shall be understood to have less than his due, and consequently to be damnified, not only in the thing it self, but in those things, which are properly the fruits arising from it, whether it be perceived or not; if he was to have perceived them, deducting the costs, which he was at in the meliorating of the thing, or the charges which he necessarily should have been at in the perceiving of them, according to that rule, that forbids us to make our selves gainers by other mens losses.

V. And to the gain that ceaseth, and how.

So also the hopes of gain, by that which is our own is valuable, not as if it were gained, but according to the nearness of our hopes to gain it; as the nearness of the Harvest to him that in hopes thereof sowed his own Land.

VI. Of Damages given Primarily.

Besides him that immediately doth the wrong, others also may be obliged to reparation, either by doing what they ought not, or by not doing what they ought to have done. By doing, and that either Primarily, or Secondarily: Primarily, as he that commands the doing of it, he that being required, gives his consent unto it, he that assists in the action, or is ready to receive what is injuriously taken away, or that shall participate of the wrong done, by any other means.

VII. Secondarily.

Secondarily, they are bound to reparation which give their advice before it be done, or that commend them that did it, being done. For as *Totilas* in his Oration to the *Goths* observes, He that commends a Malefactor, even he is to be reputed the Author of the fact: And as *Ulpian* speaks concerning an evil Servant, whom (if upon the discovery of his intentions, to run away from his Master, or to steal any thing from him) another man shall commend, That man is bound to give satisfaction; for we ought not by our commendations to encourage a Malefactor to sin. For, as *Cicero* observes in his *Philippicks*, What difference is there between him that perswades to an unjust act, and him that commends it, being done?

VIII. They that by not doing, occasion the Damage Primarily;

By not doing what he ought, a man may be bound to reparation two ways, Primarily, or Secondarily: Primarily, as when he that hath a Right properly so called, expresly to forbid the doing of it, or to defend him who hath the wrong done him, doth it not: for such a man the *Chaldee* Paraphrast calls *obfirmator*, a strengthener of wickedness, *qui non vetat cum potest, jubet*; He that hinders not when he may, commands. He is not only guilty that sets fire to his Neighbours house, but he also, who could have hindred it, but would not.

IX. And Secondarily.

Secondarily, He that doth not disswade, when he ought, or shall conceal the fact which he ought to discover. In all which cases the word *debet* (*i. e.*) ought, is to be referred to that which is a mans proper Right, strictly taken, whereunto Commutative Justice hath respect; whether that Right do arise from the Law, or from any quality in the person. For if it be due only by the rule of Charity, the omission thereof may be a sin, but not such as shall oblige to reparation; for to this it is required that there should be some proper and peculiar Right, as we have said before.

X. What is required as to this.

Where also it must be observed, that all these do so stand obliged, as we have said, if they are truly the cause of the damage given, (*i. e.*) if they do contribute any thing of moment to either the whole or any part of it. For if it ſhall evidently appear, that he that did the wrong had certainly done it, even without their act or neglect, as it often falls out in thoſe of the Second order, and ſometimes in thoſe of the Firſt, They are not bound to reparation. Which notwithſtanding is not ſo to be underſtood, that if there wanted not others that would adviſe and help, they that did ſo, are not obliged; if he that occaſioned the damage had not done it without Counſel and aſſiſtance. For even thoſe others alſo, if they had counſelled and aſſiſted, had been partakers of the ſin, and ſo obliged to reparation.

XI. In what order they are bound. But they are principally bound, who by their own command, or by ſome other means, did compel another to do the wrong: But if they fail, then he that did the fact, and after him the reſt: Every one that contributed aid or advice to the fact, are bound to make reparation, for the whole damage, if the whole fact proceeded from them, though not from them alone.

XII. The obligation extends to the Damages that are conſequent. He that is guilty of the fact, is alſo guilty of all the evil conſequences that enſue by reaſon of that fact. *Seneca* in one of his Controverſies handles this queſtion, putting the caſe in one who ſetting fire to a *Plane-Tree*, burnt thereby the houſes adjoyning, and gives his opinion thus, *Although thou didſt not intend thy Neighbour ſo great an injury, yet art thou bound to ſatisfie the whole, as if thou hadſt done it purpoſely; for he ought to be innocent, as to every part of the wrong done, that would excuſe himſelf by his imprudence.* *Ariarathes* King of *Cappadocia* damming up, in wantonneſs, the mouth of the River *Melanus*, cauſed the Waters to ſwell and rage with that violence, that forcing its way into the River *Euphrates*, did ſo ſwell that River alſo, that waſhing away a great part of the *Cappadocian* Land, it did much harm to the Inhabitans of *Galatia* and *Phrygia*: which matter being referred to the *Romans*, *Ariarathes* was adjudged to pay them 300 Talents to ſatisfie the damage thereby ſuſtained.

XIII. An example in an Homicide: For examples let theſe ſuffice. Firſt, He that kills a man unjuſtly, is bound to pay the charge of Phyſicians and Chirurgeons, if any ſuch there be; yea, and to nouriſh all that depend upon the perſon killed, for life, and lively-hood, as Parents, Wife, Children; and to give ſatisfaction proportionable to the hopes of that Aliment, conſideration being had to the Age of the perſon killed, and to other Circumſtances. As we read of *Hercules*, who the better to expiate the Murther of *Iphitus* whom he had ſlain, paid a great ſumm of money to his children, for the wrongs they ſuſtained by their Fathers death. For, as *Michael Epheſius* well obſerves, *What is ſo paid, is in a manner paid to him that is killed.* We ſpeak here of an unjuſt Homicide, (*i. e.*) of him who having no lawful power given him, ſhall commit ſuch an act of violence, that occaſions the death of the party injured; wherefore if a man ſhall have a Right to do it, but ſhall offend againſt Charity, as he that will not fly away, he ſhall not be obliged to reparation. The life of a Freeman is unvaluable, but otherwiſe of a Servant who may be ſold.

XIV. In him that maimeth another: So he that hath maimed a man, and deprived him of one of his Limbs, is bound to pay all charges, and to ſatisfie him for the loſs of his Limb, by reaſon whereof he is uncapable of making that improvement of his labour, as otherwiſe he might have done. But as I ſaid (before) of the life, ſo here I ſay of the Limbs of a Free-man, that they cannot be valued. The like may be ſaid in caſe of falſe Impriſonment.

XV. In an Adulterer: So alſo the Adulterer and Adultereſs are bound, not only to ſave the Husband harmleſs as to the Childs nouriſhment, but to repair whatſoever Damage the Children that are Legitimate, ſhall afterwards ſuſtain by any ſhare or portion, that that Child ſhall claim in the Inheritance. If a man ſhall either by force or fraud vitiate a Virgin, he ſhall be obliged to pay her ſo much as ſhe ſhall be thought to be damnified in her hopes of Marriage: and if he obtained the uſe of her body by the promiſe of Marriage, he ſtands obliged to perform his promiſe.

XVI. In a Thief or Robbers, and others: A Thief or Robber is bound to reſtore the thing taken away, together with its natural increment, and the enſuing Damage, or the ſurceaſing of his gains; but if the thing taken away do periſh, then the value of it, not to the higheſt rate, nor to the loweſt, but moderated. Among theſe, we may alſo rank ſuch as defraud Princes of their lawful Cuſtoms, and Contributions. In like manner are they bound to reparation that have wronged others, by either their unjuſt ſentence, or unjuſt accuſation, or by their falſe Teſtimony.

XVII. In him that by fear or fraud causeth a Promise.

As alſo, he that ſhall either by fraud, force or unjuſt fear urge a Contract or a Promiſe from any man, is bound to make reparation to the full: For hereby he robs the man he deals with of a double Right; Firſt, By the nature of Contracts, he had this Right, That he ought not to be deceived; And then by the natural liberty that every man ſhould have, He ought not to be enforced, or unjuſtly affrighted. And among theſe, we may likewiſe range thoſe that will not perform, what by their Office they are bound to do, without Bribes.

XVIII. What if the fear be naturally juſt.

But he that hath given juſt cauſe why he ought to be, by force or fear compelled, hath reaſon to blame himſelf. For an involuntary act ariſing from a voluntary, is naturally reckoned for a voluntary.

XIX. What if the fear be held by the Law of Nations, for juſt.

But as, by the conſent of Nations, all Wars made and denounced by the Supream power on both ſides are reputed juſt, as to the external effects (whereof we ſhall ſpeak more anon) ſo is the fear of ſuch a War, ſo far reputed juſt, That whatſoever is obtained thereby cannot be required back. In which ſenſe, that diſtinction of *Cicero's* may be admitted, which he makes between an Enemy, with whom we enjoy by the conſent of Nations many common Rights; and a Thief or Pirate. For if theſe extort any thing from us by fear, we may require it back, unleſs we are bound by Oath not to do it: But ſo we cannot do from an Enemy. Wherefore what *Polybius* writes concerning the Second *Punick* War (namely, that the *Carthaginians* had juſt cauſe to make it, becauſe the *Romans* (by denouncing War againſt them, whilſt they were engaged in another War againſt their Seditious Mercenaries) had enforced them from the Iſland of *Sardinia*, and a great ſum of money) hath indeed ſome ſhew of Equity, but is not agreeable with the Common Right of Nations, as we ſhall elſewhere prove.

XX. How far the Civil power is bound by Damages done by their Subjects, by reaſon of Letters of Mart granted them.

Kings and Magiſtrates are obliged to reparation, if they do not make uſe of ſuch remedies againſt Thieves and Pirates, to ſuppreſs them as they may, and ought to do: For which neglect, the *Scyrians* were condemned by the *Amphictyones*. I remember that this caſe was once propoſed amongſt us, when our Eſtates having granted Letters of Mart againſt our Enemies, ſome of thoſe to whom theſe Letters were granted, abuſing themſelves and us; had robbed our friends, and leaving our Country, betook themſelves to the Seas, and though recalled, would not return: whence aroſe this queſtion, Whether our States were bound to repair the damages, either becauſe they made uſe of ſuch wicked inſtruments, or becauſe they did not require from them ſufficient caution that they ſhould not tranſgreſs their Commiſſions: Whereunto I gave this anſwer, That they were obliged to no more than to puniſh them being found, or to deliver them up: And beſides, to take care that reparation ſhould be made out of the Goods of the Delinquents. For that the States were not the cauſes of the depredations, nor did they participate of them: that they had forbidden them by ſevere Laws to wrong their friends; but to require Caution from them, they were not by any Law obliged, ſeeing that they might empower all their Subjects without any Codicils, to make what ſpoil they could, of whatſoever was their Enemies, as had been anciently done: Neither was this permiſſion, the true cauſe of the wrongs done unto their friends; ſeeing that private men might arm their Ships, and put out to Sea, even without permiſſion. Neither could they foreſee that theſe men would prove wicked: Nor could they altogether avoid, the making uſe of wicked men; for then it was not poſſible for them to raiſe an Army: Neither if their Souldiers either by Sea or Land did injure their friends, contrary to the Command of the Supream Magiſtrate, were they obliged to reparation, as might eaſily be proved by the Teſtimonies of *France* and *England*. (Yet in a League between *Francis de Valois* King of *France*, and *Henry* the Eighth of *England*, it was agreed the better to prevent Depredations by Sea, that no Merchant of either Nation ſhould depart out of their Ports without giving Caution to their reſpective Admirals, that no wrong or moleſtation ſhould be done by Sea to either of their Subjects.) But that any man ſhould be bound to repair the Damages which his Servants ſhall without his fault, and againſt his command, do unto others, belongs not to the Law of Nations, by which this cauſe ought properly to be judged; but to the Civil Law, and yet not in the general, but as it is introduced for ſome particular reaſons againſt Mariners, and ſome others. And thus hath this caſe been determined by the Judges of the Supreme Aſſembly, againſt certain *Pomeranians*, and that according to Precedents of things of the like nature, two ages before.

A judged caſe.

Herbert's Henry the 8. page 54.

XXI. The owner of a Ship or Beast that hurts his Neighbour, not bound by the Law of Nature.

This also is worthy our observation, that it proceeds from the Civil Law, and not from the Law of Nature, That we deliver up our Beast, or Bond-slaves to punishment, which have endamaged our Neighbour. For the owner of them being innocent is naturally bound to nothing, as neither is he, whose Ship without his fault, falls foul and hurts another; though by the Law of diverse Nations, as well as ours, such Damages are usually divided between both, because it is very difficult to be proved.

XXII. The Damage against a mans honour how to be repaired.

But the wounds we receive in our Honour, or Fame, as by Stripes, Reproaches, Curses, and such like, must have their proper cures.* And in these no less than in Theft, and other Crimes, the hainousness of the fact is discerned by the effect. For as in those, our reparation consists in the punishment of the Thief; so in this, The Damage we sustain is repaired by confession of the fault, and by exhibiting all due Honour to him who is wronged, and the publick Testimony given both of his innocency, and our own repentance, and such like means: Although the offender in this kind may be punished in his purse, if the injured person desire it, because money is the Common Standard whereby all things tending to profit, are measured.

CHAP.

CHAP. XVIII.

Of the Rights of Embassages.

WE have hitherto discoursed of such things, as by the Law of Nature are due unto us, interserting some few things which the voluntary Law of Nations hath supperadded to the Law of Nature. It remains now that we come to such obligations, as the very voluntary Law of Nations hath of it self introduced: Whereof the chiefest head is, of the Rights of Embassages. We have in all Histories, mention made of the Sacred and Inviolable Rights of Embassages, of the Sanctimony of Embassadors: The Right of Nations peculiarly due unto them: The Rights of Embassages Sacred amongst all Nations. I. The Rights of Embassages arise from the Law of Nations.

Sanctum populis per sacula Nomen.

Ages and Nations do this name revere.

saith *Papinius*. *If any man shall strike an Embassador, though sent from an Enemy, he is said to violate the Law of Nations, because Embassadors are accounted Sacred,* saith *Pomponius*. And therefore *If whilst an Embassador from any Nation, is resident with us, War be denounced against them, it is agreeable to the Law of Nations that (if he please) he may remain with us.* Quintus Mucius *would have him that presumes to strike an Embassador, to be delivered up to that Enemy, whose Embassador he was. Josephus* also highly extolls the Sacred priviledges of Embassadors, who are honoured with the same name and title, as are the Angels, who are Gods Embassadors. *Corpora Legatorum Sancta, The persons of Legats,* saith *Varro, are Holy.* So likewise *Cicero, The Rights of Embassadors are guarded by all Laws both Divine and Humane, whose very name is so venerable, that it secures their persons not only among the Laws of their friends, but among the very weapons of their Enemies.* Wherefore to violate this Right, is not unjust only, but impious, ἔργον ἀσεβὲς, as *Plutarch* calls it. Wherewith accords that also of *Josephus*, where he saith, *That the very name of an Embassador is so Sacred, that it is able to reconcile one Enemy to another: For what can argue more impiety, than to kill Embassadors, interceeding for Peace.* And *to speak generally,* saith *Totilas, Embassadors are reverenced among all Nations, though Barbarous.* And good reason, For, *even in the midst of War, they are the sole Mediators for Peace, and he that assumes the Office of an Embassador, doth for that time put off the condition of an enemy.*

L. Si quis. D. de Legationibus. *Ant. lib. 15.* *Varro. 3.* *Vit. Æmil.* *Ant. lib. 15.* *Procop. Goth. 3.*

But

II. Among whom this Right takes place.

But yet we must in the first place, know that this Right of Nations, whatever it be, belongs to such Legats only, who are sent by such as have the Soveraign power, in both Nations between themselves. For such as are sent from Provinces, particular Cities, or other subordinate powers, are governed not by the Law of Nations, which is between diverse people, but by the Civil Law. An Embassador in *Livy* calls himself the Publick Messenger of the people of *Rome*: And in another place, the *Roman* Senate declares that the Right of Embassages was granted, not to a Citizen, but to a Foreigner: And *Cicero* to prove that they ought not to send Embassadors to *M. Anthony*, saith, *Non enim cum* Hannibale *res est, hoste reipublicæ, sed cum cive*; *For we have not now to do with* Hannibal, *a publick Enemy, but with a Citizen and a Subject.* Now what is meant by a Foreigner, *Virgil* will inform us, as well as any Lawyer can do:

A Foreign Land is that, as I suppose,
Which being free, to us no duty owes.

But they that are Confederates, though upon Terms very unequal; yet because they are *sui juris, a free people*, have likewise this Right of sending Embassages: Yea, and they also that are partly Subjects, and partly free, for that part wherein they are free. But such things as are conquered in a solemn War, and driven out of their Kingdoms do lose, together with their other goods, this Right of sending Embassadors. And therefore did *Paulus Æmilius*, (having conquered *Perseus* in open War) detain the Heralds, which he sent unto him. But yet, in Civil Wars necessity doth sometimes plead for the admittance of this Right, though irregular: As namely, when the people are so equally divided into parts, that it is an hard matter to judge, in whether part consists the Right of Empire; or when two persons with very equal titles, contend for the Succession. For in this case, one Nation for that time may be accounted as two. Thus are the *Flaviani* accused by *Tacitus*, that in their Civil discord, they had violated the Right of Embassadors, Sacred even among Barbarous Nations, in the *Vitellians*. And *Magnensius* in *Zosimus* did long debate it in his mind, whether he should dismiss *Philip*, who was sent him on an Embassy from *Constantine* without answer, or despising the priviledges of Embassadors, detain him. Pirats and Thieves being enemies to Civil Society, can have no benefit by the Law of Nations. *Spartactus* in *Appian* offered to enter into a League with *Crassus*, but was rejected with scorn; and *Tiberius*, when *Tacfarinus* sent Embassadors to him, was highly vexed, to see a Traitor and a Thief to treat with him, after the manner of Enemies: Which are the very words of *Tacitus*. Yet sometimes these also are admitted to the Rights of Embassages, upon their Faith given. As of old those Fugitives, in the *Pyrenean* Woods, were, whom *Cæsar* mentions. Yet was this a particular indulgence given at that time by him, which by the Law of Nations was not due, nor ought to be given to Subjects.

Hist. l. 3. *Zos. l. 11.* *Lib. 3. de bello civili.*

III. Whether an Embassage be always to be admitted.

There is a twofold Right due to Embassadors by the Law of Nations: First, that they be admitted; Secondly, That they be not injured. As concerning the former, *Livy* brings in *Hanno* inveighing against *Hannibal*, in the Senate of *Carthage*, thus, *Our goodly General refuseth to admit into his Camp Embassadors coming from friends, and for friends.* Jus Gentium sustulit, *He hath broken the Law of Nations*: which notwithstanding must not be understood so largely as if none should be denyed; for a Prince may deny an Embassador admittance; and he may command him to depart his Kingdom, if he behave himself seditiously, but that none should be without cause denyed: Now causes there may be, First, from him that sends, Secondly, from him that is sent, and Thirdly, from the matter of Embassage. As to the first, we read that *Pericles* dismist *Melesippus*, the *Lacedæmonian* Embassador, beyond the Territories of *Athens*, because he came from an Armed Enemy. And the *Roman* Senate denyed admission to the *Carthaginian* Embassador, because they had an Army in the heart of *Italy*. So did the *Achaians* to the Embassadors of *Perseus*, because he attempted a War against the *Romans*. The like did *Justinian* to the Embassadors of *Totilas*, and the *Goths* in *Urbin* to the messengers of *Belisarius*. And the Embassadors of the *Scythians*, because they were a people notoriously wicked, were in all places repulsed, as *Polybius* testifies. As concerning the second

Vid. Camden An. 1571. Quæst. 4. Livy l. 41. Zonaras.

cond cause (*i. e.*) from the person sent; an example we have in *Theodorus* the Atheist, to whom *Lysimachus* refused to give Audience, though he came as an Embassador from King *Ptolomy*: The like hath been done to others, for no other cause but personal hatred. The third is, when the ground or reason of him that sends is suspected to move Sedition, as was that of *Rabshakeh* rejected by *Hezekiah*, and the like: Or when the matter or form is not well suited to the dignity of the person with whom we treat, or not so well timed. So the *Romans* forbad the *Ætolians* to send out any Embassadors without their Generals permission: And *Perseus* was forbidden from sending any Embassadors to *Rome*, but only to *Licinius*; so they commanded the Embassadors of *Jugurtha* to depart out of *Italy* within ten dayes, unless they came to deliver their King and Kingdom into the power of the *Romans*. So the Emperour *Charles* the Fifth commanded the Embassadors sent to denounce War against him, from *France*, *Venice* and *Florence*, to be conducted to a place thirty miles distant from his Court, as *Guicciardine* records it. And thus may those Ordinary Embassadors which are constantly resident in most Courts, be worthily rejected as unnecessary, and a new upstart custome whereof former Ages were wholly ignorant.

Rabshakeh's Case, 2 Kings 18.

Lib. 18.

IV. Against such Embassadors as raise Sedition, our defence is lawful, but not their punishment.

Concerning the latter priviledge of Embassadors, namely, That they should not be molested, the question is more arduous and knotty; and by the best Wits of this Age, variously handled. In the stating whereof, they have respect, First, To the persons, Secondly, To their Attendants, Thirdly, To their Goods. As to their Persons, some think, that they are to be protected against all unjust force only, esteeming their priviledges to be understood of Common Right. Others are of opinion, that the persons of Emperours are not for every cause to be molested, but only when they themselves do violate the Law of Nations, which opens a door so wide, that all delinquencies are punishable in Emperours, except such as are committed against the Civil Law: For in those committed against the Law of Nations, are contained even those that are committed against the Law of Nature. Others do yet restrain this force to those, who shall be found to act any thing against the State of the Common-wealth, or against the honour and dignity of the person to whom they are sent: which some think to be of dangerous consequence; and therefore would have complaint made to him that sent them, and the Embassadors sent home, to be by him punished. Others there are, who think it fit in this case to appeal to other Kings and Free States, that are not concerned; desiring their advice therein, which indeed may stand with prudence, but not to be imposed upon us as a Law. The Arguments which every one of these do bring to strengthen their several opinions, do conclude nothing certainly: Because this Right is not grounded upon reasons that are certain, as the Law of Nature is, but it receives its bounds from the consent of Nations. Now the Nations may either altogether provide for the safety of Embassadors, or with some certain exceptions. For advantages may by either of these arise to the Common-wealth: By this latter, the punishment inflicted upon such as notoriously offend, deters others, and secures the peace of that Nation. By the former, the profit ariseth to the State by Embassies, which are the more easily and willingly undertaken, when the persons sent are encouraged thereunto, as knowing that the greatest care that can be, is taken for their security; we are therefore to observe, how far forth the Nations did agree in this point; which cannot be evinced by examples alone. For of these we have enough extant on either side; we must therefore have recourse herein, as well to the Judgement of the Wisest Men, as to our own most probable conjectures. For the Judgement of the Wisest Men are guided by two notable precedents; one out of *Livy*, the other out of *Salust*. That out of *Livy*, by the Embassadors of *Tarquine*, who pretended only to treat with the Senate about some of *Tarquine's* Goods, but were found conspiring with the Citizens to betray the City. And when it was moved in the Senate, What should be done with them, It was at length resolved on, *That though they deserved to be proceeded against as enemies*, yet *valuit Jus Gentium*, *The Law of Nations must be preserved.* Whence we may conclude, That by the Law of Nations, Protection is due unto Embassadors, though they should be found plotting against the State they are sent unto. That in *Salust*, doth more immediately respect the Concomitants of Embassadors, than Embassadors themselves; and yet by an Argument drawn from that which is less credible, to that which is more, may serve to prove, what the Law of Nations allows to Embassadors in the case aforesaid. *Salust* speaking of *Bomilcar*, who came to *Rome* as an Assistant in the Embassage, but was found stirring up the Citizens to Rebellion, saith thus, *Fit reus magis ex æquo bonoque quam ex jure Gentium*;

tium; He was made Guilty, rather by the Rules of Equity, than by the Law of Nations. Where by *æquum & bonum*, is meant the meer Law of Nature, which requires, that he that doth evil, should suffer for it being found. But the Law of Nations excepts from this General Rule, Embassadors, and such as (like them) come upon the security of the Publick Faith. Wherefore it is contrary to the Interest of the Law of Nations, that Embassadors should be held guilty, as many other things are, which are permitted by the Law of Nature. Our conjectures also may be thus guided. Most probable it is, that the priviledges granted to Embassadors, are somewhat more than what is due unto others by common right. But in case they are no longer to be secured, than whilst they live regularly, what have they more than others? Besides the benefit that accrews unto the Common-wealth by securing their persons, doth by much preponderate that which we may hope for in their punishment. For his punishment may be required of him that sent him, if he be willing: which if refused, then we can but make War upon him, as being accessary to the crime by his approving it. But some will object, That it is better that one should be punished, than a multitude engaged in a War. But if he that sent the Embassador do approve of his Fact, the punishment of the Embassador cannot free us from the Danger. (Now whether it be safest for the Common-wealth, to connive and dissemble the fact, or to run the hazard of a War, will be the question). On the other side, the safety of Embassadors, would be but slenderly provided for, if they were to give an account to any, but unto him that sent them. For since the designs of them that send Embassadors, and of those to whom they are sent, are for the most part diverse, if not contrary, it cannot possibly be, but that some of their Actions will seem to be criminous. And although some are so manifest, as not to admit of any doubt, yet is the universal danger sufficient for the equity and benefit of an universal Law. Wherefore mine opinion is, That by the Consent of Nations, that Common Custome which requires, that every man that resides in a Foreign Countrey, should conform himself to the Laws and Customes of that Countrey, should except Embassadors, who as they are imagined to be the persons of them that send them: (for so speaks *Cicero* of a certain Embassador, *Senatus Faciem secum attulerat, He brought with him the Majesty of a Senate, the Authority of a Common-wealth.*) So may they be imagined to live in their own Countrey; and therefore not bound by the Civil Laws of the place they are really in. Wherefore if the offence be such as may safely be slighted, it is either to be dissembled, or the Embassador commanded to depart the Kingdom; which (as *Polybius* tells us) was done unto him who procured the Flight of the Hostages from *Rome*. The like was done by *Stephen* King of *Poland*, to the *Muscovite* Embassadour, and by Queen *Elizabeth*, to the *Scottish* and *Spanish* Embassadors. For when *Mendoza* the *Spanish* Embassador, was found practising with *Throckmorton* and others to bring in a Foreign Power into *England*, and to depose the Queen; he being a man of a Turbulent Spirit, and abusing the priviledges of an Embassador, was commanded to depart the Realm. But when the Bishop of *Rosse* delegated Embassador from the imprisoned Queen of *Scots*, was found designing means both within the Kingdom of *England*, and without, to raise Rebellion, and to procure a Foreign Invasion: It being demanded of the most Learned Civilians of that Age, Whether an Embassador raising Rebellion against the Prince, to whom he was sent, might enjoy the priviledges of an Embassador; it was answered, That he had thereby lost his priviledge, and might be punished: as *Camden* records it *Anno* 1571. and 1584. And we may also remember, that at another time the *Romans* caused the *Tarentine* Embassadors to be whipt with Rods, for conveying their hostages out of *Rome*; but this was done, because the *Tarentines* being conquered, began then to be under the Jurisdiction of the *Romans*. So we read of *Charles* the Fifth, that he commanded the Embassador of the Duke of *Millain*, as being his Subject, that he should not depart his Court without leave, as *Guicciardine* relates it. But in case the Crime be heinous and menacing present danger to the State, then is the Embassador to be sent back to his Master, with demand, That he either punish him, or deliver him up to be punished: as we read of the *Gaules*, that they demanded the *Fabii* to be delivered up unto them. But, as I have often said before, *All humane Laws are so made, that they oblige not in extream necessity*; the same may also be said of these Rights of Embassadors. Wherefore that we may prevent some imminent danger, especially to the Common-wealth, if no fitter means can be thought on, we may both apprehend and examine him; as the *Roman* Consuls did the Embassadors of *Tarquin*, All intercourse by Letters being in the first place prevented, as *Livy* directs †. *Pelopidas* was imprisoned by *Alexander Pheræus*, for that being an Embassador, he stirred up the *Thessalians* to liberty. But in case an Embassador shall attempt to assault another man by force of Arms, surely he may be killed; not by

† *Literarum imprimis habita cura, ne interciderent.*
Plut. Vit. Pel. Off. l. 3.

by way of puniſhment, but by way of Natural Defence. So the *Gaules* might have killed the *Fabii*, whom *Livy* brands, as being the Infringers of humane Right. Wherefore when the Herald in *Euripides* attempted by force to reſcue the Suppliants, he was by force reſiſted; and when the Herald demanded of him,

Dar'ſt thou, an Herald, hither ſent, to ſmite?

He was anſwered,

Yes, if that Herald firſt begin so fight.

And becauſe that Herald did act by Force and Violence, he was ſlain by the people of *Athens*, as *Philoſtratus* records in the Life of *Herod*. By the like diſtinction, doth *Cicero* reſolve this Queſtion, Whether a Son ought to accuſe his own Father being a Traytor to his Countrey? Namely, if the Danger be great and imminent, he ought by way of prevention; but in caſe the danger be paſt, he ought not by way of puniſhment for the Fact. *The very Name of an Embaſſador*, ſaith *Theodatus* the *Goth* to the Emperour *Juſtinian*'s Embaſſador, *is with all men held as ſacred and honourable; which honour they may juſtly claim, whileſt they uphold their dignity by their modeſty. For moſt men are of opinion, that it is lawful to kill an Embaſſador, if he be injurious to the perſon of him to whom he is ſent, or ſhall defile himſelf, by violating the Rights of Marriage.* And when ſome Embaſſadors did alledge, that they were ſo far from the ſuſpicion of committing Adultery, that they could not ſtir abroad without a Guard, they prudently added, *That if an Embaſſador did deliver no other Meſſage, than what he received from his Maſter, though it were never ſo unpleaſant, he was not faulty, but he that ſent him: For there was nothing committed unto him, but that he ſhould faithfully diſcharge the Commands that were given him.*

Offic. l. 3.

Camden anno 1571.

V. He is not bound to theſe Laws of Embaſſages, to whom the Embaſſador is not ſent.

This Law of ſecuring Embaſſadors from Force or Violence, obligeth him to whom they are ſent, at leaſt when they are admitted; as if from that time, there had paſſed between them a Tacit Covenant. But before they are received, they can claim no ſuch priviledge: becauſe he to whom they are ſent, may haply declare, that they ſhall not be received: And if ſo, then they ſhall be accounted as enemies: As the *Romans* premoniſhed the *Ætolians*, and as the ſame *Romans* long ſince, by an Edict ſignified to the *Vejentine* Embaſſadors, That unleſs they departed the City, they would ſhew them no more mercy, than *Tolumnius* their King had ſhewed to the *Roman* Embaſſadors, whom he commanded to be killed. And as the *Samnites* declared to the *Romans*, namely, That if they entred into any Aſſembly in *Samninus*, they ſhould not depart in ſafety. This Law therefore, reacheth not unto thoſe through whoſe Territories Embaſſadors preſume to paſs without Licence. For if they are going to their Enemies, or coming from them, or do otherwiſe attempt any Act of Hoſtility, they may be even killed. Thus did the *Athenians* ſerve the Embaſſadors paſſing between the *Perſians* and the *Spartans*: So did the *Illyrians*, thoſe that went between the *Eſſians* and the *Romans*: Much more being taken, may they be bound and kept in Priſon; as *Xenophon* paſt Judgement upon ſome, and *Alexander* againſt thoſe which were ſent from *Thebes* and *Lacedæmon* unto *Darius*; and the *Romans* againſt the Embaſſadors ſent to *Hannibal*. But if no ſuch thing be, and yet the Embaſſadors be evil treated, the Law of Nations, whereof we now ſpeak, is not thereby violated: but the honour of thoſe Princes, either from whom they came, or unto whom they were ſent, is thereby wounded, and all friendſhip with them broken. Thus writes *Juſtine* concerning *Philip* the latter King of *Macedon*, *That he ſent his Embaſſador with Letters to contract Friendſhip with* Hannibal; *who being taken, and brought before the* Roman *Senate, was diſmiſt with ſafety. Not in honour to the King, but leſt of a doubtful Friend, they ſhould thereby make him their certain Enemy.* But it is otherwiſe in caſe any Prince ſhall lay in wait to ſurprize the Embaſſador of another Prince, without his own Territories: for this is a violation of the Law of Nations; as is plain by the Oration of the *Theſſalians* againſt King *Philip* recorded by *Livy*.

Liv. l. 27. Id. l. 4. Lib. 10.

Thucyd. l. 2.

Lib. 29.

VI. An Enemy is hereunto obliged if the Embaſſador be ſent unto him. * *Vide* §. 1. † *L. ult. D. de Legatis.* ‖ *Ann. l.* 1. *Verrin.* 1. *Lib.* 5. *c.* 2.

But on the other ſide, the Embaſſage being admitted, the Law of Nations protects the perſon ſent, even among thoſe Nations that are in Actual Arms one againſt another, much more among ſuch as are barely Enemies. It is very true, what *Diodorus Siculus* ſaith, *That Heralds enjoy Peace in the midſt of War.* The *Lacedæmonians* who killed the Heralds, ſent from the *Perſians*, are ſaid to break the Law of all Nations *. *If any man ſhall ſtrike an Embaſſador coming from an Enemy, he ſhall be judged* (ſaith *Pomponius* †) *as one that hath violated the Common Right of all Nations; becauſe their perſons are generally held as ſacred.* And *Tacitus* calls this Right ‖, whereof we now treat, *the Right of Enemies, the Sanctimony of Embaſſies, and the Law of Nations, approved by God himſelf.* So likewiſe *Cicero*, *Nonne Legati inter hoſtes incolumes eſſe debent? Ought not Embaſſadors to be ſecured, though among Troops of Armed Foes?* And *Seneca* in his Books of Anger, *He offered violence even to Embaſſadors, thereby ſpurning at the Law of Nations. A villainous Act, a wicked Cauſe, an impious Murder*, as *Livy* calls it, in the Story of the *Fidenates* aſſaſſinating the *Roman* Embaſſadors: And in another place, when their Embaſſadors were brought into great danger, he ſaith, *Ne belli quidem jura relicta ſunt; They had not left amongſt them ſo much* *Lib.* 4. *as the Rights of War.* So *Curtius*, *He ſent Embaſſadors to compel them to peace, whom the* Tyrians *killed and threw headlong into the Sea, contrary to the Law of Nations.* And deſervedly: For even in War many things fall out, which cannot be tranſacted but by Embaſſadors; and very hardly can Peace at any time be made without them.

VII. Neither are Embaſſadors liable to the Law of Retaliation.

Another Queſtion doth uſually ariſe, namely, Whether a Prince may retaliate the wrongs done unto his own Embaſſadors, upon the Embaſſadors of him who did that wrong? And ſurely, we may find in Hiſtories, many examples of revenges taken in this way. And no marvel, for Hiſtorians do uſually record, not only things that are juſtly and piouſly done, but thoſe alſo that are done unjuſtly, in heat of anger, raſhly, and impotently. But the Law of Nations doth not only carefully provide for the honour of the Perſon ſending, but for the ſecurity of the Perſon ſent. So that there is, as it were, a ſilent Contract made between the Embaſſador ſent, and the Prince to whom he goes. And therefore though there ſhould be no injuſtice done, in reſpect of the Prince that ſends his Embaſſador, as having juſtly deſerved it for the affront given him in the wrongs done unto his Embaſſador; yet to the perſon ſent there would be done a manifeſt injuſtice, becauſe by vertue of that tacite agreement he might juſtly claim his Indemnity. And therefore it was not only magnanimouſly, but juſtly done by *Scipio*, according to the Law of Nations, who though the *Roman* Embaſſadors had been very hardly uſed at *Carthage*, yet when the *Romans* brought the *Carthaginian* Embaſſadors unto him, demanding what ſhould be done with them; made anſwer, *Nihil tale quale factum fuit à* Carthaginenſibus; *Nothing of that which the* Carthaginians *did unto the* Romans. Or according to what *Livy* adds, *Nihil ſe factorum inſtitutis populi* Romani *indignum; That he would do nothing unworthy of the* Roman *Diſcipline.* Whereunto *Diodorus* adds this Reaſon, *Leſt what we blame in them, we juſtifie in our ſelves.* And the *Romans* themſelves, though they were not ignorant of what the *Carthaginians* had done, yet diſmiſt their Embaſſadors in ſafety. Thus did *Conſtantius* remit *Titianus*, being ſent unto him by *Magnentius*; though his own Embaſſador, *Philip*, ſent unto *Magnentius*, had been hy him detained, as *Zoſimon* teſtifies. And when long before the *Roman* Embaſſador, *Cornelius Aſina*, was put in Chains by the *Carthaginians*, and *Hanno* the *Carthaginian* Embaſſador, being at that time in *Rome*, was afraid of the like meaſure, the Conſuls ſtood up in the Senate, and thus beſpake him: *Iſto te metu,* Hanno, *fides Civitatis noſtra liberet; Let the Faith of our City,* Hanno, *free thee from this fear.*

VIII. The priviledge of Embaſſadors extends to their Retinue.

Not only the Embaſſadour himſelf, but his Followers and Goods are to partake of the ſame priviledge (if he pleaſe.) And therefore the Ancient Form of words uſed by Embaſſadours and Heralds unto the Kings to whom they were ſent, were theſe, *O King, doſt thou admit of me, as the Royal Meſſenger of the People of* Rome, *together with my Goods and Followers.* And by the *Julian* Law, not only they that offered violence to the perſons of the Embaſſadours themſelves, but they that injured any of their Attendants, were found guilty, *De vi publica*, Of violence done by force and arms. But

But this Sanctimony belongs unto them, but as they are Attendants to the Embassadour, and therefore no further due than he shall please: Wherefore in case any hainous crime be committed by them, they are required to be delivered up by the Embassadour to punishment, but they are by no means to be taken from him by force. Which, when once done by the *Achaians*, who seized upon some *Lacedæmonians*, who attended upon the *Roman* Embassadours, the *Romans* presently cryed out, That they had violated the Law of Nations. Whereunto also we may refer the judgemeut of *Salust* concerning *Bomilcar*, which we have formerly quoted. But if the Embassadour shall refuse to deliver him, then we are to proceed in the same manner, as is before prescribed against the Embassadour himself. But whether the Embassadour have jurisdiction over his own Family, or whether his House be a Sanctuary for all such as shall flye unto it for refuge, depends upon the pleasure of him to whom he is sent; for this belongs not at all to the Law of Nations.

IX. And to their movable Goods.

The movable Goods also of an Embassadour, and whatsoever else shall appertain to his person, are not to be received in pawn, or attached for any debt; neither by any ordinary course of Law, nor by the hands of the King himself (which some hold as the truer opinion.) For no force or compulsion must be, by any means, used against him or his; that so he may enjoy an absolute and perfect security. And if he shall have contracted any debt, and have no real Estate (as it usually falls out) he must only be fairly intreated to discharge them; which if he refuse, then is he that sent him to be likewise intreated to pay them. But if neither will do it, then in the last place we must flee to such Remedies, as are provided against such Debtors, as do reside in Foreign Countries.

Yet is it no breach of their priviledge, that their Coffers be searched at their first entrance, in case it be according to the custom of the Country whereunto they are sent: As it happened to Sir *Thomas Chaloner* in *Spain*, who complaining thereof to Queen *Elizabeth*, and desiring to be recalled, was prudently answered by that most wise Queen, *That an Embassadour should take all things in good part, so as his Prince's Honour was not directly violated.* *Cambden Eliz. Anno 1561.*

Examples where there are Obligations, but no power to compel.

Neither is there any cause to fear (as some may imagine) that if the case be thus with Embassadours, no man will trust them, or make any Contract with them: For the King himself though he cannot be compelled to any thing, yet never wants Creditors (if they give good prices.) And among some Nations, as *Damascen* informs us, it is customable, That as to such debts as are contracted upon trust, there is no remedy provided by Law, no more than there is against men that are ungrateful: So that men in those parts are compelled, either to pay readily for what they buy, and on both sides to fulfil alike all their agreements, or to content themselves with the bare faith and credit of the Debtor. *Seneca* seems to envy the happiness of those Countries, by wishing the same custom in all places: *I would to God* (saith he) *that we could perswade all people, that Moneys lent upon credit should be recovered only from those men who were willing to pay; and that no stipulation should bind the Buyer to the Seller; and that no written Contracts or Covenants under Hand and Seal, should be preserved, but rather that the performance of them should be left to the Faith and Honesty of the Debtor.* *Appian* relates of the *Persians*, *That they hated the borrowing of mony, as being an inlet to Fraud, Falshood, and Perjury.* And *Ælian* reports the very same of the *Indians*, with whom agrees *Strabo*, in these words, *Judicia non esse nisi de cæde & injuria, &c. There are no Judicatories unless it be for Murders and Injuries done, because it is not in the power of any man to avoid these: But as to Contracts and Agreements, it is in the choice of every man to make them or to refuse them; and therefore if any man break his Faith with us, we are to bear it patiently, and to learn rather to be wise, in taking heed before hand whom we trust, than by our folly to fill the City we live in with Law-suits.* It was also wisely enacted by *Charonda*, *That no man should have his Action at Law against that man, whose Faith he thought fit to take for the price of what he sold him*; which *Plato* likewise approves of. This was also observed by *Aristotle*, *In some Countries* (saith he) *there is no recovering of such Debts by Law-suits, for*

De benef. lib. 3. c. 15. *Lib. 4.* *Lib. 15.* *L. 8. de Leg. Mor. Nic. 8. 15.*

for they conceive that men ought to acquiesce, and to be contented with the faith of that Mor. l. 9. c. 1. *man whom they thought worthy to be trusted.* So in another place, *Some Countries there are where the Laws do forbid a man to recover by Law, that which he hath trusted upon the Faith of another; as if he with whom we have made any Contract, and on whose faith we have taken, were privately only to be dealt with.* Those Arguments which from the *Roman* Laws are brought against this opinion, are to be referred not unto our Embassadours, but unto such as are sent from Provinces, or from particular Cities.

XI. Prophane Histories are full of the Examples of Wars undertaken, for the affronts offered to Embassadors: And in the Sacred Story we read of a War made by King *David* against the *Ammonites* upon that ground. Neither can there be any cause more just, as *Cicero* pleads against King *Mithridates.*

CHAP.

CHAP. XIX.

Of the Right of Burial.

I. *From the same Law of Nations ariseth the Right of burying the Dead.*
II. *Whence this springs.*
III. *It is due even to Enemies.*
IV. *Whether to such as are notoriously wicked.*
V. *Whether to such as kill themselves.*
VI. *What other things are by the Law of Nations due.*

I. From the Law of Nations ariseth the right of Burial.

FRom the same Law of Nations which is voluntary, ariseth the Right of burying the bodies of the Dead. *Dion Chrysostome* amongst those Customes which he opposeth to written Laws, placeth this of Burial, next to the Rights due to Embassadors: And *Seneca* the Father, among those Laws that are unwritten, which yet are more firm and binding than those that are written, inserts this of the Interment of the dead. The *Hebrew* Historiographers, *Philo* and *Josephus*, term this *the Right of Nature*; And *Isidore Pelusiota*, *One of the Laws of Nature*: as it is very usual with them to comprehend all such Customes, as are common amongst all Nations, and agreeable to Natural Reason, under the Notion of the Law of Nature, as I have elsewhere shewed. And no marvel, seeing that (as *Ælian* speaks) *The burial of the dead is a thing commanded, even by Nature it self.* And in another place, *The Earth and Graves are to all men common and alike due.* *Eusebius* also reckons it among *the Laws of Nature.* And *Euripides*, *The Laws of Mortals.* *Aristides* calls it, κοινὸν νόμον, *A Law common to all men.* Papinius, *The Law of the whole Earth, and the general League of the World.* Tacitus, *The great Commerce of humane condition.* And *Lysias* the Orator, *The common hope of all.* He that hinders the burning of the bodies of dead men, is said in *Claudian*, *to divest himself of all humanity*; and by the Emperour *Leo*, *to reproach Nature her self*: and by *Isidore*, *to profane that which is holy.* And because the Ancients observed, that what Rights soever being common to all Civilized Nations, to the end that they might be reputed the more sacred, were attributed to the Gods as their Authors; As they did the Rights of Embassadors: So we find, that they every where ascribe unto them this Right also. In one of the Tragedies of *Euripides*, and in one also of *Sophocles*, you may find it called νόμων δαιμόνων, *A Divine Law*: and in another, you may find it reckoned among the Laws of the Gods. And *Isocrates* discoursing of the Ground of the War which *Theseus* made against *Creon*, brings in *Adrastus* (having lost his Army before *Thebes*, and by *Creon* denyed leave to bury the Dead) supplicating *Theseus* then King of *Athens*, *That he would commiserate those brave men that lay unburied before* Thebes, *and that he would not suffer the Ancient Custome to be despised, nor that Common Right violated, which all mankind might lay claim to, as being instituted, not by an humane, but by a divine power: which when* Theseus *heard, he immediately sent his Embassadors to* Thebes. The same Author exceedingly blaming the *Thebans*, for preferring their own Decrees, before the Laws of the Gods. And not only *Isocrates* in this place, but *Herodotus* in his *Calliope*, *Diodorus Siculus* in the fourth of his Histories, *Xenophon* in the sixth of his *Grecian* History, and many other Historians, do unanimously assert, That this War of *Theseus* was undertaken, for the Common Cause of all Mankind. And every where in all Authors of the best account, we read this office of burying the dead, commended unto us under the most specious names of the best Vertues. *Cicero* and *Lactantius* commend it as an Act of Humanity: *Valerius Maximus*, as an Act of Humanity and Courtesie: *Quintilian*, as an Act of Humanity and Religion: *Seneca*, as an Act of Compassion and Humanity: *Philo* attributes it to Pity and Commiseration of Common Nature: *Tacitus* calls it the Commerce of Humane Condition: And *Ulpian* ascribes it to Mercy and Piety: *Euripides* and *Lactantius* term it, an Act of Justice and of Piety. *Ultimum illud & maximum pietatis officium est Peregrinorum & pauperum Sepultura*; *To bury the Stranger and the Poor, is the last and greatest duty of Piety*, saith *Lactantius*. As on the contrary, to deny Burial to the Dead, as the *Donatists* did the bodies of the *Catholicks*, *Optatus Milevitanus* condemns as Impiety. And in *Papinus* we read

Epist. ult. edit. 491. *Lib. 12.* *Lib. 13.* *Hist. 8. 19.* *Supplic. Ajace.* *Antigone.* *Orat. pro Quintio.* *Lib. 6. c. 11, 22.* *Lib. 5. c. 1.* *Lib. 6. c. 12.*

——Bello cogendus & Armis
In mores hominemque Creon.

——By War and Arms must Creon *be*
Enforc't to Customes, and Humanity.

Vita Caracallæ. *Spartianus* brands such men with Infamy, as if they had no respect or reverence at all to Humanity: And *Livy* calls it, *A brutish Cruelty beyond the belief of Humane Anger. Homer* brings in *Jupiter* and the rest of the Gods, as being offended at *Achilles*, for abusing the body of *Hector*. And *Lactantius* condemns their wisdom, as favouring too much of Impiety, who esteem all Care in burying the Dead, superfluous.

II. Whence this custome ariseth. *Nat. Hist. l. 7. c. 54.* Upon what ground this Custome of burying the bodies of the Dead, was at first introduced, whether embalmed according to the Custome of the *Egyptians*, or burnt according to the manner of the *Grecians*, or interred as we now use, which *Cicero* approves as the most Ancient, and after him *Pliny*; (who makes this difference between *Sepultus* and *Humatus*, as if he were understood to be *Sepultus*, whose body was by any means kept and preserved; but he only to be *Humatus*, that was covered with Earth) it is not agreed upon, on all sides. *Moschion* attributes it to the savage Cruelty of the Gyants, who were wont to devour the dead bodies of men, *Cujus abolita signum est sepultura*; *The abolishing of which Brutish Custome is signified by Sepulture.* Others are of Opinion, that by this means men seem voluntarily to pay that debt which Nature will exact from us, though we were otherwise unwilling. For that all humane bodies being extracted from the Earth, should return to the Earth, was not said by God only unto *Adam*; but all both *Greeks* and *Latines*, do every where acknowledge. *Cicero* quotes this out of *Euripides*, that

Reddenda terra terra.

Earth must to Earth return.

Eccles. 12. 7. Which also are the very words of *Solomon*, Eccles. 12. 7. *Then shall the Dust return to the Earth as it was, and the Spirit shall return unto God that gave it.* Now on this subject what said *Solomon* more than *Euripides*, who in the person of *Theseus*, saith thus,

Jam sinite terra Mortuos gremio tegi:
Res unde quæque sumpserat primordium
Eo recipitur: Spiritus Cœlo redit,
Corpusque terræ: Jure, nec enim Mancupi,
Sed brevis ad ævi tempus utendum datur:
Mox terra repetit ipsa quod nutriverat:

Now let the Dead be unto Earth bequeath'd,
And each return from whence it once receiv'd
Its being; then will the Spirit soon retire to Heav'n:
The flesh to dust, from whence it came, not giv'n,
But for a short time lent: that past and gone,
The Earth what it so lent, soon seizeth on.

Lucretius speaking of the Earth, saith,

She is, of All, the Womb and common Tomb.

See Job 10. 9. *In Flaccum.* *Lib. 11. 30.* *Pliny* likewise tells us, *That the Earth receives us as soon as we are born; and being born, she nourisheth us; and being brought up, she alwayes sustains us; and at last, being forsaken by all the world, she like a tender Mother, receives us into her own Bowels again, and there hides us. Nature*, saith *Philo*, *hath ordained the Earth, as Mans proper place, not only whilest they live, but being dead also*, Ut eadem quæ primos suscepit Natales, suscipiat & ex hac vita Exitum; *That she that receives us from the womb, may, when dead, afford us a Tomb.* And yet as there is nothing that is laudably done in man, but what God hath imprinted some footsteps thereof in some Beasts; so also it falls out in this very thing. *Pliny* reports of the Pismires, *That they only of all other living creatures besides men,*

men, do bury one another. And yet he himself speaking of the Dolphins, saith, *That when they perceive one of their own kind dead, they carry him away, that he may not be devoured by Beasts.* The like doth *Virgil* record of Bees : Lib. 9. c. 8.

——Tum corpora luce carentum
Exportant tectis, & tristia Funera ducunt.

And when the Fogs of Death have clos'd their Eyes,
Their Dead th' attend with pompous Exequies.

Some are of opinion, That the first hopes of a Resurrection were by our first Parents consigned to their Posterity by this Emblem of Sepulture. So *Pliny* testifies of *Democritus*, that he taught, *That mens Bodies were deposited in the Earth, expecting the accomplishment of a promised Resurrection.* But Christians do often refer this Custome, of their decent Interment of their Dead to their hopes of a future Resurrection. So saith *Prudentius*,

Quidnam sibi saxa cavata,
Quid pulchra volunt Monumenta,
Nisi quod res creditur illis
Non mortua, sed data somno?

What means this Stately Tomb,
These Solemn Obsequies,
Surely what's in its Womb
Not dead, but sleeping lies?

But the most plain and obvious reason why Burial was introduced, is, because Man being of all other creatures the noblest, it would seem a thing very unworthy, to suffer his dead body to be torn and devoured by Beasts: Therefore was Burial invented, that this Indecency might (as far as in him lies) be avoided. This is the reason given by *Quintilian*, in commiseration of mankind, we preserve their Bodies from the incursions of Birds and Beasts. So *Cicero* in his first Book of Invention, *Being torn by Wild Beasts, he wanted in his Death the common Honour of Burial.* And God himself threatens some wicked Kings by his Prophets, *That they should be Buried with the Burial of an Ass, and that the Dogs should lick their Blood.* Neither doth *Lactantius* give any other reason for Burials than this, *We cannot suffer*, saith he, *the Image of God to lye as a prey to Fowls and Beasts.* Nor doth St. *Ambrose*, whose words sound thus, *Nothing is more excellent than to do this office for him, who cannot requite it: To defend his Body from the Beasts and from the Fowls, who is thy Companion in Nature.* But, admit there were no such injuries to be feared, yet to suffer an humane Body to be cut and torn in pieces, is far beneath the dignity of humane Nature. Not much different from this is that of *Sopater*, *To bury the dead is a very decent thing, instituted by Nature it self, lest the Bodies of men after death, being naked, should be exposed to shame and reproach. And they that indulge this Honour to the Bodies of the Dead, perform an office acceptable unto all, whether Gods or Semi-Gods. For it is not congruous to Reason, That the Secrets of Humane Nature should after Death be exposed to publick view. And therefore hath Antiquity traduced this Custome of burying the Bodies of the Dead down even unto us,* Ut Monumento condita clam & procul à conspectu tabescant; *That being deposited in their Sepulchres, they may rot and moulder away secretly and invisibly.* The like Reason is given by *Gregory Nyssen*, *We bury the Dead, that so what is the shame of Humane Nature may not lye exposed to the Sun.* Neither is this duty of Interring the Dead, due to the person of any man, but to Humane Nature it self: And therefore it ought not to be envied to any, whether publick enemies or private. As to private enemies, notable is that contest in *Sophocles*, concerning the burying of *Ajax*, where *Ulysses* thus bespeaks *Menelaus*,

Decl. 6. 1 King. 14. 11. Jer. 22. Lib. 6.

After so many things th' hast wisely said,
Take heed, O Menelau', *wrong not the Dead.*

The

Antigone. The Reason whereof is given by *Euripides* thus,

To Mortal Men death is the end of strife :
For what can Rage do to him that hath no Life?

Supplicibus. So the same Author in another of his Tragedies,

If by these Argives *ye were injured,*
It is revenge enough to see them dead.

And *Virgil,*

'Gainst Vanquished and Dead no War is made.

Which Verse being quoted by the Author to *Herennius*, he adds, *For that which is the last and greatest of Evils is already befallen them.* With whom agrees *Papinius*,

——————Bellavimus; esto:
Sed cecidere odia,& tristes mors obruit iras.

———At War we were; it is confest:
But all hate's past, when wrath's by Death supprest.

The same reason is given by *Optatus Milevitanus*, *Though your wrath were implacable whilest your Enemy lived, yet he being dead, that hatred should be appeased: For he is now silent, who haply was before litigious.*

III. It is due to publick Enemies. Wherefore it is by all confest, That this is a duty that we owe not to our private only, but our publick Enemies. *This Right* (saith *Appian*) *is common in all War: It is the usual Traffick and Commerce of War*, as *Philo* observes. So also *Tacitus*, *Our very Enemies do not envy us Graves.* This also *Dion Chrysostome* assures us, *That this Right is granted even to Enemies in War, though their hatreds before were irreconcileable. Lucan* also treating on this Subject, saith, *That Funeral Rites were observed even among Foes.* Thus also doth *Philo* plead against *Flaccus*, *Even to those who are slain in War, do men usually grant Burial: They that abound in Goodness and Humanity will do it at their own charge, and others, that extend their hatred even beyond death, will yet under some conditions deliver their Bodies, that they may not be deprived of the last Honour that the Custome of Nations hath decreed unto them.* (*Philo.*) *For what War* (saith *Sopater*) *can be so barbarous as to rob mankind of its last Honour? What enmity can protract the remembrance of injuries done so long as to violate a Law so universally binding?* (*Orat. de Lege.*) Whereunto we may add that of *Dion Chrysostome*, *For by this Law* (saith he) *no man can reckon the Dead amongst the number of his Enemies, nor doth any man extend his hatred and his reproaches to the Bodies of the slain.* Examples whereof we may find in every Author. *Hercules* (we read) buried his Enemies Bodies: *Alexander* those whom he had slain at *Issus*: *Hannibal* sought out the Bodies of *Caj. Flaminius*, *P. Æmilius*, *Tiberius Gracchus*, and *M. Marcellus*, being *Romans*, and gave them Honourable Funerals. The very same did the *Romans* to *Hanno* the *Carthaginian*: The like did *Pompey* to *Mithridates*, *Demetrius* to many of his Enemies, and *M. Anthony* to King *Archelaus*. In the War which the *Grecians* made against the *Persians*, the *Grecians* bound themselves by an Oath made in this Form, *Socios omnes sepeliam; bello victor etiam barbaros: All my fellow Souldiers I will Bury; and if I remain Conquerour in Battle, even the* Barbarians. And every where in Histories we read of leave given to carry away their dead. (*See Lib. 3. c. 20. §. 45.*) An Example we have in *Pausanias*, of the *Athenians*, who buried the Bodies of their Enemies the *Medes*; and the Reason is added, *Quia qualemcunque Mortuum terra condi fas sit: Because it was always thought an Act of Piety to inter all dead Bodies whosesoever they were.* Wherefore according to the exposition of the *Hebrew* Doctors, The High Priest, though otherwise forbidden to be present at any Funeral; yet notwithstanding, if a man were found dead and unburied, he was even himself commanded to bury him. The very same was enjoined by the Pontificial Law among the *Romans*, as *Servius* notes. Christians have so high an esteem of this duty, that for this cause, as well as for the relief of the Poor, and the redemption of Captives, they have thought it lawful to melt down their

their Consecrated Plate, and to sell it. There are also Examples that may be brought for the contrary opinion; but such as are by the Judgement of the most and best men condemned. *Hunc oro defende Furorem*, saith *Virgil*: Which *Servius* thus expounds, *O keep me from this rage, I pray, (i. e.)* from that Malice which rageth even after Death. The like we may read of in *Claudian*,

——Hominemque cruentus
Exuit, & teneum cæsis invidit arenam.

Bloody are they, wanting humanity,
Who to the slain, a little dust deny.

Wherewith agrees that of *Diodorus Siculus*, Ferinum est bellum, quod cum mortuis qui ejusdem sunt Naturæ, geritur; *To wage War with the Dead, who were lately of the same Nature with our selves, is bruitish Cruelty.*

IV. Whether to such as are notoriously wicked:

But yet as concerning such notorious Malefactors as have deserved Death, and according unto Law have suffered, there were some cause to doubt. But that the Divine Law given to the *Hebrews*, which as it was our guide and directrix to all other Vertues, so is it to this of Humanity also, did command, That such as were hanged on the Gallows, (which was a Death very ignominious among them, as appears *Numb.* 25. 4. and *Deut.* 21. 23.) should be Buried the same day. Whence *Josephus* affirms, That so great was the care that the *Jews* took of burials, that they took down the Bodies even of those that were publickly Executed before the Sun went down, and bequeathed them to the Earth. And as others of the *Jewish* Interpreters add, This they did in reverence only to the Image of God, whereunto Man was created. *Homer* records, That *Ægysthus*, who to the Sin of Adultery had accumulated another Sin, even that of the Kings Murther, being himself afterwards slain, was notwithstanding by *Orestes*, the slain Kings Son, buried. Yea, and among the *Romans*, *Ulpian* will inform us, That the Bodies of such as were put to Death as Malefactors, could not be denyed their Kinsmen if they required them: yea, they were to be given to any body else that would ask them, as *Paulus* understood it. Neither did those cruel Emperours, *Dioclesian* and *Maximilian*, forbid Burial to any, though guilty of the greatest crimes, and accordingly punished: *Hos Sepulturæ tradi non vetamus*, was the answer of both of them; *We do not forbid these to be buried.* The like Custome there was among the *Romans*, as *Philo* testifies against *Flaccus*. Yet Examples we have also of some who have been cast out unburied: But this is more frequently done in Civil, than in Foreign Wars. And though it be a Custome among us to hang notoriours offenders in Chains, to deter others; yet whether this be commendable or not, is much disputed, not only by Politicians but Divines. On the contrary, we find them highly commended, who have themselves caused those Bodies to be buried, which they would not permit others to bury: As *Pausanias*, King of the *Lacedæmonians*, who being provoked by the *Ægeneti* to retaliate what the *Persians* had before done against *Leonides*, rejected their Counsel as unworthy of him, or indeed the name of a *Grecian*. *Papinius* brings in *Theseus* bespeaking *Creon* thus,

2 Sam. 21.26.

Odyss. 3.

The hanging men in chains whether commendable.

——Vade, atra daturus
Supplicia, extremique tamen secure Sepulchri.

——Torments extreme, go and endure;
Yet of a Sepulchre be thou secure.

Josephus records it of the *Pharisees*, That they gave a most sumptuous Funeral to their King *Alexander Jannæus*, notwithstanding his barbarous cruelty exercised over the Bodies of his dead Countrey-men. And though God hath sometimes punished some persons with the loss of Burial, as he did *Jehoiakim* and *Jezebel*; yet this he did by his own most Sovereign Power which is not bound up by any Law but that only of his own Will. And whereas *David* kept the head of *Goliah*, to shew as a Monument of his Victory, it was done upon a Stranger, a contemner of the true God: And under that Law, where by the word *Neighbour* none were included but the *Hebrews* only.

Ant.l.13.c.24.

Jer. 22. 19.

1 King.21.23.

There

V. Whether to those that killed themselves. There remains yet one thing worthy our observation, concerning the Burial of the dead, namely, That the *Jews*, as zealous as they were for this duty, yet would not vouchsafe this Honour to those who killed themselves: And no marvel (as *Josephus* well observes †) since no other punishment can possibly be inflicted upon those who esteem Death it self to be none. The *Milesian* Virgins (as *Plutarch* reports) were all at once surprized with a violent fit of Melancholy, and in an humour would needs dye, no man knowing the cause why: Many of them, notwithstanding all perswasions and care taken of them, did strangle themselves, and others daily attempting to do the like, were prevented. At length, by the advice of a grave Senator, it was enacted, That all that were found so hanged, should be stript naked, and with the same cord being first dragg'd through the streets, hanged in the Market place, and exposed to publick view. The fear of shame was stronger than the fear of death: After this Law made, none was ever found so regardless of her Honour as to attempt such an Act. *Servius* upon the twelfth of *Virgil's Æneads*, tells us, That it was provided by the *Roman* Laws, *Ut qui laqueo vitam finisset, insepultus abjiceretur*; *That whosoever hanged himself should be cast out unburied.* And very frequent it is among most Nations, to inflict some brand of Infamy upon such as kill themselves, as *Aristotle* notes. Which place *Andronicus Rhodius* expounding, saith, *That they were prohibited Burial*: Which Law *Dion Chrysostome* highly commends, among many others, enacted by *Demonassa* Queen of *Cyprus*. At *Athens*, in the times of *Æschines*, he that killed himself had his Hand buried apart from his Body. Neither is it to the purpose to object with *Homer Æschylus*, and others, that the Dead feel nothing, either of pain or shame. For no malefactor is put to death simply because he hath sinned, but in regard that his death strikes a terrour into others. *Quod mortuis accidit, à vivis metuitur*; *What happens to the dead affrights the living*: and consequently, restrains them from sinning in the same kind, *which is enough to justifie the punishment.* (Yet is it worthy to be observed, That though *Plato* were somewhat favourable in his Sentence on such as killed themselves, yet doth he not think fit to leave them altogether unpunished: *What expiation,* (saith he) *or what manner of Interment they should have that kill themselves, God knows.* But then he goes on, and gives his own opinion thus, *Let them be buried*, saith he, *in some solitary and desart place, where none was ever buried but themselves; and let there be no Statue, Monument or Inscription set over them, that their Bodies, Names and Memories may rot together.*) The *Platonists* do excellently dispute against the *Stoicks*, and against all such as hold, That a man may for the avoiding either of some present slavery, or the violent assault of some dolorous and incurable disease, or out of hopes of glory for a good cause, undergo a voluntary death, by maintaining that the Soul is to be kept in the safe custody of the Body until it be unavoidably required from us by him that gave it. Much to this purpose may be read in *Plotinus*, *Olympiodorus*, and *Macrobius* upon the Dream of *Scipio*. (*Aristotle* accounted such as killed themselves to be weak and effeminate, *Fortis viri est mala perpeti*; *It is the part of a valiant man to suffer, as well as to act couragiously.* Non est virile terga Fortunæ dare; *It is but a weak and lazy refuge by a voluntary death to avoid pain or shame*, according to that of the Poet,

† *Ant. lib.* 3. *c.* 25.
* *A. Gell. l.* 15. *c.* 10.
Plut. de Mul. virt.
The *Milesian* Virgins.
Nic. 55.
Æsch. in Ctesiphontem.
Seneca.

> *Rebus in adversis facile est contemnere vitam:*
> *Fortiter ille facit, qui miser esse potest.*
>
> *Each Coward, whilest distrest, can life disdain:*
> *He valiant is, who dares encounter pain.*)

Brutus condemned the fact of *Cato*, though afterwards he wrote after the same Copy: *It is neither pious nor indeed manly*, saith he, *to turn our backs upon Fortune, and to fly away from those imminent calamities, which we should magnanimously bear.* Expectandus est vitæ exitus quem natura decrevit; *What manner of death Nature hath decreed for us, we must with patience expect*, saith *Seneca*. *It is no part of Valour or Fortitude to destroy our selves, but a madness rather*: Nonne furor est, nè moriare, mori?

Epist. 70.
Mart.

Strabo l. 15. It was well observed by *Megasthenes*, That the fact of *Calanus* was by the wisest among the *Indians* condemned, it being contrary to their Laws for any man, through impatience to kill himself. Neither did the *Persians* approve of it: Witness that of King *Darius* in *Curtius*, Alieno scelere quam meo mori malo; *I had rather perish by another mans crime than by mine own.* No, nor the *Arabians*, as may be collected from that

Lib. 5.

that of *Job*, *Who wait for death, but it cometh not, and dig for it more than for hid Treasures.* Job 3. 21. And therefore the *Hebrews* do render this word [*mori*] *To dye*, by the *Greek* word ἀπολύεσθαι, *To be let go*, or *To be dismist*, as may appear not only by *Luke* 2. 29. *Lord, now lettest thou thy Servant depart in peace*; but by the *Greek* Version of that place in *Gen.* 15. 2. and that in *Numb.* 20. towards the latter end. Which manner of Speech is familiar among the *Greeks* also, as *Themistius* testifies of them in his Book *De Anima*: *They say of the Soul of him that dyeth*, (saith he) *it is dismist*, and *death it self they call* ἀπόλυσιν, *A dismission.* *Plutarch* also in his Book of Consolation, hath the same expression, *Donec Deus ipse nos dimittat*; *Until God himself dismiss us.* It seems that the *Jews* did somewhat vary in their opinions concerning this matter, as appears by *Josephus*, where he records, and seems to commend the Generosity of *Phasacles*, who knowing that he was *Ant. l. 14. c. 25.* adjudged to death, (which he feared not,) scorning to fall at the command of an Enemy (seeing that he could not kill himself with his own Sword, being bound) dasht his Head, with all the force he had, against a Stone, and so perished. Thus the *Jews* plead to *Petronius*, as *Philo* records: *We* (say they) *mix our own Bloods by voluntary deaths, for fear lest whilest we strive at two things* (i. e.) *to reverence our Emperour, and yet to observe our Divine Law, we should incur the displeasure of God: Which danger we may avoid, if by contemning this miserable Life, we embrace a voluntary Death.* Some of these *Jews* would admit of one only case, wherein it was lawful for a man to kill himself, namely, rather than live to be a perpetual reproach and scorn to the Enemies of God. For seeing the Power over our lives is not in our selves but in God, as *Josephus* rightly instructs his Countrey-men, They presume that it is the will of God that they should put an end to that reproach by a voluntary death. And hither they refer the Examples of *Sampson*, who seeing the True Religion in, and through him, to be held in contempt, chose rather to dye than that God by him should be dishonoured. And that also of *Saul*, who fell on his own Sword, that so he might not be insulted over by such as were Gods, and his Enemies. For the *Jews* held, That immediately 1 Sam. 31. 4. after the Ghost of *Samuel* had foretold his Death he repented, and that although he *umbra Samuelis.* knew he should dye in case he did fight; yet rather than he would betray his Countrey, and the Law of God into the hands of his Enemies, he refused not to fight: Therein meriting eternal praise by the Testimony of *David.* And hence it was, that he so highly commends the men of *Jabesh Gilead* for their Piety, in bestowing an Honourable Interment upon *Saul.* A third Example we have in *Razes* a Senator of *Jerusalem*, in the History of the *Maccabees.* 2 Mac. 14. 37. Infinite Examples we may find in our Ecclesiastical Histories, of such, who lest they should be enforced by Torments to abjure their Religion, have killed themselves; and of Virgins, who to preserve their Chastity, have cast themselves into Rivers, whom notwithstanding the Church hath honoured with the Crown of Martyrdom. St. *Ambrose* doth highly extol them for it; and St. *Hierome* on the first of *Jonas*, makes an exception of this only case from that general Rule. For *no Persecution can justifie the killing of our selves* (saith he) *but where our Chastity is endangered.* But St. *Augustine* seems to be of another mind: For though he will not derogate from the Authority of the Church, which haply might be led thereunto by *De Civit. Dei lib. 1. c. 26. Epist. 61. ad Dulc.* some Divine Tradition, or those Virgins guided by some Divine Instinct, yet would he not have any Christian draw this into a Precedent; *For* (saith he) *no man must presume to offer up his own Son in Sacrifice, because* Abraham *did it in obedience to Gods express Command*: Yet this he confidently asserts, *That no man ought to destroy himself to avoid either the torments of this life, lest he incur those infinitely greater in the life to come; or to prevent Sin in another, lest he contract a worse in himself; or for Sins already past, which require a larger time to repent of; or out of an impatient thirst after immortality, because he that is guilty of his own death, must not expect hereafter a better life.* And yet elsewhere speaking of *De Civ. Dei l. 1. c. 16.* those who to preserve their Chastity killed themselves, he adds, *Who can be so void of humanity as not to forgive them.* Among the *Grecians* also there was another sort of men exempted from Burial, which custome the Locrians object against the *Phocenses*, *Diod. l. 16.* saying, *That it was generally observed through all* Greece, *that Sacrilegious persons should be cast out unburied.* The like doth *Dion Prusaensis* report of such as are Atheists, and notoriously impious. And the very same punishment was ordained at *Athens*, against such as were Traitors, as *Plutarch* testifies. But *Nicetas*, in his Third Book of *Alexius*, the Brother of *Isaacius*, having declared the death of *Joannes Comnenus Crassus*, who raised Sedition and affected the Empire, saith, That they afterward exposed his Body to be devoured by Birds and Beasts, which was an act void of humanity, and savouring too much of a Bruitish Cruelty. But that I may retreat to what was first intended, all ancient Writers do unanimously accord in this, That a War may be justly undertaken for denying Burial to the dead, as may clearly appear by the story ry of *Theseus*, which is recorded by *Euripides* and *Isocrates*, in the places before quoted.

VI. Some other things due by the Law of Nations.

There are alſo other things, which by the voluntary Law of Nations, are due: As thoſe things which have been long poſſeſt, Succeſſion to him that dyes Inteſtate, and ſuch things as we hold by Contracts, though very unequal. For all theſe, though they have in ſome meaſure their riſe from the Law of Nature, yet do they receive confirmation by Humane Laws, whether againſt the uncertainty of conjectures, or againſt ſome exceptions which otherwiſe Natural Reaſon may haply ſuggeſt: As we have already ſhewed, when we treated of the Rights of Nature.

CHAP.

CHAP. XX.

Of Punishments.

I. *The definition and original of Punishments.*
II. *That they appertain to Commutative Justice, and how.*
III. *It naturally belongs to no one person, but may by the Law of nature be exacted by any that have not alike offended.*
IV. *Among men, the end of Punishing is for some benefit; but otherwise with God, and why.*
V. *In what sense revenge is naturally unlawful.*
VI. *The profit arising from Punishment threefold.*
VII. *As it respects the good of the delinquent, it may naturally be exacted by any; yet with a distinction.*
VIII. *So also as it respects the good of the person injured, and of lawful revenge, by the Law of Nations.*
IX. *And also as it respects the good of every man.*
X. *What the Gospel requires as to this matter.*
XI. *The Argument drawn from the mercy of God, set forth in the Gospel, Answered.*
XII. *Another concerning the cutting off the opportunity of repentance, Answered.*
XIII. *An imperfect division of punishments rejected.*
XIV. *It is not safe for private Christians to exact punishment, even where the Law of Nations allows it.*
XV. *Or to accuse any man willingly.*
XVI. *Or to affect capital Punishments.*
XVII. *Whether those humane Laws that permit the killing of a man as a Punishment, give him a right, or only impunity: except by distinction.*
XVIII. *Internal acts not punishable by men.*
XIX. *Nor such external as humane infirmity cannot avoid.*
XX. *Nor such acts, as neither directly nor indirectly do hurt to humane Society: And why.*
XXI. *The opinion that Punishments are never to be remitted, rejected.*
XXII. *That they may be remitted before the penal Law be passed.*
XXIII. *Yet not always.*
XXIV. *Yea, and after the penal Law is past.*
XXV. *What probable intrinsick causes justifie the doing of it.*
XXVI. *What causes extrinsecal.*
XXVII. *The opinion that no dispensation is to be granted for any cause but what is tacitely excepted in the Law, rejected.*
XXVIII. *Punishments inflicted for some merit.*
XXIX. *Where respect is had to the causes impelling, which are compared one with another.*
XXX. *As also the causes which should withdraw us, and of the degrees of the precepts of the Decalogue that concern our neighbour, and some other matters.*
XXXI. *Of the propensity of the offender to either, which hath divers respects.*
XXXII. *That the merit of Punishment may extend to a greater harm than that which the offender intended: And why.*
XXXIII. *An harmoniacal proportion in Punishments rejected.*
XXXIV. *That Punishments ought to be mitigated out of Charity, unless a greater Charity forbid.*
XXXV. *The facility of sinning how it incites to Punishment: also custom how it incites or disswades from punishing.*
XXXVI. *Of what use clemency is in the mitigating of Punishments.*
XXXVII. *What the Hebrews or Romans had respect to in Punishments, may be referred to the places above mentioned.*
XXXVIII. *Of war made for the exacting of Punishments.*
XXXIX. *Whether war made for the punishment of injuries begun be just, explained by distinction.*
XL. *Whether it be lawful for Kings or States to make war upon such as violate the Law of nature, though they have committed nothing against them or their subjects, and that jurisdiction is not necessary naturally to the exacting of Punishments.*
XLI. *The Law of nature distinguished from civil customs largely taken.*
XLII. *And from the voluntary Divine Law not yet known to all Nations.*
XLIII. *As to the Law of nature, that which is manifest is to be distinguisht from that which is not.*
XLIV. *Whether a War may be made for sins committed against God only.*
XLV. *Of some common notions of God, which and how they are exprest in the Decalogue.*
XLVI. *The first infringers of these Punishable.*
XLVII. *But not others, as is proved by the Hebrew Law.*
XLVIII. *That War is not justly to be made upon any, only for refusing to embrace Christian Religion.*
XLIX. *War may justly be made against them that persecute Christians, as such.*
L. *But not against such Christians as do misunderstand the meaning of the Divine Law, illustrated by Authorities and examples.*
LI. *But may, and that justly, against those that are impious; against such, as they believe to be Gods.*

I. The definition of punishments.

ABOVE when we began to assign the causes of War, we considered mens deeds in a twofold respect, either as the wrong they did, might be repaired, or as it might be punished. Concerning the former we have sufficiently spoken: we come now to the latter, which is Punishments, which we shall the more accurately discuss, for as much as its Origine and nature being misunderstood, hath given occasion to many errours. Punishment in its general acceptation is, *malum passionis quod infligitur ob malum actionis*; *the evil that we suffer for the evil that we do.* And though hard labour be sometimes imposed upon some persons by way of Punishment, yet this is in respect of the pains and trouble that accompanies those works, and may therefore fitly be referred to passion. As for those inconveniencies which some men suffer without any sin committed, as by some contagious disease, or as being maimed, or for some uncleanness, to be debarred the Society of men, or to be made uncapable of some office or function, (many whereof we may read of in the Jewish Law) these are not properly Punishments, though for some resemblance they have with them, and by the abuse of the word, they are so called. Among those things that natural instinct tells us are lawful and not unjust, this is one, *ut malum qui facit, malum ferat*; *that he that doth evil should suffer evil*: which Philosophers do reckon as the most antient, and most perfect rule of justice, or as one of the Laws of *Radamanthus*; yea so antient, and indubitable, that *Plato* was so bold as to say: *That neither the Gods nor good men durst ever say otherwise, but that he that doth wrong deserves to suffer for it. Plutarch* makes justice *one of Gods immediate attendants, whose offer it is to revenge all affronts done to the Divine Law*; *which all men do naturally make use of against all men, as being fellow Citizens.* And *Hierax* describes justice by that which is its principal office, namely, *to hurt those who have first hurt others.* And *Hierocles* calls *Justice the only cure for wickedness* (as if no satisfaction could be made for wrongs done but by sufferance; neither is there any thing that so powerfully restrains us from sin, as the apprehension of some just Punishment.) *We are therefore very irrational, when we blame either God or men for their severity to us, when we are punished*: *non enim nocens dicendus qui nocentes afficit pœna*; *for he is not to be blamed that punisheth, but he that deserves Punishment.* (That which we suffer is just, because that which we do is unjust) *Omnis pœna, si justa est, peccati pœna est*; *Every just Punishment* (saith St. *Aug.*) must necessarily refer to some crime: which is true even of those that are inflicted by God himself; though sometimes by reason of our ignorance, *latet culpa, ubi non latet pœna*; *the judgment flames out, when the sin lies smothered.*

Lactantius de Ira dei c. 17.

Aug.

II. It appertains to commutative justice.

But whether it appertain to distributive, or commutative justice, divers men are of divers opinions. Some think that they that offend most are punished most, and so on the contrary: And because punishment is inflicted as it were by the whole on a part, therefore it is to be referred to attributive justice. But whereas in the first place they say, that this branch of justice takes place only where there is an equality to be assigned between terms more than two; that this holds not always true, we have already shewn in the beginning of this work: Besides that they that sin most, are punished most; and they that offend least, are least punished; this falls out by consequence only, and was not primarily and of it self intended: for that which is simply, and in the first place intended, is, that there be an equality between the offence and the punishment, whereof *Horace* thus:

> *Why doth not reason weights and measure frame,*
> *That every sin may have its proper pain?*
> ———adsit
> Regula peccatis, quæ pœnas irrogat æquas,
> Nec scutica dignum, horribili sectère flagello.

Deut. 25, 2,3. Whereunto we may refer also that of *Deut.* 25. 2, 3. where the Judge is commanded to see the malefector beaten with a certain number of stripes, according to his crime, *iniquum erit si æqualiter irascatur inæqualibus*; *to punish all sins equally is very unjust*, saith *Seneca*: for, as the Scholiast upon *Horace* observes; *If we inflict the greatest punishments upon the smallest crimes, it must necessarily follow, that the greatest will remain either (in part) unpunished, or some new punishments must be invented.* Neither is that much truer which they say, that all punishment doth proceed from the whole to its parts, as will appear by what we shall say hereafter. Besides the true intent and reason of distributive justice properly consists, neither in such an equality, nor in the procession of the whole to its part, as we have elswhere shewed; but in the respect had to the fitness and aptitude of the Delinquent to such a punishment, which doth not infer any right thereunto strictly taken, but is only preparative as giving occasion unto it; for although he that is punished, ought to be worthy of punishment: yet may we not hence infer, that he must necessarily undergo whatsoever distributive justice may impose upon him: Neither do they that refer the punishment

De Ira *l.* 11. 6.

See beneath Sect. 28. 32. and Book 3. c. 11. Sect. 1.

desert

ment of Delinquents to commutative justice, extricate themselves any better; for they consider the matter so, as if punishments were due to a malefactor in the same manner, as things are usually due upon contracts. That which deceives these men, is the vulgar manner of speaking, whereby we say that punishment is due to a malefactor, which is very improper; for he to whom any thing is properly due, hath a right against him from whom it is due. But in saying a Punishment is due unto any man, we mean only this, that it is just he should be punished: yet notwithstanding true it is, that in punishments, commutative justice is simply and by it self exercised; forasmuch as he that punisheth, that he may do it justly, ought to have a right to do it, which right ariseth from the guilt of the delinquent. And herein there is something that draws near unto the nature of contracts: Because as he that sells a thing though he mention nothing particularly, yet is presumed to stand obliged to perform all things natural to the sale: So he that transgresseth a Law, doth voluntarily oblige himself to the penalty of that Law, because it is not possible that there should be any hainous crime that is not punishable; so that he that is willing directly to transgress a Law, is by consequence willing to undergo the penalty of that Law: In which sense, some Princes do pronounce sentence against a malefactor thus, *Ipse te huic pœnæ subdidisti*; *thou hast voluntarily subjected thy self to this punishment.* And to this purpose is that of *Philo*: *Peccare cum festinatis, ad pœnam festinatis*; *whilst you make hast to sin, you do but run headlong to punishment.* That woman that would marry another mans slave is said in *Tacitus*, to consent to her own slavery; because that was the punishment ordained for such women. *Michael Ephesius* upon *Aristotle* tells us, *That in every sin, there is a kind of giving and receiving according to the nature of contracts; for he that steals or robs me of what is mine, doth for that very thing bind himself to undergo such a punishment. And a little after, under the name of contracts, the Antients comprehended not only such as were made by mutual Agreements, but such also as were forbidden by the Laws, under such a penalty.* *Vita Mosis.* *Ann.* 12. *Nicom.* 15.

III. In whom this right of Punishing is, naturally.

But yet, to whom this right of punishing offenders is due, is not by nature it self determined; this natural reason dictates, that a Malefactor may be punished, but not, who should punish him; this only nature prompts us to, that it is most convenient, that it should be done by one that is his superiour: neither doth she demonstrate this to be altogether necessary, unless, by superiour, we understand him that is innocent, and that we detrude the nocent beneath the degrees of men, and rank them with beasts which are subject unto men. Thus *Democritus* ascribes it to nature, that the better should govern the worse; and *Aristotle* observes, that in that order that nature hath placed every thing, that which is worser was had for the use and service of that which was better; which also holds true as well in artificial things, as in natural: The consequence whereof is, that he that is nocent ought not to be punished by him that is at least, equally nocent (for he that sits as Judge to punish Malefactors, should himself be free, not only from that particular crime, but from all others that may render him obnoxious to the same punishment) whence ariseth that of our Saviour to the Pharisees: *Let him amongst you that is without sin, cast the first stone at her*; which he therefore spake, because at that time, the manners of the Jews were extremely corrupted, insomuch that they who would seem to be the greatest Saints, were observed to wallow like swine in Adulteries and such like grievous Sins; as may appear by that of the Apostle to the Romans, *Rom* 2. 22. *Wherefore thou art inexcusable, O man, whoever thou art that judgest; for in that thou judgest another, thou condemnest thy self, seeing thou that judgest, doest the same things*: whereunto appertaineth that of *Seneca*, *non potest ullam authoritatem habere sententia, ubi qui damnandus est, damnat*; *that sentence can never carry any face of authority, where he that condemneth another, may as justly be condemned himself*: for as St. *Ambrose* saith in the Apology of *David*, *he that goes about to judge another, ought first to judge himself, and not rashly to condemn the errours and oversights of other men, when he daily commits far greater himself.* It is very good advice that St. *Ambrose* gives: *Judicet ille de alterius errore, qui non habet in seipso quod condemnet*, &c, *Let him be Judge of the errours of others, that hath in himself nothing condemnable: Let him be Judge, that is not guilty of the same crimes that he deemes worthy to be condemned in another*; lest whilst he judgeth another, he pronounceth sentence against himself. Let us in the first place then consider with our selves, *numquid ipsi tale commisimus? whether we our selves have not committed the like?* and the regard that every man hath to his own safety will make him more moderate in passing judgment on others. Joh. 8. 7. *Grat.* cap. 3. q. 7.

IV. To what end punishments are ordained.

Another Question here ariseth concerning the end we propose to our selves in punishing; for what we have hitherto said, amounts to no more than this, that the guilty person hath no wrong done him, in case he be punished: But from hence it doth not necessarily follow, that he must be punished; nor is it true, for both God and man, we see do pardon many men, many offences, and are highly commended for it: for as *Plato* first, and after him *Seneca* well observed; *There is no wise man that punisheth an offender simply because he hath offended, but because he should not offend again; for what is once done cannot be recalled, but what is to come may be prevented*: therefore all punishments relate to the time to

come; *Non irascitur, sed cavet. He that punisheth is not angry, but provident. Diodorus* in *Thucydides*, speaking to the Athenians concerning the Mityleneans, saith, *That they had, indeed, done very unjustly, but not so as that they should be destroyed, unless it should be found expedient.* But these things are true in punishments amongst men, because we are all link'd together in Bonds of consanguinity; so that we should not hurt one another, unless it be for a more general good: *For if one hand hurt another*, saith *Cassiodore*, *that which is hurt will not rise up in revenge against the other; no more should one man revenge himself upon another, unless it be for the prevention of some greater evil.* They therefore that punish Malefactors with Stripes, Banishment, or Fines, do it not simply out of revenge, but in pursuance of some future good that may thereby arise: But it is otherwise in God, unto whom *Plato* doth misapply those Sentences. For the actions of God may be grounded upon his very Right of Sovereignty, especially when they are applyed to some special sins of men, although they propose to themselves no end beyond themselves: and thus do some of the Hebrews expound that of *Solomon*, *The Lord*
Prov. 16. 4. *hath made all things for themselves, even the wicked for the day of wrath*; that is, Even when he punisheth the wicked, he doth it for no other end, than to shew that he can punish them;
Exod. 14. 4. (thus he is said to raise up *Pharoah*, that in him his power may be known.) And although
Rom. 9. 17. we do admit of the more vulgar Interpretation, it comes to the same sense; namely, That God is said to make all things for himself, that is, By the right of that supereminent freedom and perfection that is in himself, without seeking or regarding any thing without himself; as he is said to be αὐτοφυὴς, *of himself*, because not born of any. Certainly the Holy Scriptures do testifie that God doth sometimes inflict punishment upon some notorious Delinquents for no other reason but to shew his power. As when he is said to rejoyce at their calamity, and to mock when their fear cometh, *Deut.* 28. 63. *Isai.* 1. 24. Secondly, When in revenge for our former provocations, he is said to harden the heart, and to blind the eyes, and to stop the ears, as *Isai.* 6. 10. and thirdly, When in that last and great Gaol-Delivery, he adjudgeth them to eternal torments, after which there is no place or hopes of amendment, yea and some punishments even in this life that are inconspicuous, such as are obduration and excecation, do clearly evince the truth of that which we object against *Plato*. But when one man punisheth another man whom Nature hath made his Equal, he ought to propose some end unto hmself. And this is it that the School-men say, That the mind of him that avengeth an injury, should not acquiesce in the sufferings of the Offender. Of the same mind also were both *Plato* and *Seneca*, *Ad vindictam veniendum, non quia dulce, sed quia utile; We should affect revenge, not as it is sweet, but as it is profitable.* So likewise *Aristotle*, *Some things are simply honest, others honest out of some necessity.* And as an example of this latter, he inserts this of exacting punishments, *Exequor*, saith *Seneca*, *non quia dolet, sed quia opportet; I take revenge, not because I smart, but because it is convenient.*

V.

In what sense revenge is naturally lawful.

Thus indeed it should be with men; but for the most part it is far otherwise, for we punish in revenge, and revenge to asswage the grief of our sufferings. As if *læso doloris remedium inimici dolor; our pain were lessenned by our enemies grief.* So *Cicero* tells us, That grief is somewhat allayed and mitigated by a just revenge. But this proceeds not from the rational, but from the irascible part of the soul, being the same with us as it is with Brute Beasts. For anger, as in Beasts, so in men, is nothing else but *Æstus sanguinis circa cor, ob appetitum reponendi doloris; An inordinate heat about the heart, out of a vehement desire of revenging our own grief*, as *Eustratius* rightly defines it: which appetite is of it self so much without reason, that sometimes it mistakes the true object, and is carried violently against those that did no ways hurt us; as when we revenge our selves upon the young Whelps for the Bitches sake that bit us; and sometimes against things altogether without sence, as when a Dog bites the Staff or Stone wherewith he is beaten. Now *what can be more irrational, quam his irasci, quæ iram nec meruerunt, nec sentiunt*, saith *Seneca*, *than to be angry with those things which neither deserve our anger, nor feel it?* Like the Brasilians, a fierce and brutish Nation, who being wounded by a Sword, revenge themselves, as well on the Sword, as on the Man that weilded it. But this appetite in it self considered, agrees not with the rational part of the soul, whose Office it is to govern the passions; nor is it consonant to the Law of nature, because it thwarts that Principle of rational and social nature, as such which forbid us to do any thing whereby another may be damnified, unless it be for some greater good. But in the grief or sufferance of another, barely and in it self considered, there is nothing of good, but what is false and imaginary; as in superfluous riches, and many other things of the like nature. And in this sense it is that not only our Christian Doctors, but the ancient Philosophers, who condemn revenge as unlawful, are to be understood. So *Seneca*, *This word revenge, although it be usually taken for a thing that is just, yet it is inhumane, and differs nothing from an injury, but in order only. He that retaliates his own grief upon another, hath only this to plead for his sin, That he was first provoked.* Nay, if we will give credit to *Maximus Tyrius*, *He that revengeth, is sometimes the greater Sinner of the two; forasmuch as he that returns an injury hath more of malice, fury, and unbridled passion, than he that gave the first occasion, which is sometimes done through rashness or ignorance, and against a mans will.* Now if so, as it is against

Nature for the Stream to rise higher than the Fountain that feeds it; so is it most unjust that the punishment should be greater than the offence. Seeing then that it is unmanly, nay brutish, *remordere mordentem, to injure every man that injures us*: No one man either publick or private, can by the Law of Nature rightly punish another (merely as it is a punishment for what is past) unless it be for some future benefit, either general or particular, publick or private. *Dion* in *Plutarch*, who turned the wisdom of *Plato* into civil acts, was of opinion, That *revenge in the judgment of the Law was reckoned more just than any injury first offered; but if we look at the judgment of Nature, it springs from the very same infirmity of the mind.* It is therefore contrary to the nature of man dealing with men, to appease his own grief by occasioning another mans, barely as it is a grief. And by consequence, the less of reason any man hath, the more vindictive he is. This *Seneca* observed, *That Infants, Old men, and sick Men, are always more prone to anger than others.* And every thing that is weak and infirm, is naturally querulous and revengeful. This also was *Juvenal*'s Observation;

Revenge than life it self is sweeter far, Sat. 13.
Infants for nought, Children for trifles are
Incens'd. Chrysippus *was not of that mind,*
Nor gentle Thales; *neither do I find*
That Socrates, *who did next Neighbour live*
*To sweet-*Hymettus, *(though in Chains) did give*
Part of his Hemlock-Potion unto him,
Who (being a Slave) had his Accuser been.
Blest wisdom! first piece meal bids vice adiew;
Then, planting truth, all errours doth eschew.
To joy in those mens sufferings whom we hate,
Argues a mind weak and effeminate;
This, thus we gather, For in all mens sight
None more than Women in revenge delight.

Thus wise men define *anger to be a lasting ulcer of the mind, which usually ariseth from the weakness of the understanding, which they probably collect from this, That sick men are usually more angry than sound, women than men, old men than young, and they that are miserable than they that are happy.* Am. Marc. l. 27. The very same Observation we find in *Lactantius, Simple, and men that are unexperienced, being provoked by an injury, are carried headlong with a blind and inconsiderate fury to revenge themselves on those that hurt them.* Plain it is therefore that one man cannot be rightly punished by another, barely as such; now then let us examine what those benefits are that justifie such punishments.

VI. A threefold profit arising from punishments.

Hereunto then appertains that Partition of punishments that *Plato* gives us; and after him the Philosopher *Taurus*, recited by * *Gellius*, which is drawn from the end or scope whereunto punishments do aim, only with this difference, That whereas *Plato* proposeth but two ends, namely, for reformation and example; *Taurus* addes a third, namely, *τιμωρίαν*, *which*, (as *Clemens Alexandrinus* defines it) *is the retribution of some evil done, which looks at the profit of him that requires it, which is satisfaction.* *Aristotle*, omitting that punishment which we call exemplary, addes only this of satisfaction to that of reformation. Neither doth *Plutarch* omit it where he saith, *That the punishments that tread on the heels of wickedness do not only restrain the audaciousness of such as offend, but do much comfort such as are injured.* And this is that which the same *Aristotle* attributes *to that Justice, which* (as I have said before) *doth even the Ballance, and which he there calls commutative.* But these require yet a more strict disquisition. I say then that every punishment respects the good either of the person punished, or of the person injured, or of every man indistinctly. The first of these aims at the reformation of the person punished, and is called by Philosophers sometimes reformation, sometimes satisfaction, and sometimes admonition. *Paulus* the Lawyer calls it a punishment ordained for reformation; and *Plato*, to teach us prudence; *Plutarch*, the Souls Emperick, whereby she is amended and made better, as by Physick, which works by contraries. For because all humane acts, especially if they be frequent and deliberate, do beget a proneness in nature unto the same, which at length turns into a habit; therefore if such an act be vicious, we must as soon as we can, take away all allurements and provocations thereunto, which cannot by any means more properly be done than by allaying the sweetness of the sin by the sharpness of the punishment. The Platonists, as *Apuleius* testifies, hold, *That there is no punishment so severe as to go unpunished.* And *Tacitus* will instruct us, *That the Corrupter and the corrupted, the sick and the distempered mind, is to be restrained with no gentler medicines than are those very lusts that inflame them.* Ann. 3. And therefore as a tender Mother imbitters the Nipple when she weans her Infant, or as a *skilful Chirurgion lanceth, burns, and scarifies his Patient, whom he intends to cure; so it is the duty of a prudent Magistrate*, corrigendo mederi, *to reclaim and reform a Malefactor by sharp but seasonable punishments.* Sen. de ira lib. 2.

* Lib. 5. c. 14.

Now

VII. 1. To the offender. Now the punishment that serves to this end, may lawfully be inflicted by any man that is prudent and judicious, and not guilty of the same or of the like fault, especially if it be verbal only, as will appear by that in *Plautus*.

> *Amicum castigare ob meritam noxiam*
> *Immune est facinus, verum in ætate utile.*

> A Friend to chide, for what unjust appears,
> Is blameless sure; but most, in men of years.

But if it be by stripes or any other forceable means, then is it not equally lawful for every man; yet doth not this difference between persons lawfully, or unlawfully punishing, arise from the Law of nature (neither indeed could it, but that reason peculiarly commends the free exercise of this right to parents over their children, because they are so dearly affected toward them;) but from the positive Laws of men, which to preserve love among neighbours, and to prevent strife and discord, do restrain this common duty, and confine it to the nearest of kinn, as appears, as well by the Codes of *Justinian* under this title *de emendatione propinquorum*, as elsewhere: Apposite hereunto is that of *Xenophon* to his Soldiers: *If I shall strike any man for his good, I confess I thereby deserve a punishment; but no other than parents do from their children, or masters from their schollars: for even Physicians sometimes lance, cup, and scarify their Patients, when otherwise they cannot cure them. God himself,* (saith *Lactantius*) *commands us to keep a strict hand over our children, that is, to chastise them as often as they transgress, lest by overmuch fondness and indulgence they prove ill nurtured, and contract unto themselves vitious habits.* But this kind of punishment never reacheth unto death, because death takes away all hopes of reformation, unless it be by way of reduction, whereby negatives are reduced to their opposite positives, as in that speech of our Saviours; *It had been better for some that they had never been born*; that is, it had been less evil for them: the like may be said of incorrigible sinners, it were better for them, that is, less evil for them to dye than to live. And of such it is that *Seneca* meant, when he said, that sometimes it is good for them that dye, that they do dye: *As when a tumour or impostume is grown to suppuration, better it is to burn an hole, thereby to discharge part of that impostumated matter, than longer to imprison it; so for a man that is past hopes and desperately wicked, it is better for him to dye than to live:* for as *Plutarch* speaks of such, *they are noxious to others, but most to themselves*: so *Galen* when he had said, that some men ought to be punished by death; first to prevent the mischiefs they would do, were they suffered to live; next that by their death, others may be forewarned; adds in the last place, *that it is expedient, even for themselves to dye, being so wholly corrupted in mind and manners, that it is not possible to reclaim them.* Some there are who think, that St. *John* spake of such men, when he said, that there was a sin unto death, 1 *John* 5. 16. And St. *Chrysostome* speaking of such, saith, *that they are like men irrecoverably sick*: so *Julian* of *Constantius*; seeing that there are two kinds of offences, some that are corrigible, as not despising the means of their cure; others, of men desperately wicked, and incorrigible, for these the Laws have found out a remedy, by death, to put an end to their wickedness; not so much for their own, as for the benefit of others. But because no arguments can be brought to prove this, but what are fallacious; therefore in very charity, we are not rashly to judge any mans case to be desperate: and therefore this kind of punishment, I mean, by death, is seldome inflicted to this end, namely, for emendation.

Mark. 14. 21. — *De Ira. c. 5. interesse pereuntium ut pereant.* — *Jamblichus.* — 1 John 5. 16.

VIII. To him against whom the offence is committed. The benefit that accrues by punishment unto him, against whom the offence is committed, consists in this; that it prevents the like mischief, either by the same person, or by others. *Gellius* out of *Taurus* describes this kind of punishment thus: *when the authority or dignity of the person against whom the offence is committed, is to be upheld and maintained, then is the punishment necessary; lest if it go unpunished, that authority be held in contempt, and the honour lost.* Now what is there said concerning authority, is also to be understood of liberty, or of any thing else, wherein we may claim a just right; for he that suffers one injury to go unpunished, doth but invite another: wherefore *Tacitus* concerning one of the Roman Emperours said well, *consuleret securitati justâ ultione; he might have better provided for his own safety by a just revenge.* Now to the end that a man may secure himself against him that hath formerly injured him, there are three means:

Some resemblance of this there is in some Beasts: *Pliny* records it of the Lyon, that *in pœnam Adulteræ consurgit*; he riseth up to revenge himself of his Adulteress. *Nat. Hist.* 8. 16.

First, By putting *him* to death that did the wrong; Secondly, By taking away from him the power to do wrong: Or Thirdly, By deterring him from doing any further wrong by the sharpness of his punishment, which is conjoyned with reformation, whereof we have just now already discourst. But to be secured from others, by the punishment of him who hath offended, it is necessary that the said punishment be publick and conspicuous, which appertains to exemplary punishments, whereof more anon. Now if our desire of revenge though private, be directed to these ends only, and can be impaled within

Three ways to provide for ones safety against him that hath injur'd us.

in the bounds of equity: if we look at the bare Law of nature first abstracted from divine and humane Laws, and from those other occurrents which do not necessarily happen to the thing; it is not unlawful, whether it be done by the person injured, or by another, seeing it is natural for one man to help another. In which sense may that of *Cicero* be admitted, where he defines the Law of nature to be that which consists not in opinion or custom, but in that which nature it self suggests unto us; where also amongst other examples, he places this of vindication, which he there opposeth to grace or pardon. And lest any man should question the extent of the word, he defines it to be, *that whereby we defend both our selves, and those who ought to be dear unto us, from force and calumny by a just revenge, or whereby we punish offences. Mithridates* in that Oration which *Justin* extracts out of *Trogus*, speaks thus: *Against Thieves all men ought to draw their swords, if not for their safety, yet for their revenge*; which *Plutarch* in the life of *Aratus* calls *ἀμύνης νόμον, the law of revenge.* By this natural Law *Sampson* justifies himself against the Philistines, when they had provoked him by taking away his wife, and giving her to another: *Now* (saith he) *shall I be more blameless than they, though I do them a displeasure:* for he concluded it to be just for him to injure them, who had first provoked him by so great an injury; and according to this rule he pleads his own cause and defends himself: for being demanded by the men of *Judah* what he had done against the Philistines to provoke them; he answered, as they have done to me, so have I done to them, *v.* 11. When the *Laurentines* delivered up those that killed *Tatius* to *Romulus* to be punished, he set them at liberty, saying, *that blood was to be expiated with blood*: intimating that because *Tatius* had before slain their Embassadors, or at least connived at it; it was but just that blood should have blood: for as *Belisarius* in *Procopius* notes, *it is but natural to account him as mine enemy, who hath by an assault wounded me.* Thus likewise the *Plateans* in *Thucydides* plead for themselves in the like case: *we have deservedly punished them, say they; for by that Law that is in force amongst all men, it is lawful to be revenged on those that first make war upon us. Demosthenes* in his Oration against *Aristocrates*, saith, that this Law is common amongst all men to inforce satisfaction from them that have forceably taken away our goods from us: and *Jugurtha* in *Salust* having shewed how *Asdrubal* had laid in wait for his life, adds, *that the people of* Rome, *did that which was neither just nor right, in forbidding him that right which the Law of Nations allowed him*; that is, a just revenge: and *Aristides* the Orator proves it by the authorities both of Poets, Lawyers, Proverbs, and Orators; *that a revenge may be lawfully taken, upon such as have first injured us.* St. *Ambrose* commends the *Maccabees* for revenging the blood of their innocent Brethren, though it were on the Sabboth; and against the Jews, who bitterly complained against the Christians, for burning their Churches, he pleads thus: *if I should argue according to the Law of Nations, I should recount how many Christian Churches the Jews burnt in the time of the Emperour* Julian: thereby concluding, that to requite like for like was agreeable to the law of Nations: thus did *Jonathan*, and his associates revenge the death of their Brother *John* upon the Nabathits, as they were celebrating some great Nuptials, upon whom he unexpectedly fell, and slew both men, women, and children, as *Josephus informs us.* But because men are too partial Judges in their own causes; therefore that liberty, which nature did at first indulge unto every man in vindicating his own quarrel, is justly taken away; and Judges appointed to determine all controversies between man and man, and to help those to right, who suffer wrong. Thus *Demosthenes* pleads against *Conon: As for these injuries, it was thought fit by our Ancestors, that they should receive their punishment from the Laws, and not from the rage and violence of every mans will.* So doth *Quintillian, the compensating of an injury is not only repugnant to the Law, but unto peace; for there are Laws, Judges, and Courts whereunto any man may appeal, unless there be any that are ashamed to be vindicated by the Law.* So likewise the Emperours *Honorius*, and *Theodosius*: *for this very cause are Tribunals erected, and the defence of the publick Laws instituted, lest any man should arrogate to himself the liberty to revenge his own quarrels.* So King *Theodorick*; *from hence do the Laws challenge from us a sacred reverence, that no revenge may be taken by our own hand, nor any thing done against our enemies, by the suddain impulse of our own passions.* For how inconvenient this would be, is evident by that plea of *Tindarus* against *Orestes*:

De Invent. lib. 2.

Judg. 15. 3. 7. 11.

Plut. Rom. ad finem.

Vand. 1.

Ant. l. 13. c. 1.

Laws and Magistrates ordained to punish offenders, and why.

> *This, if thou sufferest,* Menelau', *I ask,*
> *If th' angry wife her husband*'s *blood should spill;*
> *And in revenge, the son his Mother kill:*
> *And if her blood cannot be washt away,*
> *Without fresh blood, where would these mischiefs stay?*

Which words of *Euripides*, being full of Prudence, do abundantly supply both Philosophers and Orators with matter of Argument. *Maximus Tyrius* in his dissertation concerning the retaliating of injuries speaks thus: *A good man will neither do an injury nor suffer*

suffer one; not do one, I mean, willingly; nor suffer one, because he magnanimously slights all that are done unto him: If to infer an injury be wicked, surely to return one is somewhat like it; for although he that wrongs another, in that he gives the first offence, commits the greater fault; yet he that requites that injury, because he was pleased with revenge, is alike wicked: for if he that doth his neighbour wrong, do evil; surely, he that returns that evil, is not the less evil, because he doth it in revenge. And a little after, *quis erit unquam injuriarum finis,* &c. *if it be granted,* saith he, *that a good man having received an injury may revenge it, then may he that suffers that revenge, as justly return it; for on both sides, the equity of doing the same thing is alike:* wherefore he crys out, *qualem, O Jupiter, justitiam fecisti! what manner of justice is this, that thou hast made! O Jupiter, that must necessarily arise out of injustice: quousque progreditur malum, & ubi tandem consistet? how far shall this evil proceed, and where shall it at length end?* thus likewise doth *Aristides* argue in his Oration for peace; *who of all the Grecians would be left alive, if to revenge the death of those who are already slain, those yet living should wilfully run upon their own ruine?* For prevention of which inevitable mischief, were (as I have already said) Laws instituted, Tribunals erected, and Magistrates ordained; yet doth this liberty, that nature gave us at the first, remain still in force in such places where no Laws are, or can be executed, as on the Seas and in desert places; yea, and in divers Nations, especially amongst the antient Germans, where almost all differences were ended by the Sword; as appears by that of King *Theodorick* in *Cassiodore* to his Goths: *Break off* (saith he) *this prodigious custom of single combats, where matters in differenee are much better discust with words than blows*; and in another place, *what need have we of tongues, if every slight quarrel must be ended by the Sword?* whither (haply) we may refer that act of *Cajus Cæsar*, who being then a private person, did with a tumultuary Fleet pursue and chase certain Pyrates by whom he had been formerly taken, dispersing some of their Ships and sinking others; and when he found the Proconsul negligent in punishing the Captives whom he had taken, he himself returned to the Sea and commanded them to be hanged: so likewise is it among the Umbrians, where every man is his own Judge and avenger, which at this present is usually practised among the Muscovites, and that without any restraint in some small time after their address in vain made to the Judges: from whence also before Christian Religion was planted, sprung the custom of Duels among the Germans, which is not yet utterly abolished. Wherefore the Germans in *Paterculus*, admired when they observed the form of the Roman Jurisdiction, whereby all contests and injuries were decided in a judicial way; and that that which was usually before determined by force of Arms, was now decided by Law: the Hebrew Law *permitted the kinsman of him that was murthered to kill the murtherer with his own hand, in case he overtook him without the Cities of refuge.* And it is well observed by the Hebrew Doctors, that a kinsman might exact the Law of retaliation with his own hand for the person killed; but for himself, if any violence was offered him, either by wounds, mutilation, or otherwise, he was to make his appeal to the Judges; because it is a very difficult thing to moderate our passions, when they are excited by our own personal grief. The like custom of taking private revenge for murther we find to have been among the antient Greeks, as *Homer* testifies; but examples of this kind are much more frequent among such as have no common Judge to decide controversies: whence it is, *that just wars are defined to be those, whereby injuries received are revenged*: And *Plato* doth *so long approve of contests by war, until the person injuring shall be enforced to give unto the person injured just satisfaction.*

[Margin: Duels whence they arose.]

[Margin: Aug.]

IX. [Margin: 3. To every man indistinctly.]

The profit that every man indefinitely may receive by the punishment of a Malefactor, which is the third end why they are punished, hath as many parts as that which the injured person receives by it: for he is so punished, either lest he that hath injured one, should injure another; which may be prevented, either by his death, or by disabling him from doing the like injury, as by imprisoning him; or secondly, by reclaiming him; or thirdly, lest others being encouraged by the hopes of impunity, should be alike injurious unto others, which is the end of all publick punishments which are therefore used, *ut unius pœna metus sit multorum*; *that the punishment of one, might strike a terrour into many*: Or (as *Demosthenes* speaks) that others may learn wisdom and fear. *Polybius* records that he saw some Lyons crucified for attempting the life of a man, that so the rest for fear of the like punishment, might be affrighted from committing the like crime. Now the power of executing this right also is naturally in every man: thus *Plutarch* tells us, *that nature doth design a good man to be a perpetual Magistrate*; for that man that is eminently just and honest, is by nature raised up and qualified for a Prince, as the same *Plutarch* speaks of *Philopœmen*, that he took upon himself the defence of the Citizens, who also, without regard to their Laws and times of their Elections, followed him by the bare instinct of nature which always intends the best to govern the worst: Thus *Chrysostome* speaks of *Moses, that before he led out the people by his hand, he declared himself to be their captain by his deeds; it was foolishly demanded by the Hebrew, who made thee a ruler? facta vides, & de nomine facis controversiam? thou seest his deeds, and dost thou well then to cavil about names? as if a patient being first cut, and so cured of* some

[Margin: Pliny. lib. 8. c. 16.]

[Margin: *Vit. Pelop.*]

[Margin: In 2 Cor. 7. 13.]

some desperate Disease, should cavil with his Physician, and demand of him, Who made him a Physician, or who gave him authority to cut him? To whom the Physician might very well answer, Ars mea & Morbus tuus; *My friend, it was my skill and thy Disease that made me to cut thee. So might* Moses *have answered, It was thy cruelty and manifest injustice that made me a Judge and a Ruler.* To govern well is not a dignity only, but an art, nay the greatest of arts. *Sapiens nunquam privatus est, A wise man is never a private man,* as *Cicero* proves by the example of *Nasica.* Neither is he *unius anni Consul, a Magistrate for one year only,* as *Horace* speaks of *Lollius.* Yet notwithstanding is not this liberty to be exercised in any place, but where the Laws of the Commonwealth do permit it. For these natural qualifications (as I have often said) infer no right; though they give us a capacity for it. Concerning this natural Right the opinion of *Democritus* was this, *Concerning the killing or not killing of living Creatures, the matter stands thus, If those Creatures either do or would hurt us, whosoever kills them shall be innocent; nay, he that kills them, doth much better than he that spares them.* And presently after he saith, *As for those Beasts which unjustly annoy us, it is altogether lawful for us to kill them all.* And surely it is not improbable that good men before the Flood did live much after this manner, before God had declared his will of converting the rest of the Beasts to serve a Mans nourishment. And by and by he addes, *What we have written of Foxes and other noxious Serpents, the same we suppose may be said of men.* Whereunto he presently subjoins, *Furem & Latronem qui quocunque modo occiderit, sive manu, sive jussu, sive suffragio, innocens est; He that kills a Thief or a Murtherer, whether it be with his hand, or by his command or suffrage, is to be accounted innocent.* And to these places of *Democritus*, I suppose *Seneca* had some respect in saying, *When I command an obstinate Malefactor to be* Sen. de ira l. 1.
put to death, I do it with the same mind and intent as when I command a noisom and venemous Beast to be killed. Nay, if I see a Viper or a Scorpion (saith *Philo*) *though he attempt not to bite or to wound me, yet will I kill him if I can, lest he should endanger me or some others, by that malignity that is in him. We would not kill Foxes, Wolves, and the like ravenous Beasts, could we but make them tame and serviceable, and not be endangered by them; so,* Ne homini quidem nocebimus quia peccavit, sed ne peccet, *Neither would we hurt and destroy men because they have offended, but because they should not offend again.* But since as well the strict enquiry into the nature and quality of every Fact doth often require great diligence, as also the fitting of each crime with its just punishment, much prudence and equity, lest whilst every man presuming on his own sufficiency should arrogate more unto himself than others would be content to grant him, and thereby much strife and contention should arise; therefore it was unanimously agreed upon, That in all just Societies of Men, such should be made choice of as they esteemed to be the best and most prudent amongst them, or at least whom they hoped might in time prove to be so; whom they called Magistrates, upon whom, by common consent, they transferred all that right which (by the Law of Nature) every one of them had to punish Malefactors. So the same *Democritus, The Laws would never restrain us from living as we please, but that it was evident that men went about to wrong one another. For envy is the mother of sedition.* But yet what is said before of private revenge, the same may be here also said of publick and exemplary Judgments, namely, That there doth yet remain some footsteps of that ancient Right in such places, and among such persons as are not subject to publick Judicatories; yea and among such also as are so subject in some particular Cases. As among the Jews it was lawful for any man to
kill him immediately who forsook God and his Law, or that seduced his Brother to Ido- Deut. 13. 9.
latry, which the Jews called the judgment of zeal which was first exercised by *Phineas*, Numb. 25.
and from him was drawn into a custome. Thus *Mattathias* and his five Sons fell upon a 1 Macc. 2. 24,
certain Jew, who, in obedience to the Kings Command, was sacrificing unto the Heathen- 26.
ish Gods on the Altar at *Modin*, and slew him, as *Josephus* informs us. So we read of *Ant. l. 12. c. 4.*
three hundred Jews which were killed by their own Country-men, in that Book which is 1 Macc. 2. 24.
vulgarly called the third Book of the *Maccabees*. This was the sole pretence that the Jews made for their stoning of St *Steven, Acts* 7. 57. And for their conspiracy against St *Paul, Acts* 23. many other examples we may find in *Josephus*, and in *Philo*, who in his
Book of Sacrificers to Idols saith, *That such a man as shall so sacrifice, should be punished as* Ch. 20. Sect. 9.
a publick enemy to all men, be he never so nearly related unto us. And his Motives and Arguments whereby he would perswade us to a defection from the true worship of God, are to be published unto all that love true piety, that all men may immediately run from all places to take revenge upon that impious Wretch, being fully perswaded that the desire to kill such a man is an holy thing. Yea and in many Nations, this Right doth yet remain in Masters over their Servants, and in Parents over their Children, to punish them even with death. So it was lawful for the *Ephori* of *Sparta* to put to death any of their Citizens without judgment. Now from what hath here been said we may clearly understand what the Law of Nature was concerning punishments, and how long it continued.

X. What the Evangelical Law

Let us now enquire whether this liberty of punishing or revenging an injury be restrained by the Gospel. And surely it is no wonder, as we have elsewhere said, that many things that

requires as to this.

that are consonant to the Law of Nature, and to the Civil Laws, are notwithstanding forbidden by the Divine Law, seeing that that Law is the most perfect of all Laws, and proposeth a reward far greater than humane nature, or than can possibly be given by any other Law maker; for the obtaining whereof there are deservedly required such Vertues as exceed those commanded by the sole Law of Nature. Those Chastisements that leave behind them no brand of infamy nor lasting damage, and are necessary for certain Ages and Conditions, as for Children and Servants; are no whit repugnant to the Divine Evangelical Law, especially if done by such as by humane Laws have a permission so to do, as by Parents, Tutors, Masters, *&c.* which may easily be collected from the very nature of the thing it self. For these are the Souls Physick, altogether as harmless as well-tempered Potions, though to the sense as unwelcome. But as to revenge it is otherwise: For as it only satisfies the mind that is sensible of the wrong it suffers, it is naturally unlawful, much less is it agreeable to this Evangelical Law, as we have already shewed. But the Hebrew Law did not only forbid to hate or bear any grudge against their Brethren, (that is, against their own Country-men) *Lev.* 19. 17. but it commanded them to confer on them some common courtesies, though they were their enemies, *Exod.* 23. 4, 5. Now our Saviour embowelling this Law, and shewing, That under the name of Neighbour all mankind was to be understood, doth hereby convince us, That we are not only restrained from hurting our enemies, but that we are also commanded to do them good, *Matth.* 5. 44. But yet it was permitted to the Hebrews to revenge some great injuries done them, though not by themselves, yet by their Judges. But the Evangelical Law takes away this licence also, as is evident by that opposition that he puts between the Law and the Gospel, *Ye have heard that it hath been said, An eye for an eye, and a tooth for a tooth,* saith Christ; *but I say unto you,* &c. And although the words following do properly appertain to the repelling of injuries, which licence they do at least in some measure restrain; yet much more may we think their purpose was to prohibit revenge, because they seem to be placed in direct opposition to that permission which was anciently given them, and so to imply a rejection of that licence, as being agreeable only to *Moses*'s more imperfect Discipline: *Not that a just revenge was evil, but that Christian patience was much better.* This *revenge by way of retaliation,* S[t] *Augustine* calls *the justice of the unrighteous. Not that the vengeance which the Law decrees is unjust, but that our thirst after revenge is sinful, which better befits a Judge to order, than a wise man to exact for his own satisfaction only.* Concerning which matter, thus speaks *Tertullian, God by the Prophet* Zachary *commands thus, Let no man be mindful of, or remember an injury done him by his Brother,* Zach. 7. 10. *and not by his Brother only, but by his Neighbour also, as appears by another charge given by the same Prophet, Zach.* 8. 17. *Let no man imagine evil against his neighbour,* no not *in his heart.* Whence *Tertullian* infers, *Multo magis patientiam indixit injuriæ, qui indixit oblivionem; He that commands us to forget injuries, doth much more command us to bear them patiently; and he that cleanseth the heart from thinking evil, doth much more restrain the hands from doing evil: and when he saith,* Vengeance is mine, I will repay it, *what doth he but teach us, That we should wait with patience, till God (whose Prerogative it is to revenge) will be pleased to take our Cause into his own hand? And seeing that he will not permit us so much as to remember injuries, or to imagine evil in our hearts against our Neighbour, it is plain, That he doth not require that we should exact an eye instead of an eye, or a tooth instead of a tooth, by way of revenge; but rather by permitting the second injury, his main scope was to repress the first,* Ut unusquisque recipiens licentiam secundæ injuriæ, à prima semetipsum contineret; *That every man considering with himself, that whatsoever he doth unto others, he must suffer the like from others, may be the more fearful of doing that wrong which he would not be content to suffer. For the Argument, as to men, was more forceable to restrain us from doing violence, by setting before us the Law of counter-passion, than by assuring us that he himself would avenge it. And yet both these flaming swords are set to restrain us from doing wrong,* Ut qui Deo crederet, ultionem à Deo expectaret; qui minus fideret, Leges talionis timeret: *That he who believes that God is the Avenger, might fear to offend, lest God should avenge it; and he who believes not, might yet be afraid of the Laws of men, when he assuredly knew, That what wrong soever he did unto his neighbour, he should undoubtedly suffer either from him or others. Our Saviour's Precept then of suffering injuries patiently, and of forbearing revenge, is not inconsistent with the Discipline of* Moses, *but rather strengthens and confirms it. And indeed if we look at the reason of this so perfect and exact patience that is required of us, we shall find that there would be but little of equity in the Precept, if it did not proceed from him who is the righteous Judge of the whole Earth, and who hath engaged himself by his word and promise, That he himself will revenge our wrongs. For if he that imposeth on me this grievous burthen, of not only not returning a blow that is given me, but of offering mine other cheek to the Smiter, and of not only not returning reproaches for reproaches, but of blessing those that curse me; if, I say, he that restraineth me thus from righting my self, do not right me, in vain doth he command me patience, if he give me not the reward of that patience which is a just revenge, which he ought to permit to me, if he do it not himself;* and

Vide Lactant. de ira Dei, c. 18.

Servorum Filiorùmque peccata non coercere, peccatum est.

Revenge as it proceeds from a delight in the Revenger, naturally unlawful.

Non quod iniqua est justa ultio, sed quod ei præstet patientia, Clem. Con. stitut.

Aug. in Ps. 108.

Zach. 7. 10.

Zach. 8. 17.

and if he suffer not me to do it, he himself is bound to perform it. For Disciplinæ intereſt injuriam vindicari; *It is a neceſſary part of good Diſcipline to help them to right that ſuffer wrong.* And *metu ultionis, omnis refrænatur iniquitas*; *the fear of a juſt revenge, reſtrains all acts of violence.* By this of *Tertullian* we may ſee, That it is not only unlawful for a Chriſtian to exact this Law of retaliation, but that it was not tolerated among the Hebrews as a thing ſimply, and in it ſelf commendable, but only for the prevention of a greater evil. Thus alſo doth St *Chryſoſtome* expound that Law of retaliation, *Therefore doth Chriſt urge that of* Moſes, *An eye for an eye, and a tooth for a tooth,* Ut illius manus cohibeat, non ut tuas excitet contra; *To reſtrain him that offers the wrong, not to provoke thee to revenge who ſuffereſt it; not only to preſerve Thine eye, but to keep His alſo ſafe.* That it is not lawful for a Chriſtian to exact this Law out of hatred, nor barely as a puniſhment for that which is paſt, is without all queſtion. The moſt learned amongſt the Hebrews did not apprehend it in that latitude; for they reſpected not ſo much the words of the Law, as the reaſon of it, and the intent of the Law-giver. This appears by the acknowledgment of the Jews of *Alexandria*, (as *Philo* tells the Story) who when they beheld the calamities that befel *Flaccus*, who was their bitter enemy, cried out, *Non delectamur, Domine, ultione de inimico,* &c. *We delight not, O Lord, in revenge, though on our enemy; for from thy Sacred Laws we have learned to commiſerate the man.* And to that end is that general Precept of our Saviour, To forgive every man (without diſtinction) that hath offended us; that is, Neither to do, nor to wiſh them any evil, out of the ſenſe of that evil which they have done unto us; *for he that doth ſo is cruel, arrogating that unto himſelf which is due unto the Laws:* wherefore *Lactantius* reciting thoſe words of *Cicero*, *Is vir bonus eſt qui prodeſt quibus poſſit, noceat nemini, niſi laceſſitus injuriâ*; *He is a good man that doth good to whomſoever he can, but hurts none, unleſs provoked by ſome injury*; thus deſcants upon them, *O what a plain and excellent Sentence is here ſpoiled by the addition of two words!* And St *Ambroſe*, reciting the ſame Sentence of *Cicero*, ſaith, That that Sentence wanted the authority of the holy Goſpel to confirm it, (which teacheth us, That to return an injury hath no leſs of evil than to infer one.) But what ſhall we ſay of that revenge which reſpects not the time paſt, but that which is to come? Surely Chriſt commands us to forgive even this alſo, firſt in caſe there appear any ſigns of repentance in the perſon offending, *Luke* 17. 3. And a plenary remiſſion the Apoſtle requires, *Epheſ.* 4. 32. that is, Such a remiſſion as reſtores the Offender into the ſame degree of friendſhip wherein he was before the ſin was committed; whence it follows, That nothing ought to be exacted from him by way of puniſhment. Beſides, though there be no ſuch ſigns of repentance, yet if the damage we ſuſtain be not very great, no greater than the loſs of ones Coat, Chriſt by this Precept reſtrains us from requiring any revenge at all. Of the ſame opinion were both *Plato* and *Maximus Tyrius*: The like doth *Muſonius* profeſs of himſelf, namely, That for ſmall reproaches (as a box on the ear, *&c.*) he would neither ſue any man at the Law, nor perſwade any man ſo to do; becauſe ſuch as theſe are much better forgiven or diſſembled. But in caſe we cannot paſs it by without giving encouragement to greater injuries, either to our ſelves or others; then we may provide for our own ſafety, yet with the ſmalleſt damage we can to him that hath provoked us. For even the Jews themſelves (as *Joſephus* tells us) beſides the coſts and charges of the hurt done, whereof we have a diſtinct Law, *Exod.* 21. 19 did uſually buy off their Talio with a Summ of Money. The like they did at *Rome*, as *Favorinus* in *Gellius* teſtifies. So *Joſeph* the foſter Father of *Jeſus*, believing his Wife to be with child by adultery, choſe rather to diſmiſs her privately, than to expoſe her to ſhame; and this he is ſaid to do, becauſe he was a juſt man, that is, as St *Ambroſe* expounds it, A man free not only from the cruelty of revenge, but from the ſeverity of an accuſation; for as *Lactantius* had before ſaid, *A good man ought not to accuſe any man of a crime that is capital.* Thus *Juſtin Martyr* concerning thoſe that bitterly accuſed Chriſtians, *We*, ſaith he, *would not have them puniſhed*; *for they are ſufficiently miſerable in their own wickedneſs, and in their ignorance of what is good.* Laſtly, Thoſe puniſhments that are executed, not for any private, but for the publick good, either by killing or reſtraining the perſon nocent, to deter others, or to prevent future miſchiefs; are not forbidden by Chriſt, as we have elſewhere proved by a moſt irrefragable Argument: ſeeing that when he gave thoſe Precepts, he gave alſo this Teſtimony of himſelf, That he deſtroyed no tittle of the Law: But the Law of *Moſes*, which in theſe things was certainly in force ſo long as the Jews had a Commonwealth, did peremptorily enjoin the Magiſtrate to puniſh Capital Offenders with death. And if Chriſt's Precepts could conſiſt with *Moſes*'s Law, as it exacted puniſhments, even ſuch as were capital; certainly they may conſiſt as well with thoſe humane Laws, which, in imitation of the Divine Law, do require and inflict the ſame puniſhments to the ſame end. *Joſephus* highly extols the Phariſees for their clemency and moderation in puniſhments, whence ariſe ſo many exceptions in their Laws concerning publick puniſhments; and this alſo amongſt others, That though the Offender muſt certainly be put to death, yet was the manner of his death to be gentle, and with the leaſt of torments.

In Eph. 4. 13.

Matt. 6. 14, 15.

Luke 17. 3.

The Jews might buy off their Talio.

Lib. 20. *c.* 1.

Vid. infra Sect. 15.

Lib. 6. *c.* 10.

Capital puniſhments not forbidden in the Goſpel.

Exod. 21. 14. Numb. 33. 14. Deut. 29. 13.

Vide Aug. Qu. Evang. l. 1. *c.* 10.

Talmud Tit. Keluboth.

XI. The Argument from Gods mercy in the Gospel, answered.

Yet some there are, who in defence of the contrary opinion, do thus plead; that God especially in the new Covenant, doth declare himself to be full of mercy and forbearance, which all Christian men, yea even Magistrates, as Gods vicegerents ought to imitate; which I grant to be in some measure true, but not in that large and unlimited sense as they would have it understood. For that infinite mercy of God declared in the New Covenant, doth principally respect those sins which are committed against the Laws given to *Adam* and the sons of *Noah*, or against those Laws given by *Moses* before the publication of the Gospel, as will appear, *Act*. 17. 36. *Rom*. 2. 25. *Act*. 13. 38. *Heb*. 9. 15. For those that are committed after, especially if attended with contumacy and stubborness, are threatned with Judgments of another nature, much more severe than those threatned by *Moses*, as *Heb*. 10. 29. *Matt*. 5. 21, 22, 28. Neither are they threatned with Judgments of the other life only, but very often with Judgments of this life, as 1 *Cor*. 11. 30. Neither doth he at any time indulge pardon to a sinner, *nisi ipse de se quasi pœnas exigeret*; *unless he that sins, do as it were inflict punishment upon himself*, 1 Cor. 11. 3. And that with a great deal of sorrow, 2 *Cor*. 11. 27. But here they farther object, that in imitation of Almighty God, the Magistrate should not punish those at least that are penitent. But to pass by that, it will be a difficult thing for the Magistrate to discern who are truly penitent; for if outward shews and professions of penitence would be sufficient, no man would smart for his sin: we find by the example of King *David*, that God doth not always remit all kinds of punishment, no not to the penitent: for though he do remit or abate of the severity of the Law, so that he doth not punish him with a violent, or otherwise untimely death, whereunto his sin hath subjected him; yet whilst he suffers him to be chastised with the rods of men, it plainly shews that his mercy is as well seen in the extenuation of punishments, as in the total and absolute remission of them; *there is much of mercy and lenity in the mitigation of torments, and lesser judgments deserve not the name of judgments, when we know that we have deserved greater*: even so, now God may and undoubtedly doth express his mercy to a sinner, in remitting the punishment of eternal death, which every sinner doth contract for his sin, though he do visit him with an untimely death, either immediately by himself, or mediately by the hand of the Magistrate.

XII. And that of depriving a sinner of the time of Repentance.

But others there are again that urge, that together with the life of a sinner all opportunity of repentance is quite cut off: whereunto we answer, that no man is so suddainly snatcht away, but he is allotted a certain time to make his peace with God: And although he be not permitted to make a real expression of his conversion, by his life and conversation; yet that God doth sometimes accept of the will for the deed in such cases, is most apparent by the example of the Thief upon the Cross. And if it be yet objected, That a longer life might haply conduce much to the glory of God, in the perfecting of this work of repentance in him: I answer, That God haply might as probably have received as much dishonour in his recidivation, or falling back to his accustomed wicked courses; and so that of *Seneca* might very fitly be applyed, *Quod unum bonum tibi superest, repræsentabimus, mortem*; *that only good thing that thou art capable of, we represent unto thee, which is death*. And that also of the same *Seneca*, *Quo uno modo possunt, desinant esse mali*; *there being no way left for them to cease to sin, but to cease to live*; whereunto we may add, that which the same Author saith elswhere, *Talibus ingeniis vitæ exitus remedium est, optimumque est abire ei qui ad se nunquam reverturus est*; *death is to such the only remedy, it being best for him to dye, that lives without any hopes of being cured*. Let these therefore together with what we have said in the beginning of this work, suffice for answer to those who hold that either all punishments, or at least such as are capital, are without any exceptions, prohibited unto Christians; the contrary whereunto we are taught by the Apostle, who within the duty of a King includes the power of the Sword, as being the Executioner of divine vengeance: and in another place he tells us, that we ought to pray that Kings may be made Christians, and that as Kings, they may protect the innocent; which in this general corruption and depravity of mankind, even since the times of the Gospel, cannot be done, unless by the death of some, the impudence of others be repressed; seeing that all the publick punishments that are every where inflicted upon the guilty, are not as yet found sufficient to guard or protect the innocent. Neither is it altogether impertinent, to propose unto all Christian Magistrates the example of *Sabacon* King of *Ægypt* for their imitation, a man highly famed for his Piety, by whom all capital punishments were changed into some servile works, that were profitable to the Common-wealth, and that with good success, as *Diodorus* testifies: *Strabo* relates the like of some Nations inhabiting about Mount *Caucasus*, where, saith he, *They put no man to death although they offend never so highly*: yea and among the Romans, no Citizen was ever known to be put to death or punished with stripes after the Porcian Law was made, unless for Treason, or being first condemned by the people of *Rome*. Neither is that of *Quintilian* to be slighted, *No man will doubt*, saith he, *but that if a Malefactor could be reclaimed, and become a new man, as some such there may sometimes be, it were better for the Common-wealth that he should live*

Lib. 1. *de Ira c*. 16. *c*. 15.

De Benef. *l*. 7. *c*. 10.

Lib. 1.

live than dye. It is obſerved by *Balſamon*, That thoſe Roman-Laws which condemned men to death, were moſt of them changed by the Chriſtian Emperours into ſome ſmart puniſhment, whereby both the condemned Party was more ſharply urged to repentance, and others more affrighted by their laſting puniſhment. *Nicetas* records it, That during the Reign of *Johannes Comnenus*, no Malefactor was at any time put to death. And when ſome ranting Donatiſts had killed two Catholick Prieſts, moſt barbarouſly putting out the eyes, and cutting off the fingers of one of them, St *Auguſtine* beſought Count *Marcellinus* not to puniſh them by that ſtrict Rule of retaliation, whereby *they ſhould ſuffer according to what they had done*; but that he would ſuffer them to live, and to enjoy their limbs: yet to reſtrain them from the like outrages by ſome hard, yet profitable, labour; or to reclaim them from their madneſs by ſome ſmarting puniſhment. *For this alſo*, ſaith he, *is called a condemnation. And who underſtands not this to be as well a benefit as a puniſhment, whereby neither are the Reins let looſe to licentious cruelty, nor that wholeſome Phyſick withheld, that ſhould work Malefactors to repentance?* (An Houſe of correction ſtrikes more terrour to an idle Rogue, than the Gallows; and to be chained to an Oar, than Death it ſelf.) See Chap. 24. Sect. 2. Grat. l. 23. q. 5. Circumcelliones.

XIII. The imperfect Diviſions of puniſhments rejected.

By that Diviſion which we have made of the ends for which puniſhments were ordained, it ſeems that ſomewhat was omitted by the Philoſopher *Taurus*, out of whom *Gellius* ſaith thus, *Whenſoever there ſhall appear in a Malefactor great hopes of reformation without puniſhment, or no hopes at all of his amendment, or that there is no neceſſary cauſe to fear the dignity of the Perſon againſt whom the offence is committed, ſhould be ſlighted or contemned, or that the ſin is not ſuch as requires the impreſſion of ſome neceſſary fear to preſerve others from it; then whereinſoever it is that men offend, it is not worth our ſtudy to inflict puniſhments.* For he ſeems thence to infer, That puniſhments are needleſs, if any one of theſe ends be wanting; whereas on the contrary all theſe ends muſt ceaſe, that there be no need of puniſhments. Beſides, he omits this end, namely, When an incorrigible Sinner is taken away, to the end that he may not commit more or greater ſins. And what he there ſaid concerning the loſs of the dignity of the perſon againſt whom the ſin is committed, was to be extended to other damages, which we may have juſt occaſion to fear. Much better is that Partition which *Seneca* makes, *In revenging injuries* (ſaith he) *the Law looks at three things, which every Magiſtrate ought likewiſe to purſue*: namely, *That either he whom we puniſh ſhould amend his life*; *or that by his puniſhment others ſhould be meliorated*; *or that incorrigible Malefactors being taken away, they that are innocent ſhould live more ſecurely.* The two former of theſe *Philo* commemorates, *Puniſhment oftimes corrects and amends a Malefactor; but if this fail, it doth certainly meliorate thoſe that come to the knowledg thereof. For many men are inſtructed by other mens harms, and grow more watchful over themſelves by fear of the like ſufferings.* But in that Diviſion of *Seneca*, if by thoſe that are innocent, we underſtand as well thoſe who may hereafter be injured, as thoſe who have already been injured, we have a full and perfect Partition; eſpecially if to thoſe two words, *taken away*, we adde *or ſuppreſſed.* For both exile, impriſonment, and whatſoever elſe it is whereby a man is diſabled to do wrong, may be hither referred. But that diſtribution which *Seneca* elſewhere makes, is more imperfect, where he ſaith, *That in puniſhments this Rule is to be obſerved, That ſome are inflicted to reclaim thoſe that are wicked, others to take them away.* And yet that of *Quintilian* is yet more imperfect, *That every puniſhment appertains not ſo much to the ſin, as for example.* De Clem. lib. 1. c. 21. Three ends of puniſhing. In Legatione.

XIV. Not lawful for private Chriſtians to inflict capital puniſhments, though by the Law of Nations they may.

From what hath been already ſaid, we may collect how unſafe it is for a Chriſtian, being a private man, to take revenge upon any wicked man, eſpecially by death, either for his own or for the publick good; although it be ſometimes permitted by the Law of Nations, as we have already declared *. And therefore it is a laudable cuſtom among ſome people, for ſuch as have the ſupreme power to grant Commiſſions to ſuch as put out to Sea to perſecute Pirates whereſoever they find them, whereof they may make uſe as occaſions ſerve, to ſhew (if need be) that they did it not upon any private malice, but in obedience to their Princes Commands.

* See Book 1. Chap. 3. Sect. 3. and this Ch. Sect. 8.

XV. Or to accuſe any voluntarily.

Not much unlike unto this is another cuſtom which I find in ſome Countries, where every man that will, is not permitted to prefer a Criminal Accuſation againſt another; but ſome particular men are choſen, and thereunto commiſſionated by publick Authority: ſo that no private man can attempt any thing that tends to the effuſion of humane blood, but ſuch only as are bound to do it by virtue of their Office. And to this hath that Canon of the Eliberine Council reſpect, which denies the Communion to any man that ſhall by his private ſuggeſtion or accuſation, occaſion the death or proſcription of another.

XVI. Or to affect the Office of a Judge in capital matters.

And from what hath been already ſaid, we may collect alſo how unſafe and indecent it is for a man truly Chriſtian, raſhly to thruſt himſelf into ſuch publick Offices as to have it in their power to ſentence men to death, or to conceit and to publiſh himſelf to be fit that ſuch a right of life and death ſhould be committed unto him, as to the moſt excellent of all others, and as unto a God amongſt men. For ſurely our Bleſſed Saviours advice, namely, To *take heed*, as in a caſe of danger, how we paſs ſentence upon others (becauſe, look, what Math. 7. 1.

what measure we mete unto others, we must expect from God in like cases) doth chiefly appertain unto this kind of Judgment.

XVII. Whether those Humane Laws that permit the killing of some men, do give them a true right before God, or only an impunity amongst men.

Another notable Question doth sometimes arise, namely, Whether those humane Laws which permit the killing of some men, do justifie it before God, or whether they grant only an impunity amongst men. This latter opinion was much favoured by *Covarruvia* and *Fortunius*; but on the contrary so distasted by *Vasquius*, that he calls it abominable. Without doubt, the Laws may do both in some Cases; but whether they will do so or not, may be gathered, partly, from the words of the Law, and partly, from the matter. For if the Laws have regard to the grief and sorrow of the Offender, it remits the punishment, but not the sin; as in the Case of an Husband that kills his adulterous Wife, or of the Wife her adulterous Husband. A Wife taken in Adultery might by the Law of the *Lombards* be killed by her own Husband; but not so by the Roman Laws: yet if he did kill his adulterous Wife, being so taken, he was excused and pardoned, *non à culpa vel à peccato, licet à pœna civili*; *not altogether from the sin, though from the punishment due by the Civil Law.* For as St *Augustin* observes, If *he that killeth or woundeth a Malefactor be a Magistrate, he is God's Minister, and not to be blamed for it; but if he be a private person, he shall be judged as an Homicide, because he presumes to usurp that authority which is not given him by God.* But if the Law respect some ensuing mischief that is likely to happen by the delaying of the punishment, then it is supposed to transferr publick Authority to every private man, who therein is reputed a Magistrate. And of this kind is that Law in the Codes of *Justinian* under this Title, *Quando liceat unicuique sine Judice*, &c. When it is lawful for any private man to revenge himself or the publick worship without a Judge. In which Law, licence is given unto every man, by severe punishments, to repress Souldiers when they are found straggling from the Army, and plundering the Country: And the reason of the Law is there added, *Melius est occurrere in tempore, quàm exitum vindicare*; *Better it is to prevent mischiefs in their beginning, than to revenge them when done. We therefore* (saith the Emperour) *grant you licence to avenge your own wrongs, and what is now too late judicially to punish, we shall endeavour to suppress by our Proclamation, That no man shall hereafter spare a Souldier so plundering, but shall resist and assault him with weapons, as if he were a common Thief.* And of the same kind also is the subsequent Law concerning Souldiers deserting their Colours, *Let all men know,* (saith he) *That against Robbers and Souldiers that fly from the Army, power is hereby given to every man, for the preservation of the common safety, to execute publick revenge.* And thus is that of *Tertullian* to be understood, *In reos Majestatis, & publicos Hostes, omnis homo Miles est*; *Against Traitors and publick Enemies, every man is a Souldier. There is not only in Great Commanders and other Potentates, an innate and constant purpose of doing well to the Publick; but it is both lawful and honest for every man, that will, to be troubled at the calamities that befal the Commonwealth he lives in; and to promote, as far as he is able, the publick safety and prosperity thereof.* But the right of killing Exiles (whom they also call Bannites) differs herein from those mentioned in the said Laws: For as to the former, it is necessary that they should be particularly sentenced unto death before they be killed. But as to these latter, a general Edict, together with the evidence of the Fact, is as authoritative as a Sentence particularly denounced. So thought *Quintilian*, *There are some crimes so evidently committed against the Commonwealth, that the very sight of them is enough to justifie our revenge.*

Grat. Can. 33. *Q.* 2. *inter hæc.* *Lib. de Civit. Dei.* *Grat. c.* 23. *q.* 8. *quicunque.* *Agathicas, lib.* 4. Dect. 206.

XVIII. What acts are punishable by men. The internal acts of the mind.

Now let us see whether all acts are such as ought to be punished by humane Laws. And certainly they are not: For, in the first place, the internal acts of the mind, although they afterwards come to be known unto others, as by confession, or by some other accident; cannot be liable to the punishment of men, because it is not agreeable to humane nature, that any right or obligation should arise from acts merely internal. And in this sense are the Roman Laws to be understood when they say, *Cogitationis pœnam neminem mereri,* (which we render thus, Thought is free;) yet even these internal acts, as they have their influence upon the external acts of the Body, have their estimation, not properly of their own, but as those external acts deserve more or less punishment, according to these internal ones of the mind.

XIX. Such as are inevitable to humane nature.

Those acts that are inevitable to humane nature, are not to be punished by humane Laws. For though nothing be imputed to us as a sin, but what hath the concurrence of the will, and is done freely; yet to abstain altogether, and at all times from sin, and over all temptations still to emerge Conquerours, is above the strength and condition of humane Nature: whence it is that all sorts and Sects of men have esteemed it natural for man to sin. As among Philosophers, *Sopater, Hierocles, Seneca*; amongst Jews, *Philo*; amongst Historians, *Thucydides*; and amongst Christians very many have left us their testimony upon Record. *There is no man to be found that can in all things justifie himself,* saith *Seneca.* A little before he had said, *Amongst others the calamities that attend Mortals, this is one, namely, The darkness of the understanding, which betrays us not only to a necessity of erring, but to the love of errours.* And presently after, *Quis ille est qui se profitetur omnibus Legibus innocentem?*

Sen.de ira, c. 14. ——*c.* 9. ——*c.* 17.

innocentem; *who is he that can plead his innocency to all the Laws?* and in another place, *peccavimus omnes*, &c. *we have all sinned, some more, some less; some intentionally, others haply by the perswasion of others, or violently carried away by the lewdness of another; some of us through levity, not adhereing to good counsel, and some upon the suddain approach of dangers, lose our innocency though unwillingly, and not without some reluctancy: neither do we sin only for the present, but we will continue sinning to our death; and although a man do purge his conscience never so well, so that nothing doth either disturb or deceive him, yet is it but by sinning, that we arrive at this innocency.* Thus likewise *Belisarius* in *Procopius*, *not at all to sin, falls not under the power of humane nature, neither can our weakness bear it*: *Si puniendus est, cuique pravum maleficumque ingenium est, pœna neminem excipiet*; *if* saith *Seneca*, *every man that is of a depraved nature were to be necessarily punisht, no man would go unpunished.* To the same purpose is that of *Sopater*, *He that will so punish, as if he would have men altogether without fault, must needs exceed the natural bounds of correction.* Of the same mind was *Diodorus Siculus*, *Strictly to observe whatever is done amiss, and severely to punish every offence, is a wrong done to humane frailty, and to forget the weakness that is common to all mankind.* For as the same *Sopater* saith wisely, *Our lesser and as it were, daily slips of infirmity, are rather to be connived at, than punished.* And indeed it may well be doubted, whether such as these, may properly be called sins; because though we have freedom as to this or that sin, to do it, or not to do it; yet not at all to sin in respect of our natural frailty is impossible. *Every Law then* (as *Plutarch* in *Solon* saith) *should command things possible, if it intends to punish a few profitably, and not a multitude unprofitably.* Some sins there are that are inevitable, not simply to mankind in general, but to this or that particular person, or to this or that particular time, or age, by reason of such or such a temperament of the body strongly inclining the mind, as *Seneca* observes, *Morum varietates mixtura elementorum facit*; *the variety that there is in mens manners, is occasioned by the various mixture of the elements*, or by some overgrown customs, which notwithstanding are usually punished, not so much for themselves, as for some former errours; as either for neglecting the remedies whereby they might have been prevented, or because those diseases of the mind were voluntarily contracted. *Lot*'s daughters made him drunk, and then lay with him, but he knew it not; whereupon St. *Aug.* passeth this sentence on him, *That he deserved to be punished, not for his incest, but for his drunkenness.*

De Clem. l. 1. c. 8.

Goth. 3.

Grat. Can. 15. Q. 1. c. inebriaverunt.

XX. Nor those that are neither directly nor indirectly destructive to humane Society.

Thirdly, Neither are those sins to be punished by humane Laws, which are neither directly nor indirectly against humane Society, or against any other man; because there can be no reason assigned why such offences should not be referred to the supreme Tribunal of God himself, who is most wise to understand, most righteous to perpend and weigh, and most mighty to revenge and punish them: wherefore all humane punishments as to such sins are plainly unprofitable, and therefore vain. Hence notwithstanding, we are to except such punishments as tend only to reformation, although haply it may no way concern others: neither are those sins to be punished by humane Laws, which are opposite to such vertues, as the Laws do not compel, but perswade only, and exhort us unto; as those of mercy, liberality, gratitude, &c. *Seneca* discussing this question, whether the sin of ingratitude be punishable, resolves it thus, *Cum res honestissima sit referre gratiam, desinit honesta esse si necessaria sit*; *since to be thankful is a thing eminently honest, it would cease to be so were it necessary*; which he thus explains in the subsequent words: *For* (saith he) *if to be unthankful were punishable, no man would more commend a thankful man, than he doth that man that restores what was deposited with him in trust, or that man that pays his just debts: neither whereof can with honesty be detained; and therefore are not courtesies but debts, which whoso willingly pays, we do not so properly commend, as discharge him: Non erat res gloriosa gratum esse, nisi ingratum fuisse tutum sit*; *it were not so lovely, so grateful a thing to be thankful, if to be unthankful were not safe.* (He that provides alimony for his wife and children, or that feeds and pays his servants for their labour, deserves not thereby the honour of being reputed liberal or charitable, because haply he doth it for fear of the Laws, which have power to force him to do it: But him that relieves the Poor, cloaths the naked, redeems the captive, we commonly magnifie, and extol for his charity; because these acts depend wholly upon the freedom of the will, and if he did them not, no Law can punish him.) So *Seneca* the father, *Thou wilt say unto me, we are no where commanded to do this*: whereunto he answereth, *Hujus rei æstimatio immensa est, itaque nulla vindicta est*; *because the esteem of a grateful man is so precious, for* (as *Solomon* saith of a vertuous wife, His price is above rubies) *therefore there is no punishment awarded unto the ungrateful; for such as these, are not so properly vices, as defects of vertue, for which, chidden we may be, but not punished.*

De Benef. lib. 3. c. 6, 7.

Lib. 4. Cont. 23.

Contr. l. 4. Contr. 23. Controv. 24.

XXI. Whether Magistrates may forgive offences

It follows that we enquire, whether Magistrates may sometimes forgive or pardon offences; which the Stoicks deny, but upon very slender grounds: For they say, *all sins are equal, and therefore if some, then all are equally to be punished.* Again, a wise man say they, (and such should every Magistrate be,) ought to look straight forwards to what he ought to do as a Magistrate, and not to do any thing contrary to his duty. Besides *pardon*, say they,

See *Stobæus frag. tit. de Magistratus.*

Cicero pro Murœna Sen. de clem. in fine.

they, *is the remission of punishment that is due; but a wise man will do his duty, and give unto every man what is his due:* But the fallacy lies in the word *due*; for if by *due*, we mean that which a man may lawfully do without injuring any, then it will not follow, That he that doth not punish, doth not that which he ought to do. But if by the word *due*, we understand that which we must do, then we answer, that there is not always such a necessity; for in this sense, though the offender be by the Law punishable, yet is it not always necessary that he should be punished: for thus, the punishment is not always due, but lawful only. And this may hold true as well before the penal Law is past as after; against these Stoicks *Diodorus Siculus* in his fragments argues well, *Venia melior pœnæ exactione*; *it is much better to pardon then to exact punishment.* So doth St. *Cyprian* for Christians, *There is* (saith he) *a great distance between the opinions of Philosophers and Stoicks, who hold all sins to be equal, and that a wise man must not easily be bended; and the opinion of Christians, who hold that to remit punishment is sometimes better than to exact it.*

Epist. 52.

XXII. The offender may be pardoned before the penal Law be ordained.

The Malefactor may be pardoned before the penal Law be ordained; for doubtless he that offends, lies under a punishable condition naturally: but yet it follows not that he must necessarily be punished. For as *Julian* speaks of *Eusebia*, *though some there be that deserve to be treated ill, and punished, yet is there no necessity that these should be destroyed:* Because this depends upon the coherence that there is between that punishment, and those ends whereunto punishments were ordained: wherefore in case First, these ends be not of themselves in a moral estimation necessary. Or secondly, if there occur other ends on the opposite part no less profitable or necessary. Or thirdly, if the ends proposed by punishments, may haply be by some other ways obtained; then it is plain that nothing can precisely oblige us to require punishment.

As for example, in the first case, when the offence is so privately committed, that few persons take notice of it, and the publick traduction whereof would be not only unnecessary, but haply damagable; were it not better to connive and dissemble the knowledge of it, and not at all to punish it, than by punishing it, to make it the more publick (as in the case of Scandal?) so *Cicero* of one *Zeuxis*, *Adductum in judicium, fortasse dimitti non oportuerit, conquiri vero ad judicium necesse non fuit; being brought unto judgment, he ought not to be dismist; but to have brought him unto judgment there was no necessity.* Again in the second case, sometimes the end that we propose to our selves in punishing is overballanced by some other ends which are no less profitable or necessary: As when the offence is committed by one who either in his own person, or by his parents, hath highly merited from the Commonwealth. For then as *Seneca* well observes, *Beneficium superveniens apparere injuriam non patitur; we cannot see the injury done, for the glory of his preceding merits.* Thirdly, sometimes again the end that we propose to our selves in punishing, may better be obtained by some other ways, as when reproofs will serve to reform an offender, what need is there of blows? or when a man is ready to satisfie an injury with an ingenious confession, and an humble submission, it is in vain to exact punishment; whereunto that wise Hebrew had respect when he said, *That it became the just to be merciful.* For seeing there is no punishment, especially if great, but in it self considered hath somewhat in it that is repugnant, not to justice, but to charity: Surely common reason will easily be perswaded to abstain from it, until by arguments drawn from a greater charity, and a more universal good, she be irresistably overborn, and hindered. Very apposite unto this, is that of *Sopater*, where he saith, *Justitia pars illa quæ contractus ad æqualitatem reducit, omnino respuit omne gratiæ genus: at ea pars quæ circa delicta occupatur, non recusat suavem & blandam gratiarium faciem; that that part of justice, which weighs all contracts in an equal ballance, utterly rejects all kind of favour: but that which is conversant about offences, refuseth not sometimes the meek and lovely face of the graces.* The meaning of the former part of this sentence, *Cicero* delivers in these words, *The way of dispensing this right is in some things to do nothing through favour:* And the latter part of it *Dion Prusiensis* thus explains, *Boni præsidis est ignoscere; it is the duty of a good Prince to forgive.* And in *Favorinus* also we read thus, *That which men call clemency is nothing else but a seasonable mitigation of the rigour of the Law.*

Ad. Q. fratr. 1. 21.

Ecclus. 12. 19.

Ad. Q. frat. 1, 2.

XXIII. Yet not always.

In punishment these three things do offer themselves to be considered, Either that they should be altogether exacted, as in such crimes as are of dangerous Precedents; among which, *Josephus* reckons Parricides, which as *who so commits, violates the Law of nature, and takes away the life of man; so he that doth not punish, doth himself sin against humane nature.* Or, secondly, That they should not at all be required; as when some publick good requires that it should be altogether omitted: or, thirdly, That either of these may be done lawfully. This is intended by *Seneca*, where he saith, That clemency depends upon our own free will. But then say the Stoicks, *Parcit sapiens, non ignoscit; He spares, but forgives not.* As if it were not as lawful for us (with the vulgar people, being the Masters of speech) to express that by the word *pardon*, as for them to do it by the word *spare*. But not only herein, but in many other cases we find that to be true, which *Cicero*, *Galen*, and many others have observed, That most of the disputations of the Stoicks

are

are about words only, which a Philosopher should principally avoid. For as he that wrote to *Herennius* truly notes, *Vitiosum est Controversiam intendere propter nominum mutationem*; *To heighten Controversies about the change of names, is vitious.* And as St *Augustine* argues against the Academicks, *Turpe est disputationibus in verborum quæstione immorari, cùm certamen nullum de rebus remanserit*; *It is absurd to contest about words only, when there remains no difference at all about things.* Lib. 2.

XXIV. Yea and after the penal Law.

But the pardoning of offences after the penal Law is past, seems to be more inconsistent with the integrity of a Prince; because he that is the Authour of the Law, is in some measure bound up by his own Laws, which is true as the Law-maker is a Member of the City, and as so only considered; but not as he sustains the authority, and is as it were the Body of the Commonwealth: For, as such, he may take away even the whole Law; for the nature of an humane Law is such, that it depends upon the will of the Law-maker, not in respect of its institution only, but of its continuation. But in case he do subvert or take away any Law without some probable reason or cause, he sins against the Rule of Polity. But as he may take away the whole Law, so also may he take away the condemning power of the Law, as to this or that person, or to this or that particular Fact, the same Law remaining in force as to others by the example of God himself; who, as *Lactantius* observes, *when he instituted Laws for men, did not intend to deprive himself of the power of pardoning such as should offend against those Laws. It is lawful for a Prince to revoke the sentence of death, and to absolve a person, though condemned to dye*, saith St *Augustine*; whereof he adds this as the reason, *Quia non est subjectus Legibus, qui habet in potestate Leges ferre*; *Because he is not subject unto Laws, in whose power it is to make Laws. For the condition of a Magistrate is one, and the condition of a Prince is another*; *the Magistrate is corrupt, if his Sentence be more remiss than the Law: but to mitigate the rigour of a severe Law, is sometimes the Glory of a Prince.* *Seneca* speaking in the Person of *Nero* saith, *Occidere contra Legem nemo potest, servare nemo, prater me*; *Kill contrary to Law no man can, and save none can, besides my self.* But this also must be understood so, that it ought not to be done without probable cause; but what these probable causes are, though it cannot be particularly defined, yet must we grant that they ought to be greater after the Law is past, than those that were looked at before; because unto the other causes, for which punishments are required, there is superadded the authority of the Law, which is fit should be maintained.

Vid. sup. c. 4. Sect. 12.

Humane Laws alterable by him that made them.

Symmachus, lib. 3. Ep. 63.

XXV. Causes freeing from punishment. 1. Intrinsick.

But the Causes exempting any man from the penalty of the Law, are usually either intrinsecal, or extrinsecal. Intrinsecal, as when the punishment compared with the Fact is severe, if not unjust.

XXVI. Or extrinsecal.

Extrinsecal, When a mans former merits, or some other thing commending the person offending, pleads strongly for his pardon: Or when we discern some extraordinary hopes of future good in the Delinquent: but especially if the reason of the Law do at least particularly cease in that Fact for which the punishment is to be inflicted: For although the general reason of a Law, where it is not counterballanced with a contrary reason, is sufficient to uphold the vigour of the Law; yet the failing even of that which is the particular reason of the Law, doth so far operate that the Law may more easily, and with less detriment to Authority, be dispensed with; as *Gratian* proves by many instances. And this usually falls out in such sins as are committed through ignorance, though not altogether blameless, or through infirmity of mind, which haply might (though not without much difficulty) be overcome. Whereunto a Christian Prince ought to have some regard in imitation of God himself, who in the Jewish Law did mercifully provide that most sins of this nature should by some kind of Sacrifices be expiated; as we may read in the fourth and fifth Chapters of *Leviticus*. And as in the New Testament we may find confirmed both by words and examples, wherein he declares how willing he is to pardon such sins to those that repent: as *Luke* 23. 34. *Heb.* 4. 15. 1 *Tim.* 1. 13. And by those very words of Christ, *Father forgive them, for they know not what they do.* By which words *Theodosius* the Emperour was so wrought upon, that he freely forgave the Antiochians, whom he had purposed to destroy, as St *Chrysostome* records.

C. 1. q. 7.

XXVII. Yea though no such exemption be tacitely included in the Law.

Hence then we may discern the errour of *Ferdinandus Vasquius*, who taught that the Laws were in no cases to be dispensed with, but only to such wherein the Law-maker, had he been consulted with, would have confess'd, That it was not his intent that in that Case his Law should be observed. For *Vasquius* there doth not well distinguish between the equitable interpretation of the Law, and the relaxation of it; whence it is, that in another place he reproves *Thomas* and *Scotus* for saying, That the Law was binding, though the reason of that Law did particularly cease; as if they took the Law to consist in the bare letter, which they never thought. But every relaxation of the Law, which may be, and often is, either granted or omitted freely at the pleasure of the Prince, is so far from being referred to equity properly so called, that even that relaxation which is due, either out of charity or polity, is not to be referred thither. For it is one thing to take away the efficacy of the Law, upon some probable cause, or upon some urgent occasion;

and another thing to declare that that Fact was not at the Law-making so much as thought upon by the Maker of it. But let this suffice concerning the taking away the punishments. Now let us see what may be said concerning their infliction.

XXVIII. All punishments are awarded according to mens merits.

By what hath been already said, it appears, That in punishments two things are considerable, First, The merit of the Crime; secondly, The profit that redounds by the punishment. As to the former, *Nemo puniendus est ultra meritum, No man ought to be punished beyond the merit of his offence*: for, as I said before, There ought to be an equality between the sin and the punishment, according to that of *Horace*,

Epist. 15.

——— adsit
Regula peccatis, quæ pœnas irroget æquas.

Let sins have Rules, which equal pains require,
And not plague petty faults with Rods of Wire.

See to this purpose the speech of the Melanois in *Guicc. Lib.* 17. *Vid. sup. Sect.* 11. & *lib.* 3. *c.* 11. *sect.* 1. † Leuct. 2.

Whereunto we may add that of *Cicero* to *Brutus*, *There is* (saith he) *a moderation to be used as well in punishing as in other things.* And therefore *Papinianus* calls punishment the valuation of a crime. And † *Aristides* saith, That it is agreeable to humane nature that there should be bounds prescribed, beyond which revenge should never stray, (in imitation of God himself, who when he proceeds to Judgment, is said to lay Judgment to the Rule, and Righteousness to the Ballance, as if he would retale it, as it were, by weight and measure.) But *Demosthenes* in his Epistle for *Lycurgus*'s Children, doth not approve of such an equality as is barely in weights and measures, but with respect had to the purpose and intent of the Delinquent; and then he concludes, That within the Bounds of Merit, all sins may be punished more or less, so far forth as the punishment shall be thought profitable.

XXIX. The impulsive Causes of sin are to be respected and compared together.

In the merit of the crime, three things are to be examined; First, The cause that did provoke; Secondly, The cause which ought to have restrained, and, Thirdly, The fitness and capacity of the person to either. As to the first of these, there is, doubtless, some cause that moveth every man to evil. There is hardly any man wicked, but for some end; or if there be any man that loves wickedness for wickedness sake only, surely he is not so properly a man as a Devil. The greatest part of Mankind are led unto sin by their affections; So saith St. *James*, *Lust conceiveth, and bringeth forth sin.* Where under this Notion, Lust or Appetite, I comprehend also that vehement desire of declining every thing that may hurt us, which of all others is the most natural, and so the most innocent. Oft-times a man is almost inforced upon a sin, to avoid some present danger; as when to avoid death, imprisonment, torment, or extreme poverty, he doth some act of violence or injustice, and then the fear of the evil that pursues him seems to render his sin the more excusable. Whereupon *Demosthenes* inferrs, *That if a rich man be unjust, he deserves doubly to be punished, in respect of what he suffers for the like sin who is oppressed with poverty. For before such Judges as have any sentiments of humanity, the poor mans necessity pleads strongly for pardon; whereas they who, surfeiting with abundance, sin merely out of wantonness, can have no excuse at all for their wickedness.* Thus doth *Polybius* excuse the *Acarnanæ*, that to avoid that imminent danger that threatned them, were enforced to break the Articles of their League with the Grecians against the Ætolians. The more vehement the temptation is, the more pardonable is the crime. A Woman of *Smyrna*, as *Gellius* tells the Story, was convented before Cn. *Dolabella* the Proconsul of *Asia*, for poysoning her Husband and his Son at the same time. The Fact She confess'd, alledging, That She had good cause so to do; because her Husband and his Son had betrayed and murthered her own Son by a former Husband, being a young man, innocent, and of singular hopes; which Fact was so clear that it could not be denied. *Dolabella* calls a Council, but none durst pass Sentence in so doubtful a Case; for the Womans Fact being confest, they thought, ought not to go unpunished, and yet the revenge She took, for the murder of her Son, appeared to be but just. In conclusion, *Dolabella* sent her to *Athens* to be judged by the Areopagites, as being the most knowing and experienced Judges of that Age, who upon a full hearing of the Cause, adjourned the determination of it for a hundred years; by which means they neither acquitted the Woman of her crime against the Laws, nor condemned her, though guilty; because the violence of the temptation pleaded for pardon. *The less of provocation a man hath to do evil, the greater is his sin.* Whence *Aristotle* inferrs, *That the sin of incontinence is greater than that committed through fear, because it is more voluntary; for what a man doth out of fear, is to preserve himself from destruction: and in such a Case there is a force upon the will. But lust is conceived within us, and therefore hath the more of evil, because it hath a larger share of the will.* With whom accords *Philo* upon the Decalogue, *All other vehement perturbations of the mind are occasioned by the assault of some outward temptations, which seem to happen against our will; only our lusts, be-*

Jam, 1. 15. Gell. l. 12. c. 17. See Prov. 6. 30, 31, 32.

cause they are conceived within us, can be imputed to none but our selves. All sins faith *Chrysostome, merit not the same punishment, but those deserve the greatest which might easiest be resisted.* Hence it is, that in another place he inferrs, *That the Slanderer is a greater sinner than a Fornicator, a Thief or an Homicide, because these may have vehement temptations, but the Slanderer none but his own Will. Men do not despise a Thief, if he steal to satisfie his own soul when he is hungry; but he that committeth Adultery with a Woman lacketh understanding: He that doth it destroyeth his own soul,* Prov. 6. 30, 32. All other appetites do tend to some good, either real or imaginary; those things that are really good, besides virtues and their actions which cannot entice unto sin, (being alwayes at peace among themselves) are either delectable, as pleasures; or such as are desirable in order to things that are delectable, which we call things profitable, as abundance of all outward enjoyments. Those that are imaginary only, and not really good, are either the excellency that we think we have above others, as it is separated from virtue and profit, or revenge, both which, the more devious from Nature they are, the worse they are. *(Naturalia desideria finita sunt, ex falsa opinione nascentia ubi desinant non habent; Our natural wants* (saith *Seneca) are easily summed up, but those that are grounded upon a false opinion are infinite.)* St *John* collects all the provocations to sin under these three heads, the lusts of the flesh, the lust of the eyes, or the pride of life; the first whereof comprehends the desires of pleasure; the second of profit; the third of vain-glory and anger. And *Philo* in his Exposition of the Decalogue derives all that is Evil from the desires either of Riches, Honour or Pleasure. And *Lactantius* describes the office of *Virtue to consist in the suppression of our anger, in bridling of our lusts, and in the moderating of our desires of riches. For* (saith he) *almost all our unjust and wicked actions do arise from one of these affections,* which elsewhere he repeats. 1 Joh. 2. 16. Lib. 6.

XXX. The Causes restraining from sin.

The general cause that should restrain us from sin, is, the injustice of the fact: For we speak not here of all sins, but of those which have respect to something without the person sinning. Now this injustice is so much the greater, by how much the damage thereby done to another is greater. And therefore those are the greatest injuries that are actually consummated, and those the least, which though they have made their progress through some Acts, yet are not arrived to the utmost Act: For which reason the coveting of our neighbours goods, is placed by *Moses* in the rear of the Decalogue, as being a sin of the lowest form, or, as it were, but an introduction to sin, which the farther it goes, the worse it is. In either of these kinds, that is esteemed the greatest crime, which disturbs Common Order, and thereby gives offence to most men. After this follow the injuries done to particular persons: And of these the highest is, that which touches the life of Man, exprest by *Moses* in this Precept, *Thou shalt not kill.* The next is, that injury done to a Mans Family, the foundation whereof is laid in Matrimony, contained in these words, *Thou shalt not commit Adultery.* The third and last are, such as are committed against a Mans private Estate, either directly, as by stealing; or indirectly, as when by our false Testimony we prejudice the Right of others. These may be yet more acutely divided: But it pleased Almighty God in the Decalogue to follow this Order. For under the name of Parents, which are Natural Magistrates, it is fit that Magistrates and other Rulers and Governours should be comprehended, by whose Authority Humane Society is maintained. Next unto this follows the Interdiction of Homicide; the Institution of Matrimony, and the prohibiting of Adultery; then Theft is forbidden, and false testimonies: and in the last place, such sins as are inconsummate. Neither amongst those Causes that should restrain us from sin, are we to place that single damage only, that is done directly against others; but that also which is probably consequent to it; as in firing an house, making a breach in the sea-bank, or in a bulwark wherein the lives and fortunes of many Families are concerned. Moreover that Injustice, which we put here as a general cause of restraining from sin, is sometimes aggravated by the addition of another crime; as our impiety to our Parents, our inhumanity to our Kindred, our ingratitude to our Patrons or Benefactors. Again, a sin is reputed the greater being the oftner committed; forasmuch as an habit of evil is far worse than some particular acts of evil. *Once to erre is pardonable:* but *in iisdem sæpius errare emotæ est mentis; To dash often against the same stone is folly, nay, madness; the oftner we offend, the greater punishment we deserve.* And from hence we may collect how far forth that was naturally Righteous, which was usually done amongst the *Persians*, who before they passed sentence upon a Malefactor, looked back to his former life, and compared it with the present Crime he stood convicted of; for they thought it unjust to take away the life of any man for one evil act, unless the whole course of his life had been otherwise sinfull. And indeed what *Asinius Pollio* saith, is very true; *We are not to judge of any person by some particular acts, but by his continued habits.* (None are to be accounted notoriously wicked, but they that have long persisted in a constant course of wickedness, *Nemo repente fit pessimus; No man arrives at the heighth of impudency at the first:* For our innocency leaves us not but by degrees; and boldness, that it

The Persian Custom.

it may learn not to startle at grosser villanies, gathers strength and courage by the frequent committing of lesser ones.) And yet what *Asinius Pollio* said concerning the judging of mens present Crimes by their former lives, ought to take place in such only, who being otherwise not wicked, have been on a sudden surprized by the sweetness of some particular sin: But not in those who have changed the whole course of their former lives.
Chap. 18. For of these God himself by the Prophet *Ezekiel* proclaims, that he will have no regard
Lib. 1. at all to their former deeds; whereunto that of *Thucydides* may very fitly be applyed, *They deserve doubly to be punished, because they are Apostates from goodness, and degenerate from Virtue to Vice.* And therefore it was wisely provided by the Primitive Christians in their censures of other mens failings, That no Judgment should pass barely for the crime committed, but with retrospection on their fore-past lives, and on what followed; as
Lib. 3. *de Sacerdotio.* may be seen in the Council of *Ancyra* and others: So St *Chrysostome, Punishments are not alwayes to be inflicted according to the sole measure of the Crimes: but we ought to enquire into the mind and manners of him that commits them.* But a Law being once Enacted against
Rom. 7. 13. *De vera Relig. Ob.* any one Vice, makes a sin exceeding sinfull: So St *Aug. Lex prohibens omnia delicta congeminat; The Law in prohibiting doubles all offences; for it is not a single sin when we commit not that only which is in it self evil, but that also which is forbidden us.* And *by this argument* St Paul *aggravates the sins of the Jews, in respect of those of the Gentiles, because they had the Law to direct them. We must not therefore be rash in judging, nor* (as Cicero adviseth) *in grave and serious things determine of the will and intentions of the person accused barely by the fact, but by his manner and custome of living.* (A good man may haply be ensnared by the sweetness of a sin, or by the sudden gust of temptations, and yet in the general course of his life he may retain his integrity: The heart of *Asa* is said to be upright all the dayes of his life; and yet when he was sick, it is objected against him, That he sought unto the Physician and not unto the Lord.)

XXXI. The fitness of the person offending, to both which is diversly respected.

Now before we can rightly understand how to punish, we must know the aptness and capacity of offenders to apprehend the causes which do either excite them to commit, or restrain them from committing of sin: Now this aptness or capacity of theirs, we may guess at, by either their temperament of body, age, sex, education, or some of the circumstances of the act. For it will easily be granted, that children, women, fools, illiterate persons, and ill educated, cannot so well distinguish between just and unjust, lawfull and unlawful, as they that have more perspicacity and ingenuity; and that they in whom choler predominates, are prone to anger and revenge, as they also that are of a sanguine complexion are to dalliance; so young men are propense to one passion, old men to another; insomuch that *Nature seems to plead somewhat in their excuse, as to such sins as are, as it were, congeneal with them,* as was well observed by *Andronicus Rhodius: And although it cannot exempt them altogether from punishment, yet without doubt it renders the fault the more tolerable.* So the apprehension of some imminent danger quickly begets a fear, and then we rashly adventure upon a sin to avoid that danger: In like manner, some sudden and unexpected injury sets our hot blood on boiling, and then immediately before reason can interpose, we attempt a revenge. These are the sudden irruptions of passion, and not the deliberate acts of the Will, which certainly are in themselves more excusable than those which arising meerly out of the desire of pleasure, assault us not so violently: And therefore may either be deferred, or admit of some o-
De Providentia In Epist. ad Gal. † *Nic. l.* 7. *c.* 10. ther matter wherein to delight without injury to any. So St *Chrysostome, Lust* (saith he) *seeks coition only, but not with this or that particular person:* And so † *Aristotle, Anger and cruelty are much more natural than covetousness, or an inordinate desire of things unnecessary.* For this is generally to be observed, That the more the judgment is hindered in its free choice, or in the act of discerning between Good and Evil, and the more natural the causes are exciting to sin, the less of evil the sin hath, and consequently the less it should have of punishment. *Difficilium facilis est venia; The greater difficulty there is in the thing commanded, the easier is the pardon if not performed: Quantò potestas vitandi fuit, tanto contumaciæ crimine oneratur,* saith *Tertullian*; *The more power and the greater helps we have to avoid a sin, the more contumacy we bewray in the committing it. Aristotle* likewise in the place before cited, accounts that *man less temperate, who being either not at all, or very weakly provoked with carnal desires, either seeks after enormous pleasures, or flies from some small inconveniences; than he that is urged thereunto by some vehement passion. For what would the same person do, if he felt those vehement perturbations of mind which are incident to youth, or that grief and vexation that poverty brings with it?* Pertinent whereunto is that of *Antiphanes:*

Qui cum sit opulens nequiter quicquam facit,
Hunc, si esset pauper, quid non facturum putas?

He that being opulent, unjust will be,
What will he not, if pincht by poverty?

And what we every where read in Comedians, concerning the doting love of old men. From these causes we ought to guess at the merits of mens sins, and to fit their punishments accordingly.

XXXII. Counter-passion rejected.

The Pythagoreans hold that justice requires τὸ ἀντιπεπονθός, (*i. e.*) a sufferance in the like kind by way of punishment; which is true, but not so to be understood, as if he that hurts another deliberately, and without any just cause given, should suffer just so much again and no more. For the Law of *Moses* it self, which is a perfect pattern for all other Laws, rejects this exposition; for it requires, That he that steals any thing from another, should restore four and fivefold: and the Attick Law did require, That a Thief besides a double restitution (whereunto that of St *John Rev.* 18. 6. refers) should remain in bonds for certain days, as *Demosthenes* testifies. And when the *Minyans* had without any right, extorted tribute from the *Thebans*, *Hercules* compelled them to restore it unto them double, as *Apollodorus* records it. *Aristides* also of the Grecian Laws testifies, *That the injured person is permitted to recover more than the damage sustained by way of revenge*: whereof St. *Ambrose* gives this reason, *Quo furem à detrahendo, aut pœna deterreant, aut mulcta revocent*; *that so they may affright the Thief from his pilfering by the punishment, or discourage him by the mulct.* *Seneca* speaking of judgments to be inflicted after this life, saith:

Cont. Timocr. *Lib.* 2. *Leuctr.* 2. *De offic.* 3. *c.* 3.

———*Scelera taxantur modo*
Majore nostra.

Our Crimes with greater plagues are there
Punisht, than those we suffer here.

Strabo observed a Law among the Indians, *That if one man had maimed or dismembred another, besides the common punishment of retaliation, he was to lose his hand.* And in that book which is entitled *Aristotle*'s Morals, we read, *That it is just, that he that willingly puts out another mans eye, should suffer not only in the like kind, but somewhat more.* For as *Philo* in his Special Laws observes, It is not equal that the nocent and the innocent should suffer but alike. And from hence it is, that the very attempt to commit some sins, though not consummated, and consequently have less of evil in them, than those that are perpetrated, yet are equally punished according to what they intended: as we may read, *Deut.* 19. 19. in the case of a false testimony; so *Deut* 22. 19. in the case of a Husband accusing his Wife of whoredom to defraud her of her dowry; the like we may read *Exod.* 22. 9. As also among the Roman Laws it was provided, That he that carried a weapon about him with an intent to kill a man, was to have been punished as though he had done it. And if it be objected, That if the bare attempt be punishable with death, surely the execution should be more severely punished: I answer, that because nothing can be more grievous than death, and because a man can dye but once; therefore we must necessarily aquiesce in this punishment, because we can go no further, unless we do sometimes add thereunto some kind of torments, to make death it self the more terrible.

Lib. 15. *Lib.* 1. *c.* 34.

XXXIII. In punishments regard is to be had to the person punished.

Punishments are not to be considered barely, but with respect had to the quality of him that suffers them. The same mulct or fine that is grievous to a poor man, is no punishment at all to the rich: and the Stocks or Pillory, which by the viler sort of people are slighted, are worse than death it self to the nobler. The Roman Laws did often make use of this difference of persons and punishments; and *Bodine* upon this consideration did frame a kind of harmoniacal proportion: whereas notwithstanding indeed, here is but a simple equality between the merit and the punishment, such as is in numbers, as also in all contracts between the things sold and the money, although the same Merchandises are worth in some places more, and in some less, as also is money according to its either plenty or scarcity. But we must acknowledge that oft-times among the Romans, this was not done without too great a respect had to the persons and their qualities nothing appertaining to the fact, which acception of persons *Moses* his Law did exceedingly abhor. And this is, as we have said, the intrinsick valuation of a punishment.

XXXIV. Charity mitigates Punishment.

But that which restrains us in punishing, within those bounds which the Laws permit, is the love of him who is punished, unless a greater and juster love of many perswade us otherwise, for some cause that is external; which sometimes is some extreme danger that may arise from him who hath offended, but very often, the necessity of an example. But this most usually ariseth when the encouragements to any sin are general, and cannot be prest without sharp and speedy remedies. Now the principal encouragements to sin are these two, namely Custom, and Facility.

XXXV. Custom & facility, how they add or detract from the punishment of sin.

Which two being so dangerous, ought to be provided against by sharp and severe Laws; The Hebrew Law did punish a Thief more severely for stealing Sheep or Oxen out of the field, than out of the house, *Exod.* 22. 1. 9. For he that stole out of the field, was to restore four and fivefold; but he that stole out of the house but double: The reason whereof

Orat. pro Roscio. Ea maximè animadvertenda peccata, quæ difficilimè præcaventur.

of was; because Cattle in the field are more easily driven away, and therefore had need to be secured by the severer Laws. Those crimes, saith *Cicero*, are to be fitted with the severest punishments, which cannot be prevented without great difficulty. So *Justin*, speaking of the Scythians, saith, There was no crime so heinous as Theft; because to them who had neither houses, nor inclosures to secure their herds of Cattle, or their flocks of Sheep in, what safety could there be, if it were permitted unto them to rob and steal? Much like unto that in *Aristotle*'s Problems, where speaking of such Thieves as frequented Baths, he saith, That the Law-giver, considering that the owners could not in those places look after their things wisely, committed them to the safegard of severe Laws. And accordingly we find that these Balneary Thieves were in *Athens* punished with death; if what they there stole, were above the value of ten Drachmaes, as *Demosthenes* testifies against *Timocrates*. The Custom of a fact, although it detract somewhat from the crime; (for as *Pliny* speaks in such a case, he gave him his pardon, and that not without reason; for though the fact were forbidden by the Law, yet was it commonly committed, and not punished:) yet did it require, in some sort, to have been severely punished: Because as *Saturninus* speaks, *Nimium multis grassantibus, opus exemplo est*; when a sin begins to spread, and Malefactors grow numerous, then some exemplary punishment seems necessary: (for as an hot-headed Horse hath need of a strong rein; so the more publick and customary a sin grows, the sharper should be the punishments to suppress it.) But the former that is, clemency in acquitting offenders is more to be followed in giving sentence, and should be our guide in passing Judgments; but the Laws themselves ought to be severe and impartial, yet with due regard had to the time when those Laws or Judgments were made and published, because the benefit that ariseth by punishments hath respect to the universality, as all Laws also have; but offences do vary, and are not the same in every offender, for in some, they are greater, and in some, less

XXXVI. Clemency in the mitigation of punishments.

De Clem. l. 1. c. 1.

But where there are no great or urgent causes to exact the severity of the Laws, there we should incline to mitigate punishments. For herein consists one part of clemency: the other part consisting in their total remission. *Because it is a difficult thing to find out an equal temperament between the sin and the punishment*, saith *Seneca*, *therefore let the inequality be always on the gentler side*. And in another place, *Pœnam si quis tutò poterit, condonet; sin minus, temperet: If it may safely be done, the best way is to forgive; if that cannot be, the next is to lessen the punishment.* In *Diodorus Siculus* we find one of the Kings of *Egypt* highly commended for *inflicting punishments less than the sin deserved.* So *Justin* in his Epistle to the Huns, *The manner of the Romans is not to exact punishments equal to the merits of the Offenders.* (And indeed (as I have before observed) there is a great deal of mercy even in the mitigation of punishments, the lesser lose much of their name and nature where the sin deserves greater.) It is said of *Marcus Antoninus*, *That his custom was always to award punishments somewhat lesser than the crimes deserved, or the Laws required.* And *Isæus* the Orator was wont to say, *That the Laws ought to be severe, but the punishments always milder than the Laws.* The like by way of advice we find in *Isocrates*, *To make the punishments always less rigorous than the sin was heinous.* This was it which was intended by the Emperour *Henry*, under the Symbol of a Pomegranet-Tree, with this word, *Subacre*, *Very sharp.* And *Cassiodore* reports it of a King, who was often heard to say, *Where there is danger we are severe, but where we are safe we always pardon.* When some Donatists were apprehended and brought before *Marcellinus*, for whipping a Catholick Priest, putting out one of his eyes, and cutting off one of his fingers, St *Augustine*, *fearing that he should have proceeded against them by way of retaliation, humbly besought* Marcellinus, *That he would not do so, nor suffer any such thing to be done; for nothing* (saith he) *more becomes a Prince than clemency.* And as *Macedonius* tells St *Augustine*, *It is the duty of a Priest to intercede for the guilty.*

Lib. 11. 40.

Ep. 159. Grat. c. 23. q. 5. Circumcelliones.

XXXVII. To these are referred whatsoever the Romans or Hebrews have written concerning punishments.

Thus have we, I hope, omitted nothing that may conduce to the clearing of this Argument, of it self difficult and obscure enough. For those four things which, as *Maimonides* saith, ought principally to be regarded in punishments, namely, The greatness of the sin, that is, the damage given; the frequency of such Sinners, the vehemency of the temptation, and the facility of committing it, we have referred to their proper places: no less than those seven mentioned by *Saturninus*, (though confusedly enough.) For, first, As to the person offending, he is considered principally in his aptitude to judge of the Causes exciting to, or restraining from sin, whereof we have treated before. The person suffering by that sin doth sometimes guide us to judge of the greatness of the sin. The place where it was committed doth either peculiarly aggravate it, or appertains likewise to the facility of sinning. (For *it is not the same thing*, saith *Philo*, *to offer violence to a Stranger, as to ones own Father: Nor is it the same thing to speak evil of a private man, as of a Magistrate; or to commit an unlawful thing in a common or prophane place, as in a sacred; or on an holy day, as on another day; in a private house, as in a publick assembly:* for as *Ulpian* observes, *There is great difference between an injury committed in the view of the Roman people, and the same committed in a solitary place.*) The time also is to be considered, whether long in contriving;

Sect. 31.

Sect. 30.

triving; and if so, then was the will the freer in her choice; or short and sudden, and if so, then was it done more out of rashness than out of premeditated malice. Fifthly, The quality, which may be referred, partly, to the several kinds of appetites, and partly to the Causes which ought to restrain us from sin; the greatness of the sin is likewise referred to the appetite, so must the event to the causes restraining.

That War is sometimes undertaken for the neglect of punishing offences we have already shewed, and Histories do every where teach us; whereunto is usually added the reparation of the loss sustained, when the same Fact is not only in it self vicious, but unto others damageable. From which two qualities there ariseth a double obligation; as first, That the person who hath done the wrong, be punished according to his merits: secondly, That the damage by him caused, be repaired. That we are not to fly into Arms upon every provocation, is evident enough. For even the Laws do not avenge themselves upon every one that breaks them, though they may safely do it: because they hurt none but such as hurt others. But *small and common injuries,* saith *Sopater, are better connived at and dissembled, than punished.* XXXVIII. Of War for punishment.

Another Question doth sometimes arise, Whether the purpose or intent only of doing wrong be a sufficient ground for a just War? The Rhodians sent their Ambassadours to the Romans, to urge them (by threatnings) to make peace with *Perseus* King of *Macedon*: The Senate taking this as an Argument of their evil affections towards them, (though it proceeded no further than bare words) yet thought it worthy their consultation, whether this were sufficient ground for a just War. But because the Rhodians did not break out into any hostile acts, nor had made any publick Decree against them; therefore by the advice of *Portius Cato* they were neither admitted as Friends, nor declared against as Enemies: But yet this Precedent is not always to be followed, because in some Cases the will which hath proceeded to express it self by some Overt Acts (though the internal acts of the mind be exempted from humane Laws) doth contract a kind of guilt, and so is obnoxious to punishment. *Scelera quoque, quamvis citra exitum subsederunt, puniuntur; The very first attempts only of wickedness, though they fail of success, are punishable,* saith *Seneca* the Father: *and he who purposeth and is about to do us wrong, hath already done it,* saith the other *Seneca.* So in another place, *A Thief is a Thief before he defiles his hands; neither is it the last act of killing only, that denominates a murtherer; it sufficeth that he goes out armed, with a purpose to kill and to spoil, to make him in some degree guilty.* Of the same opinion was *Philo, They only are not to be accounted Murtherers, who take away the lives of men; but they also that attempt all ways both secret and open to kill any man, although they have not, as yet, effected it.* Thus *Valerius Maximus* speaks of *Sergius Silo, That is was not his Fact that was then called in question, but his Purpose:* Plusque voluisse peccare nocuit, quàm non peccasse profuit; *And that he would have sinned was more damageable, than that he did not sin was profitable.* So *Cicero* pleads in the behalf of *Milo, Non exitus rerum, sed Concilia Legibus vindicantur; Not the event of things only, but their very purposes and intentions, are by the Laws punishable.* To the same purpose is that of *Periander* in *Plutarch, Not they only that have wronged us, but they that go about to wrong us, deserve to be punished.* The Romans thought they had just occasion to make war upon *Perseus,* unless he gave them good satisfaction why he made such warlike preparations both by Sea and Land, and had consulted about making war upon them, though they had not, as then, committed any hostile act against him. And yet it is well observed by *Livy* in that Speech which the Rhodians made to the Roman Senate, *That it did not consist with the Laws and Customs of any City in the World, to condemn a man to death only for wishing his enemy dead, unless he had also acted something in relation thereunto.* But neither is every intention of the will, though it have proceeded to some declarative act, ground sufficient for a just punishment. For if all injuries, though perpetrated, are not to be revenged, much less ought all that are only purposed or begun. *For in many* (as *Cicero* saith doubtingly) *I know not whether it be sufficient for him that provokes another, to have repented of the injury he did him.* For neither doth the Law of *Moses* award any special punishment for such sins as were inchoated against piety, nor committed against the life of a man, without judgment first pass on him; because in these, as also in Divine matters which are not clear nor conspicuous, mistakes are easie: and the passion of anger being sudden and violent, makes its effect the more pardonable. Moreover where there are such a multitude of women, whereof every man hath liberty to chuse a Wife; for any man to attempt anothers, and in so equal a distribution of Goods, so far forth as nature requires for her necessary support, to endeavour to inrich himself with the spoil of others, is no ways tolerable. For that Commandment, *Thou shalt not covet;* although if we look to the scope of the Law, that is, the spiritual sense of it, it extends it self farther, requiring the purity of the mind; yet if we look to the literal and carnal Precepts, it refers to such acts of the mind only as are declared by some outward deeds, as plainly appears by comparing that of our Saviour, *Mark* 10. 19. where he explains that very Precept by these words, *Do not defraud,* which in the very same verse he had before express'd

XXXIX. Whether War for injuries begun only or intended, be just. *Gell. l.* 7. *c.* 3. *Sen. in Controversiis. Excerpt.* 4. 7. *Sen. de ira, l.* 3. *de Benef. l.* 5. *c.* 14. *De Leg. special.* *Liv. lib.* 42. Exod. 20. 17. Matth. 10. 19.

express'd in these, *Thou shalt not steal.* The very same words we find *Mich.* 2. 2. both in the Hebrew and Greek in the same sense. Injuries begun only are not to be vindicated by Armes, unless the matter be both very weighty, and that it hath already proceeded so far, that from what is already done either a certain mischief, though not yet what was intended, hath already befaln; or some extraordinary dangers do thereby threaten: so that the vindication be either conjoined with some caution against future damage (whereof we have treated above in the Chapter of Defence) or the maintenance of our honour that seems by that act to be wounded, or to prevent it from being a pernicious example for others to follow.

XL. War for violating the Law of Nature.

This also we must know, That Kings, and such as have equal right with them, have also a right to exact punishments for offences done, not against themselves and their Subjects only, but for such injuries as do not particularly touch themselves; but against any persons, by whom the Laws of Nature or Nations have been greatly violated. For the liberty of providing for the safety of humane Society, by punishments, which at first, as we have said, was in every particular person, (Cities and Judicatories being now instituted) resides in such as have the supreme Authority, not so properly because they command all, as indeed because they are commanded by none. For that which takes away this right from private men, is their subjection to the supreme Powers, without whose Warrant they can attempt nothing of revenge. Yea, and so much the more honourable it is to revenge other mens wrongs than our own, by how much it may justly be feared; lest out of too great a sense of our own sufferings, we either exceed the just measure of punishing, or prosecute our revenge with too much malice. And upon this account it was that *Hercules* was so famous for subduing those Tyrants, *Antæus*, *Busyris*, *Diomedes*, &c. and cleansing both Sea and Land from all such noxious Creatures, which he did, not out of ambition or desire of gain, but to vindicate the cause of the oppressed, and to plague the unjust (as *Philo* testifies of him.) This Character is likewise given of him by *Diodorus Siculus*, *Many Cities he restored to an happy condition, by taking away insolent Tyrants and such like Oppressours.* For as the same Authour speaks in another place, *Orbem obiit pœnam de iniquis expetens; He travelled through the world for no other end but to scourge Tyrants.* The like testimony doth *Dion Prusiensis* give of him, saying, *That he every where plagued the wicked, destroyed the Kingdoms of the proud, and transferred them unto others.* And for the general care that he had of all Mankind, *Aristides* thought him worthy to be translated amongst the Gods. *Dionysius Halicarnassensis* records this and many more inhumane Customs which *Hercules* reformed, to the general benefit of Mankind, making therein no distinction between Greeks and Barbarians. The like doth *Pliny* testifie of the Romans, *It is not to be imagined* (saith he) *how much we owe to the Romans, for taking away those Monsters among men, who placed the principal part of their Religion to kill men, and their wholesomest food to eat them.* Thus *Justinian* commanded the Princes of the *Abasgi* to abstain from gelding their Children, as *Procopius* relates. And the King of *Incha* in *Peruana* compelled all their neighbouring Nations, that would not willingly obey him, by force of Arms to abstain from Incest, Sodomy, eating of Mans Flesh, and such like abominations; whereby they obtained the justest Empire that we have ever read of (their Religion only excepted.) The like honour is given to *Theseus*, for destroying those great Enemies of Mankind, *Sciron*, *Sinis* and *Procrustes*, who in that Age troubled all *Greece* with their barbarous inhumanity; and is therefore by *Euripides* called, *The Scourge of wickedness.*

De legat. *Lib.* 30. *c.* 1. *Goth.* 4. *Lib.* 5. *c.* 3.

My Noble Acts through Greece *are so extoll'd,*
That I the Scourge of wickedness am call'd.

For as *Valerius Maximus* reports of him, *Whatsoever Monster of cruelty that Age produced, by the strength of his Body, and the gallantry of his Mind, he subdued.* So that without doubt, a War may be justly undertaken against Parricides, whereof the Sogdians were in an high measure guilty; for till they were reclaimed by *Alexander*, they usually killed their own Parents. Against Canibals, or such as fed upon Mans Flesh, as the Scythians did, and the ancient Gauls, before the former were better instructed by *Alexander*, and the latter by *Hercules*, as *Plutarch* in *Diodorus* records. Against Pyrates, and such as live by Robberies at Sea, and the like; for against these any Prince hath power to make war, though they are not subject to his Government. For of such barbarous people, who are rather Beasts than Men, it may truly be verified what *Aristotle* sometimes said of the Persians, *Naturale in eos esse bellum, That war against such is natural.* Or as *Isocrates* notes, *The justest war is that which is undertaken against wild Beasts, and the next is that which is undertaken against such men as are bruitish. What,* saith *Seneca, though they do not infest my Country, yet if they are vexatious to their own: Though they are divided from me, yet if they infest their own people, they deserve for the pravity and corruption of their minds and manners to be destroyed.* And so far we follow the opinion of *Innocentius* and others, who hold, That war may lawfully be made against

In Panathenaic. *De benef. lib.* 7.

gainst such as do break the Laws of Nature: But we cannot approve of that which *Vasquius*, *Victoria*, *Azorius*, and *Molina* have written, namely, That to justifie a War, it is requisite, That the person that undertakes it be injured, either in himself, or in the Commonwealth, whereof he is the Supreme; or that he against whom the War is made, be under his Power and Jurisdiction. For whereas they make the right to punish to be but an effect proper to the Civil Jurisdiction: We on the other side derive it from the Law of Nature, whereof we have spoken somewhat in the beginning of the first Book. And surely, If these mens Opinions from whom we differ be admitted, one Enemy shall not now have a right to punish another, even after the War is undertaken for any cause not punishable; whereas most men do admit of this Right, and the Custom of all Nations confirms it; and that not only when the Enemy is weakned and brought under, but even whilst the War lasts, not by any Civil Jurisdiction, but by that Natural Right, which was in force even before Cities were built, and is yet in force, where the Inhabitants live dispersed in private Families, and are not congregated into Cities.

XLI. The Law of Nature is to be distinguished from Civil Customs.

But here some Cautions are to be observed, the first whereof is, That we do not mistake Civil Customs, which in most Nations are deservedly received for the Law of Nature. Such almost were those wherein the *Persians* differed from the *Grecians*, whose common pretence for their making war upon the *Persians* was to civilize them: But as *Plutarch* observed, *They did but cloak their ambition and covetousness under the title of Reformation:* As if the disagreement between themselves and others in Civil Customs, had been a violation of the Law of Nature.

XLII. And from the voluntary Divine Law not known to all men.

The second Caution is this, That among those things that are forbidden by the Law of Nature, we do not rashly interfert such things, whereof it cannot certainly be affirmed, that they are so forbidden, but are such rather as are interdicted by the Divine Law, in which number we may haply place the sin of Fornication, and some of those sins which we esteem to be Incest, Usury, &c. Thus *Asterius* Bishop of *Amasea*, They that yield obedience unto the Civil Laws of Princes only, do leave Whoredom unpunished. So likewise S[t] *Hierome* to *Oceanus*, *The Laws of Temporal Princes let loose the reins of unbridled lusts; and condemning Adultery only, suffer men to run every where to Stews and Brothel-houses without controul, as if it were the dignity that made the crime and not the will: But with us, what is unlawful for women, is likewise so for men, the same yoke binds both to the same conditions.*

Vide Hier. ad oceanum, supra, c. 5. sect. 9.

XLIII. In the Law of Nature we ought to distinguish between things that are clear, and that are obscure.

The third Caution is, That we diligently distinguish between those general maxims of Reason that are manifest of themselves, as this, That every man ought to live honestly, that is, according to the dictates of Natural Reason; and others that are nearest unto these, but so manifest, that they can admit of no doubting such as this, That we ought not to take away from another that which is his. And between those maximes which are not of themselves so clear, but must be collected from those before mentioned by consequences, whereof some are easily drawn as this, admitting Matrimony, it follows, That we ought not to commit Adultery, which was so generally received, that as *Philo* testifies in the life of *Joseph*, It was every where punished; and *Lactantius* tells us, *That to defile the Marriage-bed was condemned by the Common Law of Nations.* Others, though as true, yet are not so manifestly true, because our assent unto them cannot be gained but by the mediation of three or four consequences, as this, That that revenge that doth acquiesce in another mans grief is vicious. It is here almost as it is in the Mathematicks, wherein some things are of the first Notion, or next unto the first; some are demonstrations which are immediately both understood and assented unto: But some others, though true, yet are not so evident unto all. Therefore as by the Civil Laws, our ignorance of the Law, or of the true meaning of the Law, doth in part excuse us: So concerning the Law of Nature, there is the same Reason, That our weakness to collect what was thereby forbidden by such consequences, or what an ill education hath ingenerated in us, should also excuse us: For as St *Hierome* well observes, *Unaquæque Gens hoc Legem Naturæ putat, quod didicit; Every Nation thinks that to be the Law of Nature, which it first imbibes.* Now our ignorance of the Law, as it takes away a sin if it be inevitable, so also it diminisheth a sin, though it be caused by some neglect. And therefore those that are corrupted by some evil education, *Aristotle* compares to such, whose appetites are vitiated by some malignant distemper: And *Plutarch* observes, *That there are some diseases of the mind that violently hurry a man from his natural constitution.* Lastly, this also is to be noted, (which I say once, but shall not often repeat) That those wars which are undertaken for the exacting of punishments, unless the injuries that are done are very great, very manifest, or backt with some other cause, are alwayes suspected to be unjust. For what *Mithridates* said of the *Romans*, is oftentimes too true; *Non delicta Regum illos, sed vires ac Majestatem insequi: It was not the faults of Princes, but their Power and Majesty that they persecuted.*

In such Cases then, we ought not to be too severe chastisers of other mens infirmities, but rather pity their ignorance and their ill education, praying for them as St. *Stephen* did for his persecutors, *Father forgive them for they know not what they do.*

XLIV. Whether War may be made for offences againft God. *C. peccatum p.* 2,--9, 10.

Our propofed method now guides us to Crimes committed againft God, and to enquire whether for the punifhment of fuch, a War may juftly be undertaken. *Covarruvius* handles this queftion at large : But being fwayed by the Authority of others, he holds, That this punitive Power cannot fubfift but where there is a Jurifdiction properly fo called, which we have already rejected. Whence it follows, That as in the affairs of the Church, the Bifhops are in fome meafure faid to take upon them the care of the Univerfal Church, (for fo S[t] *Cyprian* fpeaks, *It becomes us to watch over the whole body of the Church, whofe members are difperft into feveral Provinces*; And again, *There is but one Epifcopacy, whereof every one holds his part entirely :)* So befides the charge of their particular Dominions, Kings may be faid to affume the general Care of all Humane Societies. But a better Argument brought by fuch as deny fuch a War to be lawfull, is this, That God alone is fufficient to punifh fuch fins as are committed againft himfelf; for, *Deorum injuriæ Diis Curæ, & perjurium fatis habet Deum ultorem*; *The affronts committed againft God, God takes care of*; and it *fufficeth, That God himfelf is the avenger of perjury.* But we muft obferve, That fo it may be faid of any other fins, God without doubt is fufficiently able to punifh them, and yet we fee, That the Laws are juftly and duly exercifed upon fuch offenders by Magiftrates in all Nations, none diffenting. But againft this fome reply, That thofe punifhments are inflicted not fo much for offences committed againft God, as becaufe of the damage thereby done unto men : But on the contrary, It is to be obferved, That not only thofe offences which are committed againft others directly, are punifhed by Humane Laws; but thofe alfo which may by confequence be prejudicial to others, as Self-murder, Sodomy, and the like; for though the principal end and fcope of Religion be to purchafe the Grace and Favour of God, yet hath it alfo a very ftrong influence, and works many notable effects upon Humane Society. *Plato* calls it, *The fortrefs and bulwark of all Power and Jurifdiction, and the very bond of good Difcipline : Plutarch* calls it, *the cement of all Humane Society, and the very foundation and ground-work of the Legiflative Power. Philo* faith, *It is the moft effectual charm to procure love, and that the worfhip of one and the fame God is the moft indiffoluble band of friendfhip :* Whereas on the contrary,

Heu primæ fcelerum caufæ mortalibus ægris,
Naturam nefcire Dei———

All wickednefs 'mongft Mortals hence doth flow,
That the moft Righteous God we do not know.

Every falfe Opinion concerning Religion, faith *Plutarch*, is dangerous, and if it be accompanied with perturbation of mind, moft pernicious: *But to have one and the fame Opinion concerning the worfhip of God, and to differ nothing in life and manners from each other doth produce the moft perfect harmony and agreement amongft men*, as *Jofephus* teftifies againft *Appion.* And in another place, difcourfing of the Reafons why moft Cities were fo ill governed, he adds thefe, *Becaufe their Law-givers did not at firft rightly apprehend the true Nature of God, nor did they ftudy to explain that knowledge fo far as they were able, nor to frame their Government accordingly, but paft it over flightly, as a thing of fmall moment. Jamblicus* alfo hath an excellent fentence out of *Pythagoras, That the knowledge of God is both Virtue, Wifdom, and perfect happinefs. Ariftotle* therefore placed Religion as the firft and chiefeft of all publick cares, and as *Juftine Martyr* calls it, *a work worthy of the care of all Kings*; and *Machiavel* himfelf affigns the profperity of the *Romans* to their fingular care of Religion. *Philo* feems to fumm up the whole Duty of a King in thefe three particulars, The Care of his own Eftate, the Care of the Publick, and the Care of Religion: All which are to be confidered, not only as in fome one particular City or Kingdom, in which refpect it is true, what *Cyrus* in *Xenophon* teftifies of his Subjects, that they were, *Tanto fibi addictiores, quanto Dei erant metuentiores*; The more Religious they were, the more loyal and obedient they were to their lawfull Magiftrates : but they are to be confidered in refpect of the prefervation of the common fafety of all mankind. For as *Cicero* notes, *Take away Religion, and all faithfull dealings between Man and Man, Nation and Nation, and confequently all Humane Society, and one of the four Cardinal Virtues, Juftice, will be quite loft :* whereby it clearly appears, that *Epicurus, When he denied the Divine Providence, Juftitiæ quoque nihil reliquit præter inane nomen*; *Left nothing to Juftice but an empty name*; which, faith he, as it arifeth only from contracts and agreements, fo it is no longer in force than it yields profit to both parties. *Herein (*faith *Seneca) we cannot agree with* Epicurus, *who holds, that nothing is naturally Juft, and that offences are to be avoided, becaufe they being committed, we cannot avoid fear :* As if nothing could reftrain us from injuring others, but the fear of punifhment only. Again, it is very true what *Ariftotle* obferve, That as Religion keeps Subjects in due obedience to Kings ; fo it reftrains the Tyranny of Princes, and begets a great deal of Truft and Confidence between them and their

Contr. App. lib. 1.

De Creat. Magiftrat.

Lib. 1. *de Nat. deor.*

their people. The Prince may be assured of his Subjects Loyalty, and *the people will less fear to suffer unjustly by their Prince, whom they believe to be Religious.* *Galen* observing many questions handled by *Hippocrates* and *Plato* concerning the World and the Divine Nature, which as to the meliorating of mens manners he conceived to be very impertinent, yet confesseth that of the Divine Providence to be of great efficacy and importance to the advancement of Virtues both private and publick: which blind *Homer* could very well see, as we may collect from the sixth and ninth of his *Odysses*, where *to men that were unjust and cruel, he opposeth such whose minds were seasoned with Religion.* *Justine* out of *Trogus* highly commends the Justice of the Ancient Jews, as being throughly tempered with Religion; and *Philo* in the Life of *Abraham*, *makes our love of God, and our love of men, to be congeneal, and as it were twins of the same birth:* For as *Lactantius* rightly inferrs; *If to know God be true piety, and the principal end of this knowledge be to worship him, then he that hath no knowledge of God, is likewise ignorant of true Justice; For how can he be said to know Justice, who is ignorant from whence she comes?* Now Religion is of more use and greater necessity in the common Society of Nations, than in the Civil Society of Men: Because in this Civil Society, the defect of Religion may in part be supplied by severe Laws, and the easie execution of them; but the Laws of Nations, as they are but few, so are they very difficultly executed, namely by War; wherefore these Laws have alwayes been held sacred, because God himself is the sole and immediate Judge of them, and he that violates these Laws, is said to sin against God himself. The injuries then that are done against Religion, are by all Emperours reputed as common injuries, done as it were against all mankind.

Lib. 9. de placitis Hip. & Plat.

Lib. 5.

XLV. **What are the common Notions concerning God, exprest in the four first Commandments.**

But that we may pierce a little deeper into this matter, we must observe, That the true Religion that hath been universally profest in all Ages, and in almost all places, stands erected on these four Columns: First, the acknowledgement that there is a God, and that he is but One. Secondly, That nothing of all these things we see is God, but that he is something that is yet more sublime and excellent. Thirdly, That God takes care of Humane Affairs, and that he doth judge the world righteously. And fourthly, That he is the Creator of all Things without himself. Which four Propositions are explained in the four first Precepts of the Decalogue: The first whereof shews the Unity of the Deity plainly, The Lord our God is one God: The second declares his Invisibility, which is the reason, that as we cannot liken him to any thing, so we cannot make any likeness or representation of him, *Deut.* 4. 10. Thus much doth *Antisthenes* testifie of him, *No eye ever saw him, no likeness we have of him, wherefore it is impossible by any Image or resemblance to know him.* And so doth King *Agrippa* in *Plato*, *To frame the likeness of that, either by graving or painting, which cannot be seen, is profane and ungodly.* The like we read in *Dion*; neither had the Jews any Image in *Jerusalem*, because they thought, that God could neither be seen, nor be by any words described. *Diodorus* speaking of *Moses* saith, *That he ordained no Image, because he did not believe God to be of humane shape.* And *Tacitus commends the Jews for adoring one only God, and him in their minds only; and condemns them as profane, that worship the immortal and invisible God in Images made of Wood and Stone in humane form.* *Plutarch* also gives this as the reason, why *Numa* purged the Temple from Images, *Because it was impossible any other ways to comprehend the Deity than by the mind only.* By the third Commandment we are instructed to acknowledge Gods Omniscience, which extends to our most retired thoughts, and the care he hath of Humane Affairs: for upon this foundation are Oaths built, wherein he is invoked as a witness only, if we speak truth; but if we deceive, then as a Judge and avenger, whereby also both his Justice and his Omnipotency are at once acknowledged. Lastly, That God Created the whole frame of Nature, and gave Being to all things, is confest by the fourth Commandment; in perpetual memory whereof the Sabbath was instituted, whereon he imprinted such an indelible Character of Holiness, That it is more indispensable than any other Right whatsoever: For if a man did eat of meats forbidden, or transgressed in any other case, his punishment was left as arbitrary to the Judges; but he that violated this Right was peremptorily to die the death; because he seemed thereby to renounce his belief of the Worlds Creation; *Abnegationem Mundi à Deo creati continebat Sabbathi violatio.* For as he that wrote the Answers to the Orthodox very well observes, *God did therefore give a greater honour to the seventh number than to the rest, that so the memory of the Worlds Creation might be preserved.* Now the Creation of the World doth tacitly declare both the Goodness of God, his Wisdom, his Eternity, and his Omnipotency; from which contemplative Notions these practical Duties will easily follow, That God is to be Honoured, Loved, Worshipped and Obeyed; wherefore *Aristotle* concludes, *That he that denies that God is to be honoured, or Parents reverenced, is not to be convinced by arguments, but by punishments.* To demonstrate the truth of these contemplative Notions of God, we may draw arguments from the Nature of the Things Created, amongst which the most forcible is this, That some things are made, is manifest to our sense; but these

Dion lib. 36.

Ad Quæst. 69.

Top. 1. 9.

That there is a Creator prov'd by the nature of the Creatures.

these things that are made, if we will trace them up in their direct series, will certainly at length bring us to something that was not made, which must needs be Eternal, and that is God: but for those that are not able to comprehend the strength of this argument, it may suffice to know, That these contemplative notions of God have been assented unto in all ages, and in all places (some few only excepted) and by all persons, as well gentle as simple; as well by those who have been too simple and ignorant to deceive others, as by those

Universal consent. who have been too wise to be deceived by others; which universal consent among such variety of other Laws and opinions, doth evidently witness, That this truth was delivered unto us from our first parents, and was never yet solidly confuted: and even this alone, had we no other ground to ascertain our perswasion, was enough. *Philo* argues this case

De unius imperio. thus, *Nothing made by art can come by chance; but the worlds composure is done with exquisite art, therefore it must needs be made by one, that is, the most perfect of all Artists, and that is God. And hereby ariseth this first perswasion, That there is a God.* Thus likewise *Tertullian* argues against *Marcion*, *The first knowledge of God we derive from nature, the next by doctrine; that from nature we learn by his works, that by doctrine from preaching*: whereupon *Cyprian* in his Book concerning the vanity of Idols, concludes thus, *Hæc est summa delicti, nolle agnoscere quod ignorare non possis; This is the heighth of wickedness that thou wilt not acknowledge him as God, whom thou canst not deny to be so. We are all of us, though untaught, naturally perswaded that there is a God* (saith *Julian* to *Heraclitus*) *unto whom we look, unto whom we run, and towards whom* (I believe) *our souls do as naturally turn, as our eyes to the light, (or as the needle to the North.)* Thus doth *Dion Prusiensis* ground his belief that there is a God, first upon natural reason, and

De cœlo. l. 3. then upon universal tradition. And *Plutarch* calls it παλαιὰν πίστιν, *An ancient perswasion,*

De leg. 10. *than which nothing can be more certain.* For as *Aristotle* saith, *All men have naturally some perswasion that there is a God*: Of the same opinion was *Plato*. (Now to detract from the authority of so many and so great witnesses, is not simply ignorance, but a pertinacious madness.)

XLVI. They that contradict these, may be punished.

Wherefore they are not without sin, who because they are not so quick-witted, as either to assert these notions, by arguments of their own, or to understand those framed by others, do wilfully reject them; since they do both guide us unto that which is honest, and the different opinion is not built but upon a very sandy foundation. But because we are now treating of Punishments, and those only humane, we must here distinguish between these notions themselves, and the manner of dissenting from them: These notions that there is a God, (one or more I here dispute not) and that he takes care of humane affairs, as they are most generally received; so are they to the establishment of Religion, whether true

Heb. 11. 6. or false, most necessary. He that cometh to God (saith the Authour to the *Hebrews*) that is, *He that is religious* (for Religion amongst them, is called an access unto God) *must believe that God is, and that he dispenseth rewards to those that serve him. There hath ever been, and now are,* saith *Cicero*, *some Philosophers who hold that God hath no regard to the affairs of men; which if true, Quæ potest esse pietas, quæ sanctitas, quæ religio?* saith he, *What piety can there be, what holiness, what religion? This,* saith *Epictetus*, *is the principal office of piety, to have a reverent esteem of the Gods*; as namely, that they are, and that they dispose of all

Lib. 2. c. 31. things with justice and righteousness. *Ælian* professeth that he never found any Nation, no, not amongst the Barbarians, which did wholly Apostatize unto Atheism; but that all of them did acknowledge some Divine Power that took care of them. *The first part of*

Ep. 95. *Divine worship,* saith *Seneca*, *is to believe that there are Gods; and then, to ascribe unto them all majesty, and acknowledge their goodness, without which there can be no majesty. Plutarch* in his vulgar conceptions saith, *That if we take away providence, we darken that small light that we have of God: For,* saith he, *we are to conceive of God, not only as he is immortal, and in himself most blessed; but as he is most affectionate to mankind, ever watching over us to do us good.* For otherwise, *if he will do us neither good nor hurt,* saith *Lactantius*, *to what end do we worship him?* And indeed if we look only at the influence which these notions should have upon mens manners, it is all one to deny that there is a God, and to deny that he hath any respect to humane affairs: wherefore that, in almost all Nations that are to us known, and throughout all ages, these two notions should be thus maintained, is not arbitrary, but purely

Sen. Epist. 117. necessary. *Seneca* in his 117 Epistle, pleads thus, *That there are Gods amongst other things, we may hence conclude, that nature herself seems to have insculpt this opinion in every man; neither is there any Nation in the World, so desperately wicked, as not to believe that there are some Gods.*

De Benef. lib. 4. c. 4. *Neither is it possible,* saith he in another place *that all the World should be intoxicated with so universal a madness, as to invoke, Surda numina & Deos in efficaces, such idle Gods, as can neither*

Vid. Plat. Protagora & de legibus l. 10. *hear our prayers, nor do us good.* Nay *Jamblicus* makes it as proper for a man to acknowledge a God, as for an horse to whinny. Hence it is that *Pomponius* places Religion among the Laws of Nations; and that *Socrates* in *Xenophon* saith, *That to worship the Gods, is a Law universal, being in force amongst all people*: with whom agrees *Cicero*, as we may read in his first Book of the Nature of the Gods, and in his second of Invention: And *Dion Prusiensis* calls it a perswasion both natural, and necessary to all creatures that have the use of reason. *Xenophon* likewise affirms, *That all Nations as well Greeks as Barbarians, have agreed*

greed in this, That all things are known to the Gods, whether they be present, past, or to come. Now whosoever first begins to erase these general notions of the Divine Providence out of mens minds, as they have in all well governed Cities been deservedly punished (as we read it happened to *Diagoras Melius*, and the Epicureans, who were banished out of every well-governed Common-wealth) so, I believe, they may also be now by force restrained, in the name and behalf of humane society; which, by this means (without any probable reason they endeavour to dissolve. And therefore *Moxus* the Lydian, as *Damascen* relates the story, having taken the City *Crambuz*, drowned all the Inhabitants thereof, because they neither acknowledged nor worshipped any Gods. And *Himerius* the Sophister pleads thus against the Epicures, *Dost thou suffer punishment for thine opinion; no, but for thine impiety: It is permitted to every man to deliver his opinion, but to none, to destroy Religion.* *Lydus.*

XLVII. But not others proved by the Heb. Law.

As for the other general notions; as, That there are not more Gods than one, That none of these things we see is God, not the World, not the Heavens, nor the Sun, nor the Air; That the World was not from Eternity, nor the matter whereof it is composed, but rather created by God: these cannot be so easily demonstrated, nor are they so universally received as the former. And therefore the knowledge of these, through the corruption of mens manners, and the loosness of the Laws (which did the less regard them, because, even without these there might remain some shew of Religion) have been in many places almost totally expunged. Neither did the Law of God given to the *Hebrews*, though it were confirmed by prophecies, and miracles; and though it utterly detested and abhorred the worship of false Gods, adjudge every man to death, that was convicted of such worship; but such only as by reason of some circumstances, were of dangerous consequence, as him who being a Prince or a Prophet should begin to seduce others, *Deut.* 13. 16. Or as that City that should begin to set up strange Gods, as we read *Deut.* 12. 23. Those that worshipped the Sun, the Moon, the Stars, thereby destroying the whole Law, and forsaking the worship of the true God, *Deut.* 17. 2. which St. *Paul* expounds *to be the worshipping of the creature, not the Creator* (for the word παρὰ as well here, as elswhere, hath an exclusive faculty) which was a crime punishable even among the Sons of *Esau*, as appears *Job* 31. 26, 27. So he that offered his Children to *Molock*, that is to *Saturn*, *Lev.* 20. 2. Neither did God himself adjudge the Cananites, and their neighbouring Nations to destruction, as soon as they fell to Idolatry, but suspended the Execution of his wrath, till they had contracted a vast heap of sins besides their Idolatry, *Gen.* 15. 16. So it is said of other Gentiles concerning their worship of false Gods, *That God winked at the time of their ignorance*, Act. 17. 30. It was truly said of *Philo*, *That every mans own Religion seems to him the best, because he judgeth of it, not by reason, but by affection*; like those Philosophers of whom *Cicero* spake, who liked no Discipline but their own. So we take our Religion not by choice, but by chance, being engaged to that of the Clime wherein we are born, before our judgments are awakened to discern truth from falshood; as they then are rather to be pitied, than by humane Laws punished, who having received no Laws from God, nor having any knowledge of him, shall worship either the powers of Heaven, by whose grateful heat, light and influence, all things are produced, both for delight and nourishment; or the powers of any other natural causes, or of spirits, whether in Images, or in living Creatures, or in any other things. The souls of good men, who have been eminent and exemplary for vertue or such like; especially, if they did not themselves set up that worship, but received it by tradition from others, and therefore could not properly be said to have forsaken the worship of the true God; (for we read of Sacrifices sent to the Temple at *Jerusalem* from the Kings of *Ægypt*, from *Augustus* and *Tiberius* to be offered to the true God: and though these Kings were Idolaters, yet did the Jews admit of them, as *Josephus* and *Philo* testify.) So they, on the other side, are not to be reckoned among such as are purely ignorant and erroneous, but rather among those that are impious and obstinately wicked; who worship Devils as knowing them to be such, or the names of mens vices, or that attribute Divine Honour unto men as wicked and vicious as themselves, or that honour their false Gods with humane Sacrifices; which barbarous custom we read, was practised by the Carthaginians, until they were compelled to leave it, by *Darius* the Father of *Xerxes* King of *Persia*, and by *Gelo* the Syracusian Tyrant, who stand highly commended for it. *Plutarch* also gives us an account of some barbarous people, that were to have been punished by the Romans for offering humane Sacrifices; but when they pleaded for themselves the Antiquity of those Rites, they were dismist without punishment, and only forbidden it for the future.

XLVIII. Nor against those who will not embrace Christianity.

But what shall we say of that War which is undertaken against some people, for no other Cause, but because they would not embrace Christianity when proposed unto them? I do not here question whether the Religion so proposed were such as ought to have been proposed, or in such a manner as it ought to have been. We are willing to grant both: But two things are here to be considered, first, That the truth of Christian Religion, in those Points which are superadded to that Primitive Religion which is grounded upon the Law

Two things observable.

Law of Nature, cannot be demonstrated unto any man by Arguments merely natural, because they are grounded upon matters of fact, namely, upon Christs resurrection, and upon those Miracles that were wrought by him and his Apostles, which thing being matter of fact, though of old confirmed to have been done by most irrefragable Testimonies, yet of old, so that this is a question of Fact, and that now of great Antiquity. Much more may this be questioned by such as now live so many Ages distant from that Age wherein they were done, as well as the truth of their Histories, which are as ancient as that is, especially by those who never heard of them before, nor have any of those helps either inward or outward, which are necessary to beget Faith. And therefore we say, That Faith is not by Nature, but by Grace: and that, as when God gives it, it is not as the reward of any pleading merits; so when he denies it, or gives it more sparingly, it is for Causes not indeed unjust, though unto us for the most part unknown, and so not at all punishable by humane Laws. To this purpose was that Canon of the Toletane Council made, whereby it was decreed, *That no man should be inforced (thenceforth) to Christianity:* For it is said, *He will have mercy on whom he will have mercy, and whom he will he hardeneth.* So *Josephus, Every man ought to worship God willingly and freely, and not by compulsion.* It is the custom of the Holy Scriptures, to attribute that to the will of God whereof no probable cause can be assigned by men. Wherefore, since it is not in the power of man to give a reason why some men do believe, and others not, though both have the same outward helps and means; hence it is that we resolve all such doubts in Gods will, saying, *He will have mercy on whom he will have mercy, and whom he will he hardeneth.* Neither is this the manner of the Holy Scriptures only, but it is usual with prophane Authours, who when in doubtful Cases they find not reason sufficient to inform their judgments, supply that defect with a *sic visum, Thus it seems to be.* The second thing observable is, That Christ the Authour of the New Law did never intend that any man should be compelled to receive it by temporal punishments, or driven thereunto by the fear of them. We have not received (saith St *Paul)* the Spirit of bondage to fear, *Rom.* 8. 15. So *Heb.* 2. 15. In which sense it is very true what *Tertullian* saith, *Nova Lex non se vindicat ultore Gladio, The Gospel doth not call for the Sword to avenge its injuries. Isidore* speaking of *Sisebutus* King of *Spain*, saith, *That in the beginning of his Reign, being inflamed with a zeal for Gods Glory, though not according to knowledge, he compelled the Jews to Christianity by the power of the Sword, whom he ought to have won to the Faith by meek and gentle perswasions.* And for this very Cause were the latter Kings of *Spain* highly blamed by *Osorius* and *Mariana*. In the Constitutions of *Clement* it is said of Christ, *That he left to every man the free power of his own will, not punishing the breach of his Law with temporal death, but calling them to an account for it in the life to come. So our Blessed Lord, leaving every man to his own will, makes Proclamation openly to all, If any man will come after me,* &c. And to his Apostles, *Will ye also forsake me?* as leaving it to their own choice, without laying any inforcement upon their wills. And whereas in the Parable of the Great Supper it is said, That some were compelled to come in; it is answered, That as in that Parable the word *compel* argues nothing else but a vehement sollicitation, so also is it to be understood in the Moral of that Parable; in which sense the same word is taken, *Luke* 24. 29. and not otherwise, *Matth.* 14. 22. *Mark* 6. 45. *Gal.* 2. 14. *Procopius* in his secret History tells us, That *Justinian* the Emperour was by many very wise men taxed for compelling the Samarites by force and menaces to Christianity: adding thereunto the inconveniencies that was likely to arise thereupon.

> Rom. 9.
> Jo. 6. 67. Luke 9. 54. Matth. 13. 24.
> Vid. Cypr. Ep. 55. & de Idolor. vanitate.
> Luke 14. 23.

XLIX. That war may justly be made against them that persecute Christians as such.

But they that persecute others for no other cause but because they either teach or profess the Christian Religion, are most unreasonable. For certainly our Christian Doctrine, (considered in its sincerity, without any commixture) contains nothing prejudicial to Humane Society, nay that doth not rather advance it, it shall speak for it self, and its Enemies shall confess no less. *Pliny* reports of the Christians of his time, That they had obliged themselves by oath to abstain from thefts and robberies, and not to break their faith with any man. *Ammianus*, speaking of our Religion saith, That it teacheth nothing but what is just and merciful. So doth *Arnobius*, treating of Christian Assemblies, *Wherein* (saith he) *nothing is heard but what exhorts to humanity, meekness, bashfulness, modesty, chastity, and communicating of their goods to all men, as if they were all link'd together by brotherly love.* And it is the usual Character that the very Heathen give of it, That it is *Secta nemini molesta, A Sect of Religion offensive to none. Zozimus*, though a Pagan, gives this testimony of the Christian Faith, That it *is a promise and engagement to be free from all crimes, and from all impiety.* So likewise *Tertullian, We,* saith he, *are Coadjutors and Fellow-labourers with you in establishing the peace of the Empire, instructing our Auditors that it is impossible for any man to conceal himself from God, whether he be an evil Doer, a Thief, a Traitor, or a just Person; as also that every man shall be adjudged to eternal either life or death, according to the merit of his deeds. Tertullian* also observes that it was a common by-word in his time, *Bonus vir Cajus Sejus, tantum quod Christianus, He is an honest man, only he is a Christian.* And if it be objected, That all innovations are to be feared, especially Conventicles, and

> Apolog. 2.

private

private Aſſemblies : I anſwer, That thoſe Doctrines though new, are leaſt to be feared, that teach all things that are juſt and honeſt, but principally thoſe that exact due obedience to Magiſtrates; neither ſhould the private Aſſemblies of Juſt and Innocent men be either envied or ſuſpected, eſpecially of ſuch as deſire not to abſcond themſelves, unleſs they are perſecuted. And here I might juſtly apply unto theſe Chriſtian Aſſemblies, what *Philo* records that *Auguſtus* ſaid of the Jewiſh Conventions, *Non eos Bacchanalia eſſe, aut cœtus turbandæ paci, ſed virtutum ſcholas; That ſuch meetings were not for revelling or for ſedition, but mere Academies for Virtue:* They therefore that perſecute ſuch men, and that for this only cauſe, may themſelves juſtly be perſecuted. Upon this ground it was, That *Conſtantine* made War againſt *Licinius*, and other Emperours againſt the *Perſians*. St *Auguſtine* brings in *Maximinianus* Biſhop of *Vagia* craving aid of the Chriſtian Emperours againſt the Churches Enemies, *Non tam ſui ulciſcendi cauſa, quam tuendæ Eccleſiæ ſibi creditæ; Not to revenge his own wrongs, but to defend the Church of Chriſt that was committed unto his care.* And indeed ſuch a War ſhould be undertaken more for the defence of the Innocent, than to puniſh the Nocent. *In Legatione.* *Aquin. ſecunda ſecundæ, q. 108.* *Grat. in cauſam 23. q. 3.*

L. But not againſt ſuch as erre in the interpretation of the Divine Law.

But they that eagerly perſecute thoſe that profeſs the Chriſtian Law, only becauſe they either doubt, or haply erre in ſome particulars, which either are not expreſt in our Law, or at leaſt not ſo clearly, but that it will admit of ſome ambiguity, and which have been otherwiſe underſtood by the Primitive Chriſtians are unjuſt, as may appear, partly by what we already ſaid, and partly by the example of the Ancient Jews, whoſe Religion, though ſtrongly guarded with corporal puniſhments, yet did never permit them to puniſh the Sadducees, for rejecting the Doctrine of the Reſurrection; becauſe (though moſt true) it was, as yet, but obſcurely glanced at in their Law, and not at all taught, but covertly under types and figures. But what if the Errors be ſuch, as amongſt equall Judges may eaſily be confuted, both by the authority of the Scriptures, and by the common Teſtimony of the Fathers? Yet even herein we muſt conſider how great the ſtrength is of an over-grown Opinion; and how much a mans endeavour to defend his own Sect, doth diminiſh the ſtrength and liberty of his own judgment, which as *Galen* ſaith, is *malum omni ſcabie inſanabilius; a diſeaſe more incurable than any Leproſie: A man will ſooner part with any thing than with his Opinion,* ſaith *Origen:* So S[t] *Chryſoſtome, An Opinion that hath taken deep root through Cuſtom is hardly to be removed; for there is nothing that we alter with more unwillingneſs than our Cuſtoms in Religion.* Again, how great the fault of him is that differs from us in Opinion, muſt be judged by the manner and meaſure of his illumination, and by other diſpoſitions of his mind, which is not poſſible for man to know. S[t] *Chryſoſtome makes Ambition the mother of Hereſie;* and S[t] *Auguſtine* defines *an Heretick to be one that either for Gain, Vain-glory, or Ambition, doth either ſet up, or at leaſt follow falſe and New Opinions;* where he makes a great difference between him that is an Heretick, and him that believes and follows an Heretick: *This is moſt apparent, that all Hereſies proceed from either the Ambition or Emulation of their firſt Inventers,* ſaith he that wrote the Anſwers to the Orthodox: And therefore S[t] *Auguſtine* calls it, *The frenzy of a mind obſtinately bent, or the heighth of madneſs:* And yet ſee, with what ſweetneſs and calmneſs of ſpirit, the Fathers of the Primitive Church treated the Hereticks of their times. *Salvian* ſpeaks thus of the *Arrians, Hereticks they are, but not knowingly; to us they are Hereticks, but to themſelves they are not; nay, ſo confident they are that they are in the right, That they brand us with that infamous name of Hereticks, who are Catholicks. What they are to us, the ſame are we to them. We are moſt aſſured that they diſhonour the Son by making him inferiour to the Father; and they as far condemn us, for diſhonouring the Father, in making the Son equall unto him: The Truth is on our ſide, yet they preſume it is with them, both pretend to honour God; to us they appear uncivil, but that to them ſeems to be the chiefeſt Duty of their Religion; to us they appear impious, but this they eſteem to be true piety; they erre indeed in their faith, but they do it in perfect love and charity to God; and how far puniſhable this Errour of theirs now is, or, in the day of judgment will be, none can tell but the Judge himſelf: In the mean time God* (I believe) *doth therefore forbear them, becauſe he ſees, that though they do erre in their faith, yet this errour proceeds from no other root but from the affection to a pious Opinion.* And indeed ſuch are not to be judged Hereticks by us, who do *bono animo errare, erre through an ignorant zeal: Miſeratione quàm odio digniores; they deſerve rather our pity than our hatred;* as *Agathias* ſpeaks of the ſuperſtitious *Almans: For they do not go aſtray, nor ſtumble willingly, and knowingly, they have without doubt pious intentions, but being deceived in their judgments, whatſoever they raſhly apprehend for truth, they hold obſtinately. Now in what meaſure,* ſaith *Chryſoſtome, ſuch errours are to be puniſhed, he only can without danger judge, who is the Judge of Ages, or the Eternal Judge, who alone knows both the true meaſure of knowledge, and the proportion of Faith.* Concerning the Manichees, let us hear what S[t] *Auguſtine* ſaith, who was himſelf once one of them; *Let them rage againſt you,* (ſaith he) *who are ignorant, with what labour and ſweat a man finds out the truth;* (which is but one) *and how difficult it is to de-*

In 1 ad Cor. c. 2. *Ad Gal. 5.* *Lib. de utilitate credendi.* *Grat. c. 24. q. 3. & Ep. 162.* *Script. Reſponſ. ad Orthodoxos qu. 4.* *Hom. contr. Anathematizantes.*

cline

cline errours, (which are infinite.) *Let them rage againſt you, who know not how rare and hard a matter it is to overcome all carnal conceits, by the ſerenity of a pure mind: Let them rage againſt you, that apprehend not with what difficulty the eye of our inward man is ſo ſtrengthned, as to be able to behold the beauty and ſplendor of its own Sun: Let them rage againſt you, who have not experimentally learned, how many ſighs and groans it will coſt before a man can attain to the knowledge of God in the leaſt degree. Laſtly, let them rage againſt you, who can preſume that they are without errours themſelves: As for me I neither can nor dare; for I ought to bear with you now, as others did formerly with me, and to treat you with as much patience, meekneſs and gentleneſs, as they did me, when I was blindly carried away with your errours. Athanaſius* bitterly inveighs againſt the *Arrian* Hereticks, becauſe they were the firſt that called in the Civil Power to their aſſiſtance againſt their Antagoniſt, and that endeavoured by force, ſtripes and impriſonments, to draw ſuch unto themſelves, whom they could not win by the ſtrength of arguments; *Thereby plainly declaring, how little of piety and true devotion there was amongſt the Profeſſors of that Doctrine*; alluding haply to that of St *Paul*, *Gal.* 4. 29. where it is ſaid, *That, as then, he that was born of the fleſh, perſecuted him that was born of the ſpirit, even ſo now. Nova & inaudita eſt iſta prædicatio quæ verberibus exigit fidem; It is a new and unheard of manner of preaching, to enforce Faith by ſtripes and puniſhments*, as *Gregory* Biſhop of *Rome* wrote unto the Biſhop of *Conſtantinople*. And we may read of many *French* Biſhops who were by the judgement of the Church condemned, for calling in the Civil Powers againſt the *Priſcillianiſts*, as *Sulpitius Severus* relates it; and of a whole Council in the Eaſt that was condemned, becauſe they conſented to the burning of *Bogomilus*. It was therefore wiſely ſaid of *Plato*, *Errantis pœna eſt, doceri*; *If there be any puniſhment due to errour, it is to be inſtructed:*

Grat. c. 23. *q.* 4. *qui ſecund.*

Sen. Trag.

Quis nomen unquam ſceleris errori dedit?

Who ever thought it criminous to erre?

De Ira. lib. 14. It is very true what *Seneca* ſaith, *No wiſe man ever hated thoſe that erred; for if ſo, he muſt neceſſarily ſometimes hate himſelf. He that is ignorant ought not to be ill treated nor accuſed, but it is fit he ſhould be inſtructed in that whereof he is ignorant.* And *Ammianus Marcellinus* highly commends the Emperour *Valentinian*, *That he never perſecuted any man for his Religion, never commanded this or that to be adored; nor inclined the hearts of his Subjects to enbrace his own manner of worſhip, in caſe they diſſented from it.*

Chryſoſt.

LI. But they that are openly impious and profane againſt ſuch as they believe to be Gods, may be puniſhed.

Errours in Opinion concerning the nature or worſhip of God, are not ſufficient ground for a Juſt War, but open impiety, irreverence and profaneneſs towards any that is but acknowledged as God, are (deſervedly) in all Nations to be puniſhed. This (amongſt others) is given as one Cauſe of the *Peloponeſian* War between the *Athenians* and *Lacedemonians*, and of that War which *Philip* of *Macedon* made againſt the *Phocians*; whoſe ſacriledge was ſo execrable, that as *Juſtine* ſaith †, *Orbis viribus expiari debuit; The whole world ought to have contributed to the expiation of it.* And it is St *Hierom*'s obſervation upon the ſixth of *Daniel*, *That whilſt the veſſels remained in the Idol Temple at Babylon, the Lord was not angry, for the errour was in the underſtanding, and not in the will and affections, (though they erred in their Opinion concerning God, yet were thoſe veſſels imployed to that uſe, whereunto they were primarily conſecrated,) but no ſooner were they made uſe of in a common and profane way, but the Lord breaks out into an open revenge.* St *Auguſtine* aſcribes the proſperity of the *Roman* Empire to their care of Religion, though a falſe one: And *Lactantius* ſeems to juſtifie them in part, becauſe they had a Zeal for the Worſhip of God, though not according to knowledge; though they could not exactly perform their duty, yet they ſerved him ſincerely, according to the light they had of him: *And* (as we ſaid before) *by what God ſoever we forſwear, the ſin is puniſhed by the True God, becauſe we ſwear by it as God*, ſaith *Seneca*: *And it is our opinion of him that we ſwear by, that obligeth the True God to revenge it.* And in this ſenſe we underſtand that alſo of *Seneca*, *The puniſhments of ſuch as profane Religion may vary, but in all places they are puniſhable.* And that alſo of *Plato*, who would have all ſuch as ſcoff at Religion puniſhed with death: In like manner they that falſely aſſume unto themſelves the name of Prophets, are deſervedly to be puniſhed as *Agathias* teſtifies.

Diod. lib. 16.
† *Lib.* 8.

De benef. 7. *c.* 7.
De benef. lib. 3. *c.* 6.
De legib. 10.
Lib. 5.

CHAP.

CHAP. XXI.

Of the Communication of Punishments.

I. *How punishments may pass to those that partake of the sin.*
II. *That Commonalties and their Governours are punishable for the Subjects faults, if they know of them, and do not hinder them when they both ought and may do it.*
III. *Likewise by receiving those who have been criminous elsewhere.*
IV. *Unless they either punish them, or deliver them up to be punished, illustrated by examples.*
V. *The Rights of Suppliants belong to the unfortunate, and not to the guilty, with its exceptions.*
VI. *Suppliants are to be defended till their Cause be known, and by what Law this knowledge is to be gained.*
VII. *How Subjects may partake of the faults of their Rulers, or the Members of the whole Body; and how their punishments differ.*
VIII. *How long the Right of punishing may continue against a People.*
IX. *Whether a punishment may be inflicted upon such as partake not of the faults.*
X. *A distinction between that punishment that is inflicted directly, and that which comes by consequence.*
XI. *That which comes by occasion of a fault, distinguish'd from that which is inflicted for the fault.*
XII. *Properly no man can be justly punished for the fault of another.*
XIII. *No, not the Children for the sins of their Parents.*
XIV. *Objections answered concerning Gods Dealings with the Children of guilty Parents.*
XV. *Much less should their punishments extend to their other Relations.*
XVI. *Yet some things may be denied unto these which otherwise they might have; with examples.*
XVII. *Neither can Subjects be properly punished for the defaults of their Kings.*
XVIII. *Nor the dissenting part for the crimes of the major part.*
XIX. *The Heir is not liable to the punishment of his Ancestor as it is a punishment, and why.*
XX. *Yet he shall, if what was first inflicted as a punishment, do pass under another kind of debt.*

I. How by partaking of the sin of another man, we may be liable to his punishment.

SO often as mention is made concerning the Communication of Punishments, either it concerns those that are Partakers of the sin, or some others. They that partake of the sin are not so properly punished for other mens sins as their own. And who they are that partake of other mens sins, may easily be understood by what hath been already said above concerning the damage that is occasioned by an injury done. For by the same ways, almost, whereby a man is made guilty of that damage, by the same may a man be made guilty of another mans sin: and yet not always where there is an obligation to satisfie for the damage, there is the same to satisfie for the offence; but there only where there is the concurrence of some notable malignity: whereas oft-times any offence may suffice to oblige a man to satisfie for the damage given. He therefore that commands a wicked act to be done, as *David* did *Joab* concerning *Uriah*; he that gives his consent being required, as *Saul* is said to stone St *Steven*, because he gave his consent unto it: for by the Law, *Facientem & consentientem par pœna constringit, The same punishment is due to him that commits a crime, and to him that consents to the committing of it.* They that aid and assist in the act doing, they that receive or conceal the matter, or any other way participate of the crime; so St *Hierome*, *Not only the Thief himself, but he that knowing the thing to be stoln, and where it is, conceals it or doth not declare his knowledge to the right Owner, is guilty.* (Sup. Parabolas.) So also St *Chrysostome, Not only the perjured persons, but they that knowing of it, conceal the perjury, are guilty.* (De Statuis, 14.) They that contribute their counsel and advice, for so runs the Attick Law, *He that gives his counsel to an act that is wicked, is involved in the same punishment with him that doth it.* They that countenance, encourage or commend a Malefactor; so St *Chrysostome, Pejor peccante qui peccatum laudat,* He that praiseth and applauds a wicked act, is more wicked than he that effects it. And by the Law of the Lombards, *Qui facinorosum astans hortatur, pro faciente habetur.* The By-stander that encourageth a Malefactor is equally to be punished with him. They who having full power and authority to forbid and restrain Offenders, do it not. So thought St. *Chrysostome, Not they only that commit the theft, but they also that did not hinder the commission of it when it was in their power to do it, are in the same manner to be punished.* Just as he who hinders a wounded person from being cured, is as guilty as he that wounds him even unto death. So they who being strictly bound in Duty to help those that are oppressed, and do it not. And they who do not disswade when they ought to do it. And lastly, They that conceal the Fact which they are bound by some Law to make known. All these are obnoxious

to

to the same punishment, if there be in them such a malignity of Spirit as may suffice to deserve punishment, according to what we have already said in the preceding Chapter.

II. How Princes and States are punishable by reason of the facts of their Subjects.

This will be made clearer by examples. Where offences are but personal, there the punishment is not to be national. No Community or other Civil Society of men may justly be punished for the fault of some particular persons, without either committing or omitting some fact or duty of their own, whereunto they were generally obliged. For as St *Augustine* well observes, *In every Nation those sins which are committed by particular persons, are to be distinguished from those that are done in common, as when the whole Body of the people being assembled do unanimously decree it to be done.* Hence ariseth that Clause usual in all Leagues, *Si desexerit publico Consilio, If any thing shall be done to the contrary by any publick Decree, then shall the League be adjudged as broken.* Thus the Locrians in *Livy* excuse themselves to the Roman Senate, saying, *That their defection proceeded from some ignorant and ill affected people, and not by any publick Order of the Senate.* And the Rhodians in the same Senate make their defence by the same Argument, distinguishing between the publick Acts of the City, and the private Acts of some particular persons. *There is no City* (say they) *so well governed but may sometimes have some malignant Citizens sitting even at the Stern, besides an unexperienced multitude always.* And if the attempts of every private person were ground sufficient for a just war, no City could long subsist. Thus St. *Chrysostome* likewise argues, *It was not the common crime of the City, but of some Strangers and Foreigners, who do all things rather through rashness and ignorance of the Laws, than by reason. Neither* (saith he) *is it just that so great a City should be destroyed for the indiscretion of some few, nor that the innocent should equally suffer with the nocent.* So neither are the sins of Children to be imputed to their Parents, nor Masters to be punished for the crimes of their Servants, nor others that govern for those whom they govern, unless it be for some delinquency of their own. Now of those ways or means whereby they that preside over others may be accessary to their sins, and so involv'd in their punishments, there are two of singular use, and require our strictest disquisition. As first, By connivence:

1. By Connivence.

For he that knows that such a crime will be committed, which he can hinder, and is bound to do it, but doth it not, is guilty of that crime when it is committed. Thus *Cicero* argues this Case against *Piso*, *It is not much material* (saith he) *especially in a Consul, whether he do himself stir up the people to sedition by his own pernicious Laws and wicked Speeches, and so disturb the peace of the Commonwealth, or whether by his connivence he permits others so to do.* Par est delinquere & delinquentes non prohibere, *It is the same thing* (saith *Agapetus* to *Justinian*) *to be wicked our selves, and to suffer others to be so when it lyes in our power to help it. He that suffers a Sinner to sin,* saith *Arnobius, adds unto him the strength of confidence.* Of the same opinion was *Salvian, He who having a power to prohibit a wicked act, and doth it not, doth in effect command it.* And St. *Augustine* likewise, *He that doth not resist and oppose himself against a sin when he can do it, seems to give his consent unto it.* By the Roman Laws, if a Servant did kill a man with his Masters knowledge, the main guilt was transferred to his Master, as if he himself had been the Murtherer. Even so he that suffers his Bond-slave to be prostituted, when he might rescue her, was by the same Law judged the Prostitutor. By the Fabian Law, if one Mans Servant with the consent of his Master seduced another mans Servant, the Master of the Seducer was punished for it. But, as I said before, it is requisite that besides the bare knowledg, there be also a power and authority sufficient to restrain and hinder the committing of it. And this is that which the Laws intend: for when knowledge is commanded to be punished, it is taken for connivence or toleration; so that he stands guilty who having a power to forbid the doing of a wicked act, doth it not. And in this Case knowledg is taken for that which hath the consent of the will, and so it is to be understood as if the fact were committed by his advice and counsel. And therefore as the Master is not bound by his Servants crime, though he do know thereof, if that Servant shall contemn his Masters authority, and proclaim himself a Freeman; and as Parents are not bound by their Childrens crimes, though they know of them, if those Children are not under the power and tuition of their Parents; because neither Masters nor Parents have any power and authority over them. So on the other side, although they had power and authority over them, and so might thereby prohibit the doing of such crimes; yet if they knew nothing of their purpose and intention to commit such acts, they cannot be punished for them. For both these must necessarily concur to make one man guilty of another mans crime, knowledge of the sin committed, and not restraining them when it was in their power. All which arising from natural equity may by a parity of reason be applied to Princes and their Subjects; wherefore *Proclus* upon that of *Hesiod*,

Cicero in Pisonem.

Whole Cities sometimes smart for th' crimes of one,

assigns this as the reason, *Because having power they did not restrain him from his wickedness.* So in the Grecian Army *Agamemnon* and some others being subject to a General Council of war,

it

It was deservedly said,

The Princes errours on their Subjects fall;

That is, the Grecians were plagued for the folly of their Princes, because it was in the power of that Council to have compelled *Agamemnon* and the rest, to have delivered up *Iphigenia* to the Priest to have been sacrificed. Thus doth *Cyrillus* expound this matter in his Fifth Book against *Julian*, whereupon *Ovid* thus: *Met. l.* 14.

———————— *Virgine raptâ*
Quam meruit pœnam solus, digessit in omnes:

————————The Virgin gone,
All stand engag'd, though done by one alone.

Because it was in their power to have hindered it. Thus doth St. *Chrysostome* involve all the inhabitants of *Antioch* in the crimes of the Statues, *The fact* (saith he) *though committed but by few, we all stand accused of; and the revenge which is strictly due unto those only that did it, is threatned against us all; which we might have avoided had we before expelled them the City. So might we by a timely cutting off from us those parts that were exulcerated, have wisely provided for the safety of the whole.* And a little after, *For this very thing, thou art punished and utterly destroyed, because thou wert not present to resist, because thou didst not prohibit, because thou didst not restrain their madness, that thou didst not expose thy self to danger to preserve the honour of the Emperour; 'tis true, thou didst not join with them nor partake of their crime, in this I commend thee, this I take in good part; but because thou didst not hinder them that did it, for this thou art worthily accused.* *De Statuis orat.* I. *Livy* records that as a good plea which the Vejentes and the Latines made before the Roman Senate, namely, That their Subjects had aided their Enemies without their knowledge: But on the contrary, it was not allowed unto *Teuca* Queen of the Illyrians, when she pleaded that they were her Subjects, and not her self that were the Pirates, for she knew thereof and forbad them not; for it might easily be presumed, That of what was so frequently and so publickly done, no Prince could plead ignorance. *The Laurentine Embassadors being assaulted by some of King* Tatius *his near relations, did complain that the Law of Nations was violated; but* Tatius *favouring his own kindred more than common right, drew the revenge wholly upon himself.* And hitherto may that of *Salvian* be properly applyed, *That Sovereign Princes who are able to prohibit the greatest crimes, do seem to approve of them if they permit them to be done. It is sufficient for private men to keep themselves upright, but they that are Princes must take care that others offend not,* Non est liber à consensu qui quod emendare potest, emendare negligit; *He that neglects his duty in reforming abuses, doth without doubt consent, if not approve of them,* and thereby involves himself both in the sin and punishment. *Dion in Galbâ can.* 4. *Synod. Pistensis.* *Id quod à multis fit necesse est ut à nemine ignoretur; what is done by a multitude no man can be ignorant of.* *Dion Prusæensis.* *Polybius* reproves the Ætoleans sharply, because when they would not appear to be enemies to *Philip*, yet they suffered their subjects openly to act against him in an hostile manner; yea, and preferred the principal actors to great Honours.

III. *Of receiving Malefactors into protection.* Hitherto we have shewed how they that preside over others, may be involved in their sins and punishments by toleration; now let us see how they may partake of their punishment by reception against punishments, although by the Law of nature, every innocent person hath a right to punish a Malefactor; yet since the institution of civil societies, it is generally agreed, That all each particular mans crimes, that shall be committed properly against that society, should be left to them and to their Governours, either to punish or absolve as themselves shall please: yet is not this Right so absolute and full as to those offences, which do any way appertain to humane society; but that other Cities, and their Governours may have the like power to prosecute them, in the same manner, as for some offences. Popular actions are usually granted in every City, much less have they that full power in such offences, whereby any City, or its Governour is peculiarly wronged: but that, that City or Governour hath likewise a right, either for the vindication of his own honour, or for his future security, either to require the offender to be delivered up unto him, or to require that he be punished by that City wherein he lives, according to the injuries he hath suffered by him; and of this right, he is not to be deprived.

IV. *Who ought to be either punished or delivered up.* Seeing that it is neither usual nor safe, for one Prince to permit another to enter into his Dominions, with an Army to demand Delinquents to just punishment; therefore it is fit that the injured Prince should send to him, under whose protection the Malefactor resides, to require that either he would punish him himself according to his merits, or to deliver him up to the pleasure of the Prince that is injured; and this is that dedition, whereof we find so frequent mention in all Histories. Thus did the rest of the Tribes require the Benjamites to deliver up those Sons of *Belial*, that had abused the Levites Concubine, *Judg.* 20. and the Philistines *Sampson*, *Jud.* 15. Thus did the Lacedemonians make War upon the Messenians for refusing to deliver up a man that had killed divers Lacedemonians: And at another time, for not delivering up those that had ravished some virgins that *Paus. l.* 14. *Strabo l.* 8.

Eee 2 were

were sent to perform their devotions. So *Cato* would have had the Senate to have delivered up *Cæsar* for the War he unjustly made upon the Germans. (*Plut. vit. Camilli.*) And the Gauls did in the like manner require the Fabii to be delivered up unto them, who had made war against them unjustly. Thus did the Romans demand from the Carthaginians, That *Amilcar* who had solicited the Gauls to Rebelion, should be delivered, (*Livy lib. 28.*) and afterwards *Hannibal* as *Diodorus*, and *Livy* testifie : Thus likewise they required *Jugurtha* of *Bocchus* in these words; *So shalt thou at once free us from the necessity of persecuting thee for thine errour, and him for his wickedness.* (*Salust.*) Thus the Achaians required from the Lacedemonians those who had besieged *Lanvicus*, adding, that unless they did deliver them, they would declare that they had broken the League. And thus did the Athenians make publick proclamation, That whosoever should plot any mischief against *Philip*, and fly for protection to *Athens*, *should instantly be delivered up unto him*; yet is it not necessary, that every person that is so demanded, should immediately be delivered up; but those only who upon due examination shall be found guilty : For as *Plutarch* in the Life of *Romulus* rightly observes; It is not fit, ἀκρίτως ἐκδιδόναι, to deliver up a man unheard. The King of *Scotland* (as *Camden* informs us) (*Camden, Anno 85.*) told Queen *Elizabeth*, that he would send *Fernihurst*, yea, and the Chancellor too into *England*, as soon as by sound Evidence it was proved, that they had premeditately broken the peace, and committed the murthers they were charged with : Neither is every Malefactor that is found guilty necessarily to be delivered up, for the obligation being disjunctive, binds only either to deliver up or to punish. For thus we read that the *Elians* made War upon the Lacedemonians, because they did not punish those Lacedemonians that had injured them ; that is, because they would neither deliver them up, nor punish them : sometimes they that demand the malefactor are left to their choice, but this is a favour and not a debt, unless it be so agreed in the league ; as it was between the Kings of *England* and *Denmark* recorded by *Pontanus*. Thus did the Cerites put the Romans to their choice, (*Liv. lib. 7.*) *Whether they would have the persons who had injured them delivered up or punished.* *Æschines* in his answer to *Demosthenes* declares, That treating with King *Philip* concerning the general Peace of *Greece*, he told *Philip* amongst other things, That it was fit that the Malefactors themselves, and not their Cities should pay the price of their own wickedness; and that Cities could not justly be punished, if they caused the Criminals personally to appear in judgment. (*Declam. 255.*) *Quintilian* tells us, *That the next degree to Treason, is to harbour and protect Traytors*; and *next to the Renegadoes are they that receive them.* Basilius *sent to* Cosroes *desiring him to deliver up unto him one, who being a Subject had taken up arms against him, being his Lord and Master*; *and that he would not countenance so pernicious a precedent against himself.* (*Zonaras Basil. Porphyrogenneto.*) And *Dion Chrysostom* among other mischiefs arising from the discord of Cities mentions this as one, *That it is lawfull for offenders to fly for protection from one City to another.*

Whether they who being delivered up, but not received, remain Citizens of their own City.

And here we meet with another question, namely, whether they that being so delivered up by their own City, and not received by any other, do still remain Citizens of their own City? This *Publ. M. Scævola* denies, because they that are so delivered are no less banished from their own City, than they who are interdicted fire and water. But *Brutus*, and after him *Cicero*, were of a contrary Opinion, which doubtless is the more probable, though not properly for the reason brought by *Cicero*, because as in gifts so in deditions, they cannot be compleat unless accepted ; for in every donation that is perfect, the consent of both Parties is necessary; whereas the dedition here meant is nothing else but the permitting of a Subject to be under the Arbitrary Power of another Prince or State whom he hath injured; which bare permission doth neither give nor take away any right; only it takes away that which should hinder the execution : wherefore if that other Prince or People shall not make use of that right, then doth he that was delivered, return unto the same condition as before, to be either punished or not punished, as the City whereunto he returns shall see cause, (which was the case of *Clodius* who was delivered to the Inhabitants of *Corsica*, but was not by them accepted of,) as there are many offences wherein a City may do either; but this Right of the City as both other rights and goods are not immediately by the bare fact lost, unless some publick decree or sentence first pass upon him. In the same manner, Goods also though delivered, yet if not accepted remain his, whose formerly they were; but if that Subject being delivered up shall be accepted, and afterwards happen to return, he shall lose the priviledge of his Freedom, unless by some new service done he shall be admitted. Now what we have here said of punishing or delivering offenders, is to be understood, as well of those who fly to our protection from other places, as of those who are natural and native Subjects.

V.

The right of Suppliants belong not to malefactors, but to the miserable.

Neither do those so famous rights of suppliants, and examples of sanctuaries and places of refuge, any thing derogate from what we have before said. For these belong properly to such as are wrongfully oppressed, but not unto those who do such acts as are in themselves either destructive to Humane Society, or injurious to other men. *Gylippus* the *Lacedemonian* discoursing of this right of suppliants, speaks thus; (*Diod. lib. 8.*) *They who first introduced*

duced these priviledges, intended that they who were through any misfortune miserable, should be preserved; but they that were maliciously wicked, should expect nothing but punishment; for these have nothing to blame Fortune for, neither ought they to assume to themselves the name of suppliants, which is proper to those only, Quibus innocens est animus irata fortuna, *Whom nothing but an inevitable fate or fortune have made miserable: But as for those who are constantly and professedly unjust, there remains no place either for Pity or Protection,* which two *Menander* thus distinguisheth;

Misfortune and injustice differ much,
For that's our chance, this our own choice makes such.

Wherefore as *Philo* notes, *Mercy indeed is due to the unfortunate, but they that are wilfully wretched are not unhappy, but unjust. When we behold a man that is distrest,* saith *Marcus Antoninus, we should diligently observe his mind and manners, whereby we may discover whether it were his ignorance, or his wilfulness that occasioned his misfortune, and accordingly we should administer either our advice, or our reproof.* So *Totilas* in *Procopius* doth wisely distinguish *between those injuries that are done through ignorance or forgetfulness, and those done out of a premeditated malice.* The former may plead if not for pardon, yet for mitigation of his punishment; but the latter can urge nothing, but what aggravates both the sin and judgment. Not much impertinent to this is that of *Demosthenes* which *Cicero* thus translates, *Misereri oportet qui propter fortunam, non propter malitiam in miseriis sunt; To commiserate those that are miserable is an act of humanity, but then only when such sufferings are occasioned by some misfortune, but not when occasioned by our own wickedness:* Nor that of *Antiphanes, That which is done involuntarily is from fortune, but what we do deliberately is but the fruits of our own choice.* Nor that of *Lysias, There is no man willingly unfortunate.* But when a man is made miserable either by the undeserved malice of an enemy, or by some secret fate, or some misfortune which could not be foreseen, then protection by foreign Princes, is a debt due to the frailty and inconstancy of our Humane Condition. It was a sanction of the wisest Law that ever was; *That he that had accidentally slain a man whom he hated not in times past, should fly to one of the five Cities of Refuge, and there be safe.* Because that act as to the irregularity of it had not the consent of the Will, so that it was not so properly his sin, as his misfortune: whereas the very Horns of the Altar could not secure him, who out of premeditated malice had slain an innocent person, or who out of an affectation of Soveraignty and Dominion did attempt an innovation in the State; which Law *Philo* explaining, saith, *Profanis in fanum nullum esse receptum; That no sanctuary can give protection to such unsanctified persons.* The like provision we find to have been in use amongst the Ancient *Grecians*, as *Plutarch* testifies. The *Chalcidenses* refused to deliver up *Nauplius* to the *Grecians*; and the reason is given, because he had sufficiently cleared himself of the Crimes they objected against him. The like we may read of in this latter Age, for King *Pepin* did receive into his protection, and refused to deliver up such as being tyrannically opprest, fled out of *Normandy* unto him. Yea, and the Emperour *Ludovicus Pius* received those that fled unto him, even from the Church of *Rome*, as may appear by his Decree made in the year 817, and inserted in the second Tome of the *Gallican* Councils, &c. *Cicero, Pomponius* and others relate, That there was in *Athens* an Altar called, *Ara Misericordiæ, The Altar of Mercy,* which the calamitous have sacred made, saith the Poet, and a little after:

[Margin notes: *De Judice.* — *Goth. lib.* 3. — *In Aphor.* 5. — Deut. 19. 1. 23. 15. Exod. 21. 14. 1 King. 2. 29. 2 King. 11. 13. — *Quæst. Græc.* 32.]

Where th' exil'd, and the vanquisht seek for rest,
And Kings of their own Kingdoms dispossest.

That is, all that were unfortunately distrest, *The City Athens,* as *Aristides* tells us, *was of all other Cities the most ready to protect strangers, and such as were through misfortune miserable.* And elsewhere, *This, in that age was the common Port or Haven wherein all the wrecks of fortune put in and found relief, from what part of the world, and for what causes soever they were distressed, hither they came, and here they found succour and protection:* The like Encomium *Mariana* gives of *Arragon.* The *Gepidæ* chose rather universally to perish, as *Procopius* informs us, than to deliver up *Ildigisales* either to the *Romans*, or to the *Lombards. Sophocles* in one of his Tragedies, brings in *Oedipus* supplicating the *Athenians* in these words:

[Margin notes: *Lib.* 20. *c.* 13. — *Goth.* 4.]

Ah! men of Athens, *I have suffered much;*
Suffer'd indeed: for God my witness is,
That knowingly, I have not done amiss.

And *Theseus* answering him thus,

Such Guests as thee, at all times to defend

O Oedipus

O Oedipus, *repent I never can,*
Till I forget my self to be a man.

And yet as highly as these *Athenians* delighted to protect their suppliants, whom fortune and not wilfulness had made miserable, they would not protect a known malefactor, nor give that to Vice, that was due only to Innocence; witness that in the same Tragedy:

Hunc qui facinorum conscius, nec legibus
Fidens, ad aras volvitur supplex Deûm,
Trahere ad tribunal nulla relligio mihi:
Mala semper æquum ferre qui fecit male.

From sacred Altars, who to judgment draws
A guilty Traytor, that distrusts the Laws,
Doth nothing impious: for just it is
That he should suffer, who hath done amiss.

So the same Poet elsewhere,

——————*Non enim tangi decet*
Manu nocente numina, at justum fuit
Piis patere templa contra injurias.

With hands impure the Gods to supplicate
Indecent is: yet should the Temple gate
Stand open, for th' opprest to enter at.

Lycurgus the Orator relates a story of one *Calistratus,* who having committed some hainous crime, and consulting the Oracle about his safety, received this answer; That if he would fly to *Athens, he should have right done him.* In hopes of impunity, he betakes himself to that Altar in *Athens,* which was held the most sacred, yet even from thence he was taken and put to death: So also was *Ferdinand* Lord High Chamberlain of *Portugal* forced from the Altar, and burnt, for ravishing a Noble Virgin, as *Mariana* records: So religiously did they distinguish between such as were criminous, and such as were unfortunate. *Tacitus* condemns some of the *Grecian* Cities of superstition, who thought their Gods to be pleased with their protecting of Malefactors. *Princes* (saith he) *are like Gods; for neither do the Gods themselves answer the supplications of the wicked:* and in another place, he assures us, *Neque à diis nisi justas supplicum preces audiri; That the Gods never heard the supplications of men unless they were just.* Such then as are notoriously faulty, are either to be delivered up punished, or at least banished out of their Dominions from whom they are demanded. Thus did the *Cymæi* in *Herodotus,* who though they would not deliver up *Pactyes* the *Persian,* whom notwithstanding they durst not keep, yet chose that which was safest to both, which was to suffer him to fly to *Mitylene.* Thus *Perseus* King of *Macedon* in his Apology to *Martius,* concerning those that had betrayed *Eumenes,* pleads thus, *As soon as upon your information I found these men in* Macedon, *I commanded them forthwith to depart my Kingdom, and have for ever interdicted them my Dominions.* Thus did Queen *Elizabeth* answer the *Scots* who demanded *Bothwell; That she was ready either to deliver him up, or to banish him out of* England. Yet do the European *Princes* in most places at this day, and in the age last past, connive at one another for the reception of Malefactors, unless they be such as disturb the publick peace, or that are guilty of some egregious crimes; for lesser crimes they usually pass by, unless they are directly excepted against in the Articles of any League: as it was in that made between *England* and *France,* wherein it was agreed, That Rebels and Fugitives should be delivered up: And in that made with the *Burgundians,* wherein it was provided, that all such should be expelled, as *Camden* testifies. However this is worth our observation, That notorious Thieves and Pirates, when through long and prosperous successes, they are become formidable to their Neighbours, may be protected as from punishment; because it conduceth much to the common safety, to withdraw such persons from their wicked practices, by hopes of Indemnity, in case it cannot otherwise be done, this therefore any Prince or People may undertake to do.

Lib. 21. — *Ann. lib.* 3. — *Lib.* 1. — *Camden An.* 1593. — *Anno* 1600.

VI. *Yet may they be protected until their Cause be examined, and by what Law.*

And this also is observable, that Suppliants may be defended until the equity of their case be rightly known. Thus *Demophon* tells the Ambassadors of *Eurysthius,* who demanded of him some that fled unto him for protection:

Si crimen istis aliquod hospitibus struis,
Jus impetrabis; vi quidem hinc non abstrahes.

If

If with foul crimes you can them charge, you may
What's right obtain, but not them force away.

But if the Crimes whereof they stand accused be such, as are neither against the Laws of Nature or Nation, then shall they be judged by the Civil Law of that place from whence the Suppliants came, which *Æschylus* excellently proves in his Tragedy of Suppliants, where he brings in the King of the *Argives* bespeaking a Company of *Grecians* that came out of *Ægypt* thus;

Manum tibi si immittat Ægypti genus
Quod lege patria proximos se sanguine
Dicant, quis hac objicere se contra velit?
Quare tuum est docere, natalis soli
Ex lege, nullo jure te illis subjici.

VII. How Subjects may partake of their Princes faults.

How the faults of Subjects, whether Natives or Strangers may be transferred to their Governours we have already seen. Now on the other side, Subjects also may partake of their Princes faults, in case they either consent thereunto, or act any thing at his Command, or by his perswasion that is wicked: but hereof we shall discourse more properly anon, when we treat of the Duty of Subjects towards their Prince. There may be also a communication of Crimes between the whole body of the people, and each particular member thereof; because as St *Augustine* observes, *Ubi universi, ibi & singuli*; *Universals cannot consist without individuals*; *so every single person being congregated and united in one gross body, doth constitute a body universal.* But yet the faults committed by this Body Politick, are properly transferred to those particular members only, which did yield their consents unto those publick acts, and not unto those who were over-voted by the major part of the Council: And as the faults so the punishments of singular persons, are distinct from those of the whole Nation. For as upon individual persons, the greatest punishment that can be inflicted is death; so *the death of a City is desolation*; which happens when the Body Politick is wholly dissolved; that is, when all the Laws, Priviledges and other advantages thereof do utterly fail; and by this means every single person may of a Citizen become a slave; as the *Thebans* were to *Alexander* of *Macedon*, those only excepted that contradicted the decree of dissolving the Society. So also a City or a Kingdom may be reduced into a civil servitude, by being made a Province. And every particular person may lose his propriety by confiscation; and whatsoever that City or People held in common, as their Walls, their Magazins, their Ports, Men of War, Fleets, Elephants, Treasuries, yea, and their Common Fields, all become the Conquerours. But for private men to lose their particular Estates, through the defaults of the universality, without any consent of theirs, is unjust, as *Libanius* very well observes in his Oration concerning the Antiochian Sedition. The same Author approves the fact of *Theodosius*, for punishing a common fault, with the loss of their publick Theatres, Baths, and the honour of being a Metropolis; which St *Chrysostome* also confirms in his seventeenth Oration *de Statuis.* After the very same manner were the same Antiochians of old, punished by *M. Antoninus* the Philosopher, *&c.*

Lycurgus Orat.

Sup. cap. 9. *sect.* 4.

Plut. Alex.

VIII. Whether a punishment once due may at any time be exacted.

But here we meet with a notable question, whether the punishment due for an injury done by the generality of any one City or State, may at any time afterwards be exacted: so long as that State, City or Commonwealth doth subsist, it may: for that which is justly due at all times, may at any time be exacted, because the same body politick still remains, though the individuals succeed each to other, as we have elsewhere shewed. But yet on the other side we must note, That some things are primarily and absolutely necessary to every Corporation, as to have a publick Treasury, to have Laws, and the like; others appertain thereunto derivatively only, from those individual persons that inhabit therein: In which sense a Nation or City may be said to be just, valiant, prudent, if most or many of the Inhabitants thereof be such; and of this kind are the merits of a City. For that which hath no life, cannot of it self contract any guilt, but a City is said to be guilty, in respect of those particular persons who actually offended; but they being dead, by whom the guilt was deduced to the generality of the People, the guilt dies also, and consequently the obligation to the punishment, which without merit cannot consist. Thus *Libanius* in his fore-cited Oration, *There is no place left for revenge, where all are dead that gave the offence.* Wherefore *Alexander* is highly condemned by *Arrianus*, for his too much cruelty and injustice in his revenge taken upon the Persians, there being no one person then living of those who had formerly offended the Grecians. And therefore *Julian* ascribes that War to another cause, *There was never any War*, saith he, *reputed just, that was undertaken for such a cause, neither by the Grecians against the Trojans, nor by the* *Mace-*

Constantii laudatione.

Macedonians against the Persians, as may be made clear to any child; for they never visited crimes anciently committed by Parents, on their Nephews or Children; but invaded those only, who had by force oppressed the posterity of such as had well deserved, and dispossest them of their Kingdoms. Concerning the destruction of the Branchidæ made by the same *Alexander, Curtius* gives his judgment thus, *If* (saith he) *the same punishment had been inflicted upon the Traitors themselves, it had been recorded as an act of his justice, and not of his cruelty; but the revenge fell upon the innocent, whilst their posterity (who never so much as saw* Miletum, *and therefore could not betray it to* Xerxes*) pay the price of their forefathers sin.* The like judgment doth *Arrianus* pass upon *Alexander*'s burning of *Persepolis*, in revenge for what the Persians had long before done unto the City of *Athens.* But, saith *Arrianus, In mine opinion, it was not wisely done of* Alexander; *neither could that be truly said to be a just revenge upon those Persians, who had been dead long before.* For as to that answer which *Agathocles* made to the just complaints of the Inhabitants of *Ithaca,* namely, that the Sicilians had of old suffered much more by their Countryman *Ulysses;* none that hears of it but will think it ridiculous. And *Plutarch* in his Book against *Herodotus,* saith, *That it was a thing very improbable that the Corinthians should revenge an injury done them by the Samians after three ages.* From all which we may conclude, That the memory of injuries done us, ought not to outlive the persons that did them; neither will those arguments brought by *Plutarch*, in defence of the revenge taken by God upon Posterity for the sins of their Ancestors, serve to justify the like in men; because, there is not the same right between man and man, as there is between God and man: neither will it necessarily follow, that because our Children do receive honours aud rewards, for the vertuous acts of their forefathers, therefore they may be justly punished for their faults; because such is the nature of a courtesie, or benefit, that it may be conferred upon any man without injury; but the nature of a punishment is not so.

Injuries done should not be revenged but on those that did them.

IX.

Whether a man may partake of the punishment tho' not of the crime.

Thus having shewed by what means a man may partake of the punishment, by being made accessary to the sin of another; now we intend to shew how a man may be involved in the punishment, though he be no ways accessary to his sin: And here to avoid mistake, and that we may not confound things in their own nature distinct, because they are alike in name, we must walk cautiously as to some particulars.

X.

That which comes directly, distinguisht from that wch comes by consequence.

As in the first place, we must distinguish between that damage that is purposely and directly done, and that which comes by consequence; that I account a wrong directly done, when that is taken away, whereunto a man hath a peculiar right: And that I call a wrong done by consequence, when a man is deprived of that, which otherwise he might have had, that condition ceasing without which he could have no right or title. An example whereof *Ulpian* gives us thus, If by digging a Well in my own ground, I cut off or intercept the spring that feeds my neighbours Well; the damage he sustaineth, is not occasioned directly, by any illegal act of mine, but by the lawful use of that wherein I had a proper and peculiar right as being mine own. And in another place, There is a great difference between the doing of an injury, and the prohibiting a man to make the profit, which he hath hitherto been permitted to make. And *it is very preposterous* (saith *Paulus* the Lawyer) *to account our selves rich before we have acquired those riches;* As when a Father runneth into a *præmunire* by doing that, for which his estate is justly confiscate, his Children may feel the loss, 'tis true; but the loss is not properly their punishment, because the goods could not properly be accounted theirs, unless they had continued to have been their Fathers to the hour of his death: which was well observed by *Alphenus,* when he said, The Children indeed do suffer through the default of their Father, but that they do not inherit that which should otherwise have descended unto them, is not properly the Childrens punishment, but their Parents: But those goods which accrew unto them, not from their Parents, but either from nature, custom, or education, do (notwithstanding their Fathers fault) remain perfectly theirs. *Cicero* writes that *Themistocles* his Children suffered want; nor did he think it unjust, that *Lepidus* his Children should do the like: and this he affirms to be an ancient custom, and observed in all Cities; which notwithstanding the later Roman Laws have somewhat moderated. So when through the default of the major part, which (as we have said before) represents and hath the power of the whole, the whole offends, and upon that account loseth their civil liberty *(i. e.)* their Walls, Ports, and other Commodities; those particular persons who were innocent, do indeed bear an equal share in the loss, but yet in those things only which appertained not unto them, but as they were a part of the whole.

XI

What befals us by the occasion of a crime distinguisht from that wch befals us because of the crime.

Sponde, noxa præsto est.

Besides it is to be noted, that sometimes some evil is to be imposed on a man, or some good taken from him by the occasion of anothers sin; yet so that that sin is not the immediate cause of that action, as to the very Right of doing it; as he that passeth his word for the debt of another, suffers, not by reason of the debt, but by reason of his ingagement, according to our Proverb, A Surety is a sure tye. For as he that passeth his word for a buyer, is not bound by the purchase, but by his own free promise: So he that undertakes for a delinquent may suffer, not for his delinquency, but by reason of his vadimony or susception; which

which as it was in his own free power to do or not to do; so being done, it shall no less oblige him than the offence did the delinquent. Now the ground of this is, the power and freedom that every man hath to oblige himself, and therefore the measure of his sufferings is not to be taken from the hainousness of anothers fault, but from the power he hath to oblige himself: The consequence whereof is, That no man can justly be put to death, by being a surety for another, (whose crime may happily deserve death) because no man can justly oblige himself beyond what is in his power; but this power over a mans life, either to take it away from himself, or to oblige another to take it away from him, no man hath: and therefore no man can justly be put to death by reason of such a vademony. And this I hold to be the truer opinion, though it seems, that not the ancient Romans only, but the Grecians and Hebrews also were of another mind, who believed that even the sureties also might justly be adjudged to death, as appears by that ancient story of *Damon* and *Pythias*. And by those words of *Reuben* to his Father *Jacob*, *Slay my two sons if I bring him not back unto thee* *: whereunto St *Augustine* † alludes, where he saith, *That he that is the cause of anothers death, is sometimes a greater sinner than he that kills him: As when a malefactor leaves his surety to suffer that lawful punishment which himself should undergo*; as it falls out frequently with hostages, as we shall shew anon. Neither doth this power of obliging a mans self extend to mutilation; for no man hath such a power over his bodily members as to cut them off, unless it be for the conservation of the whole body. But whatsoever any man hath a full and absolute power over, he may engage for another, and if he suffer thereby, it is not by way of punishment, but by way of equity, which requires that what is promised should be performed. Thus a man may forfeit his estate, his liberty, his goods, and the like. The same almost may be said of such things as a man enjoys, either *jure precario*, by entreaty or permission, respect being had to the propriety of the thing: Or in his own private right, respect being had to that Soveraign Right that every City or State hath over it, for the publick and general safety. Now if any of these shall be taken away by the occasion of another mans crime, it is not (as I have said before) properly as a punishment; but as the execution of that precedent right, which by promise was transferred to him that takes it. So when that Beast is put to death with whom a man hath had copulation, (as by the Law of *Moses* was decreed,) it was not by way of punishment: forasmuch as a Beast having no Law, cannot be said properly to sin, and consequently is not liable to punishment; but it is by virtue of that Right and Dominion that men have over Beasts, to do with them as they please.

Jos. Ant. lib. 2. *cap.* 3.
* Gen. 42. 37.
† *Ep.* 54. *ad Macedonium.*
See *lib.* 3. *c.* 4. §. 14.

XII. Properly, no man can be justly punished for anothers fault.

These distinctions being granted, we say, that no innocent person can be punished for the default of another; the reason whereof is, Because every punishment presupposeth an offence, and every offence must needs be personal, because it ariseth from the choice of the will; and nothing can be more truly and properly ours, than that which derives its Being from us.

XIII. No not the Children for their Parents.

It was St *Hieroms* observation, That *Neque virtutes, neque vitia parentum liberis imputantur*; *That neither the virtues nor vices of Parents are imputed unto their Children*: And St *Augustine* concludes peremptorily †, *That it stands not with the perfection of Gods Justice to punish an innocent.* *Dion Chrysostome* when he had said, That by the Athenian Laws, the Children were sometimes put to death for their Parents crimes, speaking of the Law of God; he subjoyns, *But this Law doth not like the other, punish the posterity of those that sin; but makes every man to be the author of his own misery*; according to that common Proverb, *Noxa sequitur caput*, *The punishment follows the malefactor only.* *We do Decree* (say the Christian Emperours) *That where the guilt is, there shall be the punishment: for sin, like a viper, devours its own parents; and therefore our fears should not be extended farther than our guilt. Quis locus innocentiæ relinquitur, si alienum crimen maculet nescientem? Where*, saith St *Augustine*, *shall innocence find sanctuary, if the child that is ignorant and innocent must be involved in his fathers punishment?* *Philo* in his Special Laws, abominating the custom of some Nations, in destroying the Children of Traytors and Tyrants, saith, *Justum est eorum esse pœnas quorum sunt delicta*; *It is just that they should suffer that have sinned*: And in another place, *There is nothing* (saith he) *more unjust, or of more dangerous consequence to a State, than to deny either the virtuous children of wicked parents their deserved honour, or the wicked children of virtuous parents their due punishment: For the Law judgeth every man according to his own works, and neither commends any man for the virtues, nor condemns any man for the vices of his ancestors.* And *Josephus* condemns the contrary fact in *Alexander* King of the Jews, calling it, *The exaction of punishment exceeding all humane measure.* So also doth *Dionysius Halicarnassensis*, where he confutes that common pretence of cruelty, which is that *malus corvus malum ovum*, *the child will be like the father*: For this also (saith he) is very uncertain, and an uncertain fear can be no ground sufficient to justifie a certain death. One was so bold as to tell *Arcadius*, (a Christian Emperour) that the children should also attend their guilty parents to death, if but suspected to have been infected by their example. And *Ammianus* relates a story of a Daughter, at that time very

† *Epist.* 105.
Lib. 2.

very little, that was put to death, *Nè ad parentum exempla succresceret, lest she should grow to be like her parents.* Neither is the fear of revenge any just cause to destroy the children of guilty parents, which occasioned that Greek Proverb;

Who kills the Sire and saves the Son's, a fool.

For, as *Seneca* notes, *There is nothing more unrighteous than for a child to inherit his fathers malice. Pausanias* the Greek Emperour would not do the least hurt to the Children of *Attaginus*, who had caused the *Thebans* to revolt unto the *Medes*, presuming that they were not guilty of that conspiracy. And *M. Anthony*, in his Epistle to the Roman Senate, *commands them to pardon the Sons of* Avidius Cassius, *(who had conspired against him) together with his Son-in-Law, and his Wife, adding; But what speak I of pardoning them, who have done no evil.* And *Julian* highly commends the like humanity in *Constantius*, shewing, That good Children do many times spring from wicked Parents, as Bees out of rocks, Figgs out of bitter wood, and Pomegranats from thorns.

XIV. The objection taken from Gods dealing with men answered.

But God in the Mosaical Law threatens to visit the sins of Fathers upon their Children; but he hath a full and absolute Power and Dominion, not only over our goods but lives also, as being his own gifts, which he may take away from us at any time, and that without any other cause given, than his own will. If therefore he do at any time by some violent and untimely death snatch away the children of an *Achan*, *Saul*, *Jeroboam*, *Ahab*, or the like, he doth but exercise his own right of Dominion, and not that of punishment; and yet by the same effect, he doth the more exquisitely punish the parents of those children, as some of the Jewish Doctors taught very truly. For whether the parents do survive their children, which the Divine Law did chiefly respect, and therefore extends not its threats beyond the fourth generation, which was possible for a man to see, *Exod.* 25. most certain it is, that the Parents were even therein intended to be more severely punished by so sad an example, as being thereby more deeply wounded than by their own sufferings, as *Chrysostome* well observes: wherewith agrees that of *Plutarch*, *Nullum durius supplicium quam eos qui ex se sunt ob se miseros spectare; No punishment so grievous as to see those born of us, to be for our faults miserable.* Or, whether the parents do not live so long as to see their childrens sufferings, yet doubtless to depart this life in that fear is a most dreadfull torment. *The hardness of mens hearts* (saith Tertullian) *did urge the Almighty to this severity, that so they that had any care of the welfare of their posterity, might yield the more ready obedience to the Law of God.* Whereunto we may add that of *Alexander* in *Curtius*, who being demanded what should become of their innocent children? Answered, *It is not for you to know what I intend to do with them, that you your selves may perish the more uncomfortably.* But withal we must note, That God doth not use this severity, but for such sins, as are committed properly in the reproach of himself; as for the sins of Idolatry, Sacriledge, Perjury, and the like. Neither did the Grecians themselves think otherwise. For all those sins which were thus visited on posterity, which they called stupendious, were of this sort, whereof *Plutarch* discourseth excellently in his Book, concerning the late revenge of God. And in *Ælian* we find a Delphick Oracle to this very purpose denounced against the sin of Sacriledge:

Rab. Simon Barsemi. 2 Sam. 21. 1 King. 14. 2 Kings 8, 9, 10. *Hom.* 29. *in* Gen. 9. ἄγη.

At scelerum fontes divinum persequitur jus,
Necpote vitari: non si genus ab Jove ducant:
Sed capiti ipsorum & qui nascunter ab ipsis
Imminet; inque domo cladem subit altera clades.

Vengeance, the guilty doth from Heaven attend,
Which none can 'scape, though they from *Jove* descend,
Upon themselves, and on their Children all
Plague after Plague, throughout the house shall fall.

The like we have in *Libanius*, who speaking of some Sacrilegious persons, saith, *Whereof some have already been punished, others not yet, but none shall escape; and not only they, but their Childrens Children after them.* This is also confirmed by *Strabo* and *Gellius*, in the story of the Gold stoln out of Temple at *Tholouse*. Concerning Perjury we have already given the like testimonies above; and concerning Idolatry we have a most pregnant example in *Jeroboam*, where it is also to be observed, That although God doth thus threaten to visit the sins of Parents upon their Children; yet he doth not always do it, especially if any spark of vertue appear in them, or if the Child do publickly declare his detestation of his Fathers wickedness, as *Andron Pelæologus* did; as is evident, *Ezech.* 18. and by divers examples alledged by *Plutarch*, in the place before recited. And in the New Testament, where there is a clearer discovery made of the punishments that attend us after this life, than in any of the Prophets; yet is there no commination that extends beyond the person sinning,

sinning, whereunto that of *Ezekiel* hath some respect, though but obscurely, as the manner of the Prophets at that time was. Now though God do sometimes visit the sins of Parents on their Children, yet is this no warrant for us to do the same; neither can there be the same reason, because of that absolute Power and Dominion, that he hath over our lives, to take them away at his pleasure, without any respect had unto our sins; whereas men can have no such power, but what our own crimes give them: and therefore as the sin, so the punishment should not be extended beyond our persons. And therefore the very same Law of God doth expresly in another place forbid, That either the Father should be put to death for the Child, or the Child for the Father, *Deut.* 24. 16. which some of the pious Kings of *Israel* did religiously observe, even in the case of Treason, as *Amasias* did; which Law is highly commended both by *Josephus* and *Philo*: As *Isocrates* doth the like Law amongst the Ægyptians, and *Dionysius Halicarnassensis* the same among the Romans. *Neither the sin nor punishment of the Father leaves any guilt at all upon the Children*, saith *Calistratus* out of *Plato*. For it is just that every Fox should pay his own skin unto the fleaer, and that every man should carve out his own fortunes, and no man answer for his sin before God by an Attorney. *Would any City* (saith *Cicero*) *endure such a Law, that should condemn the Son or Nephew, if the Father only or the Grandfather did offend?* Hence it is that the Roman, Grecian, and Ægyptian Laws do forbid the putting to death of Women with Child, as an act of injustice and cruelty.

XV. If not children, much less kinsmen.

And if so, then certainly the Laws of the * Persians and Macedonians, adjudging to death all the kindred and relations of Traitors, that so they might the more dolorously perish (as *Curtius* speaks) are most cruel and unjust, which *Ammianus Marcellinus* records as the severest of all Laws. *Philo* also observes, that it was usual with Tyrants to put to death together with the persons so condemned, the five Families that were of nearest kin to them; which execrable custom is not so much as heard of among Christians, being a cruelty exceeding any humane Judgment.

* *Dan.* 7. 22. *Justin.* l. 10.

XVI. Yet may children be denyed somethings wth otherwise they might have had.

But yet in case the Children of such Traitors may have, or expect to enjoy any thing whereof the peculiar Right is not in them, but in the King or People, it may be taken from them by a certain Right of Dominion, as it adds to the punishment of the offender. Hence it was that (as *Plutarch* observes) *The posterity of Traitors were held uncapable of honours*, as the Children of such as were proscribed by *Sylla* were among the Romans. So by the Law of *Arcadius*, it was provided (as a thing tolerable) against the Children of Traitors, *That they should not be admitted into any honour or office in the Commonwealth.*

XVII. Nor are Subjects properly punished for their Princes crimes.

Now what hath been here said of Children, may as well be said of such people as are truly Subjects; if the Question be put, whether they may be justly punished for the sins of their Kings or of their Governours? I mean not here, in case the people shall give their consent thereunto, or act any thing in relation to the fault of their Prince, which is in it self punishable. But we treat of that contract, which ariseth from the nature of that body, whereof the King is the Head, and the Subjects the Members: For as to those that give their consent and assistance to the sin of their Prince, it is true what *Philo* observes of *Pharaoh* in *Abrahams* time, *That the whole Family felt the smart of* Pharaohs *sin, because no man had indignation against so unjust a fact, but all of them by commending it, were as guilty almost as himself.* So *Josephus* discoursing of the judgment of *Jeroboam*, *The people*, saith he, *did likewise partake of the punishment of the Kings sin, for they also were to be expelled that good land, and to be scattered into foreign Nations, because they were his companions in the act of his sin.* But in case the people yield not their consent, yet may they partake of the punishment, by reason (as I said) of the connection that there is between them and their Prince. *David* numbred the people, and his Subjects are consumed by the Pestilence; *David* thought this to be hard dealing, because he thought the people innocent: *But God* (saith the Text) *was angry with the people, and therefore moved him* (against them) *to say, go, number the people*, 2 Sam. 24. 1. And then takes occasion by this sin of *Davids*, to punish the sins of *Israel*; and having absolute power over their lives, takes them away by the Pestilence, thereby punishing both Prince and People: for, as a good Christian Author saith well, *Kings are never more severely punished, than when they are punished in their Subjects.* And this is as just with God, as it is with men, ordinarily to be whipt on the back, for an offence committed by the hand; or as it is with a Physician, to burn a man on the great Toe, to cure him of a pain in the hip as *Plutarch* makes the comparison: But why this is not lawful for men, we have already shewed.

Quæst. ad Orthod. 138.

XVIII Nor Dissenters for the sins of the major part.

The self same may be said of the punishment of such particular persons (in those things which are properly their own) as do not consent unto those injuries that are committed by the generality of the people.

XIX. The Heir not obliged to his Fathers punishment as such, and why.

But why the Heir that is obnoxious to other debts, is not obliged to this of punishment, the true cause is, Because the Heir represents the person of the deceased, not in merits, which are meerly personal, but in his goods; whereunto that those also that are owing unto any man, by reason of the very inequality of things, should cohere, was at the first, by a general

Orat. Rhodiana. general consent introduced with dominion it self. For as *Dion Prusiensis* observes, *Whatsoever was owing by the Father, is no less due from his posterity; neither can ye justly charge it upon us, that we have renounced our inheritance.* So likewise *Cicero, There is no person so fit to succeed in the room of the deceased, as the right Heir.*

XX. Yet he is, if that punishment be changed into some other kind of debt.

Hence it follows, That if beyond the merit there appear any new cause of obligation, then even that contained in the punishment may be justly due, though not properly as a punishment: So we have seen, that sometimes after the sentence is past, and sometimes after the matter of fact is sufficiently proved, in such things as will admit of a composition; the mulct or pecuniary punishment shall be recovered from the Heir, as even that also which is drawn into that agreement, because there now appears a new cause of obligation.

CHAP. XXII.

Of Causes of War that are unjust.

I. *The difference between Causes that are just, and such as are suasory only, explained.*
II. *The War that hath neither of these, is brutish.*
III. *That War that hath causes suasory only, not justifying, is predary.*
IV. *There are some causes which seem to be just, which are not.*
V. *As uncertain fear.*
VI. *Profit without necessity.*
VII. *The denyal of Wives, where there are plenty of Women.*
VIII. *The desire to plant in a better soil.*
IX. *The finding out of such things as are preoccupyed by others.*
X. *What if those pre-occupiers be altogether mad.*
XI. *The desire of liberty no just cause, in such as are Subjects.*
XII. *Nor the desire to rule over others without their consent, though for their good.*
XIII. *Nor the title of being Universal Monarch, which some have given to the Emperour, which is refuted.*
XIV. *Which others give to the Church, which is also refuted.*
XV. *As also a pretence to fulfil some Prophecies, without a special command from God.*
XVI. *As also a pretence of some due debt, though not in strictness of Right but some other way.*
VII. *The difference between a War whose cause is unjust, and that which is some other ways unjust, and the divers effects of both.*

I. The difference between the true and the pretended causes of War. * *Lib. 2. c. 1.*

OF the causes of War, some are (as I have said above *) justifying, some suasory only; those that are unjust, have notwithstanding always some specious pretence or other, to make the War to appear just, which *Polybius* calls προφάσεις, the other he calls αἰτίας, or the true causes, which oft-times lye couchant, whilst something that is more plausible is exposed to the publick view; as in the War which *Alexander* made against *Darius*, the preface or pretence was, to revenge some wrongs which the Persians had long before done unto the Grecians; but the true cause was Ambition, and a vehement thirst after soveraignty and riches, which also was very much heightned by the facility of the enterprise, which he collected from the success, which both *Xenophon* and *Agesilaus* had before in their several expeditions. *Thucydides* distinguisheth them into the outward shew, and the inward truth; as when the Athenians made War against *Sicily*, they openly declared, that it was only to aid the *Aegestans*, but the naked truth was to gain *Sicily* to themselves. *Appian* also hath the very same expression, in the War made between the Romans and *Mithridates*; and also in his fifth Book of their Civil War, where speaking of the peace broken between *Octavius* and *Sextus Pompeius* he saith, That there were some causes which were true but latent, and others that were feigned and pretended only; the one was but as a cloak or vizard, the other was the real purpose and intention. It is true what *Procopius* in
Lib. 2. his Persian War saith, *Stultum est non libere loqui, ubi justitia dux est, comes utilitas; It is but folly to dissemble, where justice is our guide, and profit our companion.* The pretence of the second Punick War was a contest about *Saguntum*; but the true cause was, the secret disgust which the Carthaginians had against the Romans for the hard conditions they had imposed on them in the low ebb of their fortunes; and the great confidence they had in their own strength, upon some prosperous successes, they then had in *Spain*, as *Polybius* ob-
Liv. lib. 7. serves. The same distinction we find used by *Livy*, in the Oration made by the Campanes to the Romans, concerning their engagement against the Samnites, which they pretended to be only to assist the Sedicines, but their main end was their own defence; because they foresaw, that when their neighbours house was burnt, the fire would quickly reach them.

So

So when *Antiochus* made War against the Romans, his pretence was to revenge the death of *Barcilla*, and some other wrongs received; but the true cause was the great hopes he had to make some advantage to himself of the looseness of the Roman Discipline. And And *Plutarch* observes, that when *Cicero* objected against *Anthony*, That he was the cause of the Civil War, it was but a pretence; for *Cæsar* resolving to make War, took only his pretence from *Anthony*. *Lib.* 36.

II. A war without any cause is brutish.

Some there are that are carried head-long into War without either of these causes, *Periculorum propter se avidi*; *That delight only in sweat and blood, and that live wholly upon spoil and rapine.* This is a vice so much beneath the nature of mankind, that *Aristotle* calls it θηριότητα, a savageness proper to wild beasts only: And so doth *Seneca*, *Non crudelitatem sed feritatem dicimus*; *We cannot so properly call it cruelty, as a kind of savage fierceness to delight in blood: We may also call it madness, whereof as there are divers kinds*, so are there divers symptomes, *but none more certain than that which delights in humane slaughter.* Wherewith accords that of *Aristotle*, *He is cruel with a witness, who is so far transported with a thirst after humane blood, that he makes no difference between friends and foes.* And that also of *Dion Prusiensis*, *To engage our selves in unnecessary Wars, and to rush into battel without any provocation, is a meer madness.* So likewise saith *Seneca*, *There are few or none so savage, as to shed humane blood prodigally, and that for bloods sake only.* *Lib.* 2. *de clem. cap.* 7. *Orat.* 37.

III. The War that hath no justifying cause is but predatory.

Most men that make War have some Causes that move them thereto, some whereof have matter sufficient to justifie them, others none at all. Of this latter sort was that War made by the *Heruli* against the *Lombards*, a War without any pretence whatsoever. And such were the Wars made by the *Gauls*, as *Livy* testifies; who thought the best right to consist in their Arms, and that the longest sword might take all. But in the account of the Roman Laws, *Qui rogatus de possidendi causa, nullam aliam adfert, quam quod possideat, præda est*; *He who being demanded by what right he held any thing, could shew none, but that having got it he would keep it, was held to be a Thief, a Pyrate, or an Usurper of another mans Right.* So *Aristotle* of such as excite others to War, saith, *That they regard not at all whether to subdue their innocent neighbours be just or not.* Such a one was *Brennus*, who held, *That he had the best Right to All, who was strongest of All:* Such a one *Silius* thought *Annibal* to be,

> ———*pro fœdere, próque*
> *Justitia est ensis.*———
>
> Whose Sword did awe
> Both Leagues and Law.

And such was *Attila*, and all those who look not at the Cause but at the success of Wars, according to that vulgar saying of most Souldiers:

> ———*Quæritur belli exitus,*
> *Non causa.*———
>
> 'Tis not the Cause, but th' End that crowns the War.

For when once the dispute comes to blows, the vanquished Party cannot by the strength of Argument convince the Conquerour that he is in an errour, nor shall Reason be heard when the Sword hath decided the Quarrel:

> *Hæc acies victum factura nocentem est:*
>
> This battle will the vanquish't, guilty make.
> ———For let the Cause be what it will,
> The conquer'd party must be guilty still.

Whereunto that of St *Augustine* may very fitly be applyed, *To invade the Dominions of our neighbour Princes, and being encouraged by success to proceed by force of Arms to wast their Countries, and out of mere ambition to destroy those who never injured us: Quid aliud nisi grande latrocinium nominandum est? What can we call this but a grand robbery?* Of such Wars as these thus speaks *Vellejus*, *That they are made for no other cause, but for pay and plunder:* So thought *Cicero* also, *That pride and haughtiness of spirit, whereby we confront dangers, and endure all manner of hardship, is no part of true valour if justice be wanting.* To the same purpose speaks *Agathias*, *They who being transported either with an insatiable desire of Rule or of Riches, or by a violent hatred, shall without any other cause invade another mans Dominions; forasmuch as they offend those that are inoffensive, these men*, saith he, *De Civit. l.* 4. *c.* 6. *De Off. lib.* 1. *Lib.* 2.

Ferinum est ad cædes & vastationes, nulla accepta injuria, venire.
Sic Bo.2.Chap.1. §. 1.

he, *are both proud and dishonest.* Of the same mind was *Andronicus Rhodius, They who to enrich themselves, do rob others, are accounted wicked, impious and unjust, and such are Tyrants, and they who for plunder make Cities desolate.* Concerning whom, *Philo* upon the Decalogue writes thus: *They that have got the power of Thieves and Robbers, that spoil whole Cities being secured from punishment, by being above the Laws; these are men of a barbarous nature, ambitious of rule and dominion, committing great robberies, yet cloaking their villanies under the specious names of Magistracy and Empire, which may more properly be called notorious villanies.* For to waste and depopulate Countries, being by no injury provoked, is brutish cruelty.

IV. Some causes are specious but not just.

Others there are that pretend to make War upon just and warrantable grounds, which notwithstanding being throughly searched into, will be found unjust; and as *Livy* speaks, A contest not to be decided by Law or justice, but by plain force. Some Princes (saith *Plutarch*) make the same use of Peace and War, as private men do of Money; not always for just ends, but for ends suitable to their own fancies. Now tho' what causes are unjust may be in some measure known, by those that are just, *Rectum enim est obliqui judex; for by a line that is straight, we may easily discern that which is crooked*: yet for plainness and perspicuity, we shall insist upon the principal heads of them.

V. As an uncertain fear.

And First, Our fears by reason of the swelling power of our neighbour Prince, is no sufficent ground for a just War; for that our defence by Arms be just, it ought to be necessary, which it cannot be unless we are most assured, not only, that he against whom we make War, hath a power to do us wrong; but that he hath also a full purpose and resolution so to do, which certainly ought to be such as takes place in moral matters. That therefore our Neighbour, being not restrained by any former agreement, builds a Fort in any part of his own Dominions, from whence we may be hereafter annoyed, is no just ground for us to make War upon him; because, for prevention we also may do the like in any part of our own Territories, or apply our selves to other the like remedies, and not by War. Whence we may conclude, That the War made by the Romans against *Philip* of *Macedon*, and that made by *Lysimachus* against *Demetrius*, were unjust, unless warranted by the access of some other cause. I am very well satisfied with that of *Tacitus*, concerning the *Cauchi*, the noblest People of all *Germany*, *Who* (saith he) *supported their grandeur by justice, without any extraordinary affectation, either of glory, or riches, and yet without any disability or want of power to either: they lived quietly and without noise, provoked no Wars, nor were they wasted by spoil or pillage; and which was the main demonstration of their valour and strength, the credit and esteem they had before others, they got not by injuries and oppressions: every man amongst them had his Arms in readiness, and if occasion required they had an Army, both of Men and Horse they had good store; and thus they kept up the repute of being a warlike Nation, though they lived in Peace.*

Zonaras. Pausanias lib. 1.

The *Cauchi.*

Though our own uncertain fears be no sufficient ground for us to make War, yet may we use all lawful means cautiously to prevent dangers before they fall; this is that prudence that Christ commands to his Disciples, where he bids them to be wise as Serpents, but innocent as Doves. And this is the prudence of Empires, that if any one would annoy us, to take such care, and to use such means that he shall not be able to hurt us; which may be done two ways: As first, if the neighbouring Nations do see the growing power of any one Prince, so as to conceive some jealousie of him, they ought to combine in a stronger League; that if either shall be invaded unjustly, they shall all make War against the Aggressor, this being then a just cause of War. Thus the Italians being jealous of the Venetians power leagued themselves for their own defence; so that though that Republick was too strong for any of them singly, yet being far too weak for them all, it was wisely kept within its own bounds. *Livy* discoursing of the several opinions of men, concerning the War between *Perseus* and the Romans, some wishing well to one, and some to another, tells us; That the best and wisest sort wished the victory to neither; for so should they live free and secure from both. For if either of the two parties should offer to opress them, the other would be ready to secure them. And as *Spain* formerly, so *France* now, aspiring to act universal Monarchy, all European Princes have reason to be jealous of him, and to combine together to withstand him. Secondly if any Potentate being more powerful than his Neighbours, shall unjustly oppress any of them, the rest ought to confederate, and to compel the Aggressor to accept of due satisfaction, if there be cause for it; which if he refuse, his cause then being unjust, (much more if it were originally so) they may all of them make War upon him, as being the disturber of the publick peace. Thus did the Italian Princes against the French when they were invaded by *Charles* the Eighth, which occasioned the late Triple League or Alliance, when the French had seized upon the County of *Burgundy*, and invaded *Flanders*; both which belonged to the Crown of *Spain.*

VI. Unnecessary profit.

Neither hath profit the same right to make a just War, as necessity hath.

VII. The denyal of Marriages.

Neither is the denyal of Marriages, though there be plenty of Women, any just cause of a War; which notwithstanding *Hercules* made the ground of his War against *Eurytus*, who denyed him his Daughter *Iole* in Marriage; as *Darius* also did, of his War against the Scythians.

VIII. Desire to plant in a better soil.

Nor is the desire of possessing a more fruitful or more healthful soil, as it is usual for such as inhabit Fenns or Deserts, any just cause of making War, which was the case of the Ancient Germans, as *Tacitus* records *.

* *Hist. l.* 4.

IX. The discovery of things preoccupied by others.

Neither is it sufficient to justify a War, to pretend that we were the first discoverers of any place; in case it be possest, though by Pagans and Infidels, or by men of dull apprehension: For, * *Inventio est eorum, quæ nullius sunt; To entitle our selves to be the first founders, it is necessary that the land so found should belong to none.*

* *Vict. de Ind. Rel.* 1. *n.* 31.

Neither

X. What if the pre-occupants be mad.

Neither is it necessary to Propriety or Dominion, That a man should be endued with Virtues either Moral or Theological, or to be of a quick understanding; yet may this seem to be justifiable, That in case there can be found a people that have no use of Natural Reason at all, there all Right and Dominion may be taken from them: Yet ought we in charity to make them such an allowance as is necessary for their support and maintenance, as well as unto other ideots and madmen. For as to what we have already said, concerning the care which the Law of Nations takes to preserve the property of Infants and Lunaticks, it appertains to such people with whom we have any commerce, or make any contracts with, which we cannot have with such a people as are wholly and altogether destitute of Reason; and therefore of these I may very well doubt whether they have any property at all. The *Grecians* then were very unjust, in concluding the *Barbarians* to be naturally their enemies, because they differed from them in manners, and were not so quick of understanding as themselves. But how far forth a Mans Right and Property may be taken away for some hainous crimes committed against Nature, or Humane Society, is another question, whereof we have already treated, where we discour'st of the Right of Punishments.

Plato de Rep. lib. 2. *Livy lib.* 31. *Vide Supra, Ch.* 20. §. 40.

XI Nor the desire of Liberty in such as are Subjects.

Neither is it a just cause for any people or persons to take Arms to endeavour to recover their Liberty being lost; as if it did naturally and alwayes belong unto them. For when we say that Men or Cities are naturally free, we mean, that they are so by that Right of Nature, which precedes all Humane Constitutions: In which sense Liberty is taken only for a privation of Slavery, but not as it is contradictory to Servitude; so that though by Nature no Man be a Servant, yet no man hath by Nature this priviledge, that he can never be made so; for in this sense no man is free. And thus is that of *Albutius* to be understood, *Nemo natus servus est, nemo liber, hæc postea nomina singulis imposuit fortuna; To be born either Bond or Free, are the badges of Fortune, and not of Nature.* So *Aristotle, It is the Law that makes any man either a free-man or a servant.* And therefore into what Estate soever Fortune hath cast us, be it of Freedom, or of lawfull Subjection, and that either Personal or Civil, we ought therewith to be content, and in no wise to struggle, or repine against it, according to the advice of the Apostle; *Art thou called to be a servant? grieve not at it.*

Sen. lib. 3. *contr.* 21. 1 Cor. 7. 21.

XII. Nor the desire of Rule, without the consent of those whom we would rule.

Neither is it lawfull for any man by force of Arms to reduce those under his Government, who deserve to be enslaved, or as Philosophers say, are naturally slaves. For although it be expedient for them to be well governed, yet this gives no right to any man to compel them thereunto by Force and Arms; for to such as have the use of Reason, the choice of things profitable and unprofitable, should be left free to themselves, unless some one hath already got the Dominion over them. But as to Infants it is clear by another case; for seeing that it is not permitted unto them freely to dispose of their own actions, or to exercise that Right which belongs unto them, by reason of the defect or immaturity of their judgments, therefore they are committed to fit Guardians and Tutors.

XIII. The Roman Empire not Universal.

And here I should hardly mention that absurd Title, which some have given unto the Roman Emperour, as if the Right of Empire over the remotest, and as yet unknown parts of the World were already invested in him; but that I find *Bartolus* (who for a while was admired as the Prince of Civilians) so daring, as to pronounce that man an Heretick that should deny it: namely, because as well the Roman Emperours have sometimes stiled themselves Lords of the world; (as by the Council of *Chalcedon* it may appear) as also, because in the sacred story, that Empire (which later writers call *Romania*) is by way of Eminency mentioned by the name τῆς οἰκουμένης, of the world: as indeed many such hyperbolical expressions we shall meet with, not only amongst Poets, as

> *Orbem jam totum Victor Romanus habebat;*
>
> The conquering Romans held the World in awe:

and the like; which Empire, though it contained not the sixth part of the then known world, yet because it was the greatest and most eminent Empire in the world at that time, it was by way of excellency stiled the Empire of the world. Thus *Philo, I speak,* saith he, *of many, and those the most profitable parts of the earth, which a man may (by way of eminence) call the world, as it is bounded between those two great Rivers, that of* Euphrates, *and this of the* Rhine: But even in the holy Scriptures, as when *Judea* only is by the like way of eminency called the whole earth; and *Jerusalem* said to be seated in the midst of the earth, (*i. e.*) of *Judea*. For as St *Hierome* well observes, *Nomen terræ, etiam addita particula, omnis, restringi debet ad eam regionem de qua sermo est; This word, the Earth, though this particle, All, be added unto it, ought to be restrained to the Countrey whereof we discourst:* So all the world is said to be taxed, *Luk.* 2. 1. that is, all that was at that time under the Roman Jurisdiction. And in this sense *Delphos*, because it was seated on the midst of

De Legat.

Greece is said to be *Totius orbis umbilicus*, as it were, *the navel or midst of the whole earth.* Neither will it be very argumentative to say with *Dante*, That it would be expedient for all mankind, that the Roman Emperour should have such a right of Soveraignty, seeing that *Commoda quæ adfert suis compensantur incommodis*; *The conveniencies that it promises to bring with it, would be attended with many more inconveniencies that would follow it.* For as a ship may be made of that extraordinary bulk and burthen, that it cannot be well steered; so an Empire may consist of so vast a multitude of Men, and of Regions so diverse, and so far distant, as that no one man can possibly govern it: Yea, and if we should grant, that it were so universally expedient, yet would it not thence necessarily follow, that this should actually confer a Right to the Roman Emperours, because such a Right cannot possibly arise, but either by consent, or by way of punishment. Neither hath the Roman Emperour a Right to all those Countries now, which once belonged to his Predecessors: for as many of them were got by Conquest, so have they long since been lost by Conquest; as some also have been quitted by Agreement, others being deserted have fallen under the Jurisdiction of other Nations and Kings. And some Cities which heretofore were wholly Subjects, became afterwards but in part only, or admitted into a social League, upon terms only unequall. For by all, or any of these ways the Roman Empire, as well as any other might either lose or change, whatsoever Right they could formerly have or pretend unto.

XIV. But some there were that would challenge to themselves the power of the whole Church
Nor the Pope. also, even over those people who dwell in those parts of the world, which are as yet unknown; whereas St *Paul* himself openly professeth, That without the bounds of Christianity he had no right to judge, *What have I to do* (saith he) *to judge those that are*
1 Cor. 5. 12. *without?* And although that power which the Apostle had, did in its manner appertain unto earthly things, yet was not that power of Earthly, but of Divine Institution, and to be exercised not by weapons or scourges, but by the Word of God generally preached, and applyed to some particular circumstances, and by exhibiting or denying the seals of the remission of sins, as it should conduce to the salvation of every man. And in the last place, by a revenge supernatural, and therefore proceeding from God himself, as in the cases of *Ananias*, *Elymas*, *Hymenæus* and others, it evidently appeared: Yea, and our blessed Saviour himself, from whom all Ecclesiastical Power flows, and whose life was a
Joh. 18. 36. perfect Exemplar or Copy for the Church to imitate, denied *his Kingdom to be of this world*; that is, of the same nature with other Kingdom: adding this, *For if it were, then* after the manner of other Kings, *should my servants fight.* And yet even now, in case he would pray to his Father to send him an Army, it should consist not of Men, but of Angels, *Mat.* 26. 53. And whatsoever he did by the Right of his own Power, he did it not by humane strength, but by the virtue of his Divinity; and that even then when he drove the buyers and sellers out of the Temple; the whip he used was not the Instrument of Gods wrath, but the sign or symbol only; so was the spittle and the oyl, as *Abulensis*
In Mat. 9. observes, not the salve, but the sign of the cure. St *Augustine* upon that place of *John* before-cited, thus proclaims, *Hearken therefore O ye Jews and Gentiles, circumcised and uncircumcised: And hear O ye Kingdoms of the Earth, your Empires here I impede not; for my Kingdom is not of this world: Be ye not moved with vain fears, as* Herod *the Great was at the report of Christs birth, who was so far transported with jealousie, that he slew a multitude of innocent Babes, thinking thereby to secure his own Kingdoms by the death of this new born King: Timendo potius quam irascendo crudelior; being more enraged through fear and jealousie than anger. My Kingdom*, saith he, *is not of this world: What could have been said more to dispel those fears? Come, and be partakers with me of that Kingdom, which is not of this world: Come unto me by faith, and let not your fears provoke you to cruelty.* So likewise *Hilary* Bishop of *Arles*, *Christ came not into the world to invade another mans Glory, but to communicate his own, not to usurp an earthly Kingdom, but to confer an heavenly.* St *Paul* tells *Timothy*, *That a Bishop should be no striker*, 1 Tim. 3. 2. *Nor rule by constraint or compulsion*; for *to drive by force, better becomes a King than a Bishop.* Princes may ex-
De Sacerd. l. 2. ercise their Power in punishing Offenders to deter them from doing evil: *But what we do*, saith *Chrysostome*, *must be, not by coercion, but by perswasion:* whereunto he adds this Reason, *For God crowns not our forced, but our voluntary*; or as St *Paul* speaks, *our rea-*
Ad Eph. 1. 4. *sonable service.* So in another place, *It is our duty to instruct, perswade, exhort, and reprove, but not to command, or to compel: Consiliariorum locum obtinemus; We serve as Councellors to advice, and to give our Opinions, but still we leave our Auditors to their free choice, whether they will act accordingly or no: We have no such power given us, as to restrain men from sinning by severe punishments.* Whence it is evident, that Bishops, as such, have no
In Epitaphio Nepotiani. Right of Domination over men, as Kings and Princes have. St *Hierome* distinguishing between a King and a Bishop, concludes, *That the Power of a Bishop is much inferiour to that of a King, for a King may enforce to an unwilling obedience; but a Bishop hath no power but over such as are willing to obey him. Episcopus docet, ne Judex inveniat quod puniat;* *The*

The Bishop instructs and admonisheth, that the Magistrate may find no cause to punish. It was well said of *Frederick* the Emperour concerning the Pope:

> *Ecclesiam regat ille suam, divinaque jura*
> *Temperet: Imperium nobis, fascesque relinquat.*
>
> Let him his own Church rule, by Laws Divine,
> But let the Sword and Scepter still be mine.

And when *Suenno* King of *Denmark* stood Excommunicate, *William* Bishop of *Roschil*, in opposing himself against him, at his entrance into the Church with his pastoral staff, and exposing his breast naked to the officers of the King, who offered to draw upon him, did therein perform the office of a good Bishop. The like did St *Ambrose* to the Emperour *Valentinus* as we have declared above; but whether it be lawful for Kings themselves to make War upon such as have rejected Christianity by way of punishment, we have already elsewhere discourst in the Chapter of Punishments, as far as sufficeth to our purpose. *Bo. 1. ch. 4. §. 5.*

XV. The pretence of fulfilling of prophecies no cause of War.

And hereof also I shall give my advice, and that not in vain, (but because I foresee, by comparing these modern times with those long since past; much mischiefs likely to ensue, unless in time carefully prevented) that the hopes we conceive that some things are due unto us, by our own interpretation of some Divine Prophecies, can be no cause of a just War. (*Zozimus* records it of *Nicomedes* the Son of *Prusias*, that mis-appling a Prophecy of one of the *Sibyls*, by the perswasion of *Attalus* made War against his own Father; the like he and *Ammianus* relates of one *Theodorus*; so doth *Procopius* of *John* of *Cappadocia*.) For besides that those Prophecies which are not fulfilled, cannot certainly be understood without a Prophetick Spirit, the very time of the accomplishment of such as are certain may be hidden from us. And lastly the bare prediction, unless it be backed with an express command from God, gives no right to any man, seeing that God permits such things as he predicts to be sometimes brought to pass, by wicked men and by wicked actions: For the Books of the Prophets are shut and sealed up until a certain time, so that they cannot be understood, *Dan.* 12. 4. 8. 9. The Vision that the Prophet *Habbakkuk* saw concerning the judgments to fall on the *Chaldæans*, was not immediately to be inflicted on them, *But it was to be fulfilled in its appointed time*; *In the end whereof*, saith that vision, *it shall speak and not lye though it do tarry*: yet was the Prophet *to wait for it, for it shall surely come to pass and not stay*, Hab. 2. 3. Time then is the best interpreter of Prophecies. St *Jerome* upon that place of *Daniel* before-recited writes thus, *If the Prophet did hear and not understand, what will they do who presuming on their own understanding, have published this Book which is sealed up, and until the time come for its accomplishment.* So *Procopius* concerning the Oracles of the *Sibyls*, *Which*, saith he, *I believe are beyond all humane power to unfold, until the time come when they shall be fulfilled.* Let Divines therefore take heed how they undertake to unriddle Prophecies; and let Politicians beware how they give credit to over-arrogating Divines, though the things predicted were certainly to come to pass; yet are the times and means when and whereby they are to be accomplished very uncertain: and therefore it is no dishonour to profess our ignorance of them, *Eorum quæ scire nec datur, nec fas est, docta est ignorantia, scientiæ appetus insaniæ species*; *Some kind of madness it is to desire to know those things, which are therefore screened from us that we should not know them. The secret things belong unto God; but the things revealed, unto us*, Deut. 29. 29.

In the time of the Emperour *Gratian*.

XVI. Nor a debt not strictly due, but some other way.

Thus also is it to be observed, that in case any thing be owing to a man, not strictly out of justice, but arising from some other vertue; as from liberality, favour, mercy, love, or the like, as it cannot be recovered by any course of Law, so neither can it be required by War. For to either of these it sufficeth not, that what is required is for some moral reason to be done: But besides that, it is necessary that there should be in us some kind of Right unto that, such a kind of Right as the Laws both Divine and Humane do sometimes give even unto such things as are due by other vertues; which when it happens, then it becomes a debt after a new way, which now appertains to justice. But this being wanting, the War that is made for this cause is unjust; as was that War made by the Romans against the King of *Cyprus* for ingratitude. For he that doth a courtesie to another, hath no Right to exact thanks; otherwise it were not a courtesie, but a contract or debt.

XVII. Though the War be just, yet the manner of prosecuting it, may make it unjust.

It is also to be observed, that though there be a just cause of War; yet may this just cause be spoiled by the access of some vice that cleaves to the action from the mind of the Agent, either that something else, not by it self unlawful, doth more efficaciously move us to the War, than the Right it self; as when we have a greater prospect unto Glory: or when some kind of profit either publick or private, is expected to arise from the very War, being considered a part from the cause that justifies it; which vice is most dangerous, because it comes mantled with the Robe of Vertue: But as St. *Augustine* rightly adviseth, *Satius est cujuslibet inertiæ pœnas luere, quam istorum armorum gloriam quærere*; *Better it is to suffer*

suffer the punishments of any cowardice, then to seek glory by such a War. This was it that sullied all the Victories of *Alexander*, and for which all Historians declaimed against him as a Robber, because he made War only for Ambition; and to that end disquieted the whole World, vexing all Nations without any cause given, and making War upon those whom he never knew: for what could this be but as St. *Augustine* calls it, *Grande Latrocinium? A great Robbery.* Or a just cause may be spoiled when accompanied with a passion manifestly unlawful; as when we rejoice in the destruction of our Enemies barely as such, without respect to any thing that is good. So *Aristides* was of opinion that the *Phocenses* were deservedly destroyed; but withall he condemned King *Philip* for destroying them, because he did it, not upon the score of Religion as he pretended: but out of an Ambitious desire to enlarge his Empire. *Salust* ascribes *all Wars to this one, and that very ancient cause, namely, a vehement thirst after Dominion and Riches.* And it was *Tacitus* his observation, *That Gold and Wealth were ever the principal causes of making War*; which *Seneca* attributes to Covetousness and Revenge,

Mad anger and a greedy thirst for gain
The League have broke.

Whereunto we may add that of St. *Augustine, An earnest desire to make what spoil we can, the cruelty of Revenge, an unquiet and implacable Spirit, Contumacy and Rebellion, together with an ambitious thirst after Empire and Riches, these and the like are deservedly blamed in all Wars.* But yet these where a justifying cause is not wanting, though they savour rankly of a corrupt mind, yet do they not render the War properly unjust; and therefore restitution cannot justly be required of damages sustained in such a War.

CHAP. XXIII.

Of the Causes of War that are doubtful.

I. Causes of doubts whence?

IT is true, what *Aristotle* in the first of his Morals teacheth, That there cannot be the same certainty in Ethicks, as in Mathematicks; which therefore happens, because the Mathematicks abstract forms from all matter; and because the very forms themselves are such for the most part, as will admit of no mean: As between streight and crooked there is nothing intervenient. But in Morals the least circumstance varies the matter, and the forms concerning which we treat, have usually something interjacent, and of that latitude, that they sometimes approach nearer to this extreme, and sometimes nearer to that. As between things absolutely commanded, and things absolutely interdicted, there are some things that may, or may not be done: so between things exactly just, and things absolutely unjust, there are some things intermediate; whereof some encline nearer to this extreme, and some to that: From whence doth often arise some doubt and ambiguity, to whether of the two extremes they approach nearest; as we may perceive in the degrees of heat and cold in water when it is tepid, and in the degrees of light and darkness, health and sickness, &c. Insomuch that (as *Aristotle* saith) *The judgment hath sometimes an hard task to determine, which is to be preferred before the other.* But *Andronicus Rhodius* goes yet farther, affirming, *That it is a very difficult thing sometimes to distinguish between* (Realities and Resemblances) *things exactly just, and things that are only apparently so.*

But

II. *Nothing to be done against our judgment.* Rom. 14. 23.

But this Rule is in the first place to be constantly observed, That though an Act be really Just, yet if upon a serious examination we shall judge it to be unjust, to us if we do it, it is so: And this is that which St *Paul* intends when he saith, *Whatsoever is not of faith is sin.* In which place, Faith signifies the firm perswasion or judgment of the mind concerning a thing; as may easily be collected from those other expressions of St *Paul* in the same Chapter, *Let every man be fully perswaded in his own mind.* Blessed is the man that condemneth not himself in that which he alloweth: *Peccatum est quod aliter fit quam probatum est; Whatsoever any man doth,* saith St *Ambrose, otherwise than what his own conscience approveth is sin. For that a thing be well done,* saith *Plutarch, it is requisite, not only that what is done be just and honest, but that there be a firm and constant perswasion of mind in him that doth it, that what is done, is therefore done, because his conscience tells him that it ought to be so done.* For God hath endued the rational soul with a discerning faculty, to the end, that it may guide us in all our actions, which being slighted, the mind immediately becomes sensual and brutish. But yet it sometimes falls out, that the judgment wavereth and gives but a dim and uncertain light; which if upon a mature disquisition we cannot clear, then we should take the advice of *Cicero*, and *forbear to act whilst we remain doubtfull whether it be just or unjust.* The like advice *Pliny* gives, *Wherein thou doubtest forbear.* The Hebrew Doctors also give this caution, *Beware and forbear in matters that are dubious.* But this is then only seasonable where we have a free choice, either to do or not to do; but not where we are obliged to do either this or that, and yet are unsatisfied in either, whether it be just or not: for there we are to chuse that which in our judgment seems to be less evil. *Semper enim ubi electio evadi non potest, minus malum rationem induit boni; For alwayes when the will is straitned between two evils, and the choice of one of them cannot be avoided, there the lesser evil hath in it an appearance of good; because it participates more of goodness than the other doth;* and therefore, *of evils the least ought to be chosen*, saith *Aristotle:* So also *Cicero*, *De malis minimum, Of evils chuse the least.* And *Quintilian*, in comparing evils, *the less usurps the place of good.*

Ambrose. Plut. Timoleonte. De Off. lib. 1. τὰ ἐλάχιστα ληπτέον τῶν κακῶν.

III. *The judgment sometimes led by arguments drawn from the thing it self.*

But it often falls out in doubtfull Cases, That notwithstanding our strictest disquisition, yet the mind hangs as it were in a tottering condition, sometimes inclining unto this, sometimes unto that part, being poized sometimes by arguments drawn from the matter it self, and sometimes by the Authority of Grave and Learned Men, who have declared their Opinions on that very case. For as St *Augustine* in his third Book of Order well observes, *When our minds are assaulted with any difficulty, we have two wayes to extricate our selves, either by our own reason, or by the Authority of the most learned.* And herein also doth that of *Hesiod* hold true, which *Minutius* in *Livy* makes use of after a battle unsuccessfully fought, *The highest point of wisdom is to be able to manage our affairs by the strength of our own judgments: The next is to hearken to the advice of the best men; but he that is neither wise enough to govern by himself, nor willing to be led by the Counsel of wise men, is a rank fool.* Whereunto *Cicero* likewise alludes in his Oration for *Cluentius*, *He is accounted the wisest of men, that in all occurrents is able to direct himself; next unto him is he that can be content to hearken to the good counsel of others: but he that cannot do the former, and will not do the latter, is in the lowest form.* Now the Arguments from the thing it self are drawn from the causes, from the effects, or from some other adjuncts:

Lib. 22.

Ille quidem ante omnes, per se ipse quid utile, quid non
Qui videt, & longe fines prospectat agendi:
Qui bene consultis didicit parere, secundus:
At qui consiliis pollet nihil ipse, nec audit
Suadentes alios, nullos homo vivit ad usus.

Hesiod.

IV. *By the Authority of others.*

But to know these things rightly, there is required much knowledge and experience; and if either of these be wanting, whereby the judgment may be rightly informed to act by it self, then are we bound to steer our affairs by the advice and counsel of the most judicious. For that, saith *Aristotle*, is most probable which is approved of by all, or by the most, or certainly by wise men; and of these, by either all, or by the greatest part, or by the most prudent and judicious of them: And by these means do Kings, who have no leisure to be eminently learned, grow notwithstanding wise by the counsel of others:

Thus Princes by their Senators grow wise.

Thus *Aristides* in his Oration for Peace tells the *Rhodians*, *As in matters of fact, that which is attested by the most authentick and judicious witnesses is held for truth: So in matters of polity, those counsels are safest, which are approved of by men of the greatest learning and experience.* The ancient Romans never made War without consulting the Colledge of Heraulds, which consisted of men of the greatest Experience in matters of War; neither did the Christian Emperours usually undertake a War without consulting their Bishops, That so if any thing could be objected against it in point of Religion, they might be admonished of it.

And it is recorded of *Alexander* the Great, That he admitted into his Council men of the greatest Learning, but most especially Historians.

V. If the doubts be equal, the matter weighty, and one must be chosen, chuse the safest.

But in many Controversies it falls out, That the Arguments on both sides, as well from our own Reason, as from Authority, are so equally probable, that it is very difficult to judge where the Right is: And in such a case, if the matter in question be of no great moment, the judgment may be blameless, though it pass on either side. But if it be of great concernment, as in passing sentence of life and death upon a supposed offender, then by reason of the vast distance that there is between the parts eligible, that part is to be adjudged best, that is safest. And therefore *it is much better to absolve the Guilty, than to condemn the Innocent*, saith *Aristotle*; and he adds this reason, *For where the case is dubious, we should chuse that part which will infer the least danger in case we should err.* To the same purpose is that of *Antiphon*, *If we must needs run the hazard of misjudging, it is more pious unrighteously to pardon, than injuriously to condemn, for by the former we can be charged but with errour; but by the latter, with wickedness.*

Sect. 29.

VI. The safest way is to abstain from War.

To make War is a matter of the greatest consequence that can concern a Nation, whence ensues a torrent of mischiefs (as by a Sea-breach) whereby many thousands of innocent people are on both sides destroyed: And therefore amongst all our consultations the safest counsels are those that incline unto Peace. This was it for which the *Italian* Poet so highly extolled *Q. Fabius*:

> *Dangers he prudently foresaw, nor for*
> *Things mean or doubtfull, gladly would make War.*

Now three wayes there are whereby differences among Princes may be reconciled without breaking out into open War.

VII. 1. By Treaty.

The first whereof is by Treaty or Conference: *Seeing there are two wayes of debating differences*, saith Cicero, *The one by argument, the other by plain force*; whereof that is proper to men, this to beasts: *we may make the latter our refuge, if we cannot receive satisfaction by the former.* This is the method which *Dionysius Halicarnassensis* prescribes; not over-hastily to fly to blows, till we have tryed how words will prevail:

> *All means unarm'd, wise men will first assay,*
> *How know'st, if ask't, but he'l unforc'd obey?*

So *Dionysius Halicarnassensis*, *We must not proceed to blows, untill we have tryed what words can do:* Agreeable whereunto is that of *Menelaus* in *Libanius*, *It more becomes a man to make tryal how he can prevail with Reason and Arguments, before he rashly rush into War.* So also *Menelaus* in *Libanius*, *It is more agreeable to Humane Nature, to try, how far we can prevail with Reason, than suddenly to fly into arms:* The like we find in *Euripides*;

> *This I'le obtain by words, if not, by blows.*

Thus *Paneas* in *Livy*, *There are*, saith he, *many things, which men rather than make War, are willing to remit; which notwithstanding cannot be enforced from them by force of arms. Mardonius* in *Herodotus* blames the Grecians upon this account, *That being all of one Language, they did not first argue their grievances by the mediation of Heraulds and Ambassadors before they broke out into Arms.* So *Coriolanus* in *Dionysius Halicarnassensis*, *If a man*, (saith he) *without coveting anothers, do but demand his own, and being thereof denied, shall make War; that War, by the consent of all Nations is most just.* For as King *Tullus* saith in the same Author, *Quæ verbis componi nequeunt, ea armis decernenda sunt*; *Those differences which cannot by reasons be composed, must be determined by blows*: And yet, as *Vologeses* in *Tacitus* declares, *I had rather keep what mine Ancestors have left me by Equity, than by the expence of blood; by mine own Just Title, than by a doubtfull War.* For as King *Theodorick* wisely observed, *Then only is War profitable, when our Enemies will not otherwise do us Justice.*

VIII. 2. By Arbitration.

The second way to prevent War between those who have no Common Judge between them, is to put the matter in question to Arbitration: This, though much scorned by such Princes as are too confident in their own strength; yet is worthily to be prest and insisted on by all that love Peace and Equity: *To persecute him as an enemy that is willing to put his Case to an indifferent Arbiter, is impious and unjust*, saith *Thucydides.* So concerning the Kingdom of the *Argives*, *Adrastus* and *Amphiraus* were both content to refer themselves to the judgment of *Eriphyla*, as *Diodorus* testifies. The like did the *Athenians* and the *Megarenses* to three *Lacedemonians* concerning the Island *Salamis.* The same *Thucydides* records

Lib. 5.

cords this to be one of the Articles agreed on, in the League between the *Lacedemonians* and the *Argives*; *That in case any Controversie should at any time arise between their Cities, the matter in difference should amicably be referred to a third City, which should be indifferent to both, according to the ancient custome of their fore-fathers.* Thus the *Corcyreans* declare their readiness to refer their difference with the *Corinthians*, to any of the *Peloponnesian* Cities that they should agree upon. Many Great Princes and States, to save the effusion of blood, have been contented to put their grievances to Arbitration. *Aristides* commends *Pericles*, that to avoid a doubtfull War, he was willing to commit his Cause to indifferent Judges. So also doth *Isocrates* in his Oration against *Ctesiphon*, highly extol King *Philip* of *Macedon* for his readiness to refer all those Controversies which he had with the *Athenians*, to some other City that stood indifferently affected to either party. Thus do the *Samnites*, as to the differences between themselves and the *Romans*, offer to stand to the award of those States that were at Peace with both of them. *Cyrus* makes the *Indian* King Judge between himself and the *Assyrian*: So do the *Carthaginians* to avoid a War put the Cause of their Quarrel with *Masinissa*, to the Judgment of others. Yea, and the *Romans* themselves do refer their differences with the *Samnites*, to be compromised by their common Associates. *We, for our parts are ready* (say the *Gepidæ* to the *Lombards* in *Procopius*) *to refer our selves to any indifferent Arbiters.* Queen *Elizabeth* offered to refer the differences between her and the *Dane*, unto Commissioners on both sides, or unto the Elector of *Brandenburgh*, the King of *Denmark*'s Father in Law, and to the Duke of *Mechlenburgh*, and the Duke of *Brunswick* as Arbitrators. Now they that refuse this way of disceptation, by Reasons, Arguments or Arbitrements, running rashly into War, when it may be avoided, decline all Justice, Humanity, and the common practice of the best and wisest Princes. Yet, that *Philip* King of *Spain* would not admit of the Pope to be Judge between him and other Competitors, for the Kingdom of *Portugal*, I do not wonder; because the Pope claimed the decision of all such Controversies as his proper Right: wherefore that wise King was unwilling to add his own Example to some ancient ones, whereby the Pope might hereafter prove himself to be the sole Arbiter and Disposer of Kingdoms. Many other Examples may be produced, but in a Case so clear these may suffice. *Plutarch* tells us, *That it was the principal duty of the Colledge of Heraulds among the* Romans *to take care,* Nè finerent prius ad bellum veniri, quam spes omnis judicii obtinendi periisset; *That no War should be attempted, but where all hopes of receiving satisfaction for injuries done them by any other means were frustrate.* And *Strabo* testifies of the *Druides* in *Gallia*, *That anciently they were the Arbitrators between publick enemies, and that, by their mediation Peace was often made, even when the Armies were preparing for battel:* Which Office did of old in *Spain* appertain to their Priests, as the same Author records. But much more doth it concern Christian Kings and States to prevent the effusion of blood by this means. For if both Jews and Christians have thought fit to appoint Arbitrators among themselves to determine all Controversies, to the intent, *That Brother should not go to Law with Brother before unbelievers*, as St *Paul* hath also commanded; how much more reason is there that such Arbitrators or Judges should be chosen by us to prevent mischiefs far greater than going to Law, namely, spoil, rapine, murther, yea, and sometimes desolation, which are the unhappy concomitants of cruel War? From whence *Tertullian* concludes, That a Christian ought not to wage War, seeing that it is not lawfull for him to go to Law; which notwithstanding is to be understood in a qualified sense. *And indeed it is very unfit for Princes who profess themselves to be followers of Christ, to rush into arms one against the other with so much bitterness, seeing that there are other means found out to compromise their Quarrels, and to make better use of their Arms and Valour against the Common Enemy.* And for this, as well as for many other reasons, it would be very convenient, nay necessary, that constant Diets and Conventions of Christian Princes should be held, where by the prudence and moderation of such as are not interessed, all Controversies may be composed; yea, and that some expedient may be found out to enforce both Parties to accept of Peace upon equal and indifferent terms; whereof we may find Examples in *Cassiodore* *, *Gailius* †, and others, which anciently was committed to the care of the *Druides* in *France*, to whom the Bishops did afterwards by a better Right succeed: So we read of the *French* Kings, that in the division of the Kingdom, they have referred themselves to the judgment of their Peers.

Xen. Cyro, lib. 2. — *Livy lib.* 8. — *Goth lib.* 3. — *Camden. Anno* 1600. — *Aberic. Gentilis.* — *Lib.* 4. — *Lib.* 11. — *Vict. de Jure Belli, n.* 28. — *Gregor. lib.* 10. — * *Cassiod. lib.* 3. 1, 2, 3, 4. — † *Gail. de pace publ. lib.* 2. *cap.* 18. *n.* 12.

IX. 3. By Lot.

The third way to prevent War is to decide Controversies by Lots, which *Dion Chrysostome* much commends; and long before him *Solomon*, Prov. 18. 18. whereof see St *Augustine* in his first *Book*, 28 *Chap.* of *Christian Doctrine.*

X. Single Combats permitted.

Near of kin unto this are single combats between Competitors, the use whereof is not altogether to be rejected: for where two persons, standing in competition for one thing which cannot be divided, are ready to embroil a whole Nation in blood; *It were much better, and more just, that one should perish for all, than that all should perish for one only.* In which Case that of *Jocasta* in *Seneca* is good advice,

Plut. Otho.

——*Rex*

Theb.

——————*Rex sit è vobis uter,*
Manente regno, quærite.

——————Try which of you shall reign,
But let the Kingdom still remain.

And this if not justifiable in the competitors themselves, yet may it well be accepted of by the people if offered, as being of two evils by much the lesser. Thus *Metius* in *Livy* (*Lib.* 5.) bespeaks *Tullus*, *Let us agree about some way whereby it may be determined, whether of us two shall reign over the other, without the effusion of so much blood, or the slaughter of either of our people.* *Strabo* set it down as an ancient custom among the Grecians; And *Æneas* in *Virgil* accounted it a very just thing, that the quarrel between *Turnus* and him should have been thus decided:

Æn. 11. *Fitter 't had been for* Turnus *thus t' have died.*

And for this cause it was, that *M. Anthony* challenged *Cæsar* to a single combate, as *Plutarch* records. (*Vit. Ant.*) Sure it is, that amongst other customs of the Ancient Francks, *Agathias* highly commends this, whose words being worthy of Eternal Memory, are to this purpose: *No sooner did any quarrel arise between their Kings, but immediately they betake themselves to their Arms, they raise Armies and march against each other so furiously, as if nothing but an absolute conquest could end the controversie; but yet as soon as the Armies met and faced, they presently laid aside all animosity and made peace; thereby enforceing (as it were) their Kings to dispute their grievances, rather by Law than Arms; or if that pleased them not, then to end their quarrels with the peril of their own lives only, as judging it neither just nor reasonable, nor indeed agreeable to their national customs, for their Kings to sacrifice the Commonwealth to their private hatred; wherefore they instantly disband their Armies, reconcile their Princes, and make Peace:* Tanta in subditis cura justitiæ & patriæ amor, in regibus animus placidus & suis obsequens; *So great in the subjects was their esteem of justice and love to their Country; and in their Kings, their moderation of spirit, and their compliance with the people, in order to their common safety.*

XI. In cases equally dubious, the present occupant hath the best right.

Although where the equity of the cause is doubtful, both Parties are obliged to seek after conditions of peace, to prevent the miseries of War; yet doth it more concern him that demands, than him that enjoys what the other requires, as in the like equal cause, *Melior est possidentis conditio*; *The title of the present occupant is presumed to be best*, as being most agreeable not only to civil, but to natural Right; the reason whereof we have already given elswhere out of *Aristotle*'s Problems: whereunto we must here add, That War cannot be lawfully made by him, who though he know his title to what he claims to be good, yet cannot produce evidence sufficient to convince the present occupant of the illegality of his possession, because he hath not a Right to compel his Adversary to leave his possession.

XII. If neither be possest, then a partition is just.

Where the Right is equally ambiguous, and neither party in possession, or both equally, then he is to be reputed unjust, that shall refuse an equal partition of the thing controverted, being offered unto him.

XIII. Whether a war may be on both sides just, explained by many distinctions.

By what hath been herein said, it will be no hard matter to resolve that question which is so frequently controverted, Whether a War in respect of the principal promoters of it, can be on both sides just; where we must first distinguish between the various acception of the word *Just*. * For a thing may be said to be just, in respect of the cause, or according to the effects: Again, a thing a may be just in respect of the cause, either according to the special and strict acception of justice, or according to its more general acception, as it comprehends whatsoever in equity or honesty ought to be done. Again the word *Just*, taken in its special signification may be subdivided into that which respects the work done, or into that which respects the mind of him that doth it; for the agent may sometimes be said to do justly, whilst he doth not unjustly, though that which he doth be not just. As *Aristotle* * rightly distinguisheth between τὸ ἀδικεῖν and τὸ ἄδικον πράττειν, *to do unjustly*, and *to do that which is unjust*. Bonis male utuntur, qui temporali lucro juste judicant; *They make ill use of things in themselves good, who do justice for rewards sake; because it is the hopes of gain, and not the love of justice that excites them to defend the truth.* (*Greg.*) Now in this special acception of the word *Just*, and as it relates to the thing it self, no War can be on both sides just; as, neither can any other contest be: *Quia facultas moralis ad contraria non datur per rei ipsius naturam*; *Because the very nature so the thing, about which the dispute was, will not admit of a moral power to things that are contrary:* as namely, to do a thing, and yet to oppose the doing of it. But yet it may very well be, That neither of the Parties warring against each other doth unjustly; because no man can be said to do unjustly, but he that knows that which he doth to be unjust. But many men do not know that they do amiss, though

* So *Gratian* distinguisheth justice into that which respects the cause, the order, and the mind. *c.* 11. *q.* 5. *post C. Episcopus.*

* *Eth. l.* 5. *c.* 10, 11.

though that which they do, be in it self unjuſt; ſo when men go to Law, they may juſtly (that is) with a good mind, and intention do it on both ſides, becauſe they do both conceive that they are in the right; for of many things, as well in point of Right, as in matters of fact whence Right ariſeth, men are ignorant. Now in the general acception of the word *Juſt*, that is ſaid to be juſt in the doing, whereof the Agent is altogether innocent; for the act may be unjuſt, and yet the Agent blameleſs, by reaſon of his inſuperable ignorance. An example whereof we have in ſuch as being (through no default of theirs) ignorant of the Law, do not obſerve it; although haply that Law be promulgated, and time of it ſelf ſufficient allowed for the knowledge thereof: As alſo in ſuch as go to Law, both Parties may be free, not from injuſtice only, but from any thing elſe that is blameable; eſpecially when both, or either of them contend, not in the behalf of themſelves but of others; as a Tutor for his Pupil, a Guardian for his Ward, whoſe Right he is bound in duty to defend, though that Right be but uncertain. So in a wager at Law, two perſons may contend for one and the ſame thing, and yet neither of them be unjuſt: So alſo a Councellor, may plead for either of them, without the leaſt derogation to his honeſty. Nay as *Ariſtotle* well notes, to ſay of a Judge that he judgeth right, is but an Ambiguous ſpeech; for it may ſignifie either that he judgeth ὡς δεῖ, *plainly as he ought* without any ignorance, or κατὰ τὴν ἑαυτοῦ γνώμην, *according to the beſt of his knowledge, or the cleareſt evidence that is brought before him*. And therefore the ſentence which muſt paſs, according to that evidence may be (through miſ-information) unjuſt, and yet the Judge that paſſeth that ſentence may be righteous. * If it be doubtful on what ſide the Right ſtands, if both Parties contend for it, it is probable that neither doth unjuſtly. The Jews made War againſt the Canaanites juſtly, being ſo commanded by God; and the Canaanites being ignorant of that charge given againſt them, did juſtly in defending themſelves: wherefore that War was on both ſides juſt. Thus Pope *Pius* the ſecond anſwered the Hungarian Embaſſador that complained againſt the Emperour, namely, He thought that the King of *Hungary* did intend nothing diſhoneſtly, and he knew that the Emperour was a great lover of juſtice: But both contending for the Kingdom, probable it was, that neither of them thought his Cauſe unjuſt. In all controverſies this is found true, but eſpecially in War, that both Parties pretend to maintain a Cauſe that is juſt: But in War it is hardly poſſible, that either party ſhould be in that ſenſe juſt, that is, free from all blame, by reaſon of that great defect of love, and that overmuch raſhneſs, that for the moſt part inſeparably accompanies it; beſides the weightineſs of the buſineſs it ſelf which is ſuch, as being not ſatisfied with probabilities, ſtrictly requires ſuch proofs, as are demonſtrative and convincing. But if we account that to be juſt, which is permitted to enjoy ſome effects of Right; it is moſt certain, that War in this ſenſe may be on both ſides juſt, as will appear anon, when we come to treat of a publick ſolemn War: for ſo, both a ſentence though not rightly paſt, and a poſſeſſion not rightly gained, have both of them ſome effects of that which is right.

To ſome things the Right is not diſcernable whoſe it is; and then, whilſt each endeavours to take that from another, which he thinks belongs to himſelf, who can condemn either of injuſtice?

Nemo debet jus ſuum indiſcuſſum relinquere. Tentanda ſunt quæcunq; tantum ſunt, Baldus.

Again when ſomething that is very profitable, ſtands in oppoſition to what is honeſt, it is no eaſie matter to tell whether of them to follow.

When we firſt entred into War with *Niger*, ſaith *Severus* the Emperour, there was I confeſs no very plauſible pretence for War, but the Empire lay at ſtake between us, and both of us ſtrove which ſhould appropriate it to himſelf, *Herodian.*

* *Si dubium ſit à qua parte ſtet juſtitia, hanc ſi utraque pars quærit, injuſta eſſe neutra poſſit.*

In diſceptationibus fori, par eſt litigantis utriuſque jus, donec lata eſt pro altero eorum ſententia.

According to the effects of right, War may be on both ſides juſt.

CHAP.

CHAP. XXIV.

War, though Just, not to be undertaken rashly.

I. *It it better sometimes to remit our own Right, than to engage in a doubtfull War.*
II. *But especially, when undertaken to exact punishment.*
III. *And chiefly by a King that is injured.*
IV. *And that sometimes for his own and his Subjects safety.*
V. *Certain Rules guiding us to a prudent choice of things apparently good.*
VI. *An example whereby we may be guided in our endeavours after liberty or peace; whereby the miseries of War may be prevented.*
VII. *Punishment not to be exacted by War, unless by the most potent party.*
VIII. *War not to be undertaken, unless compelled by necessity.*
IX. *Or when we have some very great Cause, together with some notable advantage.*
X. *The miseries of War lively described.*

I. Better sometimes to forego our right, than to make War for it.

THough it be not properly pertinent to our purpose in treating only of the Rights of War, to shew how far other Virtues do either enjoyn or perswade thereunto, yet will it not be altogether impertinent for preventing of mistakes, to give some cautions about it, lest any man should think, that whensoever he hath a Just Cause offered him, he is bound to make War, or at least, that it is at all times lawfull for him so to do: whereas on the contrary, it is, (for the most part) much more pious to remit somewhat of our Right, than to endeavour to defend it by a dangerous War. We Christians are especially taught to expose our own lives to the greatest perils that can be, to preserve the lives, and (as much as in us lies) to procure the everlasting welfare of others, in imitation of our great Lord and Master, who laid down his own life to save ours, even then when we were strangers, nay, enemies unto him, *Rom.* 5. 6. How much more reason have we to forbear the prosecution of our Just Rights, when they cannot be obtained without the effusion of so much Christian blood, and the destruction of so many mens Lives and Estates, besides other mischiefs, which War usually brings with it? This we are forewarn'd of by *Aristotle*, and also by *Polybius*, not for every such cause to run the hazard of a War. *For the necessary defence of our Liberties, our Wives and Children, we may lawfully make War,* saith *Gallio* in *Seneca*; *but not for such things as are either superfluous, or being lost, do not much damnifie us:* This and somewhat more did *Apollonius* say to the King of *Babylon*, *We are not to contend with the Romans for a few small Villages, which many of our Ancestors being but private men did enjoy. They must be great matters indeed, that should so far provoke us, as to undertake a War, (especially with such potent enemies.)* The like *Josephus* testifies of his Countrey men, *It is not our custom to muster up our Forces, or to make War to enlarge our Dominions, but for the defence of our Laws: All other losses we can bear with patience, but being debar'd the use of our Religion, we undertake War beyond our strength, and prosecute them to the utmost of dangers.* It was prudently advised by *Dion Prusaensis* in his Oration concerning War and Peace, *We are not so much to consider whether we have been justly provoked or no, as whether the injuries we have sustained be such as will counterballance the expence of so much blood and treasure as will be expended in the prosecutiou of a War for satisfaction.*

Pol. lib. 4. *Rhet. ad Alex. c.* 3.

Suasoria 5. *Philostratus, lib.* 23.

Adv. Apion. de popul. suis.

II. Especially when undertaken for punishment only.

There are many arguments whereby we may be disswaded from exacting punishments: For first we see how many failings Parents are willing to wink at in their Children: *A Father* (saith *Seneca**) *unless highly provoked by many and those hainous offences, so that his fears swell higher than his just anger, will not proceed against his Son with the utmost rigour and severity. Augustus* sitting in Council with a Father concerning a punishment to be inflicted on his Son, being found guilty of an intended Parricide, *would not adjudge him to the Sack, the Serpent, or to Prison, but to banishment only whither his Father pleased, respecting not so much the person offending, as the person offended; as knowing that gentle punishments would best appease the wrath of a Father towards his own son.*

* *Sen. de clem. l.* 1. *c.* 14.

Pro peccato magno paullulum supplicii satis est patri;

Few stripes, for great faults, Parents will appease.

περὶ εὐγενείας.

Fathers (saith *Philo*) *do sometimes pass that sentence of exheredation on their own sons, thereby cutting them off from their own families and kindred, but never untill they grow shamelesly and incorrigibly wicked, and that their hatred of their Childrens Vices have quite overcome that great and unparallell'd Love, which Nature had at first imprinted in them.* Not much different is that

that of *Phinehas* in *Diodorus*, *No Father doth willingly punish his Sons, unless the measure of their wickedness do very much exceed the measure of his natural affection.* Nor that of *Andronicus Rhodius*, *No Father can be so unnatural as to cast of his Son, if he be not extremely wicked.* Now whosoever undertakes to punish another, assumes unto himself in a manner, the person and office of a Governour, that is, of a Father; whereunto St. *Augustine* alludes, when he thus bespake *Marcellinus*, *Perform* (O thou Christian Judge) *the office of a pious Father,* who always prefers pardon before punishment. *A merciful man* (saith *Seneca*) *is as unwilling to spill another mans blood, as he is to spill his own; knowing that nature in every man is equally solicitous to preserve its being*: And therefore, *It befits men,* who are linkt together by the bands of Consanguinity, *to be as sparing of other mens lives as of their own; for not every man that offends is to be punished, but they only that persist in their sins without repentance. Let all men that are strangers to our faith,* saith *Chrysostome*, *know, that the reverence which we bear unto Christ is so great, that it restrains all earthly powers: Servants are taught to honour their Masters, and Masters to forgive their fellow Servants; that so our Great Lord and Master may be propitious unto us in that Great Day of Judgment.* It is usual in Scripture, where mention is made of sins and punishments, to allay one word with another; and to a word that is likely to heighten our anger, to add another that may serve to qualifie it. *If a man shall commit a trespass against his neighbour* (saith *Moses*) which two words (saith St. *Augustine*) *a* [*man*] *and a* [*sinner*], *are not conjoined without a Mystery, but for this end, that if the sinner do exasperate us, the word* [*man*] *should presently becalm us: for as he is a sinner he deserves punishment; but as he is a man he deserves to be pittied. So in the new Law, thou beholdest a mote in thy Brothers eye,* Matt. 7. 13. *A mote that offends us no less than it doth our Brother, and our zeal is quickly inflamed to pull it out; but when we consider, that it is in the eye,* and which is more, *in our Brothers eye, then we go warily about it, lest whilst we endeavour to pull out the mote, we put out our Brothers eye.* So in another place, *If thy Brother offend thee,* Luk. 17. 3. *the offence provokes us presently to passion; but when we consider that he who gives it, is* Frater, *our Brother,* that is, *quasi fere alter*, *One cast in the same mold with us, and scarcely divided from our selves; this should instantly appease our swelling passion; so that though angry we may be, yet revenge we must not.* The Emperour *Julian* applauded that saying of *Pittacus, which prefered pardon before punishments. But whosoever will imitate his heavenly Father* (saith *Libanius*) *must glory more in forgiving than in punishing; for in nothing do we draw nearer to the Divine Nature* (saith *Cicero*) *than in giving life to them, who have deserved death.* Again such cases there may happen, wherein to abstain from claiming our Right, is not so much a courtesie as a debt, in regard of that love which we owe unto all men though Enemies, whether considered in it self, or in obedience to the Law of Christ: yea, and some persons there are, whose safety, though they should persecute us, we are bound to prefer, even before our own lives; because we know that their welfare is either very necessary, or very profitable to the Commonwealth. And if Christ did enjoin us to part with our Coat, rather than to contend for our Cloak, certainly he would have us to neglect much greater losses, rather than go to War; because there is no contest so destructive as War. Sometime again, the remedy brings more danger than the disease; *And* (as St. *Ambrose* observes) *to forego something of our just right, is not only liberal, but for the most part gainful. Aristides* exhorting the Grecian Cities to peace, perswades them rather to yield, than to quarrel for small matters, *In imitation of good men, who had rather sit down with loss, than go to Law for trifles.* And *Xenophon* will inform us, *That it is the part of a wise man, not to embroil himself in War, though for matters of great importance.* The like advice *Apollonius* gives unto Princes, *Not to engage in War though for great matters.*

Lib. 5.

Ep. 87.

Diod Sic. in fragm.

De Statuis l. 6.

Aug. citat. à Gratian. causa 23. q. 4. Quia peccator corripe, quia homo miserere.

Vide supra c. 20. §. 12, 26, 36.

Orat pro Antioch.

De Off. l. 2. c. 2.

Græc. Hist. l. 6.

III. Especially by a King that is injured.

As concerning punishments, our principal duty, if not as men, yet as Christians, is willingly and readily to remit them, as God in Christ doth unto us, *Eph.* 4. 32. *Seneca* concerning a good Prince, saith, *That he is more ready to forgive injuries done against himself, than those done against others; for as a magnanimous person, scorns to be bountiful of another mans purse, but had rather detract from himself what he gives unto others: so he only deserves the title of being merciful, who bears his own injuries patiently, and freely remits where he hath power to revenge.* Nec quicquam gloriosius Principe impune læso; *Neither is there any thing more glorious than an injured Prince, that disdains to revenge his own wrongs*: And therefore *Kings* (as *Quintilian* adviseth) *should be exhorted to make themselves rather famous, for their humanity and clemency, than formidable for their severity.* Amongst other the vertues that Ennobled *C. Cæsar*, this is recorded by *Cicero* as the chief, *That he never forgot any things but injuries.* Thus doth *Livia* plead with *Augustus*, *As it is the duty of Emperours, severely to punish offenders against the Commonwealth, so is it their honour to forgive their own personal injuries.* It is very true what *Antoninus* the Philosopher told the Senate, *That there was nothing so unbecoming a Prince as to avenge his own wrongs; for though the punishment be put just, yet beimg Judge in his own cause, it will seem cruelty*: And what *Themistius* said unto the Senate in the praise of *Theodosius*, *That a good Prince should excel those who had wronged him; not in power to hurt them, but in his readiness to do them good. Aristotle* denies *that Prince to be magnanimous, that is mindful*

Dion.

 of

of an injury, which *Cicero* explains thus, *For*, saith he, *there is nothing more becoming a noble person than gentleness and clemency.* When one told *Antisthenes* that *Plato* spake ill of him: he answered without passion, *Regium est benefacere, & male audire*; *To do well and hear ill, is commonly the fate of Kings.* The Holy Scriptures do furnish us with many excellent examples of clemency, as in *Moses*; who when the people began to mutinie against him for want of flesh, instead of punishing them prays for them, *Numb.* 11. 12. And when God himself branded *Miriam* with Leprosie for her seditious murmuring against him; He, instead of taking revenge, intercedes for her, healing her foul face with his devout tongue, *Numb.* 12. 13. The like we find in *David*, who being bitterly reviled by *Shimei*, crying out against him, *Come up thou man of blood*, &c. returned not reproaches for reproaches, but being urged by some to a revenge, answered meekly, *Let him alone, let him curse, for haply, God hath bidden him*, 2 Sam. 16. 7,— 10. Thus did S[t] *Stephen* intercede for his persecutors, saying, *Lord, lay not this sin to their charge*, Acts 7. 60. Now this doth in a more especial manner become those who are Soveraign Princes, *Unto whom as all things are permitted, so freely to restrain themselves, and to make the Divine Law their guide in all their actions, is the readiest way to purchase glory and immortality.* The advice therefore of S[t] *Augustine* to Count *Boniface* was worthy to be by all Kings observed, *Remember speedily to forgive him, who having injured thee, begs for pardon.* And these are the principal motives which should disswade us from entring into a bloody War, though haply justly provoked, which are drawn from that affection, which as men, we either owe, or may rightly shew, even unto our enemies.

Chrysost. in laude clem.

IV.

And that sometimes for his own and his Subjects safety.

† *Procop. Goth. lib.* 2.

Sometimes it concerns us to abstain from War, for our own and their sakes that are under us. *Procopius* † brings in the *Goths* thus bespeaking *Belisarius*, *Since these things stand thus, it is a duty incumbent upon the Governours of either Nation, not to be too prodigal of the blood of their Subjects out of an ambitious desire of their own glory; but to prefer those things that are both just and profitable, not for themselves only, but for their enemies.* *Plutarch* in the Life of *Numa* tells us, That after the Colledge of Heraulds had judged that they might lawfully make War, the Senate consulted, whether it were fit and expedient for them so to do. In the Parable of our Saviour, it is said, *That before any King entred into War, he first sate down and consulted about the charge, and whether with ten thousand he was able to encounter him that came against him with twenty thousand; and if not, he instantly sent and made peace with him.* So *Diodorus* in *Thucydides*, *Although I should pronounce them guilty of great Crimes, yet I shall not adjudge them to be slain, unless I see it expedient.* So likewise *Livy* records of the *Tusculans*, *That by suffering all things, and denying nothing, they purchased their peace with the Romans.* The very same was done by the King of *Armenia* in the times of the Emperour *Severus*, as *Herodotus* testifies *: And *Tacitus* tells us, *That the Romans sought an occasion of War with the Æduans in vain, for being commanded to send money and arms to their Camp, they sent both, and not only those, but victuals also, and that frankly.* So Queen *Amalasuntha* professed to the Ambassadors of the Emperour *Justinian*, That she would not contend with him in Arms. Sometimes an Enemy may be pacified in a moderate way; as *Strabo* informs us was done by *Syrmus* King of the *Triballi*, who at once forbad *Alexander* the *Macedonian* entrance into the Island *Peuce*, and at the same time honoured him with many rich presents: thereby shewing that it was the fear of his power, and not any hatred or contempt of his person that made him to do it. And indeed what *Euripides* sometimes said of the Cities of *Greece*, may fitly be applyed to other States:

Lib. 6.
Plut. vit. Camilli.
* *Herod. lib.* 3.
Lib. 7.

De Marte quoties itur in suffragia,
Nemo imminere cogitat mortem sibi,
Sed quisque cladem destinamus alteri:
Quod si in comitiis funera ante oculos forent,
Furiata bello non periisset Græcia.

When in full Senate Votes for War pass free,
No man his own destruction doth foresee,
But all fore-tell the others destinie:
When if its own sad fate, each had foreseen,
Greece thus by War consum'd had never been.

When we wax proud, and confident in our own strength, (saith *Livy*) *Let us then call to mind that great command that fortune hath over all sublunary things; together with the sudden changes, and uncertain events of War.* And as *Thucydides* adviseth, *Before we engage our selves too far, let us consider how many sad mischances do usually happen in War, which the most piercing eye of humane wisdom cannot foresee.*

V.

Prudent Rules about our choice of Good.

The things that usually fall under consultation, are either about the intermediate ends which may probably conduce to the last end we fully resolve on, or about those means whereby

whereby we may probably obtain those ends: The end we propose to our selves is always either some good, or doubtless the avoiding of some evil, which also falls under the notion of good. But those things that lead us hither or thither, are not expetible for themselves, but as they conduce to those ends: wherefore in all our Consultations we are to compare both those ends between themselves, and the effective power or faculty of those things which lead to the end to produce that end. For as *Aristotle* rightly observes, *The arguments that excite us to action are of two sorts, either they are drawn from the goodness of the end, or from the possibility of obtaining it*; which comparison hath these three Rules, whereby we may be guided: First, If the thing in debate seem to have (in a moral esteem) an equal efficacy to good and to evil; then if the good we hope for have somewhat more of good than the evil we fear hath of evil, we may adventure upon the action, (but if the conveniencies be not able to over-ballance the inconvenience, it is better to refrain;) for a wise man, though never so daring and magnanimous, will not run the hazard of his life for every cause; but then only when the reward is great, weighty and honourable. The second Rule is this, If the Good and Evil seem to be equal which may proceed from the thing in question, then we may thus guide our choice; if the thing it self have a greater efficacy to produce the Good than it hath to produce the Evil, then we may chuse it. Thirdly, If both the Good and Evil seem unequal, and the power or efficacy of the things no less unequal, then that thing is at length to be chosen, if its efficacy to the Good be greater, being compared with its efficacy unto the Evil, than the Evil it self is, being compared with the Good: or if the Good it self compared with the Evil be greater, than its efficacy unto Evil being compared with the Good. Thus *Narses* to *Belisarius*, *Where the dangers appear to be equal, and the damage alike if we err, there much discourse and consultation is necessary before we determine the matter in question*; *but where the difficulties are unequal, and the damages upon mistake greater or less than the hopes of gain, there the choice is very easie, and requires no great depth of judgment to determine.* What we have set down here somewhat more accurately, *Cicero* hath in a plainer way, but to the same purpose described, where he adviseth us not to expose our selves to dangers without cause, than which nothing can argue a more fool-hardiness: Wherefore in perillous cases we should imitate Physicians, who in light distempers use gentle remedies; but when the disease threatens death, then those that are more doubtfull and dangerous: Therefore it is the office of a wise man to help in a time of danger, especially when he rationally conceives, that the good he shall reap by it, if it succeed, doth over-ballance the damage that he fears if it miscarry. But as the same *Cicero* elsewhere saith, *No prudent man will endanger himself in such an enterprise, wherein the good success shall bring him little profit, but where the least miscarriage may prove fatal.* For as *Dion Prusaensis* saith, *Grant that our grievances be unjust and unworthy to be born, yet will it not follow, That whensoever we suffer any thing unjustly, we ought by striving against it, to make our condition worse. To make use of iron and steel, when more gentle remedies may prevail, or where the case is not extreamly dangerous, becomes neither a skilfull Physician, nor a Politick Statesman.* Dion Prusaensis, *When our burthens are beyond our strength, our endeavours to ease our selves of them are just and honest, because necessary*; *but if they are tolerable, and that we have cause to fear, that by struggling they may be made worse, we must arm our selves with patience.* For as *Aristides* saith well, *Where our fears are above our hopes, then it concerns us especially to beware.*

De motione animalium.

Three Rules to guide us in the choice of Good.

Procopius Goth. lib. 2. cap. 13.

De Offic. lib. 1.

Plutarch.

Aristides.

VI. Life better than Liberty.

An example whereof we will borrow out of *Tacitus*, who relates, that amongst the Cities of *France*, there arose a great debate whether were more desiderable, *Peace or Liberty*: where by Liberty, we must understand that which is Civil, namely, a right to govern by their own Laws, which in a popular estate is absolute and full; but mixt and moderate in an Aristocracy, especially in such an estate wherein no Citizen is uncapable of honours; and by Peace we mean such a Peace, whereby the destruction of a City or Nation by a cruel War may be prevented; that is, as *Cicero* explains it, *When the whole City is in danger of being lost*: or when the case of a Nation or City is so desperate, that nothing but an utter desolation can otherwise with any probable reason be expected, which was the very case of the Jews being besieged by *Titus*. No man can be ignorant of *Plato*'s Opinion in such a case, who preferred death before subjection; thereby shewing,

> ———*Quam sit non ardua virtus*
> *Servitium fugisse manu*;
>
> ———with what ease
> A man from slav'ry may himself release.

But Right Reason suggests the contrary; for the Life of Man, which is the foundation of all temporal blessings, and the occasion of eternal, is more to be esteemed than Liber-

 ty,

ty, whether we take both to be either personal or national: And therefore God himself intended it as an act of his mercy, that he delivered his people into captivity, but destroyed them not. And by the Prophet *Jeremy* he perswaded them, *To yield themselves into the hands of the King of Babylon, lest they died by the Famine or by the Pestilence.* It is a question not easily answered (saith St. *Aug.*) whether the Saguntines did well to preserve their Faith given to the Romans, so long, until the City with themselves was totally destroyed by *Hannibal.* For though *Cicero* thought nothing sufficient to justifie a War, but either the publick safety, or the publick Faith given; yet doth he not there determine the case of the Saguntines, by shewing, that if a City were driven into such a strait, that they could not possibly preserve their Faith without the ruine of themselves; nor preserve themselves without the breach of their Faith (which was the case of the Saguntines) whether of the two were most eligible: But by the Authority of the Holy Scriptures we are taught, That death is the greatest of all terrours, and that Captivity, whether of a Nation, or of some particular persons, is far more desiderable than utter destruction. Thus *Guido* the Italian Poet bespeaks the Citizens of *Milain*,

2 *Chron.* 12. 78.
Jer. 27. 13.
De Civ. Dei lib. 22. *c.* 6.
De repub. lib. 3.

> *Omnia securi pro libertate feremus:*
> *Sed libertatem contempta nemo salute*
> *Sanus amat; neque enim certæ susceptio cladis*
> *Quam vitare queas, nisi cum ratione salutis,*
> *Libertatis amor, sed gloria vana putanda est.*

It is not so properly a love to liberty, as a preposterous itch after vain Glory, that makes a man to prefer his freedom before his life. *Cicero* instances this as a case of necessity, that the Cisilinenses were necessarily to give themselves up to *Hannibal,* although this clause were added to that necessity, *Nisi malint fame perire; Unless they had rather perish by famine.* For as *Anaxilaus* in *Xenophon* apoligizeth for his surrender of *Byzantium,* being thereunto constrained for want of Bread, *Pugnandum est hominibus in homines, non in rerum naturam; Men ought to fight against men, but not against nature; neither do men commend a voluntary death, so long as their hopes are above their fears.* That sentence which *Diodorus Siculus* past against the Thebans, which lived in the time of *Alexander* the Great, stands yet upon record, namely, *That they were the authors of their own ruine; for as much as they had with more courage than prudence provoked* Alexander *to their own destruction.* And in another place, the same Author examining the ground of that War, which the Thracians undertook against *Alexanders* Army, after his death, saith, *That in the opinion of the wisest men, they had consulted well for their own glory, but not so well for their own profit, by thrusting themselves overhastily into so dangerous an enterprise, being no ways urged thereunto by any necessity; but especially being forewarned by the destruction of the Thebans.* The like censure doth *Plutarch* pass upon *Cato* and *Scipio, Whom, for refusing to submit to* Cæsar *after his victory in* Pharsalia, *he condemns, as being the cause that so many, and so gallant men, did unnecessarily perish in* Africa. Now what I have here said concerning liberty, may likewise be said concerning other things that are desiderable, when they cannot be obtained without, if not a more just, yet at least an equal expectation of some greater mischief. For as *Aristides* saith, *To preserve the ship with the loss of the goods, is usual, but not with the loss of the passengers.*

VII.
War seldom made for punishments by Princes of equal power.

This also is chiefly to be observed, That Wars are seldom or never made for exacting punishments only, by such Princes or States as are of equal power; for as the civil Magistrate, so he that undertakes to punish injuries by Arms, must always be presumed to be of power sufficient to enforce it: Neither is it prudence only, or the love we bear to our Subjects, that should disswade us from a doubtful War; but sometimes even justice, that I mean, which is essential to Government, which requires, as obedience from inferiours, so protection and preservation from superiours. And consequently as some Divines have rightly observed, If a King for any small or trifling cause, as for the exacting of punishments which are unnecessary, engage his Subjects in a dangerous War, he is bound to repair the losses they shall thereby sustain: for although to his Enemy haply he doth no wrong who hath justly provoked him; yet doth he thereby wrong to his Subjects, by involving them in a dangerous War for such slight causes, as might better have been dissembled, and is therefore bound to repair their damages; in which sense that of *Livy* holds true, *Justum est bellum quod necessarium est, & pia arma, quibus nulla nisi in armis relinquitur spes; That War is just that is necessary, and Arms are there necessary, when there is no hopes of safety but by Arms.* This was *Ovids* wish,

In what case a Prince is bound to repair his Subjects losses.

Ovid. Fast. 1.

> *Sola gerat miles, quibus arma coerceat, arma;*
>
> May then the Souldier armed be,
> When he repels his Enemy.

There

There is then one rare cause, when War either cannot, or ought not to be omitted; as namely, when (as *Flora* speaks) *Jura sunt armis sæviora*; *Laws are more cruel than War it self*: that is, when the oppressions of Tyrants are more greivious than the miseries of War. *He* (saith *Seneca*) *needs not to fear the miseries of War, that suffers the like, if not greater, living in Peace.* So *Aristides*, *When it is manifest that our condition will be worse in sitting still, then we may adventure upon the dangers of War.* Neither is that opinion of *Tacitus* much to be condemned, where he saith, *That a miserable Peace may well be exchanged for a doubtful War*; that is, as the same Author saith, *When, if we conquer, we enjoy our freedom; or being conquered our condition can be no worse*: Or, when (as *Livy* speaks) *Peace is more grievous to those that serve, than War is to those that are free.* But not (as *Cicero* puts the case) if it appear that being Conquered, we shall be proscrib'd, (*i. e.*) our estates shall be sold, and our persons banished; but being Conquerours, we change only our oppressors, but are not eased of our oppressions. VIII. War not to be undertaken but in a case of necessity.

Another time when War is to be preferred before Peace peace, is, when upon a rational debate we find that we have the best Right, and which is of greatest moment, power sufficient to defend it; that is, as *Augustus* in *Suetonius* sometimes said *, *When there is more hopes of gain than fear of loss*: Or as *Scipio Africanus*, and *L. Æmilius Paulus* were wont to say of the Battel *, *We ought not to run the hazard of a Battel, but upon some unavoidable necessity, or upon great and manifest advantage*; wherewith accords that of *Plutarch* * before-recited, *To use Iron and Steel without very great necessity, neither becomes a good Physician, nor a prudent States-man.* The like *Zonaras* records of *Marcianus*, *Kings when they may lawfully enjoy Peace, ought not to make War.* Whereunto we may add that of St. *Augustine*, *Pacem habere voluntatis est, Bellum autem necessitatis esse debet, ut liberet nos Deus à necessitate, & conservet in pace*; *Peace we should make voluntarily, War out of necessity: That so God may relieve us in our necessities, and preserve us in Peace.* But then most especially may we make War, when we have good cause to hope, that our Enemies through fear, or by the fame of our Victories, will be ready to yield without any or very little danger on our part; and this is as *Pliny* calls it, the most glorious of all Victories. IX. Or without great cause, and great advantages. * *Sueton. c.* 24. * *Aul. Gel. l.* 13. *c.* 3. *Val. Max. l.* 7. *c.* 2. * *Gracchis.*

War indeed is, as *Plutarch speaks* *, a very savage thing, and never comes unaccompanied with a torrent of mischiefs and insolencies, *Which* (saith St. *Aug.* *) *should I undertake to describe, when and where would my discourse end? But they may say, a wise man will sometimes make War; as if, when he considers himself to be a man, he doth not much more grieve to find himself enforced thereunto, though that War be just; for unless it were just, there could be no necessity to make it, because it is the iniquity of the adverse part, that thrusts a wise man into a just and necessary War; which very iniquity as proceeding from men (though no necessity of a War should thence arise) is to be lamented: whosoever therefore, shall with any remorse consider those so great, so horrid, and so direful effects of War, cannot but confess that it is miserable; but he that can feel them, or think upon them without sorrow, much more he that can glory in the success of them,* Ideo se putat beatum quia humanum perdidit sensum; *Therefore thinks himself happy because he hath lost all sentiments of humanity.* So the same Father in another place tells us, that, *Belligerare malis videtur felicitas, bonis necessitas*; *Good men make War their refuge, but wicked men make it their delight. And were there nothing of injustice in the War, yet to be enforced unto it, that is in it self miserable,* saith *Maximus Tyrius*: whereunto he adds, *Wise men never make War but by constraint, whereas fools fight for pleasure and gain.* The Lacedemonians in *Diodorus*, *considering those great enmities and animosities, likely to arise from War, thought themselves bound in duty, to declare before the Gods, and unto all good men, that they were not the Authors of it.* *Plutarch* brings in some making this objection, *But hath not* Rome *much improved her self by War? Whereunto he answers, 'Tis true indeed she hath so, in the opinion of those who place their greatest glory in Riches, in Pleasure, Wantonness, and Martial Power (which are but the dregs of Honour;) but not in theirs who place their glory in the safety of their People, in meekness, justice, and contentation.* It was therefore worthily said of *Stephanus* the Phiysician unto *Cosroes* King of *Persia*, *To thee O King who art wholly conversant in blood and slaughter, in subduing Kingdoms, and depopulating Cities, other glorious attributes may be due; but surely thou canst never hope by these ways to be esteemed good: for as no good man will greedily covet that which is anothers: so,* Non est homini homine prodigè utendum, as *Seneca* tells us; *It is no point of Honour to be prodigal of humane Blood.* *Philiscus* advised *Alexander* to be emulous of Glory, *but not by making himself like unto a Plague in depopulating Cities, and laying whole Kingdoms wast.* Nothing can add more Glory to a King, than to provide for the safety of his Subjects that they may live in Peace. *Pliny* after he had recounted so many famous Battels, gained by the Dictator *C. Cæsar*, wherein were slain (as he there computes) Eleven hundred Ninety two thousand men, adds this, *I do not reckon it as any part of his Glory, to have done so great wrong to mankind however provoked.* *Philo* in the life of *Moses* observes, *That though the killing of Enemies in War, were by the Laws permitted; yet whosoever did kill a man, though justly, though in his own defence, though compelled thereunto against his will, did notwithstanding contract some guilt unto himself, in respect of that common kindred* X. The miseries of War. * *Vit. Camilli.* * *De Civit. Dei l.* 19. *c.* 7. *Id. de Civ. Dei lib.* 4. *c.* 15. *Lib.* 13. *Ælian lib.* 14. *c.* 2. *Nat. Hist. l.* 7. *c.* 25.

kindred and alliance between man and man, which was derived from the supreme Cause; wherefore expiations and purgations were thought necessary to cleanse them from that crime which seemed to be committed by them. If then, by the Hebrew Laws, He that killed a man, though against his will, was to betake himself to one of the Cities of refuge: And if God would not permit *David* to build him a Temple, because he was a man of blood, though of his enemies; that is, as *Josephus* writes, because he had made many Wars, which by the Law was permitted: If among the Ancient Greeks, he that had slain a man, though accidentally, or in defence of himself, had need of expiation: Who cannot see, how unhappy a thing it is, and by all means to be avoided, voluntarily to engage our selves in a War, though haply not unjust? Surely among the Greek Churches, that most Christian Canon was long in force, whereby he that in what War soever had slain a man, though an enemy, was not by the space of three years admitted unto the Sacrament.

Pollutus esset, hostili quidem, attamen sanguine.

Lib. 7. cap. 4.

CHAP. XXV.

For what Causes a War may be undertaken for others.

I. *That a War may justly be undertaken by a Prince for his Subjects.*
II. *But yet it is not always to be so undertaken.*
III. *Whether an innocent Subject may be delivered up to an enemy to prevent a War.*
IV. *That a War may justly be undertaken in the behalf of our Confederates, equal or unequal.*
V. *As also for our Friends.*
VI. *Yea, and for any man.*
VII. *Yet may it also be omitted without blame, if it endanger himself, or cannot be done without the death of the invader.*
VIII. *Whether that War be just that is made to relieve another mans Subjects, this explained by a distinction.*
IX. *All those military consociations, and mercenary succours that respect not the equity of the Cause, are unjust.*
X. *To engage in War for spoil, or pay only, is wicked.*

I. A Prince may justly make War for his Subjects.

Above when we treated of such persons as had a Right to make War, it was said and shewed, That naturally every man had a power to vindicate, not only his own, but the right of another †; wherefore look what Causes do justifie a War undertaken for our selves, the very same do justifie a War made for another: But our principal, and most necessary care should be for our own Subjects, whether they be our Domesticks, or such as live under our Civil Government, for they are a part of the Governour as we there shewed. Thus *Joshua* we read made War in defence of the *Gibeonites*, who had yielded themselves unto him. *It is not sufficient to denominate a Man Just, that he wrongs no man,* saith *Procopius*, *unless he also be carefull to protect those from injuries, who for that very end have put themselves under him.* *Our Ancestors,* saith *Cicero* to the Roman Senate, *did often make Wars in the behalf of their Merchants and Mariners when they have been abused by Strangers.* And in another place, *How many Wars* (saith he) *did our forefathers undertake to revenge the wrongs done to the Citizens of* Rome, *when their Seamen have been imprisoned, and their Merchants spoiled?* Yea, and the very same *Romans* who refused to take Arms in the defence of a People that were their Confederates, thought it necessary to defend the same People when they had surrendred themselves, and so became their Subjects: Thus do the Campanes bespeak the *Romans*, *Though ye refused to assist or defend us against our enemies, whilst we were your Friends and Confederates, yet now that we are your Subjects, you will certainly protect us.* Whereupon *Florus* saith, That the Campanes made that League which they had formerly contracted with the *Romans*, more strong and inviolable by their voluntary surrender of all they had unto them; for *it agreed not with the Faith of the Romans,* saith *Livy*, *to desert such.*

† See *lib.* 1. *c.* 5.

Josh. 10. 6.

Persicor. 2.

Verr. 2.

Livy lib. 7.

II. Yet is it not alwayes convenient.

Neither is it prudence in a Governour to enter into a War always, though upon a just ground for any particular Subject, unless it may be done safely, without endangering all, or the greatest part of his Subjects. For it is the Duty of a good Prince to prefer the safety of the whole before its parts; and the greater the part is that he provideth for, the nearer it draws to the nature of the whole.

III. Whether an Innocent Subject may be delivered up to preserve the whole.

Wherefore in case the Enemy shall require any one person to be delivered to death, though that person be innocent, there is no question but that he may be forsaken, if it clearly appear, that the City is too weak to make resistance. For as *Nicephorus*, in *Zonaras*, advised rightly, concerning the delivering up of the Fugitives to the *Bulgarian* General, to purchase their peace, *We judge it much better that a few men should perish, than that so great a multitude should be destroyed.*

——*Non*

————*Non malo unius domus*
Commune vinci, sed nec æquari potest.

No one mans sufferings can equal be
Unto a general calamitie.

(When *Alexander* had destroyed *Thebes*, he came to *Athens*, threatning to destroy it, unless *Demosthenes*, *Lycurgus*, and others, who had highly exasperated the people against him, were delivered unto him. *Phocion* thereupon being urged in the Senate to deliver his Opinion in that Case, pointing to his dear friend *Nicocles*, answered, *Eo in fortunii urbem nostram isti perduxerunt, ut etiamsi hunc* Nicoclem *meum dedi* Alexander *poscat, dedi jussurus sum*; *Into such a desperate condition have these men brought this City, that if* Alexander *had demanded my dearest friend* Nicocles, *my Vote should have past for his delivery: Yea, and I should think my self happy, might my life alone be accepted, as a sacrifice to preserve it.*) It is true *Vasquius* seems to be of a contrary judgment, yet he that throughly weighs not so much his words as his intention and purpose, may perceive that all he aims at is this only, That such an innocent person is not rashly or easily to be delivered, where there remains any hopes that he may be defended. For he there brings in a story of a certain Band of Italian Foot, whom he deservedly condemns for deserting *Pompey* before his Case was desperate, upon *Cæsar*'s promise of safety and protection which he condemns, and that not unworthily. But whether an innocent Citizen may be delivered up into the enemies power to preserve his City from imminent ruine, is much disputed now amongst the learned, as it formerly was, when *Demosthenes* invented that notable Apologue of the Wolves, who were content to make peace with the sheep, upon condition that their Dogs might be delivered up unto them. Neither doth *Vasquius* only deny this, but *Sotus* also, whose Opinion *Vasquius* condemns, as being too near a neighbour to treachery: Yet *Sotus* was of Opinion, that such a Citizen ought to deliver up himself; which *Vasquius* denies, being swayed by this reason, because the nature of a Civil Society, which was at the first entred into for mutual preservation, doth not permit it. But the force of this argument reacheth no farther than this, That no Citizen is bound so to do by any right strictly taken; but it argues not, That if he do it, he transgresseth the rules of Charity: For there are many Duties, which though not by the strict rules of Justice, yet by the bonds of Charity we stand obliged to perform, which are not only laudable being done, (as *Vasquius* acknowledgeth) but which cannot be left undone without blame; whereof this is one, That every man prefers the safety of an innocent multitude before his own. *Know ye not*, saith *Caiaphas* the High Priest, *that it is better*, that is, less evil, *that one man should die, than that the whole Nation should perish.* For the destruction of no one Family can equal the destruction of the Universe. A particular mischief is much more tolerable than a general calamity. And therefore *Phocion* did wisely when he perswaded *Demosthenes*, rather to undergo death himself, than that for him his Native Countrey should be destroyed; which he urged upon him by the examples of the Daughters of *Leus*, and of the *Hyacinthides*. This was *Cicero*'s resolution in the like case, as appears by that Oration he made for *P. Sextius*, *If it should happen*, saith he, *that sailing in a ship with my friends, and being therein assaulted by many Pyrats, who peremptorily resolved to sink the ship, unless I only were delivered up unto them; I should chuse rather to cast my self into the sea to preserve my friends, than endeavour to preserve mine own life with the danger of theirs:* And so in another place, *An honest and a prudent man observing the Laws, and knowing the duties of a Civil Life, doth always prefer a general good before the advantage of any particular person, though of himself.* *Livy* speaking of certain *Molossians*, saith, *That he had often heard of men that willingly exposed themselves to death for the defence of their Countrey: But these*, saith he, *are the first that ever I heard of, that thought it fit, that their Countrey should perish for themselves only.* But here also it may be questioned, whether a Citizen (though obliged in duty to do it) may be compelled thereunto. This *Sotus* denies, by the example of a rich man, that is bound by the bonds of mercy and charity to administer to the necessities of the poor, yet cannot be compelled thereunto. But we must here note, that there is not the same reason, for the parts compared between themselves, as there is for the Superiors compared with those that are subject unto them: for equals cannot compel one another, unless it be to such things as are strictly due; whereas it is in the power of Superiors, as Superiors, to enforce their inferiors to any virtuous act for the publick good. So we read, that the *Lucans* ordained a punishment against Prodigality, the *Macedonians* against Ingratitude, and the *Athenians* and *Lucans* both against Idleness. As in a time of dearth, any one Citizen may be enforced to produce his private store of Grain, and to make it publick: So in this case, whatsoever Charity requires of us, the Magistrate for a more universal good hath a power to enforce; as *Phocion* would have delivered up his friend *Nicocles* had *Alexander* demanded him.

Plut. vit. Phocion.

Diodor. lib. 17.

De finib. lib. 3.

Next

IV. War may justly be made for our confederates, equal or unequal. *Amb. de Off. l. 1. c. 36.* *Liv. l. 34.* *Simler.*

Next unto our own Subjects, or rather equally to be defended, are our Confederates, whether they surrender themselves upon condition of protection, or whether it be covenanted for mutual aid and assistance: *Qui non repellit injuriam à socio si potest, tam est in vitio quam ille qui facit*; *He that defends not his Associate when it is in his power, is as blame-worthy as he that injures him.* Yet are not such Covenants to be so far extended, as to engage us in a War if there be no just Cause. Wherefore the Lacedemonians before they had made War against the Athenians, referred the justice of their Cause to the judgment of all their Confederates. So did the Romans before they began their War against *Nabis*, make the Grecian Cities Judges in their case. So *Simler* concerning the Commonwealth of the Switzers, *If the Lord shall make War against any man, and it be known that his cause be just, or if it be doubted whether it be so, the Vassal shall be bound to assist his Lord; but if it be manifest that the War is unreasonable, then is the Vassal bound only to defend his Lord, but not to offend another.* Whereunto we may add, That though the case of our Confederates be just, yet if his case be desperate, and that, though we should assist him with what forces we can, there are no hopes of a good end; we are not then bound to aid him, because all alliances were at first made for preservation, but not for destruction: yea, and we may defend one of our Confederates against another of our Confederates, unless we are by any Article in a former League, particularly forbidden it. Thus the Athenians might have defended the Corcyreans, if their Cause had been just, against the Corinthians their more ancient Associates.

A Confederate not to be assisted, in case his condition be desperate, and why.

V. For our Friends.

Next to our Confederates, our friends are to be assisted, to whose aid, though we stand not engaged by any League or promise; yet upon the score of common friendship, we ought to contribute towards their assistance, if we may do it with ease, and without any inconvenience to our selves. Thus *Abraham* took up Arms in defence of his Kinsman Lot. And thus the Romans farbad the Pirates of *Antium*, to rob the Grecians their Friends and Kinsmen. And thus we often read it of the same Romans, that they frequenly either made War, or at least threatned so to do; not in the behalf of their Associates only, to whom they stood obliged, but for their Friends and Neighbours also, upon no other account, but that of Love and Friendship. There is an old Oracle that serves to guide us in this case,

Non ope juvisti præsens in morte sodalem:
Effabor tibi nil, nisi, Templi finibus exi.

VI. For any man. *Cic. de Fin. l. 3. de Off. l. 2. Sen de Ira. l. 1. c. 7. de Clem. 2. 5.*

Lastly we owe our assistance to all mankind, by reason of that near conjunction that there is between us, which alone were sufficient to excite us to aid and to succour each other. *Homo in adjutorium mutuum generatus est*; *Men* (saith *Seneca*) *are born to help each other*: And again, *A wise man will as oft as he can, prevent misfortunes*: According to that of *Euripedes*,

What Beasts from Rocks, Servants from Altars have:
Cities distrest, the like from Cities crave.

And indeed, *That fortitude that defends the cause of the weak and innocent, is full of justice*, saith S[t] *Ambrose*; but of this we have treated above.

VII. Yet it may be omitted, if either it endanger our selves, or take away the invaders life. ** Diodor. l. 1.*

Here also it may be questioned, whether for one man to defend another, or for one People or Nation to protect another from violence and wrong, be a debt whereunto we stand bound. *Plato* in the fourth of his Laws affirms, *That he that doth not repel violence offered to another (if he can do it) deserves to be punished.* The like provision was made, both by the Hebrew and ÆgyptianLaws *; but this general will admit of some exceptions: for in case we cannot do this, without incurring some manifest danger unto our selves, it is most agreeable to nature that we abstain from attempting it; for every man may prefer his own before the welfare of another. And in this sense doth that of *Cicero* hold true, *He that doth not defend another, nor resist an injury when he can, is as much to blame, as he that deserts his Parents, his Country, or his Friends*; if he can, that is, with safety to himself: For he himself in another place admits, *That some, haply, may be left unprotected without blame.* *Salust* in his History gives this wholesome advice, *Let them*, saith he, *who being in prosperity, are about to engage themselves in a social War, seriously consider, First, Whether they may then live in peace; Next, Whether the War they engage in be just, safe, honourable; or otherwise, inconvenient.* Succuram perituro, sed ut ipse non peream; *I will defend him* (saith *Seneca*) *that is ready to perish; but so, that I thereby perish not my self, unless it be to rescue from death some person of great honour; or to purchase some very great advantage unto either my self, or my relations*: Bonum etiam impendio sanguinis mei tuebor; *A good man*, saith he, *though with the hazard of my life, I shall defend; and if I can rescue a bad man from Thieves, by my clamour and outcry, I shall willingly strain my voice to do him good.* But yet if that good man be so oppressed, that he cannot be relieved without the death of the oppressor, I am not bound

De benef. l. 2. c. 15.

De benef. lib. 1. c. 10.

See Book 2. ch. 1. §. 8.

bound to do it; for if what I have said above be granted, namely, That the case may so happen, that the person invaded may chuse rather to dye himself, than to be the death of the invader: He that doth believe, the invaded doth wish, or would chuse rather so to do, doth not sin, if he do not rescue him; especially when the damage that is likely to befal the invading party, is in all probability likely to be both irreparable and everlasting.

Another Question is sometimes started, Whether that War be just which is undertaken to free anothers Subjects, from the oppression of their own Prince: without doubt, as soon as civil societies were at first instituted, every Governour had some peculiar Rights over his own Subjects, according to that of *Euripides*: VIII. Whether a War may be made upon another King for oppressing his own Subjects.

Nos quotquot hujus colimus urbis mœnia,
Sufficimus ipsi nostra judicia exequi;

We that within these walls reside, suffice
Our selves to punish our Delinquencies.

To the same purpose also is that,

Spartam *tibi qua contigit orna:*
Nobis fuerint cura Mycenæ;

Let *Sparta*'s care be thine:
Mycena's shall be mine.

Thucydides amongst other marks of Soveraignty reckons this, namely, *A Power in it self to execute judgments*; and this he holds to be as necessary, *as the Power either of ordaining Laws, or creating Magistrates:* and to this we may refer that of *Neptune* concerning *Æolus*, *Virgil Æn. lib.* 1.

Non illi imperium pelagi regnumque tridentis,
Sed mihi sorte datur;

The Sea's vast Power was not by lot assign'd
To him, but me.

Whereunto not much unlike is that of *Ovid*, *Metam. lib.* 14.

——————*Rescindere nunquam*
Dis licet acta Deûm;——————

Nor can the Gods, each others Acts rescind.

So likewise *Euripides*,

——————*Mos ille est Deûm,*
Quod cupiit unus; *huic nefas obsistere:*

———The Gods their custom have,
None must oppose what any one did crave:

That is as St. *Ambrose* well expounds it, *Lest by usurping upon each others jurisdiction, they should stir up War amongst themselves.* That every State should be permitted to punish their own Subjects, was thought by the Corinthians in *Thucydides* to be just. And *Perseus* in his Oration to *Martius*, denies that he needed to make any defence for himself for what he had done against the Dolopes, saying, *Jure feci meo*; *I did but exercise mine own just Right, seeing that they were my Subjects, and so under my jurisdiction.* For as St. *Augustine* observes, *There is not the same reason, that because it is an Argument of some mens goodness, to confer courtesies on strangers; therefore it should be the like argument of their justice, to punish those that belong to anothers jurisdiction.* But rather as *Procopius* hath it, *It is more agreeable to the rules of equity, that every man should carefully govern his own Province, and not trouble himself with the affairs of others*: Yet are all these to be understood of such cases, wherein another mans Subjects have manifestly offended, or at least whereof it is doubtful whether they have or not; for to this end were Empires at first distributed: But they hold not in case Subjects apparently groan under such Tyrannies, as no just man can approve of; and therefore are precluded from those Rights that are common to humane Society. For in such a case as this it was that *Constantine* made War against *Maxentius* and *Licinius*; and other Roman Emperours against the Persians, or at least threatned so to do, unless they protected from oppression such of their Subjects as were Christians, being persecuted for no other cause but that of Religion. Yea, and although we should grant that Subjects could not *Lib. 2. de lib. Arb.*

 justly

justly taken up Arms against their Prince; no, not in case of greatest necessity (which we see is doubted, even by those, whose purpose it was to defend the Regal Power): Yet will it not thence follow, That other Princes may not take Arms in their own defence. For whensoever the impediment to any action is meerly personal, and not drawn from the thing it self, then that which is unlawful for one to do by himself, may yet be lawful for another to do for him, if the matter be such wherein one man may profit another: So a suit at Law which a Pupil, by reason of his minority cannot maintain by himself, his Tutor or Guardian may maintain for him. So a Client that cannot appear in his own person by reason of the distance of place, may notwithstanding appear by his Attorney. Now that impediment which in a Subject hinders resistance, ariseth not from the Cause which is the same in Subjects, as in those that are not; but from the condition or quality of the person, which passeth not into another. Thus thought *Seneca*, *He that being separated from my countrey is vexatious to his own, may be justly by me invaded*, as I have shewed before where we treated of punishments; which thing is often conjoined with the defence of innocents. Although we are not ignorant by those many examples we find in Histories, both ancient and modern, That Ambition, and an insatiable thirst after Gain, do too frequently disguise themselves under such specious pretences; yet may we not thence conclude, That because wicked men do sometimes usurp this Right for sinister ends; therefore to defend other mens Subjects from manifest oppression, ceaseth to be lawful. For, *Navigant & Piratæ, ferro utuntur & Latrones*; *Pyrates we see navigate the Seas, and Thieves wear swords*: yet no man will hence infer, That it is not therefore lawful for Merchants to traffick by Sea, or for Princes to make use of Arms to defend their Subjects.

IX. Of Souldiers of fortune.

But as those Warlike Confederacies, which are made to the end that succours may be promised upon any War, undertaken by whomsoever, or upon what occasion soever, be it right or wrong, are already declared to be unlawful; so is there no kind of life more wicked than that of mercenary Souldiers, who without any respect had to the equity of the Cause, fight only for plunder and pay; to whom, *Ibi fas, ubi plurima merces*: *Thats the best Cause which pays best*, which *Plato* proves out of *Tyrtæus*. (*Livy.* 32.) This was it that *Philip* upbraided the Ætolians with, and *Dionysius Milesius* condemned in the Arcadians, in these words, *Belli instituuntur nundinæ*; *They made War a trade to live by*: And, *what was the common bane of all* Greece *besides, was matter of gain and profit to them, whilst they sent out their mercenaries, sometimes to this part, sometimes to that, without any regard to justice or equity*. Surely a Souldier is a thing to be much pittied, who as *Antiphanes* speaks, *hires himself to be killed, to preserve a life that is miserable*. (*Miles qui vitæ causa se auctorat neci, Antiphanes. Bacchid.*) So *Dion Prusæensis*, *What can be more necessary, what more dear and precious than life? and yet even this, many men imprudently lose for greediness of gain*. This was *Plautus* his Character of mercenaries, *Suam qui auro vitam vendit ant*; *Their lives for gold they sell*: The like doth *Gunther*,

> *Ære dato conducta cohors, & bellica miles*
> *Dona sequens, pretioque suum mutare favorem*
> *Suetus, & accepto pariter cum munere bello*
> *Hunc habuisse, dator pretii quem jusserit, hostem.*

And yet, did they sell their own lives only, it were the less hurt; but together with their own, they sell the lives of many innocents, *Tanto carnifice detestabiliores, quanto pejus est sine causa, quam cum causa occidere*; *By so much is the condition of such Souldiers worse than that of Hangmen; by how much, it is more abominable to kill the innocent, than to destroy the guilty*: As *Antisthenes* was wont to say of Tyrants, *That they were more cruel and mercilest than common Executioners; for these hang Thieves and Murtherers only; but those murther innocents.* (*Diodor. l.* 18.) And *Philip* of *Macedon*, as truly of those who made War for gain only, *That War was to them as Peace, and Peace as War*. So likewise *Seneca*, *What may a man call this but madness, to make dangers our inseperable companions, fiercely to assault those whom we know not, to be enraged without any offence given, to destroy all we meet, and like wild Beasts to kill those whom we never hated?* Surely War is not a trade to live by; nay, it is a thing in it self so horrid, that nothing but pure necessity, or perfect charity, can denominate it just or honest. (*Quest. Nat. lib.* 5. *c.* 18.) So St. *Augustine*, *Militare non est delictum, sed propter prædam militare peccatum est*: *Simply to make War is not sinful; but to make War for plunder and pay only, must needs be wicked*. (*Grat. c.*33.*q.*1.)

X. Especially they that make War for spoil.

Nay to make War for pay or hire is likewise a sin, if that be the only or principal thing we aim at; though otherwise to receive pay for our pains, when we are lawfully called to fight, is altogether lawful: *For who*, saith St. *Paul*, *goeth to War at any time upon his own charge?*

CHAP.

CHAP. XXVI.

How War may be justly waged by such as are Subjects to anothers Command.

I. *Who they are that are under the dominion of another.*
II. *What they ought to do being admitted to debate, or being left to their free choice.*
III. *If they think the cause unjust, though commanded, they ought not to make war.*
IV. *What they ought to do in case they doubt the justice of the Cause.*
V. *If they cannot be satisfied, their persons are to be spared, but their Taxes heightened.*
VI. *In what case Subjects may justly take Arms in an unjust War.*

I. Who are said to be under anothers Dominion.

Hitherto we have treated of such as are free, and have power to dispose of their own actions. There are others that are under a more servile condition, and such are the Sons of a Family, Servants, Subjects, and each particular Citizen, compared with the whole Body of the City whereof they are.

II. What they are to do, being left to their own choice.

But these men, if either admitted to advise, or left to their own choice, whether they will either take up Armes or be quiet, ought to be guided by the same Rules, which are already set down for those who being free have power to make war either for themselves or others.

III. What if they think the cause unjust.

But if commanded thereunto, as usually they are, then if it be evident unto them that the Cause is unjust, they ought altogether to forbear; for that God is rather to be obeyed than man, was not only the judgment of the Apostle, but even of *Socrates* also, as *Plato* testifies in his Apology. So also thought the Hebrew Doctors, namely, That Kings, if they command any thing contrary to Gods Laws, were not at all to be obeyed. For this *Josephus* records of his Country-men, who being convicted before *Herod* for pulling down the Roman Eagle, which he had caused to be erected over the Great Gate of the Temple at *Jerusalem*, and demanded how they durst do it, returned this Answer, *What we have done, we did in vindication of God's honour, and of that Divine Law whereof we profess our selves to be the Disciples; neither hast thou cause to wonder if we hold the Laws which* Moses *delivered unto us from God himself, to be more sacred and indispensable than thy Decrees. Neither do we refuse to suffer death, or any other punishment thou shalt think fit to inflict upon us; as knowing that we shall not suffer as Malefactors, but as Martyrs in a good Cause.* That excellent Saying of *Polycarpus*, now ready to expire, lives still upon Record, namely, *To Princes and Potentates we owe all due honour and obedience, yet not so as thereby to endanger our eternal salvation.* It was the advice of St *Paul*, *Children obey your Parents in the Lord, for this is right*: upon which words St *Hierome* thus glosseth, *For Children not to obey their Parents, is a sin; but because Parents may haply command that which is unlawful, therefore he addes, In the Lord.* And St *Chrysostome* thus expounds them, *Children obey your Parents in the Lord,* that is, *in all things wherein you shall not disobey God.* And in another place he saith, *For it is no small reward that God proposeth to us for our obedience to Parents (and Magistrates.) For we are commanded to esteem them as our Lords, and both in words and deeds to yield them all due observance; yet so, as the works of true piety and devotion are not thereby hindred.* But if thine obedience unto God call thee forwards, then that of St *Hierome* holds true, (which he speaks declamatorily out of *Seneca*) *Per calcatum perge Patrem, Thou must go on, though thou tramplest on thine own Parents.* For our obedience unto our Parents cannot justifie our disobedience unto God. For as the same Apostle saith, *Every man shall receive from God according to his own works, whether bond or free.* The like advice doth St *Hierome* give unto Servants, where he addes, *But when our carnal Lords shall command any thing contrary to the will of him (who is the God of the Spirits of all Flesh,) then they are not to be obeyed.* Again, in another place, *In those things only are men subject unto their Lords and Masters, which are not contrary to the Commands of God.* So likewise *Chrysostome*, *Servants also have their bounds and limits prescribed them by God; and how far they may go in their obedience, is also commanded, beyond which they must not proceed. If the Lord command us nothing that is by God forbidden, he is to be followed and obeyed; but not beyond.* The like advice gives *Clemens Alexandrinus* concerning a Wife, *Let her*, saith he, *obey her Husband in all things, and do nothing against his will, but what she believes may very much conduce to vertue, and her own salvation.* So likewise *Tertullian*, *We are sufficiently instructed* (saith he) *by the Apostles Precept to be subject to Magistrates, Princes, and Powers in all obedience.* Sed intra limites Disciplinæ, *So far as they transgress not the Rules of Christian Discipline.* The like we read of *Silvanus* the Martyr, *We therefore despise the Roman Laws,*

Ant. lib. 17. c. 8.

Eph. 6. 1.

Ad Patrem Infidelem.

In Eph. 6. 1.

In 1 Cor. 7. 24.

In Martyrologio. *lest we should thereby transgress the Divine Laws.* And *Musonius, If a Son, a Servant, or a Subject, shall refuse to yield obedience unto either a Father, a Master, or a Prince in such Commands as are impious and ungodly, they shall not be accounted as disobedient, injurious or wicked.* Now as the obedience of Servants is bounded by the Divine Laws, so is that of Children to Parents. Lib. 2. c. 7. *Aulus Gellius* approves not of this opinion, *That a Father is in all things to be obeyed. For* (saith he) *what if he command his Son to betray his Countrey, to kill his own Mother?* &c. *Therefore the middle way is best and safest: in some things we must, in other some we must not obey.* So *Seneca* the Father, *Non omnibus Imperiis parendum est, All Commands oblige us not unto obedience.* So *Quintilian, There is no necessity that Children should execute all their Parents Commands; for there may be many things, which, though commanded, may not lawfully be done. As if a Father command his Son to give his suffrage, or to pass a senteuce contrary to his own judgment, or to bear witness to that whereof he is ignorant. If my Father command me to burn the Capitol, to possess my self of such a Fort or Castle; I may lawfully answer, These things I must not do.* So in another place, *We are not to execute all our Parents Commands, for otherwise nothing would be more destructive than benefits received, if they oblige us unto all manner of servitude.* To the same purpose is that of *Seneca, Neither can we command all things, nor can our servants be compelled to obey us in all our Commands:* Contra Rempublicam Imperata non facient, *They will not obey us if we command them any thing against the Commonwealth; they will not, though commanded, put their hands to any wickedness.* Of the same opinion was *Sopater, A Father* (saith he) *is indeed to be obeyed, if his Commands be according to Law, it is true; but if otherwise, it is not convenient.* To justifie Subjects for refusing to execute the wicked Commands of their Princes, we have divers examples in the Sacred Stories. *Saul* commanded his Guards to fall upon the Priests at *Nob, but they wou'd not put forth their hands to fall upon the Priests of the Lord,* 1 Sam. 22. 17. *Ahab* at the instigation of *Jezebel* persecuted the Lords Prophets to death; but *good Obadiah preserved a hundred of them, and fed them by fifty in a Cave,* 1 *Kings* 18. 4. *Ahaziah* commands a Captain and his Fifty to apprehend *Elijah*, only for pronouncing that Sentence which God passed against him; *Elijah* not only refuseth to come down, but to vindicate his Commission, *commands fire from Heaven to consume the Messengers,* 2 *Kings* 1. 10. In our Christian Stories we find *Mannel* and *Georgius* highly commended, for refusing to be instrumental in the murder of *Augusta*. And in Prophane, we have likewise two notable Examples of such who have refused to obey their Princes in their unlawful Commands; the one of *Papinianus*, that great Lawyer, who being commanded by *Caracalla* to justifie as well to the Senate as the people, the Paracide he had committed upon his own Brother Spartianus. *Geta*, readily answered, *That it was not so soon justified as done;* and for his refusal suffered Lib. 21. death. The other of *Helpodius*, both recorded by *Ammianus Marcellinus;* whereunto we may adde that of *Severus*, who would have no man exempted from punishment that should dare to take away the life of a Senator, (extrajudicially, as I suppose) though at Vid. Xiphillinum. the Emperors Command. *Stratocles* was worthily derided among the Athenians, for but offering at a Law, whereby whatsoever should please King *Demetrius*, should be reputed as Lib. 3. pious towards God, and just amongst men. *Pliny* in his Epistle to *Minutius* labours to make it appear, That the very ministry or execution of unlawful commands is sinful. For as *Tertullian* speaks, *Plus cæditur qui jubet, quando nec obsequitur qui excusatur; Surely he that commands things unjust is severely punishable, when he that but executes them cannot be excused.* Those Civil Laws which do easily pardon venial sins, are also very favourable to those who are inforced either to sin, or to disobey; and yet they are not favourable to all alike. For where the crimes are foul, and such as Nature by a secret instinct seems to abhor, they shew no favour at all. But where the offence appears not to be heinous, by any natural interpretation, but by Logical inferences may be proved to be so, there they wisely vouchsafe pardon. *Josephus* relates, *That the Jews that served under* Alexander the Great *could neither by stripes, nor any reproachful words, be inforced to carry Earth, or other materials, as the rest of the Souldiers did, towards the repair of the Temple of* Belus, *which was in* Babylon. But examples more pertinent to our purpose are the Thebean Legion, whereof we have already spoken; and the Souldiers that served under *Julian*, whereof St *Ambrose* speaks thus, *Though the Emperour* Julian *were an Apostate, yet had he many Christians that served under him; to whom if had said, Draw out for the defence of the Commonwealth, they would instantly have obeyed; but if he should have said, March out against the Christians,* tunc agnoscebant Imperatorem Cœli, *then they would have acknowledged no King but the King of Heaven.* The like we read of those Executioners, who being converted to Christianity, chose rather to dye themselves than to execute the Sentence of death pronounced against Christians. Now the Case is the very same, whensoever any man is perswaded that the thing commanded is unjust; for to such a man it is so long unjust, until he can be convinced that it is otherwise.

Christian Souldiers under *Julian* the Apostate.

IV. But what if he doubteth.

But what if he be in doubt whether it be lawful or not, is he to suspend, or to obey? The most received opinion is, That he must obey. Neither should he be startled at that notable

notable Saying, *Quod dubitas, ne feceris*; *forbear if thou doubtest*. For he that contemplatively doubteth, may, as to his practical judgment, not doubt at all; because he may be confident that in doubtful Cases he is bound to obey his Superiours. And indeed that this distinction of a twofold judgment is of necessary use in many actions, it cannot be denyed. The Civil Laws, not only of the Romans, but of other Nations, do not only indemnifie obedience in such a Case, but will admit of no civil action against them that do it in obedience. *Many Magistrates* (saith St. *Chrysostome*) *we have heard of, who being accused of unjust murthers have been punished. But no man ever questioned the Executioner, or made inquisition after him; for the necessity of obeying his Superiour, makes his fact excusable.* Is damnum dat qui jubet dare; *He*, say the Lawyers, *gives the damage that commands it*. And again, *Ejus vero nulla culpa est, cui parere necesse est*; *Neither can the fault be properly his, who being commanded must obey*. And again, *Necessitas potestatis excusat*; *That which is inforced on us by a power above us, is pardonable*. *Aristotle* himself, among those who do unjust things, but not unjustly, reckons the Servant of a wicked Master. For he is said to do unjustly from whom the action doth originally proceed. Now because in a Servant there is no full deliberative power; therefore the Servant, though he do that which is unjust, yet in doing that only which he is commanded, he doth not unjustly. According to that Proverbial Saying, *Nicom. 5. Injustum facere, sed non injuste.*

Dimidia virtute caret servire coactus;

He wants one half of goodness that must serve.

And that also,

One half of humane reason God withdraws
From those who live under anothers Laws.

And that which *Philo* makes use of,

If serve thou dost, what's reason unto thee?

Ulpian out of *Celsus* saith, *Servum nihil deliquisse, qui Domino jubenti obtemperavit*; *The Servant is not to blame, whilst he doth but what his Lord commands him.* So in another place, *Velle non creditur qui obsequitur Imperio Patris vel Domini*; *It is not believed to be his own act, if he do it in obedience either to his Father or Master.* *Mithridates* freely dismiss'd the Servants of *Attilius* without any punishment at all, though they were found guilty of the murder intended upon him. Neither would he punish the Children of those that had rebelled against him, because they were compelled to Rebellion by the Commands of others. *Themisthius* in his Ninth Oration observes, and that truly, *That Princes have always the resemblance of reason, as Souldiers the like of anger.* The like is observed by *Tacitus*, *God hath allotted unto Princes the faculty of judgment, but unto Subjects he hath left only the glory of obedience.* And as the same *Tacitus* relates, *The Son of* Piso *was by* Tiberius *acquitted of the crime of sedition, because what he did was by his Fathers command, whom he durst not disobey.* Servus herilis Imperii non Censor est, sed Minister; *The Servant is not to sit as Judge of his Masters Commands to dispute them, but to obey them.* But in this case of War let us hear what S[t] *Augustine* saith, *If a good man shall happen to war under a King though sacrilegious, he may, being commanded, fight with a good conscience, if observing the order of his Countries peace, he be either assured that what he is commanded is not repugnant to the Law of God, or doubtful whether it be or not; so that haply as the iniquity of the command may render the King guilty, so the necessity of obeying those commands for Orders sake, may likewise render the Souldier innocent.* And again, *If a Souldier under lawful Command shall in obedience thereunto kill a man, by the Laws of his City he is free from murther; nay, unless he do it, he shall be held as a Traitor to his own Country. But if he shall do it of his own accord, or without command, he shall be guilty of murder. That very Law that will punish him if he do it without command, will likewise punish him if he do it not being commanded.* And from hence ariseth that so generally received opinion, I mean as to Subjects, That a War may be just on both sides; that is, in respect of them it may be on both sides void of injustice, whereunto the Poet had respect when he said, *Annal. l. 3. De Controv. l. 3. c. 9. Cont. Faustum, lib. 22. c. 74. De Civit. Dei lib. 1. c. 26.*

——*Quis justius induat Arma*
Scire nefas——

——Who hath the juster Cause
It's hard to know——

Yet

Yet is not this opinion so generally received, but that it meets with some difficulty. For Pope *Adrian* defended the contrary; which may be confirmed not by that Argument precisely which he urgeth, but by this, which seems to be more forcible, namely, That he that doubts contemplatively, ought in his active judgment to chuse the safer part, which is, To abstain from War. The Esseni. The *Esseni* are highly commended, for *that amongst other things they bound themselves by Oath, To hurt no man, though they were commanded.* In imitation of whom the Pythagoreans did wholly abstain from War, as *being the Ringleader to destruction, commanding murder as by a Law.* Neither will it much avail to say for the other opinion, *That it is dangerous to disobey:* For whilst both are uncertain, (for if the War be unjust, it is no act of disobedience to avoid it) he is not to be blamed that chuseth the safest. But our disobedience in such things hath in its own nature less of evil than murther, especially of so many Innocents. It is storied by the Ancients, That when *Mercury* (being accused for killing of *Argus*) excused himself, for that he did it at the command of *Jupiter*; the rest of the Gods, notwithstanding, durst not acquit him: No more doth *Martial Pothinus*, an Officer of *Mark Antony*'s, when he saith,

> *Antoni tamen est pejor, quam Causa Pothini:*
> *Hic facinus Domino praestitit, ille sibi.*

> Worse than *Pothinus*'s Case is *Antony*'s;
> This for himself, that for his Lord doth dye.

Nor will that be of much greater moment which some men urge to the contrary, namely, That in case we admit that every private person may have liberty to judge of the justness of the War, and accordingly either yield or deny their obedience, the Commonwealth would soon be destroyed; because for the most part it cannot be expedient for the State, that the reasons of their counsels should be communicated to the Vulgar. For although this may be true where the causes of the War are suasory only, yet not where the War is justifiable; for there the causes thereof should be published unto all, that every man may judge of them, and be satisfied in them. What *Tertullian* sometimes said, perhaps too confusedly, of Laws in general, may very appositely be said of these of War; *No Subject so faithfully observes a Law, as he that knows the reason of that Law. For every Law ought to give testimony of its own integrity, to those from whom it requires obedience. On the contrary,* Suspecta Lex est, quæ probari se non vult; improba si non probata, dominetur: *That Law that will not endure the tryal, is held suspected; as that which being disapproved, yet exacts obedience, is held as wicked.* Thus when *Ulysses* endeavoured to perswade *Achilles* to join with the Grecian Princes in a war against the Trojans, *Achilles* urgeth them to declare the cause:

Papin.

> *What cause* Greece *hath so great a War to wage,*
> *Declare, whereby thou maist encrease our rage.*

And hence it is that *Theseus* in the same Poet thus encourageth his Souldiers,

> *Go, and fight boldly in a Cause so just.*

For as *Propertius* well observ'd, *The justice of the Cause cannot but heighten the spirits and inflame the indignation of a Souldier, whose courage droops so, that he grows ashamed of his Arms when his Cause is nought.* Josephus. *Herod* in his Oration to the Jews, after the slaughter in *Arabia*, thus bespeaks them, *I am willing to shew you how justly I have undertaken this War, being provoked thereunto by the reproaches of our enemies; which being known unto you, must needs heighten your courage to a revenge.* It is very often verified what the Panegyrist observed, *So prevalent, even amongst Armies, is a good Conscience, that the Victory seems properly to belong, not to the numbers or valour of the men, but to the justness and equity of the Cause.* And so some Learned Men have interpreted that of *Gen.* 14. 14. as if *Abraham* had before the Fight instructed his Servants fully in the justice of his Quarrel. And certainly the denunciation of War ought to be publick, and the cause express'd, that the whole Race of Mankind may judge of the equity of it. Prudence indeed, as *Aristotle* notes, is a Vertue proper to Princes; but Justice belongs to men as they are men. And therefore the reasons of their counsels as Princes are not to be communicated, but the reasons of their actions as men may be proclaimed. These things considered, we conclude with Pope *Adrian*, That where the Subject doth not only doubt the lawfulness of the War, but by very probable Arguments is induced to believe that it is unjust, especially if that War be offensive, and not defensive; *he is bound to abstain.* Nay, very probable it is, That the Executioner, whose Office it is to execute the penalty of the Law upon a condemned Malefactor, should be throughly informed in the merits of his Cause, either by being present at the whole Tryal, or by hearing the confession of the person condemned; that so he may be convinced that he whom he puts to death, hath by the Law deserved it, which in some places is observed. Neither can there any more probable reason be assigned for that Hebrew Law, whereby it was provided, That when a Malefactor was to be stoned, the Witnesses should go before the people, and cast the first stone at him. (Deut. 17. 7.) And for this Cause it was that the Kings Guards refused to fall upon the Priests of *Nob* at *Saul*'s command, (1 Sam. 22. 17.) being throughly convinced both of the sanctity of their Order, and of the equity of their Cause. And for this very reason it was, that the third Captain, being sent by *Ahaziah* unto *Elijah*, would not lay violent hands upon him. (2 Kings 1. 17.) And for the same reason it was that many publick Executioners amongst the Jews, being converted to Christianity, renounced their Offices, as being very dangerous; if we may give credit to the Martyrology, and to venerable *Bede*. (*Lib.* 1. *c.* 7.)

V. Extraordinary Taxes to be exacted, instead of obedience in this Case.

But in case the Subjects minds are not satisfied concerning the equity of the Cause by their Princes Declaration, then 'tis the Office of a good Magistrate rather to impose some extraordinary Taxes upon them, than to compel them to serve him in his Wars unsatisfied; especially when he may be supplied with men otherwise. Now whether these Souldiers do serve him with a good or evil intention, is no matter; for a good Prince may make use of both, as God himself doth of Satan and his Disciples, as Instruments to bring about his own most Sovereign purpose: or as a poor man may and doth make use of Jews and Extortioners to supply his present wants, and that without sin. Nay, though there be no doubt of the lawfulness of the War, yet it is not fit that Christians should be compelled to fight against their wills; seeing that to abstain from War, even then when it is in it self lawful, hath always been required of Church-men and Penitentials to preserve them in the greater sanctity, and is, in all others, many ways commendable. When *Celsus* upbraided the Christians for refusing to go to war, *Origen* apologized for them thus, *To those who being Unbelievers would inforce us to fight for the Commonwealth, and to destroy men, we shall give this Answer, That even their own Idol-Priests, and those that attend upon the service of their reputed Gods, do keep themselves unstained with humane blood, that so they may offer up their Sacrifices for the whole Nation with clean and unpolluted hands: Neither in case there should arise a War, are these men to be listed in their Armies. And if this be not done without reason, how much more may they be said after their manner to fight, who being Priests to the Most High God, endeavour to preserve themselves free from bloud and rapine; that so, whilst others are polluted with spoil and slaughter, they may wrestle with God himself by constant and incessant prayers for the welfare of them that make war justly, and for the safety of them that govern righteously.* Wherefore *Origen* calls all Christians Priests, by the example of the Holy Scriptures. (*Apoc.* 1. 6. 1 Pet. 2. 5.)

VI. When Subjects may justly engage in an unjust War.

But yet I believe that a Case may so fall out, that in a War not only doubtful, but manifestly unjust, it may be just for Subjects in some measure to defend themselves. For seeing that no enemy, though prosecuting a just War, can have any true and internal right to kill such Subjects as are innocent, and no ways accessary to the War, unless it be either for necessary defence, or by consequence, and not intentionally; (for such Subjects are not liable to punishment) it follows, That if it evidently appears that the enemy comes with a full purpose not to spare the lives of such hostile Subjects, when with safety to himself he may, then those Subjects may by the Law of Nature defend themselves; which right neither doth the Law of Nations take from them: neither will we say, That such a War is on both sides lawful; for we dispute not here concerning the legality of the War, but of a certain and determinate action in the War, which action (though it proceed from one that otherwise hath a sufficient right to make war, yet) is unjust, and may therefore be justly repelled.

The End of the Second Book.

BOOK

Hugo Grotius OF THE RIGHTS OF WAR and PEACE.

BOOK III.

CHAP. I.

Of certain General Rules, ſhewing what by the Law of Nature may be lawfull in War, wherein alſo he treats both of Fraud and Lies.

I. The order and method of the Book following.
II. The firſt Rule; whatſoever is neceſſary to the end is lawfull in War, explained.
III. The ſecond Rule; A Right in War may ariſe as well from Cauſes ſubſequent, as from the beginning of the War.
IV. The third Rule; that in War, ſome things may be done indirectly without injury, which if by themſelves, and intentionally done, were unlawfull with a caution.
V. What may lawfully be done to ſuch as ſupply the enemy with things needful; this explained.
VI. Whether in War Fraud be lawfull.
VII. That Fraud in its negative act is not of it ſelf unlawful.
VIII. Fraud in its poſitive act is either by ſuch outward acts, as admit of ſeveral conſtructions, or by ſuch as ſignifie as it were by arguments; fraud in the former ſenſe lawfull.
IX. Of that in the latter ſenſe, the queſtion is difficult.
X. The uſe of words in another ſenſe than that wherein we know they are underſtood, not always unlawfull.
XI. The form of a Lye as it is unlawfull, conſiſts in the repugnancy it hath with anothers Right; this explained.
XII. That it is lawfull to ſpeak that which is falſe to Children and Madmen.
XIII. So alſo when he is deceived to whom our ſpeech is not directed, and whom without ſpeech we may lawfully deceive.
XIV. And when we are aſſured, that he to whom we ſpeak is willing to be ſo deceived.
XV. And when he that ſpeaks exerciſeth that Supereminent Power that he hath over his own Subjects:
XVI. Or haply when the life of an innocent perſon, or ſomewhat that is equal unto it, cannot otherwiſe be preſerved.
XVII. That it is lawfull by falſe ſpeaking to deceive an enemy; by whom aſſerted.
XVIII. This not to be extended to words, promiſſory.
XIX. Nor to that which we affirm upon Oath.
XX. But it is more generous, and more agreeable to our Chriſtian ſimplicity to abſtain from falſehood, even to our enemies.
XXI. That it is not lawfull for us to compel another to do that which is lawfull for us to do, but not for him.
XXII. It may notwithſtanding be lawfull for us to make uſe of his ſervice, that freely offers it.

WHo may make War, and for what Cauſes, we have ſeen: It follows that we enquire what in War may be lawfull, how far forth, and by what means we may proſecute it: which we are to inſpect either ſimply, or in reference to ſome antecedent promiſe or agreement. Simply in it ſelf, and that firſt, according to what is juſtifiable by the Law of Nature, and then accord- I. The order and method of this Book.

ing

ing to what is agreeable to the Law of Nations. And in the first place, let us see what is lawfull by the Law of Nature.

II. Things necessary to the End, lawful in War.

First then, as we have often said before, in Morals, those things that conduce to the End, do receive their true intrinsick value from the End; wherefore whatsoever is necessary to the End, that is to receive or recover his own Right, (taking the word *Necessary* not physically but morally,) that we are understood to have a Right unto. A Right, I say, strictly so called, as namely, it signifies a Power or Faculty of doing in the sole respect of Society: wherefore if I cannot otherwise preserve my life, it is lawfull for me by what force soever to repell him that would take it away, though haply, he that attempts it be without fault. Because this Right of defending mine own life doth not properly arise from another mans sin, but from the Right that Nature hath granted unto me to defend my self: whereby also I am empowered to take away from another that whereby my life will otherwise be certainly endangered, without any respect at all had to his sin; and to possess my self of it, not as its right owner, for this is not indulged unto me for that end, but to keep it so long as is necessary for mine own security. So by the Law of Nature, I have a Right to take away from another that which he hath formerly taken from me; or if that cannot easily be done, yet to take that which is equivalent unto it; as also for the recovery of my just debt: and from hence will also ensue Propriety or Dominion, because that breach that is made in Equality, cannot otherwise be repaired. So where a punishment is justly due, there all manner of Force and Violence is Lawful and Just, if that punishment cannot be had without it: And so whatsoever is a part of that punishment, as the destruction of Corn, Cattel, the firing of Houses, Towns, Cities, and the like, are also just, so long as they exceed not in measure, but keep proportion with the offence.

See second Book, *Chap.* 2. §. 10.

III. A Right in War may arise from some subsequent Cause in its prosecution.

Secondly, we must know, that what is our Right is not to be adjudged by the first cause of the War only, but from other emergent causes which arise in the prosecution of it; so we have seen in our Courts of Justice, after a Cause hath been well argued, a new Right hath often arose to a Party which was not before thought on. Thus they that shall associate with him that invades me, be they either Associates, or Subjects, do give me a Right to defend my self against them. So also they that shall joyn themselves with others in a War that is unjust, especially if they may or ought to know it to be so, do oblige themselves to repair the damage, and to pay the charges of the War, because they have caused it by their own default. So likewise they that rashly thrust themselves into a War undertaken without any probable Reason, deserve to be punished according to the injustice of their actions: For so long doth *Plato* approve of the War, *Donec hi qui sontes sunt cogantur insontibus male affectis, pœnas dare*; *Until the guilty party be compelled to give satisfaction to those who being innocent, have been injured by them.*

IV. Some things may be gained without injury, indirectly, which purposely was not lawfull.

We must observe also in the third place, that whilst we execute the Right that Nature give us, either to defend our selves, or to recover our own, many things do indirectly and beyond our purpose accrew unto us, whereunto we could otherwise have no Right at all. How this Rule holds in cases of our own necessary defence we have elsewhere shewn. So in the recovery of what is our own, if we cannot get just as much as was ours, we may take more, but on condition that we restore the surplusage to the Right Owner. So a Ship wherein there are many Pyrats, or an House wherein are many Thieves, may be battered down or sunk, though it be to the endangering of many Infants, Women, and such like innocent persons that were accidentally mixt amongst them. But this must ever be observed, that *Non semper omni ex parte licitum est, quod juri, strictè sumpto, congruit*; *We are not always to extend our Right to its extremity, for not every thing that is strictly due, is always and altogether lawfull.* For sometimes our compassion towards the Innocent, and our Charity towards our Neighbours, will not suffer us to exercise our full Right: wherefore in such cases we ought to be circumspect, and (as much as in us lies) to foresee, and to avoid all such contingencies, which may fall out beyond that, which we principally aim at, unless the Good that we aim at be far greater than the Evil that we fear; or unless where the Good and Evil being equal, our hopes of obtaining the Good be greater, than our fears of the Evil can be, whereof prudence is the best Judge; yet so, that whensoever the case shall happen to be doubtfull, we always incline to that part which provideth rather for anothers safety than our own, as being much the safer, and if an errour, yet it falls on the right hand. *Let the tares grow up with the wheat,* (saith our best Master) *lest while ye pluck up them, ye pull up the wheat also.* Multos occidere & indiscretos incendii & ruinæ potentia est; *To destroy whole multitudes,* saith *Seneca, without distinction, argues a power proper to the sudden irruption of fire, or the fall of some great building,* rather than the rage of a man. And how much sorrow and penitence such a rash act cost the Emperour *Theodosius,* upon the admonition of St *Ambrose,* Histories will inform us. And although Almighty God doth so sometimes, yet ought that to be no example to us, because of that full and absolute Right of Dominion that he hath over us, which he hath not granted unto us to have

Mat. 13. 29.

one

one over another; and yet, even God himſelf, who is Lord Paramount over all Mankind, doth often ſpare a World of wicked and ungodly men for a very few that are good, thereby manifeſting his equity, as he is a Judge; as ſufficiently appears by that ſweet Colloquy between him and *Abraham* concerning *Sodom*: by which general rules, it is eaſily collected, how far our Right extends in War againſt our Enemies by the Law of Nature. Gen. 18. 23. &c.

V. What we may do againſt them that ſupply our Enemies with what they want.

And here another Queſtion is uſually ſtarted, namely, what we may lawfully do to thoſe who are not Enemies, or at leaſt will not be ſo reputed, and yet do daily ſupply our Enemies with ſuch things as they need: Great conteſts have antiently been, and now are about this matter; ſome ſtifly maintaining the rigour of the War, others as earneſtly contending for the liberty of Trade and Traffick. But firſt we muſt diſtinguiſh of the things wherewith the Enemy is ſupplyed; for ſome things there are that are of no uſe but in War, as Arms and Ammunition; ſome things there are which are of no uſe at all in War, as things ſerving for pleaſure only: And laſtly, ſome things there are that are uſeful both in Peace and War; as money, Victuals, Apparel, Ships, and materials for Shipping. (At *Athens* it was prohibited to export Flax, Bottles, Timber, Wax, Pitch, and the like.) Concerning things not uſeful but in War, it is true what *Amalaſuintha* told the Emperour *Juſtinian*, *He is to be eſteemed as an Enemy, that ſupplies the Enemy with things neceſſary for War*: as to the ſecond ſort of things there is no juſt cauſe of complaint. So *Seneca* thought, *The favour of a Tyrant I may purchaſe, in caſe that which I give him, do neither increaſe his power to do miſchief, nor confirm that which he already hath; for ſuch things as theſe a man may give without encreaſing the common calamity. I will not*, ſaith he, *ſupply him with money whereby he may keep his Army in pay; but if he require Marble, Perfumes, or coſtly Apparel, theſe being but the fuel of his luſt, can hurt no man but himſelf: Soldiers and Arms will I not furniſh; but if he will accept of the beſt Artiſts I have, to make Scenes for Masks and Plays, I ſhall willingly part with them.* (Thus did *Hyram* gladly furniſh King *Solomon* with Timber, and all kind of curious Artificers, that might encreaſe the delight he took in ſumptuous buildings, thereby to divert him from purſuing with his vaſt Riches his Fathers conqueſts in *Syria*.) So alſo St. *Ambroſe*, to contribute to him that conſpires againſt his own Country, is no commendable liberality. As to the third ſort of things which are of doubtful uſe, we muſt diſtinguiſh of the preſent ſtate of the War. For if I cannot defend my ſelf, unleſs I do intercept thoſe things which are ſent to mine Enemy, neceſſity will give me a good Right to them; yet upon this condition, that I make reſtitution, unleſs there be ſufficient cauſe to the contrary. Again, if the ſupply that is ſent in, do hinder the execution of my defence of the deſign, and he that ſends it might have known that it would ſo do: As for example, If I have beſieged a Town, and blocked up its Ports, ſo that I may juſtly expect the ſurrender of it, or a Peace; in this Caſe, he that ſhall knowingly ſend in relief, is bound to give me ſatisfaction for the loſs I ſuſtain thereby, no leſs than he that takes a Priſoner out of Cuſtody that owes me a juſt Debt, or inſtructs him how to make his eſcape thereby to defraud me: and proportionably to that loſs I ſuſtain I may ſeize his goods, and poſeſs them as mine own till I am ſatsfied; and if the damage be not already given, but intended only, then have I a Right by the detention of thoſe ſupplies, to compel him that ſent them to give ſecurity, either by pledges, hoſtages, or the like, that he will not for the future ſend any more ſupplies to the beſieged. But in Caſe the wrongs done me by mine Enemy, be manifeſtly unjuſt, and that he by thoſe ſupplies, do abet and encourage him in his unjuſt War; then he ſhall not only be bound to repair my loſs civilly, but alſo criminally, as he that reſcues a notorious malefactor, in the very preſence of a Judge: and for this Cauſe it is lawful for me to do unto him agreeable to his offence, according to thoſe rules which we have already ſet down for puniſhments. And ſo long as we contain our ſelves within theſe bounds, we may make War upon him; and for this Cauſe do they that make War uſually, ſend out Declarations, and Remonſtrances to other Nations, as well to inſinuate unto them the equity of their Cauſe, as alſo what probable hopes they have to recover their Right. Now the reaſon why we refer this matter to the Law of Nature is, becauſe we find nothing certainly determined in Hiſtories by the voluntary Law of Nations, as to it. There is a Book written in Italian, Intituled, *Liber conſulatus Maris*, concerning the Government of the Seas, wherein are recited the Conſtitutions of the Emperours of *Greece* and *Germany*, the Kings of *France*, *Spain*, *Syria*, *Cyprus*, the *Baleares*, *Venetians*, and *Genoeſe*; wherein are handled two hundred ſeventy four Queſtions upon this Subject, where we ſhall find it adjudged, That if the Ship with its freight be both the Enemies, then there is no doubt but both are lawful prize: If the Ship belong to ſuch as are at peace with us, and the goods to our Enemies, we may enforce them to put into any of our Allies or our Ports, there to unlade the goods; yet ſo, that we pay the Maſter of the Ship for the freight of them. But in Caſe the goods belong to our Friends, and the Ship to our Enemies, then is the Ship lawful prize, and to be agreed for; which if refuſed, they may be compelled into any Harbour of our Friends, and withal to pay us for the freight of thoſe goods. In the Year 1438. There being War between the Hollanders and the City of *Lubeck*, with other Cities Confederate, ſituate upon

Procop. Goth l. 1.

De Off. lib. 1. c. 30.

upon the Baltick Sea, and the River *Albis*, it was in *Holland* adjudged in full Senate, That the Goods found in an Enemies Ship, if it did appear that they belonged to others, were no lawfull prize, and this was there from thence established for a Law; and so pleaded by the Danish King in the year 1597. who thereupon sent his Embassadors into *Holland* to assert his Freedom to transport his Goods into *Spain*, notwithstanding the bloody War which the *Hollanders* then had with the *Spaniards*. The like hath always been permitted by the *French* to any Nation that were at Peace with them, and that so freely, that oftentimes the Enemies have in other mens names transported their Goods without damage; as appears by an Edict made 1543. Chapter the 42. and by another made 1584, wherein it is provided, that their Friends might freely traffick whither they pleased, so as it were with their own Ships, Men and Goods, and that those Goods were not *Belli Instrumenta*, Arms, nor Ammunition for War, whereby their Enemies might be made stronger. But in case they did so, then it might be lawfull to seize them to their own use, paying a valuable price for them. Wherein two things are observable, first, That by these Laws, Ammunition for War was not held as lawfull prize, much less were other innocent Merchandizes obnoxious to this danger. I cannot deny but that these Northern Nations have sometimes usurped anothers Right, but not constantly, being urged thereunto rather by present necessity, then by a perpetual equity. The *English* upon pretence of their War would not permit the *Danes* Freedom of Traffick, whence arose that War between those two Nations, whereby the *English* were compelled to pay a Tribute to the *Danes*, which was called the *Dane* penny, which though the Cause were changed, yet the name of it continued till the Reign of *William* the Conquerour, as *Thuanus* records it in the year 1589 Again, we find it recorded as well by *Rhedanus* in his History of *Holland* in the year 1575, as by Master *Cambden* in his History of Queen *Elizabeth* in the year following, That that most Wise Queen sent her Embassadors, Sr *William Winter* and Secretary *Beale* to Remonstrate, That the *English* could not endure that the *Hollanders* in the heat of their War then with *Spain*, should detain their Ships trading in the *Spanish* Ports. And when the *English* and the *Hollanders* being both at War with *Spain*, did disturb the Cities of *Germany* in their traffick with the *Spaniards*, with what a disputable Right they did it, appears by the eager dissertations of both Nations, which are worthy our perusal for the deciding of this Controversie. And it is observable, that the *English* themselves do in their writings acknowledge no less, whereas they principally insist upon these two Arguments to defend their Cause; namely, That the *Germans* did furnish the *Spaniards* with Instruments of War: and secondly, that it had been mutually agreed in Ancient Treaties between both Nations, That it should not be lawfull for them so to do. The like agreement we find afterwards made between the *Hollanders* and their Associates, and the *Lubeckers* and theirs, in the year 1593. That neither the one nor the other should permit the Subjects of their Enemies to traffick within their Dominions, or should aid them with either Men, Money, Ships or Victuals. And afterwards, namely, in the year 1617. It was agreed between the Kings of *Denmark* and *Sweden*, That the *Dane* should obstruct all manner of Traffick with the City of *Dantzick*, being then at Enmity with the *Swedes*; and not only so, but that they should not suffer any Merchandizes to pass through the *Sound*, or the *Baltick* Sea to any of the *Swedes* Enemies; for which the King of *Denmark* was to receive other Priviledges and advantages from the King of *Sweden*. But these are particular Contracts, from whence no general Rule can be inferred. Neither did the Cities of *Germany* only blame the *English* for denying them freedom of Traffick with their Enemies: But the *Polanders* also complained against them in the year 1597, as *Cambden* relates, That the Law of Nations was violated, because they were molested in their Commerce with *Spain*, because at that time the *Spaniards* had War with *England*: But the *French* having made Peace with *Spain*, being sollicited by Queen *Elizabeth*, (who was still at Enmity with the *Spaniard*) that it might be lawfull for the *English* to search their Ships for Arms and Ammunition, would not admit so much as this, alledging that it was but a pretence for rapine, and to disturb traffick. So in the League that the *English* made with the *Hollanders* and their Associates, it was agreed, That other Nations whom it concern'd to give check to the swelling Power of the *Spanish* Monarchy, should be sollicited to forbid all Commerce with *Spain*, which if they did not voluntarily, then that they would permit their Ships to be searched, that no Arms or Instruments for War might be thither imported; but beyond this, neither were the Goods or Ships detained, nor any hurt done under that pretence to such as traffick'd peaceably. Nay, when in the same year several *Hamburgers* were taken laden mostly with Instruments of War, those only were challenged by the *English* as prize; but for the rest of the Commodities they paid the just value. But the *French* when their Ships were seized and confiscate by the *English*, because bound for *Spain*, did declare unto Queen *Elizabeth* that they would not suffer it. It is fit therefore, as I have said, That there should be Remonstrances and publick Declarations, forbidding Traffick with our Enemies, before we seize their Goods as Prize. So Queen

Elizabeth

Elizabeth in favour to the King of *France*, against the Spaniard and those of the Holy League, sent out her Proclamation commanding that no man should carry Victuals or Provisions for War out of *England*, into any of the Ports of *France* possest by the Leaguers, or traffick with them upon pain of High Treason. And afterwards the War waxing hot, it was publickly commanded upon the like pain, That no man should carry Corn, Munition, or Provision for Shipping into *Spain*, because he professed himself an Enemy to *England*, and refused to confirm the Ancient League betwixt their predecessors. Neither is it necessary, that any Nation should be restrained from their freedom of Traffick by such Declarations; but it is left to every Nations choice to do as their own occasions and advantages shall prompt them to, there being nothing found in Histories, that may probably infer any certain determination of this controversie amongst Nations: wherefore such Declarations though published, have been sometimes observed, and sometimes not, accordingly as it stood with the respective advantages of several Nations. And for this Cause we refer the decision of this Question to the Law of Nature. When the *Hansetowns* made sore complaints against Queen *Elizabeth*, upon Her taking of Sixty Hulks Trafficking to *Spain*, then in open War with *England*, as if their Ancient Priviledges had been broken: She answered, That she had forewarned them, that they should not carry any provision for War to the Enemies of the Realm of *England*; and that carrying them she had lawfully taken them, and could do no other unless she would wilfully draw destruction upon her self and People; That Priviledges were but Private Laws, which are not to be maintained against the Publick Safety, which is the highest Law: and this she asserts to be the Law of Nations. The Carthaginians we read sometimes took the Romans Prisoners, who had carried such Warlike Provisions to their Enemies, but yet upon demand they set them at liberty. But *Demetrius* being possest of *Attica*, and having strictly begirt *Athens* both by Sea and Land, taking a Ship that was attempting to relieve it (being now ready to yield) hanged the Master of the Ship together with the Pylot; whereby others being deterred from the like attempt, the City was yielded unto him, as *Plutarch* relates in the life of *Demetrius*. Not much unlike unto this, was that which the same *Plutarch* in his Mithridatick War testifies of *Pompey*, *That he placed Guards upon the* Bosphorus, *so that if any Merchants sailed through it, they were if taken, put to death.*

> See an example of a Declaration made by the English in *Cambden* about the years 1591. and 1598.

> *Vid. Thuan. An.* 1589. *lib.* 96. *Cambd. An.* 1589. & 1595.

> *Cambd. An.* 1595.

> Many things to this purpose we may find in *Jo. Meursius* his Danish History *l.* 1. & 2. where the *Lubeckers* and the Emperour are for a free trade, the *Danes* against it.

VI. Whether fraud in War be lawful.

As to the manner of prosecuting War, it is generally granted, That Force and Terrour are the most proper ways: The Question is, Whether deceit be lawful. Both *Homer* and *Pindar* were of opinion, that an Enemy might be annoyed any way, by Fraud or Force, plainly or secretly, *clamve, palamve*: So *Virgil*,

Force or Deceit who in a Foe disputes.

No man was more famous for wisdom than *Solon*, yet he made use of both. So did *Fabius Maximus*, and is highly commended for it by *Silius*. For stratagems of War, none so celebrated as *Ulysses* amongst the Grecians; from whence *Lucian* makes this conclusion, that Deceit in War is praise-worthy. There is nothing so profitable in War as Fraud, saith *Xenophon*. *Bracidas* in *Thucydides* gives the greatest Honour unto him that overcomes his Enemy by craft and subtilty. *Hostes decipere & justum, & licitum*; *To over-reach an Enemy*, saith *Agesilaus* in *Plutarch*, *is both just and lawful.* So *Polybius*, *He that can circumvent his Enemy, by wiles and stratagems, deserves more Honour than he that overcomes him by plain force.* And from him *Silius* brings in *Corvinus* speaking thus,

> *Lib.* 15.

> *Lucian Phil. Xenoph. de Cyri Inst. lib.* 1. *Thucyd. lib.* 5. *Plut. Agesilaus.*

Bellandum est astu, levior laus in Duce dextra;

'Tis fraud, not force, commends a Captain most.

So also thought the severe Spartans, as *Plutarch* notes in the life of *Marcellus*; and therefore they offered more solemn Sacrifices to the Gods, for a Victory obtained by craft and policy, than for that which was gained by mere force. And herein it was that the same *Plutarch* commends *Lysander*, *because he used more craft than courage in destroying his Enemies*; with whom he compares *Sylla*, of whom this Character was given, *That he pieced to the Lyons skin the Foxes tail.* So likewise in that Encomium which he gives of *Philopœmen*, he inserts this, That being well instructed in the Cretensian Discipline, he did expedite that plain and generous way of fighting by wiles and stratagems. Thus *Ammianus* also, *Nullo discrimine virtutis ac doli, prosperi omnes laudari debent bellorum eventus*; *Without any distinction at all between craft or courage, all prosperous successes in War deserve commendation.* The Roman Lawyers accounted all fraud, whereby an Enemy was weakened, to be just and honest: And if a man could by any means delude the designs of his Enemy, whether it were by force or wit, he was to be encouraged. Neither amongst Divines doth S[t] *Augustine* differ in opinion from these Historians, as appears by his tenth Question on *Joshua*, *Cum justum bellum suscipitur, vi aperta pugnet quis aut insidiis, nihil ad justitiam interest*; *In case the War be just*, saith he, *it matters not to the justice of its prosecution, whether it be by force or policy.* Nay St. *Chry-*

> *Sup Josh. qu.* 10.

sostome

Sostome seems to give greater honour to those Generals that overcame their Enemies by subtilty, than to those who conquered them by pure valour. But there are opinions that seem to defend the contrary, some whereof we shall rehearse anon. The main hinge whereupon the Controversie hangs, is this, Whether deceit be universally Evil, for then it will follow, that we are not to do Evil that Good may come of it; or, Whether Deceit be to be ranked among such things as are not universally Evil in their own Nature, but that sometimes it may so happen that it may be Good.

VII. Fraud in its negative act not unlawfull.

Here therefore we are to observe, That some fraud consists in a negative act, and some in a positive. But in this question, I extend the word *Fraud* even unto those things which consist in the negative act, as *Labeo* did, who referr'd it unto that fraud which is not Evil, when a man by dissimulation preserves that which is either his own, or another mans. *Cicero* doubtless was very short in his expression, *when he laboured to explode simulation and dissimulation out of the world :* (*De Offic.* 3.) For seeing that we are not bound to reveal unto others, all that we either know, or would have; it will follow, That it is lawfull for us to dissemble some things before some men, that is, to hide from them somewhat of what we know, or of what we desire. *Licet occultare veritatem prudenter sub aliqua dissimulatione*; *The truth we may sometimes prudently conceal under some disguise*, saith S[t] *Augustine*; (*Lib. cont. Mendat. cap.* 10.) which we may do without being justly charged with lying : For as the same Author elsewhere speaks, *Aliud est mentiri, aliud verum occultare*; *It is one thing to lye, and another to conceal the truth.* As *Abraham* when he affirmed *Sarah* to be his Sister, did not therein deny that she was his Wife, but only concealed it. So S[t] *Augustine*, *Veritatem voluit celari, non mendacium dici*; *He was indeed willing that the truth should lie undiscovered, without telling a lye.* (Gen. 20.) Now if this be lawfull in others, surely it is necessary and unavoidable in Princes, as *Cicero* testifies in many places. A notable example whereof we have in the Prophet *Jeremiah*, (Jerem. 38.) where the Prophet being enquired of concerning the event of the siege, did at the Kings request prudently conceal it from the Nobles, alledging some other cause of their Conference, which notwithstanding was really true also. So *Abraham* told *Abimelech* true, when he said of *Sarah* that she was his Sister, that is, according to the custom of that speech among the Hebrews, his near Kinswoman; dissembling for that time, that she was his Wife.

VIII. Fraud in its positive acts distinguished.

But fraud which consists in a positive act, if in things, is called simulation; if in words, a lye. Some place the difference between these two in this, That words do naturally signifie the conceptions of our minds, but things not so : But on the contrary, words, of their own nature, and set aside from that sense which men have agreed to give them, signifie nothing, unless it be such an inarticulate and confused noise as pain and grief causeth us to make, which is more understood by the thing we suffer, than by the noise we utter. And if it be objected, that it is peculiar to the Nature of Man, above all other Creatures, That he is able to express the manifold conceptions of his mind unto others, to which end words and voices were invented,we do not deny it : Yet this also may be added, That such indications are not made by words only, but by becks, nods, and other signs made by the eyes, head or hand, as among such as are born dumb. (Thus *Pliny* testifies of the Æthiopians, (*Pliny lib.* 6. *cap.* 30.) *Quibusdam pro sermone, nutus, motusque membrorum est*; *That some of them instead of words, express their minds by various motions of their other members.*) Whether those becks, or other motions have naturally something common with the things signified, or whether they have a certain signification by agreement only. Consonant whereunto are those Ægyptian Hieroglyphicks, which as *Paulus* the Lawyer saith, signifie not words but things: for saith he, *It is not the figures of the letters, but the speech exprest by those letters that do oblige us so far forth as it is agreed on, That what is by any writing declared, shall be as binding, as what is exprest by word of mouth.* Where you must note, that the word *Placuit* is very emphatical, as shewing that that which gives such force and validity to words is consent and agreement. And here again we must have recourse unto that distinction, which we made use of to take away all ambiguity concerning this word, *the Law of Nations.* For we then said, that the Law of Nations signified, either that which was admitted of by every Nation without mutual obligation, or that which all Nations did mutually oblige themselves to observe. Now voices, nods, and such like indications of the mind, are admitted to signifie things by mutual obligation, which *Aristotle* calls κατὰ συνθήκην, according to agreement; whereof some are so universally agreed on to signifie such and such things, that all Nations are obliged so to understand them; which cannot be so generally understood of things. Whence it follows, that it is lawfull for me to do or use other acts, or things, though I do foresee that another man will conceive a false opinion of them : I speak of that which is intrinsick, and not of that which is accidental. And therefore we must give an instance, first of such a case wherein no detriment at all ensues; such was that of *Michal* when she deceived her Father, with an Image laid in stead of *David*. (1 Sam. 19. 16.) Thus our blessed Saviour seemed to his two Disciples, as if he would have travelled beyond *Emaus*; (Luke 24. 28.) and perhaps he intended so to do, unless they did

did importune him to abide with them, as God himself is said to will many things suppositively, which notwithstanding come not to pass, the condition being not fulfilled. And *Christ* himself made as though he would have passed by his Apostles as they were sailing on the Sea, that is, unless they should earnestly desire him to come up into their Ship. Another example may be given in St *Paul*, who doubtless when he circumcised *Timothy*, knew very well what construction the Jews would make of it, namely, That the Law of the Circumcision, though abolished by Christ, did still, even in the judgment of the Apostles, oblige the Children of *Israel*; whereas St *Paul*, dispensing with this errour, proposeth to himself another end, namely, That through that mistake he and *Timothy* might gain the advantage of a more free and friendly conversation with them. For the Ceremonial Law being abolished, neither did circumcision, by its first institution, any longer signifie a necessity of keeping that Law; neither was the evil of that errour, which from thence arose, and for a while continued, (though afterwards to be exploded) so great as was that good which *Paul* and *Timothy* then aimed at, which was a more facile insinuation of the Doctrine of the Gospel. The Greek Fathers do usually express this kind of simulation by the word οἰκονομία, signifying a dispensation. So *Chrysostome, This was no deceit nor hypocrisie, but a compliance or dispensation.* And again, upon that of St *Paul, To the Jews I became a Jew*, &c. he saith, *That St.* Paul, *to the end he might convert those that were really superstitious, at first appeared unto them to be so too, making an outward shew, as though he had been otherwise than what he was; he did such things as they did, but not with the same purpose and intention as they did.* And this is his meaning when he saith, *I became all things to all men, that I might save some.* Hither also we may refer that personated madness of King *David* in the Court of *Achish*. There is a notable Saying extant of *Clemens Alexandrinus*, who, describing the qualities of a good man, saith, *That some things he will do for his Neighbours sake, which otherwise he would not do.* Such was that act of the Romans, who when their City was besieged, threw great quantities of Bread from the Capitol into their Enemies Camp, (when in truth they had but little to spare) to the end that their enemies, despairing to take the City by Famine, might give over the Siege. Another example of such a simulation wherein the hurt or detriment that follows (setting aside the fraud) is lawful, we have in that feigned flight of *Joshua* before the Inhabitants of *Aye*, Josh. 8. which is very frequently practised by other Generals. For such a seeming flight is, questionless, lawful, as signifying nothing by consent or agreement, but according to the construction that the enemy will make of it, wherein, if they are deceived, they deceive themselves. And to this end also it is lawful for us to make use of our Enemies Armes, Colours, Garments, Sails, and the like, whereof we shall read in all Histories. For all these things every man hath liberty to make use of, though contrary to usual custom, at his own pleasure; because that very custome of using or wearing such or such a colour or fashion is in every mans particular choice, and is not appropriated to this or that Nation by common consent, and therefore obligeth none.

[Margin notes: Mark 6. 28. — Acts 16. 3. — In 1 Cor. 4. 6. — 1 Sam. 21. 12. — Josh. 8.]

IX. *Whether to ly be lawful to an Enemy.*

There is yet a more arduous Controversie concerning those notes or signs which men frequently use in their commerce one with another, of which sort the most proper and usual fraud is lying. Much may be found in Holy Writ against it, as *Prov.* 13. 5. *A good man hateth lying.* So *Prov.* 30. 8. *Remove from me all falshood and lies.* So the Psalmist, *Thou shalt destroy all those that speak lies*, Psal. 5. 7. And it was the charge of the Apostle to the *Colossians, Do not lye one to another*, Col. 3. 9. This opinion is very strenuously defended by St *Augustine*, and with him agree many, both Poets and Philosophers. Very well known is that of *Homer*,

Ille mihi invisus pariter cum faucibus Orci,
Cujus mens aliud condit quam lingua profatur.

Equal to Hell it self hateful be he,
Whose heart and tongue do always disagree.

And that of *Sophocles*,

Aliena vero proloqui nunquam decet:
At vera certam si cui pestem ferant,
Huic danda venia est, si facit quod non decet.

Uutruth to speak is an indecent thing;
Yet if to any, truth swift ruine bring,
A lye to him is not imputed sin.

And that of *Cleobulus*,

Mendacium odit quisquis animitus sapit.

He that sincerely wise doth lies detest.

Aristotle

Aristotle is on this point somewhat modest, *Simply*, saith he, *and in it self, lying is vile and reproachful, but truth fair and commendable.* But this, he saith, by it self considered, without any regard to circumstances. Yet doth not the contrary opinion want Advocates, and those of great authority. As first, In the Holy Scriptures, the examples of many good men, who though they did it upon very weighty occasions, yet are they not reproved upon record for it. Concerning which *Irenæus*, being so instructed by a certain Old Priest, gives us this Caution, *De quibus Scripturæ non increpant, sed simpliciter sunt positæ, nos non debemus fieri Accusatores*; *We ought not to be their Accusers, whose words or deeds the Scriptures do simply recite, but not blame.* Secondly, The declared opinions of many ancient Christians, as *Origen*, *Clemens*, *Tertullian*, *Lactantius*, *Chrysostome*, *Hierome*, *Cassianus*; yea, and of almost all Christian Writers, as St *Augustine* himself confesseth, herein only dissenting from them, *That he acknowledgeth it to be a very knotty question, full of intricacy, and by the learned variously disputed*; all which are his own words. Among Philosophers, the plain Assertors of this opinion are *Socrates*, and his two Disciples *Plato* and *Xenophon*; as also *Cicero*; and if we give credit to *Plutarch* and *Quintilian*, the Stoicks, who reckon this among the qualifications of a wise man, *To know where and when it is lawful to lye.* Neither doth *Aristotle* himself seem to dissent from them in some places, witness that Clause of his beforementioned [καθ' αὑτὸ] of it self, that is, commonly the thing considered in it self, without respect to other circumstances. For as *Andronicus Rhodius*, giving an instance in a Physician lying unto his Patient, saith, *He deceives indeed, but yet is no Deceiver*; and gives this reason for it, *Because his purpose and intention is not to deceive his Patient, but to preserve him.* And *Quintilian* before-mentioned, defending this opinion, saith, *That there are many things which are said to be either honest or dishonest, not simply from the fact, but from the Causes moving to that fact.* So *Diphilus*,

Plato de Rep. l. 1 & 2. & 5. Xen. lib. 4. Socrat. Plut. de Stoic. Contract. Quint. 12. 1. Arist. Nic. 7.3. l. 4. c. 8.

If by a lye mans life preserv'd may be,
What harm may thence ensue I cannot see.

When *Neoptolemus* in *Sophocles* asked *Ulysses*, Whether he were not ashamed to lye: *Ulysses* readily answered,

No, if our safety do thereon depend.

The like testimonies may be produced out of *Lisander* and *Euripides.* So in *Quintilian* also I read, *Nam & mendacium dicere, etiam sapienti aliquando concessum est*; *For it is no disparagement to a wise man sometimes to tell a lye.* *A wise man*, saith *Eustathius* upon *Homer*, *may upon a great occasion tell a lye.* And for confirmation of what he there saith, he produceth testimonies both out of *Herodotus* and *Isocrates.* There are some (saith *Donatus* upon *Terence*) that *writing concerning the Duties of a good man*, & ipsum fallere in tempore, rectum putant, *do esteem it a point of honesty sometimes to deceive.* And indeed he that would do some men good, cannot do it, unless he circumvent them; wherefore *Cicero* in his Oration for *Ligarius*, approves of such a lye as honest and charitable.

X. To use such words as may be taken in another sense, not always unlawful.

These so different opinions may haply be in part reconciled by that common distinction of lyes, taken in a stricter and in a larger sense. For we do not here take the word so largely as to comprehend all that falshood which sometimes is spoken through imprudence, as *Gellius* rightly distinguished between *mentiri, & mendacium dicere*; *To lye, and to speak that which is not truth.* But we take it here as it signifies an untruth, spoken knowingly, whereby we contradict the conceptions of our own minds, either in our understanding or our will. For whatsoever is first and immediately signified by either words or other notes, are the conceptions of our minds; wherefore he doth not lye, who though he do speak that which is false, yet conceives it (when he speaks it) to be true. But he that saith a thing is true, yet thinks it to be false, doth undoubtedly lye. For *ream linguam non facit nisi rea mens*; *The tongue is not made guilty, but by a guilty mind.* And as St *Augustine* speaks, *Quantum in ipso est, non fallit, sed fallitur*; *He that speaks an untruth, but thinks it to be true, doth not deceive, but is deceived.* And if so, then it will follow, That when any word or sentence will admit of divers significations, either by familiar use, or by the custome of art, or by any figurative expression that is intelligible; then if our inward meaning agree with any of these significations, it is not to be esteemed as a lye, though he to whom we speak is believed to understand it in a different sense. Thus did *Abraham* commune with his Servants subtilly, when he bad them to *tarry there whilst he and his Son Isaac went a little further to sacrifice*, promising *that they would both return*; which as then he intended not. But these captious and equivocal expressions are not rashly to be allowed; yet may they upon some occasions be justified: as in case we are thereby to instruct such as are committed to our charge, or to decline some pernicious questions whereby we may be insnared. Of the former Christ gives us an example in himself, when he said, *Our friend Lazarus sleepeth*; which the Apostles understood of *his taking rest in sleep.* So when he

De verbis Apost. Ser. 28.

Ambr. citat. à Gratian. l. 22. q. 2. post si quælioet.

John 11. 11.

he told the Jews, *That they would destroy the Temple, and in three days he would raise it up*; which he meant of his Body, but they of the material Temple. So again, when he promised his Apostles, *That they should sit on twelve Thrones, judging the twelve Tribes of Israel*; and *that they should drink new wine with him in his Fathers Kingdom*: He knew very well that they understood him as of a temporal Kingdom, whereof they were full of hopes, even unto the very Day of his ascension. And thus in another place *he speaks to the people in Parables, lest hearing they should understand*; that is, unless they should bring with them such reverence and attention as was requisite, in order to the right receiving of his pure Doctrine. As to the latter use of these Amphibologies, amongst prophane Authours *Tacitus* will furnish us with the example of one *Lucius Vitellius*, who being urged by *Narcissus* to unriddle himself, and to speak the truth plainly, could never prevail; but still he gave ambiguous and doubtful Answers, such as might incline them to that whereunto he would have them led. So the same *Tacitus* in another place, speaking of *Tiberius*, saith, *Ita compositus, ut ex eventu rerum adversa abnueret, vel prospera agnosceret*; *He did so artificially compose his Answers, that expecting the event, he might either renounce the Plot if it succeeded not, or owne it if it prospered.* There is a very notable Saying among the Hebrew Doctors, *Si quis norit uti perplexiloquio, recte; sin minus, taceat*: *If a man being put to answer insidious questions, can either prevent or avoid them by Amphibologies, let him; if not, let him not answer at all.* For as S[t] *Chrysostome* observes, *He is not to be reckoned as a Deceiver that useth Amphibologies to a good end, but he that useth them to a bad.* But yet, in some Cases, to use them is not allowable, as namely, when either the honour of God, or our charity to our Neighbour, when our reverence to our Superiours, or the nature of the thing it self whereof we treat, requires that we should clearly unmask our selves, and declare the truth; then to use these Amphibologies is not only indecent, but impious. So in Contracts, we have already said, Whatsoever the nature of the Contract requires to be understood, should be declared. So of Laws which should be the Guides of mens manners, it is required that they should be exprest in the plainest and most significant words that may be found. Now in the Case of Contracts may that of *Cicero* be fitly understood, *That lies ought to be excluded out of all humane commerce*; which he seems to have borrowed out of that old Attick Law, κατὰ τὴν ἀγορὰν ἀψευδεῖν; *In a Market nothing ought to be spoken but truth.* In which Cases the word *mendacium* is to be taken so largely as to comprehend all doubtful and ambiguous Phrases, which we speaking properly have hitherto excluded from this Notion of lying.

John. 11. 20, 21.
Luke 22. 30.
Matth. 26. 25.

Amphibologies.

Tacit. Ann. lib. 6.

Much like unto that of the Oracle to *Crœsus*,

If Crœsus *over Halis go,*
A Kingdom will be overthrow.

Which *Crœsus* understanding in a wrong sense, instead of conquering *Persia*, lost his own Kingdom of *Lydia*.

The like we read was sent from *Rome* to some that waited but for the Popes *fiat*, to have killed King *Edward*: *Edwardum occidere nolite timere bonum est.* Which being written without any Point or Comma, would admit of two contrary expositions.

XI. The form of a lye as it is unlawful, wherein it consists.

It is required therefore to the nature of a lye, commonly so taken, that what is either spoken or written, or by any other signs exprest, cannot otherwise be understood than in such a sense as is different from his mind that so declares it. But to a lye strictly taken, as it is naturally unlawful, there is necessarily required some peculiar difference, which if rightly understood, at least according to the common acception of Nations, can be nothing more than the violation of his existing and remaining right with whom we converse. For certain it is that in respect of himself no man can lye, let him speak never so much falshood. Where by Right, I understand not every Right, and what is extrinsick to the thing; but that which merely relates unto the matter in hand, which is nothing else but his freedom with whom we discourse, to judge at the conceptions of our minds, which as by a silent Contract, we are presumed to owe unto him. For this, and no other, is that mutual obligation which men were willing to introduce so soon as language was invented, or those other notes or signs generally received as significant of our inward thoughts; without which obligation that invention had been altogether fruitless. (And therefore amongst the Hebrews, he that deprived a man of the means of knowledg, was said *cor furari, to steal away his heart*, as *Jacob* is said to *steal away the heart of Laban*, in that he *did not acquaint him with his purpose to depart from him*, Gen. 31. 20, 26, 27. Now it is also requisite that this right or liberty to judge by such words or signs at their inward conceptions, should remain intire at that time when we discourse. For possible it is that though there was such a freedome, yet it is then taken away, or may be by some other right that is supervenient. As a Debt that was, may cease to be so, by reason either of an Acquittance given, or a failing of the performance of some Condition. Again, it is required, That the right that is violated be his with whom we discourse, and not a By-standers, or any other mans. As in a Contract there ariseth no injustice, but by the violation of the right of one of the Contractors. Hence haply it is that after *Simonides*, *Plato* refers the speaking of truth to justice. And that S[t] *Augustin* himself inserts into the definition of a lye, That it be spoken *animo fallendi, with a purpose to deceive.* And *Cicero*, *Plato*, and others would have the speaking of truth to be referred to the fundamentals of Justice. And that that lying that is forbidden, the Scriptures do often describe by bearing false

Cor furari.
Gen. 31. 20, 26, 27.

 witness

witneſs againſt our Neighbour; whereunto *Lactantius* hath reſpect where he ſaith, *That no untruth ought to be ſpoken at any time with an intent either to hurt or deceive our Neighbour.* But this right may be taken away (as I have ſaid) as by expreſs conſent of him with whom we converſe, when he declares before he ſpeaks that he will ſpeak falſe; and he to whom he declares it, doth permit it: So by a tacite conſent, or on a preſumption grounded upon juſt reaſon, or by the oppoſition of anothers right, which by the common judgment of all is moſt prevalent. From theſe premiſes rightly underſtood, many inferences may be drawn, in order to the reconciling of thoſe different opinions formerly mentioned.

XII. It is lawful to ſpeak untruth to Infants and Mad-men.

As firſt, In caſe we converſe with either a Child or a Mad man, if what we ſay be falſe, it cannot be imputed as a lye; becauſe (as *Quintilian* ſaith) it is univerſally permitted, as profitable, to inſtruct Infants by Tales and Fables. But the immediate reaſon is, Becauſe not having a freedom of judgment, they cannot be injured about that liberty which they have not.

XIII. When he to whom we direct our ſpeech is not deceived, but a By-ſtander.

Secondly, Whilſt we diſcourſe with one man who is not deceived, if another to whom we direct not our diſcourſe be thereby deceived, we cannot be juſtly charged with a lye. For firſt, It is not a lye, in reſpect of him to whom it was ſpoken; becauſe his judgment remains ſound and uncorrupted, as his doth who hearing a Romance, underſtands it to be ſo: So likewiſe doth his, who hearing a Parable or figurative ſpeech, whether it be by way of Irony or Hyperbole, whereby we arrive, as *Seneca* ſpeaks, at the knowledge of what is true by ſomething that is not true, aſſerting things incredible to gain belief to things credible. Neither is it a lye in reſpect of him that overhears it; becauſe he being not concerned in our diſcourſe, we ſtand no ways obliged unto him: but if that man do conceive an erroneous opinion by reaſon of a diſcourſe between others, he may juſtly blame himſelf if he be deceived, and not others. For to ſpeak properly, Our ſpeech one with another is no ſpeech at all in reſpect of a By-ſtander, neither doth it ſignifie to him any thing. And therefore neither was *Cato* the Cenſor to be blamed for promiſing aids to his Confederates, though falſly; nor *Flaccus* in divulging unto others, That *Emilius* had taken his Enemies City by aſſault, though it were untrue, and his enemies thereby deceived. The like *Plutarch* records of *Ageſilaus.* For nothing was therein ſaid to the Enemy; and therefore the damage that was conſequent thereunto was but extrinſick and adventitious, which to an enemy either to wiſh or procure was not unlawful. Unto this kind of falſe ſpeaking S[t] *Chryſoſtome*, *Hierome*, *Cyril*, and others, refer that ſpeech of S[t] *Paul*, reproving S[t] *Peter* at *Antioch* for too much Judaizing, as believing that S[t] *Peter* very well underſtood S[t] *Paul*, namely, That he did it not ſeriouſly, and in good earneſt; but only to prevent a ſcandal that might thence ariſe to ſuch as were weak amongſt them.

De Benef. l. 7. *c.* 23. Hyperboles, Ironies.

See *Albericus. Gent. l.* 2. *c.* 5.

Livy l. 34. *App. Hyſp.*

XIV. When our ſpeech is directed to him that is willing to be deceived.

The third Inference is this, When we are ſure that he with whom we converſe will not only not be offended, though his judgment be for the preſent deluded, but that he will alſo be thankful in regard of the profit that will thence ariſe to him. In this caſe a lye ſtrictly taken, that is, an injurious lye, cannot be imputed unto us, no more than that can be imputed unto us as theft, when upon preſumption that the Owner will not be offended, we ſpend ſomewhat that is his, thereby to procure him a much greater profit. For in caſes of ſuch certain profit, our preſumptions are as authoritative as his expreſs conſent. And *to him that is willing, is no injury done.* Wherefore a Phyſician is not preſumed to lye, when he cheers up his deſponding Patient with the feigned hopes of recovery. Or when a General in a dangerous Battel cheers up the Spirits of his fainting Souldiers, with ſome comfortable news, though falſe, whereby he procures both their ſafety and victory. *We are altogether to ſpeak truth* (ſaith *Democritus*) *where it is advantageous:* yet, as *Xenophon* obſerves, *Deceive we may even our very friends, when it redounds to their good. The Phyſician* (ſaith *Maximus Tyrius*) *deceives his Patient, the General his Souldiers, and the Pilot his Mariners; yet neither of theſe can be ſaid to injure them*: whereof *Proclus* in *Plato* gives this reaſon, *Becauſe that which is good is to be preferred before that which is true.* Hiſtories are full of examples of this nature; as that in *Xenophon*, when to encourage his Souldiers, he cauſed it to be given out, That an Army of their Confederates were coming to aſſiſt them. And that of *Ageſilaus* in *Plutarch*, *who when he came into* Bœotia, *and there underſtood that* Pyſander, *was there overthrown in a Naval Battel by* Pharnabazus *and* Conon, *cauſed the quite contrary to be publiſhed to the Army, which to confirm he came crowned into the Temple, cauſing ſolemn Sacrifices to be offered to the Gods for the Victory.* And (that *ſalubre mendacium*, as Hiſtorians call it) *that wholeſome lye* of the Conſul *Quinctius*, *who to encourage the Right Wing, gave it out, That the Left Wing had routed their Enemies.* Thus is that of *Clemens Alexandrinus* to be underſtood, who allows *of a lye as the utmoſt refuge in the time of danger.* Where we muſt obſerve, That the injury that is done unto the judgment in this kind, is ſo much the leſs as it is momentany; whereas the good that may enſue is great, general and laſting: for the victory being gained, the truth immediately appears.

Quod bonum eſt, id vero eſt melius.

Socr. 4. *Plut.*

The

The Fourth, and that which comes nearest unto the former is this; so often as he, who hath a supereminent Right over all the Rights of another, makes use of that Right, either for his own particular interest, or the publick good. And hereunto had *Plato* * respect, when he indulged unto Princes that liberty to speak untruths. And yet the same *Plato* when he seems sometimes to grant, and sometimes to take away this licence to, or from Physicians, seems to put this only difference that in giving it, he intends it to such as are publickly Authorized unto that calling; and in taking it away, he intended it from such as over arrogantly assumed it unto themselves. And yet neither did *Plato* himself think it fit to admit of lying in God, notwithstanding that Soveraign Power that he hath over men; because it is an argument of much weakness and insufficiency, to have recourse to such shifts (which to attribute to God were Blasphemy.) An example of this innocent and unblamable falshood we have in *Joseph* to his Brethren, for which *Philo* so highly commends him, who as the Kings Vicegerent, doth with a becoming severity charge his Brethren contrary to his knowledge; first, for being Spies, and afterwards, for being Thieves. Another we have in *Solomon*, who to discover the true Mother, commanded the Child to be divided, when he intended nothing less. So true is that of *Quintilian, Aliquando exigit communis utilitas, ut etiam falsa defendantur; It is sometimes expedient for the common good, that some falshoods should be maintained.*

XV. When he that speaketh, useth that soveraign power he hath over his Subjects.

* *De rep.*3.

We may add a fifth, namely, when the life of an innocent person, or some such like, cannot otherwise be preserved; or when the execution of some dishonest act cannot otherwise be prevented; such was the fact of *Hypermnestra* so much celebrated by *Horace*, As,

XVI To preserve the life of an innocent person.

Splendide mendax, & in omne virgo
Nobilis ævum.

Hor. 3. *Carm. c.* 11.

Deserving for her pious fraud
Immortal praise.

Whereupon the Scholiast hath this note, *Decenter: Pulchrum est enim pro justitia mentiri; Very decently: for to lye sometimes for justice and innocency is a lovely thing. There are* saith St *Aug.*) *two sorts of lyes not much to be blamed, though they are not altogether without blame; and these are either the jocular, or the charitable ly: The jocular is not pernicious, because it deceives no man; for he to whom it is spoken, knows, that what is so spoken is but in sport. The officious lye is so much the less dangerous, because it proceeds from charity.* And therefore *Tertullian* amongst those daily sins of infirmity, whereunto we are subject, deprecates this, *When in cases of danger we make lyes our subterfuge.* St. *Chrysostome*, doth not only excuse *Rahabs* lye, but commends it, *O pulchrum mendacium! O laudabilem dolum,* &c. *O lovely lye! O commendable fraud,* saith he, *of one that betrayed not things Divine, but to preserve true Piety.* So likewise doth St. *Augustine* of the Ægyptian Midwives, *O magnum humanitatis ingenium! O pium pro salute mendacium! O rare device of humanity, O pious lye framed only to preserve life!* For which St. *Hierome* doth not only commend them, but believes that God also did reward them, even with eternal blessedness, as will appear to any that reads his exposition on the 17. of *Ezech.* and on the 56. of *Esay*.

Vid. Eras. in Moriæ Encomio. Hæsitat. Aug. Lib. 2. *qu. super Exod.*

Some wise men are of opinion, that to an Enemy we may use falshood in a larger sense. As * *Plato* and † *Xenophon* among the Grecians, *Philo* among the Hebrews, and amongst Christians St. *Chrysostome*; who to the rules they give for not lying, add this exception, Unless it be to our Enemies. *If we call to the test the brave exploits of our noblest Captain,* saith St. *Chrysostome, we shall find that they owe most of their triumphs to fraud; and that those Victories so gained, were always more renowned, than those gained by plain force* *. And hitherto haply we may refer that Message that the men of *Jabesh Gilead*, sent unto the Ammonites, by whom they were besieged, 1 *Sam.* 11. 10. And that of *Elisha* the Prophet, when he told those that were sent to apprehend him, from the King of *Syria, That that was not the way, nor the City where Elisha was,* 2 Kings 6. 19. As also that of the same *Elisha* to *Hazael* concerning *Benhadad, Go and say to him, Thou mayest certainly recover, howbeit the Lord hath shewed me that he shall surely dye,* 2 Kings 8. 10. As that also of *Valerius Levinus*, when he boasted that he had slain *Pyrrhus*. To the third, fourth, and fifth of these inferences above mentioned, we may refer that of *Eustratius, It is not always necessary that he that gives good advice should speak true; for, haply he that rightly adviseth, may advise purposely how he may frame a lye, so that thereby, either his Enemy may be deluded, or his friends preserved.* Examples of these kinds are very frequent in all Histories. To the same purpose is that of *Quintilian, If a Thief enquiring after a Traveller, with an intent to kill him, may be misguided; or if an Enemy for the preservation of our Country, may lawfully be deluded: then that which in a servant is reproveable, is in a wise man commendable.* The Schoolmen of this latter age will not I know admit of this, who out of all the Ancient Fathers, have chosen

XVII. Lawful to Enemies.

* *Lib.* 2. *de rep.* † *l.* 2. *de Cyr. Inst.* & 5. *Socrat.*

*St. *Aug.* is very doubtful in this case.

2 Kings 6. 19.

2 Kings 8. 10.

In lib. 6. *Nicomicor.*

Tho. 2.2. *qu.* 110. *art.* 1. & 3. with others.

The Schoolmen make St. *Aug.* their guide.

ſen St. *Auguſtine* only as their guide in almoſt all things. But yet as ſcrupulous as they are and nice, in admitting of falſe ſpeaking in any Caſe, they notwithſtanding, make no ſcruple of admitting tacite interpretations, and mental reſervations, which are wholly to be rejected; inſomuch, that it is hard to determine, whether it be not better to admit of ſpeaking falſly to ſome perſons, and in ſome caſes (as thoſe before-mentioned) than ſo indifferently to diſtinguiſh between falſhood, and thoſe ſecret interpretations, and ſilent reſervations, whereof they approve; which being admitted, no man can poſſibly know, when his Neighbour ſpeaks truth, and when not: As when to a Queſtion that is asked me, I anſwer, *I know not*, I mean, *I know not ſo as to tell you that I know it*; or when I ſay to a poor man, *I have nothing*, I mean, *I have nothing to give you*, &c. which interpretations, even common ſenſe is aſhamed to own; and which being admitted, will eaſily introduce plain contrarieties: ſo that he that affirms any thing, may be underſtood to deny it; and he that denies any thing may be ſaid to affirm it. For it is moſt true what *Chryſippus* in *Gellius* maintains, *That there is ſcarce any voice that admits not of ſome ambiguity, becauſe every word beſides the ſignification, which is of its prime inſtitution, hath alſo another of the ſecond, and that divers according to the diverſity of arts, yea, and others alſo, which it borrows from tranſlations and from ſemblable figures.* Beſides as *Seneca* obſerves, *There are infinite things without names; which we are forced to deſcribe, by ſuch names as we borrow from other things.* Neither do I better approve of thoſe, who as if they quarrelled more with the word, than the thing, call that jeſt or ſport, which they utter, with a countenance and pronunciation very ſerious.

XVIII. This not to be extended to words promiſſory.

We are likewiſe to obſerve, that what we have here ſet down concerning falſe ſpeaking, is to be referred to that kind of ſpeech which is aſſertory, and that alſo ſo far forth only as it damnifies none, unleſs it be a publick Enemy, but not at all to that which is promiſſory; for every promiſe confers a new and ſpecial Right to him, to whom that promiſe is made: And this is in force, even amongſt Enemies, notwithſtanding the greateſt and moſt open hoſtility, and that, not only where the promiſe is expreſs; but where it is preſumed, as in the ſounding of a party, whereof more anon, when we come to treat of publick Faith, which is to be preſerved even amongſt Enemies, between theſe two kind of ſpeeches, I mean aſſertory, and promiſſory. *Ageſilaus* in *Plutarch* clearly diſtinguiſheth, where he ſaith, *Fœdera violare, Deos eſt contemnere; extra ea verbis hoſtem decipere, non juſtum modo eſt, ſed & gloriam habet & cum lucro voluptatem; To violate Leagues, is to deſpiſe the Gods: But otherwiſe to deceive an Enemy, which words are not only juſt, but glorious, and with delight profitable.*

XIX. Not to Oaths.

Neither is it to be extended to oaths, either aſſertory or promiſſory; for oaths have a power to exclude all exceptions, becauſe therein we have to do not with men only, but with God, to whom by our oaths we ſtand obliged, although there ariſe no Right at all to men: for (as I have already ſaid) it is not ſo in thoſe ſpeeches which are confirmed by oath, as it is in others; for in others it is ſufficient to juſtifie us from lying, if the words ſpoken be true in any ſenſe, not altogether unuſual; but in that which is ſworn, it is neceſſary that our words be plain and ſignificant, and fitted to that ſenſe, wherein he to whom we ſwear, is thought moſt probably to underſtand them, when we may diſcover the deteſtable impiety of thoſe, who affirm that it is as lawful to deceive men with oaths, as Children with dice and other toys.

XX. It is more generous and Chriſtian like to abſtain from falſhood and lies.

We know, that there are ſome kinds of fraud, which though naturally permitted, yet are by ſome people and ſome perſons decryed; not ſo much for any thing in them that is unjuſt, as out of either magnanimity of ſpirit, or ſometimes out of a preſumption on our own ſtrength. There is in *Ælian* an excellent ſaying recorded of *Pythagoras*, namely, *That there are two things wherein men draw near unto God, in ſpeaking truth always, and in doing good unto all men.* For truth (as *Jamblicus* ſpeaks) is the Captain or Guide to all vertues whether Moral or Divine. And *Ariſtotle* gives it *as the trueſt Character of a magnanimous*

Nic. 4. 1.

perſon, that he loves truth, and to ſpeak his mind freely. Whereas on the contrary, *It is*, as *Plutarch* notes, *the badge of a vile and ſervile ſpirit to lye.* And therefore (as *Arrianus* ſpeaks

Lib. 1.

of King *Ptolemy*) *It is worſe in a King to lie than in any other.* So the ſame Author ſpeaks of

Lib. 7.

Alexander, *Nothing ſo well becomes a Prince, ſpeaking to his Subjects, as truth.* And *Mamertime* ſpeaking of the Emperour *Julian*, ſaith, *Admirable is the concord that there is between our Princes tongue and his heart, as knowing, that lying argues a baſe and abject ſpirit; and whereas it is fear and poverty only, that makes men lyars, he is ignorant of his own Majeſty, who being a Prince diſdains not to lye.* It was *Plutarchs* obſervation of *Ariſtides*, *That he was ſo great an admirer of truth, that he hated lying though but in jeſt.* The like did *Probus* commend in *Epaminondas*, *Adeo veritatis diligens, ut ne joco quidem mentiretur; That he was ſo great a lover of truth, that he would not tell a lye, though but for ſport. And as for ſuch as are fallacious and deceitful, we uſually account them* (ſaith *Philo*) *as baſe and ſordid*; truth therefore ought much more religiouſly to be obſerved by us Chriſtians, by how much we

Mat. 10. 16.

are enjoined to be ſimple and innocent, and forbidden, not only falſhood and wrongful dealing,

dealing, but all idle talk and vain babling; yea, and since we have him for our Copy to write after, in whose mouth was found no guile. Wherefore as *Lactantius* saith, *That man that is truly honest, will not say with* Lucilius, *Homini amico ac familiari non est mentiri meum*; *When with my friend I talke, I do not lye: But rather will think it his duty not to lye, though he have to do with a stranger or an Enemy, and at no time to do that thing, that may occasion his tongue to speak what his heart thinks not.* Such as *Sophocles* testifies, was *Neoptolemus* the Son of *Achilles*, who being urged by *Ulysses*, *to piece the Foxes tail to the Lyons skin*, made this answer: Matt. 12. 36.

Ego audiens quæ doleo, Laerta sate,
Implere factis oderim multo magis:
Nam sic nec ego sum natus, ut fallacias
Secter, nec olim genitor, ut perhibent meus:
At sum paratus vi mera, non fraudibus
Pertrahere raptum.

So likewise *Horace* concerning his Father *Achilles*, *Carm. lib.* 4. *Ode.* 6.

Ille non inclusus equo Minervæ
Sacra mentito, male feriatos
Troas *& lætam* Priami *choreis*
Fallerat aulam:——————
Sed palam captis gravis, &c.

Whereby he intimates, *That* Achilles *though Father of* Neoptolemus, *was of that noble and generous spirit, that he disdained even victory it self, if not obtained by mere manhood.* Scholiast upon that place in *Horace.*

Thus *Euripides* also, *Rheso.*

Generosus animus hostibus furtim necem
Inferre nescit.

——————A gallant soul hath he
That scorns by stealth to kill his Enemy.

The like we read of *Alexander*, who being advised to circumvent his Enemies by some wile: answered, *Se nolle furari victoriam*; *That he scorned to steal a victory.* The like *Polybius* testifies of the Achaians, That they hated to use fraud though against their Enemies, esteeming that *the surest victory, which by the confession of their Enemies was so.* Such were the Ancient Romans until the second Punick War, insomuch that *Ælian appropriates this honour unto the Romans above all Nations*; *that they overcame their Enemies, not by craft or subtilty, but by plain force*, And when *Perseus* the *Macedonian* King, was deceived with the hopes of Peace; the old Senators disowned such Roman arts, denying that their Ancestors (who gloried more in valour than in fraud) did ever manage their Wars, with that wilines which the Carthaginians, or with such deceit as the Grecians used, with whom it was ever held more honourable to circumvent their Enemies by stratagems, than to overcome them in plain Battel; adding withal, *That sometimes wit might prevail against valour for the present*; *but that his courage was for ever quelled who was convinced, that in a pious and a just War, he was not by fraud, nor by chance, but fighting hand to hand with his whole strength in plain Battel vanquished:* Yea and in latter times, *Tacitus* testifies of them, *That the Roman people sought revenge upon their Enemies, neither by craft nor treachery, but openly and by force of Arms.* Such also were the *Tiberines*, who always proclaimed as the time, so the place, when and where they would give battel to their Enemies. And such were the Achaians, as *Polybius* testifies. The like doth *Mardonius* in *Herodotus* record of the Grecians of his time. (When *James* the fourth of *Scotland*, invaded the North of *England* with a powerful Army, *Thomas* E. of *Surrey* sent an Herald to him to let him know, that on the *Friday* following he would give him Battel in case he would stay so long in *England*; And *Thomas* his Son, sent the King word, that he would spare none save the King himself; and that he might find him in the van of his Army.) But this (as I said before) proceeds rather from magnanimity of spirit, and confidence in our own strength, than from the justice of the thing. *Herb. H.* 8.

XXI We must not enforce a man to do that wch he cannot lawfully do.

As to the manner, how the War should be prosecuted, this rule is pertinent, What is unlawful for a man to do, is also unlawful for another to compel or perswade him to do, whereof let these suffice for examples. It is unlawful for any subject to kill his Prince, or to deliver up a Town or Fort without the consent of a Council of War, or to plunder his

his fellow Subjects. And therefore it is likewise unlawful for me being an Enemy, to perswade another Prince's Subjects remaining so to do it. For evermore, He that occasioneth another man to sin, doth therein sin himself: Neither is it sufficient to say, That it is lawful for him that excites such a man to do such a villainous act, to do it himself; for it is true, that it may be lawful for him to kill him, but not to do it in that manner. For that of St. *Augustine* is very true, *Nihil interest utrum ipse scelus committas, an alium propter te admittere velis; It matters not much, whether a man do commit wickedness himself, or cause another to do it for him.*

XXII. Yet if he offer himself, we may make use of him. But it is another thing, if such a person shall freely offer himself, without any instigation from us; for it is not unlawful for us to make use of him, as an instrument to effect that, which it is lawful for us to do, as we have already proved by the example of God himself*. *Transfugam jure belli recipimus,* saith *Celsus*; that is, *It is no way repugnant to the Law of Arms, to receive Renegadoes into protection, and to make use of them.* Neither are such to be delivered up, unless it be so agreed by the Articles of Peace.

* L[illegible] c. 26. §. 5.

CHAP. II.

How Subjects Goods become liable to their Princes Debts.

I. *Naturally no man is bound by the fact of another, but the heir only.*
II. *Yet by the Law of Nations, the Goods and Acts of Subjects, are liable to the debts of the Prince.*
III. *An example whereof in the taking of men Prisoners.*
IV. *And in seizing their Goods.*
V. *Which is lawful, when the Right is denied, and when that is; where is also shewed, that though the thing be adjudged, yet it neither gives nor takes away any mans Right.*
VI. *That the lives of innocent Subjects are not liable to satisfie the Princes debt.*
VII. *The difference herein between the Civil Law, and the Law of Nations.*

I. Naturally none but the Heir obliged by the fact of another. LET us now descend to those Rights, which the Law of Nations grants unto us; some whereof appertain to every War, others to some particular kinds of Wars only. Let us now begin with generals. By the bare Law of nature no man is bound by the fact of another, but he that succeeds to inherit his Goods; for as soon as Dominion was first introduced, it was likewise agreed on, That all debts should pass, together with the Goods to the next Occupant, according to that old Law-Maxime, *Transeat fructus cum onere; Let the Estate and the Charge go together.* The Emperour *Zeno* was wont to say, That it was contrary to natural equity, that one man should be molested for another mans debt. Hence arise those titles in the Roman Laws, That the Wife shall not be sued for the Husband, nor the Husband for the Wife; the Son for the Father, nor the Father or Mother for the Son. Neither as *Ulpian* saith expresly, shall any particular person be liable to the debts of the Commonwealth; that is, if the common stock be able to discharge them; otherwise they shall, not as individual persons, but as they are a part of the whole. *If any man shall lend his money to my Country,* saith *Seneca, I shall not acknowledge my self his debtor, yet shall I willingly advance my proportion, not as my own debt, but to disengage my Country.* And again, *Singuli debebunt non tanquam proprium, sed tanquam publici partem; What the Commonwealth owes, every particular Citizen owes, not as his own debt, but as his part of the publick.* It was particularly provided by the Roman Laws, That no one of the Villagers should be obliged for another of the Villagers debts: and in another place, That no ones possessions should be destrained for the debts of another; no, not for the publick. And in *Justinians* Novels, Reprisals are expresly forbidden, and this reason added, *Because it hath no face or colour of justice, that one man should be the debtor, another enforced to pay the debt, where also such exactions are called odious.* Thus did *Theodorick* in *Cassiodore* account it, for one man to be kept as a Pledge or Hostage for another.

Vide supra B. 2. ch. 21. § 19.

De Benef. l 6. c. 20.

II. But by the Law of Nations Subjects are for their Prince. Although these things be true, yet by the voluntary Law of Nations it may be, nay as it appears, it hath been, introduced, That what debts soever any Civil Society, or their Prince shall contract, either primarily by themselves, or be engaged for by not rendring unto others that which is their right; all the Goods both corporeal and incorporeal of those that are subject to that Society or the Prince thereof, shall be liable and stand bound to discharge. Now this seems to be inforced by a kind of necessity; for otherwise the Gap would be so wide as to let in all manner of injuries. For the goods of Princes are but few, and those not so easily taken as those of private mens which are many: wherefore it is reckoned

ed by *Juſtinian* amongſt thoſe Laws which cuſtome had found requiſite to be conſtituted, for the relief of humane neceſſity. Neither will this be found ſo repugnant to nature, that it might not be introduced by cuſtom and by the tacite conſent of Nations, ſeeing that Sureties do ſtand firmly bound for other mens debts, without any other cauſe than by their voluntary ſuſception only. And very probable it is that the Members of any one Society may more eaſily be relieved one by another, than Strangers can, whoſe complaints, though never ſo juſt, are little regarded in many places. Beſides, the benefit that ariſeth from this obligation, being common to all Nations, they that find themſelves aggrieved by it at one time, may be relieved by it ſome other. Nor is this cuſtom in force only where there is a perfect and compleat War between Nation and Nation. (For what is lawful in ſuch Wars appears by the very words of their denunciation, *Againſt the ancient Latine People, and against the men of Old* Latium, *I denounce and make war*, ſaith the Roman Herauld in *Livy*. So likewiſe when the Herauld demand the peoples conſent, they ſay, *Is it your will and pleaſure that War be forthwith denounced againſt King* Philip, *and his Macedonians, and againſt all that are under his Government.* So alſo in the Decree it ſelf, *The Roman people do proclaim War againſt the Hermundulian people, and againſt the men of* Hermunduli: which is all one as what in another place he expreſſeth in theſe words, *Hoſtis ſit ille, quique intra præſidia ejus ſunt*; *Let him be declared an enemy, and whoſoever betakes himſelf to his protection.*) But this cuſtom is in force even where there is no perfect war abſolutely denounced, but where notwithſtanding a certain violent proſecution of our right is neceſſary; which is, as it were an inchoate and imperfect War. It is worth our obſervation what *Ageſilaus* anſwered to *Pharnabazus*, being a Subject to the Perſian King, *O* Pharnabazus, *when heretofore we were friends to the King of* Perſia, *we dealt friendly with all that appertained unto him; ſo now being his enemies, we uſe all his as enemies: and therefore ſince thou art willing to depend upon his protection, we may lawfully weaken him by thee.* The learned *Damaſcene* doth prudently diſtinguiſh between the taking of Prizes or Reprizals for the recovery of debts, or reparation of damages, and the making of War, which he illuſtrates by the example of King *Herod*, *For whom, though it were not lawful to make war upon the Arabians, yet was it lawful for him,* ῥύσια λαμβάνειν, *to take prizes throughout all* Arabia *for the five hundred Talents due unto him, if not paid by a certain day appointed; for ſo it was expreſly covenanted between them: and therefore* Herod *did rightly deny that to be the making of War, which was but a juſt and lawful way to recover his own right.* Liv. lib. 1. Plut. Ageſ. & Xenoph. Hiſt. Græc. 4. Joſ. Antiq. 6.

III. An example in taking of men Priſoners.

A branch of the execution of this right was that which the Athenians called ἀνδροληψίαν, *the making men Priſoners*; concerning which the Attick Law was this, *If any man had been by forcible aſſault killed by a Stranger, the next of kin had a right to take any three men Priſoners, but no more, and to detain them until the Murderer were either puniſhed, or delivered up to be puniſhed.* Hence we may perceive, That there is a kind of incorporeal right of Subjects (that is, a liberty to live where, and to do what they pleaſe) engaged for the debts of every Society, which ought to puniſh ſuch of their own Society as ſhall dare to injure thoſe of another Society; ſo that any of the Members of that Society that ſhall neglect or refuſe to do it, if taken, may be held in bondage until that Society do what they ought; that is, until they either puniſh or deliver up the Offender. For although the Egyptians (as *Diodorus* teſtifies) did maintain, That it was not juſt to impriſon a man for debt; yet is there nothing in it repugnant to nature. And the general practice not only of the Grecians, but of moſt other Nations, is ſufficient to warrant the contrary. *Ariſtocrates*, who was Contemporary with *Demoſthenes*, demanded, That a Decree might paſs, That whoſoever ſhould kill *Charidemus*, ſhould be taken away from what place ſoever; and that whoſoever ſhould make reſiſtance, ſhould be held as an enemy. In which Decree *Demoſthenes* obſerves theſe errours: Firſt, that *Ariſtocrates* did not diſtinguiſh between the putting to death of *Charidemus* juſtly or unjuſtly, ſeeing that poſſible it was that he might deſerve death; next that he did not require that judgment ſhould firſt be demanded againſt him: And thirdly, that not they amongſt whom he ſhould be killed, but they that ſhould receive the murtherer being eſcaped into protection ſhould be proſecuted as enemies. *Demoſthenes* his words are to this purpoſe, *If a murther be committed amongſt any people, and they refuſe either to puniſh or to deliver up the murtherer, the Law allows the apprehenſion of three men; but* Ariſtocrates *leaves theſe men untoucht, and not ſo much as mentions them; but would have thoſe perſecuted as enemies who have according to the Common Right of Nations concerning ſuppliants received him that hath eſcaped by flight, for ſo I put the caſe, into protection, unleſs they deliver him.* The fourth thing that he reproves, is, that *Ariſtocrates* would inſtantly bring it to an abſolute War; whereas the Law requires only the detention of three men. Of theſe four exceptions, that *Demoſthenes* takes againſt *Ariſtocrates* his Decree, the firſt, the ſecond, and the fourth are not altogether without reaſon; but for the third, unleſs reſtrained to the ſole event of the murther done, either accidentally, or in the defence of himſelf, I cannot perceive why it ſhould be mentioned, unleſs it were like an Orator for arguments ſake, rather than truly or juſtly: for as we

ſaid

Vid. lib. 2. *cap.* 21. *Sect.* 7. said before, That Right which all men challenge of receiving and defending Suppliants, doth concern those only whom Fortune, and not their own crimes have made miserable; for otherwise there is the same Law for those amongst whom the crime is committed, as for those who refuse either to punish or deliver the guilty. And surely either the Law it self cited by *Demosthenes* hath through custom been thus interpreted, or against such cavils was afterwards more liquidly exprest; the truth of one of these, none will deny, that

Lib. 8. *c.* 6. reads that of *Julius Pollux*, whose words are these, *The taking of men prisoners is then lawfull, when a man having demanded Homicides, (who have fled for safety to others) cannot receive them: For the right of apprehending three men lies against those, who having received malefactors into protection, refuse either to deliver them, or to punish them according to Law.* The like we find in *Harpocration*, *The Right of taking prisoners is a Right to snatch away some men from some other City: For it was an ancient custom against such Cities as received Malefactors, and refused either to punish them, or to deliver them to be punished, to make use of this Right of Pignoration.* The like may be done by any City whose Citizen hath been manifestly and injuriously taken away and detained from them. Thus we read, that at *Carthage* there were some that opposed the taking of *Ariston* the Tyrian prisoner upon this

Liv. l. 34. ground, *That the like would be done against the* Carthaginians, *both at* Tyre, *and at other Mart Towns, where the* Carthaginians *used to traffick*.

IV. Reprizals lawful. Another kind of forcible execution of this Right, is the taking of Goods between the People of divers Nations, which our Modern Lawyers call Reprizals, or a violent seizing and detention of each others Goods, which the *English* and the *Saxons* call *Withernam*, and the *French*, (even where it is wont to be obtained from the King) Letters of Marque: which also are frequently granted, and are of force, as Lawyers say, where Right is denied.

V. Our right being first denyed, and when that is. *Vid. Gailius de pace publ. l.* 2. *c.* 8. *n.* 7. *Vasq. Cont. illust. c.* 10. *sect.* 41. And this may be presumed, not only when they cannot in any reasonable time obtain judgment against a delinquent or a debtor: But when in a Case that will hardly admit of any doubt, sentence shall pass plainly against Right; for Cases that are ambiguous, the definitive power is supposed to be in the Delegates, as persons publickly chosen to do Justice, whose Authority notwithstanding is not of the same force to oblige strangers, as their own Subjects; nay, even between their own Subjects, it makes not a debt void that was justly due: For as *Paulus* the Lawyer observes, *Verus debitor, licet absolutus sit, Natura tamen debitor permanet*; *He that owes a real debt, though he be discharged by the sentence of the Judge, yet by the Law of Nature stands still obliged. And when by the injury of the Judge, a Creditor had taken away from the right Owner something that had not been the Debtors, as if engaged unto him: the question being put, Whether the debt being paid, that thing were to be restored to the debtor*; Scævola *proved that it ought to be restored.* But between a Subject and a Stranger, there is this difference, Subjects are bound up by the Sentence of the Judge, though it be unjust, so as they can neither resist the execution of it lawfully; nor by Force recover their own Right against a Sentence unjustly given, by reason of the efficacy of that power they live under: But Strangers have a coercive power, though it be not lawfull for them to use it so long as they may recover their Right in a Judicial way: wherefore in such a Case, that both the Persons, and the moveable Goods of his Subjects that refuse to restore what is violently taken away, may be by the like violence taken, is not introduced by Nature, but by Custom generally received in all Nations. The most ancient Example of this we may read of in *Homers Iliads*, where *Nestor* is said to drive away the Cattle of the *Elidenses*; because they had before plundered his Fathers Horses: whereupon as the story goes on, Proclamation was made, That every man to whom the *Elidenses* did owe any thing, should come and partake of the spoil, in such a manner, as that every man might have his just proportion. Another Example we have of this in the Roman History, where *Aristodemus Tarquin*'s heir, seizeth the Roman Ships lying in Harbor at *Cumæ*, which he detained for the Goods of the *Tarquines* detained in *Rome*. And in *Aristotle* we find a Decree against the *Carthaginians* to seize all foreign ships, if any man had a Right so to do.

VI. This Right reacheth not to the life of him that is taken. Book 1. Ch. 1. Sect. 12, 13. It hath haply been believed among some people, that the lives of innocent Subjects do stand engaged upon the like account, and that haply upon this presumption, that every man hath an Absolute Power over his own life, which Power may be transferred unto the Common-wealth, which is very imbrobable; and as we have already said, not consistent with sound Divinity: yet it may fall out, that such Subjects may be killed, though not intentionally, yet accidentally, namely, when they shall attempt by force to impede the execution of this Right. But yet if such a mischief may be foreseen, we are obliged by

VII. The distinction that is herein made between the Law of Nations, and the Civil Law. the Law of Charity to forbear the prosecution of our Right, as we have elsewhere shewed; since by that Law, we that are Christians especially ought to set a greater value upon the life of a Man, than upon our Goods, as we have elsewhere proved.

Moreover as well in this, as in several other Cases, we must take heed, That we distinguish between those things that are properly due by the Law of Nations, and those that

that are due by the Civil Law, or by a mutual agreement between some people. By the Law of Nations, all Subjects that are injurious unto the Subjects of another Prince are liable to this Law of Reprizals, especially if they have occasion to reside there, whether they be Natives or Strangers; but not if they be only Travellers, or sojourn there but for a little time. For these Pignorations are of the same nature with Taxes, which being raised for the discharge of publick debts, are imposed on such as are constant Inhabitants, and not on such as are Sojourners, and so subject to the Laws of the place for a while only. Neither are the Persons or the Goods of Embassadors, being not sent to our Enemies, any wayes liable to this right of Pignorations by the Law of Nations; as also in many places the persons of Women and Children are by the Civil Law often exempted: But even the Goods of such as addict themselves to Learning or to Merchandizing, may by the Law of Nations be taken by any, as their persons also were at *Athens*. But by the Civil Law of many places, this Right of seizing Goods or Persons, must first be demanded from the Supreme Power, but in other places from the Judges. By the Laws of Nations the Propriety of things taken passeth immediately to him that takes them to the value of his principal debt, together with his charges, so as the remainder ought to be restored. Thus did the *Venetians* to the *Genoese*, as *Gregoras* relates; *Whose ships*, saith he, *being taken at* Galata, *laden with Wheat, Barly, and Salt for Fish, whereof the Lakes of* Copais, *and* Mæotis, *and the River* Tanais *affords great plenty, they did not diminish the least part of the Goods, but took great care to preserve them, until having received their just debts, they restored all they had taken entirely.* By the Civil Law they that have any share in the Prizes taken are usually cited, and being adjudged lawfull, they are by publick Authority sold and divided among such as are concerned in them. But to be better informed in these and the like Cases we must consult such as have treated of the Civil Law, especially *Bartolus*, who hath written much concerning the matter of Reprizals. One thing I shall here add, because it serves somewhat to allay and qualifie the severity of this Law, in it self too rigid, namely, That they who either by the non-payment of what they owe, or not doing that which is Right to such as they have wronged, do occasion the seizing of their fellow-subjects Goods, are bound by the Laws both of God and of Nature to make satisfaction for those losses, which other men through their faults have sustained. Thus *Plutarch* of the *Syrians*, *Many of them*, saith he, *would not contribute money, but commanded those that had either received or taken away other mens Goods to repair their loss.*

Gregor. lib. 9.

Cymon.

CHAP. III.

Of a Just or Solemn War, according to the Law of Nations; and of its Denunciation.

I. *That a Solemn War by the Law of Nations ought to be between divers people.*
II. *A distinction between a Nation, though doing unjustly, and a company of Thieves and Pyrats.*
III. *Yet sometimes there happens to be a change.*
IV. *It is requisite to a Solemn War, That he that makes it should have Soveraign Power; and how this is to be understood.*
V. *And that the War be solemnly denounced.*
VI. *Whereunto what by the Law of Nature, and what properly by the Law of Nations is required, is handled distinctly.*
VII. *The denunciation of War is sometimes conditional, sometimes simple and absolute.*
VIII. *In denunciations, what belongs to the Civil Law, and not to the Law of Nations.*
IX. *War being denounced against a Prince, is denounced also against his Subjects and Associates, so far forth as they follow him.*
X. *But not as by themselves considered; this illustrated by examples.*
XI. *The reason why denunciation is requisite to some effects of War.*
XII. *That these effects are not to be found in other Wars.*
XIII. *Whether a War may be made as soon as it is denounced.*
XIV. *Whether against him that hath violated the Rights of Embassadors a War may be made, though not denounced.*

I. A Solemn War ought to be between two diverse Nations. * *Lib.* 1. *cap.*3. *sect.* 4.

WE have already said *, That according to the Opinion of the best Authors, a War is oft-times said to be Just, not from the Cause that excites it, nor from those Heroick Actions that are done in it, but from some peculiar effects of Right which one War hath more than another. But what manner of War this is, is best understood by the definition which the *Romans* give of an enemy, *Hostes sunt qui nobis, aut quibus nos publicè bellum decernimus*; *They are Enemies*, saith *Pomponius*, *against whom we publickly denounce War, or who do the like against us*; the rest are but Pyrats and Robbers: to the very same purpose speaks *Ulpian*: Wherefore as he there adds, He that is taken by Robbers, is not a slave to those that take him, neither need he recover his freedom by the Right of Postliminy, as one that returns out of Captivity doth. *A Piratis aut latronibus captus, liber permanet*, saith *Paulus* the Lawyer; He that is taken prisoner by a Robber or a Pyrat loseth not thereby the priviledge of a Citizen, as he doth, that is taken prisoner in War by the *Germans*, or by the *Parthians*. Whereunto we may add that of *Ulpian*, In Civil Dissentions, although the Common-Wealth be dangerously wounded, yet doth not the Contest extend to the ruine of the State; they that betake themselves to either part are not such mortal Enemies, as they are to whom the Right of captivating men, and of Postliminy belong: And therefore though they be taken and sold, yet whensoever they shall recover their liberty, they shall not need to petition their Prince to restore them to their Freedom, because they never lost it by a just Captivity. This only is to be observed, That under the Example of the People of *Rome*, whosoever in any City or Common-wealth hath the Supreme Power, hath a Right to make a Just War; according to that of *Cicero*, *Ille hostis est, qui habet Rempublicam, Curiam, Ærarium, &c.* He is accounted an Enemy who enjoys a Common-Wealth, a Court, a Treasury, the Consent and Concord of Citizens, with some regard had, if the matter require it to Peace and Leagues: The word *Hostis*, signifies properly an Equal, which Pyrats and Robbers cannot be to Soveraign Princes; and therefore they cannot be said to make a Just War.

L. Postliminium, sect. 2. *D. de Cap. L. si quis ingenuam.*

Philip. 4.

II. A distinction between a Nation doing things unjustly, and Pyrats, and Robbers. * *Vand.* 2.

Neither doth a Common-wealth cease to be a Common-wealth, because some Acts of Injustice are publickly and generally committed by them; nor are Robbers or Pyrats to be deemed a Civil Society, because haply they do observe some kind of equality between themselves, without which no Society can possibly long subsist: For these latter are not (as *Procopius* speaks *) *Turba hominum, Lege congregata, sed injustitiæ causa, in unum coacta*; *A company of men associated under a Law, but forced to unite, to defend themselves against the Law*: whereas the former, though guilty sometimes of some injustice, and so not without some faults, yet do they associate for the defence of their own Right, and do Right unto Foreigners, though haply not in all things according to the Law of Nature, which in many places is almost obliterated; yet certainly according to those Covenants and Agreements which they have made with every Nation, or according to the Customs by them used. This the Scholiast upon *Thucydides* observes, That whilst the *Grecians* preached Pyracy as a lawfull Calling, they at the same time abstained from Murther, from robbing

Lib. 1.

robbing by night, and from driving away the Oxen that ploughed the earth. And *Strabo* records it of divers other Nations, who though they lived by Piracy; yet as soon as they returned home, would send to the right Owners, that if they would they might redeem their Goods at indifferent prizes. And hitherto we may also refer that of *Homer*: *Lib.* 2.

Ipsi etiam rapti avidi, qui aliena pererrant
Littora, concessu Superûm si præda reperta est,
Navibus impletis abeunt, & vela retorquent.:
Quippe Deos metuunt, memores fandi atque nefandi.

Greedy of Gain to foreign Coasts they stray;
If by their starry Guides they find a prey,
With sails retort they go, their Ships full fraught,
Fearing the Gods, minding what's good, what's nought.

The Ancient Normans accounted Piracy an honourable Trade to live by. And *Plutarch* notes of the *Scipii*, that they were extremely corrupt (yet a Commonwealth) although they robbed even such Merchants, as came in a friendly way to traffick with them; but in Morals the principal part gives form to the whole: And as *Cicero* well observed, *Because it contains the most parts, and spreads farthest, therefore it gives denomination to the whole.* *De finibus.* 5. To the same sense is that also of *Galen*, *In temperaments the denomination is always taken from that which is the greatest portion.* Wherefore *Cicero* is very crude in his expression in saying, That when the King is unjust, the Nobles unjust, and the generality of the People so, it is not so properly a corrupt Commonwealth, as none at all: which sentence of *Cicero's*, St. *Augustine* thus corrects, *Neither can I therefore say truly, that that people are no people, or that Commonwealth no Commonwealth, so long as there remains any society of a rational multitude, unanimously congregated for the mutual defence of such things as they love.* *De Civit. Dei lib.* 19. *c.* 24. A Body though diseased yet remains a Body; and a City is still a City so long as it hath Laws, and executes judgments, and hath other means necessary for both natives and strangers, to preserve or recover their just Rights. That which *Dion Chrysostome* observes, comes much nearer to truth, who tells us, That the Law (especially that of Nations) is in a City, as the Soul in an humane Body; which being taken away, it remains no longer a City. So likewise *Cicero* in another place, *There were neither Laws nor judgments, nor any sign to shew that there was a Commonwealth.* *Lib.* 10. *Ep.* 1. *Aristides* in his perswasive Oration to the Rhodians for Peace, proves that many good Laws may very well consist even with Tiranny. And *Aristotle* informs us, That he that strains the power, either of the Nobles or of the People, to too high a key, marrs the Harmony of good Government; and first corrupts the Commonwealth, and then destroys it. *Lib.* 5. *de rep.* Let us illustrate this by examples: That they who are taken by Robbers, are not made slaves, was (as we have said) the opinion of *Ulpian.* But if a Roman Citizen was taken by the Germans or Parthians, he lost his freedom; and yet among the Germans, the Roberies that were done without the bounds of the City were blameless, which are *Cæsars* own words. *Lib.* 6. *Tacitus* records it of the *Garamantes*, that they were, *Gens Latrociniis fœcunda, sed Gens tamen*; *A Nation wholly addicted to Roberies, but yet a Nation though.* The Illirians spoiled all they met at Sea without regard; but yet to him that subdued them, was a triumph granted; which was denied to *Pompey* who had purged the Sea of Pirates. So great is the difference between a Nation though corrupt, and a company of men combined only to do mischief.

III. Yet there often happens a change.

Yet a change doth sometimes happen, not in particular persons only; as in *Jephtha*, *Arsaces*, *Variatus*, who of Captains over Thieves and Robbers, became lawful Commanders; but in Societies also: As when a company of Robbers or Pirates shall forsake that wicked kind of life, and unanimously betake themselves to a Civil Government, an example whereof we have in the Mamertines. St. *Augustine* concerning Robberies speaks thus, *When this mischief by the concourse of men of desperate fortunes, grows so great, that they betake themselves to some certain place to inhabit, and there build Cities, raise Forts, and thereby are able to subdue Nations; then it assumes the title of a Kingdom or free State: Not,* as St. *Augustine* goes on, *that they cease to be what before they were; but because what they formerly did through fear, and therefore secretly, they now do with boldness and confidence.* *De Civit. Dei, l.* 4. *c.* 4. *It was a bold answer, that* Diomedes *the Pirate made to* Alexander *the Great, when he demanded of him the reason why he so troubled the Seas; For the same* (saith he) *that thou dost the World: But because I rob with one single Ship, I am called a Pirate; whereas thou, because with a great Fleet, art therefore stiled an Emperour.* But that which makes this change according to what is here intended, is not so much their impunity as their repentance. For this St. *Augustine* requires, that deserting their wicked courses, they live together under some wholsom Laws, according unto which, justice may be administred, as well to strangers, as natives.

IV. A solemn War ought to be between such as have Sovereign Power.

Who they are that have soveraign Power we have already shewed, from whence we may also collect, That he that hath that power but for a part, may for that part make a just War; much more, they who are not Subjects but Confederates, though on Articles very unequal. Thus were all the Wars between the Romans and their Confederates, the Volscians, Latines, Spaniards, and Carthaginians, just; though their Confederacies were made on very unequal terms, as we may collect out of Histories.

V. A solemn War must be denounced. *Jos. Ant. l. 15.* *Camd. Eliz. an. 1582.*

Neither is it sufficient to denominate a War, in this sense just, that it is made between such as have soveraign Power: But as we have heard before, it must be publickly declared; yea so publickly, that both parties may have equal knowledge thereof, which *Ennius* calls the proclaiming of War, *Bellum inferre non ante denuntiatum, injustum est; To make War before it be denounced is unjust:* to exercise Hostility without denouncing War or requiring satisfaction, is not done like a Christian, nor allowable by the Law of Nations; as the English Ambassador told the Emperour of *Russia*. And therefore as *Cicero* well observes, *To determine of the equity of a War, was a Right proper to the Colledge of Heralds which was amongst the Romans held very sacred; thereby giving us to understand, that no War could be just, but that which was made, either for the recovery of things unjustly taken away, or publickly decreed and solemnly proclaimed.* Not so clear is that of an Ancient Writer, quoted by *Isidore, That War is just which is made by publick Edict, either for the recovery of our own, or for repelling an invading enemy. Livy* describes a just War thus, *That War which is openly decreed by publick Edict, and solemnly denounced, is just;* that is, if it be so done by such persons as have the supreme Authority. And the same Authour having first declared, That the Epirots had wasted the Territories of *Athens*, saith, *That the Athenians were first highly incensed against the Epirots, and afterwards by the Decrees of their Cities, first voluntarily denounced, and then waged against them a just War.*

VI. Wherein what is required by the Law of Nature, and what by the Law of Nations.

For the clearer understanding of this and the like places, which concern the denuntiation of War, we must accurately distinguish what things are due by the strict Law of Nature; and what things are honest and commendable, though not by nature due; Thirdly, What things are by the Law of Nations required to the obtaining of the proper effects of the right of Nations; and lastly, What things do arise from the peculiar Laws and Customs of some people. By the Law of Nature, where force cannot be repelled but by force, and where punishment cannot be demanded but of him who is the Offender; there the denouncing of War is needless. *Sthenelaidas* in *Thucydides* pleads thus †, *Non est quod verbis & judiciis disceptemus ultra verba læsi; 'Tis vain to contest with words and arguments, when the wrongs which we manifestly sustain, are more than verbal.* Thus likewise do the Plateans in the same Authour plead *, *By that Law that is received by all Nations, it is lawful to repel him by force that shall invade us like an enemy.* So *Flaminius* in *Diodorus* †, *calls all, both Gods and men, to witness, That according to this Law, the King, and not himself, was the Aggressor.* And if so, then as *Latinus* in *Halicarnassensis* notes, *Every man that is by a War damnified, may right himself upon him that began it.* And as *Ælian* out of *Plato, Quod ad propulsandam vim suscipitur Bellum, non à Caduceatore, sed à natura indicitur; That war that is made against an Invader, needs no other Herald to proclaim it than nature it self.* And herein is that of *Dion Chrysostome* verified, *That many wars are made, which were never denounced.* Neither is there any thing else that *Livy* blames in *Menippus* King *Antiochus*'s General, but that he had slain certain Romans before any war was denounced, or any hostile act had proceeded so far as either to the drawing of a weapon, or the effusion of bloud in any place; intimating thereby, That in either of these cases that fact of *Menippus* had been justifiable. Neither doth the Law of Nature necessarily require, That the right Owner being to apprehend what is his own, should first denounce war, or declare his intention before he do it. But so often as one thing is to be taken in lieu of another, or the Goods of a Debtor attached for a Debt; there a predemand is necessary: much more is it necessary when the Goods of Subjects are to be seized for the Debt of their Prince, that thereby it may appear, That we had no other means or way left, but by war to recover either our own, or what is due unto us. For the right that we have in the things so seized, is no primary, but a surrogated right, as we have elsewhere declared. The like may be said of him who hath the supreme Authority, who cannot justly be invaded for either the debts or the faults of his Subjects, until satisfaction hath been demanded; which if denied, renders the Prince also culpable, either by participating with them in the wrong done, or at least by omitting what he ought to do, according to those Rules which we have elsewhere given. Nay farther, even where the Law of Nature doth not require any such demand to be made, yet may it be done both honestly and honourably, to the end that men may be more careful to abstain from giving offence; and that those already given, may be expiated by confession and satisfaction: according to those Rules which I have already prescribed for the prevention of those mischiefs which do usually accompany War, whereunto even that also appertains:

1. The Invader may be repelled without the denouncing of War. † *Lib. 1.* * *Lib. 3.* † *Excerp. Peiresianis. Lib. 1.*

So may the right Owner apprehend his own without declaring his intention. But to recover a Debt, or one thing for another, a predemand is necessary.

2. What in these cases Nature requires not, yet may be done honestly and laudably. *Vid. lib. 2. c. 23. sect. 7.*

Extrema

Extrema primo nemo tentavit loco.

No man at first unto extremes will flye.

When all Israel were ready to fall on the Gibeonites to revenge the outrage done to the Levites Wife, *the Elders restrained them, urging, That it was not fit that they (who were forbidden by the Law, rashly to make war upon Strangers, though justly provoked, till by their Ambassadours they had sought all means to induce them to do them justice) should unadvisedly fall upon their Brethren, until they had first heard their grievances and denied satisfaction.* And as to that Command which God gave unto the Israelites, *Deut.* 20. 2. namely, *That before they fought against any City, they should offer them peace.* It was peculiarly given to that Nation, and therefore not at all to be confounded with the Law of Nations. Nor was that peace which was so offered an absolute peace, but on this Condition, That they would submit and pay tribute. When *Cyrus* had march'd with his Army into *Armenia*, he forbore all hostile acts till he had sent Ambassadours to the King to require of him the Tribute and Succours by the League due; *esteeming it* (as *Xenophon* speaks) *more friendly thus to proceed, than to act farther, until he had declared the ground of the War.* Nevertheless by the Law of Nations, as to those peculiar effects of a just War, a publick denunciation is in all cases requisite, if not on both sides, yet on one.

Deut. 20. 11. *Jos. Ant. l.* 5. 2.

Xenoph. Hist. l. 2.

VII. War denounced sometimes conditionally, and sometimes absolutely.

This denunciation of War is sometimes conditional, and sometimes absolute. Conditional, when restitution or satisfaction is demanded at the same time when the War is denounced. Now the Fecial Law (whereby the Heralds are guided) do under the Notion of things demanded, comprehend not only a vindication of what is due by the right of dominion, but the persecution also of whatsoever is due, either upon any civil account, or by reason of any crime committed, as *Servius* rightly expounds it. Hence it is, that in all such Conditional Denunciations we read either of some things to be restored, of some damages to be repaired, or some Offenders to be delivered up; unless they from whom such Offenders are demanded, shall chuse rather to punish them themselves, as we have elsewhere said. And that this solemn Demand of things was called *Clarigationem*, or a *proclaiming of War*, *Pliny* testifies in these words, *Et Legati cùm ad Hostes clarigatum mitterentur, id est, res raptas clare repetitum, unus utique Verbenarius vocabatur; And Ambassadours, when sent to their enemies to demand with a loud voice restitution of things taken away by force, one of them was called* Verbenarius, *an Herald, because he was always crowned with Vervin.* And in another place, speaking of Vervin, he saith, *That it is that Herb which Ambassadours and Heralds do usually carry with them to their enemies, as we have elsewhere shewed.* One example of this conditional denouncing of War we have in *Livy*, in these words, *Which injuries, unless redressed by those that occasioned them, they are resolved with all their power to revenge.* Another we have in *Tacitus*, *Ni supplicium in malos præsumant, usurum promiscua Cæde; Unless punishment be inflicted on the Malefactors, they will seek their revenge by War.* And of this kind of proclaiming War we have an ancient Precedent in *Euripides*, where *Theseus* gives this Charge to his Ambassadours:

Lib. 22. 2.

Lib. 25. *c.* 9.

Lib. 8.

Ann. l. 1.

Vicina Theseus qui tenet Regni sola
Humare poscit mortuos; quod si datur,
Sit amica faciet Gens Erechtidûm tibi.
Hæc si probantur, tam refer retro pedem;
Sin nemo paret, verba sint hæc altera:
Jam mox ut Arma pubis expectent meæ.

All which *Papinius*, rehearsing the same Story, abreviates in this Verse;

Graves for the slain, or War 'gainst Thebes *proclaim.*

A pure or absolute denunciation is that which is especially called an Indiction or Proclamation, which is either when the other Party hath already begun the War (which is that which in *Isidore* is called a War to repel the force of an invading Enemy;) or when he himself hath committed that which deserves to be punished. Sometimes after a denunciation that is conditional, there follows another that is pure and absolute, though not necessarily, yet redundantly. Hence ariseth that usual Form, *Testor hunc Populum injustum esse, neque jus reddere; I declare this Nation to be unjust, neither will they do right.* And this other Form, *Concerning which matters, differences and causes, Remonstrance hath been given by the Chief Herald at Arms of the People of* Rome, *to the Chief Herald at Arms of the Ancient Latines, and of the People of the Ancient Latines; but yet neither have they paid, given or done any of those things which they should have paid, given or done: wherefore I do judge, agree and ordain, That satisfaction be sought by an open and a just War.* Whereunto we may add a third

The Greeks calls this ῥύσια καταγγέλλειν, to declare Reprizes lawful.

third Form, which follows, *Because the people of the Ancient Latines have injured the people of* Rome, *and failed in what they ought to have done, and because the people of* Rome *have decreed to make war against the Ancient Latines; therefore I and the people of* Rome *do denounce and make war against the Ancient Latines.* But yet that the denouncing of War is not in this case (as I have said) precisely necessary, is plain by this, That it is sufficient if it be proclaimed but at the next Garrison. For thus it was adjudged by the Heralds, as well in the case of *Philip* of *Macedon*, as afterwards in the case of *Antiochus*; Since *he is first to denounce the War that seeks satisfaction by the War.* Nay, the War that the Romans made against *Pyrrhus* was denounced but to one of his Souldiers, and that in the Flaminian Cirque only. Besides, this also gives an occasion to another needless Observation, That War is sometimes solemnly denounced on both sides; as that Peloponesian War, which was made between the Corcyrians and the Corinthians; whereas had it been proclaimed but on one side only, it had been sufficient.

Livy lib. 31. 36.

VIII.

3. In denouncing War what is required by the Civil, and what by the law of Nations.

Caducaeus, whence derived, see *Plinys Nat. Hist. l.* 29. *c.* 3. and *Servius* upon the 4th and 8th of *Virg. Æneads.*

That Heralds were usually sent to denounce War among the *Grecians*, clad with party-coloured Coats, and armed with a bloody Javelin by the *Æquicoli* first, and afterwards in imitation of them by the *Romans.* That there should be a solemn renunciation of all former friendship and alliance, (if any such there were) after thirty dayes demand of reparation for damages received; And that the King of the Heralds should again thrust his Spear into the enemies ground, as *Servius* upon the ninth of *Virgils Æneads* records, and the like, are not dictates of the Law of Nations, but are Ceremonies arising from the Customs and Institutes of some particular Nation, many of which *Arnobius* confesseth, were antiquated in his time, and some of them grown out of use even in *Varro*'s. The third Punick War was as soon made as denounced, and it was the Opinion of *Mecœnas* in *Dion*, that some of those Ceremonies were peculiar to popular States only.

IX.

War denounced against a Prince, is denounced against all that adhere unto him.

Livy lib. 35.

War being denounced against him that hath the Supreme Power in any Nation is presumed to be denounced also against not only all his Subjects, and against all that shall afterwards adhere unto him, as being his Associates. And this is the meaning of our Modern Lawyers, when they say, *Diffidato Principe, diffidati sunt omnes adhærentes; War Proclaimed against a Prince, is proclaimed also against all that shall side with him:* For *Diffidare* with them is *to proclaim War*, which is to be understood of that very War which is made upon him against whom it is denounced: As when the *Romans* denounced War against *Antiochus*, they thought it needless to denounce it against the *Ætolians* also seperately, who had publickly espoused *Antiochus* his quarrel; for say the Heralds, *The Ætolians have spared us that labour, by denouncing War against themselves.*

X.

But not by themselves considered.

Livy lib. 35. *cap.* 42.

But that War being ended, If any other either Prince or People are to be invaded for Succours sent unto our Enemies during that War, we ought to denounce that War anew, if we expect the effects proper unto a Just War by the Law of Nations: For such a Prince or State are not then to be looked at as Accessaries, but as Principals. Neither is it the prosecution of the old War, but the beginning of a new: Whereunto, as the Law of Nations requires a solemn indiction, so by the Civil Law of the *Romans* was it not to be undertaken, untill it had the Warrant of a new Decree from the People. Wherefore the War that *Manlius* made against the *Gallo-Græcians*, and that which *Cæsar* made against *Ariovistus* were not justifiable by the Law of Nations. And whereas when the consent of the People of *Rome* was asked to make War against King *Antiochus*, the question was put in this form, *Is it your Will and Pleasure, that War be made against King* Antiochus, *and against all that shall side with him?* (Which was also the form used in the Decree against King *Perseus.*) It ought to be understood with this limitation, namely, so long as that War shall continue with those two Kings, and with those who are truly and really engaged in it with them.

XI.

4. Why denunciation is necessary to some effects of War, in a Solemn War.

† *Alb. Gent, lib.* 1. *cap.* 2.

The Turks two dayes before Battle make many great fires.

Chalcoc. lib. 7.

Lib. 3. *de Ira. cap.* 2.

Now the reason why a Solemn Denunciation is so necessarily required unto such a War as by the Law of Nations is Just, is not (as some think) to prevent deceit and treachery; for this is better referred to Magnanimity than to Justice. Thus have we read of some Nations so confident of their own strength, that they have appointed the time and place long before, when and where they would give their Enemies battle: As *Plutarch* tells us, that the *Romans* did to King *Porsenna* †. Thus *Thomas* Earl of *Surrey* sent an Herald to *James* the fourth King of *Scotland*, to let him know, that on the *Friday* following he would give him Battle, if he would stay so long in *England*; and *Thomas* his Son, then Lord Admiral sent the King word, that he might find him in the Van of his Army; as *Herbert* Records it in his History of *Henry* the Eighth, *pag.* 43. But the true reason is to remonstrate unto all Nations, That the War is made not rashly or upon any private ends, but with the Consent and Approbation of both Nations, or at least of those who have the Supreme Power on both sides. For from hence ariseth those effects proper to a Just War, which in a War made with Pyrats and Robbers, or in a War made by a Prince against his own Subjects will not be allowed. And therefore *Seneca* did well distinguish between *a War denounced against Foreigners, and that made against Subjects or Citizens.*

Now

Now where some note, and by examples teach, that even in such Wars as these, whatsoever is taken away immediately becomes his that takes it: I answer, That this is true but on one side only, and that likewise by the Law of Nature, but not by the voluntary Law of Nations, which makes provision for the safety of Nations only, and not of those who are either no Nation, or but a corrupt part of one. They likewise are in an errour, who conceive, that in a War undertaken for the defence either of our own persons or our Goods, there needs no Denunciation; for even in such a War Denunciation is altogether necessary, though not simply, yet to the obtaining the effects proper to a Just War, as we have already hinted, and shall hereafter more fully explain. XII. Which are not in other Wars. *Ayala. l. 1. c. 5. Alb. Gent. l. 2. c. 2.*

Neither are they in the right who hold, That War cannot justly be as soon made as it is denounced, which *Cyrus* did against the *Armenians*, and the *Romans* against the *Carthaginians*, as I said before. For the Law of Nations requires not that any time should be allowed, the War being denounced; yet notwithstanding the nature and quality of the business may haply require that some time be given, as in case Restitution be demanded, or punishment against an Offender, but not as yet denied: For in these Cases convenient time is to be granted for the doing of it. XIII. Whether a War may be as soon made as denounced.

Nay, though the Rights of Embassadors should be violated, yet it will not thence follow, That to the attaining those Effects, which are proper to a just War, Denunciation is not necessary; for it is sufficient if it be done either by Citation, Declaration, Proclamation, or any other safe way or means, as is customarily done in such places, whereunto we cannot without danger approach. XIV. Whether it be to be denounced, in case the Right of Embassadors be violated.

CHAP. IV.

That in a solemn War, the Right of killing Enemies is by the Law of Nations granted.

I. *The effects of a solemn War generally explained.*
II. *The word Lawful distinguisht, into what may be done without blame, though it may be more commendably otherwise; and what is done is unpunishable.*
III. *That the effects of a solemn War generally considered, are therefore lawful because unpunishable,*
IV. *Why such effects were introduced.*
V. *Divers testimonies concerning those effects.*
VI. *In this sense it is lawful to kill, or any other ways to distress all that reside in an Enemies Territories.*
VII. *What if they came thither before the War.*
VIII. *That the Subjects of an Enemy may in any place be assaulted, unless protected by the Laws of a foreign Prince.*
IX. *That this licence extends to Women and Infants:*
X. *Yea, and to Captives, and that at all times:*
XI. *Yea, even unto such as are willing to yield themselves, if not accepted of:*
XII. *Also unto such as surrender themselves without condition.*
XIII. *That this Right ought not to be refered to any other cause, as to Retaliation, Obstinacy,* &c.
XIV. *That this licence may be extended even to Hostages.*
XV. *By the Law of Nations it is forbidden to kill by Poyson.*
XVI. *Or to Impoison either Waters or Weapons.*
XVII. *But not any other ways to corrupt their Waters.*
XVIII. *Whether the Law of Nations will admit the killing of an Enemy by a private Murtherer, explained.*
XIX. *Whether the ravishing of women be permitted by the Law of Nations.*

SERVIUS upon this Verse of *Virgils*, I. The Right of killing Enemies in a solemn War.

Tum certare odiis, tum res rapuisse licebit.

Then lawful 'twas to fight, to kill and spoil.

deriving the fecial Laws from *Ancus Martius*, and so upwards from the *Æquicolæ*, tells us, *That when any great injuries were done unto the Romans by any other Nation, the* Pater patratus, *or President of the Colledge, with some other of the Heralds, whose office it was to contract Leagues, and denounce War, went to the borders of that Nation, and there with a loud voice proclaimed the cause of the War; and if they did not restore the things taken, or deliver up the Offender*

offender within thirty days, then he cast a Javelin into their Territories, which was the beginning of the War; that done, it was lawful for them to kill and spoil. He had before said, *That the Ancients under* Res rapere, *comprehended all manner of injuries; and under* Res reddere, *the restoring things, all manner of satisfaction, though there were nothing at all of rapine in the case:* Whence we learn that a War solemnly denounced between two Nations, or their chief Magistrates hath some peculiar effects; which War in its own nature cannot challenge, all which are very agreeable to what we have already quoted from the Roman Lawyers.

Crantzius Saxonicorum 2. 5.

II. The word lawful distinguisht.

Which words of *Virgil* that we may the better understand, we must note, That the word *Lawful* is taken in a twofold sense; for in the first place, that is said to be lawful which is altogether just and honest, though haply some other thing may be more commendably done; in which sense St *Paul* speaking of things in themselves indifferent, saith, *All things are lawful for me, but all things are not expedient:* As for example, to marry is lawful, but to contain if it be with a pious intention is more laudable. For as *Tertullian* well observes, *Continence would lose her best evidence, if to marry were unlawful. Virgins,* saith St. *Hierome, deserve the greater honour, because what they may do without sin, they voluntarily disdain.* And again, *All those supereminent vertues that lead to perfection, are left as Arbitrary to our Auditors*: Nulla tibi imponitur necessitas, ut voluntas præmium consequatur; *No necessity is imposed on thee, that what thou dost truly, may receive the greater reward.* St. *Chrysostome* speaking of Matrimony shews, *That although it be lawful, yet it is better to abstain*; and yet in his exposition on the seventh to the *Romans,* he saith, *That to them that do not what they are commanded, Hell is denounced; thereby shewing, that things absolutely commanded, are not of the same nature with those that are left to their own free choice: As Virginity and the renouncing of our possessions, because those that are commanded must of necessity be done.* And therefore in his second Oration concerning Fasting, *He placeth Virginity without the lists; and above that which we are commanded to strive for; unto which, as he that can attain, shews his Christian magnanimity; so he that shall fall short of, easily obtains pardon.* And in this sense also are second Marriages lawful, although to have been contented with one only were much better, as *Clemens Alexandrinus* rightly states the Question; where speaking of a man that had contracted a second Marriage, he saith, *That although therein he sinned not, because there was no Law that forbad it; yet could he never attain unto that perfection of holiness, that the Gospel seemed to commend unto us.* So for a believing Husband to put away his unbelieving Wife is lawful, as St. *Augustine* affirms, (which with what circumstances is to be verified, it is not to our purpose in this place to discuss) but yet he may, and that haply more laudably retain her: Wherefore he adds, *Both are equally lawful, according to the rules of Divine Justice; for neither of them are prohibited by God, but yet both are not equally expedient. Ulpian* concerning him that having sold his Wine, and covenanted with the buyer, that if he fetcht it not by such a day, it should be lawful for him to pour it out, saith, *That although he may do it, yet if he do it not, he is the more to be commended.* Secondly, this word *Lawful* may be taken for that which is not punishable by humane Laws, although it consist not with Piety, or the rules of Morality; thus in many Countries fornication is lawful, that is, not punishable. Amongst the Lacedemonions and Ægyptians theft was lawful. And in *Quintilian* we read, *That there are some things, which though not in their own nature commendable, yet that are by the Laws tolerated;* as by the Laws of the twelve Tables, *The body of the Debter might de divided among the Creditors;* all which, though in themselves unfit and unseemly, yet are by some Lawgivers permitted to avoid greater inconveniencies: *Licentia plerumque est tentatio Disciplinæ; Licence,* saith *Tertullian, is for the most part but the touchstone of Discipline. All things,* saith S. *Paul, are lawful, but all things edify not.* Now this acception of the word *Lawful* is somewhat improper, as *Cicero* testifies in his Tusculans, where speaking of *Cinna,* who had been four times Consul, and had caused divers of the chiefest of the Roman Nobility to be slain, saith thus, *Shall we esteem this man happy; nay, on the contrary, I think him miserable, not because he committed these things, but because he so governed the Commonwealth, that he might lawfully commit them: not that it is lawful for any man to sin (Sed sermonis errore labimur, dum id licere dicimus, quod cuique conceditur;) But we are misled through the common errour of speech, whilst we pronounce that lawful which is only permitted.* Whence *Columella* concludes, *That we ought not to prosecute our revenge to the utmost of what we may, for extreme severity is too near a Neighbour to extreme cruelty:* Yet notwithstanding, though this acception of the word *Lawful*, be not so proper, yet is it among the Romans very frequent, as will appear by the same *Cicero,* who thus bespeaks the Judges, *Quid deceat vos, non quantum liceat vobis, spectare debetis; Ye that are Judges ought to consider, not so much what in strictness of Law ye may do, but what in every case is most fit and convenient to be done; for if you regard your own power only, ye may put to death even whom you will.* In the same sense, as it is usually said of Kings, *That they may do even what they please, because they are exempted from the lash of humane Laws;* yet is that advice which *Claudian* gives unto his Prince, much more worthily to be by all Princes received:

1 Cor. 6. 17.
Adv. Marcion.
Ad Helv.
Ad Pammach.
Ad 1 Cor. 7.
Strom. 4.
See *Grat.* out of St *Aug. c.* 14. *q.* 1.
Ad Pollent. lib. 1. *c.* 15.
Grat. c. 28. *q.* 1.
Lib. 5.
Summum jus summa injuria.
Orat. pro Rabirio Posthumo.

Nec

Nec tibi quid liceat, sed quid fecisse decebit,
Occurrat.————

————Resolve to do,
Not what you may, but what becometh you.

Musonius highly blames those Princes who study more their own Prerogatives, than the Good of their Subjects, and that say, thus and thus I can do, rather than thus and thus I ought to do. Hence it is, that we find these two words, *Licet* and *Oportet*, *it is lawfull*, and *it behoves*, placed sometimes in opposition one to the other: As in *Ammianus Marcellinus*, *Sunt aliqua quæ fieri non oportet, etiam si licet; Some things there are which are not fit to be done, though lawfully we may do them.* So in *Pliny*'s Epistles, *Things that are dishonest we must avoid, not as they are unlawfull, but as they are shamefull.* And as *Cicero* himself affirms the same, *Est enim aliquid, quod non oporteat, etiamsi licet, Somethings are not fit to be done, though lawfull.* And in his Oration for the defence of *Milo*, he distinguisheth between *fas* and *licet*, attributing to the former, that which is agreeable to the Law of Nature, and to the latter, that which was agreeable to the Laws of particular Countries. So *Quintilian* the Father in one of his Declamations tells us, That *It is one thing to look strictly to what is a mans Right,* (i. e.) *to what a man may do; and another thing to respect that which is just: Aliud est spectare jura, alind justitiam.* [Declam. lib. 3. cap. 5. — Lib. 30. — Orat. pro Balbo. — Orat. 251.]

III. In War the effects are lawfull generally, that is, not punishable.

In this sense therefore it is lawfull for one Enemy to hurt another, both in his Person, or in his Estate; It is lawfull, I say, not only for him that makes War upon a Just ground, and that in the prosecution of that War contains himself within those bounds, which by the Law of Nature are prescribed him, as we have already said, but for both parties, and that without distinction. So that he that doth thus injure his Enemy, though he be apprehended in another Princes Dominion, yet can he not be proceeded against as an Homicide, or as a Thief; neither can any other Prince for this only Cause make War upon him, and in this sense is that of *Salust* true: *By the Law of Arms all things are lawfull to the Conquerour.*

IV. Why such effects were introduced.

Now the Reason of this so great a licence granted by all Nations, is this, because when two Nations are at War, for any other Nation to judge, where the Right is, had been dangerous; for by that means, that Nation may quickly be intangled in the others War, as the Marseillians pleaded in the Cause of *Cæsar* and *Pompey*: And therefore they confest, That they had neither Wisdom nor Power sufficient to determine, whether of them had the Juster Cause. Besides even where the War is manifestly Just, it is a very nice thing by any outward token to judge which is the Just Rule or Measure, either of defending our selves, of recovering our own Right, or of exacting punishments: So that it is agreed, that it is much better to leave it to the Honesty and Conscience of the Princes engaged to determine of these things among themselves, than to refer it to the arbitrement of others. Thus did the Achaians demand of the Roman Senate, *How it came to pass, that what had formerly been acted by the Right of War, should now fall into debate?* Now besides this of licence and impunity, there is another effect of a Just and Solemn War, namely *Dominion*, whereof we shall treat hereafter.

V. Testimonies of these effects.

But the licence that a Just War gives to one Enemy against another, extends either to his person, or his Estate: And first to the person of an Enemy, and hereof we have many testimonies recorded in the most approved Authors: The Greek Proverb acquitteth the Souldier for what he doth against the person of an Enemy in the time of War, in that it saith,

He guiltless is that doth his Enemy kill. Euripides.

The custom of the ancient Grecians was not to wash nor to eat with an Homicide, much less to joyn with him in any Duties that were holy, and yet with him that in the War had killed an Enemy it was lawfull. And in all Authors we read, That to kill was *Jus Belli, the Right of War.* *Marcellus* in *Livy* justifies himself by this Right, *Quicquid in hostibus feci, jus belli defendit; Whatever I did among mine Enemies, the Law of Arms doth defend me in.* And so doth *Alcon* justifie himself and his Soldiers to the Saguntines, *Suffer your Wives and your Children to be dragged about and ravished before your faces, according to the licence given in Wars, for better it is with patience to endure those out-rages, than that they should put you all to the sword.* And the same *Livy* having declared, the general Massacre of the *Astapenses* adds, *That it was done by the Right of War.* *Cicero* likewise in his Oration for King *Dejotarus* pleads thus, *And why, O* Cæsar, *should he be suspected as thine enemy, who could not forget, that whereas thou mightest have adjudged him even to death by the Law of Arms, thou madest both him and his Sons also Kings?* And in another place he confesseth, *That whereas* Cæsar, *by the Right of a Conquerour might have sentenced them all to death,* [Livy 26. — Id. 21. — Lib. 28. — Pro M. Marcel.]

Lib. 7. *death, he out of his Princely Clemency had preserved them.* *Cæsar* in his Commentaries acquainted the State of the *Hedui*, *That he saved their people, whom by the Law of Arms he might have slain.* *Josephus* also in his Jewish War, *accounts it an honourable death to dye in the War; but he means to die by the Law of Arms, or at the Will and Pleasure of the Conquerour:* Of the same mind was *Papinius*,

Non querimur cæsos; hæc bellica jura, vicesque
Armorum.———— ——.

———Nor for our slain we grieved are;
This is the Law of Arms, the chance of War.

Yet we must observe, That when these Authors seem to justifie such acts of cruelty by the Right of War, they do not altogether free them from sin, but from being punishable as sins, as will appear by other places in the same Authors. It was well said of *Tacitus*, *In pace, causas & merita spectari, ubi bellum ingruat innocentes ac noxios juxta cadere; Peace doth usually distinguish of Causes and Merits, (and accordingly dispenseth rewards and punishments) but in War the nocent and innocent do fall alike.* And in another place, speaking of a Common Trooper, who demanded of his Captains a Reward for killing his own Brother in the head of his Enemies Troops, he saith, *Nec illis aut honorare eam cædem jus hominum, nec ulcisci, ratio belli permittebat; Neither would the Laws of humanity suffer them to reward so unnatural a murther, nor the Law of Arms permit them to punish it.* For that which *Seneca* observes is very true; Annal. lib. 1.

Quodcunque libuit facere, victori licet.

What e're he will, that may a Victor do.

Troad. See the second Book, chap. 1. sect. 1.

Epist. 96. And what he notes in his Epistles, *Quæ commissa capite luerent, tum quia paludati fuerunt, laudamus; What in another we punish with death, that in a Souldier under command we commend:* wherewith accords that of St *Cyprian*, *Homicidium cum admittunt singuli, crimen est, virtus vocatur cum publicè geritur; That which in a time of peace is a capital crime, in the time of War is accounted valour; but it is not the nature of their fact, but the exorbitancy of their cruelty, that renders Souldiers unpunishable:* And a little after he adds, *Consensere jura peccatis, & cœpit esse licitum quod publicum est; The Laws do connive at sin, which is therefore sometimes reputed innocence because licensed by publick authority.* And in this sense it is true what *Lactantius* saith of the Romans, that they did *Legitimè injurias inferre; Infest others lawfully:* As that also of *Lucan*, *Jusque datum sceleri*, which we may translate in the words of *David*, *Wickedness is practised as by a Law.* Epist. 2. Institut. 4. c. 9. Pharsal.

VI. All that are found among enemies are liable to the effects of War. Livy lib. 37.

But this Right of licence or impunity in War extends it self very far, for it reacheth not only to such as are actually in Arms, nor unto such only as are Subjects to these Princes against whom the War is made, but unto all such as reside within their Territories or Dominions; as may appear by that form so often used in *Livy*, *Hostis sit ille, quique intra præsidia sunt ejus; Let him, and all that live under his protection be held as enemies.* And no marvel, seeing that by all such we may be damnified, which in a War that is lasting and universal, is sufficient to justifie the licence here spoken of; otherwise than in Reprizals or Pignorations, which, as I have said, was at the first introduced after the manner of Taxes for the payment of publick debts. Wherefore it is not to be wondered at, if, as *Baldus* notes, This licence in War, be much greater than that in Pignorations: Nor is there any question, but that Strangers coming into the Enemies Territories after the War is proclaimed and began, may be persecuted as Enemies.

VII. Though they come before the War began. Liv. l. 25. Thucyd. lib. 1.

But as for those that went thither before the War was proclaimed, it is thought fit by the Law of Nations, that they should have some time allowed them to depart thence with their Goods; for so we read of the Corcyræans, That before they laid close siege to *Epidamnum*, they gave warning to all strangers to depart, or to be held as Enemies.

VIII. But natural Subjects every where, unless protected by another Prince.

But such as are true and natural Subjects, if we have respect only to their persons, they may in all places whatsoever be persecuted, because, as we have already shewed, when War is decreed and denounced, it is declared to be against a Prince or Nation, and the People thereof: So the Romans in their Decree against King *Philip*, *did Will and Command that War should be proclaimed against him and the Macedonians under his Dominions.* Now he that is an Enemy may by the Law of Nations be every where persecuted, according to that of *Euripides*;

Ubicunque prensum jura lædi hostem sinunt.

A Foe where ever found destroy'd may be.

And

And that of *Marcianus*, Renegadoes where ever they are met, may be killed as Enemies: And therefore, whether it be in their own Country, or in the Enemies, in a desart that belongs to none, or on the Sea, where ever it be, if found, they may lawfully be killed. But yet, that it is not lawful to kill them, or to spoil them in a Country that is in peace, this ariseth not from any Right that belongs properly to their persons, but from the Right of that Prince under whose Power and Protection they are. For all Civil Societies have a Right to Ordain, That no force or violence be offered against any in their Dominions, unless the differences be first examined in a judicial way; as we have already proved out of *Euripides*:

> *Si crimen istis aliquod hospitibus struis,*
> *Jus impetrabis : vi quidem hinc non abstrahes.*

> If charge thou can'st these Guests with great offence,
> Thou may'st have Right, but shalt not force them hence.

Where Laws flourish, and Courts of Justice are open, there every man is punished according to his deserts; and then this promiscuous licence of injuring each other ceaseth, which was only granted amongst Enemies in times of War only. Whilst the War raged between the Romans and the Carthaginians, it hapned that seven of the Carthaginian Gallies rode in a Port belonging to *Syphax*, who at that time was in League with both Nations; At which time *Scipio* with two of the Roman Gallies was by storm driven into the same Harbour before the Carthaginians could weigh anchor. It had been lawfull for the Carthaginians to have taken or sunk them before they had entred the Port: But being entred into the Kings Chambers, they durst not assault them lest thereby they should have violated the League with *Syphax*. The like we read of the Venetians, who would not suffer the Grecians to injure the Turks in any Port belonging unto them.

IX. *This Right extends to Women and Infants.*

But to return to what we have in hand, how far this licence of Murther, Spoil, and Rapine, extends it self in the time of War will appear, in that Women and Infants are subject thereunto. I shall not hitherto refer the slaughter that the Israelites made of the Women and Children at *Heshbon*, *Deut.* 11. 34. Nor that which they were commanded to do against the Canaanites, and their Associates, the Amalakites; whereof *Josephus* (speaking of the Acts of *Saul*) writes thus, *He proceeded even to the slaughter of Women and Children, accounting nothing therein too cruel or inhumane*: First, because they were Enemies; and Secondly, because it was done at the special command of God, whose Right over men is far greater and more unquestionable, than that which men claim to have over beasts, as we have elsewhere said. No, rather, that which comes nearer to testify the manners and customes of the Nations as to this, is that of the Psalmist, *Blessed is he that taketh thy children and casteth them against the stones*: Agreeable to that of *Homer*, Psal. 136.

> ——————*Illisa corpora terræ*
> *Infantum, sævus dum concutit omnia Mavors.*

> When dreadful War, whole Nations doth lay wast,
> Then Infants bodies 'gainst the Earth are dasht.

And that also which *Severus* out of the same *Homer* applied to the Britains,

> ————*Nec qui latet abditus intra*
> *Viscera Matris adhuc, fugiet crudelia fata.*

> ————Nor can the Babes unborn,
> Escape Wars rage, being from their Mothers torn.

The Thracians of old having taken the City *Mycalessus* put all to the Sword, both Women and Children, as *Thucydides* relates. So did the Macedonians when they took *Thebes*, as *Arianus* tells us. Thus did the Romans also when they had taken the City *Ilurgis* in *Spain*, destroy all without distinction of Age or Sex, as *Appianus* testifies. The like did *Scipio* when he took *Numantia*. The Emperour *Julian* having taken by storm the City *Majozamaltha*, destroyed all, making no distinction of Age or Sex: *Quicquid impetus reperit, potestas iratorum absumpsit*; *Whatsoever force found, was sacrificed by the Swords of the enraged.* *Germanicus Cæsar* is said in *Tacitus* to depopulate all the Villages of the *Marsi*, a people of *Germany*, with Fire and Sword, so that neither Sex nor Age could find pity. And the Emperour *Titus* when he conquered the Jews, exposed their Women and Children to be devoured by Beasts in their publick shews; and yet were neither of these two Princes esteemed

ſteemed to be of a fierce and cruel nature, but were only carried away with the cuſtomes of thoſe times: No marvel then, if old men did ſometimes undergo the ſame fate, as *Priamus* did who was killed by *Pyrrhus*.

X. And to Captives. Neither were Captives exempted from the rage of the Conquerours: when *Eliſha* the Prophet had led the Syrians blindfold to the Gates of *Samaria*, as *Joſephus* relates the ſtory, King *Joram* demanded of the Prophet whether he ſhould kill them; but the Prophet anſwered, that it was not lawful for the King ſo to do, *Solus enim Bello ſuperatos hoſtes occidi fas eſt*; *For thoſe Enemies only may be lawfully killed that are taken in War.* *Pyrrhus* in *Seneca* according to the cuſtome of the Nations then in uſe, pleads thus,

Troad. *Lex nulla capto parcit aut pœnam impedit.*

No Law from puniſhment doth ſlaves protect.

Neither doth this licence extend to Men only, but even to Women if taken in War, according to that of *Scylla*, concerning a Woman taken Priſoner:

At Belli ſaltem captivam lege necâſſes.

By th' Law of Arms, thy ſlave thou mightſt have kill'd.

To the ſame purpoſe is that of *Seneca* before quoted to be underſtood; for it was ſpoken of *Polyxena*, who being taken Captive might have been ſlain: yet is the advice of *Horace* to be preferred,

Vendere cum poſſis captivum, occidere noli.

Kill not thy ſlave, in caſe thou canſt him ſell.

Wherein he takes it as granted, that kill him he might, though to ſell him were better; hence it is, that they are called ſervants, becauſe they are ſaved alive, whereas by the Law of Arms they might have been killed: thus were all the Captives taken in *Epidamnum* put to death by the Corcyræans, as *Thucydides* relates; and ſeventy thouſand Sclavonians we read of that were put to the Sword by the Emperour *Otto*, and of five thouſand Captives that were at once put to death by *Hannibal*. And *Hirtius* in his African War, brings in a Cæſarean Captain giving thanks unto *Scipio* for ſparing his life in theſe words, *Tibi gratias ago, quod mihi vitam incolumitatemque belli jure capto polliceris*; *I thank thee noble* Scipio, *for that being thy ſlave, thou art pleaſed to engage thy word for my life and ſafety.* Neither is this licence of killing our Captives confined to any ſpace of time, although by Municipal Laws it be reſtrained in ſome places more, in ſome leſs.

Terence Adelph. Act. 2. Scen. 1.

Dion. 47.

XI. Yea, and to Suppliants. No nor Suppliants as we are inſtructed by many examples in all Hiſtories; as namely, by the example of *Achilles in Homer*, of *Mago* and *Turnus* in *Virgil*; which do therefore ſtand yet upon record, to juſtifie the like practice hereafter by the Right of War: For St. *Auguſtine* himſelf commending the Goths for ſparing Suppliants, and ſuch as fled unto Temples for protection, yet ſaith, *That which by the Right of War they might do, they thought unlawful for them to do:* Neither are they always received to mercy that beg it, witneſs the Grecians that ſided with the Perſians againſt *Alexander*, at that great Battel fought at the River *Granicum*. And the Uſpenſes in *Tacitus*, *Who craving leave but to depart their City with their Bodies free, were rejected by the Conquerours, becauſe it would have been thought cruelty to have killed them in cold blood after they had yielded themſelves, and hard to keep a Guard upon ſo great a multitude, therefore they choſe rather to let them periſh by the Sword according to the Law of Arms.* Obſerve here alſo the Right of War.

De Civit. Dei. c. 2.

Ann. 12.

XII. Yea, and to ſuch as yield without conditions. Neither do they always find mercy that ſurrender themſelves without any condition at all, but even theſe are ſometimes put to death, as the Princes of *Pomeria* were by the Romans, the Samnits by *Sylla*, the Numidians, yea, and *Vercingentoriges* himſelf by *Cæſar*: Nay, it was almoſt the perpetual practice of the Roman Generals upon the dayes of their Triumph, to put to death all the Captains and other Commanders (whether they were taken Priſoners during the War, or had yielded themſelves) as *Cicero* in forms us in his fifth Oration againſt *Verres*; which, both *Livy* and *Tacitus* confirm: Nay, the ſame *Tacitus* records it of *Galba*, That he cauſed the tenth Man to be killed of thoſe, whom upon ſubmiſſion he had received to mercy. And *Cæcina* upon the ſurrender of *Aventicum*, cauſed *Julius Alpinus* to be put to death, as being the principal inſtigator of the War; but the reſt of the Citizens he left to, either the mercy, or the ſeverity of *Vitellius*.

Dion. 45. Livy. 2. Cicero in Ver. 5. Livy lib. 28. Annal. 1.

It

It is the usual custome of Historians to ascribe the cause of this cruelty and outrage against Captives, or Suppliants; either to the like cruelty done by them unto others, or to their obstinacy in resisting them: But these are rather pretences than just causes; for Retaliation (properly so called) is not to be executed, but upon the same persons that offended (as hath been already said, where we discourst concerning the Communication of Punishments.) But contrariwise in War, this Right of Retaliation is often exercised on those, who were in no measure guilty of the crime, for which they are said to be punished. This custome is thus described by *Diodorus Siculus*, *The chance of War being on both sides equal, neither party can be ignorant of this; that in case they be vanquished, what they intended to do against their Enemies had they been Victors, that they must be contented to suffer from them.* Thus did *Philomelus* the Phocensian General *perswade his Enemies to refrain from a proud and insolent revenge, by threatning to exact the like in case the Victory fell on his side.* But as to the other pretence which is usually pleaded, namely, an obstinate endeavour to defend their own party; it is so far from being punishable as a crime (as the *Neapolitans* alledged to *Belisarius* in *Procopius*) that according to the Ancient Roman Discipline, it was ever accounted a capital crime to do otherwise, especially if we were engaged therein, either by some natural obligation, or by an honest and deliberate choice; for in these cases they seldome admitted of any excuse, were the fear or danger never so great, *Præsidio decedere apud Romanos capitale est*; *To desert a Garrison*, saith *Livy*, *was ever accounted among the Romans a capital crime.* Every man therefore may make use of this rigour and severity, so far as he sees it may conduce to his own advantage, and is therein justified before men, by that common right and licence of Nations, whereof we here treat.

XIII. This right not to be referred to other causes.

Goth. l. 1.

Polyb. l. 1. & 5.
Liv. lib. 24.

This right or licence doth sometimes extend it self to hostages; and that not only to those who voluntarily give themselves as Pledges for the performance of Articles agreed upon, but unto those also who are delivered up by others. Thus we read of two hundred and fifty hostages slain by the Thessalians, and of three hundred slain by the Romans; where also by the way we may observe, That sometimes Children are admitted as Hostages, as by the example of *Simon* the Maccabite we may learn; and sometimes Women, as by the Romans in the time of *Porsenna*, and by the Germans in *Tacitus*.

XIV. It extends also to Hostages.
Plut. de claris Mulierib.
Dionys. 16.
Tac. An. 12.
1 Mac. 13. 17.
Hist. 4.

As there are many things tolerated by the Law of Nations in this sense that we now speak of, which by the Law of Nature are prohibited; so are there many things forbidden by the former, which by the latter are tolerated. For if we respect the Law of Nature only, if a man have deserved to be put to death, it matters not much whether it be by the Sword or by Poyson: by the Law of Nature, I say, though otherwise it be far more noble so to invade another mans life, as to give him an equal power to defend himself. But this is not due unto every man that hath deserved to dye. But by the Law of Nations, (if not of all, yet of the greater and better part of them) it is not lawful to take away the life, no not of an Enemy, by poyson; which Custom was introduced for a general good, lest dangers, which are too rife and frequent in War, should be beyond all measure multiplied. And very probable it is that this Law was first enacted by Kings and Emperours, whose lives, as they are principally guarded by Arms, so are they most easily endangered by poyson, were it not for the severity of the Laws, and the fear of infamy. This *Livy* calls *a clandestine villany*, speaking of *Pyrrhus*. And *Claudian*, concerning the design of *Pyrrhus*'s Physician, who offered *Fabritius* to poyson him, calls it *a detestable act*, not fit to be spoken; so doth *Cicero*, glancing at the same Story: which offer of the Physician, the Consuls not only rejected, but discovered unto *Pyrrhus*; not so much for his sake, as to prevent the reproach and scandal that might ensue to themselves, lest it should be said of them, That whom they could not conquer by true valour, they had by treachery destroyed. Or as *Aulus Gellius* recites the Epistle of the Consuls out of *Claudius Quadrigarius*, *Communis exempli & fidei ergo, visum est*; *We think it not fit for common examples, and our own honour's sake, to admit of so great a wickedness.* For as *Valerius Maximus* well observes, *Armis Bella, non Venenis geri debent*; *Wars should be waged by Arms, and not by Poyson.* Insomuch that when the Prince of the *Catti* made offer to poyson *Arminius*, *Tiberius* rejected it, therein equalling himself in honour to the old Roman Emperours. They therefore that hold it lawful to destroy an Enemy by poyson, as *Baldus* by the authority of *Vegetius* did, do regard the mere Law of Nature, but overlook that Law which is established by the voluntary consent of Nations.

XV. To kill by poyson, unlawful.

Lib. 42.

Offic. l. 3.

Plut. vit. Pyrrhi.

Lib. 3. *c.* 8.
Lib. 5. *c.* 5.
Annal, 3.

Somewhat different from this manner of poysoning (because it hath something of force in it) is the anointing the Heads of Spears with poyson, thereby to enforce death upon a double account; which, as *Ovid* records, was much in use among the *Getæ*. The like testimony doth *Pliny* give of the Scythians, *For they anointed their Arrows*, saith he, *with poison, compounded of the putrified Gore of Vipers, and humane bloud*: immedicabile id scelus; *a mischief incurable, because it made every slight hurt mortal.* *Lucan* testifies the same of the

XVI. As also by imposoning Waters or Weapons.
How this was prepared, we may learn out of *Rhodoginus*, c. 10. 23. See *Lyps. Ann.* upon *Plin. l.* 11. *c.* 53.

Parthians;

Parthians; so doth *Silius* of some of the Africans; and *Claudian* particularly of the Ethiopians. It was observed, that in *India Alexander*'s Soldiers being wounded by these impoysoned Arrows dyed immediately. Yet was this also contrary to the Law of Nations; though not

Salisburiensis, lib. 8. c. 20.

of all, yet of these of *Europe*, and of such others as are civilized like them; *amongst whom the use of poyson was never by any Law allowed, although among Pagans and Infidels it hath sometimes been usurped.* Therefore in *Silius*'s account this was but *ferrum infamare veneno, the shame and reproach of valour.* And therefore *Ilus Mermerides* in *Homer* denied poyson to *Ulysses*'s Spears, for fear of a revenge from the Gods Immortal. So also the impoysoning of Springs, *Florus* reckons to be unlawful, being repugnant not only to the Constitutions of men, but to the Laws of God. Where we may note, (as we have already elsewhere) That prophane Authours do usually ascribe the Laws of Nations unto the Gods. Nor will it seem strange that there should be such a tacite agreement amongst Nations, for the lessening of the dangers that attend the Wars, when we find it anciently covenanted

Strab. l. 10.

between the Chalcidenses and the Eretrienses, That during the War between them, *it should not be lawful to cast or to dart any thing.*

XVII.
But not otherwise to corrupt Waters.

Proc. Goth. l. 2.
De Piscatu. l. 4.

But it is otherwise where waters are (without poyson) so corrupted, that they cannot be drunk; as by throwing Carrion into them, and dead Bodies, or *asbestus*, which *Belisarius* made use of in the Siege of *Auximum*; or Lime, which the Turks did at *Dibibras*, or such like. For this was approved of by *Solon*, the Amphictyones, and others, against the Barbarians; and as *Oppianus* records, was usually done in his Age: it being no more than if the Current of a River, or the Veins of Water that feed a Well, should be cut off or turned some other way, which by the Law of Nature and the general consent of Nations are held lawful.

XVIII.
Whether it be against the Law of Nations to use Murtherers.

But whether the Law of Nations do justifie the killing of an Enemy privately, that is, by sending one purposely to kill him in his own Quarters, is often questioned. For the resolving of which doubt, we must distinguish of the persons sent: for in case he be such a one as hath any ways given his faith, either expresly or tacitely, unto him whose life he attempts; as if he be a Subject that shall be hired to kill his Sovereign, a Vassal his Lord, or a Souldier his General, or if he be received by him in protection as a Suppliant, a Stranger, or a Renegado; yea if the person sent owe any faith to him whom he is sent to kill; then the Law of Nations doth not only condemn the person that is the instrument for his treachery and perfidiousness, but those also that make use of him. For although in other matters he that makes use of wicked instruments, though against an enemy, may be found guilty before God; yet is he not so before man. For he is not thereby said to violate the Law of Nations, because in this Case, *Mores Leges perduxerunt in potestatem suam; Custom hath prevailed above the Laws.* Et decipere, pro moribus temporum, prudentia est:

Lib. 8. Epist. ad Rufinum.

And to deceive (as *Pliny* saith) *if it accord with the manners and customs of the Age we live in, is not a crime, but a Vertue; no knavery, but commendable policy.* Yet doth not this custom extend it self so far as to the killing of an enemy: For he that shall make use of another mans treachery in such a case, doth not only sin against the Law of Nature, but of

Curtius l. 4.

Nations. This is plain by what *Alexander* wrote to *Darius*, *Impia Bella suscipitis, & cum habeatis Arma, licitamini hostium capita; It is an impious War that ye wage against me; for having Weapons to fight, ye chuse rather to purchase with money the lives of your enemies.*

Lib. 14.

And presently after he complains, *That they did not observe the Law of Armes.* And in another place, *I ought to persecute him even unto death, not as an open Enemy, but as a secret*

Liv. l. 42.

Murtherer. Hither we may refer that of *Livy* concerning *Perseus*, of whom he complains, *That he waged not a just and open war with a mind becoming a Prince, but that he used all*

Marcius Philipus, Liv. l. 44.

manner of base and clandestine ways to destroy his Enemies, like a Thief or a Poysoner. All which, how odious they are to the Gods themselves, would at length be seen by the event of his Fortunes. Agreeable hereunto is that of *Valerius Maximus* concerning the murder of

Lib. 9. c. 7.

Viriatus, which gave occasion to a double accusation of perfidiousness, the one by his friends, by whose hands he was killed; the other in Quintus Servitius Cæpio *the Consul, who by encouraging them to do it by his promise of impunity, became himself the Authour of the fact, and did therefore justly lose the glory of the Victory.* For *Victoriam non meruit, sed emit; He deserves not the honour of a Triumph that buys the Victory.* Wherefore when the Murtherers demanded the reward promised them by the Consul *Cæpio*, it was answered, *That it was never thought*

Eutropius.

a meritorious act by the Romans for Souldiers to kill their General, as *Eutropius* testifies. Now the reason why the Law of Nations, that allows us to make use of the treachery of others in all other cases, doth not allow of it in this case, is the very same that was before given in the case of poyson; namely, To restrain the dangers that attended Kings and Princes.

Just. lib. 14.

When one told *Eumenes*, That his Enemies had hired one to kill him, *He would not believe that any General or inferior Captain would give so ill an example against himself.* And in

Just. Lib. 12.

another place the same *Justine* declares, *That when* Bessus *had killed King* Darius, *it was not to be endured for examples sake; because it was the common cause of all Kings.* For as *Seneca* well observes,

Regi

Regi tuenda est maxime Regum salus.

A Kings chief care is the defence of Kings.

In a solemn War, and amongst those who have a right to denounce a solemn War, it is not lawful by the Law of Nations privately to kill an Enemy; but where there is no solemn War, it is by the same Law of Nations accounted lawful, that is, unpunishable. *Tacitus* denies peremptorily, That the Plot that was laid against the life of *Gannascus*, was at all, degenerous; because he was a Traitor. And *Curtius* was of opinion, That the guilt of *Bessus* in killing *Darius*, did make the treachery of *Spitamenes* appear the less odious; for that *nothing could be thought wicked that was done against a Regicide*. So likewise *Ammianus* concerning *Florentius* and *Barchalba*, who had surprized *Procopius* the Traitor, *Si Principem legitimum prodidissent, vel ipsa Justitia jure cæsos pronunciaret; si rebellem & oppugnatorem internæ quietis, ut ferebatur, amplas ei memorabilis facti opportuerat deferri mercedes: If it had been their lawful Sovereign that they had betrayed, the Laws had justly sentenced them to death; but if he were a Rebel, or a Disturber of the peace of his own Country, (as was said) ye ought to give him a reward worthy of so memorable a fact*. Thus is *Artabanes* highly commended in *Procopius* for killing *Gontharides*, as we may read at the latter end of the second of his Vandal History. So perfidiousness or treachery against Thieves and Pyrates, though it be not altogether blameless; yet is it not by the Law of Nations punishable, because committed against such as are Enemies to humane Society.

Annal. l. 11. *Lib.* 7.

But what if they, that are sent to kill an enemy privately, do owe him no faith, nor are any ways obliged unto him? Surely then by the Law of Nations it is lawful for them to kill him if they can, even in his own Quarters. Thus *Pipin*, Father to *Charles the Great* of *France*, attended with one only of his Guard, passed the Rhine, and killed his enemy even in his own Chamber. The like was attempted by one *Theodotus* an Etolian upon *Ptolomy* King of *Egypt*, which *Polybius* commends as no unmanly attempt. Such also was that Heroick enterprize of *Q. Mutius Scævola*, who was in *Plutarch*'s esteem, *A man accomplished with all vertuous endowments*, which attempt he thus defends, *Hostes hostem occidere volui; I being an Enemy would have killed an Enemy*. *Porsenna* himself acknowledged this to be an act of true valour. *Valerius Maximus* commends it for *a brave and gallant resolution*. So doth *Cicero* in his Oration for *Publius Sextus*; because to kill an Enemy wheresoever we find him, is lawful both by the Laws of Nature and Nations; neither doth it make any difference, how many they are that either thus act or suffer. Six hundred Lacedemonians we read of that with *Leonides* their King, marched directly through the Camp of five hundred thousand of their Enemies, even unto the Kings Pavilion; the same may be done by fewer. A reward was promised by the Emperour *Valens* to him that should bring in the head of any Scythian, whereupon a Peace immediately ensued. They were not many that circumvented *Marcellus* and his fellow Consul and slew them, and that had likely to have killed *Petilius Cerealis* even in his Bed. *Ambrose* highly commends *Eleazer*, who seeing a mighty Elephant higher than all the rest, assaulted him, supposing that he that sate upon him had been the King. Not much unlike was that attempt that *Theodosius* made upon *Eugenius*, recorded by *Zozimus*. Nor that of the ten Persians against the Emperour *Julian* attested by *Ammianus*. Neither are they only that make these attempts excusable by the Law of Nations, but they also that imploy them. Those Roman Senators that were so renowned for their Wars, were reputed the Authors of that gallant attempt made by *Scævola*. Neither is it to the purpose to object, that such men being taken are put to exquisite torments; for this happens, not for that they violate the Law of Nations, but because by the Law of Nations, every thing is lawful that is done against an Enemy; and all Conquerours are more or less severe, according as it shall conduce to their future advantage, for thus are spies dealt withal; yet notwithstanding, it is held lawful by the general consent of Nations, to send out such, as *Moses* did *Joshua* into the land of *Caanan*. *It is the custom of all Nations to kill spies*, saith *Appian*, and that justly sometimes by such as have apparently a just Cause to make War; but by others, it is only lawful by that licence which the Law of Arms sometimes gives: But if there be any that will not make use of such instruments, though offered, this proceeds rather from the Magnanimity, and the confidence of him that makes the War in his own strength, than from an opinion he hath that by the Law of Nations it is unjust.

But not if he owe him no faith. But not, if the person sent owe no faith to him whom he is sent to kill.

Livy. l. 2. *Lib.* 3. *c.* 3. *Just. l.* 2. *Zozimus l.* 4. *Livy* 27. *Tacit. Hist. l.* 5. *De Off. l.* 1. *c.* 40. & *Jos. Ant.* 15. *Lib.* 4. *Lib.* 24. *Livy l.* 2.

XIX. Whether ravishment be in such a War lawful.

The ravishing of Women is by the Law of Nations sometimes permitted in War, and sometimes forbidden. They that permit it do respect only the injury done to the body of an Enemy, which by the Law of Arms they think ought to be subject to the Will of the Conquerour: But others much better, look not unto the sole injury done unto the body of an Enemy, but to the very unbridled act of Lust, which conduceth nothing either to the security of the Conquerour, or to the punishment of the Enemy; and therefore

fore ſhould be no more unpuniſhable in War, than in Peace, and this is the Law if not of all Nations, yet at leaſt of the better and more civilized amongſt them. *Marcellus* before he took *Syracuſe* took ſpecial care of the preſervation of the Chaſtity, even of his Enemies. And *Scipio* (as *Livy* teſtifies) told his Souldiers, *That it much concerned his own honour, and the honour of the people of* Rome, *That nothing that was any where, (that is among ſuch Nations as were civilized) reputed ſacred, ſhould be by them profaned or violated. Diodorus Siculus* complains againſt *Agathocles* his Souldiers, *That they abſtained not from that foul ſin of raviſhment.* The like doth *Appian* in his Mithridatick War, concerning the Captives taken in *Chius*, *That both Women and Children were barbarouſly raviſhed by thoſe that led them away priſoners. Ælian* ſpeaking of the inſolencies of the Sicyonians, being Conquerours in raviſhing the Pellenæan Virgins, and Matrons crys out thus, *Theſe by the Gods of Greece are ſuch acts of cruelty and inhumanity, as were never to my remembrance, allowed of by the very Barbarians.* And ſurely it is but reaſonable, that this ſhould be generally obſerved among the Chriſtians, not only as a part of our Military Diſcipline, but as a part of the Law of Nations: namely, *That he that ſhall forcibly abuſe a Woman, though in the War, ſhall every where be puniſhable. Beliſarius* always obſerved this Rule: So did *Totilas* when he had taken *Cumæ*, and at *Rome* alſo, as *Procopius* leaves it upon Record. Neither did the Hebrew Law ſuffer this wickedneſs to go unpuniſhed, as may be collected from that part of it, which ſo provides for a Virgin taken Captive, That he that takes her might marry her, and if afterwards he liked her not, he might diſmiſs her, but not ſell her: *Thou ſhalt not take money for her, becauſe thou haſt humbled her,* ſaith the Law, *Deut.* 21. 12. Upon which words one of the Hebrew Doctors thus gloſſeth, *God would have the Camp of Iſrael to be holy, and not like the Camp of the Gentiles, polluted with Whoredom, and ſuch like abominations. Joſephus* likewiſe *highly extolls the Jewiſh Law for its care of priſoners taken in the War, to preſerve them from ſhame and reproach, eſpecially of women. Arrianus* highly commends that fact of *Alexander*, who being taken with *Roxana*'s beauty, *refuſed to abuſe her as his Captive, but did her the honour to marry her:* So doth *Plutarch* alſo, *He diſdained to force her as a Conquerour, but wedded her as a Philoſopher.* The ſame *Plutarch* relates it of one *Torquatus*, That he was baniſhed by the Romans into the Iſle of *Corſica*, for forcing a Virgin whom he had taken Captive: But *Coſroes* King of *Perſia* was more ſevere, for he cauſed one that had raviſhed a young Maid to be Crucified; as *Procopius* informs us in the ſecond of his Perſian Wars.

Aug. de Civit. Dei, lib. 2.

Lib. 26.

Goth. lib. 3.

Bacchai.

Contra App.

CHAP.

CHAP. V.

Of Spoil and Rapine committed in War.

I. *That the Goods of an Enemy may be ſpoiled or taken away.*
II. *Even thoſe that are ſacred, which how to be underſtood.*
III. *Yea, and thoſe that are Religious, where ſome caution is added.*
IV. *How far forth fraud may be uſed in this caſe.*

Cicero in the third of his Offices gives this Rule, *Non eſt contra naturam ſpoliare eum, quem honeſtum eſt necare*; *It is no whit repugnant to the Law of Nature, to ſpoil and plunder him, whom it is lawfull to kill.* It is not then to be wondered at, That the Law of Nations permits the ſpoil and devaſtation of an Enemies Land and Goods, ſeeing that it permits him to be killed. *Polybius* tells us *, That by the Right of War, It is lawfull either to take away or to deſtroy the Forts, Ports, Cities, Subjects, Ships, Corn, Cattle, and ſuch like things of an Enemy. And in *Livy* we read, *That there are certain Rights in War, which as we may ſafely do unto an Enemy, ſo we muſt with patience ſuffer from them; ſuch are the burning of our Corn, the pulling down of our Houſes, the taking away of our Men and Beaſts.* He that is vers't in Hiſtories, will find almoſt every page filled with theſe dreadfull effects of War, the demoliſhing of Cities, the razing and throwing down their Walls, the ſpoiling and laying waſt of the Enemies Countrey with Fire and Sword; yea, and we may obſerve, That all theſe are lawfull to be done, though the Enemy do voluntarily ſurrender themſelves. *The Townſmen,* ſaith *Tacitus, ſet open their Gates of their own accord, and ſubmitted themſelves, and all they had to the Romans, whereby they ſaved themſelves: But the Romans burnt the City* Artaxata *and laid it level with the ground, becauſe they could neither keep it with ſafety, nor leave it with honour.*

I. That the Enemies Goods may be waſted and taken away.

* *Lib.* 5.

Neither are things ſacred, that is, conſecrated to any one or more Gods, exempted from theſe Out-rages of War, meerly by the Law of Nations, ſetting aſide the conſideration of other Duties: for, *Cum loca capta ſunt ab hoſtibus, omnia deſinunt eſſe ſacra*; *As ſoon as any place is taken from the Enemy, every thing in it ceaſeth to be ſacred,* ſaith *Pomponius.* And ſo ſaith *Cicero*, *Sacra Syracuſarum victoria profana fecerat*, *The victory made all the ſacred things in* Syracuſe *profane.* *Tertullian* in his Apologeticks confeſſeth, *That War and Victory cannot conſiſt without the ſubverſion of Cities; which alſo cannot happen without ſome injury done to their tutelar Gods. For Temples undergo the ſame fate that their Cities do, and their Prieſts have an equal ſhare in publick Calamities as other Citizens; neither do their conſecrated veſſels eſcape better than their profane.* Tot Sacrilegia Romanorum, quot Trophæa; tot de diis, quot de gentibus triumphi: *Look how many Victories the Romans had, ſo many Sacriledges they committed; and as often as they conquered their Enemies, they ſpoiled and rifled their Gods.* The cauſe whereof is this, becauſe thoſe things which are ſaid to be ſacred, are not in truth exempted from humane uſes, but are made publick, as *Marſilius Patavinus* obſerves in his Defence of Peace: But they are called Sacred, from the end whereunto they are deſtin'd, which appears by this, That when any People give themſelves up to another People, or to any King, they deliver up that alſo which is called Sacred; as is manifeſt by the uſual form in *Livy*, *We the People of* Campania, *do deliver up into your Power and Poſſeſſion, O Fathers Conſcript, our City* Capua, *our Fields, the Temples of our Gods, together with all that we have whether Humane or Divine*: (the like we read in *Plautus* his Amphitryo.) And therefore as *Ulpian* concludes, *There is a publick Right even in things that are ſacred.* And *Pauſanias* tells us, That it was a Cuſtom common as well with the Grecians as Barbarians, that things Sacred ſhould be diſpoſed of, at the Will and Pleaſure of the Conquerour. So when *Troy* was taken, the Image of *Jupiter Hercæus* was given to *Sthenelus*, and many other Examples he there brings. And *Thucydides* confirms this, ſaying, *That it was a Law among the Græcians, That look whoſe the Empire was of any City or Countrey, whether great or ſmall, theirs alſo were the Temples*: Wherewith accords that of *Tacitus*, where he ſaith, *That all the Ceremonies, Temples and Images, that were in any of the Cities of* Italy, *were at the diſpoſe, and under the Juriſdiction of the Romans.* Wherefore it is plain, That the People themſelves changing their minds, may make any thing profane that was holy; and this is not obſcurely proved by thoſe great Lawyers *Paulus* and *Venulejus.* We may alſo obſerve, That in times of War, and in caſes of neceſſity, thoſe things which have been conſecrated, have by thoſe that conſecrated them been converted to uſes of War; as was done by the Syracuſians in the time of *Timoleon*, as *Plutarch* teſtifies. So the *Chii* raiſed the tribute impoſed on them by *Mithridates* by the ſale of the conſecrated

II. Though Conſecrated.

Chap. 5. §. 1.

Lib. 4.

Annal. l. 12.

 Veſſels

Bell. Mithrid. Vessels of the Temple, as *Appian* testifies. *Pliny* speaking of *Portius Cato* tells us, *That he suffered the consecrated Trees and Groves to be cut down, having first offered sacrifices. Sulla* in his War against *Mithridates* robb'd the Temple at *Delphos* of those rich Presents, sent thither by *Olympia* and *Epidaurus*, as it is storied in *Plutarch*; the just price whereof he afterwards restored, as *Diodorus* informs us. *Augustus* we read borrowed all the Treasures of the Temple in a time of necessity, as *Appian* writes. And *Agapetus* pawned all the Consecrated Vessels, as *Cassiodore* relates. The Emperour *Heraclius* in his great necessity, turned all the Vessels of the Church into Money, the price whereof he afterwards restored, as *Theophanes* writes. The like was done by *Pericles*, but with a promise of restitution; by *Mago* in *Spain*, by the Romans in their War against *Mithridates*, by *Sulla, Pompey, Cæsar*, and many others. *There is nothing so Sacred, so Holy, as those things that are Consecrated to the Worship of the Gods*, saith *Tiberius Gracchus* in *Plutarch : And yet there is none that can hinder the people from using them, or removing them as they please.* *Contr. in excerptis 4. 4.* *Our Churches*, saith *Seneca*, *are sometimes spoiled for the defence of the publick, and what was given to the Gods, we often take to pay our Souldiers.* Whence *Servius* upon *Virgil* tells us, *Eclog. 7.* *That whatsoever is given to the Gods is so long holy, as it continues unprofaned.* And therefore *Trebatius* the Lawyer in *Cæsars* time saith, *That is said to be profane, which is taken from an Holy and Religious use, and converted to the use of private men.* Thus *Germanicus* having conquered the Marsians destroyed all things both Sacred and Profane, levelling *Lib. 8.* with the ground that Temple so famous among those Nations called *Tanfanæ*, as *Tacitus* relates it. It is acknowledged by *Pausanias*, That whatsoever was Consecrated to *Verr. 3.* the Gods, was lawful prize to the Conquerour. And *Cicero* speaking of *Publius Servilius* saith, *That the Images, and other Ornaments of the Enemies Cities, which by force and valour he had conquered, He by the Law of Arms, and by the Right of Conquest took and carried away.* So *Plutarch* speaking of *Fabius*, saith, That the Image of *Hercules* which he took at *Tarentum*, he sent to be placed in the Capitol at *Rome*, leaving the rest of their Gods as enraged against the Tarentines. So also *Livy* concerning the Ornaments taken out of the Temples at *Syracuse* by *Marcellus*, and brought to *Rome*, saith, That they were *Parta Jure Belli, Got by the Right of War.* Thus *Fulvius* also in his Oration, calls the spoilings of Temples, *the Rights of War.* The like we read in *Salust* of *Cato*, who recounting the miseries that usually befall the Conquered, brings in this amongst others, the robbing of their Churches. But yet in case it be believed, That there is any thing of a Deity in this or that Image, then to break it, to spoil or deface it, is in them that are of that perswasion, great impiety. And upon this presumption, that both Parties agree in this belief, it is, That they that commit such robberies, are so often branded with impiety, and accused for violating the Law of Nations. But in case the Enemy be of another perswasion, then it is otherwise. As to the Jews it was not *Deut. 7. 5.* only permitted but commanded, That they should utterly abolish the Idols of the Gentiles, but that they should not assume them to themselves: the reason was, to instill into them the greater detestation of their superstitions, by begetting this conceit in them, That the very touching of them was not without pollution; and not that what was con- *Antiq. lib. 4. cap. 8. & lib. 2. Contr. App.* secrated to strange Gods was to be spared, as *Josephus* seems to expound it, therein doubtless flattering the Romans no less, than in the Exposition of another Precept, namely, of not naming the Gods of the Gentiles, which he so interprets, as if it were therefore prohibited to name them lest they should reproach them: whereas their Law did expresly forbid to name them with any Honour or Reverence, nay, without some shew of detestation. For the Hebrews most assuredly knew, that in those Images there was nothing sacred, neither Angel, nor Spirit, nor any virtue of the Stars, as the Gentiles dreamed, unless they were such Evil Spirits as are usually destructive to Mankind. And therefore as *Tacitus* rightly observed, in his description of the Manners and Institutes of the Jews, *Profana illis omnia, quæ apud nos sacra*; *All things that are holy to us, are unto them profane.* It is no wonder then, that we read of so many Idol Temples burnt by the Macchabees, 1 *Mac.* 5. and 10.

That *Nebuchadnezzar* should sack the Temple at *Jerusalem* was not to be admired; but for *Joaz* (though an Idolater) yet one that acknowledged the Eternal True God, and that had worshipped him that was Lord of the Temple: That he, I say, should lay his hands on the Consecrated Vessels, and call the Family of *Obed-Edom*, whose Children had the Hereditary charge of its Treasures to a strict account, as if they had been Officers of his own Exchequer; this was an execrable sin, which hastened his destruction.

Xerxes when he demolish'd all the Idols of the Grecians, did nothing contrary to the Law of Nations, though all their Historians did bitterly inveigh against him. For the Persians could not believe, that there was any Divinity in them, because they adore the Sun only as God, and the fire as a spark or ray of the Deity; and therefore as *Diogenes Laertius* tells us, did their *Magi* abhor Images. By the Hebrew Law, *None must enter into the Temple but the Priests only*; *Tacit.* yet *Pompey the Great entred into it by the Right*

of

of a Conquerour, as *Tacitus* thought : Or, as St *Augustine* relates it, *Non devotione supplicis, sed jure Victoris*; *Not as a Suppliant, but as a Victor*. He did well to ſpare the Temple, and to reſtrain his Souldiers from the pillage of it, though, as *Cicero* wiſely conjectured, it was more out of ſhame, and to avoid ſcandal, than out of any true piety; but he did ill in entring thereinto in contempt of the True God, for which the Prophets did ſo bitterly inveigh againſt the Chaldeans, and for which cauſe it was ſo ordered by the Divine Providence, That *Pompey* ſhould afterward be killed at *Caſſium* a Promontory in *Ægypt*, as it were, in the ſight of thoſe Jews, whoſe Temple he had ſo profaned. But yet, if we regard the Opinion of the Romans, there was nothing done by *Pompey* that was contrary to the Law of Nations. So when *Joſephus* had declared the deſtruction of the ſame Temple by *Titus*, he likewiſe adds, That it was done by the Right of War. *De Civit. Dei lib. 18. cap. 45. Pro Flacco. Dan. 5. 23.*

III. *Yea, and things that are Religious.*

What hath been ſaid of things Sacred, may alſo be ſaid of things Religious. For theſe are not ſuch as belong to the dead, but to the living, whether of ſome People, or of ſome Families : Wherefore as *Pomponius* well obſerves, as places being taken by the Enemy, though holy; ſo whatſoever is Religious in thoſe places ceaſeth to be ſo after the victory. *Sepulchra hoſtium religioſa nobis non ſunt, ideoque lapides inde ſublatos in quemlibet uſum convertere poſſumus*; *The Sepulchres of our Enemies are not unto us Religious*, ſaith *Paulus* the Lawyer; *and therefore we may take away the ſtones, and convert them to what uſe we pleaſe :* Which notwithſtanding muſt be underſtood ſo, that no violence be offered to the bodies of the dead, which by cuſtom is admitted among the Laws of Nations. *With caution to the dead.*

IV. *And that not only by force but by fraud.*

This alſo we muſt here repeat, That the Goods of our Enemies may be taken away from them, not only by plain force, but even by fraud alſo, ſo it be without perfidiouſneſs; nay, we may by the Law of Nations be permitted to excite the treachery of others; (that is to ſay) the ſaid Law of Nations begins ſo to connive at ſuch petty and ordinary ſlips, as the Civil Law doth at whoredom, and griping uſury.

CHAP. VI.

Of the Right to things taken in War

I. What the Law of nature decrees concerning things gained by War. * *Vide lib.2.ch.7. §.2. Lib.2.ch.20.* † Gen. 14. * Heb. 7. 4.

BEsides the licence that a just War gives to commit such acts against men, whereof we have treated hitherto; there is also another effect, which by the Law of Nations is proper to a solemn War. And indeed, even by the Law of Nature, those things may be acquired by a just War, which are, either equivalent to that *, which though due, cannot otherwise be obtained; or which causes them to suffer who have done wrong, so as it exceeds not the bounds of a just punishment. By vertue of this Right of acquiring things by a just War, *Abraham offered unto God the tenth of the spoil he got from the five Kings* †, as the Author to the Hebrews seems to expound the story *. So also did the Grecians, the Carthaginians, and the Romans unto their Gods; as to *Apollo*, to *Hercules*, to *Jupiter Feretrius*, and others. The Patriarch *Jacob* leaving to *Joseph* an e-
Gen. 48. 22. special Legacy above his Brethren, saith, *Lo I give thee one part above thy Brothers, which I took from the Amorites with my Sword and with my Bow*: where the word, *cepi, I took*, seems to be Prophetically spoken for, *certo capiam, I shall surely take*, (for so the Chaldee Paraphrast expounds it, as if it had already been done by *Jacobs* Prayers to God, who by his special favour preserved *Sichem* for *Jacob* and his Posterity:) Where note also, that that is attributed unto *Jacob* which was done afterwards by his Posterity, who were called by his name, as if he and they were but one and the same person; which place is better thus expounded, than to wrest it (as the Hebrews do) to the spoil taken from the Sichemites, which was long before done by the Sons of *Jacob*. For that, as being somewhat perfidiously done, the old Patriarch did consciensciously disclaim, as may be yet seen upon record, *Gen.* 34. 30. and *Gen.* 49. 6. Now that this Right, which *Abraham* and others had unto the spoils taken in a just War, was approved of by God, so long as it was limited within the natural bounds prescribed, will appear, not by this only, but by other the like places of the Scripture. God in the Law which he gives, *Deut.* 20. 14. concerning that City that should refuse to surrender, but was afterwards taken by the Sword, orders thus, *Thou shalt take the spoil of it to thy self, and thou shalt enjoy the prey of thine Enemies which the Lord hath given thee.* Again, *The Rubenites, the Gadites, and a part of the*
1 Chron. 5. 20, 21, 22. *Tribe of* Manasses, *are said to have conquered the Itureans, and their Neighbours, and to have taken much spoil from them*; this being given as the reason, *because in the fight they called upon*

upon God, and he was propitious unto them. The like is said of that good King *Asa*, who being provoked by an unjust War made against him by the Æthiopians, and *calling upon God, obtained the Victory, and by it much spoil*, 2 Chron. 14. 13. Which is the more notable, because that War was not undertaken by any special command from God, but only out of common Right. *Joshua* also pursuing the same Rubenites, Gadites, and part of the Manassites in their prosperous successes, saith, *Divide the spoil of your Enemies with your Brethren*, Josh. 22. 8. And when *David* sent to the Elders of *Israel* the spoil taken from the Amalekites, he gave this honourable Character of it, *That it was a present sent them out of the spoil of the Enemies of the Lord.* And no marvel; for, as *Seneca* observes, *To enrich any man with the spoils of an Enemy is honourable.* There are also certain Divine Laws extant concerning the dividing of such spoils, as *Numb.* 31. 27. And *Philo* the Jew reckons it among the Curses of the Law, *That their fields should be reaped by their Enemies*, whereby must necessarily ensue, Famine to themselves and Plenty to their Enemies: Whereunto we may add, *That God gave the spoil of* Tyre *to* Nebuchadnezor *for the pay of his Army*, Ezech. 29. 19, 20. because that by him God punished the Pride of the Tyrians for insulting over *Jerusalem*, *Ezech.* 26. 2. 1 Sam. 30. 26. *De Benef.* 37.

II. What the Law of Nations.

Moreover by the Law of Nations, not only he that makes War for a just cause, but every man in a solemn War, is without either end or measure owner of whatsoever he can take from an Enemy; namely, in that sense, that both he, and whosoever claims from him are to be defended in their possessions of the things so gained by all Nations: which, according to the external effects thereof may be called Dominion. *This*, saith *Xenophon*, *is an everlasting Law with all men, that a City being taken by force, all the goods and riches are the Conquerours.* *Plato* likewise was of the same opinion, *All that was the Conquereds, become after the Victory, the Conquerours.* And elswhere amongst divers kinds of natural acquisitions, he placeth this also which he calls sometimes *Polemical*, sometimes *Predatory*, and sometimes *Certatory*: Therein agreeing with *Xenophon*, who brings in *Socrates* by divers interrogations drawing *Euthydemus* to this confession, That it was not at all times unjust to spoil and to destroy; as for example, when done against an Enemy. *Aristotle* in the first of his Politicks, saith, *That the Law of Nations, as by an universal agreement had ordained, that whatsoever is conquered from an Enemy by War becomes immediately the Conquerours.* To the like purpose is that of *Antiphanes*, *We ought to wish our Enemies abundance of riches without valour; for so those riches will quickly find other Masters, not those that possess them, but those that can conquer them.* For as *Plutarch* observes in the life of *Alexander*, *What was the vanquisheds, both is, amd ought to be accounted the Conquerours.* And elsewhere the same *Plutarch*, *The goods of those that are by War overcome, are proposed as the reward of the victory*; which are the very words of *Xenophon*. *What is gained by Arms*, saith *Diodorus*, *or got by the right of War, ought not easily to be lost.* Thus *Philip* in his Epistle to the Athenians, saith, *All of us possess Cities, which were either left us by our Ancestors, or being subdued became ours by the right of War.* Thus *Æschines* also, *If by making War against us, thou hadst subdued our City, thou mightest lawfully have possest it by the Law of Arms.* *Marcellus* in *Livy* justifies himself in taking the spoil of *Syracuse* by the Right of conquest. And the Goths in *Agathias*, do by the same Law, justifie King *Theudorick* who had first conquered *Odoazer*, saying, *Quæ ejus fuerant omnia tenuit jure belli*; *Whatsoever* Odoazer *had*, Theudorick *possest by the right of War.* Thus the Roman Embassadors told *Philip* concerning the City of *Thrace* and some others, That if he had taken those Cities by War, they had been his by the Law of Arms, as being the reward of his victory. And thus *Massanissa* pleads, saying, The land that his Father conquered by War from the Carthaginians, he held by the Law of Nations. So also *Mithridates* in *Justine* saith, *That to please the Romans he had withdrawn his Son out of* Cappadocia, *which as a Conquerour he was rightly possest of by the Law of Nations.* *Cicero* tells us that the City *Mitylene* became the Romans by the Right of War and by Conquest. And in another place he tells us, That propriety in some things may be gained either by preoccupancy, or by War, as in those things that are gained by Victory. Of the same mind was *Dion Cassius*, All that was the Conquered's immediately becomes the Conquerours: *Quæ ex hostibus capiuntur jure gentium statim capientium fiunt*; *Whatsoever*, saith *Cajus* the Lawyer, *is taken from an Enemy by the Law of Nations, immediately is made his that takes it.* And this kind of acquisition *Theophilus* calls a *natural possession*. So likewise *Aristotle*, because it hath respect to no other cause than the bare fact it self; from whence ariseth a kind of natural Right, as the Dominion of all things at first began by Preoccupancy: an impression whereof, we have yet remaining in such Creatures as are naturally wild, whether they live on the Earth, in the Sea, or in the Air, which for the most part are theirs that first take them. As those things also which are taken in War: Besides those things are presumed to be taken from an Enemy, that are taken from the Subjects of an Enemy: As *Dercyllides* in *Xenophon* argues, since *Pharnabazus* was an Enemy to the Lacedemonians, and *Mania* subject to *Pharnabazus*, therefore were the goods of *Mania* lawful prize by the Law of Nations.

Bona quæ victus habuit omnia victoris fiunt.

Instit. Cyri. l. 2.

Lib. 38.

Or. 2. *contra Rullum.*

Offic. 1.

Arist. l. 1. *de rep. c.* 8.

Hist. &c. *l.* 3.

Moreover

III. When moveable Goods are said to be taken.

Moreover, by the Law of Nations things are then said to be taken in War, when they are so detained from us that we are deprived of any probable hopes to recover them, and are no longer able to pursue them; as *Pomponius* determines the like Question. And this, in things moveable, is to be presumed as soon as they are carried into the Enemies Garrisons. A thing may be said to be lost in the same manner as it is said to return after it hath been lost; but may be said to return as soon as it comes within the Bounds of the Empire from whence it was taken, that is, as soon as it comes within our Garrisons. Nay, *Paulus* the Lawyer doth plainly averr that man to be taken that is carried out of our Bounds. And *Pomponius* declares that man to be taken in War whom our Enemy, having apprehended from out of our Garrisons, had led into their own. For until he be secured within their Garrisons, he remains a Citizen or Subject of ours. Now by this Law of Nations there is the same reason for Goods as there is for Persons, whereby we way easily conclude, That in some places things taken in War are presently said to be his, or theirs, that take them, that is, upon this condition, That they continue in their possession for such a time. Whence it seems to follow, That at Sea, Ships and other Goods are then said to be taken when they are carried into our Enemies Harbours, or to such a place where their whole Navy rides; for then their remains no hopes of recovery. But by a later Law of Nations, especially of these of *Europe*, it is thus judged, namely, If the things taken continue in the possession of the Enemy twenty four hours, then are they accounted for lost.

IV. When Lands.

But it is not so with Lands. For they are not said to be taken as soon as the enemy sets down upon them. For though it be true that that part of the Land which an enemy with a strong Army encamps upon, is by them for the present possest, as *Celsus* observes; yet is it not every possession that is sufficient to alienate the Title of Land, but such a one as is firm and lasting. The Romans were so far from thinking that part of their Land lost whereon *Hannibal* encamped, that at that very time they sold it for as much as it would have given before. But that Land only is said to be lost that is so immured or secured with Walls, Forts, Rampires, and such like Muniments; that unless the enemy that holds them can be driven away, there can be no possible access unto it by the former Owners. And this derivation of the word Territory, which *Siculus Flaccus* gives, namely, *A terrendis hostibus, From deterring the enemy from approaching unto it*, seems to be as probable as either that assigned by *Varro, à terendo, from wearing*; or that of *Frontinus, From the soil or earth*; or that of *Pomponius* the Lawyer, From the power that the Magistrate of the place hath to affright all persons within those bounds by removing or driving them out of it. Thus *Xenophon* in his Book concerning Contribution saith, That the possession of Lands is held in the time of war by Muniments, which he there calls Walls and Frontier Garrisons.

V. Things not the Enemies cannot be acquired by War.

Whence this also may be gathered, That before the War can transfer a Right unto us in any thing so taken, it is requisite by the Law of Nations, that that Right should first be in our enemies. For things deposited or laid up within our Enemies Towns or Garrisons, whose right Owners are neither Subjects to our Enemies, nor have any hostile mind towards us; cannot by War be made lawful prize, though we do conquer the place; as is sufficiently proved, among many others, by that of *Æschines*, where he shews, That *Amphipolis*, being a City belonging to the Athenians, could not be lawful prize to King *Philip* by that War which he made with the Amphipolitans. First, because no reason could be given why the Athenians should lose their right, being no Enemies at that time to King *Philip*; and then, Because this Right of changing properties by mere force would prove a matter of so dangerous a consequence, that it ought not to be largely interpreted.

VI. Concerning Goods found in an Enemies Ship.

Wherefore that which is commonly said, That Goods found in the Ships of our Enemies are adjudged to be the Enemies Goods, and consequently are lawful prize, is not so to be understood as though it were a certain Law made by the Right of Nations, but because it gives occasion to a very great presumption that they are so, which notwithstanding by pregnant and evident proofs to the contrary may be dash'd. And so it was long since adjudged in *Holland* in a full Senate during the War with the *Hans-towns* in the Year 1338. and from thence hath since past into a Law. Neither are the Ships of our Confederates forfeited, though the Goods in them be an Enemies, unless it be so agreed with the consent of the Masters of the Ship. And so are the Laws of *France*, as I suppose, to be understood, which adjudge the Goods lawful prize, if the Ship be so; and the Ship lawful prize, if the Goods be so. But otherwise the Goods only are prize, but not the Ship. So in the War between the Venetians and the Genoese, the Ships of the Grecians being searched, those Enemies that lay hid in them were taken and made Prisoners.

Greg. l. 9.

VII. Things taken from our enemies are ours by the Law of Nations, tho' they took them from others.

This also is most certain, That if we look no farther than the Law of Nations, whatsoever is taken by War from our Enemies, cannot justly be claimed by those from whom those Enemies won it, by the Right of War; because, The Law of Nations first made our Enemies Lords of it, (as to an external Right) and afterwards the same Law made it ours. Thus *Jephtha* pleads his Title against the Ammonites, because the Land in question, as also another part of the Land of the Moabites were, by the right of Conquest first won from the

the Ammonites and so, invested in the Amorites; and from the Amorites, by the same 1 Sam. 30. 20.
Right of War, was transferred unto the Israelites, *Judg.* 11. 23, 24, 27. Thus did *David*
claim and divide as his own, the Lands that he took from the Amalekites, notwithstanding
that the Amalekites had before taken it from the Philistines. *Titus Largius* (as *Dionysius* *Lib. 6.*
Halicarnassensis records the Story) did thus adjudge this Case in the Roman Senate, when
the Volscians laid claim to some of those Lands which the Romans had then lately won by
the Right of War, because anciently they had been Lords thereof, saying, *We Romans do
account the possession of those Lands which we have won by the Sword to be most just and honest;
neither can we be so easily perswaded to erase the Monuments of our Ancestors valour, by resto-
ring that back unto those, who when they had them were not able to keep them. Nay those Lands
that we thus gain, we conceive our selves bound not only to communicate to those Citizens that are
now living, but to leave to those who shall hereafter succeed us. So far are we from adjudging
that against our selves (by a voluntary surrender of what we have gained by the Sword) which is
usually adjudged against Enemies.* This *Plutarch* relates *to be the ground of the War between*
the Romans and the Vejans, who demanded of the Romans the City Fidonæ, *as anciently belonging* *Vit. Rom.*
*unto them; which demand was not thought by the Romans to be unjust only, but ridiculous; to
wit, that they who would not aid and assist the Fidenates whilst they were contending against the Ro-
mans, and in great danger; but suffered the Citizens thereof to be destroyed, should now lay claim
to their Houses and Lands when the were possest by the Romans by the Right of Conquest.* This also
is plain by that Answer which the Romans gave unto the *Arunci*, *We Romans do conceive
that whatsoever any man wins by his valour from his Enemies, he may bequeath to his Posterity,
as being by the best of titles his own.* So in another place they return this in answer to the
Volsci, *We account that which we conquer from our Enemies to be the best Estate we have, seeing* *Dionys. Hali-*
that this is not only adjudged ours by our own Laws, but by a title derived more truly from the gods *car. l. 7.*
*than from men, and approved of by the constant practice of all Nations, both Greeks and Bar-
barians; we shall not therefore yield up any thing cowardly of that which we have gotten by va-
lour, nor calmly forego what by the Sword we have gained.* Maximum hoc probrum foret, quæ *Livy lib. 7.*
virtute ac fortitudine quæsita sunt, ea per formidinem aut stuporem amittere; *For this
would be the greatest dishonour unto us, if either through fear or stupidity we should lose that which
by virtue and mere manhood we have acquired.* And this is also confest in that Answer of the
Samnites, *We have gained this by Conquest, which Law is of all acquisitions the justest.* By
this Right the Romans held *Syria*, as *Appianus* notes, without restoring it to *Antiochus* *Lib. 12.*
Pius, from whom *Tigranes*, that great enemy to the Romans, had formerly taken it; *ad-
judging it more equal that* Syria *should be governed by the Romans, who had expelled* Tigra-
nes; *than by the* Seleucidæ, *who had been ejected by* Tigranes. Yea, and *Antiochus* himself was
of opinion, *That that was the most just and lasting possession that was got by the sword. Justine* *Polyb. in ex-*
brings in *Pompey* answering the same *Antiochus* (who, after the recession of *Tigranes* into *Ar-* *cerpt. Legat. n.*
menia, demanded the Kingdom of *Syria*, out of which he had been by the same *Tigranes* dri- *72.*
ven, and into which after eighteen years he had been restored by *Lucullus*) in these words, *Mithrid. Ci-*
That he would neither with nor without the consent of the Syrians set such a King over them as could *vil. 1.*
be content to hide himself in a corner of Cilicia *all the while that* Tigranes *held* Syria. *And* *Justin lib. 40.*
now the same Tigranes *being vanquished by the Romans, would demand the reward due to other
mens labours.* And therefore *as he had not taken the Kingdom from him, so that Kingdom
which himself had left unto* Tigranes *he refused to give him, because he knew not how to defend it.*
So also those parts of *Gallia* which the *Cimbri* took from the Gauls, the Romans afterwards
taking, held as their own. Nor did the French restore to the Romans that part of *Italy*
which they took from the Goths.

VIII. That things taken from the Enemies are not always theirs that take them.

But here a more knotty Question ariseth, concerning the persons to whom the spoils
taken from the enemy in a solemn War belong, whether to the State, or to every person
of, or among the people. The Modern Lawyers do vary exceedingly in their opinions
concerning this Point; for most of them finding it in their Civil Law, That *capta sunt ca-
pientium*; *Things thus taken, are theirs that take them.* And in the Body of the Canon
Law, That the spoil is to be distributed by publick Authority, do one from another (as is
usual) deliver their opinions thus, That primarily, and by original Right, he that first appre-
hends them hath the best title to them; but notwithstanding that they are all to be brought
to the General, who may distribute them amongst his Souldiers. But this opinion is not
more common than false; and therefore that we may hereby learn how unsafe it is in such
doubtful cases to be biassed by so weak an Authority, I shall the more accurately confute
this opinion. We cannot indeed deny but that by the consent of Nations this Question
may be determined either way, namely, That the Spoil may belong either to the people,
or to him that bears the charge of the War, or to those particular persons that with the
hazard of their lives do first lay hands on it. But the Question here is, Not what they
may determine in this Point, but what they have or do determine of it; whereunto I an-
swer, *That the things of an enemy, by the consent of Nations, are no otherwise their enemies that
take them, than as they belong to none*; as we have already explained it from that Saying of
Nerva the Son.

But

IX. That possession and dominion may be gained for us by another. *L. ea qua D. de acq. dom.*

But the things that are no Bodies, are indeed theirs that first take them. But they may be said to take them that employ others to take them, as well as they who take them for and by themselves. So they that are employed by others to catch Fish, Fowl, Deer, or Pearls, whether they be Children, Servants or Freemen, do not appropriate them unto themselves, but take them for those that employ them. It was well said of *Modestinus* the Lawyer, *Whatsoever is naturally gained, as possession is, may be gained by any man whomsoever we will appoint to do it for us.* So likewise *Paulus* the Lawyer, *Possession is gained by the mind, and by the body, but then the mind must be our own; but the body may be either our own or anothers.* And in another place, *Possession may be taken for us by either a Proctor, an Attorney or Guardian; that is, if it be done by them with that mind and purpose as to make it ours.* Thus it was among the Grecians, they that overcame in the Olympian Games, obtained indeed the prize; but not for themselves, but for those that sent them. And the reason is, because naturally one man may make use of another as his Instrument, if both are willing. Wherefore the difference that is said to be between persons bond and free, as concerning acquisitions, respects only the Civil Law, and appertains properly to civil acquisitions; as appears by that place of *Modestinus* before cited. And yet the Emperour *Severus* drew these nearer to the pattern of natural acquisitions, not only for profit, as out of Jurisprudence, as he himself acknowledgeth. Setting then aside the Civil Law, that saying will hold good, That what a man may do for himself by himself, that he may also do by another; and it is the same thing to do it by another, as to do it by himself.

X. A distinction of Acts done in War into publick and private. *Lib. 30.*

Here then we must distinguish between those acts which in a War are truly publick, and those private acts that are done by the occasion of a publick War. By these private acts the Goods of an Enemy may primarily and directly belong to the private Souldier; but whatsoever is gained from an Enemy by such acts as are publick, is due to the people, or to him that maintains the War. Upon this Right of Nations *Scipio* grounds his Plea against *Massanissa* in *Livy*, Syphax, *by the good conduct of the Roman people, is conquered and taken; and therefore He, his Wife, his Kingdom, Lands, Towns, with their Inhabitants, yea and in a word, whatsoever* Syphax *had, is thereby become lawful prize to the people of* Rome. And in the same manner doth *Antiochus* the Great argue, That *Cœlosyria* did of right belong to *Seleucus*, and not to *Ptolomy*; because it was *Seleucus* that maintained the War, to whom *Ptolomy* was but an Auxiliary, as *Polybius* relates. *Lib. 5.*

XI. The Land that is taken is his that maintains the War.

The Soil, and whatsoever is fixed thereon, are not usually taken but by some publick Acts, as by the introducing of an Army, by placing of Garrisons in Strong Holds, Towns and Castles; and therefore, as *Pomponius* saith, *Publicatur Ager qui ex Hostibus captus est; Lands taken from an Enemy fall to the State*, that is, (as he expounds himself) *præda non cedit, is no part of the prey or booty* strictly taken, (which is sometimes granted to the common Souldiers.) So *Salomo* in *Procopius*, *That Prisoners and some other Moveables should be given as a prey to the Souldiers, is not without some reason*, (so as it be done by publick Grant, as we shall anon explain it;) *but that the Lands should altogether belong to the Prince, or to the Roman Empire that defrays the charge of the War, is but just*; though the Emperor *Severus* gave the very Lands conquered from his Enemies unto the Captains and Souldiers of his Frontier Garrisons. Among the Hebrews and Lacedemonians the Land taken by War was divided by Lots amongst the Tribes; yet so, that amongst the Hebrews the Kings Lot was equal to that of each single Tribe. Among the Romans, the Lands taken in War were either kept to be let out, some small portion thereof being sometimes left for honours sake to the former Owners; or alienated and sold, or assigned over to Husbandmen to be ploughed or made tributary, whereof we have divers testimonies in their Histories, Laws and Commentaries. *The Romans*, (as *Appian* tells us) *when they subdued* Italy, *took away part of their Fields by way of punishment.* And elsewhere he tells us, *That the Romans having conquered their Enemies did not take away all their Lands, but a part only.* *Cicero* also in that Oration that he made to the Chief Priests for his own house, notes, That their Emperours having subdued an Enemies Country, did sometimes consecrate their Fields, but it was always by the Decree of the people.

Vand. l. 2. *Lampridius.*

XII. Things moving themselves and moveable, being taken by private Acts, are theirs that take them.

But as to things moving themselves or moveable, they are taken either in publick service, or out of it. If they are such as are not taken upon publick Duty, they are theirs that take them. And hither we may referr that of *Celsus*, *Quæ res hostiles apud nos sunt, non publicæ, sed occupantium fiunt*; Whatsoever is found amongst us that was the enemies, belongs not to the Commonwealth, but to them that apprehend them; that is, the War being begun. For the very same was observed even of Men and Women at such time as they in this case were equally valued with Goods. We have a notable Saying in *Tryphonius* to this purpose, *But they who in times of peace come to sojourn in anothers dominions (as friends) the War suddenly breaking out, were made Slaves with them amongst whom they were by their own hard fate apprehended as enemies.* Where we may note, That the Lawyer ascribes *this* unto Fate, because they were brought into bondage without any merit of their own; for all such were anciently ascribed to Fate. So *Servius* upon that of *Virgil*, *Acti*

fatis,

fatis, observes, That the Poet endeavours to attribute nothing to the merits of the Trojans, but all to Fate. So *Nævius* concerning the *Metelli*, *Fato fiunt Romæ Metelli consules*; *The* Metelli *were made Consuls at* Rome (as it were) *by Fate*, that is, without any merit of their own. In like manner it is, when Souldiers take any thing from their enemies whilst they are not upon Duty, nor executing the Commands of their Captain, but by permission of their Commanders, or by a promiscuous licence that Souldiers do usually take on each side one against another; what, I say, is so taken is lawful prize to him that takes it; because it is not taken in order to any Command, but voluntarily, and is therefore given them as the reward of their valour. As when in pickeering a Souldier overcomes, disarms or kills his Enemy, the spoil of that enemy is due unto him in recompence of his Virtue; so when a Party shall make an excursion freely without Command into an enemies Country, so as it be beyond ten miles from the Camp, according to the Roman Discipline (as we shall see anon) whatsoever they shall so take is theirs that take it.

XIII. Unless the Civil Law do otherwise ordain.

And whereas we say, That by the Law of Nations whatsoever is thus acquired becomes directly his that takes it, we are so to understand it, that this was the Law of Nations before any thing in this Case was decreed by the Civil Law. For every State or people may among themselves otherwise determine of it, and prevent the right and dominion of him that takes it, as we may perceive it done in many places where Fowl and Deer are taken. So also the Civil Law may ordain, That whatsoever is found amongst us of or belonging to our enemies, the War being begun, shall be confiscate to the use of the Commonwealth.

XIV. What is taken by a publick act is his that maintains the War.

But as yet as to those things that any man takes by any publick Act of a solemn War, there is another reason why those things should not be theirs that take them. For herein every private Souldier represents the Body of the Commonwealth, and what is done by any one is taken to be done by the publick State that employs him; and therefore whatsoever, whether possession or dominion, any of them do thus take, (unless the Civil Law do otherwise determine) the people may be said to acquire; and therefore they may transfer their right thereunto to whom they please, and to what uses they please. But because this seems to be repugnant to the common opinion, therefore I shall endeavour to confirm it with more than ordinary proofs, which I shall draw from the examples of the noblest Nations. I shall begin with the Grecians, whose custom, in this case, *Homer* in several places describes.

Omnia jam divisa, quibus spoliavimus Urbes.

Their Cities sack'd, the spoils divided are.

Achilles in the same Poet, speaking of the Cities which he himself had stormed, saith,

Omnibus his ingens pretio numeróque suppellex
Nostra rapta manu: Regi sed Victor Atridæ
Cuncta tuli, celeres residens qui pone carinas,
Divideret cum pauca aliis, sibi multa tenebat.

From which Cities *Achilles* brought to *Agamemnon* all the rich plunder which he divided, distributing some few things for others, but reserving the greatest part to himself. For here we look at *Agamemnon*, partly, as he was at that time Prince of all *Greece*, and so representing the whole Body of the people; by which right he divided the spoil, but with the advice and consent of his Council: and partly as a General, and so out of that which was publick he claimed a greater share than others to himself; and therefore *Achilles* thus bespeaks *Agamemnon*,

Nam neque me tecum prædæ pars æqua sequetur,
Si Danaûm virtus Trojanum everterit Urbem.

My part of th' prey with thine must not compare,
Though by our valour *Troy* subverted were.

And so in another place *Agamemnon* by the advice of his Council offers unto *Achilles* a Ship laden with Brass and Gold, with twenty Women, which he might take first out of the Spoil. *Troy* being taken, *Virgil*, speaking of King *Priamus*'s Palace, saith,

Custodes Lecti Phœnix & dirus Ulysses
Prædam asservabant: huc undique Troïa gaza,
Incensis erepta adytis, Mensæque Deorum,
Cratéresque Auro solidi, captiváque vestis
Congeritur.

Æn. l. 2.

> There *Phœnix* and *Ulysses* guard the Spoil,
> And from all parts *Troy*'s precious things do pile,
> Snatcht from burnt Temples, and from Altars rare,
> Goblets of Gold, and sacred Vestments are.

Plut. Aristid. Herod. l. 9. *Plut. Lysand.* λαφυροπῶλαι. *Homer. Iliad.* 10. *Pliny lib.* 23. *c.* 3. *Plut. Alex. Curt. Diod. l.* 17. *Strab.* 15. *Greg. Turon. l.* 2. *c.* 27. *Æn. l.* 3. *Servius. Liv. l.* 23.

Thus we read, That in after Ages *Aristides* preserved the Spoil at *Marathon* intire. And after the Battel at *Platææ* it was severely forbidden that any man should presume to take to himself any part of the spoil; afterwards the spoil was preserved and distributed among the people, according to each mans deserts. After this, when *Athens* was conquered, *Lysander* caused the spoil of the City to be brought into the open Market. And the Lacedemonians had *publick Officers* who were appointed to make Portsale of all their prizes taken in the War. If we look into *Asia*, *Virgil* will inform us, That the Trojans were wont to divide the spoil by lot, as is usual; where things held in common are to be divided amongst many. In other places the spoil was divided by the General, by which right *Hector* at the special instance of *Dodonis* promised to give him *Achilles*'s Horses, whereby we may understand, That this Right of gaining propriety was not always in the bare taking of the thing. So the spoil taken in *Asia* was brought to *Cyrus* the Conqueror, and not distributed but by his order, whose whole care was to chuse out such things to offer unto the Gods as the *Magi* thought most acceptable to them. If we look into *Africa*, we shall find the same custom there. So whatsoever was taken at *Agrigentum*, or in the Fight at *Cannæ*, or in other places, was sent unto *Carthage*. Among the ancient Francks, whatsoever was taken in War was divided by lot; neither had the King himself any other share than what fell to him. *Captivi & Prædæ inter Victores sorte dividebantur*; *The Conquerours divided by lot both the Captives and the Spoil*, saith *Servius* upon *Virgil*. But look how much more excellent the Romans were than other Nations in Military Discipline, so much the more worthy they are of our imitation. *Dionysius Halicarnassensis*, a most exact Observer of their Manners and Customs, thus instructs us in this Case, *Whatsoever is taken from the Enemy by valour in War, is decreed by the Law to be publick: so that not only the private Souldier was forbid to claim any propriety in it, but even the General himself could claim no interest therein; but the Quæstor received it, and in an open Market exposed it to sale.* These are the very words of those that undertook to accuse *Coriolanus* to the people of *Rome*; which words, though true, yet smelt too rankly of envy and distraction.

XV. Yet was some power herein always granted to the General. *Liv. l.* 37. *Liv. l.* 5.

For that the people were the right Owners of the Spoil, was most true (as *Simler* testifies in his History of the Switzers:) and yet it is as true, that the power of disposing thereof was allowed in every free State to the General, yet so that he was to render an account thereof unto the people. *Polybius* concerning *L. Æmilius Paulus* testifies thus, *Being possest of the whole Kingdom, and having it thereby in his own power to dispose of all things at his pleasure, he yet coveted nothing.* So doth *Livy* concerning the same *Æmilius*, *It is in the power of the General to destroy those Cities that are taken by the sword, but not those that are surrendred; yet even in these also the disposition of the spoil is in his power, and not in the Souldiers.* But notwithstanding this power that custom hath given to Generals, some of them to the end that they might free themselves from all manner of suspicion, have wisely transferred it back to the Senate, as *Camillus* did. And they that have claimed it, have been observed to have disposed of the spoil to several uses, according to their several designs, to the promoting of either Religion, Honour, or Ambition.

XVI. Who have either brought into the publick Treasury, *Lib.* 13. *c.* 23. *Vit. Æmil. Lib.* 2. *Lib.* 2. *Ep.*

But those amongst them who desired to be, or to appear, most holy, would not at all enrich themselves with the spoils of the enemy; but whether it were in money, the Quæstor of the people was commanded to receive it; or in other Goods, he was commanded to make Portsale of them: and the money for which they were sold, went under the name of *Manubiæ*, as *Favorinus* in *Gellius* notes, and was by the Quæstor brought into the Treasury. But in case there were matter for a triumph, then it was first ostentously shewed to the people. Manius Curius *called the Gods to witness, That he had not so much as touched any of the spoil, but only one poor Beechen Cup, wherewith to sacrifice to the Gods.* But that of *Æmilius Paulus*, which *Plutarch* records, is admirable, and for which all men did extol him for his magnanimity, namely, *That when he had collected from the enemy an infinite mass of Gold and Silver*, nec inspicere voluisset, *he would not be tempted with the sight of it. But delivered it to the Quæstor for the publick use.* The like did *Pompey*, of whom *Vellejus* writes thus, *The money that he took from* Tigranes, *he caused to be delivered to the Quæstor, as his custom was, and to be publickly registred.* So also *Marcus Tullius* in his Epistle to *Salust*, gives this testimony of his own integrity, *De præda mea præter Quæstores Urbanos, Teruntium nec attigit, nec tacturus est quisquam*; *Besides the Quæstors of the City, no man hath or shall touch the least part of the spoil that I have got from the enemy.* And this indeed was the general practice of the Romans in their most ancient and best days; whereunto *Plautus* alluding, saith,

Nunc

Nunc hanc prædam omnem jam ad Quæstorem deferam.

Now all this ſpoil I'll to the Queſtor bring.

The like he ſaith of Priſoners taken,

Whom from the Queſtors of the ſpoil I bought.

But others of the Roman Generals, did without the Queſtors make Portſale of the ſpoil taken from the Enemie by themſelves, as may be gathered from the enſuing words of *Halicarnaſſenſes.* Thus we read that the Sabines being vanquiſhed by King *Tarquin*, he ſent the Priſoners together with the ſpoil unto *Rome*. So likewiſe *Romulius* and *Veturius* being Conſuls, the ſpoil was ſold to ſupply the publick Treaſury, which was then almoſt exhauſted, the whole Army repining at it. But in a caſe ſo clear and ſo beaten, what need we any more teſtimonies? But yet this is worthy to be obſerved, That the ſpoil, or part thereof at leaſt, was ſometimes given to the Gods, ſometimes to the Souldiers, and ſometimes to others; to the Gods were given, either the ſpoils themſelves, as thoſe which *Romulus* was ſaid to hang up in the Temple of *Jupiter Feretrius*; or being reduced into Money, that Money was imployed to religious uſes: Thus was the Temple of *Jupiter* built on the Hill *Tarpeius*, with the Money raiſed out of the Pometine ſpoils by *Tarquin* the Proud. *Liv. l. 1. Liv. l. 3. Dion. Hal. l. 2. Liv. l. 1.*

XVII. Or divided it to the Souldiers, and how.

To give the ſpoil to the Souldiers, was by the Ancient Romans accounted as proceeding from Ambition. So *Sextus* the Son of *Tarquin* the Proud, but driven unto the Gabians, is ſaid to diſtribute the prey amongſt the Souldiers, that thereby he might render himſelf the more powerful. *Appius Claudius* in the open Senate condemned ſuch kind of largeſſes to Souldiers, as ſavouring too much of novelty, raſhneſs, and prodigality: The ſpoil given to the Souldiers, was either divided amongſt them, or taken, as when each man had what he could catch; when it was divided, either it was in lieu of their pay, in caſe it could not conveniently be reduced to money, and ſo brought into the publick Treaſury, and this was never oppoſed by *Appius Claudius*; or elſe it was divided according to every mans merits for ſervices then done. The order and method of this diſtribution is excellently deſcribed by *Polybius*, namely, the leſſer part of the Army was ſent out daily to fetch in the ſpoil, who were commanded to bring whatſoever they found into the Camp, where the Tribunes were equally to divide it. They that had the charge of the Camp, which from the practice of King *David* grew into a Law; and they that through ſickneſs, or by reaſon of ſome publick employment were abſent, had equal ſhares with thoſe that were preſent: ſometimes the ſpoil was reduced into money, which in lieu thereof was diſtributed among them; which in Triumphs was uſually done. The proportions I find to be thus divided, ſometimes to a Foot Souldier a ſingle ſhare, to a Captain of Foot a double, to an Horſe-man a treble; and ſometimes to a Foot-man a ſingle, and to an Horſe-man a double proportion; elſwhere, a ſingle to a Foot Souldier, a double to the Captain: but to a Tribune, and to a Horſe-man (or rather to a Captain of Horſe, as *Appianus* relates) a quadruple ſhare. There was alſo ſometimes a reſpect had to the merits of Souldiers. Thus was *Cajus Marcius*, who had behaved himſelf gallantly, at the taking of *Corioli* highly rewarded for his valour out of the ſpoil of that City, before it was diſtributed among the Souldiers; but which way ſoever the ſpoil was to be divided, it was lawful for the General to take of the principal part of it, what he pleaſed uuto himſelf, that is, as much as was fit: which alſo hath ſometimes been granted unto others, as the reward, or an encouragement to valour. As *Euripides* ſpeaking of the Trojan Ladies ſaith, *Liv. l. 5. Loco dicto. Lib. 10. 1 Sam. 30. 24. Liv. 45.*

——Quæ principibus eximiæ datæ
Erant Achivis.

——They that were moſt fair
Unto the Grecian Princes given were.

And of *Andromacha* he tells us, That *Pyrrhus* the Son of *Achilles* choſe her to himſelf. *Fabricius* in his Oration to *Pyrrhus*, challengeth to himſelf this priviledge, ſaying, *That of the things taken in War, it was lawful for him as General, to take what and as much as he pleaſed*; whoſe example *Julian* propoſeth both to himſelf and his Army, as *Ammianus* teſtifies. Whereunto *Iſidore* hath reſpect, where treating of the Right of War, *He divides the ſpoil into that part which was equally to be diſtributed among the Souldiers, with regard had to the quality of their perſons and to their hard ſervice, and into that which was the Princes or Generals portion.* *Tarquin* the Proud, as *Livy* teſtifies, would both enrich himſelf with the beſt *Dion Hal. l. 4. Lib. 1.*

best, and pacifie the minds of the people with the rest of the spoil. *Servilius* in his Oration to *Lucius Paulus*, saith, That it was in his power to have made himself rich in the division of the spoil. And there are some of opinion, that it is that part only that falls to the General, which is signified by the word *Manubiæ*, amongst whom we find *Asconius Pedianus*. But much more commendable are those Generals, who can be content to forgoe their Right in this case, and assume nothing of the spoil unto themselves, but the *Honour* of the Conquest; among whom was that *Fabricius* before named, *who preferred his own honour before riches though justly got*, which he confesseth he did in imitation of *Valerius Publicola* and some few others; whose example *M. Porcius Cato* also followed in his Spanish Victory, denying that he kept any thing to himself of the spoil he had taken from the Enemy, besides what he had eaten and drank: yet adding withal, that he did not thereby blame those Generals that had, or hereafter should enrich themselves by the spoil of their Enemies; but that *he chose rather to emulate the best of men in their vertues, than the wealthiest in their riches.* Next unto these are to be commended those Generals, who took somewhat of the spoil to themselves, but very sparingly. Such was *Pompey* whom *Cato* in *Lucan* commends, for that *he brought into the publick treasury much more than he kept himself.* In the division of the spoil, regard was sometimes had to such as were absent from the fight, as it was ordained by *Fabius Ambustus* at the taking of *Anxur*; and sometimes no regard at all was had of some, though present: As when *Cicinnatus* was Dictator, no respect was had in the division of the spoil to that part of the Army, that was commanded by *Minutius*. But look what Right the Emperours had in the Ancient Commonwealth, the same was translated when the Commonwealth was setled to the Generals of the Armies, as appears by *Justinians* Code; where from an insinuation of acts done, all donations of thing moving themselves and moveable were discharged, which their Generals gave unto the Souldiers out of the spoil of the Enemies, whether they were then occupied in the War, or in what places soever they were known to abide. But this division gave frequent occasion of calumny, as if those Captains did by that means purchase favour to themselves only, which was the crime charged upon *Servilius*, *Corolianus*, and *Camillus*, as if they obliged their friends and clients by their liberality out of the publick stock; whereunto they plead that they had done it for the publick good, namely, *That they that were present at the work done, receiving the fruits of their own labours, might thereby be encouraged the more willingly to adventure themselves in other expeditions*, which are the very words of *Halicarnassenses.*

Verr. 3. *Plut. M. Cato.* *Magistri militum.* *C. de donationibus.* *Dion. l. 6. & 7.* *Livy lib. 5.* *Dion. Hali.*

XVIII. Or by plunder.

Thus much for Division, now we come to Direption, when every private Souldier held what he could catch; which licence was granted unto the Souldiers, either in wasting the Enemies Country, or after a set Battel, or at the storming of a City that had been long besieged: for then commonly upon a sign given, every man ran in and took what he could get; this licence was very rarely given anciently, yet doth it not want some precedents. For *Tarquin* we read gave the spoil of the City *Suessa* to his Souldiers. So did *Q. Servilius* the Dictator, the rifling of the Camp of the *Æqui*. The like did *Q. Fabius*, having defeated the *Volsci*, and taken the City *Ecetra*, and afterwards some others did the same very often. *Perseus* being put to flight, *Paulus* the Consul gave the spoil of those that were slain or maimed upon the spot to his Foot Souldiers; but to the Horse, the spoil of the Country adjoining. So also by the decree of the Senate, did he give the spoil of the Cities of *Epirus* to the Souldiers. The like did *Sulla* the City of *Athens*. *Lucullus* having vanquished *Tigranes*, did for a while restrain his Souldiers from gathering the spoil; but at length being assured of the Victory, he suffered them to take it: He gave also the plunder of *Tigranocerta*, as *Plutarch* records, to the Souldiers. The like did the Emperour *Severus* the spoil of *Ctesiphon* to his; yea, and commanded his Tribunes, Captains, and common Souldiers to plunder all the Villages about it. *Mahomet* the second to encourage his Army, promised them all the spoil and Captives they could find in *Constantinople*. That which some men do object against this is, That it oftens comes to pass, through this licence given to every Souldier to catch what he can, that they that are greedy of plunder, do deprive those that are truly valiant, of the reward of their valour. For it is frequently seen, that *they that are most backwards to fight, are most forwards to plunder; whereas they that have magnanimously exposed themselves to the greatest labour and danger, have reason to expect the best part of the prey*, which are the very words of *Appius* in *Livy*. Whereunto not very impertinent is that of *Cyrus* in *Xenophon*, *In this way of partition*, I mean by plunder, *I very well know that the worst Souldiers get most*: But unto this, it is commonly answered, That what any man takes from his Enemy with his own hands, is ever more acceptable unto him, than that which is assigned him by others, though in value it be much less. Sometimes again it is permitted Souldiers to plunder, because indeed it cannot easily be prevented. So it was in the winning of *Cortuosa* a Town of the *Hetruscians*, *The Tribunes ordered the spoil to be sold*: *but* Imperium quàm consilium segnius fuit; *The command came too late*; *for the*

Liv. l. 4. *Dion l. 5, 6. 9. 10.* *Livy l. 46.* *Lib. 6.*

the Souldiers had already got it, which could not without envy be retrieved.

Now whereas I said, that the spoil, or the mony raised out of it, was sometimes divided among such as were no Souldiers; this often happens, when to the maintenance of the War, some men have liberally contributed, unto whom restitution hath been promised to be made after the Victory to the full value: yea, and sometimes Plays and Interludes have been ordained out of the money raised by the spoil of the Enemy. XIX. Or grant it to others.

Neither is the spoil thus diversly disposed of only where the Wars are divers, but the same prey in one and the same War, is often set apart for divers uses, distinguishing it either by its parts, or by its kinds. So *Abraham* gave the Tenth of the spoil to *Melchisedeck*. The like did *Camillus* to *Apollo Pythius* in imitation of the Greeks, who also learned it from the Hebrews; at which time under the vow of decimating the spoil, the Chief Priests did adjudge, That not only things moveable, as Money, Jewels, Cattel, and the like; but Towns, and Fields, and the like immoveable things were also comprehended. The same *Camillus* having conquered the *Falisci*, allotted the greatest part of the spoil to the Questor, yet reserved some small part of it to to the Souldiers. So did *Lucius Manlius* also *sell part of the spoil which he reduced into the publick treasury; and yet took great care that part thereof should be divided among his Souldiers, as it was most just.* The spoil of the Enemy may also be divided by its several kinds, which are these; either they are Captives, Droves, or Herds of Cattel (which the Grecians when they speak properly, call, λείαν, *the prey*) Money, things moveable, and these either common and ordinary, or such as are more rare and precious. *Q. Fabius* when he had overcome the Volsci, commanded the prey and spoil to be sold; but for the Silver, he reserved that for himself. And when he had subdued the *Volsci* and *Æqui*, the Prisoners he led beyond the Territories of *Tusculum*, and distributed them to the Souldiers; but the common people, and the Cattel, he left in the fields of *Ecetra* for pillage and plunder. *Lucius Cornelius* when he had taken *Antium*, brought all the Money, whether Gold, Silver, or Brass, into the publick Treasury, caused the Prisoners and spoil to be sold, reserving for the Souldiers such things only as sufficed for food and clothing. Neither was that of *Cincinnatus* much unlike, who having taken *Corbio*, a Town belonging to the *Æqui*, sent the most precious part of the spoil to *Rome*, the rest he divided among the Souldiers by their Centuries. *Camillus* having taken *Veji*, brought nothing to the publick Treasury, but the Money he had raised by the selling of the Captives: But having Conquered the *Hetrusci*, and made sale of the Captives; out of the Money so raised, he restored to some Roman Matrons the Gold they had contributed to maintain the War, and laid up three Cups of Gold in the Capitol. *Fabricus* having conquered the Lacanes, the *Brutii*, and the Samnites, did very much enrich the Souldiery, restored to every Citizen his Taxes, and brought into the Treasury Four hundred Talents besides. So did *Fabius*, when he had taken *Tarentum*, brought the Money raised by the sale of Prisoners into the Treasury; but the rest of the spoil he disperst among his Souldiers. Thus did *Q. Fulvius*, and *Appius Claudius*, when they had taken *Hanno*'s Camp, they sold the spoil and divided it, rewarding every man that had done any signal service in that fight. *Scipio* having taken *Carthage*, gave the spoil of the City to his Souldiers, reserving only the Gold and Silver to gratifie his friends. *Acilius* upon the taking of *Lamia*, divided among the Souldiers one part of the spoil, and sold the other. *Cn. Manlius* having subdued the *Gallogrecians*, and according to the then Romish superstition, burnt their Arms, sold the rest of the Prey; part whereof as his own he brought into the Treasury, the rest he divided among his Souldiers with singular care as was most fit. XX. Or being divided it is diversly disposed of. *Livy l. 5.* *Livy l. 5.* *Lib. 38.* *Dion. lib. 8.* *Idem lib. 10.* *Ibidem.* *Liv. l. 10.* *Liv. l. 5.* *L. 6.* *Liv. lib. 37.* *Lib. 25.* *Liv. l. 37.* *Id. l. 38.*

Whence we may collect, That no less among the Romans, than among other Nations, the spoil did belong to the people of *Rome*, though the disposition thereof was sometimes granted to their Generals; yet so, that they were to give account thereof to the people: which we may learn amongst others, by the example of *L. Scipio*, who as *Valerius Maximus* relates it, having conquered King *Antiochus*, and added *Asia* to the Roman Empire, was afterwards (as *Livy* reports) condemned for enriching himself with the spoil that belonged to the Commonwealth, for he had received Four hundred and eighty Talents of Silver from the Enemy, more than he had brought into the Treasury. *Cato* in his Oration concerning the spoil taken from the Enemy, bitterly and resolutely complains of the licence and impunity granted unto their Generals in his time, in imbezelling the spoils of the Enemy, and so robbing the publick Treasury: A fragment of which Oration is recorded by *Aulus Gellius* in these words, *Fures privatorum furtorum in nervo atque compedibus ætatem agunt: Fures publici in auro atque purpura. Private Thieves we usually load with bolts and fetters: But they that rob the Commonwealth, are clad in Gold and Purple (and are indeed the only Gallants of our age.)* So elsewhere the same *Cato* wonders, *That any man should dare to hang up in his own house those Ensignes that were taken in Wars, as if they were a part of his own houshold-stuff.* Neither are Generals only guilty of this crime, but even private Souldiers, XXI. Oft-times it was embezelled. *Lib. 5. c. 3.* *Livy lib. 45.* *L. 11. c. 18.*

Souldiers, in case what they so take from the enemy, they do not forthwith produce in publick. For *they were all of them bound by Oath*, saith *Polybius*, *that they should not purloin or convey away any thing of the prey, but that they should faithfully discharge their trust in regard of their Oaths.* The Form whereof we find recorded by *Aulus Gellius*, *whereby they were obliged not to take away any thing, either within the Army, or within ten miles of it, that was more worth than a small piece of Silver: or if they did, then they were to bring it to the Consul, or within three days to make open profession of what they had done*: which gives some light to that of *Modestinus*, *Is qui prædam ab hostibus surripuit Peculatus tenetur*; *He that stealeth away any of the spoil and keeps it to himself, is guilty of robbing the publick Treasury.* And this one thing is sufficient to admonish those that expound the Law not to believe that the spoils taken from the enemy are peculiar unto those that take them; but unto the State that bears the charges of the War. For there can be no robbing of the Commonwealth but in those things that are either publick, sacred or religious. The result of all this is to shew, That, setting aside the Civil Law, and primarily, whatsoever is, in the publick acts of a Just War, taken from the enemy, belongs to the Prince or people who are at the charge of making the War.

Lib. 16. c. 4.

XXII. That somewhat may be changed of this common right by any Law or Act of the Will.

We add *setting aside the Civil Law, and primarily or directly.* The former, because the Law, whether made by the people, as among the Romans, or by the King, as among the Hebrews and other places, may dispose of these things that are not actually possest to the benefit of the Commonwealth. And here under the word Law we understand also Custom, if rightly introduced. The latter I add, that we may know that it is in the power of the people to grant the spoils of the enemy to others, as well as they may dispose of other things. And that not only after they are got, but before; so that immediately upon the taking of them, Actions are commenced, *brevi manu*, as the Lawyers speak, that is, compendiously, declining the dilatory Forms of Suits. Which Grant may be made not only nominally, but generally also, as to Widows, to the aged and impotent, and to poor Orphans; as part of the spoil was thus given in the times of the Maccabites: or unto uncertain persons, in imitation of those *Sportulæ* which the Roman Consuls and other Princes cast among the people, whereof every man had liberty to catch what he would. Neither is the translation of this Right, either by Law or Grant, unto others always a mere donative. For sometimes it is due by some former Covenant or Agreement, sometimes in discharge of some Debt, or as a recompence for some loss received, or some extraordinary charge men have been at in the War either by purse or pains. As when a man serves in the War without pay, or for less than his pains deserves. For in these cases it is usual, we see, to grant either all, or some part of the spoil unto others.

2 Mac. 8. 28, 30.

XXIII. Some of the spoil may be due to our Associates.

It is also observed by Civilians, That Custom hath so far prevailed almost every where, that whatsoever either our Associates or Subjects that serve without pay, and at their own cost and peril, shall take in the Wars, is their own. As to our Associates, the reason is manifest, because by the Law of Nature, they that are associated in a War, are bound to repair each others losses, which shall be occasioned by reason of the War which is common and publick. Besides, there are very few that will expose themselves to labour and danger for nothing; for this reason (saith *Seneca*) we usually reward Physicians, though they cure us not, *Quod à rebus suis avocati nobis vacant*; *Because we call them from their own affairs to serve ours.* And the same reason likewise serves for Lawyers, as *Quintilian* notes, Because they tear out their time, and employ their whole study to defend other mens Estates, thereby neglecting all other means to improve their own. The very same is given by *Tacitus*, *Omittit res familiares, ut quis se alienis negotiis intendat*; *That he casts off all care of his own domestick affairs, that he may the better intend the good of others.* It is therefore very credible (unless there shall appear some other cause, as namely, mere kindness, or some former Contract) that it was the bare hope of gain by the spoil of the enemy, which they expected as a compensation for their loss of time and of their labour, that made them to expose themselves to so great dangers.

De benefic. 4. c. 15.

Ann. l. 9.

Vid. Plut. Marcell.

XXIV. And often to Subjects.

But as to Subjects, the reason is not so evident; because Subjects and Citizens owe their help and assistance to the Country or City whereof they are. But yet seeing that all Citizens either cannot or will not expose themselves to those hazards and hardships that attend War; therefore it is but reasonable that retribution be made by the whole Body of the people, unto such as shall sustain the toil or the charges of it, but much more the damage that shall be thereby occasioned; in full recompence whereof, the hopes of the whole prey, or of an uncertain part thereof, is by the people easily (and that not without reason) granted unto them. So thought the Poet,

Propert.

Præda sit hæc illis quorum meruere labores.

Theirs be the prey whose pains deserv'd it have.

As

As to our Associates, an example we have in the League that was made between the Romans and the Latines, wherein it was agreed, That in all the Wars wherein the Romans *Liv. l. 4. c. 24.* should engage them, the spoil taken from the Enemy should be equally divided between them. So in the Wars wherein the Ætolians engaged the Romans, it was agreed, That *Dionys. l. 6.* the Cities and Territories should be the Ætolians, but the Prisoners and all Moveables *Polyb. l. 6.* should be granted to the Romans. To the ancient Latines the Romans gave a third part of the spoil, as *Pliny* testifies. And proportionable to the succours sent, the free Towns of the Switzers received their share of the spoil, as *Simler* relates. In a War against the *Paruta l. 8.* Turks, the Pope, the Emperor and the Venetians, divided the spoil according to their respective charges that they had been at in making the War. And *Pomponius* gratified *Deiotarus* King of *Galatia* with the lesser *Armenia*, because he had been his Companion in the War against *Mithridates*. St *Ambrose*, upon the Story of *Abraham*, demonstrates the equity of *Lib. 1. de Abra.* this custom, *Abraham*, saith he, *perhaps thought it but just, that they that came up to his assistance in that War, should likewise partake with him of the spoils, as being the reward of their labour.* But as to Subjects, an example we have in the Nations of the Jews, where God *Numb. 31. 27.* commands *Moses* to divide the spoil of the Midianites into two parts, that is, between them that undertook the War and went out to Battel, and between all the Congregation. And in ver. 47. he subdivides that part which belonged to the Congregation, and gave the fiftieth part thereof to the Levites, that had the charge of the Tabernacle. Thus *David* divided the spoil taken from the Amalekites equally, between them that went down to Battel, and them that guarded the Stuff. Sometimes the Jews would divide the spoil, and *1 Sam. 30. 24.* grant half to the Souldiers; and as to the other part, they admitted the maimed, the Widows and the Orphans to have share with them. So we read of *Alexander*'s Souldiers, that they al- *2 Mac. 28. 30.* ways challenged the spoil taken from private men unto themselves, only the most precious things they reserved and presented to the King. Wherefore we find them accused for robbing the publick Treasury, who had conspired to assume all the prey taken at *Arbela* to themselves, so as to bring nothing to the Treasury. But yet those publick things that belonged to the enemy, or to the King against whom they fought, were exempted from this Licence. Thus it was with the Macedonians when they brake into *Darius*'s Camp, they carried away an infinite Mass of Treasure, leaving no place unrifled, but the Kings Pavilion only; *it being a custom received amongst them* (as *Curtius* notes) *as well as amongst most Nations, to receive the Conquerour in the Pavilion of the conquered.* The custom of the Hebrews was not much unlike this of the Macedonians; For they always set the Crown of the vanquished King upon the *2 Sam. 12. 30.* head of the Conqueror, assigning all the Furniture of the Kings Palace or Pavilion unto him, as his share of the spoil. And amongst the Acts of *Charles the Great* we find that having conquered the Hungarians, *Whatsoever was taken from private men, he gave to the Souldiers; but what was the vanquisht Kings, was brought into the Emperour's Treasury.* The Grecians distinguished them by their several names, calling the publick λάφυρα, but the private σκῦλα; as also they did those taken in the Battel σκῦλα; but those taken after Battel, being publick, λάφυρα; which distinction was afterwards approved of by other Nations. But it is plain, by what hath been already said, That the Romans during their ancient Commonwealth did not allow to their Souldiers so much; yet they began to be more indulgent to them in their Civil Wars. Thus you may read *Æquilanum* given to the Souldiers for pillage by *Sulla*. And *Cæsar* after the Battle of *Pharsalia*, gave *Pompey*'s Camp to be pillaged by the Souldiers, with this Complement,

> ———— *superest pro sanguine merces,*
> *Quam monstrare meum est, nec enim donare vocabo*
> *Quod sibi quisque dabit.*
>
> For loss of bloud, a recompence I'll make,
> Not what I'll give, but what each man shall take.

And in another Civil War, the Flavians being led against *Cremona*, made all the haste they *App. Civil. 1.* could the Night approaching, to storm the City, lest the pillage thereof should fall unto their Commanders and Legates; having, it seems, been sufficiently instructed by *Tacitus*, *Tacit. Hist. 3.* *Expugnatæ Urbis prædam ad militem, deditæ ad Ducem pertinere; That the Plunder of a Town, if stormed, belonged to the Souldiers; but if surrendred, unto the General.* But afterwards *Ne manente periculo omissis hostibus præda manus impediret, quod plurimas sæpe Victorias corrupit.* as the Discipline grew more remiss, so this Licence of pillage was more willingly granted to the Souldiers upon this ground, lest whilst the Victory was yet doubtful, the greediness of the Souldiers should make them neglect their Enemies, and over-hastily fall upon the prey, which hath often proved fatal to the Conquerour. When the Castle *Volandum* in *Armenia* was taken by *Corbulo*, *Tacitus* tells us, *That the common people were sold, but the rest of the spoil was the Conquerours*, The same *Tacitus* brings in *Suetonius* encouraging his *Sub Corona.* Souldiers to pursue their Enemies, and not at all to mind the pillage, assuring them that the Victory being ascertained, the spoil should be their own. So in *Procopius* we read that *Goth. 2.*

all

all the pillage taken at *Picenum* was brought to *Belisarius*, that he might divide to every man according to his merits; the cause whereof is added, *For*, saith he, *it is most unreasonable, that whilst some with much toil and valour are killing the Drones, others without any labour or peril should devour the honey.* [*Vand. l. 2.*] And in another place he tells us, That the Souldiers were much incensed against *Salomon* when he warred against the *Levatæ*, because he detained from them the prey, who excused himself, in that he did it for no other reason than that at the end of the War he might therewith reward every man according to his deserts. There are some things of so small value, that they are not worth the publication, or exposing to sale, these are usually granted to those that take them: such in the old Roman Commonwealth were a Spear, a Javelin, Fodder, Fuel, a Bottle, a Pair of Bellows, a [*Lib. 16. c. 14.*] Torch, and any thing else of less value than a small Piece of Silver. For all these are expresly excepted in the Military Oath given to the Souldiers, as we may read in *Gellius*. Not much unlike is that which is allowed to Sea-men and Mariners, although they are un- [*Gall. Constitut. lib. 20. tit. 13.*] der pay. The French call this the spoil or pillage, wherein are comprehended Apparel, Bedding, Fuel, Gold also and Silver, under ten Scutes, sometimes the fifth part, some- [*Leges Hisp.*] times the third, sometimes half the prize, belongs to the King, as it doth in *Spain*; and the seventh, and sometimes the tenth to the General of the Army; the rest belongs to them that take it, except Men of War with all their Tackle, which are always the Kings, [*Jo. Magn.* in his Sweed. Hist.] and so are all Engines of War amongst the Swedes. In some places again, regard is also had to the labour, peril and charge that any man hath been at, and allowance is made in [*Consulatus Maris Cap. 285.*] the partition of the spoil accordingly. In *Italy*, a third part of the Ship taken in Fight is the Masters of the Ship that took it, and as much belongs to them whose Goods the conquering Ship is laden withal, and another third is theirs that fought and took her. And sometimes it falls out, that they who at their own charge and peril maintain the fight, do not carry away the prize; but some part thereof is due to the State, or to him, at least, [*Leg. Hisp.*] that derives it from the State. As in *Spain*, they that set out the Ship upon their own charge, yield a part of the spoil taken to the King, and a part to the Admiral of the Seas. In *France* the Admiral claims the tenth part; so also in *Holland*: But there the State first takes the fifth part to themselves. Thus it is at Sea, but at Land in the sacking of Towns, and in Battels, every man usurps that which he takes to himself. And in excursions into the Enemies Country by Parties, whatsoever is so taken is divided among them that take it, according to every mans merit and dignity.

XXV. To what use these serve.

What hitherto hath been said, serves to this end, That if in any Nation, not embroiled with War, any Suit or Controversie arise concerning any thing taken in War, the things shall be adjudged unto him to whom the Laws and Customs of that people from whose parts they were taken, shall determine. But if nothing can be thereby proved, then by the common right of Nations the thing so taken shall be adjudged to the State or people themselves, if at least it were taken in the act of War. For by what we have already said it [*Lib. 5. c. 8.*] is plain, that what *Quintilian* sometimes said in the behalf of the Thebans doth not always prove true. As to what may be brought under *the tryal of the Law*, the right of War avails nothing; neither is it a good Plea to say, It was gained by Arms, unless by Arms we can retain it.

XXVI. Whether things taken without the Territories of either Party, be lawful prize. [See above Ch. 4. Sect. 7. and this Ch. Sect. 5. *Livy lib. 55.*]

But whatsoever is not the enemies, though it be found with the enemy, shall not be adjudged to them that take it. For this, as I have already said, is neither agreeable to the Law of Nature, nor was introduced by the Law of Nations. So the Romans in *Livy* answer *Prusias*, *If the Lands in question were not King* Antiochus's, *neither could it by Conquest belong to the Romans.* But if the Enemy had any right or interest in those things which were annexed to the possession, as if it were taken by him as a Pledge for some Debt, or if it were retained by him for the performance of some Covenants, for service or the like, that was for the advantage of the Enemy. In all or any of these Cases, I see no reason but that whatsoever was the Enemies is transferred unto the Conquerour. This also is sometimes controverted, Whether persons or Goods taken without the Territories of either of those Princes or people that are at War against each other, be theirs that take them. Whereunto it is answered, That if we respect the Law of Nations only, no place can give an Enemy protection: for as we have already said, *Every where an enemy being found, may be killed.* But yet he that hath the supreme power in that place, may at his pleasure prohibit the prosecution of an Enemy within his own Dominions; and in case of disobedience, may require satisfaction as for an injury done against himself. The like may be said concerning Deer taken in another mans Ground, That they are his that takes them; but it is lawful for him whose Ground it is, to prohibit his access unto them.

XXVII. This Right, how proper to a solemn War.

But this external Right of gaining things taken in War, is by the Law of Nations so peculiar to a Solemn War, that in other Wars it can take no place. For in other Wars amongst Foreigners the Right to a thing is not gained by force of the War, but only in compensation of some Debt, which cannot otherwise be recovered. But in Civil Wars, whether they be great or small, there is no change of Dominion, but by the Authority of a Judge.

CHAP.

CHAP. VII.

Of the Right over Captives taken in War.

I. Captives in a solemn War naturally slaves.

THERE is no man by nature servant to another, that is, no man in his primitive state or condition considered, without any fact done by himself, whereby his natural liberty is impeached, as I have elsewhere shewed *; in which sense our Lawyers may be understood, when they say, that to be another mans slave is against nature: But that this kind of slavery might at first be introduced by some fact done; namely, by some voluntary agreement, or for some crime committed, is not repugnant to natural justice, as we have elsewhere also shewed. But by that Law of Nations, whereof we now treat, the word *Servitude* is of a larger extent, both as to persons, and as to its effects; for as to the persons, not only they that surrender themselves to the will of the Conquerour, or that oblige themselves by promise so to do, but all persons whatsoever that are taken in a solemn War, as soon as they shall be brought within our Garrisons, are altogether accounted Captives or Slaves, as *Pomponius* hath well observed. Neither is it to any purpose to plead, that they never bare Arms against us, nor declared themselves Enemies by any Hostile Act, seeing that in this case, *Par est omnium fortuna*; *Every mans condition is alike*: yea, even the condition of those, who by mere fate happen to be found in the Enemies Territories, at such time as the War unexspectedly brake forth. *Polybius* speaking of Captives taken in actual Arms, puts the Question thus, *Quid patiendum est his ut justa supplicia pendant? What must these men suffer that their punishment may be just? If any man say they may be sold with their Wives and Children, he answers,* At hæc belli lege etiam illis ferenda sunt, qui nihil impii commiserunt; *But so,* saith he, *may they be by the Law of Arms, who never did us hurt. Philo* notes the very same where he saith, *That many good men lose their natural liberty, by occasions that are involuntary, and merely accidental. Dion Prusæenses* recounting the several ways whereby a man may get Dominion, *assigns this as the third, When a man hath taken a Prisoner in time of War, that never did any act of hostility, and by that means makes him his slave:* So Children being taken in War may be led away and made slaves. *Servius* upon the first of *Virgils* Æneads speaking of *Hesione* the Daughter of *Laomedon*, whom *Hercules* slew as he was going out of *Troy*, saith, *That she was taken Prisoner by the Law of Arms, and given to* Telemon, Hercules *his companion.* And in another place he tells us, *That the Grecians refused to deliver her back to the Trojans*, saying, *she was a Prisoner of War.*

* *Vide lib. 2. ch. 22. §. 11.*

Book 2. ch. 5. §. 27.

Lib. 2.

Oppianus de piscatu l. 2.

II. Yea and their posterity.

Neither are the persons of Men and Women only, thus taken made slaves, but their posterity for ever; for whosoever is born of a Woman after her Captivity, is a slave born; for, *Partus sequetur ventrem*; *The Child will follow the condition of the Mother. Martianus* accounts all those for slaves by the Law of Nations, who are born of Bond-women. And *Tacitus* speaking of the Wife of *Arminius* a German Prince, who had been taken Prisoner by *Germanicus*, saith, That she had *Utrum servitio subjectum*; meaning, *that whatsoever Children were born of her were bond-slaves.*

III. Whatsoever is done unto such is unpunishable.

The effects and consequences of this Right are infinite so that there is nothing so unlawful but the Lord may do it to his slave, as *Seneca* the Father notes *, there are no Torments but what may with impunity be imposed on them, nothing to be done but what they may be forced to do by all manner of rigour and severity; so that all kinds of cruelty may by the Law of Nations, without controul or appeal be exercised upon Captives, were it not that this licence is somewhat restrained by the Civil Law. *It is universally indulged by all Nations, to the Lord to have power of life and death over his slave,* saith *Cajus* the Lawyer; but he tells us withal, That the Roman Laws did limit otherwise unbridled power within their own Territories. *Quid non justum Domino in servum? What may not the Lord do unto his slaves,* saith *Donatus* upon *Terence*? yea, not only the person, but all that is taken with him are lawful prize, *Ipse servus qui in potestate alterius est, nihil suum potest habere*; *He that is a slave,* saith *Justinian*, *and under the power of another, can have right to nothing that was his before.* So likewise *Philo*, *He that is a*

* *1. Controv. 5.*

Andr. Act 1. Scen. 1.

Libro omnem virum bonum liberum esse.

Captive loseth his right to all other things, no less than the power over himself.

IV. Even the things incorporeal of the slave are transferred to the Lord.

Hence then, their Opinion may be confuted, or at least restrained, who hold that things incorporeal cannot by the Law of Arms be acquired. * *Val. Maximus* records it of *Scipio Nasica, That whereas being Consul he was taken prisoner by the Carthaginians at* Lipara, *and so by the Right of War had lost all; yet fortune afterwards smiling upon him, he recovered all, and was again created Consul.* It is true, that primarily, and by it self, things incorporeal cannot by War be gained, but they may be lost as to the person whose they formerly were. But yet we must here except all things that do proceed from some singular propriety in the person taken, which by no means can be alienated, as the right of a Father to his Son, for such Rights, if they do not remain with the person are altogether extinct.

* *Lib. 6. cap. 9. 2.*

V. The reason why this Instituted.

Now all this unlimited Power is by the Law of Nations granted for no other Cause than that the Conquerour being allured by so many advantages might be willing to forbear that utmost cruelty which they may lawfully use by killing their Captives, either in the heat of fight, or afterwards in cold blood. *The name of servant*, as *Pomponius* tells us, *did at first arise from the custom of Generals who sold their Captives, and thereby preserved them from being slain; (Servi quasi servati:)* That they may be the more willing to forbear, I say, for it is no bargain or agreement, whereby they stand obliged to save them, if we respect the Law of Nations; but a perswasive argument drawn from profit, it being far more beneficial to the Conquerour to sell his Prisoner then to kill him. And therefore he hath the same power to transfer his Right in his Captive to another, as he hath to assign over unto others the Right and property he hath in any of his own Goods or Chattels. This Power is also extended to the Children that are born after Captivity, because if the Conquerour had used his power to the utmost, they had not been born. From whence it follows, That the Child that is born before that Captivity, in case he be not taken Prisoner, remains free. Therefore by the Law of Nations, the Children born of such Captives follow the Mothers condition, because their Chastity is not provided for by any Law, nor is there any strait guard kept upon them; and therefore no presumption how great soever is sufficient to prove who is the Father. And thus is that of *Ulpian* to be understood, *Lex Naturæ hæc est, ut qui nascitur, sine legitimo matrimonio matrem sequatur; The Law of Nature is this, That he that is born without lawfull marriage, should follow the condition of the Mother*: that is, General custom grounded on some Natural Reason hath moulded this into a Law (* abusively sometimes so taken, as we have already elsewhere shewn) they that are born out of wedlock should retain the name and quality of the Mother, and not of the Father, because of the certainty of the one, and the uncertainty of the other. But that this unlimited Power over Captives was not introduced by the general consent of Nations in vain, we may collect from the usual practice of Civil Wars, wherein all Prisoners are commonly put to the sword, because they cannot be sold for slaves, which was well observed by *Plutarch* in the life of *Otho*; and by *Tacitus*, who speaking of the Captives taken at *Cremona*, saith, *Irritam prædam militibus fecerat consensus* Italiæ; *That it was agreed throughout all* Italy, *that no quarter should be given*: whereby no booty came to the Souldiers by the sale of Prisoners. *Moreover*, whether the Prisoners taken should belong to the people, or to them that take them, must, by what hath been said of the spoil, be determined. For the Law of Nations hath in this case equalled the condition of men with goods: So *Cajus* the Lawyer, *Those things that are taken from the Enemy are by the Law of Nations theirs that take them; so that even such as were free men are by this Law reduced into bondage.*

* See second Book, ch. 13. §. 26.

Lib. Hist. secundo & tertio.

VI. Whether such as are taken may fly.

Neither can I concur in Opinion with those Divines who hold, That Captives taken in an unjust War, or such as are born of them, are obliged in conscience not to make their escape, unless it be to their own Garrisons, for herein I believe they err; surely in this lies the difference, if they can fly and make it good to their own Garrisons, whilst the War lasts, by the Right of Postliminy they recover their liberty, and all things consequent to it. Of *M. Sergius Pliny* reports, that being twice taken by *Hanibal*, he both times made his escape out of his chains. But in case they make their escape to others, or unto their own Country after the Peace made, being re-demanded they are to be delivered. But yet from hence it follows not, that the Captives themselves are bound in conscience to return; for there are many Laws which bind only as to the outward judgement, which do not at all restrain the conscience; and such are these of War whereof we now discourse: neither is it much to the purpose to say, that the very nature of Dominion doth of it self induce such an obligation; because there being many kinds of Dominion, possible it is, that such there are as are of force only in humane judgement, and so long only as the coercive Power lasts, which is frequently seen in other kinds of Right. Such in some sort also is that Law that makes void some Testaments, because, forsooth, they want some formalities which the Civil Law requires; whereas the more probable Opinion is, that what is bequeathed by such a Testament, may with a good conscience be retained,

See Chap. 9th of this Book §. 5, 6.

Plin. Nat. Hist. lib. 7. c. 28.

tained, so long (at least) as nothing appears to contradict it. And not much different is his Right, who hath according to the Civil Laws unfaithfully prescribed to anothers Estate; for by the judgment of those Laws, even this mans Title shall be defended, untill it be made void by another sentence of the same Law. And thus is that riddle of *Aristotles* resolved, *Is it not just* (saith he) *that every man should enjoy his own, but whatsoever the Judge hath according to his understanding decreed, is by Law confirmed (though in it self it be false) therefore will the same thing be both just and unjust.* But in this question of ours, there is no cause imaginable why the Nations should respect any other Right than that which is external, and meerly humane. For the Right of laying claim to a Captive, of forcing him, of binding him, and possessing what he hath, or can do, is of it self motive sufficient to perswade the Conquerours, that it is a greater advantage to them to keep them alive than to kill them. But in case this cannot move the Conquerours, surely, no obligation that can be laid upon the conscience can do it, which notwithstanding he may impose, by requiring either his verbal or sacramental engagement, if he think it necessary: Yet *if the Captive can make an escape, and carry with him some Goods, his Conscience cannot be charged with theft, so as he carry away nothing but what was before his own.* In such Laws as arise not out of natural equity, but are purposely made to avoid a greater mischief, we must not rashly admit of such an interpretation, as makes that act to be sinfull, which is otherwise lawfull. *Nihil interest quomodo captivus reversus est, utrum dimissus, an vi, aut fallacia potestatem hostium evaserit*; *It matters not much* (saith *Florentinus*) *which way a Captive gets loose from his enemy, whether he be freely dismist, or make his escape either by force or fallacy.* Because the right of holding a man Captive is so a Right, that in another sense, it is for the most part an injury; for which reason *Paulus* the Lawyer calls it, *a Right as to some certain effects*; but an injury as to the intrinsick nature of the thing it self. From whence this also appears, That a man being taken in an unjust War, and brought within the Power of the Enemy, cannot in his conscience be guilty of theft, though he do, as I said before, carry away with him somewhat that was his own; or though not his own, yet that is due unto him as the reward of his labour: If at least he have reserved any thing besides his sustenance, provided that he himself owe nothing unto either his Lord, or him from whom his Lord claims his Right unto him. Pertinent hereunto are those Testimonies of *Irenæus* and *Tertullian*, concerning the departure of the Israelites out of *Ægypt*, and their carrying away their Goods with them; which fact *Irenæus* seems to defend by the Law of Nature, as being but the recompence of so many years hard labour: for saith he, *The Ægyptians were indebted unto the Hebrews, not only for their Goods, but for their lives.* *Tertullian* also handling the same subject speakes thus, *The Ægyptians demand of the Hebrews their vessels of Gold and Silver*; *the Hebrews on the other side alledge, That the Ægyptians owed them much more as due unto them for their long and hard service.* Thus also *Philo* pleads for his own Countrey men, *That they spoiled not the Ægyptians out of Covetousness, but first as the reward of their long labour, and then as a gentle mulct or punishment, far inferiour to their great oppression.* Neither is it much to the purpose to say, that such an escape and taking away of Goods is usually severely punished, if the Prisoner be apprehended; because such, and far greater acts of injustice are usually done by men of Power against their Inferiours, *Non quia æqua sunt, sed quia ipsis expedit*; *Not because they are just and equitable, but because they are for themselves expedient.* Now whereas some Canons do prohibit any man from perswading any servant to forsake his Masters service: I answer, That in case such prohibition be referred to such Servants, as are deservedly punished with the loss of their Liberty, or have by some voluntary covenant or bargain made themselves servants, then it is just: but in case it be referred to such as are made slaves by the misfortune of an unjust War, or to such as are born of them; it only argues, that Christians ought to perswade Christians to Patience and Sufferance, rather than to such courses, which though lawfull, yet may give offence unto others. In like manner, are those admonitions of the Apostles to Servants to be understood, unless we had rather say, that those admonitions seem only to perswade Servants to strict obedience whilst they do serve; which indeed is but consonant to Natural Equity, for their labour is but equivalent to their sustenance.

Lib. 2. de cavillat. c. 5. *Bemb. lib. 10.* See the second Book, seventh Chap. §. 2. *Lib. 2. Cont. Marcion.* *Vita Mosis.* *Synod. Gangr.* See second Book, 5. chap. towards the end.

VII. Whether they may resist their Lords.

But whereas the same Divines hold, That a Captive ought not to resist his Lord in the execution of that external Power that he hath over him without injustice; therein I agree with them. But yet between those things which before I denied, and this that I here assert, there is this manifest difference, That external Right which a Lord hath over his Slave, which consists not in a bare licence of doing what he pleaseth to him, but in the protection of the Laws for doing it, were altogether vain; if on the other side it were lawfull to resist it. For if it were lawfull for a Servant by force to resist his Lord or Master, it would be lawfull for the same Servant to resist the Magistrate that defends his Master, seeing that it is from the Law of Nations that that Magistrate ought to defend the Lord in that Right, and in the exercise of it. This Right therefore is like unto that which we have elsewhere granted unto the Supreme Magistrate in every City, whom forceably to resist is unlawfull, nay, impious. And therefore St *Augustine* unites these two Powers, saying, *That Subjects should so bear with their Princes, and Servants with their Masters, that in the exercise of their patience they may preserve their temporal estates, and hope after eternal.*

VIII. This not in force in all Nations. But this also we must observe, That even this Law of Nations as to Captives hath not at all times, nor amongst all Nations been received; though the Roman Lawyers are pleased so to understand it, taking perhaps the Customs of those Countries which were then most known to them, for the Universal Custom of all Nations. Among the Hebrews (who did at little mix their Customs with those of other Nations, as they did themselves in Marriages) there were places of refuge for Slaves, namely, for such as became such by fate or misfortune, rather than by any fault of their own; whereupon seems to be grounded that priviledge which among the Francks is given unto Slaves, to proclaim themselves at Liberty, which is also now indulged, not only to such as are taken in the War, but to all other Slaves whatsoever. (Deut. 23. 15.) (*Bod. de rep. l.* 1. *c.* 5.)

IX. Nor now amongst Christians, and what is introduced in its stead. But even among Christians it is universally agreed, That being at War amongst themselves, they that are taken Prisoners are not made Slaves so as to sell them, or to enforce them to servile offices, or to impose upon them such things as they usually do on Slaves: And there is good reason for it, for they either are, or at least should be better instructed in the Principles of Christian Charity, than not to abstain from the shedding the blood of those whom misfortune only hath made miserable, unless it be granted them, that they may be permitted to use a little less cruelty. It is a Custom generally received among Nations of the same Religion, *That what Goods or Chattels soever are taken in War, are lawful prize; And for men taken in War, they neither make them Slaves, nor kill them in cold blood*, as *Gregoras* testifies. *Boerius* also makes mention of this Custom, whereunto he adds, That it is observed in *France*, in *England*, and in *Spain*, That in case a Duke, a Baron, or an Earl be taken in War, they are not their Prisoners that take them, but the Prince's that maintains the War. And this at least (though but a small matter) hath Christian Religion brought to perfection, which *Socrates* attempted to have done among the Grecians but could not. The same Custom which Christians observe among themselves, do the Mahumetans likewise observe among themselves; yet notwithstanding even among Christians this custom still remains entire, That such as are taken in the Wars are kept in safe custody till their ransom be paid, which commonly is set as the Conquerour pleaseth, unless otherwise agreed before hand: which Right of keeping Prisoners is usually granted to those that take them, unless they be persons of honour, who are always kept and maintained at the charge of the Common-wealth, or of the Supreme Magistrate, according to the Custom of Nations. (*Lib.* 4.) (*Plat. de rep. lib.* 5.)

CHAP.

CHAP. VIII.

Of Empire over the Vanquished in War.

I. *That a Civil Empire, whether in a King or a people, may be acquired by War, and what the effects are of such an acquisition.*
II. *Such an Empire may be gained over a people as is merely despotical, and then they cease to be a City.*
III. *Sometimes a mixt Government is acquired.*
IV. *Sometimes even the incorporeal things of the people may be acquired by War, where also is handled the Bond given by the Thessalians to the Thebans, forgiven by* Alexander.

IT is no marvel that he who can bring into subjection every particular person, can also subdue the Body Politick, whether it be a City, or part of a City, and whether that subjection be merely civil, or merely despotical, or mixt. This Argument we shall find used by *Seneca* in that Controversie which is *de Olynthio*, where he brings in one pleading thus, *He is my Slave whom I bought by the right of War; and very expedient it is for you, O ye Athenians, not only to acknowledge my Title to be just, but to defend it; otherwise notwithstanding all your great Conquests, your Empire also must be confined within your ancient Territories.* Wherefore *Tertullian* acknowledgeth, That Empires are gained by Armes, but enlarged by Conquests. So likewise *Quintilian*, Kingdoms, Nations, and the Bounds of Cities and Countries, are determined by the Rights of War. *Alexander* in *Curtius* claims by this Right, saying, That Laws are usually given by the Conquerour, and received by the Conquered. Thus *Minio* in his Oration to the Romans, *Why do ye Romans send every year your Prætor with the Ensigns of your Empire, the Rods and Axes into* Syracuse, *and other the Grecian Cities in* Sicily; *for which ye can give no other reason but this, That having conquered them by your Armes, you impose upon them what Laws you please.* *Ariovistus* in *Cæsar's* Commentaries saith, *That by the Law of Armes, the Conquerour may govern the Conquered in what manner he pleaseth; and that the custom of the Romans was to govern those Cities which they had by their Armes subdued, not after other mens prescriptions, but according to their own will and pleasure.* *Justine* likewise out of *Trogus* tells us, That before *Ninus*, Princes that made War, fought not Empire but Glory; and therefore were contented with the honour of the Victory, but fought not to enlarge their Kingdoms: and that this *Ninus* was the first that ever incroached upon another mans dominions, and from him it became a custom. *Bocchus* in *Salust* pleads, *That he took up Arms only to defend himself; for that part of* Numidia, *from whence he had driven* Jugurtha, *was made his by the Law of Armes.* But a Right may be gained by a Conquerour, either so far only as it was in the King or some other Governour; and then he succeeds in his Right only, and no farther. So *Alexander* after the Battel at *Gaugamela* was saluted King of *Asia*. And the Romans also claimed unto themselves all that was *Syphax's* by the Right of War. But when the Huns pleaded to the Romans, That the Country of the *Gepidæ* was theirs, because they had taken their King Prisoner: the Romans denied it, because the *Gepidæ* were governed by a Prince rather than by a King; for that the Kingdom was not Patrimonial. And therefore they conclude, That he could not lose more than what was his own. Or it may also be gained, as it is in the people; and then the Conquerour hath as much power to alienate it as the people had; and thus do some Kingdoms become Patrimonial, as I have elsewhere said. Thus the Persians in *Menander* plead for the Territories of the City *Daras*, *For*, say they, *since the City* Daras *it self is by the Right of War subdued by us, it is but reasonable that what belonged to that City should likewise be ours.* So *Belisarius* having conquered the Vandals, would have had *Lilybæum* in *Sicily* yielded up to the Romans; because, as they pretended, the Goths had before given it to the Vandals, which the Goths denied.

> I. That the Civil Empire, as well in a King as people, may be gained by War.
> *Liv. l.* 35.
> *De Bello Gallic.*
> *Lib.* 1.
> Book 1. Ch. 3. Sect. 2.
> *Procop. Vand.* 2.

Or an Empire may be yet more absolutely gained. For such a Government may by War be gained, as that which was before a City, may cease to be any more a City, but be rather reduced (as it were) into a Family; which may be done either by adding it unto another City, as Kingdoms were by the Romans annexed to their Empire as Provinces; or by annexing it to no other City, (but by destroying its Charter, and nulling the Government thereof:) As for example, When a King maintaining the War at his own proper charge, doth so enslave the people, that in his Government over them he minds his own private gain and interest only, but neither their profit nor safety; which kind of Government is Despotical, and not Civil. *Aristotle* thus distinguished them, *Of Empire*, saith he, *some are altogether fitted to the profit of the Prince, others for the profit and safety of the Subjects; this is proper to Monarchy, that to Tyranny.* Now the people that are held under this kind of Government, are no longer Citizens, but a multitude of Servants in a great Family. It was well said of *Anaxandrida*,

> II. Such an Empire may be gained over the people as is merely despotical.
> *De Repub. lib.* 7.

—Servorum

——————*Servorum nulla est usquam Civitas.*

A multitude of Slaves can never constitute a City. Which distinction is allowed of by *Tacitus*, (Annal. lib. 12.) *He did not carry himself,* saith he, *in his Government as a Lord over his Slaves, but as being chief among his Fellow Citizens.* So *Xenophon* of *Agesilaus, What Cities soever he reduced under his obedience, he made free by exempting them from the slavery which Captives pay unto their Lord, and by contenting himself with that obedience that a free people do willingly yield unto their natural Prince.*

III. A mixt Government is sometimes got by War.

Whence we may understand the nature of a mixt Monarchy, that is, between that which is Despotical, and that which is Civil; as namely, when our servitude is mixt with some kind of personal liberty. Thus we read, that to some people the use of Armes are forbidden by the Conquerour, and that no Iron shall be wrought into any thing, but such Instruments only as are necessary for ploughing the Earth, and such like. So some people being conquered, are enforced to change their language, others to alter the whole course of their lives, and the like.

IV. That even the incorporeal things of the people, may be by a War gained. See Book 1. Chap. 4, Sect. 8. Book 2. Ch. 5. Sect. 31. Book 3. Ch. 5. Sect. 2. and Ch. 20. Sect. 49. *Vid. Ch. 7. Sect. 8.*

Now as whatsoever any particular Prisoner had when he was taken, was by the Law of Arms his or theirs that took him; so whatsoever belongs to the people in general is his or theirs that subdue them, if they will take it. For what *Livy* saith of such as surrender themselves, namely, *All are given up to the Conquerour; so that what he will take to himself, and wherein and how far forth he will punish the Conquered, is wholly in his own power.* The very same in a Solemn War may be said of those that are conquered. Thus *Polybius, They that yield themselves up to the Romans, do yield up in the first place their Country, and what Towns and Cities soever are therein, together with all their Men and Women that are in them; then all their Rivers and Ports, and generally all things sacred and religious: so that the Romans are Lords of all, and they that thus surrender themselves have nothing left.* And the self same Right hath the Conquerour over those that are actually conquered in a solemn War. For dedition doth but voluntarily yield up that which otherwise would be taken away by force. *Hannibal* encourageth his Souldiers, being ready for Battel, with this Argument, *Whatsoever the Romans have by so many Conquests got and heaped up, shall together with themselves be ours after the Victory.* Thus all that *Mithridates* had by force of Armes added to his own, *Pompey* by subduing him annexed to the Roman Empire; wherefore even those incorporeal Right which formerly belonged to the whole Body of the people, are now by the Law of Armes the Conquerours, so far forth as he pleaseth. Thus *Alba* being subdued, what Rights soever the Albans enjoyed were claimed by the Romans. Whence it follows, That the Thessalians stood fully discharged of the hundred Talents for which they stood bound to the Thebans, when *Alexander the Great* conquering the Thebans, had by the Right of Conquest forgiven the Debt. Neither is that altogether true that *Quintilian* urgeth in the defence of the Thebans, namely, That that only is the Conquerours which he can lay hold on. But that Right which is incorporeal cannot be apprehended by any mans hand; and again, That the condition of an Heir is one thing, and that of a Conquerour is another; because to the Heir may pass the Right, but to the Conquerour the thing: For he that is Master of the persons, is also Master of the Estate, and of all the rights belonging to the persons. He that is himself possest as a Slave, cannot be said to possess any thing to himself; neither can he have any thing in his power to dispose of, who hath no power to dispose of himself: yea, though the Conquerour do grant unto the conquered *Jus Civitatis, The Right of being a City*; yet may he take away and reserve to himself whatsoever he pleaseth out of what was the Cities. It is in his own power to prescribe what bounds he will to his own bounty. Thus *Cæsar*, in imitation of that Fact of *Alexander*'s to the Thessalians, forgave a very great Debt to the Dyrrhachines, which they owed to another City of the adverse part. But here it might have been objected, That that War of *Cæsar*'s was not of the same kind with that concerning which this Law of Nations was instituted. So also we read that *Mark Anthony* commanded the Tyrians to restore unto the Jews what belonged unto them, as not being granted unto them by the Roman Senate, and whereof they were possest before the War made with *Cassius*; as *Josephus* relates it.

CHAP.

CHAP. IX.

Of the Right of thoſe that return out of Captivity.

THERE are none of our modern Lawyers, who have written any thing ſolidly, either concerning things taken from the Enemy, or concerning the Rights due unto them, who having been taken Priſoners, yet have either by favour, force, or fraud, eſcaped and got home again. The Ancient Romans have handled this Queſtion ſomewhat more accurately, but yet oft-times ſo confuſedly, that the Reader cannot diſtinguiſh between what is due by the Roman Civil Law, and what is due by the Law of Nations. Concerning the word *Poſtliminium*, that opinion of *Servius* is to be exploded, who held, that the latter part of the word ſignified nothing. That of *Scævola* pleaſeth better, who makes it a compound word, of *poſt* which ſignifies a return, or coming from beyond, and *Limen*, or *Limes*, which ſignifies properly the threſhold of an Houſe, or the utmoſt bounds or frontiers of a Country: for *Limen* and *Limes*, though they differ no leſs in flection, than in termination, as *Materia* and *Materies*; yet are they both derived from that old Verb *Limo*, which ſignifies tranſverſe or overthwart, as *Servius* upon *Virgil*, and *Donatus* upon *Terence* obſerve; from whence *Limes oculis aliquem intueri*, is, *to look a ſquint upon a man*: Though by the latter uſe of the word, *Limen* be referred to things private, and *Limes* to things publick, as to the bounds or borders of Kingdoms. For, as *Iſidore* notes, all oblique or croſs-ways, the Ancients called *Lima*: from whence, *the threſholds of doors* over which we go in and out, are called *Limina oſtiorum*. So the Ancients when they baniſhed any man, were ſaid *eliminare, to thruſt him beyond their marches*; and baniſhment they called *Eliminium, a thruſting out of their bounds and Territories.* *Poſtliminium what it is.* *Ænead. l. 12.* *Eunuch.*

II. Poſtliminy therefore is a Right that ariſeth unto a man that was a Captive upon his return from Captivity; that is, upon his entring within the Frontiers of his own Country. So *Pomponius*, He is ſaid to be returned out of Captivity that begins to be within our own Garriſons; or as *Paulus* ſaith, that enters within the bounds of our Territories. But by a parity of reaſon, it is by the general conſent of Nations granted, That the Right of Poſtliminy takes place, as ſoon as the perſon that was a Captive, or any other thing that is capable of this Right, ſhall come within the Guards or Garriſons of our friends and Aſſociates, as *Pomponius* ſpeaks; or as *Paulus* expounds it by way of example, as ſoon as he ſhall enter into any Garriſon that belongs unto ſuch a King or State, as are our friends and companions in the ſame War. For ſo indeed are theſe words (Friends and Aſſociates) here to be underſtood, not of any Nation or King with whom we are at peace, but of ſuch only as are ſo Confederate with us that they are parties in the ſame War, into whoſe Garriſons whoſoever enters out of Captivity, ſhall enjoy his former Rights, and be defended upon the publick account. It matters not much whether they that ſo return are men or things, or whether they come into our Garriſons, or the Garriſons of our Aſſociates: But in caſe they that are taken Captives, ſhall fly into the Dominions of our Neighbour King, who though at Peace with us, is not aſſociated with us in the ſame War, they ſhall not change their condition of being Priſoners; unleſs it were before ſo expreſly agreed, as it was between the Romans and the Carthaginians in their ſecond League, That if any of the friends of the Romans, being taken by the Carthaginians,

thaginians, could escape out of any peoples Territories that were friends to the Romans, into any of their Ports or Cities that were Subjects to the Romans, they might enjoy their liberty; the like provision being made for the friends of the Carthaginians. And therefore when some of the Romans, being taken in the second Punick War, were sold by way of Traffick into *Greece*; they were not admitted to enjoy this Right of Postliminy, because the Grecians in that War stood Neuters: and therefore it was necessary that they should be first ransomed before they could be set at liberty; yea, and although *Flaminius*, having conquered King *Philip*, had set all the Cities of *Greece* at liberty, yet would he not take away from their Masters by force those Roman Captives, which had been formerly sold by the Carthaginians unto the Grecians; but the Achaians to gratifie him for their liberty, bought Twelve hundred of them who were dispersed though *Greece*, and presented them to *Flaminius*, who received them as a Present of great value. So did the Rhodians buy the Athenian Captives, taken in the War that King *Philip* made in *Greece*, and frankly restored them to the Athenians. And in *Homer* we read of divers persons taken in War, that were sold into such Countries that were in Peace.

Val. Max. lib. 5. c. 2. 6. Diod. Sic. exc. Leg. n. 3. Plut. Vit. Flaminii. Polyb. except. Leg. n. 3.

III. Some things return, and some are received by the Right of Postliminy.

The Ancient Romans did always account those that were received out of Captivity as freemen. *Gallus Ælius* in his first Book of the significations of Law Terms, saith, *That he who being free of one City did voluntarily depart to another, and afterwards did return back into that City, whereof he was at the first made free, was said to be* Postliminio receptus; *that is, admitted to his old freedom by that Law, which provides for such as return out of Captivity. As also in case a servant being taken from us, and carried Captive into our Enemies Garrison, should afterwards return unto us, he may by this Law of Postliminy place himself under his old Master. So Horses, Mules, and Ships, by a parity of reason, had the same right of reception as servants. And look what kind of things do teturn unto us by this right, the very same may return from us to our Enemies.* But the Ancient Roman Lawyers have more discreetly admitted but of two sorts of Postliminy; as namely, when we either return, or receive something that is returned.

IV. It is of use as well in Peace as War.

Neither may we altogether reject that of *Trophonius*; namely that this Right of returning out of Captivity into Freedom, may be of use as well in Peace as War, though in a little different sense than as *Pomponius* expresseth it. This Right of Postliminy in Peace, appertains unto those who were not conquered in War by force of Arms; but were through misfortune surprised within the Enemies Territories, when the War unexpectedly brake forth. But to other Captives there belongs no such Right in times of Peace, unless it be otherwise agreed on by both parties at the making of the Peace, as it was at the conclusion of the War between *Jonathan* and *Bacchides* recorded by *Josephus*. *Polybius* among other Articles of the Peace concluded and agreed on between King *Philip* and *Antiochus*, recites this, That all Prisoners taken on either side (the Ætolians only excepted) should be set at liberty. Thus we read that *Probus* made Peace with the Vandals and Burgundians, upon this condition, *That all the prey they had taken, together with the Prisoners should be restored.* Nay sometimes it is agreed, That not only those Prisoners that belong to private men, but those that belong to the Commonwealth are to be discharged, as *Thucydides* testifies. Now this is plainly evinced, as well by the subsequent reason, as by its opposite member, *The Peace was concluded, and the Prisoners released, for,* saith *Zonaras*, *so it was agreed.* It was then by vertue of the agreement, and not simply by their making of Peace, that their Captives were dismist. So *Pomponius*, *If the Captive concerning whom it was agreed in the Articles of the Peace, that he might return home, shall notwithstanding chuse to remain with the Enemy, he shall not afterwards claim this right of Postliminy.* So also *Paulus*, *If a Prisoner taken in War when the Peace is made, shall fly away and come home, he shall be made to return back to him, who in the War took him Prisoner; because in the Articles of Peace it was not mentioned, that the Prisoners should be released.* Now the reason why the Romans seemed so to neglect their Prisoners, is *because they would have them to place all their hopes of returning back in their valour, rather than in a Peace.* For thus doth *Livy* testifie of them, That *Rome* was a City, that of old was in *Captivos minime indulgens, very regardless of their Captives.* But this reason being proper only to the Romans, could not of it self constitute the Law of Nations; it might notwithstanding serve as one cause amongst others, for which the Romans did the more willingly embrace that Law which was before introduced by other Nations. But a truer reason may be this, because all Princes and States making War would willingly be believed that there Cause was just; and on the contrary, that they that took Arms against them did the wrong. Now whilst both parties are thus perswaded, it would not be safe for any other Prince or State that would live in peace to judge between them; therefore they conclude it better to sit still, and to esteem whatsoever should be done in that War to be just, and so the Prisoners on either side taken in actual Armes to be lawfully taken. But now against those Prisoners, that have been by misfortune surprized through the suddain eruption of the War, no such thing can be alledged; for they have neither advised nor attempted

Ant. l. 13. c. 2.

Why the Romans neglected their Citizens taken Prisoners.

attempted any hurt to us. Neverthelesſs to weaken the power of the enemy, becauſe poſſible it is that they might be inticed to injure us, it hath been thought not unjuſt to detain them during the War; but the War being ended, there can be nothing alledged why they ſhould not be releaſed: and therefore it is generally conſented unto by all Nations, That ſuch Priſoners, when the Peace is made, ſhould be enlarged, as being confeſt by both parties innocent. But as to other Priſoners, every man that uſurps a Right over them, is willing that he ſhould be believed that he hath juſtly gained them, unleſs by ſome preceding Agreements he be limited. And for this Cauſe neither Captives nor any thing elſe taken in War, is to be reſtored in Peace, unleſs it be ſo expreſt in the Articles of Peace, becauſe the Conquerour would be thought to have a juſt Title to them, which to contradict, were to renew the War: and therefore *Totilas* in *Procopius* charges *Pelagius*, who was ſent unto him from the Romans, that he ſhould not mention the releaſing of the Sicilian Captives; urging that it was not equitable that the Romans ſhould redeliver their Fellow-Souldiers to their old Maſters. Wherefore the Agreement brought by *Quintilian* in the behalf of the Thebans, is rather witty than ſolid, namely, That Priſoners if they can make their eſcape into their own Country, the War being ended, are to be reckoned as Freemen; becauſe what is gotten by force, is no longer ours than we can keep it by force. Concerning thoſe that make their eſcapes after the Peace is concluded, we have hitherto treated: now in the time of War they are ſaid to return by Poſtliminy to their former freedom, who were free before they were taken Captives in the War; but they are ſaid to be received, who before were not free, as Servants and other things.

V. The War laſting, when a Freeman may be ſaid to return.

He that was a Free-man returns ſo by this Right, in caſe he return to this purpoſe, That he may follow the Fortune of that City whereunto he returns, as *Trophoninus* delivers it; becauſe, as the Servant that is to be made free, ought firſt to be *ſui juris*, of and for himſelf, that ſo his act may be voluntary: ſo he that would be admitted as a Citizen after captivity, muſt reſolve to incorporate himſelf with that City, and become one with it, or as a Member of it. Moreover, Whether the Captive be retaken by force of Armes, or whether he have made his eſcape by fraud, it is all one, as *Florentinus* obſerves; and the Caſe is the ſame if he be freely diſmiſs'd by the Enemy. But what if he be ſold by way of Contract to another, and that he thence eſcape into his own Country? This Queſtion is handled by *Seneca* in his Controverſie concerning the Olynthians, whom *Parrhaſius* bought. For when the Decree was paſt by the Athenians, whereby it was ordained, That the Olynthians ſhould be free, he made this doubt, Whether by that Decree it was meant that they might be made free; or that they were adjudged thereby to be free: which latter opinion was the trueſt. Thus *Chi dubius* in *Procopius* pleaded, *That being returned into his own Country, he was by the Law thenceforth a free man.*

VI. What Rights he may receive, and what not.

But a Freeman being returned Home, doth not only recover his own freedom, but all things elſe that were his in any Nation that is at peace, whether they are things corporeal or incorporeal; becauſe, though people that are at peace, as they do not enquire into the juſtneſs of the War, but take every thing that is done to the Captive to be juſt: ſo when they ſee the Captive to be at liberty, they diſpute not the manner how, but take it as granted that he was releaſed juſtly, whereby they ſhew themſelves indifferent to both parties. Wherefore he that by the Law of Arms is poſſeſt of a Captive, hath not an abſolute and indubitable Right unto all things that belong to him. For it is poſſible that his right may ſurceaſe without or againſt his will, that if the Priſoner can make his eſcape, and return into his own Country; for then juſt ſo as he loſeth his right to the Man, doth he loſe his title to thoſe Goods which were his. But what if thoſe Goods be alienated, Whether ſhall he that derived his title to them from him who at that time was by the right of War the Owner of them, be defended by the Law of Nations, or ſhall the ſame thing ſo alienated be recovered? Thoſe Goods, I mean, that are extant among ſuch people as ſtand Neuters in the War. Here then we are to diſtinguiſh between ſuch things as may return by Poſtliminy, and ſuch as are uncapable of this right; the difference whereof we ſhall preſently explain, That the former may appear to be alienated during their Cauſe only, and under this Condition, That the perſon be ſtill held in cuſtody: theſe latter, ſimply and abſolutely. By things alienated, I underſtand even thoſe things that are given or received.

VII. All Rights againſt him are reſtored.

As he that returns home hath a Right unto all things by the Law, that were his before he was taken; ſo are the Laws in force againſt him as fully as if he had never been under the power of the Enemy.

VIII. Why they that yield themſelves are not capable of this Right.

But unto this Rule, as it concerns ſuch as are Freemen, *Paulus* allows of this exception, *Poſtliminio carent, qui Armis victi hoſtibus ſe dederant*; *They that being conquered by Arms had yielded themſelves up to the will of their enemies, have no benefit by their return home.* The reaſon whereof is, Becauſe all agreements with enemies are, by the Law of Nations, to be obſerved, as we ſhall ſhew anon. Neither is this Right of Poſtliminy to be admitted againſt thoſe agreements; and therefore thoſe Romans in *Gellius*, who being taken by the Carthaginians,

Lib. 7. c. 18.

Carthaginians, and ſent back to *Rome* to procure exchanges, did acknowledge, *That the Right of Poſtliminy was not due unto them, becauſe they were bound by Oath to return.* From whence alſo it is rightly obſerved by *Paulus*, That during the time of a truce there is no Right claimed by Poſtliminy; yet *Modeſtinus* is of opinion, That if they that delivered themſelves up to their enemies were bound by no Covenant or Promiſe made, they might be admitted to their freedom by Poſtliminy.

IX. How a people may obtain this Right. That which hath been ſaid of particular perſons, may alſo be ſaid of Cities and people, That if they were free they may recover their freedom. If the power of their Friends and Aſſociates be able by force of Arms to releaſe them from the power of their enemies. But if the very Body of the people that conſtituted that City be diſſolved, I believe that they that ſucceed are not to be accounted the ſame people; neither are thoſe things that formerly belonged to that City to be reſtored unto them by this Right of Poſtliminy, according to the Right of Nations; becauſe a Nation, like a Ship, by the diſſolution of its parts, doth abſolutely periſh: for that its whole Nature conſiſts in the perpetual Conjunction of all its Members. Wherefore it was not the ſame City of *Saguntum*, though the place where it formerly ſtood were reſtored unto the ancient Inhabitants eight years after its diſſolution. Neither was *Thebes* the ſame City after that *Alexander* had ſold the Citizens for Slaves: whence it follows, That what the Theſſalians owed unto the Thebans before ſuch diſſolution, could not juſtly be claimed by thoſe Thebans by Poſtliminy; and that for a double reaſon, Firſt, Becauſe they were then a new people; ſecondly, Becauſe *Alexander* whilſt he was Lord over them, had a power to alienate that Right, and accordingly had done it: and laſtly, A Debt is not to be reckoned among thoſe things which return by Poſtliminy. Not much unlike to what we have ſaid concerning Cities, is that which the ancient Roman Laws concluded of Marriages, namely, That they were by captivity diſſolved, neither could they be reſtored by poſtliminy, but muſt be redintigrated by the firſt conſent of both parties. But it is otherwiſe among Chriſtians, witneſs that of Pope *Leo* unto *Nicetas*, Biſhop of *Aquileia*, concerning ſuch Marriages, namely, *That as in Slaves or Fields, or even in Houſes and Poſſeſſions, the right and title of them is preſerved for thoſe that are Captives, in caſe they ſhall return out of captivity; ſo alſo in Wedlock, if either party be married to another, let them be reformed.* See what *Hincmar* hath written to this purpoſe in his Tract concerning the Divorce of *Lotharius* and *Terberga*, to the thirteenth Interrogatory; and the Anſwer of Pope *Stephen*, in the ſecond Tome and nineteenth Chapter of the Councils of *France*.

X. To thoſe that return, what Rights ariſe from the Civil Law. By what hath been already ſaid, it is no hard matter to underſtand what manner of right by the Law of Nations, Poſtliminy gives to free men. Moreover, this very ſame right may by the Civil Law, ſo far as it belongs to things agitated within the City, be both reſtrained by adding ſome exceptions or conditions, and alſo enlarged unto other profits and advantages, as occaſion ſerves. As by the Roman Civil Law Fugitives are exempted out of the number of thoſe that were capable of this right; ſo were alſo the Sons of a Family, over whom the Father was conceived not to have loſt that Paternal power and authority which was peculiar to the Romans; and that for this reaſon, as *Paulus* obſerves, Becauſe to Roman Parents their Military Diſcipline was ever dearer than their own Children; whereunto agrees that which *Cicero* records of *Manlius*, *That he ſtrictly upheld the Diſcipline of the Roman Empire, though to his own grief, that ſo he might the better provide for the ſafety of the City, wherein was alſo bound up his own; which made him prefer the Sovereign Right of Majeſty, which was then in himſelf, before the bonds of Nature, or the tenderneſs of a Father towards his own Son.* Again, ſome diminution of this Right of Poſtliminy, is that which was ordained, firſt, by the Athenians, and afterwards by the Romans, namely, *Ut qui redemptus eſt ab hoſtibus, Redemptori ſerviat donec pretium reddiderit; That he that was redeemed, ſhould ſerve his Redeemer until he ſhould have repaid his ranſome.* But this was made in favour to the poor Captives, leſt if there ſhould be no proviſion made for the recovery of the money ſo paid, many Priſoners ſhould have been left in perpetual ſlavery among their enemies. But yet even this very ſlavery was many ways mitigated by the Roman Laws, and at length by the laſt Law of *Juſtinian*, it was limited to five years ſervice; neither could the money paid for his redemption be recoverable after the death of the party redeemed. So alſo by any Contract of Marriage between the perſon redeemed, and the perſon redeeming, it was adjudged to be forgiven. So if it were a Woman that was redeemed, if the Redeemer did proſtitute her Body, the ranſome was loſt. There were many other Laws made among the Romans in favour to thoſe that would redeem Priſoners, and to puniſh their Kinſmen for neglecting them. Again, this Right of Poſtliminy was by the Civil Law much enlarged, in that not only thoſe Rights in Poſtliminy which are allowed of by the Law of Nations, are granted unto him that ſo returns; but generally all things and all Rights are as intirely his, as if he had never been within the power of the enemy. And this was alſo the Attick Law: for as we read in *Dion Pruſaenſis*, A certain man pretending to be the Son of *Callias*, who had been taken Priſoner in the Slaughter at *Acanthus*,

Acanthus, and, as he said, been kept as a Prisoner in *Thrace*, when he had made his escape to *Athens*, claimed by Postliminy his inheritance from those that then had the possession thereof after his Father; we do not read that any thing was pleaded against his Right, only it came in issue, Whether he were the Son of *Callias*, or not. The same Authour likewise relates, That the Messenians after long captivity, at length returning, received both their liberty and Country. Yea, and those things which either by usucapion or redemption seemed to be taken away out of the Goods, or through disuse, to be deserted, are all of them recovered by a Rescissory Action. For under the Edict of making restitution to Ancestors, he also who is under the power of Enemies, is comprehended. Nay farther, the Cornelian Law provides for the Heirs of such as dye in captivity, and conserves all their Goods as lawfully as if he that returned not, were at that very time when he was taken, dead. Now were it not for these Civil Laws, without doubt as soon as any man were taken Prisoner by the enemy, his Goods would presently be theirs that had them in possession; because, *Qui apud hostes est, pro nullo habetur*; *He that is under the enemies power is held for none.* And then, if he that was taken should return, he should receive nothing but such things as by the Law of Nations were due unto him by Postliminy. But that the Goods of a Captive were confiscate and brought into the Treasury, in case he had no Heir, was a Law peculiar to the Romans only. Hitherto we have treated of things that return, now we shall speak of such things as are received by Postliminy.

XI. How Servants are received by Postliminy, how Fugitives, and how they that are redeemed.

Amongst which, in the first place, are Bondmen and Bondwomen, yea even such ofttimes as have been alienated, and such as have been set at liberty by the enemy; because (as it is very well noted by *Tryphoninus*) it is not just that his former Master being our Citizen, should be damnified by the Right of an Enemy. By an Edict of King *Theuderick* it was ordained, *That Servants and Tenants being taken by the enemy, and returning home, should be restored to their own Lords, if they were not before bought by some other from the enemy by way of traffick.* But by the wise Gothick Law, a Servant recovered by War was restored to his Master, he paying unto him that took him the third part of his just price. But in case the Servant were sold by the Enemy, then was the Lord to pay the full price for which he was sold with some advantage. Therefore that a Servant may be capable of reception, it is necessary that his old Master should be either actually possest of him, or at least that the Servant be where he may easily have him, if he so pleaseth. And therefore whereas in other things it may suffice, That they are brought within the Bounds of our own Territories, this is not sufficient in a Servant to receive the right of Postliminy, unless it be also made known to his Master that he is there. For as *Paulus* saith, If he lye sculking in *Rome*, and will not be seen nor known to be there, he is not yet received by this Law. And as herein Servants differ from things inanimate, so do they from the case of a Freeman in this, That it is not required in them to make them capable of being received, that they should return with an intent to follow the fortune of the City whereunto they return; for this is required from him only that is to receive his own freedom, and not of him that is to be received by another. For *every man hath a free power to make himself a Member of what City he pleaseth, but not of the Right of Dominion.* Neither do the Roman Laws exempt Fugitive Servants from this right of reception: for even in these may their old Masters claim their Right, as *Paulus* notes, lest if we should admit the contrary, it should prove injurious not to the Servant, who nevertheless is still to remain a Servant, but to the Master who would want his service. But generally, concerning such Captives as are redeemed by the valour of Souldiers, that may be truly said by their Generals, which some would so wrest, as if it were meant of all things, *Receptos eos non captos judicare debemus, & Militem nostrum defensorem eorum decet esse non dominum*; *We are to esteem of these not as taken, but received, whom we ought rather to defend and protect, than insult over.* Those Captives that are ransomed from the enemy, are by the Roman Laws theirs that redeem them; but the Summ paid being tendered, they are understood to be by Postliminy received. But by the more recent Laws some things have been changed; and that Servants being taken may be encouraged to return, they now propose present liberty to such as have been maimed in their service, and to the rest after five years, as appears by their Military Laws, collected by *Rufus*.

Sabinus. Fugitives.

XII. Whether a people, being subjected by another, may be received by Postliminy.

But unto us (that are Dutch-men) this Question is more pertinent, Whether those people that were once subjected to the power of another Prince, may return back to their former state and condition; which will admit of a Dispute, in case not he whose the Empire had been, but some other of their Associates, had recovered them from the enemy, whereunto the same Answer, I conceive, may serve that was before given concerning Servants, unless by some Social League it be otherwise agreed.

XIII. Whether lands may be said to be received.

Among things that are received by this Right of Postliminy, the first that offer themselves are Lands; whereof *Pomponius* speaks thus, *Expulsis Hostibus ex Agris quos ceperint, Dominia eorum ad priores Dominos redeunt*; *The Enemy being driven out, the Lands return to their former Owners.* Now the Enemy is then said to be driven out, when it appears plainly that they are not able to recover it again. Thus the Island *Ægina* which the Lacedemonians took from the Athenians, they restored to their Associates who were the Ancient Lords thereof. And the Goths and Vandals being expelled; *Justinian*, and the Emperours succeeding, restored the Lands unto the Heirs of those who anciently possest it, notwithstanding those prescriptions which in other cases the Roman Laws did admit of against them. The very same was confirmed by a Law made by *Honorius*, who though *Spain* had been in the possession of the Vandals for Three hundred Years, yet would not permit that any prescription should be pleaded in Barr against the Ancient occupants, as *Procopius* testifies; which Law we find also recited in the Council of *Sivil*, where this is added as the reason, *Non enim erit objicienda præscriptio temporis, ubi necessitas interest hostilitatis*; *For no prescription of time is to be pleaded which is enforced by open hostility.* Now look what Right they have to the Lands, the same also they have to every thing that is affixt to the soil; for even those places, which had been formerly held as Sacred or Religious, being taken by Enemies if they do escape that calamity; they also as if returned by a kind of Postliminy, shall be restored to their former condition, as *Pomponius* notes. Wherewith agrees that of *Cicero* concerning *Diana* in *Segesta*, P. Africani *virtute Religonem simul cum loco recuperavit*; *By the valour of* Scipio Africanus, Diana *recovered both her Temple and worship*: wherefore the fruits and profits of the ground thus received, are likewise to be restored, according to what *Pomponius* writes concerning Lands first drowned, and afterwards recovered. So in *Spain* it is provided by a Law, that as well the honour and dignity, as all the hereditary jurisdictions thereunto belonging, may return by Postliminy; the greater at any time, the lesser if claim be laid unto them within four Years after their reception, unless it be some strong fort, which if lost and recovered again is the Kings.

Compare this with what was said above *ch.* 6. §. 7.

Vand. l. 1.

Concil. Hispal.

XIV. What difference was anciently made between things moveable.

Concerning moveables the general rule is quite contrary; for they do not return by Postliminy, but are utterly lost, as being lawful prize, and may therefore be bought and sold; wheresoever they are found, they are adjudged his that bought them: neither hath the first owner any Right at all to them, though he find them either abroad among Neuters, or at home in his own Country. But from this general rule we find, that in Ancient times, such things as were of use in War, were excepted; which seems to be agreed unto by the Nations for this reason, that the hopes of recovering such things to themselves, might render them the more cheerful and industrious in regaining them. For the Laws of most Cities in those times were made for the encouragement of valour, and in favour to military affairs, wherefore their consent was easily gained. What things were accounted useful in War we have already summed up out of *Gallus Ælius*, but we find them more accurately set down, as well by *Cicero* in his Topicks, as by *Modestinus*: As, namely, Ships that are long and fit for burden, but not such as are made for pleasure; Mules, but such as are accustomed to the Pack-Saddle; Horses and Mares, but such as will abide the Bit, and are fit for service: Armes also and Apparel are of necessary use in War, but these do not return by Postliminy; because they were thought to merit no favour at all, who would suffer their Weapons and Garments to be taken from them: nay, it was accounted as a crime that deserved punishment, as may every where appear in Histories. And herein we may observe the difference they made between Horses and Armes; the one being capable of reception, the other not; because possible it was that an Horse may break loose of himself, and so fall within the Enemies power, without any default of his Rider, but so could not Arms. And this difference between moveables seems to have continued in use from the Goths until *Boëtius* lived, who expounding *Cicero*'s Topicks, seems to speak of this Right, as if it were in force at that Day.

XV. What at this Day.

But in these latter times, if not before, this difference is taken away; for now no moveables do return by Postliminy, as hath been observed by those who are most expert in the Customs of Nations; and the same Custome is for Ships, as we may perceive in many places.

XVI. What things are received that need no Postliminy.

But those things, which though taken by the Enemy, yet were never within their Garrisons, have no need of Postliminy; because by the Law of Nations, the owner never lost his property in them: The like may be said of such things as are taken by Thieves and Pyrates; Because (as *Ulpian* and *Javelinus* answer) the Law of Nations never granted unto them a power to alter the property of what they got: upon which ground it was, that the Athenians were willing to accept of the Island *Halonesus*, which some Pyrates had taken from them, as King *Philip* did from those Pirates, as of a thing restored by *Philip*; but not as of a thing given them, as will appear by the very Epistle of King *Philip* recorded by *Demosthenes*. And therefore things so taken, wheresoever they are found may be claimed, only (what out of equity we have already concluded to be just) so much ought to be allowed him, who at his own charge hath possest himself of them, as may be conceived, it would have cost the first owners themselves to have recovered them.

Now

XVII. Some alterations may be made by the Civil Law, as to their own Subjects.

Now though it be thus by the Law of Nations, yet may the Civil Law otherwise determine it; as in *Spain*, the Ships that are taken from Pyrates are theirs that take them; so also they are among the Venetians. Neither is it unreasonable that a private thing should give way to publick profit, especially where the recovery of them must necessarily be accompanied with so much difficulty. But yet this Law can be no Plea against Strangers, who may notwithstanding challenge their own things.

XVIII. How Postliminy is observed among such as are not Enemies, but Strangers.

But that which is more to be admired, is that which the Roman Laws do testifie, namely, That this Right of Postliminy took place, not only between enemies, but even between the Romans and Strangers. But surely this, as I said elsewhere *, was but a Relique of that barbarous Age, wherein the general corruption of mens manners had taken away all sense of that natural Society that should be between all Mankind: and therefore among Nations that had no publick War one against another, there was practised among private men a certain licence of War, which their different language and manners seemed to denounce; which licence, that it might not swell so high as to kill each other, it pleased the Nations to limit, and to agree, That they that were taken on either side, being Strangers, should be held as Slaves; and consequently they introduced the Law of Postliminy, which puts a difference between Strangers and Robbers or Pyrates; because Strangers do usually agree upon equal Conditions, which Pyrates and Robbers disdain. It seems that of old it hath been a Case much controverted, Whether if the Subjects of a Confederate Nation, being Slaves here, should escape from us and get home, They may be said to return by Postliminy. This Question we find proposed by *Cicero*, concerning which *Gallus Ælius* delivers his opinion thus, *We*, saith he, *observe the same Right of Postliminy with a free people, with Confederates and with Kings, as we do with Enemies.* But *Proculus*'s opinion was quite contrary, *I doubt not*, saith he, *but that both our Confederates, and they that are a free Nation, are all Strangers unto us; between them and us there is no Postliminy.* We are therefore to distinguish of Leagues; for if any Leagues be made on purpose only to put an end, or to prevent open War, those Leagues do not for the time to come hinder either the taking of Prisoners, or the Right of Postliminy. But if in the Articles of the League it be exprest, That the Subjects of either Nation may upon the publick Faith safely travel or sojourn in the others Dominions, then it is not lawful to take Prisoners on either side, and so there is no place for Postliminy. And this I take to be the meaning of *Pomponius*, where he saith, If there be a Nation with whom we have neither friendship nor hospitality, nor League made for friendships sake; these indeed are not enemies: But yet whatsoever of ours comes to them is theirs; and a man that is free with us, being taken by them, is made their Slave: and it is the same if any thing come from them to us, and therefore in this case Postliminy is granted. In mentioning a League made upon the account of friendship, he shews that there may be Leagues that have no Right either of friendship or hospitality. And *Proculus* sufficiently declares, That by a people confederated, he understood such a people as had promised friendship and safe hospitality, where he subjoined these words, For what need is there of Postliminy between us and them, when they may equally retain as well their own liberty as property in their own things with us, as they do among themselves; and we may enjoy the same liberty and dominion with them as with our selves. Wherefore that which follows in *Gallus Ælius*, namely, With those Nations that are under our jurisdiction, there is no Postliminy is to be understood with this supplement: nor with those with whom we have contracted any League of friendship.

* See second Book, ch. 15. §. 5.

Lib. 1. de Orat.

XIX. How the same may now take place.

But in our days, not only amongst Christians, but even amongst Mahometans, this Right of Captivity without the time of War, as also that of postliminy, are worn out of use. The necessity of both being taken away by virtue of that cognation or affinity wherein Nature hath linked us, which is now re-acknowledged to be between all Mankind. Yet may that ancient Right of Nations be now in force, in case we have to do with any Nation so barbarous as to conceive it lawful for them to invade in an hostile manner the persons and properties of all Strangers without any provocation or denouncing of War. And even whilst I am writing this, thus it is adjudged in the High Court of *Paris*, *Nicholaus Verdunius* being President, That the Goods which have been the Subjects of *France*, but were afterwards taken by the Pyrates of *Argier*, who live upon the spoil of all that traffick by Sea, were by the Right of War justly alienated; and therefore being recovered by others, were theirs that recovered them. And in the same Court this also was adjudged, which I said even now, That Ships are not to be at this day reckoned among the number of those things that are received by Postliminy.

CHAP. X.

Admonitions concerning things done in an unjuſt War.

I. Modeſty forbids what the Law permits.

I AM now to look back, and to take away from thoſe that make War almoſt all thoſe Rights which I may be thought to have granted them, though indeed I have not. For when I began to explain this part of the Law of Nations, I alſo declared, That many things were ſaid to be right and lawful, becauſe they were not puniſhable by Law, partly becauſe they derive their authority from Military Councils, which notwithſtanding either ſwell beyond the Bounds of honeſty, whether we confine it to Right ſtrictly taken, or place it in the Precepts of other Vertues; or elſe they are ſuch as may more religiouſly, and amongſt good men, more commendably be left undone. *Seneca* brings in *Pyrrhus* pleading thus,

Lex nulla capto parcit, aut pœnam impedit.

No Law ſpares Slaves, nor them from ſtripes defends.

To whom *Agamemnon* replies,

Quod non vetat Lex, hoc vetat fieri pudor.

What Law forbids not, Modeſty commends.

For the word *Pudor* in this place reſpects not ſo much a mans fame and reputation, as what is in it ſelf right and honeſt; or at leaſt what is better and more laudable than that which the Law permits. Thus we read in *Juſtinian*'s Inſtitutions, Things are ſaid to be committed to a mans truſt, when they have no tye of the Law to ſecure them, but *the honeſty and integrity* of the perſon entruſted: So in *Quintilian* the Father, The Creditor cannot with any *honeſty or conſcience* require his Debt of the Surety, unleſs it be when he cannot get it from the Principal; and in this ſenſe we find that *Pudor* and *Juſtitia*, Equity and Juſtice, are very often conjoined.

Salvo pudore.

Nondum Juſtitiam facinus mortale fugârat.
Ultima de Superis illa reliquit humum.
Próque metu populum ſine vi pudor ipſe regebat.

Juſtice as yet did amongſt Mortals dwell,
She was the laſt that bid the Earth farewel.
'Twas ſhame, not force, that then the people aw'd.

Plato calls Juſtice the Companion of modeſty; and in another place he tells us, That God fearing the deſtruction of mankind, had ſent Equity and Juſtice amongſt men, as Ornaments to Cities, and as Bonds to contract love and friendſhip between them. *Plutarch* alſo in the life of *Theſeus* terms Juſtice an Inmate or Cohabitant with Righteouſneſs. And in another place he joins them together as Companions. But *Cicero* aſſigns them their diſtinct Bounds, ſaying, *It is the Duty of Juſtice not to hurt our Neighbour, but of Modeſty not to offend him*; *Juſtitiæ eſt non violare homines, Verecundiæ non offendere.* With that Verſe above quoted of *Seneca* agrees that of the ſame *Seneca* in his Philoſophy, *Quam anguſta eſt innocentia ad Legem bonum eſſe*; *How ſcant is that innocency that is meaſured by the Law only? Juſtice and faithfulneſs require ſuch things of us as no Law can oblige us unto.* Where we may obſerve that he puts a difference between *Jus* and *Juſtitia*, attributing to the former that which the Law enjoins, but unto the latter that which right reaſon and conſcience dictates. *Of how much larger extent are the Bounds of our Duty one to another, than what is contained within the Hedg of the Law; How many things do piety, humanity, liberality, juſtice and fidelity require of*

De Offic. lib. 1. *De ira l.* 1. *c.* 27.

of us, which fall not under the Commands of the publick Laws: Which the same *Seneca* doth in
another place excellently illustrate, by the Right of a Lord over his Slave, *As to our Bondser-* Orat. 15.
vants, saith he, *we should consider, not what we may impose upon them with impunity to our selves, but* Lib. 1. de Clem.
what we ought in right reason and equity to do unto them, which commands us to shew mercy even c. 18.
to our Slaves, and to those whom we have bought with our money. And again, *Cum in servum om-*
nia liceant, est aliquid quod in hominem licere commune Jus animantium vetat; *Whereas all things*
are by the Law tolerated that are done to a Slave, there are notwithstanding some things that the
common Right of living Creatures forbids us to do unto him, as he is a man. Where also we may
observe the twofold acception of the word *licet*, the one being referred to the judgment
of the Law, the other to the dictates of right reason. *There are many things*, saith *Seneca*, De Benef. l. 5.
that are not enjoined us by any Law, neither will the omission of them bear an Action, notwithstand- c. 21.
ing we are led unto by the mere custom of our lives, which is far more forcible than any humane
Law. *Quintilian* tells us, *That there are some things, which though granted by the Law, yet* Instit. l. 3.
in their own nature are not very commendable; *as by the Law of the twelve Tables, it was lawful*
for the Creditors to divide the Body of the Debtors (if insolvent) *between themselves, which Law*
common custom did abhor. So likewise *Cicero* in the third of his Offices, *Aliter Leges, aliter* De Offic. l. 3.
Philosophi tollunt Astutias; *Leges, quatenus manu tenere possunt*; *Philosophi, quatenus ratione &*
intelligentia: *The Laws take away fraud one way, Philosophy another*; *the former by pinnacling*
the hands, the latter by clearing the understanding, and informing the judgment.

II. This appliedto what the Laws permit.

To the same purpose is that of *Marcellus* in his Oration to the Roman Senate, *That*
which comes here to be discust, saith he, *is not what I have done against the Syracusians*; *for what*
ever I have done against them as enemies, the Law of Armes will justifie me in; *but what those*
men, being overcome, ought in reason and equity to suffer. *Aristotle* discussing this Question,
Whether Captivity arising from War be just, seems to owne this distinction, *Some* (saith Pol. l. 1. c. 6.
he) *looking only at that which the Law permits* (for the Law it self also is something that is Vid. sup. c. 4.
just) *do hold, That Captivity in War is just*; *but yet they deny it to be so absolutely, because pos-* § 2.
sible it is that the cause of that War may be unjust. *Others there are*, saith *Seneca*, *that create*
unto themselves a Right by Arms in anothers Territories: where these two words [*a Right, and*
in anothers Territories] do seem no less to clash than the Arms whereby that Right was got.
But that is there called Right which the Law of Nations permits only. Consonant where-
unto is that of *Thucydides* in that Oration which the Thebans made to the Roman Senate,
As for those, saith he, *that were slain during the Conflict, we complain not*; *for this was in*
some sort just. Nay, the very Roman Lawyers themselves do often call *That the Right of Ca-*
ptivity, which in another place they term *an injury*, and place it in oposition to natural equi-
ty. And *Seneca*, respecting that which often falls out (namely, when the War is unjust)
accounts the very name of Slave as a badge of injustice. The Italians in *Livy*, detaining from Ep. 32.
the Syracusians that which they had gained by War, are said to be obstinate in the detention
of that which they had gained unjustly. And *Dion Prusaensis*, having declared such Captives
free as could make their escape home, addes this, *As being unjustly brought under bondage.*
So *Lactantius* observes, *That the Philosophers in all their Discourses concerning Military Affairs,*
always fitted their Orations rather to the publick customs of the Age they lived in, than to justice
and true valour. And St *Augustine* in an Epistle of his to *Marcellinus*, tells him, *That if* Ep. 4.
in this World the Precepts of Christianity were duly kept, no War could be made without some mercy. De diversis Ec-
And in another place, *Among the true Worshippers of God, even their very Wars are peace-* clesiæ Observ.
able.

III. What is done in an unjust War, an unjust, as to internal Justice.

We conclude therefore in the first place, That the ground of the War being unjust, al-
though it be solemnly undertaken as to the manner, yet are all those acts that are done in
it unjust, if we understand injustice, not as it is repugnant to the Law of Arms; but ac-
cording to its natural acception, as it is repugnant to right reason, equity and conscience.
So they that shall knowingly either commit such acts, or assist in the doing of them, are
included in the number of those, *who without repentance cannot enter into the Kingdom of Hea-* 1 Cor. 6. 10.
ven: for repentance, if true, necessarily requires from such as have time and estates suffici-
ent, That he that hath done wrong, either by killing men, spoiling Goods, driving away
Cattel, or the like, should make satisfaction. And therefore did God himself renounce Es. 58. 6.
the solemn Feasts of the hypocritical Jews, *because they did not suffer their Captives unjustly ta-* Numb. 5. 6.
ken to go free. And the King of *Niniveh* proclaimed a Fast throughout the City, and com- Jonah 2. 10.
manded all his Subjects to turn every one from his evil way, and to empty their hands from
all things got by rapine and violence; as being by the very dictates of natural reason taught
to acknowledge, That without restitution all their humiliations were but vain and ficti-
ous. *Non differtur ultionis sententia, si non redduntur universa*; *Vengeance will not be long de-* Hier.
layed, unless restitution be made to the full, saith *Hierome*: with whom agrees S[t] *Augustine*,
If that wherein we have sinned be not restored, being in our power, we do not repent, but dissem-
ble. Neither is this the judgment of Jews and Christians only, but of the Mahometans al- Turcicor. 5. c.
so, as *Leunclavius* informs us. 17.

Now

V.
Who and how far forth they are obliged to reſtitution.

Now they that are obliged to make reſtitution, according to what we have elſewhere delivered in general, are in the firſt place the Authours of the War, whether as having the ſupreme power, or as counſelling and perſwading thereunto; and theſe are bound to make ſatisfaction as well for all damages that are uſually done in War; as alſo for all thoſe unuſually done, if they were done by their either order or perſwaſion, or by their permiſſion, in caſe it were in their power to have hindred it. Thus alſo are Captains bound to make reſtitution for thoſe things that are either ſpoiled, or taken away by any under their Command; yea, and the whole Army in general, that ſhall run headlong to any one common outrage, as to fire a Town, or the like; and for particular acts, every particular Souldier ſhall ſatisfie for that loſs whereof he was the Authour, either ſolitary, or concurrent with others.

V.
Whether things taken in an unjuſt War are to be reſtored by him that took them.

Neither may we herein admit of that exception which by ſome is brought of ſuch as are only Auxiliaries, if they be any ways guilty of the crime; *To oblige any man to reſtitution without guilt, the bare crime ſufficeth.* Some alſo are of opinion that though the War be never ſo unjuſt, yet the things taken in it are not to be reſtored; becauſe, both Parties, when the War began, were preſumed to agree to this, That their Goods ſhould be theirs that could take them. But on the contrary, it cannot eaſily be granted that any man will raſhly give away his Right; and the nature of War is much different from that of Contracts. But to the end that Nations being once at peace, ſhould reſt ſo, and not involve themſelves in endleſs War againſt their will; it was thought ſufficient to introduce this external Right of Dominion, whereof we have already ſpoken, which notwithſtanding may very well conſiſt with that internal obligation to reſtitution. Nay, theſe very Authours ſeem to aſſert as much in their Diſcourſes concerning the Right of taking Priſoners; wherefore the Samnites in *Livy* declare, *That the ſpoil which they had taken from their Enemies, and which by the Law of Armes ſeemed to be theirs, they had reſtored*: Which, he ſaith, ſeemed to be theirs, becauſe the very Samnites themſelves had before acknowledged that War to have been unjuſt. Not much unlike is that power which the Law of Nations gives in a Contract made without fraud, wherein there is ſome inequality to compel the Contractor to fulfil his Contract; yet neverthelſs he that receives more in value than what he gives, is bound, though not by Law yet, in honeſty and conſcience, to even the ballance by reducing the Contract to an equality.

See Book 2. Chap. 11.

Lib. 9.
Lib. 8.

See Book 2. Chap. 9.

VI.
Or whether by him that detains it.

Yea farther, as though the damage be not done by our ſelves, or if it be yet without any fault of ours; yet if the thing taken away in an unjuſt War by another, be in our poſſeſſion, we are bound to reſtore it; becauſe there can be no reaſon given naturally juſt, why the right Owner ſhould be deprived of it: for he never conſented to its alienation, nor was their any crime committed by him, nor did he receive any recompence for it; appoſite whereunto is that of *Valerius Maximus*, *The people of* Rome, ſaith he, *when* Claudius *had publickly ſold ſome Camerine Priſoners taken in the War, although they ſaw their Treaſuries thereby filled, and their Empire enlarged; yet being convinced, That their General had not dealt very faithfully in their Conqueſt, they with great diligence ſought out thoſe Captives, and redeeming them, reſtored them unto their Lands.* So alſo is that which *Joſephus* records of *Mark Anthony*, who commanded the Tyrians to reſtore to the Jews thoſe Parts of *Judæa* which they withheld from them, to releaſe their Priſoners, and to return the ſpoil to the right Owners. Thus we may read of the Phocians, That by the Decree of the Roman Senate, even their publick liberty together with their Lands formerly taken from them, were reſtored. So likewiſe were the Lygurians ſold by *M. Pompilius*, but redeemed by the Romans, and, together with their Goods, ſet at liberty. The ſelf ſame Decree paſt for the Abderites, the reaſon being added, Becauſe the War made againſt them was unjuſt. Thus *Macrinus* releaſed all the Parthian Priſoners, and reſtored all the ſpoil, Becauſe the Romans had unjuſtly broken the peace. And *Mahomet* the Turk diſmiſt upon this account, all the Captives taken at *Sancta Maria* in *Achaia*. Yet may the preſent Poſſeſſor of ſuch Goods or Perſons deduct ſo much for his either charge or labour, as in probability it would have coſt the right Owner to have recovered them: but if he who without any default was thus poſſeſt of any thing ſo taken, hath either conſumed or alienated it; he is not bound to make any farther ſatisfaction, than he ſhall be thought to have been made the richer thereby.

Lib. 6. c. 5. Sub Haſta.

Ant. l. 14. c. 22.

CHAP.

CHAP. XI.

Moderation to be used in killing of men in a Just War.

NEITHER is that generally true that is commonly said, I. In a just War some acts are not internally just.

He hazards all, who what is just denies.

That of *Cicero* is much better, *There are some good offices to be performed, even to those who have injured us; there is also some moderation to be used even in revenge and punishments.* And even in the sharpest War, there ought to be some grains of mildness and clemency, if it be regulated according to Christian Discipline. Nay the very Philosopher hath already pronounc'd them cruel, *who though they have cause, yet know no measure in punishing.* *Cicero* commends that golden age of the Roman Empire, the end of whose Wars were mild and gentle, and never otherwise but upon necessity. *Aristotle* notes, *That the punishment taken on the Thebans and Heracleans, favoured more of cruelty than equity.* And *Thucydides* speaks of some, *that suffered punishments greater than what were fit.* So *Tacitus* taxeth *Pompey*, *for exacting punishments far greater than the crimes deserved.* And in the same Book he blames *Aug. Cæsar*, that in punishing Adulteries he was more cruel than any of his Ancestors; yea, oft-times than his own Laws. Although as *Juvenal* speaks in this Case:

Offic. l. 1. *Vide lib. 2. ch. 20. §. 2.—28.* *Sen. de Clem. lib. 2. c. 4.* *De Off. l. 2.* *Pol. 5, 6.* *Lib. 3.* *Annal. l. 3.*

——————————Exegit autem
Interdum ille dolor plus quam lex ulla dolori
Concessit.——————

This Grief sometimes far greater licence pleads,
Than any Law to other grief concedes.

So *Quintilian*, *A punishment beyond what is humane, is not to be exacted from any, unless it be from the very worst of Parricides.* And therefore *M. Antoninus* the Emperour did well when he wrote to the Senate, *To be careful that their proscriptions were not too severe, nor their punishments too cruel.* Whereof *Ammianus* likewise complains, *Their rage against many was much greater, than either their errours or crimes deserved.* *It is possible*, saith *Aristides*, *that they who take revenge for an injury done to themselves, may be unjust, if they shall exceed in measure; for he that in this case, proceeds beyond his just bounds, is the Author of a new quarrel.* And he that punisheth a Malefactor beyond what he hath deserved, deserves himself to be punished. This was *Ovids* opinion of a King: *Lib. 26.*

——————————Cæde nocentum
Si nimis ulciscens extitit ipse nocens.

He that for Blood too great revenge doth take,
Doth (sure) himself the greatest Murtherer make.

The Platæans in *Isocrates* demand, *Whether it be fit or reasonable, to require for so small faults, so great and grievous punishments.* And in his second Oration for Peace, the same *Aristides* gives this wholesom advice, *Look not so much at the crimes, as at the persons to be punished; and at your own frailty and propensity to fall, that are about to punish: and lastly, at the measure how far you may with equity punish. Minos* in *Propertius* is highly commended in that,

Ovid Trist. lib. I. Eleg. I.

Victor erat quamdiu æquus in hoste fuit.

Though Victor he even to his foes was just.

So he in *Ovid*, who,

In giving Laws to's Captives was most just.

II. According to internal justice who may be killed.

But when we may justly kill our Enemies in a just War, according to that which we call internal justice, and when we may not, may easily be understood by what we have already said in the first Chapter of this Book. One man may be said to kill another, either accidentally or purposely; no man may justly be killed purposely, unless it be for some crime that deserves Death, or because we cannot otherwise defend our own lives or fortunes: And although to take away the life of a man, for things of small value, do not swerve from the rules of justice strictly taken; yet it doth from the rules of Charity. Now that the punishment may be just, it is necessary that he that is killed should offend, and that in so high a measure, as that by the sentence of an upright Judge, he may be condemned to Death; whereof we shall now speak the less, because we have already sufficiently done it in the Chapter of *Punishments.*

III. No man may justly be killed for being unfortunate.

Heretofore when we treated of Suppliants (for such there are as well in War as Peace) we distinguisht between misfortune and injustice. *Gylippus* the Lacedemonian, discoursing about the Right of Suppliants, states the Case thus; they who at the first introduced that Right, did certainly intend mercy and compassion to those whom fortune had made miserable; but as to such as were fallen into misery, through their own deceitful dealings, or out of a desire to usurp another mans Right, these have no reason to blame fortune, nor ought to assume unto themselves the name of Suppliants. Whence we may observe, That whereas there are two sorts of men, that usually cry for protection, they that are unfortunate, and they that are malefactors: *Gylippus* places the Athenians amongst these latter, because unprovoked by any injury, they made War upon the Syracusians; whereupon he infers, that since they voluntarily began the War, it was but just that they should feel the evil consequences that attended the War. Examples of such as are unfortunately miserable, are those who being no Enemies, are notwithstanding unhapily found, and thereby blocked up amongst Enemies, although they bear no malice against us: Such were the Athenians, when *Aristion* their Tyrant forced them to side with *Mithridates* against the Romans; of whom *Paterculus* writes thus, *If any man shall impute that to the Athenians as an act of Rebellion, when being close besieged by* Sulla, *they were enforced by* Aristion *their Governour, to defend themselves and their City against him in favour to* Mithridates, *he will find himself mistaken, as well in the truth, as in the Ancient Histories; for the Athenians were so fast friends to the Romans, that at all times, and upon all occasions, whatsoever was faithfully performed, the Romans would usually say was done* (fide Attica) *with as much fidelity, as if done by the Athenians. Nevertheless being miserably opprest by the forces of* Mithridates *within, who held their City in despiet of them, and straitly besieged by the Romans, their friends without, whilst their hearts were without their walls, they were compelled to keep their bodies within.* The latter part of which sentence seems to have been borrowed from *Livy*, who speaking of *Indibilis*, saith, That with his Body he served the Carthaginians, but with his mind the Romans. For as *Cicero* rightly observes, *They who hold their lives at the mercy of others, do more consider their power what they may do, than their justice what they ought to do.* So the same *Cicero* elsewhere, *The third time was,* saith he, *when after the coming of* Varus *into* Africk, *he remained therewith, if it were a crime*: Necessitatis non voluntatis fuit; *It was rather inevitable than voluntary.* And this very course took *Julian* in the case of the Aquileians, as *Ammianus* testifies; who when he had described the punishment of some few, adds, *The residue he dismist without any hurt done them*: Quos in certaminum rabiem necessitas egerat, non voluntas; *Who,* saith he, *fought more through compulsion, than by choice or election.* Thus did this merciful Prince upon very equitable considerations. Thus also did

Lib. 2. Lib. 26. Pro Quintio. Pro Ligario. Lib. 21.

did *Cleon* in *Thucydides* freely forgive them who being enforced by the enemy, did serve against him. So *Pertinax* speaking of *Lætus* and others, whom *Commodus* compelled to serve under him; *They*, saith he, *obey* Commodus *with an unwilling mind; but whensoever they have a power and opportunity to serve us, they never wanted a will to do it.* Necessity is a strong and violent thing, not to be resisted; wherefore *Cassius Clemens* in *Xiphilinus*, treating concerning the affairs of the Emperour *Severus*, pleads thus, *For my part*, saith he, *I never knew thee, nor yet* Niger; *but being unfortunately left in that part which he had obtained, I did what necessity urged me unto, and obeyed the present Power; not that I was willing to make War against thee, but that I was desirous to repel* Julian *for mine own safety.* Thus also *Aurelianus*, when he made his entry into *Antioch*, set out a very gracious Proclamation, referring all that was done rather to an impulsive necessity, being over-awed by *Zenobia*, than to any enmity they bare unto him. And *Belisarius* in *Procopius* thus excuseth the Africans, *That what they did was against their wills, being then under the power of the Vandals.* So likewise *Totilas* told the Neapolitans, *That he knew them to be under the Command of their Enemies unwillingly.* An ancient Commentator upon that part of *Thucydides*, where he discourseth concerning the selling of the Corcyræan Captives, thus glosseth, *He shewed therein a Princely clemency, every way agreeable to the honour of the Grecians; for to kill men in cold bloud is barbarous, especially Servants, who fight not upon their own choice, but at the command of their Masters.* The Platæans in *Isocrates* do thus plead for themselves, *We did not serve the Lacedemonians voluntarily, but by compulsion; for we durst not do otherwise.* The same Plea doth he make for the other Grecians, *Illorum partes Corpore sequi cogebantur, animo vero nobiscum erant; They were compelled with their Bodies to serve the Lacedemonians, but their hearts were with us.* So likewise of the Phocians *Herodotus*, *That they followed the Medes, but by compulsion, not willingly.* Upon which account *Alexander* forgave the *Zeldi*, as *Arrianus* testifies, *Because they were enforced to take part against him with the Barbarians.* And *Diodorus* brings in *Nicolaus* the Syracusian thus pleading for the Captives, *They that are Confederates with our Enemies, are by force driven to make War upon us; therefore as it is but just that they that studiously and industriously make War against us, be severely punished; so to pardon those who unwillingly offend us, is alike conscientious.* So *Antigonus* alledged, That he made War indeed against *Cleomenes*, but not against the Spartans, as *Justine* reports it.

Lib. 3. — *Vand. l. 1.* — *Goth. l. 1.* — *Lib. 1.* — *Lib. 38.*

IV. Nor for an intermediate fault between fraud and misfortune.

This also is to be observed, That between a plain and manifest injury, and an injury done by a mere mischance, there intercedes sometimes something of a middle nature, as if participating somewhat of either; so as the action is neither merely or altogether voluntary, nor yet done merely through ignorance or against our will. *Aristotle* calls these acts ἁμαρτήματα, slips or failings, as the Latines do trespasses or offences. *Of actions*, saith he, *that are spontaneous, some are done deliberately, others rashly, and without consideration. Now whereas in humane Society injuries may be done three several ways; those done merely through ignorance are called mischances, as when a mischief lights upon a man against whom no hurt was ever intended, (as for example, if a Son by forcing open a Door should accidentally wound his own Father, whom he could not suspect to be behind;) or if a greater hurt or damage befal a man than what was intended, (as if a Fencer, for the tryal of skill, and only intending to draw bloud, should kill his Adversary,) it might be called a mischance, but not a mischief. For whatsoever happens besides what a man proposeth to himself, is to be attributed to misfortune: for haply* vellicare voluit non vulnerare, *He intended to beat him, not to wound him; or if he did intend to wound, yet haply not this man, but another; or it may be not in that manner, or in so great a measure, as it fell out: if therefore any such hurt or damage do arise, besides what was intended, or might probably be expected, it shall be esteemed as a mischance, not a mischief. But secondly, If the wrong done might have been foreseen and prevented, though it were not done* improbo animo, *with a wicked intention, it shall be accounted as a fault* (ἁμάρτημα, as *Aristotle* terms it) *for* culpæ affinis est qui in se habet agendi principium; qui vero extra, infœlix: *He must needs be accessary to the sin or fault committed, that acts by a principle within him; but he that is passive and over-ruled by something without him, is unhappy. But when a man doth what he doth knowingly, though not deliberately, it is confest that an injury is done; as he that in a Forest shoots at a Deer, but kills a man whom he saw not, is unfortunate: but he that discharges a Musquet in a populous Street, though with no mischievous intention, yet if he kill a man, he sins; because he did it freely and voluntarily (though not considerately:) As also they that through anger, or any other perturbation of the mind, either natural or necessary, shall hurt a man, cannot be faultless; and yet we cannot account them wicked or malicious. But yet if a man should knowingly and premeditatedly do the same thing, he may justly be accounted wicked. Wherefore whatsoever is done, through anger suddenly, may very well be said to be unadvisedly done; for it is not he that doth the wrong through anger that begins the fray, but he that first provokes that anger: Hence it is that before judgment in such Cases can be given, the Query is not so much after the fact as after*

Mor. l. 5. c. 10.

Non incipit is qui ex ira quid facit, sed is qui iram provocavit. *Arist.*

after the occasion, namely, Who gave it, and how great the provocation was. For anger usually ariseth from hence, when a man thinks himself to be injured; and therefore in such differences as do arise about wrongs done through anger, the Question is not as in ordinary Contracts, An hoc factum sit, *Whether done or not; for therein, unless excused by forgetfulness, one of the Parties must of necessity be unjust; as namely, He that fulfils not the Contract. But the Question should be, Whether the wrong done were justly done, considering the provocation. For he that first gave the occasion, did it knowingly; it is no marvel then if the one Party may think himself to be injured; and the other not, it may notwithstanding so happen, That he that through anger doth the wrong may be unjust; if, namely, the revenge swell higher than the provocation; or the wrong we do, bear not a just proportion with what we before suffered. For* justus est qui deliberatò justè agit, *He is a just man who knowingly and deliberately doth justly; for possible it is that a man may do justly knowingly, but not deliberately. Moreover, of such wrongs as are spontaneous, some deserve pardons, others not. Those injuries are pardonable which are done not only by such as know not but that they may lawfully do them. But these also that are done through ignorance, that is, when their ignorance is the cause of the offence. But if injuries be committed by ignorant persons, but not through their ignorance, but with such an affection of mind as exceeds the common bounds of humanity, such Offenders deserve no pardon.* Thus far *Aristotle*, whose very words, because the matter is of great use, I have therefore, saith *Grotius*, intirely turned into Latine, because usually being but ill translated, they are not easily understood, *Quod sponte non fit, omne dignum venia; Whatsoever is unwillingly done,* saith *Dionysius Halicarnassensis*, *is pardonable.* So likewise *Procopius*, *They who have wronged others, if through ignorance, that is, when their ignorance is the cause of the wrong, ought in equity to be forgiven by those whom*
Nic. 7. 2. *they have wronged. Michael Ephesius* interpreting that place of *Aristotle*, where he speaks of an injury that may be done beyond the expectation of him that did it, places that which I have before-recited as an instance in a Son, who forcing open a Door wounds his own Father. And of that which might have been foreseen, he puts that of a man that without any malice shoots an Arrow at random in an High-Way; and of that done by necessity, he instanceth in him who being opprest with hunger or famine is constrained to be injurious to others to preserve himself; an example of faults committed out of natural perturbations, he puts in love, grief, fear. That is said to be done through ignorance when the fact is unknown, as when *Abimilech* would have taken *Sarah*, not knowing that She was *Abraham*'s Wife. An injury is said to be done by a person ignorant, but not through ignorance, where the Law is unknown. And this very ignorance of the Law is sometimes excusable, and sometimes inexcusable. All which do very well agree with what our Civilians tell us. Not unlike unto this is another place of the same *Ari-*
De Arte Oratoria. *stotle, It is equity,* saith he, *that distinguisheth as well between manifest injuries and trespasses, as also between these trespasses and mischances. Whatever hurt is done without an ill intention, and that could not be foreseen and prevented, is merely a mischance; that which might have been foreseen, yet is done without any prepensed malice, is a fault or oversight: But what is done purposely, and with a wicked intent, is a manifest mischief, or an open injury, which deserves no pardon.* The Ancients digested all wrongs done into these three Forms, as proceeding from either ignorance, improvidence, or wilfulness. And *Homer* in the last of his Iliads, speaking of *Achilles*, saith,

Οὔτε γὰρ ἔστ' ἄφρων, οὔτ' ἄσκοπος, οὔτ' ἀλιτήμων,

i. e. That he was neither ignorant, inconsiderate, nor mischievous. The like distinction also we find in *Marcian, Delinquitur, aut proposito, aut casu, aut impetu; We commonly offend either purposely, or casually, or rashly: Purposely, as Thieves, whose Trade it is to rob and kill men for what they have; casually, as when a man in hunting shoots at a Deer, and kills a man; rashly, when men, being drunk with wine or anger, do usually fall out from words to*
De Offic. l. 1. *blows.* The first and last of these *Cicero* thus distinguisheth, *In all acts of injustice,* saith he, *it is very considerable whether they be done by a too hasty eruption of passion, which usually lasts not long, and then ends in repentance; or by judgment and premeditation. For what proceeds from the former are like Mushrooms, hasty in their birth, and sudden in their fall; and are therefore much more pardonable than those that grow up leisurely by premeditation. A wise man will ea-*
De ira l. 1. c. 16. *sily remit injuries,* saith *Seneca*, *if he understand that they proceed not from a deep rooted hatred, but from some sudden puff of passion.* And a little after, *Sometimes he sooner remits greater injuries, than he doth lesser; that is, if the former be committed through rashness, and not cruelty; and the latter proceed from a long lingring and inveterate malice. Neither will he punish the same sin in two several persons in one and the same manner, if what the one did unadvisedly, the other did wilfully.* Thus also *Philo* in his Exposition of some certain Laws, *Dimidiatum est facinus ubi non antecessit longa animi deliberatio; That injury abates one half of its punishment that is unpremeditated:* of which kind are those that we are provoked unto by pure necessity, which

which if it do not altogether justifie, yet it extenuates the fault. Thus the Samians in *Thucydides* told *Alcidas* the Lacedemonian, when he would have put the Captives taken at *Chios* to death, That *it was not probable that he came to set* Greece *at liberty, as he pretended, who killed men no ways obnoxious unto him; but only as they were associated with the Athenians, whereunto also they were compelled by necessity.* See Book 2. Chap. 20. Sect. 29. and Sect. 3. in this Chapter. So also S[t] *Chrysostome, Strangers can forgive Strangers, and one Enemy another, if the wrongs done by them, though never so great, were involuntary, and done by mere compulsive.* Lib. 5. de Prov. For as *Demosthenes* pleads against *Aristocrates, So strong and impulsion an Orator is necessity, that it robs us of our freedom in judging what is and what is not to be done in any thing that lies before us; wherefore such Cases are not to be too nicely sifted in a Court of Equity.* Concerning which Point, the same *Demosthenes* doth much enlarge himself in his Oration concerning false witnessing, against *Stephanus.* To the like purpose is that of *Thucydides* also, *It is very probable,* saith he, *that God himself is ready to forgive whatsoever is involuntarily committed, either in War, or in such other like cases of necessity. For the Altars of the Gods have ever been as so many Sanctuaries for such to fly unto as have offended against their will; for they only are to be persecuted as Malefactors, who are willingly and professedly so; but not they whom extreme necessity hath enforced to transgress.* Lib. 4. Thus it is by the Hebrew Laws, as we may collect from that place, wherein it is provided, That he that had ravished a Damosel in the Field was to be put to death, but in the Damosel there was found nothing worthy death; because there was a force upon her. Deut. 22. 26. The Cærites in *Livy* humbly besought the Romans, *That they would not call that an act of counsel, which was an act of pure necessity.* Lib. 7. And *Justine,* speaking of that execrable act of Sacriledge committed by the Phocians, saith, *That the scandal thereof did more properly belong to the Thebans, by whom they were reduced to that extreme necessity, than to the Phocians.* It was the opinion of *Isocrates, That he that was enforced to steal or else to starve, had an excellent Advocate to plead his Paodon,* meaning necessity. Of the same opinion was *Aristides* in the like Case, *Difficilia tempora excusationem aliquam dant desciscentibus, The difficulty of the times is some excuse for those that fly away; as the dangers of a close Siege, a Famine, or Plague, are the best Pleas for Fugitives.* Leuct. 2. *Philostratus* excuseth the Messenians for not entertaining those that were banished *Athens* upon this ground, *That they durst not do it for fear of* Alexander, *whom they and all* Greece *at that time stood in awe of.* The like doth he in *Aristotle, who being compelled through necessity to do some unjust act, confesseth himself that he was ἡμιπονηρὸς, half wicked; but neither altogether unjust, nor at all malicious.* Thus *Cleon* in *Thucydides* aggravates the crime of the Mityleneans, *The injuries they have done us were not casual nor compulsory, but voluntary, nay malicious; but those injuries only are pardonable that are done unwillingly.* *Philo* therefore instructs his Prince thus, *That whensoever he was provoked to revenge or to punish, he should learn how to distinguish between such as were notoriously and professedly wicked, and those who were only overtaken with a sin, or overborn by some violent temptations; for to kill all that have in the least degree offended, is brutish and savage.* *Themistius* in his Panegyrick upon the Emperour *Valens*, thus applieth these distinctions to our purpose, *Thou,* saith he, *hast wisely distinguished, O Emperour, between acts of prepensed malice, acts of humane frailty, and acts of inevitable misfortune. And although thou hast not at all conversed with* Plato, *nor read* Aristotle; *yet hath thy practice been much according to their Precepts, whereby thou hast justified their Sayings. Thou hast not inflicted the same punishment upon all sorts of Offenders, upon those who were the first Authours of the War, and upon those who in process of time were enravelled in it, and upon those who have since yielded themselves, as unto the Conquerour; but* illos damnâsti, hos castigâsti, & postremos miseratus es; *The first thou hast condemned, the next thou hast chastised, and on these last thou hast had compassion.* And the same Authour in another place thus instructs a young Emperour, *Observe,* saith he, *what a vast difference there is between an act done through misfortune, an act done through imprudence, and an act done out of obstinate malice: Now accordingly it becomes a Prince to pardon the first, correct the second, but to persecute these last, even unto death.* Thus did the Emperour *Titus,* as *Josephus* records it, *punish the Leaders of the people severely and exemplarily, but for the multitude he only rebuked them with sharp and menacing words.* Those injuries that are done by misfortune only, and that could not be avoided, neither deserve to be punished, nor are liable to restitution. Those that are wilful and malicious do both deserve punishment, and are liable to restitution. But those of a middle nature that are done through rashness or imprudence, do engage us to restitution; yet are not always punishable: but if they be, yet not unto death. What *Themistius* said of the Emperour *Valens, Xiphilinus* testifies of that most excellent Emperour *Trajan, That though he were not capable of much bookish Learning, yet what concerned himself, and matters of Government, he both knew and practised.* The like Testimony *Herodian* gives of *Marcus Aurelius, That he was the only Prince whose wisdom consisted not in Discourse or in speculative knowledge; but in a grave, constant and sober habit both of life and manners.* The like Character doth *Xiphilinus* give of the Emperour *Macrinus, Leges non tam norat exactè, quàm fideliter exequabatur; He was not so skilful in the Laws, as he was exact and faithful in the execution of them. God grant such Princes unto us in our days.*

Every

V.
The Authours of the War to be distinguished from them that follow them.

Every History will furnish us with Examples of the different punishments inflicted on the principal Authors of a War, and those who have been seduced into it. *Herodotus* tells us, That the Grecians did severely punish the chief Authors of the Revolt of the Thebans, to the Medes. So doth *Livy*, That the chief Citizens of *Ardea* were beheaded. And when *Agrigentum* was taken, he tells us, *That* Valerius Levinus *took the principal Leaders of the people, whom having first whipped with Rods, he afterwards beheaded; but the rest, together with the spoil of the City, he sold.* (*Lib. 4.*) And in another place he tells us, *That* Atella *and* Calasia *being taken by surrender, the Leaders of the people were put to death.* And elsewhere he thus bespeaks the Roman Senate, (*Lib. 26.*) *Seeing that the principal Authors of this Rebellion are deservedly punished by the Immortal Gods, and by you, O Fathers Conscript, what doth it please you shall be done with the innocent people? Whereupon it was at length decreed, That they should not only be pardoned, but that their City should be restored unto them, that so,* as he there speaks, *Unde orta culpa esset, ibi pœna consisteret; Where the crime began, the punishment should cease.* *Euripides* highly commends *Eteocles* the Argive, for that,

> *Culpam ferebat semper illo Judice*
> *Reus ipse; non Urbs Patria, quæ passim mali*
> *Rectoris ergo sustinet calumniam.*
>
> Whilst he was Judge, the guilty person still
> Bare his own punishment; nor was't his will
> That Princes crimes their Subjects bloud should spill.

Lib. 3. And the Athenians, as *Thucydides* tells us, repented of that Decree which they had past against the Mitylenians, *whereby the whole City, rather than the principal Authors only of their destruction, should be put to the sword.* And when *Demetrius* took *Thebes*, he put ten of the Leaders of the people to the sword, and spared the rest; as *Diodorus* testifies.

VI.
And in them the Causes, whether probable or improbable.

But even in the Authors of the War distinguish we must of the Causes; for some causes there may be, which though not just, yet are such as may easily delude men not otherwise wicked. The Author to *Herennius* sets done this as a most equitable Plea for Pardon, when to those injuries we have done, we have been provoked, not by any hatred to the adverse part, nor by our own cruelty, but by the Bonds of love and faithfulness to others. (*Lib. 2. de clem. c. 7.*) *Seneca's Wise-man will sometimes dismiss his enemies with safety, yea and sometimes commend them too for their fidelity, when he is convinced that their engagement in that War was upon just and honest grounds; as to express their loyalty towards their Prince, to assert their own liberties, or to keep faith with their Friends and Confederates, whereunto they stood obliged.* (*Lib. 7.*) The Cærites in *Livy* beg pardon of the Romans, for assisting their Kinsmen the Phocians and others, who according to the League which, with the good leave of the Romans, they had entred into, had helped *Antiochus*. (*Leuct. 2.*) *Aristides*, concerning the Thebans, who had under the Conduct of the Lacedemonians made War upon the Athenians, saith, *That they were engaged in an unjust action, but not without a plausible excuse, being thereunto induced by their fidelity to the Prince of their League.* (*De Offic.*) *Cicero* also concludes them to be pardonable, who neither begin the War through hatred, nor prosecute it with cruelty: Besides, that War which is undertaken merely for Glory and Empire, is not to be prosecuted with too much severity: which King *Ptolomy* seems to insinuate to *Demetrius*, when he tells him, (*Lib. 3.*) *That he did not make War for Plunder and Spoil, but for Glory and Empire only.* So *Severus* in *Herodian* confesseth, *That when he first entred into a War with* Niger, *he had no very plausible pretence to quarrel with him; but the Empire lying at stake, and the Title as then dubious, each of them endeavoured to gain it to himself.* What *Cicero* observed in the War between *Pompey* and *Cæsar*, (*Ep. ad Brut. 2.*) doth very often fall out, *That the thing in question was very obscure, the Contest among Commanders very great: insomuch that many of us know not which Cause is best.* But in his Oration for *Marcellus* he thus pleads, *We may* perhaps *be guilty of some failings, being as men subject to errour; but we are certainly clear from all wickedness.* Thus also doth the same *Cicero* excuse *Deiotarus* to *Cæsar*, for *that he followed* Pompey, *not out of any hatred to* Cæsar; *but being misled by vulgar errour.* So likewise *Salust* in his History, *The residue of the multitude, led more by popular reports than by their own judgment, do one follow another, every one thinking his Leader wiser than himself.* What *Brutus* sometime said of Civil War, may also be said of all other Wars, namely, *That they should be more discreetly managed, than to suffer the common Souldiers to satiate their anger with the bloud of the Conquered.*

VII.
Even Enemies deserving death, may be sometimes pardoned.

Yea though in strictness of justice they have deserved death; yet oft-times it is more agreeable to the Goodness, Modesty, and Magnanimity of a Conquerour to forgive than to revenge. Of this mind was King *Theuderick* in *Cassiodore*, *Those Wars have always succeeded well to me,* saith he, *which have ended moderately; for he can never want the victory, that knows how to use it with temperance and clemency.* (*Lib. 2. c. 41.*) *Salust* ascribes the prosperity of the Romans and the greatness of their Empire, to nothing more than to their promptness

promptness to forgive. And it was the advice of *Tacitus*, *Quanta pervicacia in hostem, tanta benificentia adversus supplices*; *To shew as much love and kindness to poor Suppliants, as courage and resolution towards Enemies.* Yea and *Seneca* tells us, *That the most generous of Beasts did disdain to tear and prey upon things vile and abject*; *Elephants and Lyons scorn things that are prostrate, and pass by what they have overcome.* The Author to *Herennius* hath an excellent saying to this purpose, *Our Ancestors*, saith he, *did very wisely observe this custome, never to put any King to death whom they had taken in War*; *but why? because*, saith he, *it would seem unreasonable to use that power which fortune hath now given us, to destroy them whom the same fortune not long before had so eminently favoured: And why should I now punish them? because they have led their Armies against me? This having now got the victory, I am willing to forget*, Quia viri fortis est, qui de victoria contendant eos fortes putare; qui victi sunt, eos homines judicare, ut possit Bellum fortitudo minuere, Pacem humanitatis augere: *Because it is the part of a valiant Commander, to esteem men as Enemies whilst they are able to contend for victory; but being overcome, then to pity them as men; that so valour may end the War, and humanity confirm the Peace. But you will haply say, what if he had overcome you, would he have done so? wherefore then should you spare him? I answer*, Quia talem stultitiam contemnere, non imitari consuevi; *Because it is my custome to contemn, and not to imitate such folly.* Now if this Author did mean this of the Romans (which is very uncertain, because he intermixes many strange, and indeed Romantick stories, with some true ones) it manifestly contradicts that which we read in the Panegyrick of *Constantine* the Son of *Constantius*, *He acts the part of a prudent man, who having conquered Rebels can bind them to himself by a free pardon; but he, of a valiant man, who having vext them, can trample upon them. Thou hast revived, O Emperour, that ancient confidence of the Roman Empire, who triumphed in the death of those great Commanders whom they had taken in the War; for in those days their Captive Kings, after they had graced their triumphs, by attending the Conquerours Chariot from the Ports to the most publick place of the City, as soon as he turned his Chariot towards the Capitol, were hurried away to Execution. Only* Perseus *upon the intercession of* Paulus Æmilius, *to whom he had yielded himself, escaped the severity of this custome; but the rest having their eyes put out, remained for ever after in Chains: teaching thereby other Kings rather to preserve their faith and friendship with the people of Rome, than to exasperate their justice.* But these things are written somewhat too loosely. *Josephus* in his History concerning the death of *Simon Bar-joræ*, testifies the same severity of the Romans; but he speaks it of such Captains and Commanders only as was *Pontius Samnis*, but not of such as carried the titles of Kings, whose words sound thus, *The conclusion of the triumph was after that the triumphant Chariot was come to the Capitol; for there by the Ancient custome the Conquerour was to stay till tidings were brought of the death of that great Commander, whom he led in triumph; who having an halter cast about him, was presently drawn into the Market-place, his Keepers whipping him forward: for in that place by the custome of the Romans, such as were condemned for Capital crimes, were put to death, and there executed. So soon then as it was declared unto the Emperour, that his Enemy was dead, they immediately proceeded to perform all other the Rites that were in those cases provided very joyfully.* The very same ceremonies doth *Cicero* also recite in his Oration concerning Punishments. Concerning great Commanders thus Executed, Histories afford us examples enough, and some few of Kings also, as of *Aristonicus*, *Jugurth*, *Artabasdus*; I should be loth to revive this obsolete custome, yet we read that *Joshua* put to death those Kings that he took Captives. And *Dion* relates of *Sossius*, *That he whipt* Antigonus *with rods after he had fastned him to his Cross.* But withal the same Historian wisely adds, *Which no King ever suffered by any of the Roman Conquerours.* The same History we may also read in *Josephus*. *Eutropius* likewise records it of *Maximianus Herculius*, that having slain the Francks and Almains, and taken their Kings Captives, *He exposed them to be devoured by wild Beasts.* So doth *Ammianus* concerning a King of the Almains, who being taken Captive was crucified. Yet even among the Romans there were divers Kings besides *Perseus*, that escaped the severity of that custome, as *Syphax*, *Gentius*, *Juba*, and in the time of the *Cæsars*, *Caractius*, and others: Whence it may appear that the Romans (though as *Cicero* and others blame them for being too severe in this case) had always some respect both to the causes of the War, and also to the manner of its prosecution, when they thus punish'd them: And therefore it was no ill advice that *M. Æmilius Paulus* gave to the Roman Senate in the case of *Perseus*, *Si nihil humani metuerent, at divinam vindictam timerent iis imminentem qui victoriâ insolentius utuntur*; *Though they stood not in awe of any humane power, yet they should do well to fear the anger of the Gods, who never failed to avenge themselves on those who abused their favours, with too much pride and insolency.* *Plutarch* in the life of *Agis* observes, that in the Grecian Wars such reverence was born unto the office and dignity of a King, that their very Enemies durst not offer violence to the Lacedemonian Kings. An Enemy therefore that considereth not what humane Laws permit to be done, but what in equity he ought

Annal. l. 12.

Lib. 4.

Orat. in Ver.

Jos. Ant. l. 5. c. 1.

Dion.

Ant. l. 15.

ought to do, or what Religion and Piety requires to be done, forbears the shedding of the blood even of his Enemies; neither will he sentence any man to death, unless it be to preserve life or livelyhood to himself, or for such personal crimes as by the Laws of God or Man deserve death; yea, and though some of them do deserve it, yet in consideration of humane frailty, and of the instability of fortune or some such probable reasons, he either altogether omits, or at least contents himself with such a punishment as is not capital. It is an excellent observation that *Diodorus* makes, *That whosoever succeeds prosperously in War, whether it were the expugnation of Cities or victory in Battel,* Sæpe fortunæ magis quam virtuti debentur; *are for the most part rather the gift of fortune, than the necessary effect of true valour.* But to shew mercy unto such as they have conquered, is the work of Providence only. Thus *Alexander* in *Curtius, Though he was highly incensed against the Authors of the War, yet he thought it prudent to forgive them all.*

VIII. The innocent not to suffer for the nocent. *Lib.* 5.

Concerning such as may occasionally or accidentally, but not intentionally be killed, mine opinion is (as I have already said) that if not for justice sake, yet for pity, we ought not to attempt any such design, wherein the safety of so many innocents may be concerned, unless it be for some very great cause, or for the necessary preservation of a multitude. Of the same mind was *Polybius, It is a good mans duty not to prosecute a mortal War, though against such as are not just, any longer than till they have given satisfaction for the wrong done, and reformed what is amiss, but not to involve the innocent with the nocent in the same punishment, but rather to spare the nocents for the innocents sake.*

IX. Children and Women to be spared. * *De Ira l.* 3. *c.* 24. Deut. 20. 14. Num. 31. 40. Jon. 4. 2. *De Ira l.* 2 *c.* 9.

These things being granted, it will be no hard matter to determine those things that are more special; for (as *Seneca* in those Books, wherein he seems to be angry with himself, observes,*) *Puerum ætas excusat, Fœminam sexus; Children by their non-age, and Women by their sex are to be excused.* God himself in the Wars of the Hebrews, even after the Peace was offered and refused, took special care for the preservation of Women and Infants; some few Nations only being by a particular Law excepted, against whom the War that was made, was not in the behalf of man but of God; and therefore it was called *the War of the Lord.* And when he commanded the Midianitish Women to be slain for crimes properly their own, he excepts those who were pure Virgins; yea, and when he threatned imminent destruction to the Ninivites for their crying sins, he suffered himself to be moved, to retract that sentence by the compassion he took *on so many thousands of Infants, who knew not good from evil.* Very like whereunto is that of *Seneca, Num quis irascitur pueris, quorum ætas nondum novit rerum discrimina; Will any man be angry with an Infant, whose age is not yet capable of understanding the difference of things.* So also is that of *Lucan,*

Crimine quo parvi cædem potuere mereri.

For what crimes may poor Infants slaughtered be.

If God then, who without any cause at all, may without violation of his justice, destroy any of what Sex or Age soever, as being Lord and giver of life; do thus, not only spare Women and Children himself, but command us also so to do: How doth it befit men, to whom God hath given no such Right over the lives of others, but what is necessary for the conservation of humane safety and society, to destroy in our rage so many innocent persons, who can neither resist nor deserve our anger. Let us therefore in the first place observe, what the judgment of those people and of those times was concerning Infants, wherein Religion and Piety were in greatest esteem. *We,* saith *Camillus* in *Livy, come not armed against Women and Children, for though we destroy their City, yet we spare them; but our Arms we use against such only as are armed.* And *Plutarch* handling the same Subject, tells us, *That good men observe some Laws even in War*: Where we must note that he saith, among good men, that so we may distinguish between this moderation, and that licence which is supported only by custome and impunity. And *Livy* speaking elsewhere of Children saith, *A qua ætate etiam hostes irati abstinerent; Whom in respect of their age an Enemy though enraged would spare.* And in another place, describing the more than humane cruelty committed in War, he saith, *Usque ad infantem cædem ira crudelis pervenit; Their cruelty was such that they spared neither infants nor sucklings.* *Pliny* in his natural History discoursing of the Lyon, saith, *That when he roameth about he preys upon Men rather than Women, but never upon Infants unless extremely opprest with hunger.* *Horace* passionately complains of the brutish cruelty of *Achilles,* who was so mercilesss, that he spared not Infants, no not in the Womb.

Plut. vita Camilli. *Lib.* 24. *Lib.* 8. *c.* 16.

Nescios fari pueros Achivûm
Ureret flammis etiam latentes
Matris in alvo.

The

The Trojan Babes but lately born,
And those that from the Womb were torn,
In fire be burnt.

Philo also in his Special Laws tells us, *That there may be a thousand specious pretences for men to quarrel with men; but for men to quarrel with infants and sucklings,* Ne calumina quidam quod dicat, habet; *Even malice it self can have no pretence,* they are so very innocent. *Josephus* likewise speaking of *Manaemus,* saith, *That he that in War destroys, leaves nothing undone that cruelty can do.* And he records it of *Judas* the Maccabite, that upon the taking of *Bosra* and *Emphronè, He destroyed all the Males amongst them, and whomsoever he found in them able to fight.* And in another place, he calls that punishment which *Alexander* surnamed *Thracidas* inflicted upon the Jewish Women and Children, *A revenge more than humane.* *Agathias* also concerning this Subject writes thus, *Forasmuch as piety forbids us to exercise our rage upon infants newly born, who must needs be ignorant of their Fathers crimes, therefore shall this sin be surely and severely visited upon you.* *Nicetas* also, or whosoever else continued that story unto the times of King *Henry,* writing of the Scythians, who took *Athira,* saith, *Neither were their Babes as yet sucking at their Mothers breasts, exempted from their outrage; but were either mowed down by the sword like grass, or suffered to pine and wither like blossomes for want of nourishment. A most barbarous act of men void of humanity, and having no sense of the wrong done unto nature herself, nor of the breach they made of the Laws both of God and Man, by extending their cruelty beyond what was necessary in subduing their Enemies.* Whereunto we may add those Pious Mandates given by Queen *Elizabeth,* recorded by Mr. *Cambden* in the Year 1596. who when she sent out her Fleet against the Spaniard, gave charge that if they took any Towns, they should spare the Female Sex, and those of feeble Age; and offer violence to none but to such as resisted. Now that compassion which seems to have been in all Ages taken of Infants, and such as have not yet attained to the use of reason, is for the most part shewed unto Women, that is, if they have done nothing in their own persons that may particularly deserve punishment; or if they have not personally performed such service, as properly belongs to Souldiers only. For as *Statius* notes, It is *Sexus rudis insciusque ferri; A sex that is ignorant and unfit for War.* As the Captain in *Seneca*'s Tragedies demanded of *Nero,* who had termed *Octavia* an Enemy, *Fœmina hoc nomen capit? Can a Woman be so called?* For which Cause *Tucca* and *Varus,* thought it fit to expunge those two Verses in the second of *Virgils* Æneads, where *Æneas* consults about the putting of *Helen* to Death. It was a magnanimous speech of the great *Alexander* in *Curtius, It is not my custome to make War against Captives and Women,* Armatus sit oportet quem oderim; *He must be armed whom I look at as an Enemy.* So *Grypus* in *Justine denies, that either he or any of his Ancestors, in all their Wars foreign or civil, did ever after the Victory obtained, exercise their cruelty upon Women, whom their very sex did sufficiently guard, as well from the perils of War, as from the rage of the Conquerour.* And so doth he in *Tacitus* profess of himself, *That he never made War against Women, nor against any others, but such as he found armed to resist him.* *Valerius Maximus* relating the barbarous outrage, which *Munatius Flaccus* exercised on Women and Children, calls it *Efferatam crudelitatem, & auditu etiam intolerabilem; A savage cruelty and not with any patience to be heard.* The Carthaginians, as *Diodorus* testifies, at *Salinæ* destroyed not the Women and Infants only, *without the least sense of humanity;* but their very Beasts also, which he elswhere calls, *an act of cruelty.* Now what *Latinus Pacatus* said of Women, that they were, *Sexus cui Bella parcunt; A sex alway favoured in War.* The like doth *Papinus* say of old men, that they are,

Camden 1596.

L. 9. c. 1.

Lib. 13.

Nullis violabilis armis
Turba, senes.

A sort of People that no Arms can hurt.

X. Priests and Students to be spared.

What we have said of Women and Children, may also be said of all men generally, whose manner of life is altogether abhorrent from deeds of Arms, *Jure Belli in armatos repugnantesque cædes; By that Right of War which is most agreeable to the Law of nature, they only are to perish by the sword, who have actually taken up the sword.* Where there is no power to resist, there can be no cause of revenge. So *Josephus, It is but just and equal that they that take up arms, should be punished by Arms, but the innocent should always be indemnified.* Thus *Camillu* in *Livy* when he had taken *Veji,* commanded his Souldiers to spare every man whom they found unarmed. And among these, they are in the first place to be spared, who are conversant about things sacred and holy: for anciently, it

Livy l. 28. Ant. 12. c 3. Lib. 5.

was the general cuſtom of all Nations to exempt ſuch from bearing Armes; and for that
1 Sam. 10. 5. 10. cauſe were they alſo priviledged from the Force of Armes. For ſeeing they could do no
violence, therefore was no violence done unto them. Though the Philiſtines were mortal Enemies to the Jews, yet did they forbear to uſe any violence to the College of the Prophets at *Gaba.* So we read of *David,* that he fled with *Samuel* to another place, where
there was ſuch another Colledge of Prophets, as to a place of refuge againſt all hoſtile violence, 1 *Sam.* 19. 18. *Hircanus,* when he beſieged *Hieruſalem,* ſent Sacrifices to the Temple; as the Jews teſtifie. And the Goths are commended by *Procopius* for ſparing the
Prieſts that belonged to the Church of St *Peter* and St *Paul,* being ſituate without the
Quæſt. Græc. Walls of *Rome.* *Plutarch* records it of the Cretians, That though they were embroiled in
Civil Wars, yet did all Parties carry themſelves inoffenſively towards their Prieſts, and to-
Lib. 8. wards thoſe that had the charge of burning the Dead. It is obſerved by *Strabo,* That when all
Greece was haraſſed with Inteſtine Wars, the Æleans being conſecrated to *Jupiter,* together
with thoſe that came to ſojourn with them, lived in great peace and ſecurity. And *Servius* upon the ſeventh of *Virgil's* Æneads, ſpeaking of a Reverend Old Prieſt, ſaith, *Eum defendebat à Bello, ſi non Ætas, ſaltem Religio Sacerdotis; That he was priviledged from all vi-*
Polyb. l. 4. *olence, if not by his Age, yet in reſpect of his Prieſthood.* In like manner alſo they that went
up to try their Fortunes at the Olympian, Pythian, Nemæan and Iſthmian Games, though
Thucyd. l. 5. & 8. it were in the time of War, were on all ſides protected. The like Priviledges and Immunities from the calamities of War were due unto ſuch as, though no Prieſts yet, do
Plut. Arat. voluntarilily ſequeſter themſelves from worldly Affairs, giving themſelves up wholly to
piety and devotion. For whom the Eccleſiaſtical Canons (grounded upon natural equity)
do make the ſame proviſion as they do for Prieſts. To theſe alſo we may add thoſe who
ſpend their time in either the invention or perfection of ſuch arts as are uſeful or neceſſary for humane Society. Wherefore *Protogenes* being demanded by *Demetrius,* How he
durſt truſt himſelf without the Walls of *Rhodes?* Anſwered, That he knew *Demetrius*
warred againſt the Rhodians, not againſt Arts.

XI. And Husbandmen. Next unto theſe are Husbandmen, who are alſo provided for by the Canons. *Diodorus Siculus* records this in honour of the Indians, *That in their Wars they that are Souldiers do kill and deſtroy one another without mercy; but ſuch as were employed in Husbandry they never mo-*
Lib. 2. *leſted, as being Benefactors in common to all Parties.* The like doth *Plutarch* teſtifie of the
ancient Corinthians and Megarenſes, *Nemo Agricolas ullo afficiebat malo; Not one of them*
Cyropæd. l. 5. *would wrong an Husbandman.* Thus favourable was *Cyrus* in *Xenophon,* as appears by the
Meſſage he ſent to the King of *Aſſyria,* wherein he tells him, *That he was very willing that Husbandmen ſhould follow their Callings without any diſturbance.* And it is a very honourable
teſtimony that *Suidas* gives of *Beliſarius,* and worthy of all mens imitation, *That he was ſo great a friend to Huſbandmen, and took ſuch care for their indemnity, that whilſt he com-*
Goth. l. 3. *manded the Army, no Souldier durſt ever injure them.* The like Teſtimony doth *Procopius*
give of him.

XII. And Merchants and the like. Next unto Husbandmen, the Canon provides for Merchants, and not only for ſuch as are Factors and Sojourners in the Enemies Country for a while, but for ſuch as are perpetual Subjects; becauſe the courſe of theſe mens lives are altogether averſe from War: where alſo we muſt note, That under this general name of Merchant are comprehended all kinds of Tradeſmen and Artificers, who for their gain do uſually prefer Peace before War.

XIII. And Captives. Let us now proceed to ſuch as have born Armes: That of *Pyrrhus* in *Seneca* we have already quoted, namely, That though the Law permits us to do what we pleaſe to Captives; yet equity and conſcience forbid us to take away their lives. Of the like opinion was
Alexander, who (as we have ſaid) places Captives in the ſame condition with Women:
Epiſt. 1. whereunto we may add that of S[t] *Auguſtine* to *Boniface, Hoſtem pugnantem neceſſitas perimat, non voluntas; It is not cruelty, but neceſſity, that makes us deſtroy a fighting Enemy. As force and violence is properly uſed againſt thoſe that are armed againſt us; ſo to thoſe whom the chance of War hath left naked and unarmed, mercy and compaſſion is peculiarly due; eſpecially to thoſe who can no ways endanger the publick peace.* *Xenophon* writes of *Ageſilaus, That he gave command to his Souldiers not to deſtroy their Priſoners as Malefactors, but rather to preſerve them for humanity ſake.* And *Diodorus* teſtifies of the Greeks, *That they always fought valiantly where they found reſiſtance: But to thoſe that were ſubjected they were very merciful.* *Saluſt* in his Jugurthine Hiſtory, ſpeaking of ſome young men, who having yielded themſelves,
were put to death, ſaith, *That it was done contrary to the Law of Armes,* that is, contrary to
Lib. 5. equity and the cuſtom of civilized Nations. *Lactantius* of the times he lived in, ſaith, *Parcitur victis & eſt locus inter Arma clementiæ; We ſpare thoſe whom we have conquered, and*
Hiſt. l. 4. *there is clemency to be uſed, even in Armes.* *Tacitus* commended *Primus Antonius* and *Varus,*
two Flavian Commanders; for *that they never committed any act of cruelty, beyond the place*
De pace ſecunda. *where the Battel was fought.* So likewiſe *Ariſtides, It is the cuſtom of our Age by force of Armes to ſubdue thoſe that reſiſt us, but to deal mercifully with thoſe that ſubmit unto us.* Concerning ſuch as were taken Priſoners in the War, the Prophet *Eliſha* puts this Queſtion to
the

the King of *Samaria, Wouldst thou kill those whom thou hast taken Captive with thy Sword and with thy Bow?* When one in *Euripides* demanded, Whether the Grecian Laws did forbid the killing of an enemy, he as readily answered, *Quem Mars reliquit Prælio superstitem; That they did, if that Enemy survived the Fight.* And therefore *Erysthеus*, being taken Prisoner, comforts himself in this, 2 Kings 6. 22.

He that kills me guiltless shall never be.

Plutarch comparing *Marcellus* with *Pelopidas*, seems to condemn *Marcellus* for his cruelty in shedding bloud unnecessarily after the Victory, whereas *neither* Pelopidas *nor* Epaminondas *did ever put any to the Sword whom they had overcome, neither did they take away the liberty of any City that they took; neither would the Thebans (as it was believed) have exercised that cruelty upon the Orchomenians, had either of these Commanders been present.* Besides, when *Scipio* would have put all the Inhabitants of *Utica* to the Sword, without regard of Age or Sex; because they had taken part with *Cæsar*, *Cato would not suffer him: But protesting against it as an act of inhumanity, and calling the Gods to witness in open Council, with great difficulty he saved them from so great a slaughter.* *Procopius* in the first of his Persian Wars, which he also repeats in his second, saith, *That to use cruelty to the Conquered, is repugnant to the Rules of Piety; so that when* Cabadas *King of* Persia, *after he had taken the City* Armada *by storm, had made great slaughter among the Inhabitants, a certain old Priest told him, That to kill so many Captives, was not Kingly.* And the same *Procopius* elsewhere records an excellent Speech of *Belisarius* to his Souldiers, upon the taking of *Naples*, disswading them from the unnecessary effusion of bloud; *Do not* (saith he) *extend your hatred of your enemies beyond measure: No Conquerours continue to hate the Conquered: If you kill them now, you do not abate the number of your Foes, but of your Subjects. Do not therefore prosecute your revenge too far; but consider, that having subdued them, to become now Slaves to your own passions, is ignoble.* When *Alexius* the Emperour was perswaded by one of his Council to kill his Scythian Captives, he made this noble Answer, *Though they be Scythians, yet are they men; though they be enemies, yet do they deserve pity: It is the chance of War only that puts the difference between us and them.* It is a most excellent Observation that we read in *Gregoras*, *Whatsoever is done in the heat of Fight is pardonable, because the faculties of Discourse and Ratiocination is (as it were) block'd up; so that the hands, being as it were drunk with anger and revenge, and wanting the guidance and manuduction of Reason, do even they know not what. But when by our strength and courage our dangers are over, and our Reason enjoys her liberty to examine and judge of what we are about, and to issue out her Mandates to the hands for execution; then if any things be done unjustly or unseemly it plainly shews the perverseness of the mind.* *Julian* in his second Panegyrick on *Constantius*, under whose Person he describes a vertuous Prince, saith, *That having conquered his enemy by force of Arms, he makes no farther use of the Sword, esteeming it impious to kill him who is no longer able to defend himself.* And therefore *Diodorus Siculus* condemneth the Byzantines and Chalcedonians of notorious cruelty, for killing a multitude of Captives taken in War. And in another place he tells us, That it was a Law generally observed to spare Captives, and that he that violates this Law doth, doubtless, sin against God and man. And hence it is, that in all Stories we find those Commanders highly commended, who having taken a multitude of Captives, whom they could not without danger and charge keep, have chose rather freely to dismiss them, than to kill them.

Plut. in Cat. Uticens.

Goth. l. 1. c. ib.

Ann. Comnenas.

Lib. 4.

See Chap. 7. towards the end.

XIV. They are to be spared that surrender on equal Conditions.

Wherefore they that in a Battel shall cry for Quarter, or in a Siege shall offer to yield upon Conditions to save their lives, are neither of them to be rejected. The Romans (as *Procopius* testifies *) thus bespeaks the Persians whom they held closely besieged in the Fort of *Petra*, *We*, say they, *do extremely commiserate your hard condition, and would gladly spare you, though ye wish to dye; and that life which ye so nicely disdain, we would save, as it becomes Christians and Citizens of the Roman Empire.* And therefore *Arrianus* speaking in that Slaughter, which the Thebans made of their Captives that had yielded to mercy, saith, *That it was not according to the custom of the Grecians.* The like we read of *Thucydides*, *Ye did accept of us, who willingly and with lifted up hands begged to be received to mercy, and it is not the custom of the Grecians to kill such.* The Syracusian Senators in *Diodorus* tell us, *That to spare a Suppliant is the sign of a truly noble and magnanimous spirit.* And *Soparer* confesseth, That it was the custom of the Grecians to save such as begged for life in the Wars. In Towns that were besieged this custom was generally observed by the Romans, That if they yielded before the Battering Ram toucht the Walls, the lives of the Citizens were saved. *Cæsar* signifies to the *Advatici*, That he was willing to preserve their City, in case they would surrender before his Ramms approached their Walls: Which custom is yet observed, with this difference, In places meanly fortified before the Cannons begin to batter; but in places of great strength, before a breach be made in their Works. Howbeit, *Cicero* respecting not so much what may lawfully be done, as what in equity ought to be done, gives his opinion in this Case thus, *Seeing that we ought to provide for the*

* Goth. 4.

Lib. 3.

the safety of those whom we conquer, it is fit that we receive them into protection, who shall surrender themselves, though our Ramms have battered their Walls. The Jewish Interpreters note, That it was a custom among their Ancestors, when they had laid close Siege against any Town, not to incircle it with a Ditch quite round, but to leave one part thereof open for such to fly, as would save themselves by flight; whereby the Town might be taken with the least effusion of bloud. Thus *Scipio Æmilianus* being commanded to destroy *Carthage*, made Proclamation, That they that would provide for their own safety by flight, might do it freely; as *Polybius* testifies.

XV. They also that surrender without conditio . The same equality bids us to spare those who are willing to surrender themselves to the will of the Conquerour, without any Conditions at all. *Trucidare deditos sævum*, *To kill those who are at our mercy is cruelty*, saith *Tacitus* †. So also *Salust*, rehearsing that bloudy fact of *Marius* in putting to death those young men among the Campsans that had delivered themselves to mercy, saith, That it was *facinus contra Jus Belli*, *A cruelty scarce justifiable by the natural Right of War.* And in another place he complains of the like cruelty, saying, *That he was so far transported with rage, that he put to the Sword not only men armed, and such as were in Battel, which he might do by the Law of Armes; but even Suppliants also that begged for mercy.* So also *Livy*, *Qui deditis contra Jus, ac fas Bellum intulisset*; *He made War even against those that yielded themselves, contrary to the Laws of God and good men.* Nay, the principal design of a General should be rather to force his enemy through fear to surrender, than to kill them. And herein is *Brutus* to be commended, *who would seldom fall on his enemy by assault, but chose rather to encompass them with his Horse, commanding his Souldiers to spare them, who e're long would be his own.*

† *Tac. Lib.* 12. *Bello Jug. lib.* 1. *de Rep. ord.*

XVI. Unless some very great crime do hinder. Against these Rules of natural Right and Equity, are usually brought these specious Exceptions, which notwithstanding have little of solidity in them: as namely, What if such acts of cruelty be done by way of retaliation? what if they be done by way of example, to deter others? or what if it be done against such as have been notoriously obstinate? None of these are sufficient to justifie an unnecessary or an unjust Slaughter, as is easily to be collected by what we have already written concerning the just causes of killing Enemies. For from Captives and such as actually deliver themselves or desire so to do, there can be no danger. That therefore they may justly be put to death, there ought to precede some such crime, as to an impartial Judge should deserve death. And thus we may haply read of cruelty sometimes used unto such as have either been taken Prisoners, or yielded without Conditions of life, if being convicted of the injustice of the War, they have still persisted in Armes, or if they have reproached or defamed the Conquerour with bitter invectives, or have broken their faith, or somewhat of the Law of Nations, as the priviledges of Ambassadours, or have been Traitors, Renegadoes, or the like. But as to the Objection of retaliation, Nature doth not admit thereof, unless it be against those numerical persons, who have done the wrong. Neither will it suffice to say, That the Enemies do all of them make but one Body by their combination against us, as may easily be gathered by what hath been already said, when we treated concerning the communication of punishments. For, as we read in *Aristides*, *Is it not a shame to imitate that as just, which we condemn in others as unjust.* Upon which account it was that *Plutarch* blames the Syracusians for putting to death the Wives of *Hicetas*, and his Children; for no other cause, but because *Hicetas* had before put *Dion*'s Wife, his Sister and little Son to Death. But as to the profit which may hereafter be expected by putting a terrour into others, this gives no positive Right to put any man to death that yields himself Prisoner. But if there be just cause of death before given, this may be one cause amongst others why the punishment due may not be remitted. Again, an obstinate endeavour to maintain our own Party, if our cause be not altogether unjust or dishonest, doth not at all deserve punishment, as the Neapolitans argue in *Procopius*; or if it do, surely that punishment cannot amount to death, if equity may be the Judge. When *Alexander* had commanded all the Youth in a certain Town to be put to death, because they defended it so resolutely against him, the Indians told him, *That he made War like a Thief or a Murderer*; *Latronum more bellare Indis visus est*, saith the Authour: whereupon to preserve his own honour he ever after used his Victories with more clemency. Much more for his honour it was, that he would have spared some Milesians, *because he perceived them to be very generous and faithful to their own Party*; as *Arrianus* records. When *Phyto* the Prætor of *Rhegium* was dragged out to tortures and death, because he had resolutely defended his City against *Dionysius*, as they dragged him along he cried out, That the Tyrant had thus punished him, for no other reason than because he would not betray the City to him. For which cause the Gods would certainly revenge his death upon the Tyrant within a short time. Such punishments as these *Diodorus* calls *unjust*. For mine own part, I am highly pleased with that wish of *Lucan*'s,

Plut. Tim. & Dion.

Terror.

Goth. lib. 1.

Polyan. Lib. 4.

——*Vincat*

——Vincat quicunque necesse
Non putat in victos sævum distringere ferrum,
Quique suos Cives, quod signa adversa tulerunt,
Non credit fecisse nefas——————

His be the Day, who can contented be
To conquer, but not kill his Enemy;
That can believe his Neighbour honest, though
He march against him as an Armed Foe,

So that we understand the word *Cives*, not for Neighbours inhabiting the same Town or Country, but Citizens of the same Universe. Much less can the griefs we conceive for the like loss we have sustained in War, make the unnecessary shedding of bloud to be just and lawful, as we may read of *Achilles*, *Æneas*, and *Alexander*, who were wont to celebrate the Funeral of their friends whom they had lost in the War (thinking thereby to make an atonement for them) with the bloud of their Prisoners, and such as had yielded themselves to the mercy of the Conquerour; which *Homer* deservedly condemns as an unjust act; and which after Ages adjudged as cruelty, as *Servius* notes upon *Virgil*. *Æn. l. 10.*

XVII. A multitude offending may be justly pardoned.

Yea, and where their crimes are such as to deserve death, yet is it the property of mercy to abate somewhat of the extremity of our Right, by reason of the multitude of Offenders; an example whereof we have even in God himself, *who commanded the Hebrews to tender Peace to the Canaanites, and other bordering Nations*, though exceedingly wicked, that *so paying an Annual Tribute to the Conquerour they might enjoy Peace*. Pertinent to this purpose is that of *Seneca*, *When some particular Souldiers in an Army mutiny, the severity of a General is necessary; but if the whole Army threaten a revolt, then is a General Pardon seasonable*. And again, *Quid tollit iram sapientis? Turba peccantium; What is it that sooner appeaseth the wrath of a Wise-man, than the multitude of Offenders?* Quicquid multis peccatur inultum est, *When the people generally offend, there revenge is not so proper as pardon.* For as *Livia* in *Xiphilinus* observes out of *Dion*, *He that will punish all Offenders according to the utmost rigour of the Law, will be enforced to destroy the greatest part of Mankind.* That of St *Augustine* is very seasonable advice in this Case, *He that would reform the errours of a multitude, must do it* magis monendo quam minando, *more by perswasion than by threatnings. For severity is then seasonable when the number of Delinquents are but few.* But when they are numerous, then that of *Lucan* holds true: *De ira l. 2. c. 10.*

Tot simul infesto juvenes occumbere Letho,
Sæpè Fames, Pelagique furor, subitæque ruinæ,
Aut Cœli Terræque Lues, aut Bellica clades,
Nunquam pœna fuit.

Sadly at once so many Youths to slay,
Sometimes a Famine, or a Sea-breach may,
A sudden Fall of Buildings, or a Plague
From Heaven and Earth, or Wars unbridled rage;
(But in cold bloud to shew such ire and teen)
By way of punishment was never seen.

And therefore to avoid the effusion of much bloud was the invention of Lots, or casting of Dice, (as *Cicero* testifies) whereof *Salust* gives this reason, where speaking of such bloudy and inhumane punishments, he saith, *Quibus vastatur Civitas magis quàm corrigitur, Whereby a City is rather wasted and depopulated, than reformed.* *Orat. pro Cluent.*

XVIII. Hostages to be spared, unless in themselves criminous.

By what hath been already said, it may easily be gathered what the Law of Nature doth determine concerning Hostages. In Ancient times when it was generally believed, that every man had as much right over his own life, as he had in any other thing wherein he claimed a propriety; and that this right, was either by explicite or implicite consent transferred into that Commonwealth or City wherein he lived, it was not to be wondred at; if, as we may read, those hostages, though in themselves innocent, were sometimes put to death for the offences of those Cities whereunto they belonged, whether they were delivered by their own peculiar consent, or by the publick, wherein theirs also was included: But since a purer light hath discovered unto us, that the soveraign power over mens lives is reserved in God alone; it follows, that no man can by his own consent only, give unto another this power, either over his own life, or over the life of his fellow Citizen. Wherefore that noble Captain *Narses* (as *Agathias* relates) did abominate it as an act of cruelty, to put to death such hostages, as were no ways

ways guilty of those crimes that were committed against him. So also have others done in like cases, even by the example of *Scipio* (perhaps) who was wont to say, *That he scorned to take revenge on the innocent hostages, but he would severely punish the Delinquents themselves*, Nec ab inermi sed ab armato hoste pœnas expetiturum; *Disdaining* (it seems) *that revenge that was taken upon an unarmed foe.* The very same answer do we read of, given upon the like occasion by the Emperour *Julian*, as *Eunapius* testifies. That which our modern Lawyers, and those no mean ones hold forth, namely, That such conventions and agreements are valid, in case they are confirmed by ordinary and general practice; I also condescend unto, in case they will understand by right, that which is not punishable; for so, in this argument it is usually taken: but in case they imagine, that they that shall take away the life of any, by vertue of such a pact or agreement only, do not sin, I fear that they are both deceived themselves, and by their perilous examples deceive others. But plainly, if he that comes as an hostage be at that time, or at any time before hath been a notorious offender, or hath afterwards in any matters of moment satisfied his faith given in any of these cases, his punishment may be without injury. But the flight of *Clelia* over *Tiber*, when she made her escape to King *Ethruseus*, was not only safe, but to use *Livys* own words, an honourable attempt; because she came as an hostage, not by any voluntary act or consent of her own, but by the command of the City she was sent from.

XIX. All needless and unprofitable combatings are to be avoided.

This one thing is yet to be added, that all Duels and Tryals by Combitants, seeing that they are of no use, either to the decision of right, or the ending of a War, but merely for ostentation of strength, are not only repugnant to our Christian profession, but to the Laws of humane society. And therefore all Commanders in all Armies should carefully provide against such unprofitable effusion of Blood, as being lyable to render an account thereof to those whose Vicegerents they are; because, as *Salust* observes, it is the honour of a General, *Incruento exercitu victoriam deportare*; *To conquer with the least effusion of blood that may be. Tacitus* writing of the *Catti*, a Nation at that time eminent for their Valour and good Conduct, saith, *Rari excursus, & fortuitæ pugnæ; They made but very few excursions, and fought as few Battels but upon advantage.* Upon which account it was that *Plutarch* deservedly censured *Demetrius, Who rashly exposed his Army to unnecessary dangers, rather out of vain ostentation, than hopes of gain.*

CHAP.

CHAP. XII.

Moderation in the ſpoiling of an Enemies Country.

I. *What waſt is juſt, and how far forth it is ſo.*
II. *Things profitable unto us, and out of the Enemies power not to be waſted.*
III. *Nor in caſe there be great hopes of a ſpeedy victory.*
IV. *Nor if the Enemy may ſuſtain themſelves without them from other parts.*
V. *If the things to be deſtroyed are of no uſe to the maintenance of the War.*
VI. *As thoſe things that are ſacred or thereunto belonging.*
VII. *So likewiſe thoſe that are Religious.*
VIII. *The benefit that attends ſuch a moderation obſerved.*

I. What ſpoil is juſt and how far forth.

THAT one man may deſtroy the things of another without injuſtice, it is neceſſary that one of theſe three things ſhould proceed: Either ſuch a neceſſity as may be preſumed to have been excepted in the inſtitution of primary Right or Dominion, as when a man merely to avoid ſome imminent danger to himſelf, ſhall caſt the Sword of a madman into a River; yet even in ſuch a caſe, there remains an obligation to make reſtitution to the full value, according to the opinion of the beſt Authors, as we have elſewhere declared: Or ſecondly, there proceeds ſome debt, which aroſe from ſome inequality; and then that which is waſted is ſo underſtood, as if it had been taken in ſatisfaction of that debt, for otherwiſe it would not be juſt: Or thirdly, there muſt proceed ſome crime or wrong done that may deſerve ſuch a puniſhment; or which, ſuch a puniſhment doth not in proportion exceed. For as it is well obſerved by a Judicious Divine, *It cannot ſtand with equity or right reaſon, that a whole Kingdom ſhould be waſted, becauſe ſome herds of Cattel have been driven away, or ſome houſes or villages burnt*: which alſo is acknowledged by *Polybius*, who would not have puniſhments by War multiplied without end or meaſure; but rather that all injuries ſhould be expiated by puniſhments proportionable. And for theſe cauſes, and within theſe bounds and limits, an Enemies Country may be ſpoiled and waſted without injuſtice; but otherwiſe, unleſs it be for ſome great advantage to do another man hurt, and to gain thereby nothing, is but mere folly. Therefore wiſe men are uſually ſwayed by matters of profit, whereof the principal is that noted by *Oneſander*, *Where he adviſeth a Prince to deſtroy, burn, and lay waſt his Enemies Country, becauſe*, ſaith he, *a ſcarcity of money and victuals will ſoon ſhorten the War, as plenty will prolong it.* Conſonant whereunto is that of *Proclus*, *It is the duty of a good General to cut off forage from his Enemy, and proviſions from every ſide.* So thought *Curtius* of *Darius*, *That having nothing to feed himſelf and his Army with, but what he muſt get by rapine and ſpoil, he muſt needs at length be overcome by want and famine.* Now, that ſpoil and devaſtation may eaſily be diſpenſed withal, which ſooneſt enforceth an Enemy to ſue for Peace. *Philo* the Jew in his Book of a contemplative life, ſaith, *They that are in Arms do uſually deſtroy and lay waſt their Enemies Country*, Ut hoſtes eo facilius ſe dedant rerum neceſſarium penuria; *That ſo being puniſhed by famine, they may without the hazard of a Battel be compelled to yield themſelves to the Conquerour.* After this manner did the Halyattes make War upon the Mileſians, the Thracians againſt the Byzantines, the Romans againſt the Campanes, Capenates, Spaniards, Legurians, Nervians, and others. But if we would diligently obſerve how our modern Wars are managed, we ſhall find that ſuch devaſtations are now a days made more out of hatred, than any prudent council: for it ſo falls out oft-times, that either thoſe reaſons which would perſwade us thereunto do ceaſe; or thoſe that diſſwade us from it, are more forceable.

Lib. 2. *c.* 2. §. 9.

Vict. de Jure Belli n. 52. &c. 56.

Strat. c. 6.

Herod. lib. 1. *Pol. lib.* 4. *Front. Strat.* 3. *c.* 4.

II. No waſting of things profitable to us, and without the reach of the Enemy.

And this in the firſt place happens, when that part of the Country which yields profit is ſo in our poſſeſſion, that the Enemy can reap no benefit by it. And hereunto doth the Divine Law properly look, when it permits wild and unfruitful trees to be cut down to make engines for War, but commands ſuch as are fruitful to be preſerved for food *; adding this reaſon, becauſe trees cannot riſe up in Arms againſt us as men may: which precept, *Philo* by a parity of reaſon enlargeth to fields and other lands that are fruitful, affixing theſe words thereunto, *Quid rebus inanimis quæ & mites ſunt, & mites fructus ferunt, iraſceris? Why art thou angry with things inanimate, eſpecially with ſuch as are in themſelves gentle, and that yield ſweet and delectable fruit unto others? Do they like men expreſs any menacing ſigns of hoſtility againſt thee, for which they deſerve to be eradicated? Are they not much more profitable to the Conquerour whilſt they live and bear fruit, than when they ſhall be torn up? Do they not yield thee plenty of things, not only for neceſſity, but for delight and pleaſure? For trees and fields as well as men, do in their reſpective ſeaſons pay tribute to the*

* Deut. 20. 19.

De Creation. Magiſt.

the Conquerour, yea and much better, being so necessary, that we can no ways live without them. And in another place, he commends the equity of *Moses*, in restraining the licence of Souldiers, from destroying Trees bearing Fruit or Corn before it be ripe, adjudging it very unjust, *Iram in homines conceptam erogari in ea quæ causa mali nullius sunt; That our indignation against men should be exercised upon things that do no ways hurt us; besides, seeing that all sublunary things are mutable, and that nothing long continues in the same state wherein now it is, some provision ought in prudence to be made for the future. Possible it is, that they that are now most bitterly enraged against us, may upon debate and conference had, become our Friends and Allies. And then we will easily confess, That* Amicos necessariis fraudare, durum est; *To defraud our Friends of necessaries, is very hard. It is very true what from our Ancestors we have received, We ought so to trust our friends, as if at some times or other they may be our Enemies; that is, that every man ought to reserve something within his own breast of what nearest concerns himself, whereby to provide for his own safety; and not so wholly to discover himself by his words or actions, as that he may one day repent himself by reason of the vehemency of either passion, and blame his own rashness when it is too late to help it. This in all Cities is observed as an Oracle, That in times of Peace they ever provide for War; and in times of War they lay the foundations of a firm and lasting Peace: we should neither place too much confidence in our friends, because they may prove our enemies; neither should we appear too diffident of our enemies, because they may hereafter prove our friends. But if the hopes of our enemies conversion cannot prevail with us to do them civil offices, yet let us remember, That there is no hostility at all against us in those things which an enemies Country produceth. For all things there are serviceable, all things profitable, all things pleasureable, or very necessary to our selves. All its fruits affording unto us, either nourishment, or somewhat that is equivalent unto it. Again,* Non opportet Bellum inferre Belli nesciis; *We ought not to make War upon those things that are so amicable, so innocent, that they know not what War means. To burn, cut down, and utterly to extirpate those things which Nature by heat from above and moisture from beneath, hath so tenderly brought up and nourished, to no other end but to pay their yearly Tribute unto men, as unto Kings, savours of too much inhumanity.* Thus far *Philo*; wherewith agrees that of *Josephus*, *If Trees*, saith he, *could speak, they would certainly upbraid us with injustice, for inflicting upon them the plagues and miseries of War, who are in no wise guilty of the causes thereof.* Neither hath that Saying of *Pythagoras* any other ground than this, where he tells us, *That to cut down or to hurt tender Plants or Trees that bear Fruit, is a sin against Nature, and not justifiable before God.* *Porphyry* likewise describing the manners of the Jews, taking (as I suppose) their Customs to be the best Interpreters of their Laws, extends this Custom or Law to all Beasts that are serviceable for Tillage. Their Talmuds and their Interpreters do yet stretch out this Law somewhat farther, even to all things that may causelesly perish, as the firing of Houses, the poysoning of Springs, or the spoiling of any thing that may afford nourishment to Mankind, unless it be such Trees or Houses, as being near unto the Walls may thereby hinder Souldiers in the performance of their Military Duties. Agreeable with this Law was that prudent moderation of the Athenian General, *Timotheus*, *Who would not suffer his Souldiers to destroy any House or Village, nor cut down any Plant that bare Fruit.* There is the like Law extant in *Plato*, *prohibiting the laying of any Lands waste, or the demolishing of any Houses.* And if we may not waste the Country of an Enemy, much less when by Conquest we have made it our own. *Cicero* did not approve of the demolishing of *Corinth*, though the Citizens had unhandsomly treated the Roman Ambassadours. And in another place he calls that War *an ugly, horrid and malicious War, that was made against Houses, Walls, Pillars, and Posts.* *Livy* highly commends the lenity of the Romans, for that having taken *Capua*, they did not pull down the Walls, nor set on fire the innocent Houses. There is a most excellent Epistle upon this Argument extant in *Procopius*, which *Belisarius* writes to *Totilas*, *It hath been*, saith he, *reputed in former Ages the Glory of wise men to raise fair and magnificent Structures, to preserve their Names and Memories; but to rase and demolish them being built was ever esteemed the badge of folly and madness, as not blushing to transmit to Posterity the Monuments of their own vileness. It is confest by all men, That* Rome *is the most magnificent and beautiful City of all that the Sun beholds: Neither did it arise to this height of splendour by the bounty or industry of any one man, or in few years; but many Kings and Emperours, and a vast series or succession of Noble-men, many Ages, and a stupendious Mass of Treasure, have drawn hither, as other things, so the most expert Artificers in the World, whereby having by little and little brought this City to that perfection, wherein we now see it, they have bequeathed it to future Ages, as an everlasting Monument of their Vertue and Magnanimity; wherefore to rase this City, were to be injurious to Mankind in all Ages; to our Ancestors, in sacrilegiously burying in its Ruines the memory of their noble Acts; to our Posterity, enviously depriving them of the very sight of those noble Structures, whereby they may be excited to the imitation of their Vertues. And if it be thus, then consider that one of these two must necessarily fall out, either the Emperour must vanquish, or you: If you be Conquerour, then in destroying this City you destroy not what is your Enemies, but your own; and in preserving it, you enjoy the richest and most beautiful place on*

De non edendis, lib. 4.

De Repub. l. 5.

Offic. l. 1.

Pro domo sua.

Lib. 26.

on the Earth. But in case thou be worsted, thy clemency in preserving this great City shall plead strongly to the Emperour for mercy; but in destroying it, all hopes of favour lye buried in the ruines of it: and thou shalt not only lose whatever thou canst gain by the Spoil, but an eternal brand of shame and infamy shall cleave unto thy Name throughout all Ages, according to thy dealings herein. For fame is equally ready to report either good or evil of us. Potentum quales sunt actiones, talis existimatio; *According to the lives and actions of Grandees, so is their fame to the Worlds end.* Thus far *Procopius.* It is true, that God himself in the sacred Scriptures did not only command, that some Cities should be destroyed by fire, but also that the Trees of the Moabites, contrary to this General Rule, should be cut down. But this was not done out of an hostile malice, but out of a pure detestation of their sins, which were either publickly known to deserve such a punishment, or at least were so reputed in Gods account. Josh. 6. 2 Kings 3. 19.

III. If there be great hopes of Victory.

Secondly, We should forbear to waste an enemies Country, where the possession of it is in question, especially if there be any probable hopes of a speedy Victory, whereby both the Land and the profits thereof are likely to become the reward of the Conqueror. So *Alexander the Great* (as *Justine* tells us) prohibited his Souldiers from depopulating *Asia*, telling them, *That they ought rather carefully to preserve their own, and not to destroy that which they came to possess.* Thus *Gelimer* with his Vandals besieging the City *Carthage*, made no spoil, nor took any pillage; but secured the Country to himself as his own. The like Speech I find in *Helmoldus, Nonne Terra quam devastamus nostra est? Is not the Land that we waste, ours? and the people whom we destroy, our Subjects? Wherefore then are we become Enemies to our selves? wherefore do we drive away those who should serve us with food, and pay us Contributions?* So *Quintius*, when *Philip* over-ran *Thessaly*, wasting all before him, perswaded his Souldiers so to march, as if the whole Country were now their own. Thus likewise *Crœsus* perswades *Cyrus*, not to give *Lydia* to be spoiled by his Souldiers, by this very Argument, *Non Urbem meam, non res meas diripies; nihil enim ad me ista pertinent: Tua sunt: Tua isti perdent. No sober man will voluntarily destroy his own. This Country, these Cities, these Goods, are no longer mine, but thine; The fortune of the War hath left me nothing: All are thine by the Right of Conquest: Whatsoever then the Souldiers thus waste and consume, is not mine, but thine.* And to those who after the Conquest shall so waste and spoil what they have conquered, may that of *Jocasta* to *Polynices* be not unfitly applied, Proc. Vand. 2. Lib. 1. c. 66.

Petendo Patriam perdis: ut fiat tua
Vis esse nullam: quin tuæ Causæ nocet
Ipsum hoc, quod Armis vertis infestis solum,
Segetésque adultas sternis, & totas fugam
Edis per Agros. Nemo sic vastat sua.
Quæ corripi Igne, quæ meti Gladio jubes,
Aliena credis. Sen. Theb.

Whilst thou seekest to regain thy Country, thou destroyest it; by endeavouring to make it thine, thou makest it none. It is a good Argument against thy Title, that thou labourest to destroy it. No man doth so to his own; that which we wilfully consume by Fire and Sword, we confess to be not ours, but our enemies. To the same sense are those words of *Curtius, Quicquid corrupissent hostium esse confessi; Whatsoever they had wasted they confess to have been their Enemies.* Nor very discrepant are those Arguments which *Cicero* in his Epistle to *Atticus* useth against that Counsel that *Pompey* gave, namely, To destroy his own Country by Famine. Lib. 9. Ep. 7. 9, 10.

IV. If the Enemy may be elsewhere supplied.

Thirdly, We ought to forbear the wasting of an Enemies Country, if we see that they may be otherwise supplied with necessaries, either by Sea or Land. *Archidamus* in *Thucydides*, in that Oration wherein he disswades the Lacedemonians from making War against *Athens*, enquires what hopes they had to subdue the Athenians; If by wasting and destroying their Country, they might do well to remember, That the Athenians had other Lands and Countries under their Dominion, which confined not on their Cities (as *Thrace* and *Ionia*) and that they wanted neither Ships nor Ports, whereby they might be supplied with necessaries from any other Coasts. In which Case it was best to cherish and protect the Husbandman, even to the Enemies Quarters; that upon payment of their Contributions to either Party, they might enjoy Peace in the midst of War: which we have seen done, not only in our own late Civil Wars in *England*, but (not long since) in the Wars of the *Netherlands*; which also is very agreeable to the practice of the Indians, among whom, as *Diodorus* writes, *Their Husbandmen enjoy the very same Priviledges and Immunities, as do their Priests; insomuch that they follow the Plough without danger, even in the midst of their Troops, and to the very Skirts of their Camp.* And a little after he adds, *There is no enemy that will willingly wrong Husbandmen, but will rather preserve them from all injuries, as being the common Benefactors to both Parties.* Wherefore it was agreed and concluded in the War between *Cyrus* and the Assyrian, as *Xenophon* records it, That, *Cum agricolis pax esset, cum armatis bellum*; *Though the souldiers might fight, yet the Husbandmen should live in peace.* Neither do the Indians, as *Diodorus* testifies, either burn their Enemies Corn, or cut down their Trees. *Polyænus* reports the same of *Timotheus*, namely, that he set the fruitfullest part of the Country to Farmers and Husbandmen; yea, and as *Aristotle* adds, sold the Corn even to his Enemies, and with that money paid his Souldiers. So did *Viriatus* in *Spain*, as we read in *Appian*. And *Totilas*, *Whilst he besieged* Rome, *gave no disturbance to the Husbandmen throughout all* Italy, *but commanded them to follow their business without fear, so as they sent their annual contributions unto him.* This is the Glory of a Conquerour to defend what he hath won, and not to destroy it. And this we have seen in our days to be practised by the Hollanders, who ordinarily sold their Corn and other provisions even to their Enemies, and with the money so raised paid their own Army, with as much equity as profit, even to the admiration of foreign Nations. These manners and customs do our Canons commend to our Christian imitation; because as we profess to be more civilized, so ought we to express more humanity in our Wars, than was practised among the Heathens; whereof they enjoin us not to spare not the husbandmen only, but the Oxen and Horses wherewith they plow, and the seed which they carry out to sow their ground. For the self same reason doth the Civil Law forbid to take in pawn any of those instruments that belong to the plough. The Cyprians and Phrygians of old, and since them, the Athenians and Romans did condemn it as an heinous Act, to kill an Oxe that plowed up the Earth, because the Oxe was Mans companion and fellow labourer in tilling of the Ground; it was therefore forbidden by the Laws of *Athens*, that the Oxe should be offered in Sacrifice. And *Suetonius* in the life of *Domitian* testifies, That in the beginning of his Raign, he so far abhorred murther, that in his Fathers absence, remembring that Verse in *Virgil*,

Oecon. 2.

Procop. Goth. l. 3.

Ælian. Hist. l. 5. 14.

Rhodog. c. 26. 19.

An imp'ous people wh' on slain bullocks feast.

Vid. Plin. Nat. Hist. l. 8. c. 45. cum Lipsii Annot. Lit. D.

He forbad by an Edict the killing of Oxen. And *Aratus* in his *Phænomena* assures us, that it was not lawful to eat of an Oxe that plowed the ground, until the Brazen Age of the World began, nor that their Gods in their bloody Sacrifices should be worshipt by them.

V. Nor if the things be of no use in War.

Fourthly, there are some things of so innocent a Nature, that they neither cause a War, nor prolong it; which things, though the War continue, yet common reason should perswade us to spare. Thus do the Rhodians plead with *Demetrius*, who in mere envy had besieged their City, and threatned to burn it for that exquisite piece of Art, the Picture of *Jalysus* drawn by *Protogenes*, as it is recited by *Aulus Gellius*, whose words found to this sense, *What reason* (say they) *canst thou give for destroying so famous a Picture, by firing the house wherein it is? If thou canst conquer us, the whole City, together with that Picture safe and unblemished, will by thine own; but if thou fail in that design, consider what a dishonour it will be to thee, when it shall be said, that although thou couldst not conquer the Rhodians, yet thou hadst made War against* Protogenes *a dead Painter.* *Polybius* thought it an Act of the highest madness to seek to destroy those things, which being destroyed weakned not the Enemy, nor brought any advantage to those that destroyed them; such as are Churches, Statues, Schools, and Religious Houses. *Cicero* highly extols *Marcellus* for the care he took to preserve all the fair Buildings in *Syracuse*, both publick and private, *Quasi ad ea defendenda cum exercitu non expugnanda venisset*; *As if he had been sent with his Army to defend the City and not to take it.* And a little after he gives this reason, *Our Ancestors did ever leave unto the Conquered such things as to them were pleasant, but to the Conquerours of no great use or benefit.*

Lib. 15. c. 31.

Lib. 5.

Ver. 2.

VI. Especially things sacred or thereunto belonging.

And although this also may be pleaded in the behalf of other publick ornaments, yet a more special reason may be added; for those things that are dedicated to sacred uses, although these also are in some sort publick, and so not exempted from the outrages of War; yet if there be no great danger that may justly be feared by them, the very reverence that we owe to those holy places, and to the things thereunto appertaining, should plead strongly for their preservation, especially with those that agree in the worship of one and the same God, though they do differ in opinion concerning some outward rites and ceremonies. It was observed as a Law among the Grecians in the time of *Thucydides*, that when they invaded one another as Enemies, they should always forbear to use violence to holy places. And *Livy* tells us, that when the Romans had sackt and destroyed *Alba*, they spared the Temples of their Gods. And when *Capua* was taken, the Poet *Silius* writes thus of the Romans:

Ecce repens tacito percurrit pectora sensu
Relligio, & sævas componit numine mentes;
Ne flammam tædasque velint, ne templa sub uno
In cinerem sedisse rogo.

Livy tells us, that it was objected against *Qu. Fulvius* the Censor, *That by the spoil and ruine of Churches, he had made the people of* Rome *guilty of Sacriledge, as if the immortal Gods were not in every place the same, but that the Gods of one place delighted in the spoil of the Gods of another.* But *Marcius Philippus* coming to encampe about *Dium*, under the Temple, gave special command that no violence should be offered to that Holy place. *Strabo* relates it of one *Tectosages*, That having (with some others) robbed the Temple at *Delphos* of some treasure, thought he had sufficiently appeased the Gods by consecrating that Money, with some addition, to the Gods at home (supposing it to be no sacriledge, to despoile the Temple at *Delphos* to adorn his own Temple, both haply being consecrated to one and the same God.) But let us descend to such as were Christians. *Agathias* tells us, That the *Francks* spared the Temples in *Greece*, as being of the same Religion with them: Nay it was usual not only amongst the Heathens (whereof Historians give us many examples, and do therefore call it the common custom of the Grecians) but amongst Christians also, to spare the persons of such as fly for sanctuary to the Temples, even for the reverence they bear unto the places; which St. *Augustin* highly commends in the Goths, having taken *Rome*: *who* (as he there tells us) *had so great a regard to the Temples dedicated to the memory of the Apostles and Holy Martyrs; that in that miserable devastation all that fled thither found protection, whether natives or strangers: Hitherto* (saith he) *might the fury of the Enemy rage without restraint: But here as by a divine power, it was suddenly checkt: Hither do the commiserating Souldiers bring their distressed Captives, lest they should be destroyed by their fellow Souldiers that had no remorse: And they, who elsewhere were inexorably bloudy, no sooner approached to these places, where the licence which the right of War gave them was interdicted, but instantly all manner of Cruelty and all desires of revenge wholly vanished.* We give such reverence to holy places, saith *Appian*, That we use no manner of hostility against them amongst our Enemies, though Foreigners. For as *Polybius* observes, *It is the greatest folly and madness in the world to behave our selves impiously towards God, because we are enraged against our Enemies who are but men:* For *much better it is*, that *God should in those places, after any manner be worshipped, than that they should be made tippling-houses.* It is written of *Agesilaus, That not in* Greece *only, but amongst the Barbarians, he spared with holy reverence whatsoever was consecrated unto the Gods; as well their Altars and Images, as their Churches,* Mirarique se prædicabat eos non sacrilegorum numero haberi, qui supplicibus eorum nocuissent; *Admiring how they could be excused from Sacriledge that had violated the priviledges of those places, by oppressing them who fled thither for protection.* The very same testimony doth *Plutarch* give of him. The like he doth also of diverse Roman Generals, who in their Conquests, as well in *Greece* as in *Macedonia*, did not only spare the Temples of their Gods, but honoured them with presents, and enlarged both their immunities and priviledges. *Procopius* records it of one *Cabao* a Moor, who (though no Christian) yet commanded, That all honour and reverence should be given to Christian Temples: The neglect whereof by the Vandals themselves, he hoped that the God of the Christians (who ever he was) would severely revenge on them. And in the Second Book of his Persian Wars he testifieth the same of *Cosroes* the Persian King, who, though no Christian, yet took special care to preserve the Christians Church at *Antioch*. Neither durst the Emperour *Justinian* keep the spoils of the Temple at *Jerusalem*, which *Vespasian* brought to *Rome*; but they being found at *Rome*, were transported by *Gizerich* into *Africa*; as the same *Procopius* testifies in the Second Book of his Vandal Wars. Nor can I here omit that memorable fact of King *Alarick*, who *having ignorantly received some vessels, which his Souldiers had taken out of a Temple dedicated to St.* Peter, *and being afterwards informed thereof, commanded the same vessels to be restored by the same persons, adding others of a very great value unto them, to expiate the crime.*

Lib. 42. *Livy l.* 44. *Lib.* 2. *De civit Dei l.* 1. *c.* 1. *In excerpt. Peiresc.* *Severus.* *Vita Ages.* *Vand. l.* 1. *Cassiodor. l.* 12. *c.* 20.

What hath been already said of things Sacred, may likewise be said of things that are Religious; even of such as are erected as Monuments for the Dead. For though the Law of Nations do expose these also to the will of the Conquerour, yet ought they for humanities sake to be spared. Our Lawyers do assert, That to be the best and highest Reason which advanceth Religion. There is an excellent saying in *Euripides* which makes as well for Religious things, as for things Sacred.

VII. Yea and things that are Religious.

Homo quisquis urbes vastat & dis Manibus
Sedes sacratas, templaque, haud recte sapit:
Nam similis ipsum pestis excidii manet.

Who conquered Cities rashly do erace,
And Temples with their Monuments deface,
Do not foresee the like may be their case.

Apollonius Tyanæus doth thus interpret that Fable of the Giants fighting against Heaven, *When audacious men presume to violate the Temples and Images of the Gods.* It is said of *Scipio*, That having taken *Carthage* he inricht all his Souldiers with the spoil, *excepting only those who had before invaded the Temple of Apollo*; neither durst *Cæsar* himself (as *Dio* relates) demolish the Trophies of *Mithridates*, being consecrated to the Gods of War. *Cicero* speaking of *Marcus Marcellus*, thus testifies of him, *Quæ victoria profana fecerat, religione impeditus, non attigit*; *What the victory had made common and profane, that his Conscience would not permit him to touch.* Adding withal, That there were some Enemies who voluntarily observed the Rights of Religion and of Customs, even in the midst of War. And in another place, he declaims against the War made by *Brennus* against the Temple of *Apollo* as wicked and impious. So doth *Livy* against that act of *Pyrrhus* in Plundering the Treasury of *Proserpine*, which he calles *Fœdum, & in deos superbum facinus*; An act of high insolency against the Gods. The same *Livy* bitterly inveighs against the War which *Philip* made as being wicked, and as if it had been made against all the Gods: *Ultra enim jus victoriæ in Templa, in Aras, in Sepulchra sæviit*; *For that he spared neither their Temples, nor their Altars, no nor the Sepulchres of the dead:* Whereat *Polybius* also glancing, adds his own judgment in these words, *Wilfully to destroy those things which can be of no use unto us in War, nor doth much incommodate our Enemies, especially Temples, Images and such like ornaments, who can deny to be an act of brainsick madness?* Neither doth he herein admit of that common excuse of retaliation.

In Ver. 4.

VIII. The advantages that accrue by this moderation.

Although to speak properly it was not our intention in this place to enquire what is now most in use, but to reduce that loose and inordinate licence in making War, to that which is most agreeable to natural equity, or to that which among things lawful is best; yet will vertue her self, being but little valued in our age, plead mine excuse: If seeing her by her self so despised, I endeavour to set a much greater price upon her, by proposing what great profits and advantages may by her be reaped. In the first place therefore this moderation which spares such things as do not protract the War, doth so far weaken the Enemy, as it disarms him of one of the most forceable engines he hath to destroy us, which is desperation. *Archidamus* in *Thucydides* would needs perswade his Souldiers, *That the Enemies Country whereof they were possest, was no other than an hostage or pawn, which the better it was stockt with Corn and Cattle, was the richer and so the better: great reason therefore we have to spare it*, ne desperatio hostes redderet invictiores; *Lest desperation should make them to redouble their valour.* The same Counsel did *Agesilaus* in *Plutarch* follow, when contrary to the opinion of the Acarnanians, he gave the Achaians a free liberty to sow their Corn; saying, *That the more they sowed, the sooner they would harken to Peace.* This is the meaning of the Satyrist, when he tells us, That *spoliatis arma supersunt*; *They are compelled to live by force and arms, that have nothing else to live by.* This was the usual practice of the Gaules, as *Livy* notes, who *when they had taken a City, would not burn all their houses, that so they might pacifie the minds of their Enemies by giving them some things, when it was in their power to have destroyed all.* Whereunto we may add, That our preserving the Enemies Country during the War, begets in the Souldiers a great assurance of the victory. For what a man intends, and can make his own, he will not be easily perswaded to destroy. Again, Clemency is in it self apt to soften the resolutions and animosities of Enemies, and to draw them to a submission. *Hannibal spares all the fields and territories of the Tarentines, but not* (saith *Livy*) *out out of modesty or conscience; but rather that thereby he might the sooner gain them to a voluntary surrender.* (For to a Conqueronr, *utilis est clementiæ fama*; *Nothing is more advantageous than the same of being merciful*, especially if the Enemy be any ways diffident of his own strength.) Thus did *Augustus Cæsar* abstain from all Plunder and Rapine in *Pannonia*, *Because* (as *Dio* gives the reason) *he hoped to conquer them without the least effusion of bloud.* The like doth *Polybius* testifie of *Timotheus*, That by taking care to spare the Country wherein he marched, *He got much love and the good opinion of his Enemies.* Thus *Plutarch* commemorating the same care in *Quintius Flaminius* when he made war in *Greece*, adds this as the effect of it, *Not long after* (saith he) *did* Quintius *reap the fruits of his moderation and clemency; for as soon as he came out of* Thessaly, *the Cities yielded unto him: And the Grecians that dwelt in* Thermopilæ *did earnestly long for his coming: yea and the Achaians renouncing their Confederacy with King* Philip, *entered into League with the Romans against*

Xenoph. Hist. Græc.

Lib. 49.

Lib. 3.

gainst him. We read in *Frontinus*, that a City of the *Lingones*, having unexpectedly escaped a general devastation in a War made by *Domitian* the Emperour, under the conduct of *Cerealis* against *Civilis* the *Batavian*; because they had contrary to their fears lost nothing, being reduced to obedience, supplyed him voluntarily with an Army of seventy thousand Men, well armed. Whereunto also we may add, That from the contrary Counsels have usually arose clean contrary effects: An example whereof *Livy* gives in *Hannibal, who was*, as he describes him, *exceeding prone to covetousness and cruelty, insomuch that what Cities or Towns he could not keep, he would totally spoil and burn*; which *Livy* there calls *wicked counsel, as well in respect of the cause as of the success of it. For he did not only thereby alienate the hearts of those who were the immediate Sufferers, but he deterred others; and so enforced them the more to strengthen themselves against him; because*, Ad plures exemplum quam calamitas pertinebat, *More were frighted by the example than felt the calamity it self.* And therefore what some Divines have observed and taught, I must needs assent unto, That it is the Duty of such Commanders as would be thought Christians, (as far as in them lies) to intercede for and hinder the sacking and pillaging of Towns and Cities, especially of such things in them as add but little to the Conquest, being taken away; and yet whereby many innocent persons are or may be damnified: so that such acts as these Christian clemency doth always almost, and Justice it self also doth for the most part abhor. Surely there is a greater tye and obligation among Christians, than there ever was anciently amongst the Grecians; yet we find a Decree made by the Amphictiones, *Ne qua Urbs Græca Bello exscinderetur, That none of the Cities of* Greece *should ever be burnt down by War.* And it stands yet recorded by some ancient Writers, That *Alexander the Great* never repented any thing more, than he did the destroying of *Thebes*.

Lib. 5. c. 3.

Lib. 26.

CHAP. XIII.

Moderation concerning things taken in War.

I. *The Goods even of our Enemies Subjects being taken in War are to be detained only after the manner of some just Debt.*
II. *But not for the punishment of another mans crime.*
III. *By Debts here, all the charges and damages occasioned by a just War, are also included.*
VI. *Not to exact the utmost of our Right, is an Argument of humanity.*

I. Subjects Goods taken in War, detained in the manner of a just Debt.

THE taking of our Enemies Goods in a Just War is neither altogether blameless, nor is it exempted from all Obligations of restitution. For if we respect that which is done rightly, we can neither take nor detain more from our Enemies than what is justly due from him, unless it be such things as (beyond what is due) we are enforced to detain for our necessary safety, which are likewise to be restored (the danger being past) either in kind, or to their full value, (as we have already declared.) For what is lawful for us to do to the Goods of such as are at peace with us, is much more lawful to the Goods of those that are our Enemies. But in the times of Peace, what is necessary for our preservation, may be taken so as it be with a purpose to restore it, as is already proved; this necessity creating a kind of Right to take that wherein we have otherwise no propriety at all. But whereas Debts may arise either by reason of some inequality that there is in things, or by reason of some punishment due for some acts of injustice done unto us, we may in either of those cases possess our selves, if we can, of the Goods of our Enemies; but yet with this difference, namely, In the former of these cases: The Goods, not of the principal Debter only, but those of his Subjects also, by the Law of Nations (as it were by way of Suretiship) stand obliged. Which Right of Nations we conceive to be of another kind than that which consists either in a bare impunity, or by virtue of external Judgments. For as by our own private consent or agreement, he that deals with us for what is ours, seeks to have not only an external or judicial Right, but an internal and equitable also, in that which he deals for; so is it by a kind of common consent or agreement, wherein is virtually contained every particular mans. In which sense the Law is called the *common Pact or Agreement of the whole City*. Now it is so much the more credible that it pleased the Nations that such a Right should be thus acquired, because this Law of Nations was at first introduced, not only for the prevention of greater mischiefs, but also as a way whereby every State and Nation might recover their own.

Lib. 2. c. 2.

Lib. 2. c. 2. § 6, 7, 8.

But

II. But not for the punishment of anothers crime.

But if the Debt wherein a Foreign Prince ſtands obliged unto us be penal only, I do not perceive that by the conſent of Nations ſuch a Right is given to detain his Subjects Goods barely for his neglect. For ſuch a tye upon another mans Goods would be odious, and therefore ſhould not extend it ſelf farther than the perſon offending. Neither is there the like profit ariſing from theſe latter Debts, as from the former; for the former Debts require ſome reparation for the loſs of Goods, but ſo do not theſe latter: and therefore the proſecution of them may without damage be omitted. Neither doth that which we have already ſaid concerning the Attick Law, contradict this. For there men ſtood obliged, not for that properly, becauſe the City might have been puniſhed; but only to compel the City to do what it ought to do, that is, to inflict puniſhments upon Offenders; the neglect whereof is referred to the former, and not unto theſe latter ſort of Debts. For to owe a Duty in puniſhing Offenders is one thing, and to lye obnoxious to puniſhment for the non-performance of that Duty is another. The omiſſion of that doth uſually induce this, yet ſo that the former is the cauſe and the latter the effect. And therefore the Goods of an Enemies Subjects cannot lawfully be poſſeſt by way of puniſhment. For this were to puniſh the innocent for the nocent; but ſuch things only are liable to this Debt, that belong to the perſons who are Delinquents, amongſt whom are the Magiſtrates themſelves, whoſe Duty it was to puniſh, but did it not. (*Lib. 3. c. 2.*)

III. By Debt is underſtood the ſubſequent charges alſo.

Beſides, the things belonging to our Enemies Subjects may be taken and kept, not only to reimburſe our ſelves of our original Debt, which was the ground of the War; but to repair our loſſes and expences in the War, according to what hath been already ſaid in the beginning of this Book. And thus muſt we underſtand that which ſome Divines have written, namely, That things taken in War are not to be equalled with the principal Debt, that is, until ſatisfaction be made, according to ſound judgment, for the damage done in the War it ſelf. Thus the Romans, in their Treaty with *Antiochus*, adjudged it equitable, *That the King ſhould bear the charges of the War*, through whoſe default it was that the War began. So *Juſtine*, *Impenſas Belli Lege Juſta ſuſcepturus, qui Belli Author eſt*; *He that is the Author of the War, ought by the Law of Arms to bear the charges of it.* The like we find in *Thucydides*, where the Samians *are condemned to defray the charges of the War*. Now whatſoever is juſtly impoſed on the vanquiſhed, may by the Conquerour be exacted by force of Armes.

IV. For humanities ſake we ought not to exact our utmoſt due.

Moreover, this alſo muſt be remembred, which I have elſewhere delivered, That the Rules of Charity are of larger extent than thoſe of Juſtice. That man hath but little of mercy in him, who, being opulent, uſeth the extremeſt rigour of the Law to inforce from his poor Creditor the utmoſt Farthing of what the Law permits, eſpecially if that Debt were contracted by his kindneſs to his friend only, in being Surety for him. *Very lamentable were the condition of ſuch a Surety*, ſaith *Quintilian* the Father. But yet ſuch a Creditor doth nothing herein but what he may do by Right, ſtrictly taken; whereunto he adds, *Salvo pudore, ad Sponſorem non aliter Creditorem venire, quàm ſi recipere à Debitore non poſſit*; *The Creditor cannot for ſhame ſue the Surety, unleſs the Principal be inſolvent.* Wherefore it behoves us for humanities ſake, to ſpare their things, who have no ways offended, either as Authors or as Promoters of the War; nor are any other ways concerned than as by way of Suretiſhip, and who can worſe endure the loſs of them than we can. But eſpecially if it do ſufficiently appear unto us, That they ſhall receive no reparation for what we ſhall ſo take away from that Prince or City whereof they are a part. King *Ptolomy* having overcome *Demetrius* the Son of *Antigonus*, and taken his Camp, ſent back his Money and his Apparel, with this Meſſage, *That the Conteſt between them was for honour and Empire only, and not for private gain.* (*Plut. vit. Demetrii.*) Thus doth *Cyrus* beſpeak his Souldiers when they had taken *Babylon* and plundered it, *What ye have got from your Enemies, ye may without any injuſtice poſſeſs; but if you will leave them ſome things, it will teſtifie your humanity.* This alſo is to be noted, That ſince this Right of ſeizing the Goods of innocent Subjects for their Princes Debt, is but ſubſidiary, or by way of Suretiſhip, in caſe there be any hopes of recovering our Debts from the original Debtors, or from them who by not doing us Right, have voluntarily made themſelves Debtors, then to fall upon them who are no ways acceſſary to the injury done us, though it may ſtand with the Rules of Juſtice ſtrictly taken, yet it cannot ſtand with the Rules of humanity. *The Ancient Romans having conquered their enemies, never made ſale of all their Lands, but left them ſome part thereof to till for their ſuſtenance.* (*Appian. Civil. l. 2.*) So did the Vandals in *Africa*, and the Goths in *Italy*, as *Procopius* informs us. Hiſtories do plentifully ſupply us with ſuch like examples of humanity; as when the Romans having overcome their Enemies, granted them their Fields back, upon Condition, That they ſhould be from thenceforth held of the City they had conquered, or when ſome ſmall portion of thoſe Lands were for honour's ſake left unto the ancient Occupants. Thus *Romulus* puniſhed the *Vejentes* with the loſs of a part of their Territories. So *Alexander* reſtored the Lands

Lands he had conquered to the *Uxii*, under a certain Tribute. The like we read in ſeveral Hiſtories of Cities taken, but reſtored, and not deſtroyed; and of not the perſons only of Husbandmen, but their Goods laudably reſtored, at leaſt under a certain Tribute: as alſo under the like Tribute, immunity from War we may read of uſually granted to Merchandiſes.

CHAP. XIV.

Moderation concerning Captives.

I.
How far forth men may be enſlaved by internal Juſtice.

IN ſuch places where this Right is yet in force, of taking men Priſoners, and making them Slaves, if we reſpect internal Juſtice, it is to be reſtrained in the ſame manner as the Right of taking things is; that is to ſay, It is ſo far lawful, until we are ſatisfied our original Debt, together with the ſubſequent Charges thereof, unleſs the perſons ſo taken ſhall be found guilty of ſuch particular crimes as in common equity deſerve to be puniſhed with the loſs of liberty. Hitherto therefore, but no farther, hath he that wageth a juſt War a Right in the Captives taken from his Enemy, and a power to transfer that Right firmly unto others. But here alſo the ſame equity and humanity ſhould perſwade us to put the like difference as before we obſerved, when we diſcourſed concerning the killing of our enemies. *Demoſthenes*, in that Oration which he wrote concerning *Licurgus*'s Children, extols the clemency of *Philip* of *Macedon*, for that he made not all that were found amongſt his Enemies, Slaves; *but weighing, as in a juſt Ballance, all circumſtances, he proceeded rather as a Judge than as a Conquerour.* Thus likewiſe did *Alexander* his Son, who having taken *Thebes*, ſet at liberty both their Prieſts, and ſuch of their Citizens as had not aſſented to the Decree that the City paſt againſt him. *Plut. vit. Alex.*

II.
What may be juſtly done unto Captives in equity.

But here it is in the firſt place to be obſerved, That this Right of making men Slaves, which ariſeth as by Suretiſhip for that City, whereof they were Members, doth not extend it ſelf ſo far as that which ariſeth directly from perſonal delinquency, and are therefore made Slaves by way of juſt puniſhment. And therefore a reſolute Spartan being commanded to do ſome ſlaviſh Office, pleaded, That *he was indeed a Captive, but no Slave.* *Captivum ſe, non Servum dicebat.* *Philo* obſerves, *That ſometimes Parents are taken and made Slaves for their Childrens faults, and ſometimes Children for their Parents crimes; as when they are taken either by Pirates or in the Wars, whom notwithſtanding the Law of Nature, much more vigorous than any humane Law, ſets free.* And indeed, if we look directly into that general Right which a juſt War gives over Captives, it is much like unto that which a Lord hath over ſuch Servants, as being reduced to poverty have ſold themſelves unto him; only herein lyes the difference, That the condition of thoſe taken in War is the more to be pitied, becauſe this calamity befel them, not through any crime which was *properly* their own; but through the default of their Governours. *To be made a Slave by the Right of War, is* (as *Iſocrates* accounts it) *a bitter thing.* For this kind of bondage is a perpetual Obligation to all kinds of labour and hardſhip, for a perpetual ſupply of Food and Rayment. *Chryſippus*'s definition doth very well agree with ſuch kind of Slaves, who ſaith, That a Slave is a perpetual Hireling. And thus doth the Moſaick Law eſteem of him whom poverty hath compelled to ſell his liberty, as we read *Levit.* 25. 18, 40, 53. And his Redemption ſhall be paid by his work, as the Fruits of Lands ſold or mortgaged, ſhall redeem it to them that ſold it, *Lev.* 25. 50. There is therefore a main difference between that which by the Law of Nations may be done unto a Slave without puniſhment, and that which natural reaſon and equity doth allow to be done unto him. So ſaith *Seneca*, in the place before cited, *Cum in ſervum omnia liceant, eſt aliquid quod in hominem licere, commune jus animantium vetat; Although whatſoever is done to a Slave be lawful, yet are there ſome things which the very Law of Nature prohibits to be done unto him, as he is a man. For whoſoever is born a man, though he be a Slave, yet doth he not thereby ceaſe to be a man.* So *Seneca*, *Are they Servants? yet are they men; Are they Servants? yea, and our Companions? Are they Servants? yea, and our humble Friends; Are*

De Clem. l. 1. c. 18.

Philem. Epiſt. 47.

Are thy Servants? yea, and our fellow Servants, if we do but consider what power fortune hath over either of us. And a little after in the same Epistle, *Consider that he whom thou callest thy Servant, is born of the same nature, equally to enjoy the same common air, equally to breathe, live and dye as thy self; and if it had so pleased fortune, might as well have seen thee a Slave, as he now sees thee a Freeman.* And what we may read in *Macrobius*, is but

Coll. 4. 1. the same advice that St. *Paul* commends unto us, *Masters do unto your Servants that which is just and honest, as knowing that ye also have a Master in Heaven.* And in another place he admonisheth us, *not to terrifie them with menaces and threatnings*; which he presseth upon us by the same argument, *because we also have a Master in Heaven, who*

Lib. 7. c. 14. *regards not such distinction of qualities.* In the constitutions of *Clemens Romanus* we have this advice, *Govern not thy man nor thy maid-servant with too much austerity*: The reason whereof is given by *Barnabas* in his Epistle, *Lest thereby thou testifie against thy self, that thou fearest not him who is the supreme Lord both of them and thee. Clemens Alexandrinus* also exhorts us to use our Servants as our second selves, *Seeing that they are men as well as we*, imitating therein that wise Hebrew, *If thou hast a Servant use him as a Brother, for he is such a one as thy self.*

III. That it is not lawful to kill an innocent.

Let us now admit that the Lord hath over his Slaves the power of life and death to uphold his Domestick Discipline; but then, let that jurisdiction be used with that religious moderation, as the Magistrate useth in the publick. This was the advice of *Seneca*,

De Clem. lib. 1. cap. 18. & Ep. 47. *In thy Bondman thou art to consider, not what thou maist inflict on him without the restraint of the Law, but what in equity and good conscience thou oughtest to do unto him, which requires sometimes to favour even thy Captive and thy Slave, whom thou hast bought with thy money.* And in another place comparing Subjects with Servants, he saith,

De. Benef. lib. 3. c. 18. *Though they have different titles, yet is the licence over both, the same*; which certainly holds true in this particular, in taking away the life of either, *Majores nostri domum nostram pusillam Rempublicam esse voluerunt*; *Our Ancestors*, saith *Seneca*, *did reckon every family as a little Commonwealth.* So also *Pliny*,

Ep. 43. *Every mans house as to Servants is as a City.* Insomuch that *Cato* the Censor, as *Plutarch* informs us, *would not punish any of his Servants for never so great a fault*, Nisi postquam damnatus esset etiam conservorum judicio; *Until he had been found guilty by his fellow Servants.* Whereunto we may add that of *Job*,

Job. 31. 13, 14, 15. *If I did despise the cause of my man-servant or of my maid-servant, when they contended with me, what then shall I do when God riseth up and when he visiteth, what shall I answer him? Did not he that made him make me, and did not one fashion us both?*

IV. Nor unmercifully to punish him.

Yea, and to lesser punishments, as stripes and blows, *&c.* much of equity and favour is to be shewed to Captives and Bondmen, *Thou shalt not oppress him or rule over him with rigour*, saith the Divine Law concerning the Hebrew Servant; which since the

Levit. 25. coming of our Saviour, by reason of that affinity that there is between all mankind, ought to extend to all Servants: upon which Law *Philo* thus glosseth, *Servants in respect of the goods of fortune are our inferiours, but in respect of our common nature our equals. But the rule of Divine justice*, saith he, *is not that which is agreeable to fortune but to nature. Masters therefore are not to behave themselves towards their Servants insolently, nor to abuse that power which the Law permits them, thereby to grow cruel. For these are signs not of a meek and calm, but rather of a froward and intemperate mind, domineering over their Ser-*

In excerp. Legationum. *vants in a tyrannical way. Priscus* comparing the Romans with other barbarous Nations, tells us, *That they treated Captives with much more mildness than others did, performing unto them rather the offices of Fathers and Tutors than of Conquerours: For as they studiously withdrew them from those things, which in respect of their own customes were unlawful; so if they did offend, they only corrected them as sons; but to kill them (as the Scythians did) they esteemed utterly unlawful. There are divers kinds of liberty indulged unto them by their Lords, and that not only whilst they lived, but at their deaths: for whatsoever dying, they ordain or appoint to be done, with that which is their own, hath the power and force of a Law. Philo* in his second Book of Special Laws, as also St. *Cyprian* in his Epistle to *Demetrian*, highly blames this severity towards Servants, *If thou art not readily obeyed in all things* (say they) *if thy will be not executed as a Law, thou growest presently imperious and cruel; thou tormentest thy slave with whips and scourges, thou afflictest him with hunger, thirst, nakedness, and oft-times woundest him and throwest him into Prison; and yet, wretched man that thou art, whilst thou thus abusest thy power towards thy captivated slave, thou forgettest thy duty to, and thy fear of the Lord thy God. Now what can be more foolish and absurd*, saith *Se-*

Seneca. *neca, than to make the condition of a Servant worse than that of a Beast: He that would skilfully manage an Horse, will not provoke and exasperate him with many stripes; for unless he be gently handled at the first, he grows fearful and headstrong.* And again, *What can be more unseemly* (saith the same *Seneca*) *than to exercise that cruelty upon a man though our Slave, which we would be ashamed to exercise over Doggs or Oxen.* To restrain which brutish cruelty, it was wisely provided by the Hebrew Law, That if a Master did strike out the eye or tooth of his Servant injuriously, he was for that eye or tooths sake, to let him go free,

free, *Exod.* 21. 26, 27. *Whereby it falls out,* saith *Philo, that the Master undergoes for his cruelty a double punishment in the loss of his Servants, both labour and ransome: whereunto we may add a third more grievous than both the former, namely, That thereby he is compelled by the Law against his will to do good in a matter of the greatest concernment to a person whom he hates, and whom he wisheth it were in his power everlastingly to vex and torment; whereas the Servant for the wrong he hath suffered, receives this double comfort, first that he enjoys what of all things he most desires, to wit, his liberty, and then that he is for ever freed from the commands of so cruel and severe a Master.*

Neither are we to impose upon them too hard labour, without regard had to their strength and health. To this end with some others was the Sabbath by the Mosaical Law instituted, namely, That Servants as well as Beasts might enjoy some refreshment from their labours. *Do ye not observe,* saith *Seneca* *, *how careful our fore fathers were, as well to prevent all occasions of envy to Masters, as of reproach to Servants, when they stiled the Lord,* Pater Familias, *The Father of the Family; And his Servants,* Familiares, *His familiar Friends.* So in another place he bitterly inveighs against the too strict exaction of Servants labours; where speaking of such, he saith, *Nos non tanquam hominibus sed tanquam jumentis abutimur; Whom we abuse not as Men but as Beasts.* And *Dion Prusæensis* describing a good King, saith, *That he is so far from usurping the title of Lord over his Subjects, being Freemen, That he will hardly admit of it over his Servants. Ulysses* in *Homer* professeth, That those of his Servants whom he found faithful were as dear unto him as his own Son *Telemachus, Gratius est nomen pietatis, quam potestatis; Much more graceful is that name which imports Piety than Power; and better it is to be called the Father than the Lord of a Family. Neither is there any other reason,* saith *Lactantius, why we call each other Brethren, but because we believe that we are all by nature equal. For since we esteem all humane things, not from or by their Bodies but their Spirits, though the condition of the bodies be diverse, yet are they not unto us Servants; but we both esteem of them, and call them in spirit Brethren, but in Religion our fellow-servants.* Thus also St *Augustin* concerning the customs of the Catholick Church, *Thou (i. e.* the Church) *teachest Servants to adhere to their Masters, not as prest thereunto by necessity, but out of delight they should take in doing their duty. Thou teachest Masters in imitation of God, who is the supreme Lord and Master of all, to be gentle and merciful to their Servants, and to be always more propense to exhort and admonish them than by force to compel them to do their duty: And in case they transgress, rather to correct them as Sons, than to rage and tyranize over them as Slaves.* The like advice doth St *Hierome,* or *Paulinus,* give unto *Celantia* concerning Servants, *So order and govern thine House, as though thou wert rather a Mother than a Master in it: And invite thy Servants to reverence thee, not by thy sharpness, but by thy meekness and benignity.* And St *Augustin* observed, That in antient times *good Parents governed their Families in this order: As to temporal things the condition of their Children was much better than that of their Servants; but as to Religious duties they made no distinction, but Servants as well as Children were with the same affection instructed in the true worship of God: From whence every Master was called* Pater Familias, *which in time grew so common, That even they that lorded it over their Servants with the greatest severity, would not willingly be called Lords.* And for the very same reason were Servants called Children, as *Servius* notes upon that of *Virgil, Claudite jam rivos pueri, &c. Tacitus* commends the *Germans,* That they made the same account of their Servants as they did of their Farmers or Tenants. And *Theano* in an Epistle of his, prescribes a just measure for Servants, namely, *That they should neither be tired with over much labour, nor weakned through want or poverty.*

V. Nor to impose too hard labour upon him. Exod. 20. 10. 23. 14. Deut. 10. 14. * Ep. 47. Ep. 107. Od. 1. Tertul. Lib. 5. c. 15. De moribus Eccl. De Civit. Dei l. 19. c. 16.

To Servants for their Labour we owe Aliment; So saith that wise Son of *Syrach, Bread, correction and work are due to a Servant.* Of the same opinion was *Aristotle* *, *The reward of a Servants work is Aliment.* Neither are they much out who command us to use our Servants as we do Mercenaries, *Operam exigendo, justa præbendo; By exacting their work, and withal paying what is their due. So provide for thy family,* saith *Cato, that they be not pined through hunger, nor starved through cold. There is somewhat,* saith *Seneca* †, *that a Master owes unto his Servant, that is, Food and Rayment.* And in another place *, *Familia vestiarium petit victumque; A Family requires Food and Rayment.* For this it is that the Roman Captives plead unto *Bessus* †, *Give us,* say they, *at the least Food, as we are thy Slaves, not as much as sufficeth, though our necessities require it, yet so much as may keep us alive.* St *Chrysostome* gives this advice to the Master of a Family *, *If thy Servant perform his dayly labour for thee, do thou feed him; and besides his food, provide that he be well clad and well shod: and this is some kind of service that we owe unto our Servants; for unless thou do this office for him, neither will he do his duty to thee, but will remain free,* Neque ulla eum lex constringit si non alatur, operas præstare; *For there is no law to enforce him to perform his duty, if thou neglect to perform thine.* The proportion allowed to every Captive amongst the Romans, was four Roman Bushels of Corn for every Month, (every such Bushel containing of our measure about three Pints and ten Ounces above our Peck) as *Donatus*

VI. The Stock of the Servants, how far the Lords, and how far his own. Ecclus 33. 24. * Oecon. l. 5. † De benef. l. 2. * Idem de tranquilitate. † Procop. Goth. 3. * In Eph. 5. 2. Phorm. Act. 1, scen. 1.

natus upon *Terence* informs us. Thus alſo *Martianus* the Lawyer, Some things there are which of neceſſity the Lord muſt do for his Servant, namely, to provide for him
Thucyd. l. 7. meat and cloathing. The Sicilians ſtand condemned by all Hiſtorians for their cruelty
Diod. l. 11. 1. in famiſhing the Athenian Captives. So alſo doth *Iſaacus Angelus*, for the like cruelty to
Lib. 1. the Sicilian Captives, as *Nicetas* records: who alſo recites an Epiſtle ſent by the King of *Sicily* to the Grecian Emperour concerning this matter. Beſides, *Seneca* in the place before quoted proves, That Servants are in ſome ſort free, and in ſome things able to oblige their Maſters by ſome courteſies; as when they do more than is impoſed on them, or when they do ſome profitable acts, being not commanded, but voluntarily and freely and beyond their duty; wherein, though ſervants, they perform the office of Friends. As alſo when a Servant or Slave ſhall out of his *dimenſum* or allowance pinch his own carkaſs to ſave ſomewhat every day, or by improving his ſpare time gain ſomething to himſelf: This is in a manner his *peculium*, which is (as *Theophilus* defines it) his natural Patrimony; as if thou ſhouldſt call the Marriage of a Bond-man with a Bond-woman a natural Marriage. Which ſtock *Ulpian* calls, *Puſillum Patrimonium*; *A ſmall Patrimony*. Such was that which *Ulyſſes* propoſeth to *Eumæus* and *Philætus*.

Veſtrum utrique thori ſocias dabo, largiar & rem
Vicinaſque domos noſtræ.

Wives for you both, and Goods will I provide,
And Houſes where, near us, you may reſide.

Thus alſo *Varro* ſpeaking of Servants ſaith, *That by treating them liberally, as by enlarging their proportion in dyet and cloathing, by remitting ſomewhat of their hard labour, or by granting them ſome little ſtock of their own to be kept with thoſe of their Maſters, they may be made more ſedulous, careful and induſtrious than they would be.* Neither will it be much to the pur-
Peculium. poſe to ſay, That ſuch a little ſtock may at the will of the Lord be either taken away or diminiſhed at pleaſure: For in caſe he doth ſo without juſt cauſe, he deals very unrighteouſly with them. But a juſt cauſe there may be, not only when it is done by way of puniſhment, but when it is done to ſupply the neceſſity of his Lord; for the Servants profits are more ſubject to the neceſſities of his Lord, than the goods of Citizens to the Ci-
Lib. 7. *de Ben.* ty they inhabit. Very pertinent hereunto is that of *Seneca*, *It will not follow that a Servant hath nothing, becauſe his Lord may chuſe whether he ſhall have any thing.* And again in the ſame place, *Who can doubt but that the Servant, together with his ſtock, is the Lords; yet may the Servant preſent his Lord with a gift.* And hence it is that the Lord cannot re-demand that debt which being due unto his Servant in the time of his ſervitude, he pays him after his manumiſſion. For as *Trophoninus* teſtifies, *Debiti, vel non debiti ratio, in condidictione naturaliter intelligitur*; *In perſonal actions, the conſideration of what is due or not due is to be underſtood naturally.* But poſſible it is, That the Lord may be indebted to his Slave naturally: As therefore Clients may confer ſomething to the uſe of Patrons, and Subjects to the uſe of Kings; ſo we may read of ſome Servants who have out of
Dionyſ. lib. 1. their own ſmall ſtock contributed ſomething to the uſe of their Lords: As in caſe he be to
Lib. 8. raiſe a Portion for the marrying of his Daughter, or to redeem a Son out of Captivity, or
Ep. 16. upon ſuch like accidents. *Pliny* indulged this favour to his Slaves, That they might make their Wills, and give or bequeath what they had got unto any, ſo they were of his own Family. Among ſome Nations we read, That a fuller right of acquiring things was granted unto them according to the ſeveral degrees of ſervitude; as we have elſe-
Lib. 2. *c.* 3. where deſcribed. And many nations have corrected their Laws, reducing their external right of Lords over their Servants unto that internal juſtice, which we have heretofore expounded: For even among the Grecians it was lawful for Slaves, being too rigorouſly treated, to demand, That they might be ſold. And even at *Rome* they might *ad Statuas confugere*; *Fly to the Statues*, or implore the aſſiſtance of the Magiſtrates in caſes of Famine, Cruelty, or any ſuch unſufferable injuries done them. And this alſo is now allowed, though not in the ſtrictneſs of right, yet as proceeding from the goodneſs and humanity, and ſometimes ſuch as may be in equity due; as, That after long and very hard ſervice, they have rewarded that ſervice with liberty. So ſaith *Ulpian*, After that Captivity by the Law of Nations came to be in force, manumiſſion became a courteſie. An example whereof *Terence* gives us:

Thou waſt my Slave, till I enfranchiz'd thee,
Becauſe thou didſt thy duty cheerfully.

In ſome places it is cuſtomary to ſet a Slave at liberty if he can procure eight times as
Lib. 3. much as he was bought for. *Salvianus* obſerves, that in his time it was of frequent uſe,

That

That Servants, though not of the best, yet at least not of the worst kinds of servitude, were rewarded with liberty. And as he adds, *Were permitted to carry away with them whatsoever they had got in the time of their service.* Whereof we have many examples yet extant in our Martyrologies. And here I cannot but commend the generosity of the Hebrew Law, which commanded, *That the Servant having served out his time prefixt, should be altogether free, and that he should not go away empty handed:* That is, as their customs expound it, That his Gifts should not be less worth than thirty Sicles, (which in our Money amounts to about three pounds ten shillings.) Against the contempt of this Law, the Prophets do bitterly complain. The like doth *Plutarch* of *Cato Major*, for *selling his Captives, who had faithfully served him until they were almost worn out with Age, forgetting the common condition of mankind.* Deut. 15. 13.

VII. Whether Captives may fly.

But here falls in another Question, namely, Whether a Captive taken in a just War may lawfully make his escape? I do not speak of him that for some particular fault of his own had deserved to be deprived of his liberty; but of him who in the publick discharge of his duty falls into this calamity: Whereunto the best Answer is, That he ought not; because as I have said, by the general consent of all Nations, upon the account of the City he owes his labour. Which notwithstanding is so to be understood, unless to avoid some intollerable cruelty he be enforced so to do.

VIII. Whether they that are born of Slaves are obliged to the Lord, and how far.

We have elsewhere started another Question, Whether or no, and how far forth, the Children that are born of such Captives are by an internal Right bound to him whose Bond-men the Parents are? Which Question in regard of the persons so taken in War, cannot be well omitted. For if their Parents did for their own crimes deserve to be put to death; Children that were expected to be born of them are bound to serve for giving them their lives, which otherwise they had never had. For otherwise also even for want of Food and Rayment their Parents had power to have sold them for Slaves, as we have elsewhere shewed. Such a Right it was that God himself gave unto the Hebrews, over the Children of the Cannanites. So for the publick Debts of a City, Children already born, as being a part of that City, may stand no less obliged than their Parents. But for those that are unborn, this reason sufficeth not, but some others are requisite: As the express consent of Parents, together with the necessity of nourishing them, and that even for ever; or for affording them aliment, and that so long only until their labour shall fully satisfie the charge of their maintenance. If any Right beyond this be given to a Lord over such Children, it proceeds from the too great indulgence of the Civil Law to the Lords themselves. *Lib. 2. c. 5.* Deut. 15. 13.

IX. What may be done where Bond-slavery is not in use.

But in such places where this Right of making Men Slaves is not in use, there the best way is to exchange Prisoners: And next to this is to release them paying their ransoms, which likewise should not be over great but moderate; Neither can any man set down a certain rate; but common humanity instructs us that it should not be so excessive as that the Prisoner being released should thereby want necessaries: which are allowed by the Civil Law, even unto such as through their own peculiar fact are fallen into debt. In other places the ransome of Prisoners is prefixt, either by mutual covenants, or by the customs of the Countries. Amongst the Græcians of old, the ransome of a common Souldier was *Mina*, a Pound, that is of our Coin about three pounds two shillings and six pence. We now a days require for every Souldier a Months pay. In the War between *France* and *Spain* in *Italy*, the ransome of every Horse-man was the fourth part of a Years pay, unless he were a Captain or some other eminent Commander, or that he was taken in a just Fight, or at the storming of a Town, as *Mariana* testifies. *Plutarch* records it of the Corinthians and the Megarenses, *That the War between them was prosecuted mildly, and as it became Neighbours and Kinsmen.* If any man were taken Prisoner, he that took him entertained him as his guest, and taking his word for his ransom dismist him friendly: whence arose the name Δορύξενος, for one that by the courteous usage of his Enemy taken in the War, makes him his friend. But much more magnanimous was that of *Pyrrhus*, so highly extolled by *Cicero*: *Lib. 27. c. 18.* *Quest. Græc.*

> *No wealth I ask, nor ransome will I take,*
> *'Tis Steel, not Gold that must the Victor make:*
> *Yet, whoso after Fight shall chance to live,*
> *To him his liberty I'll freely give.*

Pyrrhus thought no doubt that his cause was good; but yet he was content to restore them to liberty, whom some probable reason had induced to fight against him. The like fact of *Cyrus*, *Xenophon* highly commends: As *Polybius* doth that of King *Philip*: And *Curtius* that of *Alexander*: *Plutarch* also records the same of King *Ptolomy*, and of *Deme-* *Cyropæd. l. 2.* *Vit. Demetr.*

trius, that they strove whether of them should excel, not so much in Arms, as in clemency and benignity towards the vanquished. And *Dromichates* King of the *Getes*, having taken *Lysimachus* Prisoner in War, entertained him friendly as his Guest; and understanding by the King how poorly, and yet how obligingly the Getick Nations lived, he chose ever after rather to make them his Friends than his Enemies.

Strabo l. 7.

CHAP. XV.

Moderation in the acquiring of Empire.

I. *How far internal justice permits the acquiring of Empire.*
II. *That by this Right to spare the Conquered is laudable:*
III. *Either by mixing the Conquered amongst the Conquerours:*
IV. *Or by leaving them under their Government, who before had it.*
V. *Yet sometimes placing Garrisons amongst them.*
VI. *Or by imposing on them tributes and such like charges.*
VII. *The benefit that ariseth from such moderation.*
VIII. *Examples, and of the change of Government over such as are conquered.*
IX. *The Empire though gained, yet some part thereof ought to be left to the vanquished:*
X. *Or at least some kind of liberty:*
XI. *Especially in matters that concern Religion.*
XII. *At least the vanquished are to be treated with much clemency: and why.*

I. How far Empire may be gained by internal justice.

WHAT in equity is requisite, or in humanity commendable, being done to single persons, is so much more being done to a Nation or any parts of it; by how much the good or evil that is done to a multitude, is more notorious than the same done to particular men. Surely by a just War, as other things, so also the Right of soveraignty over the people, and the very Right that the people have in the Government may be lawfully acquired; that is to say, so far as the greatness either of the punishment due to their crime, or of some other debt doth warrant it. Whereunto we may add so far as is necessary to secure the Conquerour from some great and imminent danger that otherwise may befall him. But this Cause is for the most part mixed with others, which notwithstanding as well in making of peace, as in prosecuting the Victory is principally aimed at. For in the other cases that the Conquerour remits the punishment or debt, it is from his mercy. But that security which in publick dangers exceeds moderation is cruelty. Thus doth *Isocrates* advise *Philip*, *It will suffice thee so far to subdue the Barbarians, that thou mayest secure the Peace of thine own Country.*

II. To abstain from it, commendable. *Jugurth.* *De Rep. l. 7. c. 14, 15.& c.10.* *De Off. l. 1.*

That which *Salust* records of the Ancient Romans is worthy of our imitation, namely, that they were so Religious, *That they they took nothing away from the conquered, but the licence they took to do them wrong.* And in another place he tells us, *That wise men make War for Peace sake, and sustain labour in hopes of rest*; Sapientes pacis causa Bellum gerunt, & laborem spe otii sustentant. Not much discrepant is that of *Aristotle*, *The end of War is Peace, as the End of Motion is rest.* To the same purpose is that notable saying of *Cicero*, *Bellum ita suscipiatur, ut nihil aliud nisi Pax quæsita videatur*; *War should be so made, as if nothing else were thereby intended but Peace.* And in another place, *War should be undertaken for this cause only, that we may live in Peace and not be injured.* Nor is this much different from what our Christian Divines teach us, *The end*, say they, *of War is to remove those things that disturb Peace.* Before *Ninus* his Raign, Kings were studious to preserve the bounds of their own Empires, but not to enlarge them. Thus *Alexander* wrote to *Artaxerxes* the Persian, *Manendum cuique intra fines suos nihil novando*; *Every King ought to confine himself within his own Dominions, and not encroach upon anothers; neither should any man, out of an uncertain hope invade the right of another, but rest contented with his own.* All Kingdoms were at first limited with their own bounds, neither were Kings so Ambitious of Empire to themselves, as of glory to their People; and if they did make War it was not for Dominion, but for the honour of the Conquest. Now unto this Ancient Custome it is, that St. *Aug.* laboured as much as in him lay to reduce us, *Let Princes* (saith he) *consider, that it belongs not to good Kings to take pride in the enlargeing their Dominions*; for as he there adds, *Major est fœlicitas vicinum habere concordem, quam malum subjugare bellantem*; *It is greater happiness to have a good Neighbour that is peaceable, than to subdue a bad one that is troublesome.* Upon which account it was that St. *Cyril* commends the Hebrew Kings who always contented themselves

De Civit. Dei l. 4. c. 15.

Lib. 5. cont. Julian.

ſelves with their own bounds, without encroaching on their Neighbours; which was the very ſin for which the Prophet *Amos* did ſo ſeverely reprove the Ammonites.

III. Which may be done either by intermixing the Conquerors with the Conquered;

Neareſt unto this original draught of innocence, comes that prudent moderation uſed by the old Romans: *What*, ſaith *Seneca* *, *had our Empire been, had not a wholeſome providence taught us to intermix the Conquered with the Conquerours? Our great founder* Romulus, as *Claudius* in *Tacitus* tells us †, *did ſo prevail by his wiſdom, that many people, whom the riſing Sun ſaw His Enemies, the ſetting Sun ſaw his Subjects and Citizens.* Neither was there any thing that did more ruine the Lacedemonians and the Athenians than this, That they always drove away the vanquiſhed as Strangers. *Livy* informs us that the Commonwealth of *Rome* was much augmented by the reception of the Conquered into their City, whereof Hiſtories afford us plenty of examples: As of the Sabines, the Albanes, the Latines, and ſo of the reſt of the Italian Nation; till at length *Cæſar* firſt led the Gaules in triumph, and afterwards admitted them to be of his Court and Council. *Cerialis* in *Tacitus* thus beſpeaks the Gauls, *Ye your ſelves are uſually admitted to command our Legions; Ye are they that govern not this only, but others of our Provinces, there are no places of truſt from which ye are excluded; wherefore* (as he there infers) *ye ought in all reaſon to endeavour all you can to preſerve that life and Peace; which ye, though vanquiſhed, do equally enjoy with us the Victors.* Nay, which is yet more admirable by the decree of the Emperour *Antoninus*, all that lived within the Circle of the Roman Empire were made Citizens of *Rome*, which are the very words of *Ulpian*: whereupon *Rome* was then accounted, as *Modeſtinus* affirms, *Communis Patria*; *The common City*, or every mans Country. Whereof *Claudius* thus,

* *Lib. de Ira c.* 34.
† *Annal. l.* 5.
Lib. 1.

> *Hujus pacificis debemus moribus omnes,*
> *Quod cuncti gens una ſumus.*

> To th' honour of this Prince it may be ſaid,
> That of the World he but one Nation made.

IV. Or by leaving the Government to the vanquiſhed.

Another kind of moderation uſed in Victory, is when the Government is left in the ſame hands, either of King or People who hold it before the Conqueſt. Thus *Hercules* beſpeaks King *Priamus*,

Sen. Troad.

> *Hoſtis parvi victus lacrymis,*
> *Suſcipe dixit, rector habenas,*
> *Patrioque ſede celſus ſolio:*
> *Sed ſceptra fide meliore tene.*

> By a weak Enemies tears ore'tane,
> Take, ſaith he, thy Crown again,
> Aſcend thy Fathers Throne on high:
> But henceforth rule more moderately.

So alſo the ſame *Hercules*, having conquered *Neleus*, gave his Kingdom to *Neſtor* his Son. Thus the Perſian Kings were wont to leave their Kingdoms to the Kings whom they had conquered, contenting themſelves with the bare Victory. Thus did *Cyrus* to *Armenius*, *Alexander* to *Porus*. And this is it that *Seneca* highly commends in a Conquerour, *Nihil ex rege victo præter gloriam ſumere*; *To take nothing from the Conquered beſides the honour of the Conqueſt. This is triumph over Victory it ſelf; and to declare that there was nothing to be found among the Conquered worthy of the Conquerours acceptance, but the Conqueſt it ſelf.* Thus *Pompey* having overcome *Tigranes*, left him a part of his Kingdom to govern, as *Eutropius* informs us. And herein is *Antigonus* extold by *Polybius*, That having brought *Sparta* under his abſolute power, he gave the Citizens *the free uſe of both their Ancient Laws and Liberties*; for which Act his praiſes were highly celebrated throughout all *Greece*. Thus did the Romans give unto the Cappadocians whom they had conquered, a power to uſe what form of Government they pleaſed; and many Nations we may read of, which being Conquered, were notwithſtanding left free. Thus was *Carthage* left at liberty *to live under their own Laws*, as the Rhodians pleaded to the Romans after the ſecond Punick War. And when the *Ætolians* told *Quintius*, that there could be no firm Peace until *Philip* of *Macedon* were driven out of his Kingdom: He anſwered, That they were too ſevere in their cenſures, as being unmindful of the common cuſtome of the Romans; who for the moſt part ſpared thoſe whom they had in their power, adding this withal, *Adverſus victos mitiſſimum quemque maximum animum habere*; *That he who was mildeſt towards the Conquered was ever held moſt magnanimous.*

De Clem. lib. 1. *c.* 21.
Lib. 6.
Livy lib 33.

Sometimes

V. Sometimes by keeping of Garisons. Sometimes though the Empire be reſtored, yet the Conquerours ſecurity is alſo provided for. Thus it was ordained by *Quintius*, That the City of *Corinth* ſhould be reſtored to the Achaians; but withal; That there ſhould be left a Gariſon in *Acrocorinth*, which alſo was afterwards withdrawn; and that *Chalcides* and *Demetriades* ſhould be detained, until all fear concerning *Antiochus* ſhould ceaſe.

IV. Sometimes by impoſing Tribute. The impoſition of Tribute is oft-times, not only for the defraying the charges of a War but, for the mutual ſecurity of both the Conquerour and the Conquered for the time to come. *Cicero*, in his Epiſtle to his Brother *Quintus* concerning the Grecians *, writes thus, *Let* Aſia *alſo conſider, That unleſs She be ſecured by the Roman Power, She can never be without a Foreign War, or Domeſtick Broils: And ſince this Power that ſecures her cannot poſſibly ſubſiſt without Tribute, good reaſon it is that She ſhould be contented, with ſome part of her wealth, to purchaſe to herſelf perpetual Peace.* Thus doth *Petilius Cerealis* in *Tacitus* plead for the Romans, with the *Langres* and other Gauls, *We*, ſay they, *though often provoked, yet by the Right of Conqueſt do offer unto you one only Condition of Peace, namely, That ye pay your Tribute.* For *Peace among Nations cannot be defended without Armes, nor Armes without Pay, nor can we pay our Souldiers without Contributions.* Hereunto likewiſe we may refer thoſe other things mentioned before, where we diſcourſed concerning unequal Laws, as the Delivery of Armes, of Fleets, of Elephants, the prohibiting the uſe of Weapons, the raiſing of Armies, and ſuch like, whereby the Conquerour may be ſecured.

* *Lib.* 1. *ad Quintum Fratrem. Epiſt.* 1.
Hiſt. l. 4.
Lib. 2. *c.* 15. § 7.

VII. What profit ariſeth from this Moderation. But that the Conquerour ſhould leave the Conquered poſſeſt of his own Kingdom, ſtands not with humanity only, but ſometimes with policy. Among *Numa*'s Laws this is commended for one, That in thoſe Sacred Rites wherewith they worſhipped their God *Terminus*, he would have no bloud ſpilt; thereby intimating, That nothing could more conduce to a laſting Peace between Neighbour Princes, than to content to live themſelves within their own Bounds. It was very well ſaid of *Florus*, *Difficilius eſt Provincias obtinere, quam facere; viribus parantur, jure retinentur: It is much more difficult to keep Provinces, than to make them; for they may be gained by force, but they muſt be kept by juſtice.* Not much unlike is that of *Livy*, *Facilius parari ſingula quàm teneri univerſa; Particulars are more eaſily gained than Univerſals kept.* Nor that of *Auguſtus* in *Plutarch*, *It is better to govern our own well, than to be poſſeſt of a greater Empire.* Whereunto we may add that Saying of *Darius*'s Ambaſſadour to *Alexander*, *A foreign Empire is full of danger: Thou wilt find it very difficult to hold what thou canſt not graſp: Some things may be eaſily gained, yet not ſo eaſily kept. How ready are our hands to catch at that, which when they have, they cannot hold?* Which *Calanus* the Indian, and before him *Oebarus*, *Cyrus*'s Friend, did very well emblem out by a dryed Oxe's Hide, which being preſt down with our feet on the one ſide, riſeth inſtantly on the other. And *Titus Quintius* in *Livy* by a Tortoiſe, who whilſt he gathers himſelf up within his Shell is ſafe, but as ſoon as he thruſts out any one part he is expoſed to danger. *Plutarch* thus relates, That when the Achaians conſulted about the taking of the Iſland *Zant*, he diſſwading from it, told them, That it was a dangerous attempt, if like the Tortoiſe they thruſt their head beyond *Peloponneſus*. And herein is that of old *Heſiod* verified, which *Plato* likewiſe thus applies, *Dimidium plus toto*, That ſometimes *it is better to take up with the one half, than to covet the whole.* When ſome Nations, as *Appian* notes, would willingly have annexed themſelves to the Roman Empire, they were refuſed: And over other Nations they thought it fitter to appoint Kings, than to unite themſelves as Provinces. And in the judgment of *Scipio Africanus*, the Roman Empire was in his time of ſo large an extent, that as to effect more might well be thought greedineſs; ſo if they could but keep what they had, they might be abundantly happy. Wherefore that Prayer, whereby in their ſolemn purgations they invoked the Gods to proſper and enlarge their Empire, he ſo changed, that he prayed only, That they would preſerve it in perpetual peace and ſafety: which the Emperour *Auguſtus* thought worthy his imitation; and is therefore commended by *Dion*, for that he did never attempt any new Conqueſt, eſteeming that which he had already got to be ſufficient.

Plut. Quæſt. Rom. qu. 15.
Lib. 37.
Plut. vit. Alex.
Lib. 27.
Val. Max. 4. 1.
Plato de Leg. 3.

VIII. Examples of the change of Government among the Conquered. The Lacedemonians, yea and the Athenians alſo, in their Golden Age, never challenged the Sovereign Power over any City that they took by War; only they required that they ſhould mould their Government according to their own Form. For the Lacedemonians uſed an Ariſtocratical Government, wherein a few of the beſt governed the reſt. But the Athenians uſed a Democratical, whereby the Government was wholly ſetled in the People; as *Thucydides*, *Iſocrates*, and *Demoſthenes* teach us. Nay *Ariſtotle* himſelf confirms as much in ſeveral places. *Tacitus* records the like done by *Artabanus* at *Seleucia* *, *Who aſſigned the Government of the Common People to the Noble-men, according to his own uſe and cuſtom: For he judged it the next way to Liberty to leave it in the People, as to leave it in a few was the next way to Tyranny.* But whether theſe alterations in Government do conduce any thing to the ſecurity of the Conquerour, is not our purpoſe in this place to determine.

Lib. 4. *de Rep. cap.* 11. *lib.* 5. *cap.* 7.
* *Ann.* 6.

But

IX. *If the Empire be assumed, to leave some part thereof to the Conquered;*

But in case it be not thought safe for the Conquerour to leave the Conquered altogether free, yet may the matter be so moderated, that some part of the Government may be left to them, or their King, with a reservation of some other part to the Conquerour. *Tacitus* tells us, That it was the manner of the Romans to make use of Kings themselves as Instruments of subjection. *Antiochus* is said to be, *Romanis inservientium Regum ditissimus, The richest of all the Kings that were subject to the Romans.* The like we read in the Commentaries upon *Musonius*, namely, Of some Kings that were subject to the Romans. So in *Lucan,*

Atque omnis Latio quæ servit purpura Ferro.

And every King whom *Rome*'s vast Power commands.

Thus did the Scepter continue amongst the Jews in the Sanhedrim after *Archelaus*'s confiscation. And *Evagoras* King of *Cyrus* (as *Diodorus* testifies) told the King of *Persia, That he would obey him, but as one King obeyed another.* And when *Darius* was overcome, *Alexander* was willing to restore him to his Kingdom, but upon this Condition, That he might command others, but obey him only. Such Kings there were also antiently in *Italy*, who though they ruled others, yet were themselves subject to other Kings. So in *Æschylus* we read, That among the Persians, there were, *Reges, Regis magni subices*; *Petty Kings, that were subject to the Great Kings*: As there are now also among the Turks. Now as concerning the manner how an Empire may be mixt, we have already treated; but sometimes a part of a Kingdom being taken away, the rest is left to the Conquered, as is usual after the Conquest to take away some part of the Fields, and to leave another part to the ancient Occupants.

Lib. 15. *Lib. 17.* *Leunclav. lib. 18.* *Lib. 1. c. 3. § 17.* *Lib. 3. c. 8. § 3.*

X. *Or at least some liberty;*

Yet when the Conquered are altogether deprived of their Empire, may there be left unto them power over their private Estates, and some smaller things that are publick; as their own Laws, Customs and Magistrates. Thus *Philo* in his Embassy to *Caius* saith, *That* Augustus *was no less careful to preserve the Laws peculiar to every Nation, than to preserve the Laws proper to the Romans.* So we read also in *Pliny*, That in *Bithynia*, being a Proconsulary Province, the City *Apimæa* retained this priviledge, That they governed their Commonwealth at their own pleasure. And in another place he tells us, That it was granted them that they might chuse their own Magistrates, and their own Senate. The City *Sinope*, though under the Persian Monarchy, was yet permitted to live under a popular Government; as *Appianus* testifies. Such another shadow of liberty the Grecians enjoyed under the Romans. And *Cicero* confesseth, That though the Romans had conquered *Cyprus*, yet it was not lawful for the Romans to call the Cypriots out of their own Island. So likewise in *Pontus*, The City of *Amisenes*, by the favour of *Lucullus*, retained the use of their own Laws. And the Goths, though they had conquered the Romans yet they, changed not the Roman Laws.

Lib. 10. Ep. 56. & 14. Lib. 3. Ep. 113.

XI. *Especially in Religion:*

Another favour may also without danger be granted to the vanquished, namely, The free exercise of their Religion, and not at all to withdraw them from it; unless it may be done by perswasion: which, as *Agrippa* in his Oration to the Emperour *Caius* proves, is both grateful to the Conquered, and no ways prejudicial to the Conquerour. And this was it that, as well *Josephus* himself as, the Emperour *Titus* objected against the rebellious Jews at *Hierusalem*, That through the Indulgence of the Romans they might exercise their own Religion with so great a right and freedom, that they might drive Strangers out of their Temple, even with the peril of their lives. But in case the Religion of the Conquered be false, yet may the Conquerour make it his care that the true Religion be not oppressed. As the Emperour *Constantine* did, by weakening *Licinius*'s Party; and as the Francks and other Kings did after him. And although we cannot perswade them to the worship of the true God, yet must we not drive them from the worship of their own. For, to use the words of *Severus, Melius est ibi aliquem coli Deum, quàm nullum*; *Better it is that any God be there worshipped, than none at all.* Thus the Goths in *Procopius* profess, That they would not compel any man to embrace their Religion, but leave them to their own.

XII. *At least to use the Conquered gently, and why.*

The last Premonition is this, That where the Empire is fully and absolutely got, the Vanquished should be treated with much kindness and clemency, and so as may stand with the mutual good both of the Conquerour and Conquered. *Cyrus* in *Xenophon* bids the Assyrians, whom he had overcome, to be of good cheer, for their condition should be the same as before; for they should only change their King, but their Houses, Fields, Wives, Children, *&c.* should as fully remain theirs, as they were before. And if any man should wrong either them or theirs, he and his would revenge their injuries. We read in *Salust*, *That the Romans always sought to ingage men as their friends, rather than as their Slaves; thinking themselves more safe in a free than in a compulsory obedience.* Thus we read

read of the Lacedemonians in *Thucydides*, *We*, say they, *are of opinion*, *That our worst Enemies may thus be made our best Friends*, *not if the one Party thirsting only for revenge*, *and abusing his good fortune*, *shall endeavour to bind the other Party by Oaths*, *to Conditions manifestly unequal*; *but if (though he may so do) he shew no less equity in conquering his own passions*, *than he did courage and conduct in conquering his Enemies*; *using his Victory with as much moderation as may stand with his own security*. The Britains in *Tacitus*'s days did readily make their Levies, pay their Tributes, and perform all Duties enjoined them by the Romans, so long as they were not provoked by manifest injuries; but such they bare very impatiently, *Jam domiti ut parerent*, *nondum ut servirent*; *Being already so far conquered as to be Subjects*, *but not so far as yet*, *as to be Slaves*. That *Pincernas* in *Livy*, who was asked in the Roman Senate, What manner of Peace it was that the Romans might expect from him? answered readily, *Si bonam dederitis*, *& fidam & perpetuam*; *si malam*, *haud diturnam*: *If on reasonable Conditions*, *that which is firm and lasting*; *if otherwise*, *not very durable*. Adding this Reason, *No Nation*, *and indeed no man*, *will remain longer in such a Condition whereof he repents that he is fallen into*, *than necessity shall inforce him*. So *Camillus* was wont to say, *That was the most lasting Empire under which the Subjects rejoyced*. Thus the Scythians answered *Alexander*, *Between the Lord and his Slave there can be no true friendship*; *for though they live in peace*, *yet there still remains some Rights of War*. Thus likewise *Hermocrates* in *Diodorus*, *To overcome is not so glorious as to use the Victory with clemency and moderation*. Whereunto we may refer that excellent Saying in *Tacitus*, *Bellorum egregii fines*, *quoties ignoscendo transigitur*; *The effects of those Wars are notable which are shut up with a General Pardon*. For as *Cæsar* observes, *Hæc nova sit vincendi ratio*, *ut misericordia & liberalitate nos muniamus*; *This is a new way of conquering*, *when we secure our selves by our acts of mercy and liberality*.

Vit. Agr. — *Lib. 8.* — *Curt. lib. 9.* — *Lib. 13.*

CHAP. XVI.

Moderation concerning such things as by the Law of Nations want the benefit of Postliminy.

I. Things taken in an unjust War ought to be restored.

HOW far forth in a Just War things taken away may be his that takes them, hath been already declared; from which are to be deducted such things as are received by the Right of Postliminy: for these are as if they had not been taken. But the things taken in an unjust War (as we have said before) are to be restored, not only by those that took them, but by others also unto whomsoever they shall by any means come. *Nemo plus Juris ad alium transferre potest*, *quam ipse habuit*; *No man can transfer more Right to another than he hath himself*; say the first Founders of the Roman Laws, which *Seneca* thus briefly explains, *Nemo potest dare quod non habet*, *No man can give what he hath not*. But he that first took them had no internal Right or Property in them; wherefore neither shall he have any that hath no Title to them, but what he derives from him. Now that Dominion which the second or the third Occupant hath gained, we call external; that is, such an advantage that he is every where to be defended in it, by all judiciary Power and Authority, as if he were the first Owner. But yet, if he plead this Right against him, from whom the thing was at first unjustly taken, he deals not honestly. For look what Answer some eminent Lawyers have given concerning a Servant, who being first taken by Robbers did afterwards escape unto the Enemy, namely, That it was true that he was taken away, neither was his having been amongst Enemies, nor that he did return back by Postliminy, any impediment unto him as to that thing. The very same Answer from the Law of Nature may serve concerning him who being taken in an unjust War, and afterwards either in a just War, or by some other means, comes under the power of another. For, as to that which we here call internal Right, there is no difference between an unjust War, and Piracy or Robbery. And according to this opinion did *Gregorius Neocæsariensis* frame his Answer, being consulted with concerning the Goods of some of his Citizens, which after they had been taken away by the Barbarians, were received by some of the Inhabitants of *Pontus*.

Lib. 5. de Benef. — *L. Latrones. D. de Captivis.* — *Ægid. Regius de Act. supern. dist. 31. dub. 7. n. 122.* — *Can. 10.*

Wherefore

II. Examples.

Wherefore things so taken ought in honesty and conscience to be restored to their first Owners, as being unjustly taken away, which we see frequently done. *Livy* having declared how the *Volsci* and *Æqui* had been conquered by *Lucius Lucretius Truipitinus*, saith, That the spoil was brought and exposed to publick view in the Field of *Mars*, that every man might within the space of three days find out his own, and take it away. The same *Livy* in another place, having related the Victory got over the *Volsci* by the Dictator *Posthumius*, tells us, That *he restored a part of the spoil to such as knew their own, of another part whereof he made Portsale*: And elsewhere he tells us, *That two days were allowed for every man to come in, and to lay claim to his own Goods.* And in another place, *Having recited the joyful Victory which the Samnites got over the Campanes, wherein there were taken seven thousand four hundred of them Prisoners, and a very great Booty from their Associates.* He likewise tells us, That *the right Owners were summoned by Proclamation to come in by a certain day, to find out and receive back their own Goods.* The like fact he records of the Romans, For *the Samnites, endeavouring to possess themselves of* Interamna, *a Colony of the Romans, but not able to keep it, having plundered the City and depopulated the Country, and driving away before them an infinite number of Men, Cattel, and other things; fell unexpectedly into the hands of the Roman Consul in his return from* Luceria, *who recovering the spoil, and pursuing the Samnites with great Slaughter, at last exposed all he had got to open view, sending out his Edict, That every man might come in and receive his own.* The same Authour speaking of the Prey taken by *Cornelius Scipio* at *Ilippa*, a City in *Portugal*, saith, *All which being exposed to view before the City, every man had leave granted to search out and take away what was his own; the rest was delivered to the Questor to make sale of; which was presently done, and the money divided among the Souldiers.* So again, after the Battel fought by *Titus Gracchus* at *Beneventum*, *The whole Prey, except the Prisoners, was divided among the Souldiers; but the Cattel were preserved, which the right Owners had liberty given them within thirty days to find out and to recover.* The like doth *Polybius* record of *L. Æmilius, Who having conquered the Gauls, restored all the spoil to them from whom it had been taken.* The very same doth *Plutarch*, *Appian* and *Diodorus* testifie of *Scipio* the African, who having taken *Carthage*, refunded their many rich Presents which the Carthaginians had taken from the Cities of *Sicily*, and elsewhere, and brought thither: With whom agrees *Valerius Maximus* concerning the same *Scipio*, *Whose humanity*, saith he, *was such, that having taken* Carthage *he sent Letters to all the Cities of* Sicily, *That they might by their Ambassadours receive back all the Ornaments of their several Churches, which the Carthaginians had taken from them; which he desired them to take care of, and to set them up in their former stations.* The like testimony doth *Cicero* give of him, *The Carthaginians*, saith he, *did formerly possess themselves of* Himera, *one of the beautifullest and best adorned Towns in* Sicily; Scipio *esteeming it an act worthy of the Roman People, took care that, the War being ended, and* Carthage *taken, all the ancient Ornaments taken at any time from the Sicilians should be restored unto them.* Thus did the Rhodians restore four Ships to the Athenians, which they had recovered from the Macedonians, who had formerly unjustly taken them from the Athenians. So likewise *Peneas* the Ætolian, as *Livy* records it, thought it fit that all that before the War began had been the Ætolians, should be restored unto them: which *Titus Quintius* did not deny, had the demand been only of Cities taken in War, and had not the Ætolians first broken the Laws of friendship. Nay even those Goods that were at first consecrated to the Temple at *Ephesus*, which afterwards their Kings made their own, the Romans caused to be restored to their former condition.

Lib. 3. *Lib.* 10. *Lib.* 24. *Hist l.* 2. *Plut. Apotheg. Appian Puni. Lib.* 1. *c.* 1. *n.* 6. *Orat. Ver. Lib.* 31. *Lib.* 31. *Lib.* 33. *Strab. l.* 13.

III. Whether any thing may be deducted.

But what if such Goods so taken shall come unto us by way of Commerce, may we not charge him from whom they were taken with so much as they cost us? We may, as we have already said *, so far forth as the recovery of the possession of things so desperately lost, would probably have cost him from whom they were taken. And if the charges may be required of him, why may not our labour and peril also be valued, as if a man should recover some precious Jewel of another mans out of the Sea, by diving unto the bottom? Very pertinent unto this is the Story of *Abraham*'s return from the Conquest of the five Kings, *Reduxit omnes illas res, He brought back all those things*, saith *Moses* (*i. e.*) which the Kings had taken away. Neither can we refer that Offer which the King of *Sodome* made unto *Abraham*, of restoring the men, and detaining the Goods to himself, to any other cause than this, That those Goods should be the reward of his pains and peril. But that *Abraham* refused to take any thing to himself of the Prey, was an Argument of his, no less piety than, magnanimity; which was very well observed by *Jacchiades* on the fifth Chapter of *Daniel*. Nevertheless, of the things so recovered, he gave the tenth to God, as being due to himself by the reason of his necessary charges, and some portion thereof he was willing should be given to his Companions. St *Ambrose*, speaking of this generous fact of *Abraham*, saith, *The reward which he refused from men he received from God.* And *Sulpitius* speaking of the rest of the spoil, saith. *That* Abraham *restored it to those from whom it was taken.* Not much inferior to this of *Abraham*'s was that Heroick Act of

* *Lib.* 2. *c.* 10. § 9. Gen. 13. 16. Vers. 20, 21, 22, 23, 24. Dan. 5. 17.

Lib.6.c.5.n.1. See above Book 2. Chap. 14. Sect. 6. Book 3. Chap. 4. Sect. 1.

Pittacus the Mytilenean, recorded by *Valerius Maximus*, *Who being offered by the general consent of his Country-men the one half of the Land taken from the Athenians for his good conduct, utterly refused it; accounting it a dishonour to sully the Glory of his Victory, by receiving so large a part of the spoil.*

IV. The people or any part of them, to be restored, if unjustly possest. * Liv. lib. 2. —— lib. 73. Xenoph. Hist. Græc. lib. 3. † See above Ch. 10. Sect. 6. * Liv. lib. 34.

As things taken in an unjust War are to be restored to their right Owners, so a people or any part of a people ought to be restored to him or them who had the Right of Government over them, or even to themselves, if before any unjust force was used against them, they were a free people. Thus we read of the exiled Saguntines, That after six Years they were restored by the Romans *. So *Anthony* in the War of *Cassius* set at liberty all those that were made Bondmen, and commanded their Goods to be restored unto them. Thus also was *Calatravia* restored by the King of *Castile* and others to the Souldiers, from whom the Moors had before taken it †. And so also was *Sutrium* taken and restored in *Camillus*'s time, as *Livy* testifies *. The *Æginetæ* and *Melii* were likewise restored to their Cities by the Lacedemoniaes. The Cities of *Greece*, which had been subdued by the Macedonians, were set at liberty by *Flaminius*; who in the Treaty he had with *Antiochus*'s Ambassadour, insisted on this as a Point of Equity, That the Asian Cities, which were called by Greek Names, should be restored to their liberty; which *Seleucus*, the Great Grandfather of *Antiochus*, had taken by force, and which afterwards, being lost, were re-taken by the same *Antiochus*: *For*, saith he, *those Grecian Colonies were not sent into* Æolia *and* Ionia *to be enslaved by the King; but for the encrease of the Greek Race, and to propagate that ancient Nation throughout the World.*

V. In what time the obligation to restitution ceaseth.

It is sometimes questioned, How long a time is required before this Obligation to restitution ceaseth? But this Question, if it happen to arise between Subjects of the same Empire, is best determined by their own Laws; that is, in case those Laws will admit of this Internal Right, and not of that only which is External: which by a prudent inspection into the words and purpose of those Laws may be collected. But in case it be between such as are Strangers to each other, then it must be determined by a sole conjecture of the former Owners dereliction, whereof we have sufficiently spoken as far as is fit for our purpose.

Lib. 2. c. 4.

VI. What if the Right of War be dubious. * Mariana lib. 29. c. 14.

But if the Right of War be very ambiguous, it is best to follow the Advice of *Aratus* the Sicyonian (as King *Ferdinando* did *) who in part perswaded the new Occupants to accept of present money, and to yield up their possessions; and in part perswaded the ancient Lords to accept of the value of their Lands, rather than to hazard the recovery of them.

CHAP.

CHAP. XVII.

Of Neuters in War.

I. *From Neuters nothing is to be taken away, but in extreme necessity; nor then without restoring the full value.*
II. *Examples and Precepts of such abstinence.*
III. *What the Duty of Neuters are to such as are at War.*

Though it may seem impertinent here to treat of such as are not concerned in War, because against these it is plain, That War hath no Right at all; yet seeing that many outrages are committed, and many injuries done against such, if Borderers, (by reason of the War) upon pretence of necessity; it will not be much amiss briefly to repeat here what hath elsewhere been delivered more at large *. In the first place therefore we must remember, That it is required that that necessity that gives us a kind of Right to that which is properly anothers, must be extreme; Secondly, That there be not a like necessity in the right Owner of the thing; Thirdly, If there be such an extreme necessity, it is plain that we ought to take no more than what our present necessity requires. As for example, If the bare custody be sufficient, we ought to forbear the use; if the use be necessary, we ought to forbear the abuse; if the abuse be necessary, we ought to give the full value of it to the right Owners. I. From Neuters nothing must be taken but upon pure necessity. * Book 2. Ch. 11. Sect. 10.

Moses being necessitated to pass with his Israelites through *Idumaea*, promises first to pass only through their High-ways, and not to hurt either their Fields or Vineyards; and in case they should want water, they would pay for it. Those famous Generals, both of the Greeks and Romans, did the same. The Greeks in *Xenophon* under *Clearchus* promise the Persians, That in passing through their Country they would offend no man. And if they might be supplied with necessaries for their money, they would not forceably take either Meat or Drink from any man. Thus did *Dercyllides pass with his Army through Countries that were quiet, without offence given to the Provincials.* *Livy* testifies the same of King *Perseus, That he passed into his own Dominions through* Phthiotis, Achaia *and* Thessaly, *without any damage or injury done to the Country through which he past.* The self same doth *Plutarch* testifie concerning the passage of the Army led by *Agis* the Spartan into *Peloponnesus, It was a pleasant Spectacle*, saith he, *to all the Cities of* Greece *to see how civilly and inoffensively they marched, and almost without noise.* The like Testimony doth he give to *Titus Quintius Flaminius.* Thus *Vellejus* writes of *Sylla, That he led his Army through* Calabria *and* Apulia *into* Campania, *so orderly, and with such singular care of their Fruits, Fields, Cities and People, as if he had come into* Italy, *not as one meditating revenge, but as a Peace-maker.* *Tully* speaking of the Great *Pompey*, saith thus, *Whose Legions came into* Asia *so inoffensively, that neither the hands of so great a multitude, nor the print of their feet, were observed to hurt any that lived peaceably.* And understanding that some of his Souldiers had misbehaved themselves in their March, *Sigillum Gladiis eorum imposuit, quod qui non custodisset, is puniebatur; He sealed up their Swords in their Scabbards, which Seal whosoever brake was severely punished.* *Frontinus* thus testifies of *Domitian, That being about to raise new Forts and Castles upon the Frontiers of the* Ubii, *he caused all the Fruits growing within the places which he intended to intrench, to be first apprized and paid for, and thereby got himself so great a fame for his Justice, that every man was willing to trust him.* So likewise *Lampridius* concerning the Parthian Expedition of *Alexander Severus*, tells us, *That his Army was so well disciplined, and bore so great a reverence to his Person, that they seemed rather Senators than Souldiers. For the Tribunes were so ready, the Captains so modest, and the Souldiers themselves so friendly, that the Country-people wheresoever he came, for those many and great benefits they received from him, honoured him as a God.* The Panegyrist, speaking of the Goths, Vandals and Alanes that served under the Emperour *Theodosius*, saith, *That in that Army there were no such tumults, nor such confusions, nor such robberies committed, as were among the Barbarians; but if at any time there happened to be a scarcity of provision, they sustained it patiently, lessening every mans* dimensum *or proportion, as either their numbers encreased, or their Stores decreased*; which very praise *Claudian* gives unto *Stilico*: II. Examples of abstinence, and some Precepts. Xenophon. Lib. 2. Pro Lege Manilia. Plut. Pomp. Lib. 2. Strat. c. 2.

> *Tanta quies, tantúsque metus, Servator honesti,*
> *Te moderante fuit, nullis ut Vinea furtis*
> *Aut seges erepta fraudaret Messe Colonum.*

The Army thou in so much awe didst leave,
That no mans Vineyard was of Fruits bereav'd,
Nor Farmer of his Harvest hopes deceived.

Concerning the singular modesty of the Goths in their Wars, we find many rare testimonies in *Cassiodore*, but especially in the twenty fifth Epistle of the eleventh Book, where he brings in the Emperour giving his charge to his Souldiers, *Ye shall destroy neither the Corn nor the Meadows in your march towards us; but ye shall hasten hither without giving offence to any, that so your access unto us may be acceptable, who for this very reason do freely undergo the whole charge of the War, that so you may preserve the reputation ye have gained by your civility, unblemished.* The like testimony doth *Suidas* give of *Belisarius*, whose admirable Discipline is so celebrated by *Procopius* (as being both his Companion in Arms, and a witness and strict observer of all his Actions) whose excellent speech to his Souldiers, as they were marching into *Africk*, is worthily recorded by *Procopius* in the first of his Vandal Wars. But that which he records of him in the third of his Gothicks, deserves to be here inserted, whose words sound to this sence, *So great was his care of Husbandmen, that no violence was at any time offered unto them, whilst* Belisarius *was their General; but on the contrary, the Provincials grew rich whithersoever he came with his Legions; for they sold them necessaries at their own Rates, and when the Corn grew ripe, his care was doubled, that the Horse-men should not spoil it, nor were any of his Souldiers permitted to pluck so much as an apple from the trees.* The like Discipline *Gregoras* extols among the Venetians, *Where justice and magnanimity seemed to contend for mastery, no man being permitted to straggle from the Army, or to take away any thing but what he bought with his money*: which might easily be done where there was plenty of Provision, the Army well paid, and a strict Discipline constantly observed, whose principal Law is, *That the Countries with whom we have Peace should not be wasted.* *Wherefore,* saith *Pliny* *, *did the Roman Generals make it their greatest care in their Wars that there should be freedom of commerce?* Whereunto *Cassiodore* gives this answer †, *Ut habeat miles quod emat, ne cogatur cogitare quod auferat; That what the Souldier wants he may buy, which otherwise he should be enforced to steal.* *Vopiscus* brings in the Emperour *Aurelian* giving this charge to his Souldiers *, *Nemo pullum alienum rapiat; Let none of you presume to take away a Chicken or a Sheep of another mans; let none of you presume to trample down the Corn, to pluck a Grape, or forceably to require from any man either Oyl, Salt, or Wood, &c.* So likewise in *Cassiodore*, *Vivant cum Provincialibus, jure civili; nec insolescat animus qui se sentit armatum: Let the Souldiers live with the Provincials according to the rules of the Civil Law; neither let them grow insolent because they know themselves to be armed, for the shields of our Army ought to protect our friends in Peace.* Apposite whereunto is that of *Xenophon*, *No City that is at Peace can be compelled to give us any thing against their will.* By all which wise precepts, we may the better understand those cautions which the great Prophet gave unto the Souldiers, who demanded of him what they should do, *Luke* 3. 14. namely, *Offer violence to no man, accuse no man falsly, and be content with your wages.* Where, by the way we may observe, that the words here translated *accuse no man*, may as well be translated (as it is elsewhere) Oppress no man, or, Defraud no man, as will appear by the Greek Version of the same word, *Job* 35. 9. and other places. And by the vulgar Latine, *Luke* 19. 8. Agreeable whereunto is that of *Aurelian* in *Vopiscus*, *Let the Souldier be content with his allowance, and let him chuse rather to enrich himself with the spoil of his Enemies, than with the tears of Strangers.* There are many excellent Penal Laws in *Gregory Turonensis* to this purpose. That of *Frederick* the first, *Gunther* thus translates,

Lib. 5. 10.
Lib. 11. *c.* 13.
Procopius.
Goth l. 3.
Lib. 9.
Ammianus. Pacatorum tellus non debet calcari.
* [illegible] *Nat. l.* 26. *c.* 4.
† *Cassiod.* 14. *c.* 13.
* *Vopis. lib.* 18. *Aurel.*
Exped. l. 6.
Luke 3. 14.
Accuse no man: for, oppress or defraud no man.
Psal. 118. 121.
Prov. 14. 33. 22. 16.
Levit. 19. 11.

Si quis pacificæ plebis villasve domosve
Usserit, abrasis signabitur ora capillis,
Et pulsus castris, post verbera multa recedet.

Who peaceful Countries waste or Houses burn,
B'ing branded in the front with Hair all shorn,
And smartly whipt, shall from the Camp be turn'd.

Neither is there any reason that any man should think that these things thus generously spoken cannot be done; for neither would so holy a man as St *John* was, advise, nor so many wise Law-makers command that which they believed to be impossible. Besides, what we have seen done, we must needs grant may be done; but that it hath been done we have already proved by many examples. Whereunto we may add that notable one of *Frontinus* (recited out of *Scaurus*) *Of an Appletree hung full with fruit, which happening*

An Appletree in a Camp.

happening to stand within the compass of ground whereon the Camp was that day pitcht, was the next day, the whole Army being gone, left with all her fruits untoucht. And that exemplary punishment taken by *Niger* on a Souldier of his, for but taking away of a Dunghil Cock, as it is related by *Spartianus*. *Livy* having declared how dissolutely *Lib.* 28.
the Roman Souldiers lived in their Camp at *Sucro*, when straggling from the Camp by Night, they robbed and pillaged the Countries round about that lived at Peace: Adds this as the Cause, That all things were done loosly and licentiously, without order or military discipline. Another notable place we find in *Livy* to this purpose, where description is made of *Philips* march through the Territories of the *Denthelatæ*, *Lib.* 40.
These (saith *Livy*) *had been* Philips *Associates, but yet the Macedonians pressed by want, wasted their Country as if it had been the frontiers of their Enemies, robbing and pillaging every where as they went, first great Houses and small Villages, afterwards laying waste some Towns, to the no little shame of the King, who from all parts heard his friends and confederates imploring in vain the Gods and him for redress.* *Pelignus* we find branded by *Tacitus* with in- *Ann.* 12.
famy, for that he did more hurt to his Friends than to his Enemies. And the Vitellian Souldiers were notorious throughout all *Italy* for their sloth and Thievery, and for this cause were only terrible to those that entertained them. And here I cannot but insert the opinion of some Divines which I conceive to be very right, namely, *Ægid. Regius de act. supernat. disp.* 31. *dub.* 7. *n.* 95.
That the King who pays not his Army, stands obliged not to the Souldiers only, but to his Subjects and Neighbours for the injuries they sustain by them, who without pay cannot live, but by rapine and plunder.

III. The duty of those that are at Peace. *Lib.* 3. *c.* 1.

On the other side, it is the duty of those that are not concerned in the War, to do nothing whereby he that foments an ill cause may be strengthened, or whereby he that moves in the defence of a good cause may be hindered, according to what hath been already said: But where the cause is doubtful, to shew themselves equally civil to both parties, whether it be by suffering them to go through their Country to pass and repass with their Legions, or by not relieving either, being closely besieged. The Corcyrenses in *Thucydides* tell the Athenians, That it concerned them if they would be thought Neuters, neither to suffer the Corinthians their Enemies, nor themselves to raise forces in *Attica*. For this, the Romans objected against *Philip*, that he had doubly violated his League with them; first, in wronging their Friends, and again, in assisting their Enemies with Men and Money. The very same objections *T. Quintius* makes in his Treaty with *Nabis*, *Thou say'st* (saith *Quintius*) *that thou hast not directly violated thy league with us: How often shall I convince thee that thou hast? I shall not use more arguments, but shall draw to this issue; By what means thinkest thou may friendship be broken? certainly by these two chiefly; if thou persecutest our Associates as thine Enemies, or joinest thy self with our Enemies against us.* *Agathias* tells us, that he is an Enemy who *Lib.* 3.
doth that which pleaseth an Enemy. And *Procopius* reckons him to be in the Enemies *Goth lib.* 1.
Army, who supplies the Army of an Enemy with things properly appertaining to War. Queen *Elizabeth* tells the Hansetowns, complaining that their priviledges were broken by her seizing of some hulks carrying warlike provisions into *Spain*, who had then open War with *England*, *That the right of neutrality is in such sort to be used, that* *Camden Ann.*
whilst we help the one we hurt not the other. And so on the contrary, as *Amalasuntha* in 1589.
Her Epistle to *Justinian* pleads, *He is a friend and companion, who though he stand not in a readiness to fight, yet readily and openly supplies us with all things requisite for War.* Of the same opinion was *Demosthenes* of old, *Qui ea facit aut machinatur quibus ego capi possim, etiamsi nec feriat, nec jaculum emittat, hostis mihi est; He that makes or contriveth such things whereby I may be taken, though he neither strikes me, nor throws a dart at me, is mine Enemy.* *M. Acilius* tells the Epirots, who though they sent no supplies of Souldiers to *Livy lib.* 36.
Antiochus, yet were accused for supplying him with money, that he knew not whether he should rank them among Neuters or Enemies. And *L. Æmilius* the Prætor re- *Lib.* 37.
proves the *Teji*, for that they had victualled the Enemies Fleet, and promised them wine; adding withal, that unless they did the like for them, they should be held as Enemies. We shall conclude with that of *Augustus Cæsar* recorded by *Plutarch*, *Pacis jus* *Plut. Brut.*
amittit Civitas, quæ hostem recipit; That City hath lost its right to Peace, that receives and protects an Enemy. It would be very commodious for us therefore, if such a League could be made with both parties engaged in War, that with their consents we might sit still as wellwishers to both; and yet, that it may be lawful for us to perform the common duties of humanity to either of them. So *Livy*, *Pacem, quod medios decet ami-* *Lib.* 35.
cos, optent; Bello se non interponant: It behoves those that are friends to both parties, to endeavour to make Peace, but not to engage themselves in War on either side. *Archidamus* King of *Sparta* perceiving the Elians inclining to take part with the Arcadians, wrote an Epistle unto them, wherein were contained these words only, καλὸν ἡσυχία, *It is good to be quiet.*

CHAP.

CHAP. XVIII.

Concerning things privately done in a publick War

I. *Whether it be lawful to hurt a publick E-nemy privately, explained by a distinction.*
II. *What they may lawfully do against an Enemy by internal justice, that make War at their own private charge* (i. e.) *as Privateers; first in respect of the Enemy:*
III. *Secondly in respect of the State or City under whom they fight.*
IV. *What the Laws of Christian Charity require of them.*
V. *How a private War may be mixt with a publick.*
VI. *Unto what he stands obliged, who without order damnifies an Enemy, explained with a distinction.*

I. Whether to hurt a publick Enemy privately, be lawful.

WHAT we have hitherto said doth mostly appertain unto such as have the supreme Authority in an Army, or unto such as are to execute publick commands. Now we are to see what in a publick War may privately be done, whether we respect the Law of Nature, Nations, or the Divine Law. *Cicero* in the first of his Offices relates, that when *Marcus* the Son of *Cato* the Censor, had listed himself in the Army under *Pompilius* the General, that Legion in which he served being disbanded; yet he for the delight he took in Arms, continuing still in the Army, *Cato* wrote to *Pompilius*, desiring him in case his Son would continue there, to give him a second Oath; adding this reason, because the former Oath being with that Legion discharged, it was not lawful otherwise for his Son to fight the Enemy. Whereunto the same *Cicero* adds the very words of *Cato* recited out of his Epistle to his Son, wherein he adviseth him, *To take heed how he engaged in Battel, for that it was not lawful for him to kill an Enemy being then no Souldier.* So we read in *Plutarch* of one *Chrysantas* a Souldier under *Cyrus*, who having his Sword lifted up to kill his Enemy, and hearing the Trumpet sound a Retreat, withdrew his hand and would not hurt him (as if it were only the necessity of obeying his General, that could justifie a Souldier in killing his Enemy, without which it would be no better than Homicide.) *Seneca* tells us, *That that Souldier is useless that neglects the sound of a Retreat.* Now they that conceive this to proceed only from the external Right of Nations are mistaken. For if we respect that Right only, it is lawful for any man as to possess himself of his Enemies Goods (as hath been said) so to take away his life also; for by that Right, *Hostes pro nullis habentur; Enemies are not reckoned as men.* This therefore that *Cato* adviseth, proceeds from the Roman Military Discipline, which provided, That he who being a Souldier observed not the word of Command, though the success were good, should notwithstanding be put to Death (as *Modestinus* observes:) But he that without order or command should engage in fight with an Enemy, was so understood as if he wilfully disobeyed his Generals command; as we are taught, as well by the severity of *Manlius* to his own Son, as by the like proceedings of *Epaminondas* against his. Because in case such things may rashly be done, it may happen that Souldiers may sometimes desert their own stations; which licence encreasing, the whole Army or some part thereof, may happen to be unexpectedly engaged on terms very unequal, which by all means is to be avoided: which is the reason why *Acidius Cassius* past the sentence of Death in the like case, *Evenire potuit ut essent insidiæ; It might have so happened,* saith he, *that ambushes had been laid to the destruction of the Army.* And therefore *Salust* in his description of the Roman Discipline, tells us, *That in War, as well they who contrary to command had fought the Enemy, as they who being called back made not their return in time, were frequently punished.* A certain Spartan being just about to kill his Enemy whom he had in his Power, hearing the Trumpet sounding a Retreat, suddenly staid his hand, giving this reason for it, *Præfectis parêre satius est quàm hostem occidere; Better it is to obey our Commanders than to kill our Enemy.* And *Plutarch* gives this as the reason, why he that is dismist the Army, hath no Right to kill an Enemy, because he is not bound by any Military Laws, which they that are to fight the Enemy are obliged to observe. *Epictetus* in *Arrian*, reciting the fact before-mentioned of *Chrysantas*, adds, *Tanto illi potius videbatur Ducis quam suam voluntatem exequi; That he thought it much better to execute the commands of his Captain than to humour his own passion.* But if we respect that Right which is internal and natural, it seems lawful in a just War for any man to do those things whereby the innocent party may receive benefit, so as he exceed not the just measure of making War: not that it is lawful for him to make any thing that he takes from the Enemy his own; for to him there is not any thing owing, unless haply it be in the nature

Plut. Quæst. Rom. 39. & de Marcello.
De Ira. c. 9.
Bo. 3 ch. 6. *Supra l. 3. c. 7.*
Livy lib. 7. Plut. paral. Rom. &. Græ. paral. 12.
II. 6.

ture

ture of a puniſhment, which he exacts by that Right which is common to all mankind, which in what meaſure it is by the Evangelical Law reſtrained, may eaſily be underſtood by what we have ſaid above. *Lib. 2. c. 17.* Now a command in War may be either General, or Special: General as when in a tumult among the Romans, the Conſul cryed out, *Qui Rempublicam ſalvam volunt, me ſequantur*; *Let them that wiſh the ſafety of the Commonwealth follow me.* *Serv. ad 8. Æneid.* Nay, ſometimes this power of killing is granted to every Subject, beyond what is done in our own defence, if it be expedient for the publick ſafety,

II. What Reformadoes and Privateers may do by internal Right againſt an Enemy. † Bo. 3. ch. 6.

A ſpecial charge or command to kill an Enemy may be given, not only to them who receive pay, but to thoſe who go to War on their own charge; or (which is yet more) who adminiſter upon their own charge a part of the War, as they that build, ſet out, and maintain men of War at their own private charge, who inſtead of pay, gain to themſelves whatſoever they can take from the Enemy, as is elſewhere declared †: which how far it is agreeable to that which we call internal juſtice, is worthily diſputed. This juſtice hath reſpect, either to the Enemy, or to the City, with which we make our Contract. From an Enemy, the poſſeſſion of all things that may conduce to the maintenance of the War, may for our own ſecurity be taken away, but this muſt be under a condition of reſtitution; but the Dominion or property in thoſe things muſt be no farther retained, than will ſerve to compenſate the coſts and damages which that City that maintains the War hath been at, either from the beginning, or in the proſecution of the War; whether the things ſo taken, belong to the Commonwealth that is at enmity with us, or ſome private Citizens thereof, though haply of themſelves they are innocent: but the goods of ſuch of their Subjects as are nocent, or in actual Arms againſt us, may be taken and detained by way of juſt puniſhment. Things therefore taken from the Enemy may be theirs, who at their own charge maintain part of the War in reſpect of the Enemy, ſo far forth as to ballance their damages and expences, with ſome allowance for the peril they undergo, which alſo ought to be valued by equal Arbitrators.

III. What in reſpect of their own City.

But as to the City with whom we contract, the ſame will be internally juſt, if at leaſt there be an equality in the Contract, that is, in caſe the charge and peril we undergo, be but equivalent to the Body we take or may hope to gain. But if the Booty hoped for, do in value ſurmount the charge and danger, the overplus ought to be reſtored to the City; juſt as he that buying at a low prize, the caſt of a Net, which though uncertain, yet is eaſily made, and yet of great hopes (if it anſwer his expectation, is bound to give to him with whom he did contract, ſo much as to make the ballance even.)

IV. What Chriſtian charity requires.

But ſuppoſe that what we do thus take, be no more than what in ſtrictneſs of juſtice we may keep, yet may we thereby break the bonds of charity, wherein, as Chriſtians we ſtand obliged; as in caſe it appear, that the Booty ſo taken, doth not impoveriſh the Commonwealth or the King that maintains the War, or thoſe particular perſons that are in actual Arms againſt us; but rather ſuch particular perſons as are innocent, who likewiſe are thereby reduced into ſo miſerable a condition, that in caſe we ſhould caſt thoſe who are privately indebted unto us into the like, we ſhould be thought unmercifully cruel. Whereunto if we likewiſe add, that the ſpoil we take from theſe, contributes little or nothing, either to the finiſhing of the War, or to the enfeebling of the Enemies ſtrength, it will eaſily convince us that it would ill become an honeſt man, much leſs a Chriſtian, to make an advantage to himſelf by the ſole infelicity of the times. For which very thing it was that *Plutarch* ſo highly blamed *Craſſus*, ſaying, *Pleraque horum ex igne belloque rapuit, nihil magis lucro habens quam communes calamitates*; *The greateſt part of whoſe riches he gained by Fire and by War, raiſing his private fortunes by nothing more than by publick calamity.*

V. How a private War may be mixt with a publick.

But it ſometimes happens, that by the occaſion of a publick War there ariſeth a private; as if a Man fall by accident amongſt his Enemies, and is thereby in danger of his life or Goods, in which caſe, ſuch means as we have already granted *, may lawfully be uſed in defence of our lives and fortunes. ** Lib. 2. c. 1.* We read that ſometimes in War, private profit is warranted by publick Authority; as when a man having ſuſtained ſome extraordinary damage by the Enemy, obtains of his Prince a Commiſſion to repair his loſſes by what he can get from the Enemy, which alſo is to be limited in the ſame manner, *Lib. 3. c. 2.* as pledges, and ſuch like things are that are left in gage.

VI. How far he ſtands obliged, who without command hurts an Enemy.

But in caſe any Souldier or others, ſhall in a juſt War ſet fire to an Enemies Houſe, or deſtroy his Fields, or commit ſuch and ſuch like Acts, whereby the Enemy is damnified without ſpecial order or command from his Superiours, whereunto we muſt add, unleſs it be in caſe of neceſſity, or for ſome other juſt cauſe, That man according to the opinion of our beſt Divines, ſtands obliged to make ſatisfaction. I have here added what they have omitted, unleſs it be for ſome other juſt cauſe; becauſe if there be any ſuch cauſe, he may haply be bound to anſwer for it to his own Prince or State,

whoſe

whose Laws he hath transgrest; but not to his Enemy, to whom he hath done no wrong. Not much unlike was that Answer which a certain Carthaginian made to the Romans, who demanded, That *Hannibal* should be delivered to them: *We*, saith he, *are not to dispute with you, Whether* Saguntum *were besieged by the private command of* Hannibal, *or by the publick Decree of the Carthaginian Senate; but whether it were justly or unjustly done, for it belongs unto us only to call him to an account, being our Subject, whether he did it by his own Authority, or by ours. This only concerns you to enquire, Whether it were lawful to be done by that League which we have made with you.*

CHAP. XIX.

Concerning Faith to be kept between Enemies.

I. That faith is to be kept wth Enemies of all sorts.

WE have already shewed, What and how much may lawfully be done in War, simply and in it self considered. We are now to consider what and how much may be done, as considered in relation to some foregoing promise, namely, Concerning the faith which Enemies ought to keep one with another. It was notably said by *Silius*, an Italian Poet, concerning a Roman Consul:

——————Optimus ille
Militiæ, cui postremum primúmque tueri
Inter Bella fidem.

He amongst Generals the best praise deserves,
Who first and last in Wars his faith preserves.

Xenophon in his Oration concerning *Agesilaus*, from his Example concludes thus, *So great and excellent a thing it is for every man, but especially Generals, to be just, and to be so accounted in the performance of their Oaths and Promises.* So *Aristides*, *In the preservation of Peace and of all other publick Agreements, they are ever most to be regarded that are most just.* There is no man, as *Cicero* well observes, but approves of and commends that affection of mind by which no profit is sought after, but rather faith is preserved against profit. It is the publick faith only, as *Quintilian* the Father rightly observes, that makes Truces even among armed Troops, and that conserves the Right of surrendred Cities. *Faith*, saith the same *Quintilian*, *is the strongest and most indissoluble Bond of humane Society.* Sacra laus fidei inter Hostes, *Its reputation is great, even amongst Enemies.* Fides sanctissimum humani pectoris bonum; *Faith*, saith *Seneca*, *is the most precious Ornament of the rational soul, the best gift that God bestows upon Men, the strongest support of humane Society.* It is the Cement that binds

Leuct. 4.

Lib. 2. c. 29.

binds up all Traffick and Commerce between man and man,

> *Qua ſine non Tellus Pacem, non Æquora norunt,*
> *Juſtitiæ Conſors, tacitúmque in pectore Numen.*
>
> ——————without her
> No Peace is firm either by Land or Sea,
> She's Juſtice's Mate, an inward Deitie.

The Romans placed her in their Capitol next to *Jupiter* himſelf; and deſervedly, for a great cauſe of their proſperity may be attributed to their faith, which they religiouſly kept both with their Friends and Enemies. *Though all other Laws ſleep in War, yet muſt Faith and Juſtice be ſtrictly obſerved,* ſaith *Ambroſe.* Of the ſame mind was St *Auguſtine, Fides quando promittitur etiam hoſti ſervanda eſt, contra quem Bellum geritur; When our word is paſt, it muſt be kept, though with an Enemy, againſt whom we wage War.* (Ep. 203. ad Bonif.) *Fœdera juraſtis, dexteras dediſtis, quæ etiam inter Hoſtes valent; Ye have ſworn Leagues with us,* ſaith *Archelaus* the Philoſopher in *Appian, Ye have plighted unto us your Faith, all which are in force even amongſt Enemies.* (Appian. Civil. 4.) For in being Enemies they ceaſe not to be rational men, but by being men endowed with reaſon they are capable of a Right by virtue of a promiſe. *Camillus* in *Livy* profeſſeth, That there was between him and the *Faliſci* ſuch a Society as was common with all Mankind; but even from this common Society of diſcourſe and reaſon, there naturally ariſeth that obligation from a promiſe, whereof we now ſpeak. Neither muſt we think that becauſe (as many Authours hold) it is lawful, or at leaſt blameleſs, to deceive an Enemy by falſehood; therefore by a parity of reaſon the ſame may be done, though we have given our faith. For the obligation of ſpeaking truth proceeds from a cauſe long preceding any War, and which may haply be in ſome meaſure relaxed by War; but a promiſe doth of it ſelf confer a new Right: which difference was clearly diſcerned by *Ariſtotle,* who treating of veracity thus diſtinguiſheth, *I ſpeak not of him who ſpeaketh truth in ordinary Contracts and Agreements, and in thoſe which appertain unto Juſtice and Injuſtice; which are indeed Branches of another Vertue. Pauſanias,* ſpeaking of *Philip* of *Macedon,* gives of him this Character, *No man,* ſaith he, *can well ſtyle him a good Emperour, as being (indeed) always regardleſs of his Oaths, though made by the Immortal Gods, and upon every ſlight advantage faithleſs in his promiſes; ſo that, though a King, no man was leſs to be believed, either upon his Word or Oath, than himſelf.* The like teſtimony doth *Valerius Maximus* give of *Hannibal,* namely, *That as profeſt an Enemy as he was to the people of* Rome *and all the Italians, yet was he a much greater Enemy to faith and ſincerity, rejoycing always in falſhood and lies, as if they had been commendable Vertues; whereby it came to paſs, That whereas he had otherwiſe bequeathed unto the World an honourable memory of himſelf, he hereby left it diſputable, Whether his Vices did not exceed his Vertues.* Thus the Trojans in *Homer,* being prick'd in conſcience by reaſon of their perfidiouſneſs, condemn themſelves:

> ——————*rumpentes Fœdera ſacra,*
> *Juratamque fidem, pugnamus; non quibus fas eſt.*
>
> Breaking our ſacred Leagues, and Faith, though ſworn,
> We fight 'gainſt thoſe who ſuch falſe Dealings ſcorn.

II. Faith to be kept with Thieves and Tyrants.

Neither, as we have already ſaid *, may we admit of that of *Cicero, Nulla nobis Societas cum Tyrannis,* That *no Society is to be held with Tyrants.* No, nor of the ſame *Cicero, Pirata non eſt perduellium numero, cum hoc nec fides eſſe debet, nec juſjurandum commune; A Pyrate is not to be reckoned as any mans particular Enemy, with whom neither faith nor common Oath is to be kept.* Nor that of *Seneca,* who ſpeaking of a Tyrant, ſaith †, *All Obligations to him are cancelled, if he cut off from that which is the common Right of all Mankind.* From which impure Fountain proceeded that errour of *Michael Epheſius* *, who taught, That it was not Adultery that was committed with the Wife of a Tyrant. *Non putans Adulterium Uxorem Tyranni polluere; ſicut nec homicidium, Tyrannum occidere: Suppoſing it,* ſaith *Seneca* †, *no Adultery to pollute the Wife of a Tyrant, nor Murder to kill him.* Thus *Julius Clarus* * conceived that a Woman who ſtood out-lawed might be lain withal, without being puniſhed as an Adulterer. And thus did ſome of the Jewiſh Doctors maintain the like errour concerning Strangers *, whoſe Marriages they reckoned as none at all. But *Pompey* finiſhed a great part of that Naval War which he made againſt Pyrates, by covenanting to preſerve their lives, and to aſſign them a Country wherein they might live without rapine. And of *Didius* we read, That he was condemned as perfidious, for breaking faith with the Celtibrians, who lived by robbery. *Cæſar* alſo in the third of his Civil Wars, writes of a compoſition made by the Roman Captains, with the Tories and Renegadoes, who lay lurking in the Pirenæan Mountains. Now who can ſay, That ſuch a compoſition being

* *Lib. 2. c. 13. Sect. 5.*
† *Lib. 7. de Benef.*
* *Ad 5. Nicom.*
† *Sen. in excerp. 4. 7.*
* *In Sect. Homicid. n. 56.*
* *R. Levi Ben. Gerſon. in Levit. 20. 10.*

 made

made is not binding? 'Tis true indeed that ſuch Agreements do not produce ſo friendly a Communion, as that which the Law of Nations hath introduced between Enemies engaged in a Solemn and Juſt War: But yet, being men, it may induce ſuch a Communion as natural Right affords them; as *Porphyry* rightly argues, which is ſufficient to prove that ſuch Contracts are to be performed. Thus did *Lucullus* keep his faith given to *Apollonius*, who was Captain of the Renegadoes; as *Diodorus* records. And thus did *Auguſtus* pay the ranſome impoſed on him by *Crocata* the Thief, being by him apprehended, rather than he would ſatisfie his word; as *Dio* teſtifies.

III. This Objection, That ſuch deſerve puniſhment, anſwered. *Offic. lib. 3.*

But let us now ſee what more probable Argument than thoſe brought by *Cicero* may be produced. The firſt whereof is this, That ſuch as are notoriouſly wicked, and are no part of a Civil Society, may by the Law of Nature be by any man puniſhed, as we have elſewhere ſhewed. But they that may lawfully be puniſhed, even with death, may alſo be lawfully diſpoiled of their Goods, and diſpoſſeſt of their other Rights: as the ſame *Cicero* well obſerves, *Non eſt contra Naturam ſpoliare eum ſi poſſis, quem honeſtum eſt necare; It is no violation of the Law of Nature to deſpoil him of his Goods if we can, whom it is lawful to kill.* But among thoſe things wherein he claims a Right, even thoſe which accrew unto him by virtue of any promiſe that is made to him, may be included; and therefore even thoſe, by way of puniſhment, may lawfully be taken from him. Whereunto I anſwer, That all this may be very true, if we did not knowingly treat with him as ſuch: But in caſe we treat with a Thief, as ſuch, we are ſo to be underſtood as if we were contented to remit the puniſhment due, as to that offence; becauſe, as we have elſewhere ſaid, promiſes are always to be taken in ſuch a ſenſe, as that we make not the act void. Thus the old Pimp in *Terence*,

Leno ſum, fateor; Pernities communis Adoleſcentûm;
Perjurus, Peſtis; tamen tibi à me nulla eſt orta injuria.

A Bawd I am; Youth's Common Peſt, 'tis known;
Perjur'd; yet wrong by me Thou haſt had none.

It was no ill Plea then that *Nabis* (in *Livy*) made, when his tyranny was objected againſt him by *Quintius Flaminius, Concerning the name* Tyrant, *I anſwer, That whatſoever I am, I am the very ſame I was when thou, O* Titus Quintius, *entredſt in League with me.* And by and by, *Theſe things, whatſoever they are, I did when ye contracted friendſhip with me.* Whereunto he preſently adds, *Si quid ego mutâſſem, mihi inconſtantiæ meæ; cum vos mutetis, vobis veſtræ ratio reddenda eſt: If I had changed, I ought to have given the reaſon of my inconſtancy; but ſeeing it is you that change, you ought to give the reaſon of yours.* Not much unlike unto this is the Anſwer that *Pericles* in *Thucydides* gives unto his Subjects, *Our Confederates we ſhall permit to enjoy their own freedom, and to live by their own Laws, if they did ſo when they firſt entred into League with us.*

IV. Fear not to be objected, if the Promiſer were not himſelf affrighted. * *Lib. 2. c. 11. § 7.*

Another Objection may be made, which I have heretofore hinted *, namely, That he that by fear hath extorted a promiſe, ought in Juſtice to releaſe the Promiſer; as having by his injuſtice damnified him, that is, by ſuch an act as is repugnant both to the nature of humane Liberty, and to the nature of the act it ſelf; for all promiſes that bind ought to be free. This, though in ſome caſes true yet, is not to be extended to all promiſes that are made to Thieves; for that the Promiſed be bound to free the Promiſer, it is requiſite that he to whom the promiſe was made ſhould have extorted the promiſe by an unjuſt fear: But in caſe a man ſhall come and promiſe to pay the ranſome of his Friend, and thereby deliver him out of Bondage, he is bound to perform it; becauſe there was no impreſſion of fear upon this man, who in the behalf of his Friend came voluntarily to make this Contract.

V. What if the promiſe were bound by Oath.

Whereunto we may add, That he that is compelled, even by an unjuſt fear, to make a promiſe, may be obliged to perform it, if he confirm that promiſe with an Oath; for thereby (as we have ſhewed before) he ſtands bound, not unto men only, but unto God, againſt whom no exceptions can be admitted. But true it is notwithſtanding, That by ſuch a ſole promiſe, though confirmed by Oath, the Heir of the Promiſer ſtands not obliged; for thoſe things only deſcend to the Heir which by the original Right of Dominion may paſs from man to man in ordinary Traffick. But thoſe things that are due unto God, cannot, as ſuch, be included amongſt theſe. Moreover, here we muſt again repeat what we before delivered, That if a man do haply break his faith with a Thief, whether ſworn or unſworn, he ſhall thereby incur no puniſhment amongſt other Nations: For generally all Nations, in deteſtation of theſe men, whom they account as common enemies to humane Society, are pleaſed to connive at whatſoever is (though unjuſtly) done againſt them.

Lib. 3. c. 4. § 10.

But

But what ſhall we ſay concerning the War that Subjects make againſt their King, or againſt ſuch as have the Supreme Authority? Though they may haply have a cauſe not in it ſelf altogether unjuſt, yet that they can have no Right to act by force againſt their Prince, we have elſewhere ſhewed*. But yet, it ſometimes ſo happens, That either their Cauſe is ſo notoriouſly unjuſt, or their obſtinacy in reſiſting ſo great, that it may be ſeverely puniſhed. But yet, if they be treated with as Rebels or Traitors, and therein any promiſe made unto them, the puniſhment though juſtly due for their Treaſon ought not to be pleaded in Bar to the performance of that promiſe. For ſuch was the piety of the Ancients, that they durſt not break their faith, no not with their very Slaves; as may appear by the Lacedemonians, who were generally believed to have been juſtly puniſhed for putting their Tenarenſian Priſoners to death, contrary to their Covenants. And it is likewiſe obſerved by *Diodorus*, That the faith given to Slaves in the Temple of the *Palici* was never broken by any of their Lords. Neither will any exceptions of fear be allowed of in this Caſe, if the faith given be by Oath confirmed: as we may collect from *M. Pomponius*, the Tribune of the People, who being bound by Oath, punctually performed what he had, though compelled by fear, promiſed to *L. Manlius*.

> VI. This applied to Subjects that make War.
> * *Lib.* 1. *c.* 4.
> *Ælian.* 6,7.
> *Lib.* 11.
> *Sen. de benef. l.* 3. *c.* 37.

But a greater difficulty than any before mentioned may ariſe from the Legiſlative Power, and from that ſupereminent Right of Dominion which every City hath over the things of their Citizens, and which is exerciſed in its name by him who hath the Supreme Power therein: Which ſupereminent Right, if it extend it ſelf to all that is the Subjects, why ſhould it not likewiſe unto that Right which ariſeth from any promiſe made in War? Which being granted, then it ſhould ſeem that all ſuch Promiſes and Agreements may be null'd, and ſo all hopes of concluding a War, unleſs by Victory, would be loſt. But on the contrary, we muſt obſerve, That this ſuperlative Right is not fit to be put in execution promiſcuouſly, at all times; but ſo far forth as it is commonly expedient to the preſervation of the publick ſafety in a Government not Tyrannical, but Civil, yea even Regal. But for the moſt part it is commonly expedient, That all ſuch Promiſes and Agreements ſhould be fulfilled. Very appoſite to this purpoſe is that which we have already written concerning the defence of the preſent Government; adding thereunto, That where the *publick ſafety* requires that this Sovereign Right ſhould be made uſe of, ſatisfaction ought to be given out of the publick to ſuch particular perſons as ſhall be thereby damnified, as ſhall be hereafter more fully explained.

> VII. Of Promiſes made by Sovereign Princes unto their Subjects.

Moreover, Agreements may be confirmed by Oath, and that not by the King or Senate alone, but by the whole Body Politick; as *Lycurgus* bound the Lacedemonians, and *Solon* the Athenians, by Oath to obſerve the Laws they had given them. And leſt the change of Citizens ſhould in time relax the binding power of this Oath, (and ſo at length it be forgotten, or left arbitrary) this Oath may be every Year renewed; which if done, the Citizens could by no means recede from their Engagements, no though it were for their publick profit. For a City hath power to grant away even what is her own. Now the words of the Oath may be ſo clear and ſo full as not to admit of any exceptions, *Lege Legem, quæ te jurejurando obſtrictum tenet*; *Read over your own Law*, ſaith *Valerius Maximus* to the City of *Athens*, *whereunto ye ſtand bound by your Oath.* And ſuch Laws the Romans held as ſacred, becauſe the people of *Rome* were obliged by Oath to keep them, as *Cicero* teſtifies. We find in *Livy* a very pertinent Diſcourſe as to this matter, though of it ſelf more obſcure, where (as the opinion of the beſt Expoſitors of the Laws) he aſſerts, That the Tribunes of the people were *ſacroſanct*, that is, ſo holy, that they could not be injured without perjury. But ſo were neither the *Ædiles*, Judges, nor *Decemviri*; and yet to injure either of theſe was puniſhable by the Laws. The ground of which difference was this, Becauſe theſe latter were thought ſufficiently defended by the ſeverity of the Laws alone. But that which was in the laſt place enacted by the people was moſt inviolable, yet whilſt the Law remained in force, no man could pretend to a Right to act contrary to the Laws. But that which defended the Tribunes, beſides the Law, was the publick Religion of the Romans; for they were all bound by a ſolemn Oath not to offer violence unto them, which they that took, could not break without giving a publick ſcandal to their Religion. This light we receive from a place in *Dionyſius Halicarnaſſenſis*, where it is thus recorded, Brutus *calling the Aſſembly together, propoſed it to the People of* Rome, *That the Tribunes of the People might thenceforth be rendred inviolable, not by the Laws only, but by a publick Oath, whereunto all the People gave conſent.* And hence it was that this Law was called *ſacred*. And therefore that fact of *Tiberius Gracchus* in depoſing *Octavius* from the Tribuneſhip, (alledging that the Tribunitial Power had its ſanctimony from the people, but not to be exerciſed againſt them) was much condemned by all honeſt men. And therefore, as I have ſaid, as well a City as a King may be bound up by Oath in ſuch Agreements as they make with their own Citizens or Subjects.

> VIII. That ſuch promiſes may be confirmed by the Oath of the City.
> *Lib.* 5. *c.* 3.
> *Orat. pro Balbo.*
> *Lib.* 3.
> *Plut. vit. Gracchi.*

IX. Or if the promise be made to a third person, for the Subjects——

But yet farther, A Promise or Agreement made by Princes or States to their own Subjects shall be valid, being made to a third person, who hath given no cause of fear. But wherein and how far forth that third person may stand interessed in that promise, being one of the niceties of the Roman Law, we shall not here search into. For naturally it concerned all men to provide (as much as in them lyes) for the safety of others. Thus we read, That King *Philip* having made his Peace with the Romans, bound himself by promise, Not to revenge himself on those Fugitives, who during the War had sided with the Romans.

X. How the publick State may be changed.

But yet possible it is, as we have elsewhere proved, that a State may sometimes become mixt; and as from an Absolute Monarchy it may pass into an Absolute Aristocracy or Democracy, so also it may by Covenants and Agreements be transferred from any one of these simple, into one mixt, of any two, or of all. So as they which before were Subjects, may begin to settle the Government in themselves, or at least some part thereof, even with a liberty to defend and protect their own Party by Force of Armes.

XI. That fear in a Solemn War, by the Law of Nations, is no Just Exception.

But a Solemn War, that is, such a War as is on both sides publick and denounced, among many other things which (by that Right which we call external) it peculiarly enjoys, hath this also, That all promises made in that War, or that conduce to the concluding of it, are so firm and valid, that though they were caused through a fear unjustly brought, yet can they not be null'd or made void without the consent of him to whom they were made; because, as many other things, though in themselves not altogether just, yet are by the Law of Nations reputed so, so fear, though it be in either side unjustly caused, yet shall it in such a War by the same Law be accounted just: Which unless granted, it would follow that such solemn Wars, which are indeed but too frequent, could be neither moderated nor ended; both which are very expedient for the conservation of Mankind. And this we have reason to believe is that Right in War which *Cicero* tells us is to be kept even with Enemies, to whom also it was elsewhere said, That there were some Rights which an Enemy might retain, though in War, namely, Not such only as are allowed of by the Law of Nature, but some such also as are introduced by the consent of Nations. Neither doth it hence follow, That he who in an unjust War hath extorted any such thing may without the breach of piety or honesty retain what he hath thereby got, or compel another to perform such a promise sworn or unsworn. For internally, and in the very nature of the thing it still remains unjust. Neither can this internal injustice of the act be otherwise removed than by the new and absolutely free consent of the Promiser. Again,

De Offic. l. 3. Ver. 4.

XII. This to be understood of such a fear as is allowed by the Law of Nations.

Whereas that fear is said here to be just which is caused in a Solemn War, it is to be understood of such a fear as the Law of Nations doth not disallow: As for example, A promise wrested from an Ambassadour that is taken Prisoner, shall not yield the least advantage to him that extorts it; as *Mariana* testifies. So in case any thing be extorted through the fear of Ravishment, or through any other the like terrour or affrightment, contrary to our faith given; this ought to be judged by the Law of Nature, because the Law of Nations takes no cognizance of any such fear. Again,

XIII. That faith is to be kept with the perfidious:

That faith ought to be kept with such as are notoriously perfidious, we have in a more general Treatise already proved: Which also we may learn from St *Ambrose*, which without doubt reacheth even unto such enemies as are altogether faithless. Such as the Carthaginians were unto the Romans, who notwithstanding kept their faith inviolably with them. For, as *Valerius Maximus* well observes, *The Roman Senate regarded not what the Carthaginians deserved, but what in honour became the People of* Rome; which is the Testimony that *Salust* gives of them, *In all the Wars*, saith he, *between* Rome *and* Carthage, *though the Carthaginians, as well in times of Peace as during their Truces, committed many outrages, yet would not the Romans upon any provocation permit that the like should be done unto them.* And concerning that fact of *Sergius Galba*, who, in revenge upon the Portuguese for so often breaking their League with him, first deceived them with a new League, and then slew eight thousand of them; *Appian* gives this Answer, *Perfidiâ perfidiam ultus, contra Romanam Dignitatem, Barbaros imitabatur*; *In revenging one treachery with another, he wounded the Majesty of the people of* Rome, *imitating therein the Barbarians.* For which he was afterwards worthily accused by *Labo*, a Tribune of the People, whereof *Valerius Maximus* gives his opinion thus, *It was not equity, but compassion, that pleaded in that Cause: For that absolution which his own innocency could not challenge, was given to his innocent Babes:* which also is confirmed by *Cato*, *He had certainly died for his treachery, had not his own tears, and the innocency of his Children, procured his pardon.*

Lib. 6. c. 6.

But

XIV. But not if the Condition be not performed, or if either Party stand not to the Agreement:

But this also we may observe, That there are two ways whereby a man, though he perform not that which he promised, yet may avoid perfidiousness, as namely, If the Condition be not performed whereupon that promise was grounded, or if some other compensation be made for it; for want of the Condition the Promiser is not really discharged: But it will appear by the event, That there had been no obligation but what was contracted upon Condition; therefore that Condition being not performed, there needed no discharge. Whereunto we may refer another Case, namely, If the other do not perform that which he was first bound on his part to fulfil. For the particular Heads of one and the same Agreement seem to be complicated each with other in the manner of a Condition, as if it had been thus exprest. Thus will I do, if you do so or so, which he hath promised. Wherefore *Tullus* in his Answer to the Albans, *calls the Gods to witness, Whether of the two Nations were the first Aggressors; praying earnestly, That all the miseries of the War might befal that Nation.* For as *Ulpian* notes, *He breaks not the League, who therefore renounceth his Associates, because they do not perform some Articles, whereupon the League was at the first made.* For which Cause, where it is otherwise intended, it is usually thus exprest, *That if either Party shall transgress in this or that Article, yet shall the rest remain firm and inviolable.*

XV. Nor when there is otherwise a just compensation made: * Book 2. Ch. 7. § 2.

The original of compensation or recompence we have elsewhere declared *, namely, When we cannot otherwise recover either what is our own, or what is justly owing unto us, we may take away from him that either detains it or owes it the full value, thereof in any thing else; whence it follows, That whatsoever is actually in our possession, whether it be Corporeal or Incorporeal, we may much more lawfully detain and keep. Whatsoever therefore it is that we have promised, it is in our power not to perform; if it be of no greater value than that which being once ours, he to whom the promise was made injuriously keeps from us. *Comparatio nulli invidiosa est, ubi aut Gratiæ aut Injuriæ communis est ratio; That comparison is to no man odious, wherein a common regard is had to either courtesie or injury.* (Tertul.) *Thus in a wager at Law,* saith *Seneca, the Debtor doth sometimes cast the Creditor, when he hath upon some other account got more from him than his Debt amounted unto. For between the Creditor and the Debtor only the Judge sits as an equal Arbitrator, who may say to the Creditor, It was thy money that thou lentest, how camest thou then by the Land which thou possessest, but never boughtest? wherefore upon a just valuation, Thou that camest in a Creditor, Depart hence a Debtor.* (De benef. lib. 6. cap. 4.)

XVI. Although due by another Contract: * Eod. Lib. c. 6, 7.

The Case is the same if he with whom we have to do owes me as much upon any other Contract, which I cannot otherwise recover but by detaining that which I have promised to him. In Courts of Justice there are, saith *Seneca* *, some separate Actions, neither is the form confounded. But those Precedents, as it is there said, are contained within certain Laws, which are necessarily to be followed. One Law is not mixed with another. We must walk as every Law doth lead us. But the Law of Nations admits of no such distinctions, namely, Where there is no other hopes of recovering what is our own.

XVII. Or some damage done. * Eod. lib. c. 4.

The like may be said where he that exacts a promise hath damnified the Promiser to the value of the thing promised. Thus the same *Seneca* *, *The Farmer is not bound to his Landlord, though his Lease be not cancelled, in case he wilfully trample down his Corn, and cut down his Fruit-trees; not because he hath received what he agreed for, but because he hath hindred his Tenant from receiving the Fruits of his Grounds, whereby he shou'd have paid his Rent.* Where also he subjoins another Example, *Pecus abegisti, Servum occidisti; Thou hast haply driven away his Cattel, or slain his Servant.* And a little after, *It is lawful for me to compare the good that any man doth me, with the hurt that he doth me; and thereby to pronounce my self his Debtor, or him mine.*

XVIII. Or for some punishment justly due.

Lastly, Whatsoever also is due to the Promiser by way of punishment, may be emballanced with what he hath promised; which *Seneca* in the same place thus clearly illustrates, *Beneficio Gratia debetur, injuriæ ultio; Thanks is due for a courtesie, revenge for an injury: If therefore I pay him no thanks, nor require that punishment from him that I lawfully might; there is nothing at all due to either, for the one acquits the other.* And anon, *By comparing the good turns I receive with the wrongs I receive, I shall easily discern whether I am indebted unto him, or he to me.* (Ib. c. 6.)

XIX. How these take place in War.

But as whatsoever is contended for by a wager at Law cannot whilst the Suit depends be counterballanced against that which is promised, whether it be the thing sued for, or the costs and damages sustained in the Suit; so neither can the injuries that first occasioned the War, nor any of the losses or expences which are usually through the licence in War caused, be recompenced as long as the War lasts. For the very nature of this business, lest nothing at all be done, shews that setting a part on either side the controversies of the War, they are agreed. For otherwise there can be no Agreement so firmly made, that may not be avoided. Whereunto may that of *Seneca* not unfitly be applyed, *Our Ancestors would admit of no excuses* (De Benef. lib. 7. cap. 15.)

ſes at all for the breach of promiſes, that ſo they might teach us that our faith was altogether to be kept: For better it was not to admit of ſome excuſes, though juſt, from a few, than to encourage all to make what excuſes they would for the breach of their faith. But what things are thoſe which may countervail that which is promiſed? Surely in the firſt place, Whatſoever by any other Contract made ſince the War is owing unto us by him to whom our promiſe was made, or whatſoever damages we have ſuſtained by him in the times of Truces, or in caſe the Perſons or Rights of Ambaſſadors have been by him violated, or, in brief, if he have done any other thing which between Enemies is not juſtifiable by the Law of Nations, where this alſo is to be underſtood, That the ſatisfaction be made between the ſame perſons, and that the Right of no third perſon be thereby injured; but yet with this allowance, That the Goods of Citizens may ſtand obliged for the Debts of their own City, as thoſe of Subjects may for the Debt of their Prince; as we have already ſhewed. Whereunto we may add, That it is the ſign of a generous Soul ſtrictly to obſerve his faith in Leagues given, notwithſtanding all provocations to the contrary by injuries received: Upon which account it was that that wiſe Indian *Jarchas* ſo highly commended that King, who being much injured by his Confederates, yet would never break his faith given, ſaying, *Tam ſanctè ſe juraſſe, ut alteri ne poſt acceptam injuriam nociturus eſſet*; *That the Oath he had taken was ſo ſacred, that he durſt not injure him to whom he had given his faith, though he were ſufficiently provoked.* Now look what other Queſtions uſually ariſe concerning our faith given to Enemies, may almoſt all of them be reſolved by applying them to thoſe Rules heretofore preſcribed, concerning the Obligatory Power, as of Promiſes in general, ſo of thoſe ſpecial promiſes made by Oaths, Leagues, Sponſions, and of the Right and Obligation of Kings, and concerning the interpretation of ſuch promiſes as are ambiguous. But yet notwithſtanding for the better uſe of what hath been already ſaid, and for the clearing of any other doubts which may happen to ariſe, it ſhall not at all be troubleſome to me briefly to unfold ſuch of theſe ſpecial Caſes as are moſt notable, and as do moſt frequently occur.

Lib. 2. c. 2.

Philoſt. l. 3. c. 6.

Lib. 2. c. 11. & ſeq.

CHAP.

CHAP. XX.

Concerning the publick Faith, Treaties, Lots, ſet Combats, Arbitrements, Surrenders, Hoſtages, Pledges.

I. *The diviſion of Faith among Enemies in order to that which follows.*
II. *In Monarchies, it is in the Kings power to make Peace.*
III. *What if the King be an Infant, Mad, a Priſoner, or an Exile.*
IV. *In other Governments this power is in the major part.*
V. *How an Empire, or a part of it, or the goods of a Kingdom, may be firmly alienated to obtain Peace.*
VI. *How far by a Peace made with a King, his People and Succeſſors may ſtand bound.*
VII. *That what is the Subjects, may in Peace be granted away for the publick good, but with condition of repairing damages.*
VIII. *What may be ſaid of things already loſt by War.*
IX. *No diſtinction here between things got by the Civil Law, and things got by the Law of Nations.*
X. *With Foreigners, what a King doth, is held to be for the publick good.*
XI. *A general rule whereby to interpret Articles of Peace.*
XII. *In doubtful caſes it is credible, that it is agreed, that things ſhould remain in the ſtate they are at preſent: how this is to be underſtood.*
XIII. *What if it be agreed, that all things ſhall be reſtored to the condition they were in before the War began.*
XIV. *Then they who being before free, and had voluntarily enſlaved themſelves, were not to be made free.*
XV. *That damages occaſioned in War, if left dubious, are preſumed to be forgiven.*
XVI. *But not thoſe, which before the War were due to private men.*
XVII. *Puniſhments alſo before the War publickly due, if left doubtful, are believed to be remitted.*
XVIII. *What is to be ſaid concerning the Right that private men have to require puniſhment.*
XIX. *That Right which before the War, though publickly claimed, was controverted, is eaſily believed to be forgiven.*
XX. *Things taken after Peace made, to be reſtored.*
XXI. *Of agreements, whereby things taken in War are to be reſtored: ſome certain rules.*
XXII. *Together with the things, the fruits and profits are to be reſtored.*
XXIII. *Concerning the names of Countries.*
XXIV. *Concerning the relation that is had to ſome precedent agreements.*
XXV. *Of delay.*
XXVI. *Where the words are doubtful, the interpretation muſt be made againſt him that gives Laws.*
XXVII. *Diſtinction muſt be made between the giving of a new cauſe of War, and the breaking of Peace.*
XXVIII. *How a Peace may be broke, by doing contrary to that which is preſumed to be in every Peace.*
XXIX. *What if we be invaded by Aſſociates.*
XXX. *What if by Subjects? and how their fact may be judged as approved.*
XXXI. *What if Subjects engage under another Prince.*
XXXII. *What if Subjects be invaded? explained by diſtinction.*
XXXIII. *What if Aſſociates? who are likewiſe diſtinguiſhed.*
XXXIV. *How a Peace may be broken by doing contrary to that which was ſaid in the Peace.*
XXXV. *Whether any diſtinction is to be made between the Articles of Peace.*
XXXVI. *What if to the breach of the Articles there be ſome puniſhments added.*
XXXVII. *What if we are hindred by an unavoidable neceſſity.*
XXXVIII. *The Peace ſhall ſtand firm, if he that is injured be willing thereunto.*
XXXIX. *How a Peace may be broken, by doing that which is contrary to the ſpecial nature of every Peace.*
XL. *What under the name of friendſhip may be comprehended.*
XLI. *Whether it be enough to break friendſhip, to receive Subjects and Exiles.*
XLII. *How War may be ended by lots.*
XLIII. *How by a ſet combate, and whether lawful.*
XLIV. *Whether the fact of the King do in this caſe oblige the People.*
XLV. *Who is to be judged the Conquerour.*
XLVI. *How War may be ended by Arbitrement, and how it muſt be underſtood, if it admits of no appeal.*
XLVII. *Arbitrators in caſes doubtful, muſt be ſo underſtood as bound to do Right.*
XLVIII. *That Arbitrators are not to determine of poſſeſſions.*
XLIX. *How far forth the force of a pure dedition extends.*
L. *What a Conquerour ought to do as to ſuch as ſurrender.*
LI. *Of a ſurrender upon conditions.*
LII. *Who may and ought to be given in Hoſtage.*
LIII. *What Right is given againſt Hoſtages.*
LIV. *Whether an Hoſtage may awfully eſcape*

scape by flight.
LV. *Whether an Hostage may be lawfully detained upon any other account.*
LVI. *Upon the death of him, for whom an Hostage is given, the Hostage is to go free.*
LVII. *The King dying who sent the Hostage, whether the Hostage may lawfully be detained.*
LVIII. *Hostages may sometimes be principally obliged, and that one of them is not bound for the fact of another.*
LIX. *What obligation lies upon pledges.*
LX. *When the Right of redemption of things engaged, is to be judged as lost.*

I. The Division of Faith in order to what follows.

ALL agreements between Enemies depend upon Faith, either exprest or understood. Faith exprest is either publick or private. Publick, is either that given by supreme, or that given by subordinate power. That given by the supreme power, either puts an end to the War, or is of some force, the War continuing. Among those things that conclude a War, some things are looked at as Principals, and some Accessaries. The principals are those very things that finish it, either by their own act, as the Articles of agreement; or by consent on both sides, that it shall be determined by some other thing; or by Lots, by the event of some Combats, the award of Arbitrators: whereof that by Lots is altogether fortuitous, the other two moderate the case by the strength of the mind, or of the body, or by the discerning faculty.

II. The power to make Peace is in the King if the Government be Kingly. * See Bo. 2. ch. 15. §. 3.

They that have power to begin a War, have also a power by Articles of agreement to end it *, for every man is the best moderator of his own affairs; whence it follows, that in a War on both sides publick, the power of making Peace belongs to them who are entrusted with the Supreme Authority, as in a Government truly Monarchical to the King, so as he be no ways disabled to exercise that Authority.

III. What if the King be an Infant. * Bo. 1. ch3. §. 24. *Francis* King of *France* (being Prisoner to *Charles* the Fifth Emperour and King of *Spain*) his case about the Dutchy of *Burgundy*. See Lord *Herberts* Hist. of *H.* the 8th pag. 193.

For in case a King be not at Years of discretion (which in some Kingdoms is determinable by Law *, but in others by probable conjectures) or if he be not of sound mind, he is not capable of making Peace. The like may be said of a King that is in Captivity; in case that Kingdom had its first rise from the suffrages of the People, it being incredible that the People should ever consent to entrust their Government into such hands, as were not at liberty to exercise it; wherefore in this case also, though not the full power, yet the exercise of that power, and as it were the Guardianship of it is in the people, or those whom the people shall surrogate in their stead. Thus when *Rodolfus* the Palatine fled through fear into *England*, and when the Bishop of *Mentz* was driven out of his Territories, by the Bishop of *Tryers*; neither the one nor the other lost their Electorship. But yet as to those things that are privately his own, a King though a Captive may make any Contract good, after the example of those things that we shall say concerning private agreements. But what if the King be an exile (as *Camillus* was when he lived amongst the Vejans of whom *Lucan* writes thus,

> *Vejos habitante* Camillo,
> *Illic* Roma *fuit.*)

is it in his power to make Peace? yea surely, if it appear that he lives free, obnoxious to none; for otherwise the condition of an exiled King is not much different from that of another Captive, a banished man being but a Prisoner at large. Thus *Cicero* speaks concerning *Regulus*, that he refused to give his opinion in the Senate; alledging, that so long as he stood bound to his Enemies by Oath, he was uncapable of voting as a Senator.

IV. In other States it lies in the major part. Bo. 2. ch. 5. §. 17. * *Lib.* 32.

But where the Supreme Authority is seated, either in the Nobles or in the People, it is in the power of the major part of them to make Peace: The Decrees either of the publick Senate in the former, or of the Citizens in the latter, being to be pronounced by such as by use and custome have a Right thereunto, according to what we have elsewhere delivered. And therefore what is thus agreed upon shall oblige the whole, yea, even those that dissented from them. Thus *Livy* *, *Whatsoever is once upon a full debate decreed, is to be defended by all, even by those who had been before against it.* Wherewith accords that of *Dionysius Halicarnassensis, Parendum est his quæ pars major decreverit*; *Whatever the major part thinks fit, must by all be obeyed.* So likewise *Appian, Omnes decreto obsequi tenentur, nulla admissa excusatione*; *What is so decreed is by all men to be observed, no excuse being admitted of to the contrary.* With whom agrees *Pliny, Quod pluribus placuisset, cunctis tenendum*; *What pleaseth the greater part obligeth all: But those whom Peace obligeth, it also profiteth*; *Iisdem & volentibus prodest.*

V. How an Empire or any part thereof may be alienated for Peace. *See above Bo. 2. ch. 6. §. 3. and what follows.

Now let us see what manner of things they are that are subject to such agreements; most Kings now a days, because they hold not their whole Kingdoms, nor any part of them in propriety, but in respect of their fruits and profits only, cannot by any Contract or Agreement alienate them *. Yea, and before they receive that great charge of the Empire upon them (during which time the People are as yet above them) all such acts of alienating the Kingdom or any part thereof, may by a publick Law for the future be made absolutely void, so that as to what concerns That, they shall not be binding

binding at all. And credible it is that the People were generally thus minded, *Ne alioqui si ad id quod interest salva esset actio contrahenti, subditorum bona pro debito regis caperentur*; *Lest otherwise if as to that which is so provided against the action should hold good to the person contracting, the goods of the Subjects might be taken for the Debt of the King*: And consequently this caution of not alienating the Kingdom would be in vain. But that the whole Empire may be firmly alienated, the whole body of the People must yield their consents, which may quickly be done by their Representatives, which are the three Orders or States of a Commonwealth; namely the Clergy, Peers, and the Commons: But that any part of the Empire may be firmly alienated, a twofold consent is requisite; first of the whole, but more especially of that power which is to be alienated, which cannot be severed from the body whereunto it grew against its will. This was the French Kings Plea why he would not deliver *Burgundy* as he had upon his Oath agreed and promised. But yet in a case of extreme necessity, and otherwise unavoidable, That very part may firmly conveigh away the Government over themselves unto any other without the consent of the People; because credible it is, that when that society was instituted, this power was reserved. But in Kingdoms that are Patrimonial, what should hinder a King from alienating his Kingdom I know not; but yet such the case may be, that such a King hath no power to alienate any part thereof, as if he received the whole as his propriety upon this condition that he should not divide it. But as concerning those things which are called the goods of the Kingdom, these may also become the Kings Patrimony two ways, either as separable from the Kingdom, or as inseparably united unto it: if this latter way, they may be transcribed, but not unless with the Kingdom; if the former, they may be alienated without it. But such Kings, whose Kingdoms are not patrimonial, can hardly be permitted to alienate the Goods of the Kingdom, unless it evidently appear by some Primitive Law, or by a continued and uninterrupted custome that they may do it.

See Bo. 2. ch. 15.

VI. How far the people and successors are obliged by a Peace made by the King.

But how far forth the promise of a King shall bind his Subjects and Successors, hath already been declared *; namely, so far as the power obligatory is comprehended in that Government, which should be neither infinite nor impaled within in too narrow bounds, but to extend so far only as in probable reason it shall be found convenient. But in case the King be absolute Lord * over his People, as having at his own charge conquered him, and so holds them under a Government merely Despotical and not Civil; or if he have gained the Dominion, not over their persons but over their things, as *Pharaoh* bought all that the Ægyptians had, for Corn; or as they that admitted of Strangers into their Houses, to whom they prescribe what Laws they please: if, I say, the Government be thus absolute, then it is another thing. For in this case, besides that Right which is regal, there is an access of another Right which makes that justifyable, which a bare regal power could not.

* See Bo. 2. ch. 3. §. 10, *&c.*

* See Bo. 3. ch. 8. §. 2.

VII. What power a King hath over his Subjects goods to the making of Peace.

But here there usually ariseth another Question, namely, What Right Kings have over the Estates of private men in order to the establishing of Peace, as having no other Right to that which particularly belongs to his Subjects, than what he hath as a King. That the things belonging to Subjects are under the supereminent power of the Commonwealth, whereof they are a part we have already proved, so that that Commonwealth, or he that exercises the supreme power in it, hath a Right to make use thereof, either by even destroying them, or by alienating them, and that not only in a case of extreme necessity, which is even between private men justifyable; but when it extends even to the good of the publick, which is always to be preferred before any private mans, by the general consent of those who first entred into civil society: Which notwithstanding is so to be understood, that the whole Commonwealth is obliged to repair the damages, that shall befal any of her Subjects or Citizens, by reason of any such spoil or alienation, out of their publick stock, or by a publick contribution; whereunto even he who hath sustained the loss, shall (if need be) pay his proportion. Neither shall that City or Commonwealth stand discharged from this obligation, although at present it be not able to satisfie it; for whensoever that City shall be enabled, this sleeping obligation may rise up against it.

VIII. But what if the things be already lost by War.

Neither can I here generally admit of the opinion of *Vasquius*, namely, that the City is not obliged to repair the damages of her Citizens sustained by the War, because such damages are by the licence of War permitted. For this Right of War hath only respect to the People of several Nations as we have elsewhere explained it *; and partly to such as were in open hostility amongst themselves, but not to Citizens amongst themselves, who being mutually associated, and equally engaged in the defence of their City, should in equity esteem every mans to be the common loss. But yet doubtless, it may by the Civil Law be so ordained, that no Action shall lye against such a City for any damages sustained by the War, to the end that every man may be the more watchful and resolute to defend his own.

* Bo. 3. ch. 6. §. 2.

IX. No difference between things got by the Civil Law, and things got by the Law of Nations.

Some there are that place a vast difference between those things which belong to Subjects according to the Law of Nations, and those things which are theirs by the Civil Law, granting a larger Right to the King in taking away these, without either cause or recompence; but not so in the former, but erroneously. For a Right of Dominion, however lawfully gained, hath always by the Law of Nature its proper effects; that is to say, that it cannot be taken away, unless it be for such causes as are naturally inherent in Dominion it self, or such as arise from some fact done by him that is the right owner.

X. What is done by a King, is taken by Foreigners to be done for a publick good.

Now this care and inspection that the things of private persons be not alienated, unless it be for a publick benefit, appertains to the King and to the Subjects, as that of repairing of damages doth to the City, and each particular Citizen: For the bare fact of the King, is sufficient to Strangers that contract with him, not only in respect of the presumption, which the Dignity of his person brings with it; but also in respect of the Law of Nations, which permits the Goods of Subjects to stand obliged by the fact of the King.

XI. A general rule for the interpreting of Articles of Peace. * See Bo. 2. c. 16. §. 12.

But as to the right understanding of the Articles of Peace, what we have said before, must here also be observed *, *The more of grace and favour any Article contains, the more extensively it should be taken, and the more of rigour it hath, the more restrictively it should be understood.* If we look at the bare Law of Nature, the greatest favour that can be granted, seems to be this, *That every man should enjoy his own:* wherefore where the Articles are ambiguous, such an interpretation should be admitted as may lead us to this sence, That he that undertakes a just War should receive what he fights for, together with his costs and damages; but not that he should get any thing more by way of punishment, for this savours of rigour which ought to be restrained. But because a bare acknowledgment of wrongs done, seldome procures a lasting Peace, therefore in Articles of Peace, such an interpretation should be admitted, as may according to the justice of War make the ballance on both sides even, which may be done two ways; either by an equal composure of all such things, as the Sword hath not as yet determined, according to the form of Ancient Right (which are the very words of *Menippus* in his Oration, wherein he discourseth of the several sorts of Leagues) or otherwise, as the Greeks say, ἔχοντες ἃ ἔχουσι, *That every man should keep what he hath.* (*Livy, lib.* 34.)

XII. In dubious cases it is to be believed that things should remain as they are. See ch. 9.

Of which two ways of pacification, the latter, if the case be doubtful, is the rather to be believed; because as it is more facile, so it requires no alteration. Upon which that of *Triphoninus* seems to be grounded, where he saith, That in Peace such Captives only are to return by Postliminy, as are comprehended in the Articles of agreement; as also where he saith, That Fugitives are not to be restored, unless it be so expresly agreed on, as we have already proved by irrefragable arguments. For by the Law of Arms we may receive such, and muster them among our own Troops: All other things by such an agreement remaining his that at present holds them; where the word [Hold] is meant of a natural not of a civil possession; for in War a possession in fact only is sufficient, neither is any other required. Fields (as we have already said) are then soppos'd to be possest, when they are strongly secured by fortifications; for such as are for a while only encampt upon (as in Leaguers or Sieges) are not here to be regarded. *Demosthenes* in his Oration for *Ctesiphon*, saith, That *Philip* made hast to get into his possession what places he possibly could, as knowing that the Peace being concluded, whatsoever he could get, he should keep; but things incorporeal cannot be kept, unless either by the things whereunto they adhere (as the services of Tenants that are annexed to Mannors) or by detaining the persons whose they are, that whilst in a Country that is their Enemies, they shall not be exercised. (*Lib.* 3. *c.* 6. §. 4. *Lib.* 3. *c.* 7. §. 4.)

XIII. Of the restoring all things as before the War.

In that other kind of pacification, whereby the possession of things not yet determined by War are to be restored, we are to understand, That restitution is to be made to those who held the possession thereof last before the War began; yet so, that those private men that were cast out, might lawfully appeal to the Judge for either injunction or vindication.

XIV. This reacheth not unto such as have voluntarily yielded themselves. *Thucyd. l.* 3. *Thucyd. l.* 5. *Livy lib.* 33.

But if any free People do voluntarily subject themselves to either Party that were in Arms, this Article of restitution shall not extend unto them, because it was intended only to such things as were done either by force, fear, or otherwise by such kind of fraud as is not lawfully used but against Enemies. Thus the Peace being concluded among the Grecians, the *Thebans* detained *Platæa*, alledging, *That they were possest thereof neither by force nor treachery, but by the voluntary surrender of the Citizens.* And in another place the same Author urgeth, *That* Platæa *ought not to be restored because it submitted it self to the Thebans of its own accord.* By the same Law *Nisæa* was detained by the Athenians. And the same distinction is used by *Titus Quintius* against the Ætolians, who urging that the Cities of *Thessaly* might be set at liberty, was answered, *That as to the Cities taken by force, that indeed was the Law; but the Cities of* Thessaly *did freely submit themselves to the Roman jurisdiction.*

If

XV. Damages by War, if in doubt, are believed to be remitted:

If nothing elſe be agreed on, yet this in every Peace ought to be preſumed, that no Action ſhall be commenced for damages done in War, which is alſo to be underſtood of ſuch damages as are received by private perſons; for theſe alſo are the effects of War. For where the cauſe of the War is doubtful, neither party will be willing ſo to agree as to condemn themſelves of injuſtice.

XVI. But not thoſe done by private perſons, before the War began.

Yet muſt not thoſe Debts, which were due to private men when the War began, be accounted as pardoned: For theſe were not contracted by the Right of War, but forbidden to be exacted during the War; and therefore the War (which only hindred the exacting of them) being ended, the Debts remain in force as before. For although it ought not eaſily to be believed, That that which was a man's Right before the War ſhould be taken away, (for for this cauſe chiefly, as *Cicero* obſerves, were Commonwealths and Cities at firſt inſtituted, That every particular man might be defended in what was his Right) yet ought this to be underſtood of that Right only, which ariſeth from the inequality of things. *De Offic. lib.* 2.

XVII. Puniſhments, if in doubt, though publickly due before the War, are preſumed to be remitted.

But as to puniſhments, it is not ſo; for this Right of exacting puniſhments, ſo far as it concerns thoſe very people or Kings that have contracted Peace, is therefore preſumed to be remitted, leſt if any old grudge ſhould remain unforgiven, there could be no firm or laſting Peace. Wherefore even thoſe injuries which are as yet unknown to the Party injured, are uſually comprehended in general words; as that fact of the Carthaginians in drowning ſome Roman Merchants was remitted by the Romans, before it was made known unto them; as *Appian* tells us. *Optimæ conciliationes quæ iram & offenſarum memoriam delent, Thoſe are the beſt reconcilements that pacifie all anger, and leave nothing in the memory unremitted.* For as *Iſocrates* very diſcreetly, *In Pace non decet ante peccata exequi; After Peace is ratified, to revenge former injuries is unſeemly.* *Dionyſ. Hal.*

XVIII. Not ſo as to puniſhments due to private men.

But there is not the ſame reaſon that this Right of exacting puniſhment ſhould alſo be remitted by private men, becauſe theſe may without War be judicially required; yet foraſmuch as this Right is not ſo properly ours, as that which proceeds from inequality, and that the very exacting of puniſhments argues ſomewhat of hatred; therefore any ſlight interpretation of words will ſuffice to ground our conjectures, that this alſo was intended to be remitted.

XIX. That Right which though publickly claimed before the War, but controverted, is preſumed to be remitted.

Now whereas we ſaid, That the Right which we had, before the War ought not eaſily to be believed to be remitted, this holds very true as to that Right which belongs to private men. But as to that which belongs to Kings and Nations, it will be more eaſily granted, if the words will but afford us whereupon to raiſe any probable conjectures to that purpoſe; eſpecially if it were not a clear, but a controverted Right that was in Debate. For to believe that to be done whereby all occaſions of a new War may be prevented, is generous; becauſe, as the ſame *Dionyſ. Halicarneſſenſis* excellently obſerves *, *Non tam cogitandum eſt de ſarcienda in præſens amicitia, quam id curandum ne Bello iterum impliecmur; neque enim ad differenda, ſed ad auferenda mala convenimus: We are not ſo much to conſider how to piece up a broken friendſhip for the preſent, as how to provide that we be not again intangled in the ſame War hereafter. For our main deſign in this Treaty is not to put off the miſeries of War, but to take them quite away.* Which laſt words are borrowed from *Iſocrates*.

* *Lib.* 3. *Orat. pro pace.*

XX. Things taken after the Peace is made, are to be reſtored.

The Peace being once concluded and ratified, it is expedient that whatſoever is taken away afterwards muſt be reſtored; for from thenceforth all licence of War is taken away.

XXI. Some cautions concerning the reſtoring of things taken in War.

But among thoſe Articles that concern the reſtitution of things taken in War, thoſe in the firſt place will admit of a larger interpretation that are mutual, than thoſe that concern one Party only; and next, thoſe that reſpect Priſoners are to be conſtrued with more allowance of favour than thoſe that reſpect things: And among thoſe that reſpect things, thoſe that have relation to Lands ought to be more favourably underſtood than thoſe that relate to Moveables; and even among theſe, ſuch as are in the poſſeſſion of the Commonwealth than thoſe in the poſſeſſion of private men. And among thoſe Articles that command the reſtitution of things in the poſſeſſion of private men, thoſe are to be taken in the larger ſenſe that are poſſeſt under a gainful than thoſe under a chargeable title, as things bought with our money, and things held in Dowry by Marriage. *Cic. de Offic. l.* 2.

XXII. The profits reſtored with the things.

To whomſoever any thing is granted by Articles of Peace, to him alſo is granted all the fruits and profits thereof, from the time of that conceſſion, but not before; which *Auguſtus* juſtly defends againſt *Sextus Pompeius*, who having *Peloponneſus* granted unto him, claimed all the Tributes that were in Arrears for ſome years paſt, before the time of that Grant.

XXIII. The names of Countries.

The names of Countries are to be taken, as they are at preſent uſed, not ſo much by the common people, as by ſuch as are learned; for by ſuch only are theſe Affairs negotiated.

XXIV. Reference to ſome former Agreements.

The aforeſaid Rules are of frequent uſe, as often as reference is had to ſome precedent or ancient Agreement, for ſo often the Qualities and Conditions, expreſt in that Agreement

Quintil. Dec. 248. ment, are supposed to be repeated. And he shall be deemed to have performed his Agreement, who was willing to have performed it, had he not been hindred by another, in whose power it was to obstruct the performance of it.

XXV. Of delay. But whereas some are of opinion, That excuses may be admitted for some short delay in the performance of an Agreement, this holds not true, unless that delay be occasioned by an unexpected and unavoidable necessity. That some of our Canons do seem to favour such purgations, is no wonder; seeing that it is their design to perswade Christians to such things as promote mutual Charity. But in this Question that concerns the interpretation of Agreements, we enquire, not what is best, no nor what either piety or Religion require of us but, what we may lawfully be compelled unto. All which is to be determined by that Justice which we call external.

XXVI. The interpretation of words doubtful ought to favour the weaker. But where the words will bear a double sense, that interpretation is most to be favoured which makes against him that imposeth Laws; because he is usually the most potent Party. (The power, saith *Hannibal*, is in him that gives, not in him that demands Conditions of Peace.) As in other Contracts that are doubtful, the interpretation ought to favour the Buyer; for the Seller may blame himself that he did not fully express himself. But the other, receiving Conditions in words that will admit of divers sences, hath a Right to accept of what is offered in that sense which is most favourable to himself. *Persa.* *Tua merx, tua judicatio est*, saith *Plautus*; *It is in him to set the price that ownes the Goods.* In War, he prescribes first that is most powerful; but in demanding Conditions, he first speaks that is the weaker. So *Sulla* in *Plutarch*, *Eorum est prius loqui qui opus habent Pace*; *Victori satis est tacere: Let them speak first that stand in need of Peace; it is enough for the Conquerour to be silent.*

XXVII. Great difference between giving cause of a new War, and breaking the Peace. Peace broken three ways. It it also frequently disputed when a Peace may be said to be broken; for it is not one and the same thing to give a cause of War, and to break a Peace. But between these two the difference is great, as well to require punishment from the Delinquent, as to vindicate the Faith of him against whom the offence was committed in other matters. Now a Peace may be broken three several ways, first, By doing that which is contrary to all Peace; secondly, In doing contrary to that which is plainly and exprefly said in that Peace; thirdly, In doing contrary to that which from the nature of every Peace ought to be understood.

XXVIII. The first way of breaking Peace. First, The Peace is broken when that is done which is contrary to all Peace; as when we are invaded by Force of Armes, there being no new cause of War; which if with any probability it may be alledged, better it were so to understand it as if the War were simply unjust, than that it should be both unjust, and also treacherous: *Thucyd.* *Pacem rumpunt non qui vim vi arcent, sed qui priores vim inferunt*; *They break not the Peace who repel force with force, but they who first offer violence.* *Lib. 29.* Therefore *Ammianus*, speaking of the Romans, saith, *That they purposely gave back, because they would not be thought the first Aggressors; yet afterwards, being urged thereunto by necessity, they gave Battel willingly.* *Pers. 2.* So likewise *Procopius*, in that Oration which *Armenius* makes to *Cosroes*, *They*, saith he, *are not always to be accounted the Peace-breakers that are first in Armes, but they who during the League, are found treacherous to their Confederates.* *Vand. lib. 2.* Thus also do the Moors in *Procopius*, *They break not their League, who being first injured, and publickly complaining thereof (in vain) fly for succour unto others; but they who first wrong those whom they owne as their Associates: Neither do they make God their Enemy, who taking nothing with them but their own, fly unto others for protection; but they who invading other mens Rights do inforce them into War to defend their own.* This being granted, let us now examine by whom and upon whom, an invasion being made, the Peace is dissolved.

XXIX. What if we are invaded by the Associates of those that are at Peace with us. There are some of opinion, That if they that shall forceably invade us were but their Associates, with whom we have made Peace, that Peace is broken. I deny not but that such a League there may be made, not properly, That one man should be punished for the fact of another; but because that Peace seemed not to be fully and absolutely made, but rather under some Condition, partly potestative, and partly casual. And yet that such a Peace should be made, unless it evidently so appear, is scarce credible; because it is irregular, and inconsistent with the common design of those that make Peace. Wherefore they that do actually invade, being no ways assisted therein by others, they only, and not their Associates, shall be judged the Peace-breakers; and against these it shall be lawful to make War. *Pauf. lib. 9.* Contrary unto which, the Thebans did sometimes plead against the Associates of the Lacedemonians.

XXX. What if by their Subjects, and when it may be imputed unto their Prince. But what if they be Subjects that make such an invasion without publick Warrant or Authority? Then we ought to consider whether such a fact of private men be publickly approved of. For the better understanding whereof, three things are requisite (as elsewhere we have declared *) First, The knowledge of the fact; secondly, A power to punish; thirdly, A neglect in them that could and ought to have done it. Their knowledge may easily be evinced, if the fact be publick and declared. A power to restrain or punish it is

* *Lib. 2. c. 21. § 2. & seq.*

to be presumed, unless it appears that they are Rebels. The neglect will appear by the space of time which Cities usually take to punish Malefactors; and such a neglect is equivalent to a publick Command. Neither is that of *Agrippa* in *Josephus* otherwise to be understood, in saying, *That the Parthian King had broken the Peace, for suffering his Subjects to march armed against the Romans.*

XXXI. What if those Subjects fight under the command of another Prince.

Another Question is here usually started, Whether the Case be the same if Subjects take Armes, not by themselves but, under the Command of others. Surely the Cerites in *Livy* do thus excuse themselves †, That their Subjects took Armes without any publick Warrant or Commission from them. The like defence do the Rhodians make for themselves *. But that opinion which favours more of truth is, That neither should this be permitted, unless it appear by very probable Arguments that it hath been otherwise customarily done, as it is sometimes used now amongst us, in imitation of the ancient Ætolians, amongst whom it was accounted lawful, *Ex omni Præda Prædam sumere*; *To take Armes on either side.* Which custom, saith *Polybius*, was of that force, *That although they were not at War themselves, but their Friends or Associates only; yet it was lawful for the Ætolians without any publick Decree of their Senate to list themselves on either side, and consequently to pillage both Parties.* This is likewise the Testimony that *Livy* gives of them, *They suffer their Youths without any publick Order to serve in the Wars, with their Associates, or against them: so that oft-times in two contrary Armies, the Ætolians serve as Auxiliaries on both sides.* Thus the Ætrurians of old, although they denyed aid to the *Vejentes*, yet if any of their Youths would serve them voluntarily, they would not hinder them.

† *Lib.* 7.
* *Aul.Gel. l.* 7. *c.* 3.
Lib. 17.
Livy l. 5.

XXXII. What if our Subjects be invaded.

Again, the Peace is broken, not only when the whole Body of a State or Kingdom, but if any of its Subjects shall by force of Armes be invaded, unless there be some new Cause of War given. For for this Cause is every Peace made, That the Subjects on both sides might live secure; it being an act of the City or Commonwealth, in behalf of the whole, and of every of its parts; yea and although there were a new cause of War, yet by Peace it shall be lawful for every man to defend both himself, and whatsoever is his. *By Armes to defend our selves against Armes*, saith *Cassius*, *is that Right which Nature hath given us:* Which Right cannot easily be presumed to be renounced amongst Equals. But to revenge our own private Quarrels, or to recover by force what hath been taken away, is not lawful, unless judgment be first denied us: for this will admit of delay, but that of none. But if Subjects make it their continual trade of life to rob and pillage, contrary to the Law of Nature, so that it be apparent that what they do is contrary to the will of their Governours, and that no Court of Judicature can reach to punish them, such as are Pyrates, Robbers, or the like; from these, as if they were surrendred up unto us, we may both recover our damages, and revenge our selves of them by force of Armes. But to do the like to those that are innocent for that cause, is to break the Peace.

XXXIII. If our Associates be invaded, the Peace is broken.

Although we are not as yet invaded, yet if our Associates be, the Peace is broken; that is, if they be such as are comprehended in the Peace, as hath been already proved in the Case of the Saguntines †. This the Greeks in *Xenophon* alledge *, *Omnes nos omnibus vobis juravimus*; *We have all of us sworn this Peace to all of you.* Yea, though those Associates do not contract for themselves, but others do in their behalf, it is all one, in case it do sufficiently appear that they have ratified it. But so long as this is uncertain, they are to be held as Enemies. But for the rest of Associates, that are not expresly comprehended in the Peace, and for our Kinsmen and Allies, that are neither Subjects nor nominated, the Case is otherwise. Neither can an invasion of them amount to the breach of Peace. But yet it will not hence follow, as we have elsewhere said, That it is unlawful for us in this Case to make War, but that the War so undertaken is not grounded upon the breach of Peace, but upon a new cause given.

† See Book 2. Ch.16. § 13.
* *Græc.Hist.l.6.*

XXXIV. The second way of breaking a Peace.

The Peace is also broken, as we have said before, by doing contrary to that which is expressed in the Peace: Where, under the word [doing] we are to comprehend the not doing of what we ought to do, and when we ought to do it.

XXXV. All the Articles of Peace are alike to be observed.

Neither may we here admit of any distinction between the Articles of Peace, as if some were of greater concernment than others. For what is thought worthy to be inserted, is also thought worthy to be observed. Yet should goodness and common humanity prevail with all men, but especially Christians; to pass by small faults, but chiefly if repented of: For as the Poet speaks,

> *Quem pœnitet peccâsse, pene est innocens.*
>
> He's almost guiltless who is penitent.

Yet small offences are to be referred;

But yet to the end that the Peace may be the better preserved, to these of smaller concernment, this Clause ought be added, That in case any of them should be broken, it should not amount so high as to the breach of the peace: But that such things should be first put to to reference, before it ſhould be lawful to take Arms, which we find added to the Peloponneſian League recorded by *Thucydides*.

XXXVI. Or ſome puniſhment for them inflicted. *Lib. 3. c. 19. §. 14.*

And I am clear of opinion that the ſame may be done in caſe ſome ſpecial puniſhment be inſerted in thoſe Articles; not that I am ignorant that ſuch an agreement there may be, That it ſhall be in the choice of the Party injured, either to accept of ſome puniſhment, or to null the Peace: But that the nature of the offence may be ſuch, as requires rather that, than this. Beſides, what I have formerly ſaid and proved by the Authority of Hiſtory is evident, That he that fulfils not his promiſe, being firſt failed, breaks not the Peace, for he is not bound but under condition.

XXXVII. What if hindered by neceſſity.

But if the nonperformance of what is agreed unto be occaſioned through neceſſity, as if the thing promiſed be taken away or periſhed; or if what was agreed to have been done, be by any chance or caſualty rendred impoſſible, the Peace ſhall not be deemed as broken: For (as we have ſaid before) Peace doth not uſually depend on ſuch conditions as are caſual. But the other Party ſhall be at his choice, whether he had rather expect the performance of that promiſe hereafter, if there remain any hopes that it may be done though late; or receive to the value of the thing promiſed; or laſtly, whether he had rather be diſcharged from ſome other thing mutually promiſed, and anſwerable to that in this Article, and that is thought equivalent to it.

XXXVIII. Yet if the innocent party will, the Peace is not broken.

It is certainly an argument of great integrity in the innocent party to preſerve the Peace, even with thoſe who have often broken their Faith as *Scipio* did with the Carthaginians, notwithſtanding their many perfidious dealings with them; becauſe no man can poſſibly cancel his obligation by doing contrary unto it: For although it be expreſt that by ſuch a contrary fact, the Peace ſhall be broken; yet is this ſo to be underſtood, that it ſhall ly in the choice of the innocent perſon, whether he will make ſuch an advantage thereof or not.

XXXIX. The third way of breaking Peace.

Laſtly we ſaid, That the Peace may be broken by doing that which is contrary to the ſpecial nature of every Peace.

XL. What falls under the notion of Friendſhip. *Pro Gabin.*

Thus thoſe things that are done contrary to Friendſhip, do break that Peace that was contracted under condition of Friendſhip; for look what the duty of friendſhip may require from others, ought alſo to be performed by the Right of this agreement. And to this, though not to every Peace (*for ſome there are that are not tyed up to this condition*, as *Pomponius* obſerves) may we refer many of thoſe diſſertations, which Civilians handle concerning ſuch injuries and contumelies as are committed without force of Armes, and particularly that of *Tully*, *If after Peace made any thing be committed, it ſhall not be accounted as a bare neglect, but as a wilful breach; neither ſhall it be imputed to impudence, but unto perfidiouſneſs.* And even here alſo (as much as in us lies) we are to take care that we judge not of the fact invidiouſly; if therefore an injury be done againſt either our Allies, or Subjects, it ſhall not be imputed to him with whom we have made Peace, unleſs it be evident that it was done by his inſtigation. According to which natural equity, do the Roman Laws proceed concerning ſuch acts of cruelty as are done againſt Servants; as Adultery and Raviſhment are imputed rather to acts of unbridled luſt than of hatred; and ſo the invading of another mans Right is adjudged as an act of Covetouſneſs, rather than of Treachery. Cruel threatnings whether by words or ſigns, unleſs it be upon ſome new cauſe given, cannot conſiſt with friendſhip, no more than can the erecting of new Forts and Bulwarks upon the Frontiers, when it is manifeſt that they are not ſo much for defence as offence; ſo alſo, the more than ordinary preparations for War, either by Sea or Land, if he with whom the Peace is made have ground enough to believe that they are made againſt none, but againſt himſelf.

XLI. To receive Exiles whether contrary to friendſhip. * *Lib. 2. c. 5. §. 24.* † *Lib. 42.* * *Leuctr. 2.*

The reception of ſuch particular perſons as are willing to tranſplant themſelves from one Princes Dominions to another, is no breach of Friendſhip, for this freedom is not only natural but benign; whereunto we may likewiſe add the receiving of Exiles: for as I have elſewhere proved out of *Euripides* *, over ſuch the City or Prince that baniſhed them, can have no power. *What advantage is it*, ſaith *Perſeus* in *Livy* †, *that every man hath power to baniſh himſelf, if there be no place left him to fly unto?* And this *Ariſtides* calls *a right common to all mankind to receive perſons baniſhed* *. Solon *would not admit that any Strangers ſhould be enrolled among his Citizens, but ſuch as had been for ever baniſhed their own Country, or ſuch as came with their whole Families to* Athens, *there to exerciſe ſome Craft or Manufacture.* *Perſeus* in *Appian* pleads thus with the Romans, concerning his receiving of ſome fugitives, *What I did*, ſaith he, *was juſtifiable by the common right of* *of all mankind, which you your selves also do sometimes:* which likewise is usually confirmed by mutual Covenants, as may appear by that Peace made between the Romans and the Persians. The like doth *Strabo* testifie of the Aradii, who whilst the Kings of *Syria* were at War among themselves, obtained this liberty, That they might receive what Fugitives they pleased, but send away none. But as to walled Towns, or any great Multitudes, that did constitute any one entire part of a City, that it is not lawful for any Prince to receive these, we have already proved. This was the cause of the War between the Persians and the Romans, because King *Lazus* at the sollicitation of the Consul had revolted to the Romans. Neither is it lawful to receive such as are bound, either by Oath, or otherwise to perform duty or service to another Prince. The like hath sometimes been introduced by the Law of Nations among some people concerning such as have been by the chance of War made Slaves; but as concerning the dedition of such, who are not banished, but do fly to avoid condigne punishment, we have elsewhere treated. *Lib. 2. c. 5. §. 24.* *Lib. 2. c. 21. §. 3. & seq.*

XLII. War sometimes ended by lot.

To determine a War by lots is not always lawful, but then only when we have an absolute propriety in the thing contended for; for Cities are to be defended for the preservation of the Lives, Goods, Chastities, and such like of their Citizens. And Kings are more strictly bound to defend the general safety of their Kingdoms, than to omit those means which for their own and others defence are most natural; but yet in case, he that is unjustly invaded, shall upon due examination find himself too weak to make any considerable resistance, it may seem lawful for him to refer the quarrel to the chance of a lot, that so by exposing himself to a danger that is uncertain, he may avoid one that is certain, of which two evils the lesser is to be chosen.

XLIII. Whether it may be determined by the event of a set number of Combatants.

But here follows a case very much disputed, namely, Whether it be lawful to determine a War by the success of a Battel fought by an appointed number of Combatants, as between on each side one, as that between *Turnus* and *Æneas*, *Menelaus* and *Paris*; or between on each side two, as between the *Ætolians* and the *Ælians*; or between on each side three, as that between the *Roman Horatii* and the *Alban Curatii*; or between on each side three hundred, as that between the Lacedemonians and the Argives: Whereunto I answer, That if we look no farther than unto the Law of Nations, which is external, without doubt, such a decision is lawful; for by that Law every man may destroy his Enemy any way: But if according to the opinion of the Ancient Grecians, Romans, and other Nations, every man hath an absolute power over his own life, then surely there is nothing therein repugnant to internal justice. But this opinion (as we have often said) is contrary not only to right reason but to Gods precepts; for to kill a man for his detaining of such things as we may well spare, is as we have already proved, to transgress the rules of Charity. Whereunto let us now add, That if he to whom God hath given life as a blessing, shall set so meanly by it, as to cast it away for a trifle, he sins both against God and his own Soul. If the thing contended for be worthy of a War, as if it be undertaken to preserve the lives of many innocent persons (as *Charles* the fifth Emperour pretended when he challenged *Francis* the first King of *France* to a single Combat) in this case we ought with all our power to endeavour it; but to make use of a set Combat, either as a tryal of the goodness of our Cause, or as an instrument of Divine judgment, is vain and abhorrent from true Piety. There is but one only case which renders such a Combate just and innocent, and that too but on one side only, which is when nothing can reasonably be expected, but that he who maintains an unjust cause, will otherwise be certainly the Victor, and will prosecute his Victory to the destruction of a multitude of Innocents. Now he that shall in this case adventure his life by any means, whereby he conceives any probable hopes to prevail, must needs be innocent, or at least so reputed. But yet we cannot deny, but that many things, though not exactly done, yet may be by others, if not well approved of, yet permitted for the prevention of greater mischiefs, which could not otherwise be avoided. Like as in many places, griping Usury and publick Stews are at this Day tolerated. Wherefore in that case formerly put, of two persons pretending with equal titles to one Kingdom which cannot be divided, if they shall offer to try their fortunes in such a Combate, the people may safely permit them for the prevention of a more general calamity, which must otherwise necessarily ensue. The like may be said where such a Combate may put an end to any bloody War. Thus did *Cyrus* challenge the King of *Assyria*; and *Metius* in *Dionysius Halicarnassensis* thus concludes, That seeing that the contest did not concern the power or dignity of the Nation but of their Princes only, it was but reasonable that they only who were concerned should decide the quarrel by Armes between themselves. Thus did the Adrianopolitans answer *Mahomet*, when he and *Musa Zilebes* contested for the Ottoman Empire. *Lib. 2. c. 7. §. 12. & lib. 2. c. 19. §. 5. c. 21. §. 1.* *Aq. 2. 2. c. 95. Art. 8. & ibi Cajetan.*

And

And so we read of sundry challenges made by several Pretenders to one and the same Kingdom, as of that which *Charles* the Fifth sent to *Francis* the first King of *France*; and of many Duels fought in such Cases, as that of *Heraclius* the Emperour with *Cosroe* Son to the King of *Persia*.

XLIV. Whether the fact of a King do oblige the people.

Where also we must note, That they that cast their Fortunes upon the Tryal of such Combates, may haply lose their own Right, if any they had, to the thing contended for. But they cannot transfer any Right to another, unless the Kingdom contended for be Patrimonial. And therefore, for the confirmation of such Agreements, the consent, not only of the people but, of such as have any Right to the Succession, if there be any then born, would be necessary. And so it is the consent of the chief Lord in those Estates that are not free.

XLV. Who is to be adjudged the Conqueror. * *Lib.* 3. *Guic. lib.* 1. *Herod. lib.* 1. *Thucyd. lib.* 1. *Lib.* 16. *Lib.* 29. 40.

It is likewise frequently disputed (where such Combats are permitted) which is the conquering Party, seeing that neither of them can be said to be absolutely conquered, unless all the Combatants on one side be either killed or put to flight. As in *Livy* *, he that forsaking his ground shall retreat either within his own Bounds, or unto places of strength, is said to be conquered. Amongst those three famous Historians, *Herodotus*, *Thucydides*, and *Polybius*, we read of three Questions proposed concerning Victory; the first whereof concerns this of set Combats. But he that judiciously weighs it, shall find that both Parties departed the Field without any true Victory. For the Argives were not put to flight by *Othryades*, but marched away by Night, stedfastly believing, and as confidently proclaiming themselves Conquerours to their own Country-men. Neither were the Corinthians routed by the Corcyreans, but having fought it out gallantly, and perceiving a strong Fleet of the Athenians near them, without endangering their Forces with the Athenians; they made a safe retreat. But *Philip* King of *Macedon* having taken a single ship of *Attalus*, forsaken by her Mariners, though he were far enough from destroying his whole Fleet; yet thereupon (as *Polybius* notes) rather carried himself like a Conquerour, than thought himself one. And as to those other things which, as well *Livy* in several places as, the Authours before recited, do set down as signs of Victory; as the taking of the spoil, the granting leave to bury the dead, and the offering Battel a second time: These though they carry some shew of Victory, yet of themselves prove nothing; but as they are backt with other more demonstrative Aguments of the Enemies Flight. *Plutarch*, concerning *Agesilaus*, writes thus, *Having given the Enemy leave to bury their dead, and thereby gained to himself the honour of being Conquerour, he went to* Delphos. So the same *Plutarch* in the life of *Nicias* proves both by Law and Custom, *That he who craves leave to bury his dead, seems thereby to disclaim the Victory. Neither had they that craved this leave any Right at all to erect Trophees.* But this (as I have already said) is no infallible sign of Victory; and yet where the Victory is otherwise doubtful, he that first departs the Field may more probably be thought to fly, than he that keeps it. But where there are no certain signs of Victory, there every thing is to remain as before the Fight; and so both Parties are either to prosecute the War, or to draw to a new Agreement for Peace.

XLVI. War sometimes determined by Arbitration. *Lib.* 2. *c.* 22. *Præf. Nat. Hist.*

Concerning Arbiters, *Proculus* informs us, That they are of two sorts, whereof the one he makes so Authoritative; that whether his award be just or unjust it must be obeyed: which (saith he) is to be observed whensoever both Parties do engage themselves to stand to the determination of a third person. The other he makes to be less binding; as when both Parties are content to refer their Case to be moderated by some indifferent person: An example whereof we have in that Answer of *Celsus*, *If the Servant, being made free, shall swear to perform such services as his Patron shall think fit to impose upon him, the imposition of the Patron shall not be binding, unless what he imposeth be equal.* But this interpretation of an Oath, though haply it might be warranted by the Roman Laws, yet can it not agree with the plain and genuine sense of the words simply taken. But yet this is very true, That the word [Arbiter] may be taken in both senses, either for a Moderator only, such as the Athenians were between the Rhodians and *Demetrius*; or for an absolute Judge, whose Sentence must be obeyed. And in this sense we here take it, as also we did elsewhere, treating of the means how to prevent a War. And yet even against such Arbiters, to whose award both Parties have mutually promised to stand, it may be provided by the Civil Law, as in some places it is, That Appeals shall be granted and Bills of complaint admitted. But this cannot be between Kings or between Nations, for here can be no superiour Power that can either hinder or dissolve the obliging power of the promise. And therefore whether the Sentence be right or wrong, we must be concluded by it. So that what *Pliny* sometimes said may very fitly be applied hither, *Summum quisque Causæ suæ Judicem facit, quemcunque elegit*; *Every man makes him to whom he refers himself, the supreme Judge of his own Cause.* This also we must add, That it is one thing to discourse concerning the Duty of an Arbiter, what he ought to do; and another thing to treat of their obligation that are content to refer their Cause to such an Arbitrement. For as though there were a Law among the Cities of *Italy*, That one Kinsman should not go to Law with another

ther, but that all differences ſhould be determined by Arbiters choſen on purpoſe ; yet notwithſtanding this Law, there were ſome Caſes wherein they might refuſe ſuch a reference. So alſo there may be ſome Caſes and ſome Reaſons why Princes may refuſe to put their differences to Arbitrement. Amongſt which, this is not the leaſt, When no aſſurance can be given that the perſons referring will ſtand to the award, *Quis alterutrum coget noſtrum, qui conventis ſtare noluerit ?* ſaith *Auguſtus* to *Mark Anthony* ; Who ſhall compel him (of us two) that refuſeth to be determined by the Sentence of our common Judge or Arbiter ? Private men may be compelled to ſtand to an Agreement by the publick Magiſtrate, but who ſhall compel Princes that have no Superior ? Other Reaſons alſo there may be ; as that of *Philip* King of *Spain*, who refuſed the Pope to be Arbitrator between himſelf and other Competitors, for the Kingdom of *Portugal* ; becauſe the Pope claimed the deciſion of all ſuch Controverſies as his Right : wherefore that prudent King was unwilling to add his own example to ſome ancient ones, whereby the Pope might prove himſelf to be the ſole Arbiter of Kingdoms. *Albericus Gentilis.* See pag. 335.

XLVII. Arbiters in Caſes dubious, tied up to Law.

That which is to be conſidered in an Arbiter is, Whether he be choſen as a Judge or as a Moderator, which was the proper Office of an Arbiter, as *Seneca* thought where he tells us *, *That a good Cauſe is better referred to a Judge than to an Arbiter : Melior videtur conditio bonæ Cauſæ ſi ad Judicem, quam ſi ad Arbitrum mittitur ; Becauſe a Judg hath a conſtant Rule to walk by which he muſt not tranſgreſs ; whereas an Arbiter being freed from the Shackles of the Law, hath liberty to judge according to equity and good conſcience ; and therefore can either add or detract from the rigour of the Law, and give Sentence, not always as Juſtice ſhall exact, but ſometimes as pity and humanity ſhall direct. Ariſtotle* reckons it as a Duty of an honeſt and a frugal man to refer his Cauſe to an indifferent Arbiter, rather than to a ſevere Judge, *Arbiter id quod æquum eſt reſpicit, Judex Legem ; For an Arbiter looks at that which is righteous, but a Judge at that only which is legal.* And therefore is an Arbiter made choice of, to the end he may rebate the edge of the Law, or otherwiſe ſupply that wherein the Law is defective. For equity in this place doth not ſignifie (as elſewhere) that part of Juſtice that expounds the general words of the Law, neareſt to the mind of the Law-maker ; for even this alſo is the Office of a Judge ; but every thing that is better done than not done, although it be not according to the ſtrict Rules of Juſtice properly ſo called. But ſuch Arbiters as they are very frequent among private men, that are Fellow-Citizens or Subjects to the ſame State, and are highly commended, eſpecially to us Chriſtians, by St *Paul*, 1 *Cor.* 6. ſo in ſuch Caſes as are ambiguous, we are not to allow them ſo much power as to determine of them. For in theſe we are to follow that ſenſe that hath the leaſt of doubt in it ; but eſpecially when the diſpute ariſeth between two Sovereign Princes, who having no common Judg between them, may be preſumed to reſtrain the power of Arbiters within thoſe ſtrict Rules of Juſtice which Judges are uſually confined to.

* *Lib.* 2. *de benef. c.* 7. *Rhet.* 1. *c.* 19. Equity, what.

XLVIII. Arbiters, not to judg of poſſeſſions.

Where this alſo is to be noted, That ſuch as are choſen Arbiters by a People, or ſuch as have the Sovereign Power over them, ought to give Sentence on the principal matter, but not to intermeddle with Poſſeſſions ; For the judgment of theſe belong to the Civil Law. By the Law of Nations, Dominion follows the Right of Poſſeſſion ; and therefore till the Cauſe be tryed, no innovation ought to be made, as well to avoid prejudice, as becauſe the recovery of things out of poſſeſſion is difficult : Wherefore *Livy* in his Book of Pleas between the Carthaginians and *Maſſiniſſa*, hath this Obſervation, *Legati jus poſſeſſionum non mutarunt, Ambaſſadours do never alter the Right of Poſſeſſions.*

XLIX. What the power is of a pure Dedition.

There is alſo an aſſuming of an Arbiter, but of another kind ; when a man yields himſelf up to the judgment of his very Enemy, which is a pure and abſolute ſurrender, whereby he makes himſelf a Slave, and gives his Enemy Sovereign Power over him. Thus the Ætolians in *Livy* were demanded in the Senate, Whether they would ſubmit themſelves to the Judgment of the Romans. This was the advice of *L. Cornelius Lentulus*, as it is recorded by *Appian* about the end of the ſecond Punick War, concerning the affairs of *Carthage*, *Let the Carthaginians*, ſaith he, *ſubmit themſelves to our cenſures, as the Vanquiſhed uſually do, and as many others have formerly done ; then we ſhall ſee how thankful they will be for what we ſhall give them. Neither ſhall they call this a League, for the difference between a League and this is great. For if we enter into a League with them, they will never want ſome plauſible excuſe to break it, alledging, That they had been firſt injured in ſome part of it ; for ſeeing that many words in that League will admit of a doubtful interpretation, they can never want a pretence that have a mind to cavil. But when we ſhall have diſarmed them as Priſoners, and made them our Slaves, then at length they will perceive, That they have nothing that is properly their own ; and then they will deſpond, and whatſoever we ſhall afterwards give them they will thankfully accept of, as of a mere gratuity.* But here alſo we muſt diſtinguiſh between what the Conquered ought to ſuffer, what the Conquerour by the Right of his Conqueſt may do, and laſtly, what moſt of all becomes him. The Conquered Party having yielded themſelves, ought to ſuffer whatſoever the Conquerour will impoſe upon them ; for being perfectly inſlaved, if we reſpect that Right of War that is external, they have nothing

Lib. 37. *Lib.* 14.

but what may be taken from them, even their lives and personal liberty, much more their Goods, whether they be those that are publick, or those that belong unto them, as private men. *The Ætolians,* saith *Livy, having yielded themselves to the will of their Enemies, dreaded nothing more than corporal punishments.* And, as we have elsewhere said, *When all things are surrendred, it rests in the choice of the Conquerour what he will take away, and wherein and how far he will punish the Conquered.* Pertinent whereunto is that of *Livy, It was the ancient custom of the Romans, when they had to do with a people or a King with whom they were not joined in friendship, either by League, or by equal Laws, not to use their Sovereign Power over them, as being at peace with them, until they had first delivered up unto them all things both Divine and humane, and until they had received their Hostages, taken away their Armes, and had placed Garrisons in their Cities.* Yea, and sometimes they that thus surrendred themselves might be killed, as we have elsewhere shewed *.

Lib. 37.

Above, Book 3. Chap. 8. Sect. 4.

* Above, Book 3. Chap. 11. Sect. 18.

L.

The Duty of a Conqueror towards the Conquered.

See Book 2. Chap. 15. in finem.

But the Conquerour, that he may do nothing unjustly, ought in the first place to take care that no mans life be taken from him, unless it be for some crime that deserves death. As also that no mans Goods be taken from him, unless it be by way of a just punishment. For in the Conqueror there is nothing so honourable, nor in some Cases so necessary, as in this manner to extend his clemency and liberality to the Conquered, so far forth as it may stand with his own security. When *Cyrus* had subdued the Assyrians, he comforted them by this assurance, *That their Condition should be the same that before it was, their Houses, Lands, Wives and Children, they should freely enjoy; and in Case any personal injuries were offered them, both he and his would readily defend them.* Admirable are the effects of those Wars that are concluded with a general pardon. Thus did *Nicholas* the Syracusian plead in *Diodorus* in the behalf of those that had yielded to mercy, *They have,* saith he, *yielded themselves, and given up their Armes, relying wholly on the Conquerours clemency:* Quare indignum foret, eos decipi spe nostræ humanitatis; *Wherefore it would be an everlasting dishonour to us to suffer them to be deceived in their confidence they have of our clemency.* And a little after, *Who amongst all the Grecians did ever inexorably condemn them to punishment, who yielded themselves to the Conquerours mercy. Appian* brings in *Octavius Cæsar* thus bespeaking *L. Antonius,* when he came to surrender himself, *If the end of thy coming hither had been to purchase thy Peace only, thou hadst found me, not only a Conquerour, but such a Conquerour as was throughly incensed by the wrongs thou hast done; but since thou art come to yield thy self, thy Friends, and thine Armes to our discretion, thou hast appeased mine anger, and taken away from me that power I had to have enforced thee to have accepted of what Conditions I pleased. For I am now to weigh, not so much what thou deservest to suffer, as what becomes me to grant; wherefore I shall chuse rather to consult mine own honour by forgiving, than to gratifie my passion by a just revenge.* We do often meet with these expressions in the Roman Stories, namely, That the Conquered do yield themselves sometimes to the faith, sometimes to the mercy or clemency, of the Conqueror. As in *Livy, To those Ambassadours that were sent from the Neighbour Provinces to surrender their Cities to the faith of the Romans, he gave a gracious Audience.* So in another place, speaking of King *Perseus,* he saith, Paulus *earnestly labouring that he might be permitted to surrender both himself and whatsoever was his, to the faith and clemency of the People of* Rome: Whereby nothing else is to be understood but an absolute rendition. For the word [Faith] in this and the like places, signifies nothing but the bare honesty and goodness of the Victor, unto which the Vanquished submits himself. There is a notable Story extant both in *Livy* and *Polybius,* concerning one *Phanea* an Ætolian Ambassadour, who in his Speech to the Consul *Manius* let fall these words, *That the Ætolians did freely surrender themselves and all they had to the faith of the same People of* Rome: Which (being thereunto urged by the Consul) he re-affirmed in the very words. But when the Consul demanded the principal Authors of the War to be immediately delivered unto him, *Phanea* readily answered, *That it was only to the faith, and not to the subjection, of the Romans that they submitted themselves:* Adding, That it was not the custom of the Grecians to be commanded; whereunto the Consul replied, That he cared not what the manner of the Grecians was, but the custom of the Romans was to impose Laws upon those who by their own concession had surrendred themselves: And immediately commanded the Ambassadour to be clapt up in Chains. *Polybius*'s words are to this sense, *Do ye, having newly surrendred your selves unto our trust, teach us what we must or ought to do?* By which words it is evident what he to whose faith any people do commit themselves may do with impunity, and without violating the Law of Nations. But yet the Roman Consuls did not make use of their power so as these Historians have reported, They only dismist the Ambassadours, and gave the Ætolians longer time to consult about it. Thus did the people of *Rome* answer the *Falisci,* as *Valerius Maximus* informs us, *That they very well understood that the* Falisci *had surrendred themselves not unto the power, but unto the faith of the Romans:* And of the *Campanes, That they had put themselves under the Romans, not by any League but, by a voluntary surrender.* Now

as

as concerning his Duty unto whom ſuch a ſurrender is made, that of *Seneca* is very pertinent, *Clementiæ liberum arbitrium habet*, *The Conquerour may ſhew what clemency he pleaſeth; but yet he ought to give Sentence not as a Judge according to the rigour of Law, but according to equity and good conſcience, he may either abſolutely forgive, or he may exact whatever ſatisfaction he pleaſeth.* Nor do I think it much material in what form of words ſuch a ſurrender is made, whether to the Conquerour's wiſdom, or to his moderation, or to his mercy and clemency. All theſe being but palliations, the main thing intended is, That the Conquerour muſt be Judge.

LI. Of a Conditional Surrender. *Lib.* I. *c.* 3. § 17.

Yet there are alſo Conditional Surrenders, which make proviſion either for every perſon, as when their lives, liberties, or ſome part of their Goods are expreſly excepted; or for the generality, and amongſt theſe ſome may amount even unto a Mixt Government, whereof we have elſewhere diſcourſed.

LII. Who may and ought to be given as Hoſtages.

To the Articles agreed upon for ſuch a Surrender, there ſucceeds in the next place Sureties for their performance; and theſe are either Hoſtages or Pledges. Hoſtages are either ſuch as freely give themſelves, or ſuch as are ſent by the Prince or State. For in all Civil Governments, he that hath the Sovereign Civil Power hath a Right as well to the actions, as to the Goods of his Subjects; but ſo that the Prince or State that ſends them are obliged to ſatisfie either them or their Relations, for the loſſes and damages they ſhall thereby ſuſtain. And in Caſe there be many nominated to be ſent, and it be indifferent to the Commonwealth whether of them goes, it is beſt to determine it by Lots. But yet he that is only Lord of the Fee hath no ſuch Right over his Vaſſal, as to ſend him, unleſs he be alſo his Subject; for the reverence and obedience due unto him doth not extend ſo far.

LIII. What Right is given over Hoſtages.

That an Hoſtage may be put to death by that Right of Nations which we call external, we have elſewhere ſhewed. But not by that which is internal, unleſs for ſome crime of his own, he hath deſerved it. Neither can they be made Slaves: Nay farther, they may by the Law of Nations enjoy and leave their Goods to their next Heirs; although by the Roman Laws it is provided, That their Goods being confiſcated, ſhould be brought into the publick Treaſury.

LIV. Whether they may make their eſcape.

But whether it be lawful for an Hoſtage to make his eſcape, would be likewiſe enquired. Certainly it is not, if either at his firſt entrance, or at any time after, to the end that he might live under a more gentle reſtraint, he engaged his word, That he would not. Otherwiſe it was not the purpoſe of the City or State in ſending their Citizen to oblige him not to flye; but to empower the Enemy to keep him in ſuch a ſtrict cuſtody, that though he would, yet he could not fly. And thus may that Fact of *Clælia* be defended, who made her eſcape from *Porſenna*, to whom She was ſent, with other Ladies, as Hoſtages. But admit that *Clælia* had not at all offended in making her eſcape, yet could not the City of *Rome* juſtifie her reception and detenſion. Which made *Porſenna* declare plainly, *That unleſs they ſent back his Hoſtage, he would take it to be a breach of their League.* Whereupon the Romans immediately reſtored her, as a Pledge of their Peace. *Liv. lib.* 2.

LV. Whether an Hoſtage may for any other cauſe be detained.

But this kind of aſſurance by Hoſtages is to thoſe who are ſent very odious, as well by reaſon that it deprives them of their liberty, as becauſe it is occaſioned by the fact of another. Wherefore in all Caſes that are dubious, we are to underſtand it in the ſtricteſt ſenſe; as that they that are ſent as Hoſtages in one Caſe, cannot be detained as Hoſtages in another. Which is ſo to be underſtood, That when the latter Agreement was made, there was no mention at all made of thoſe Hoſtages. But if we have already broken our faith in any other Agreement, or if there be any Debt juſtly due, then thoſe Hoſtages may be detained, yet not then as Hoſtages, but as Subjects, which by the Law of Nations may be taken and kept as Priſoners for their Sovereign's Debt. Which very thing may alſo be eaſily prevented, by inſerting this Clauſe amongſt thoſe Articles, That ſo ſoon as that, for which they were ſent, ſhall be performed, thoſe Hoſtages ſhall be freely ſent back.

LVI. The Principal being dead, the Hoſtage is to be ſet free.

He that is ſent as an Hoſtage to releaſe for a while either a Priſoner or another Hoſtage, this dying, the other ſhall be releaſed. For when the perſon dyed that was the Hoſtage, all the Right that any man had in him as an Hoſtage, dyed with him; as *Ulpian* ſpeaks in the Caſe of a redeemed Captive. Wherefore as in *Ulpian*'s Caſe, the ranſome is not due, if the Captive dye before it be paid; ſo in this Caſe, the perſon ſubſtituted cannot lawfully be detained, if the principal Perſon be defunct. It was then no unreaſonable Demand that *Demetrius* made to the Roman Senate, in deſiring to be diſmiſt, as being no longer an Hoſtage for *Antiochus*, he being dead. *Appian.* Which very Plea, *Juſtine* alſo out of *Trogus* records and approves of, where he ſaith, *That as ſoon as* Demetrius *heard that his Brother* Antiochus *(for whom he remained as an Hoſtage in* Rome*) was dead, he immediately addreſs'd himſelf to the Senate, telling them,*

That whilſt his Brother lived he was contented to be his Pledge; but he being dead, he would gladly know whoſe Hoſtage he then was.

LVII. The King dying, whether the Hoſtage may be detained. * Book 2. Ch. 16. Sect. 18.

But what if the King dye that made the Hoſtage, ſhall his Hoſtage be detained? Of this the Anſwer depends upon that which we have heretofore handled *, namely, Whether the League ſo made be perſonal only, or real. For Acceſſaries cannot juſtifie us in receding from that general Rule which we ought to walk by in the interpretation of Principals, whoſe nature they themſelves ought to follow.

LVIII. An Hoſtage may ſometimes be principally obliged. * See Book. 3. Ch, 15. § 18. *Alb. Gent. l.* 2.

But here by the way we muſt add, That Hoſtages are not always bare Sureties in the Obligation, but ſometimes the principal Parties; as when in an Agreement one man engageth himſelf for the fact of another, which if not performed, he himſelf is to make it good: and thus Hoſtages in his ſtead may ſtand obliged. Thus it was adjudged in that Sponſion made at *Caudys*, as we have elſewhere declared *. But their opinion who hold, That Hoſtages may ſtand obliged one for the fact of another, though done without their conſent, is not only rigorous, but unjuſt.

LIX. Pledges, how engaged.

Pledges have ſome things common with Hoſtages, and ſome things they have peculiar to themſelves. That which they have in common is, That they may be detained for another Debt, at preſent due, unleſs faith be given to the contrary. That which they have peculiar is, That what Contract ſoever is made concerning theſe, will admit of a larger conſtruction than thoſe made concerning Hoſtages. Neither is the one ſo diſtaſteful as the other: for that things ſhould be kept ſtrictly is natural; but that men ſhould be ſo kept, is not ſo.

LX. The Right of Redemption, how loſt. * Book 2. Ch. 4. Sect. 17.

Laſtly, That length of time cannot prejudice the Right of Redemption as to things ſo engaged, if that be performed for which they were originally depoſited, we have elſewhere proved *. For that act that was done upon an ancient and known Agreement cannot eaſily be believed to proceed from a new one; and therefore that the Debtor forbears to redemand his Pledge, is no good Argument to prove his dereliction of it, unleſs ſome other ſtrong conjectures do induce us to believe otherwiſe: As in Caſe a man being by ſome means hindred when he would have redeemed it, had paſt it over in ſilence ſo long as was ſufficient for him that detained it to ground his conjectures that we had forſaken it.

CHAP.

CHAP. XXI.

Of Faith during War, of Truces, Safe-Conduct, and the Redemption of Prisoners.

I. Whether a Truce be a time of Peace or War.

THERE are some things which Soveraign Princes even in the midst of War, do usually grant one to another, which *Virgil* and *Tacitus* call, *Belli Commercia, The Traffick of War*; and in *Homer* are said to be συνημοσύναι, *Mutual Agreements or Covenants of War*. Such are Truces, Safe-Conducts, and the redemption of Prisoners. A Truce is an agreement, whereby though, the War continue yet, all acts of hostility do for a while cease, though (as I said) the War continue. For, as *Cicero* speaks, between War and Peace there is no *Medium*; it may be called a War, although at present its operations are intermitted: As, *A man may be said to be wise or prudent, though he be asleep; and vertuous, though for a while he be void of action.* The distance of place, saith *Aristotle, doth not dissolve friendship it self, but interrupts the exercise of it.* An habit there may be, though at present it operates not. For, as *Eustratius* well observes, *An habit being compared with an ability simply taken, is called an act; but being compared with action it self, or the exercise of that ability, is called power; as a man may be an excellent surveyor, or a skilful Architect, though at present he be fast asleep:* Est disertus etiam qui tacit; *A man may be eloquent though for a while he be silent*: and a good Workman, though he have no tools to work with. So then as *Gellius* sometimes said, *Neque Pax est inducia; Bellum manet, pugna cessat: A Truce cannot be called a Peace; for though the fight cease, the War continues.* So *Pacatus* in his *Panegyrick*, *Inducia Bella suspendebant; A Truce is but the suspension of the acts of War.* Which I here the rather mention, that we may understand, That whatsoever is agreed upon to be of force during the War, is also of force during the time of a Truce; unless it plainly appear, that it was not the state of War that was so much looked at, as the exercise of it. On the contrary, If any thing be agreed upon as concerning Peace, that is of no force in the time of a Truce: Neither am I ignorant that *Virgil* calls a Truce, *Pacem sequestram; An indifferent Peace, or a thing between Peace and War:* And that *Servius* upon that place calls it a *temporary Peace.* As also doth the Scholiast upon *Thucydides*: *Varro* calls it

Nic. 8.

Ad 6. *Nic.*

The

The Peace of Camps for a few days, all which are rather descriptions than definitions, and those also but figurative; such as was that of the same *Varro*, who calls a Truce Wars Holyday, who might as well have call'd it Wars napp or short sleep. As *Papinius* calls those Days whereon there are no pleadings, Days of Peace. And as *Aristotle* called sleep, *Vinculum sensuum*; *The lock or chain of the senses*: By whose example we may rightly call a Truce the fetters of War. Which exposition of *Varro* (which

Ad Ter. Eun. Act. 1. Scen. 1.

also *Donatus* follows) *Gellius* deservedly blames for adding thereunto, *for a few days*, as if there could not be a Truce made for a few Hours. Whereunto also I may add, for Years; nay, for twenty, thirty, forty, yea a hundred Years: Examples whereof we may find in *Livy*, which serves also to confute that definition of *Paulus*, *Induciæ sunt cum in breve, & in præsens tempus convenit, ne invicem lacessant*; *A Truce is when by an agreement, neither party shall at present, or for a short time prefixt, provoke each other to acts of hostility.* But yet possible it is, that if it shall evidently appear, that an absolute cessation from all Hostile Acts, was the solitary reason simply and wholly moving both Parties to make such an agreement, that then whatsoever is said concerning a time of Peace, may also be said concerning the time of such a Truce, not simply by vertue of the word [*Truce*,] but by a certain conjecture that it was the mind and intention of both

Lib. 3. c. 16. §. 20.

Parties, that that Truce should be equivalent to a Peace, whereof we have already treated in another place.

II. The word *Induciæ* whence derived.

This word *Induciæ*, which signifies a Truce, is not (as *Gellius* would have it) derived from *Inde uti jam*; *from thence, as it is now*: Nor (as *Opilius* thought) from the word *Endoitus*, or *Endoitium*, which signifies *an Entrance* into, or a beginning of; but rather

Gell. l. 19. c. 8.

from these words, *Quod inde*, that is, *That there should be rest from such a time*; or as the Greeks call it, *A cessation of Armes from thenceforth*. For it is confest both by *Gellius* and *Opilius*, that the word, *Induciæ*, was by the Ancients wrote with a [*t*,] and not with a [*c*,] thus, *Induciæ*; and that what they now use in the plural, was doubtless of old used in the singular number, the Ancient word being *Endoitia*: As, for *Otium*, *Rest*, they then pronounced, *Oitium*, from the word *Oiti*, which we now pronounce *Uti*: As also of the word *Poina* (for which we now use, *Pœna*, *Punishment*) is made *Punio*, and of *Poinus* (now *Pœnus*) is made *Punicus*: So of that word, *Ostia*, *Ostiorum*, is now made *Ostia*, *Ostiæ*; and of *Ostrea*, *Ostreorum*, is now made *Ostrea*, *Ostreæ*; so of *Endoitia*, *Endoitiorum*, is made *Endoitia*, *Endoitiæ*, and from thence *Indutia*; whereof the plural number is now only in use. Neither was *Donatus* much amiss, who would have *Indiciæ*, to be derived from *In dies otium*, *A rest for some Days*. A Truce then in War

Livy, Plut. Justine.

is a rest or cessation, and not a Peace: Therefore some Historians do exactly distinguish them, when they say (as they often do) *Pacem negatam, inducias datas*; *That though a Peace was denyed, yet was a Truce granted.*

III. The Truce ended, War need not be re-denounced.

Wherefore this time of a Truce being expired, there needs no new denouncing of War, for that which for a time hindred it, being taken away, the War presently starts up and enjoys its own Rights, being during that time not dead, but asleep, just as the Dominion or Jurisdiction that a State hath over a madman, doth, as soon as he recovers from his madness. But yet we may read in *Livy* of a War, that by the judgement of the Colledge of Heralds was denounced after the expiration of a Truce: But then we must know, that it was the custome of the Ancient Romans to make use of these unnecessary cautions and premonitions, to shew how much they loved Peace, and how unwillingly they made War though their Cause were just, it being usual with them, *Bellum indicere ne inferrent*; *To proclaim War to the end that they might make Peace.* And

Livy l. 4.

this *Livy* himself seemed to hint, where he saith, *That after a pitcht Battel had been fought with the Vejentes at* Nomentum *and* Fidenæ, *there was indeed a Truce granted, but no Peace made*; *which Truce being ended, though they had before broken it, yet were the Heralds notwithstanding sent, who receiving no satisfaction to their demands, denounced War.*

IV. How the time of a Truce is to be composed.

The time assigned for a Truce is either continual, as when it is made for an hundred Days; or by prefixing a time when it shall end, as until the Calends of *March*. In the former, the account must be to the last moment; for this is most natural. For that account which is made by days Civil, depends upon the several Laws and Customs of Nations. In the other kinds of assignments, it is usually questioned, Whether the Day, the Month, or the Year, whereon any Truce is to determine, ought to be included or excluded the time of the Truce. Surely all natural things have two Bounds whereby they are terminated, the one within, or adhering to the things themselves, as the Body is terminated by the Skin, being the utmost part of it: The other outward, as a River is the Bound of the Land. Now according to either of these two ways, may those Bounds that depend upon the will be assigned. But yet those are most natural, that are a part

Met. lib. 2. c. 17.

of the thing bounded. So saith *Aristotle*, *Terminus dicitur, quod ultimum cujusque est*; *That is said to be the end of any thing which is the extreme part of it.* Neither is this repugnant to com-

mon

mon use, *For if a man promise to do a thing before the day of his death, it shall include that very day whereon he died.* *Spurina* forewarned *Cæsar* of some danger that should not be protracted beyond the Ides of *March*; and being upbraided by *Cæsar* as a false Prophet, because the Ides of *March* were already come, yet no danger had befaln him; he replied, *Venisse quidem eas, sed non præteriisse, That they were indeed come, but not past.* Wherefore much more should the interpretation of Truces be thus understood, the production whereof deserving so much the more of favour, as it is sparing of humane blood. But yet that Day from whence any Truce is to commence is not to be reckoned as one of the number, because such is the force of this Preposition [*from*] that it serves not for Conjunction, but for separation. Suet. in Cæs. c. 81.

V. When they begin to bind.

But this also I may add on the by, That Truces and such like Conventions do immediately oblige both Parties consenting, as soon as they are perfected; but the Subjects on either side are not bound until the Truce receives the Form of a Law by a publick Proclamation: which done, The Subjects on either side are obliged to observe it. But yet this Proclamation being made in one place only, shall not from that instant extend its obliging power through all parts of that Nation. But sufficient time must be allowed, that every part may receive knowledge thereof. And in the mean time, if any thing be by those Subjects done contrary to that Truce, they are not at all punishable for it. Neither are the persons contracting notwithstanding any thing the less bound to repair those damages. Wherefore that fact of the Spaniards in *Italy*, recorded by *Mariana*, cannot be defended. Lib. 28. cap. 7.

VI. What may lawfully be done during a Truce.

What may lawfully be done, and what not, may easily be collected from the very definition of a Truce. All hostile Acts are unlawful, whether they be done against persons or things. For whatsoever is by force of Armes done against an Enemy during a Truce is contrary to the Law of Nations, as *Lucius Æmilius* in *Livy* tells his Souldiers. Nay, whatsoever shall come from the Enemy accidentally into our Quarters, although it had been formerly ours, yet must it be restored; because by that external Justice, whereby such things ought to be tryed, they are the Enemies. And therefore, as *Paulus* the Lawyer observes, the Right of Postliminy in the time of a Truce, is, as it were, out of date; because unto this Right it is required that there should precede another Right, namely, A Right to take from an Enemy by force what we can; which during a Truce cannot be admitted. To go and come hither or thither, as we please, so arrayed as not to threaten danger, is lawful. This *Servius* notes upon the words of *Virgil*,

Trojans, with Latines mixt, in safety go. Ænead. lib. 11.

Where also he relates this Story, That the City being besieged by *Tarquin*, and a Truce agreed upon between *Porsenna* and the Romans, whilst the Circean Games were celebrating within the City, the Latine Captains were permitted freely without any restraint, not only to try their Fortunes among the Romans, but, being Victors, to be crowned also.

VII. Whether to retreat back, to repair breaches, or the like.

For an Enemy to retreat back with his Army, as *Livy* informs us that *Philip* did *, is no breach of a Truce: No more is it to make up our breaches, to levy Souldiers, and the like, unless it be particularly agreed to the contrary.

* Liv. lib. 31.

VIII. To surprize places of strength, unlawful.

But on the contrary, by corrupting a Garrison to surprize places held by them during a Truce, is utterly unlawful; for it is not possible that such places should be justly gained but by the Right of War. The like may be said of Subjects, who during a Truce, cannot, if they would, revolt to the Enemy. An example whereof we may read in *Livy* *, *For when the Inhabitants of* Coronæa *and* Haliartus, *in favour to Monarchy, sent their Ambassadours to* Macedonia *to desire a Garrison, whereby the better to defend themselves against the insolent pride of the Thebans; they received this Answer from the King, That having lately made a Truce with the Romans, he could not at present answer their desires.* We may indeed read in *Thucydides*, That *Brasidas* took the City *Menda*, revolting from the Athenians, to the Lacedemonians, in the time of a Truce; but withal he excuseth himself by the like formerly done by the Athenians. And yet to possess places altogether deserted is lawful, that is, if they be truly so, with a purpose never to owne them again; but not if they be left only without Guards or Garrisons, whether those Guards were omitted before any Truce was made, or whether they were withdrawn upon the Truce-making only. For *where the propriety is retained, another mans usurpation is unjust*: whereby that cavil which *Belisarius* urged against the Goths, is easily refuted; who in the time of a Truce seized on some places being ungarrisoned, upon this pretence of being forsaken. Proc. Goth. 2.

* Lib. 42.

IX. Whether he that being forcibly detained during the

Here also it may be questioned, Whether he who during the Truce is forcibly detained, and that Truce being ended is found among Enemies, hath by the Law of Nations a Right to return. If we look only to that Right which is external, this mans condition is the same with his, who coming in Peace only for Traffick, the War breaking out unexpectedly

Truce, hath a Right afterwards to return. * Book 3. Ch. 9. *Cic. l. 2. de inv.*

pectedly is unfortunately found amongſt Enemies, whoſe doom (as we have already declared *) is, To be kept Priſoner during the War. Neither is this repugnant to internal Juſtice, ſo far forth as the Goods and actions of Enemies ſtand obliged for the Debt of the City they inhabit, and may be taken in diſcharge thereof. Neither hath this man any more reaſon to complain, than many more innocent perſons have, who occaſionally ſuffer by that War. Neither are we to refer hither that Caſe which *Cicero* puts in his ſecond Book of Invention, concerning that Ship armed with an Iron Beak, which contrary to the Rhodian Law was found driven by a violent Tempeſt into Harbour, and according to that Law confiſcate, and by the Queſtor demanded to be ſold. For there the force of the Tempeſt did excuſe the puniſhment. But here we diſcourſe not of puniſhment, but of a Right that for a certain time only lay, as it were, aſleep. Yet without all doubt to releaſe ſuch a man were far more generous.

X. Of ſome ſpecial reaſons, for which a Truce is granted, and ſome Doubts thereupon.

There are alſo ſome things that during a Truce are unlawful, not ſimply of themſelves, but as they are repugnant to that end for which only the Truce was granted. As for example, If a Truce were granted only for the Burial of the Slain, there ought nothing to be altered; ſo if the Truce be made, That the Beſieged ſhould not in ſuch a time be aſſaulted, as that made by *Totilas* with the Neapolitans; then to receive freſh Supplies, or to go and come freely, is unlawful. For ſeeing that ſuch a Truce is granted in favour to one ſide only, it ought not to be made uſe of to the detriment of the other. Sometimes it is agreed, That during the Truce it ſhall not be lawful to come and go at pleaſure. Sometimes again ſafety to our perſons is granted, but not to our things; in which Caſe, if any mans perſon ſhall be hurt in the defence of his Goods, nothing ſhall be judged done contrary to the Truce. For ſince it is lawful for us to defend our Goods, perſonal ſafety is here to be referred to that which is principal, and not to that which comes by conſequence only.

XI. A Truce broken on one ſide, may diſcharge the other. * Book 3. Ch. 19. Sect. 19. & Ch. 20. 36.

If the Truce be broken on one ſide, there is no doubt but the injured Party may take Armes without any other ſolemn Denunciation; for every Article implies a Condition, as we have elſewhere ſaid *. Some examples we may find in Hiſtories where the breach of a Truce hath been connived at, even to the end of it; but we may likewiſe read of the War made againſt the *Hetruſci* and others, for doing things contrary to the Truce agreed on. From both which different examples we may collect, That the injured Party may lawfully take Armes. But whether he will make uſe of this Right or not, lyes in his own choice.

XII. What if a puniſhment be added.

But this is evident, That if the puniſhment agreed upon, being required, be accordingly inflicted on him that breaks the Truce, then the Party injured hath no Right to make war upon that account. For to this end is the Offender puniſhed, That all others may be ſecured; ſo on the contrary, If the injured perſon ſhall chuſe rather to make war, then is the Offender acquitted of puniſhment.

XIII. When private acts break the Peace.

But yet what is done by a private perſon breaks not a Truce, without the acceſs of ſome publick Act, that is, of command or approbation. But if he that doth it be neither puniſhed, nor delivered, nor reſtitution made, it ſhall be reputed as done by the publick Order of the State.

XIV. Free Paſſage without a Truce, how to be underſtood. * Book 2. Ch. 16. Sect. 12.

A freedom to paſs to and fro when no Truce is agreed on, is a kind of priviledge, and will therefore admit of ſuch an interpretation as is already declared *, where we treated of priviledges. Now this priviledge being neither prejudicial to any third perſon, nor grievous to him that granted it, is not to be underſtood in the ſtricteſt ſenſe, but with ſome allowance of favour, yet ſo that the propriety of the words will bear it; but eſpecially if it were freely offered and not granted at the requeſt of him that hath it. But much more when, beſides that which is private, there is any publick advantage to be gained thereby. We are therefore to forbear rigorouſly to interpret any ſuch Paſſes, though the words may perhaps warrant it, unleſs otherwiſe ſome great abſurdity will enſue, or that we are thereunto led by very probable conjectures, That it was ſo intended by him that gave them. On the contrary, A favourable conſtruction, even beyond the proper ſignification of the words, ſhall take place, rather than any ſuch like abſurdity ſhall be admitted, eſpecially if we ſhall be thereunto induced by any ſuch probable conjectures.

XV. Who may be admitted under the name of Souldiers.

From whence we may collect, That a ſafe Paſs given unto Souldiers comprehends not inferiour Captains only, but even chief Commanders; becauſe the propriety of the word will admit of ſuch a conſtruction. Although alſo it may admit of another more ſtrict, ſo under the name of a Clerk may be underſtood a Biſhop; as under that of Souldiers, Mariners employed in a Ship may be comprized, and all ſuch as in that War are engaged by a Military Oath.

XVI. Leave given to come, implies leave given to return.

Leave given to come, ſhall be underſtood as if it were alſo given to return; yet not through the force of the word, but to avoid ſomewhat that would otherwiſe be abſurd. For that which is intended as a courteſie, ſhould not by any conſtruction be rendred unprofitable; wherefore it implies alſo a ſafe return, ſo far until we ſhall arrive thither, where

we

we may be in safety. It was therefore but treachery in *Alexander* to cause those persons to be killed in their journey homewards, to whom he had indulged the favour to depart. Concerning which fact *Plutarch* gives his censure thus, *Hæc velut macula adhæsit bellicis actionibus regis, cætera in Bello agere & juste & regaliter soliti*; *This was a great blemish to the actions of a King, otherwise just and magnanimous.* But on the other side, if licence be given to depart, it shall not be so understood as if it were also given to return; neither doth that which is given us to come, give us a Right to send; for these are two divers and distinct things: neither is there any reason why we should seek after a sense beyond that which is natural to the words; but yet an errour herein committed, though it confer no right, yet certainly it mitigates somewhat of the punishment, if any such be added. But even he, to whom leave is given to come, may come once, but not again, unless the time limited in the Pass be such as may induce us to believe otherwise. *Diod. Sic. lib. 17.*

XVII. How far it extends to persons:

The Son shall not be permitted to follow his Father, nor the Wife her Husband, unless it be with a purpose to cohabit with him: for it is usual to dwell, but not to travel with our Families; a Servant or two though not exprest, yet may be presumed to be allowed to such as cannot well travel without them: for he that grants the principal, may well be thought to grant the necessary consequents, which yet is to be morally understood.

XVIII. How far to Goods:

Where licence is granted to persons, Their goods are also comprehended, though haply not all, yet such as are useful for travellers to carry with them.

XIX. To Attendants.

Under the word [Companions,] we are not to understand such whose condition is more hateful than his, to whom the licence of Safe-coming is granted, as Pyrates, Robbers, Fugitives, and Rebels, if the Nation from whence they come, be in the Pass-port exprest, it evidently excludes all Foreigners from protection.

XX. A Pass dyes not with him that gave it: * *Lib.2. ch.13.*

Licence to pass freely, being granted by vertue of the supreme power, is not in a case that is dubious, made void by the death of him that granted it, according to what hath been already said * concerning the grants of Kings and Soveraign Princes.

XXI. During pleasure, how to be understood.

It is likewise frequently questioned what is meant by this clause in a Pass, *during my pleasure*; whereunto the best answer is, that this priviledge shall last until some new declaration of the will of the Donor shall rescind it; for in a dubious case, that which was deemed sufficient to give a Right, shall be presumed sufficient to continue it: But yet not, if he that granted it be disabled any longer to declare his pleasure; as in case he be dead, for then whatsoever depended barely upon the uncertainty of his will, shall likewise cease, as accidents do when the substance fails.

XXII. A Pass implies protection. Bo. 3. ch. 4.

A Safe-pass being granted, protection is due even beyond the Territories of him that grants it, because it ought to protect us against all the licence of War, which of it self is not confined within the bounds of any one Princes Dominion, as we have elsewhere shewed.

XXIII. The redemption of Prisoners. Matt. 25. 36. 39. *De Offic. l. 2. c. 28.*

The redeeming of Captives is very much favoured, especially among Christians, it being an especial act of mercy commended unto us by the Law of God. *Redemptio magnum & præclarum justitiæ munus*, were the words of *Lactantius*; *The redeeming of Prisoners is a great and singular part of justice.* And in case it be from Barbarians, it is by St. *Ambrose* reckoned as the best and greatest liberality in the World; and in that Apology he makes for himself and his Church, for the breaking in pieces the consecrated Vessels, thereby to redeem the Captives, he affirms, that, *Ornatus Sacramentorum est redemptio captivorum*; *The chiefest ornament to Christian Sacraments, is the redeeming of Slaves*: where also he hath many other such excellent sayings to the same purpose. St. *Aug.* following the example of St. *Ambrose* did the like, though contrary to the carnal sense of some who therein opposed him, as *Possidius* relates. The very same is recorded by *Hincmarus* in the life of *Remigius*. And *Adamus* in his Ecclesiastical British History, makes honourable mention of the like fact done by *Rimbertus* Archbishop of *Breme*. And we likewise find it approved of by the sixth general Synod, whose decree is recited by *Gratian*, namely, That no Bishop shall presume to alienate any of the consecrated Vessels of their Churches, unless for such causes as were of old approved of by the Ancient Canons of the Church, as for the redeeming of Captives and the like. *Causa. 12.q. 2.*

XXIV. Whether the redemption of Prisoners may by any Law be forbidden.

Being thus awed by so great Authorities, I dare not absolutely approve of those Laws, which forbid the Redemption of Slaves, without a distinction, such I mean as we may read of among the Romans, *Nulli Civitati viliores Captivi quàm nostræ*; *There is no City so regardless of Captives as ours*, saith a wise Roman in open Senate. For which cause *Rome* is called in *Livy*, *Civitas Captivis minime indulgens*; *A City shewing little favour to Captives.* That Ode of *Horace* is very well known, where he condemns the ransoming of Prisoners as an opprobrious act, an example of dangerous consequence, and is an execrable fact encouraged with a reward. But what *Aristotle* blames in the Laconian, is also usually blamed in the Roman Government, namely, that all their Polity tended only to the advancement of their Military Discipline, as if in this alone consisted the safety of their Commonwealth; whereas, if we will but duly consider it as rational men, with the allowance of some grains of compassion, it would seem much better to rebate somewhat of that rigour, which the licence of War permits, than to leave so many of, perhaps, our Kinsmen and Countrymen in an everlasting slavery. I cannot therefore conceive how such a Law can be reputed just, unless it shall appear that such a severe course is necessary for the prevention of far greater, and morally inevitable calamities, which will otherwise in all humane probability fall upon us: for in such a case of necessity, as the Prisoners themselves ought by the rules of Charity, patiently to bear their hard fortune; so may this punishment be justly imposed upon them and threatned against others, to deter them from the like cowardize, according to what we have elsewhere written concerning any one Citizen, which for the publick safety of the City may be delivered up.

XXV. That a man may transfer his Right in a Captive.

True it is, that to make Slaves of such as are taken in War, is not agreeable to our Laws and Customes; yet doubtless may that Right of exacting a ransome from him that is so taken, by him that took him, justly be transferred to another: For by the Law of Nature things even incorporeal may also be alienated.

XXVI. The ransome may be due to more than to one.

And possible it is that the same ransome may be due to several persons; as in case a Prisoner being discharged by one, the ransome not paid, be apprehended by another, and after that by another, these must needs be distinct debts, because they arise from distinct causes.

XXVII. Whether an agreement for a ransome be null'd, his estate or quality being not then known.

The ransome agreed upon, shall bind the Contractors, though the Prisoner be found richer than he was thought to be, when the Contract was made; because by that Right of Nations which is external, whereby we are in this case to be judged, no man can be compelled to give a greater price than what was first agreed on, although undervalued, if there were no fraud in the Contract, as may easily be understood by that which hath been already delivered in the Chapter of Agreements *.

* *Lib.* 2. *c.* 26.

XXVIII. What Goods of Captives are his that takes them.

From what hath been already said, that Captives are not now to be made Slaves, it follows, That the Dominion that we have over their persons, doth not give us an universal Right to all that is theirs, as hath been elsewhere said *: for he that takes a Prisoner hath a Right to nothing but what he particularly lays hold on; so that if the Prisoner can conceal any thing he hath from him, he cannot be said to get it, because he is not thereof possest. Thus *Paulus* the Lawyer pleads against *Brutus* and *Manlius*, He that takes a Field into his possession, cannot be said to be possest of the treasure, which he knoweth not to be there buryed; for no man can be said to possess that which he knows not of: Whence it will likewise follow, that what the Prisoner can so conceal, he may make use of for his Redemption.

**Lib.*3.*c.*7.§.4.

XXIX. Whether the ransome agreed on be chargeable upon the Heirs.

Another Question is like to arise, namely, whether a ransome agreed on, the Prisoner dying before it be paid, may be recovered from his Heir? Whereunto the answer is easie, for if the Captive dye in Prison, doubtless the ransome is not due; because the promise was made upon condition that the Prisoner should be set at liberty, but he that is dead cannot be said to be at liberty: But on the contrary, if being at at liberty, he shall dye, the ransome shall be recovered, because he enjoyed that for which the ransome was promised; yet I confess the Contract may be so made that the ransome shall be due simply, and immediately from the time of the Contract, and then the person taken shall not from thenceforth be held as a Prisoner of War, but as one that doth freely engage himself as a Surety for the payment thereof: So on the contrary, the Contract may be so made that the ransome shall not be due, unless the Prisoner live and be at liberty upon a Day prefixt; but these things being less natural, shall not be presumed to be done, unless evidently proved.

XXX. Whether he that is freed to free another, ought to return, the other being dead.

It may likewise be questioned, whether he that is released on condition, that he shall release another, if that other dye before he be released, is bound to return into Captivity. I have elswhere * proved that a promise freely made for the Fact of a third, is sufficiently performed if nothing be omitted by the Promiser, in order to its accomplishment; but if a promise be made upon a valuable consideration, the Promiser stands obliged to the full value of what he promised. Just so it is in this case, for he that is released is not bound to return into Captivity, because it was not so agreed upon; nor will that indulgence that is given to liberty, admit it so to be tacitly understood, neither ought any man to make a gain of another mans liberty; but yet he that is so dismist out of Prison, ought to pay the value of that which he could not perform. For this cause was *Balionius* much blamed by *Mariana*, who being released upon his promise to release *Carvailius*, *Carvailius* dying before he could be released, refused to pay the value of his ransome. This answer I conceive to be more agreeable to the naked and simple truth, than that which is delivered unto us by the Interpreters of the Roman Laws.

* Bo. 2.ch.11. §. 22. & 15. and in this Book ch. 20.§. 58.

CHAP.

CHAP. XXII.

Concerning Faith given by inferiour Commanders in War.

I. *Of the several kinds of Commanders.*
II. *How far an agreement by them made, binds the supreme power :*
III. *Or gives occasion to such an obligation.*
IV. *What if any thing be done contrary to commands : this explained by distinctions.*
V. *Whether in such a case the contrary party be obliged.*
VI. *What the Commanders in War, or the Magistrates may do concerning their inferiours, or for them.*
VII. *It is not in the power of a General to make Peace*
VIII. *Whether he may grant a Truce ; this cleared by a distinction.*
IX. *What security of persons, and what of things may be granted by them.*
X. *Such Agreements are to be strictly understood : and why.*
XI. *A surrender accepted by a General, how to be understood.*
XII. *The addition of this caution, if the King or the People shall think fit, secures the General.*
XIII. *How the promise of delivering up a Town is to be interpreted.*

AMONGST publick agreements this is reckoned by *Ulpian* as one, when the Generals of each Army do agree about some things between themselves : We declared before that when we had sufficiently discourst of Faith given by the supreme Powers, we would likewise say somewhat of Faith given by subordinate Powers, and that either between themselves or unto others, whether those powers were next immediately to the supreme : As that of Generals, to whose Conduct the Army is committed ; whereunto we may fitly refer that of *Livy*, *Nec Ducem novimus, nisi cujus auspicio Bellum geritur* ; *We acknowledge no other Captain, but him to whom the management of the whole War is committed* : Or whether they are such as are Commanders under them, between whom *Cæsar* in his Commentaries distinguisheth thus, *The office of a private Captain is one thing, and the office of a General is another ; the former doth but execute particular orders, but this latter ought freely to consult and provide for the safety of the whole.* I. The several kinds of Commanders. Lib. 4. Lib. 3.

As concerning these mens engagements, there ought to be a twofold inspection, first, Whether the supreme powers are thereby engaged ; and secondly, Whether they themselves are bound by them. The former of these may be determined by what we have already said, namely, That Princes may be obliged by such as they depute to declare their wills, whether particularly exprest, or collected from the nature of their office ; for he that grants a power, grants as much as in him is, all things necessary to that power, which in moral things is morally to be understood : whence we may collect, That subordinate Commanders may oblige their Soveraigns two several ways, first, by doing that which in all probability belongs to their place or office ; secondly, by doing that which belongs not to their office , yet which they have a special Commission to do, in case that Commission be either publickly known, or at least unto those with whom they have to do. II. How far agreements by them made, bind their Soveraigns :

There are also other ways whereby a Soveraign Prince may be bound by the facts of his Officers, yet so, that that fact is not the proper and immediate cause of that obligation, but the occasion only, which may be done two ways, either by consenting unto it when done, or by the thing it self. Their consent will appear by their approbation, which may be given not only expresly but tacitly ; that is, when the supreme power had knowledge thereof, and yet permitted them to be done, which cannot with any probability be referred to any other cause ; and how this may proceed we have elsewhere shewed. By the thing it self he may be so far obliged, as not to enrich himself by anothers loss ; as if by an agreement made by his Ministers, a Prince receives any benefit, he is thereby bound to perform that part of the said agreement which concerns himself to perform ; or if he refuse to do it, then he is bound to forego the benefit, which he either hath or may receive by that agreement : for this is that equity which as we have often elsewhere said, evens the scales of justice. And hitherto and no farther is that saying true, *Si quid utiliter gestum sit, valet* ; *Whatsoever contract brings profit, binds the Contracter.* And therefore we cannot but condemn them of injustice, who refusing to fulfil the agreement, yet are resolved to detain that, which but by that agreement they could never have had ; as the Romans did when they refused, either to confirm the agreement made by *Cnæus Domitius*, or to set at liberty King *Bituitus*, whom *Domitius* had first invited as his Guest, and then perfidiously taken and sent bound to *Rome* : which fact as *Valerius Maximus* testifies, *Senatus nec ap-* III. Or give occasion to such an obligation. Bo. 2. ch. 4. §. 5. &. ch. 15. §. 17.

 probare

probare potuit, nec rescindere voluit; *The Roman Senate neither could approve of, nor would for Reasons of State rescind.* Many other such like examples we may find in Histories.

IV. What if any thing be done contrary to Command.

And here also we must repeat what we have formerly delivered, namely, That a Sovereign Prince may be obliged by the fact of his General, in case he transgress not the bounds of his publick Office, though he act contrary to his private instructions; this equity was well observed by the Roman Pretor, in such actions as concerned Factories. For it is not every Contract made with a Factor that shall be binding to him that employs him; but such only as are made concerning such Goods for which he is appointed his Factor. But in Case it be publickly proclaimed, That no man shall thenceforth treat or make any Agreement with such a man, that man shall no longer be treated with as a chief Minister: Nay, though such a Proclamation be made, yet if it appear not so to the Contractors, whatsoever shall be by him agreed on, shall bind the Prince that first employed him. Moreover, the condition of his Preposition ought to be observed; for he that is willing to be treated with under such a certain condition, and by the mediation of such a person, whatsoever is agreed upon by that person, in reference to the business for which he was commissionated, ought in all equity to be observed. Whence it follows, That some Princes or People are more, and some less, bound by such Contracts as are made by their Generals, if their several Laws and Constitutions are sufficiently known. But in Case these be not well known, then must we be guided by the most likely conjectures, which always presume that to be within their power, without which they cannot well discharge the Office of a General. But yet if any such inferior Officer shall transgress his Commission, and promise more than he can perform, he himself shall be bound to the full value, unless some Law sufficiently known shall hinder it. So likewise if there shall be found any fraud in the Case, as if such a principal Commander shall pretend to have a greater power given him by his Prince than indeed he hath, he shall then be obliged to satisfie for the damage thereby sustained; yea, and if through his crime some great injury do arise to the adverse Party, he shall be bound to suffer punishments answerable to his crime. In the former Case, his Goods shall make satisfaction; and if those fall short, his service, or his Corporal Liberty: In the latter, his person, or his Goods, or both, according to the greatness of his crime. Neither will it suffice in the Case of fraud to declare before-hand, that he will not oblige himself: For as well satisfaction for the damages done, as punishment for a crime committed, are both of them due, not by a voluntary, but by a natural obligation.

V. In which Case the other Party stands obliged.

Now because in all such Contracts, either the Prince or his Principal Minister, doth stand obliged; therefore it follows, That the other Party is thereby obliged; for the Contract cannot be said to halt. And by this we may discern the power that subordinate Commanders have to oblige their Superiours.

VI. What power they have over their Inferiors.

Now let us see what power they have over their Inferiours. And surely it is not to be doubted but that a General hath a power over his Souldiers, and a Magistrate over his Citizens, as to those Acts that are usually subject to their Command; but not otherwise, without their consent. On the contrary, an Agreement made by a General or a Magistrate in such things as are merely profitable, shall wholly bind their Inferiours. For this is sufficiently warranted by their Office and Authority; yea, and in such things also as are burthensome and chargeable, so as those burthens be such only as have been usually exacted; but as to those that are extraordinary, they stand not obliged without their own consents and acceptance: Which things are very agreeable to what we have already from the very Law of Nature proved, concerning a stipulation made in the behalf of a third person. But these Generals will receive a clearer light in the handling of these Particulars.

Lib. 2. *c.* 12. § 18.

VII. It is not in the power of Generals to make a Peace;

It belongs not to a General to look into the Causes or consequences of a War, it being his Duty carefully to manage the War, but not to conclude it; yea, though he have the greatest power that can be given him by his Commission, yet shall it be understood of the conduct of the War only, *Neque enim nos Jus habemus ordinandi res Imperatoris, For neither have we any power to dispose of what only belongs to the Emperour* (saith *Belisarius* to the Goths.) Thus *Agesilaus* answered the Persians, *De Pace constituendi Jus est penes Civitatem, It is only in the power of the Commonwealth to make Peace.* And therefore the Peace which *Albinus* made with *Jugurtha*, withour Order from the Senate, the Senate broke, as *Salust* informs us. Thus likewise *Livy*, *Quî rata ista pax, quam non ex authoritate Senatus, non jussu populi Romani peregerimus? What stability can there be in that Peace which is made without any Order or Decree, either of the Senate or People of* Rome? And therefore neither did that Promise made at *Caudis*, nor that made at *Numantia*, bind the people of *Rome*, as we have elsewhere said. And thus far is that of *Posthumius* verified, *If there be any thing whereunto a People may be obliged, they may be also obliged to all things*; that is, to all things that concern not the Conduct of War. And this is apparent by what hath been already said about Surrenders, and about Sponsions made for the leaving or burning of Cities, and concerning the change of Government.

To

To grant Truces is in the power, not of a General only but, of inferiour Commanders; that is, to such as they either assault or hold besieged, so far forth I mean as it shall concern themselves and their Forces. For other Commanders are not thereby obliged, as we may learn from the examples of *Fabius* and *Marcellus*, recorded by *Livy*.

VIII. But it is to grant Truces: *Lib.* 24.

On the other side, to dispose of Men, Empires or Lands is not in the power of Generals; and therefore was *Tigranes* dispossest of *Syria* by the Senate, although it had been given him by *Lucullus* *. Neither was it in the power of *Massinissa* to release *Sophonisba*, whom he had taken in War; because (as *Scipio* pleaded) She was under the power, and at the discretion of the people of *Rome* †. But over the rest of the spoil the General hath some kind of Right, yet not so much by virtue of his Authority as by the custom of Nations, whereof we have discoursed sufficiently before. But as to such things as are not actually possessed, they are wholly in the Generals power to forgive; because it is frequently seen, that both Men and Cities are willing to surrender themselves upon condition of their lives or their liberties, or sometimes that their Goods may be preserved; concerning which, the present state of things will not permit so much delay, as to expect the Prince or the Peoples pleasure. And by a parity of reason, the same power may be granted to an inferiour Commander concerning such things as are particularly committed to his Conduct. There were some Roman Souldiers that had escaped out of the Battel at *Thrasymenes*, to whom *Maharbal* in *Hannibal*'s absence had granted leave to depart, not with life only, but, laying down their Armes, unstript; whom notwithstanding *Hannibal* detained, pretending, That *Maharbal* had no power to grant such a Pass without his knowledge. Upon which fact of *Hannibal Livy* gives his censure thus, *Punica Religione servata Fides*, That he kept his Faith like a Carthaginian: Wherefore we must consider *Cicero* rather as an Orator than a Judge, who pleading before the Senate for *Rabirius*, endeavoured to perswade them, That *Saturninus* was lawfully killed by him, notwithstanding that *Marius* the then Consul had drawn him out of the Capitol with the promise of life. For, saith he, without a Decree of the Senate, who could give indemnity? as if the Faith given by *Marius* did oblige himself only. Not considering that *Marius* by his Commission was empowred to use all lawful means, whereby as well the Majesty as the Empire of the Romans might be preserved. Neither can it reasonably be denyed, That the Right of pardoning Offenders, if by that means the Commonwealth may be secured, must needs be comprehended under the Consular Power, which among the Romans was ever accounted the greatest; as *Salust* testifies in the Wars of *Catiline*.

IX. But not to dispose of Men, Empires or Lands.
* *Just. l.* 40.
† *Liv. l.* 30.

Moreover, in these Agreements made by principal Commanders, because they govern not their own, but the Affairs of the State, the strictest interpretation that the nature of the Contract will bear is to be followed, lest thereby Princes be bound to grant more than haply they would, or their Generals damnifie themselves in the execution of their Office.

X. Such Agreements are to be taken in a strict sense.

So he that is accepted of upon an absolute Surrender, shall be judged to submit himself wholly to the will of the Conquerour, whether it be of the King, or of the People that maintain the War; Examples whereof we have in *Gentius* King of *Illyrium*, and *Perseus* King of *Macedonia*, of whom the former yielded himself to *Anicius*, the latter to *Paulus*.

XI. How a Surrender accepted by a General is to be understood.

Wherefore, if this Clause may be added to the Contract, namely, *That it shall stand good if the Prince or the People shall think fit*; as of such we may read in divers Histories, divers Sponsions. It will so far provide for the Generals safety, that in Case that Agreement shall not be confirmed by the Supreme Power, he himself shall be indemnified, unless it be in that wherein he shall clearly be enriched.

XII. How that caution, If the King or the people please, is to be understood.

And they who have engaged themselves to deliver up a Town, may dismiss their Garrisons; as we read in *Livy* the Locrians did.

XIII.

CHAP.

CHAP. XXIII.

Of Faith given in War by private Men.

I. Faith to be kept even with Enemies by private men:

THAT Saying of *Cicero* is very well known, *Etiam, si quid singuli, temporibus adducti Hosti promiserint, est in eo ipso Fides servanda; Whatsoever any private person, being urged by the necessity of the times, shall promise to his Enemy, even in that very thing ought he to preserve his Faith.* Now whereas he saith [*any private person*] it is plain that it matters not whether he be a Souldier or a Citizen; for Faith ought to be kept with an Enemy by both. Strange it is then that any man, expert in the Laws, should averr, That *Faith in publick Agreements ought strictly to be kept, but not in private.* For if private men have Rights peculiar to themselves, which they may dispose of as they please. And if an Enemy be capable of those Rights, what should hinder but that these private men may for their lives or liberties engage those? Whereunto we may add, That unless this be granted, many Murders would daily be committed; yea, and many men kept in perpetual bondage: For neither could the lives of many men be otherwise preserved, nor their liberty procured, if no Faith privately made were to be kept with Enemies.

Bartol. in L. Conventio.

II. Even with Pyrats & Thieves, and how far forth.

Yea, and not only with such as the Law of Nations accounts Enemies, but even with Pyrates and Thieves, are we to keep our private Faith no less than if it were publick; as we have elsewhere proved *, with this only difference, That in Case any promise shall be extorted from us by an unjust fear, imprest by him to whom the promise is made, the Promiser may demand restitution; which if refused, he may take by himself: which by the Law of Nations we cannot do, if that fear proceed from a publick War. But in Case such a promise be confirmed by an Oath, it must necessarily be kept, if we would avoid the sin of perjury; which if committed against a publick Enemy, is punishable by man; but if against Pyrates or Thieves, it is connived at; yet not that it is then justifiable, but merely in detestation of their condition of life, who are to receive the benefit thereof.

* Book 3. Ch. 19. Sect. 2.

III. Minors not herein exempted.

Neither may we in this Case exempt Minors, if they be of such capacity as to understand what they promise; for the priviledges indulged unto them spring only from the Civil Law, whereas we respect only the Law of Nations.

IV. Whether an errour do excuse us.

As to those promises made through errour or misbelief, we have already declared, That we have a power to retract them, when that which was erroneously believed was, as it were, the Condition of the promise; as when a man believing his own Son to be dead, adopts another to be his Heir.

B.2.ch.11.§6.

V. The Objection drawn from publick profit, answered.

But how far forth the power of private men extends in making any Contract with an Enemy, is a Question of greater difficulty. Certain it is, That no private man can alienate that which is publick. For if so great a power be not to be given to a General, much less to private men; as is elsewhere proved *. And yet what Contracts private men may make with an Enemy concerning their own private affairs, whether actions or things, may very well be doubted; because we cannot well grant these to our Enemies without endamaging our own Party: Whence it will appear, That all such Contracts made are unlawful, as well with Citizens, in respect of that supereminent power their City hath over them, as with mercenary Souldiers, in respect of their Military Oath. But yet we must know,

* Ch. 22. Sect. 7.

know, That such Agreements being made to prevent a greater or more certain mischief, are to be reckoned rather as beneficial than destructive, even to the Publick. For always a lesser evil being comparted with a greater, hath the appearance of good; according to that Saying of him in *Appian*, *Of evils the lesser is most eligible.* And yet neither can that bare Faith whereby a man doth not utterly renounce all power that he hath over himself, and all that he hath; nor can the publick benefit, without the Authority of a Law, be of that efficacy as to make void that which is done, so as it shall have no effects of a just Right, though we should grant, That that which was promised was contrary to his Duty that promised it. The Law indeed may take away this power from its Subjects, whether they be Natives or Sojourners; but it doth not always do so, for it spares Citizens. Neither indeed can it always do it; for humane Laws (as we have already said) do then bind when made after an humane way: but do lose their binding power when they impose such things as are either altogether unreasonable, or unnatural. For those Laws or particular Mandates which do manifestly enjoin such things, are not to be either held or obeyed as Laws. For all general Laws are to be construed with so much favour to humanity, as not to bind in Cases of extremity. But if that act which by any Law or Precept was prohibited, and though done, declared to be void, might with equal Right be so prohibited; then shall that act of a private person be altogether void, yet may that man be justly punished, because he promised that which he had no Right to perform, especially if being bound by Oath he shall do it.

Book 1. Ch. 4. Sect. 7. 21. Book 2. Chap. 14. Sect. 12.

VI. This applied to a Captive promising to return into Captivity:

A promise made by a Prisoner to return into Prison is deservedly binding, because it renders not his Condition worse than it was: and therefore that fact of *Regulus* was not only glorious, but just; for as *Cicero* well observes, Regulus *ought not by his perjury to interrupt that general Traffick and Commerce of War, or to break those mutual Covenants and Conventions made between Enemies*; yea although, as *Horace* speaks,

> ———— *He could not chuse but know*
> *The tortures threatned by his Barb'rous Foe.*

For even when he did engage himself by promise to return, he was not ignorant what they might do. So of those ten Captives sent to *Rome*, eight of them denyed, *That they had any Right to recover their Estates by Postliminy, being bound by Oath to return back*; as we may read in *Gellius*. *Lib. 7. c. 18.*

VII. Or to such a place, or not to take Armes.

Some Prisoners are set at liberty upon their promise, That they will not return to such a place, or that they will never more bear Armes against them, under whose power they then are: An example of the former we may find in *Thucydides*, where the *Ithomenses* engaged themselves to the Lacedemonians to depart out of *Peloponnesus*, and never to return thither again. And of the latter, Examples are now very frequent; an ancient Example whereof is left us by *Polybius*, where we find that the Numidians were dismist by *Amilcar*, upon Condition, *That none of them should ever engage in War against the Carthaginians.* The like Condition we find imposed on the Heruleans in *Procopius*; yet there are that hold such an Agreement to be void, as being contrary to the Duty we owe unto our Countrey. But to this I answer, as before, That not every thing that we do contrary to our Duty is presently void. Besides, it is not against our Duty to procure our own liberty by such a promise; because, being already under the power of the Enemy until we are dismist, we are as useless to our Countrey as if we were dead: wherefore our Countries condition cannot be made worse by such a promise.

Goth. l. 2.

VIII. Not to flye.

Some there are that engage themselves not to make their escape; and herein also Faith is to be kept, though when we made that promise we were under restraint: though some there are that hold otherwise. For by this very promise either our lives are sometime preserved, or we enjoy the more liberty. But yet if after this promise made, we are still kept under a closer restraint, we are thereby discharged of our promise, if it were made upon Condition that we should not be so bound.

IX. A Captive taken by one, cannot yield himself to another.

It is but a foolish Question that some make, Whether he that is taken Prisoner by one, may yield himself Prisoner to another. For it is too clear, That no man can take away that Right which another man hath gained by any Contract that he can make: For by the very Right of War, or partly by the Right of War, and partly by the Grant of him that maintains the War, according to what we have already said, A Prisoner taken in War is his that takes him.

X. Whether private men may be compelled by their Prince to perform what they have promised.

As concerning the effects of such Agreements there is a notable Question, namely, Whether private men, in Case they neglect to perform what they have promised, may be compelled thereunto by their superior Power? Whereunto the best Answer is, That they may, but in a solemn War only; because they that make War, are bound by the Law of Nations each to other to do that which is right and just, even concerning the facts of private men; as if an Ambassadour being publickly sent from an Enemy, should by a private person be be assaulted. Wherefore, that motion which *Cornelius Nepos* made, was assented unto by many of the Roman Senators, as *Gellius* testifies, namely, That those two of the ten Captives, who being bound by Oath to make their returns, refused, should by a strong Guard be conducted, and delivered up to *Hannibal*, especially considering that the same Senate had, not long before, compelled those to return whom King *Pyrrhus* had dismist upon the like Conditions.

XI. What interpretation we should give to such a Contract.

Concerning the interpretation of some words in such an Agreement, we are to be guided by those Rules which we have often recited, that is to say, We ought not to recede from the proper signification of the words, unless it be to avoid some absurdity that would from thence follow; or that we be induced thereunto by some other very strong conjectures: and where the words are ambiguous, that we incline to that sense that makes most against him who gives the Law.

XII. How these words [Life, Garments, the coming of Aids] are to be understood.

As he that covenants for his life only, hath no Right to his liberty; under the name Apparel we are not to comprehend Armes: Aids are then said to come when they are in sight, though they do nothing; for their appearance hath some kind of efficacy.

XIII. Who may be said to return to the Enemy.

But he cannot be said to return to the Enemy, who returning privately, presently departs: For our promise to return is not fulfilled, until we have put our selves under the same power of the Enemy as we were when we promised to return. The contrary interpretation *Cicero* accounts to be merely delusive, and foolishly crafty, introducing fraud, and sometimes perjury. And *Gellius* calls it a fraudulent Cheat, always branded by the Censors with reproach, and the persons that made use thereof rendred intestable.

XIV. Succors, when said to come. *Goth. l.* 3.

In Agreements made, Not to surrender in case just succours should come within such a time to their relief, such succours are to be understood as are sufficient to repel the Enemy, and secure us from farther danger; four Examples whereof are recorded by *Procopius*.

XV. That which relates to the manner of the execution is no Condition.

This also deserves to be observed, That if any thing shall be agreed on concerning the manner of the execution, that shall be annexed unto the Agreement as a Condition. As for example, In Case a Safe-Conduct be granted to such a place, and that place before we can arrive thither, happen to be in the possession of the Enemy, the Agreement is not fulfilled until we come where we may be in safety.

XVI. Of Hostages to perform such Covenants.

As to Hostages, we are to be guided as abovesaid; sometimes they are but Sureties for the acts of their Principal; but yet it may be so agreed that the Obligation should be disjunctively understood, that is to say, That either such a thing shall be done, or the Hostages may be detained. But if the meaning be doubtful, we must incline unto that which is most natural, which is, That they shal be held as Sureties only, until such things shall be performed.

CHAP.

CHAP. XXIV.

Of Faith tacitely given.

I. Faith given by silence.

THAT some things are by silence agreed on was not ill observed by *Javolenus*, for this is usual in most agreements, whether they be publick, private or mixt; the reason whereof is, because it is our consent only however signified and accepted that hath the power to transfer our Right. But this consent of ours may be otherwise exprest than by voices or letters, as we have already shewed: for some signs are naturally included in the act it self.

II. As in him that desires to be admitted unto protection;

As for example, He that coming from an Enemy, or as a Stranger, commits himself to the Faith of another King or People, doth without doubt tacitely oblige himself, not to act any thing against that State under which he desireth protection; we cannot then agree with them, who justifie that act of *Zopyrus*, who not being able to conquer *Babylon* by force, cut off his own Nose, Ears, and Lips, and so mangled, fled into the City, and perswaded the Citizens that *Darius* his Master had done it in revenge for speaking somewhat in their behalf; and having thereby got into some place of eminent trust, betrayed the City unto *Darius*: For *Zopyrus* his fidelity unto his Prince, could not justifie his perfidious dealings with them to whom he fled, and by whom he was received into protection. The like may be said of *Sextus* the Son of *Tarquin*, who betook himself for safety to the *Gabii*. *Virgils* censure upon the like fact of *Sinon* was this,

> *Now Græci'an Treacheries view, and from this one,*
> *Learn to avoid the rest.*——————————

III. And in him that craves a Parly.

So he that demands or admits of a Parly, gives his Faith tacitely, that during that Parly both Parties may be secure. * *Agathias* condemns *Ragnaris* the Hun, for attempting to kill *Narsetes* in his return from a Conference whereunto he had invited him. This *Livy* concludes to be a manifest breach of the Law of Nations, when Enemies under the colour of a Treaty, shall lay wait to destroy each other, which he there stiles, *Colloquium perfide violatum*; *A treaty most perfidiously broken.* Upon that fact of *Cnæus Domitius* before-mentioned in treacherously seizing upon King *Bituitus*, whom he had first invited to a Parly, and afterwards entertained as his Guest, *Valerius Maximus* gives this censure: *Nimia gloriæ cupiditas perfidum existere coegit*; *His immoderate thirst after glory constrained him to be perfidious.* Wherefore I cannot but admire why he that wrote the eighth Book of *Cæsars* Gallick Wars, rehearsing the like fact of *T. Labienus*, adds these words, *Infidelitatem* Comii *sine ulla perfidia judicavit comprimi posse*; *He conceived that* Comius *his disloyalty might be thus supprest without any imputation of Treachery.*

* *Lib.* 1. — *Liv.* 38. — *Lib.* 10. *c.* 6.

IV. During a Parly each may promote his own interest, not hurting the other.

Neither may we wrest this tacite consent beyond what I have said; for if carrying themselves inoffensively one towards another during the conference, they can under the colour of that conference divert their Enemies from their Warlike Counsels, and in the mean time strengthen themselves and promote their own affairs, this shall not be accounted treachery but policy, such as in times of War are not lawful only but commendable: wherefore they that blamed King *Perseus* for suffering himself to be deluded through hopes of Peace, had not so great a regard to justice and fidelity, as to the generosity of a mind emulous of Martial Glory, as may be sufficiently collected from what hath been already said concerning the deceits and stratagems usual in War. Such was that stratagem wherewith *Asdrubal* preserved himself and his Army out of the Ausetane Forests. And that also whereby *Scipio African* the Elder, discovered the situation of *Syphax* his Camp, both which we find recorded by *Livy*, whose

Liv. l. 42. — See Bo. 3. c. 1. §. 6. &c. — *Livy l.* 26. *lib.* 30.

example *L. Sulla* alſo followed in the ſocial War at *Eſernia*, as *Frontinus* informs us.

V. Of dumb Signs which by cuſtom are ſignificant.

There are alſo ſome dumb ſigns, which through cuſtome are ſignificant, as teſtifying the conſent of the will; as of old the branches of Olives, and among the Macedonians the erection of Pikes; among the Romans the covering of their heads with their Shields, theſe were then the uſual ſigns of ſubmiſſion and rendition: So alſo was the folding of the hands behind them among the Perſians; and the turning of their Shields and Enſigns downwards among the Romans, as *Ammianus* teſtifies. The Germans, and from them ſome other Nations, expreſs their ſubmiſſion by the holding forth of Herbs or Graſs, as *Pliny* tells us. And they that yield themſelves to the Conquerour, do uſually caſt away their Armes, and beg mercy, as *Servius* notes upon *Virgil*. But he that would ſignify his acception of a ſurrender, whether he be bound to give quarter, and how far forth, we may inform our ſelves by what hath been ſaid above. In our days the hanging forth of a white Flagg is a tacite ſign that a Treaty is demanded: So among the Northern Nations is the kindling of a fire, as *Johannes Magnus* relates. The like doth *Pliny* write of the Laurel, all which according to the cuſtomes of ſeveral Nations, are no leſs ſignificant, and conſequently as obligatory, as if they were expreſt by words and voices.

Lib. 18. *Lib.* 26. *Lib.* 22. *Pliny l.* 15. *c.* 30.

VI. Of a tacite approbation of ſomething demanded.

A Sponſion made by a General, how far forth it may be believed to be tacitely approved of by the Prince or People, we have already declared *; as namely when both the act is ſufficiently known, and thereupon ſome thing done or not done, whereof no other reaſon can be given, but what proceeded from their conſent to that promiſe or agreement.

* Bo. 3. ch. 4. §. 15. & Bo. 2. ch. 15. §. 17.

VII. Puniſhments when tacitely remitted

We cannot conclude that a puniſhment is remitted, becauſe it is for a time diſſembled or connived at; but ſome other act muſt neceſſarily intervene, which either by it ſelf may argue, either a perfect reconciliation, as when a League of friendſhip is made with ſuch a man; or at leaſt that the perſon offended hath ſo great an opinion of the vertue or the valour of the perſon puniſhable, that what he formerly did, deſerves to be pardoned, whether this opinion be by words expreſt, or by ſuch other means as are uſually taken to ſignifie as much.

VIII. Whether the actors being pardoned, the inſtigators be alſo acquitted.

Another Queſtion we find diſcuſt by *Polybius*, namely, Whether a puniſhment being remitted to them that did the miſchief, may be judged to be remitted to them that commanded it to be done; which I conceive it ought not, for, *Singulos tenent ſua delicta*; *Every Fox ought to pay his own ſkin to the fleaer, and every offender bear his own puniſhment.*

CHAP.

CHAP. XXV.

The Conclusion, with certain admonitions to preserve Faith and Peace.

I. *An exhortation to Princes to keep their Faith.*
II. *The end of War is to settle a firm Peace.*
III. *That Peace is to be embraced, though with loss, especially by Christians.*
IV. *That to make Peace is profitable to the Vanquished*;
V. *And no less to the Conquerours*;
VI. *And to those also whose condition is doubtful.*
VII. *That Peace being once made, ought religiously to be kept.*
VIII. *The Authors wish, and the Conclusion of this Treatise.*

AND here I conceive I may make an end, not that I have said all that might have been said; but that what hath been here said, may suffice for a foundation, whereupon if any other will build more speciously, I am so far from envying him, that I shall heartily thank him. Yet before I dismiss my Reader, as before when I began to discourse of War, I gave some arguments to perswade all men (so far as in them lay) to prevent it; so here, I shall only add some few motives to excite Princes, both in and after the War, to keep their Faith and maintain Peace; but especially to preserve their Faith, as for many other reasons, so especially for this, lest being observed to be faithless, there remain no hopes at all of Peace. *For it is by Faith*, saith *Cicero*, *that not Commonwealths only, but that Grand society of Nations is maintained. Take away this*, saith *Aristotle*, *and all Humane Commerce fails.* It is therefore an execrable thing to break Faith, upon which so many lives depend. It is, saith *Seneca*, *Sanctissimum humani pectoris bonum*; *The best ornament wherewith God hath beautified the rational soul*: which ought so much the more inviolably to be kept by Soveraign Princes, by how much they may sin with greater licence and impunity than other men: Wherefore take away Faith, and men are more fierce and cruel than Savage Beasts, whose rage all men do horribly dread. Justice indeed in all other of her parts hath some thing that is obscure: But that whereunto we engage our Faith, is of it self clear and evident; yea, and to this very end do men pawn their Faith, that in their Negotiations one with another, all doubts may be taken away, and every scruple removed. How much more then doth it concern Kings to keep their Faith inviolable, as well for Conscience sake, as in regard to their Honour and Reputation, wherein consists the Authority of a Kingdom. Wherefore let all Princes know, that they that endeavour to instill into them such fallacious Principles, do themselves practise what they would teach others: And that it is impossible that those practices should always prosper, which render men unsociable with men, and detestable to God himself.

I. Exhortation to keep our Faith. Off. l. 3. Rhet ad Theod. l. 1. c. 15. Ep. 88. Cic. pro Q. Rosc.

Moreover it is not possible, that any Soul should (throughout the whole course of the War) rest secure, and contain it self within its Duty toward God, that doth not always aim at Peace. It was very truly said of *Salust*, *Sapientes pacis causa Bellum gerunt*; *That wise men in making War, aim at Peace.* Wherewith agrees that of St. *Aug. We seek not Peace, that we may make War*; *but we make War, to establish Peace.* Nay, *Aristotle* himself often condemns those Nations that make War their trade of life, and propose it to themselves not as their refuge, but as their choice: for, *Ferinum quiddam vis est*; *Force in it self is brutish*, yet is it the very Soul of War: it ought therefore to be the more carefully carryed on, and attempted with Clemency and Humanity, *Ne nimium feras imitando, dediscamus hominem*; *Lest*, like *Nebucadonozer*, *by living too long like Beasts, we at length forget our selves to be men.* It was an excellent Speech that *Justinians* Embassadors made to *Cosroe*, recorded by *Procopius*, *Were it not*, say they, *that we are in thy presence, O King, we could not have believed that* Cosroe *the Son of* Cabada *would have entred into the Roman Territories with an Army*; *not only in contempt of the Oath he hath taken, which is the strongest pledge of truth and faithfulness that can be given amongst men*; *but contrary to the League made between us, which was the only hope of those, who by reason of the outrages committed in War, could not otherwise live in safety*: *what else can be said of this, but that the lives of men are hereby changed into the lives of wild Beasts. For take away the force and power of Oaths and Leagues, and it will necessarily follow, that men must eternally make War one upon another*: *and the consequence of endless War is, That it holds men perpetually as if banished from their own Nature.*

II. The end of War is Peace. Orat. ad Caes. Ep. ad Bonif. 7 Pol. 2. & 14. Pers. l. 2.

III. Peace to be embraced, even with loss, especially by Christians: * Rom. 12. 18. Cujac.

A safe and honourable Peace is not too dearly bought, if it may be had by forgiving, as well the Offenders as the charges and damages of the War; especially by us Christians, to whom our great Lord and Master hath bequeathed Peace as his last Legacy: whose best Expositor St *Paul** would have us, *if possible, and as far as in us lies, to live peaceably with all men.* A good man, saith *Salust*, will not enter into a War unless enforced, nor willingly prosecute it to the utmost, although he be provoked. Is it not a shame for men the mildest of all Creatures, to delight in shedding each others bloud, and to make War and bequeath it to their Children, when they see dumb Beasts to live quietly and peaceably together?

IV. Profitable to the Vanquished;

It is enough, if we can obtain Peace, though with loss; but for the most part the common interest of all Parties invites, nay draws us to this Point: As first, That Party that is weakest. For to cope long with an Enemy stronger than our selves, must needs be dangerous: wherefore, as in a violent Storm, we esteem it a good purchase if we can redeem our lives with the loss of our Goods; so being over-powered by an Enemy, it will be no ill Bargain, if with the loss of some part we can secure the whole, leaving those vain Arguments drawn from hope and revenge to their deluding Authors. Which *Aristotle* delivers thus, *Much better it is for them that think themselves strongest, to forgo somewhat of their Right, than to hazard all (together with their lives) to an uncertain Victory*: Wherefore *Philo*, in his Institutions of a vertuous Prince, tells him, That *Pax quamvis cum maximo detrimento est Bello utilior*; *Peace, though with some very great damage, is far more profitable than War*.

V. And to the Conquerour.

Yea, and to that Party that is most powerful, is Peace most profitable; because they enjoy Peace, with plenty and prosperity, which is much better and more lasting than an hoped for Victory. For we must remember, That the success of War is uncertain, and many changes and chances do frequently happen which cannot be foreseen. *Diodorus*, in an Oration he makes for Peace, blames them that boast of their great Exploits done in War; as if it were not usual for Fortune sometimes to favour one side, and sometimes another. And the bold attempts of desperate Men are more to be feared than the sharp Teeth of dying Beasts.

VI. The best time to make Peace.

But what if both Parties seem to be of equal strength? Then (if *Cæsar* may be believed) is the fittest time to treat of Peace, whilst each Party is confident of his own power.

VII. Peace once made is religiously to be kept.

But Peace being once made, whatever the Articles are, they ought strictly to be observed, to preserve our Faith. For very careful we ought to be, not only to avoid perfidiousness, but whatsoever else may provoke or exasperate the adverse Party. For what *Cicero* sometimes said of private friendship, may very fitly be applied to publick. If all friendships are to be faithfully and religiously preserved, surely these most especially, that from an open hostility are redintegrated and made new again by making Peace.

VIII. The Authours Prayer.

God, who alone can do it, instil these things into the hearts of those who manage the Affairs of *Christendom*, giving them a mind throughly instructed in all Rights both Divine and humane, and always remembring that She is chosen by God as his Vicegerent on the Earth to govern Men, the best and (as *Chrysostom* notes) the most beloved of all his Creatures.

All Glory be given unto God alone.

Joinvil's *Testimony of St.* Lewis *King of* France, Chap. 89.

HIS Grand Counsellors did often blame him, for taking so much pains in composing the Quarrels of his Neighbour Princes, and for not rather suffering them to make War one against another, which might turn to his advantage: but the King told them, they did not well advise him; for, saith he, in case those Princes and Governours, do once perceive that I foment the War betwixt them, they will presently say, the *French* King deals craftily in suffering us to War one against another, thereby to promote his own designs; whereupon they will immediately turn all their hatred against me, and with joint forces make War upon me to the great damage of my Kingdom; and haply I shall thereby provoke Gods wrath against me, who hath pronounced a Blessing to the Peace-maker. This I do confidently affirm, That the Burgundians and the Lorrainers did so highly honour this King for his goodness and justice, that they made him their Common Arbitrer to decide all their differences: I have often seen them addressing themselves unto him, sometimes at *Paris*, sometimes at *Rhemes*, and sometimes at *Melun*, and sometimes at other places where the King was resident.

His Charge to his Son.

IF any Controversie or Suit arise against thee, search into the truth whether it be for thee or against thee. And if thou possessest any thing that is thy Neighbours, which either thou or thine Ancestors have unjustly gotten, restore it presently. Beware how thou makest War against any of thy Christian Neighbours, without the advice of many, and unless prest thereunto by unavoidable necessity. In thy Wars spare the Priests, and such as are inoffensive. If War or Suits arise among thy Subjects, appease it and reconcile them with all speed possible. Have a watchful eye over thy Bayliffs, Governours, and other Officers, and enquire strictly into their acts, that what is amiss may be speedily amended, and see that no crying sin raign within thy Kingdom.

FINIS.

A TABLE put Alphabetically, guiding to the PRINCIPAL MATTERS and WORDS contained in the TREATISE.

B.

C.

Of

D.

G.

K.

L.

Magistrates

N.

O.

Philip

P.

S.

T.

In

X.

Y.

Z.

The End of the TABLE.

www.ingramcontent.com/pod-product-compliance
Lightning Source LLC
LaVergne TN
LVHW081345011026
849161LV00013BB/3011